HEALTH PSYCHOLOGY
A Biopsychosocial Approach

SIXTH EDITION

Richard O. Straub

University of Michigan, Dearborn

worth publishers
Macmillan Learning

New York

Senior Vice President, Content Strategy: Charles Linsmeier
Program Director, Social Sciences: Shani Fisher
Senior Associate Editor: Sarah Berger
Development Editor: Elsa Peterson
Editorial Assistant: Dorothy Tomasini
Executive Marketing Manager: Katherine Nurre
Marketing Assistant: Chelsea Simens
Director of Media Editorial and Assessment, Social Sciences: Noel Hohnstine
Media Editor: Stefani Wallace
Media Project Manager: Jason Perkins
Director, Content Management Enhancement: Tracey Kuehn
Senior Managing Editor: Lisa Kinne
Senior Content Project Manager: Kerry O'Shaughnessy
Senior Project Manager: Vanavan Jayaraman, Lumina Datamatics, Inc.
Senior Workflow Project Manager: Lisa McDowell
Senior Photo Editor: Cecilia Varas
Photo Researchers: Kerri Wilson, Lumina Datamatics, Inc.; Krystyna Borgen, Lumina Datamatics, Inc.
Director of Design, Content Management: Diana Blume
Design Services Manager: Natasha Wolfe
Cover Designer: John Callahan
Art Manager: Matthew McAdams
Composition: Lumina Datamatics, Inc.
Printing and Binding: King Printing Co., Inc.
Cover: Ted Horowitz/Alamy Stock Photo

Library of Congress Control Number: 2018959646

ISBN-13: 978-1-319-16981-7
ISBN-10: 1-319-16981-3

Printed in the United States of America
2   3   4   5   6   23   22   21

Worth Publishers
One New York Plaza
Suite 4500
New York, NY 10004-1562
www.macmillanlearning.com

For Pam ... *we've only just begun*

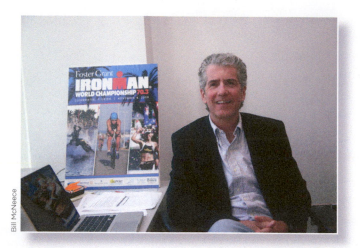

Bill McNeece

About the Author

Richard O. Straub is professor of psychology and founding director of the graduate program in health psychology at the University of Michigan, Dearborn. After receiving his PhD in experimental psychology from Columbia University and serving as a National Institute of Mental Health fellow at the University of California, Irvine, Dr. Straub joined the University of Michigan faculty in 1979. Since then, he has focused on research in health psychology, especially mind–body issues in stress, cardiovascular reactivity, and the effects of exercise on physical and psychological health. His research has been published in such journals as *Health Psychology*, the *Journal of Applied Social Psychology*, and the *Journal of the Experimental Analysis of Behavior*.

A recipient of the University of Michigan's Distinguished Teaching award and the Alumni Society's Faculty Member of the Year award, Dr. Straub is extensively involved in undergraduate and graduate medical education. His professional devotion to health psychology dovetails with his personal devotion to fitness and good health. Dr. Straub has completed hundreds of road races and marathons (including multiple Boston Marathons, Ironman Triathlons, and the 2010 IRONMAN Hawaii World Championship).

Brief Contents

Contents

Preface

Not so long ago, *health* and *psychology* were separate disciplines, each aware of the other but unable to connect in any meaningful way. Then, in 1978, the field of *health psychology* was born, and it has grown explosively since then. Now, four decades since *health psychology* emerged as a specific focus of study, an overwhelming and growing body of evidence continues to demonstrate that good health is more than just a physiological state. From the earliest research linking Type A behavior to increased risk for cardiovascular disease, to the most current discoveries regarding psychosocial influences on gene expression and the inflammatory processes involved in cardiovascular disease, cancer, and other chronic diseases, health psychology already has accomplished much.

More important than individual research findings has been the ongoing refinement of the *biopsychosocial model* as an interdisciplinary template for the study of health issues. Increasingly, researchers are able to pinpoint the physiological mechanisms by which anger, loneliness, and other psychosocial factors adversely affect health, and by which optimism, social connectedness, and a strong sense of self-empowerment exert their beneficial effects.

Experiencing these exciting and productive early years of health psychology inspired me to write this textbook—to share with aspiring students this vitally important field. My goals in *Health Psychology: A Biopsychosocial Approach* have been to present current, relevant, well-supported summaries of the main ideas of the field and to model a scientific way of thinking about those ideas. Understanding human behavior and teaching students are my two professional passions, and nowhere have these passions come together more directly for me than in writing about how psychology and health are interconnected.

WHAT'S NEW IN THE SIXTH EDITION?

In this thoroughly revised sixth edition, my aim continues to be to present the science of health psychology clearly, accurately, and in an accessible voice that helps students make meaningful connections with their own lives. Yet I've introduced a number of significant changes:

- Hundreds of new research citations that provide a complete and up-to-date picture of the field
- A new, full-color design with new photos and figures
- New learning outcomes at the beginning of each chapter
- Significant streamlining to emphasize the most important topics and make room for cutting-edge research in health psychology
- A broader, global, evidence-based perspective that incorporates information from diverse sources like the World Bank, the Institute for Health Metrics and Evaluation, and the World Health Organization

- A new section on Interactions Among Body Systems, with coverage of the microbiota-gut-brain axis

- A new section on mHealth—research investigating the use of smartphones and other mobile technologies to promote health and well-being

- Thoroughly revised and updated material on stress and coping, including these new sections: Biological Differences in the Stress Response (or Gender and the HPA Axis); Prenatal Stress and Adverse Childhood Experiences; Negative Affect, Depression, and the Type D Personality; and new research on how gratitude, humor, pets, and spirituality can be used to cope with stress

- New coverage of the effects of trauma, including new research on eating disorders and trauma and new *Diversity and Healthy Living* boxes on Neighborhood Violence, Brain Development, and PTSD

- New material on electronic cigarettes and the health concerns associated with "vaping"

- New material on the resurgence of marijuana use, including growing support for legalization of both medical and recreational use, and information on marijuana's long-term impacts on health and brain function

- New discussion of spirituality and the research evaluating its health benefits

- New material on nutrition and weight, including coverage of implicit weight bias, food security, genetics and the risk of developing an eating disorder, the "health at every size" movement, and the fat–sugar dietary controversy

- Updated data on substance use among teenagers, including the increased use of inhalants

- Updated data on prescription and nonprescription opioid use and abuse and its economic burden

- Updated coverage of communicable and noncommunicable diseases around the world

- Updated discussion of the neuromatrix of pain and the factors that influence the experience of pain

- New material on the health effects of poor sleep, including risk of chronic health disorders and cognitive decline

- A new *Diversity and Healthy Living* box: HIV Stigma and Living with AIDs Around the World

- New *Your Health Assets* boxes: The Brief Cope scale, allowing readers to assess their coping style in response to stressful events; and Social Media Addiction, encouraging readers to examine the role of social media in their lives

- Updated coverage of the status of the Affordable Health Care Act, including cross-cultural comparisons of how other countries address the basic human right of health care

- Updated coverage of positive psychology, resilience, mindfulness, and cognitive-behavioral interventions

TABLE 1 Coverage of Culture and Multicultural Experience

Coverage of culture and multicultural experiences can be found on the following pages:

Acculturation, p. 338
    in U.S. government nutrition guidelines, p. 239
African American adolescents and psychological control, pp. 141, 145
African Americans and hypertension, pp. 101, 145, 317, 319–320, 325–326
Alcohol use, p. 287
Antismoking campaigns, pp. 175–176, 298
Body mass and hypertension among African Americans, p. 37
Cancer
    and age, p. 350
    and diet, pp. 353–354
    screening interventions, p. 350
    survival rates, p. 362
Cardiovascular disease
    racial and ethnic differences in, pp. 21, 317, 319–320

Childbirth pain, pp. 457, 465
Death rates among racial/ethnic groups, pp. 5, 20–21, 227
Diabetes, p. 334
Eating disorders, pp. 254, 265–266
Food deserts, pp. 256–257
Health care use, pp. 418, 424–426
Health insurance, pp. 171–173
Health system barriers, pp. 171–173, pp. 423–427
HIV
    counseling and education, p. 403
    intervention, pp. 397, 399, 402–405
    transmission and AIDS, pp. 387–388
Immigrants, p. 21
LGBT issues, pp. 101, 130, 378
Microaggressions, pp. 101, 128–129
Obesity, pp. 254–257

Pain, pp. 456–458
Personal control, pp. 189–190
Smoking cessation programs, pp. 299–302
Sociocultural perspective in health psychology, pp. 20–21
Socioeconomic status
    and cancer, p. 350
    and cardiovascular disease, pp. 317–319
    and health care providers, pp. 426–427
    and health care use, p. 418
    and obesity, p. 224
    and patient communication problems, pp. 426–427
    and provider communication problems, p. 424
Substance abuse, pp. 285–287
Tobacco use, pp. 294–295

TABLE 2 Coverage of Life-Span Issues

Life-span issues are discussed on the following pages:

Adolescence
    and exercise, p. 206
    and hypertension, p. 319
    and perceived vulnerability to risky behaviors, pp. 165, 169
    and tobacco use, pp. 296–297
Age differences in sick role behavior, pp. 416–418
Age–pain relationship, p. 455
Age-related conditions and cortisol, pp. 110–111
Ageism and compliance, p. 416
Alcohol, pp. 150, 285–287
Asthma and childhood, pp. 72–73
Cancer
    and age, pp. 349–350

    and children, pp. 349, 360, 371
Children coping with pain and medical procedures, pp. 445, 458, 459
Cigarette advertising and children, p. 296
Cigarette antismoking campaign and children, p. 298
Community and wellness, pp. 170–176
Diabetes and age, pp. 334–335, 336
Eating disorders, demographics and genders, pp. 263–264
    treatment of, pp. 266–269
HIV/AIDS and age-appropriate counseling, pp. 402–403
Life-course perspective, p. 16

Longevity and lifestyle, p. 170
Obesity–health relationship
    and age, pp. 251–252
    and gender, pp. 250–251
Optimism and children, pp. 139–140
Reactivity and hypertension in children, p. 125
Research methods, p. 42
Resilience in children, pp. 142–143
Seeking health services, pp. 416–418
Shaping pain behavior in children, pp. 14–19
Sleep and health, pp. 211–212
Stress and social support, pp. 145–148
Workplace, pp. 179–182

TABLE 3 Coverage of the Psychology of Women and Men
Coverage of the psychology of women and men can be found on the following pages:

AIDS and HIV
  and psychosocial barriers to intervention, p. 407
  and transmission, pp. 387–388
Alcohol
  and behavior and personality traits, p. 26
  and dating behavior, p. 289
  gender and drinking contexts, p. 287
Cancer, p. 349
Cardiovascular disease, pp. 317–318
Coping styles, pp. 135–137
Gender, stress, and taste, p. 254

Gender and obesity, pp. 250, 254–255
Gender and use of health services, pp. 416–417
Gender bias in medicine, pp. 21–23
Gender perspective, pp. 21–23
Hostility and anger, pp. 323–325
Male-pattern and female-pattern obesity, p. 250
Pain, pp. 455–456
Reactivity and hypertension in men, p. 125
Reproductive system, pp. 80–83
Role overload and conflict, p. 103

Sexism in health care, pp. 22–23, pp. 424–425
Sexual practices, pp. 403–404
Sexually transmitted infections, pp. 359, 384–388
Sick role behavior, pp. 416–418
Smoking cessation programs, p. 302
Social support and effects on PSA, p. 147
Stress response, pp. 107, 111–112
Substance abuse, p. 287
Use of health care services, 416–418

TABLE 4 Coverage of Women's Health
Coverage of women's health can be found on the following pages:

AIDS, pp. 398–99
Alcohol and pregnancy, pp. 276, 288–289
Body image and the media, pp. 239, 266
Body image dissatisfaction, pp. 262–264
Breast cancer
  and diet, p. 355
  and emotional disclosure, pp. 372–373
  and ethnic differences, pp. 349–350
  and exercise, p. 355

  and heredity, pp. 355–356
  and Nurses' Health Study, pp. 354, 355–356
  and obesity, p. 355
  and relationship to alcohol, p. 354
  and social support, p. 371
  coping with, pp. 367, 369
Caregiving role and stress, p. 103
Childbirth, pp. 380–381, 385, 457, 465
Eating disorders, pp. 262–269
  treatment of, pp. 266–269
Employment and health, pp. 101–106

Fertilization, pp. 81–83
HIV transmission
  during pregnancy, p. 387
  with breast feeding, p. 387
Lung cancer, pp. 349, 352
Medical treatment, in comparison to males, pp. 21–23
Pregnancy, pp. 81–82, 276, 288–289, 296, 382, 385, 387
Reactivity, p. 125
Self-efficacy and high-risk sexual behaviors, pp. 403–405, 406
Smoking and miscarriage, p. 296

TABLE 5 Coverage of Positive Health Psychology

Coverage of positive health psychology can be found on the following pages:

Alcohol abuse prevention programs, pp. 292–294

Behavioral control, pp. 432–434

Cancer-fighting foods, pp. 353–354

Daily uplifts and stress, p. 100

Dispositional affect, pp. 138–139

Education programs, pp. 174–176, 293–294, 298–299, 403–404

Explanatory style, pp. 139–140, pp. 414–415

Family therapy, p. 267

Health behaviors, pp. 162–168

Health psychology interventions, defined, p. 27

Heart and healthy diets, pp. 321, 330–331

Hospitalization, increasing perceived control prior to, pp. 430–431

Hostility and anger, control of, pp. 332–333

Hypertension, control of, pp. 329–330

Nutrition, pp. 236–243

Optimism
  and coping with cancer, p. 367
  and immune system health, pp. 138–139

Personal control and self-efficacy, pp. 189–190

Reducing cholesterol, pp. 330–331

Relaxation, pp. 150–151

Resilience, pp. 141–143

Self-efficacy beliefs in safer sex behaviors, pp. 403–404, 406

Self-regulation, pp. 140–141, 489

Smoking
  and effects of, pp. 295–296
  inoculation programs, p. 299

Social support
  and cancer, p. 371
  and cardiovascular disease, p. 328
  and health and mortality, p. 146
  and physiology, p. 156

Work site wellness programs, pp. 181–182

TRADEMARK FEATURES OF THIS TEXT

In an effort to communicate the excitement and value of the field, I have maintained my focus on ensuring that students understand—rather than just memorize—the concepts that make up health psychology. The sixth edition retains the following key features:

- **Biopsychosocial approach.** The book follows the biopsychosocial model as the basic organizing template. Throughout, I have strived to convey how the components of this model interact dynamically in influencing the well-being of the *whole* person. Each chapter dealing with a specific health problem—cardiovascular disease, diabetes, cancer, or substance use/abuse, for example—presents a critical analysis of what we know to be the underlying biological, psychological, and social factors in the onset of the health problem, as well as how these factors affect the course of the disease and the outcome. My commitment to this interdisciplinary *systems* perspective on behavior stems from my eclectic graduate training (or, some would say, my inability to make up my mind as to which career path I would follow!) as a student of learning theorist Herbert Terrace, physiological psychologist Richard Thompson, and social psychologist (and health psychology pioneer) Stanley Schachter.

- **Up-to-date coverage.** Few psychological disciplines generate more research each year—and from such a wide variety of related fields—than does health psychology. I have retained the field's classic studies and concepts, but I have also presented the most important recent developments. More than 25% of the references cited in this sixth edition are from research published since 2015. Across the chapters, health statistics have been updated with the most recent demographic and prevalence information available.

- **Fully integrated gender and cultural diversity coverage.** One of my major goals has been to promote understanding of and respect for differences among groups of people—and how these differences affect health and illness. This effort extends beyond merely cataloging ethnic, cultural, and gender differences in disease, health beliefs, and behaviors. I have made an in-depth effort to stimulate students' critical thinking regarding the origins of these differences. For example, many differences in health-related behaviors are the product of restrictive social stereotypes and norms, economic forces, and other overarching ecological processes. Whenever possible, the text digs deeply into diversity issues by considering the origins of these behaviors and their implications for health-promoting treatments and interventions. Examples of this integrated coverage are provided in Tables 1, 3, and 4 on pages xv–xvi. The *Diversity and Healthy Living* boxes found throughout the text expand the integrated coverage of gender and multicultural issues by highlighting specific health issues. For example, students will explore why children born to low-SES immigrants seem to do better in health and cognition than native-born children of the same ethnicity and income, and they'll learn about cultural differences that become apparent as people adapt to Type 2 diabetes interventions.

- **The life-course perspective.** In integrated coverage throughout the text, students will learn about the special needs and health challenges of people in every season of life. As with gender and diversity, my approach is to teach students to think critically about aging and health. Increasingly, researchers are realizing that much of what was once considered normal aging is actually disease. Many older people who have made healthy lifestyle choices are "rewriting the book" on successful aging. The choices people make as children and adolescents may determine their fate in later years. Table 2 on page xv directs readers to examples of coverage of life-span issues.

- **Coverage of complementary and alternative medicine.** Nearly half of all Americans use acupuncture, massage therapy, naturopathy, or some other form of nontraditional medicine. Chapter 15 carefully explores the validity of these high-interest, alternative interventions.

In addition, the sixth edition retains these effective pedagogical features:

- *Your Health Assets* boxes give students self-testing opportunities to connect the material to their own experiences.

- *Interpreting Data* boxes help students become more comfortable with the crucial quantitative component of research in a health psychology context.

- The *Weigh In on Health* feature at the end of each chapter emphasizes critical thinking to help students assess their understanding of material and make meaningful connections between the course and their own life experiences.

■ **Helpful study aids.** This text is designed to bring health psychology alive and reinforce learning at every step. The book's clean, student-friendly visual appeal is enhanced by numerous clear graphs of research findings, useful and interesting photos, and compelling artwork that illustrates anatomical structures as well as important concepts and processes. In addition, each chapter includes the following learning aids:

— An engaging **case study** or **vignette** at the beginning of each chapter connects the world of health psychology to some concrete experience and weaves a thread of human interest throughout the chapter. All of these case studies describe real situations. For example, Chapter 11 describes my own family's life-changing battle against the cancer that threatened my young son's life.

— Specific **learning outcomes** are listed at the beginning of each chapter.

— All important **terms** are boldfaced in the body of the text and are defined concisely and clearly in the margins near their first appearance, to enhance students' study efforts. All **key terms** and **concepts to remember** are listed, with their page numbers, at the end of each chapter.

— **End-of-chapter summaries** distill the important points, concepts, theories, and terms discussed in the chapters.

THE MULTIMEDIA SUPPLEMENTS PACKAGE

As an instructor and a supplements author, I know firsthand the importance to a textbook of a good, comprehensive teaching package. Fortunately, Worth Publishers has a well-deserved reputation for producing the best psychology supplements around, for both faculty and students. The *Health Psychology* supplements package includes several valuable components, described next.

Instructor's Resource Manual

The digital ***Instructor's Resource Manual*** accompanying *Health Psychology,* Sixth Edition, features chapter-by-chapter previews and lectures, learning objectives, suggestions for planning and teaching health psychology, ideas for projects, new iClicker questions, and more. The *Instructor's Resource Manual* is available for download at www.macmillanlearning.com/psychology

Downloadable Computerized Test Bank in Diploma

The comprehensive ***Test Bank***, based on my classroom experience and testing, contains well over 1,000 multiple-choice and short-answer essay questions, each keyed to the American Psychological Association's goals for the undergraduate psychology major and Bloom's Taxonomy. The Test Bank contains a wide variety of applied, conceptual, and factual questions, and each item is keyed to the topic and page in the text on which its answer can be found. The Test Bank is available for download at www.macmillanlearning.com/psychology

Illustration and Lecture Slides

The *Lecture Slides* to accompany *Health Psychology*, Sixth Edition, focus on key terms and themes from the text, and they feature tables, graphs, and figures.

The *Illustration Slides* include all the illustrations, photos, and tables featured in the text. All slides can be used as they are or customized to fit course needs. All slides are available for download at www.macmillanlearning.com/psychology

LaunchPad for *Health Psychology*

The LaunchPad for *Health Psychology* offers a variety of simulations, tutorials, and study aids organized by chapter, including the following:

- **NEW e-book.** The Health Psychology LaunchPad now offers the complete sixth edition mobile compatible e-book for students to access anywhere.

- *Health Psychology video activities.* These are a collection of video clips spanning the topics in the book, with each clip followed by brief questions assessing students' understanding of the clip.

- **Check Your Health.** These inherently interesting, automatically tallying self-assessments allow students to examine their own health beliefs and behaviors. For example, students will learn about their stress-management style, their ability to control anger, and potential high-risk health behaviors. Each exercise also gives specific tips that encourage students to manage their own health more actively.

- **Online quizzing.** This helpful feature offers multiple-choice quizzes tied to each of the book's chapters.

- **Critical thinking exercises.** The text has two major goals: (1) to help students acquire a thorough understanding of health psychology's knowledge base and (2) to help students learn to think like health psychologists. The second goal—learning to think like psychologists—involves critical thinking. To support this goal directly, the LaunchPad Solo for *Health Psychology* includes a complete exercise for each chapter, designed to stimulate students' critical-thinking skills. These skills include asking questions, observing carefully, seeing connections among ideas, and analyzing arguments and the evidence on which they are based.

- **Interactive flashcards.** Students can use these flashcards for tutoring on all text terminology, and then to quiz themselves on those terms.

- **PsychSim: Interactive Exercises for Psychology.** Key modules from these series (by Thomas Ludwig, a psychology professor at Hope College) allow students to explore research topics, participate in experiments and simulations, and apply health psychology to real-world issues.

- **Concept Practice.** Key selections from the Concept Practice collection offer dynamic, interactive mini-tutorials that teach and reinforce foundational ideas.

LaunchPad for *Health Psychology* is available for packaging with the sixth edition of *Health Psychology*. Alternatively, LaunchPad for *Health Psychology* can be previewed and purchased at launchpadworks.com

ACKNOWLEDGMENTS

Although as the author my name is on the cover of this book, I certainly did not write the book alone. Writing a textbook is a complex task involving the collaborative efforts of a large number of very talented people.

Many of my colleagues played a role in helping me develop this text over the years. I am indebted to the dozens of academic reviewers who read part or all of this book, providing constructive criticism, suggestions, or just an encouraging word. Their input made this a much better book, and I hope they forgive me for the few suggestions not followed.

I begin by thanking the following reviewers for their excellent advice and encouraging words in the creation of this thoroughly revised **sixth edition** and its multimedia supplements:

Judith Andersen
University of Toronto Mississauga

Karen L. Baker
University of Memphis Lambuth

Austin Baldwin
Southern Methodist University

Devin E. Banks
Indiana University—Purdue University Indianapolis

Jessica Barnack-Tavlaris
The College of New Jersey

Olivia Bogucki
University of Maine

Brittany M. Brothers
Indiana University Bloomington

Alison Buchanan
Henry Ford College

Michele Camden
Stetson University

Ellen-ge Denton
City University of New York—College of Staten Island

Marc A. Dingman
The Pennsylvania State University

Angela Duncan
Washburn University

Deborah Flynn
Nipissing University

Aaron J. Godlaski
Centre College

Christine Guardino
Dickinson College

Charlie L. Harris
Clayton State University

Rob Hoff
Mercyhurst University

Bianca Jardin
Francis Marion University

Sasha Karnes
University of Wisconsin

Glenn P. Kent
Jefferson College of Health Sciences

Mukti Khanna
The Evergreen State College

Colleen Lewy
Portland State University

Raylene Paludneviciene
Gallaudet University

Crystal Park
University of Connecticut

Scott Perkins
Abilene Christian University

Michael Rader
Johnson County Community College

Jenna L. Scisco
Eastern Connecticut State University

Barbara Stetson
University of Louisville

Melanie Tabak
Kent State University

Holly Tatum
Randolph College

Amy B. Wachholtz
University of Colorado Denver

Michelle Williams
Holyoke Community College

Ilona Yim
University of California, Irvine

At Worth Publishers—a company that lets nothing stand in the way of producing the finest textbooks possible—a number of people played key roles. Chief among these are Vice President of Content Management Catherine Woods, whose initial interest, vision, and unflagging support gave me the push needed to start the project and sustained me throughout; Senior Associate Editor Sarah Berger, whose hands-on approach and attention to detail were key factors in building our new team and the conceptualization and execution of this edition; Director of Content Management Enhancement Tracey Kuehn, Senior Managing Editor Lisa Kinne, Senior Content Project Manager Kerry O'Shaughnessy, Senior Project Manager Vanavan Jayaraman, and Senior Workflow Project Manager Lisa McDowell, who all worked wonders throughout production to keep us on course; Art Manager Matthew McAdams, Design Services Manager Natasha Wolfe, and Cover Designer John Callahan, whose creative vision resulted in the distinctive design and beautiful art program that exceeded my expectations; Editorial Assistant Dorothy Tomasini, who meticulously prepared manuscript for production and commissioned reviews and surveys to inform the revision; Executive Marketing Manager Katherine Nurre, who has championed *Health Psychology* since its second edition; and Senior Photo Editor Cecilia Varas and Photo Researcher Kerri Wilson, who researched the photos that help give the book its tremendous visual appeal. Finally, credit is due to Development Editor Elsa Peterson. Her skillful editing can be observed on virtually every page.

As ever, my heartfelt thanks go to Pam for her unwavering confidence and support, and to the many students who studied health psychology with me and assisted in the class testing of this book. They are a constant reminder of the enormous privilege and responsibilities I have as a teacher; it is for them that I have done my best to bring the field of health psychology alive in this text.

To those of you who are about to teach using this book, I sincerely hope that you will share your experiences with me. Drop me a line and let me know what works, what doesn't, and how you would do it differently. This input will be vital in determining the book's success and in shaping its future.

Richard O. Straub
University of Michigan, Dearborn
Dearborn, MI 48128
rostraub@umich.edu

Part **1** FOUNDATIONS OF HEALTH PSYCHOLOGY

Introducing Health Psychology

Chapter 1

Caiaimage/Getty Images

LEARNING OUTCOMES

Once you have studied this chapter, you will be able to:

- Describe how views of health and illness have changed over the course of human history,
- Identify and define the various perspectives from which health psychologists work, and
- Describe the training health psychologists receive and the kinds of work they do.

Caroline Flynn stepped aboard a 32-ton steamer on what must have been an uncertain morning in the early 1880s. Bound for the United States, she began her journey of hope in Liverpool, England, in a desperate attempt to escape the economic distress and religious persecution that she and her family suffered in Ireland. The country's troubles had begun decades earlier with a famine caused by the potato fungus that destroyed the primary—and often only—food of most Irish families.

Caroline's journey was hardly unique. Between 1861 and 1926, four million Irish left the country for similar reasons. After a harrowing five- to six-week voyage across the Atlantic, crowded with other emigrants into a steerage compartment that was rarely cleaned, they endured the humiliating processing of immigrants upon landing in New York. Many of those who were sick, or who lacked financial means or sponsors, were forced to return to their homeland.

As Caroline resolutely made her way in her adopted country, first north to upstate New York and then west to Chicago, she found that things were better, but life was still hard. Like everyone of her generation, she was vulnerable to the dangers of drinking impure water; eating contaminated foods; or becoming infected with typhoid fever, diphtheria, or one of the many other diseases that were prevalent in those days. Medical treatment was expensive, if available at all. Despite Caroline's vigilance, her survival (and later that of her husband and newborn baby) remained uncertain. Life expectancy was

Fotosearch/Getty Images

About 12 million immigrants to the United States would pass through lower Manhattan, including the author's great-grandmother.

less than 50 years, and one of every six babies died before his or her first birthday. "It would keep you poor, just burying your children," wrote one Irishwoman to her family back home (Miller & Miller, 2001). Equally troubling was the attitude of many native-born Americans, who viewed the Irish as inferior, violent, and drunken. Most of the new immigrants toiled as laborers in the lowest-paid and most dangerous occupations, and they were banished to ghettolike "Paddy" towns that sprang up on the outskirts of cities such as New York and Chicago.

More than a century later, I smile as my mother recounts the saga of my great-grandmother's emigration to the United States. Her grandmother lived a long, productive life and left a legacy of optimism and "indomitable Irishy" that fortified her against the hardships in her life—and carried down through the generations. "How different things are now," I think as our phone call ends, "but how much of Caroline's spirit is still alive in my own children!"

Things are very different now. Advances in hygiene, public health measures, and microbiology have virtually eradicated the infectious diseases that Caroline feared most. Women born in North America today enjoy a life expectancy of over 81 years, and men on average reach the age of 77. This gift of time has helped us realize that health is much more than freedom from illness. More than ever before, we can get beyond survival mode and work to attain lifelong vitality by modifying our diets, exercising regularly, and remaining socially connected and emotionally centered.

health psychology The application of psychological principles and research to the enhancement of health and the prevention and treatment of illness.

My great-grandmother's story makes clear that many factors interact in determining health. This is a fundamental theme of **health psychology,** a relatively new field that applies psychological principles and research to the enhancement of health and the treatment and prevention of illness. Its concerns include social conditions (such as the availability of health care and support from family and friends), biological factors (such as family longevity and inherited vulnerabilities to certain diseases), and even personality traits (such as optimism).

The word *health* comes from an old German word that is represented, in English, by the words *hale* and *whole,* both of which refer to a state of "soundness of body." Linguists note that these words derive from the medieval battlefield, where loss of *haleness,* or health, was usually the result of grave bodily injury. Today, we are more likely to think of health as the absence of disease rather than as the absence of a debilitating battlefield injury. Because this definition focuses only on the absence of a negative state, however, it is incomplete. Although it is true that healthy people are free of disease, complete health involves much more. A person may be free of disease but still not enjoy a vigorous, satisfying life. **Health** involves physical as well as psychological and social well-being.

health A state of complete physical, mental, and social well-being.

We are fortunate to live in a time when most of the world's citizens have the promise of a longer and better life than their great-grandparents, with far less disability and disease than ever before. However, these health benefits are not universally enjoyed. Consider the following:

- The number of years a person born today can expect to live differs substantially from country to country, ranging from about 79 to 81 years in high-income countries such as the United States and Canada to well under 50 years in very poor countries such as Sierra Leone and Chad (World Bank, 2018).

- In general, people who live in cities and are members of ethnic majorities enjoy better health than those who live in rural areas and are members of disadvantaged minority groups (Meit and others, 2014; Centers for Disease Control [CDC], 2017e).

- Women continue to face a number of unique challenges to their health, as do lesbian, gay, bisexual, and transgender individuals (LGBT) and those who belong to other marginalized groups (Logie, James, Wangari, & Loutfy, 2012).

- At every age, these and other **health disparities** abound. Among American men and women, those of European ancestry have a longer life expectancy than African Americans, but both groups have shorter life expectancies than people in Japan, Canada, Australia, the United Kingdom, Italy, France, and many other countries (Kochanek, Murphy, & Xu, 2015). It is estimated that nearly 1 million deaths each year in the United States (among all age groups) are preventable (see Table 1.1).

- Beginning in middle age, women have higher disease and disability rates than men (U.S. Census Bureau [USCB], 2012).

- Despite having the world's most expensive health care system, the United States ranks worst among 11 wealthy nations as measured by such factors as life expectancy, efficiency, and accessibility to quality health care by all individuals (Schneider, Sarnak, Squires, Shah, & Doty, 2017).

health disparities Preventable differences in the burden of disease, injury, violence, or opportunities to achieve optimal health that are experienced by socially disadvantaged populations.

These statistics reveal some of the challenges in the quest for global wellness. Health professionals are working to reduce the 30-year discrepancy in life expectancy between developed and developing countries; to help adolescents make a safe, healthy transition

---

TABLE 1.1 Preventable Injury and Death

- Control of underage use and excess use of alcohol could prevent 100,000 deaths from automobile accidents and other alcohol-related injuries.
- Elimination of public possession of firearms could prevent 35,000 deaths.
- Elimination of all forms of tobacco use could prevent 400,000 deaths from cancer, stroke, and heart disease.
- Better nutrition and exercise programs could prevent 300,000 deaths from heart disease, diabetes, cancer, and stroke.
- A reduction in risky sexual behaviors could prevent 30,000 deaths from sexually transmitted diseases.
- Full access to immunizations for infectious diseases could prevent 100,000 deaths.

Data from: U.S. Department of Health and Human Services, *Healthy People 2020*. Retrieved from www.healthypeople.gov.

to adulthood; and to achieve a deeper understanding of the relationships among gender, ethnicity, sociocultural status, and health.

In the United States, the Department of Health and Human Services report entitled *Healthy People 2020* identifies specific actions and targets for improving access to health services, eliminating health disparities, reducing chronic diseases such as cancer and diabetes, improving health in people of all ages, preventing injuries and violence, and taking steps in 32 other areas (see Table 1.2). Specifically, the overarching goals are to do the following:

- attain high-quality, longer lives free of preventable disease, disability, injury, and premature death;
- achieve health equity, eliminate disparities, and improve the health of all groups;
- create social and physical environments that promote good health for all; and
- promote quality of life, healthy development, and healthy behaviors across all life stages.

TABLE 1.2 Select Topic Area Goals and Targets of *Healthy People 2020*

Adolescent Health

- Increase the proportion of adolescents who have had a wellness checkup in the past 12 months (target: 75.6%)
- Reduce the proportion of adolescents who have been offered, sold, or given an illegal drug on school property (target: 20.4%)

Physical Activity

- Increase the proportion of adults who engage in aerobic physical activity of at least moderate intensity for at least 150 minutes/week, or 75 minutes/week of vigorous intensity, or an equivalent combination
- Increase the proportion of the nation's public and private schools that require daily physical education for all students

Nutrition and Weight Status

- Increase the proportion of schools that do not sell or offer calorically sweetened beverages to students (target: 21.3%)
- Increase the proportion of adults who are at a healthy weight (target: 33.9%)

Injury and Violence Prevention

- Reduce unintentional injury deaths (target: 36.0 deaths per 100,000 population)
- Reduce motor vehicle crash–related deaths (target: 12.4 deaths per 100,000 population)

Sleep Health

- Increase the proportion of adults who get sufficient sleep (target: 70.9%)
- Reduce the rate of vehicular crashes per 100 million miles traveled that are due to drowsy driving (target: 2.1 vehicular crashes per 100 million miles traveled)

Data from: U.S. Department of Health and Human Services, *Healthy People 2020*. Retrieved from www.healthypeople.gov.

To help the nation meet these goals, on March 23, 2010, President Barack Obama signed the **Patient Protection and Affordable Care Act (PPACA),** the most significant overhaul of the U.S. health care system in nearly 50 years. The primary goals of the law are to decrease the number of people who do not have health insurance and to lower the costs of health care. Other reforms are aimed at improving health care outcomes and streamlining the delivery of health care. In addition, under PPACA, insurers are required to cover certain types of preventive care at no cost to the consumer, including blood pressure and cholesterol tests, mammograms, colonoscopies, and screenings for osteoporosis. In late 2017 Congress passed a bill, to become effective in 2019, repealing the requirement that people who do not have health insurance must pay a tax penalty.

With the foregoing background material kept in mind, this chapter introduces the field of health psychology, which plays an increasingly important role in meeting the world's health challenges. Consider a few of the more specific questions that health psychologists seek to answer: How do people's attitudes, beliefs, self-confidence, and personality affect their physiology and their overall health? What role do social support, positive emotions, and relationships play in optimal health and well-being? Why are so many people turning to acupuncture, yoga, dietary supplements, and other forms of alternative medicine, as well as do-it-yourself preventive care? Do these interventions really work? Why do so many people ignore unquestionably sound advice for improving their health, such as quitting smoking, moderating food intake, and exercising more? Why are certain health problems more likely to occur among people of a particular age, gender, or ethnic group? Why is being poor, uneducated, or lonely a potentially serious threat to a person's health? Conversely, why do those who are relatively affluent, well educated, and socially active enjoy better health?

Health psychology is the science that seeks to answer these and many other questions about how people's wellness interacts with how they think, feel, and act. We begin by taking a closer look at the concept of health and how it has changed over the course of history. Next, we'll examine the biopsychosocial and systems theory perspectives on health. Finally, we'll take a look at the training needed to become a health psychologist and what you can do with that training.

Patient Protection and Affordable Care Act (PPACA) A federal law aimed at reducing the number of people in the United States who do not have health insurance, as well as lowering the costs of health care.

HEALTH AND ILLNESS: LESSONS FROM THE PAST

Although all human civilizations have been affected by disease, each one has understood and treated it differently (Figure 1.1).

From Ancient Times Through the Renaissance

Our efforts at healing can be traced back 20,000 years. In southern France, for example, a cave painting that is believed to be 17,000 years old depicts an Ice Age shaman wearing the animal mask of an ancient witch doctor. In religions based on a belief in good and evil spirits, only a shaman (priest or medicine man) can influence these spirits.

MIGUEL MEDINA/Getty Images

Science Source/Science Source

ANCIENT GREECE Illness caused by an imbalance of bodily humors; good diet and moderation in living would cure it.

PREHISTORIC PERIOD Illness caused by evil spirits and treated by trephination.

MIDDLE AGES (476–1450) Disease was divine punishment for sins, cured by miraculous intervention, invoking of saints, as well as bloodletting.

1800s Disease caused by microscopic organisms. Treatment was surgery and immunization.

TWENTY-FIRST CENTURY Biopsychosocial causes of disease. Modern, flexible methods of treatment.

B.C.E. | 10,000 | 5000 | 2000 | 1000 | C.E. | 200 | 500 | 1000 | 1100 | 1400 | 1500 | 1600 | 1700 | 1800 | 1900 | 1960 | 1980 | 2000

ANCIENT EGYPT Demons and punishment by the gods caused illness. Sorcery and primitive forms of surgery and hygiene were treatments.

ANCIENT ROME (200 B.C.E.) "Pathogens" such as bad air and body humors caused illness. Treated by bloodletting, enemas, and baths.

1920s Disease influenced by mind and emotions and treated by psychoanalysis, psychiatry, and other medical methods.

ANCIENT CHINA (1100–200 B.C.E.) Unbalanced forces of nature caused illness. Treated with herbal medicine and acupuncture.

RENAISSANCE Disease was a physical condition of the body, which was separate from the mind. Surgical techniques first used.

FLHC 20/Alamy Stock Photo

ADRIAEN BROUWER/akg-images

FIGURE 1.1 A Timeline of Historical and Cultural Variations in Illness and Healing From the ancient use of trephination to remove evil spirits to the current use of noninvasive brain scans to diagnose disease, the treatment of health problems has seen major advances over the centuries. A collection of treatments across the ages is shown (from left to right): trephination (on an ancient Peruvian skull); acupuncture from China; early surgery in seventeenth-century Europe; and English physician and pioneer of vaccination Edward Jenner vaccinating his young child.

For preindustrial men and women, confronted with the often-hostile forces of their environment, survival was based on constant vigilance against these mysterious forces of evil. When a person became sick, there was no obvious physical reason for it. Rather, the stricken individual's condition was misattributed to weakness in the face of a stronger force, to bewitchment, or to possession by an evil spirit.

During this period of time, sick people were often treated with rituals of sorcery, exorcism, or even a primitive form of surgery called *trephination*. Archaeologists have unearthed prehistoric human skulls containing irregularly shaped holes that were apparently drilled by early healers to allow disease-causing demons to leave patients' bodies. Historical records indicate that trephination was practiced in Europe, Egypt, India, and Central and South America.

Ancient healers did search for a more rational understanding of how the human body functioned. Given the importance of the Nile River, it is not surprising that Egyptian healers drew parallels with how its channels were used to irrigate farmers' fields. The Nile Theory reflects their belief that the body had similar channels carrying air, water, and blood, and that people became sick when blockages occurred.

In Greece, the philosopher and physician Hippocrates (460–377 B.C.E.) also rebelled against the ancient focus on mysticism and superstition. Hippocrates, who is often called the father of Western medicine, was the first to argue that disease is a natural phenomenon and that the causes of disease (and therefore their treatment and prevention) are knowable and worthy of serious study. In this way, he built the earliest foundation for a scientific approach to healing. Historically, physicians took the Hippocratic Oath, with which they swore to practice medicine ethically. Over the centuries, the oath has been rewritten to suit the values of various cultures that were influenced by Greek medicine.

Hippocrates proposed the first rational explanation of why people get sick. According to his **humoral theory,** a healthy body and mind resulted from equilibrium among four bodily fluids called humors: blood, yellow bile, black bile, and phlegm. To maintain a proper balance, a person had to follow a healthy lifestyle that included exercise, sufficient rest, a good diet, and the avoidance of excesses. When the humors were out of balance, however, both body and mind were affected in predictable ways, depending on which of the four humors was in excess. People suffering from headaches and anxiety, for example, might have been considered choleric, with an excess of yellow bile and a fiery temperament. They might have been treated with bloodletting (opening a vein to remove blood), liquid diets, enemas, and cooling baths.

humoral theory A concept of health proposed by Hippocrates that considered wellness a state of perfect equilibrium among four basic body fluids, called *humors*. Sickness was believed to be the result of disturbances in the balance of humors.

Although humoral theory was discarded as advances were made in anatomy, physiology, and microbiology, the notion of personality traits being linked with body fluids still persists in many folk and alternative medicine traditions, including those of Asian and Native American cultures. Moreover, as we'll see in Chapter 2, we now know that many diseases involve an imbalance (of sorts) among the brain's neurotransmitters, so Hippocrates was not too far off. Hippocrates was also interested in patients' emotions and thoughts regarding their health and treatment, and thus he called attention to the psychological aspects of health and illness. "It is better to know the patient who has the disease," Hippocrates said, "than it is to know the disease which the patient has" (quoted in Wesley, 2003).

At the same time that Western medicine was emerging, different traditions of healing were developing in other cultures. For example, more than 2,000 years ago, the Chinese developed an integrated system of healing, which we know today as *traditional Chinese medicine (TCM)*. TCM is founded on the principle that internal harmony is essential for good health. Fundamental to this harmony is the concept of *qi* (sometimes spelled *chi*), a vital energy or life force that ebbs and flows with changes in each person's mental, physical, and emotional well-being. Acupuncture, herbal therapy, tai chi, meditation, and other interventions are said to restore health by correcting blockages and imbalances in *qi*.

Ayurveda is the oldest-known medical system in the world, having originated in India around the sixth century B.C.E., coinciding roughly with the lifetime of the Buddha. The word *ayurveda* comes from the Sanskrit roots *ayuh,* which means "longevity," and *veda,* meaning "knowledge." Widely practiced in India, ayurveda is based on the belief that the human body represents the entire universe in a microcosm and that the key to health is maintaining a balance between the microcosmic body and the macrocosmic world. The key to this relationship is held in the balance of three bodily humors, or doshas: vata, pitta, and kapha, or, collectively, the tridosha. We'll explore the history, traditions, and effectiveness of these and other non-Western forms of medicine in Chapter 15.

The fall of the Roman Empire in the fifth century C.E. ushered in the Middle Ages (476–1450), an era characterized by a return to supernatural explanations of health and disease in Europe. Religious interpretations colored medieval scientists' ideas about health and disease. Illness was viewed as God's punishment for evildoing; and **epidemic** or **pandemic** diseases, such as the two great outbursts of plague (a bacterial disease carried by fleas that infest rats and other rodents) that occurred during the Middle Ages, were believed to be a sign of God's wrath. Medical "treatment" in this era often involved attempts to force evil spirits out of the body. There were few scientific advances in European medicine during these thousand years.

In the late fourteenth century, a new age—the Renaissance—was born. Beginning with the reemergence of scientific inquiry, this period saw the revitalization of anatomical study and medical practice. The taboo on human dissection was lifted sufficiently that the Flemish-born anatomist and artist Andreas Vesalius (1514–1564) was able to publish an authoritative, seven-volume study of the internal organs, musculature, and skeletal system of the human body. Descended from a family of physicians and apothecaries and himself the recipient of a medical degree, Vesalius was fascinated by nature, especially the anatomy of humans and animals.

One of the most influential Renaissance thinkers was the French philosopher and mathematician René Descartes (1596–1650), whose first innovation was the concept of the human body as a machine. He described all the basic reflexes of the body, constructing elaborate mechanical models to demonstrate his principles. He believed that disease occurred when the machine broke down, and the physician's task was to repair the machine.

Descartes is best known for his beliefs that the mind and body are autonomous processes that interact minimally, and that each is subject to different laws of causality. This viewpoint, which is called *mind–body dualism* (or *Cartesian dualism*), is based on the doctrine that humans have two natures, mental and physical. Descartes and other great thinkers of the Renaissance, in an effort to break with the mysticism and superstitions of the past, vigorously rejected the notion that the mind influences the body. Although this viewpoint ushered in a new age of medical research based on confidence in science and rational thinking, it created a lasting bias in Western medicine against the importance of psychological processes in health. As we'll see, this bias has been rapidly unraveling since the 1970s.

epidemic Literally, *among the people*; an epidemic disease is one that spreads rapidly among many individuals in a community at the same time.

pandemic A pandemic disease is one that affects people over a large geographical area, such as multiple continents or worldwide.

First Anatomical Drawings
By the sixteenth century, the taboo on human dissection had been lifted long enough that the Flemish anatomist and artist Andreas Vesalius (1514–1564) was able to publish a complete study of the internal organs, musculature, and skeletal system of the human body.

From Post-Renaissance Rationality through the Nineteenth Century

Following the Renaissance, physicians were expected to focus exclusively on the biological causes of disease. English physician William Harvey (1578–1657) offered the first detailed description of the circulation of blood, and he also noted that emotions were often associated with how the heart functioned. Physician and Quaker preacher John Fothergill (1656–1745) was noteworthy for being the first to identify diseases that affect the nerves and also for emphasizing the importance of practicing temperance and self-control in maintaining health. Surgeon John Hunter (1728–1793), one of the most distinguished scientists of his day, was an early advocate of careful observation and the importance of applying the scientific method in medicine. Although a ground lens had been used for magnification in ancient times, the first practical microscopes were developed in this era. This made it possible to view blood cells and the structure of skeletal muscles.

Once individual cells became visible, the stage was set for the *germ theory* of disease—the idea that bacteria, viruses, and other microorganisms that invade body cells cause them to malfunction. In the mid-nineteenth century, the French biologist and chemist Louis Pasteur conducted groundbreaking research in support of this concept. Germ theory forms the theoretical foundation of modern medicine and was followed by rapid advances in medical knowledge and procedures.

In 1846, William Morton (1819–1868), an American dentist, introduced the gas ether as an anesthetic. This great advance made it possible to operate on patients, who experienced no pain during procedures and thus remained completely relaxed. The German physicist Wilhelm Roentgen (1845–1943) discovered x-rays 50 years later, making it possible for the first time for physicians to directly observe internal organs in a living person. Before the end of the nineteenth century, researchers had identified the microorganisms that caused malaria, pneumonia, diphtheria, syphilis, typhoid, and other diseases that my great-grandmother's generation feared. Armed with this information, medicine began to bring under control diseases that had plagued the world since antiquity.

Gianni Dagli Orti/Shutterstock

Louis Pasteur in His Laboratory Pasteur's meticulous work in isolating bacteria in the laboratory, then showing that life can come only from existing life, paved the way for germ-free surgical procedures.

The Twentieth Century and the Dawn of a New Era

As the field of medicine continued to advance during the early part of the twentieth century, it looked more and more to physiology and anatomy, rather than to the study of thoughts and emotions, in its search for a deeper understanding of health and illness. Thus was born the **biomedical model** of health, which maintains that illness always has a biological cause. This model became widely accepted during the nineteenth century and continues to represent the dominant view in medicine today.

The biomedical model assumes that disease is the result of a **pathogen**—a virus, bacterium, or some other microorganism that invades the body. The model makes no provision for psychological, social, or behavioral variables in illness. In this sense, the biomedical model embraces *reductionism,* the view that complex phenomena (such as health and disease) derive ultimately from a single primary factor. The biomedical model is consistent with the doctrine of *mind–body dualism* that, as we have seen, considers the mind and the body as separate and autonomous entities that interact minimally.

biomedical model The dominant view of twentieth-century medicine that maintains that illness always has a physical cause.

pathogen A virus, bacterium, or some other microorganism that causes a particular disease.

Finally, according to the biomedical model, health is nothing more than the absence of disease. Accordingly, those who work from this perspective focus on investigating the causes of physical illnesses rather than on those factors that promote physical, psychological, and social vitality.

Psychosomatic Medicine

The biomedical model advanced health care significantly through its focus on pathogens. However, it was unable to explain disorders that had no observable physical cause, such as those uncovered by Sigmund Freud (1856–1939), who was initially trained as a physician. Freud's patients exhibited symptoms—such as loss of speech, deafness, numbness, and even paralysis—that could not be explained physiologically. Freud labeled such illnesses *conversion disorders,* as he believed they were caused by unconscious emotional conflicts that had been "converted" into a physical form.

In the 1940s, Franz Alexander advanced the idea that an individual's psychological conflicts could cause specific diseases. When physicians could find no infectious agent or other direct cause for rheumatoid arthritis, Alexander became intrigued by the possibility that psychological factors might be involved. According to his *nuclear conflict* model, each physical disease is the outcome of a fundamental, or nuclear, psychological conflict (Alexander, 1950). For example, individuals with a "rheumatoid personality," who tended to repress anger and were unable to express emotion, were believed to be prone to developing arthritis. Alexander helped establish **psychosomatic medicine,** a subfield of psychiatry named from the root words *psyche,* which means "mind," and *soma,* which means "body." Psychosomatic medicine is concerned with the diagnosis and treatment of physical diseases thought to be caused by faulty processes within the mind.

Psychosomatic medicine was intriguing and seemed to explain the unexplainable. However, it had several weaknesses that ultimately caused it to fall out of favor. Most significantly, psychosomatic medicine was grounded in Freudian theory. As Freud's emphasis on unconscious, irrational urges in personality formation lost popularity, the field of psychosomatic medicine faltered. Psychosomatic medicine, like the biomedical model, was also based on reductionism—in this case, the outmoded idea that a single psychological problem or personality flaw is sufficient to trigger disease. We now know that disease, like good health, is based on the combined interaction of multiple factors, including heredity and environment, as well as the individual's psychological makeup.

Although Freud's theories and psychosomatic medicine were flawed, they laid the groundwork for a renewed appreciation of the connections between medicine and psychology. This was the start of the contemporary trend toward viewing illness and health as *multifactorial.* That is, many diseases are caused by the interaction of several factors, rather than by a single, invading bacterial or viral agent. Among these are *host factors* (such as genetic vulnerability or resiliency), *environmental factors* (such as exposure to pollutants and hazardous chemicals), *behavioral factors* (such as diet, exercise, and smoking), and *psychological factors* (such as optimism and overall "hardiness").

Health Psychology Emerges

In 1973, the American Psychological Association (APA) appointed a task force to explore psychology's role in medicine, and in 1978, the APA created the division of health psychology (Division 38). Four years later, the first volume of its official journal, *Health*

psychosomatic medicine
A branch of psychiatry that developed in the 1900s and focused on the diagnosis and treatment of certain diseases believed to be caused by emotional conflicts.

TABLE 1.3 Twentieth-Century Trends That Shaped Health Psychology

Trend	Result
Increased life expectancy	Recognize the need to take better care of ourselves to promote vitality through a longer life
Rise of lifestyle disorders (for example, cancer, stroke, and heart disease)	Educate people to avoid the behaviors that contribute to these diseases (for example, smoking cigarettes and eating a high-fat diet)
Rising health care costs	Focus efforts on ways to prevent disease and maintain good health to avoid these costs
Rethinking the biomedical model	Develop a more comprehensive model of health and disease—the biopsychosocial approach

Psychology, was published. In this issue, Joseph Matarazzo (1982), the first president of the division, laid down the four goals of the new field:

- *To study scientifically the causes or origins of specific diseases,* that is, their **etiology.** Health psychologists are primarily interested in the psychological, behavioral, and social origins of disease. They investigate why people engage in *health-compromising behaviors,* such as smoking or unsafe sex.

- *To promote health.* Health psychologists consider ways to get people to engage in *health-enhancing behaviors,* such as exercising regularly and eating nutritious foods.

- *To prevent and treat illness.* Health psychologists design programs to help people stop smoking, lose weight, manage stress, and minimize other risk factors for poor health. They also assist those who are already ill in their efforts to adjust to their illnesses or comply with difficult treatment regimens.

- *To promote public health policy and the improvement of the health care system.* Health psychologists are very active in all facets of health education, and they consult frequently with government leaders who formulate public policy in an effort to improve the delivery of health care to all people.

As noted in Table 1.3, a number of twentieth-century trends helped shape the new field of health psychology, pushing it toward the broader **biopsychosocial model,** which is the focus of this text.

etiology The scientific study of the causes or origins of specific diseases.

biopsychosocial model The viewpoint that health and other behaviors are determined by the interaction of biological mechanisms, psychological processes, and social influences.

THE BIOPSYCHOSOCIAL MODEL

As history tells us, looking at just one causative factor paints an incomplete picture of a person's health or illness. As depicted in Figure 1.2, the biopsychosocial model recognizes that *bio*logical, *psycho*logical, and *sociocultural* forces act together to determine an individual's health and vulnerability to disease; that is, health and disease must be explained in terms of multiple contexts.

FIGURE 1.2 The Biopsychosocial Model According to the biopsychosocial perspective, all health behaviors are best explained in terms of three contexts: biological processes, psychological processes, and social influences. This diagram illustrates how these three processes could promote symptoms of anxiety.

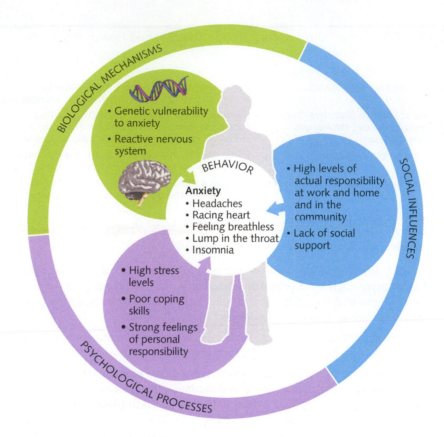

BIOLOGICAL MECHANISMS

- Genetic vulnerability to anxiety
- Reactive nervous system

BEHAVIOR

Anxiety
- Headaches
- Racing heart
- Feeling breathless
- Lump in the throat
- Insomnia

SOCIAL INFLUENCES

- High levels of actual responsibility at work and home and in the community
- Lack of social support

PSYCHOLOGICAL PROCESSES

- High stress levels
- Poor coping skills
- Strong feelings of personal responsibility

The Biological Context

All behaviors, including states of health and illness, occur in a biological context. Every thought, mood, and urge is a biological event made possible because of the characteristic anatomical structure and biological function of a person's body. Health psychology draws attention to those aspects of our bodies that influence health and disease: our genetic makeup and our nervous, immune, and endocrine systems (see Chapter 3).

Our genetic makeup has much to do with how healthy we are and what diseases we get. For example, a person can inherit the genetic component of a disease such as breast cancer that has multiple causes. As another example, the tendency to abuse alcohol has long been known to run in some families (see Chapter 9). Research has shown that alcohol dependency is at least partly genetic, although it does not seem to be linked to a single, specific gene. Instead, some people may inherit a greater sensitivity to alcohol's physical effects, experiencing intoxication as pleasurable and the aftermath of a hangover as minor. Such people may be more likely to drink, especially in certain psychological and social contexts.

The complete set of genetic instructions that make a living organism is called its *genome*. Rapid advances in the field of **genomics** (the study of genomes) reflect the increasing scientific evidence supporting the benefits of using genetic tests and family history to improve health. For example, women with high-risk family health history patterns for breast cancer may benefit from genetic testing for specific mutations, such as in the BRCA1 and BRCA2 genes; such testing would enable medical interventions to reduce the women's

genomics The study of the structure, function, and mapping of the genetic material of organisms.

risk of developing cancer. As genomic evidence mounts, these benefits have been incorporated as new target areas that appear in the U.S. Department of Health and Human Services' *Healthy People 2020* report (Healthy People 2020, 2013, 2014). One new goal is to "improve health and prevent harm through valid and useful genomic tools in clinical and public health practices" (Office of Disease Prevention and Health Promotion [ODPHP], 2018).

The Evolutionary Perspective

A key element of the biological context is our species' evolutionary history, and an *evolutionary perspective* guides the work of many health psychologists. Our characteristic human traits and behaviors exist as they do because they helped our distant ancestors survive long enough to reproduce and send their genes into the future. For example, natural selection has favored the tendency of people to become hungry in the presence of a mouthwatering aroma (see Chapter 8). This sensitivity to food-related cues makes evolutionary sense in that eating is necessary for survival—particularly in the distant past when food supplies were unpredictable and it was advantageous to have a healthy appetite when food was available.

At the same time, biology and behavior constantly interact. For example, some individuals are more vulnerable to stress-related illnesses because they react to daily hassles and other environmental "triggers" in an angry fashion (see Chapter 4). Among men, such reactivity is correlated with aggressive reaction related to increased amounts of the hormone testosterone. This relationship, however, is reciprocal: Angry outbursts can also lead to elevated testosterone levels. One of the tasks of health psychology is to explain how (and why) this mutual influence between biology and behavior occurs.

It is also important to recognize that biology and behavior do not occur in a vacuum. At first, the remarkable success of the Human Genome Project (International Human Genome Sequencing Consortium [IHGSC], 2001) in mapping all the genes that make up a person seemed to suggest that genes might determine everything—that every aspect of you, including your health, will become whatever you are biologically destined to be. We now know otherwise. It is true that genes influence all traits, both psychological and physical. But even identical twins, who share identical genes, do *not* have identical traits. Increasingly, we're learning that most important traits are **epigenetic.** Epigenetic effects occur throughout our lifetimes. Some "epi-" influences impede our chances for optimal health (e.g., environmental toxins, child abuse, and poverty), and some improve them (e.g., nourishing food, safe places to grow up, and education). One example of this type of gene–environment interaction comes from research on the *MAOA* gene, which codes for an enzyme that affects key neurotransmitters in the brain. Boys who inherit one variation of the gene and girls who inherit a different variation of the same gene are more likely to engage in high-risk delinquent behavior as adolescents, but only if they were exposed to the "epi-" effect of maltreatment as children (Aslund and others, 2011). The variations in question are *gene promoters,* regions of DNA that regulate the expression of that gene.

> **epigenetic** The effects of environmental forces on how genes are expressed.

As another example, consider *DNA methylation,* a biochemical process that occurs in cells and is essential to the healthy functioning of nearly every body system. Occurring billions of times each second, methylation helps regulate the expression of genes that repair DNA, keep inflammation in check, and promote healthy blood vessels. A breakdown in methylation may promote the development of cancer, diabetes, and cardiovascular disease, and it may even accelerate aging (Alashwal, Dosunmu, & Zawia, 2012). The degree of methylation changes over the life span and is also influenced by "epi-" effects such as diet, tobacco use, and exposure to environmental toxins (Davis & Uthus, 2004).

These examples of epigenetic research demonstrate that *gene–environment* effects are always important. Some genes are *expressed* and affect our health, while some genes are *silenced* and remain unnoticed from one generation to the next unless circumstances, such as the quality of nurturing during childhood, change (Riddihough & Zahn, 2010; Skipper, 2011).

Life-Course Perspective

Within the biological context, the *life-course perspective* in health psychology focuses on important age-related aspects of health and illness. This perspective would consider, for example, how a pregnant woman's malnutrition, smoking, or use of psychoactive drugs would affect her child's lifelong development.

The life-course perspective also considers the leading causes of death in terms of the age groups affected. In high-income countries such as the United States and Canada, the top three leading causes of death are stroke, heart disease, and lung cancer (Institute for Health Metrics and Evaluation [IHME], 2018). However, the profile of leading causes of death varies by age group. The chronic diseases that are the leading causes of death in the overall population are more likely to affect middle-aged and elderly adults. Young people between the ages of 1 and 24 are much more likely to die from external causes that include accidents, homicide, and suicide, followed by cancer and heart disease (see Figure 1.3).

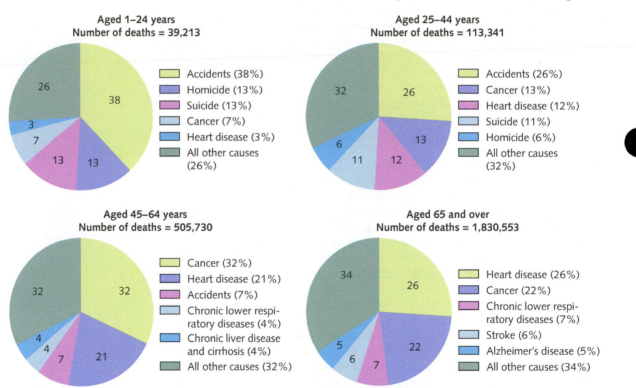

FIGURE 1.3 The Leading Causes of Death in the United States by Age Group The five leading causes of death in young people include external causes (accidents, homicide, and suicide), followed by cancer and heart disease. This pattern of external causes accounting for more deaths than chronic conditions changes as people get older. In older age groups, chronic conditions account for more deaths than do external causes. For example, accidents account for more than one third of all deaths among persons aged 1–24 years. Accidental deaths are rarer in older age groups and do not even rank as one of the five leading causes of death in people 65 years and older.

Data from: Murphy, S. L., Kochanek, K. D., Xu, J. Q., & Heron. M. (2015). Deaths: Final data for 2012. *National Vital Statistics Reports*, 63(9). Hyattsville, MD: National Center for Health Statistics.

The Psychological Context

The central message of health psychology is, of course, that health and illness are subject to psychological influences. Our personal health practices and behaviors are key determinants of our health. These, in turn, are strongly influenced by our beliefs and attitudes. Our diet, sexual activity, and use of tobacco and other drugs may contribute to the development of heart disease, sexually transmitted infections, cancer, and other unhealthy conditions.

A key factor in how well a person copes with a stressful life experience is how the event is appraised or interpreted (see Chapters 4 and 5). Events that are appraised as overwhelming, pervasive, and beyond our control take a much greater toll on us physically and psychologically than do events that are appraised as minor challenges that are temporary and surmountable. Indeed, some evidence suggests that, whether a stressful event is actually experienced or merely imagined, the body's stress response is nearly the same. Health psychologists think that some people may be more susceptible to certain health problems because they replay stressful events over and over again in their minds, which may be functionally equivalent to repeatedly encountering the actual event. The field of *positive psychology* has given rise to many studies of the importance of **subjective well-being**—our feelings of happiness and sense of satisfaction with life (see Table 1.4). Throughout this book, we will examine the health implications of thinking, perception, motivation, emotion, learning, attention, memory, and other topics of central importance to psychology.

Psychological factors also play an important role in the treatment and management of chronic conditions. The effectiveness of all health care interventions—including medication and surgery, as well as acupuncture and other alternative treatments—is powerfully

subjective well-being The cognitive and emotional evaluations of a person's life.

TABLE 1.4 Testing Yourself: Subjective Well-Being

The WHO-5 Well-Being Index (WHO-5) is a self-report mood questionnaire developed by the World Health Organization's Collaborating Center in Mental Health.

For each statement, please indicate which is closest to how you have been feeling over the last two weeks. For example, if you have felt cheerful and in good spirits more than half of the time during the last two weeks, put a tick in the box with the number 3 beside it.

	Over the Last Two Weeks	All of the Time	Most of the Time	More Than Half of the Time	Less Than Half of the Time	Some of the Time	At No Time
1.	I have felt cheerful and in good spirits.	☐5	☐4	☐3	☐2	☐1	☐0
2.	I have felt calm and relaxed.	☐5	☐4	☐3	☐2	☐1	☐0
3.	I have felt active and vigorous.	☐5	☐4	☐3	☐2	☐1	☐0
4.	I woke up feeling fresh and rested.	☐5	☐4	☐3	☐2	☐1	☐0
5.	My daily life has been filled with things that interest me.	☐5	☐4	☐3	☐2	☐1	☐0

The raw score is calculated by totaling the figures of the five answers. The raw score ranges from 0 to 25, 0 representing worst possible and 25 representing best possible quality of life. A score below 13 indicates poor subjective well-being and may indicate the need for additional testing for depression.

Data from: Bech, P. (2004). Measuring the dimensions of psychological general well-being by the WHO-5. *Quality of Life Newsletter, 32,* 15–16.

The field of *positive psychology* has given rise to many studies of the importance of our feelings of well-being and our sense of satisfaction with life.

influenced by a patient's attitude. Patients who believe a drug or other treatment will only cause miserable side effects may experience considerable tension, which can actually worsen their physical response to the treatment. This reaction can set up a vicious cycle in which escalating anxiety before treatment is followed by progressively worse physical reactions as the treatment regimen proceeds. On the other hand, patient who are confident that a treatment will be effective may actually experience a greater therapeutic response to that treatment.

Psychological interventions can help patients learn to manage their tension, thereby lessening negative reactions to treatment. Patients who are more relaxed are usually better able, and more motivated, to follow their doctor's instructions. Psychological interventions can also assist patients in managing the everyday stresses of life, which seem to exert a cumulative effect on the immune system. Negative life events such as bereavement, divorce, job loss, and relocation have been linked to decreased immune functioning and increased susceptibility to illness. By teaching patients more effective ways of managing unavoidable stress, health psychologists may help those patients' immune systems combat disease.

The Social Context

Turn-of-the-century Irish immigrants like my great-grandmother surmounted poverty and prejudice in the United States by establishing Irish American associations that strongly reflected an ethic of family and communal support. "Each for himself, but all for one another," wrote recent immigrant Patrick O'Callaghan to his sister back home (Miller & Miller, 2001), as he described this system of patronage. In placing health behavior in its social context, health psychologists consider the ways in which we think about, influence, and relate to one another and to our environments. Your gender, for example, entails a particular, socially prescribed role that represents your sense of being a woman or a man. In addition, you are a member of a particular family, community, and nation; you also have a certain racial, cultural, and ethnic identity, and you live within a specific socioeconomic class. You are influenced by the same historical and social factors as others in your **birth cohort**—a group of people born within a few years of each other.

Each of these elements of your unique social context affects your experiences and influences your beliefs and behaviors—including those related to health. For example, people who lived 100 years ago were more likely to die from *communicable diseases* that we in developed countries today consider preventable, such as tuberculosis and diphtheria (Table 1.5), and infant mortality in the United States has dropped significantly (Figure 1.4). These are **acute disorders** that are caused by infection and spread from person to person. Now, however, slowly developing **chronic illnesses,** such as heart disease and cancer, are the main causes of death and disability. Many are *noncommunicable diseases* that are not spread by infection and that people live with and manage with the help of health care providers, for years. The greatest burden of disease is predominantly

birth cohort A group of people who, because they were born at about the same time, experience similar historical and social conditions.

acute disorder An illness or other medical problem that occurs over a short period of time.

chronic illness An illness that lasts a long time and is usually irreversible.

TABLE 1.5 Leading Causes of Death in the United States, 1900 and 2015

Disease in 1900	Percent of All Deaths	Disease in 2015*	Percent of All Deaths
Pneumonia	11.8	Heart disease	23.4
Tuberculosis	11.3	Cancer	22.0
Diarrhea and enteritis	8.3	Chronic lower respiratory disease	5.7
Heart disease	5.2	Accidents	5.4
Liver disease	5.2	Cerebrovascular disease	5.2
Accidents	4.2	Alzheimer's disease	4.1
Cancer	3.7	Diabetes	2.9
Senility	2.9	Influenza and pneumonia	2.1
Diphtheria	2.3	Kidney disease	1.8

*Note that the leading causes of death in 2015 were not new diseases; they were present in earlier times, but fewer people died from them then, or they were called something else.

Data from: Murphy, S. L., Xu, J., Kochanek, K. D., Curtin, S. C., & Arias, E. (2017). Deaths: Final data for 2015. *National Vital Statistics Reports, 66*(6). Hyattsville, MD: National Center for Health Statistics.

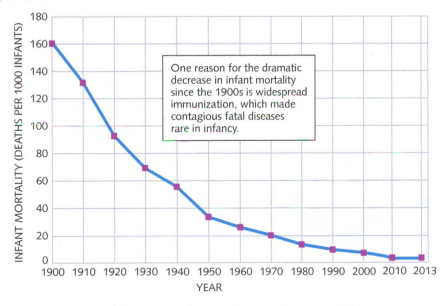

One reason for the dramatic decrease in infant mortality since the 1900s is widespread immunization, which made contagious fatal diseases rare in infancy.

FIGURE 1.4 Infant Mortality in the United States Less than a century ago, 15% of babies born in the United States died before their first birthday. For those who survived, life expectancy was only slightly more than 50 years. With improved health care, today more than 99% of newborn babies survive to at least 1 year of age.

Information and Data from: *Historical Statistics of the United States: Colonial Times to 1970*, by U.S. Bureau of the Census, 1975, Washington, DC: U.S. Government Printing Office, p. 60; Matthews, T. J., MacDorman, M. F., & Thoma, M. E. (2015). Infant mortality statistics from the 2013 period linked birth/infant death data set. *National Vital Statistics Reports, 64*(9). Hyattsville, MD: National Center for Health Statistics.

noncommunicable in all parts of the world except sub-Saharan Africa (where communicable diseases remain the leading causes of death).

Consider the social context in which a chronic disease such as cancer occurs. A spouse, significant other, or close friend provides an important source of social support for many cancer patients. Women and men who feel socially connected to a network of caring friends are less likely to die of all types of cancer than are their socially isolated counterparts (see Chapter 11). Feeling supported by others may serve as a buffer that mitigates the output of stress hormones and keeps the body's immune defenses strong during traumatic situations. It may also promote better health habits, regular checkups, and early screening of worrisome symptoms—all of which may improve a cancer patient's odds of survival.

Sociocultural Perspective

Within the social context, the *sociocultural perspective* considers how social and cultural factors contribute to health and disease. When psychologists use the term *culture,* they're referring to the enduring behaviors, values, and customs that a group of people have developed over the years and transmitted from one generation to the next. Within a culture, there may be two or more *ethnic groups* –large groups of people who tend to have similar values and experiences because they share certain characteristics.

In multiethnic cultures such as those of the United States and most large nations, wide disparities still exist between the life expectancy and health status of ethnic minority groups and the life expectancy and health status of the majority population. These disparities were even greater among previous cohorts, such as the ethnic groups of my great-grandmother and others who emigrated to America. Some of these differences undoubtedly reflect variation in **socioeconomic status (SES),** which is a measure of several variables, including income, education, and occupation. As we'll see in later chapters, low SES is a potent health risk factor, and the highest rates of chronic disease occur among people who are at the lowest socioeconomic level. Conversely, people who are in poor health often have difficulty performing well in high-functioning jobs (or, sometimes, any job), so that chronic disease can be a cause of low income. Evidence also suggests that bias, prejudice, and stereotyping on the part of health care providers may be factors. Racial and ethnic minority individuals tend to receive lower-quality health care than whites do, even when insurance status, income, age, and severity of conditions are comparable (Schpero and others, 2017).

Sociocultural forces also play an important role in the variation in health-related beliefs and behaviors. For example, traditional Native American health care practices are *holistic* (see Chapter 15) and do not distinguish separate models for mental and physical illnesses. As another example, Christian Scientists traditionally reject the use of medicine in their belief that sick people can be cured only through prayer. And Judaic law prescribes that God gives health, and it is the responsibility of each individual to protect it.

In general, health psychologists working from the sociocultural perspective have found wide discrepancies not only among ethnic groups, but also within these groups (see, for example, *Diversity and Healthy Living: The Immigrant Paradox*). Latinos in the United States, for example, are far from homogeneous. The three major nationality groups—Mexicans, Puerto Ricans, and Cubans—differ in education, income, overall health, and risk of disease and death (Angel, Angel, & Hill, 2008). Socioeconomic, religious, and

socioeconomic status (SES)
A person's position in society as determined by education, income, and occupation.

Feeling supported by others may serve as a buffer that mitigates the effects of stress. Here, a cohort of adults supports one another while studying English as a second language.

Joe Raedle/Getty Images

Diversity and Healthy Living

The Immigrant Paradox: SES and the Health of Immigrants

A dramatic example of research stemming from the sociocultural perspective concerns the surprising health of Latinos in the United States, considering their generally lower incomes and lower education levels. In general, low SES correlates with poorer health outcomes. This is true for low birth weight, the rate of which increases worldwide as income falls. Immigrants to the United States, especially those from Spanish-speaking countries, have an average lower SES than native-born Americans. Logically, then, researchers would expect babies born to immigrants to weigh less than those born to native-born women. But, paradoxically, babies born to U.S. immigrants are healthier in every way, including birth weight, than babies of the same ethnicity whose mothers, like their babies, were born in the United States. This surprising finding—which was first documented among Mexican Americans and is also true for U.S. immigrants from other Spanish-speaking countries, from the Caribbean, and from parts of Eastern Europe—continues after birth.

Throughout childhood, children born to low-SES immigrants seem to do better in health and cognition than native-born children of the same ethnicity and income (García Coll & Marks, 2012). Remarkably, the **immigrant paradox** (also called the *Hispanic paradox* or *Latino paradox*) is found throughout the life span. Although Latinos in the United States generally have lower SES, are less likely to have health insurance, use health care less often, and receive less in the way of high-level care when they are sick, they appear to have lower rates of heart disease, cancer, and stroke—the biggest killers of Americans.

Carry this out a generation or two, however, and things change. The children and grandchildren of immigrants typically surpass their elders in income and education, but as SES increases, so does the prevalence of virtually every illness and chronic condition, including obesity, diabetes, cardiovascular disease, and cancer (García Coll & Marks, 2012). By the time an immigrant family has been in the United States for two generations, the "playing field" has been leveled: The grandchildren of immigrants die at the same rate as those of native-born Americans (Barger & Gallo, 2008).

Even within the life span of a single person, the immigrant paradox can be observed. Adults who immigrated to the United States within the past year are one tenth as likely to be obese as are their counterparts who arrived as children and who have lived in this country for 15 years or more (Roshania, Narayan, & Oza-Frank, 2008). Similar disparities exist for diabetes, cardiovascular disease, and many other chronic conditions.

One possible explanation for the immigrant paradox, called the *healthy migrant effect*, is that people who choose to leave their native country are healthier to begin with, despite being poor. Although it may be true that some people do not emigrate because they are too sick to make what is often a hazardous journey, this effect is not sufficient to explain the immigrant health advantage (García Coll & Marks, 2012). The immigrant paradox remains a rather remarkable mystery.

other cultural patterns also may explain why variations in health are apparent not just among ethnic groups, but also from region to region, from state to state, and even from one neighborhood to another. For example, out of every 1,000 live births, the number of infants who die before reaching their first birthday is greater in Mississippi (9.38) and Delaware (8.71) than in Alaska (3.75) and Iowa (4.74) (Kochanek and others, 2015). In terms of your overall health, the way you age seems to depend on where you live.

immigrant paradox The finding that, although low socioeconomic status usually predicts poor health, this is not true for some ethnic groups, such as Hispanics, in the United States.

Gender Perspective

Also within the social context, the *gender perspective* in health psychology focuses on the study of gender-specific health behaviors, problems, and barriers to health care. With the exceptions of reproductive-system problems and undernourishment, men are more vulnerable than women to nearly every other health problem. Although biology certainly plays a part in gender differences in health, masculinity norms have also been implicated (Gough, 2013). Compared to women, men are more likely to

- make unhealthy food choices,
- be overweight,
- exceed guidelines for alcohol consumption and engage in binge drinking,
- ignore illness symptoms and avoid seeing doctors,
- engage in risky competitive sports where there is a higher rate of injury, and
- be at greater risk for nearly all the major diseases that affect both sexes.

The idea that masculinity is bad for men's health is a strong theme in health psychology. The effect is cumulative, so that by age 80, women outnumber men 2 to 1.

As another example of research guided by the gender perspective, consider that the medical profession has a long history of treating men and women differently. For example, women treated for heart disease are more likely to be misdiagnosed (Chiaramonte & Friend, 2006); they are less likely than men to receive counseling about the heart-healthy benefits of exercise, nutrition, and weight reduction (Stewart, Abbey, Shnek, Irvine, & Grace, 2004) or to receive and use prescription drugs for the treatment of their heart disease (Vittinghoff and others, 2003).

Historically, women's health seems to have been viewed primarily in terms of reproductive health (Chilet-Rosell, 2014). As a result, knowledge has often been limited, leading to misdiagnosis and unnecessary delays in treatment. Consider *endometriosis,* a painful chronic condition suffered by an estimated 6% to 10% of women of reproductive age worldwide, in which tissue that normally lines the uterus begins growing elsewhere in the body (Rogers and others, 2013). Unless a woman is trying to conceive, the disease is often overlooked and may take years to be diagnosed. One United Kingdom study reported that it took an average of 7.5 years after the onset of symptoms before women received a formal diagnosis of endometriosis (North, 2011). Delays in accurate diagnosis and treatment cause women to unnecessarily suffer agonizing pain that impacts their lives, relationships, and other aspects of health and well-being.

Research also suggests that women's pain is generally taken less seriously by health care professionals, who take longer to address it and treat it less aggressively, even when the symptoms are the same as those in men (Fassler, 2015). One study reported that, nationwide in the United States, women were less likely to receive an analgesic, and waited an average of 65 minutes in the emergency room before being treated for acute abdominal pain compared to men, who waited only 49 minutes (Chen and others, 2008).

Problems such as these, and the underrepresentation of women as participants in medical research trials, have led to the criticism of *gender bias* in health research and care. Historically, the medical community's understanding of many chronic illnesses, such as cardiovascular disease, has been based on male physiology and has failed to recognize that women may have altogether different symptoms than men for the same condition (Nabel, 2000). In response, the National Institutes of Health (NIH) issued detailed guidelines on the inclusion of women and minority groups in medical research (U.S. Department of Health and Human Services [USDHHS], 2001). In addition, in 1991 the NIH

Sociocultural Bias in Diagnosis Physicians were told that a group of supposed "heart patients" were identical in occupation, symptoms, and every other respect except age, race, and gender. Although catheterization was the appropriate treatment for the described symptoms, the physicians were more likely to recommend it for the younger, white, male patients than for the older, female, or black patients (Schulman and others, 1999).

launched the Women's Health Initiative (WHI), a long-term study of more than 161,000 postmenopausal women, focusing on the determinants and prevention of disability and death in older women. Among the targets of investigation in this sweeping study were osteoporosis, breast cancer, and coronary heart disease. The clinical trials that formed the basis of the WHI tested the effects of hormone therapy, diet modification, and calcium and vitamin D supplements on heart disease, bone fractures, and breast cancer (Women's Health Initiative [WHI], 2010).

Despite the significance of such sociocultural and gender influences, it would be a mistake to focus exclusively on this, or any one context, in isolation. Health behavior is not an automatic consequence of a given social, cultural, or gender context. For example, although as a group cancer patients who are married tend to survive longer than unmarried persons, marriages that are unhappy and destructive offer no benefit in this regard and may even be linked to poorer health outcomes.

Applying the Biopsychosocial Model

As these examples indicate, the **biopsychosocial model** emphasizes the mutual influences among the biological, psychological, and social contexts of health. More broadly, it is also based on an **ecological-systems approach.** Applied to health, this approach is based on the idea that our well-being is best understood as a hierarchy of systems in which each system is simultaneously composed of smaller subsystems and part of larger, more encompassing systems (Kazak, Bosch, & Klonoff, 2012).

One way to understand the relationship among systems is to envision a target with a bull's eye at the center and concentric rings radiating out from it (Figure 1.5). In this model, the individual is at the center. Now consider each of us as a system made up of interacting systems such as the endocrine system, the cardiovascular system, the nervous system, and the immune system. (Also keep in mind that, within each of our biological systems, there are smaller subsystems consisting of tissues, nerve fibers, fluids, cells, and genetic material.) If you move out from the individual at the center and into the radiating outer rings, you can see larger systems that interact with us—and these rings include our families, our schools and workplaces, our neighborhoods, our communities, our societies, and our cultures.

Applied to health, the model emphasizes a crucial point: A system at any given level is affected by and affects systems at other levels. For example, a weakened immune system affects specific organs in a person's body, which affect the person's overall biological

ecological-systems approach
The viewpoint that nature is best understood as a hierarchy of systems, in which each system is simultaneously composed of smaller subsystems and larger, interrelated systems.

FIGURE 1.5 Ecological-Systems Approach and Health The systems potentially influencing an individual's headache, shortness of breath, sleeplessness, racing heart, and other symptoms of anxiety include the body's internal biological systems (immune, endocrine, cardiovascular, and nervous), as well as an individual's family, neighborhood, and culture.

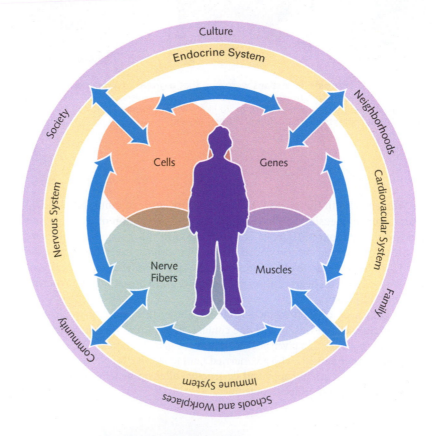

health, which in turn might affect the person's relationships with family and friends. Conceptualizing health and disease according to a systems approach allows us to understand the whole person more fully. Recognizing the importance of this approach, a growing number of health psychologists are investigating *biopsychosocial health* as a specific outcome measure in their research (Ferris, Kline, & Bourdage, 2012).

To get a better feeling for the usefulness of biopsychosocial explanations of healthy behaviors, consider the example of *alcohol use disorder (AUD),* which is a maladaptive drinking pattern characterized by the presence of 2 or more of 11 criteria that include uncontrolled drinking, preoccupation with alcohol, and continuing to use alcohol even when it causes problems (American Psychiatric Association, 2013). Like most disordered behavior, AUD is best explained in terms of several mechanisms that include both genetic and environmental components (Figure 1.6). Research studies of families, identical and fraternal twins, and adopted children clearly demonstrate that people (especially men) who have a first-degree biological relative who was alcohol-dependent are significantly more likely to abuse alcohol themselves. In fact, children of alcoholic parents are four times more likely than the general population to develop alcohol problems themselves (National Institute on Alcohol Abuse and Alcoholism [NIAAA], 2012). In contrast, people who inherit a gene variant that results in a deficiency of a key enzyme for metabolizing alcohol are more sensitive to alcohol's effects and far less likely to become problem drinkers (Zakhari, 2006).

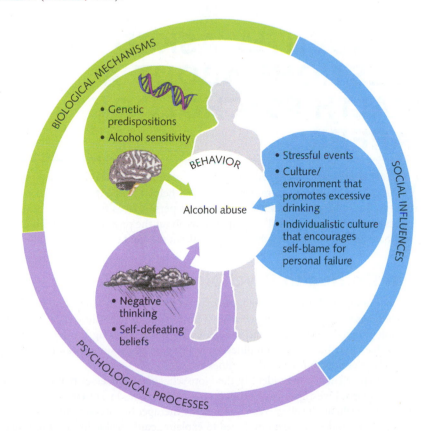

FIGURE 1.6 A Biopsychosocial Model of Alcohol Abuse
Alcohol abuse is best understood as occurring in three contexts: biological, psychological, and social.

On the psychological side, although researchers no longer attempt to identify a single "alcoholic personality," they do focus on specific personality traits and behaviors that are linked with alcohol dependence and abuse. One such trait is poor *self-regulation,* characterized by an inability to exercise control over drinking (Hustad, Carey, Carey, & Maisto, 2009). Another is *negative emotionality,* marked by irritability and agitation.

On the social side, alcohol abuse sometimes stems from a history of drinking to cope with life events or overwhelming social demands. Peer pressure, difficult home and work environments, and tension reduction also may contribute to problem drinking. And more generally, as many college students know, certain social contexts promote heavy drinking. Research studies have shown that college students who prefer large social contexts involving both men and women tend to be heavier drinkers than those who prefer smaller mixed-sex contexts. In addition, men who often drink in same-sex groups (whether large or small) report more frequent drunkenness than men who drink more often in small mixed-sex groups. This suggests that college men who drink heavily may seek out social contexts in which this behavior will be tolerated (LaBrie, Hummer, & Pedersen, 2007). Fortunately, researchers have also found that heavy college drinking does not necessarily predict similar postcollege drinking behavior. Students tend to stop heavy drinking sooner than nonstudents—*maturing out* of hazardous alcohol use before it becomes a long-term problem (NIAAA, 2006; White, Labouvie, & Papadaratsakis, 2005).

FREQUENTLY ASKED QUESTIONS ABOUT A HEALTH PSYCHOLOGY CAREER

We have seen how views regarding the nature of illness and health have changed over the course of history, examined trends that helped shape the new field of health psychology, and discussed the various theoretical perspectives from which health psychologists work. But you may still have questions about the profession of health psychology. Here are answers to some of the questions about the field that students often ask.

What Do Health Psychologists Do?

Like all psychologists, health psychologists may serve as *teachers, research scientists,* and/or *clinicians.* As teachers, health psychologists train students in health-related fields such as psychology, physical therapy, and medicine. By understanding the biopsychosocial processes that contribute to certain illnesses, health care professionals can have a clearer understanding of how to prevent those illnesses.

As research scientists, they identify the biopsychosocial processes that contribute to health and illness, investigate issues concerning why people do not engage in healthful practices, and evaluate the effectiveness of specific therapeutic interventions. Because the biopsychosocial model was first developed to explain health problems, until recently the majority of this research has focused on diseases and health-compromising behaviors. Historically, if you weren't a patient, you were considered healthy. However, as part of the positive psychology movement, an increasing amount of research centers on **positive health,** the scientific study of *health assets* that produce longer life and optimal human functioning (American Psychological Association, 2010). The premise of this movement is simple but critical: The absence of disease and distress is *not* the same thing as health and happiness. The scope of this research—covering assets as diverse as optimism and happiness, psychological hardiness, and the traits of people who live to a ripe old age—shows clearly that the biopsychosocial model guides much of it (see "Your Health Assets").

Clinical health psychologists, who generally focus on treating individuals, are licensed for independent practice in areas such as clinical and counseling psychology. As clinicians, they use the full range of diagnostic assessment, education, and therapeutic techniques in psychology to promote health and assist the physically ill. Interventions are not limited to those who are already suffering from a health problem. Healthy or at-risk individuals may be taught preventive healthy behaviors.

Community health psychologists center their work on the health of a community as a whole. They investigate the prevalence of diseases in specific geographical regions and the various factors that might cause the diseases. More broadly, *public health psychologists* investigate the impact of public health programs. They might work to change government health policies to reduce health disparities in low-income and other marginalized groups. They also help organize public health campaigns to prevent the spread of infection, reduce violence, and in other ways promote wellness.

Occupational health psychologists are concerned with the health of people in the workplace. They might work with a business to change workplace policies or counsel individual employees to improve their subjective well-being.

Where Do Health Psychologists Work?

Traditionally, many psychologists accepted teaching or research positions at universities and four-year colleges. Employment opportunities for health psychologists with applied or research skills also include working in government agencies that conduct research, such as the National Institutes of Health (NIH) and the Centers for Disease Control and Prevention (CDC).

In clinics and hospitals, the work of health psychologists falls into several categories. One type of service involves teaching health care providers, conducting research, and becoming involved in policy development. Another type of service involves helping patients cope with illness and the anxiety associated with surgery and other medical interventions. Other clinical health psychologists may administer psychological or neuropsychological tests, or they may intervene to promote patients' adherence to complicated medical regimens. In this capacity, clinical health psychologists often work on interdisciplinary hospital teams.

In addition, medical residency programs in the United States now have a clear mandate to improve physician training in areas such as sensitivity and responsiveness to patients' culture, age, gender, and disabilities. Increasingly, health psychologists are helping physicians become better listeners and communicators. As we'll see, this mandate stems from mounting evidence that this type of care results in better health outcomes and helps control health care costs (Novotney, 2010a).

Health psychologists may also be found working in health maintenance organizations (HMOs), medical schools, pain and rehabilitation clinics, and private practice. A growing

positive health The scientific study of health assets, which are factors that produce longer life, reduce illness, and increase overall well-being.

Your Health Assets

College Does a Mind and Body Good

Depending on what your day has been like, it may be difficult for you to believe that attending college is most likely good for your health. To be sure, college can add additional sources of possible stress. Your hectic schedule may include squeezing in an online course between jobs or after putting children to bed at night, leaving you in a sleep-deprived state, with little time for exercising and maintaining a healthy diet. Some group settings on campus may also promote high-risk activities such as binge drinking, violence, and dangerous sexual behaviors. Despite these potential barriers to a healthy lifestyle, women and men who have attended college are healthier than those who have not. Those who graduate from college have lower death rates from all causes, including accidents, infectious diseases, and chronic illness, and they live about 10 years longer than those without a high school diploma (National Center for Health Statistics [NCHS], 2017).

What factors might explain why higher education is a valuable health asset? One is the impact of college on cognition. According to one classic study (Perry, 1999), thinking advances through nine levels of increasing complexity over a typical four-year college experience. A first-year student may think in simple, dualistic terms (yes/no, right/wrong) on many issues. Over the next three years of college, thinking tends to become broader, with the student increasingly recognizing the validity of multiple perspectives on issues. Intelligent, educated people thus are more likely to develop higher **health literacy** and become better-informed consumers of information, doing their own research and becoming more knowledgeable and empowered when it comes to their health.

A second factor in the college–health relationship is higher income. College students, especially those who graduate, generally find better jobs and have greater average incomes than those who do not. This gives them greater access to health care and the sometime costly choices of a healthy lifestyle that includes nutritious food, flexible work and leisure time, and safe places to exercise. In 2015, U.S. college graduates, on average, earned 56% more than high school graduates (Rugaber, 2017).

A third factor is healthier lifestyle. Higher education is associated with better health habits, including avoiding tobacco, eating nutritious food, and exercising regularly. This may partly explain why among U.S. adults, the rate of obesity is 21.7% for those with a college degree, compared to 34% for those without. Children of parents with less than a high school degree have an obesity rate 3 times higher than those whose parents completed college (Robert Wood Johnson Foundation, 2018).

Throughout the world, the leaders of many nations have accepted the idea that increasing the number of students enrolled in college is an effective way to promote health and increase productivity. This has resulted in **massification,** the idea that higher education benefits everyone (i.e., the masses) (Altbach, 2010). As a college student, you have an opportunity to acquire many assets that may be reflected in a long, healthy life—including higher income potential; greater health literacy; a social context in which you are surrounded by like-minded, health-conscious friends; and good lifestyle habits.

health literacy The ability to understand health information and use it to make good decisions about one's health.

massification The transformation of a product or service that once was available to only the wealthy such that it becomes accessible to everyone. Applied to education and health, it is the idea that college can benefit everyone.

number of health psychologists can be found in the workplace, including corporations, nonprofit organizations, and government sectors, where they advise employers and workers on a variety of health-related issues, such as helping employees lose weight and learn adaptive ways of managing stress (see Figure 1.7).

How Do I Become a Health Psychologist?

Preparing for a career in health psychology usually requires an advanced degree in one of several different educational programs. Some students enroll in medical or nursing school and eventually become nurses or doctors. Others train for one of the allied health professions, such as nutrition, physical therapy, social work, occupational therapy, or public health. An increasing number of interested undergraduates continue on to graduate school in psychology and acquire research, teaching, and intervention skills. Those who ultimately hope to provide direct services to patients typically take their training in clinical or counseling psychology programs.

Most health psychologists eventually obtain a doctoral degree (PhD or PsyD) in psychology. To earn a PhD in psychology, students complete a four- to six-year program, at the end of which they conduct an original research project. PsyD programs generally provide slightly more clinical experience and clinical courses, but less research training and experience, than PhD programs.

Graduate training in health psychology is generally based on a curriculum that covers the three basic domains of the biopsychosocial model. Training in the biological domain includes courses in neuropsychology, anatomy, physiology, and psychopharmacology. Training in the psychological domain includes courses in each of the major subfields (biological, developmental, personality, etc.) and theoretical perspectives (social-cultural, cognitive, behavior, neuroscience, etc.). And training in the social domain includes courses on group processes and ways in which the various groups (family, ethnic, etc.) influence their members' health. Some health psychologists also complete specialized training in medical subspecialties such as neurology, immunology, and epidemiology.

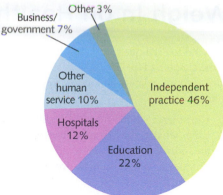

FIGURE 1.7 Where Do Health Psychologists Work? Besides colleges, universities, and hospitals, health psychologists work in a variety of venues, including corporations, HMOs, medical schools, pain and rehabilitation clinics, and independent practices.

Data from: *2009 Doctoral Psychology Workforce Fast Facts.* Washington, DC: American Psychological Association.

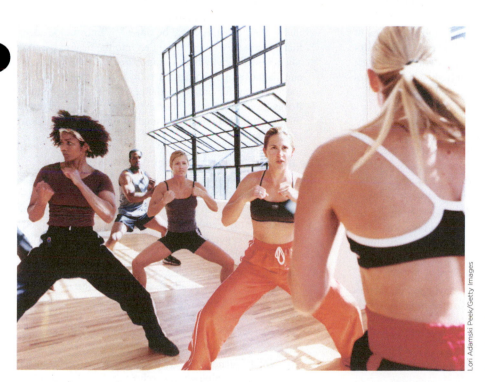

Lori Adamski Peek/Getty Images

Those who pursue graduate training in health psychology are more likely to understand the biopsychosocial benefits of participating in a vigorous group activity, such as a martial arts and boxing class.

Weigh In on Health

Respond to each question below based on what you learned in the chapter. (**Tip:** Use the items in "Summing Up" to take into account related biological, psychological, and social concerns.)

1. Considering how views of health have changed over time, what would be a good description of health for an individual today? How do gender, culture, and the practice of health influence your description?

2. How does the overall health of your school population benefit when different contexts, systems, models, and theories about health are taken into consideration?

3. Your friend Tran is thinking about pursuing a career in health psychology. What general advice would you give him, and how would you suggest he choose a specific career in the field?

Summing Up

1. Health is a state of complete physical, mental, and social well-being. The goals of health psychology are to promote health; prevent and treat illness; investigate the role of biological, behavioral, and social factors in disease; and evaluate and improve the formulation of health policy and the delivery of health care to all people.

2. Although many of the world's citizens have the promise of a longer and better life than their ancestors, these health benefits are not universally enjoyed. Health disparities such as ethnic and socioeconomic group differences in the rates of disease occur in every nation.

Health and Illness: Lessons from the Past

3. In the earliest-known cultures, illness was believed to result from mystical forces and evil spirits that invaded the body. Hippocrates developed the first rational approach to the study of health and disease. Non-Western forms of healing, including TCM and ayurveda, developed simultaneously.

4. In Europe during the Middle Ages, scientific studies of the body (especially dissection) were forbidden, and ideas about health and disease took on religious overtones. Illness was viewed as punishment for evildoing, and treatment frequently involved what amounted to physical torture.

5. French philosopher René Descartes advanced his theory of mind–body dualism—the belief that the mind and body are autonomous processes, each subject to different laws of causality. Descartes's influence ushered in an era of medical research based on the scientific study of the body. This research gave rise to the anatomical, cellular, and germ theories of disease.

6. The dominant view in modern medicine is the biomedical model, which assumes that disease is the result of some pathogen invading the body. Because it makes no provision for psychological, social, or behavioral factors in illness, the model embraces both reductionism and mind–body dualism.

7. Sigmund Freud and Franz Alexander promoted the idea that specific diseases could be caused by unconscious conflicts. These views were expanded into the field of psychosomatic medicine, which is concerned with the treatment and diagnosis of disorders caused by faulty processes within the mind. Psychosomatic medicine fell out of favor because it was grounded in psychoanalytic theory and predicated on the outmoded idea that a single problem is sufficient to trigger disease.

The Biopsychosocial Model

8. Health psychologists approach the study of health and illness from several overlapping perspectives. The life-course perspective in health psychology focuses attention on how aspects of health and illness vary with age, as well as how birth cohort experiences (e.g., shifts in public health policy) influence health.

9. The sociocultural perspective calls attention to how social and cultural factors, such as ethnic variations in dietary practice and beliefs about the causes of illness, affect health. The gender perspective calls attention to male–female differences in the risk of specific diseases and conditions, as well as in various health-enhancing and health-compromising behaviors.

10. The biopsychosocial model combines these perspectives, recognizing that biological, psychological, and social forces

act together to determine an individual's health and vulnerability to disease.

11. The new field of epigenetics focuses on environmental factors near and around genes that affect their expression. An evolutionary perspective guides the work of many health psychologists.

12. According to the ecological-systems model, health is best understood as a hierarchy of systems in which each system is simultaneously composed of smaller subsystems and part of larger, more encompassing systems.

Frequently Asked Questions about a Health Psychology Career

13. Health psychologists are engaged in three primary activities: teaching, research, and clinical intervention. Health psychologists work in a variety of settings, including hospitals, universities and medical schools, health maintenance organizations, rehabilitation clinics, private practice, and, increasingly, the workplace.

14. A growing body of research in health psychology focuses on positive health, the scientific study of health assets that produce longer life and optimal well-being.

15. Preparing for a career in health psychology usually requires a doctoral degree. Some students enter health psychology from the fields of medicine, nursing, or one of the allied health professions. An increasing number enroll in graduate programs in health psychology.

Key Terms and Concepts to Remember

health psychology, p. 4
health, p. 4
health disparities, p. 5
Patient Protection and Affordable Care Act (PPACA), p. 7
humoral theory, p. 9
epidemic, p. 10
pandemic, p. 10
biomedical model, p. 11

pathogen, p. 11
psychosomatic medicine, p. 12
etiology, p. 13
biopsychosocial model, p. 13
genomics, p. 14
epigenetic, p. 15
subjective well-being, p. 17
birth cohort, p. 18

acute disorder, p. 18
chronic illness, p. 18
socioeconomic status (SES), p. 20
immigrant paradox, p. 21
ecological-systems approach, p. 24
positive health, p. 27
health literacy, p. 28
massification, p. 28

 LaunchPad macmillan learning   To accompany your textbook, you have access to a number of online resources, including quizzes for every chapter of the book, flashcards, critical thinking exercises, videos, and *Check Your Health* inventories. To access these resources, please visit the Straub Health Psychology LaunchPad at **launchpadworks.com**

Janine Wiedel Photolibrary/Alamy Stock Photo

Research in Health Psychology

LEARNING OUTCOMES

Once you have studied this chapter, you will be able to:

- Define *critical thinking* and demonstrate how to apply it;
- Differentiate the major research methods in health psychology;
- Describe how epidemiologists study health, illness, and risk factors; and
- Discuss ethical issues in research and explain how study participants are protected.

Darryl Andrew Kile, the 33-year-old pitching ace for the St. Louis Cardinals, died of coronary disease on June 22, 2002. As news of his sudden death spread, the collective reaction was disbelief. How could an elite athlete die suddenly at such a young age? Kile's death was (wrongly) taken by many as proof that exercise offered no protection against cardiovascular disease. After several weeks of public speculation about drug use or other causes, the coroner attributed Kile's death to a massive heart attack caused by a strong family history of heart disease (his father died of a heart attack at age 44) and 90 percent blockage in two coronary arteries.

About two decades earlier, the world had similarly been shocked by the sudden death of another high-profile athlete—52-year-old running guru Jim Fixx, who helped launch the running boom in the United States. As with Kile, Fixx's sudden death while running was, regrettably, taken by many as proof that exercise has no real impact on preventing cardiovascular disease. However, this quick explanation was wrong, too. For most of his life, Fixx was overweight and consumed a high-fat, high-cholesterol diet. In addition, he had been a chain smoker, smoking three to four packs of cigarettes a day, and a workaholic, working 16 hours or more each day and getting only a few hours of sleep each night. Fixx was also at high risk of heart disease because his father had died from a heart attack at the young age of 43 years.

Fixx ignored early warning symptoms as well. His fiancée said that he complained of chest tightness during exercise and traveled to Vermont to see whether the fresh air there would alleviate his symptoms, which he believed to be due to allergies. The change of air did not help, and Fixx died while running on his first day in Vermont.

Fixx's autopsy showed severe coronary artery disease, with near-total blockage of one coronary artery and 80% blockage of another. There was also evidence of a recent heart attack. On the day Fixx died, more than 1,000 other American men and women succumbed to heart attacks. There is overwhelming evidence that heart attacks occur most commonly in males who have high blood pressure, smoke heavily, have high cholesterol levels, and maintain a sedentary lifestyle. Fixx's midlife change to a healthy lifestyle may very well be what allowed him to outlive his father by nine years.

Beware of the trap of believing easy, untested explanations for the causes of diseases or seemingly unexpected physiological events. Medical researchers and health psychologists investigate such cases, comparing situations and considering all relevant factors. Researchers must adopt a formal, systematic approach that has a proven ability to find reliable explanations. This approach is called the scientific method. In this chapter, we will consider how the scientific method is applied to answer questions about health psychology.

CRITICAL THINKING AND EVIDENCE-BASED MEDICINE

Health psychology touches on some of the most intriguing, personal, and practical issues of life. Does my family history place me at risk of developing cancer? Which of my lifestyle choices are healthy and which are unhealthy? Why can't I quit smoking? Every day, we seem to be bombarded with new, "definitive" answers to these and countless other vital health questions. Sorting things out can be difficult. Consider, for example, the never-ending controversy surrounding coffee. Almost every day, a study comes out showing that daily (caffeinated) coffee consumption decreases the risk of Alzheimer's disease. Or heart disease. Or Type 2 diabetes. Coffee drinkers rejoice and order a celebratory latte. Then another study is released showing that daily consumption of coffee increases gastrointestinal problems, or anemia, or depression. So, is caffeine safe? What are you to believe?

To make good decisions, health psychologists, students, physicians—indeed, every one of us—need a "lens" through which to examine the information we are bombarded with. **Evidence-based medicine,** is an approach to health care intended to optimize decision making in treating patients by integrating the best research evidence with clinical expertise and patient values (Masic, Miokovic, & Muhamedagic, 2008). This means that all medical interventions are first subjected to rigorous testing and evaluation of their *efficacy* before they are adopted as a *standard of care*.

evidence-based medicine The use of current best evidence in making decisions about the care of individual patients or the delivery of health services.

critical thinking A skeptical attitude that encourages health care providers and researchers to evaluate evidence and scrutinize conclusions.

At the heart of evidence-based medicine is a skeptical attitude that encourages health care providers to evaluate evidence and scrutinize conclusions. This attitude is called **critical thinking,** and it involves a questioning approach to all information and arguments. Whether listening to the news, reading a journal article, or pondering a friend's opinion, critical thinkers ask questions. What am I being asked to believe? How did they arrive at that conclusion? What is the evidence supporting the claim? Is there an ulterior motive? Is there another explanation for the results? Until you have critically considered these and other questions, you should be skeptical of all persuasive arguments, including health reports that appear in the media. Learning which questions to ask will make you a much more informed consumer of health information.

The Dangers of Unscientific Thinking

In our quest for greater understanding of healthy behavior, we draw on the available information to formulate *cause-and-effect relationships* about our own and other people's behaviors. If this information derives solely from our personal experiences, beliefs, and attitudes, then we may be like the quick-reacting reporters who tried to make sense of the deaths of Darryl Kile and Jim Fixx—making snap judgments with little attention to accuracy. It is dangerous to base our explanations on hearsay, conjecture, anecdotal evidence, or unverified sources of information. For example, upon seeing a lean, statuesque female gymnast or dancer, we may admire what we believe to be her healthy eating and exercise habits, wishing that we too could possess such willpower and well-being. But we may be shocked to learn that she is actually anorexic and suffering from a stress fracture related to poor diet and excessive, exercise-induced skeletal trauma.

Examples of faulty reasoning unfortunately abound in all fields of science. In the early twentieth century, for example, thousands of Americans died from *pellagra,* a disease marked by dermatitis (skin sores), gastrointestinal disorders, and memory loss. Because the homes of many pellagra sufferers had unsanitary means of sewage removal, many health experts believed that the disease was carried by a microorganism and transmitted through direct contact with infected human excrement. Although hygienic plumbing was certainly a laudable goal, when it came to pinpointing the cause of pellagra, the "experts" fell into a faulty reasoning trap—failing to consider alternative explanations for their observations. This type of leaping to unwarranted (untested) conclusions is an example of **confirmation bias,** a tendency to pay attention only to evidence that confirms what we already believe. Confirmation bias is one of several unscientific thinking patterns that can help to explain why two people can look at the same situation (or data) and draw starkly different conclusions.

confirmation bias A form of faulty reasoning in which our expectations prevent us from seeing alternative explanations for our observations.

Testing a Common Belief

Fortunately, U.S. Surgeon General Joseph Goldberger's critical thinking skills allowed him to observe that many pellagra victims also were malnourished. To identify the cause of the disease, in 1914 Goldberger conducted a simple, if distasteful, empirical test: He mixed small amounts of the feces and urine from two pellagra patients with a few pinches of flour and rolled the mixture into little dough balls, which he, his wife, and several assistants ate! When none of them came down with the disease, Goldberger then arranged for a group of Mississippi prisoners to be fed a diet deficient in niacin and protein (a deficiency that he suspected caused the disease), while another group continued to consume the normal, more balanced prison diet. Confirming Goldberger's hypothesis, the former group developed symptoms of pellagra within months, while the latter remained disease free (Stanovich & West, 1998). As this example illustrates, seeking information that confirms preexisting beliefs causes researchers to overlook alternative explanations of observed phenomena.

Goldberg's study was conducted before there were rules that researchers were required to follow and would not be permitted today. Apart from the "yuck factor," the study violates ethical standards that all scientists, especially those studying humans, today must uphold. Today colleges, universities, and most medical institutions have an *Institutional Review Board (IRB)* that protects research participants from harm by permitting only studies that follow a strict *code of ethics*—a sort of moral code that provides researchers with guidelines about where to draw the line between what is "right" and what is "wrong." We'll take up the topic of research ethics in more detail at the end of the chapter.

HEALTH PSYCHOLOGY RESEARCH METHODS

Health psychologists use various research methods in their search to learn how psychological factors affect health. The method used depends in large measure on what questions the researcher is seeking to answer. To answer questions regarding how people cope with medical procedures or cancer, for example, a psychologist might observe or ask questions of a large sample of cancer patients. On the other hand, researchers investigating whether lifestyle factors contribute to the onset of cancer might conduct laboratory studies under controlled conditions.

There are two major categories of research methods in psychology: descriptive and experimental (Table 2.1). Health psychologists also borrow methods from the field of **epidemiology,** which seeks to determine the frequency, distribution, and causes of a particular disease or other health outcome in a population. This section describes the research methods employed by psychologists and the tools they use to gather, summarize, and explain their data.

epidemiology The scientific study of the frequency, distribution, and causes of a particular disease or other health outcome in a population.

Descriptive Studies

Think about how a health psychologist might set about answering the following three questions: What are the psychological and physiological health outcomes for victims of a grave national crisis, such as catastrophic Hurricane Harvey, which caused extreme flooding in the Houston, Texas, area in September 2017, or the 2015–2016 European refugee crisis? How can hospital staff reduce the anxiety of family members waiting for a loved one to come out of surgery? Does binge drinking occur more often among certain types of college students? Clearly, the answers to each of these important questions will not be found in a research laboratory. Instead, researchers look for answers about the behavior of an individual or a group of people as it occurs in the home, at work, or wherever people

TABLE 2.1 Comparing Research Methods

Research Method	Research Setting	Data Collection Method	Strengths	Weaknesses
Descriptive studies	Field or laboratory	Case studies, surveys and interviews, focus groups, naturalistic observation	In-depth information about one person; often leads to new hypotheses; detects naturally occurring relationships among variables	No direct control over variables; subject to bias of observer; single cases may be misleading; cannot determine causality; correlation may mask extraneous variables
Experimental studies	Usually laboratory	Statistical comparison of experimental and control groups	High degree of control over independent and dependent variables; random assignment eliminates preexisting differences among groups	Artificiality of laboratory may limit the generalizability of results; certain variables cannot be investigated for practical or ethical reasons
Epidemiological studies	Usually conducted in the field	Statistical comparisons between groups exposed to different risk factors	Useful in determining disease etiology; easy to replicate; good generalizability	Some variables must be controlled by selection rather than by direct manipulation; time-consuming; expensive
Meta-analysis	No new data are collected	Statistical combination of the results of many studies	Helps make sense of conflicting reports; replicable	Potential bias due to selection of studies included

descriptive study A research method in which researchers observe and record participants' behaviors, often forming hypotheses that are later tested more systematically; includes case studies, interviews and surveys, focus groups, and observational studies.

spend their time. In such a **descriptive study,** the researcher observes and records the participants' behavior in a natural setting, often forming hunches that are later subjected to more systematic study. Several types of descriptive studies are commonly used: case studies, interviews, surveys, focus groups, and observational studies.

A *case study* is a descriptive study in which one person (or, sometimes, one group) is studied in depth in the hope of revealing general principles. Although case studies are useful in suggesting hypotheses for further study, they do have one serious disadvantage: Any given case may be unusual and not representative of others in the population, limiting the generalizability of the results.

The *interview* is often used by clinical health psychologists as a start for developing supportive working relationships with patients. Clinicians also often use *surveys* for diagnostic assessment as a first step in developing intervention programs. For example, chronic-pain patients may be asked to complete a questionnaire related to their problem that sheds light on the effectiveness of previous treatments and the impact of their condition on their daily functioning. *Focus groups,* in which a small number of participants gather to discuss a specified topic or issue, are sometimes used as an alternative to one-on-one interviews.

Survey and interview responses may change with the sequence and wording of the questions. For instance, "global warming" and "climate change" are two ways of wording the same phenomenon, yet survey respondents are more likely to say they believe in climate change than in global warming (McCright & Dunlap, 2011). This is one reason why two surveys that seem to focus on the same issue may reach opposite conclusions.

Another limitation of survey and interview data is that respondents sometimes answer questions in ways that they would like to be perceived or that they believe the investigator expects. For instance, every two years since 1991, a representative sample of all high school students in the United States has been surveyed regarding six categories of health-risk behaviors. The most recent Youth Risk Behavior Surveillance (YRBS) survey included 15,713 students from all 50 states and from schools large and small, public and private (Kann and others, 2016). Among many other topics, students are asked whether they had sexual intercourse before age 13. In the most recent survey, more tenth-grade students said they'd had sexual intercourse before age 13 compared to twelfth-grade students. Why might this be? Have students simply forgotten by the time they reach twelfth grade? Are tenth-graders trying to show that they are "grown up" or more mature than they really are?

Focus groups, such as this one, are increasingly being used in health research.

Observational Studies

In **observational studies,** the researcher observes participants' behavior and records relevant data. For example, a researcher interested in the physiological effects of everyday hassles might have participants wear a heart-rate monitor while commuting to and from school or work in rush-hour traffic.

Observational studies may be structured or unstructured. Those studies that feature structured observations often take place in the laboratory and involve tasks such as role-playing or responding to a certain stimulus. In unstructured observations, referred to as *naturalistic observation,* the researcher attempts to be as unobtrusive as possible in observing and recording the participants' behaviors. For example, a health psychologist might observe family members visiting a parent in a nursing home to gain insight into how people cope with watching a parent decline. These observations may be audiotaped or videotaped and then quantified through rating methods or frequency scores.

observational study A nonexperimental research method in which a researcher observes and records the behavior of a research participant.

Correlation

Descriptive studies often reveal information about two variables that may be related, such as caffeine consumption and high blood pressure, or hypertension. To determine the extent of a suspected relationship between two variables, psychologists often calculate the **correlation coefficient.**

Suppose, for example, that you are interested in the relationship between body weight and blood pressure. Perhaps you are testing your theory that a lean build lowers a person's risk of cardiovascular disease by reducing hypertension, a documented risk factor. To test your theory with an experiment would require manipulating the body-weight variable and then recording blood pressure. Although measuring blood pressure is certainly possible, manipulating body weight would be unethical. So, instead, you calculate a correlation coefficient. Sara Shuger and her colleagues (2008) did just that, measuring body mass index, or BMI (a measure of weight-to-height ratio), in 5,296 women who had

correlation coefficient A statistical measure of the strength and direction of the relationship between two variables, and thus of how well one predicts the other.

In an observational study, the researcher observes participants' behavior and records relevant data, such as the facial expressions this newborn makes while sleeping.

scatterplot A graphed cluster of data points, each of which represents the values of two variables in a descriptive study.

normal blood pressure, and subsequently monitoring these participants to see if they developed hypertension. Figure 2.1 displays a **scatterplot** of the results of their study. Each point on the graph represents two numbers for a sample of participants from one country: average BMI and prevalence of hypertension. Notice that the relationship between the two variables appears to be both fairly strong (the points fall roughly along a straight line) and positive (the points sweep upward from the lower left to the upper right). So, body mass and hypertension tend to increase together.

It is tempting to draw cause-and-effect conclusions from the results of this study. However, even when two variables are strongly correlated, one does not necessarily cause the other. Maybe high blood pressure and a high BMI are both caused by a third factor, such as not enough exercise. Correlations do not rule out the possible contributions of other variables. Even if two variables *are* causally related, correlations do not indicate directionality—in this case, whether a high BMI elevates blood pressure or vice versa (see *Interpreting Data: Association versus Causation*).

Despite certain limitations noted in this section, the use of descriptive studies—including case studies, interviews, surveys, focus groups, and observational studies—is often an important first step in research. In health psychology, correlations identify relationships, often among several variables, that later may be studied more closely with experiments.

FIGURE 2.1 The Relationship between Body Mass Index and Hypertension Body mass index (BMI) measures a person's weight-to-height ratio; BMIs over 25 are generally considered a sign of being overweight. In this study researchers found that as BMI increased, so did the prevalence of hypertension. The scatterplot reveals a strong positive correlation between BMI and hypertension. The solid line confirms this, showing an upward slope and tight clustering of the data points.

Data from: Shuger, S. L., Sui, X., Church, T. S., Meriwether, R. A. & Blair, S. N. (2008). Body mass index as a predictor of hypertension incidence among initially healthy normotensive women. *American Journal of Hypertension, 21*(6), Table 2, p. 616.

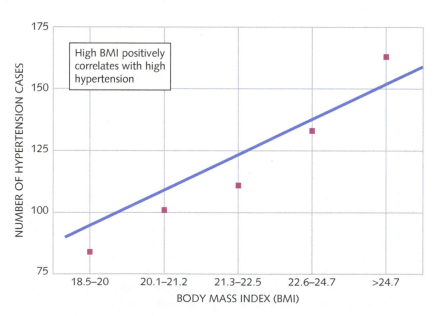

High BMI positively correlates with high hypertension

Interpreting Data...

Association versus Causation

Statistical literacy is the ability to read and interpret statistics in graphs, tables, surveys, and research studies, and to think critically about arguments that use statistics as evidence (Schield, 2010). It focuses on the skills of understanding what is being asserted in a research report, asking good questions, and evaluating evidence.

A common error in reasoning about the results of research is mistaking statements of association for statements of causation. Consider three claims from a hypothetical observational study of body weight and height:

1. People who weigh more tend to be taller than people who weigh less.
2. Weight is positively associated with height.
3. If you gain weight, you can expect to get taller.

Statement 1 is clearly an example of an association between the variables weight and height. Statement 2 may be misinterpreted as implying causation; that is, changes in weight are mistakenly viewed *as a physical change within one participant in the study*. Statement 3, which is obviously false, is an example of an implied causal relationship. In this example, it is easy to see that the truth of statement 2 doesn't mean that statement 3 is also true. A common mistake, however, is to conclude that if statement 3 is false, then statement 2 also must be false.

Let's look at another example:

1. Teenagers who play violent video games are more likely to engage in antisocial behavior.
2. Playing violent video games is positively associated with antisocial behavior.
3. If juveniles played fewer violent video games, they would exhibit less antisocial behavior.

In this context, it is more likely that a person will conclude that if statement 2 is true, then statement 3 also must be true. To be statistically literate, one must understand that the difference between the two statements is the difference between association and causation. If the results of an observational study demonstrate that statement number 2 is true, this finding is *evidence* for the possible truth of statement 3.

Experimental Studies

Descriptive studies are useful, but they cannot tell us about the causes of the behaviors that we observe. To test causal relationships, researchers conduct experiments. Considered the pinnacle of the research methods, experiments are commonly used in health psychology to investigate the effects of health-related behaviors (exercise, diet, etc.) on an illness (e.g., heart disease).

Unlike descriptive studies, experiments test hypotheses by systematically manipulating (varying) one or more *independent variables* (the "causes") while looking for changes in one or more *dependent variables* (the "effects") and *controlling* (holding constant) all other variables. By controlling all variables except the independent variable, the researcher ensures that any change in the dependent variable is *caused* by the independent variable rather than by another extraneous variable.

Typically, the researcher randomly assigns a sample of participants to two or more study groups and administers the condition or treatment of interest (the independent variable) to one group, the *experimental group,* and a different or no treatment to the other group, the *control group*. For example, one experimental study examined the impact of a texting and gaming intervention to encourage physical activity (Thorsteinsen, Vitterso, & Svendsen, 2014). The participants were healthy adults recruited through ads

statistical literacy The ability to read and interpret statistics and to think critically about arguments that use statistics as evidence.

in local newspapers. Researchers *randomly assigned* participants to the intervention or to a control group for comparison. Participants in the intervention group received daily text messages and interactive gaming elements that promoted the health benefits of physical activity. Compared to control group participants, who received text messages and gaming elements unrelated to health and exercise, those in the intervention group reported significantly more minutes of physical activity at higher intensity levels over the three-month study.

Health psychology is somewhat unique among the subfields of psychology in that it studies a variety of variables as cause and effect. As possible causes, health psychologists examine internal states (e.g., optimism and feelings of self-efficacy), overt behaviors (e.g., exercise and cigarette smoking), and external stimuli (e.g., a stressful job or a therapeutic program to promote relaxation). As possible effects, they investigate overt behaviors (e.g., coping reactions to stressful employment), physiological measurements (e.g., blood pressure or cholesterol levels), and psychological states (e.g., anxiety levels). See Figure 2.2 for an example of how psychological research methods may be used to investigate the relationship between exercise and depression.

Quasi-Experiments

Recall the experiments described earlier in the chapter, in which the U.S. Surgeon General consumed flour balls contaminated with urine and feces and arranged for a group of prisoners to be fed a nutrient-deficient diet. As noted, these procedures were unethical and would not be allowed today. Many research questions have similar constraints, whether for ethical reasons or practical ones (budget, schedule, etc.). In cases like this, when health psychologists cannot manipulate the variable of interest or randomly assign participants to experimental and control groups, they have another option: quasi-experiments. A quasi-experiment (*quasi* means "resembling") is similar to an experiment in that it involves two or more *comparison* groups. A **quasi-experiment** is not a true experiment, however, because it uses groups that differ from the outset on the variable under study (the *subject variable*). Therefore, no cause-and-effect conclusions can be drawn. (Notice that we refer to a *comparison group* rather than a *control group* because the group naturally differs from the experimental group and no variable is being controlled.)

For example, suppose that researchers wish to investigate the effect of exercise on academic achievement. In a quasi-experiment, the subject variable would be a sedentary lifestyle, with the group consisting of students who by their own admission get little or no exercise. The comparison group would be students who exercise regularly. Health psychologists would collect data on the participants' base levels of daily physical activity over a defined period of time and then identify separate "active" and "sedentary" groups. The researchers would follow these comparison groups for a period of years, regularly reassessing the groups' activity levels and academic achievement.

Subject variables commonly used in quasi-experiments include age, gender, ethnicity, and socioeconomic status—all variables that are either impossible or unethical to manipulate. Researchers also cannot manipulate variables to produce extreme environmental stress, physical abuse, or natural disasters. In such cases, the researcher finds events that have already occurred and studies the variables of interest.

quasi-experiment A study comparing two groups that differ naturally on a specific variable of interest.

FIGURE 2.2 Does Exercise Reduce Depression? A psychologist interested in studying the relationship between exercise and depression might follow these steps:

1. Using observation, surveys, interviews, and case study results, determine that there is a *negative correlation* between the amount of exercise and depression levels. Higher exercise levels predict lower levels of depression.

2. Use an *experiment* to test the *hypothesis* that exercising more will lower depression levels in mildly depressed individuals.

   Independent variable: exercise
   Dependent variable: depression levels

Administer surveys to volunteer participants that assess depression levels.	→ Randomly assign the mildly depressed participants to either the experimental or the control conditions for 10 weeks.	→ A. Experimental condition: Exercise aerobically for 20 minutes, three times per week. B. Control condition: No aerobic exercise.

3. Re-administer surveys that assess depression levels. Compare depression levels before and after for each participant, and calculate any differences between the experimental and control conditions.

Ammentorp Photography/Alamy Stock Photo

A growing body of research evidence demonstrates that symptoms of depression often improve with exercise.

Developmental Studies

Health psychologists working from the life-course perspective are interested in the ways that people change or remain the same over time. To answer questions about the process of change, researchers use two basic research techniques: *cross-sectional studies* and *longitudinal studies*.

In a **cross-sectional study,** data are collected on the whole study population (e.g., comparing groups of people of various ages) at a single point in time. For example, in the Youth Risk Behavior Surveillance (YRBS) study mentioned earlier, researchers compared six types of risky health behaviors (the dependent variables) among ninth- through twelfth-grade students in the United States. A challenge in cross-sectional research is to make sure that the various groups are similar in ways other than different levels of the independent variable—such as socioeconomic status—that might affect the characteristic being investigated. If the groups are similar, then any differences in early patterns among them may be attributed to the variable of interest—in the YRBS example, age-related processes.

Matching different age groups for all subject variables other than age is difficult to do. Another limitation of cross-sectional studies is that they do not reveal information about changes in people over a period of time. If researchers want to be very sure that age, rather than some other variable, is the reason for differences in the characteristics of different age groups, they may conduct a **longitudinal study,** in which a single group of individuals is observed over a long span of time. This allows information about a person at one age to be compared with information about the same person at another age, revealing how this person changed over time.

Suppose you want to study age-related changes in how people cope with stress. If you choose a cross-sectional approach, you might interview a sample of, say, 25 adults at each of five ages—for example, 20, 30, 40, 50, and 60 years—and gather information about the ways in which they handle job stress, family quarrels, financial problems, and so forth. On the other hand, if you choose a longitudinal study to explore the same span of years, you (or, more likely, the researchers who will continue your study 40 years from now) would interview a group of 20-year-olds today and again when they are 30, 40, 50, and 60 years of age. The longitudinal study thus eliminates confounding factors, such as differences in the types of stress encountered.

Longitudinal studies may be the design of choice from the life-course perspective, but they have several drawbacks. Such studies are very time consuming and expensive to conduct. More important, over the span of years of longitudinal studies, it is common for some participants to drop out because they move away, die, or simply fail to show up for the next scheduled interview or observation. When the number of dropouts is large, the results of the study may become skewed. Another potential problem is that people who remain in longitudinal studies may change in the characteristic of interest, but for reasons that have little to do with their advancing age. For example, our study of age-related coping responses to stress may show that older people cope more adaptively by not allowing everyday hassles to get to them. But suppose that a large number of the participants dropped out of the study midway (or perhaps died of stress-related illnesses!), and those who remained tended to be those employed in low-stress occupations. Can the researcher conclude that age has produced the results? Despite these drawbacks, longitudinal studies are relatively common in health psychology because they afford a unique opportunity for researchers to observe health changes that occur gradually over long periods of time.

cross-sectional study A type of observational study in which data are collected from a population, or representative subset, *at one specific point in time.*

longitudinal study A study in which a single group of people is observed over a long span of time.

EPIDEMIOLOGICAL RESEARCH: TRACKING DISEASE

When researchers consider the role of psychological and behavioral factors in health, among the first questions asked are these: Who contracts which diseases, and what factors determine whether a person gets a particular disease? Such questions are addressed by the field of epidemiology.

Although health recordkeeping can be traced back to ancient Greece and Rome, epidemiology was not formalized as a modern science until the nineteenth century, when epidemic outbreaks of cholera, smallpox, and other infectious diseases created grave public health threats. As with efforts to investigate the causes of more recent conditions, such as the increase in resistant bacterial infections, these diseases were conquered through the work of epidemiologists whose painstaking research gradually pinpointed their causes.

The modern era of epidemiology began with the work of John Snow during an outbreak of cholera in London in 1848 (Frerichs, 2000). Snow laboriously recorded each death from cholera throughout the city, and he noticed that death rates were nearly 10 times higher in one part of the city than elsewhere. In some instances, residents on one side of a residential street were stricken with the disease far more often than were their neighbors on the opposite side of the street. Like a good detective solving a mystery, Snow kept looking for clues until he found something different in the backgrounds of the high-risk groups: polluted drinking water. Although two separate water companies supplied most of the residents of south London, their boundaries were laid out in patchwork fashion, so residents living on the same street often received their water from different sources. By comparing the death rates with the distribution of customers getting polluted and nonpolluted water, Snow inferred that the cholera came from an as-yet-unidentified "poison" in the polluted water, and thus the field of epidemiology was born.

One incident during this epidemic became legendary. In the neighborhood at the intersection of Cambridge Street and Broad Street, the incidence of cholera cases was so great that the number of deaths exceeded 500 in 10 days. After investigating the site, Snow suspected that the cause was centered on the Broad Street pump, and convinced city officials to remove the pump handle so that water could not be drawn there. Soon after, the number of new cases of cholera in the neighborhood dropped dramatically. Although the bacterium responsible for transmitting cholera would not be discovered for another 30 years, Snow's intervention—making contaminated water unavailable—broke the citywide epidemic.

Since Snow's time, epidemiologists have described in detail the distribution of many different infectious diseases. In addition, they have identified many of the *risk factors* linked to both favorable and unfavorable health outcomes. In a typical study, epidemiologists measure the occurrence of a particular health outcome in a population and then attempt to discover why it is distributed as it is by relating it to specific characteristics of people and the environments in which they live. For example, some forms of cancer are more prevalent in certain locales than in others. By investigating these geographical areas, epidemiologists have been able to link certain cancers with toxic chemicals found in these environments.

DEATH'S DISPENSARY.
OPEN TO THE POOR, GRATIS, BY PERMISSION OF THE PARISH.

The Granger Collection, New York

The Pump Handle—Symbol of Effective Epidemiology Since John Snow's pioneering efforts to eradicate cholera in nineteenth-century London, the pump handle has remained a symbol of effective epidemiology. Today, the John Snow Pub, located near the site of the once-contaminated water pump, boasts of having the original handle. This cartoon was published in 1866 in the London periodical *Fun,* with the caption "Death's Dispensary, Open to the Poor, Gratis, By Permission of the Parish."

morbidity As a measure of health, the number of cases of a specific illness, injury, or disability in a given group of people at a given time.

mortality As a measure of health, the number of deaths due to a specific cause in a given group of people at a given time.

incidence The number of new cases of a disease or condition that occur in a specific population within a defined time interval.

prevalence The total number of diagnosed cases of a disease or condition that exist at a given time.

etiology The scientific study of the causes or origins of specific diseases.

Epidemiologists record **morbidity,** which is the number of cases of a specific illness, injury, or disability in a given group of people at a given time. They also track **mortality,** which is the number of deaths due to a specific cause, such as heart disease, in a given group at a given time. Morbidity and mortality are outcome measures that are usually reported in terms of *incidence* or *prevalence*. **Incidence** refers to the number of new cases of a disease, infection, or disability, such as whooping cough, that occur in a specific population within a defined period of time. **Prevalence** is defined as the *total* number of diagnosed cases of a disease or condition that exist at a given time. It includes both previously reported cases and new cases at a given moment in time. The prevalence of a chronic disorder such as hypertension is much greater than the incidence because people can live for many years following diagnosis. Thus, if epidemiologists wished to know how many people overall have hypertension, they would examine prevalence rates. If, however, they sought to determine the frequency with which hypertension is diagnosed, they would look at incidence rates.

Objectives in Epidemiological Research

Epidemiologists use several research methods to obtain data on the incidence, prevalence, and **etiology** (origins) of disease. Like research methods in psychology, epidemiological research follows the logical progression from description to explanation to prediction and control. Epidemiologists have three fundamental objectives:

1. Identify the etiology of a particular disease in order to generate hypotheses.
2. Evaluate the hypotheses.
3. Test the hypotheses by assessing the effectiveness of specific preventive health interventions.

Epidemiologists start by counting current cases of an illness (prevalence) or measuring the rate at which new cases appear (incidence) in order to describe the overall health status of a population. Then they analyze this information to generate hypotheses about which subgroup differences are responsible for the disease, just as John Snow found water source differences that affected cholera prevalence in different groups.

Once epidemiologists have identified the origins of a disease or health condition and have generated hypotheses about its causes, they evaluate those hypotheses. For example, some doctors have noted that lung cancer is more likely to develop in women who smoke than in men who smoke. Could hormonal differences, or some other factor linked to gender, allow the cellular damage that cigarette smoking causes to occur more rapidly in women than in men? Indeed, large-scale epidemiological studies have reported this very finding (Iarmarcovai, Bonassi, Botta, Baan, & Orsiere, 2008; Hakim and others, 2012).

Epidemiologists test new hypotheses by attempting to predict the incidence and prevalence of diseases. If the predictions are borne out by the epidemiological data, researchers gain confidence that their understanding of the etiology of the disease is increasing. The emerging science of molecular epidemiology, which relates genetic, metabolic, and biochemical factors to epidemiological data on disease incidence and prevalence, also promises to improve researchers' ability to pinpoint the causes of human disease.

The final goal of epidemiological research is to assess the effectiveness of intervention programs created to test the researchers' hypotheses. For example, epidemiologists assessed AIDS intervention programs, such as needle-exchange and safer-sex initiatives, in large groups of high-risk participants and determined that the programs are effective in reducing the incidence of new cases of AIDS in targeted groups (see Chapter 12).

Research Methods in Epidemiology

To achieve their purposes, epidemiologists use a variety of research methods, including *retrospective studies, prospective studies,* and *clinical trials*. Like research methods in psychology, each epidemiological method has its strengths and weaknesses.

Retrospective studies begin with a group of people who have a certain disease or condition and then look backward in time in an attempt to reconstruct the characteristics that led to their condition and that distinguish them from people who are not affected. For example, retrospective research played an important role in identifying the risk factors that led to AIDS. Initially, researchers observed a sharp increase in the incidence of a rare and deadly form of cancer called Kaposi's sarcoma among gay men and intravenous drug users. By taking extensive medical histories of the men who developed this cancer, epidemiologists were able to pinpoint unprotected anal sex as a common background factor among the first men to die from this deadly form of cancer. This was years before the AIDS virus, the human immunodeficiency virus (HIV), was isolated (see Chapter 12).

As another example of a retrospective study, INTERHEART was a Canadian-led global study of risk factors for acute myocardial infarction, commonly known as heart attack. This study compared thousands of patients who were admitted to the coronary care unit at 262 hospitals in 52 countries with a comparison group of people matched by age and sex but with no history of heart disease (Yusuf and others, 2004). Retrospective studies such as this one are also referred to as **case–control studies** because "cases" (here, people who have had a heart attack) are compared with "controls" (people who have not had a heart attack). In comparing the two groups, the researchers identified nine risk factors (smoking, lipids, hypertension, diabetes, obesity, diet, physical activity, alcohol consumption, psychosocial factors) that account for over 90% of the risk of having a heart attack.

In contrast, a **prospective study** begins with a group of disease-free participants and follows them over a period of time to determine whether a certain condition or behavior, such as obesity or cigarette smoking, is related to a later health condition, such as heart disease or lung cancer. Recall the study by Shuger and colleagues, mentioned earlier in the chapter, that measured BMI and monitored the participants for later occurrence of hypertension—this was a prospective study.

As another example, there is some evidence that alcohol consumption may contribute to breast cancer. In one large prospective study that has followed a multiethnic cohort of 70,033 healthy women in the San Francisco Bay area for more than 20 years, researchers found that women who consumed one to two drinks per day (one drink equals 12 ounces of regular beer, 5 ounces of wine, or 1.5 ounces of 80-proof liquor) were 1.21 times more likely to be diagnosed with breast cancer than were women who did not drink. Among those who consumed three or more drinks a day, the relative likelihood risk rose to 1.38, whereas those who consumed one drink or fewer each day had a relative likelihood risk of only 1.08 (Li and others, 2009).

Prospective studies can yield more specific information than retrospective studies about potential causal relationships between health behaviors (or risk factors) and health

retrospective study A longitudinal study that looks back at the history of a group of people, often one suffering from a particular disease or condition.

case–control study A retrospective epidemiological study in which people with a disease or condition (cases) are compared with people who are not affected by the disease or condition (controls).

prospective study A forward-looking longitudinal study that begins with a healthy group of subjects and follows the development of a particular disease in that sample.

outcomes. Suppose we know through retrospective research that men who have suffered recent heart attacks tend to score high on measures of hostility. Although it is tempting to assume that their hostility contributed to heart problems, causality could be in the opposite direction—perhaps suffering a heart attack increases one's feelings of hostility. A prospective study would allow researchers to follow hostile men with healthy hearts over time to see whether they eventually develop cardiovascular disease at higher rates than do nonhostile men.

Clinical Trials

randomized clinical trial (RCT) A true experiment that tests the effects of one independent variable (such as a particular drug or treatment) on individuals or on groups of individuals (community field trials).

The gold standard of biomedical research is the **randomized clinical trial (RCT).** This type of study is a true experiment, so it allows researchers to draw conclusions about cause-and-effect relationships. RCTs test the effectiveness of treatments or interventions over time.

Although many variations are possible, the most common clinical trial for individuals involves measurement of a *baseline* (starting point) level of a condition, followed by a measure of the effectiveness of a treatment. For example, in testing the effectiveness of an analgesic drug on migraine headaches, the researcher first records each participant's pretrial level of headache pain, perhaps using a self-report pain scale. Once the baseline establishes a pretreatment reference value in the dependent variable (the subject's pain), treatment (the drug), which is the independent variable, is administered, and the dependent element (pain) is assessed once again. If the treatment data show improvement over the baseline data, the researcher concludes that the treatment is likely to be effective in the future. To be sure that the treatment itself, rather than some extraneous factor (such as the mere passage of time), produced the improvement, the researcher removes the medication and then observes whether the baseline condition returns and symptoms reappear. If they do, the researcher can be even more confident in accepting the hypothesis that the drug produces a significant (clinical) improvement.

In the most common type of clinical trial involving groups, baseline measures are taken, and participants are then randomly assigned to either an experimental group that receives the treatment of interest, such as a new headache medication, or a control group that receives a placebo. If outside variables have been controlled properly, then differences in the groups can be attributed to differences in the treatment.

Meta-Analysis

Traditionally, when a researcher began investigating a phenomenon, the first step was a thorough review of the relevant research literature. Although the *literature review* has a long and respected history in the annals of science, such reviews are subject to bias in how they are interpreted. No matter how skilled the person reviewing the literature may be, the way that various results are interpreted essentially remains a subjective process, in which the reviewer's own biases, beliefs, overconfidence, and so forth may influence the outcome.

meta-analysis A quantitative technique that combines the results of many studies examining the same effect or phenomenon.

To assist researchers in sifting through the sometimes dozens of research studies that pertain to a particular hypothesis, statisticians have developed **meta-analysis,** a quantitative technique that combines the results of studies examining the same effect or phenomenon. Just as an experiment examines the consistency in the responses of individual participants, a meta-analysis determines the overall consistency of individual studies

Interpreting Data...

Tables and Graphs

The ability to interpret information presented in tables and graphs is a key element of statistical literacy. Lacking *graph literacy*, for instance, makes us more likely to rely on the interpretation of others, including those who may present information in carefully chosen ways that support a particular point of view (Gaissmaier and others, 2012). It may be a politician arguing against a policy on climate science, a pharmaceutical company representative presenting evidence for the efficacy of a new drug for the treatment of cancer, or simply a person debating a social problem such as gun control. The information may be presented via printed material in books and journals, during an evening news program or a political speech, on Web sites, or in survey or opinion-poll data. Whatever the source, learning to scrutinize such information carefully will help you to understand that all statistics should be subject to careful scrutiny (Best, 2002). The following is a *five-step framework* that you can use for interpreting tables and graphs.

Step 1: Getting started

Carefully examine the title; the labels of columns, rows, and graph axes; legends; footnotes; and other details of the table or graph.

Step 2: WHAT do the numbers mean?

Make sure that you know what all the numbers represent. Find the largest and smallest values in each category of the graph or table to get an overall impression of the data.

Step 3: HOW do they differ?

Look at the differences in the values of the data in a single row, column, or part of a graph or table. This may involve changes over time, or comparison with a category, such as male and female.

Step 4: WHERE are the differences?

What are the relationships that connect the variables being presented in the table or graph? Use information from step 3 to help you make comparisons across two or more categories.

Step 5: WHY do they change?

If you see differences in the data, why do you think they are occurring?

Now let's apply the framework to actual data that are illustrated in Figure 2.3. Make sure that you understand the importance of—and answers to—each of the questions listed in column 2.

Step 1: Getting started

Scope
  What topic is being examined?
  From the vertical axis, what is being measured?
  What do the columns (bars) represent?
Data quality
  What is the source of the data? Is it trustworthy?
Definitions
  What do the terms *HIV, heterosexual,* and *IDU* mean?

Step 2: WHAT do the numbers mean?

  What is the number of new HIV infections among white heterosexual women?
  What is the number of new HIV infections among Hispanic men?

Step 3: HOW do they differ?

  What subpopulation has the highest number of new HIV infections?
  What subpopulation has the lowest number of new HIV infections?

Step 4: WHERE are the differences?

Compare the values for African American men who contracted HIV through heterosexual contact to those who contracted HIV through male to male sexual contact, which involve individuals of the same gender. Why might these values be different?

   Compare the values for white women and Hispanic women who contracted HIV through heterosexual contact, which also involve individuals of the same gender. Why might these values be different?

Step 5: WHY do they change?

  What subpopulations are missing in the figure? Why are they missing?
  What other observations can you make about what you see in these data?

Reprinted with permission from Kemp, M., and Kissane, B. (2010). A five-step framework for interpreting tables and graphs in their contexts. In C. Reading (Ed.), *Data and context in statistics education: Towards an evidence-based society. Proceedings of the Eighth International Conference on Teaching Statistics.* Voorburg, The Netherlands: International Statistical Institute.

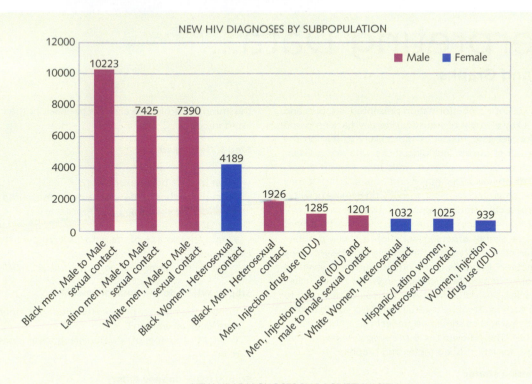

NEW HIV DIAGNOSES BY SUBPOPULATION

NEW HIV DIAGNOSES BY RACE/ETHNICITY

FIGURE 2.3 Estimated Number of Diagnoses of HIV Infection, 2016 The latest estimates of new HIV infections (HIV incidence) in the United States indicate that HIV remains a serious health problem. Certain groups continue to be disproportionately affected by HIV, including men who have sex with men and intravenous drug users.

Data from: Centers for Disease Control and Prevention. (2017f). *HIV Surveillance Report, 2016* (Vol. 28).

that address the same topics. A meta-analysis does not replace individual studies; rather, it provides a systematic procedure for summarizing existing evidence about focused research hypotheses that already appear in the health psychology literature.

Meta-analysis has a number of advantages. First, by pooling the results of many studies, meta-analysis often reveals significant results simply because combined studies have more participants. Second, demonstrating that a finding holds up across different studies conducted by different researchers at different times and places and with different participants gives researchers greater confidence in the finding's validity. Finally, as with good experiments, meta-analysis is subject to replication. That is, other researchers may repeat the series of statistical steps and should reach the same conclusions.

All of the research methods described typically involve data that can be represented in tables and graphs. To boost your expertise in working with these data tools, read *Interpreting Data: Tables and Graphs.*

Inferring Causality

No matter which research method epidemiologists use, certain basic conditions must be met before a cause-and-effect relationship can be inferred between a particular risk factor and a particular disease or other adverse health outcome (Bonita, Beaglehole, & Kjellstrom, 2006):

- *The evidence must be consistent.* Studies that report an association between a risk factor and a health outcome must be replicated. When evidence is not entirely consistent (as is often the case in health research), a convincing majority of the evidence must support the alleged association. If not, causality cannot be inferred.

- *The alleged cause must have been in place before the disease actually appeared.* This may seem obvious, but the importance of this criterion cannot be overstated. For example, if a woman suddenly increases her consumption of alcohol after her breast cancer is diagnosed, drinking alcohol could not have caused the disease. You would be surprised at how often this criterion is overlooked.

- *The relationship must make sense.* This means that the explanation must be consistent with known physiological findings. In the case of the relationship between alcohol and breast cancer, for example, a wealth of other evidence suggests several plausible biological links between alcohol and other forms of cancer, including that alcohol increases hormone levels or that alcohol makes cells more vulnerable to other cancer-causing compounds because of the way it is metabolized in the body.

- *There must be a dose–response relationship between the risk factor and health outcome.* Dose–response relationships are systematic associations between a particular independent variable, such as cigarette smoking, and a particular dependent variable, such as breast cancer. Such relationships pinpoint the relative risk associated with specific levels, or dosage, of an independent variable. Thus, the morbidity rate of breast cancer is higher among women who drink heavily, somewhat less for women who drink moderately, less still for light drinkers, and lowest among non-drinkers (LoConte, Brewster, Kaur, Merrill, & Alberg, 2018).

- *The strength of the association between the alleged cause and the health outcome (relative risk) must suggest causality.* **Relative risk** refers to the ratio of the incidence

relative risk A statistical indicator of the likelihood of a causal relationship between a particular health risk factor and a health outcome; computed as the ratio of the incidence (or prevalence) of a health condition in a group exposed to the risk factor to its incidence (or prevalence) in a group not exposed to the risk factor.

Interpreting Data...

Measuring Risk

Let's look at an actual example of how measures of risk are used to estimate the impact of an actual risk factor on chronic disease. Table 2.2 displays the results of a classic 20-year study of death rates due to lung cancer and heart disease among British physicians. The researchers examined death rates due to both diseases among doctors who smoked at least one pack of cigarettes per day, comparing them to the death rates among those who did not smoke. For smokers, the incidence or absolute risk of developing heart disease during the course of the study (669 per 100,000 people) was much higher than the absolute risk of developing lung cancer (140 per 100,000 people). In contrast, the data demonstrate a very strong *relative* association between smoking and lung cancer (RR = 14.0), and a much smaller association between smoking and heart disease (RR = 1.6).

RR for lung cancer = incidence (smokers)/incidence (non-smokers) = 140/10 = 14.0
RR for heart disease = incidence (smokers)/incidence (non-smokers) = 669/413 = 66 = 1.6

Thus, cigarette smoking is a much stronger risk factor for mortality from lung cancer than for heart disease. On the face of it, these data seem to offer powerful support to the idea that smoking causes lung cancer, but they leave plenty of doubt as to whether there is a causal relationship between smoking and heart disease. Given that there is a large body of evidence that smoking *does* cause both lung cancer and heart disease (see Chapters 10 and 11), how can we make sense of these differences in relative risk?

The explanation is that death from lung cancer is a relatively rare event among nonsmokers, accounting for only 10 deaths per 100,000 people. Because the background rate of lung cancer is very low, a small difference in absolute risk among those who smoke leads to a very high relative risk. In contrast, the annual death rate for heart disease among nonsmokers is much larger (413 per 100,000), so a much larger difference in the *absolute risk* among smokers would be needed before the *relative risk* changed substantially.

It is important to remember that these data are evidence of an *association* between a risk factor (smoking) and two health conditions (lung cancer and heart disease). Assuming that smoking is a causal factor in both diseases, eliminating smoking would prevent far more deaths from chronic heart disease than from lung cancer. A third measure or risk brings this to our attention. **Attributable risk** measures the actual amount of a disease that can be attributed to exposure to a particular risk factor. Attributable risk is determined by subtracting the incidence rate of a disease in people who have been exposed to a risk factor from the incidence rate of the disease in people who have not been exposed to the risk factor.

AR for lung cancer = incidence (smokers) – incidence (non-smokers) = 140 − 10 = 130
AR for heart disease = incidence (smokers) − incidence (nonsmokers) = 669 − 413 = 256

In this study, differences in attributable risk demonstrate that the actual *public health impact* of smoking is twice as large for heart disease mortality as it is for lung cancer mortality. For every 100,000 people, there are 256 additional deaths from heart disease in smokers, compared to 130 additional deaths over the background rate among nonsmokers from lung cancer.

TABLE 2.2 Relative Risk of Mortality From Lung Cancer Among Cigarette Smokers

	Annual Mortality Rate per 100,000	
	Lung Cancer	**Heart Disease**
Cigarette smokers	140	669
Nonsmokers	10	413
Relative risk	14.0	1.6
Attributable risk	130/year	256/year

Data from: Doll, R., Peto, R., Boreham, J., & Sutherland, I. (2004). Mortality in relation to smoking: 50 years' observations on British male doctors. *British Medical Journal, 328,* 1519–1528.

or prevalence of a disease in a group exposed to a particular risk factor to the incidence or prevalence of that condition in a group not exposed to the risk factor. A relative risk value of 1.0 means there is no difference in risk between the two groups. A relative risk value above 1.0 indicates that there is a positive association between the risk factor and the health condition; that is, the exposed group has a greater risk than the unexposed group. For example, a relative risk of 2.0 indicates that the exposed group is twice as likely to develop a health outcome as an unexposed group is. Conversely, a relative risk of 0.50 means that the incidence or prevalence rate of the condition in the exposed group is only half that of those in the unexposed group; that is, there is a negative association between the risk factor and the condition (see *Interpreting Data: Measuring Risk*).

- *The incidence or prevalence of the disease or other adverse health outcome must drop when the alleged causal factor is removed.* Although dose–response and relative risk relationships are necessary to infer causality, they are not sufficient. Before we can infer that drinking causes breast cancer, we must have evidence that women who reduce or eliminate their consumption of alcohol have a reduced risk of this disease. Research has shown this very thing to be true, in fact, thus meeting our fifth criterion (World Cancer Research Fund International [WCRFI], 2017). When all conditions are met, epidemiologists are able to infer that a causal relationship has been established, even when a true experiment cannot be conducted.

While working to meet these conditions, health psychologists need to evaluate individual research studies very carefully. Quality rating forms, such as the one in Figure 2.4, are very helpful means of achieving this standard. In medicine, too, there is a new emphasis on the importance of basing patient care on the "best available evidence" for a given health condition. Medical residency programs today are required to train new physicians in evidence-based medicine, which involves virtually all of the principles we have discussed in this chapter, including learning how to appraise research critically for its validity, reliability, and usefulness in clinical practice (Accreditation Council for Graduate Medical Education [ACGME], 2017).

In this chapter, we have introduced a variety of research methods for studying biological, psychological, and social factors in health. It is natural to ask, which one is best? Some researchers might answer quickly that the laboratory experiment is most desirable because only in such studies are the variables of interest directly manipulated while all other variables are controlled. But we also have seen that some questions of vital interest to health psychologists do not, for ethical and/or practical reasons, lend themselves to experimentation. Moreover, experiments are often criticized for being artificial and having little relevance to behavior in the real world.

Increasingly, researchers are combining experimental and nonexperimental methods in order to make their investigations more comprehensive. For example, suppose that a researcher is interested in determining whether an educational campaign about safer sex would induce college students to modify their behavior. The researcher might design an experiment in which a randomly assigned group of students who received educational materials related to this issue was compared to a control group that received unrelated materials. The students would be compared on their stated intentions to practice safer sex. However, the researcher surely would want to know whether students' actual behavior reflected their stated intentions, and nonexperimental means would need to be used

attributable risk The actual amount that a disease can be attributed to exposure to a particular risk factor. Attributable risk is determined by subtracting the incidence rate of a disease in people who have been exposed to a risk factor from the incidence rate of the disease in people who have not been exposed to the risk factor.

FIGURE 2.4 Putting Health Psychology into Practice: Evaluating Scientific Evidence Health psychologists use quality rating forms similar to this to evaluate research studies. For each criterion, they rate the study by assigning a number from 0 (no evidence that the criterion was met) to 3 (strong evidence that the criterion was met). Overall scores on the rating system can range from 0 to 21, with higher scores justifying greater confidence in the study's conclusions.

3 = Good, 2 = Fair, 1 = Poor, 0 – No evidence that the criterion has been met

Criterion	Evidence	Score
1. Problem or Question Studied: *(clearly stated hypothesis, significant or relevant issue, operational definitions included)*		
2. Sampling: *(representative of population, random selection and assignment, sample characteristics identified, group differences controlled, low dropout rate)*		
3. Measurement: *(clearly stated methodology)*		
4. Reliability: *(test yields consistent results, even among multiple raters; questions measure single construct, such as anxiety or degree of disability)*		
5. Validity: *(constructs clearly explained, independent and dependent variable levels clear, generalized to appropriate populations)*		
6. Statistical Significance: *(inferred relationships, accurate and appropriate significance supported by data)*		
7. Justification for Conclusions: *(warranted by data and research design)*		
Total		

to observe behavior. The researcher would likely also want to know if the educational campaign was equally effective with women, men, members of various ethnic minorities, and so forth—variables that cannot be manipulated experimentally. Together, however, experimental and nonexperimental methods complement one another, giving health psychologists a larger tool kit with which to study their subjects.

In addition to favoring experiments, health psychologists generally have also favored *quantitative research* studies of health phenomena where measurement, prediction, and control are prioritized. However, when data are presented in numbers, some information may be lost. Many health psychologists thus turn to **qualitative research** to complement quantitative data—asking open-ended questions and reporting responses in narrative, rather than numerical, form (Gough & Deatrick, 2015).

For example, a recent study of 18- to 25-year-old New Zealanders used multiple qualitative methods (focus groups, interviews using images from social media, and online

qualitative research Research that focuses on qualities instead of quantities. Participants' expressed ideas are often part of qualitative studies.

materials) to explore the influence of corporate marketing on young people's drinking behavior (Lyons, Goodwin, McCreanor, & Griffin, 2015).

Research Ethics and Scientific Misconduct

The most important concern for all scientists, especially for those studying human behavior, is to uphold ethical standards in their research. Responsible researchers design their studies to ensure that participation is voluntary, harmless, and confidential. Many professional associations, including the American Psychological Association (APA) and the National Science Foundation (NSF), have research guidelines to protect the well-being of research participants. The ethics codes of the APA mandate that research participation must be completely voluntary, that researchers must (1) obtain human participants' **informed consent** beforehand—that is, participants must understand and agree to the research procedures and know what risks are involved—(2) protect participants from harm and discomfort, (3) keep information about individual participants confidential, and (4) fully **debrief** people (explain the research afterward). Moreover, as noted at the beginning of the chapter, university ethics committees and IRBs screen research proposals to make sure safeguards are in place before approving them (American Psychological Association [APA], 2017).

  Scientific misconduct is the violation of accepted codes of scholarship and ethical behavior in research. In addition to the mistreatment of research participants, the NSF defines three types of misconduct: fabrication, falsification, and plagiarism. *Fabrication* means "making up results and recording or reporting them." *Falsification* means "manipulating research materials or changing data and results such that the research is not accurately represented." *Plagiarism* means "appropriating another person's ideas, results, or words without giving appropriate credit."

  As an example, the University of Connecticut reported that one of its researchers, who studied the link between aging and a substance found in red wine, committed more than 100 acts of data fabrication and falsification, throwing much of this work into doubt (Wood, 2012). Although reports of this type of outright fraud are rare, experts say unethical or sloppy researchers take advantage of a system that sometimes allows them to operate in secrecy and manipulate data to find what they want to find without much fear of being challenged.

  Even research that has been conducted under rigorous standards of quality may produce results that are not reproducible. A group called the Reproducibility Project at the Center for Open Science conducted replications of 100 experimental and correlational studies published in three psychology journals (Open Science Collaboration, 2015). Despite the use of high-powered study designs and original materials wherever possible, the researchers found that over 60 percent of the studies failed to replicate—that is, the original findings did not hold up the second time around.

informed consent Permission granted by a client, patient, or research participant with full knowledge of the potential risks involved in a treatment, procedure, or research study.

debrief The process in which research participants are given more details about the study following its completion.

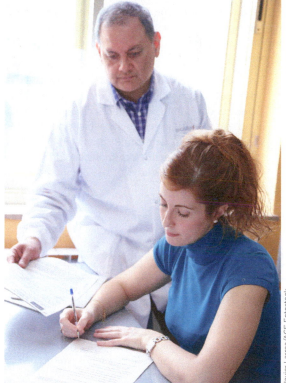

The American Psychological Association requires researchers to make sure health study participants understand and agree to research procedures as well as know what risks are involved prior to participating.

Javier Larrea/AGE Fotostock

Although *reproducibility of results* is a defining feature of the scientific method, some experts say researchers pay too little attention to this issue because the incentives for individual scientists place higher value on novel findings. Journal reviewers and editors may dismiss a study that replicates already published findings for being unoriginal, and therefore unworthy of publication. As the authors of this landmark study concluded, "there is still more work to do to verify whether we know what we think we know" (Open Science Collaboration, 2015, p. 950).

This chapter has presented you with the basic tools of the health psychology trade—(1) critical thinking that guards against faulty everyday reasoning and (2) scientific methods that guide researchers in their quest for valid and reliable answers to health-related questions. Armed with this information, you are now ready to begin to address those questions.

Weigh In on Health

Respond to each question below based on what you learned in the chapter. (**Tip:** Use the items in "Summing Up" to take into account related biological, psychological, and social concerns.)

1. Recently, you read about a study that indicated a link between taking a vitamin supplement and lessening the chance of developing Alzheimer's disease in older adulthood. As a health psychologist, what kinds of questions would you ask to determine the merits of this study? What kinds of unscientific thinking should you be aware of as you review the study?

2. For each of the following methods of research in health psychology, develop a question that would provide focus for a study: a descriptive study, an experimental study, a quasi-experiment, and a developmental study. Why is the method of research that you chose well suited to each question?

3. In the past, several health psychology professors at your school were involved in epidemiological research to help reduce the incidence of sexually transmitted infections. They were involved in retrospective studies, clinical trials, meta-analysis, and intervention. In what way could each of these epidemiological research methods have helped?

Summing Up

Critical Thinking and Evidence-Based Medicine

1. Our everyday thinking is prone to bias, including making snap judgments and inferring cause and effect inappropriately. Using scientific research methods to search for evidence will help you become a more careful consumer of health psychology reports.

2. An important aspect of critical thinking in health psychology is statistical literacy, the ability to read and interpret statistics and to think critically about arguments that use statistics as evidence.

Health Psychology Research Methods

3. Descriptive studies, which observe and record the behavior of participants, include case studies, interviews and surveys, focus groups, and observation.

4. The strength and direction of a relationship between two sets of scores are revealed visually by scatterplots and statistically by the correlation coefficient. Correlation does not imply causality.

6. In an experiment, a researcher manipulates one or more independent variables while looking for changes in one or

more dependent variables. Experiments typically compare an experimental group with a control group.

6. When health psychologists study variables that cannot be manipulated, they may conduct a quasi-experiment in which participants are assigned to comparison groups on the basis of age, gender, ethnicity, or some other subject variable.

7. Developmental studies focus on the ways people change or remain the same over time. In a cross-sectional study, data are collected on the whole study population (such as comparing groups of people of various ages) at a single point in time.

8. In a longitudinal study, subjects are followed over a long span of time. To compensate for the problem of subjects dropping out over a lengthy span of years, researchers have developed a cross-sectional study, in which different age groups are tested initially and then retested later at various ages.

Epidemiological Research: Tracking Disease

9. Epidemiological research studies measure the distribution of health outcomes, seek to discover the etiology of those outcomes, and test the effectiveness of health interventions. Among the commonly used epidemiological statistics are morbidity, mortality, incidence, and prevalence.

10. Epidemiologists use several basic research designs, including retrospective and prospective studies.

11. Epidemiologists use several measures of risk: absolute risk, relative risk, and attributable risk.

12. Meta-analysis analyzes data from already published studies, statistically combining the size of the difference between the experimental and control groups to enable researchers to evaluate the consistency of findings.

13. In order to infer causality in epidemiological research, research evidence must be consistent and logically sensible and exhibit a dose–response relationship. In addition, the alleged cause must have been in place before the health outcome in question was observed and must result in a reduced prevalence of the condition when removed.

14. Ethical research entails ensuring certain protections for participants, and avoiding fabrication, falsification, and plagiarism in conducting studies and reporting results.

Key Terms and Concepts to Remember

evidence-based medicine, p. 33
critical thinking, p. 34
confirmation bias, p. 34
epidemiology, p. 35
descriptive study, p. 36
observational studies, p. 37
correlation coefficient, p. 37
scatterplot, p. 38
statistical literacy, p. 39

quasi-experiment, p. 40
cross-sectional study, p. 42
longitudinal study, p. 42
morbidity, p. 44
mortality, p. 44
incidence, p. 44
prevalence, p. 44
etiology, p. 44
retrospective studies, p. 45

case–control studies, p. 45
prospective study, p. 45
randomized clinical trial, p. 46
meta-analysis, p. 46
relative risk, p. 49
attributable risk, p. 50
qualitative research, p. 52
informed consent, p. 53
debrief, p. 53

 LaunchPad macmillan learning   To accompany your textbook, you have access to a number of online resources, including quizzes for every chapter of the book, flashcards, critical thinking exercises, videos, and *Check Your Health* inventories. To access these resources, please visit the Straub Health Psychology LaunchPad at **launchpadworks.com**

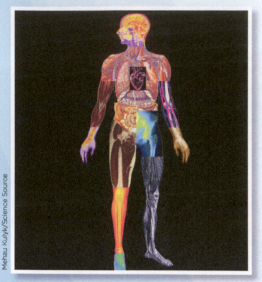

Mehau Kulyk/Science Source

Biological Foundations of Health and Illness

LEARNING OUTCOMES
Once you have studied this chapter, you will be able to:

- Describe the structure and function of cells and the nervous system,
- Identify the major endocrine glands and their functions,
- Explain why the cardiovascular and respiratory systems are important to survival,
- Explain how the digestive system functions,
- Summarize what is known about the immune system, and
- Identify other bodily systems and explain how bodily systems interact.

Lakeesha's life began with a difficult birth. Her mother had to be given strong anesthetics, and the delivery staff had to use forceps to pull her tiny body into the world. Together, these medical procedures choked off the supply of oxygen to Lakeesha's young brain. Although she survived, Lakeesha's complicated delivery, combined with her low birth weight and her mother's heavy use of alcohol during pregnancy, meant that her problems were just beginning. Lakeesha was born with mild spastic cerebral palsy (CP), a movement disorder that results from damage to the brain's motor centers.

This biological condition cast a lifelong shadow over Lakeesha's health, affecting her continuing physical, psychological, and social development. Among her challenges were mild intellectual disability, visual and hearing impairments, slight deformities in her teeth and joints, and scoliosis (curvature of the spine). Later, when her same-age peers were learning to speak, Lakeesha experienced speech difficulties caused by her muscular problems.

Like most children with disabilities, Lakeesha needed extra self-confidence and persistence to master tasks that were routine for other children. During early childhood, Lakeesha often found that she couldn't do the same things as other children, look the way they did, or keep up with them. Realizing that her disability was permanent caused Lakeesha to become depressed and angry.

Lakeesha's condition also challenged her parents, who experienced grief, guilt, and disappointment. They found that it took more time and effort to raise Lakeesha than it did to raise her older sister, and other people were often insensitive in their comments and behavior toward Lakeesha.

Fortunately, interventions were available. Dental treatments and orthopedic surgery corrected most of Lakeesha's facial and posture problems. Speech and behavior therapy helped her improve her muscular control, balance, and speech.

By age 8, Lakeesha was able to attend her neighborhood elementary school for the first time. In some areas, her skills were poor. Writing with a pencil, for example, was extremely difficult, and vision problems hampered Lakeesha's efforts to learn to read. In other areas, however, her skills were average or even advanced. She was one of the first in her class to understand multiplication and division.

Throughout her childhood, Lakeesha had high emotional and psychological needs, but they were met. She worked with a psychotherapist to address her anger, low self-esteem, and perception of herself as damaged or different. Similarly, her parents joined a support group and worked with a cognitive-behavioral therapist to recognize and cope with their feelings.

Today Lakeesha is an adult living independently, working part-time in an electronics store and attending classes at a community college. She maintains a close, warm relationship with her parents, who live nearby, and she has a small but close-knit circle of friends. Most important, she feels good about herself and has confidence in her ability to overcome life's obstacles.

Lakeesha's story illustrates the importance of the biopsychosocial perspective. Factors in the realms of biology (difficult birth, prenatal alcohol exposure), psychology (dealing with being "different"), and social relations (struggling to connect with others) all contributed to Lakeesha's challenges, and all three areas were addressed as part of her successful survival. The biopsychosocial perspective is effective because it advocates thinking of the human body as a system made up of many interconnected subsystems (including, for Lakeesha, the abilities to walk and talk) and externally related to several larger systems, such as society and culture.

Lakeesha's story also makes clear one of health psychology's most fundamental themes: The mind and body are inextricably intertwined. Whether they are focusing on promoting health or treating disease, health psychologists are concerned with the various ways our behaviors, thoughts, and feelings affect—and are affected by—the functioning of the body.

This chapter lays the groundwork for our investigation into health psychology by reviewing the basic biological processes that affect health. These processes are regulated by the nervous system, the endocrine system, the cardiovascular system, the respiratory system, the digestive system, the immune system, the reproductive system, the integumentary system, the muscular system, the skeletal system, and the urinary system.

For each system, we will consider its basic structure and its interdependence with the other systems for healthy functioning. Later chapters will discuss the major diseases and disorders to which these various systems are vulnerable.

Because every thought, feeling, and action is also a biological event, the material in this chapter is fundamental to understanding the specific aspects of health and illness discussed in later chapters. So study this chapter carefully, and be prepared to refer to it frequently throughout the course.

CELLS AND THE NERVOUS SYSTEM

cell The basic unit of structure and function in living things.

All living things are made up of **cells**, the basic building block of tissue, organs, and bodily systems. The human body contains about 10 trillion cells consisting of 200 specialized types. The cells of the nervous system play a crucial role, as they transmit electric impulses throughout the body, enabling the brain, the spinal cord, the heart and lungs, and other bodily systems to function. For this reason, the nervous system is referred to as the body's primary communication system. Without the nervous system, our muscles would not expand or contract, our pancreas would not release insulin, and consciousness would not be possible.

The nervous system is just one of several specialized bodily systems. Although each of the major bodily systems is described separately, we'll see later in the chapter that each interacts with, and depends on, the others to keep the body functioning well.

Cells

Cells first became known in the mid-1600s when Robert Hooke examined thin slices of cork and other plants with a compound microscope. Each cell has a structure consisting of an outer *membrane*, which serves as a boundary defining the cell into a sort of package, and a water-based interior called the *cytoplasm*.

There are two basic types of cells: *prokaryotic*, which make up bacteria and other single-celled organisms, and *eukaryotic*, which are found in all other living things. Eukaryotic cells contain specialized, membrane-bound internal structures called *organelles*, one of which—the *nucleus*—contains the cell's hereditary material and serves as its control center. Other cellular organelles perform different functions, such as protein synthesis.

TABLE 3.1 Nervous System Connections

See how the nervous system is involved in health psychology issues covered in many later chapters, including coverage of the following:

- Physiology of Stress (in Chapter 4)
- Coping Interventions for Stress (in Chapter 5)
- Obesity (in Chapter 8)
- Substance Abuse (in Chapter 9)
- The Physiology of Pain (in Chapter 14)

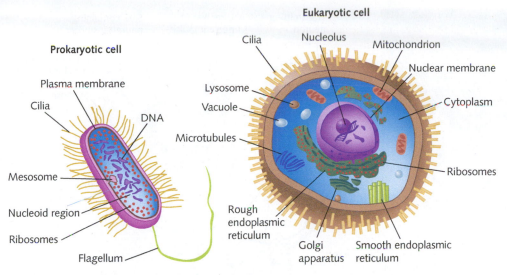

FIGURE 3.1 Prokaryotic versus Eukaryotic Cells Prokaryotic cells do not have nuclei or other organelles. Eukaryotic cells contain nuclei and many other types of organelles.

Prokaryotic cells do not have nuclei or any other organelles. Figure 3.1 illustrates the differences between a prokaryotic and a eukaryotic cell.

A group of similar cells that perform the same function is called a **tissue**. Most tissues in humans and other animals are one of two types. *Epithelial tissues* are sheets of closely packed cells covering body organs and other surfaces. They also form *glands* that secrete hormones, breast milk, and other substances. *Connective tissues* are made up of more widely separated cells that function to bind together and support organs and other body tissues. Bone is a type of connective tissue, as is *cartilage*, found in the joints between bones, and *tendons*, which connect bone to muscle. Blood, nerve, and muscle are specialized tissues that do not belong to either the epithelial or connective tissue group.

A group of tissues that work together to perform a specific function, such as the stomach, is an **organ**. Organs have their own blood vessels, nerves, and muscles. Organs and tissues that work together to serve a common purpose are said to form a functional unit, or bodily system, such as the nervous system, discussed next.

Divisions of the Nervous System

The human **nervous system** contains billions of *neurons* (nerve cells) that send and receive signals across trillions of *synapses* (communicating connections between neurons), via chemicals called **neurotransmitters**. Traditionally, these neurons (Figure 3.2) are grouped into two major divisions: the *central nervous* system *(CNS)*, which consists of the brain and the spinal cord, and the *peripheral nervous* system *(PNS)*, which contains the remaining nerves of the body.

The PNS is further divided into two subdivisions: the *somatic nervous system*, which includes the nerves that carry messages from the eyes, ears, and other sense organs to the CNS, and from the CNS to the muscles and glands; and the *autonomic nervous system*, the nerves that link the CNS with the heart, intestines, and other internal organs.

tissue A group of similar cells organized into a functional unit.

organ A group of tissues working together to perform a specific function.

nervous system Consists of all the neurons in the body; the central nervous system includes the brain and spinal cord, and the peripheral nervous system includes the body's other nerves.

neurotransmitters Chemical messengers released by a neuron at synapses that communicate across the synaptic gap and alter the electrical state of a receiving neuron.

(a)

(b)

FIGURE 3.2 The Neuron (a) The scanning electron micrograph shows neurons in the human brain. (b) A neuron may receive messages from other neurons on any of its dendrites, and then it transmits each message down the long axon to other neurons. Nerve impulses travel in one direction only: down the axon of a neuron to the axon terminal. When a nerve impulse reaches the axon terminal, chemical messengers called *neurotransmitters* cross the synapse and bind to receptor sites on the receiving neuron's dendrite—similar to the way a key fits into a lock.

Because the skeletal muscles that the somatic nerves activate are under voluntary control, the somatic nervous system is often referred to as the *voluntary nervous system.* In contrast, the autonomic, or involuntary, nervous system controls the organs over which we normally have no control. As we'll see in the next chapter, involuntary responses play a critical role in how we react to environmental challenges and stressful situations.

The autonomic nervous system is also composed of two subdivisions (Figure 3.3). The *sympathetic nervous system* consists of groupings of neuron cell bodies called *ganglia* that run along the spinal cord and connect to the body's internal organs. The sympathetic division prepares the body for "fight or flight," a response generated when a person experiences performance stress (preparing for the big football game or an important job interview) or perceives a significant threat (see Chapter 4). It does so by increasing the heart rate and breathing rate, decreasing digestive activity (this is why eating while under stress can lead to a stomachache), increasing blood flow to the skeletal muscles, and releasing energizing sugars and fats from storage deposits. Because all the sympathetic ganglia are closely linked, they tend to act as a single system, or "in sympathy" with one another.

Unlike the ganglia of the sympathetic division, the ganglia of the *parasympathetic nervous system* are not closely linked and therefore tend to act more independently. This system has effects opposite those of the sympathetic ganglia: It helps the body to recover after arousal by decreasing heart rate, increasing digestive activity, and conserving energy.

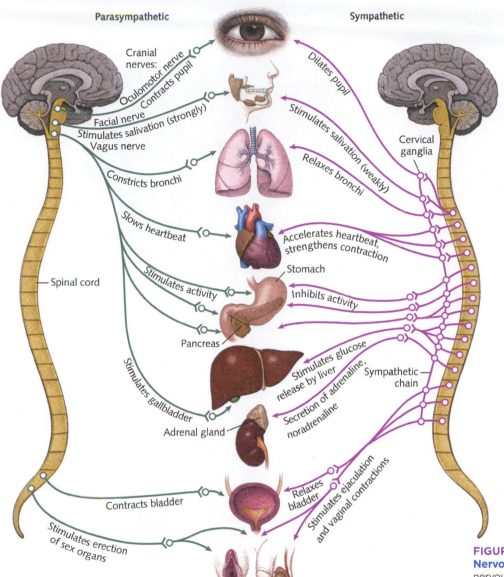

Parasympathetic

Sympathetic

Cranial nerves:

Oculomotor nerve

Contracts pupil

Dilates pupil

Facial nerve

Stimulates salivation (strongly)

Stimulates salivation (weakly)

Vagus nerve

Cervical ganglia

Constricts bronchi

Relaxes bronchi

Slows heartbeat

Accelerates heartbeat, strengthens contraction

Spinal cord

Stimulates activity

Stomach

Inhibits activity

Pancreas

Stimulates glucose release by liver

Sympathetic chain

Stimulates gallbladder

Secretion of adrenaline, noradrenaline

Adrenal gland

Relaxes bladder

Stimulates ejaculation and vaginal contractions

Contracts bladder

Stimulates erection of sex organs

FIGURE 3.3 The Autonomic Nervous System The autonomic nervous system is split into the sympathetic and parasympathetic divisions. The sympathetic division prepares the body for action, accelerating the heartbeat, stimulating the secretion of adrenaline, and triggering other elements of the "fight-or-flight" response. The parasympathetic division calms the body by slowing the heartbeat, stimulating digestion, and triggering other restorative activities of the body.

The Brain

The human brain weighs about 1,400 grams (3 pounds) and is thought to comprise some 40 billion individual neurons. This lump of tissue, which has the consistency of a soft cheese, is the control center of our nervous system and the storage vault for our memories. Without it, we couldn't think, move, speak, or breathe. Let's consider the brain's structure and functions so that we can better understand the role of the brain in achieving good

FIGURE 3.4 The Brain This cross section of the human brain shows its three principal regions: the brainstem, which controls heartbeat and respiration; the cerebellum, which regulates muscular coordination; and the cerebrum, which is the center for information processing. Surrounding the central core of the brain is the limbic system, which includes the amygdala, the hippocampus, and the hypothalamus. The limbic system plays an important role in emotions, especially those related to sexual arousal, aggression, and pain.

health. We'll be considering the three principal regions of the brain: the brainstem, the cerebellum, and the cerebrum (Figure 3.4).

Lower-Level Structures

brainstem The oldest and most central region of the brain; includes the medulla, pons, and reticular formation.

Located at the point where the spinal cord swells as it enters the skull, the **brainstem** evolved first in the vertebrate brain; it is remarkably similar in animals ranging from fish to humans. The brainstem contains the medulla, the pons, and the reticular formation. Together, they control basic and involuntary life-support functions via the autonomic nervous system. (This is why a blow to the head at the base of the skull is so dangerous.) The brainstem is also the point at which most nerves passing between the spinal cord and the brain cross over, so that the left side of the brain sends and receives messages from the *right* side of the body, and the right side of the brain sends and receives messages from the *left* side of the body.

medulla The brainstem region that controls heartbeat and breathing.

The **medulla** controls several vital reflexes, including breathing, heart rate, salivation, coughing, and sneezing. It also receives sensory information about blood pressure and then, based on this input, varies the constriction or dilation of blood vessels to maintain an optimal state. Damage to the medulla is often fatal. An overdose of an opiate drug such as morphine or heroin may disrupt (or even arrest) breathing because of the drug's effects on the medulla.

Located just up from the medulla, the *pons* consists of two pairs of thick stalks that connect to the cerebellum. The pons contains nuclei that help regulate sleep, breathing, swallowing, bladder control, equilibrium, taste, eye movement, facial expressions, and posture.

reticular formation A network of neurons running through the brainstem involved with sleep, alertness, and arousal.

As the spinal cord's sensory input travels up through the brain, branch fibers stimulate the **reticular formation**, a brainstem circuit that governs arousal and sleep. The reticular formation is also responsible for alerting the brain during moments of danger and for prioritizing all incoming information. If a person suffers injury to the reticular formation, he or she may lapse into a coma and never awaken.

thalamus The brain's sensory switchboard; located on top of the brainstem, this brain structure routes messages to the higher brain regions.

Above the brainstem is the **thalamus**. Consisting of two egg-shaped groups of nuclei, the thalamus sorts sensory information received from the brainstem and routes it to the higher brain regions that deal with vision, hearing, taste, and touch.

Located at the back of the brain, the **cerebellum**, or "little brain," is shaped like a small-scale replica of the larger brain. Its main function is to maintain body balance and coordinate voluntary muscle movement. Damage to the cerebellum produces a loss of muscle tone, tremors, and abnormal posture. In addition, some studies suggest that specialized parts of the cerebellum contribute to memory, language, and cognition. Children with *dyslexia* or *attention deficit hyperactivity disorder (ADHD)*, for example, often have smaller cerebella or reduced activity in this region of their brains (Kibby, Pavawalla, Fancher, Naillon, & Hynd, 2009; McAlonan and others, 2007).

The Limbic System

Surrounding the central core of the brain is the **limbic system**, which includes the amygdala, hippocampus, hypothalamus, and septal area. The limbic system is believed to play an important role in emotions, especially those related to sexual arousal, aggression, and pain.

The limbic system includes an almond-shaped structure called the **amygdala** that is associated with emotional responses. In 1939, neurosurgeons Heinrich Kluver and Paul Bucy surgically lesioned (destroyed) the amygdala in the brain of an especially aggressive rhesus monkey; the operation transformed the violent creature into a docile one. Other researchers have discovered that electrical stimulation of the amygdala will reliably trigger rage or fear responses in a variety of animals.

Some scientists believe that a range of behaviors associated with *autism*, such as a reluctance to make eye contact and other deficits in social functioning, may be linked to abnormal size or functioning of the amygdala. Using brain scans, researchers in one study found that among toddlers diagnosed with autism the amygdala was, on average, 13% larger at age 2, compared with control children without autism (Mosconi and others, 2009).

Another limbic circuit involves areas within the **hippocampus**, thought to be involved in spatial orientation, learning, and memory. When the hippocampus is injured, people typically develop *anterograde amnesia*, a form of amnesia in which they are unable to form new memories but retain their memory for previously learned skills. In a famous case, a talented composer and conductor, Clive Wearing (2005), suffered damage to his hippocampus in 1985. Since then he has lived from one moment to the next, always feeling as though he has just awakened and not remembering the moment before, yet he has retained his musical skills.

Lying just below (*hypo*) the thalamus, the **hypothalamus** interconnects with numerous regions of the brain. Neuroscientists have pinpointed hypothalamic nuclei that influence hunger and regulate thirst, body temperature, and sexual behavior. Neuroscientists James Olds and Peter Milner made an intriguing discovery in 1954 about the role of the hypothalamus in the brain's reward system. The researchers were attempting to implant electrodes in the brainstems of laboratory rats when they accidentally stimulated an area in the hypothalamus. Much to the researchers' surprise, the rats kept returning to the precise location in their cages where they had previously been stimulated by the errant electrode. Recognizing that the animals were behaving as if they were seeking more stimulation, Olds and Milner went on to conduct a series of experiments that validated their discovery of the brain's reward circuitry. Indeed, rats have been known to "self-stimulate" their hypothalamic reward centers as many as 7,000 times per hour. As you will see in Chapter 9, some researchers believe that certain addictions—perhaps to food, alcohol, and other drugs—may stem from a genetic *reward deficiency syndrome* in which the brain's reward circuitry malfunctions and leads to powerful cravings.

cerebellum Located at the rear of the brain, this brain structure coordinates voluntary movement and balance.

limbic system A network of neurons surrounding the central core of the brain; associated with emotions such as fear and aggression; includes the hypothalamus, the amygdala, and the hippocampus.

amygdala Two clusters of neurons in the limbic system that are linked to emotion, especially aggression.

Hypothalamus
Hippocampus
Septal area
Amygdala

Limbic system

hippocampus A structure in the brain's limbic system linked to spatial orientation, learning, and memory.

hypothalamus Lying just below the thalamus, the region of the brain that influences hunger, thirst, body temperature, and sexual behavior; helps govern the endocrine system via the pituitary gland.

The Human Brain The cerebrum, which is covered in a network of blood vessels and made up of extensive folds and convolutions, is divided into two hemispheres.

The Cerebral Cortex

The *cerebrum*, which represents about 80% of the brain's total weight, forms two hemispheres (left and right) that are primarily filled with synaptic connections linking the surface of the brain to its other regions. The thin surface layer of the cerebrum, called the **cerebral cortex**, is what really makes us human. This 3-millimeter-thick sheet of some 20 billion nerve cells contains neural centers that give rise to our sensory capacities, skilled motor responses, language abilities, and aptitude for reasoning.

The cortex in each hemisphere can be divided into four principal regions, or lobes; each lobe carries out many functions, and in some cases, several lobes work together to perform a function (Figure 3.5). The *occipital lobe*, located at the back of the cortex, receives visual information from the retina of each eye. The *parietal lobe*, in the center of the cortex, receives information from the skin and body. Auditory information from the ears projects to the *temporal lobes*. The *frontal lobes*, lying just behind the forehead, are involved in reasoning, planning, and controlling body movement.

In the parietal lobe, on the edge of the frontal lobe, the **sensory cortex** processes body sensations such as touch. The **motor cortex**, at the back of the frontal lobes, lies just in front of the sensory cortex. Remember Lakeesha from the chapter introduction? Her cerebral palsy was caused by damage to her motor cortex.

In 1870, German physicians Gustav Fritsch and Eduard Hitzig discovered that electrical stimulation of the motor cortex triggers movement in the limbs of laboratory animals.

(a)   (b)

FIGURE 3.5 The Cerebral Cortex (a) Each of the four lobes, or regions, of the cerebral cortex performs various functions—sometimes separately, but more often in conjunction with another region. (b) Within these regions are the neural centers that give rise to our sensory capacities, skilled motor responses, language ability, and reasoning ability.

Many decades later, neurosurgeon Wilder Penfield (1952) mapped the motor cortex in conscious patients during surgery to remove brain tumors. In addition to mapping the cortex according to the body parts that it controlled, Penfield made the remarkable discovery that the amount of motor cortex devoted to a specific body part is proportional to the degree of control that we have over that body part. The muscles of the face and fingers, for example, have much more representation in the motor cortex than does the thigh muscle. Penfield also mapped the sensory cortex and similarly found that the amount of cortical representation was proportional to the sensitivity of a given body part (see Figure 3.6).

The basic functional organization of the primary sensory and motor areas of the cerebral cortex is virtually identical in all mammals, from the rat to the human. However, the sensory and motor areas account for only about one fourth of the total area of the human cerebral cortex. Researchers are just beginning to understand the functions of the remaining areas, called the **association cortex**, which are responsible for higher mental functions, such as thinking and speaking. Interestingly, humans are not the species with the the largest brains proportionate to their body size: Porpoises, whales, and elephants have much larger brains. Yet in ascending the evolutionary scale, it is clear that the more intelligent animals have much greater amounts of association cortex.

cerebral cortex The thin layer of cells that covers the cerebrum; the seat of conscious sensation, skilled motor responses, language, and information processing.

sensory cortex Lying at the front of the parietal lobes, the region of the cerebral cortex that processes body sensations such as touch.

motor cortex Lying at the rear of the frontal lobes, the region of the cerebral cortex that controls voluntary movements.

association cortex Areas of the cerebral cortex that integrate multisensory information and higher mental functions such as thinking and speaking.

Primary motor cortex

Somatosensory cortex

FIGURE 3.6 Topographic Organization of the Somatosensory and Primary Motor Areas Proportionately more cortical tissue is devoted to the primary (more sensitive and delicately controlled) body parts than to other (somatosensory) parts (information from Penfield, 1952).

endocrine system Consists of glands that secrete hormones, chemical messengers that regulate bodily functions.

hormones Chemical messengers, released into the bloodstream by endocrine glands, which have an effect on distant organs.

FIGURE 3.7 The Endocrine Glands and Feedback Control (a) Under the direction of the brain's hypothalamus, the pituitary releases hormones that, in turn, regulate the secretions of the thyroid, the adrenal glands, and the reproductive organs. (b) A complex negative feedback system regulates the production of many hormones. As the levels of hormones produced in target glands rise in the blood (stimulation), the hypothalamus and the pituitary decrease their production of hormones, and the secretion of hormones by the target glands also slows (inhibition).

THE ENDOCRINE SYSTEM

The second of the body's communication systems, the **endocrine system** (Figure 3.7), is closely connected to the nervous system in regulating many bodily functions. Whereas the nervous system communicates through neurotransmitters, the endocrine system communicates through chemical messengers called **hormones**. Unlike the much speedier nervous system, which is chiefly responsible for fast-acting, short-duration responses, the endocrine system primarily governs slow-acting responses of longer duration, stimulating or inhibiting various bodily functions. As we'll see in later chapters, these responses play key roles in our health, including our moods and sleep, as well as suggesting why, for some people, stressful situations may promote overweight and obesity.

Endocrine glands secrete hormones directly into the bloodstream, where they travel to various organs and bind to receptor sites. Binding either stimulates or inhibits organs, depending on the type of receptor and hormone. In this section, we'll consider the activity of four important endocrine glands—the pituitary, adrenal, and thyroid glands and the pancreas.

(a)   (b)

The Pituitary and Adrenal Glands

The **pituitary gland** secretes a number of hormones that influence other glands. These include hormones that influence growth, sexual development, reproduction, kidney functioning, and aging.

Although the pituitary gland is often referred to as the *master gland* of the endocrine system, the brain's hypothalamus more properly deserves this title because it directly (and rigidly) controls pituitary functioning. Together, the hypothalamus and pituitary act as a master control system. For example, during a stressful moment, the hypothalamus secretes the hormone *corticotropin-releasing hormone (CRH)*, which travels in the bloodstream to the anterior pituitary, where it stimulates the pituitary to secrete *adrenocorticotropic hormone (ACTH)*. ACTH binds to receptor cells on the adrenal cortex, causing this gland to release cortisol into the bloodstream. The increased level of cortisol in the blood acts back on the hypothalamus and pituitary gland to inhibit the release of additional CRH and ACTH. This example of *feedback control* is similar to the mechanism by which a household thermostat regulates temperature by turning a furnace or air conditioner on or off as needed.

Located atop the kidneys, the **adrenal glands** secrete several important hormones that play a crucial role in the body's response to stress and emergencies. In a moment of danger, for example, the innermost region of the gland (the adrenal medulla) releases the hormones *epinephrine* and *norepinephrine*, which travel through the bloodstream to receptor sites on the heart. These hormones increase heart rate, blood pressure, and blood sugar, providing the body with a quick surge of energy. The outermost region of the gland (the adrenal cortex) consists of three regions, each of which produces a different group of steroid hormones: The *gonadocorticoids* include the male androgens and female estrogens. The principal glucocorticoid is *cortisol*, which helps to reduce swelling and inflammation following an injury. The *mineralocorticoids* include aldosterone, which helps maintain normal blood pressure. As the biopsychosocial model notes, each of these hormones represents one way in which our bodies react biologically to the social and psychological events of our lives.

pituitary gland Controlled by the hypothalamus, this gland releases a variety of hormones that act on other glands throughout the body.

adrenal glands Lying above the kidneys, the pair of endocrine glands that secrete epinephrine, norepinephrine, and cortisol, which are hormones that arouse the body during moments of stress.

The Thyroid Gland and the Pancreas

Located in the front of the neck, the *thyroid gland* is shaped like a butterfly, with the two wings representing the left and right thyroid lobes, which wrap around the windpipe. The thyroid gland produces the hormone thyroxin, which helps regulate the body's growth and metabolism (energy use). Located just behind the thyroid are four parathyroid

TABLE 3.2 Endocrine System Connections

See how the endocrine system is involved in health psychology issues covered in many later chapters, including the following:

- Mood and Depression (in various chapters)
- Sleep (in Chapter 7)
- Overweight and Obesity (in Chapter 8)
- Diabetes (in Chapter 10)

glands. The hormones secreted by these glands regulate the level of calcium in the body within a narrow range so that the nervous and muscular systems can function properly.

Overactivity in one or more of these glands (*hyperparathyroidism*) may trigger a host of problems, the symptoms of which have been described as "moans, groans, stones, bones, and psychiatric overtones." "Moans and groans" refers to the aching bones, fatigue, and weakness that patients often experience. "Stones" refers to kidney stones that can result when excess calcium circulating in the bloodstream gets caught in the kidneys. "Bones" refers to the possible development of osteoporosis, which occurs when the overactive parathyroid takes calcium from bones, decreasing their density and making them brittle. The "psychiatric overtones" come from the difficulty concentrating and depression that may occur.

Another endocrine gland, the *pancreas*, produces glucagon and insulin, two hormones that act in opposition to regulate the level of the sugar glucose in the blood. Glucagon raises the concentration of glucose in the blood, while insulin controls the conversion of sugar and carbohydrates into energy by promoting the uptake of glucose by the body's cells (see Chapter 8).

THE CARDIOVASCULAR AND RESPIRATORY SYSTEMS

cardiovascular system Consists of the heart, blood, and blood vessels that supply oxygen to the body.

respiratory system Consists of the lungs and airway through which we inhale air and exhale carbon dioxide.

Long before stethoscopes were invented, heartbeat and respiration were recognized as indicators of health—and, indeed, of being alive. The **cardiovascular system** consists of the heart, blood, and blood vessels that supply every tissue in the body with oxygen. Where does that oxygen come from? From the **respiratory system**, which consists of the lungs and the airway (including the nose and mouth, pharynx, larynx, trachea, and bronchial tubes) through which we inhale air and exhale carbon dioxide. Let's examine the major components of these two vital bodily systems.

Blood and Circulation

Human blood is a living tissue; it contains three types of cells that perform different functions. Red blood cells, or *erythrocytes*, carry oxygen from the lungs to the cells of the body. Red blood cells are formed in the bone marrow and contain *hemoglobin*, the iron-rich substance that gives blood its reddish tint. The blood uses hemoglobin to pick up oxygen in the lungs while releasing the carbon dioxide it has carried in from the cells. Blood also carries nutrients from the digestive system to cells and transports cellular waste to the kidneys for excretion in urine.

The white blood cells (*leukocytes*) carried by the blood are part of the immune system, and the *platelets* are small cell fragments that stick together (coagulate) when necessary to form clots along the walls of damaged blood vessels. Without leukocytes, we would have no defenses against infection. Without platelets, we would bleed to death from a wound or even from a small cut.

Blood is transported throughout the body by the *circulatory system*, which consists of several types of blood vessels. **Arteries** carry blood from the heart to the other organs and tissues. The arteries branch into increasingly narrower blood vessels called *arterioles*, which eventually connect with *capillaries*. Capillaries are the smallest of the blood vessels and carry blood directly to the individual cells. **Veins** return blood from the capillaries to the heart.

The vessels of the circulatory system move blood throughout the body by dilating and contracting as needed. When arteries narrow (constrict), resistance to blood flow increases. Blood pressure is a measure of the force exerted by blood against the blood vessel walls. This force is highest during *systole*, when the heart contracts in order to force the blood out. During *diastole*, the heart relaxes as blood flows into the heart and blood pressure drops. Thus, diastolic blood pressure is lower than systolic blood pressure (see Figure 3.8).

arteries Blood vessels that carry blood away from the heart to other organs and tissues; a small artery is called an *arteriole*.

veins Blood vessels that carry blood back to the heart from the capillaries.

FIGURE 3.8 The Cardiac Cycle The beating of the heart occurs in two phases. In the *systolic phase* the heart muscle contracts, blood is pushed out, and blood pressure increases. The *diastolic phase* occurs between contractions, as the heart muscle relaxes, blood flows in, and blood pressure drops to its minimum.

Blood Pressure Systolic blood pressure (BP) less than 120 mmHg (millimeters of mercury), and diastolic BP less than 80 mmHg, is considered normal. When blood pressure rises above these levels, it is categorized as "elevated" (systolic between 120 and 129 or diastolic less than 80), as Stage 1 hypertension (systolic between 130 and 139 and diastolic between 80 and 89), as Stage 2 hypertension (systolic above 140 or diastolic above 90), or as hypertensive crisis (systolic above 180 and/or diastolic above 120) (Whelton and others, 2017).

Javier Larrea/Getty Images

TABLE 3.3 Cardiovascular System Connections

See how the cardiovascular system is involved in health psychology issues covered in many later chapters, including the following:

- Coping with Stress (in Chapter 5)
- Overweight and Obesity (in Chapter 8)
- Smoking and Alcohol Use (in Chapter 9)
- Cardiovascular Disease and Diabetes (in Chapter 10)

The Heart

The human heart is a muscular organ about the size of a clenched fist. It weighs only about 11 ounces, yet it pumps 5 or more quarts of blood through your circulatory system every minute of every day. Through the heart's pumping action, the blood vessels carry blood to our cells and tissues and remove waste products through the lungs, liver, and kidneys.

In birds and mammals, the heart is separated into four parts, or chambers: the right and left *atria*, in the upper section of the heart, and the right and left *ventricles*, in the lower section of the heart. These chambers work in coordinated fashion to bring blood into the heart and then to pump it throughout the body (Figure 3.9). Blood returning

① Oxygen-depleted blood returns to the heart from the body through the superior and the inferior vena cava. . . .

② This blood is pumped from the right atrium into the right ventricle. . . .

③ And from there, through capillaries of the lungs, where it picks up fresh oxygen and disposes of carbon dioxide. . . .

④ The freshly oxygenated blood is pumped through the pulmonary vein into the left atrium and from there into the left ventricle, from which it flows into the arterial system.

FIGURE 3.9 The Human Heart The heart is separated into four parts, or chambers: the right and left atria, in the upper section of the heart; and the right and left ventricles, in the lower section of the heart.

from the body enters the *right atrium* through two large veins. After expanding to receive the blood, the right atrium contracts, forcing the "used" blood into the *right ventricle*. Depleted of oxygen, this "used" blood is sent into the pulmonary artery (*pulmonary* refers to lungs), then through the capillaries of the lungs, where it picks up oxygen for later distribution to cells and disposes of carbon dioxide (CO_2, which will be exhaled) as waste. The now oxygen-rich blood flows into the pulmonary vein, and the pumping action of cardiac muscles forces that blood into the left atrium and then into the left ventricle. The left ventricle propels the oxygen-rich blood into the aorta, from which it flows into the arterial system, carrying nutrients to all parts of the body. If you listen to your heartbeat, the "lubb-dup, lubb-dup" sound represents the closing of the valves between the atria and ventricles ("lubb"), followed by the closing of the valves between the ventricles and the arteries ("dup").

The Lungs

From the foregoing description of the heart's action, it's clear that the heart is closely related to the respiratory system. The most important organs in the respiratory system, of course, are the lungs (Figure 3.10). After air enters the body through the mouth or nose,

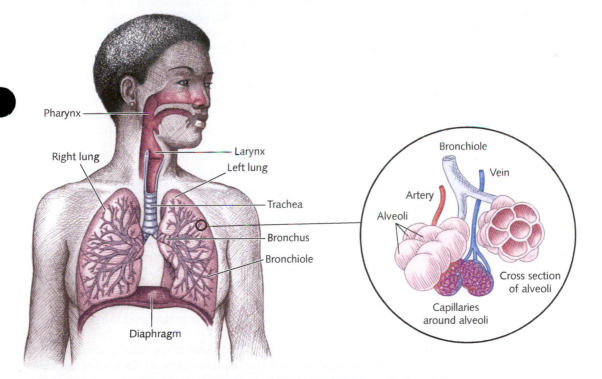

FIGURE 3.10 The Respiratory System Air enters through the nose and mouth, passes into the pharynx, past the larynx (voice box), and into the trachea, bronchi, and bronchioles to the alveoli. The alveoli are the sites where oxygen and carbon dioxide are exchanged.

Diversity and Healthy Living

Asthma

The rapid rise of chronic **noncommunicable diseases (NCDs)** represents one of the major global challenges to health. By 2020, it is estimated that over 70% of the global burden of disease will be caused by NCDs—especially cancer, diabetes, cardiovascular disease, and chronic respiratory diseases such as asthma (World Health Organization, 2015f).

Most childhood cases of asthma are triggered by animal dander, pollens, dust, indoor mold, or damp conditions in homes and buildings (National Center for Environmental Health, 2017a). In the nonallergic form of asthma (which is more likely to affect adults), cold air, viral infections, secondhand smoke, and household chemicals trigger asthma attacks. There are an estimated 6 million chemicals in the environment, and 2,800 of these have allergenic properties. Many people with asthma find that strong emotions, stress, or anxiety can make symptoms of asthma worse, especially during a severe attack.

An asthma attack occurs when the immune system produces an antibody that activates the body's defensive cells, causing the muscles surrounding the bronchi in the lungs to constrict and obstruct the flow of air. In addition, the bronchi become inflamed and filled with mucus, further reducing the supply of oxygen. The major symptoms of an asthma attack include wheezing, a whistling sound that may occur throughout the chest or in a local area where the airway has become blocked; coughing as the body attempts to rid itself of any foreign substance (mucus) or irritant (smoke); and shortness of breath caused by fast, shallow breathing as the body attempts to take in sufficient oxygen through narrowed airways.

Although asthma can develop at any age, it usually begins in childhood. It now affects 8.4% of children under age 18, making it the most common chronic childhood disease in the United States. It affects more boys (9.9%) than girls (6.9%), more children in families living below the federal poverty level (11.1%) than children in families that are not poor (8.4% or less), and more non-Hispanic black children (13.4%) than Hispanic children (8.0%) or non-Hispanic white children (7.4%) (National Center for Environmental Health, 2017b).

Asthma was rare in 1900, but now it has grown into an epidemic and is on the rise everywhere: About 25 million people have asthma in the United States (7.8%) and nearly 10 times that many around the world (World Health Organization, 2017a). The prevalence of asthma is highest in Western countries, particularly English-speaking ones; the disease is rare in parts of rural South America and Africa. Each year in the United States, there are nearly 2 million visits to the emergency room for asthma, 10 million outpatient visits to private physician offices, 500,000 hospitalizations, and nearly 5,000 asthma-related deaths, mostly in older adults. Worldwide, there were 383,000 asthma deaths in 2015 (World Health Organization, 2017a).

---

noncommunicable disease (NCD) A chronic disease, such as cardiovascular disease, cancer, or diabetes, that is not passed from person to person.

bronchi The pair of respiratory tubes that branch into progressively smaller passageways, the bronchioles, culminating in the air sacs within the right and left lungs (the alveoli).

it passes to the lungs through the *pharynx* and *trachea*, from which it travels through the **bronchi** that branch into smaller tubes, called *bronchioles*. Each bronchiole ends in a cluster of small, bubble-like sacs called *alveoli*. The membranous wall of each alveolus is thin enough to permit the exchange of gases, allowing oxygen to be exchanged for carbon dioxide. Alveoli are surrounded by millions of capillaries so that gases can be transferred efficiently to and from the bloodstream.

The word *respiration* has two meanings. At the level of the individual cell, it refers to energy-producing chemical reactions that require oxygen. At the level of the whole organism, it refers to the process of taking in oxygen from the environment and ridding the body of carbon dioxide. The first of these meanings addresses the question How do the muscles that control lung expansion "know" when it's time to breathe? The answer is that sensors in capillaries monitor the chemical composition of the blood. As the

The cause of asthma, which may not be one disease but rather a number of different diseases that have common symptoms but different underlying pathologies, is not understood. Although having one parent—or both—with asthma increases a child's risk, environmental and lifestyle factors probably have a greater influence on risk than genetic factors do. Among the candidates for risk factors is the tendency of children to spend more time indoors today than they did in earlier generations, thus increasing their exposure to household allergens, including dust mites, animal dander, and indoor pests such as cockroaches. According to another theory, the immune systems of Western children, unlike children in developing countries, are weaker because Western children are not conditioned to live with parasites, so the children become more vulnerable to asthma and other respiratory conditions such as allergic rhinitis (commonly called hay fever).

In the largest study of its kind ever conducted, researchers at the National Institute of Allergy and Infectious Diseases studied more than 1,500 children, ages 4 to 11, living in inner cities. In a powerful validation of the biopsychosocial model, the researchers found that many factors, rather than a single cause, were responsible for the recent increase in asthma morbidity. Among these factors were environmental toxins, such as indoor allergens and passive smoke; psychological problems of both the children and their caretakers, such as defensiveness and panic disorder; and problems with access to medical care.

In addition to shortness of breath and wheezing, asthma attacks often trigger anxiety and even panic as the person feels unable to breathe. Health psychologists play a role in helping patients manage these symptoms by teaching them how to monitor their symptoms, avoid triggers, use medications properly, and devise a self-management plan. Patient education is the most prominent behavioral intervention for asthma, beginning with instruction about basic asthma facts and medications. Some programs also focus on stress management; muscle relaxation techniques that improve breathing; and navigating the health care system, including how to find a doctor, prepare for medical visits, and pay for medical care. Environmental interventions include removing carpeting, draperies, curtains, and upholstered furniture; sealing mattresses and pillows in dustproof enclosures; finding new homes for pets; and installing high-efficiency particle-arresting (HEPA) filters. The goal of these programs is to eliminate or reduce symptoms, minimize the need for emergency interventions, and improve the overall quality of the asthma sufferer's life.

As you'll see in subsequent chapters, new research is offering a better understanding of the link between stress and the respiratory system, and research is demonstrating the effectiveness of new treatments, including *heart-rate variability biofeedback* and cognitive-behavior therapy. Behavioral interventions often result in improved pulmonary function and significant reductions in symptoms and in the need for medical treatment (Clark, Mitchell, & Rand, 2009).

level of carbon dioxide rises, via the chemical reactions of respiration, this information is relayed to the brain's medulla, which signals the muscles of the *diaphragm* to contract and cause you to inhale. Sensing that the level of carbon dioxide is low, the medulla signals the muscles to slow the rate of breathing until the carbon dioxide level returns to normal.

The respiratory system also has protective mechanisms that eliminate airborne dust particles and other foreign matter from the body. The two reflex mechanisms are sneezing when the nasal passages are irritated and coughing when the larger airways of the throat are irritated. In addition, the air passages in the nose, mouth, and trachea are lined with tiny hairs called **cilia** that trap germs. Moving in a wavelike fashion, the cilia force the mucus that coats them gradually up toward the mouth, where it is either expelled in a cough or swallowed.

cilia Tiny hairs; those that line the air passageways in the nose, mouth, and trachea move in wavelike fashion, trapping germs and forcing them out of the respiratory system.

The Diversity and Healthy Living box discusses asthma to give an example of what can happen when the respiratory system malfunctions and how health psychology contributes to the care and well-being of sufferers.

THE DIGESTIVE SYSTEM

Digestion is the breaking down of food into molecules that can be absorbed by the blood and distributed to individual cells as nutrients for energy, growth, and tissue repair. The **digestive system** consists primarily of the *digestive tract* or *gastrointestinal (GI) tract*—a long, convoluted tube that extends from the mouth to the anus (Figure 3.11). The digestive system also includes the salivary glands, the pancreas, the liver, and the gallbladder.

Asthma Most childhood cases of asthma are triggered by animal dander, pollen, dust, indoor mold, or damp conditions in homes and buildings.

digestive system The body's system for digesting food; includes the digestive (gastrointestinal, or GI) tract, salivary glands, pancreas, liver, and gallbladder.

FIGURE 3.11 The Digestive System *Digestion* is the process of breaking food down into simpler chemical compounds to make it absorbable in the digestive tract. The process begins in the mouth, where food is chewed and ground up by the teeth. From the mouth, food passes through the esophagus to the stomach, where it is churned and proteins are chemically digested. From there, food passes into the large and small intestines, where chemical digestion of carbohydrates and proteins is completed. Waste products of food are stored as feces in the rectum and eliminated from the body through the anus.

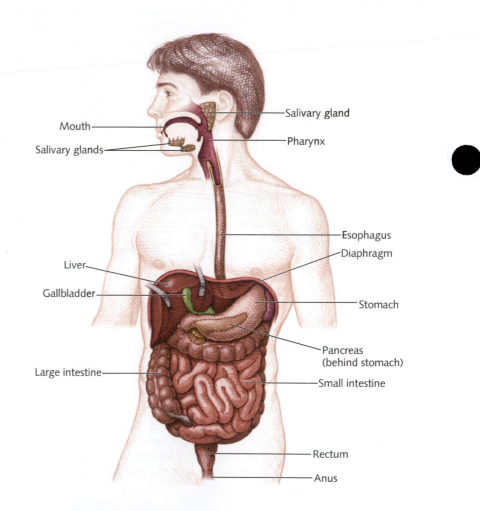

How Food Is Digested

Digestion begins in the mouth, where chewing and the chemical action of salivary enzymes begin to break food down. Like most mammals, humans have teeth that assist in the tearing and grinding of food. As food is chewed, it is moistened by saliva so that it can be swallowed more easily. Saliva contains a digestive enzyme called *amylase* that causes starches to begin to decompose.

Once food is swallowed, it passes into the *esophagus*, a muscular tube about 9.3 inches (25 centimeters) long in the typical adult. The muscles of the esophagus contract rhythmically, propelling the food downward in an involuntary reflexive motion called *peristalsis*. This reflex is so efficient and strong that you are able to swallow food and water even while standing on your head.

In the stomach, the food is mixed with a variety of gastric juices, including hydrochloric acid and *pepsin*, an enzyme that breaks down proteins. At this point, the food has been converted into a semiliquid mass. The secretion of gastric juices (including saliva) is controlled by the autonomic nervous system. Food in the mouth—or even the sight, smell, or thought of food—is sufficient to trigger the flow of gastric juices. Conversely, fear inhibits digestive activity. When you are in danger or under stress, your mouth becomes very dry, and food remains an uncomfortable, undigested lump in your stomach.

Stomachs vary in capacity among different species. Depending on their success in hunting, carnivores such as hyenas may eat only once every few days. Fortunately, their large-capacity stomachs can hold the equivalent of 30% to 35% of their body weight. In contrast, mammals that eat more frequent, smaller meals typically have much smaller stomachs. The capacity of the average college student's stomach is roughly 2 to 4 liters of food—about 2% to 3% of the average person's body weight—though it can stretch to hold much more.

By about four hours food is eaten, the stomach has emptied its contents into the small and large intestines. Digestive fluids from the pancreas, liver, and gallbladder are secreted into the *small intestine* through a series of ducts. These fluids contain enzymes that break down proteins, fats, and carbohydrates. For example, the *liver* produces a salty substance called *bile* that emulsifies fats almost as effectively as dishwashing liquid, and the pancreas produces the hormone *insulin*, which assists in transporting glucose from the intestine into body cells.

The breakdown of food that began in the mouth and stomach is completed in the small intestine. The inner lining of the small intestine is composed of gathered circular folds, which greatly increase its surface area. Fully extended, an average adult's small intestine would be almost 20 feet (approximately 6 meters) in length, with a total surface area of 3,229 square feet (300 square meters)—roughly the size of a basketball court. This vast area is lined with tiny, fingerlike projections of mucus, called *villi*, through which water and nutrient molecules pass into the bloodstream. Once in the bloodstream, nutrients travel to individual cells.

Food particles that have not been absorbed into the bloodstream then pass into the *large intestine*, or *colon*, where absorption (mainly of water) continues. In the course of digestion, a large volume of water—approximately 7 liters each day—is absorbed. When this process is disrupted, as occurs in diarrhea and other gastric disorders, dehydration becomes a danger. Indeed, dehydration is the reason that diarrhea remains the leading cause of infant death in many developing countries.

FIGURE 3.12 The Immune System Positioned throughout the body, the organs of the immune system are home to lymphocytes, white blood cells that are the basis of the body's immune defense against foreign agents, or antigens. Other components of the system are the bone marrow, where lymphocytes are produced; lymph nodes, which are glands that help your body fight infection; and the thymus, spleen, and tonsils. The lymph nodes produce the fluid lymph, which travels throughout the body via the lymphatic capillaries and filters impurities.

Tonsil

Thymus

Spleen

Lymph nodes

Bone marrow

Lymphatic capillaries

The process of digestion is completed when food particles that were not absorbed earlier are converted into feces by colon bacteria such as *Escherichia coli*. (*E. coli* has gotten a lot of press for causing sickness in people who eat foods infected with it, but that is actually a different strain than the one that occurs naturally in the colon.) Fecal matter is primarily composed of water, bacteria, cellulose fibers, and other indigestible substances.

THE IMMUNE SYSTEM

At this moment, you are surrounded by countless numbers of microorganisms. Most are not dangerous. Indeed, many, such as those that assist in digestion and the decomposition of waste matter, play an important role in health. However, **antigens**—foreign substances that can be bacteria, viruses, fungi, parasites, or any foreign microorganism—are dangerous to your health, even deadly. Defending your health against these invaders is the job of the immune system.

You may be exposed to antigens through direct bodily contact (handshaking, kissing, or sexual intercourse) or through food, water, insects, and airborne microbes. Antigens may penetrate body tissue through several routes, including the skin, the digestive tract, the respiratory tract, or the urinary tract. Their impact depends on the number and virulence of the microorganisms and the strength of the body's defenses.

Structure of the Immune System

Unlike most other systems, the immune system is spread throughout the body in the form of a network of capillaries, lymph nodes (glands), and ducts that make up the *lymphatic system*, along with the bone marrow, thymus, and tonsils (Figure 3.12). Lymphatic capillaries carry *lymph*, a colorless bodily fluid formed by water, proteins, microbes, and other foreign substances that are drained from the spaces between body cells. Lymph takes its name from the billions of white blood cells it circulates, called **lymphocytes**. These cells, which are produced in the bone marrow, patrol the entire body, searching for bacteria, viruses, cancerous cells, and other antigens.

The lymph nodes contain filters that capture infectious substances and debris; as lymph passes through the lymph nodes, the lymphocytes destroy the foreign particles collected there. During an immune response, the lymphocytes expand, which produces swelling and inflammation. You may have noticed how your lymph nodes swell when you are fighting an infection.

Two structures play a role in the activity of lymphocytes: the thymus and the tonsils. The *thymus*, which also functions as part of the endocrine system, secretes *thymosin*, a hormone that helps control the maturation

---

TABLE 3.4 Immune System Connections

See how the immune system is involved in health psychology issues covered in many later chapters, including the following:

- How Does Stress Make You Sick? (in Chapter 4)
- Diabetes (in Chapter 10)
- Immunocompetence in Relation to Cancer (in Chapter 11)
- HIV and AIDS (in Chapter 12)

antigen A foreign substance that stimulates an immune response.

lymphocytes Antigen-fighting white blood cells produced in the bone marrow.

and development of lymphocytes. Interestingly, the thymus is largest during infancy and childhood and slowly shrinks throughout adulthood, which may partially explain why immune responses are generally more efficient during childhood and why aging is associated with reduced immune efficiency. Finally, the *tonsils* are masses of lymphatic tissue that seem to function as a holding station for lymphocytes, as well as a garbage can for worn-out blood cells.

The Immune Response

The body's immune reactions can be divided into two broad categories: nonspecific immunity and specific immunity. *Nonspecific immune defenses* fight off any foreign substance, including those never before encountered. *Specific immune defenses* occur only when a particular invader has been encountered before, creating a kind of immunological *memory* for the intruder.

Nonspecific Immune Responses

The body's first line of defense consists of the several layers of tightly knit cells that make up the skin. Chemicals found in perspiration, such as the oily *sebum* secreted by glands beneath the skin, prevent most bacteria and fungi from growing on the skin.

The nose, eyes, and respiratory tract—although they lack the tough, protective barrier of the skin—also provide a first line of defense. The mucous membranes of the nose and respiratory tract are armed with hairlike cilia, which, as noted earlier, catch dust, microbes, and other foreign matter. A powerful enzyme in tears and saliva destroys the cell walls of many bacteria. Similarly, gastric acids are able to destroy most foreign substances that enter the digestive system.

When a foreign substance penetrates the skin cells, it encounters a second line of defense, called *phagocytosis*, in which two specialized lymphocytes—phagocytes and macrophages—attack the foreign particles. *Phagocytes* are large scavenger cells that prowl the blood and tissues of the body for invaders, destroying them by engulfing and digesting them. *Macrophages* ("big eaters") are phagocytes found at the site of an infection, as well as in the lymph nodes, spleen, and lungs. These specialized white blood cell "sentries" pass into body tissues, where they hunt antigens and worn-out cells. A single phagocyte can digest 5 to 25 bacteria before it dies from an accumulation of toxic wastes.

Suppose, for instance, that a splinter has punctured your skin. Neighboring cells in the area of the wound immediately release several chemicals—particularly *histamine*, which increases blood flow to the area. Circulating phagocytes and macrophages, attracted by these chemicals, rush to the site of the wound, where they begin to engulf the inevitable

Eye of Science/Science Source

The Immune System in Action: A Macrophage Attacks Macrophages ("big eaters") are specialized white blood cell "sentries" that pass into body tissues, where they hunt antigens and worn-out cells. A single macrophage can digest 5 to 25 bacteria before it dies from an accumulation of toxic wastes.

bacteria and foreign particles that enter the body through the wound. At the same time, blood clots form, sealing off the wound site, and additional histamine is released, creating a hot environment unfavorable to bacteria.

As a consequence of this sequence of nonspecific immune reactions, collectively referred to as the *inflammatory response*, the injured area becomes swollen, red, and tender to the touch. In addition, some lymphocytes release proteins that produce *systemic effects* (effects throughout the entire body), such as fever, in the most serious cases of invasion (for example, food poisoning). In addition to its role in destroying invading microorganisms, inflammation helps restore bodily tissues that have been damaged (Figure 3.13). Inflammation is essential for survival because it isolates injured tissue, mobilizes our immune response, and promotes healing. However, inflammation can also be out of proportion to a health threat, or directed toward otherwise healthy tissue. This overreaction, called *chronic inflammation*, can be damaging. Allergies and *autoimmune diseases* such as arthritis are common examples of chronic inflammation.

In addition to the phagocytes and macrophages, the immune system's nonspecific defenses include smaller lymphocytes called *natural killer* (NK) cells, which patrol the body for diseased cells that have gone awry. NK cells destroy their targets by injecting them with lethal chemicals. They also secrete various forms of *interferon*, an antimicrobial protein that inhibits the spread of viral infections to healthy cells. Interferons, which differ from species to species, work by preventing viruses from replicating. Interferons are the

FIGURE 3.13 The Inflammatory Response When an infection or, as in this case, an injury breaches the body's first line of defense, histamine and other chemicals are released at the site of the disturbance. These chemicals increase blood flow to the area; attract white blood cells; and cause a clot to form, sealing off the site. Some of the white blood cells engulf foreign particles, while others release a protein that produces fever.

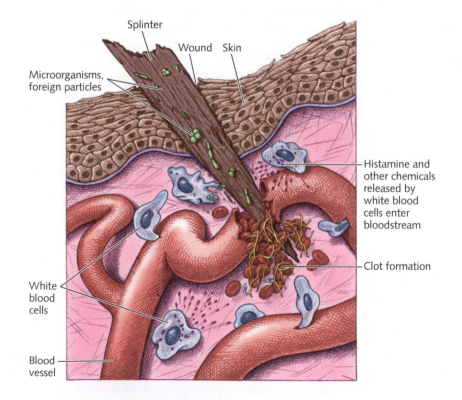

subject of intensive biomedical research; they show potential for treating influenza, the common cold, and other diseases.

Specific Immune Responses

Some invaders either elude the body's nonspecific defenses or are too powerful to be handled by phagocytes, macrophages, and NK cells alone. In such cases, the immune system calls upon its strongest line of defense: specific immune responses. These reactions occur when a particular substance has been encountered before. Some specific immunities are acquired, for example, when a nursing mother passes a specific immunity to her child through breast milk. Others develop when a person successfully weathers a disease such as measles or is *immunized*.

Specific immunity is also conferred by vaccines, which use a killed or nonvirulent form of a specific virus or other antigen to stimulate the body's responses. In response, the body acquires immunity by developing a "memory" of the antigen. Pediatric care includes early childhood vaccinations against mumps, chicken pox, whooping cough, polio, and other diseases, making the body artificially resistant to these diseases should the child ever be exposed to them. In 2016, about 86% of infants worldwide received the recommended 3 to 4 doses of the diphtheria–tetanus–pertussis (DTP3) vaccine, protecting them against infectious diseases, disability, and even death (World Health Organization, 2018). Still, more than 19 million children missed out on these routine, life-saving vaccinations, including about 15% of preschoolers in the United States (National Center for Health Statistics, 2017). Adults are encouraged to be immunized against influenza during the flu season; strains of influenza that are most expected to be contagious in a given season are used to develop that year's vaccine. Vaccination is an important public health measure because it not only protects the individual, but also reduces the risk of spreading disease to others who may not have been vaccinated, a phenomenon called *herd immunity*.

Specific immune responses involve two special lymphocytes, called *B cells* and *T cells*, which recognize and attack specific invading antigens. When a B cell is activated by a particular antigen, it divides into two types: a plasma cell and an antibody-producing memory cell (Figure 3.14). The rapid response of memory cells, called the *primary response*, is the basis of immunity to many infectious diseases, including polio, measles, and smallpox. Memory cells may last a lifetime, producing a stronger, faster antibody reaction should the particular antigen be encountered a second time. When a memory cell encounters the same antigen during a subsequent infection, the *secondary immune response* is triggered.

For many years, scientists believed that circulating antibodies produced by B cells were the sole basis of immunity. They now know that the immune system has a second line of defense, called *cell-mediated immunity*, in which T cells directly attack and kill foreign substances without the aid of antibodies.

How does the brain know there is an infection in the first place? The information is conveyed by chemical messengers called **cytokines**. One group of cytokines, called *anti-inflammatory cytokines*, reduces inflammation and promotes healing. Another group, called *proinflammatory cytokines* because they accelerate inflammation, includes several types of *interleukins* that have been linked to fatigue, depression, and social withdrawal (Eisenberger, Inagaki, Mashal, & Irwin, 2010; Irwin, 2008). Cytokines are produced in the blood by macrophages, which, as described earlier, are the first immune cells on the scene of an infection.

cytokines Protein molecules produced by immune cells that act on other cells to regulate immunity (including the interferons, interleukins, and tumor necrosis factors).

FIGURE 3.14 Primary and Secondary Responses of the Immune System (a) When a B cell is activated by an antigen, it divides into plasma cells, which manufacture antibodies, and memory cells. (b) When memory cells encounter the same antigen during a subsequent infection, the secondary immune response occurs. Memory cells release antibodies that attack the antigen and also divide, producing a new generation of plasma cells and memory cells.

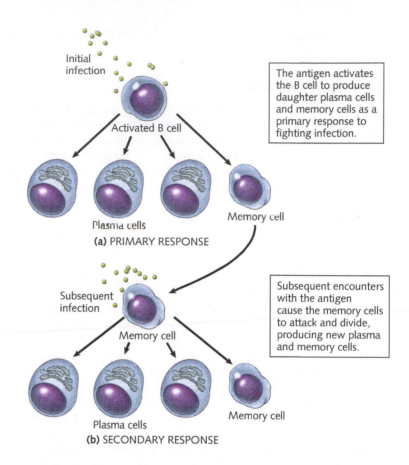

Initial infection

Activated B cell

The antigen activates the B cell to produce daughter plasma cells and memory cells as a primary response to fighting infection.

Plasma cells   Memory cell

(a) PRIMARY RESPONSE

Subsequent infection

Memory cell

Subsequent encounters with the antigen cause the memory cells to attack and divide, producing new plasma and memory cells.

Plasma cells   Memory cell

(b) SECONDARY RESPONSE

THE REPRODUCTIVE SYSTEM AND BEHAVIOR GENETICS

reproductive system The organs that make procreation possible; includes the male and female gonads and genitals.

The human **reproductive system** is where life and health begin (see Figure 3.15); it consists of the organs that make procreation possible. The separate development of the female and male reproductive systems begins during prenatal development, when a hormonal signal from the hypothalamus stimulates the pituitary gland to produce the *gonadotropic hormones*, which direct the development of the *gonads*, or sex glands—the ovaries in females and the testes in males. One of these hormones in particular, *GnRH* (gonadotropin-releasing hormone), directs the ovaries and testes to dramatically increase the production of sex hormones, especially *estrogen* in girls and *testosterone* in boys.

Ovaries and Testes

On either side of the female's uterus are two almond-shaped *ovaries*, which produce the hormones estrogen and progesterone. The outer layer of each ovary contains the *oocytes*, from which the *ova* (eggs) develop. The oocytes begin to form during the third month

FIGURE 3.15 The Reproductive System In the female, the left and right ovaries make eggs and secrete the sex hormone estrogen. In the male, the testes produce sperm cells and the sex hormone testosterone.

of prenatal development. At birth, an infant girl's two ovaries contain some 2 million oocytes—all that she will ever have. Of these, about 400,000 survive into puberty, and some 300 to 400 reach maturity and are released, generally one at a time, approximately every 28 days from the onset of puberty until menopause, which typically occurs around ages 45 to 55. If the released ovum is not fertilized by a sperm, it remains in the uterus for approximately 14 days, after which it is flushed out of the system with the uterine endometrium during menstruation.

The ovaries also produce two important hormones: *estrogen*, which triggers development of secondary sex characteristics, and *progesterone*, which is produced during the second half of the menstrual cycle to prepare the female body for possible pregnancy and declines if pregnancy does not occur.

In males, testosterone produced in the testes stimulates development of secondary sex characteristics and brings about the production of sperm. From puberty until old age, the testes of a human male produce an average of several hundred million sperm each day. The testes form during prenatal development and are subdivided into some 250 individual compartments, each of which is packed with coiled *seminiferous* ("seed-bearing") *tubules*. Sperm cells form in the tubules.

Fertilization and the Mechanisms of Heredity

Each of us started life as a single fertilized cell, called a *zygote*. At the moment of conception, a *sperm cell* from the male finds its way upward from the *uterus* into the *fallopian tubes*, where it fertilizes an ovum. Within a few hours, the nuclei of the egg and sperm fuse. Pregnancy is counted from the first day of the woman's last menstrual cycle, which is also the starting point of gestational (prenatal) age. Full-term pregnancies last 38 weeks, or nine months. Although obstetricians assign a due date based on the woman's last menstrual period, only about 5% of babies are born on that exact date. Babies born between three weeks before and two weeks after that date are considered "full term." Babies born earlier are called *preterm*; babies born later are called *post-term*.

Pregnancy is divided into three trimesters. During the first trimester, the woman may not even know she is pregnant, as menstrual periods sometimes continue to occur. Yet the first trimester is the time when the developing embryo is most sensitive to harm from substances such as drugs, alcohol, and environmental chemicals, collectively called *teratogens*. Many women experience "morning sickness" (nausea and vomiting) as an early symptom of pregnancy. During the second trimester, the baby—now referred to as a *fetus*—undergoes most of its development of organs and limbs; it also gains weight, as does the pregnant woman, for her weight comprises not just the growing fetus but also increased blood and other body fluids necessary for nourishing the fetus. In the third trimester, the expectant mother may experience intermittent discomfort as the fetus "kicks" and shifts position. Eventually she will go into labor, which may be signaled by "water breaking" (rupture of the amniotic sac, in which the fetus has been encased) and/or by strong cramp-like contractions of the uterus. The cervix dilates to allow the baby's head to "crown" and, if all goes well, after a few more pushes a new life is welcomed into the world.

Chromosomes and the Genome

A few hours after fertilization, the single-celled zygote travels down the fallopian tube, where the first cellular divisions take place. The zygote contains inherited information from both parents that will determine the child's characteristics. Each ovum and each sperm contain 23 *chromosomes*, the long, threadlike structures that carry our inheritance. At conception, the 23 chromosomes from the egg and the 23 from the sperm unite, bequeathing to the newly formed zygote a full complement of 46 chromosomes. As the cells of the developing person divide, this genetic material is replicated over and over, so that the nucleus of every cell in the person's body contains the same instructions written at the moment of conception.

The 23rd pair of chromosomes determines the zygote's sex. The mother always contributes an X chromosome; the father can contribute either an X or a Y chromosome. If the father's sperm also contains an X chromosome, the child will be a girl; a Y chromosome from Dad will produce a boy. Y chromosomes contain a single gene that triggers the *testes* to begin producing testosterone, which in turn initiates the sexual differentiation in appearance and neural differentiation during the fourth and fifth months of prenatal development.

Each chromosome is composed of strings of *genes*—the basic units of heredity that determine our growth and characteristics. Genes are discrete particles of *deoxyribonucleic acid (DNA)*. Each cell in the body contains over 20,000 genes that determine everything from the color of your hair to whether you have a tendency toward schizophrenia, a major psychological disorder.

Human Chromosomes At conception, 23 gene-carrying chromosomes from each parent unite to form a zygote with a full complement of 46 chromosomes and all the information needed to create a complex new being nine months later.

Adrian T Sumner/The Image Bank/Getty Images

Within the zygote, the 23 pairs of chromosomes carrying the genes from the mother and the father duplicate, forming two sets of the **genome**, the complete genetic instructions for making an organism. These two sets move toward opposite sides of the zygote, and the cell splits into two cells, each containing the original genetic code. These two cells duplicate and divide, becoming four, which duplicate and divide, becoming eight, and so on—each cell identical to the first. The first cells are **stem cells**, which have the potential to develop into many different types of cells in the body. About once in every 250 conceptions, at the two-cell stage the organism splits and *monozygotic* (identical) twins develop, each of which has the same DNA.

Tom Collins/Alamy Stock Photo

Genes and Environment

Behavior genetics is the study of the relative power and limits of genes and environment on our behavior. Most human characteristics are not determined by genes alone; rather, they are *multifactorial*—influenced by many different factors, including environmental factors. Human traits also tend to be *polygenic*—influenced by many different genes.

The sum total of genes that a person inherits is that person's **genotype**. The observable physical and nonphysical traits that are actually expressed constitute the person's **phenotype**. This distinction is important because each of us inherits many genes in our genotype that are not expressed in our phenotype. In genetic terminology, we are *carriers* of these unexpressed bits of DNA; although we may not manifest them in our own phenotype, they may be passed on to our offspring, who then will have them in their genotype and may or may not express them in their phenotype. Eye color inheritance is among the most straightforward and therefore often is used to help us understand this distinction. For most traits, a person's phenotype is determined by two patterns of genetic interaction: gene–gene and gene–environment.

Gene–Environment Interaction: Epigenetics

As we saw in Chapter 1, the field of *epigenetics* explores the ways in which genes interact with a person's environment. When behavior geneticists refer to "environment," they are referring to everything that can influence a person's genetic makeup—from the beginning of prenatal development until the moment of death. Environmental influences include the direct effects of nutrition, climate, and medical care, as well as indirect effects brought on by the particular economic, cultural, and historical context in which the individual develops (see Figure 3.16).

Understanding these processes is part of epigenetics. Access to the genes is controlled by the epigenome, a layer of additional DNA, and another molecule, ribonucleic acid (RNA), attached to the genome. In a process called *DNA methylation*, this material transcribes, activates, silences, and in other ways alters the expression of genes and guides cells to their specialized roles. Once considered "junk," this nongenetic material is the subject

Monozygotic Twins About once in every 250 conceptions, one fertilized egg divides into two, producing identical twins: two individuals with the same genetic makeup.

genome The complete instructions for making an organism, including all the genetic material found in that organism's chromosomes.

stem cells Early, undifferentiated biological cells with the potential to develop into any other type of specialized cell.

genotype The sum total of all the genes present in an individual.

phenotype A person's observable characteristics; determined by the interaction of the individual's genotype with the environment.

FIGURE 3.16 Epigenetics: Guiding Cells to Their Specialized Roles An organism's genome is a sort of how-to manual for all the tasks individual cells need to perform in order to function. The *epigenome*—a layer of proteins that packages the genome and points cells to specific instructions—is affected by many things, including food, stress, and toxic chemicals. Beginning before birth, life experiences lay down epigenetic marks, which can block the expression of any gene in the DNA segment they affect. So far, more than 100 kinds of epigenetic marks have been found, but researchers are still studying how different parts of the epigenome adjust to the environment.

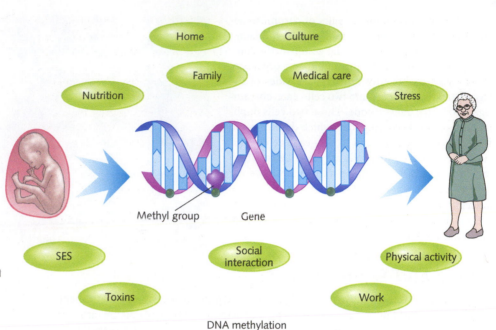

Home   Culture   Family   Medical care   Nutrition   Stress

Methyl group   Gene

SES   Social interaction   Physical activity   Toxins   Work

DNA methylation

of intense research as scientists seek to discover exactly what these biological molecules do, and how they respond to stress, pollution, poor diet, and other environmental experiences (Xu and others, 2015).

Methylation begins before birth and continues throughout life, altering how genes are expressed in response to environmental events, even after we are born. Because DNA methylation patterns seem to be set largely during the *perinatal* period (immediately before and after birth), long-term gene expression programming is especially vulnerable to environmental insults that occur early in life. In this way, epigenetics contributes to the development of many multifactorial diseases (Elsing, Datson, van den Maagdenberg, & Ferrari, 2013). For instance, DNA methylation appears to be one of the biological mechanisms responsible for the development of asthma in children who are exposed to air pollution at a young age (Jiang and others, 2012). DNA methylation also may mediate the effect of early stress in increasing an individual's vulnerability to depression, by causing the reprogramming of a key neuroendocrine circuit for functioning in a harsh environment (Booij, Wang, Levesque, Tremblay, & Syzf, 2013).

OTHER BODILY SYSTEMS

In addition to the seven major systems described thus far, four others protect our bodies from the outside world, filter excess fluid and other substances from the bloodstream, and perform many other important functions.

The **integumentary system** consists of the skin, hair, nails, and sweat glands. In humans, the skin consists of two layers that together cover a surface area of almost two square meters, forming our body's largest organ. The outer layer, called the *epidermis*, cushions underlying tissues and keeps skin supple. The inner layer, called the *dermis*, is home to two types of tiny glands that secrete protective oils and provide a barrier to infections. *Sebaceous glands* secrete a fat-based substance (*sebum*) that keeps our skin supple; it also forms ear wax. *Sweat glands* produce the watery, salty secretion that helps regulate body temperature (*thermoregulation*) by providing an evaporative cooling effect, whether we are fighting a fever or in the middle of a hard workout. Sweat glands also excrete wastes from the body.

The **muscular system** is made up of three types of tissue that, together, make up half your body weight. Each muscle is an organ itself, consisting of cells that contract and relax, blood vessels, tendons, and nerves that move the body and help transport materials through the body. *Skeletal muscle*, which is the only muscle under voluntary control, derives its name from the fact that it is connected to the skeleton, usually attached by *tendons* between two bones. Skeletal muscles create movement by shortening their length, pulling the attached tendons and bones closer together. *Cardiac muscle* is found only in the heart and, as we've seen, pumps blood throughout the body. Cardiac muscle is not under our conscious control, so it is an involuntary muscle. *Visceral muscle*, another involuntary type, is found inside the stomach, intestines, and blood vessels. The weakest of the three types of muscle tissue, visceral muscle moves food, waste, and other substances through the body.

The adult human **skeletal system** consists of 206 bones and a network of cartilage, ligaments, and tendons that support our bodies, facilitate movement, protect internal organs, and store and release fat and minerals. The interior of most bones contains a soft connective tissue (*bone marrow*) that produces red blood cells, white blood cells, and the platelets that help the body form clots to stop bleeding.

The **urinary system** (also called the **renal system**) consists of the kidneys, bladder, ureters, and urethra. The primary function of the kidneys is to maintain a stable internal environment in the body (homeostasis). They do this by filtering excess water and waste products from the blood—producing urine—while conserving water, salts, and electrolytes. Urine flows from the kidneys to the bladder through two thin tubes called *ureters*. When the bladder is full, urine leaves the body through another tube (the *urethra*).

Interactions Among Bodily Systems

Although each of the bodily systems has a unique function, each depends on all the others, whether directly or indirectly, to function well. As we saw earlier in the chapter, the respiratory system relies on the circulatory system to deliver the oxygen it has taken in, while the heart muscle cannot function without oxygen from the lungs. The bones of the skeletal system protect the brain and spinal cord, but the central nervous system regulates the position of the body by controlling the muscles.

Even bodily systems that may seem unrelated are connected. The integumentary system, for example, contains one type of cell that secretes *melanin* to protect the skin from ultraviolet rays, and another that works with the immune system to form the body's first line of defense against infection. The integumentary system also works with the circulatory and digestive systems through a network of capillary cells that help our bodies

integumentary system Includes the skin, hair, nails, and sweat glands.

muscular system Includes the body's skeletal, cardiac, and visceral muscle tissues.

skeletal system Consists of 206 bones and the body's network of cartilage, ligaments, and tendons.

urinary (renal) system Includes the kidneys, bladder, ureters, and urethra.

synthesize and absorb vitamin D from the sun (vitamin D is essential for bone health and absorption of calcium from the foods we eat). In turn, the stomach and intestines support the integumentary system by digesting foods that contain the fats and oils required to produce the protective oils that keep hair and skin supple. The integumentary system is also home to a variety of *somatosensory receptor* cells that sense touch, pressure, heat, and cold—providing input to the nervous system and serving as warning sensors that allow the body to steer clear of painful environmental stimuli that might cause harm.

Thus, the systems of the body work closely together to maintain homeostasis. Disease or disturbance in one system can disrupt this internal stability and cause problems elsewhere. Health psychologists are increasingly aware of the interrelationship of our thoughts, emotions, digestive processes, and health. If you've ever followed your "gut instinct" to make a decision or felt "butterflies" in your stomach before an exam, you have experienced the workings of the **microbiota-gut-brain axis (MGBA)**, a bidirectional communication network that connects the emotional and cognitive centers of the brain to gastrointestinal functions via neural, endocrine, and immune signals (Zhu and others, 2017; Carabotti, Scirocco, Maselli, & Severi, 2015).

How does this communication take place? An estimated 100 million neurons and two thirds of the body's immune cells can be found in the gut, lining the walls of the 9-meter-long gastrointestinal (GI) tract. In fact, there are more neurons in the GI tract than in the spinal cord or the peripheral nervous system! The network is so extensive that it is sometimes referred to as the "second brain," and it has even been designated as a separate division of the nervous system called the *enteric system* (Hadhazy, 2010).

In addition to this network of neurons and immune cells, the GI system hosts a complex ecosystem of trillions of bacteria, fungi, parasites, and other microorganisms—together called **microbiota,** or **microbiome**—that assist in breaking down and absorbing nutrients from food, expelling wastes, and acting as a barrier that prevents toxins from entering the blood. Microbiota communicate directly with the central nervous system (CNS) by means of neural, endocrine, and immune links and thus influence our cognitive functions, behavior, and health (Monteil-Castro, Gonzalez-Cervantes, Bravo-Ruiseco, & Pacheco-Lope, 2013). As Figure 3.17 illustrates, much of this communication occurs through the vagus cranial nerve, which, as we have seen, can trigger the release of cytokines that affect activity in our immune system. Disorders in the composition and number of gut microbiota can thus affect health, and may be linked with CNS disorders such as Parkinson's disease, Alzheimer's disease, multiple sclerosis, and schizophrenia (Zhu and others, 2017). The state of the gut microbiome may also be a factor in obesity (Manco, 2012), inflammatory bowel disease (Bonaz and Bernstein, 2012), anxiety and depression (Foster & McVey Neufeld, 2013), and cardiovascular risk (Tang and others, 2013).

A variety of factors can have a significant impact on your gut microbiota and health, including age, diet, and other health behaviors. Health is also influenced by genetic predispositions and by the physiological states associated with the interdependent bodily systems. Biopsychosocial research on the interactions among bodily systems reminds us, however, that health is also influenced by our thoughts and emotions. Subsequent chapters will present additional evidence of how the body's physical systems combine with psychological and sociocultural factors to determine our overall states of wellness or illness.

---

microbiota-gut-brain axis (MGBA) A bidirectional communication system that links the central nervous system with the enteric nervous system.

microbiota (microbiome) The bacteria and other microorganisms of a particular habitat, such as the gastrointestinal tract.

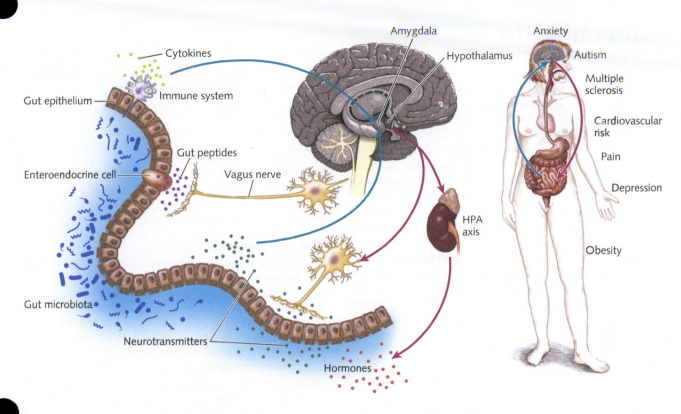

FIGURE 3.17 The MGBA In the microbiota-gut-brain axis, microbiota communicate directly with the central nervous system (CNS) by means of neural, endocrine, and immune links. Much of this communication occurs through the vagus nerve, which can trigger the release of cytokines in our immune system.

Weigh In on Health

Respond to each question based on what you learned in the chapter. (**Tip:** Use the items in "Summing Up" to take into account related biological, psychological, and social concerns.)

1. What would you say to help a classmate distinguish between neurotransmitters and hormones? In your explanation, discuss where and/or how these substances are produced, as well as their functions and the role they play in issues that concern health psychologists.

2. Since your childhood, what are three different ways in which your immune system has been able to overcome pathogens that could have harmed your health? As a college student, what are three things (physical, psychological, and/or social) that you might do to keep your immune system as strong as possible?

3. If a friend asked you why it's important to study the human reproductive system and behavior genetics in a course on health psychology, how would you answer?

4. Give several examples of the interdependence of the physical systems of the body.

5. Explain why people might take dietary supplements in an effort to restore the composition of their gut microbiome.

Summing Up

Cells and the Nervous System

1. There are two types of cells: eukaryotic, which contain nuclei and other organelles, and prokaryotic, which do not. Cells of similar structure and function form a tissue. Tissues working together form an organ.

2. The central nervous system consists of the brain and the spinal cord. The peripheral nervous system has two main divisions: the somatic nervous system, which controls voluntary movements, and the autonomic nervous system, which controls the involuntary muscles and endocrine glands through the sympathetic and parasympathetic nervous systems.

3. The brainstem controls basic life-support functions via the autonomic nervous system. The limbic system includes the medulla, which controls heart rate and breathing; the amygdala, which plays an important role in aggression and other emotions; the hippocampus, which is involved in learning and memory; and the hypothalamus, which influences hunger, thirst, body temperature, and sexual behavior.

4. The cerebral cortex includes areas specialized for triggering movement (motor cortex), sensing touch (sensory cortex), speaking and decision making (frontal lobe), vision (occipital lobe), hearing (temporal lobe), and spatial orientation (parietal lobe).

The Endocrine System

5. Controlled by the hypothalamus, the pituitary gland secretes hormones that influence growth, sexual development, reproduction, kidney functioning, and aging. Other glands help to regulate heart rate and blood pressure (adrenal medulla), growth and metabolism (thyroid), and blood glucose levels (pancreas), and to reduce inflammation (adrenal cortex).

The Cardiovascular and Respiratory Systems

6. Oxygen-depleted blood returning from the body is pumped from the right atrium into the right ventricle, and from there through the capillaries of the lungs, where it picks up fresh oxygen and disposes of carbon dioxide. The freshly oxygenated blood is pumped through the pulmonary vein into the left atrium of the heart, and from there into the left ventricle, from which it flows into the arterial system.

7. Inhaled air travels to the lungs via bronchial tubes that branch into the smaller bronchioles and air sacs of the lungs (the alveoli). The thin walls of the alveoli permit the exchange of oxygen and carbon dioxide.

The Digestive System

8. Digestion begins with chewing and salivary enzymes that begin to break food down. Rhythmic movements of the esophageal muscles then propel food downward to the stomach, where it is mixed with gastric enzymes. Digestive fluids from the pancreas, liver, and gallbladder are secreted into the small and large intestines, where—several hours after eating—the breakdown of food is completed.

The Immune System

9. The body's first line of defense against health-threatening pathogens includes the protective barrier provided by the skin, the mucous membranes of the nose and respiratory tract, and gastric enzymes of the digestive system. Lymphocytes filter out infectious substances and debris with the passage of fluids through the lymphatic system. Other nonspecific immune defenses include the action of phagocytes, macrophages, and natural killer (NK) cells.

10. Specific immune reactions occur when B cells and T cells attack specific foreign substances. B cells accomplish this when memory cells produce specific antibodies that kill previously encountered antigens, whereas T cells directly attack and kill antigens by injecting them with lethal toxins. Immune functioning improves throughout childhood and early adolescence and declines in old age.

The Reproductive System and Behavior Genetics

11. The reproductive system directs the development of primary and secondary sex characteristics. The sum total of all the genes that a person inherits is the person's genotype. How those genes are expressed in the person's traits is the phenotype. DNA methylation is a key epigenetic process that may mediate the biological effects of environmental factors by causing a reprogramming of neuroendocrine circuits in the body.

Other Bodily Systems

12. The integumentary system consists of the skin, hair, nails, and sweat glands. Its primary functions are to act as a barrier to protect the body from the outside world, to regulate body fluids and temperature, and to eliminate waste products.

13. The muscular system is made up of three types of tissue—skeletal muscle, visceral muscle, and cardiac muscle—that

help move the body, and that move blood and other materials through the body. The skeletal system consists of bones, cartilage, and joints. Its primary functions are to provide shape and form for the body, protect internal tissues, enable movement, produce blood cells, and store fats sand minerals.

14. The urinary system consists of the kidneys, bladder, ureters, and urethra. Its primary functions are to filter excess fluid and wastes from the bloodstream; the fluid and wastes are then expelled as urine.

15. The microbiota-gut-brain axis (MGBA) is a bidirectional communication network that connects the brain's emotional and cognitive centers to the digestive system. Microbiota communicate directly with the central nervous system by means of neural, endocrine, and immune links, and thus influence our cognitive functions, behavior, and health.

Key Terms and Concepts to Remember

cell, p. 58
tissue, p. 59
organ, p. 59
nervous system, p. 59
neurotransmitters, p. 59
brainstem, p. 62
medulla, p. 62
reticular formation, p. 62
thalamus, p. 62
cerebellum, p. 63
limbic system, p. 63
amygdala, p. 63
hippocampus, p. 63
hypothalamus, p. 63
cerebral cortex, p. 65
sensory cortex, p. 65

motor cortex, p. 65
association cortex, p. 65
endocrine system, p. 66
hormones, p. 66
pituitary gland, p. 67
adrenal glands, p. 67
cardiovascular system, p. 68
respiratory system, p. 68
arteries, p. 69
veins. p. 69
noncommunicable disease (NCD), p. 72
bronchi, p. 72
cilia, p. 73
digestive system, p. 74
antigen, p. 77

lymphocytes, p. 77
cytokines, p. 79
reproductive system, p. 80
genome, p. 83
stem cells, p. 83
genotype, p. 83
phenotype, p. 83
integumentary system, p. 85
muscular system, p. 85
skeletal system, p. 85
urinary (renal) system, p. 85
microbiota-gut-brain axis (MGBA), p. 86
microbiota (microbiome), p. 86

 LaunchPad macmillan learning   To accompany your textbook, you have access to a number of online resources, including quizzes for every chapter of the book, flashcards, critical thinking exercises, videos, and *Check Your Health* inventories. To access these resources, please visit the Straub Health Psychology LaunchPad at **launchpadworks.com**

Part **2** STRESS AND HEALTH

E+/Getty Images

Stress

Chapter 4

LEARNING OUTCOMES

Once you have studied this chapter, you will be able to:

- Summarize the basic concepts of stress,
- Describe some common stressors,
- Explain the physiology of stress, and
- Compare various models of stress and illness.

In 1934, Hungarian-born Hans Selye (1907–1982) was a promising young endocrinologist employed in a laboratory at Montreal's McGill University. Working with an ovary extract in an effort to identify a new hormone, Selye devised a simple plan: Give daily injections of the extract to a sample of laboratory rats and watch for changes in their behavior and health. Easier said than done! Selye quickly learned that rats, like people, are not fond of being injected. Often, as he was about to insert the needle, a rat would squirm, causing Selye to miss the injection site. Squeezing an uncooperative rat more tightly sometimes caused it to nip at the experimenter, who then would drop the animal and be forced to chase it around the laboratory before eventually completing the injection.

After several months of these sessions, Selye made an extraordinary discovery: Most of the rats had developed bleeding ulcers, shrunken thymus glands (the gland that produces disease-fighting lymphocytes), and enlarged adrenal glands. At first he was elated, believing he had discovered the physiological effects of the as-yet-unknown ovarian extract. Being a careful scientist, however, Selye realized that without a control group, this conclusion was premature. So other groups of laboratory rats were given daily injections of extracts of kidney or spleen, or injections of a saline solution, instead of the ovarian extract. Otherwise, these control animals were treated the same: They were often squeezed, dropped, and chased around the lab before receiving their injections!

Much to Selye's surprise, at the end of the experiment, these control rats had the same enlarged adrenal glands, shrunken thymus glands, and bleeding ulcers. Because the same changes occurred in both groups of rats, the changes could not have been caused by the ovarian extract. What,

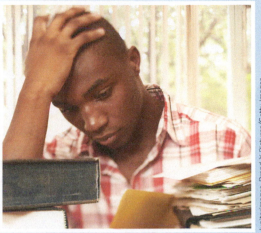

Jupiterimages, Brand X Pictures/Getty Images

then, could have caused the changes? What else did the two groups have in common? In a moment of insight (and humility), Selye correctly reasoned that his hapless handling of the animals had triggered some sort of nonspecific response. The rats were stressed out!

We now know that Selye had discovered the *stress response*, and his breakthrough helped forge an entirely new medical field: *stress physiology*. Although he was not the first to use the term *stress*, Selye is credited with two important new ideas:

- The body has a remarkably similar response to many different stressors.
- Stressors sometimes can make you sick.

The second of these ideas—that persistent, or *chronic*, stress influences a person's vulnerability to disorders—is especially important and has become a major theme in health psychology. As discussed in this and other chapters, researchers have established links between stress and many physical and psychological disorders: cancer, heart disease, diabetes, arthritis, headaches, asthma, digestive disorders, depression, and anxiety, among others. At the same time, stressful experiences that are weathered successfully can ultimately have positive influences on our lives, better equipping us for coping in the future.

STRESS: SOME BASIC CONCEPTS

Stress is a part of life, and without some stress, life would be dull. But when stress overtaxes our coping resources, it can damage our health. We encounter stress from many sources, including school, family and friends, interactions with strangers, and work. Stress often comes from daily hassles, such as the ever-changing demands of school, work, family, and friends. In other cases, stress persists for a long time, as when a person loses a loved one or is forced to retire.

Despite the pervasiveness of stress, it has been challenging for psychologists to find an acceptable definition of the word. *Stress* can describe a threatening situation or *stimulus*, or it can describe a *response* to a situation. Health psychologists generally agree that **stressors** are demanding events or situations that trigger coping adjustments in a person, and that **stress** is the *process* by which a person both appraises and responds to events that are judged to be challenging or threatening (i.e., we must judge a challenging event or situation to be threatening or even beyond our ability to cope with before we will be stressed by it). Stress arises less from events themselves than from how we appraise them. A significant stressor for one person may be no big deal for another.

When we appraise a stressor—especially a short-lived one—as a challenge, it can have positive effects, such as mobilizing our immune system to fend off infection and promote healing (Dhabhar, 2014). Champion athletes, musicians, actors, and successful leaders all learn that their best efforts often come when they have been aroused by a challenge. We will examine this individual appraisal process later in this chapter. In Chapter 5, we will

stressor Any event or situation that triggers coping adjustments.

stress The process by which we perceive and respond to events, called *stressors,* that we appraise as threatening or challenging.

consider effective ways to cope with stress. In this chapter, we will take a *biopsychosocial* approach to understanding stress and its impact on the body, as follows:

- *Biological* processes that occur when we experience stress can differ according to each individual's physiology and levels of physiological reactivity, but the same basic processes affect us all. For example, the body's response to challenging, potentially stressful events is partially under the control of sex hormones, including estrogen and testosterone (Pasquali, 2012; Verma, Balhara, & Gupta, 2011).

- *Psychological* influences, such as our individual personalities and life experiences, affect how we *appraise* challenging situations—either as manageable (not stressful) or unmanageable (stressful). Gender also plays a role in whether we fight or flee, or seek social support when under pressure.

- *Sociocultural* factors affect how we respond to stress from many different sources, including major life events, daily hassles, work, and family.

Let's turn first to the types of stressors people experience.

STRESSORS

Everyone experiences stress. How and why we experience stress may change as we journey through life, but none of us escape. Each of us experiences the events of life in a unique way. Research has focused on several types of stressors: significant life events, daily hassles, work, and sociocultural factors.

Significant Life Events

What impact do major life events—such as leaving home, changing jobs, having a child, or losing a loved one—have on the quality of our health? In the late 1950s, psychiatrists Thomas Holmes and Richard Rahe of the University of Washington substantially advanced our understanding of how the events of our lives affect our health. They interviewed more than 5,000 people to identify which events forced people to make the most changes in their lives. Then they assigned each event a value in *life change units* (LCUs) to reflect the amount of change that was necessary to affect health. For example, a divorce disrupts many more aspects of one's life than does taking a vacation, and thus it is assigned a larger number of LCUs. The range of events Holmes and Rahe investigated was broad, even including occasions that called for celebration, such as marriage or a promotion. They then ranked these events and devised the Social Readjustment Rating Scale (SRRS), the first systematic attempt to quantify the impact of life changes on health. Table 4.1 shows the College Undergraduate Stress Scale, a variation of the original SRRS that is directed specifically at college students.

Holmes and Rahe theorized that the total number of LCUs that a person had accumulated during the previous year could be used to predict the likelihood that the person would become sick over the next several months. In one study (Rahe, Mahan, & Arthur, 1970), researchers obtained SRRS scores of naval crewmen who were about to depart

TABLE 4.1 The College Undergraduate Stress Scale

Copy the "Stress Ratings" number into the "Your Items" column for any item that has happened to you in the last year. Then add up the numbers.

Event	Stress Ratings	Your Items	Event	Stress Ratings	Your Items
Being raped	100		Change in housing situation (hassles, moves)	69	
Finding out that you are HIV-positive	100		Competing or performing in public	69	
Being accused of rape	98		Getting in a physical fight	66	
Death of a close friend	97		Difficulties with a roommate	66	
Death of a close family member	96		Job changes (applying, new job, work hassles)	69	
Contracting a sexually transmitted disease (other than AIDS)	94		Declaring a major or concerns about future plans	65	
Concerns about being pregnant	91		A class you hate	62	
Finals week	90		Drinking or use of drugs	61	
Concerns about your partner being pregnant	90		Confrontations with professors	60	
Oversleeping for an exam	89		Starting a new semester	58	
Flunking a class	89		Going on a first date	57	
Having a boyfriend or girlfriend cheat on you	85		Registration	55	
Ending a steady dating relationship	85		Maintaining a steady dating relationship	55	
Serious illness in a close friend or family member	85		Commuting to campus or work, or both	54	
Financial difficulties	84		Peer pressures	53	
Writing a major term paper	83		Being away from home for the first time	53	
Being caught cheating on a test	83		Getting sick	52	
Drunk driving	82				
Sense of overload in school or work	85				
Two exams in one day	80		Concerns about your appearance	52	
Cheating on your boyfriend or girlfriend	77		Getting straight A's	51	
Getting married	76		A difficult class that you love	48	
Negative consequences of drinking or drug use	75		Making new friends; getting along with friends	47	
Depression or crisis in your best friend	73		Fraternity or sorority rush	47	
Difficulties with parents	73		Falling asleep in class	40	
Talking in front of a class	72		Attending an athletic event (e.g., football game)	20	
Lack of sleep	69		Total		

Note: Of 12,000 U.S. college students who completed this scale, scores ranged from 182 to 2,571, with a mean score of 1,247. Women reported significantly higher scores than men, perhaps because most of the students used in pretesting items were women. This being the case, items that are stressful for women may be overrepresented in the scale.

Information from: Renner, M. J., & Mackin, R. S. (1998). A life stress instrument for classroom use. *Teaching of Psychology, 25,* 47. Vol. 25(1) pp. 46–48. Copyright (c) 1998 by Society for the Teaching of Psychology. Reprinted by permission of SAGE Publications, Inc. Holmes, T. H., & Rahe, R. H. (1967). The social readjustment rating scale. *Journal of Psychosomatic Research, 11*(2), 213–221.

on a six-month mission. Over the course of the voyage, the researchers found a positive correlation between LCUs and illness rates. Those sailors who reported the highest LCUs were more likely to fall ill than those who reported the lowest LCUs. The message: When life brings many changes at once, the stress that results may make us more vulnerable to health problems.

Although the research by Holmes and Rahe was groundbreaking and influential, the value of the SRRS and other scales for predicting stress and illness has been criticized for several reasons:

- Many of the items are vague, subjective, and open to interpretation. "Change in living conditions" or "Revision of personal habits," for example, can mean almost anything.

- Assigning specific point values to events fails to take into consideration individual differences in the way events are appraised (and therefore experienced). A divorce, for example, may mean welcome freedom for one person but a crushing loss to another.

- The SRRS and other scales lump all events together—whether positive or negative, by chance or willfully chosen. Many studies have found that unexpected or uncontrollable negative events, such as the premature death of a family member, are much more stressful than are events that are positive, expected, or under one's control, such as getting married, changing jobs, or taking a vacation.

- Many inventories do not differentiate between resolved and unresolved stressful events. There is evidence that stressors that have been resolved successfully have substantially weaker adverse effects on the person's health than events that linger unresolved (Dhabhar, 2014).

- Life event scales tend to underestimate the stress that African Americans and other minorities experience (Balsam, Molina, Beadnell, Simoni, & Walters, 2011; Turner & Avison, 2003).

One measure of a good theory, however, is that it generates research that leads to new understanding, even if it also leads to its own demise. If nothing else, the many studies conducted using the SRRS have revealed that there is no simple, direct connection between life stress and illness: Subjected to the same stressors, one person will get sick, while another will not. The health consequences of stress depend upon our appraisal of the stressors. A good example of this is how people respond to challenging events that tend to mound up at certain points in the lifespan.

The Stress of Emerging Adulthood

In past generations the transition from adolescence to adulthood was marked by completing school, leaving home, becoming financially independent, marrying, and having a child. In 1960 more than two thirds of Americans age 30 and over (77% of women and 65% of men) had reached all five milestones (Henig, 2010). Today, however, millions of young people are postponing these roles. For example, the average age at first marriage in the early 1970s was 21 for women and 23 for men; by 2017, it had climbed to 27 for women and 29 for men—an increase of more than five years within one generation (U.S. Census Bureau, 2018) (see Figure 4.1).

This shift in the timetable for adulthood is so prominent that *emerging adulthood*—the period between 18 and 25 years of age—has been called out as a distinct new stage of

FIGURE 4.1 Average Age at First Marriage, 1890–2015 The average age at first marriage has increased by about five years, for both women and men, within one generation.

Data from: U.S. Census Bureau (USCB). (2015). Decennial censuses, 1890 to 1940, and current population. Survey, annual social and economic supplements, 1947 to 2015.

Age (years)

Data only available every 10 years prior to 1947

Men

Women

1890 1900 10 20 30 40 1950 60 70 80 90 2000 10 15

TABLE 4.2 How Does It Feel to Be an Emerging Adult?

% Agree (Somewhat or Strongly) with Each Statement	
This time of my life is fun and exciting	83%
This time of my life is full of changes	83%
Overall, I am satisfied with my life	81%
At this time of my life, I feel I have a great deal of freedom	73%
This time of my life is stressful	72%
This time of my life is full of uncertainty	64%
I often feel anxious	56%
I often feel depressed	32%
I often feel that my life is not going well	30%

Data from: Arnett, J. J., & Schwab, J. (2012). The Clark University Poll of emerging adults: Thriving, struggling & hopeful (p. 5).

life, and researchers are identifying its distinctive features. In 2012, researchers at Clark University began an annual survey of a large, diverse group of emerging adults. The results indicate that emerging adulthood is a fascinating transitory period, frequently evoking mixed emotions. Most participants see this time of life as "fun and exciting," as well as a time with "a great deal of freedom." On the other hand, 72% say this time of life is stressful, 56% say they often feel anxious, and 33% report feeling depressed (see Table 4.2).

Why does stress increase at this stage of life? One reason may be the upheavals that often characterize these years. Emerging adults frequently

■ move (slightly more than 30% move every year),

■ change jobs (averaging seven jobs during their twenties),

- have not made as much progress in their careers as they had hoped (70%),

- move back in with their parents (more than 40% do so at least once during their twenties), and/or

- spend time living with a romantic partner (66%).

Emerging adulthood is also a time when major life questions are asked, such as Who am I? Who and what means the most to me? What do I want to do with my life? All of this can be stressful and take its toll on physical and mental health. Indeed, except for dementia, emerging adults experience more of every diagnosed psychological disorder than any older age group—almost double that of adults over age 25 (Center for Behavioral Health Statistics and Quality, 2015). Further, emerging adults have a heightened risk for alcohol and drug abuse. Because of brain development during emerging adulthood, addiction can be particularly harmful at this time and have long-lasting effects on cognitive development and other aspects of health.

Researchers point to several cultural changes that have led to emerging adulthood, including the need for more education to survive in today's information-based economy and the fact that there are fewer entry-level jobs available after all that schooling. As a result, emerging adults are the age group most likely to be unemployed. Lacking the steadiness of work and often experiencing rejection after rejection, emerging adults who are still struggling to form an identity can find this time of life to be especially stressful.

Despite these areas of concern, however, emerging adults are also more optimistic than people of any other age group. In this respect, the decade of the 1920s has been called the "stem cell of human development" (Henig, 2010), as it is a time filled with possibilities, when countless outcomes are possible.

Adverse Childhood Experiences and Prenatal Stress

Before reaching emerging adulthood or even adolescence, we encounter the potential stresses of infancy and childhood. Fortunately, most children thrive in safe, nurturing environments. However, the landmark Adverse Childhood Experiences (ACE) Study uncovered a link between childhood trauma (i.e., abuse or neglect) and the onset in adulthood of chronic diseases, including cardiovascular disease, diabetes, certain types of cancer, and autoimmune disease; as well as depression, suicide, and violence. In the original study, conducted between 1995 and 1997, over 17,000 participants completed confidential surveys regarding their current health status and their memories of childhood experiences (Felitti and others, 1998; see Table 4.3). It is important to note that the ACE participants were mostly middle- and upper-middle-class, college-educated adults who had good jobs and high-quality health insurance; thus the findings are unlikely to be attributable to adverse circumstances such as living in poverty or living in a high-crime neighborhood (discussed later in this chapter). Dozens of follow-up research studies continue to confirm the association between childhood trauma and morbidity in adulthood (Morey, Boggero, Scott, & Segerstrom, 2015; Wadhwa, Entringer, Buss, & Lu, 2011).

Exposure to stress even earlier in the lifespan can also have adverse consequences. Research suggests that children whose mothers experienced high levels of stress during pregnancy may be at increased risk for a range of problems, including impaired cognitive

TABLE 4.3 Adverse Childhood Experience (ACE) Questionnaire

While you were growing up, during your first 18 years of life:

1. Did a parent or other adult in the household **often** … Swear at you, insult you, put you down, or humiliate you? **or** Act in a way that made you afraid that you might be physically hurt?	Yes	No	If yes enter 1 _____
2. Did a parent or other adult in the household **often** … Push, grab, slap, or throw something at you? **or** **Ever** hit you so hard that you had marks or were injured?	Yes	No	If yes enter 1 _____
3. Did an adult or person at least 5 years older than you **ever** … Touch or fondle you or have you touch their body in a sexual way? **or** Try to or actually have oral, anal, or vaginal sex with you?	Yes	No	If yes enter 1 _____
4. Did you **often** feel that … No one in your family loved you or thought you were important or special? **or** Your family didn't look out for each other, feel close to each other, or support each other?	Yes	No	If yes enter 1 _____
5. Did you **often** feel that … You didn't have enough to eat, had to wear dirty clothes, and had no one to protect you? **or** Your parents were too drunk or high to take care of you or take you to the doctor if you needed it?	Yes	No	If yes enter 1 _____
6. Were your parents **ever** separated or divorced?	Yes	No	If yes enter 1 _____
7. Was your mother or stepmother … **Often** pushed, grabbed, slapped, or had something thrown at her? **or** **Sometimes or often** kicked, bitten, hit with a fist, or hit with something hard? **or** **Ever** repeatedly hit over at least a few minutes or threatened with a gun or knife?	Yes	No	If yes enter 1 _____
8. Did you live with anyone who was a problem drinker or alcoholic or who used street drugs?	Yes	No	If yes enter 1 _____
9. Was a household member depressed or mentally ill or did a household member attempt suicide?	Yes	No	If yes enter 1 _____
10. Did a household member go to prison?	Yes	No	If yes enter 1 _____

Reprinted with permission from Felitti, V. J., Anda, R. F., Nordenberg, D., Williamson, D. F., Spitz, A. M., Edwards, V., Koss, M. P., & Marks, J. S. (1998). Relationship of childhood abuse and household dysfunction to many of the leading causes of death in adult. The Adverse Childhood Experiences (ACE) Study. *American Journal of Preventive Medicine, 14*(4), 245–258.

and emotional development. The impact of prenatal stress was seen even in studies that controlled for possible confounding variables such as birthweight, gestational age, and maternal smoking and alcohol consumption (Suurland and others, 2016; Glover, 2011).

Furthermore, a mother's own history of stress can affect her children's health. A number of research studies have reported lower levels of vagal tone (a stress indicator discussed later in the chapter) in infants whose mothers reported high levels of trauma during their own childhoods (see Table 4.3). In one recent study, the mothers of 167 four-month-old infants reported on ACEs and prenatal stress in their own lives. Infant vagal tone was then measured during a standard laboratory social stressor test widely used with infants—the Still-Face Paradigm (Tronick, Als, Adamson, Wise, & Brazelton, 1978), in which mothers are asked to hold a "still face" while facing their babies, and not react to their child's behavior. Infants of mothers who had experienced higher levels of adversity during their childhoods had lower vagal tone, and higher levels of prenatal stress (reported by the mothers as they remembered their pregnancies) were associated with slower recovery of heart rate variability following the social stressor paradigm (Gray, Jones, Theall, Glacken, & Drury, 2017).

These research studies underscore the potential benefits of providing the best possible emotional care for families with young children and for women during pregnancy. This begins with greater public health education about the effects of prenatal and childhood trauma. Parents and parents-to-be need to be encouraged to look after themselves emotionally, and to seek help if needed. Sadly, anxiety, depression, and distress related to pregnancy and parenting are often undetected and untreated.

Daily Hassles

For people of all ages, everyday hassles happen all the time and thus are generally the most significant sources of stress. These minor annoyances range from missing a commuter train to work, to not having the required answer booklet for an exam, to losing a wallet, to arguing with a professor, to living with an aggravating roommate (Repetti, Wang, & Saxbe, 2009). The impact that such hassles have on health depends on their frequency,

Daily hassles and background stressors such as traffic jams or a crowded commute seem to be a better predictor of health problems than either major life events or the frequency of daily uplifts.

Kumar Sriskandan/Alamy Stock Photo

duration, and intensity. In addition, our reactions to minor hassles are influenced by our personality, our individual style of coping, and how the rest of our day has gone.

The counterpart to daily hassles is daily *uplifts*: mood-lifting experiences such as receiving an approving nod from the boss, hearing your favorite song at just the right moment, or even getting a good night's sleep. Just as hassles may cause physical and emotional stress that may result in illness, uplifts may serve as buffers against the effects of stress.

Richard Lazarus (whose transactional model of stress is discussed later in the chapter) and his colleagues devised a scale to measure people's experiences with day-to-day annoyances and uplifts (Kanner, Coyne, Schaefer, & Lazarus, 1981). The Hassles and Uplifts Scale consists of 117 events that range from small pleasures to major problems (Kanner and others, 1981). Table 4.4 shows the 10 most frequent hassles and uplifts as reported by this sample of adults, together with the percentage of time each event was checked.

Recurrent, persistent hassles seem to be a stronger predictor of health problems than either major life events or the frequency of daily uplifts. This finding has been confirmed many times. Studies have found, for instance, that the Hassles and Uplifts Scale (Table 4.4) does a better job than the Social Readjustment Rating Scale in predicting headaches, inflammatory bowel disease episodes, and other disorders (Searle & Bennett, 2001). Other studies have shown that daily hassles are associated with a worsening of symptoms in people who are already suffering from illnesses such as lupus (Peralta-Ramirez, Jimenez-Alonzo, Godoy-Garcia, & Perez-Garcia, 2004).

Critics have argued, however, that some of the items listed in the scale as hassles may actually be *symptoms of* stress rather than stressors. Items relating to appearance, for example, may tap into lowered feelings of self-esteem that *result from* rather than

TABLE 4.4 Common Hassles and Uplifts

Hassles	Percentage of Times Checked over Nine Months		Uplifts	Percentage of Times Checked over Nine Months
1.	Concern about weight	52.4	1. Relating well with your spouse or lover	76.3
2.	Health of family member	48.1	2. Relating well with friends	74.4
3.	Rising prices of common goods	43.7	3. Completing a task	73.3
4.	Home maintenance	42.8	4. Feeling healthy	72.7
5.	Too many things to do	38.6	5. Getting enough sleep	69.7
6.	Misplacing or losing things	38.1	6. Meeting responsibilities	68.8
7.	Yardwork or outside home maintenance	38.1	7. Eating out	68.4
8.	Property, investment, or taxes	37.6	8. Visiting, phoning, or writing someone	67.7
9.	Crime	37.1	9. Spending time with family	66.7
10.	Physical appearance	35.9	10. Home pleasing to you	65.5

Information from: Kanner, A. D., Coyne, J. C., Schaefer, C., & Lazarus, R. S. (1981). Comparison of two modes of stress measurement: Daily hassles and uplifts versus major life events. *Journal of Behavioral Medicine, 4*(1), 1–39.

contribute to stress. In addition, some items refer to alcohol and drug use, sexual difficulties, physical illness, and personal fears—all possible consequences of stress.

In addition, other researchers have suggested that individuals who have trouble "letting go" of unattainable goals (Miller & Wrosch, 2007), as well as people who perceive low levels of social support (Fiksenbaum, Greenglass, & Eaton, 2006), will find daily hassles more stressful. This suggests that an overly anxious or socially isolated person may overreact to daily hassles in a way that magnifies their impact.

Daily hassles also have been demonstrated to interact with *background stressors,* such as job dissatisfaction (Wang, Lesage, Schmitz, & Drapeau, 2008), having a long commute to work or school (Gottholmseder, Nowotny, Pruckner, & Theurl, 2009), and crowded living conditions (Regoeczi, 2003). In impoverished areas—where many people routinely live with inadequate income, unemployment, and the demands of single parenting—such stressors are part of daily life.

For minority populations, daily hassles are compounded by perceived discrimination (Pascoe and Richman, 2009) and racism, which has been linked to hypertension in African Americans (Mays, Cochran, & Barnes, 2007). Discrimination is also experienced regularly by other ethnic groups (Edwards & Romero, 2008) and by lesbian, gay, bisexual, and transgender people (Wu, 2015; Centers for Disease Control and Prevention, 2015d). The Daily Hassles Microsystem Scale was designed for poor, urban, and culturally diverse adolescents (Seidman and others, 1995), and the LGBT People of Color Microaggressions Scale assesses stress and life events in lesbian, gay, and bisexual individuals who are also racial/ethnic minorities (Balsam and others, 2011). The *Diversity and Healthy Living* box later in this chapter discusses this issue further.

A dramatic illustration of the interaction of daily hassles with chronic stress comes from studies of the aftermath of unpredictable large-scale events such as earthquakes, floods, and other catastrophes. In the New York City area, repeated exposure to media images of the September 11, 2001, terrorist attacks turned the event into a *collective trauma.* One line of research assessed the mental and physical health records of 1,322 participants before and after the 9/11 attacks, along with information about their media exposure. People who watched four or more hours of 9/11-related television per day were significantly more likely to report health problems—even over the next two to three years (Silver and others, 2013). It is suspected that persistent background stress during this difficult period caused many people to overreact to everyday stressors that they would normally have shrugged off.

Work

Because busy people generally are happier (Hsee, Yang, & Wang, 2010), and because satisfaction with work feeds satisfaction with life (Bowling, Eschleman, & Wang, 2010), an extensive amount of research has been devoted to examining the causes and consequences of job-related stress. These studies are important for two reasons. First, almost all people at some time experience stress related to their work. Second, because work-related stress may be one of the most preventable health hazards, it provides a number of possibilities for intervention.

For most of us, job stress is brief in duration and does not pose a serious threat to our health. For some people, however, job stress is chronic, continuing

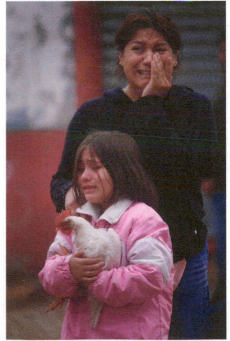

Significant Stress Catastrophic events, such as the 8.8-magnitude earthquake that struck central Chile in 2010, provide tragic, real-world examples of stress as both a stimulus and a response. The event that triggers coping behavior is the stressor (the stimulus), and the person attempting to flee the event or trying to compensate for the destruction that it causes illustrates the response.

Roberto Candia/AP Images

for years. Data from the massive 2010 Canadian Community Health Survey found that respondents with the highest level of perceived work stress had higher odds of being treated for an emotional or mental-health problem at any point and higher odds of being treated in the previous 12 months. These high-stress respondents also had higher odds of being diagnosed for mood and anxiety disorders than their less-stressed counterparts (Szeto & Dobson, 2013).

Changing jobs can be stressful. Between ages 18 and 50, the average worker in the United States holds 11.9 jobs, with nearly half of those jobs held before age 25 (U.S. Bureau of Labor Statistics, 2017). One study found that people who frequently changed jobs before age 36 were more likely to have a variety of health problems by age 42 (Kinnunen, Kaprio, & Pulkkinen, 2005). However, there are several reasons why a job change is even more stressful for older workers (Rix, 2012): loss of seniority, need to learn new job skills, and age discrimination in hiring and promotion. For those who need to relocate to find a new job, disrupting one's social network is especially stressful for older workers.

Next, let's take a look at some of the factors that can make certain jobs more stressful than others.

Social-Evaluative Threat

social-evaluative threat A stressor in which people fear negative evaluation by others of their appearance or ability.

Even a job environment to which a person is well matched can present momentary stressors. One is the threat of negative evaluations from others; these can range from direct criticism to more subtle negative messages, and can come from subordinates, colleagues, or superiors. Although **social-evaluative threat** is not limited to the workplace—it is a central stressor in many models of stress and health (Dickerson, Gruenewald, & Kemeny, 2004)—evaluations are a frequent, and explicit, experience in many jobs. Feeling accepted, liked, and included by others is a basic social motive, as are the prospects of achievement, protection of status, and gaining respect (Kenrick, Griskevicius, Neuberg, & Schaller, 2010). When social evaluation is negative, it poses a threat to these positive health resources and, not surprisingly, has been associated with increased physiological arousal in the workplace, classroom, and other environments (Smith, Birmingham, & Uchino, 2012; Taylor and others, 2010).

stereotype threat
The experience of stress in a situation where a person's ability, appearance, or other characteristic has the potential to confirm a negative viewpoint about his or her social group.

A notable example of this fear of negative evaluation is **stereotype threat**, first described by Claude Steele, an African American researcher and psychologist who called it a "threat in the air." Stereotype threat begins with the thought that other people hold prejudices against one's social group, and then that thought becomes a stressor. In reality, those other people may not hold those stereotypes, but the possibility that they do may be stressful (Inzlicht & Schmader, 2012).

Overload

Even a job environment to which a person is well matched can become a stressor if there is *work overload.* People who feel they have to work too long and too hard at too many tasks feel more stressed. They also have poorer health habits, experience more accidents, and suffer more health problems than do other workers (CDC, 2015d). As one example, chronic activation of the part of the neuroendocrine system that controls reactions to stress, which has been linked to overcommitment, increases the risk of cardiovascular disease (Steptoe, Siegrist, Kirschbaum, & Marmot, 2004), as does incomplete rest during weekends and vacations (Kivimaki and others, 2006).

A key factor in the relationship between the number of work hours and worker satisfaction is whether employees can choose their own schedules. Workers who volunteer for paid overtime, for example, are usually more satisfied than workers who are required to work overtime (Klaus, Ekerdt, & Gajewski, 2012).

Combining Work and Family

A related form of stress occurs when people attempt to balance several different jobs at the same time and experience *role overload*. A large study of adult Canadians found that about half of the variation in their self-reported stress was related to employment (working conditions, support at work, occupation, job security), but at least as much was related to family (having children younger than age 5 or inadequate amount of support at home) and feeling personally incompetent (Marchand, Durand, & Lupien, 2012).

The problems associated with juggling multiple roles simultaneously have been particularly great for women. Today, most mothers, even those with the youngest children, participate in the labor force (Department for Professional Employees, 2009). Studies have supported two competing hypotheses. One, the *scarcity hypothesis,* maintains that because they have only so much time and energy, women with competing demands suffer from role overload and conflict. The other, the *enhancement hypothesis*, argues that the benefits of meaningful work in enhancing a worker's self-esteem outweigh the costs.

Although some early research seemed to support the scarcity hypothesis, researchers have generally found that the multiple roles of employee, wife, and mother offer health benefits for women (Schnittker, 2007). Moreover, for many working mothers, employment is an important source of self-esteem and life satisfaction. Whether multiple roles are associated with adverse or beneficial health effects depends heavily on the resources people have available to them. Women who are raising children without a partner are especially likely to feel stressed (Livermore & Powers, 2006); they also may be at risk for health problems (Hughes & Waite, 2002).

From studies such as these, researchers have concluded that what matters most is not the number of roles that a person occupies, but the quality of the experience in those roles. Having control over one's work, a good income, adequate child care, and a supportive family combine to reduce the stress of multiple role demands. Similarly, although people often complain that working long hours creates stress, researchers consistently find that stress symptoms, sick days, and overall life satisfaction are more likely to be influenced by other workplace characteristics, such as job autonomy, learning opportunities, supportive supervisors, and scheduling flexibility.

Workers with a spouse or partner often find ways to adjust to each other's work, which helps them function well as a unit. If there are children, partners adjust their work and child-care hours. When mothers work full time, fathers often spend far more time with their children, and mothers do less housework (Abele & Vollmer, 2011).

Role Overload The task of managing multiple roles affects both men and women, but the increase in employment of women has triggered more research on role overload and job-related stress in women. Some research findings regarding the stress of role overload have been contradictory; however, the overall conclusion seems to be that what matters most is the quality of a working mother's experiences in her various roles.

E+/Getty Images

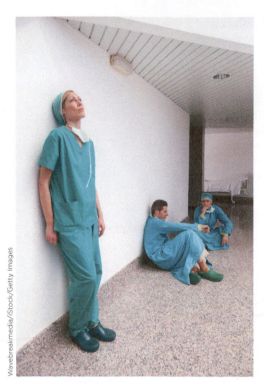

Wavebreakmedia/iStock/Getty Images

Burnout Jobs that involve responsibility for other people, rather than responsibility for products, appear to cause high levels of burnout. Physicians have stressful jobs, partly because of their responsibility for other people's lives, which makes them especially susceptible to burnout. Firefighters and other first responders are also especially susceptible to this type of job stress.

burnout
A job-related state of physical and psychological exhaustion.

Burnout

Burnout has been defined as a job-related state of physical and psychological exhaustion (Maslach, 2003). Jobs that involve responsibility for other people (especially people who are needy in some way), rather than responsibility for products, appear to cause high levels of burnout (Sears, Urizar, & Evans, 2000). Health care workers, dentists, paramedics, air traffic controllers, and firefighters are especially susceptible to job-related burnout (Koinis and others, 2015).

Although burnout typically develops over a period of years, its warning signs and symptoms may appear early on (i.e., soon after the person begins working in the stressful job). These include feelings of mental and physical exhaustion; absenteeism; high job turnover (Schernhammer, 2005); abnormal stress hormone levels (Mommersteeg, Keijsers, Heijnen, Verbraak, & van Doornen, 2006); changes in immune and sympathetic nervous system functioning; an increase in stress-related ailments, such as headaches, backaches, and depression; and irritability (Zanstra, Schellekens, Schaap, & Kooistra, 2006).

Burnout is not, however, an inevitable consequence of employment in certain professions. As the biopsychosocial model reminds us, susceptibility to most health conditions is the product of overlapping factors in every domain of health. For instance, nurses on chronic care wards who have high self-esteem, a strong sense of personal control, and a hopeful, optimistic view of life are much less likely to experience burnout than their more pessimistic counterparts, a finding that highlights the protective function of certain personality styles (Browning, Ryan, Greenberg, & Rolniak, 2006).

Job Demands and Lack of Control

Workers who have little or no control over the procedures, pace, and other aspects of their jobs are prone to stress. The relationship between lack of control and illness was clearly revealed in Marianne Frankenhaeuser's (1975) classic study of Scandinavian sawmill workers. Compared with workers who had more say over aspects of their jobs, those working at dull, repetitive, low-control jobs had significantly higher levels of stress hormones, higher blood pressure, more headaches, and more gastrointestinal disorders, including ulcers. Even a little bit of control goes a long way to produce beneficial health effects (Montpetit & Bergeman, 2007).

Other studies have confirmed the relationship between perceived control and work-related stress, especially in Western cultures that emphasize individual autonomy and responsibility. The *demand-control model* for work stress focuses on the balance between job requirements and workers' perception of autonomy (Karasek, 1979; Kain & Jex, 2010). People who experience high demands with little control over their jobs are more likely than other workers to feel stressed. For example, baristas working in a busy coffee shop is at risk of feeling stressed because they must fill orders quickly and accurately (high demand), while having little or no say about how or when the coffee is made (low control). This type of *job strain* has been linked to increased risk of cardiovascular disease and other health problems (Kivimaki and others, 2012).

Lack of control has also been linked to anger and the development of coronary artery disease (Davidson & Mostovsky, 2010; Fitzgerald, Haythornthwaite, Suchday, & Ewart, 2003), as well as an increased overall risk of death (Amick and others, 2002).

Office workers, restaurant staff, factory workers, and middle managers are among those with the most stressful occupations, marked by repetitive tasks and little control over events. Common to these jobs are complaints of too many demands with too little authority to influence work practices. The sense of powerlessness that results often creates crushing stress. Control issues contribute to the experience of stress among others in our society who have felt powerless, including the impoverished, immigrants, and women.

Other Sources of Job-Related Stress

Several other aspects of jobs can also increase stress among workers. Among these are the closely related phenomena of role ambiguity and role conflict. *Role ambiguity* occurs when workers are unsure of their jobs or the standards used to evaluate their performance. *Role conflict* occurs when a worker receives mixed messages about these issues from different supervisors or coworkers.

Shiftwork, which involves working a schedule other than the traditional "day job" (e.g., swing shift, graveyard shift, or rotating shifts) is another stressful aspect of work. Shiftwork is considered necessary to ensure round-the-clock care in hospitals and nursing homes, as well as for police officers, firefighters, and many other workers in various industries. It has been the subject of a great deal of research. Among the findings is that shift workers face disruption to their family and domestic lives, as well as to their *biological rhythms*. Most human functions have a rhythm that ebbs and flows over a regular 24- to 25-hour cycle. Shiftwork desynchronizes these rhythms and may lead to health complaints, including headaches, loss of appetite, fatigue, sleep disturbances, gastrointestinal problems, and heart disease (Ferri and others, 2016).

Downsizing, layoffs, mergers, and bankruptcies cost thousands of workers their jobs each year. Job loss can have a serious impact on a worker's well-being, putting unemployed workers at risk for physical illness, anxiety, depression, and even suicide (Vinokur, Schul, Vuori, & Price, 2000). Similarly, job insecurity and the threat of unemployment have been linked to lowered immunity (Cohen, F., and others, 2007) and higher levels of several health-compromising risk factors. One study of healthy workers who lost their jobs due to factors out of their control, such as the closing of a factory, found that 80% were diagnosed with a new health problem—ranging from high blood pressure and heart disease to diabetes—within 18 months (Strully, 2009). Other studies have reported increased smoking, alcohol consumption, use of prescription drugs, body weight, and hospital admissions among laid-off workers (Wanberg, 2012). Adults—especially adults under age 40—who can't find employment are 60% more likely to die than their same-age peers (Roelfs, Davidson, & Schwartz, 2011). On the other hand, having job security appears to protect health, and reemployment can reverse the effects of job loss (Cohen, F., and others, 2007).

Lack of fairness and inadequate career advancement also contribute to stress, for the sense of fairness is universal and even encoded in the brain (Hsu, Anen, & Quartz, 2008). Workers who feel they have been denied a promotion or recognition they deserve experience more stress and have higher rates of illness (Semmer, 2007), and workers are more likely to quit if they believe their salary ranking is unfair (Brown, Gardner, Oswald, & Qian, 2008). Conversely, workers who have a direct role in setting fair salary levels report higher levels of satisfaction (Choshen-Hillel & Yaniv, 2011). Perceiving fairness in health insurance coverage and other benefits is also very important (Bianchi & Milkie, 2010).

As an extreme example of work-related stress in a particular culture, the Japanese language has a term, *karoshi,* to describe death that results from work overload. Under Japanese labor laws, bereaved family members may be entitled to special financial compensation if they are able to prove that the cause of their family member's death was *karoshi* ("Editorial," 2016).

Although job-related stress is difficult to avoid, there are ways to buffer its negative impact. Better ways of responding include knowing what to expect from certain aspects of work (and coworkers), expressing your feelings to increase your perception of control, keeping things in perspective, and avoiding self-defeating thoughts and overreactions. Coping with stress is covered much more fully in Chapter 5.

Social Interactions

Social support is beneficial to our health throughout the life span (Hale, Hannum, & Espelage, 2005). At work and elsewhere, social relationships help us deal with stress, often serving as a buffer against low control and other work stress (Fitzgerald and others, 2003). Over time, our relationships with family members even shape how we cope (Slatcher, Selcuk, & Ong, 2015), and physically respond to stressful events. (Laws and others, 2015).

The biopsychosocial mechanisms for the effects of social support on illness include enhanced cellular, immune, endocrine, and cardiovascular functioning (Taylor, 2011). One study of 98 workers in Japan reported a positive correlation between the level of perceived social support and natural killer cell levels (Miyazaki and others, 2003). Social support has also been linked to reduced cortisol responses to stress (Turner-Cobb, Sephton, Koopman, Blake-Mortimer, & Spiegel, 2000), less accumulated wear and tear on the body due to stress (Brooks and others, 2014), and even less cellular aging as measured by longer telomere length in white blood cells (Carroll, Roux, Fitzpatrick, & Seeman, 2013). People who are not lonely or socially isolated also have better health habits (Shankar and others, 2013) and report less pain and other adverse symptoms (Wolf & Davis, 2014). Small wonder, then, that social support may lower the likelihood of illness, speed recovery from treatment (Krohne & Slangen, 2005), and lower the risk of mortality due to illness (Rutledge, Matthews, Lui, Stone, & Cauley, 2003).

Social support is a two-way street, of course: We receive it and we give it. Although providing social support to others is often beneficial for the giver (Brown, Nesse, Vinokur, & Smith, 2003), some such situations can be overwhelming for the giver, resulting in *social stress.* The caregiving role, in which one person provides the bulk of care for a loved one with a chronic illness, also can be stressful and adversely affect physical health (Vitaliano, Zhang, & Scanlan, 2003).

Social Support Social relationships are an important factor in how we deal with stress, often serving as a buffer against low control and other work stress.

Ghislain & Marie David de Lossy/Getty Images

One study of parents who were full-time caregivers of adult children with a serious mental illness found higher self-reported stress levels and abnormalities in the daily production of the hormone cortisol (Barker, Greenberg, Seltzer, & Almeida, 2012). Caregiving stress has also been linked to poor immune functioning. In a series of studies, Janice Kiecolt-Glaser and colleagues demonstrated that family members who provide care for a relative with Alzheimer's disease report more depression and lower life satisfaction than those in the control group (matched family members with no caregiving responsibilities). Caregivers also have lower percentages of T cells and other measures of immunosuppression, as well as concurrent *overproduction* of proinflammatory cytokines (Kiecolt-Glaser and others, 2003). Overproduction of cytokines has been associated with a broad array of adverse health conditions, including cardiovascular disease, arthritis, Type 2 diabetes, and certain cancers. Ethnic minorities, immigrants, those who are poor, and women often experience the most intense social stress.

THE PHYSIOLOGY OF STRESS

A decade before Hans Selye's discovery (described in the chapter opening), physiologist Walter Cannon introduced the term *stress* to medicine (Cannon, 1932). Cannon observed that extremes of temperature, lack of oxygen, and emotion-arousing incidents all had a similar arousing effect on the body. He was the first to call this effect *stress,* and he believed it was a common cause of medical problems.

In one of Cannon's studies, cats were frightened by the sound of a barking dog. Afterwards, Cannon discovered large amounts of the hormone epinephrine in the cats' blood. Cannon called this response to stressful events the body's *fight-or-flight response.* An outpouring of epinephrine, along with cortisol and other hormones, helps prepare an organism to react to a threat, either by attacking or by running away.

From an evolutionary perspective, this emergency response system seems highly functional and adaptive. It undoubtedly was essential for survival in our evolutionary past, when humans faced numerous physical threats. Today, our stressors are apt to be psychological as well as physical, but we still react as though we are facing a wild animal. According to neuroscientist Robert Sapolsky, this explains why humans and their primate cousins get more stress-related diseases than any other member of the animal kingdom. All vertebrate animals respond to stressful situations by releasing hormones such as adrenaline and cortisol, but they do not appear to suffer the same health consequences as humans and other primates. In Sapolsky's words, primates, like humans, "are super smart and organized just enough to devote their free time to being miserable to each other

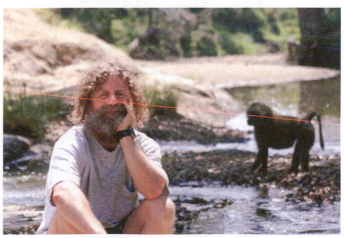

Robert Sapolsky, a Stanford University professor of neurology and neurological sciences, spent more than 30 years studying baboons in the wild. In this 2007 photo he is observing them at the Talek River in Masai Mara National Reserve, Kenya.

©John Heminway

and stressing each other out. We've evolved to be smart enough to make ourselves sick" (Sapolsky, 2004b, 2010; Shwartz, 2007).

Many of Sapolsky's insights come from his 30-year field study of wild African baboons, highly social and intelligent primates that often have elevated resting levels of stress hormones despite facing a relatively low level of threat from predators, lack of food, or other life-threatening problems. Baboons that have the lowest rank in the troop and those that are socially isolated are most likely to show stress-induced changes in their physiology. In addition to having elevated resting levels of epinephrine and cortisol, these baboons have reproductive systems that function poorly, blood pressure that is elevated, and wounds that heal more slowly than those of other baboons. High-status baboons that frequently have to defend their dominant position physically are also likely to show these adverse physiological changes (Sapolsky, 2005). What that means, says Sapolsky, is that if you are a baboon living in a troop in the Serengeti, you "only have to work three hours a day for your calories, predators don't mess with you much … and you've got nine hours of free time every day to devote to generating psychological stress toward other animals in your troop" (Shwartz, 2007).

As noted at the beginning of the chapter, however, stressors can have positive effects if they are short-lived and are perceived as challenges rather than threats. Momentary stressors mobilize the immune system for fighting off infections and healing wounds (Segerstrom, 2007). In addition, many experts—from champion athletes to professional entertainers—find that their performances improve under pressure (Blascovich, Seery, Mugridge, Norris, & Weisbuch, 2004). Hans Selye himself recognized this in his concept of *eustress* (from the Greek prefix *eu-,* meaning "good" or "well"), meaning that challenging events can lead to growth if they enhance our functioning, just as working the body by lifting weights ultimately improves a person's muscular strength.

The Role of the Brain and Nervous System

The body's overall reaction to stress is regulated by the central nervous system. Recall from Chapter 3 that the nervous system consists of two parts: the *central nervous system* (the brain and spinal cord) and the *peripheral nervous system.* The peripheral nervous system is divided into two major branches: the *autonomic nervous system* (ANS) and the *somatic nervous system.* Finally, the ANS is further divided into two branches: the *sympathetic nervous system* (SNS) and the *parasympathetic nervous system* (PNS).

When an external event is first perceived by your sense organs, sensory neurons in the somatic nervous system transmit nerve impulses to lower-level brain regions announcing the impending threat. The *reticular formation,* which runs like a rope through the middle of the brainstem (see Chapter 3), plays a central role in alerting the brain to an impending threat or challenge.

The reticular formation coordinates two neural pathways of brain–body communication. Through the first, it routes information about the existence of a potential stressor to the *thalamus,* which sorts this sensory information and relays it to the *hypothalamus,* the *limbic system,* and higher brain regions in the cerebral cortex that interpret the meaning of the potential stressor. Through the second pathway, the reticular formation carries neural instructions back from the higher brain regions to the various target organs, muscles, and glands controlled by the SNS; as a result of these instructions, the body is mobilized for defensive action.

Under instructions from the SNS, the adrenal glands release hormones that cause the fight-or-flight response, in which heart rate increases, the pupils dilate, stress hormones are secreted, and digestion slows. In addition, SNS activation increases blood flow to the muscles and causes stored energy to be converted to a form that is directly usable by the muscles. The region of the brain that most directly controls the stress response is the hypothalamus, which reacts to a variety of stimuli, from actual threats to memories of stressful moments to imagined stressors, and interacts with nearly every region of the brain. The hypothalamus also coordinates the activity of the endocrine system; as we will see, the endocrine system's hormones play a key role in how we respond to stress.

The Role of the Endocrine System: The SAM and HPA Axes

As we saw in Chapter 3, the endocrine system is the body's relatively slow-acting communication system consisting of a network of glands that secrete hormones directly into the bloodstream. This communication system is involved in our stress responses in two key ways. First, under stress, the hypothalamus orders the pituitary gland to secrete *adrenocorticotropic hormone* (ACTH), which is taken up by receptors in the *adrenal glands,* a pair of small endocrine glands lying just above the kidneys. Each of these remarkable structures consists of two nearly independent glands: a central region called the *adrenal medulla* and an outer covering called the *adrenal cortex.* When the hypothalamus sends stress signals via the pituitary gland, the adrenal medulla launches a counterattack by secreting *epinephrine* (also called *adrenaline*) and *norepinephrine* (also called *noradrenaline*) into the blood. These endocrine reactions, which help trigger the fight-or-flight response, last much longer than those generated directly by the SNS. Taken together, the interaction of the SNS and adrenal medulla is called the **sympatho-adreno-medullary (SAM) axis** (Figure 4.2).

The endocrine system is involved in stress in a second, equally important way. This second way involves the hypothalamus, the pituitary gland, and the adrenal cortex, or what has been called the **hypothalamic-pituitary-adrenocortical (HPA) axis.** While the SAM axis is the body's initial, rapid-acting response to stress, the HPA is a delayed response that functions to restore the body to its baseline state, a process known as **homeostasis.** The HPA axis is activated by messages relayed from the central nervous system to the hypothalamus, which in turn secretes *corticotropin-releasing hormone* (CRH). CRH stimulates the production of ACTH by the pituitary gland, which then activates the adrenal cortex to secrete **corticosteroids,** steroid hormones that reduce inflammation, promote healing, and help mobilize the body's energy resources.

Just as the hypothalamus initiates the stress response, it also shuts it down—normally before the body is damaged. The mechanism involves cortisol, a corticosteroid hormone that has a potent effect on all the body's tissues, including raising glucose levels in the blood, stimulating the breakdown of proteins into amino acids, and inhibiting the uptake of glucose by the body tissues but not by the brain (Kemeny, 2003). In a finely tuned *feedback* mechanism, cortisol acts on the hippocampus, which has a high density of cortisol receptors and neurons that project to the hypothalamus, signaling the pituitary to suppress the further release of CRH and ACTH. As the amount of ACTH in the blood decreases, the adrenal cortex shuts down its production of cortisol.

The rate of cortisol secretion, which is remarkably sensitive to psychological factors and peaks about 30 minutes after a stressor occurs, is so closely linked to stress that health

sympatho-adreno-medullary (SAM) axis The body's initial, rapid-acting response to stress, involving the release of epinephrine and norepinephrine from the adrenal medulla under the direction of the sympathetic nervous system.

hypothalamic-pituitary-adrenocortical (HPA) axis The body's delayed response to stress, involving the secretion of corticosteroid hormones from the adrenal cortex.

homeostasis The tendency to maintain a balanced or constant internal state; the regulation of any aspect of body chemistry, such as the level of glucose in the blood, around a particular set point.

corticosteroids Hormones produced by the adrenal cortex that fight inflammation, promote healing, and trigger the release of stored energy.

SAM and HPA: Hypothalamus secretes corticotropin-releasing hormone (CRH).

SAM and HPA: CRH causes the pituitary gland to secrete adrenocorticotrophic hormone (ACTH).

SAM: ACTH causes the sympathetic ganglia to stimulate the adrenal medulla to release a mixture of epinephrine and norepinephrine that triggers the physiological fight-or-flight responses: increased heart rate, breathing, blood pressure, etc.

HPA: ACTH causes the adrenal cortex to secrete corticosteroids, including cortisol, that combat inflammation, promote healing, and mobilize the body's energy resources.

FIGURE 4.2 The Body's Response to Stress During a moment of stress, the hypothalamus secretes releasing factors that coordinate the endocrine responses of the pituitary and adrenal glands. As part of the sympatho-adreno-medullary (SAM) axis, the adrenal medulla releases the stress hormones epinephrine and norepinephrine as the body's initial, rapid-acting response to stress. Epinephrine and norepinephrine increase heart rate, breathing, and blood pressure; slow digestion; and dilate the pupils. A second, delayed response involves the hypothalamic-pituitary-adrenocortical (HPA) axis, which triggers secretion of corticosteroids from the adrenal cortex. These steroid hormones fight inflammation, promote healing, and trigger the release of stored reserves of energy.

psychologists frequently use the level of this hormone circulating in the blood or saliva as a physiological index of stress. For some people, even a seemingly ordinary event such as boarding an airplane can trigger a large increase in cortisol, which means, of course, that CRH has already been released from the hypothalamus and ACTH from the pituitary (Thompson, 2000).

All of these endocrine system actions help the organism deal with stress. When an organism is faced with a threat, its brain needs energy in the form of glucose, which cortisol helps provide. But too much cortisol can have negative consequences, leading to hypertension, weakened immune function, and perhaps psychological problems. When Robert Sapolsky studied wild-born vervet monkeys that farmers had trapped and caged in groups to protect their crops, he found that a number of the monkeys became sick and died, especially those that were caged with other monkeys that were especially aggressive. Autopsies of the monkeys showed high rates of bleeding ulcers, enlarged adrenal glands, and something else: pronounced damage to the hippocampal regions of their brains, perhaps as the result of prolonged high cortisol levels triggered by the prolonged stress (Sapolsky, 2004a).

Normally regulated by the hippocampus, cortisol levels can spiral upward when, in response to unrelenting stress, more and more cortisol is secreted and the hippocampus is damaged, leaving it unable to signal the hypothalamus to shut off the stress response (Morgan and others, 2001). This condition of *hypercortisolism*, as well as a more prolonged activation of the HPA system, has been linked to the rate of cognitive decline in individuals with Alzheimer's disease (Suhr, Demireva, & Heffner, 2008). It's associated with a disruption in the brain's production of new neurons (Mirescu & Gould,

2006), observed in patients suffering from anorexia nervosa (Haas and others, 2009), and described as evidence of premature aging (Sapolsky, 1990).

In a less well understood phenomenon, the HPA axis may become underactive in some individuals in the face of chronic stress, creating a state of adrenal exhaustion and chronically low levels of cortisol (*hypocortisolism*) (Heim, Ehlert, & Hellhammer, 2000). Immune diseases such as fibromyalgia, rheumatoid arthritis, and asthma have all been associated with this state of blunted cortisol production.

Sex Differences and the HPA Axis

The body's physiological response to stress is shaped by many factors, including our biological sex. Although some differences in how women and men respond to stress depend on the type of stress being experienced, between puberty and menopause females generally have lower, and more variable, HPA and autonomic nervous system reactivity to stressful events than males of the same age (Van der Voorn and others, 2017). To pinpoint the cause of these differences, research has focused on the close connection between the HPA and the *hypothalamic-pituitary-gonadal (HPG) axis*, through which the nervous system and the endocrine system regulate development, reproduction, and aging via the production of testosterone and estrogen by the testicles and ovaries (gonads).

Although *fight-or-flight* characterizes the primary physiological response to stress in both females and males, when females are under pressure they may be more likely than males to **tend and befriend**—that is, to nurture others in their care, especially children, and to seek the company of other people. Like the fight-or-flight response, tend-and-befriend behaviors depend on underlying physiological mechanisms—in particular the hormone *oxytocin*, which releases rapidly in response to stressful events (Taylor and others, 2006). The tend-and-befriend pattern, which may have evolved because women and men faced somewhat different adaptive pressure over the course of time, appears to involve the blunting of SNS responses geared toward aggressing or fleeing. This gender difference was apparent among 634 mothers and fathers who had lost a child during its first months of life (Christiansen, 2015). While the men were more likely to "flee" by sometimes spending hours away from home, the women were more likely to seek social support from other people.

Oxytocin, the key tend-and-befriend hormone, is strongly influenced by estrogen, which may partly explain women's and men's different responses to stressful events. Circulating levels of cortisol, and HPA reactivity, vary with estrogen levels across the menstrual cycle, with higher levels of estrogen being associated with lower cortisol and blunted HPA activity (Herman and others, 2016). Gender differences in HPA activity, which are already present during childhood, may increase during puberty, along with increases in gonadal hormones (Goel, Workman, Lee, Innala, & Viau, 2014). In adults, testosterone seems to increase HPA reactivity, while estrogens decrease HPA activity (Goel and others, 2014).

Overall, research studies suggest that men respond to psychological stress with greater increases in cortisol and HPA reactivity than women. This difference is of interest to health care professionals because differences in HPA responsiveness to stress may partially explain gender differences in the development of chronic illness. Illnesses and chronic conditions that are more prevalent in males than females, such as cardiovascular disease and diabetes, are also associated with higher levels of cortisol and HPA

tend and befriend The human tendency to respond to stress by seeking the company of other people and nurturing offspring.

activity. Conversely, conditions that are more prevalent in females—including lupus, multiple sclerosis, certain forms of arthritis, and other autoimmune illnesses—are associated with hypocortisolism and HPA underactivity (Bellavance & Rivest, 2014). Some researchers believe that HPA axis functioning might be a general, biological marker of the cumulative, long-term effects of the body's physiological response to stress (Kudielka & Kirschbaum, 2005).

Measuring Stress

Health psychologists have used a variety of approaches to measure stress, most of which fall into two categories: self-report inventories and physiological measures. Self-reports such as life events inventories and daily hassle scales are the most common, but as we have seen, they have many limitations in their reliability and validity.

A major disadvantage of self-reports is that information that is recalled long after significant events have occurred is often inaccurate. To overcome this limitation, health psychologists increasingly rely on self-reports made closer in time to the events being investigated. This approach, called **ecological momentary assessment (EMA)**, involves repeated sampling of people's behaviors and experiences in real time and in their natural environments (Shiffman, Stone, & Hufford, 2008). EMA can take several forms (Wenze & Miller, 2010). One is the collection of information at specified time intervals, such as via daily journal entries. This approach asks research participants to look back, at the end of the day, and report about mood, stressors, social interactions, and other variables. To reduce the reliance on memory even further, EMA may require the reporting of information several times a day. One example of this type of measurement is *signal-contingent recording* (also called an ambulatory diary record), in which reports are requested in response to a signal that comes randomly several times per day from a pager, smartphone, or other device (Smith and others, 2012).

ecological momentary assessment (EMA) A method of measuring stress that involves repeated sampling of people's behaviors and experiences in real time and in their natural environments.

Physiological Measures

Given the limitations of self-report measures, many researchers have relied on physiological measures of stress instead. In the laboratory, the autonomic nervous system response can be provoked by many different stressors, including physical, mental, and psychosocial tasks. Physiological measures include changes in heart rate, blood pressure, respiration rate, and the electrical conductance of the skin (a measure of sweating). Changes in these measures occur in response to stress- or emotion-induced activation of the sympathetic division of the autonomic nervous system. With advances in technology, many of these measures can be taken outside the laboratory with ambulatory monitoring equipment that allows research participants to go about their daily activities. For example, *ambulatory blood pressure* (ABP) is recorded via a cuff worn under participants' clothing and a small control box attached to their belts (Smith and others, 2012).

Health psychologists also measure stress via its association with hormones such as cortisol, epinephrine, and norepinephrine (Eller, Netterstrom, & Hansen, 2006). Epinephrine and norepinephrine levels are typically measured in either blood or urine samples, and cortisol is measured via a sample of saliva. These measures have several advantages, including being highly reliable and easily quantified. They are not, however, problem-free.

Blood levels of hormones decrease quickly (within minutes) after a stressful experience, so researchers must be very quick to obtain accurate measurement. Hormone levels generally persist longer in urine, but these are also influenced by factors unrelated to stress.

Cardiovascular Reactivity

Because of the relationship between self-control and physical arousal, researchers are exploring the use of blood pressure, heart rate, and other measures of **cardiovascular reactivity (CVR)** to identify individual differences in how people cope with stress (Quigley, Barrett, & Weinstein, 2002). Situations that are appraised as threatening may be associated with a different pattern CVR than situations that are appraised as challenging. Threat appraisals have been linked with enhanced *vascular* responses, as reflected by increases in diastolic blood pressure and *total peripheral resistance* (the cumulative resistance of all the body's blood vessels), whereas challenge appraisals have been linked with increased *myocardial* reactivity, as reflected by increases in heart rate and cardiac output (Maier, Waldstein, & Synowski, 2003).

Physiologically, our reactivity to stressful situations seems to be quite stable. In one study, researchers measured participants' blood pressure while the participants completed stressful tasks. Years later, follow-up studies demonstrated that those whose blood pressure had increased most during the initial phase of the study were most likely to have chronic hypertension (Matthews, Raikkonen, Sutton-Tyrrell, & Kuller, 2004).

Cardiovascular reactivity to psychological stressors, if exaggerated or prolonged, may be harmful. According to the **reactivity hypothesis**, individuals who are "hyperreactors" (those who show large changes in blood pressure and vascular resistance to stress) have an increased risk of developing heart disease (Phillips & Hughes, 2011). In one illuminating study, Karen Matthews and her colleagues (Matthews, Woodall, & Allen, 1993) found that children who showed larger CVR to a combination of mental and physical challenges had higher resting blood pressure. Results such as these suggest that CVR to stress may have a role in the development of hypertension. Interestingly, other researchers have reported that CVR is influenced by the quality of our diet, sleep, and other lifestyle factors. One study reported that participants displayed increased CVR during stress tasks, such as public speaking, following a single high-fat meal in comparison with a low-fat meal (Jakulj and others, 2007).

Despite findings such as these, the reactivity hypothesis remains controversial (Phillips & Hughes, 2011). One question is whether a person's reactivity to acute stress in a laboratory setting also reflects his or her reactivity to stress in real life. Another question is whether the reactivity hypothesis can be extended to health outcomes other than those directly associated with the heart, as some researchers have suggested (Carroll, 2011).

Most changes in heart rate, such as those that occur in response to challenging physical and emotional demands, are controlled by the tenth cranial nerve (i.e., vagus nerve), which is the longest in the body, extending into each limb all the way from the brain. The *vagus* (which means "wandering" in Latin) plays an important role in the parasympathetic nervous system's calming response; its main function is to lower blood pressure and heart rate. When a healthy person inhales, for instance, the vagus becomes less active, increasing heart rate; when he or she exhales, vagal activity increases, and heart rate decreases. In response to stress, the autonomic nervous system speeds heart rate

cardiovascular reactivity (CVR) An individual's characteristic reaction to stress, including changes in heart rate, blood pressure, and hormones.

reactivity hypothesis The hypothesis that individuals who show large changes in blood pressure and vascular resistance to stress have increased risk of developing heart disease.

respiratory sinus arrhythmia
(RSA) Variability in heart rate in
synchrony with breathing.

(to meet the metabolic demands of the body's emergency response system) by decreasing vagal action on the heart.

Respiratory sinus arrhythmia (RSA), or vagal tone, is a measure of how the interval between heart beats synchronizes with breathing, and it is shorter when we inhale than when we exhale. RSA reflects the balance of activity between the sympathetic and parasympathetic divisions of the autonomic nervous system, and it is used to measure both baseline heart rate variability and how people react to environmental events. People who have high RSA tend to have better emotional well-being than those with lower RSA (Mather & Thayer, 2018). Low RSA has been linked to a variety of poor health outcomes, including cardiovascular disease, obesity, and diabetes (Thayer & Lane, 2007).

Cardiovascular reactivity may partly explain individual and group differences in coronary disease morbidity and mortality rates. Individuals who face repeated threats and challenges in their daily lives and have weaker cardiac autonomic control may be at a substantially greater risk for coronary artery disease than those who have greater regulatory control (Sloan, Bagiella, & Powell, 1999). Researchers at Harvard University's School of Public Health reported that Caribbean Americans and African Americans, two of the largest Black ethnic groups in the United States, display different patterns of cardiovascular reactivity to laboratory stressors than European Americans do (Arthur, Katkin, & Mezzacappa, 2004). In response to a mental arithmetic task, for instance, African Americans displayed larger decreases in heart period variability (i.e., lower vagal tone) than European Americans, but smaller decreases than their Caribbean American counterparts.

How Does Stress Make You Sick?

Biomedical researchers who study mind–body connections in disease were once ostracized from the scientific community. Harvard University's Herbert Benson notes that when he began doing his research decades earlier, he was told he was jeopardizing his medical career (Sternberg, 2001). Things began to change with two remarkable discoveries that would forever transform the face of medicine. The first was an accident. Working in a laboratory at the University of Rochester, psychologist Robert Ader had been conducting a classic Pavlovian learning experiment, attempting to condition laboratory rats to avoid saccharin-flavored drinking water. The design of the study was simple. After the rats were given a drink of the artificially sweetened water (a neutral stimulus), they received an injection of a drug (unconditioned stimulus), which made them nauseous (unconditioned response)—sick enough so that a single pairing of the two stimuli should have been sufficient to establish a *conditioned aversion* to the sweetened water.

But Ader discovered a problem. Over the course of several weeks of training and testing, a number of the rats became very sick and died. Puzzled by this development, Ader found that the number of virus- and infection-fighting T lymphocytes was reduced significantly in the bodies of the experimental animals. The nausea-inducing drug apparently had a more serious impact on the rats—it suppressed their immune responses (Figure 4.3).

What was most remarkable in Ader's experiment was that when these same rats were given saccharin-flavored water alone, without the drug, their immune systems responded as if the drug were actually circulating in their bloodstream. Classical conditioning had created a learned association between the taste of the water as a conditioned stimulus and

FIGURE 4.3 Conditioning the Immune Response After Robert Ader and Nicholas Cohen paired saccharin-flavored water with an immune-suppressing drug, the taste of the sweetened water alone elicited a conditioned response (immune suppression) in laboratory rats.

the suppression of T cells as a conditioned response. Over time, conditioned responding made the animals increasingly susceptible to disease as their immune reserves were weakened with each drink of sweetened water.

Before Ader's study, most biomedical researchers believed that the mind and body were, for the most part, independent systems that had no influence on one another. So entrenched was this belief that Ader himself had difficulty accepting the results of his own research. Good science demands replication of findings, so Ader teamed up with immunologist Nicholas Cohen to see if his initial findings were a fluke. They were not. In a subsequent series of experiments, Ader and Cohen (1985) demonstrated that the immune system could be conditioned, just as Ivan Pavlov had demonstrated that the salivary response could be conditioned in hungry dogs.

The second key discovery that changed medicine was neuroscientist Candace Pert's demonstration that the brain has receptors for immune molecules that enable the brain to monitor, and therefore influence, the activity of the immune system (Pert, 2003). As an example of this communication network, consider that when antigens induce an immune response, cells in the hypothalamus become more active. This may occur when T cells that have been activated by antigens release proinflammatory cytokines.

Cytokines (see Chapter 3) are protein molecules produced by immune cells that have a multitude of biological effects, including serving as a means of intercellular communication. They attract macrophages and stimulate phagocytosis at wound and infection sites. They are similar in structure to neurotransmitters (the chemical messengers in the process of neural communication); in fact, they look enough like neurotransmitters to bind to receptor sites on brain cells and trigger nerve impulses. The apparent interchangeability between neurotransmitters and cytokines suggests that the immune system's lymphocytes may, in effect, act as circulating "language translators," converting information from their direct contact with pathogens into the language of the central nervous system so that the brain can monitor and regulate the immune response.

The work of Ader, Cohen, and Pert gave credibility to an article that had been published a decade earlier by George Solomon, in which he coined the term **psychoneuroimmunology (PNI)**, referring to a "speculative theoretical integration" of the links among emotions, immunity, and disease (Solomon & Moos, 1964). This word describes a great deal about its focus: *psycho* for psychological processes, *neuro* for the neuroendocrine system (the

psychoneuroimmunology (PNI) The field of research that emphasizes the interaction of psychological, neural, and immunological processes in stress and illness.

nervous and hormonal systems), and *immunology* for the immune system. Focusing on three areas of functioning that were formerly believed to be relatively independent, PNI researchers investigate interactions between the nervous and immune systems, and the relationship between behavior and health (Figure 4.4). An important goal of PNI is to conduct basic research that can be applied to health care (Psychoneuroimmunology Research Society, 2010).

Since the publication of these watershed studies, the evidence for coordinated interactions among the brain, the neuroendocrine system, and the immune system has mounted quickly. There are hundreds of published studies examining the relationship between stress and immune functioning in humans (Segerstrom & Miller, 2004). Taken together, these studies demonstrate that short-term stressors, such as loud noises and electric shocks in the laboratory (or, in the real world, being called on by a professor in class), can have a positive effect by triggering an increase, or *up-regulation,* of natural immunity. Longer-lasting, chronic stressors, however, can have damaging effects by suppressing immunity.

Reduced immune functioning (*immunosuppression*) has been demonstrated following a divorce, bereavement, unemployment, and stressful bouts of exercise or military

FIGURE 4.4 Research Themes in Psychoneuro- immunology The goal of psychoneuroimmunology research is to reveal the many ways that behaviors and health are interrelated, with a focus on the immunological mechanisms that underlie these interactions.

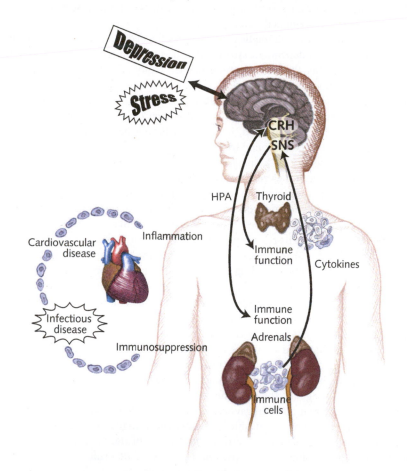

training; during exam periods; and when one is experiencing workplace stress. Among the changes observed are reduced numbers of natural killer cells, T cells, and total lymphocytes. And there seems to be a "dose–response" relationship between stress and immunosuppression. College students with the highest levels of overall life stress or the tendency to overreact to stressful events, for instance, show the greatest deficit in their immune response during exam weeks (Segerstrom & Miller, 2004).

Stress is also linked to lowered immune resistance to viral infections. In one study, 47% of participants living stress-filled lives developed colds after being inoculated with a rhinovirus, compared to only 27% of those inoculated who reported relatively stress-free lives (Cohen, Alper, Doyle, Treanor, & Turner, 2006). Other studies demonstrate that, compared to their counterparts experiencing only minor or short-term stress, both children and adults who are under chronic stress suffer more bouts of flu, herpes virus infections (cold sores and genital lesions), chicken pox, mononucleosis, and Epstein-Barr virus (Cohen, Doyle, Turner, Alper, & Skoner, 2003). Psychological stress has been linked with autoimmune disorders such as rheumatoid arthritis (Straub & Kalden, 2009), as well as coronary artery disease with accelerated progress. This connection occurs as the immune system reacts to stressful events by releasing cytokines that promote inflammation (Steptoe, Hamer, & Chida, 2007).

In addition, stress delays the healing of wounds (Walburn, Vedhara, Hankins, Rixon, & Weinman, 2009). In one study, married couples who received standardized punch biopsy wounds just prior to a 30-minute argument took a day or two longer to heal than did unstressed couples (Kiecolt-Glaser and others, 2005). In another study, 47 adults were given a standard questionnaire assessing psychological stress before undergoing hernia surgery. Patients who reported higher levels of preoperative stress had significantly slower rates of healing and reported a slower, more painful recovery (Broadbent, Petrie, Alley, & Booth, 2003).

Pathways from Stress to Disease

How stress influences the immune system is the subject of a great deal of ongoing research. Two hypotheses have been suggested. According to the *direct effect hypothesis*, stress directly influences the nervous, endocrine, and immune systems; stress on any of these systems can lead to disease. Alternatively, the *indirect effect hypothesis* suggests that immunosuppression is an aftereffect of the stress response (Segerstrom & Miller, 2004).

The Direct Effect Hypothesis Stress may directly affect immune efficiency through the activation of the HPA and SAM axes. T cells and B cells have receptors for corticosteroid "stress" hormones (which produce immunosuppression), and lymphocytes have catecholamine (epinephrine and norepinephrine) receptors. Stress activates these systems; the hormones released attach to the receptors of T cells, B cells, and lymphocytes, suppressing the immune response.

A growing body of research supports the direct effect hypothesis. In one study, Timothy Smith and his colleagues at the University of Utah (Smith and others, 2012) explored the direct cardiovascular effects of social stress in daily experience in 94 married, working couples (mean age 29.2 years). The participants completed a daily protocol from 8 a.m. to 10 p.m. that included the working hours and an evening at home with their spouse on the same day. During the 14-hour period of the protocol, each participant wore an ambulatory blood pressure (ABP) monitor that took a reading at random, averaging once every 30 minutes. After each ABP assessment, participants completed an *ambulatory diary record* (ADR) on a smartphone consisting of a battery of questions. The ADR questions were divided into two sections. The first assessed the participants' posture (sitting, standing, lying down); recent consumption of nicotine, caffeine, alcohol, or a meal (no, yes); temperature (too cold, comfortable, too hot); and other factors that might influence their ABP. The second section included items related to negative affect ("sad," "frustrated," "upset"); social-evaluative threat ("Worried about what others think about me" and "Concerned about the impression I am making"); appearance concerns ("Pleased about my appearance right now," "Feel satisfied with the way my body looks right now"); and ability perceptions ("Confident about my abilities" and "Feel as smart as others").

In both women and men, momentary reports of social-evaluative threat were associated with higher systolic blood pressure (SBP). This effect was mediated by negative affect. In other words, SBP increased when participants were worried about how their appearance or abilities were being perceived, but only if they also were frustrated or upset. Social-evaluative threat was also associated with higher diastolic blood pressure, but only in women, suggesting that gender may play a role in the extent to which evaluative threat has specific physiological effects that might have an adverse effect on health. Other studies have shown that ABP is linked to the development of future cardiovascular problems (Chida & Steptoe, 2010).

As another example of the direct effects of stress, consider the mounting evidence that family conflict early in life is associated with a variety of later health problems (Miller, Chen, & Parker, 2011). In one study, Richard Slatcher and Theodore Robles (2012) investigated the associations between conflict in family environments and daily cortisol levels in preschool children. Each child participant wore an ambulatory assessment device called the Child EAR for one full weekend day. The EAR records ambient sounds while participants go about their daily lives, allowing the researchers to note examples of interpersonal conflict (e.g., Child: "No! I don't want to!" Parent: "You are going to shut your mouth and be quiet!"). Parents also collected saliva samples from their children at six specified times each day.

The results showed that greater conflict at home was associated with children having a lower *cortisol awakening response* and flatter cortisol responses throughout the day, both of which have been linked to negative health consequences in adulthood, including earlier mortality (Kumari, Shipley, Stafford, & Kivimaki, 2011). Flatter cortisol levels are also a marker of the cumulative long-term effects of the body's physiological response to stress (McEwen, 2007).

Stress and Blood Clotting In addition to increasing blood pressure, SAM and HPA activation can also influence blood clotting. When you cut yourself, proteins and platelets in your blood stick together (coagulate) to stop the bleeding and start the healing process. However, blood shouldn't clot when it's just circulating through the body. When blood clots too much, it is referred to as being in a hypercoagulable state (blood clotting disorder). In this state, people have an increased risk for blood clots developing in their arteries and veins, which, in turn, can increase the risk of heart disease and stroke.

Overcommitment, overload, and other forms of job stress have been linked to hypercoagulable states (Austin, Wissman, & von Känel, 2013). Blood clotting disorders have also been reported among caregivers (von Känel and others, 2006) and teachers (von Känel,

Bellingrath, & Kudielka, 2009) who feel high levels of stress. Researchers at the University of Bonn (2008) found increased coagulation among 31 patients with anxiety disorders, which may explain why such patients are 3 to 4 times more likely to die from heart disease.

The Indirect Effect Hypothesis According to the indirect effect hypothesis, stress-induced delays in healing and other adverse health outcomes may occur because stress alters immune processes *indirectly* by encouraging maladaptive behaviors. Among the behavioral risk factors that could delay wound healing through their effects on the immune system are smoking, alcohol and drug abuse, fragmented sleep, not enough exercise, and poor nutrition, each of which has been associated with increased stress (Krueger & Chang, 2008). Smoking, for instance, slows healing by weakening the normal proliferation of macrophages at wound sites and by reducing the flow of blood through vasoconstriction (McMaster and others, 2008). In addition to healing more slowly, smokers are more likely to develop infections following surgical procedures, perhaps because nicotine and other toxins in cigarette smoke suppress both primary and secondary immune responses by reducing the activities of white blood cells.

As another example of how stress indirectly alters immune processes, consider that deep sleep is associated with the secretion of growth hormone (GH), which facilitates wound healing by activating macrophages to kill bacteria at the wound site (see Chapter 3). Loss of sleep, or fragmented sleep, results in reduced GH secretion and delayed healing (Leproult, Copinschi, Buxton, & Van Cauter, 1997; Sander, 2009).

Duration of Stress

The ability to recover after a stressful experience strongly influences the total burden that the experience has on an individual. The neuroendocrine system plays an important role in the concept of **allostatic load** (or **allostasis**), which refers to the cumulative long-term effects of the body's physiological response to stress (McEwen, 2011). Stressors that are unpredictable, uncontrollable, of longer duration, and difficult to cope with cause a buildup of allostatic load, which manifests in many ways, including decreased immunity, elevated epinephrine levels, increased abdominal fat, decreased hippocampal size and functioning (leading to problems with thinking and memory), and the overproduction of interleukin-6 and other proinflammatory cytokines.

Interestingly, many of these changes also occur with aging, leading some researchers to characterize a high allostatic load as a form of accelerated aging in response to stress. These adverse responses have been observed, for example, among those with lower socioeconomic status (SES) (Dowd, Simanek, & Aiello, 2009), unemployed adults (Ala-Mursula and others, 2013), and hurricane survivors (Bourgeois & Owens, 2014). Links between allostatic load and a variety of chronic illnesses have also been established—including cardiovascular disease, diabetes, and chronic obstructive pulmonary disease—as well as a general decline in cognitive and physical health (Shiels, Stenvinkel, Kooman, & McGuinness, 2017). Unchecked, allostatic overload is associated with increased risk of illness and even mortality (Robertson, Beveridge, & Bromley, 2017; Karlamangla, Singer, & Seeman, 2006).

In clinical settings, allostatic load is increasingly being viewed as a useful tool that physicians, nurses, and other health care providers can use to measure physiological "wear and tear" in their patients, with the goal of being able to intervene, and improve health outcomes, at various stages of the stress response (Rosemberg & Seng, 2017).

allostatic load (allostasis) The cumulative long-term effects of the body's physiological response to stress.

Stress, Inflammation, and Disease

Investigations of the direct and indirect effect hypotheses have given rise to an immuno-suppression model of the relationships among stress, immunity, and disease that nicely summarizes what we've discussed thus far. According to this model, stress suppresses the immune system, which leaves the individual vulnerable to opportunistic infection and disease (Miller, Cohen, & Ritchey, 2002) (Figure 4.5).

The immunosuppression model offers a plausible explanation for the influence that stress has on wound healing, infectious diseases, and some forms of cancer (see Chapter 11). But it does not explain how stress might influence diseases whose central feature is excessive inflammation. These include many allergic, autoimmune, rheuma-tologic, neurologic, and cardiovascular diseases—all of which are exacerbated by stress. Parkinson's disease, for instance—a neurodegenerative disease that affects more than 1 million Americans—involves a loss of brain neurons that produce dopamine and sero-tonin (Parkinson's Disease Foundation, 2010). People with Parkinson's suffer muscular tremors, rigidity of movement, and a gradual deterioration in overall health. Inflamma-tion accelerates the development of Parkinson's, which is why ibuprofen may lower the risk of developing the disease (Gao, Chen, Schwarzschild, & Ascherio, 2011).

To account for the impact of stress on inflammatory diseases, researchers have proposed a **glucocorticoid receptor (GCR) resistance model**, the basic premise of which is that chronic stress interferes with the body's ability to regulate the inflammatory response. Runaway inflammation, in turn, can promote the development and progres-sion of many diseases (Cohen, S. and others, 2012). Specifically, chronic stress disrupts

glucocorticoid receptor (GCR) resistance model The idea that chronic stress promotes the development and progression of disease by reducing the sensitivity of immune system receptors to glucocorticoid hormones such as cortisol, thereby interfering with the body's ability to regulate the inflammatory response.

FIGURE 4.5 Summary of the Physiology of Stress: Immunosuppression Model These conditions compromise the immune system's capacity to mount an effective response to infection or injury.

Stress reduces immunity by:

(a) Activating autonomic nervous system fibers that descend from the brain to immune tissue.

(b) Triggering the secretion of hormones that bind to white blood cells and alter their functioning.

(c) Inducing immunosuppressive coping behaviors, such as poor diet and substance abuse.

the sensitivity of immune system receptors to glucocorticoid hormones such as cortisol, which normally terminate the inflammatory response. In a test of the model, Gregory Miller and his colleagues measured the perceived stress and immune responsiveness of 25 healthy parents of children undergoing active treatment for cancer, in comparison to 25 healthy parents of medically healthy children. Parents of cancer patients reported higher levels of psychological stress than parents of healthy children *and* were found to have diminished sensitivity to a synthetic glucocorticoid hormone, as revealed by higher levels of cytokine production. Remember that glucocorticoid hormones function as *anti-inflammatory* signals by suppressing the production of *proinflammatory cytokines* by immune cells. Parents of cancer patients showed significantly *less suppression* of cytokine production in response to an administered glucocorticoid compared with parents of healthy children (Miller, Cohen, & Richey, 2002). These findings are significant because overproduction of cytokines has been linked with a spectrum of chronic inflammatory diseases and adverse conditions, including cardiovascular disease (discussed in Chapter 10), osteoporosis, arthritis, Type 2 diabetes, Alzheimer's disease, periodontal disease, and the general weakening or frailty associated with aging (Kiecolt-Glaser and others, 2003).

In another study, Sheldon Cohen and his colleagues administered a comprehensive stress interview to 276 healthy adults who were then exposed to a rhinovirus that causes the common cold. The participants were held in quarantine for five days and monitored for signs of infection and illness. The results demonstrated that those who had recently experienced a prolonged stressful event were more likely to have immune cells that were unable to respond to hormonal signals that normally regulate inflammation. They were also more likely to develop colds when exposed to the virus. "When under stress, cells of the immune system are unable to respond to hormonal control, and consequently, produce levels of inflammation that promote disease," Cohen said. "Because inflammation plays a role in many diseases such as cardiovascular, asthma and autoimmune disorders, this model suggests why stress impacts them as well" (Carnegie Mellon University, 2012).

OTHER MODELS OF STRESS AND ILLNESS

Thus far we have discussed the immune suppression and glucocorticoid resistance models of stress and illness. These models developed from many years of research and are based on or inspired by other important models, including Selye's general adaptation syndrome, the transactional model, and the diathesis–stress model. We will consider Selye's work first.

Selye's General Adaptation Syndrome

Surely the most significant contribution to our understanding of stress and illness comes from the research of Hans Selye, introduced in the chapter-opening story. Selye devised the concept of stress as a "nonspecific response of the body to any demand" (1974, p. 27). The body's reaction to stress was so predictable that Selye called it the **general adaptation syndrome (GAS)**.

general adaptation syndrome (GAS) Selye's term for the body's reaction to stress, which consists of three stages: alarm, resistance, and exhaustion.

FIGURE 4.6 **The General Adaptation Syndrome** Under stress, the body enters an alarm phase during which resistance to stress is suppressed temporarily. From this, it rebounds to a phase of increased resistance to stress. The body's resistance can last only so long. In the face of prolonged stress, the stage of exhaustion may be reached. During this final stage, people become more vulnerable to a variety of health problems.

As Figure 4.6 shows, GAS consists of three stages. Stage 1, the *alarm reaction,* is essentially the same as Cannon's *fight-or-flight* response, which we considered earlier. The strength of the alarm reaction depends on the degree to which the event is perceived as a threat.

When a stressful situation persists, the body's reaction progresses to Stage 2, the *resistance stage.* In this stage, physiological arousal remains high (but not as high as during the alarm reaction), as the body tries to adapt to the emergency by replenishing adrenal hormones. The individual's ability to cope with everyday events and hassles decreases, and people often become irritable, impatient, and increasingly vulnerable to health problems.

If the stressful situation persists and resistance is no longer possible, the body enters the final stage of the GAS—the *stage of exhaustion.* At this point, the body's energy reserves are depleted. Hypocortisolism (depletion of cortisol), for instance, is consistent with this final stage of the syndrome. If stress persists, disease and physical deterioration or even death may occur. For example, one result of exhaustion is increased susceptibility to what Selye referred to as *diseases of adaptation.* Among these are allergic reactions, hypertension, and common colds, as well as more serious illnesses caused by immune deficiencies.

Numerous studies have reinforced Selye's basic point: Prolonged stress exacts a toll on the body. People who have endured the prolonged stress of combat, child abuse, or a chronic disease may suffer enlarged adrenal glands, bleeding ulcers, damage to the brain's hippocampus, and abnormalities in several other cerebral areas. More generally, stress disrupts *neurogenesis,* the brain's production of new neurons (Mirescu & Gould, 2006) and the process by which cells divide. In one study, women who reported high levels of stress as caregivers for children with serious chronic illnesses also displayed a remarkable symptom of premature aging—shorter DNA segments, called *telomeres,* at the ends of chromosomes. Caregivers who reported the highest levels of stress had cells that appeared 10 years older than their true age (Epel and others, 2004). In another study, participants who reported a higher number of ambivalent relationships in their social networks also had shorter telomeres, even after control variables such as age, medication use, and health behaviors were ruled out (Uchino and others, 2012). Telomere shortening, which causes cells to die because they can no longer reproduce, is associated with a wide range of age-related diseases (Starr and others, 2008).

Cognitive Appraisal and Stress

Selye's model has been criticized for largely ignoring how psychological factors contribute to stress. There now is clear evidence that *how* potential stressors are appraised, or perceived, strongly influences their impact on the individual. The most influential model describing the importance of conscious appraisal in stress is the **transactional model**, proposed by Richard Lazarus and Susan Folkman (1984). The fundamental idea behind this model is that we cannot fully understand stress by examining environmental events (stimuli) and people's behaviors (responses) as separate entities; rather, we need to consider them together as a transaction, in which each person must continually adjust to daily challenges.

According to the transactional model, the *process* of stress is triggered whenever stressors exceed the personal and social resources that a person is able to mobilize in order to cope. If a person's coping resources are strong enough, there may be no stress, even when—to another person—the situation seems unbearable. On the other hand, if a person's coping resources are weak or ineffective, stress occurs, even when—to another person—the demands of a situation can easily be met.

As shown in Figure 4.7, appraising an event as stressful means seeing it as a potential challenge, a source of harm, or a threat to one's future well-being. A *challenge* is perceived when a situation is demanding but ultimately can be overcome, and the person can profit from the situation. Appraisals of harm–loss or threat refer to less positive outcomes. *Harm–loss* is the assessment that some form of damage has occurred already as a result of a situation. An event may be appraised as a *threat* when the person anticipates that a situation may bring about loss or harm at some point *in the future*.

When the demands of an event or a situation do create stress, our response is not static but instead involves continuous interactions and adjustments—called *transactions*—between the environment and our attempts to cope. Each of us is an active agent who can dramatically alter the impact of a potential stressor through our own personal resources.

According to Lazarus, transactions between people and their environments are driven by *cognitive appraisal* of potential stressors. Cognitive appraisal involves assessing (1) whether a situation or event threatens our well-being, (2) whether there are sufficient personal resources available for coping with the demand, and (3) whether our strategy for dealing with the situation or event is working.

When we confront a potentially stressful event, such as an unexpected pop quiz, we engage in a **primary appraisal** to determine the event's meaning. In effect, we ask, "Is this situation going to mean trouble for me?" In the primary appraisal, we interpret an event in one of three ways: *irrelevant, benign-positive,* or *threatening* (challenging or harmful) (Figure 4.7). If the event is appraised as irrelevant or benign-positive, no physiological arousal—and no stress—occurs.

Once an event has been appraised as a challenge or threat, **secondary appraisal** addresses the question "What can I do to cope with this situation?" At this point, we assess our coping abilities to determine whether they will be adequate to meet the challenge or avoid the potential harm, loss, or threat. If these resources are deemed adequate, little or no stress occurs. When a threat or challenge is high and coping resources are low, stress is likely to occur.

Lazarus's transactional model has three important implications. First, any given situation or event may be appraised (and experienced) as stressful by one person but not by another. Second, cognitive appraisals are extremely susceptible to changes in mood,

transactional model Lazarus's theory that the experience of stress depends as much on the individual's cognitive appraisal of a potential stressor's impact as it does on the event or situation itself.

E+/Getty Images

K What does "k" mean in this text conversation? Appraising it as a negative comment could lead to stress and potentially to responding with a message that would be perceived negatively by the other person in the conversation.

primary appraisal A person's initial determination of an event's meaning, whether irrelevant, benign-positive, or threatening.

secondary appraisal A person's determination of whether his or her own resources and abilities are sufficient to meet the demands of an event that is appraised as potentially threatening or challenging.

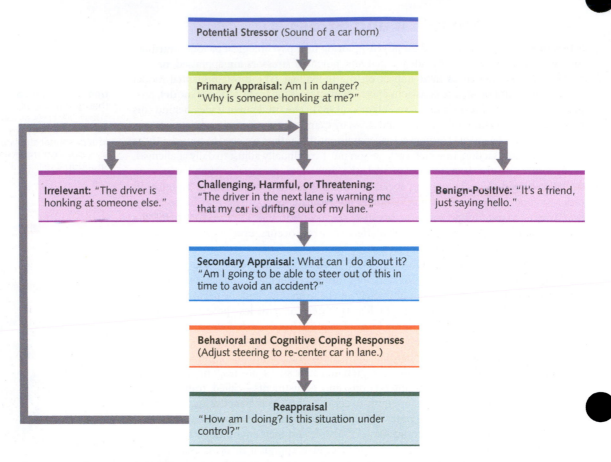

FIGURE 4.7 The Transactional Model of Stress The impact of a potential stressor, such as the startling sound of a honking horn, depends on a three-step process of cognitive appraisal. During primary appraisal, events perceived as neutral or benign pose no threat as a source of stress. Events perceived as challenging, harmful, or threatening are subjected to a secondary appraisal, during which the individual determines whether his or her coping resources are sufficient to meet the challenge posed by the stressor. Finally, in the reappraisal process, feedback from new information or ongoing coping efforts is used to check on the accuracy of both primary and secondary appraisals.

health, and motivational state. Being stuck in traffic may be a minor annoyance on most days; on the day when you are late for an exam, it may seem an insurmountable obstacle. Third, some evidence suggests that the body's stress response occurs whether a situation is actually experienced in the here and now, remembered from the past, or merely imagined.

How might this work? Recall that the HPA axis and homeostasis are central players in the stress response. When the hypothalamus receives signals from its various inputs (including the cerebral cortex) about conditions that deviate from an ideal homeostatic state (such as reliving an emotionally charged event), corticotropin-releasing hormone is secreted, which in turn causes the pituitary gland to release ACTH. Then ACTH can stimulate the adrenal cortex to release cortisol, and in this way, the stress-response cascade is triggered by an alarming event, whether real and present, recalled, or imagined.

The Diathesis–Stress Model

Knowing that the stress response varies with how a particular stressor is perceived has led researchers to propose several other models that highlight the interaction of biological and psychosocial factors in health and illness. The **diathesis–stress model** proposes that two continuously interacting factors jointly determine an individual's susceptibility to stress and illness: *predisposing factors* that establish a person's vulnerability and *precipitating factors* from the environment (Steptoe & Ayers, 2004). The predisposition can result from genetic factors or from prior environmental factors, such as chronic exposure to secondhand tobacco smoke. In most cases, the precipitating environmental factors (stress) are not believed to be specific for a given health condition, whereas predisposing genetic factors (diathesis) are.

For instance, some individuals are more vulnerable to illness because their biological systems show greater **reactivity**—they respond more strongly to specific environmental triggers. As one example, Jennifer McGrath (2003) found stable individual differences (diathesis) in children's blood pressure and heart rate during a stressful mirror-image tracing test. Interestingly, children who displayed the strongest cardiovascular reactivity were more likely to have a family history of hypertension and cardiovascular disease than less reactive children. Other studies have shown that cardiac reactivity to stress is linked to the risk of heart attack and stroke. For example, researchers studied the responses of 901 Finnish men on a simple test of memory that was designed to elicit a mild state of mental stress. The men under age 55 who displayed the strongest blood pressure reaction during the test also had the most severe blockages in their carotid arteries. The researchers speculate that, over time, blood pressure reactions to stress may injure coronary vessels and promote coronary disease (Kamarck & Lichtenstein, 1998).

diathesis–stress model The model that proposes that two interacting factors determine an individual's susceptibility to stress and illness: predisposing factors in the person (such as genetic vulnerability) and precipitating factors from the environment (such as traumatic experiences).

reactivity Our physiological reaction to stress, which varies by individual and affects our vulnerability to illness.

Post-Traumatic Stress Disorder (PTSD)

The diathesis–stress model highlights the fact that different people have different vulnerabilities, resulting in many possible health consequences due to stress combined with diathesis. An extreme case in point is **post-traumatic stress disorder (PTSD)**, which historically was diagnosed when a person experienced an overwhelming event so fearful as to be considered *outside the range of normal human experience*. PTSD has been expanded to include "exposure to an extreme traumatic stressor involving direct personal experience of an event that involves actual or threatened death or serious injury" (American Psychiatric Association, 2018b).

Although the traumatic event most often studied with regard to PTSD is military combat, researchers now also focus on physical attack; diagnosis of a life-threatening illness; or a catastrophic environmental event such as an earthquake, flood, or act of terrorism (Klein & Alexander, 2007). In the month following the September 11 terrorist attacks, an estimated 8.5% of Manhattan residents experienced symptoms of PTSD (Galea, Nandi, & Vlahov, 2005). Having a child or adolescent diagnosed with a serious disease such as cancer may put parents at increased risk for PTSD (Dunn and others, 2012). Car accidents are the most frequent cause of trauma in men, and sexual assault is the most frequent source of trauma among women. Children who live in violent or disordered neighborhoods, or in one of the world's war zones, may also show symptoms of PTSD.

post-traumatic stress disorder (PTSD) A psychological disorder triggered by exposure to an extreme traumatic stressor, such as combat or a natural disaster. Symptoms of PTSD include haunting memories and nightmares of the traumatic event, extreme mental distress, and unwanted flashbacks.

Diversity and Healthy Living

Neighborhood Violence, Brain Development, and PTSD

A growing body of research suggests that PTSD may be a significant problem among people who merely live in a violent neighborhood, even if they have not directly experienced a violent act. Residents of poor, urban neighborhoods such as those in Detroit, Atlanta, Chicago, and Philadelphia—where high rates of violent crime have persisted despite a national decline—display disproportionately high rates of PTSD (National Center for PTSD, 2018).

When researchers at trauma centers in Chicago began screening patients for PTSD in 2011, they found that over 40% had signs of PTSD (Reese and others, 2012). Similarly, researchers have reported higher rates of PTSD among the residents of violent Atlanta neighborhoods than among a comparison group of war veterans (Rothbaum and others, 2014). One survey of 21 hospital emergency departments in U.S. cities with high rates of violence reported that trauma surgeons view PTSD as a serious problem in their patients (Beckett, 2014). Just like combat veterans, these civilian patients experience flashbacks, nightmares, and social withdrawal. Even the perception that a neighborhood is violent seems to cause some of its residents to develop symptoms of PTSD (Gapen and others, 2011).

People who grow up with violence as a backdrop to their lives may also suffer impaired neural, cognitive, and emotional development. Neuroscientists at USC, for example, have been conducting a longitudinal study of 73 southern California teenagers in order to understand how exposure to violence, chaos at home, and other conditions often associated with poverty affect neural, cognitive, and emotional development (Hayasaki, 2016). In the laboratory, the teens first watch an inspirational video while an MRI scanner records their brain activity. One video tells the story of Malala Yousafzai, who at age 15 survived being shot in the head and went on to receive the Nobel Prize for her peacemaking work. Two years later the participants return to the laboratory, watch the videos again, and receive another brain scan to track possible neural changes over time.

Preliminary results from this research suggest that those who have grown up with higher levels of violence may develop progressively weaker neural connections in brain areas that regulate decision making, emotion processing, and ethical reasoning. The affected brain areas included the hippocampus (memory), the temporal lobe (language and auditory processing), and the frontal cortex (decision making, judgment, problem solving, impulse control, and social and emotional behavior) (Immordino-Yang & Gotlieb, 2017). Results such as these are part of the emerging field of **affective neuroscience**, which explores the neural mechanisms of emotion and their impact on the brain. A key finding is that human brain development is inherently social: Our nature (biology) is organized by our nurture (experiences).

Health psychologists have long known that neighborhoods strongly influence the social, psychological, and emotional experiences of residents. They are now learning how these experiences may become biologically embedded and impact brain development.

affective neuroscience The scientific study of the neural mechanisms of emotion.

Eric Clark/Tribune News Service/chicago/IL/USA/Newscom

Merely living in a neighborhood where violent crime frequently occurs can be a risk factor for PTSD.

Among the symptoms of PTSD are intrusive memories and nightmares of the traumatic event; sleep disturbances; excessive guilt; impaired memory; and extreme mental and physical distress in the form of muscle pains, sensitivity to chemicals and sunlight, and gastrointestinal problems. People experiencing PTSD show an increase in inflammatory processes that could promote illness (Shirom, Toker, Berliner, & Shapira, 2008); their bodies produce increased epinephrine, norepinephrine, testosterone, and thyroxin activity that lasts over an extended period of time, and they respond to audiovisual reminders of their trauma with elevated heart rate, blood pressure, and muscle tension. In terms of glucocorticoid secretions, PTSD is often associated with hypocortisolism (unnaturally low levels of cortisol) (Yehuda, 2000).

PTSD has also been associated with poor health behaviors that may play a role in the relationship between PTSD and chronic illnesses such as cardiovascular disease (CVD). Data from the prospective Heart and Soul Study of 1,024 adults with CVD found that those with PTSD (9%) were more likely to be physically inactive, to fail to take medications properly, and to use tobacco (Zen, Whooley, Zhao, & Cohen, 2012).

The concept of vulnerability, or diathesis, is important to keep in mind with PTSD. Several major studies show that, on average, the prevalence of PTSD varies from about 10% among members of the U.S. military who did not see combat in Vietnam, Iraq, or Afghanistan to over 30% among those who experienced heavy combat (Dohrenwend and others, 2006; Hoge, Terhakopian, Castro, Messer, & Engel, 2007). Similar prevalence rates have been found among victims of natural disasters, torture, and sexual assault (Stone, 2005).

Biological and familial risk factors have also been implicated in the disorder. For instance, PTSD has been linked to an overly sensitive limbic system, which causes disruptions in the HPA axis, leading to dysregulation of cortisol levels and atrophy of the hippocampus as the traumatic event is "relived" time and time again (Gill, Saligan, Woods, & Page, 2009). In addition, there is a higher prevalence of PTSD among adult children of family members who themselves have PTSD than among children in families without a history of the disorder, even though these adult children, as a group, do not report a greater exposure to traumatic events (Yehuda, 2000). It is difficult to know, of course, to what extent this is due to biological, genetic, or experiential phenomena because of the large degree of shared environment in families.

Post-Traumatic Stress Disorder (PTSD) can result from exposure to a life-threatening event. Among workers in high-risk occupations, some are more prone than others to experience PTSD. Health psychologists study the factors that influence such individual differences.

The Minority–Stress Model

Stressful experiences are especially common among many ethnic minority families. Racial discrimination and perceived discrimination are significant stressors that can adversely affect physical and mental health (Luo, Xu, Granberg, & Wentworth, 2012). Compounding the stress associated with discrimination is poverty. In 2015, 69% of African American infants and toddlers under age 3 lived in low-income families (Jiang, Granja, & Koball, 2017). Poverty rates for American Indian and Hispanic American children were nearly as high (64% and 63%, respectively), with low-income rates for both groups nearly twice as high as rates for White (33%) and more than twice as high as for Asian American children (29%). (See Figure 4.8)

Impoverished families experience more pollution, substandard and overcrowded housing, crime, and dangerous traffic than do more affluent families. They also suffer poor nutrition, limited education, low-paying work, and a lack of health insurance and

FIGURE 4.8 Family Income by Race/Ethnicity African American, American Indian, and Hispanic American children are disproportionately poor.

Data from: Jiang, Y., Ekono, M., & Skinner, C. (2016). Basic facts about low income children: Children under 6 years 2014. New York, NY: National Center for Children in Poverty, Mailman School of Public Health, Columbia University.

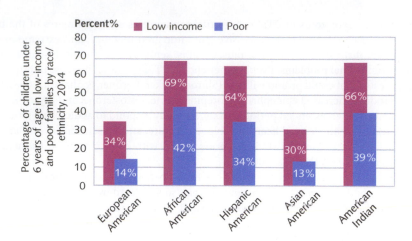

access to health care (Johnson and others, 1995). Moreover, children from low-SES homes are more likely to experience divorce, frequent school transfers, and harsh and punitive parenting—events that have been linked with a variety of behavioral and emotional difficulties (Aughinbaugh, Robles, & Sun, 2013).

Although household income is a powerful predictor of stress, coping, and health behaviors among women and men in virtually every group that has been studied, the relationship varies with ethnicity. For instance, while SES is inversely related to self-reported stress levels among most groups, including African American women, the Pitt County, North Carolina, study found SES to be positively related to stress in African American men (James, Van Hoewyk, & Belli, 2006). Another study of a culturally diverse group of adolescents reported that Hispanic Americans, Asian Americans, and African Americans reported higher levels of social stress than European-Americans (Choi, Meininger, & Roberts, 2006).

David Williams (2000) has identified three factors that help explain the interactions of socioeconomic status, gender, and ethnicity among African Americans. First, middle-class African American men report higher levels of racial discrimination than African American women (Forman, 2002). Significantly, the more years of education an African American male has completed, the stronger his perception of racial discrimination. A particularly insidious type of discrimination that people of color experience daily are **microaggressions**, which are insults, indignities, and marginalizing messages conveyed by people who seem unaware of the hidden messages they are sending (Sue, 2011). *Microaggression fatigue* has been noted among African American men who live or work in environments that are predominantly White (Smith, Hung, & Franklin, 2011); see Table 4.5.

Second, the attainment of middle-class status may be tenuous and marginal for some African Americans. For instance, college-educated African Americans are more likely than European Americans to experience unemployment and job insecurity, both of which are associated with higher levels of stress, illness, disability, and mortality (U.S. Census Bureau, 2004). African Americans are also less likely to convert their socioeconomic achievements into more desirable housing and community living conditions (Alba, Logan, & Stults, 2000). And even when they do, the outcome is not necessarily rosy. One study found that living in the suburbs predicted *higher* mortality risk for African American men than living in an urban or rural environment (House and others, 2000).

microaggressions Insults, indignities, and marginalizing messages sent by well-intentioned people who seem unaware of the hidden messages that they are sending.

TABLE 4.5 Examples of Racial Microaggressions

Theme	Microaggression	Message
Alien in own land When Asian Americans and Latino Americans are assumed to be foreign-born	"Where are you from?" "Where were you born?" "You speak good English." A person asking an Asian American to teach him or her words in the Asian person's native language	You are not American. You are a foreigner.
Ascription of intelligence Assigning intelligence to a person of color on the basis of his or her race	"You are a credit to your race." "You are so articulate." Asking an Asian person to help with a math or science problem	People of color are generally not as intelligent as whites. It is unusual for someone of your race to be intelligent. All Asians are intelligent and good in math/sciences.
Color blindness Statements that indicate that a white person does not want to acknowledge race	"When I look at you, I don't see color." "America is a melting pot." "There is only one race, the human race."	Denying a person of color's racial/ethnic experiences Assimilate/acculturate to the dominant culture. Denying the individual as a racial/cultural being
Criminality/assumption of criminal status A person of color is presumed to be dangerous, criminal, or deviant on the basis of the person's race	A white man or woman clutching purse or checking wallet as a black or Latino approaches or passes A store owner following a customer of color around the store A white person waits to ride the next elevator when a person of color is on it	You are a criminal. You are going to steal/You are poor/ You do not belong. You are dangerous.
Denial of individual racism A statement made when whites deny their racial biases	"I'm not racist. I have several black friends." "As a woman, I know what you go through as a racial minority."	I am immune to racism because I have friends of color. Your racial oppression is no different from my gender oppression. I can't be a racist. I'm like you.
Myth of meritocracy Statements that assert that race does not play a role in life successes	"I believe the most qualified person should get the job." "Everyone can succeed in this society, if they work hard enough."	People of color are given extra, unfair benefits because of their race. People of color are lazy and/or incompetent and need to work harder.
Pathologizing cultural values/communication styles The notion that the values and communication styles of the dominant/white culture are ideal	Asking a black person: "Why do you have to be so loud/animated? Just calm down." To an Asian or Latino person: "Why are you so quiet? We want to know what you think. Be more verbal." "Speak up more." Dismissing an individual who brings up race/culture in work/school setting	Assimilate to dominant culture. Leave your cultural baggage outside.
Second-class citizen Occurs when a white person is given preferential treatment as a consumer over a person of color	Person of color mistaken for a service worker Having a taxi cab pass a person of color and pick up a white passenger	People of color are servants to whites. They couldn't possibly occupy high-status positions. You are likely to cause trouble and/or travel to a dangerous neighborhood.

Reprinted with permission from Sue, D. W., Capodilupo, C. M., Torino, G. C., Bucceri, J. M., Holder, A. M. B., Nadal, K. L., & Esquilin, M. (2007). Racial microaggressions in everyday life: Implications for clinical practice. *American Psychologist, 62*(4), 271–286.

Third, African American males may experience a unique source of stress because the educational attainment associated with their higher SES has not been rewarded with equitable increases in income. At every level of education, African American men have lower incomes than European American men. Moreover, the pay gap between African Americans and European Americans is larger for men than for women (Yang, 2010).

Stigma, prejudice, and discrimination often create a stressful social environment for other minorities, including the lesbian, gay, bisexual, and transgender (LGBT) population. This may come in the form of familial rejection, work discrimination, and even interpersonal violence (Lewis, Derlega, Berndt, Morris, & Rose, 2002). Although researchers have not given the physical health of LGBT individuals the same level of attention as other groups, a growing body of evidence suggests that sexual minorities have heightened risk for many physical health conditions, including cancer, cardiovascular disease, diabetes, allergies, and chronic gastrointestinal problems (Lick, Durso, & Johnson, 2013).

minority stress theory The concept that proposes that health disparities among minority individuals are due to chronically high levels of stress experienced by members of stigmatized groups.

Minority stress theory proposes that health disparities among populations such as that of gay men can be explained in large part by stressors induced by a hostile, homophobic culture (Meyer, 2003). These stressors may include the perception of prejudice, stigma, rejection, and the internalized homophobia that can occur when gay and bisexual individuals apply negative attitudes toward themselves. This hostile environment contributes to a greater likelihood than in the general population for a number of risk-taking behaviors, including avoidant coping strategies, cigarette smoking, drug use, and risky sexual behavior (Proxmire, 2015; Cochran, Mays, & Sullivan, 2003). Having multiple minority statuses (e.g., being African American and gay, or Hispanic American and lesbian) increases the likelihood of feelings of rejection and isolation, along with heightened risk of substance abuse and other hazardous forms of coping (Dentato, 2012).

As this chapter concludes, it is worth remembering that although stress is inescapable, it does offer mixed blessings. Some stress arouses and motivates us and, in the process, often brings out our best qualities and stimulates personal growth. A life with no stress whatsoever would be boring and leave us unfulfilled. The price we pay, though, is the toll that stress may take on our physical and psychological health. Too much stress can overtax our coping abilities and leave us vulnerable to stress-related health problems. Fortunately, there are many things we can do to keep stress at a manageable level. We turn to this topic in the next chapter.

Weigh In on Health

Respond to each question below based on what you learned in the chapter. (**Tip:** Use the items in "Summing Up" to take into account related biological, psychological, and social concerns.)

1. Describe a situation or event on your campus that can cause students stress. What are the biological, psychological, and sociocultural influences in that situation that contribute to stress?

2. Provide a hypothetical situation to explain each of the models of stress and illness: GAS, the transactional model of stress, the diathesis–stress model, and the tend-and-befriend theory. In each situation, what are some biological, psychological, and social or cultural influences?

3. Reconsider the situation or event that you identified in response to Question 1. What have you learned about the psychosocial sources of stress that might help you better understand this situation and advise those who experience stress from it?

Summing Up

Stress: Some Basic Concepts

1. Researchers distinguish among stimulus events that are stressful (stressors), the physical and emotional responses of a person to a stressor, and the overall process by which a person perceives and responds to threatening or challenging events (stress).

Stressors

2. Sources of stress include significant life events, daily hassles, and job-related stress. At various stages of the lifespan, such as childhood and emerging adulthood, people are likely to experience stress.

3. Work is a potential source of stress for many people. Among the factors that make work stressful are work overload, burnout, role conflict or ambiguity, perceived unfairness, inadequate career advancement, lack of control over work, and the challenge of juggling work and family. The caregiving role also can be stressful and impair physical health.

The Physiology of Stress

4. The sympatho-adreno-medullary (SAM) axis is the primary or first response to stress. Activation of the SAM axis leads to increased blood flow to the muscles, increased energy, and higher mental alertness.

5. The hypothalamic-pituitary-adrenocortical (HPA) axis is a slower-reacting response to stress that is activated by messages from the central nervous system. HPA activation functions to restore homeostasis to the body. Excessive cortisol production (hypercorticolism) from the adrenal glands may impair immune efficiency.

6. The body's physiological response to stress is shaped by many factors, including gender. The HPA is strongly influenced by the hypothalamic-pituitary-gonadal (HPG) axis. Testosterone seems to increase HPA reactivity, whereas estrogens decrease HPA activity.

7. The field of psychoneuroimmunology (PNI) focuses on the interactions among behavior, the nervous system, the endocrine system, and the immune system.

8. According to the direct effect hypothesis, immunosuppression is part of the body's natural response to stress. The indirect effect hypothesis maintains that immunosuppression is an aftereffect of the stress response.

9. Stressors that are unpredictable, uncontrollable, of long duration, and difficult to cope with cause a buildup of allostatic load, which manifests in many ways, including decreased immunity, elevated epinephrine levels, increased abdominal fat, decreased hippocampal size and functioning, and the overproduction of proinflammatory cytokines.

10. Stress exacerbates many inflammatory diseases, including allergic, autoimmune, rheumatologic, neurologic, and cardiovascular conditions. The glucocorticoid resistance model suggests that this is due to chronic stress interfering with the immune system's sensitivity to glucocorticoid hormones, such as cortisol, which normally terminate the inflammatory response.

Other Models of Stress and Illness

11. Hans Selye outlined the concept of general adaptation syndrome (GAS) to describe the effects of chronic stress. This syndrome consists of an alarm reaction, a stage of resistance, and a stage of exhaustion. Persistent stress may increase a person's susceptibility to a disease of adaptation.

12. According to the transactional model, a key factor in stress is cognitive appraisal. In primary appraisal, we assess whether an event is benign-positive, irrelevant, or a potential threat or challenge. In secondary appraisal, we assess the coping resources available for meeting the challenge.

13. The diathesis–stress model suggests that some people are more vulnerable to stress-related illnesses because of predisposing factors such as genetic weakness.

14. Post-traumatic stress disorder (PTSD) is prevalent among people who have been exposed to violent, life-threatening events. Individuals growing up with higher levels of violence may develop progressively weaker neural connections in brain areas that regulate decision making, emotion processing, and ethical reasoning.

15. Members of minorities who experience discrimination often report higher levels of stress. A particularly insidious type of discrimination is microaggressions—hidden negative messages from people who often seem unaware of their bias.

Key Terms and Concepts to Remember

stressor, p. 92

stress, p. 92

social-evaluative threat, p. 102

stereotype threat, p. 102

burnout, p. 104

sympatho-adreno-medullary (SAM) axis, p. 109

hypothalamic-pituitary-adrenocortical (HPA) axis, p. 109

homeostasis, p. 109

corticosteroids, p. 109

tend and befriend, p. 111

ecological momentary assessment (EMA), p. 112

cardiovascular reactivity (CVR), p. 113

reactivity hypothesis, p. 113

respiratory sinus arrhythmia (RSA), p. 114

psychoneuroimmunology (PNI), p. 115

allostatic load (allostasis), p. 119

glucocorticoid receptor (GCR) resistance model, p. 120

general adaptation syndrome (GAS), p. 121

transactional model, p. 123

primary appraisal, p. 123

secondary appraisal, p. 123

diathesis–stress model, p. 125

reactivity, p. 125

post-traumatic stress disorder (PTSD), p. 125

affective neuroscience, p. 126

microaggressions, p. 128

minority stress theory, p. 130

  To accompany your textbook, you have access to a number of online resources, including quizzes for every chapter of the book, flashcards, critical thinking exercises, videos, and *Check Your Health* inventories. To access these resources, please visit the Straub Health Psychology LaunchPad at **launchpadworks.com**

Coping with Stress

Chapter 5

LEARNING OUTCOMES

Once you have studied this chapter, you will be able to:

- Describe a variety of personal resources that people can use to cope with stress,
- Explain how several external factors influence people's coping with stress, and
- Identify several stress management strategies and how researchers can assess their effectiveness.

As soon as he graduated from high school, Kristofer Goldsmith fulfilled his childhood dream of serving his country by enlisting in the army. He completed basic training in 2005 and was deployed to Iraq, where he was assigned to document Iraqi-on-Iraqi violence during the U.S. occupation of Sadr City. "I was a 19-year-old kid taking pictures of mutilated men, women, and boys and little girls," he recalled. "Those are the type of images that never really go away" (Gajilan, 2008).

After less than a year in Iraq, Goldsmith returned to the United States to serve out his military contract, but he found himself a changed man. He began drinking heavily, sleeping too little or too much, and displaying an uncontrollable and violent temper. Despite a promotion to sergeant and receiving the Army Commendation Medal for his service in Iraq, Kris counted the days until he could return to civilian life. "I just wanted to get out of the army," Kris said, "and I figured all my problems would go away once I got out of the service."

His breaking point came when, the very week he was supposed to get out of the army, he and his unit received "stop-loss" orders that automatically extended their service past their commitments as volunteers. The orders scheduled an immediate redeployment to Iraq. Before this could take place, however, Kris began experiencing heart attack–like symptoms.

After extensive testing, the doctors at the army hospital said Kris most likely had suffered a panic attack, and they ordered him to report to the behavioral health clinic on the base. There he was told he had an "adjustment disorder with

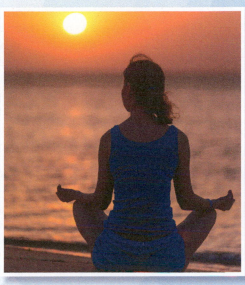

iStock/Getty Images

Personal Factors Affecting the Ability to Cope
Coping Style
 Your Health Assets: The Brief Cope
Dispositional Affect
Optimism
Psychological Control
Resilience

External Factors Affecting the Ability to Cope
Socioeconomic Status
Social Support

Managing Stress
Relaxation Therapies
Mindfulness-Based Stress Reduction
Cognitive-Behavioral Therapy
 Your Health Assets: Try Mindfulness-Based Stress Reduction for Yourself
Cognitive Behavioral Stress Management
Emotional Disclosure
Other Coping Tools and Techniques

disturbance of emotions and conduct." He saw a psychiatrist, who further diagnosed chronic severe depression, prescribed group therapy and an antidepressant, and then cleared Kris for duty.

Feeling helpless and out of options, Kris Goldsmith tried to kill himself the night before he was supposed to return to Iraq. "… So I took a black Sharpie magic marker and I wrote across my arms 'Stop-loss killed me. End stop-loss now.' I took my half-bottle of Percocet and … a liter-and-a-half bottle of vodka and downed the Percocet and I chased it with the vodka and drank until I couldn't drink anymore."

Remarkably, Goldsmith survived his attempted suicide. He was discharged from the army, moved in with his parents, and became eligible for disability assistance of $700 per month after his diagnosis was changed to post-traumatic stress disorder (PTSD).

Why was Kris Goldsmith's response to military service so life-disrupting and nearly fatal? As you saw in Chapter 4, experiencing a stressful situation or event does not inevitably lead to an adverse physiological and psychological response. In fact, *how* people cope with stressful events is at least as important as the stressors themselves in determining health or illness.

In this chapter, we will take a biopsychosocial approach in considering the factors that affect how people deal with stress. Those factors include biological influences, such as inherited personality traits and our physiological reactivity level; psychological and social influences, such as coping strategies, outlook on life, and perception of control; and external psychosocial factors, including socioeconomic status and social support. We will also evaluate practical strategies for managing stress. Through our journey into the biology and psychology of responding to stress, we will see ample evidence supporting the connection between mind and body. At every turn, biological, psychological, and social forces interact in our ability to cope with stress.

PERSONAL FACTORS AFFECTING THE ABILITY TO COPE

We all know that certain life stresses (such as final exams) tend to give us headaches, queasy stomachs, and other ailments, whereas exhilarating or uplifting experiences (such as a ski weekend or a new intimate relationship) make us feel on top of the world. In this section, we explore several personal biopsychosocial factors that affect how well we cope with potential stressors and, by extension, how this affects our health. Keep in mind that no one factor, by itself, determines your well-being. Health is always a result of biopsychosocial factors interacting in various ways.

Coping Style

Coping refers to the cognitive, behavioral, and emotional ways that people deal with situations that are appraised as stressful (Taylor & Stanton, 2007). Coping is not a one-time reaction, but rather a dynamic process—a series of responses involving our interactions with the environment. For example, after breaking up with a romantic partner you may experience physical and emotional reactions such as overall sadness, inability to sleep or eat, and even nausea. It is not just the initial incident but also continuing interactions with the environment, such as hearing sympathetic comments from friends, or visiting a place that holds poignant memories, that affect your responses. Together, these responses form our style of coping with stress.

Not all coping strategies are equally effective. Some provide temporary relief but tend to be maladaptive over time. For example, although psychological defenses like Kris's belief that his problems would go away when he left military service may allow us to distance ourselves from a stressful situation, they do not eliminate the source of stress. Similarly, alcohol or other drugs temporarily push the stress into the background but can make matters worse in the long run.

The many ways in which people cope with threatening events have been categorized in several ways. One useful distinction is between **approach coping**—taking action and confronting a source of stress—and **avoidance coping**, also called **disengagement**, which is aimed at ignoring or escaping from it. Disengagement can be cognitive in nature (denying distress, wishful thinking, fantasizing), or behavioral (excessive sleeping, taking drugs, shopping, playing video games). Although disengagement is sometimes effective in dealing with short-term events, such as the mild distress associated with a dentist appointment, it is less likely to work for chronic sources of stress, such as job stress or financial problems. Research demonstrates that approach coping is generally more effective in the long run (Taylor & Stanton, 2007).

One type of approach coping, **problem-focused coping**, calls for dealing directly with the stressful situation, either by reducing its demands or by increasing our capacity to deal with the stressor. For instance, a student who tackles a seemingly overwhelming course load by breaking her assignments into a series of smaller, manageable tasks is using problem-focused coping, as is someone recovering from an alcohol problem who joins a support group to share experiences.

When we employ **emotion-focused coping**, we attempt to regulate our emotional reaction to a stressful event rather than the stressor itself. We tend to rely on emotion-focused coping when we believe that little or nothing can be done to alter a stressful situation or when we believe that our coping resources or skills are insufficient to meet the demands of the stressful situation. Examples of emotion-focused coping include keeping yourself busy to take your mind off a stressful event, disclosing your emotions by talking with a friend, or journaling in a gratitude diary.

Note that emotion-focused coping can be either approach-oriented or avoidance-oriented. **Emotional-approach coping (EAC)** involves working through our emotional reactions to a stressful event, such as by using cognitive strategies to change the way that we appraise a stressor (see Chapter 4) (Stanton, 2010). In addition to reducing emotional distress, EAC often leads to better problem-focused coping (Carver & Connor-Smith, 2010).

coping The cognitive, behavioral, and emotional ways in which we manage stressful situations.

disengagement (avoidance coping) A coping strategy aimed at distancing oneself from a stressful situation.

problem-focused coping A coping strategy for dealing directly with a stressor, in which we either reduce the stressor's demands or increase our resources for meeting its demands.

emotion-focused coping A coping strategy in which we try to control our emotional response to a stressor.

emotional-approach coping (EAC) The process of working through, clarifying, and understanding the emotions triggered by a stressor.

Shopping can be a behavioral form of avoidance coping Also called disengagement, this may be a useful short-term strategy for ignoring or escaping from a stressor, but it can also lead to higher stress—for example, in spending more than one can afford or buying things one does not really need.

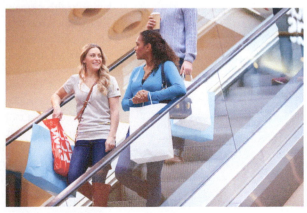
MBI/Alamy Stock Photo

rumination Repetitive focusing on the causes, meanings, and consequences of stressful experiences.

emotional cascade Becoming so focused on an upsetting event that one gets worked into an intense, painful state of negative emotion.

repressive coping An emotion-focused coping style in which we attempt to inhibit our emotional responses, especially in social situations, so we can view ourselves as imperturbable.

Sometimes people overreact in an approach-based attempt to control their emotional reactions to a stressor. **Rumination** refers to thinking repetitively about an upsetting situation and how it relates to past and future problems. This may spiral out of control into an **emotional cascade**, a vicious cycle in which intense rumination makes the person more upset, which in turn causes more rumination (Moberly & Watkins, 2008). The end result is a self-amplifying feedback loop of rumination and negative emotion that ultimately may lead to self-destructive behaviors such as binging and purging, self-injury, self-medicating with alcohol or drugs, or impulsive shopping (Selby, Franklin, Carson-Wong, & Rizvi, 2013). According to the emotional cascade model, these self-damaging behaviors, which to the outside observer would only seem to make a bad situation worse, are used to distract from rumination through intense physical sensations (Selby, Anestis, Bender, & Joiner, 2009).

People sometimes use an avoidance mechanism to control their emotional reactions by repressing them. **Repressive coping** is an avoidance coping style in which the person inhibits or avoids information and emotional responses. Is repression healthy? Accumulating evidence suggests not. Emotional repression activates the sympathetic nervous system, functioning much like a stressor in elevating blood pressure and triggering the fight-or-flight response (Butler and others, 2003; Myers, 2010). Inhibited emotional expression contributes to greater cortisol reactivity in people with cardiovascular disease, increasing the incidence of adverse cardiac events and cardiac-related death (Whitehead, Perkins-Porras, Strike, Magid, & Steptoe, 2007). It has also been shown that heart rate variability—the time between two subsequent heartbeats, which depends on sympathetic and parasympathetic activity (see Chapter 4)—differs between repressors and nonrepressors in a way that is associated with cardiac problems.

Repressive coping has also been associated with the development of cancer, asthma, and diabetes (Myers and others, 2008). Although the empirical evidence for a "cancer personality" is mixed, differences in immunological markers do suggest that repressors are more cancer-prone than nonrepressors. The same is true for asthma and diabetes, which are both linked to several immune markers. Repressors have a higher number of white blood cells called *eosinophiles*, which become active in allergic diseases and infections. Research on diabetes shows that repressors have an increased level of both insulin and glucose—biomarkers that can signal an emerging resistance to insulin and the development of Type 2 diabetes (Mund & Mitte, 2012).

Although coping research studies generally have linked problem-focused strategies with better health outcomes than emotion-focused strategies, it is increasingly clear that this conclusion is too simple. For one thing, which coping strategy is likely to work best depends on the duration and perceived controllability of the stressor. With school- or work-related stressors, we are more likely to be successful if we apply problem-focused coping, whereas for some health-related problems, distancing oneself through emotion-focused coping may be beneficial. Of course, many health-related problems also benefit from the direct action of problem-focused coping, as when, for example, a dietary change or regular exercise regimen improves a person's ability to manage her diabetes. As these examples demonstrate, we often use problem-focused and emotion-focused coping together, or at different times for different situations. Some researchers have suggested that people develop a type of *coping intelligence* from their previous experiences of success and failure in how they have attempted to manage life stress (Libin, 2017). (See Your Health Assets: The Brief COPE to get a feeling for how a health psychologist might investigate your own coping style.)

Your Health Assets

The Brief COPE

This questionnaire has been used by researchers to assess the various ways people cope with stressful events. Think about a threatening event in your own life, such as a health issue, financial difficulties, or even an upcoming exam, and rate how you have been dealing with things according to the following scale:

1 = I haven't been doing this at all. 2 = I've been doing this a little bit. 3 = I've been doing this a medium amount. 4 = I've been doing this a lot.

1. Self-distraction

I've been turning to work or other activities to take my mind off things.
I've been doing something to think about it less, such as going to movies, watching TV, reading, daydreaming, sleeping, or shopping.

2. Active Coping

I've been concentrating my efforts on doing something about the situation I'm in.
I've been taking action to try to make the situation better.

3. Denial

I've been saying to myself, "This isn't real."
I've been refusing to believe that it has happened.

4. Substance Use

I've been using alcohol or other drugs to make myself feel better.
I've been using alcohol or other drugs to help me get through it.

5. Emotional Support

I've been getting emotional support from others.
I've been getting comfort and understanding from someone.

6. Instrumental Support

I've been getting help and advice from other people.
I've been trying to get advice or help from other people about what to do.

7. Behavioral Disengagement

I've been giving up trying to deal with it.
I've been giving up the attempt to cope.

8. Venting

I've been saying things to let my unpleasant feelings escape.
I've been expressing my negative feelings.

9. Positive Reframing

I've been trying to see it in a different light, to make it seem more positive.
I've been looking for something good in what is happening.

10. Self-Blame

I've been criticizing myself.
I've been blaming myself for things that happened.

11. Planning

I've been trying to come up with a strategy about what to do.
I've been thinking hard about what steps to take.

12. Humor

I've been making jokes about it.
I've been making fun of the situation.

13. Acceptance

I've been accepting the reality of the fact that it has happened.
I've been learning to live with it.

14. Religion

I've been trying to find comfort in my religion or spiritual beliefs.
I've been praying or meditating.

Information from: Carver, C. S. (1997). You want to measure coping but your protocol's too long: Consider the Brief COPE. *International Journal of Behavioral Medicine, 4*, 92–100. Table 1, p. 96.

Dispositional Affect

dispositional affect A person's coping style or personality dimension consisting of a tendency toward chronic negative emotions and distress (negative affectivity), or positive emotions and subjective well-being (positive affectivity).

Similar to mood, but more stable, **dispositional affect** is our general approach to life—the tendency to respond to situations in a predictable way. People with high *positive affectivity (PA)* tend to be happy, cheerful, optimistic, and energetic, whereas people who score high on measures of *negative affectivity (NA)*, or neuroticism, are tense, anxious, insecure, jealous, hostile, and less emotionally stable. Positive affect and negative affect are relatively independent dimensions that seem to differ in etiology, with PA influenced more by our situational experiences and NA more by heredity (Zheng, Plomin, & von Stumm, 2016). Table 5.1 presents the Positive and Negative Affect Schedule (PANAS), a widely used 20-item test that measures PA and NA (Watson, Clark, & Tellegen, 1988).

Negative affectivity is linked to poorer health, including chronic disorders such as arthritis, diabetes, hypertension, and coronary artery disease (e.g., Pressman, Gallagher, & Lopez, 2013). This may be due in part to the fact that people with NA tend to have a

---

TABLE 5.1 PANAS Questionnaire

This scale consists of a number of words that describe different feelings and emotions. Read each item and then list the number from the scale below next to each word. Indicate to what extent you feel this way right now, that is, at the present moment; OR indicate the extent to which you have felt this way over the past week (circle the instructions you followed when taking this measure).

1 Very Slightly or Not at All

2 A Little

3 Moderately

4 Quite a Bit

5 Extremely

_____ 1. Interested	_____ 11. Irritable
_____ 2. Distressed	_____ 12. Alert
_____ 3. Excited	_____ 13. Ashamed
_____ 4. Upset	_____ 14. Inspired
_____ 5. Strong	_____ 15. Nervous
_____ 6. Guilty	_____ 16. Determined
_____ 7. Scared	_____ 17. Attentive
_____ 8. Hostile	_____ 18. Jittery
_____ 9. Enthusiastic	_____ 19. Active
_____ 10. Proud	_____ 20. Afraid

Scoring Instructions:

Positive Affect Score: Add the scores on items 1, 3, 5, 9, 10, 12, 14, 16, 17, and 19. Scores can range from 10 to 50, with higher scores representing higher levels of positive affect.

Negative Affect Score: Add the scores on items 2, 4, 6, 7, 8, 11, 13, 15, 18, and 20. Scores can range from 10 to 50, with lower scores representing lower levels of negative affect.

Information from: Watson, D., Clark, L. A., & Tellegen, A. (1988). Development and validation of brief measures of positive and negative affect: The PANAS Scales. *Journal of Personality and Social Psychology, 54*(6), 1063–1070.

higher allostatic load than people characterized by greater positivity, as indicated by elevated heart rate (Daly, Delaney, Doran, Harmon, & MacLachlan, 2010), inflammation (Roy and others, 2010), and cortisol (Polk, Coen, Doyle, Skoner, & Kirschbaum, 2005).

In contrast, PA seems to predict better physical and mental health, lower risk of disease, and reduced mortality in patients with renal failure and HIV-infection (Cohen & Pressman, 2006; Wiest, Schüz, Webster, & Wurm, 2011; Chida & Steptoe, 2008). PA is associated with lower chronic levels of stress hormones such as cortisol (Low, Matthews, and Hall, 2013) and a stronger immune response to environmental challenges such as exposure to the flu virus (Steptoe, de Oliveria, Demakakos, & Zaninotto, 2014).

Interestingly, just how bad NA is for health depends on culture. In individualistic cultures such as the United States, negative emotions tend to be viewed as the individual's responsibility and as harmful. In collectivist cultures such as Japan, negative emotions tend to be viewed as rooted in relationships and as natural. In one large cross-cultural study of the relationship between NA and health, negative affect more strongly predicted poor physical and mental health in the United States than in Japan (Curhan and others, 2014).

Although research on dispositional affect suggests that some people are genetically driven to feel more or less negative than others, it is important to remember that heritability does not mean immutability (see Chapter 2). Individual differences in the average level of positive emotions are strongly influenced by environmental factors, such as family, friends, school, work, and community. Further, each of us can make a conscious effort to notice and nurture the positive emotions we experience. Health psychologists can use what we know about emotions and coping to promote positive affect and, in turn, improved health among their clients. In addition to its association with biological indicators of well-being, PA also fosters the development of other personal resources that have a beneficial effect on coping. These resources include physical activity and other healthy lifestyle behaviors (Sin, Moskowitz, & Whooley, 2015), as well as other psychosocial resources (Taylor & Broffman, 2011) such as optimism, psychological control, and social support. We'll discuss each of these in turn.

Optimism

People with an optimistic nature cope more effectively with stress and tend to lead healthier, longer lives than their more pessimistic counterparts (Segerstrom, 2006). Among college students, optimists—those who agree with statements such as "In uncertain times, I usually expect the best" and "I always look on the bright side of things"—report less fatigue and fewer aches, pains, and minor illnesses (Carver & Scheier, 2002).

Why is optimism beneficial to health? One meta-analytic study that investigated the relationship between optimism and physical health reported beneficial effects for a variety of health outcomes and the cardiovascular, endocrine, and immune system indicators that often predict them (Rasmussen, Scheier, & Greenhouse, 2009). Optimism and positive emotions in general are associated with reduced levels of stress hormones such as cortisol, lower blood pressure, and reduced levels of biological markers of inflammation such as *C-reactive protein* (Steptoe, O'Donnell, & Badrick, 2008). By shortening the duration of negative emotional arousal, positive emotions such as optimism may stave off stress-related elevations in hypertension, inflammation, immunosuppression, and other disease-promoting processes (Jobin, Wrosch, & Scheier, 2014; Roy and others, 2010). One study found that people who consistently experienced positive emotions as children,

FIGURE 5.1 Optimism and Immune Function Two months after beginning law school, optimistic law students showed a 13% increase in the blood level (estimated total number) of CD4 cells in the bloodstream, compared with a 3% drop in the number of cells in the bloodstream of pessimists. Similarly, natural killer (NK) cell cytotoxicity, a measure of cell activity level, rose by 42% in the optimists, but by only 9% in pessimists.

Data from: Segerstrom, S. C., Taylor, S. E., Kemeny, M. E., & Fahey, J. (1998). Optimism is associated with mood, coping, and immune change in response to stress. *Journal of Personality and Social Psychology, 74*(6), 1646–1655. Copyright 1998 by the American Psychological Association.

psychological control The belief that we make our own decisions and determine what we do and what others do to us.

and again as adults, were half as likely as their peers to display high levels of allostatic load, a measure of cumulative wear and tear on the body (Figure 5.1; see Chapter 4) (Ryff, Singer, Wing, & Love, 2001).

Optimists and pessimists not only have different physical reactions to stress; they also differ in how they cope with stress. Optimists are more likely than pessimists to try to alter stressful situations with direct problem-focused action against a stressor, including seeking treatment when illness strikes (Segerstrom, 2006). In contrast, pessimists are more likely to disengage or to ruminate (Carver & Connor-Smith, 2010).

Pessimism can be changed into *learned optimism,* a set of consciously cultivated habits that entail viewing life's setbacks and misfortunes as external (due to forces or influences outside of oneself), temporary, and specific (limited in scope) (Seligman & Csikszentmihalyi, 2000). Martin Seligman, founder of the *positive psychology* movement, recommends learning the "ABCs" of optimism, which stand for Adversity, Beliefs, and Consequences. Let's consider how the ABCs might help Kris Goldsmith, whom we met in our opening vignette, to develop a more optimistic outlook.

■ Adversity: Kris can learn to interpret difficulties in terms that are *external* ("It was the military's policies, not me, that caused my troubles."), *temporary* ("This will be a difficult year, but I will get through this."), and *specific* ("My career and family plans are still on hold, but I know that other parts of my life have been positive and will continue to go well.").

■ Beliefs: Practicing such optimistic explanations mindfully will lead Kris to get into the habit of holding healthier, more upbeat beliefs.

■ Consequences: Healthier, more optimistic beliefs will prompt more positive health consequences for Kris.

Martin Bolt (2004, p. 176) explains that when we are faced with adversity, "Learning to counter argue, to offer alternative causes for the disappointment, to recognize that you are overreacting, and even to show that the belief is factually incorrect undermine the pessimistic explanation and enable you to cope with setbacks more effectively."

Psychological Control

Healthy children gradually develop a sense of control over their surroundings. Albert Bandura and other researchers have called this belief in our ability to deal with potentially stressful situations *self-efficacy* (Bandura, 1997). **Psychological control** is the belief that we make our own decisions and determine what we do or what we allow others to do to us. Psychological control and self-efficacy both help people to cope more effectively with stressful events (Wrosch, Schulz, Miller, Lupien, & Dunne, 2007).

When faced with repeated, uncontrollable stress, people sometimes learn that they cannot affect what happens to them. Low perceived control may be one reason racial and ethnic minorities are high-risk groups when it comes to health. Particularly in Western cultures—where men are socialized under norms emphasizing achievement and competence—discrimination, economic marginalization, and an absence of employment opportunities can have a devastating impact on self-efficacy and on the way that men appraise and respond to potentially stressful situations. When African American college students in one study overheard European American classmates negatively evaluating African American performance on a task, those who attributed their poor evaluation to racism and discrimination displayed the strongest stress reactions (King, 2005).

How does the perception of psychological control influence health? One way is by buffering our physiological response to stressful situations. One meta-analysis of 200 separate research studies reported that laboratory stressors that are perceived as uncontrollable, such as performing under impossible time pressure, led to the greatest, and most prolonged, activation of the hypothalamic-pituitary-adrenocortical axis (see Chapter 4), as measured by cortisol levels (Dickerson & Kemeny, 2004). Other research studies have shown that the perception of psychological control in stressful situations improves immune system functioning (Paquet, Dube, Gauvin, Kestens, & Daniel, 2010), fosters greater physical activity (Infurna, Gerstorf, Ram, Schupp, & Wagner, 2011), and contributes to better overall health (Infurna & Gerstorf, 2014). Small wonder, then, that a sense of control has been linked to a lower risk of mortality, primarily due to lower levels of risk factors for cardiovascular disease (Paquet and others, 2010).

Have you ever been so angry with a rude driver that you felt like exploding, yet you didn't? Or perhaps you've been at a religious service when you found something hysterically funny, but you needed to stifle your laughter? In such situations, we strive to control which emotions are merely experienced and which are actually expressed. **Regulatory control**, which refers to our capacity to modulate thoughts, emotions, and behaviors, is a part of everyday life.

regulatory control The various ways in which we modulate our thinking, emotions, and behavior over time and across changing circumstances.

Controlling your responses and emotions has broad implications for your health (de Ridder, Bertha, & de Wit, 2006). Self-regulation is associated with success in dieting, quitting smoking, and maintaining good interpersonal relationships. In addition, children who have good self-control are calmer, more resistant to frustration, better able to delay gratification (an important factor later in resisting substance abuse), and less aggressive.

Individual differences in regulatory control are also related to how people cope with stressful events and experiences. People with good self-control are less likely to resort to maladaptive coping responses such as angry venting of emotions or avoidant coping (Aronoff, Stollak, & Woike, 1994). Similarly, children and adults with good self-control are likely to use constructive, problem-focused coping responses and are unlikely to use avoidant or aggressive coping responses in stressful situations (see Figure 5.2; Fabes & Eisenberg, 1997; Mann & Ward, 2007).

Think back to our opening story: What happened to Kris Goldsmith's feelings of psychological control when his service contract was extended? What impact did this have on his ability to cope with the stress of his service in Iraq?

Resilience

Resilience is "the process of adapting well in the face of adversity, trauma, tragedy, threats or significant sources of stress" (APA, 2018). In its online brochure "The Road to Resilience," the American Psychological Association explains:

resilience The quality that allows some people to bounce back from difficult events that might otherwise disrupt their well-being.

A combination of factors contributes to resilience. Many studies show that the primary factor in resilience is having caring and supportive relationships within and outside the family. Relationships that create love and trust, provide role models and offer encouragement and reassurance help bolster a person's resilience.

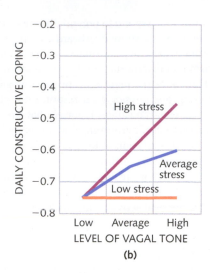

High vagal tone is inversely related to negative emotional arousal and positively related to constructive coping.

FIGURE 5.2 Vagal Tone and Coping with Stress (a) Students with a high vagal tone were less likely than students with a lower vagal tone to experience high levels of negative emotional arousal in response to everyday hassles and stress. (b) Students with a high vagal tone were also more likely to rely on constructive coping measures.

Data from: Fabes, R. A., & Eisenberg, N. (1997). Regulatory control and adults' stress-related responses to daily life events. *Journal of Personality and Social Psychology, 73*(5), 1107–1117. Copyright 1997 by the American Psychological Association.

Several additional factors are associated with resilience, including:

- The capacity to make realistic plans and take steps to carry them out.
- A positive view of yourself and confidence in your strengths and abilities.
- Skills in communication and problem solving.
- The capacity to manage strong feelings and impulses. (American Psychological Association, 2018)

Research on resilience has identified contributing factors that can be divided into two groups. One group relates to individual traits, the other to positive life experiences and social support. Resilient children have well-developed social, academic, or creative skills; easy temperaments; high self-esteem; self-discipline; and strong feelings of psychological control (Dunkel Schetter & Dolbier, 2011; American Psychological Association, 2018). These elements of *social-emotional competence* foster healthy relationships with others who help such children adjust to adverse conditions.

Studies of resilient children point to the importance of at least one consistently supportive person in the life of a child at risk. This person can be an aunt or uncle, older sister or brother, grandparent, family friend, or teacher. This supportive person, often a caring parent, is a model of resilience who plays a significant role in convincing at-risk children that they can and will beat the odds.

Although early studies of resilience implied that there was something remarkable about these children, recent research suggests that resilience is a more common phenomenon that arises from the ordinary resources of children, their relationships, and positive community experiences. Echoing the theme of the positive psychology movement (see Chapter 1), resilience research now focuses on understanding how these adaptive processes develop, how they operate under adverse conditions, and how they can be protected or restored. Using data from the Fragile Families and Child Wellbeing Study, which is following nearly 5,000 low-income children who were born between 1998 and 2000 in large U.S. cities, Columbia University researchers have identified several parental resilience characteristics as being particularly important in inhibiting externalizing and internalizing behaviors in children. These included parental supervision, parental attendance at important events, and parental fair treatment (Wilson-Simmons, Jiang, & Aratani, 2017).

Until recently, research studies of resilience focused mostly on children. Today, however, researchers increasingly focus on resilience in their investigations of the well-being of adults. In medicine, for instance, biological resilience refers to various protective factors (genetic, demographic, social-cultural, psychological, gender-linked, and environmental) that contribute to positive outcomes in the elderly (Alfieri, Costanzo, & Borgogni, 2011). Resilience is associated with many specific characteristics among adults, including forgiveness (Broyles, 2005), sense of coherence and purpose in life (Nygren and others, 2005), and self-efficacy (Caltabiano & Caltabiano, 2006). Based on decades of research focused on military veterans, psychiatrists Steven Southwick and Dennis Charney (2018) have developed the following list of attributes and habits associated with resilience: optimistic outlook; facing one's fears; moral compass and ethics; religion and spirituality; social support; role models; physical fitness; cognitive fitness through lifelong learning; cognitive and emotional flexibility; and seeking meaning, purpose, and growth in one's life. Resilience is characterized by lower incidence of depression, anxiety, and perceived stress (Wagnild, 2008). As more studies reveal the positive relationships between resilience and aging well, health psychologists are increasingly interested in recognizing and strengthening the ability to bounce back following challenge and adversity among the growing elderly segment of the population (Prince-Embury & Saklofske, 2013).

EXTERNAL FACTORS AFFECTING THE ABILITY TO COPE

So far, we have focused on a person's internal resources for dealing with stress. These resources—coping style, dispositional affect, optimism, psychological control, and resilience—certainly play important roles in our response to stress. Yet external factors are also important, especially family, friends, education, employment, time, and money. People who have more resources available typically cope with stressful events more successfully than those who are lacking in such resources.

Socioeconomic Status

One of the most influential factors with respect to health is *socioeconomic status (SES)*, which you will recall from Chapter 1 is a measure of a person's economic and social position relative to others. People who are low in SES have increased risk for chronic disease, disability, and premature mortality (Stowe and others, 2010). It is important to note, though, that access to health care does not completely explain the relationship between SES and health. The association between lower SES and poor health is found even in countries that have universal health care (Cohen, Doyle, & Baum, 2006).

Health disparities increase with each step down the SES ladder (Adler & Rehkopf, 2008). Older adults who never completed high school and those with an annual household income less than $15,000 have more than twice as many unhealthy days as do women and men with a college degree and an annual household income of $50,000 or more (Figure 5.3). This is cause for concern given the fact that U.S. children who are African American, American Indian, or Hispanic children are disproportionately likely to be growing up in a low-SES family. One longitudinal study found that children with highly reactive emotional styles who grew up in low-SES environments had higher levels of chronic inflammation as adults than did similar children raised in higher-SES environments (Appleton and others, 2012). Chronic inflammation is associated with the risk of a number of age-related diseases, including hypertension, heart disease, and diabetes (Singh & Newman, 2011). Another study found that SES also predicts whether supportive personal relationships confer health benefits. Among women who were either awaiting further evaluation from an abnormal mammogram or newly diagnosed with breast cancer, those with higher SES had a stronger cellular immune response than women with lower SES (Fagundes and others, 2012).

Low levels of education and income and high levels of distress tend to be associated with a maladaptive coping style (Roohafza and others, 2009; Poetz, Eyles, Elliott, Wilson, & Keller-Olaman, 2007). These circumstances may cause people to develop a feeling of hopelessness and to believe that they have little or no psychological control over events in their lives. So, with repeated exposure to stress and no way to break the cycle, their only recourse is to try to control their emotional responses to stress—because they've learned that they can't control the situation itself. This is important because people who believe that they can determine their own behavior and influence the environment to bring about desired outcomes cope more effectively with stressful events (Wrosch, Schulz, Miller, Lupien, & Dunne, 2007). A strong perception of control has also been associated with a healthier lifestyle, a stronger immune response to allergens (Chen, Fisher, Bacharier, & Strunk, 2003), and a lower overall risk of death (Surtees, Wainwright, Luben, Khas, & Dy, 2006). No wonder, then, that psychological control may be especially important for people who are vulnerable to

FIGURE 5.3 Unhealthy Days by Socioeconomic Status and Sex Older adults who never completed high school and those with an annual household income less than $15,000 (Low SES) have more than twice as many unhealthy days—defined according to a composite measure of physical, mental, social well-being—compared to women and men with a college degree and an annual household income of $50,000 or more (High SES).

Data from: Moriarty, D. G., Kobau, R., Zack, M. M., & Zahran, H. S. (2005). Tracking healthy days—A window on the health of older adults. *Preventing Chronic Disease, 2*(3), 5.

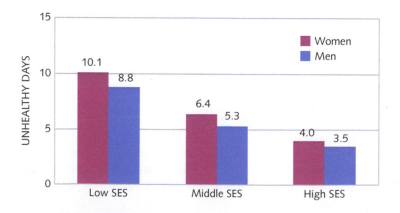

health problems, including children, the elderly, and those who are already being treated for medical conditions (Wrosch and others, 2007).

Socioeconomic status is also a powerful predictor of both health and health behaviors. One study of health behaviors and outcomes in Pitt County, North Carolina, reported that SES was inversely related, among both African American women and men, to alcohol consumption, cigarette smoking, and risk of hypertension (James and others, 2006). The same study found that low-SES African Americans perceived weaker levels of emotional support when under stress than did their higher-SES counterparts. Compared with those of high SES in both childhood and adulthood, low-SES men were also seven times more likely to suffer from hypertension as adults.

Interestingly, socioeconomic indicators at the level of individual neighborhoods predict the health of residents in relationship to smoking and other harmful health behaviors, even after individual differences in SES, lifestyle behaviors, and other risk factors are taken into consideration (Kendzor and others, 2009; Paul, Boutain, Manhart, & Hitti, 2008). Pamela Feldman and Andrew Steptoe (2004) believe that neighborhood SES is linked to health because it strongly influences the social and psychological experiences of residents living in a particular neighborhood. The researchers compared 19 low-SES neighborhoods and 18 high-SES neighborhoods in London on four measures: *social cohesion* (trust and solidarity with neighbors), *social control* (confidence that neighbors would take action to maintain the well-being of the neighborhood), *neighborhood problems* (community-wide stressors such as litter and traffic noise), and *neighborhood vigilance* (a measure of feelings of threat and vulnerability in the neighborhood). Londoners living in lower-SES neighborhoods perceived greater *neighborhood strain* (weaker social cohesion, more neighborhood problems, and greater vigilance) than people living in more affluent neighborhoods, which in turn was associated with poorer individual health, poorer social relationships, and lower levels of perceived control among residents. In other studies, community violence has been linked to increased stress symptoms, depression, and anxiety among inner-city African American adolescents and to the use of negative coping strategies, such as avoidance and aggression (Dempsey, 2002).

Social Support

Another important external factor in how we cope with threatening events is the degree of social support that we receive. Social ties and relationships with other people powerfully influence us, in both positive and negative ways. In stressful situations, people who perceive a high level of social support may experience less stress and may cope more effectively.

Evidence for the Effects of Social Support

Multiple studies over several decades have found positive associations between social support and various emotional and physical health benefits. Let's examine some of this evidence.

Faster recovery and fewer medical complications Social support has been associated with better adjustment to and/or faster recovery from surgery, rheumatoid arthritis, childhood leukemia, and stroke (Brembo, Kapstad, Van Dulmen, & Eide, 2017; Martin & Brantley, 2004). In addition, women with strong social ties have fewer complications during childbirth (Collins, Dunkel-Schetter, Lobel, & Scrimshaw, 1993), and both women and men with high levels of social support are less likely to suffer heart attacks (Holahan, Holahan, Moos, & Brennan, 1997).

Lower mortality rates Having a number of close social relationships is associated with a lower risk of dying at any age. The classic example of this association comes from a survey of 7,000 adults in Alameda County, California (Berkman & Syme, 1994). The researchers found that having a large number of social contacts enabled women to live an average of 2.8 years longer and men an average of 2.3 years longer than those who don't have such social contacts (Figure 5.4). These benefits to longevity remained even when health habits such as smoking, alcohol use, physical activity, obesity, and differences in SES and health status at the beginning of the study were taken into account. Similarly, a 15-year prospective study of mortality rates among Swedish men who were 50 years old at the start of the study revealed that social support was inversely related to mortality. Men with a large circle of friends whom they saw regularly were half as likely to develop heart disease or die compared with men who had little social contact or support. The impact of low levels of social support on mortality was comparable in magnitude to that of cigarette smoking (Rosengren, Wilhelmsen, & Orth-Gomer, 2004). Another study showed that cancer patients with the fewest contacts each day were 2.2 times more likely to die of cancer over a 17-year period than were those with greater social support (Spiegel, 1996).

Less distress in the face of terminal illness Patients who perceive a strong network of social support experience less depression and hopelessness when undergoing treatment for AIDS, diabetes, and a variety of other chronic illnesses than do patients lacking social support (Kiviruusu, Huurre, & Aro, 2007; Varni, Setoguchi, Rappaport, & Talbot, 1992).

How Social Support Makes a Difference

As the foregoing evidence indicates, the support of others can benefit our health, but how? According to the **buffering hypothesis**, social support mitigates stress indirectly by helping us cope more effectively (Cohen & McKay, 1984; Cohen & Wills, 1985). For instance,

buffering hypothesis A theory that social support produces its stress-busting effects indirectly by helping the individual cope more effectively.

FIGURE 5.4 Social Isolation and Mortality The Alameda County Study was the first to establish a strong connection between social support and long life. Over a nine-year period, women and men with the fewest social ties were two to four times more likely to die than those who were not socially isolated.

Data from: Berkman, L. F., & Syme, S. L. (1979). Social networks, host resistance, and mortality: A nine-year follow-up of Alameda County residents. *American Journal of Epidemiology, 109*(2), 190.

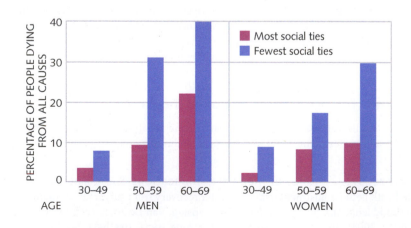

people who perceive strong social support are less likely to ruminate. Rumination tends to lead to more negative interpretations of events, triggering recall of unpleasant memories, interfering with problem solving, and reducing the ruminator's interest in participating in enjoyable activities (Lyubomirsky, Caldwell, & Nolen-Hoeksema, 1998; Spasojevic & Alloy, 2001). As another example, happily married people live longer, healthier lives than those who are unmarried (Kaplan & Kronick, 2006).

According to the **direct effect hypothesis**, social support enhances the body's physical responses to challenging situations (Pilisuk, Boylan, & Acredolo, 1987). Support for the direct effect hypothesis comes from an investigation of the relationships among self-reported stress levels, the availability of social support, and circulating levels of prostate-specific antigen (PSA) in men being screened for prostate cancer (Stone, Mezzacappa, Donatone, & Gonder, 1999). Men with the highest levels of self-reported stress also had significantly higher levels of PSA—a biological marker of prostate malignancy—than their less-stressed counterparts. Although stress was positively associated with PSA levels, there was an inverse correlation between PSA levels and the participants' perceived level of social support, as demonstrated by their scores on the six-item Satisfaction with Social Contacts (SSC) scale (see Figure 5.5). The SSC includes items such as "How has the number of people that you feel close to changed in the past six months?" and "How satisfied are you with the amount of social contact you have?"

The issue of how social support benefits health continues to be hotly debated. It may be that social support makes potentially stressful events more benign by diffusing or minimizing their initial impact. For example, having a supportive friend may make you less likely to interpret a low exam grade as evidence that your intelligence is low. Or perhaps the belief that other people care about you increases your self-esteem and gives you a more positive outlook on life. The result? Greater resistance to disease and a greater chance of adopting health-enhancing habits.

Who Receives Social Support?

Why are some people more likely than others to receive social support? The answer is predictable: People with better social skills—who relate well to others and who are caring and giving—create stronger social networks and thus receive more social support. Some evidence comes from a study of college freshmen who were categorized according to their social competence, social anxiety, and self-disclosure skills (Cohen, Sherrod, & Clark, 1986). Over the course of the study, the researchers discovered that students with greater social skills were the most likely to form strong social networks.

Other studies have found that angry or hostile people receive less social support than agreeable people do. They also report more negative life events and make people around them feel more stress (Hardy & Smith, 1988; Wager, Fieldman, & Hussey, 2003). Results such as these suggest an obvious intervention: To help people increase their social support, help them learn to be friendlier and less hostile.

It would seem, then, that the secret to a long, healthy life is to construct a large social network. But can a person be too socially connected? Can some social connections adversely affect our health?

direct effect hypothesis
A theory that social support produces its beneficial effects during both stressful and nonstressful times by enhancing the body's physical responses to challenging situations.

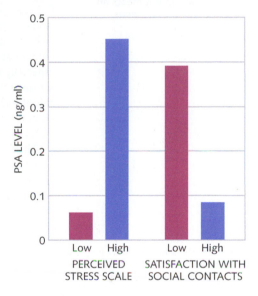

FIGURE 5.5 Stress, Social Support, and Prostate-Specific Antigen (PSA) Level of PSA was positively associated with stress and inversely related to satisfaction with social contacts. Participants who perceived low levels of stress and high satisfaction with social contacts had significantly lower levels of PSA, a biological marker of prostate malignancy.

Data from: Stone, A. A., Mezzacappa, E. S., Donatone, B. A., & Gonder, M. (1999). Psychosocial stress and social support are associated with prostate-specific antigen levels in men: Results from a community screening program. *Health Psychology, 18*(5), 485.

When Social Support Is Not Helpful

Sometimes social support does not reduce stress and benefit health. In fact, it may produce the opposite results. There are several reasons for this surprising fact. First, although support may be offered, a person may not perceive it as beneficial (Wilcox, Kasl, & Berkman, 1994). This may occur because the person does not want the assistance, thinks the assistance offered is inadequate, or is too distracted to notice that help has been offered. For example, in the first hours of coping with the loss of a loved one, a person may want only to be alone with his or her grief.

matching hypothesis The idea that social support is beneficial to the extent that it meets an individual's specific needs.

Second, the type of support offered may not be what is needed at the moment. According to the **matching hypothesis**, different stressful situations create different needs, and support that is responsive to these differences is most effective (Maisel & Gabel, 2009). For example, a single mother who is struggling to complete her college degree may feel stress during exam weeks. Although what she may need most is *instrumental social support,* such as assistance with child care or household chores, all that may be offered is emotional support, such as encouragement to study hard. Instrumental social support is especially valuable for controllable stressors, whereas emotional support is more helpful for uncontrollable stressors, such as a cataclysmic event or the loss of a loved one. The role of social support in promoting health, then, is quite specific. It is also subject to social and cultural norms concerning the types of support that are helpful (Abraido-Lanza, 2004).

Third, too much social support may actually increase a person's stress. Perhaps you know someone who is a member of too many organizations or is overwhelmed by intrusive social and family relationships. During periods of stress, this person may feel under siege in the face of all the advice and "support" that is offered. The critical factor appears to be having at least one close friend to confide in and share problems with. Having five, six, or even a dozen more may convey no more—and perhaps may give even less—benefit than having one or two.

Instrumental social support is sometimes more valuable than emotional support.

MANAGING STRESS

E ach of us has coping skills that we have acquired over the years. These include strategies that have worked in the past, techniques that we have read about, and behaviors that we have observed in other people. In most situations, these skills are probably adequate to keep us from experiencing undue stress. Sometimes, however, the demands of a situation may exceed our coping resources. Health psychologists have played a prominent role in developing interventions that help people cope with stress. Some of these techniques, such as biofeedback and meditation, are considered forms of complementary and alternative medicine (Barnes, Bloom, & Nahin, 2008), which is explored in Chapter 15. However, the growing evidence base for the effectiveness of relaxation training, cognitive-behavioral therapy, cognitive behavioral stress management, and emotional disclosure has led to the incorporation of a number of stress management techniques into conventional medicine.

Stress management describes a variety of psychological methods designed to reduce the impact of potentially stressful experiences. These techniques were originally introduced in clinical settings to help patients adapt to chronic illnesses and stressful medical procedures, but now they are used widely. For example, occupational groups (especially health care providers, emergency services personnel, students, and teachers) and people in disadvantaged personal circumstances (e.g., family caregivers, single parents, the unemployed, and victims of assault or abuse) all benefit from stress-management techniques.

So do students making the transition from high school to college. Consider how stressful the college experience can be. You might be living away from home for the first time, perhaps crammed into a crowded dorm room with people who have very different backgrounds, personalities, and habits. Your professors may seem gruff, and the coursework may be more challenging and accelerated than you expected. You're forced to study more than ever, often under noisy circumstances and with inadequate sleep and campus food that doesn't sit well in your stomach.

To help new students cope with these challenges, many colleges make stress-management programs available. A typical program involves three phases: education, acquiring skills, and practicing skills. In the first phase, participants learn what stress is, how it takes a toll on health, and that stress is more a process of their own cognitive appraisal than a characteristic of situations themselves.

Next, the participants are trained to monitor stress in their everyday lives using some of the techniques of ecological momentary assessment. For instance, they learn to observe their own behavior closely and to record when, and under what circumstances, they feel stress. Participants are also encouraged to keep track of their emotional, physical, and behavioral reactions to the stressors they've identified. By charting this information, students can learn to recognize, and then focus on, events and people that seem to be regular "triggers" of their stress. They also may begin to see an unhealthy pattern in their own behavioral responses to these circumstances, such as emotional eating, oversleeping, or using alcohol and other drugs.

The third phase of stress management involves learning new skills to either eliminate potential stressors or to reduce the experience of stress in healthy ways. There are many techniques and resources available to help people manage stress more effectively. We will consider relaxation training first.

stress management The various psychological methods designed to reduce the impact of potentially stressful experiences.

Relaxation Therapies

Although relaxation techniques have been used since antiquity, modern use is usually traced to Edmond Jacobson (1938), whose **progressive muscle relaxation** technique forms the cornerstone for many modern relaxation procedures. In progressive relaxation, you first tense a particular muscle (such as the forehead) and hold that tension for about 10 seconds. Then you slowly release the tension, focusing on the soothing feeling as the tension drains away. In similar fashion you tense, then relax other major muscle groups, including the mouth, eyes, neck, arms, shoulders, thighs, stomach, calves, feet, and toes. After practicing the relaxation technique for several weeks, you will identify the particular spots in your body that tense up during moments of stress, such as the jaw or fists. As you become more aware of these reactions, you can learn to relax these muscles at will.

progressive muscle relaxation A form of relaxation training that reduces muscle tension through a series of tensing and relaxing exercises involving the body's major muscle groups.

Relaxation Response

In another training technique, the **relaxation response**, participants assume the meditative state described below, in which metabolism slows and blood pressure lowers. Cardiologist Herbert Benson (1996) became intrigued with the possibility that relaxation might be an antidote to stress when he found that experienced meditators could lower their heart rate, blood lactate level (a byproduct of physical exercise that creates the "burn" of muscular exertion), blood pressure, and oxygen consumption. Benson identified four requirements for achieving the relaxation response:

relaxation response A meditative state of relaxation in which metabolism slows and blood pressure lowers.

- a quiet place in which distractions and external stimulation are minimized;
- a comfortable position, such as sitting in an easy chair;
- a mental device, such as focusing your attention on a single thought or word and repeating it over and over; and
- a passive, nonjudgmental attitude.

There is considerable evidence that relaxation training can help patients cope with a variety of stress-related problems, including hypertension, tension headaches, depression, lower back pain, adjustment to chemotherapy, and anxiety (Smith, 2005). Underlying the effectiveness of these techniques is their ability to reduce heart rate, muscle tension, and blood pressure, as well as self-reported tension and anxiety. Moreover, these techniques generally have been found to be more effective than placebos in reducing pain and alleviating stress. Relaxation training also has been shown to be an effective intervention following surgery, including by reducing hormonal stress responses (Phillips and others, 2011) and promoting faster healing (Broadbent and others, 2012).

Diaphragmatic Breathing and Visualization

When we're stressed, our breathing is often short and rapid. Simply slowing it down by taking long, deep breaths can help induce relaxation. You can try this yourself. Inhale slowly, and then exhale slowly. Count slowly to five as you inhale, and then count slowly to five as you exhale. As you exhale, note how your body relaxes. The keys to deep breathing are to breathe with your diaphragm, or abdomen, rather than your chest, and to take at least as long to exhale each breath as you did to inhale. Imagine a spot just below your navel. Breathe into that spot, expanding your abdomen as it fills with air. Let the air fill you from the abdomen up, then let it out, like deflating a balloon. Each long, slow exhalation should make you feel more relaxed.

Diaphragmatic breathing relaxation (DBR) has proven effective in reducing the perception and symptoms of anxiety (Chen, Huang, Chien, & Cheng, 2016). DBR has also been shown to improve lung functioning in patients with asthma, heart failure, and chronic obstructive pulmonary disease (Seo and others, 2016), and to reduce levels of pain following surgery (de Jong & Gamel, 2006). DBR offers many advantages over some of the conventional therapies for treating anxiety, including ease of learning, safety, and avoiding possible side effects and other hazards of the use of medication (Kim, Roth, & Wollburg, 2015). DBR seems to stimulate the parasympathetic nervous system, stabilizing heart rate and blood pressure, and the body's autonomic stress response (Kim, Roth, & Wollburg, 2015).

In Eastern cultures, breathing techniques such as DBR are often involved in yoga, meditation, and qi gong (see Chapter 15). These techniques sometimes combine DBR with matching visualization (guided mental imagery), which is a form of focused relaxation used to create peaceful images in your mind—a "mental escape." In guided imagery, the person is directed to recall or create a pleasant, relaxing image, focusing attention on sensory details such as sensations of color, sound, and touch. Visualization is powerful enough to reduce, or even to trigger, stress reactions in the laboratory. In one study, participants spent five minutes imagining scenes typical of their relationships with a romantic partner. Those who had earlier reported being in an unhappy relationship had significantly greater increases in salivary cortisol following the imagery (indicating higher stress) than those in happier relationships (Berry & Worthington, 2001).

To try visualization for yourself, find a comfortable place where you can close your eyes and begin breathing deeply, in a natural rhythm. Now visualize relaxation entering your body as you inhale and tension leaving your body as you exhale. As you breathe, visualize your breath coming into your nostrils, going into your lungs, and expanding your chest and abdomen. Then visualize your breath going out the same way. Continue breathing, but each time you inhale, imagine that you are breathing in more relaxation. Each time you exhale, imagine that you are getting rid of a little more tension.

Finally, breathing techniques and visualization can be combined with positive self-affirmations, or self-talk, as you relax. The goal is to identify negative self-talk and convert it into healthier, positive self-talk. Here are a few positive statements you can practice:

- I am healthy and strong.
- There is nothing that I cannot handle.
- I am safe.

Mindfulness-Based Stress Reduction

Is there a link between effective coping and being more consciously present? **Mindfulness-based stress reduction (MBSR)** was developed at the Stress Reduction Clinic at the University of Massachusetts as an adjunct to medical treatment for people with a variety of chronic health problems. Jon Kabat-Zinn, who developed MBSR, has described mindfulness as "falling awake," "coming to our senses," and "knowing what you are doing as

mindfulness-based stress reduction (MBSR) A form of therapy that focuses on using structured meditation to promote mindfulness—a moment-to-moment, nonjudgmental awareness.

you are actually doing it" (2005). A basic premise of mindfulness training is that in most aspects of life, people function on "automatic pilot"—a mode of behavior characterized by habit. Proponents of mindfulness training believe that stress can be reduced, and quality of life improved, by overriding "autopilot" mode and instead focusing on the present moment.

MBSR interventions have been used to decrease stress, depression, and anxiety in cancer patients (Zainal, Booth, & Huppert, 2013); to reduce distress and possibly slow disease progression in people living with HIV (Riley & Kalichman, 2015); and help patients suffering from low-back pain (Cramer, Haller, Lauche, & Dobos, 2012). Among cancer patients, MBSR interventions have also been associated with lower stress hormone levels and blood pressure (Hughes and others, 2013), and improved immunity (Carlson, Speca, Faris, & Patel, 2007). Some researchers have suggested that MBSR interventions are effective because they tend to reduce people's tendency toward rumination over stressful experiences (Gu, Strauss, Bond, & Cavanagh, 2015).

Neuroimaging studies have begun to explore the neural mechanisms underlying MBSR with techniques such as functional magnetic resonance imaging (fMRI). Mindfulness training seems to increase activity in the prefrontal cortex of the brain, an area important in regulating activity in the amygdala and other parts of the limbic system related to anxiety and other negative emotions (Creswell, Way, Eisenberger, & Lieberman, 2007). One study found that college students who scored high in measures of dispositional mindfulness had lower resting neural activity in the amygdala (Way, Creswell, Eisenberger, & Lieberman, 2010).

Using fMRI, another study found increased tissue density in the brain's hippocampus among participants who completed an eight-week MBSR course compared with a control group (Holzel and others, 2011). The hippocampus is believed to play a central role in mediating some of the benefits of mindfulness training due to its involvement

Mindfulness can be applied to a variety of activities, from silent meditation to taking a walk in nature to contemplating a work of art.

Andrea De Martin/Alamy Stock Photo

in regulating cortical arousal and emotion (Milad and others, 2007). Structural changes in the hippocampus therefore may reflect improved function in regulating emotional responses to potential stressors. In contrast to these increases in tissue density, decreased density of the hippocampus has been associated with several pathological conditions, including major depression (Sheline, 2000) and post-traumatic stress disorder (Kasai and others, 2008).

Mindfulness training may also improve immune functioning and reduce the risk of a number of chronic medical conditions (Hofmann, Sawyer, Witt, & Oh, 2010). One prospective study found that hypertension patients who received MBSR had a 30% lower cardiovascular death rate over the next two decades compared to members of other treatment groups (Schneider and others, 2005). Other studies have established the efficacy of mindfulness-based interventions in reducing symptoms of generalized anxiety disorder (Roemer, Orsillo, & Salters-Pedneault, 2008), depression (Teasdale and others, 2000), substance abuse (Bowen and others, 2006), eating disorders (Tapper and others, 2009), and chronic pain (Grossman, Niemann, Schmidt, & Walach, 2004). For an easy primer on how MBSR works, see *Your Health Assets: Try Mindfulness-Based Stress Reduction for Yourself.*

Cognitive-Behavioral Therapy

Cognitive-behavioral therapy is based on the view that our way of thinking about the environment, rather than the environment itself, determines our stress level. If thinking can be changed and skills acquired to make positive changes in behavior, stress can be reduced. There are a variety of clinical interventions that use cognitive strategies, including distraction, calming self-statements, and cognitive restructuring. In distraction procedures, people learn to direct their attention away from unpleasant or stressful events. Use of pleasant imagery (also called visualization), counting aloud, and focusing attention on relaxing stimuli (such as a favorite drawing, photograph, or song) are examples of distraction.

cognitive-behavioral therapy The use of principles from learning theory to change unhealthy patterns of thinking and behavior.

Your Health Assets
Try Mindfulness-Based Stress Reduction for Yourself

Mindfulness-based stress reduction (MBSR) has been shown to have many benefits, including increased attention, an improved immune response to disease, reduced stress hormones, and perhaps even a higher quality of life. Following are a few suggestions for how to try MBSR:

- Next time you are outside, take several deep breaths. What is the air like? Is it warm, or is it cold? How does the air feel on your body? Try to accept that feeling and not resist it.

- Eat your next meal in silence. Don't do anything but focus on your food. Eat slowly, and savor each bite.

- One morning when you can, take time at the beginning of the day to sit alone and think. Focus on your breathing. Open the window a little way, gaze out, and listen to the sounds outdoors.

- At work or school, try to stop for a few moments each hour. During those moments, note how your body feels. Let yourself regroup, and allow your mind to settle before you return to your work or school task.

FIGURE 5.6 The Negative Stress Cycle Stressful events interpreted through a pessimistic, self-defeating style create a negative mood that leads to stress-related physical symptoms and fuels additional stress. Fortunately, this vicious cycle can be interrupted at any point.

cognitive behavioral stress management (CBSM) A multimodal intervention that combines relaxation training, visualization, cognitive restructuring, reinforcement, and other techniques to help people cope with a range of stressors.

stress inoculation training A cognitive behavioral treatment in which people identify stressors in their lives and learn skills for coping with them so that when those stressors occur, the people are able to put those skills into effect.

appraised meaning How a particular stressor is cognitively perceived—for instance, as a challenge or threat.

Individuals can also be taught to silently or softly make calming, relaxing, and reassuring self-talk statements that emphasize the temporary nature of a stressor ("Let it go, that rude driver won't get to me."), are aimed at reducing autonomic arousal ("Stay calm now, breathe deeply, and count to 10"), or are directed at preserving a sense of psychological control ("I can handle this"). In our opening story, Kris Goldsmith's therapist might have helped him to learn self-calming techniques and to maintain a sense of self-control.

Cognitive restructuring is a generic term that describes a variety of psychological interventions directed at replacing maladaptive, self-defeating thoughts with healthier adaptive thinking. These interventions aim to break the vicious cycle of negative thinking, which pessimistically distorts perceptions of everyday events and prevents adaptive coping behaviors (Belar & Deardorff, 1996) (Figure 5.6). Therapists teach clients to reinterpret their thoughts in a less negative way and to raise awareness of distorted and maladaptive thinking.

This reciprocal relationship between maladaptive thinking and unhealthy behaviors is well documented. For example, focusing on a negative experience at work can affect your mood and lead to a tension headache. Having a tension headache can sour your mood, which in turn can make your thoughts more pessimistic.

Cognitive Behavioral Stress Management

Cognitive behavioral stress management (CBSM) is a multimodal intervention that combines relaxation training, visualization, cognitive restructuring, reinforcement, and other techniques; it has helped people cope with a range of stressors. CBSM often begins by teaching people to confront stressful events with a variety of coping strategies that can be used before the events become overwhelming. In this way, individuals are able to "inoculate" themselves against the potentially harmful effects of stress (Antoni, Ironson, & Scheiderman, 2007). Many stress inoculation programs offer an array of techniques so that a client can choose the strategies that work best for him or her.

Stress inoculation training is a three-stage process that uses the same principle as medical vaccination, with the therapist using a weakened dose of a stressor in an attempt to build immunity against the full-blown stressor (Meichenbaum, 2007). The stages are as follows:

- Stage 1: Reconceptualization. Patients reconceptualize the source of their stress, changing its **appraised meaning** (Chapter 4). Imagine that you are agonizing over an upcoming dental procedure, such as a root canal. During the first stage of stress inoculation training, you would learn that your discomfort is at least partially the result of psychological factors, such as dwelling on how much the procedure is going to hurt. Once you are convinced that some of your pain is psychological in nature, you will be more likely to accept that cognitive behavior therapy can offer some relief.

- Stage 2: Skills acquisition. Next, you will be taught relaxation and controlled breathing skills. The logic is inescapable: Being relaxed is incompatible with being tense and physically aroused. Therefore, learning to relax at will is a valuable tool in managing pain. Other techniques that you might learn include the use of pleasant mental imagery, dissociation, or humor.

- Stage 3: Follow-through. Now you will learn to use these coping skills in everyday life, beginning with how you might apply them to the imagined upcoming root canal. You will be encouraged to increase your physical activity and to take pain medication on a timed daily schedule, rather than waiting until you feel pain. Your family members may be taught ways of reinforcing your new healthier behaviors.

CBSM has proved to be effective in helping people cope with a variety of stress-related problems, including job stress (Kawaharada and others, 2009), hypertension (Amigo, Buceta, Becona, & Bueno, 1991), post-traumatic stress disorder (Ponniah & Hollon, 2009), depression associated with breast cancer (Antoni and others, 2009), prostate cancer (Penedo and others, 2004), and AIDS (Antoni and others, 2001). CBSM also has been shown to reduce HPA axis hormones (see Chapter 4) among men who are infected with symptomatic human immunodeficiency virus (HIV) (Antoni and others, 2001).

Emotional Disclosure

In the 1980s, psychologist James Pennebaker began a fascinating series of studies with college students, most of whom followed this simple protocol: Students were asked to write about an assigned topic for 15 minutes a day for four days. Half of the participants wrote about everyday, ordinary experiences—describing their dorm rooms, for instance. The other students were told to write about their deepest thoughts and feelings regarding a stressful or traumatic experience. Students in the emotional disclosure group took immediately to the task and wrote intimate, gripping stories, sometimes crying and displaying other strong emotional reactions. At the end of the study, most reported that the experience had helped them find new meaning in the traumatic experience. The most striking result, however, came six months later, at the end of the school year, when Pennebaker discovered that those who had written about stressful experiences had visited the university health center far less often than did the students who had written about everyday things (Pennebaker & Susman, 1988).

expressive writing A technique that promotes emotional disclosure through writing, or journaling, about our feelings.

Over the decades, Pennebaker's finding has been repeated in dozens of settings with scores of people from different walks of life, ethnicities, and cultural backgrounds. The participants instructed to use **expressive writing** or, alternatively, to confide verbally to a confidante have included prison inmates, crime victims, chronic pain sufferers, Holocaust survivors, college students, bereaved widows and widowers, business executives, and laid-off workers. In almost every instance, emotional disclosure is related to some positive health benefit.

When people write or talk about traumatic events, their skin conductivity, heart rate, and systolic and diastolic blood pressure all decrease (Ernst, 2017). Over time, keeping a daily journal of thoughts and feelings has been associated with decreased absenteeism, fewer medical visits, and even improved immune functioning and wound healing (Ernst, 2017). In one recent study, 122 healthy participants

Expressive Writing Journal writing and other techniques that promote emotional disclosure can have a variety of health benefits.

were randomly assigned to write about traumatic events (expressive writing) or control topics (neutral writing) before or after receiving a small punch biopsy wound. After 10 days, those assigned to the expressive writing group showed significantly greater healing of their wounds than those in the neutral writing group (Robinson, Jarrett, Vedhara, & Broadbent, 2017). This study, and another that explored the benefits of expressive writing for reducing test anxiety, demonstrated that emotional disclosure is most beneficial when performed before the threatening event occurs (Shen, Yang, Zhang, and Zhang, 2018).

There are many reasons why **emotional disclosure** may help us cope with stress. Interestingly, people who have been diagnosed with alexithymia, or difficulty in identifying and expressing their own emotions, have been linked to increased cardiovascular mortality (Tolmunen, Lehto, Heliste, Kurl, & Kauhanen, 2010). Writing or talking about stressful experiences may help lower this risk. Confiding in others may allow us to gain helpful advice. It also may provide a source of reinforcement and social support, as well as eliminate the need to ruminate about and inhibit a stressful event, which may reduce the physiological activity linked to the event (Stanton, 2010). Finally, writing or talking about a stressful experience may encourage cognitive reappraisal as we gain a new perspective on the event or develop a plan to deal with a stressful situation (Lestideau & Lavallee, 2007). In support of this latter idea, Pennebaker has found that people who write the most coherent, persuasive, and well-organized stories tend to experience the greatest health benefits (Niederhoffer & Pennebaker, 2002). Similarly, women who had recently lost a close relative to breast cancer and who were asked to write daily about the death were most likely to demonstrate a bolstered immune response (increased natural killer cell cytotoxicity) when daily written disclosure enabled them to find positive meaning from the loss (Bower, Kemeny, Taylor, & Fahey, 2003). A meta-analysis of studies indicates that emotional disclosure may be more effective in helping people cope with physical rather than psychological challenges (Frisina, Borod, & Lepore, 2004).

Other Coping Tools and Techniques

Research has identified additional ways in which people can cope with stress. Here we will discuss gratitude, humor and pets, and spirituality and meaning.

Gratitude

Gratitude has been categorized in many different ways: as a temporary emotional state, a stable personality trait, a coping response, and an attitude. Most often, *gratitude* is defined as the recognition of a positive outcome from an external source, including a sense of wonder and thankfulness for benefits received (Nelson & Lyubomirsky, 2016). People who maintain a grateful outlook on life cope better with stress, perceive greater social support in their lives, sleep better, and have better physical and mental health (Emmons & Mishra, 2011).

Cultivating gratitude is also an effective way to develop positive affectivity. One way to begin cultivating gratitude is by catching yourself when you complain or grumble about a stressor and trying to think of three or four related things for which you are grateful. When you are feeling stressed at work, for example, try to shift your focus to a few things that you like about your job. Another effective technique is to begin keeping a *gratitude journal* in which you write down, two or three times a week, things for which you are grateful.

---

emotional disclosure A therapeutic activity in which people express their strong, often stress-related, emotions by writing or talking about the events that triggered the emotions.

Journaling combines the benefits of emotional disclosure—as you explore your thoughts and feelings about the events in your life—with an active problem-focused strategy to develop a more positive mindset. In one study, people who kept gratitude journals exercised more regularly, reported fewer physical symptoms, and felt better about their lives, compared with those who recorded hassles or neutral life events (Emmons & McCullough, 2003).

Humor and Pets

Laughter and a sense of humor help many people cope with stress (Fritz, Russek, & Dillon, 2017). In addition to boosting mood, laughter reduces epinephrine and cortisol secretion, boosts the immune system, reduces the risk of coronary disease, lowers blood pressure, and generally promotes vascular health (Heo, Kim, Park, & Kil, 2016; Miles, Tait, Schure, & Hollis, 2016).

How can you bring more humor and laughter into your life? Here are some simple things to try.

- Practice smiling more and laughing more. Smiling, which is the beginning of laughter, is contagious. Laugh at yourself.

- Spend time with fun people, and when you hear laughter, move toward it. Sometimes humor is private, but in most cases people are happy to share a funny experience. Share a joke or funny story of your own.

- Try simulated laughter by laughing out loud even when nothing funny is happening. There are laugh yoga and laugh therapy groups that make this technique a focus.

- Create additional opportunities to laugh. Watch a funny film or video. Go with friends to a comedy club. Keep an amusing toy, picture, or poster in view at the location where you study or work.

In addition to human friends, pets are a source of fun and affection. Pet ownership can reduce loneliness, help lower blood pressure, decrease secretion of cortisol, and increase secretion of dopamine, oxytocin, and serotonin—three hormones associated with feelings of well-being. If your living arrangements make pet ownership impractical, try visiting any of the many Web sites that feature amusing animal videos.

Spirituality and Meaning

For many people, spirituality may promote well-being and health. People who are spiritually active tend to eat healthier, exercise more, smoke less frequently, and generally have healthier lifestyles. Because spirituality is often communal, those who participate in spiritual or religious groups often benefit from increased social support. Spiritual activity may also promote health by fostering more positive emotions, including optimism, feelings of acceptance, and a sense that life is meaningful.

People who receive a diagnosis of a serious illness such as cancer, or experience a traumatic environmental event, sometimes show improved psychological adjustment and better health outcomes by using **meaning-focused coping** (Updegraff, Silver, & Holman, 2008). In this process, people don't try to change a situation or the distress associated with it, but rather search for its personal meaning by asking questions such as "Why did this happen?" and "How has this changed me?" (Haynes and others, 2017; Gan, Zheng, Wang, & Li, 2017).

meaning-focused coping
A coping strategy in which a person attempts to find meaning in a stressful situation or traumatic event, rather than trying to change the situation or event or alter the distress associated with it.

Weigh In on Health

Respond to each question below based on what you learned in the chapter. (**Tip:** Use the items in "Summing Up" to take into account related biological, psychological, and social concerns.)

1. Your roommate, a pre-med student who is heavily invested in the medical model, doesn't believe that personality traits, such as a person's general approach to life and feelings of control over their decisions and choices, affect their health. What evidence can you offer to change her thinking on this issue?

2. How would you describe yourself in terms of coping style, psychological control and choice, social support, and any other factors discussed in this chapter? From what you have read, can you list a few ways in which you might improve your stress responses and possibly improve the way in which you cope with stressful situations?

Summing Up

Factors Affecting the Ability to Cope

1. Coping refers to the various ways—healthy or unhealthy—in which people attempt to prevent, eliminate, weaken, or simply tolerate stress.

2. Dispositional affect refers to a person's tendency toward negative emotions and distress (negative affectivity) or positive emotions and subjective well-being (positive affectivity).

3. Coping can involve dealing directly with a stressor (approach coping), or distancing oneself from the distress associated with a threatening event (avoidance coping).

4. Problem-focused coping applies problem-solving skills to anticipate and prevent potential stressors or confront the source of stress. Emotion-focused coping refers to controlling one's emotional response to a stressor, either by distancing oneself from it or by appraising it differently.

5. Emotional-approach coping (EAC), which involves working through our emotional reactions to a stressful event, is adaptive and healthy.

6. Rumination refers to thinking repetitively about an upsetting situation and how it relates to past and future problems associated with a stressor. This may spiral out of control and make the person more upset, which in turn causes more rumination.

7. How people cope with a stressor is influenced by a number of external resources: family, friends, education, employment, time, money, the presence of other stressors, etc. People with access to more resources typically cope more successfully because they have more options.

8. Socioeconomic status (SES) has a significant effect on coping and on health. People who are low in SES have increased risk for chronic disease, disability, and premature mortality.

9. People of higher SES are more likely than those of lower SES to use problem-focused coping strategies in dealing with stress. Low SES is often accompanied by a stressful lifestyle that limits a person's coping options.

10. The perception of psychological control plays a crucial role in determining a person's response to a stressful situation. The perception of control is a buffer against stress-related arousal and enhances immune activity.

11. People who perceive a high level of social support may cope with stress more effectively than people who feel alienated. Along with companionship, social ties can provide emotional support, instrumental support, and informational support.

12. People with better social skills—who relate well to others and who are caring and giving—create stronger social networks and thus receive more social support. Social support does not always reduce stress, however. It may be perceived as intrusive, or the type of support offered may not be what is needed.

Managing Stress

13. Relaxation techniques such as progressive muscle relaxation and the relaxation response (meditation) can help people cope with a variety of stress-related problems, including hypertension, headaches, chronic pain, and anxiety. Mindfulness-based stress reduction focuses on using

structured meditation to promote mindfulness, a moment-to-moment, nonjudgmental awareness.

14. Cognitive-behavioral therapy is based on the view that the appraised meaning of a potential stressor, rather than the situation itself, determines our stress level.

15. Cognitive behavioral stress management is a multimodal form of therapy that helps people to confront stressful events with coping strategies that can be put in place before stressors become overwhelming. Expressive writing and other techniques that promote emotional disclosure have a variety of health benefits.

Key Terms and Concepts to Remember

coping, p. 135
disengagement, p. 135
problem-focused coping, p. 135
emotion-focused coping, p. 135
emotional-approach coping (EAC), p. 135
rumination, p. 136
emotional cascade, p. 136
repressive coping, p. 136
dispositional affect, p. 138

psychological control, p. 140
regulatory control, p. 141
resilience, p. 141
buffering hypothesis, p. 146
direct effect hypothesis, p. 147
matching hypothesis, p. 148
stress management, p. 149
progressive muscle relaxation, p. 150
relaxation response, p. 150

mindfulness-based stress reduction (MBSR), p. 151
cognitive-behavioral therapy, p. 153
cognitive behavioral stress management (CBSM), p. 154
stress inoculation training, p. 154
appraised meaning, p. 154
expressive writing, p. 155
emotional disclosure, p. 156
meaning-focused coping, p. 157

 To accompany your textbook, you have access to a number of online resources, including quizzes for every chapter of the book, flashcards, critical thinking exercises, videos, and *Check Your Health* inventories. To access these resources, please visit the Straub Health Psychology LaunchPad at **launchpadworks.com**

Part 3 BEHAVIOR AND HEALTH

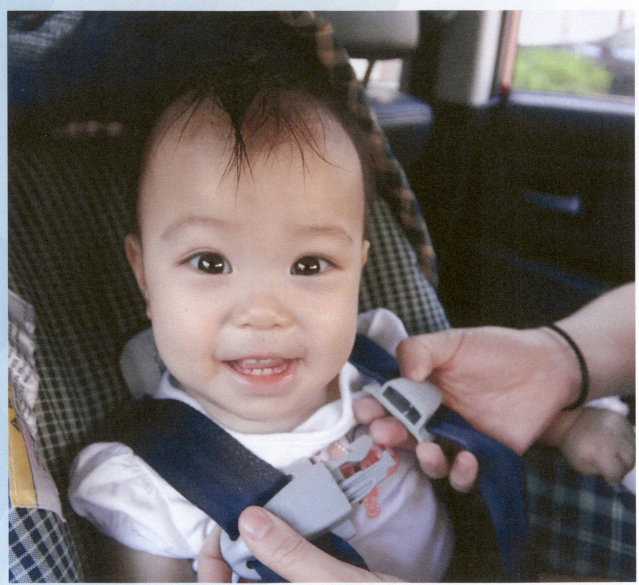

Staying Healthy: Primary Prevention and Positive Psychology

Chapter 6

Andre Schoenherr/Getty Images

LEARNING OUTCOMES
Once you have studied this chapter, you will be able to:
- Summarize the main theories of health behavior,
- Identify several strategies and interventions that are used to prevent health problems, and
- Describe the principles of positive psychology and apply them to health.

When Sara Snodgrass found a lump in her breast, her first thoughts were of her aunt and mother, both of whom died after battling breast cancer. Sara recalled that after her aunt was diagnosed with cancer, she "went home, pulled all the curtains closed, refused to leave the house except for chemotherapy treatments, and allowed very few visitors. She waited for death" (Snodgrass, 1998, p. 3). Unlike her aunt, Sara was determined to continue her work as a university professor throughout her cancer treatment. Resolving that cancer would not interfere with her life, she also continued scuba diving, skiing, and other activities that flowed from her natural optimism, sense of self-mastery, and confidence.

Sara's treatment began with a biopsy, followed by a lumpectomy (removal of the malignant tumor) and two months of radiation treatments. Although she and her doctor were hopeful that she was cured, less than one year later metastasized (widely spread) cancer was found in her abdomen. In her words, she has been "submerged in cancer" ever since, having undergone three surgeries, five different courses of chemotherapy, two types of hormone therapy, three months of radiation, a bone marrow transplant, and a stem cell transplant. Throughout her treatment, she also has battled unpredictable, debilitating pain 10 to 14 days per month. Throughout these experiences Sara has taken charge of her health care, learning everything she can about her treatments, making her own decisions, and refusing to work with doctors who do not treat her with respect and honor her desire to maintain a sense of control over her life.

Perhaps most remarkable is Sara's conviction that her cancer has led to a reorganization of her self-perception, relationships, and philosophy of life. It has taught her to live more in the present rather than to be concerned about the future. She stopped worrying about whether she would find the right romantic partner, whether her students would give her good evaluations, and whether she would have enough money to live comfortably in retirement. She realized that relationships with friends and family are the most important part of her life. When thinking about dying, she asserts, "I will not say I wish I had written more articles. However, I might say I wish I had seen or talked to more friends or acquaintances with whom I had lost contact." So that is what she is doing—corresponding, telephoning, and traveling to renew old relationships, and reveling in new ones that have extended her network of social support throughout the country.

Sometimes illness cannot be prevented, as in Sara's case. Yet even in such extreme cases, building our human strengths may allow us the capacity to thrive. In this chapter, we consider the connection between behavior and health. We then explore how health psychology's biopsychosocial approach to prevention, first, and positive psychology, second, can help build healthy individuals, families, and communities.

HEALTH AND BEHAVIOR

It is difficult to imagine an activity or behavior that does not influence health in some way. **Health behaviors** are actions that people take to improve or maintain their health. Exercising regularly, using sunscreen, eating a healthy diet, sleeping well, practicing safe sex, and wearing seatbelts are all behaviors that help "immunize" you against disease and injury, while activities such as meditation and laughter help many people manage stress and remain upbeat.

health behavior A health-enhancing behavior or habit.

Because they occur on a continuum, some health behaviors can have both a positive and a negative impact on health. For example, exercise and dieting are often beneficial, but if carried to the extreme, they can actually be hazardous to health. Other behaviors influence health indirectly, through their association with behaviors that have a direct impact on health. Many people who drink coffee excessively, for example, also smoke and engage in other risky behaviors that increase the risk of heart disease (Cornelis, El-Sohemy, Kabagambe, & Campos, 2006). Health behaviors that have become firmly established and are performed automatically have become **health habits**.

health habit An automatic health behavior that has become a firmly established part of everyday life.

Some behaviors (e.g., not wearing a seatbelt) affect health immediately, whereas others (e.g., eating a healthy diet) have a long-term effect. Still others (e.g., exercising or smoking) have both immediate *and* long-term effects on health. Health behaviors also interact and are often interrelated. For example, the combined interactive effect of smoking, drinking alcohol, and consuming too much coffee is stronger than that of only one such behavior. Similarly, exercising, eating healthy foods, and drinking a lot of water also tend to come together, but in a positive way.

Studying Healthy and Risky Behaviors

As part of its *Youth Risk Behavior Surveillance* project, the Centers for Disease Control and Prevention identified six risky health behaviors—often begun while young (and therefore habits)—that put people at risk for premature death, disability, and chronic illness (Youth Risk Behavior Surveillance System [YRBSS], 2018):

1. Tobacco use
2. Unhealthy dietary behaviors
3. Inadequate physical activity
4. Alcohol and other drug use (including prescription drugs)
5. Sexual behaviors related to unintended pregnancy and sexually transmitted diseases (STDs)
6. Behaviors that contribute to unintentional injuries and violence

What is the potential impact of adopting a healthier lifestyle? In one classic epidemiological study begun in 1965, Lester Breslow and Norman Breslow (1993) began to track the health and lifestyle habits of male residents of Alameda County, California. Although this landmark study was carried out more than two decades ago, the salutary effects of seven healthy habits—sleeping seven to eight hours daily, never smoking, being at or near a healthy body weight, using alcohol in moderation, getting regular physical exercise, eating breakfast, and avoiding between-meal snacking—are still part of what makes the human body function in a healthy way (Figure 6.1).

Theories of Health Behavior

Health psychologists have developed a number of theories to explain why people engage (or do not engage) in healthful or unhealthful behaviors. Let's examine several of the most influential theories.

The Health Belief Model (HBM)

According to the **health belief model (HBM)**, decisions about health behavior are based on four interacting factors that influence our perceptions about health threats (see Figure 6.2) (Strecher & Rosenstock, 1997):

■ *Perceived susceptibility.* Some people worry constantly about health threats such as HIV; other people believe that they are not in danger. The greater the perceived susceptibility, the stronger the motivation to engage in health-promoting behaviors. Adolescents especially seem to live their lives following an *invincibility fable,* which gives them little motivation to change risky behaviors.

health belief model (HBM) A nonstage theory that identifies four factors that influence decision making regarding health behavior: perceived susceptibility to a health threat, perceived severity of the disease or condition, perceived benefits of and barriers to the behavior, and cues to action.

FIGURE 6.1 Health Behaviors and Death Rate Follow-up assessments both 9 and 12 years into the famous Alameda Health Study found that the mortality of men who regularly practiced all seven health habits (sleeping seven to eight hours daily, never smoking, being at or near a healthy body weight, using alcohol in moderation, getting regular physical exercise, eating breakfast, and avoiding between-meal snacking) was 28% of the mortality of those who had practiced three or fewer healthy behaviors. Women who practiced all seven behaviors had a 43% lower mortality than others.

Data from: Housman, J., & Dorman, S. (2005). The Alameda County study: A systematic, chronological review. *American Journal of Health Education, 33*(5), 302–308.

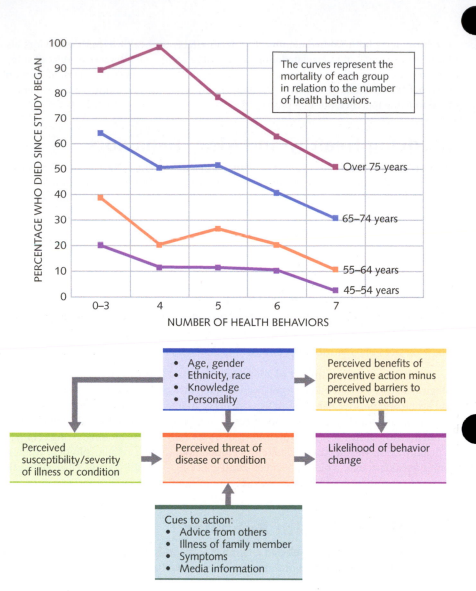

FIGURE 6.2 The Health Belief Model This nonstage theory emphasizes the interacting factors that influence our decision making about health behaviors. If we believe that an available course of action will reduce our susceptibility to or the severity of the condition, then we will engage in that health behavior.

Information from: Strecher, V. J., & Rosenstock, I. M. (1997). The health belief model. In A. Baum, S. Newman, J. Weinman, R. West, & C. McManus (Eds.), Cambridge handbook of psychology, health, and medicine (pp. 113–117). Cambridge, UK: Cambridge University Press.

- *Perceived severity of the health threat.* Among the factors considered are whether pain, disability, or death may result, as well as whether the condition will have an impact on family, friends, and coworkers.

- *Perceived benefits of and barriers to treatment.* In evaluating the pros and cons of a particular health behavior, a person decides whether the perceived benefits of the behavior exceed its barriers. For example, someone may overlook the huge advantages of quitting smoking due to concerns about becoming overweight and unattractive.

- *Cues to action.* Advice from friends, media health campaigns, and factors such as age, socioeconomic status, and gender also will influence the likelihood that the person will act.

In summary, the HBM is a commonsense theory proposing that people will take action to ward off or control illness-inducing conditions if they believe or perceive that (1) they themselves are susceptible, (2) the condition has serious personal consequences, (3) a course of action will reduce either their susceptibility or the severity of the condition, (4) the benefits of the action outweigh the costs, and (5) environmental influences are encouraging change.

The HBM has been subjected to extensive research. People are more likely to have regular dental checkups, practice safe sex, eat in a healthy way, obtain health screenings for colorectal and other forms of cancer, and engage in other health-protective behaviors if they feel susceptible to the various health problems that might stem from failure to do so (Deshpande, Basil, & Basil, 2009). Importantly, interventions aimed at changing health beliefs increase health-protective behaviors.

Despite these successes, some studies have found that health beliefs predict health behaviors only modestly and that other factors, such as perceived barriers to action, are also important determinants (Chen, Fox, Cantrell, Stockdale, & Kagawa-Singer, 2007). One such barrier occurs when people don't believe they are capable of changing their behavior. *Protection Motivation* Theory *(PMT)* adds *self-efficacy* as a separate component, focusing not only on how people appraise threats to their health, but also on their ability to manage these threats by acting more healthfully (Rogers, 1983). Two meta-analyses of research on PMT found that increases in self-efficacy worked hand in hand with threat severity in promoting a range of behaviors (Sommestad, Karlzen, & Halberg, 2015; Floyd, Prentice-Dunn, & Rogers, 2000).

Other critics have argued that the HBM focuses too heavily on attitudes about perceived risk rather than on emotional responses, which may more accurately predict behavior (Lawton, Conner, & Parker, 2007). The HBM represents an important perspective, but it is incomplete. Let's look at another theory that focuses on the role that intentions and self-efficacy play in the practice of health behaviors.

Cigarette? Health psychologists have developed a number of theories to explain why people smoke and engage (or do not engage) in other unhealthy behaviors.

Theory of Planned Behavior

Like the health belief model, the **theory of planned behavior (TPB)** specifies relationships among attitudes and behavior (see Figure 6.3). The theory maintains that the best way to predict whether a health behavior will occur is to measure **behavioral intention**—the decision to either engage in or refrain from a health-related behavior. Behavioral intentions are shaped by three factors: (1) *attitude toward the behavior,* which is determined by the belief that engaging in the behavior will lead to certain outcomes; (2) the **subjective norm**, which reflects our motivation to comply with the views of other people regarding the behavior in question; and (3) *perceived behavioral control,* which refers to our expectation of success in performing the health behavior. So, for instance, we may decide that reducing the amount of sugar in our diet is a good thing to do because (1) we believe that doing so will lead to weight loss; (2) our relatives and friends are following similar diets; and (3) we are confident that we will be able to shop for healthy ingredients, make the time to prepare meals, and still enjoy the flavor of food even though our diet is more restricted.

The specific intention to adopt or change a health behavior (what, when, where) can, indeed, help to bring it about (McEachan, Conner, Taylor, & Lawton, 2011). People's self-reported attitudes and intentions predict a variety of health-promoting actions,

theory of planned behavior (TPB) A theory that predicts health behavior on the basis of three factors: personal attitude toward the behavior, the subjective norm regarding the behavior, and perceived degree of control over the behavior.

behavioral intention In theories of health behavior, the rational decision to engage in a health-related behavior or to refrain from engaging in the behavior.

subjective norm An individual's interpretation of the views of other people regarding a particular health-related behavior.

FIGURE 6.3 Theory of Planned Behavior This theory predicts that a person's decision to engage in a particular health behavior is based on three factors: personal attitude toward the behavior, the subjective norm regarding the behavior, and perceived degree of control over the behavior.

Information from: Sutton, S. R. (1997). The theory of planned behavior. In A. Baum, S. Newman, J. Weinman, R. West, & C. McManus (Eds.), Cambridge handbook of psychology, health, and medicine. Cambridge, UK: Cambridge University Press.

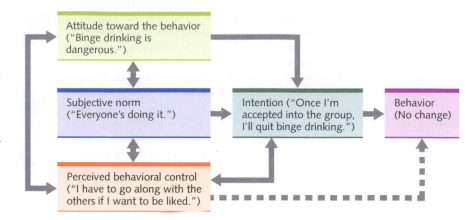

transtheoretical model (TTM) (stages of change model) A stage theory that contends that people pass through five stages in altering health-related behavior: precontemplation, contemplation, preparation, action, and maintenance.

including genetic testing for diseases, taking medication (Goldring, Taylor, Kemeny, & Anton, 2002), reducing consumption of soft drinks among teens (Kassem & Lee, 2004), healthy eating (Conner, Norman, & Bell, 2002), condom use (Davis and others, 2016; Montanaro & Bryan, 2014), and not smoking (Van de Ven, Engels, Otten, & Van Den Eijnden, 2007), among others.

Given its emphasis on planning, it is not surprising that the TPB is most accurate in predicting intentional behaviors that are goal-oriented and fit within a rational framework, such as physical activity and diet (McEachan and others, 2011). In some cases, such as substance abuse (Morojele & Stephenson, 1994), risky sexual behavior (Cha, Doswell, Kim, Charron-Prochownik, & Patrick, 2007), and drunk driving (Stacy, Bentler, & Flay, 1994), the model has been less successful, perhaps because these behaviors are often reactions to social situations. For example, young people may attend a party where others are consuming alcohol or marijuana, or may give in to peer pressure to have sex.

The Transtheoretical Model

The theories of health behavior that we have considered thus far attempt to identify variables that influence health-related attitudes and behaviors and combine them into a formula that predicts the probability that a particular individual will act in a certain way in a given situation. In contrast, the **transtheoretical model (TTM)** (also called the **stages of change model**) maintains that behavior often changes systematically through distinct stages (Rothman, 2000).

The TTM contends that people progress through five stages in altering health-related behaviors. The stages are defined in terms of past behavior and intentions for future action.

Stage 1: Precontemplation. People are not seriously thinking about changing their behavior. They may even refuse to acknowledge that their behavior needs changing.

The Power of the Social Situation For many teenagers and young adults, health behaviors are often reactions to social situations. Young people may swim because their friends are swimming, not because they have made a conscious decision to exercise. Social situations can foster both healthy and unhealthy behaviors.

The Image Bank/Getty Images

Stage 2: Contemplation. People acknowledge the existence of a problem (e.g., smoking) and are seriously considering changing their behavior (quitting smoking) in the near future (typically within six months).

Stage 3: Preparation. People engage in both thoughts and actions. In preparing to quit smoking, for example, a person obtains a prescription for a nicotine patch, joins a support group, enlists family support, and makes other specific plans.

Stage 4: Action. People have actually changed their behavior and are trying to sustain their efforts.

Stage 5: Maintenance. People continue to be successful in their efforts to reach their final goal. Although maintenance can last indefinitely, its length is often set arbitrarily at six months.

The TTM recognizes that people move back and forth through the stages in a non-linear, spiral fashion (Velicer & Prochaska, 2008). Figure 6.4 illustrates a smoker's progression through the five stages of change in quitting smoking. Many recently reformed ex-smokers relapse from *maintenance* to *preparation,* cycling through stages 2 to 5 one or more times until they have completed their behavioral change.

Although the TTM is more successful in predicting some behaviors than others, research has generally confirmed that people at higher stages are more successful at improving health-related behaviors, such as smoking cessation (Rosen, 2000), adopting a healthier diet (Armitage, Sheeran, Conner, & Arden, 2004), exercising regularly (Hellsten, Johansson, Dahlman, Sterner, & Bjartell, 2011), using sunscreen (Adams, Norman, Hovell, Sallis, & Patrick, 2009), and testing for colorectal and breast cancer (Champion

FIGURE 6.4 The Transtheoretical Model
The transtheoretical, or stages of change, model assesses a person's readiness to act on a new, healthier behavior. The model also identifies strategies and processes to guide the individual through the stages of change to successful action and maintenance. Critics point out that the stages are not mutually exclusive, and people do not always move sequentially through discrete stages as they strive to change health behaviors.

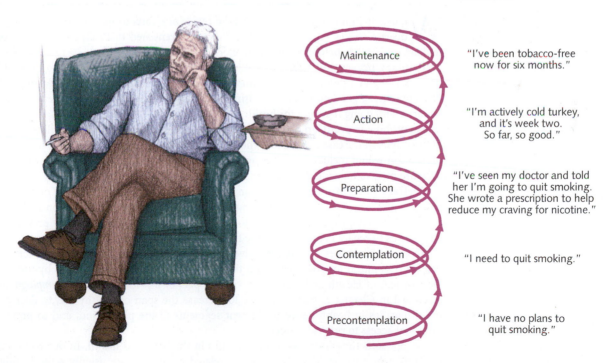

Maintenance — "I've been tobacco-free now for six months."

Action — "I'm actively cold turkey, and it's week two. So far, so good."

Preparation — "I've seen my doctor and told her I'm going to quit smoking. She wrote a prescription to help reduce my craving for nicotine."

Contemplation — "I need to quit smoking."

Precontemplation — "I have no plans to quit smoking."

and others, 2007; Lauver, Henriques, Settersten, & Bumann, 2003). When the model's predictions have failed, it may be due to problems with how researchers have classified participants into stages (Cahill, Lancaster, & Green, 2010; Herzog, 2008).

Theories with fewer stages may, indeed, be more useful in designing interventions that accurately predict behavior change (Armitage, 2009). One such theory is the *Health Action Process Approach (HAPA)*, which specifies only two stages: a goal-setting, *motivational phase* in which a person forms the intention to change a health behavior, followed by a goal-pursuit, *volitional phase* in which a plan to change the behavior in question is created and then put into place (Schwarzer, 2008, 2016). Before behavior can change, HAPA specifies that during the motivational phase people must perceive a health risk, believe that taking the action in question will have a favorable outcome, and have confidence in their ability to make the change (self-efficacy).

A growing body of research supports the fundamental principles of HAPA, especially the importance of planning in promoting successful behavior change (Schwarzer, 2016; Craciun, Schuz, Lippke, & Schwarzer, 2012). Although HAPA has not yet been studied as extensively as other theories, health psychologists are increasingly using the model to design interventions to promote a wide range of health behaviors, including diabetes self-management, physical activity, healthy dieting, and sunscreen use (Arbour-Nicitopoulos, Duncan, Remington, Cairney, & Faulkner, 2017; Schwarzer & Luszczynska, 2015).

PREVENTION

We usually think of prevention solely in terms of efforts to modify one's risk *before* disease strikes. In fact, researchers have differentiated three types of prevention that are undertaken before, during, and after a disease strikes.

primary prevention Health-enhancing efforts to prevent disease or injury from occurring.

secondary prevention Actions taken to identify and treat an illness or disability early in its course.

tertiary prevention Actions taken to contain damage once a disease or disability has progressed beyond its early stages.

Primary prevention refers to health-promoting actions that are taken to prevent a disease or injury from occurring. Examples of primary prevention include wearing seatbelts, practicing good nutrition, exercising, avoiding smoking, maintaining healthy sleep patterns, and going regularly for health screening tests.

Secondary prevention consists of actions taken to identify and treat an illness early in its course. In the case of a person who has high blood pressure, for example, secondary prevention would include regular examinations to monitor symptoms, the use of blood pressure medication, and dietary changes.

Tertiary prevention involves actions taken to contain or retard damage once a disease has progressed beyond its early stages. An example of tertiary prevention is the use of radiation therapy or chemotherapy to destroy a cancerous tumor. Tertiary prevention also strives to rehabilitate people to the fullest extent possible.

Table 6.1 illustrates a comprehensive program of primary, secondary, and tertiary disease prevention for AIDS based on the national health goals established by the U.S. Department of Health and Human Services as part of its *Healthy People Campaign*. As discussed in Chapter 1, these goals are to increase the span of healthy life, to decrease the disparities in health between different segments of the population, and to provide universal access to preventive services.

We are sometimes our own worst enemies in the battle for health. In our teens and twenties, when we are developing health-related habits, we are usually quite healthy.

TABLE 6.1 Levels and Timing of Prevention for HIV/AIDS

Level	Timing		
	Primary	Secondary	Tertiary
Individual	Self-instruction guide on HIV prevention for HIV-positive people Designing an immune-healthy diet	Screening and early intervention for an uninfected, lower-risk, HIV-positive person	Seeking medical treatment to suppress the virus
Group	Parents gather to gain skills to communicate better with teens about risky behaviors	Needle exchange program for low-SES, high-risk, IV drug users	Rehabilitation programs for groups of AIDS patients
Work site	Work-site educational campaign focusing on how HIV is transmitted	Work-site safer-sex incentive program (e.g., free condoms, confidential screening)	Extending leave benefits so employees can care for HIV-positive relatives
Community	Focused media campaign to promote safe-sex behaviors	Establishing support network for HIV-positive people	Providing better access to recreational facilities for those with AIDS
Society	Enforcing felony laws for knowingly infecting another person with HIV	Enacting antidiscrimination policies for HIV-positive people	Mandating the availability of HIV medications for uninsured AIDS patients

Information from: Winett, R. A. (1995). A framework for health promotion and disease prevention programs. *American Psychologist, 50*(5), 341–350.

Smoking cigarettes, eating junk food, and avoiding exercise seem often to have no effect on health at this time, so young people have little immediate incentive for practicing good health behaviors and correcting poor health habits. Many health-enhancing behaviors are either less pleasurable or require more effort than their less healthy alternatives. If engaging in a behavior (such as eating when you are depressed) causes immediate relief or gratification, or if failing to engage in this behavior provides immediate discomfort, the behavior is difficult to eliminate.

High-risk sexual behaviors that may result in HIV or other sexually transmitted infections are a tragic example of this principle. The far-removed potential negative consequences of risky behavior too often are overshadowed by the immediate pleasures of the moment.

Compressing Morbidity

The "fountain of youth" myth is present in the histories of nearly every culture and finds its current expression in the allegedly rejuvenating elixirs, creams, and gadgets that are advertised on television, on alternative medicine Web sites, and in drugstore displays.

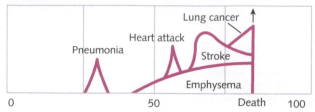

(a) Brother One

Pneumonia
Heart attack
Lung cancer
Stroke
Emphysema

0   50   Death   100

(b) Brother Two

Pneumonia
Heart attack
Stroke
Lung cancer
Emphysema

0   50   Death   100

AGE (YEARS)

FIGURE 6.5 Compression of Morbidity In focusing on the individual's quality-adjusted life years, health psychologists seek to limit the time that a person spends ill or infirm, as illustrated in this diagram of the illnesses and eventual deaths of identical twin brothers. Although the brothers carry the same disease vulnerabilities and life-span-limiting genetic clocks, the healthy lifestyle of one (b) keeps disease and disability at bay until primary aging is well advanced. In contrast, the unhealthy lifestyle of his brother (a) takes its toll at a much younger age.

Data from: Fries, J. F. (2001). Living well: Taking care of your health in the middle and later years. New York: Perseus Publishing.

Claims that people will soon live to be 200 years old because of megadoses of antioxidants, vitamins, herbs, or some other "magic bullet" have resulted in confusion about *longevity* (long duration of life). For decades, scientists have systematically investigated people's claims of having vastly exceeded the normal life span, and in every instance, the claims could not be verified. However, even without a magic bullet, people today can expect to live much longer than previous cohorts. The major diseases of our ancestors, such as polio, smallpox, tetanus, diphtheria, and rheumatic fever, have been eradicated almost completely. Even so, in many parts of the world life expectancy has begun to get shorter due to factors like obesity and opioid addiction.

In focusing on healthy life expectancy, health psychologists aim to shorten the amount of time older people spend in *morbidity* (disabled, ill, or in pain). To illustrate, consider twin brothers who, although genetically identical and exposed to the same health hazards while growing up, have had very different health experiences since adolescence. The first brother smokes two packs of cigarettes a day, is obese, never exercises, has an angry and pessimistic outlook on life, and eats foods containing high amounts of animal fat and sugar. The second brother pursues a much healthier lifestyle, avoiding tobacco and excessive stress, exercising regularly, watching his diet, and enjoying the social support of a close-knit circle of family and friends. As Figure 6.5 shows, although the two brothers have the same genetic vulnerabilities to lung, circulatory, and cardiovascular disease—and both die at the same age—the unhealthy lifestyle of the first brother dooms him to an extended period of adulthood morbidity, beginning at about age 45. In contrast, the healthier brother's lifestyle postpones adverse health events (i.e., heart attack and stroke) until much later in life. Illnesses he contracts are likely to be less severe, and recovery will be quicker. In some cases, the illness, such as lung cancer, may be "postponed" right out of his life.

Promoting Healthy Families and Communities

The factors that influence health are not limited to individuals. Preventive health psychology research is increasingly focused on the various external systems that also promote or impair our well-being. Chief among these systems are the family and the community.

Family Behaviors

Health habits are typically acquired from parents and other family members who model health behaviors. When children see others routinely caring for their health, social learning pushes them to follow suit. Establishing good health habits before adolescence is vital for two reasons. First, adolescent egocentrism and rebellion often lead young people to engage in high-risk behaviors. This is especially dangerous for adolescents with chronic illnesses, who may ignore special diets, medication, and other treatments unless they have already incorporated these habits into daily life (Dean, Walters, & Hall, 2010). Second, epigenetic factors in childhood come into play, such that people who have poor health during childhood are at risk throughout their lives, even if their environmental circumstances later improve (see Chapter 3).

In addition to healthy behaviors, children also acquire expectancies about risky behaviors by observing family members, especially older siblings. Rena Repetti and her colleagues (Repetti, Taylor, & Seeman, 2002) have argued that certain family characteristics start a "cascade of risk" that begins early in life by "creating vulnerabilities (and exacerbating preexisting biological vulnerabilities) that lay the groundwork for long-term physical and mental health problems" (p. 330). These risky family characteristics fall into two categories: *overt family conflict,* manifested in frequent episodes of anger and aggression; and *deficient nurturing,* including relationships that are unsupportive, cold, and even neglectful. Other family variables linked with risky health-related behaviors among adolescents include absence of parental supervision, absence of the father, homelessness, coercive parent–child relationships, and parental drug and alcohol use (Bracizewski, 2010).

Health System Factors

Historically, medicine focused on treating conditions that had already developed (secondary and tertiary care), and early warning signs of disease and contributing risk factors often went undetected. Doctors were oriented toward correcting conditions rather than preventing future problems, and people who were not experiencing symptoms of illness were not encouraged to seek advice regarding potential risk factors.

Today's health care system puts much greater emphasis on prevention, and defines *health* as not just the absence of disease, but as thriving. In fact, as discussed further in Chapter 13, the World Health Organization (WHO) defines a *health care system* as "all activities whose primary purpose is to promote, restore, or maintain health (World Health Organization, 2006). Similarly, in 2010 when the U.S. Congress passed the Patient Protection and Affordable Care Act (ACA) (often called "Obamacare"), the Act's cornerstone was stated as "strengthening health care." This multifaceted legislation is built around the objective of emphasizing primary and preventive care linked with community prevention services (Calsyn & Rosenthal, 2013).

The best-known facet of the ACA is undoubtedly its overhaul of the health insurance system, making insurance more accessible for many, adding regulations to make insurance policies more consistent, and instituting the *individual mandate*—a requirement for most Americans to have insurance or pay a tax penalty. In 2010, the Congressional Budget Office estimated that without successful implementation of the ACA, the number of Americans without health insurance—44 million at that time—was expected to increase to about 54 million in 2019 (Congressional Budget Office, 2010). People who lack medical insurance receive about half of the medical care of people with insurance, which leaves them sicker and likely to die at a younger age. Because they cannot afford regular doctor visits and screening that could catch serious illnesses early, such as cancer and heart disease, many uninsured patients are diagnosed too late to affect the outcome. Although Hispanics, African Americans, and Native Americans are at much higher risk of being uninsured than non-Hispanic whites, the uninsured don't fit any stereotype. They come from every race and ethnic group, every community, and every walk of life (see *Interpreting Data: Which Americans Are Uninsured?*).

Interpreting Data...

Which Americans Are Uninsured?

The percentage of Americans without health insurance declined sharply after the passage of the Affordable Care Act (ACA), and declined even more so in 2014, the first full year after the ACA's *individual mandate*—its provision requiring most Americans to carry health insurance—took effect (Goldstein, Clement, & Guo, 2015). For this reason, we focus here on 2014 data as displayed in the pie graphs of Figure 6.6.

An important question to ask when encountering data is, "Which population(s) are you referring to?" As indicated in the title, Figure 6.6 refers to nonelderly persons: infants, children, and adults from birth through age 64. This makes sense considering that U.S. citizens age 65 and older are eligible for low-cost insurance under the federal Medicare program. But, you might ask, what about noncitizens? The data in the graphs are from the U.S. Census Bureau, which counts all U.S. residents including citizens, legal noncitizen residents, and undocumented immigrants. Thus, the graphs in Figure 6.6 tell us about all American residents who were under age 65 in 2014.

Now that we have clarified who is included in the data graphs, would it surprise you to know that nearly 33 million people living in the United States, or 10.4% of the population, went without health insurance in 2014? Who were they? Would you guess that most of them belonged to certain groups? As with many statistics, it is easy to leap to conclusions based on lack of information, political bias, or attitudes about people who are different than you.

Here is a more detailed profile of the uninsured people ages 0–64 in the United States.

- A large majority of the uninsured (79%) are U.S. citizens.
- The majority of the uninsured come from working families. More than 70% have at least one full-time worker in their family, and another 12% have one or more part-time workers. Uninsured workers are more likely to have low-wage or blue-collar jobs and to work for small firms or in service industries.
- People with low incomes are at the highest risk of being uninsured (in 2015, the federal poverty level [FPL] for a family of four was $24,250). More than 80% of those without health insurance are in low- to mid-income families (incomes between 100% and 400% of the FPL).
- Although 45% of the uninsured are non-Hispanic whites, people of color have a higher risk of being uninsured than non-Hispanic whites. People of color account for 40% of the total population of the United States but for over half of the uninsured. This disparity in coverage is particularly high for Hispanics, who comprise 19% of the population but 34% of those who are uninsured. Hispanics and non-Hispanic blacks have higher uninsured rates (20.9% and 12.7%, respectively) than whites (9.1%).

FIGURE 6.6 Characteristics of the Nonelderly Uninsured As with many statistics, people often harbor misconceptions about the uninsured. As one example, the majority of uninsured U.S. residents ages 0–64 are in families with one or more full-time workers.

Data from: Kaiser Family Foundation. (2015). Key facts about the uninsured population.

Since becoming law, the Affordable Care Act (ACA) has largely succeeded in delivering on its main promises. First, under the new law the number of uninsured nonelderly Americans decreased from 44 million in 2010 to less than 28 million in early 2017 (Auter, 2018). Second, about 85% of those who signed up during the ACA enrollment period qualified for federal subsidies, which reduced the cost of their insurance by an average of 76% (Sanger-Katz, 2014). Third, the ACA has contributed to a significant slowdown in health care spending. Across most measures, including the cost of hospital care, prescription drugs, and per capita Medicare spending, the national cost of health care has been increasing by smaller margins than it had in the years before the ACA was passed (Altarum Institute, 2014).

However, the ACA continues to have its detractors, including those who point to the economic consequences of the new law's requirement that insurers provide a wider range of benefits and cover people with pre-existing conditions. This has meant that insurance premiums have actually increased for some people who already had coverage. To keep insurance premiums affordable, enrollment in *high-deductible health* plans *(HDHPs)* has also increased. HDHPs are of concern because they create their own financial barrier and can result in personal financial hardships when care is needed.

Efforts to repeal or fundamentally alter the ACA are threatening the gains of recent years. In December 2017, Congress passed a tax reform bill that effectively eliminated the individual mandate beginning in 2019. Without this mandate, experts predict that 4 million more people will go without insurance in 2019, and insurance premiums will increase 10% each year (Sarly, 2017).

Being uninsured can have a devastating impact on a person's health and financial security. Medical bills can wipe out a family's savings, and fear of high bills is a barrier that prevents many uninsured people from seeking health care. One in five uninsured adults in 2016 went without needed medical care due to cost (Kaiser Family Foundation, 2017). Because people without health coverage are less likely to receive regular outpatient care, they are more likely to be hospitalized and to experience declines in their overall health. As an example, only 16% of uninsured women have mammograms each year, compared with 42% of insured women (Morbidity and Mortality Weekly Report [MMWR], 2012). Is it any wonder that uninsured women are 40% more likely to be diagnosed with late-stage breast cancer and 40% to 50% more likely to die from breast cancer than insured women?

Robert Gauthier/Getty Images

Health System Barriers Not having health insurance can have a devastating impact on a person's health and financial security. People without insurance are less likely to have a regular doctor, more likely to rely on emergency room care, and more likely to have chronic health problems.

Jim West/Newscom/ZUMAPress/Detroit/Michigan/U.S.

Health Insurance Reform in the United States In Detroit, Michigan, a volunteer "navigator" helps a young man sign up for insurance under the Affordable Care Act.

Community Influences

The community can be a powerful force for promoting or discouraging healthy living. People are more likely to adopt health-enhancing behaviors when these behaviors are promoted by community organizations, such as schools, governmental agencies, and the health care system. As one example, psychologists at the University of Minnesota asked 17 school districts to start high school at 8:30 a.m. or later, citing evidence that teen sleep deprivation is associated with poorer cognitive processing, increased anxiety, depression, the use of drugs to stay awake or go to sleep, and driving accidents (Mueller, Bridges, & Goddard, 2011). Three years of data showed that the later start times resulted in increased likelihood of students eating breakfast, improved attendance, less tardiness, greater alertness in class, a calmer school atmosphere, fewer disciplinary referrals to the principal, and fewer student trips to counselors and the school nurse for stress-related and other health problems (National Sleep Foundation, 2013).

Social pressures, however, can exert powerful negative influence, as evidenced by drug abuse—particularly of alcohol and marijuana—which is more prevalent among college students than among their peers who do not attend college (Johnston, O'Malley, Miech, Bachman, & Schulenberg, 2015). Surveys reveal that binge drinking among college students also is associated with other social risk factors. For some students, the excitement of being together in a largely unsupervised environment seems to trigger such risky behaviors.

Fortunately, most peer-inspired risk taking is a short-lived experiment that is outgrown before irreversible, long-term consequences are felt. Although drinking rates increase significantly in the transition from high school to the college freshman year, heavy drinking declines as students grow older, assume increased responsibilities, and display a pattern called *maturing out* (Bartholow, Sher, & Krull, 2003).

Community Health Education

AP Images/AL HARTMANN

Culturally Competent Health Care A physician assistant and nurse examine a member of the Navajo Nation near Bluff, Utah.

There is a greater emphasis on health promotion today than at any other time in history. Substantial effort is devoted to shaping the public's views on health issues through educational campaigns in advertisements, on public transportation, in magazines and newspapers, and on television, radio, and Web sites. An excellent example of community health education is embodied in *Promotores de salud* ("promoters of health")—a 2011 initiative of the U.S. Department of Health and Human Services Office of Minority Health (OMH). Under the Affordable Care Act, an estimated 9 million Latinos have or will obtain health insurance. *Promotores* are lay health workers, patient navigators, and health advocates who work in Spanish-speaking communities in a culturally competent and linguistically appropriate fashion to promote health care delivery, education and prevention—particularly for groups that have been historically underserved (Office of Minority Health [OMH], 2015).

The importance of campaigns such as this is revealed in research controversies over how information should be presented—for example, should campaigns for the prevention of sexually transmitted infections (STIs) concentrate on both safer sex and abstinence? According to the *precede/proceed model*, planning for health education begins by identifying specific health problems in a targeted group (Yeo, Berzins, & Addington,

2007). Next, lifestyle and environment elements that contribute to the targeted health problem (as well as those that protect against it) are identified. Then, background factors that predispose, enable, and reinforce these lifestyle and environmental factors are analyzed to determine the possible usefulness of health education and other interventions. During the final implementation phase, health education programs are designed, initiated, and evaluated.

Let's examine how the precede/proceed model would apply to a health education campaign for lung cancer. First, health psychologists would identify the target group for the intervention. Next, they would investigate environmental factors that might affect the target group because the disease might result from unhealthy working or living conditions in which people are exposed to hazardous pollutants. In addition, health psychologists would consider behavioral, psychological, and social factors. They would begin by determining who smokes. When did they start smoking? Why? Researchers have found that smoking typically begins during adolescence in response to social pressures (Rodriguez, Romer, & Audrain-McGovern, 2007). These pressures include the imitation of family members, peers, and such role models as well-known celebrities and athletes. Many adolescents find it very difficult to resist social pressure. Being accepted by one's peers is an extremely important source of reinforcement. There are also strong enabling factors: Cigarettes are generally very easy to obtain, and sanctions against smoking are minimal.

Having identified a major factor contributing to the health problem (i.e., smoking contributing to lung cancer), health psychologists would design a health education program to counteract smoking. For example, if social pressure was found to be a major factor, they might design a health education program that focuses on improving the ability of teens to resist social pressure to smoke. Such programs might involve role models urging teens not to smoke, adopting antismoking policies in public buildings, imposing stricter sanctions against the sale of cigarettes, levying higher taxes on cigarettes, or a combination of these measures.

Antismoking Campaign in China Although the number of smokers in the United States has decreased recently, the reverse seems to be occurring in other countries, such as China. Everyone, no matter what their native language, can understand billboards such as this one.

How Effective Are Health Education Campaigns?

Researchers have found that education campaigns that merely inform people of the hazards of health-compromising behaviors are typically ineffective in motivating people to change long-held health habits (Kaiser Foundation, 2010). For example, antismoking messages and other drug education programs by themselves often have little effect—or a negative effect. Simply finding out that one's lifestyle is not as healthy as it could be often is insufficient, because many people believe they are invulnerable to the negative consequences of their risky behavior.

Michael Siluk/Alamy Stock Photo

Message Wording Makes a Difference In the culture of the Ojibwe tribe, tobacco use is a ceremonial tradition. A public billboard acknowledges that tradition while discouraging smoking in other contexts.

Multifaceted community campaigns generally work better than "single-shot" campaigns. For example, a long-term antismoking campaign that combined school intervention programs with communitywide mass media messages resulted in a significant decrease in smoking, a shift in viewing smoking as more addictive and less socially desirable among seventh through eleventh graders (Chassin, Presson, Sherman, & Kim, 2003). As another example, a skin cancer prevention program focused on children using sunscreen, wearing hats and sunglasses, and following other sun-protection habits during swimming lessons at 15 swimming pools in Hawaii and Massachusetts. In addition to targeting the children, the Pool Cool program, which combined education, interactive activities, and environmental changes (providing free sunscreen, portable shade structures, and sun safety posters), was a randomized, controlled trial intervention targeting parents, lifeguards, and swim instructors. Compared with children in a control group at 13 other pools who received a bicycle and inline skating safety intervention, children in the intervention group showed significant positive changes in use of sunscreen and shade, overall sun-protection habits, and a reduced number of sunburns (Glanz, Geller, Shigaki, Maddock, & Isnec, 2002). Similarly, other researchers have found that multicomponent sun-protection behavior interventions are particularly effective with adult beachgoers (Pagoto, McChargue, & Fuqua, 2003).

Community programs are on the rise and have several advantages. First, they can promote changes that are difficult for individuals to accomplish, such as creating bike paths and other public exercise facilities or banning smoking in public buildings. Second, unlike interventions that concentrate on high-risk individuals, community programs are directed to a broader cross section of the public, potentially reaching those in the lower- to moderate-risk categories earlier in the process of disease. Third, community programs combine information with the social support of friends, neighbors, and family members.

One of the earliest community campaigns was initiated for residents of a rural county in Finland with a very high incidence of coronary heart disease (Puska, 1999). Launched in 1972 by the Finnish government and the World Health Organization, the North Karelia Project had one major goal: to reduce smoking, cholesterol, and blood pressure levels through informational campaigns. When the program began, the Finns had the highest coronary mortality rates in the world. The initial five-year follow-up study demonstrated a 17.4% reduction in these coronary risk factors among men and an 11.5% reduction among women. In addition, coronary disability payments had declined by approximately 10%, much more than enough to pay for the entire community program. Most significant of all, over three decades, deaths among the working-age population from heart disease dropped by 82% (Templeton, 2004).

Message Framing

An important factor in the effectiveness of health education is how information is worded, or *framed*. Health messages generally are framed in terms of the benefits associated with a particular preventive action or the costs of failing to take preventive action (Salovey, 2011).

Gain-framed messages focus on the positive outcome from adopting a health-promoting behavior ("If you exercise regularly, you are likely to look and feel better") or on avoiding an undesirable outcome ("If you exercise regularly, you decrease your risk of obesity and a number of chronic diseases"). **Loss-framed messages** emphasize the negative outcome from failing to take preventive action ("If you don't exercise, you increase the risk of an undetected, potentially life-threatening disease"). Loss-framed messages also may emphasize missing a desirable outcome ("If you don't exercise, you will miss out on the extra energy that physical fitness brings").

Tailored Messaging A growing body of literature attests to the importance of tailoring health messages and interventions to individual characteristics of participants instead of giving everyone identically framed information. For instance, the effectiveness of gain- or loss-framed messages appears to vary with whether a person tends to be *avoidance oriented* or *approach oriented*. Approach-oriented individuals are highly responsive to rewards and incentives, while avoidance-oriented individuals are highly responsive to punishments or threats. In one study, Traci Mann and her UCLA colleagues (Mann, Sherman, & Updegraff, 2004) found that when college students received loss-framed messages promoting dental flossing, avoidance-oriented students reported taking better care of their teeth, and when given a gain-framed message, approach-oriented students reported flossing more than avoidance-oriented students. These results suggest that tailoring health messages to individuals based on their dispositional motivations is an effective strategy for promoting behavior change.

Loss-Framed Fear Appeals Are fear-arousing messages effective in promoting attitude and behavior change? To find out, Irving Janis and Seymour Feshbach (1953) compared the effectiveness of messages that aroused various levels of fear in promoting changes in dental hygiene. Messages that aroused moderate levels of fear were more effective than more extreme messages in getting junior high school students to change their dental hygiene habits. In accounting for their results, the researchers suggested that individuals and circumstances differ in the optimal level of fear for triggering a change in attitude or behavior. When this level is exceeded, people may resort to denial or avoidance coping measures.

A key factor in determining the effectiveness of threatening health messages is the recipient's perceived behavioral control. Before they can be persuaded, people must believe that they have the ability to follow through on recommendations. In one study, Carol Self and Ronald Rogers (1990) presented highly threatening messages regarding the dangers of sedentary living with or without information indicating that the subjects could perform the health-enhancing behavior (such as exercise) and succeed in enhancing their health. What did they the researchers find? Threat appeals worked only if participants were convinced that they could cope with the health threat; attempts to frighten participants without reassuring them were ineffective.

Heike Mahler and her colleagues (Mahler, Kulik, Gibbons, Gerrard, & Harrell, 2003) found college-age beachgoers were particularly responsive to an educational campaign promoting sunscreen use and other sun-protection behaviors when it focused on the dangers of sun exposure to each participant's appearance. The intervention began with a

gain-framed message A health message that focuses on attaining positive outcomes or avoiding undesirable ones by adopting a health-promoting behavior.

loss-framed message A health message that focuses on a negative outcome from failing to perform a health-promoting behavior.

RICHARD B. LEVINE/Newscom

These young protesters recognize the power of tailored messaging—in this instance, tobacco advertising that targets their demographic group.

12-minute slide presentation that included graphic photos of extreme cases of wrinkles and age spots. Afterward, each participant's face was photographed with an ultraviolet (UV) ray–filtered camera that accentuated brown spots, freckling, and other existing skin damage from UV exposure. A one-month follow-up indicated that the intervention resulted in a significant increase in sun-protective behaviors and substantially lower reported sunbathing.

However, scare tactics that arouse tremendous fear, such as photographs of grossly decayed or diseased gums, tend to upset people. As a result, such messages may backfire and actually *decrease* people's likelihood of changing their beliefs and hence their behavior (Beck & Frankel, 1981). Such messages increase people's anxiety to such a level that the only coping avenue that they perceive as available is a refusal to face the danger.

In conclusion, research on the framing of health messages reveals a basic pattern: Gain-framed messages are effective in promoting prevention behaviors, while loss-framed ones are effective in promoting illness-detection (screening) behaviors (Salovey, 2011).

Cognitive-Behavioral Interventions

cognitive-behavioral interventions Health interventions that focus on the conditions that elicit health behaviors and the factors that help to maintain and reinforce them.

Cognitive-behavioral interventions are those that focus on the conditions that elicit health behaviors and the factors that help to maintain and reinforce them (Dobson, 2010). Typically, the health psychologist identifies a target behavior to be modified (e.g., consumption of soft drinks), measures the current status of the behavior (including the context in which it occurs and its antecedent cues), and examines its consequences. Many programs use **self-monitoring** as the initial step in promoting behavior change. In our earlier example, doing so might include keeping track of the number of soft drinks consumed each day, the situation and time of day, and any cravings or other feelings that occurred before and after each beverage was consumed. In this way, the individual can get a clearer sense of the target behavior, including its initial baseline rate of occurrence. This allows the establishment of specific goals for the intervention—goals that are both objective and realistic. Interestingly, many people find that self-monitoring itself produces a change in the target behavior (Quinn, Pascoe, Wood, & Neal, 2010).

self-monitoring People keeping track of their own target behavior that is to be modified, including the stimuli associated with it and the consequences that follow it.

Two key aspects in cognitive-behavioral interventions are *stimulus-control* and *contingency contracting*. Habitual behaviors such as cigarette smoking and overeating are often triggered by environmental signals that communicate to the brain that certain behaviors will be followed by reinforcement; these signals are known as **discriminative stimuli**. For example, the sights and smells of a batch of cookies in the oven can serve as discriminative stimuli for overeating. And the various sights, sounds, and smells a former smoker encounters upon entering a noisy bar can be potent discriminative stimuli that trigger the urge to light up.

discriminative stimuli Environmental signals that certain behaviors will be followed by reinforcement.

One reason self-monitoring is an effective step in modifying behavior is that it points out the various discriminative stimuli that have come to control the target behavior. **Stimulus-control interventions** aimed at modifying a health behavior involve two strategies: removing discriminative stimuli for the behavior from the environment, and establishing new discriminative stimuli signaling the availability of reinforcement for healthier response choices. For people who are trying to reduce snacking on calorie-dense, low-nutrient junk foods, a good first step is to eliminate the presence of such foods in their homes and to avoid activities that trigger snacking. One such activity is

stimulus-control intervention A behavioral intervention aimed at modifying the environmental discriminative stimuli that control a target behavior by signaling its reinforcement.

watching television, particularly since exposure to food advertising is likely. In one study, elementary school children received a snack while they watched a cartoon that contained either food advertising or advertising for other products. Children consumed 45% more snack foods when exposed to food advertising (Harris, Bargh, & Brownell, 2009). Turning off the television can be an effective step in gaining control over this type of automatic, mindless snacking. Another effective strategy to gain stimulus control over eating behavior is to restrict its occurrence to one location, say, at the dining room table. As we'll see in Chapter 8, researchers have found that many people who struggle to control unhealthy eating behaviors are especially sensitive to food-related discriminative stimuli.

However, it is not always possible to completely eliminate all discriminative stimuli that have become associated with a target behavior. A former professor of mine had successfully quit a 20-year smoking habit until he took a cross-country trip as a passenger on a train. When he returned from his trip, he had resumed smoking, complaining that the urge to smoke while he was aboard the train was irresistible. "The last time I took a train ride," he lamented, "I was still a smoker." To forestall this type of occurrence, many **relapse prevention** programs deliberately bring participants into contact with discriminative stimuli that are likely to evoke the target behavior. Doing so gives participants the opportunity to learn and practice coping skills that increase their feelings of self-efficacy and decrease the likelihood of lapsing into old and unhealthy patterns of behavior.

People who are striving to change a health behavior may choose to enter into a **contingency contract**, a formal agreement with another individual, such as a therapist, regarding the consequences of target behaviors. The agreement establishes the specific reinforcements or punishments that will be contingent on the participant's behavior. For example, a person who wants to quit smoking might deposit a sum of money and arrange to receive the price of a pack of (unsmoked) cigarettes as a reward for each successful day of not smoking. A contingency contract might also specify that each occurrence of an unwanted target behavior will result in a monetary fine.

relapse prevention Training in coping skills and other techniques intended to help people resist falling back into old health habits following a successful behavioral intervention.

contingency contract A formal agreement between a person attempting to change a health behavior and another individual, such as a therapist, regarding the consequences of target behaviors.

Promoting Healthy Workplaces

Occupational health psychologists are leading the way in designing healthy workplaces. Four dimensions of healthy work have been identified: *stress, work–family relations, violence prevention,* and *relationships at work* (Quick & Quick, 2004). Because job stress is a health epidemic in this country, psychological research and intervention are vital tools for promoting the health of workers. Increasingly, insurers are recognizing that the causes of disabilities in the workplace are shifting from injuries to job stress.

The workplace has a profound psychological effect on all aspects of our lives and on the lives of our family members. For instance, job stressors may result in family social interactions that are less sensitive and supportive and more negative and conflicted. Such interactions can, in turn, adversely affect children's biological responses to stress, emotional regulation, and social competence (e.g., Perry-Jenkins, Repetti, & Crouter, 2000). Two behavioral *crossover effects* have been observed between a worker's experiences of job stress and the well-being of other family members. *Negative emotion spillover* occurs when work-related frustrations contribute to greater irritability, impatience, or other negative behaviors at home. *Social withdrawal* occurs when one or more working adult parents or caregivers withdraw behaviorally and emotionally from family life following especially stressful days at work.

In recent decades there has been a significant shift in how we think about the relationship between work and family life; specifically, the issue of *work–life balance* has attracted significant attention. This shift in thinking occurred between the 1960s and 2000, a time when the labor force participation rates of women increased steadily (see Figure 6.7). This workforce trend persisted despite several economic downturns and became increasingly diverse, with more Hispanic, Asian, and African American women pursuing full-time career jobs than ever before. As employers and governmental agencies began to recognize that all employees face complex challenges in balancing work and family roles, these changing views triggered an explosion of work–life or work–family research.

Among the most consistent findings of this research is the fact that in the United States, many employees find little support and have little say in the policies of work that affect them and their families. Consequently, they are left on their own to arrange child care, balance work schedules, stave off work stress, and so forth. The 1993 Family and Medical Leave Act (FMLA) helps some workers by protecting their jobs as they care for new babies and for family members who are ill, but many workers are not covered by this legislation, and FMLA does not provide for income to replace lost time at work. Moreover, FMLA applies only to immediate family—a newborn or adopted child, or a parent or spouse (including spouses in legal same-sex marriages) with a serious health condition.

A healthy workplace can be threatened by violence, an issue that continues to receive considerable media attention. By some estimates, homicide has become the second-leading cause of occupational injury death, exceeded only by motor vehicle deaths. Most of these deaths occur during robberies, but about 10% can be attributed to aggrieved coworkers or former employees. Nearly 2 million American workers report having been victims

FIGURE 6.7 Women's Labor Force Participation Rate, 1950–2015 and Projected to 2024 Between the 1960s and 2000, the workforce participation rates of women increased steadily, leading to an explosion of research on the issue of work-life balance.

Data from: Toossi, M., & Morisi, T. L. (2017). Women in the workforce before, during, and after the great recession. Spotlight on Statistics. U.S. Bureau of Labor Statistics.

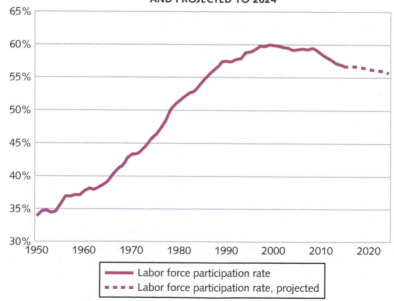

WOMEN'S LABOR FORCE PARTICIPATION RATE, 1950–2015 AND PROJECTED TO 2024

— Labor force participation rate
••••• Labor force participation rate, projected

of workplace violence each year (U.S. Department of Labor, 2015). A number of factors increase a worker's risk of being a victim of violence, including contact with the public; exchange of money; delivery of passengers, goods, or services; having a mobile workplace; working with unstable or volatile people; and working alone, late at night, and in high-crime areas (Occupational Safety and Health Administration [OSHA], 2016).

Work-Site Wellness Programs

The workplace is an ideal site for promoting health, for several reasons. First, workers find such programs convenient to attend. Some employers even permit their employees to participate in prevention programs during the workday. In addition, the workplace offers the greatest opportunity for continuing contact, follow-through, and feedback. Finally, coworkers are available to provide social support and help motivate each other during difficult moments. The same is true of wellness programs on university and college campuses.

Work-site programs emerged rapidly with the advent of the wellness movement during the 1980s. In the United States today, more than 80% of organizations with 50 or more workers offer some sort of health-promoting program. Work-site wellness programs offer a variety of activities, including weight management, nutrition counseling, smoking cessation, preventive health screenings, educational seminars, stress management, lower back care, fitness centers, immunization programs, and prenatal programs (see Figure 6.8).

At the heart of the wellness movement was the realization that preventing disease is easier, cheaper, and far more desirable than curing disease. Case in point: the H1N1 vaccination campaign on college campuses during the 2009–2010 flu season. Worldwide, health care costs have risen from about 3% of world gross domestic product (GDP) in 1948 to about 10% today (World Health Organization, 2015b). The United States currently spends 17.9% of its GDP on health care (Centers for Medicare and

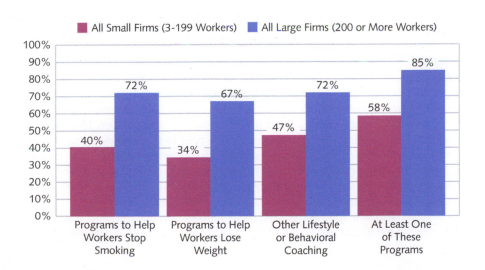

FIGURE 6.8 Percentage of Employers Offering Various Types of Health Promotion Programs Among firms offering health benefits, 52% of large companies provide workers the opportunity—and financial incentive—to complete a health risk assessment covering their medical history, health status, and lifestyle, along with access to biometric screening of body weight, cholesterol, blood pressure, stress, and nutrition. Of large firms today, 85% offer programs in smoking cessation, weight management, and/or behavioral or lifestyle coaching.

Data From: Kaiser Family Foundation (2017). 2017 Employer Health Benefits Survey.

Medicaid Services, 2018), and an ever-increasing proportion of these costs has been passed along to both employers and employees. According to a William B. Mercer study, 97% of corporate health benefits costs are spent on treating preventable conditions such as cardiovascular disease, lower back problems, hypertension, stroke, bladder cancer, and alcohol abuse (Arnst, 2009). Employers have realized that work-site programs that are even modestly successful in improving employees' health can result in substantial savings.

Are such programs effective? A large number of careful studies reveal that they are. The cost of the programs is more than offset by reductions in work-related injuries, absenteeism, and worker turnover. The U.S. surgeon general's *National Prevention Strategy* (Office of the Surgeon General, 2011) concluded that medical costs are significantly reduced by $3.27 and worker absenteeism costs by $2.73 for every dollar spent on work-site wellness programs. Clearly, prevention is the best buy when it comes to health.

POSITIVE PSYCHOLOGY AND THRIVING

In 2001, the American Psychological Association (APA) modified its 60-year-old mission statement to include the word *health* for the first time. Over 95% of the organization's membership endorsed the bylaw change, underscoring its awareness that within each person are not just physical and psychological elements that contribute to illness and disability, but also other elements that contribute to health, wellness, and thriving. The bylaw change was part of APA's Healthy World Initiative, which aligned with the **positive psychology** movement described in Chapter 1 to promote a *strength-based, preventive approach* to research and interventions rather than psychology's more traditional approach of attacking problems after they have occurred (Seligman, 2002). As APA President Norine Johnson (2004) stated, "We must bring the building of strength to the forefront in the treatment and prevention of illness, for the promotion of wellness and health" (p. 317).

positive psychology The study of optimal human functioning and the healthy interplay between people and their environments.

This new emphasis has generated an upswing in research on such topics as personal growth, positive affect, optimism, meaning, gratitude, spirituality, and resilience; their relationship to health; and their potential for interventions that promote healing and health (Korb, 2015). No single term has been accepted as the best way to describe the co-occurrence of human strengths in the positive psychology literature, as is the case with *comorbidity* when multiple states of disease occur simultaneously. The terms *flourishing* and *psychological capital* have been used to refer to the combined effects of hope, optimism, self-efficacy, and resilience to predict wellness and success in the workplace (Luthans, Avolio, Avey, & Norman, 2007). Other researchers have recently used the term *covitality* to describe the relations among the positive traits of well-being, self-confidence, and general health among college students (Jones, You, & Furlong, 2013).

A central theme of the positive psychology movement is that the experience of adversity, whether physical or psychological in nature, can sometimes yield benefits, as it did for

Sara Snodgrass, whom we met at the beginning of the chapter. As Charles Carver (Carver and others, 2005) noted, when we experience physical or psychological adversity, there are at least four possible outcomes: (1) a continued downward slide, (2) survival with diminished capacity or impairment, (3) a gradual or rapid return to the pre-adversity level of function, and (4) the emergence of a quality that makes the person somehow better off than before.

Thriving refers to this paradoxical fourth outcome, in which adversity somehow leads people to greater psychological and/or physical well-being. This is a step beyond *resilience,* the capacity to withstand stress and catastrophe. It is the difference between bouncing back and bounding ahead. How can this be? According to neuroscientist Bruce McEwen (2011), who introduced the concept of *allostatic load,* "Under conditions of stress, one would expect a physically weakened system, but positive physiological changes can occur—often in the context of psychological thriving. In physiological terms, this translates into greater restorative processes than destructive processes at work" (p. 195). Using the analogy of athletes strengthening their muscles by first breaking them down through exercise, allowing recovery, and then repeating this pattern over time to produce muscles that are stronger and capable of doing more work, positive psychologists point to evidence that adversity can similarly trigger "psychological bodybuilding" (Pearsall, 2004).

thriving A paradoxical outcome in which adversity somehow leads people to greater psychological and/or physical well-being.

Allostasis and Neuroendocrine Health

As we saw in Chapter 4, in response to a stressor, activation of the hypothalamic-pituitary-adrenal (HPA) axis causes a change in the body's overall metabolic state. Most of the time, the cells of the body are occupied with activities that build the body (*anabolism*). When the brain perceives an impending threat or challenge, however, anabolic metabolism is converted into its opposite, *catabolism,* which breaks down tissues to be converted to energy. Catabolic metabolism is characterized by the release of catecholamines, cortisol, and other "fight-or-flight" hormones that help the body quickly mobilize energy. To counteract these neuroendocrine reactions, the parasympathetic nervous system triggers the release of anabolic hormones, including growth hormone, insulin-like growth factor (IGF-1), and sex steroids. Anabolic metabolism counters arousal and promotes relaxation, energy storage, and healing processes such as protein synthesis.

Recall from Chapter 4 that allostasis refers to the body's ability to adapt to stress and other elements of rapidly changing environments (McEwen, 2011). One measure of *physical thriving* is a fluid allostatic system that flexibly shifts from high to low levels of sympathetic nervous system arousal, depending on the demands of the environment. Catabolic hormones, for instance, are essential to health over the short term. However, when people are in a constant state of arousal, prolonged elevations of catabolic hormones can damage the body and promote chronic illness. As an example, repeated stress can strongly affect brain function, especially in the hippocampus, which has large concentrations of cortisol receptors (McEwen, 2011). The consequences of long-term elevations of catabolic hormones, when taken together, look very much like aging. Hypertension, wasted muscles, fatigue, and increased risk of chronic disease are common signs of both aging and chronic stress. This state, which has been called **allostatic overload**, is indicated by a predominance of catabolic activity at rest. An elevated resting level of salivary or serum

allostatic overload The consequences of long-term elevations of stress-related catabolic hormones, including hypertension, wasted muscles, ulcers, fatigue, and increased risk of chronic disease.

cortisol is one biological indicator of allostatic overload and the general functioning of the HPA system. Conversely, a predominance of anabolic hormones at rest reflects enhanced health and a low allostatic load.

Neurobiology of Resilience

Evolutionary biologists point out that the primary function of all living creatures—from single-celled organisms to humans—is to survive, reproduce, and ensure that genetic material is successfully passed to future generations. In mammals, the *need* to maintain homeostasis is essential for survival and triggers *drives* that range from regulating body temperature to getting adequate food and sleep. Threats to survival engage a host of physiological and behavioral responses meant to defend homeostasis by removing the threat if possible and coping otherwise if not (Karatoreos & McEwen, 2013). As we saw in Chapter 4, in some animals, and especially in humans, internally generated threats, such as ruminating on problems, constantly thinking about disappointments, or blaming oneself for mishaps, also threaten homeostasis and health.

resilience The capacity of the brain and body to withstand challenges to homeostasis.

Considered in these terms, **resilience** can be thought of as the capacity of the brain and body to withstand challenges to homeostasis. The brain is the central organ of adaptation to a stressor since it determines which behavioral response is needed (e.g., fleeing or fighting). The brain also regulates the body's neuroendocrine, autonomic, and metabolic systems. Overuse or *dysregulation* of these systems can lead to allostatic overload and the development and acceleration of many chronic illnesses, from depression to cardiovascular disease.

Positive psychologists are discovering that exposure to certain events early in life may promote the development of resistance to allostatic overload. In recent years, various neural, molecular, and hormonal mechanisms related to this type of resilience have been studied extensively in humans and laboratory animals (Russo, Murrough, Han, Charney, & Nestler, 2012). These mechanisms involve the HPA axis, which regulates the stress response. This work has demonstrated that resilience is mediated by distinct biological adaptations that can blunt stress-induced HPA activation to promote normal functioning, even in the face of adversity.

Neuroendocrine adaptations are an important aspect of resilience. For example, the hormone *dehydroepiandrosterone (DHEA)*, which is normally released from the adrenal cortex along with cortisol in response to stress, has antioxidant and anti-inflammatory effects. Research studies with soldiers undergoing the extreme stress of military survival training have found that individuals with a higher DHEA-to-cortisol ratio have been shown to have fewer negative symptoms during the extreme stress of military survival training (Rasmusson, Vythilingam, & Morgan, 2003).

biological embedding The processes by which the structure and functioning of the brain are shaped by feedback from neuroendocrine systems as they are engaged as part of the body's effort to maintain homeostasis.

The brain also responds to hormonal and neural feedback from neuroendocrine systems as they are engaged as part of the body's effort to maintain homeostasis. This feedback, which has been called **biological embedding**, seems to shape the structure and function of the brain throughout life (McEwen & Gianaros, 2011). For example, animal studies have shown that chronic stress leads to a dramatic shrinkage and loss of connectivity among neurons in one region of the prefrontal cortex (PFC). Often called the "CEO [chief executive officer] of the brain," the PFC is responsible for cognitive analysis, planning, impulse control, and the modulation of intense emotions. Interestingly, neurons in a different region of the PFC often display an *increase* in complexity in response to environmental stress, thus demonstrating how early experiences seem to sculpt the brain (Liston and others, 2006). Four somewhat overlapping periods seem to be especially sensitive to the biological embedding of environmental events. These events include prenatal development, the neonatal period (the first four weeks after birth), the years of early childhood (ages 2 through 6), and adolescence (Karatoreos & McEwen, 2013).

Hormones appear to be the agents of adaptation and change in the brain's response to environmental events. They do so by altering the complexity of dendrites and the turnover of synapses in the PFC, the amygdala, and the hippocampus. For example, research studies have found that the type of maternal care experienced by rat pups affects the expression of glucocorticoid stress hormone receptors in the brain, and ultimately, the adult response of the HPA stress axis. This occurs as a result of changes in the *methylation* (see Chapter 3) of promoter genes for these receptors, ultimately changing the sensitivity of the hippocampus to cortisol and other glucocorticoid hormones (Zhang and others, 2010; Bagot and others, 2012).

Thus, researchers are beginning to understand how changes in early life experiences can alter neural circuits and environmental responses through epigenetic changes (see Figure 6.9). Multiple pathways interact to shape the brain and body's physiological and

FIGURE 6.9 The Neurobiology of Resilience
The interaction of genes and early environmental experiences can induce physiological and neurobehavioral changes that alter the way an individual responds to stressors later in life. These changes alter the structure and function of brain areas involved in cognition and the regulation of emotion, especially the prefrontal cortex (PFC), the amygdala, and the hippocampus.

Information from: Karatoreos, I. N., & McEwen, B. S. (2013). Annual research review: The neurobiology of resilience and adaptation across the life course. *Journal of Child Psychology and Psychiatry, 54*(4), 337–347.

neurobehavioral responses to early life experiences. Gradually, epigenetic research is building a picture of how the mechanisms of gene–environment interaction can alter the resilience of the brain (Russo and others, 2012).

Psychosocial Factors and Physiological Thriving

Elsewhere in this book, we have seen how psychosocial factors can modify immune functioning in ways that impair health. In this section, we focus on evidence that psychosocial factors also can have beneficial effects on immune functioning and other bodily systems.

A number of psychological variables have been linked to lowered stress hormones, enhanced immunity, lower levels of inflammation, and healthier patterns of heart rate variability in response to stress. These variables include optimism (Segerstrom & Sephton, 2010), self-esteem, and perceptions of personal competence and control over outcomes (O'Donnell, Brydon, Wright, & Steptoe, 2008), self-efficacy (Bandura, Taylor, Williams, Mefford, & Barchas, 1985), and a sense of coherence in one's life (Myrin & Lagerstrom, 2006).

Self-Enhancement

Until recently, health research focused almost exclusively on the unhealthy impact of negative emotions such as hostility, stress, and depression. Yet a growing body of evidence demonstrates that people who generally have more positive affect are healthier and live longer than those with more negative emotions (Pressman & Bowlin, 2014).

Even positive mental states that are unrealistic seem to be linked to healthier physiological functioning. This phenomenon appears to occur in people who lean toward *self-enhancement,* a tendency to recall positive over negative information, to see oneself more positively than do others, and to feel personally responsible for good outcomes. Contrary to early views in psychology, which considered this type of inflated self-perception as evidence of narcissism, self-centeredness, and poor mental health, recent studies have suggested that self-enhancement is indicative of health, wellness, and the ability to feel good about oneself. Self-enhancement has also been linked to the ability to develop and sustain relationships, to be content, and to thrive in environments that are changing or threatening (Taylor, Lerner, Sherman, Sage, & McDowell, 2003).

Erroneous but positive views of our medical condition and of the perception of our control over it appear to promote health and longevity. Although these correlational findings do not prove causality, researchers speculate that *self-enhancing cognitions* might blunt physiological and neuroendocrine responses to stress and thus lessen HPA responses to stress (Taylor and others, 2000).

In one study, Shelley Taylor and her colleagues (2003) asked 92 college students to complete the How I See Myself Questionnaire, a measure of self-enhancement on which participants rate themselves in comparison with their peers on academic ability, self-respect, and 19 other positive qualities, as well as on selfishness, pretentiousness, and 19 other negative characteristics.

In the study by Taylor and colleagues (2003), students also completed personality scales tapping psychological resources such as optimism, extraversion, and happiness. One week later, the participants reported to a UCLA laboratory, where they first provided a saliva sample for cortisol analysis and then performed several standard mental arithmetic tasks that reliably induce stress. As they did so, their heart rates and systolic and diastolic blood pressures were monitored. Following completion of the stress-challenge tasks, a second cortisol measure was taken.

The results showed that self-enhancers had lower baseline cortisol levels at the start of the study *and* lower heart rate and blood pressure responses during the stress-challenge tasks. The baseline cortisol results suggest that self-enhancement is associated with lower resting HPA axis levels, indicating a chronically healthier neuroendocrine state. The blunted heart rate and blood pressure responses suggest that positive self-perceptions help people manage acute stressors. Over time, self-enhancers may experience less stress-related wear and tear on their bodies. Equally interesting were the participants' responses to the psychological resources questionnaire, which suggested that the relationship between self-enhancement and neuroendocrine response was mediated by higher self-esteem, optimism, extraversion, stronger social support, and greater work and community involvement than that found in participants who scored low on measures of self-enhancement.

Because most of the data from such studies comes from research participants in affluent regions of the developed world, Sarah Pressman and her colleagues (Pressman, Gallagher, & Lopez, 2013) wondered if the connection between positive emotions and health was a problem only in highly developed countries. In other words, in parts of the world where people might not have adequate food or safety, are emotions still strongly tied to health? To find out, they surveyed over 150,000 people in 142 different countries, asking them about recent emotions and health concerns, as well as about their safety and access to food and shelter. Importantly, the results showed that the relationship between emotions and health not only held true globally, but also was even stronger in poorer countries.

Social Integration

Sara Snodgrass (from the chapter-opening vignette) feels that a key feature of her psychological thriving is the extent to which she has reorganized her life's priorities around her relationships with friends and family. Indeed, the importance of **social integration**—the number of social roles one participates in—has been demonstrated by studies showing that people who maintain strong social ties are more likely to retain better mental and physical health, and to live longer (Berkman, Buxton, Ertel, & Okechukwu, 2010). One recent study of over 1,000 adults between the ages of 70 and 79 found that the more social roles people engaged in, the better their lung function (Crittenden and others, 2014). Other studies have demonstrated that interventions that include some form of social support have enhancing effects on natural killer (NK) cell cytotoxicity, lymphocyte proliferation, and cell-mediated immunity (Miller & Cohen, 2001).

Social integration also applies to one's experience at work, and many companies offer their workers opportunities to promote the psychosocial aspects of thriving. Some workplaces are designed with creative play areas or "power nap" zones, offer the option

social integration The number of social roles a person participates in.

monkeybusinessimages/Getty Images

Social Engagement People who maintain strong social ties are more likely to retain health and live longer.

of working at a standing or treadmill desk, or have "bring your dog to work" policies, while others offer employee "laugh clubs," intramural sports, field trips, wilderness outings, yoga classes, or paid community service days.

Relaxation

Wakeful relaxation is also associated with decreases in negative emotions and alterations of neuroendocrine functions (Daruna, 2004). Relaxation can be achieved through meditation, listening to music, simple breathing exercises, yoga, and a variety of other simple means. For instance, research studies have shown that relaxation promotes decreased leukocyte counts, enhanced NK cell activity, and, in the case of students who regularly practice relaxation, improved immune functioning during stressful exam periods (Davidson and others, 2003). The most consistent finding associated with relaxation is an increase in secretory IgA, an anabolic hormone. Interestingly, hypnosis, which is also thought to induce relaxation, also produces reliable increases in secretory IgA (Johnson, Walker, Heys, Whiting, & Eremin, 1996).

Spirituality

Spirituality has been defined as the sense of connection to something bigger than ourselves, such as the belief in an ultimate purpose or meaning in life, and a higher calling to compassion for others (Debnam, Milam, Mullen, Lacey, & Bradshaw, 2018). Spirituality is unusual in that health psychologists have actually evaluated its efficacy using the standards of evidence-based medicine (Knabb & Vasquez, 2018) (see Chapter 2). Spiritual beliefs appear to convey several health benefits, including elevating mood (Horton & Luna, 2016), protecting against stress by promoting problem-focused coping strategies (Krok, 2015), and reducing unhealthy lifestyle behaviors and promoting better health practices (Schieman, Bierman, & Ellison, 2013). We discuss spirituality and its connection to health further in Chapter 15.

Curiosity

A growing body of research reveals that an attitude of curiosity contributes strongly to psychological thriving. *Curiosity* refers to a person's orientation or attraction to novel stimuli. Research suggests that curiosity in older people is associated with maintaining the health of the aging central nervous system. In examining the relationship between curiosity in older men and women and survival rates, researchers in one classic study found that after 5 years, those with the highest levels of curiosity survived longer than those with lower levels (Swan & Carmelli, 1996).

Curiosity may enhance healthy aging because it enables older adults to meet daily environmental and physical challenges successfully. Thus, curious older adults use active coping strategies (see Chapter 5) to approach potential problems and impediments, and in this way, manage to reduce the strain on their physical and mental resources. It seems that such individuals stand a better chance of being physically and mentally healthy in later life. In addition, people with greater curiosity tend to be more responsive to healthy opportunities for growth and cognitive stimulation. In one study, over a 3-week period, people who scored high on a measure of curiosity reported more frequent opportunities to demonstrate persistence at goals in the face of obstacles and to express gratitude to others, along with greater sensitivity to these opportunities for growth (Kashdan & Steger, 2007).

It's important to note, however, that this correlational evidence does not indicate that curiosity automatically increases older people's chances of survival; it may be simply a sign that their central nervous system is operating properly. In some individuals, age-related declines in curiosity reflect declining mental functioning. Because certain brain structures known to be involved in Alzheimer's disease also are involved in directed attention and novelty-seeking behavior, diminished curiosity may be one of the earliest signs of abnormal aging of the central nervous system.

More research is needed into the mechanisms linking curiosity to outcomes such as mortality. Several hypotheses have been suggested as to why highly curious people should live longer than their less curious peers (Kashdan & Silvia, 2008). Among these are greater *neurogenesis* from continued novel and cognitive pursuits, greater willingness to try less traditional treatments and health strategies, and the health benefits of responding to stressors as challenges rather than threats (including a less overactive hypothalamic-pituitary-adrenal axis).

Perceived Control and Self-Efficacy

A sense of control over one's life is another factor that contributes significantly to psychological thriving. In one major prospective study of personality traits and health, researchers in the Netherlands interviewed 8,723 late-middle-aged and older persons living independently or in adapted housing for elderly people (Kempen, Jelicic, & Ormel, 1997). Three measures of personality were investigated: mastery or personal control, general self-efficacy, and neuroticism (emotional instability). *Mastery* concerns the extent to which one regards one's own life changes as being under one's own control, as opposed to being fatalistically ruled. *Self-efficacy* refers to the belief that one can perform specific behaviors successfully. *Neuroticism* is related to a constant preoccupation with things that might go wrong and a strong emotional reaction of anxiety to these thoughts. Research participants with lower levels of neuroticism and higher levels of mastery and self-efficacy reported significantly higher levels of functioning and well-being.

Why should a sense of control and mastery improve health? Both behavioral and physiological explanations are viable. Those who have a greater sense of control are more likely to take action, to engage in health-promoting behaviors, and to avoid health-damaging behaviors. Because individuals with a high sense of control believe that what they do makes a difference, they behave in healthier ways. In a recent study of 3,352 people with Type 2 diabetes, patients' mastery and perceived autonomy correlated positively with their self-management skills (Raaijmakers and others, 2014). Findings such as these have significant practice implications for health care providers, since a greater sense of mastery is likely to increase patients' motivation to actively cope with and manage their health challenges. In contrast, those who feel helpless and fail to see a relationship between actions and outcomes may be more prone to illness and disease because they fail to engage in health-promoting practices or because they tend toward health-compromising behaviors ("I could get lung cancer no matter what I do, so I might as well smoke").

Having a sense of control also seems to show positive physiological effects. For instance, research has shown that people with a high sense of control have lower cortisol levels and return more quickly to baseline levels after stress (see Hansen, Blangsted, Hansen, Sogaard, & Sjogaard, 2010, for a review).

Additional evidence comes from research involving people at different socioeconomic levels. Margie Lachman and Suzanne Weaver of Brandeis University (1998) examined three large national samples of various social classes and found that for all income groups, higher perceived control was related to better health, greater life satisfaction, and fewer negative emotions. Although the results showed that, on average, those with lower incomes had lower perceived control as well as poorer health, control beliefs played a moderating role: Participants in the lowest-income group, but with a high sense of control, showed levels of health and well-being comparable to those of the higher-income groups. The results provide some evidence that psychosocial variables such as sense of control may be useful in understanding social-class differences in health.

Beyond Positive Psychology

During the decades since positive psychology was introduced, there has been a strong push to study various psychological traits, such as those considered in this chapter, that are presumed to be beneficial for well-being. Some critics have suggested that positive psychologists have not paid enough attention to the interpersonal context in which individual traits are displayed (Fincham & Beach, 2010). When the social context is considered, some studies have found that psychological traits are not inherently positive or negative but depend on the context in which they operate.

James McNulty and Frank Fincham (2012) offer the example of a person involved in a physically abusive relationship. They note that a large body of research suggests that people and relationships benefit in the following situations:

- Any negative behaviors in the relationship can be attributed to external causes rather than to dispositional traits in the offending partner.
- Partners in a relationship are optimistic about their future interactions.
- Partners forgive one another.
- Partners remember their positive experiences in the relationship and forget their more negative ones.
- Partners remain committed to one another.

However, these findings are primarily based on research conducted with participants who were not involved in abusive relationships. McNulty and Fincham suggest that applying these principles to a woman living in a physically abusive relationship may be unhealthy. Such women may, instead, benefit from (1) attributing their partner's abuse to his dispositional qualities rather than to external sources, (2) expecting the abuse to continue, (3) not forgiving the abuse, (4) remembering the abuse, and (5) being less committed to the relationship. In other words, so-called positive traits and processes sometimes can be harmful, whereas traits and processes often thought to be negative can be beneficial for well-being.

Other critics of positive psychology call for researchers to move beyond labeling traits as positive or negative. Doing so, they argue, imposes values on psychological science that influence what researchers choose to study, what they expect to find, and how they interpret results. Although science is never completely value-free, critics argue that positive psychology needs to be thought of as just plain psychology before we can have a fuller understanding of the human condition, and that psychological traits and processes are not inherently positive or negative.

In this chapter, we have explored the connection between behavior and health. We have seen how health psychology's biopsychosocial focus on strength-based approaches to prevention promotes healthier individuals, families, workplaces, and communities. As this healthier, more positive model takes hold, we are also witnessing a tipping point in which health care similarly shifts from its historical emphasis on tertiary prevention to a more balanced delivery system favoring primary prevention.

Weigh In on Health

Respond to each question below based on what you learned in the chapter. (Tip: Use the items in "Summing Up" to take into account related biological, psychological, and social concerns.)

1. When Sonia, a student in your health psychology course, moved into off-campus housing, she discovered that many of the residents smoked cigarettes. How would she explain this behavior in terms of the HBM, TPB, and TTM theories of health behavior?

2. Suppose you were asked by your college or university to design a health campaign to reduce risky health-related behaviors among students. Based on the research discussed in this chapter, what types of interventions are likely to be effective? What types of interventions are likely to be ineffective?

3. What health situation do you and other students at your college face that could benefit from greater awareness of positive psychology? How would positive psychology help make your student population healthier? What are some findings that support your response?

Summing Up

Health and Behavior

1. Most behaviors affect health in some way: for better (healthy behaviors) or worse (health-risk behaviors), directly or indirectly, and immediately or over the long term.

2. The health belief model (HBM) assumes that decisions regarding health behavior are based on (1) perceived susceptibility to a health threat, (2) perceived severity of the threat, (3) perceived benefits of and barriers to treatment, and (4) cues to action. The theory of planned behavior (TPB) maintains that the best way to predict whether a health behavior will occur is to measure people's behavioral intention, which is shaped by their attitude toward the

behavior, the subjective norm, and their perceived behavioral control.

3. The transtheoretical model (TTM) outlines five stages through which people progress in changing health-related behaviors: precontemplation, contemplation, preparation, action, and maintenance. The health action process approach (HAPA) comprises two stages: a goal-setting phase followed by a goal-pursuit phase.

Prevention

4. Primary prevention refers to actions to prevent a disease or injury from occurring. Secondary prevention involves actions to treat an illness early in its course. Tertiary prevention involves containing damage once a disease has progressed beyond its early stages. In focusing on healthy life expectancy, health psychologists aim to shorten the amount of time that older people spend disabled, ill, or in pain (morbidity).

5. Family connectedness, conflict, and nurturance are powerful influences on the individual's health behavior, as are the health habits and attitudes of other family members. At the community level, people are more likely to adopt health-enhancing behaviors when these behaviors are promoted by community organizations, such as schools, government agencies, and the health care system.

6. Message framing is a critical factor in the effectiveness of health education. Messages can be framed to emphasize either the positive outcomes from adopting a health-promoting behavior (gain-framed messages) or the negative outcomes from failing to do so (loss-framed messages). Tailoring health messages to individuals is an effective strategy for promoting behavior change. Fear-arousing messages may backfire and actually decrease a person's likelihood of adopting a certain health behavior.

7. Behavioral interventions focus on the conditions that elicit health behaviors and the factors that help to maintain and reinforce them. Self-monitoring is often the initial step in promoting behavior change. Stimulus-control interventions aimed at modifying a health behavior involve two strategies: removing discriminative stimuli from the environment and establishing new discriminative stimuli linked to reinforcement for healthier response choices.

8. Most organizations with 50 or more workers offer some form of work-site wellness program. The cost of such programs has proved to be more than offset by reductions in work-related injuries, absenteeism, and worker turnover.

Positive Psychology and Thriving

9. A central theme of the positive psychology movement—which promotes a strength-based, preventive approach to research and interventions—is that adversity can lead people to greater psychological and/or physical well-being.

10. Although catabolic hormones are essential to our short-term health, when we are in a constant state of arousal (allostatic load), prolonged elevations of catabolic hormones can weaken our immunity and promote illness.

11. Resilience can be thought of as the capacity of the brain and body to withstand challenges to homeostasis. Overuse or dysregulation of the neuroendocrine systems that maintain homeostasis can lead to the development and acceleration of many chronic illnesses, from depression to cardiovascular disease.

12. Neuroendocrine adaptations are an important aspect of resilience. The brain also responds to hormonal and neural feedback from neuroendocrine systems, as they are engaged as part of the body's effort to maintain homeostasis. This feedback (biological embedding) seems to shape the structure and function of the brain throughout life.

13. Psychosocial factors that have been linked to enhanced immunity in response to stress include self-esteem, perceptions of personal competence and control, self-efficacy, self-enhancement, social engagement, wakeful relaxation, spirituality, curiosity, and a sense of control over one's life. Curiosity may enhance healthy aging because it helps older adults use active coping strategies to meet daily challenges.

14. Critics suggest that positive psychologists should pay more attention to the interpersonal context in which individual traits are displayed. When the social context is considered, some studies have found that psychological traits are not inherently positive or negative but depend on the context in which they operate.

Key Terms and Concepts to Remember

 LaunchPad
macmillan learning   To accompany your textbook, you have access to a number of online resources, including quizzes for every chapter of the book, flashcards, critical thinking exercises, videos, and *Check Your Health* inventories. To access these resources, please visit the Straub Health Psychology LaunchPad at **launchpadworks.com**

Adam Hester/Getty Images

Exercise, Sleep, and Injury Prevention

LEARNING OUTCOMES
Once you have studied this chapter, you will be able to:
- Explain how physical activity, exercise, and fitness benefit the body and mind;
- Describe the effects of sleep and sleep disorders; and
- Identify ways in which injuries can be prevented or controlled at different stages of the life span.

At 7:00 a.m. on October 9, 2010, I had been treading water in the Pacific Ocean for nearly 20 minutes. I was about 200 meters offshore from Dig Me Beach and the small town of Kailua-Kona, on the Big Island of Hawaii. Since 1981, Kona has been the seat of the Ironman World Championship, a 140.6-mile triathlon consisting of a 2.4-mile swim, followed by a 112-mile bike ride, and finally a 26.2-mile marathon. I was holding my place at the watery starting line of this incredible event, along with 1,500 others who had qualified to be there, amid network news helicopters hovering overhead, race officials floating on paddleboards, a full-size SUV that served as a floating advertisement for the race's major sponsor, and a flotilla of outrigger canoes, pontoon boats, and other small watercraft.

As I waited for the cannon to signal the start of the race, my mind flashed on several vivid memories along my journey to earn this coveted qualifying spot—one of only 50 for men my age, worldwide. I thought of the day 27 years earlier when I took my first painful, wheezy steps as a "jogger" and reformed smoker. I had started exercising on the advice of cardiologist and running enthusiast George Sheehan, MD, who had written that people who want to improve their fitness through exercise should find a form of play: movement that, above all, is fun—so much so that the desire to smoke is pushed aside because it is incompatible with being the "runner" I wanted to be.

My memory fast-forwarded several years to the start of the 1987 Boston Marathon, a race I'd earned the right to enter by finishing the 26.2-mile Detroit Marathon in under three hours. It had taken thousands of miles run in training, dozens of pairs of running shoes, and hundreds of 5K, 10K, and half-marathon road races to earn my entry—a feat of which I was so proud that my dad made the trip with me in celebration.

My hard-won identity as a serious runner came with many benefits, including excellent physical fitness, increased self-esteem, and lower levels of stress. However, the smile that briefly crossed my face at this thought vanished at the next "scene" in my memory movie—the rather dark period in which my competitiveness as a serious runner took over my life, at times hurting the ones I loved, affecting my work, and ultimately leading to one injury after another as I pushed my running to an average of over 70 miles each week for several years. I remembered the day in 1999, when, 24 hours after partially tearing my right Achilles tendon in the USA Track and Field National Championship 10K, I painfully hobbled a mile in order to keep my four-year streak of daily running intact.

That streak soon ended, along with my ability to walk—much less run—without limping, and I began a new, medical journey, intent to find a "cure" for my foot pain. Medicine had three things to offer, only one of which proved the right prescription. It wasn't the various surgical procedures or anti-inflammatory drugs recommended by health care providers; being specialists in tertiary care, they didn't know what to make of the extremely fit, yet obviously unhealthy, guy who sought one referral after another in his quest to continue running.

No, these remedies didn't work at all. What worked was rest and, eventually, embarking on a healthier exercise regimen that was a balance of cross training, swimming, cycling, and moderate amounts of running. I thought of my first days back in the pool, trying not just to regain the swimming form I'd had as a child, but merely to make it one length of the pool without stopping! I remembered recapturing the joy and freedom I'd found as a kid riding my Schwinn Stingray around the neighborhood, but this time on a sleek new carbon fiber time-trial bike that was steeply angled to keep my upper body down in an aerodynamic position.

As the Kona Ironman cannon boomed, I "found the toes" of the swimmer just ahead of me and wondered if he, and the rest of the 1,500 triathletes wearing the gold Ironman Championship wristband, had been "watching" their own memory movies. One thing I knew was that this event would surely have a scene in my own movie's sequel.

My journey to the starting line of the Ironman World Championship highlights the potential benefits and hazards of exercise. Motivation to start exercising can promote more general lifestyle changes, as it did when it helped me quit smoking and, later, take steps to improve my eating habits. And although exercise can enhance physical functioning and reduce anxiety, it poses hazards to physical and psychological health when taken too far. This chapter explores the role that physical activity plays in people's health, along with two other important lifestyle issues: healthy sleep and injury prevention.

Exercise improves sleep, and sleep improves athletic performance and many other facets of our well-being. Today, however, more than one quarter of adults in the United States report not getting enough sleep, and about 10% experience chronic insomnia (Centers for Disease Control and Prevention [CDC], 2015c). Poor sleep undermines health in many ways, not just by draining our energy, but also by making us more prone to unintentional injuries, which are the leading causes of death from ages 1 to 44 and a leading cause of disability for all ages, regardless of gender, socioeconomic status, and race/ethnicity. Despite popular belief, most injuries are not "accidents" but instead are predictable and preventable. Promoting increased physical activity and healthier sleep habits and reducing the prevalence and consequences of injuries are the subject of this chapter.

PHYSICAL ACTIVITY, EXERCISE, AND FITNESS

physical activity Bodily movement produced by skeletal muscles that requires expenditure of energy.

physical exercise Physical activity that is planned, repetitive, and purposeful in the sense that it is intended to improve or maintain one or more aspects of physical fitness.

aerobic exercise Light- to moderate-intensity exercise performed for an extended period of time; examples include swimming, cycling, and running.

anaerobic exercise High-intensity exercise performed for short periods of time; examples include weight training and sprinting.

basal metabolic rate (BMR) The minimum number of calories the body needs to maintain bodily functions while at rest.

calorie A measure of food energy equivalent to the amount of energy needed to raise the temperature of 1 gram of water 1 degree Celsius.

Physical activity, defined as bodily movement produced by skeletal muscles that requires expenditure of energy, is natural for humans. Our bodies were designed for it, and staying active is essential for good health. Physical inactivity, on the other hand, is the fourth-leading risk factor for global mortality, each year causing an estimated 3.2 million (6%) deaths worldwide. In addition, physical inactivity is a key risk factor for noncommunicable diseases such as cardiovascular disease, cancer, and diabetes (World Health Organization [WHO], 2015b).

Physical exercise is physical activity that is planned, repetitive, and purposeful in the sense that it is intended to improve or maintain one or more aspects of physical fitness. **Aerobic exercise**, often called "cardio," is light- to moderate-intensity exercise performed for an extended period of time; examples are swimming, cycling, and running. "Aerobic," which means "living in air," refers to the use of oxygen to meet energy demands adequately during this type of exercise. This type of exercise can be contrasted with **anaerobic exercise**, such as strength training and short-distance sprinting. This type of exercise is generally performed at a higher intensity than aerobic exercise but for shorter periods of time. Any exercise lasting longer than about two minutes is largely aerobic.

Do you exercise regularly? How active should you be? About 50% to 70% of the total energy that your body burns involves the functioning of cells and vital organs. This is your **basal** (resting) **metabolic rate (BMR)**. Although BMR is not easily determined—because it depends on a number of variables, including your age, gender, current weight, and activity level—a rough estimate of your daily calorie needs to maintain your current weight can be calculated by multiplying your body weight (in pounds) by 13. About 7% to 10% of the energy that your body uses serves to break down the food you eat. The rest is the result of physical activity, including the things you have to do every day, such as showering, getting dressed, vacuuming, and engaging in leisure activities such as dancing, playing sports, and walking. The more physical activities you choose to do, the more energy you expend.

Energy expenditure is typically measured in **calories**, a measure of food energy equivalent to the amount of energy needed to raise the temperature of 1 gram of water 1 degree Celsius. Table 7.1 lists the calories burned by people in three different weight groups as those people perform different activities (Harvard Heart Letter, 2015).

TABLE 7.1 Calories Burned by 30 Minutes of Activity

This table lists the calories burned by performing 30 minutes of the following activities, listed by category (such as gym activities, training and sports activities, and home repair). In each category, activities are listed from least to most calories burned.

	125-pound person	155-pound person	185-pound person
Gym Activities			
Weight lifting: general	90	112	133
Stretching, hatha yoga	120	149	178
Calisthenics: moderate	135	167	200
Stair step machine: general	180	223	266
Circuit training: general	240	298	355
Rowing, stationary: vigorous	255	316	377
Elliptical trainer: general	270	335	400
Aerobics, step: high-impact	300	372	444
Bicycling, stationary: vigorous	315	391	466
Training and Sport Activities			
Bowling	90	112	133
Dancing: slow, waltz, foxtrot	90	112	133
Frisbee	90	112	133
Volleyball: noncompetitive, general play	90	112	133
Golf: using cart	105	130	155
Gymnastics: general	120	149	178
Horseback riding: general	120	149	178
Walking: 3.5 mph (17 min/mile)	120	149	178
Badminton: general	135	167	200
Skateboarding	150	186	222
Walking: 4.5 mph (13 min/mile)	150	186	222
Dancing: disco, ballroom, square	165	205	244
Swimming: general	180	223	266
Rollerblade skating	210	260	311
Soccer: general	210	260	311
Tennis: general	210	260	311
Basketball: playing a game	240	298	355
Bicycling: 12–13.9 mph	240	298	355
Football: touch, flag, general	240	298	355
Running: 5 mph (12 min/mile)	240	298	355
Skiing: cross-country	240	298	355
Running: 5.2 mph (11.5 min/mile)	270	335	400
Running: cross-country	270	335	400
Jumping rope	300	372	444
Running: 6 mph (10 min/mile)	300	372	444
Swimming: laps, vigorous	300	372	444
Running: 6.7 mph (9 min/mile)	330	409	488
Swimming: crawl	330	409	488
Bicycling: 16–19 mph	360	446	533
Running: 7.5 mph (8 min/mile)	375	465	555

Jayden is 20 years of age, stands 5 feet 3 inches, weighs 120 pounds, and has a moderately active lifestyle that includes 1 to 2 miles of walking to and from classes each day and a daily 30-minute yoga workout. Jayden's basal metabolic rate (BMR), which represents about 60% of the calories her body uses each day just to breathe, stay warm, and maintain other vital functions, is about 1,300 calories. Due to her lifestyle (see Table 7.1), Jayden's body needs 2,000 to 2,200 calories each day to remain healthy.

	125-pound person	155-pound person	185-pound person
Outdoor Activities			
Raking lawn	120	149	178
Gardening: general	135	167	200
Mowing lawn: push, power	135	167	200
Carrying and stacking wood	150	186	222
Digging, spading dirt	150	186	222
Laying sod/crushed rock	150	186	222
Mowing lawn: push, hand	165	205	244
Chopping and splitting wood	180	223	266
Shoveling snow by hand	180	223	266
Home and Daily Life Activities			
Sleeping	19	23	28
Watching TV	23	28	33
Reading while sitting	34	42	50
Cooking	75	93	111
Childcare: bathing, feeding, etc.	105	130	155
Food shopping with cart	105	130	155
Heavy cleaning: washing car, windows	135	167	200
Playing with kids: vigorous effort	150	186	222
Moving: household furniture	180	223	266
Moving: carrying boxes	210	260	311
Occupational Activities			
Computer work	41	51	61
Light office work	45	56	67
Sitting in meetings	49	60	72
Desk work	53	65	78
Sitting in class	53	65	78
Truck driving	60	74	89
Bartending/server	75	93	111
Operating heavy equipment	75	93	111
Being a police officer	75	93	111
Theater work	90	112	133
Welding	90	112	133
Carpentry work	105	130	155
Coaching sports	120	149	178
Construction, general	165	205	244
Firefighting	360	446	533

Data from: *Harvard Men's Health Watch*, January 2009. © 2009 Harvard University. Updated 2016. www.health.harvard.edu.

Benefits from Physical Activity

Regular physical activity is the closest thing we have to a fountain of youth. It becomes even more important as people age, promoting both physical and psychological well-being and possibly helping to slow down or even reverse many of the effects of aging. Regular exercise can reduce the risk of premature disability and many chronic illnesses, including those related to stress. Many of the benefits of physical activity are optimized when people pursue physical fitness.

How physically fit are you? **Physical fitness** has been defined as a set of attributes or characteristics that people have or achieve that relates to the ability to perform physical activity. The most important attribute is **cardiorespiratory endurance**, or *aerobic fitness,* which refers to the ability of the heart, blood vessels, and lungs to supply oxygen to working muscles during physical activity for prolonged periods of time. The amount of oxygen your body uses is referred to as *oxygen consumption* or VO_2, which stands for "volume of oxygen." As your intensity of exercise increases, VO_2 rises and eventually reaches its peak value, known as VO_2max. VO_2max, also known as *aerobic capacity,* is the measure of cardiorespiratory endurance. The other components of physical fitness include the following:

- Muscular strength—the amount of force that a muscle or group of muscles can exert against heavy resistance,

- Muscular endurance—the ability of a muscle or group of muscles to repeat a movement many times or to hold a particular position for an extended period of time,

- Flexibility—the degree to which an individual muscle will lengthen, and

- Body composition—the amount of fat in the body compared to the amount of *lean mass* (muscle and bones).

The costs of an inactive lifestyle are high. One study of more than 26,000 American adults reported that those who exercised at recommended levels paid $2,500 less in health care costs each year than those who did not exercise (Valero-Elizondo and others, 2016). Globally, physical inactivity costs $67.5 billion dollars each year in health care and lower workplace productivity (Ding and others, 2016).

Sitting too much and spending too much time watching TV and computer screens are powerful predictors of health problems. One study of nearly 2,000 middle-aged Scottish men found that those spent two or more hours a day sitting had two times the risk of myocardial infraction and other heart problems (Stamatakis, Hamer, & Dunstan, 2011). Men who spent four or more hours a day engaged in *recreational sitting* (screen-based entertainment) had higher levels of inflammation and other metabolic risk factors and were 50% more likely to die of *any* cause—even if they also exercised—than were less sedentary men!

With "sitting disease" on the rise, a growing number of businesses are outfitting their offices with *active workstations*—treadmills, standing desks, and even fit-under-the-desk elliptical trainers set up so that workers are able to use a screen and keyboard and move at the same time. Active workstations, which are not intended to be a substitute for aerobic exercise, allow users to approximately double their resting metabolism (Torbeyns, Bailey, Bos, & Meeusen, 2014).

Research has shown that a person's degree of physical fitness is an excellent predictor of not only quality of life but also life expectancy. Improving physical fitness

physical fitness A set of attributes relating to the ability to perform physical activity that includes muscular strength, endurance, flexibility, and healthy body composition.

cardiorespiratory endurance The ability of the heart, blood vessels, and lungs to supply oxygen to working muscles during physical activity for prolonged periods of time.

Active workstations, such as this treadmill desk, can give employees an alternative to "sitting down on the job"

may also help prevent age-associated diseases for healthy people and for those with chronic conditions such as cardiovascular disease (Carnethon and others, 2003); it holds true for both women (Gulati and others, 2003) and men (Kurl and others, 2003). Improving one's physical fitness can reduce the risk of death by 44% (I. M. Lee and others, 2013). In addition, improving physical fitness has a favorable influence on self-image and self-esteem and has been shown to reduce depression, anxiety, and panic syndromes (Kirkcaldy, Shephard, & Siefen, 2002). It has even been reported that while antidepressant medication may produce a more rapid initial response, exercise is just as effective at reducing depression over a period of several months (Harvard Health Publications, 2013).

Appropriately undertaken, physical exercise may be the best means available for delaying and preventing the consequences of aging. Evolutionary biologists define *aging* as an age-progressive decline in intrinsic physiological function, leading to an increase in the age-specific mortality rate (Fabian & Flatt, 2011). Aging can be influenced for the better (delaying it) or worse (accelerating it) by lifestyle factors such as diet and physical activity, regardless of the age, gender, health, or physical condition of the person who undertakes to improve physical fitness. Simply put, the body's cells age faster with a sedentary lifestyle. A recent study of nearly 1,500 participants in the Women's Health Initiative that evaluated the relationship between activity level and *leukocyte telomere length* estimated that physically inactive women were biologically older than their same-chronological-age peers by about 8 years (Shadyab and others, 2017). A sedentary lifestyle also accelerates age-related changes in physical appearance and risk of disability and disease (Castillo-Garzon, Ruiz, Ortega, & Gutierrez, 2006).

Weight Control

Preventing weight gain and actually losing weight, particularly when combined with reduced calorie intake, are notable benefits of regular physical activity. Obesity has been recognized as one of the chief threats to overall health and well-being (see Chapter 8). Sedentary lifestyles are partly to blame—nearly 80% of American adults don't get the minimum recommended amount of aerobic and muscle-strengthening physical activity (Clarke, Norris, & Schiller, 2017).

Broom and colleagues (Broom, Batterham, King, & Stensel, 2009) compared the effects of aerobic and resistance exercise on feelings of hunger and the circulating levels of appetite-regulating hormones. In the study, a group of healthy men completed three trials in a counterbalanced design: 60 minutes of treadmill running at 70% maximal oxygen uptake (aerobic exercise), a 90-minute free-weight-lifting session that included 10 different exercises, and a resting control trial in which no exercise was performed. Blood was sampled before, during, and after the exercise sessions to compare levels of three appetite-regulating hormones (ghrelin, peptide tyrosine-tyrosine [PYY], and insulin). Perceived hunger was assessed using a visual scale in which participants rated their hunger from zero (not hungry) to 15 (very hungry). The results showed that ghrelin (high levels of which stimulate hunger) was lower during both aerobic and resistance exercise than for the control. In contrast, PYY (high levels of which signal satiety) was significantly elevated after aerobic exercise compared to both resistance exercise and the resting control. These hormonal changes were accompanied by reduced feelings of hunger after both aerobic and resistance exercise compared to the control condition, with the response being slightly greater with aerobic exercise.

Although exercise is helpful in maintaining a healthy body weight, a persistent myth is that fat can be targeted for reduction from a specific area of the body (spot reduction). Advertisers exploit this common, yet mistaken, belief when hawking the latest device or pill. Most experts do not believe it is possible to reduce fat in one area by exercising that body part alone. Instead, fat is lost from the entire body as a result of diet and regular physical activity.

How much physical activity is needed? The most recent recommendation is that healthy adults between the ages of 18 and 64 years need, at minimum, moderate intensity physical activity for at least 30 minutes, five days each week, or at least 75 minutes of vigorous intensity physical activity throughout the week (WHO, 2015h). For additional health benefits, moderate intensity physical activity should be increased to about 300 minutes per week. In addition, muscle-strengthening activities should be done involving major muscle groups on two or more days each week.

Most important to maintaining vitality is aerobic exercise, in which the heart speeds up in order to pump larger amounts of blood, breathing is deeper and more frequent, and the cells of the body develop the ability to extract increasing amounts of oxygen from the blood, among other benefits (see Table 7.2). In addition, weight-bearing aerobic exercises such as walking, jogging, and racquetball help preserve muscular strength and flexibility, promote healthy body composition, and maintain bone density.

For most people, light daily activities such as shopping, cooking, and doing laundry do not count toward the guidelines. Examples of moderate-intensity exercise are brisk

---

TABLE 7.2 Health Benefits of Aerobic Exercise

- Promotes the growth of new neurons in the brain (neurogenesis)
- Decreases resting heart rate and blood pressure
- Improves regulation of blood sugar
- Increases maximum oxygen consumption (VO_2max)
- Increases strength and efficiency of the heart
- Increases slow-wave (deep) sleep
- Increases HDL (good) cholesterol and reduces LDL (bad) cholesterol
- Decreases the risk of cardiovascular disease
- Decreases obesity
- Promotes relaxation
- Decreases menstrual cycle length
- Increases longevity
- Decreases risk of some cancers
- Improves immune system functioning
- Improves mood

Information from: Mayo Clinic. (2011). Aerobic exercise: Top 10 reasons to get physical.

walking, water aerobics, ballroom dancing, and playing tennis. Examples of vigorous-intensity exercise are race walking, jogging, running, swimming laps, jumping rope, and bicycling 10 miles per hour or faster.

Protection Against Chronic Illness

osteoporosis A disease of the bones involving a loss of bone mineral density that leads to an increased risk of fracture.

Physical exercise has been demonstrated to protect against a number of chronic conditions, including **osteoporosis**, a disorder characterized by declining bone density due to calcium loss. This is especially true for those who were active during their youth, when bone minerals were accruing (Hind & Burrows, 2007). Although osteoporosis is most common in postmenopausal women, it also occurs in men, as does the protective effect of exercise. Roughly one woman in four over age 60 has osteoporosis, with European American and Asian American women being at higher risk than African American women. In the United States alone, every year osteoporosis results in more than 1 million bone fractures, the most debilitating of which are hip fractures.

In addition to increasing physical strength and maintaining bone density, regular exercise reduces an older person's risk for several of the most common chronic illnesses of adulthood: cardiovascular disease, certain cancers, diabetes, and metabolic syndrome. Exercise helps fight heart disease by strengthening the heart, increasing blood flow, keeping blood vessels open, and lowering both blood pressure and the blood pressure reaction to stress (Eijsvogels, Molossi, Duck-chul, Emery, & Thompson, 2016). Even moderate exercise, such as gardening and walking, can result in significant increases in HDL—the so-called "good cholesterol"—and decreased total serum cholesterol. Regular exercise is linked to lower triglycerides, which have been implicated in the formation of atherosclerotic plaques, as well as lower levels of low-density lipoprotein (LDL), or "bad" cholesterol, and higher levels of high-density lipoprotein (HDL) (Szapary, Bloedon, & Foster, 2003). Due to these and other benefits, people who exercise suffer only half as many heart attacks as do those who are inactive (Visich & Fletcher, 2009).

Several extensive review studies have reported that physical activity also offers protection against cancers of the colon and rectum, breast, endometrium, prostate, and lung (National Cancer Institute [NCI], 2015d). Regular physical activity may reduce cancer risk by influencing proinflammatory cytokines (Stewart and others, 2007), which, in turn, have beneficial effects in blocking the development and growth of tumor cells (Rogers, Colbert, Greiner, Perkins, & Hursting, 2008). In addition, physical activity promotes healthy immune functioning by delaying some age-related declines in white blood cells. For example, endurance-trained athletes preserve telomere length in their white blood cells—which otherwise systematically decrease in aging, sedentary adults (LaRocca, Seals, & Pierce, 2010).

metabolic syndrome (MetS) A cluster of conditions—including increased blood pressure, high blood sugar level, abdominal obesity, low HDL ("good") cholesterol level, and high triglyceride level—that occur together and increase a person's risk of heart disease, stroke, and diabetes.

Diet and exercise are especially important for people living with diabetes mellitus, as they are the best nonpharmacological means by which patients may improve and manage their blood glucose levels significantly. Sedentary behavior, measured objectively with accelerometers and heart rate monitors, and TV viewing time, measured by self-report, have been associated significantly with **metabolic syndrome (MetS)**, a cluster of conditions that occur together: increased blood pressure, elevated blood-sugar, excess body fat around the waist (abdominal obesity), low HDL cholesterol level, and high triglyceride level (a type of fat found in the blood). Those with MetS are at increased risk of diabetes, heart disease, and stroke (Thorp and others, 2010).

The risk of having metabolic syndrome is closely linked to lack of physical activity and to insulin resistance, a condition in which the body can't use insulin properly. Insulin is a hormone that helps move blood sugar into cells, where it's used for energy. Metabolic syndrome is more common in African American women and Mexican American women than in men of the same racial/ethnic groups. The condition affects white women and men about equally. Adults who report engaging in regular physical exercise—especially resistance exercises such as weight-lifting, push-ups, and sit-ups—have significantly lower prevalence estimates of MetS (Churilla, Johnson, Magyari, & Crouter, 2012). Diabetes and metabolic syndrome are discussed more fully in Chapter 10.

How does fitness help protect the body from MetS? Exercise increases insulin sensitivity (over both the short and long term), lowers blood sugar levels, reduces body fat, and improves cardiovascular function (Zisser, Sueyoshi, Krigstein, Sziglato, & Riddell, 2012). Exercise also promotes greater **metabolic flexibility**—the body's ability to switch fuel sources when it needs to, from using carbs to fats. *Metabolic inflexibility*, which occurs when the body doesn't expend as much energy as the fuel consumed could support, contributes to the development of insulin resistance and MetS (Tarpey, 2017).

metabolic flexibility The body's ability to switch fuel sources, from carbohydrates to fats, when needed.

Cognitive and Emotional Well-Being

The benefits from exercise extend to our psychological well-being. Regular exercise is associated with improved mood and elevated well-being after even a single workout (Anderson & Brice, 2011). Studies show that over time, exercise may serve as an effective buffer against anxiety and stress (Conn, 2010; Windle, Hughes, Linck, Russell, & Woods, 2010), boost self-esteem and self-efficacy (McAuley, Jerome, Marquez, Elavsky, & Blissmer, 2003), help people feel more vigor and less fatigue (Mead and others, 2010), and offer protection against depression (Daley, 2008) and anxiety (Wipfli, Rethorst, & Landers, 2008). In a massive, 21-country survey of university students, physical exercise was a "strong" and consistent predictor of life satisfaction (Grant, Wardle, & Steptoe, 2009).

The psychological benefits of physical activity are particularly pronounced among older adults who perceive high levels of stress. The four-year Montreal Aging and Health Study of adults over age 60 found that among participants with high baseline levels of perceived stress, those who frequently engaged in physical activities experienced a reduction of perceived stress over two years and fewer increases in physical health symptoms over four years (Rueggeberg, Wrosch, & Miller, 2012).

Regular exercise also predicts better cognitive functioning, including improved reaction time and memory, in both the young and the old (Hindin & Zelinski, 2012). Cognitive benefits can be observed in children as young as 7 years of age. In one study, 171 overweight children between 7 and 11 years of age were randomly assigned to three months of low-dose (20 minutes/day) or high-dose (40 minutes/day) aerobic exercise, or a no-exercise control group. Each day, the participants were transported to an after-school exercise program that included running games, jumping rope, and playing modified basketball and soccer. Neuroimaging data revealed that aerobic exercise was associated with increased prefrontal cortex activity. The prefrontal cortex plays a key role in planning, emotional regulation, and other so-called executive cognitive functions. Animal studies show that aerobic exercise also increases growth factors in the brain that lead to increased capillary blood supply to the cortex and growth of new neurons and synapses (neurogenesis), resulting in better learning and performance (Dishman and others, 2006a; Reynolds, 2009).

Neuroimaging data vividly demonstrate one benefit of aerobic exercise: increased activity in the prefrontal cortex, the part of the brain that plays a key role in planning and emotional regulation.

Figure 2 from Davis, C. L.; Tomporowski, P. D.; McDowell, J. E.; Austin, B. P.; Miller, P. H.; Yanasak, N. E.; . . . Naglieri, J. A. (2011). Exercise improves executive function and achievement and alters brain activation in overweight children: A randomized, controlled trial. *Health Psychology, 30*, 91–98. doi:10.1037/a0021766. Copyright © 2011 by the American Psychological Association. Reproduced with permission.

functional plasticity The brain's ability to move functions from damaged areas to undamaged ones.

The cognitive benefits of exercise are especially important for older adults. Regular exercise predicts better cognitive functioning and reduced risk of dementia and Alzheimer's disease among the elderly (Weinstein and others, 2012). One randomized controlled trial reported that 12 months of twice-weekly strength training improved **functional plasticity** (the brain's ability to move functions from a damaged area of the brain to other undamaged ones) in a group of senior women (Liu-Ambrose, Nagamatsu, Voss, Khan, & Handy, 2012).

Is It Ever Too Late to Begin Exercising?

The answer to the question "Is it ever too late to start exercising?" is no. Aging can be associated with declines in physical function that make it more difficult for older adults to complete regular activities, such as bathing, dressing, and cooking. Regular exercise is essential to minimizing this decline. The Centers for Disease Control and Prevention recommend that older adults get 75 to 150 minutes of moderate- to vigorous-intensity aerobic exercise each week, plus muscle-strengthening resistance activities at least twice a week. Unfortunately, only 12% of American adults over age 65 meet these recommendations (Ward, Clarke, Nugent, & Schiller, 2016).

Older adults benefit from regular exercise in many ways, including decreased risk for cardiovascular disease, diabetes, osteoporosis, osteoarthritis, depression, and early death (Kohn, Belza, Petrescu-Prahova, & Miyawaki, 2016). Although it's never too late to begin exercising, during late adulthood, the intensity of exercise must be adjusted to reflect declines in cardiovascular and respiratory functioning. For some adults, this means that walking replaces jogging; for others, such as former world-class marathoner Bill Rodgers, now in his sixties, this means training at a 6-minute-per-mile pace rather than a 5-minute pace.

Why Don't More People Exercise?

Despite the well-documented physical and psychological benefits of lifelong exercise, the percentage of people who exercise regularly declines with age and varies significantly across socioeconomic and ethnic groups (WHO, 2015h). Although some children get regular exercise through school programs, the level of physical activity has declined substantially by adolescence, especially among girls (Davison, Schmalz, & Downs, 2010) and among boys not involved in sports programs (Crosnoe, 2002).

Globally, one in four adults aged 18 and over are not active enough (WHO, 2015i). An estimated 32% of men and 42% of women in the United States describe themselves as sedentary. Minority group members consistently seem to have lower physical activity levels than majority group members, with minority women being among the least active subgroups in the United States (Cassetta, Boden-Albala, Sciacca, & Giardina, 2007). Why would this be? People choose not to exercise for many reasons, such as lack of time, money, or energy (Ruby, Dunn, Perrino, Gillis, & Viel, 2011). In several large surveys, physical activity was found to be lowest among people with low incomes and lower levels of education.

Some older adults are reluctant—even fearful—of exercising too much due to myths associated with exercise. These myths include the idea that exercise can accelerate the loss of bone density, lead to arthritis, and even increase the risk of dying from a heart attack. In fact, the body is far more likely to fail from lack of use than it is to wear out. As the saying goes, "Use it or lose it!"

It's never too late to begin exercising. Physical activity is one of the most important things older adults can do to prevent health problems and to promote healthy aging.

Exercising behavior also is related to an individual's beliefs regarding its health benefits, confidence in his or her ability to perform certain physical skills correctly (known as *exercise self-efficacy*), and self-motivation. Believing that exercise will help one to live a longer, healthier life is a strong stimulus for initiating exercise. Believing that exercise is difficult, useless, or unsafe, or that declines in health are inevitable and irreversible with increased age, on the other hand, will almost certainly have the opposite effect.

There are several reasons why older adults might lack exercise self-efficacy. For one, they typically have less experience with exercise and have fewer exercising role models than younger people. Older people are also faced with ageist stereotypes about what constitutes appropriate behavior; vigorous exercise, especially for women, is contrary to stereotypes of old age. Many older adults view old age as a time of rest and relaxation and are less likely to initiate and maintain regular exercise. Older adults will be less likely to begin an exercise regimen if they believe they are unable to do even basic exercises, so intervention efforts should include some basic instruction. Finally, age-appropriate programs, with exercises such as tai chi, have been shown to reduce older adults' fears of hazards, especially of falling (Zijlstra and others, 2007).

To the list of reasons why people don't exercise, you can add that people fail to appreciate how much they will enjoy it. I'm reminded of chatting with cardiologist George Sheehan many years ago before the start of the Boston Marathon. Sheehan, himself a dedicated runner, said, "People won't do something very long just because it's good for them. They've got to find some activity that, for them, is play." This bias sometimes stems from *forecasting myopia*, in which people contemplating an exercise routine place disproportionate emphasis on the beginning of a workout, which may be unpleasant. (Getting out the door with stiff legs on a cold winter morning for my daily run comes to mind.)

Another reason why people don't exercise is that environmental barriers make doing so more difficult. The neighborhood environment has emerged as an important area of focus in predicting individual activity levels. Consider, for example, *neighborhood walkability.* A walkable neighborhood allows travel from home to key destinations on foot. Adults who

JAG IMAGES/AGE Fotostock

When people feel their neighborhood affords safe opportunities to exercise, such as by having traffic-free bike lanes or well-lit jogging paths, participation levels increase.

live in low-walkable neighborhoods are less physically active and more likely to be overweight and obese, and to engage in more obesity-related sedentary behaviors than their peers living in more walkable communities (A. C. King and others, 2010; Kozo and others, 2012).

When people feel their neighborhood is safe, when they are not socially isolated, and when they know about exercise facilities that are available to them, they are more likely to be physically active (Hawkley, Thisted, & Cacioppo, 2009). The absence of convenient and easily accessible exercise settings leads to lower rates of participation (Humpel, Marshall, Leslie, Bauman, & Own, 2004). For example, having few or only distant safe playgrounds, traffic-free bike lanes, well-lit jogging paths, and other community resources makes it difficult for urban children and working adults who must fit exercise in around busy schedules. Improving these options increases rates of exercise, and when communities have facilities such as these available, the prevalence of overweight and obesity in the neighborhood is reduced (Dowda, Dishman, Porter, Saunders, & Pate, 2009).

Lack of resources for exercising is a particular barrier for people low in socioeconomic status (SES) (Feldman & Steptoe, 2004). Recent studies have strongly suggested that neighborhood SES has an influence on health, in part because of differences in physical activity (Boone-Heinonen and others, 2011). Neighborhood health disparities are associated with neighborhood SES, which determines the availability of resources for activity such as parks, walking/bike paths, and sports facilities, which in turn are linked to differences in physical activity (Schuz and others, 2012).

Another factor in sedentary lifestyles is the decline in physical education classes in schools due to mounting economic pressure. This means that, for many children, a lifelong habit of healthy physical activity and exercise is hard to establish. The U.S. Department of Health and Human Services recommends that young people between the ages of 6 and 17 participate in at least 60 minutes of physical activity daily. Yet in 2015, only 27.1% of high school students surveyed had participated in

Rawpixel.com/Shutterstock.com

For children, exercise means playing and being physically active. In addition to promoting healthy physical development, regular physical activity is associated with cognitive and academic benefits. Ideally, children and teenagers should have at least 60 minutes of exercise every day.

at least 60 minutes per day of physical activity on all seven days before the survey (Kann and others, 2016).

The Centers for Disease Control and Prevention (CDC, 2011b) conducted a meta-analysis of 50 studies of physical activity and academic performance among schoolchildren. Its findings included the following: Regular physical activity in childhood and adolescence improves strength and endurance, helps build healthy bones and muscles, helps control weight, reduces anxiety and stress, increases self-esteem, and may improve blood pressure and cholesterol levels. Physical activity can have a positive impact on academic achievement (including grades and standardized test scores) and more generally on cognitive skills, attitudes, and academic behavior (e.g., improved concentration, attention, and classroom behavior), all of which contribute to children's academic performance. In terms of time dedicated to physical education, increasing or maintaining that time commitment in school does not appear to adversely affect academic performance, and doing so may have a positive effect.

Another way to look at the issue of why more people don't exercise is to ask who *is* most likely to exercise. Research suggests that people are most likely to stick with exercise programs if they

- enjoy exercise;
- have already formed the habit of exercising regularly;
- grew up in families that exercised;
- have social support for exercising from relatives, friends, and coworkers;
- have a favorable attitude and a strong sense of self-efficacy toward exercising;
- perceive themselves as being somewhat athletic; and
- believe that people should take responsibility for their health (Floyd & Moyer, 2010).

Exercise Interventions

Health behavior theories identify factors that predict physical activity in the individual. Among these are social cognitive factors, such as attitudes and intentions toward exercise; socioeconomic factors, such as education, which determine the ability to find and understand health-related information; and the financial resources needed to facilitate physical activity. A number of studies have shown that interventions aimed at the individual work best when they are matched to the stage of readiness of the participants and employ a variety of **behavior change techniques (BCTs)** (Vancampfort and others, 2014; Gawwad, 2008).

In one study of 2,790 adults participating in seven hour-long fitness classes, researchers found that participants significantly underestimated how much they would enjoy exercising. Recall from Chapter 6 that the *theory of planned behavior* maintains that attitudes toward a given behavior, along with subjective social norms and perceived behavioral control, shape our behavioral intentions, which in turn guide our behavior. The researchers found that a simple intervention, in which participants were prompted to consider all phases of the workout before starting, increased their expected enjoyment of the exercise routine and boosted their intention to exercise in the future (Ruby and others, 2011).

Also at the level of the individual, interventions that help people develop positive but realistic expectations for a new exercise program (Dunton & Vaughan, 2008) and those that focus on increasing participants' motivation, intentions, and perceptions of behavioral control and exercise self-efficacy can be successful in changing behavior (Conroy, Hyde, Doerksen, & Riebeiro, 2010). Interventions that combine this emphasis on changing social cognitions with behavioral techniques such as teaching self-monitoring skills have been particularly successful (Michie, Abraham, Whittington, McAteer, & Gupta, 2009; van Stralen, De Vries, Mudde, Bolman, & Lechner, 2009). One meta-analysis found that programs that emphasized behavioral strategies over cognitive strategies were the most effective (Conn, Hafdahl, & Mehr, 2011).

behavior change technique (BCT) A theory-based method for changing one or more determinants of a health behavior, such as self-efficacy.

Because many people find it easier to begin an exercise program than to keep it going as part of a permanent lifestyle change, relapse prevention techniques are important in promoting long-term adherence. These include "inoculating" participants against the temptation to skip exercise by increasing their awareness of obstacles such as work and family obligations, stress, and fatigue. For some, simple reminders sent via text messages, phone, or e-mail can help prevent relapse (Scholz, Keller, & Perren, 2009; Blanchard and others, 2007).

As we have seen, facilitating and impeding factors for physical activity also can be found in the environment. Neighborhood SES can determine the availability of exercise resources, and urban planning and local policies can facilitate or impede the ability to engage in physical activity (Schuz and others, 2012). The most effective interventions designed to promote increased physical activity in a community integrate individual and environmental factors, including demographic, biological, psychological, social/cultural, and public policy.

The World Health Organization (2015h) has set a global target of increasing physical activity by at least 10% by 2025. To reach this target, the WHO's *Global Action Plan* (2013b) promotes policies to ensure that

- walking, cycling, and other forms of active transportation are accessible and safe for all;

- labor and workplace policies encourage physical activity;

- schools have safe spaces and facilities for students to spend their free time actively;

- quality physical education supports children to develop behavior patterns that will keep them physically active throughout their lives; and

- sports and recreation facilities provide opportunities for everyone to do sports.

mHealth

People today are more likely than ever to be connected to the world of digital information via a smartphone or handheld tablet rather than a stationary computer. An estimated 77% of Americans own smartphones today, up from 35% in 2011. Of these, 62% have used their smartphone to find help or information about a health condition (Pew Research Center, 2018). Research investigating ***mHealth***, defined as the use of smartphones and other mobile technologies to promote health and well-being, is on the rise, and health psychologists are teaming up with software developers to create and test new apps. In 2015, an entire issue of the journal *Health Psychology* focused on the range of health behaviors targeted by mHealth platforms. These included smoking cessation, substance abuse, stress management, sleep, medication adherence, and physical activity.

A recent meta-analysis of 21 randomized controlled trials of 1,700 participants tested effectiveness of mHealth interventions in promoting physical activity (PA) and reducing sedentary time (ST) (Direito, Carraca, Rawstorn, Whittaker, & Maddison, 2017). Across the studies, the mHealth interventions included listening to podcasts, SMS text messaging, and the use of wearable activity-tracking devices such as wristband accelerometers and other biosensors. Interventions that delivered information included goal setting, self-monitoring of behavior, social support, feedback, instruction on how to perform the target behavior, and information about health consequences, among others. The intervention frequency among studies varied from one text message per day to one podcast

mHealth The use of smartphones and other mobile technologies to promote health and well-being.

each week. The mHealth intervention groups were compared to non-technology-based control groups that used print materials or counseling to promote physical activity. Outcome measures included total physical activity duration, metabolic/caloric "cost" of activity, walking step count, and sitting duration. Despite the wide variation in content, frequency of intervention, and other variations across the studies, the results demonstrated that mHealth interventions, after an average follow-up duration of 9 weeks, were associated with a small overall decrease in sedentary behavior and a moderate increase in physical activity levels.

Promoting Physical Activity During Cancer Treatment

In the past, people being treated for chronic illnesses such as cancer were often advised to rest and to reduce their physical activity. Today, however, it is recognized that being physically active is safe and has benefits for many cancer patients, including slowed disease progression, reduced recurrence and better prognosis, lower levels of fatigue and distress during treatment, and higher quality of life (NCI, 2018). Despite this, exercise levels among cancer patients are often very low, and as many as 75% report decreased physical activity after their diagnosis (Romero, Li, & Mao, 2017).

As members of health care teams, health psychologists often work with nurses and other providers to design educational interventions for patients. A diagnosis of cancer can be a *teachable moment*; the perception of increased vulnerability to a health threat can motivate increased receptivity to lifestyle changes (McBride & Emmons, 2003). Although nurses are well positioned to speak with patients about healthy lifestyle behaviors, research has shown that awareness of the benefits of physical activity to cancer patients is not universal. One survey found that 28% of nurses did not think that discussing exercise with their patients was critical, 41.5% were unaware of recommended guidelines for exercise, and only 9% actually did talk to their patients about exercise (Webb, Foster, & Poulter, 2016).

One widely used scheme for designing educational interventions in health care is the COM-B behavior change model (Michie, van Stralen, & West, 2011). This model proposes that for a desired change in behavior (B) to occur, a person must be physically and psychologically capable (C) of the behavior, have the opportunity (O) to engage in the behavior, and be motivated (M) to do so. If a desired behavior is not occurring (or an undesirable behavior is occurring), an intervention should target one or more of these elements, after an analysis to determine what specific *behavior change techniques (BCTs)* are needed. Frequently employed BCTs in intervention groups include goal setting and self-monitoring of target behaviors; information about health consequences; instruction, social support, and feedback for target behaviors; and the provision of prompts or cues for performing the target behavior.

Using the COM-B model, a team of UK researchers recently designed a 60-minute educational intervention to improve the capability, opportunity, and motivation of nurses to deliver brief, accurate advice on the benefits of physical activity to their cancer patients

AndreyPopov/Getty Images

Goal setting and self-monitoring of target behaviors can help make exercise a habit that is maintained over the long term.

(Webb, Foster, & Poulter, 2016). The intervention began with an analysis of what needed to change in order to bring about the desired outcome in the targeted nursing practice behavior. This analysis focused not only on the nurses' knowledge and attitudes, but also on institutional policies and the practicality, acceptability, and affordability of the desired change in the standard of care with cancer patients. Next, the researchers prepared a 60-minute training module, delivered either face-to-face or online, incorporating seven behavior-change techniques that research studies have shown to be effective in changing nursing practice. These included measuring baseline levels and monitoring of the target behavior, instructing nurses on the importance of delivering lifestyle advice and the patient-outcome benefits of promoting physical activity, setting specific goals for asking and advising patients about their physical activity, and providing script cards and an actual demonstration of how to deliver exercise advice to patients.

Now that the intervention has been designed, the researchers are conducting a feasibility study in several UK hospitals; they hope to follow the study with a full clinical trial, evaluating the effectiveness of the intervention in changing nursing practice. The COM-B has been the basis of many other health psychology interventions—including efforts to improve medication adherence, implement smoking cessation programs, and improve hearing-aid use—and in many other health behavior contexts (e.g., Gould and others, 2017; Barker, Atkins, & de Lusignan, 2016; Jackson, Eliasson, Barber, & Weinman, 2014).

Hazards of Exercise

Although exercise can promote health, it also poses some hazards if done to excess. Musculoskeletal injuries are common, and are directly associated with the intensity and frequency of exercise (Powell, Paluch, & Blair, 2011). Fortunately, supervised training, proper warm-up routines, appropriate clothing and other exercise gear, and adequate caution go a long way in reducing the probability of exercise-related injury.

What about the risk of death during exercise? Recall the story of Jim Fixx (see Chapter 2), the running guru who helped launch the 1970s jogging craze in the United States. Fixx's sudden death at age 52 while running was taken by many as proof that exercise has no real impact on preventing cardiovascular disease, and can even promote its development. As we saw, however, Fixx's death was likely caused by his unhealthy lifestyle prior to becoming a runner, and his existing and advanced coronary artery disease.

Most cases of *sudden cardiac death* during exercise in athletes with no known disease are related to inherited heart conditions such as hypertrophic cardiomyopathy (Wasfy, Hutter, & Weiner, 2016). Although exercise *can* increase the risk of sudden cardiac death, or SCD, the risk is very low for any specific episode of exercise (about one death per 1.5 million bouts of activity in one study). Moreover, the benefits of exercise in reducing the overall risk of death significantly outweigh the risks of SCD (Albert and others, 2000).

Compulsive Exercise

As my personal story at the beginning of the chapter illustrates, some athletes become so involved with exercise that they over train, ignore injuries, and allow their training to interfere with other parts of their lives. In some people, what started as a healthy commitment to exercise may come to resemble an *exercise addiction*. Distinguishing healthy exercise from addictive exercise is difficult, and gambling disorder is the only nonsubstance disorder that is recognized in the *Diagnostic and Statistical Manual of Mental Disorders,* 5th edition, or *DSM–V* (Potenza, 2014). Even so, **compulsive exercise** (also called obligatory exercise) resembles this form of *behavioral addiction* when it becomes obsessive and causes dysfunction in a person's life (Villella and others, 2011). As I did, obligatory runners become compulsive about their training regimen; show strong emotional attachment to exercise; and even exhibit symptoms of withdrawal, such as anxiety and depression, when they are unable to exercise (Landolfi, 2013).

Compulsive exercisers tend to use exercise as a way to manage negative emotions or personal problems (Warner & Griffiths, 2006). Many come to define their self-worth through their athletic performance, and they attempt to deal with feelings of depression or anger by pushing their bodies to the limit. Obligatory exercisers share many of the characteristics of people with eating disorders, especially anorexia, and many people with anorexia also have a compulsion to exercise excessively (Klein, Bennett, Schebendach, Devlin, & Walsh, 2004). These characteristics include perfectionism, neuroticism, denial of physical discomfort, and obsessive-compulsive traits (Lichtenstein, Hinze, Emborg, Thomsen, & Hemmingsen, 2017).

compulsive exercise Physical activity that becomes obsessive and causes dysfunction in a person's life.

SLEEP

If exercise is the "fountain of youth," healthy sleep habits may be the "elixir of health" (Grayling, 2009). Adults need 7 hours or more of sleep each day for the best health and well-being (Watson and others, 2015). Unfortunately, 35.2% of adults in the United States fail to get enough sleep, and they experience **short sleep duration**, defined as less than 7 hours of sleep each day (Ford, Cunningham, & Croft, 2015). As Table 7.3 shows, the prevalence of short sleep duration varies by age group and race/ethnicity, but is about the same in women and men.

short sleep duration Sleeping less than 7 hours each night.

For some 70 million Americans, a **sleep disorder** such as insomnia, narcolepsy, sleepwalking, or sleep apnea is the cause of short sleep duration. For others, stress or a demanding work or study schedule contributes to their poor sleep habits. Adolescents, who need 8 to 10 hours of sleep each night, now average less than 7 hours—a full 2 hours less than that averaged by their grandparents as teenagers (Paruthi and others, 2016). More than two thirds of high school students report getting less than 8 hours of sleep on school nights, and nearly one third admit that they routinely fall asleep in class (Wheaton, Olsen, Miller, & Croft, 2016).

sleep disorder Any problem with sleeping.

Our bodies are approximately synchronized with the 24-hour cycle of night and day by an internal biological clock called the **circadian rhythm**. The rhythm is clearly linked to the light–dark cycle, because animals, including humans, kept in total darkness for extended periods eventually develop a more free-running rhythm. Daylight and other environmental cues reset our circadian rhythm when, for instance, we travel across several time zones; these cues are called *zeitgebers* ("timekeepers").

circadian rhythm A biological clock that operates on a 24-hour cycle.

Our thinking and memory are sharpest when we are at our peak in the daily circadian cycle. Try working out a difficult math problem in the middle of the night, and you'll understand this immediately. This is why many people who travel extensively have learned to arrive at their destination a day or two before important meetings or other events where

TABLE 7.3 Short Sleep Duration (less than 7 Hours) by Sex, Age, and Race/Ethnicity

Characteristic	Percent (%)
All Adults[a]	35.2
Sex[a]	
Men	35.5
Women	34.8
Age (Years)	
18–24	32.2
25–34	37.9
35–44	38.3
45–54	39.0
55–64	35.6
≥65	26.3
Race/Ethnicity[a]	
White	33.4
Hispanic	34.5
Black	45.8
Asian	37.5
American Indian/Alaska Native	40.4
Native Hawaiian/Pacific Islander	46.3
Other/Multiracial	44.3

[a]Age-adjusted to the 2000 U.S. standard population.

Data from: CDC (2017). Short sleep duration among U.S. adults. Centers for Disease Control and Prevention.

their thinking needs to be sharp. Doing so gives them a chance to use local *zeitgebers* to reset their internal biological clocks. Bright light, which activates light-sensitive proteins in the retinas of our eyes, is the most important factor in setting our 24-hour biological clock. It signals the brain's *suprachiasmatic nucleus* to decrease its production of the sleep-inducing hormone *melatonin*. Our body temperature also responds to day–night light cycles, rising in the morning, peaking during the day, and decreasing in the evening.

Age alters our circadian rhythm. During adolescence, we are likely to be "night owls," energized during the evening, with cognitive performance improving as the day wears on. This is a key reason why school districts around the country have pushed back school start times for high school; research suggests that later start times improve mood and alertness among adolescent students (Perkinson-Gloor, Lemola, & Grob, 2013). After about age 20 (slightly earlier for women), we begin to shift from being owls to being morning-loving "larks" and feel our energy and performance declining through the day (Roenneberg and others, 2004). Women become more lark-like as they have children (Leonhard & Randler, 2009). There is some evidence that people who are at their best in the morning tend to do better in school and to be less vulnerable to depression (Randler & Frech, 2009).

Sleep Stages

Once asleep, the brain operates according to a 90-minute biological rhythm, cycling through four distinct sleep stages (see Figure 7.1). There are two broad types of sleep: non–rapid eye movement (NREM) and **rapid eye movement (REM)**, distinguished by different brain wave patterns, changes in breathing and muscle tension, and a few other bodily changes.

When you are awake and alert, the brain generates fast, low-amplitude beta waves. As you begin to relax and your eyes close, your brain begins to generate the slower *alpha waves* of the awake but relaxed state. As you fall asleep, your breathing slows, and your brain generates the irregular waves of NREM stage 1 sleep (Silber and others, 2008). This is the briefest and lightest stage of sleep, during which loud sounds and other stimuli can awaken you easily.

As you relax more deeply, about 20 minutes of NREM-2 occurs, distinguished by periodic bursts of rapid brain waves called *sleep spindles,* which alternate with large K-complex waves. During this stage, breathing and heart rate even out and body temperature drops. You still can be awakened without much difficulty, but you are clearly asleep. About half of each night's sleep is spent in NREM-2.

Next, you transition to the deep, *slow-wave sleep* of NREM-3, in which your brain emits large (high-amplitude) and very slow (low-frequency) delta waves. During this stage of sleep, you will be much harder to awaken. This stage of deep sleep, marked by delta waves, is most important for restoring energy levels, strengthening the immune system, and stimulating the release of growth hormone.

About one hour after falling asleep, you shift from NREM-3 back to NREM-2 and then enter REM. For 10 minutes or so, your eyes dart back and forth, heart rate and breathing become more irregular, and vivid dreams often occur. REM is also marked by faster beta brain waves and is believed to be important for consolidating memory and other cognitive functions. During REM, the brain's motor cortex is also active, but the brainstem blocks its messages, leaving the muscles relaxed.

The sleep cycle repeats itself about every 90 minutes, but as the night wears on, NREM-3 sleep stages grow shorter and REM and NREM-2 get longer. By the time we awaken, we have spent about 100 minutes (25% of sleep) in REM.

Sleep Patterns

Sleep patterns differ greatly from one stage of the life cycle to another. Newborns sleep 15 to 17 hours a day, in segments lasting 1 to 3 hours, because their brain areas that regulate sleep are immature. The number of hours that babies sleep decreases rapidly as their brains continue to develop—down to a little over 14 hours for the first 2 months, 13 and one-quarter hours for the next 3 months, and 12 and three-quarters hours for the 6th through 17th months. Full-term newborns sleep more than low-birth-weight babies, who are hungry every 2 hours. As parents soon learn, the environment has a direct effect on infant sleep behaviors: If parents respond to early morning cries with food and stimulating play, their infant will continue wake up early each morning (Sadeh, Mindel, Luedtke, & Wiegand, 2009).

(b)   6 sec

FIGURE 7.1 Sleep Stages The small, fast beta waves of an alert state and the larger alpha waves of a relaxed state differ from the slower, large delta waves of NREM-3 sleep.

Data from: Davis, C. L., Tomporowski, P. D., McDowell, J. E., Austin, B. P., Miller, P. H., Yanasak, N. E., Allison, J. D., & Naglieri, J. A. (2011). Exercise improves executive function and achievement and alters brain activation in overweight children: A randomized, controlled trial. *Health Psychology, 30*(1), 91–98.

rapid eye movement (REM) Rapid eye movement sleep; a sleep stage during which vivid dreams occur.

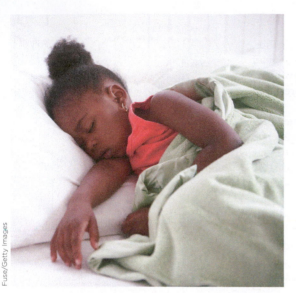

Sleep patterns change as we grow older. The American Academy of Pediatrics recommends that school-age children sleep 9 to 12 hours per night.

It is not just the amount of time spent sleeping, but also the time in the various stages of sleep that changes during infancy. About 50% of the sleep of full-term newborns is REM sleep, with flickering eyes, rapid brain waves, and dreaming. REM sleep declines over the first few weeks, as does "transitional sleep," the dozing, half-awake NREM-1 stage. At three or four months, NREM-3 (slow-wave sleep) increases, as does time spent alert and wide awake.

Although genes play an important role in determining our individual sleep patterns (Hor & Tafti, 2009), lightbulbs, work schedules, the Internet, and other diversions mean that people today sleep less than their counterparts did 100 years ago. This phenomenon has been called *social jet lag*, underscoring the fact that it occurs when our body's internal biological clock is out of sync with our social clock, which is set by the demands and distractions of modern life. In one study of 65,000 European adults, 69% of participants reported suffering from at least one hour of social jet lag each week, and a third regularly suffered at least two hours (Roenneberg, Allebrandt, Merrow, & Vetter, 2012).

Sleep researchers also have found that insufficient sleep is related to socioeconomic status, race and ethnicity, workplace, neighborhood, and other social factors (Cunningham, Wheaton, Ford, & Croft, 2016). A survey of 9,714 adults reported a significant *sleep disparity* among participants (Patel, Grandner, Xie, Branas, & Goooneratne, 2010). Overall, minority respondents reported poorer sleep quality than majority group respondents. However, among those with the lowest income levels, majority respondents reported the most sleep problems.

Another study of 500 healthy U.S. adults reported that African Americans slept an average of only 6.8 hours per night, compared with 7.4 hours, on average, for European Americans. Asian Americans and Hispanic Americans slept an average of 6.9 hours per night (Carnethon and others, 2012). The differences in average sleep time persisted even after the researchers adjusted for weight, high blood pressure, diabetes, and other factors known to interfere with sleep. The authors suggest that social environmental factors such as pollution, noise levels, and crime rates may account for these group differences.

Other researchers have directly investigated the associations among sleep quality, health, and neighborhood conditions. Participants who reported living in neighborhoods with more physical and social disorder also reported having poorer sleep quality, more symptoms of depression, and poorer perceived health (Patel and others, 2010).

Work Schedules and Stress

People who work long hours, at multiple jobs, and those who do shift work report poor sleep. Nearly 15 million Americans work full time on evening shift, night shift, rotating shift, or other irregular schedules. Nearly one in five work 48 hours or more each week. Shift work is commonly found in industries providing services 24/7, such as health care, food services, transportation, and police work. Both shift work and long work hours are associated with fatigue, sleep loss, and a host of health and safety risks. These include cognitive impairments, on-duty injury, Type 2 diabetes, cardiovascular disease, metabolic syndrome, certain cancers; autoimmune disorders, and even death (National Institute for Occupational Safety and Health [NIOSH], 2018). One study of over 3,000 participants reported that people who had worked rotating shifts for 10 or more years had lower overall cognitive and memory scores than those who had never worked irregular shifts—the equivalent of 6.5 years of age-related decline (Marquié, Tucker, Folkard, Gentil, & Ansiau, 2015). Another study reported a significantly increased death rate due to cardiovascular disease and all causes among nurses with 5 or more years of rotating night shift work, compared to those who never worked night shifts (Gu and others, 2015).

Why might irregular work schedules promote cognitive decline and disease? Some researchers suspect that shift workers' bodies may not always be able to adapt to the circadian rhythm disruption that accompanies an irregular work schedule, a number of metabolic risk factors that are indicative of physiological stress and higher allostatic load (see Chapter 4). These include vitamin D deficiency as a result of reduced exposure to sunlight, which may promote cognitive decline; insulin resistance, which is linked to Type 2 diabetes; suppressed production of melatonin, which may affect sex hormones and increase the risk of several cancers; and changes in intestinal microbiota and increased inflammation, which has been linked with many diseases (Proper and others, 2016).

People who are coping with stressful events at work or in the home also report poorer sleep (Shockey & Wheaton, 2017; Cunningham, Wheaton, & Giles, 2015). This is especially true when stressors are appraised as uncontrollable (see Chapter 4). One study of health care workers found that those who had less supportive managers got 29 minutes less sleep daily and were twice as likely as those with more supportive bosses to have

One in five adults fails to get enough sleep. Our body's internal biological clock is often out of sync with our social clock, which is set by the demands and distractions of modern life. As a result, people today sleep less than their counterparts did a century ago.

Working shifts that disrupt normal circadian rhythms exposes the body to physiological stressors. Police and other first responders, medical professionals, and food service workers are among those who often work night and "graveyard" shifts.

several risk factors for cardiovascular disease (Berkman, Buxton, Ertel, & Okechukwu, 2010). People who react to stressful events by ruminating (see Chapter 5) and people who have high levels of hostility or arousal (Fernandez-Mendoza and others, 2010) are more prone to insomnia than are people who use strategies to blunt the impact of stressors (Zoccola, Dickerson, & Lam, 2009).

Pain also can disrupt sleep. Parents of children with chronic arthritis pain rate their children as having significantly more sleep anxiety, night awakenings, and other sleep disturbances (Bromberg, Gil, & Schanberg, 2012). In turn, poor sleep can increase the intensity of pain experienced the next day by adolescents and adults with chronic pain (Lewandowski, Palermo, De la Mott, & Fu, 2010). Other studies have shown that sleep loss leads to exaggerated pain perception, perhaps by increasing blood levels of *interleukin-6,* a signaling cytokine that contributes to inflammation and pain sensitivity (Haack & Mullington, 2007).

Sleep Loss

After a few nights of sleep loss, people have accumulated a *sleep debt* that cannot be repaid by one long sleep (Cohen and others, 2010). College students are among those most likely to be sleep-deprived—70% in one national survey (Hershner & Chervin, 2014). (See *Your Health Assets: How Good Is Your Sleep?* to determine whether the amount and quality of the sleep that you are getting is adequate.) Students who don't sleep enough also report more conflicts in their friendships and social relationships (Gordon & Chen, 2014).

Sleep loss slows our reaction times and increases errors on visual attention tasks, which may explain why driver fatigue is linked to an estimated 20% of traffic accidents (Caldwell, 2012). Remarkably, when the high schools in one Virginia city pushed back their starting times 75 to 80 minutes, over a two-year period, the number of student traffic accidents was 25% lower than the number in another city in the same state that kept its earlier starting time (Vorona and others, 2011).

Sleep loss also is a predictor of depression. In one study, students who reported sleeping five hours or less a night had a 71% higher risk of depression than others who slept eight hours or more (Gangwisch and others, 2010).

Sleep Disorders

About one third of adults experience sleep problems occasionally. Poor sleep is enough of a problem that *Healthy People 2020* (2014) (see Chapter 1) established the national goal of increasing the proportion of people who get sufficient sleep. Poor sleep, as noted earlier, takes a toll on both physical and psychological well-being. Although early research focused on the devastating effects of total sleep deprivation, far more common is what researchers today call *partial sleep loss, sleep restriction,* or *short sleep*—routinely cutting one's sleep short by just an hour or two each night (Carpenter, 2013).

insomnia A persistent problem in falling or staying asleep.

The most commonly reported sleep problem is **insomnia**—a persistent problem in falling asleep, staying asleep, or getting restful sleep; it affects 10% to 15% of adults and as many as 25% of older adults (Khurshid, 2015). Although chronic insomnia can be a serious problem, waking occasionally during the night is the norm for adults from middle age onward and does not necessarily need to be treated with medication (Vitiello, 2009).

Your Health Assets

How Good Is Your Sleep?

Cornell University sleep researcher James Maas has reported that 65% of people are sleep deprived. To find out if you are in that group, answer the following true–false questions. If you answered "true" to three or more items, you probably are not getting enough sleep.

Please indicate true or false for the following statements:

1. I need an alarm clock in order to wake up at the appropriate time.
2. It's a struggle for me to get out of bed in the morning.
3. Weekday mornings, I hit the snooze button several times to get more sleep.
4. I feel tired, irritable, and stressed out during the week.
5. I have trouble concentrating and remembering.
6. I feel slow when doing critical thinking, problem solving, and being creative.
7. I often fall asleep watching TV.
8. I often fall asleep in boring meetings or lectures or in warm rooms.
9. I often fall asleep after heavy meals or after a low dose of alcohol.
10. I often fall asleep while relaxing after dinner.
11. I often fall asleep within five minutes of getting into bed.
12. I often feel drowsy while driving.
13. I often sleep extra hours on weekend mornings.
14. I often need a nap to get through the day.
15. I have dark circles around my eyes.

Information from: Quiz reprinted with permission from Maas, J. B. (2013). *Sleep to Win!* Bloomington, IN: AuthorHouse.

People who experience insomnia may get short-term relief from sleeping pills and other medications, but these may not be the best long-term solution because of bothersome side effects and concerns about developing dependency on drugs. Ironically, the use of sleeping pills, alcohol, and other "quick fixes" often makes the situation worse by suppressing REM sleep and leading to *tolerance,* in which increased doses are needed to produce any sleep-inducing effect.

Unlike pills, **cognitive behavioral therapy for insomnia (CBT-I)** targets the underlying causes of insomnia instead of its symptoms. CBT-I is a structured intervention that aims to first improve sleep quality and later improve sleep quantity. CBT-I is a stepwise procedure that helps people identify thoughts and behaviors that cause or aggravate sleep problems and replace them with healthier ones that promote restful sleep. This often includes learning how to control or eliminate sleep-interfering thoughts and worries, manage stress, and calm an active mind that won't "shut off" when its owner is trying to fall asleep. A comparative meta-analysis of research studies reported that CBT-I is an effective treatment for insomnia, and its effects may be more durable than those of medications (Mitchell, Gehrman, Perlis, & Umscheid, 2012).

cognitive behavioral therapy for insomnia (CBT-I) A structured treatment for insomnia aimed at replacing thoughts and behaviors that cause or worsen sleep problems with habits that promote sound sleep without the use of medication.

Poor sleep takes a toll on both physical and psychological well-being.

Most people with insomnia have very unpredictable sleep patterns. The behavioral element of CBT-I promotes the development of a "pro-sleep" routine that establishes a strong connection between the bedroom and restful sleep. Over time, practicing this routine means that falling asleep and staying asleep become more natural and automatic.

CBT-I is typically delivered over the course of 6 to 8 weekly sessions with a trained health psychologist. Treatment is typically tailored to individual needs, and may include the following:

- *Stimulus control therapy* to remove factors that condition the mind to resist sleep. These factors include irregular bedtimes and waking times. The therapist might coach a client to set a consistent bedtime and wake time, avoid naps, use the bed only for sleep and sex, and leave the bed if unable to fall asleep within 20 minutes.

- *Relaxation training* to help calm the mind and body. Various approaches are used, including meditation, imagery, and muscle relaxation.

- *Sleep environment improvement.* This focuses on creating a comfortable sleep environment by keeping the bedroom dark, cool, and quiet; not having a television or other devices in the room; and keeping any clocks out of view.

- *Sleep restriction.* Lying in bed when you're awake can quickly become a habit that interferes with restful sleep. This technique reduces the time clients spend in bed, causing partial sleep deprivation designed to make them more tired the next night. As sleep improves, the time in bed is gradually increased.

- *Biofeedback.* This technique, discussed more fully in Chapter 15, enables people to monitor their heart rate, muscle tension, or other physical signs and shows people how to adjust those responses to calm the body.

- *Sleep hygiene* focuses on improving lifestyle behaviors that influence sleep, such as drinking too much alcohol, consuming caffeine late in the day, or not getting regular exercise. It also includes training in ways to wind down before bedtime.

narcolepsy A sleep disorder characterized by uncontrollable sleep attacks.

In addition to insomnia, *DSM-V* identifies 10 other sleep–wake disorders (see Table 7.4). People with **narcolepsy**, a neurological disease that usually begins between 15 and 25 years of age, don't have difficulty falling asleep. Rather, they experience excessive daytime sleepiness that results in episodes of falling asleep suddenly, typically lasting less than 5 minutes. These sleep attacks may occur during any type of activity and at any time of day. Other symptoms of narcolepsy include abnormal REM sleep—for example, experiencing dreamlike hallucinations and feeling physically weak or even paralyzed for a few seconds.

Researchers have identified genes that appear to trigger the disorder by causing the body's immune system to attack brain cells that signal sleep and awake cycles (De la Herrán-Arita and others, 2013). One promising hypothesis is that narcolepsy may be due

TABLE 7.4 Major Sleep-Wake Disorders

This table lists the major sleep-wake disorders included in *DSM-V*. Sleep disorders are often accompanied by anxiety, depression, and other cognitive changes.

Disorder	Symptoms
Insomnia disorder	Persistent difficulty falling asleep or staying asleep
Hypersomnolence disorder	Excessive daytime sleepiness or prolonged nighttime sleep
Narcolepsy	Neurological disorder involving poor control of sleep-wake cycles, excessive daytime sleepiness, and brief, involuntary sleep episodes
Obstructive sleep apnea or hypopnea	Brief, involuntary pauses in breathing, or shallow breathing while asleep; caused by an airway that collapses or becomes blocked during sleep
Central sleep apnea	Less common form of apnea (brief pauses in breathing while sleeping) caused by the brain's failure to send correct signals to breathing muscles
Sleep-related hypoventilation	Breathing disorder characterized by abnormal oxygen/carbon dioxide exchange while sleeping
Circadian rhythm sleep-wake disorders	A family of sleep disorders that affects the timing of the sleep-wake cycle
Non–rapid eye movement (NREM) sleep arousal disorder	Episodes of incomplete awakening from sleep; may involve sleepwalking or nightmares
Nightmare disorder	Recurrent dreams that are horrifying or threatening in nature
Rapid eye movement (REM) sleep behavior disorder	Behavioral arousal during rapid eye movement sleep; dreamer may kick, grab, punch, and in other ways seem to be acting out a dream
Restless legs syndrome	Neurological disorder characterized by a desire to move the legs and uncomfortable sensations such as crawling, tingling, burning, or itching

Information from: American Psychiatric Association. (2013). *Diagnostic and statistical manual of mental disorders—DSM-V* (5th ed.).

to a deficiency of cells in the hypothalamus that produce *hypocretin*, a neurotransmitter that regulates arousal, wakefulness, and appetite (Han and others, 2013).

Narcolepsy is most often treated with drugs, including stimulants that manage sleepiness and antidepressants that relieve the symptoms of abnormal REM sleep, enabling most patients to regain about 80% of normal function (Stanford Center for Narcolepsy, 2015).

Sleep apnea is a potentially serious disorder in which breathing repeatedly starts and stops hundreds of times each night, depriving people of slow-wave sleep. Apnea sufferers typically don't recall these waking episodes and so are often unaware of their disorder. Compared to people with a healthy body mass index, people who are obese have four times the risk of sleep apnea. As the prevalence of obesity has increased, so too has this sleep disorder, particularly among men (Keller, Hader, De Zeeuw, & Rasche, 2007). People with thicker necks (17 inches or larger for men, and 15 inches or larger for women) may

sleep apnea A sleep disorder characterized by temporary cessations of breathing.

Gentle air pressure administered in the form of a nasal continuous positive airway pressure (CPAP) device is often effective in the treatment of sleep apnea.

have narrower airways and have increased risk of sleep apnea. Snoring loudly, morning headache, excessive daytime drowsiness (*hypersomnia*), attention problems, insomnia, and feeling irritable after a full night's sleep are other warning signs for the disorder (Mayo Clinic, 2015).

There are several types of apnea. Most common is *obstructive sleep apnea,* which occurs when throat muscles relax, causing the airway to narrow and preventing the sufferer from getting an adequate breath. As the level of oxygen in the blood drops, the brain briefly rouses the sleeper to reopen the airway, sometimes causing a snorting, choking, or gasping reflex that is repeated 5 to 30 times each hour of the night (Mayo Clinic, 2015).

Mild cases of sleep apnea are often managed through healthy lifestyle changes, including losing weight, quitting smoking, and treating allergies. If these measures aren't effective, symptoms can often be relieved by wearing a continuous positive airway pressure (CPAP) device, a mask connected to an air pump that keeps the airway open during sleep. For more severe cases, surgery to straighten the partition between the nostrils, remove tissue from the back of the mouth and top of the throat, or reposition the jaw may be necessary.

Research studies on sleep loss have found that adults who are short-duration sleepers (less than 7 hours per night) are more likely to be obese, to be physically inactive, and to smoke. In addition to these health risk factors, sleep-deprived adults are more likely to report at least one of the 10 most recognized chronic health conditions, including arthritis, depression, asthma, diabetes, and cancer (MMWR, 2015, January 9) (see Table 7.5).

TABLE 7.5 Chronic Health Conditions and Sleep Duration

Percentage of sleep-deprived adults who are more likely than other adults to report at least one of the following 10 most recognized chronic health conditions.

Chronic Condition	Short Sleep (<7 hours)	Sufficient Sleep (≥7 hours)
Heart attack	4.8%	3.4%
Coronary heart disease	4.7%	3.4%
Stroke	3.6%	2.4%
Asthma	16.5%	11.8%
COPD (chronic obstructive pulmonary disease)	8.6%	4.7%
Cancer	10.2%	9.8%
Arthritis	28.8%	20.5%
Depression	22.9%	14.6%
Chronic kidney disease	3.3%	2.2%
Diabetes	11.1%	8.6%

Data from: CDC (2017). Short sleep duration among U.S. adults. Centers for Disease Control and Prevention.

One researcher concluded that sleep restriction leads to "substantial and clinically significant changes in appetite regulation, hunger, food intake, glucose metabolism and blood pressure control" (Carpenter, 2013). Increased body mass index (BMI) can result from chronic sleep debt. One study reported that healthy men and women who were restricted to just 4 hours of sleep per night over six nights consumed more calories, particularly from fat, than their well-rested counterparts in a control group (St-Onge and others, 2011). Another study found that adults who were allowed to sleep only 5.5 hours per night for two weeks ate more snacks than control participants (Nedeltcheva and others, 2009). Sleep complaints such as difficulty falling asleep, difficulty staying asleep, and daytime sleepiness have been linked to increased total calorie intake; and children and adults who sleep less have a higher percentage of body fat than those who sleep more. One study reported that as average nightly sleep duration decreased from 8 hours to 5 hours, BMI increased more than 3% (from 31.3% to 32.4%) (Taheri, Lin, Austin, Young, & Mignot, 2004). In terms of the endocrine system, poor sleep stimulates an increase in the hunger-triggering hormone *ghrelin* and a decrease in the appetite-suppressing hormone *leptin* (Shlisky and others, 2012). Sleep loss also elevates levels of the stress hormone cortisol, which promotes the storage of calories into body fat (Chen, Beydoun, & Wang, 2008). This effect may help explain why chronically sleep-deprived college students often gain weight.

Sleep loss promotes insulin resistance, a key factor in the development of diabetes. Fat cells in people who experience sleep restriction are 30% less able to respond to insulin. Fortunately, this biochemical process may be reversible if sleep loss is not chronic. The same study found that when teens who normally got only six hours of sleep per night were allowed just one extra hour of sleep, insulin resistance improved by nearly 10% (Matthews, Dahl, Owens, Lee, & Hall, 2012). A more general condition, *cardiometabolic disease*, is a complex of chronic conditions that include obesity, diabetes, and cardiovascular disease; it is linked to sleep deprivation.

Sleep deprivation also suppresses immune functioning (Moller-Levet and others, 2013). Immunological signaling molecules such as tumor necrosis factor, interleukin-1, and interleukin-6 play an important role in sleep regulation. Elevated levels of these cytokines, which can occur with poor sleep, also are associated with diabetes, cardiovascular disease, inflammation, pain sensitivity, and a number of chronic illnesses (Motivala & Irwin, 2007). Other research has associated sleep loss with chronic inflammation (Motivala & Irwin, 2007) and has found adverse effects on our body's metabolic, neural, and endocrine functioning in ways that mimic accelerated aging (Pawlyck, Ferber, Shah, Pack, & Naidoo, 2007). Older adults who are *not* sleep deprived actually may live longer than people who have trouble falling or staying asleep (Dew and others, 2003).

At the cognitive level, research studies suggest that the brain uses sleep to repair damage, replenish energy stores, and promote *neurogenesis,* or the formation of new nerve cells (Winerman, 2006). As such, effects of poor sleep include impaired concentration, memory, and creativity, as well as increased reaction time, errors, and accidents (Lim & Dinges, 2010; Stickgold, 2009). Driver fatigue contributes to an estimated 20% of traffic accidents in the United States (Brody, 2002).

The American Academy of Sleep Medicine [AASM] (2017) offers the following tips for improving sleep:

- Keep a consistent sleep schedule. Get up at the same time every day, even on weekends or during vacations.

- Set a bedtime that is early enough for you to get at least 7 hours of sleep.

- Don't go to bed unless you are sleepy.
- If you don't fall asleep after 20 minutes, get out of bed.
- Establish a relaxing bedtime routine.
- Use your bed only for sleep and sex.
- Make your bedroom quiet and relaxing. Keep the room at a comfortable, cool temperature.
- Limit your exposure to bright light in the evening.
- Turn off electronic devices at least 30 minutes before bedtime.
- Don't eat a large meal before bedtime. If you are hungry at night, eat a light, healthy snack.
- Exercise regularly and maintain a healthy diet.
- Avoid consuming caffeine in the late afternoon or evening.
- Avoid consuming alcohol before bedtime.
- Reduce your fluid intake before bedtime.

If you are having sleep problems or regular daytime sleepiness, consider keeping a sleep diary. In it, record your sleep patterns and the amount of sleep that you get. The diary will help you examine some of your health and sleep habits so that you and your doctor can pinpoint any causes of poor sleep.

INJURY PREVENTION AND CONTROL

One of the many potential consequences of sleep deprivation is an increased risk of human error–related accidents. Sleep deprivation has been shown to produce cognitive, perceptual, and motor impairments equivalent to those caused by alcohol consumption at or above the legal limit. Motor-vehicle accidents related to fatigue, drowsy driving, and even falling asleep at the wheel are far too common, and they have a fatality rate and injury severity level similar to alcohol-related crashes (Durmer & Dinges, 2005).

One of health psychology's most important goals is to forestall the development of problems through primary prevention—a much more effective way of improving health than treating disease and disability that has already developed. In 2015, 214,008 deaths in the United States were classified as injury-related, mostly due to motor-vehicle crashes, poisoning, firearms, and falling (Murphy, Xu, Kochanek, Curtin, & Arias, 2017). Most of these fatalities were classified as **unintentional injuries**, or accidents, because the injured person didn't intend for it to happen. Most of the remaining deaths were **intentional injuries**, meaning that the person who caused the injury meant for it to happen. These deaths included suicides, homicides, and fatalities that occurred as part of war or another "legal intervention." In addition to these fatalities, nearly 43 million Americans were treated in hospital emergency departments (CDC, 2014a). One of the major goals of

unintentional injury Harm that is accidental, not meant to occur.

intentional injury Harm that results from behaviors designed to hurt oneself or others.

Healthy People 2020 is to reduce the overall rate of unintentional injuries to the target of no more than 36 deaths per 100,000 and to reduce motor-vehicle-crash–related deaths to no more than 12.4 per 100,000 Americans.

Although overall injuries are the fifth leading cause of death (after heart disease, cancer, stroke, and chronic obstructive pulmonary disease), the risk of injury, as well as the likelihood of dying from an injury, varies considerably across the life span (see Figure 7.2). When all people between ages 1 and 44 are considered as a group, unintentional injury is the *leading* cause of death, ahead of cardiovascular disease and cancer (Murphy and others, 2017). Not until age 40 does any specific disease overtake accidents as a cause of mortality.

The five leading causes of death in young people include several *external causes* (accidents, homicide, and suicide), followed by cancer and heart disease. This pattern of external causes accounting for more deaths than *chronic conditions* changes as people get older. In older age groups, chronic conditions account for more deaths than do external causes. For example, accidents account for more than one third of all deaths among persons aged 1 to 24 years. Accidental deaths are less prevalent in older age groups and do not even rank among the five leading causes of death in people 65 years of age and older.

FIGURE 7.2 10 Leading Causes of Death by Age Group The leading causes of death for those aged 1 to 24 years include a number of external causes (accidents, homicide, and suicide), followed by cancer (malignant neoplasms) and heart disease. This pattern shifts as age increases. In older age groups, chronic conditions account for more deaths than do external causes.

Data from: CDC (2016). Ten leading causes of death and injury. Centers for Disease Control and Prevention, National Center for Injury Prevention and Control.

10 Leading Causes of Death by Age Group, United States – 2016

Rank	<1	1–4	5–9	10–14	15–24	25–34	35–44	45–54	55–64	65+	Total
1	Congenital Anomalies 4,816	Unintentional Injury 1,261	Unintentional Injury 787	Unintentional Injury 847	Unintentional Injury 13,895	Unintentional Injury 23,984	Unintentional Injury 20,975	Malignant Neoplasms 41,291	Malignant Neoplasms 116,364	Heart Disease 507,118	Heart Disease 635,260
2	Short Gestation 3,927	Congenital Anomalies 433	Malignant Neoplasms 449	Suicide 436	Suicide 5,723	Suicide 7,366	Malignant Neoplasms 10,903	Heart Disease 34,027	Heart Disease 78,610	Malignant Neoplasms 422,927	Malignant Neoplasms 598,038
3	SIDS 1,500	Malignant Neoplasms 377	Congenital Anomalies 203	Malignant Neoplasms 431	Homicide 5,172	Homicide 5,376	Heart Disease 10,477	Unintentional Injury 23,377	Unintentional Injury 21,860	Chronic Low. Respiratory Disease 131,002	Unintentional Injury 161,374
4	Maternal Pregnancy Comp. 1,402	Homicide 339	Homicide 139	Homicide 147	Malignant Neoplasms 1,431	Malignant Neoplasms 3,791	Suicide 7,030	Suicide 8,437	Chronic Low. Respiratory Disease 17.810	Cerebro-vascular 121,630	Chronic Low. Respiratory Disease 154.596
5	Unintentional Injury 1,219	Heart Disease 118	Heart Disease 77	Congenital Anomalies 146	Heart Disease 949	Heart Disease 3,445	Homicide 3,369	Liver Disease 8,364	Diabetes Mellitus 14,251	Alzheimer's Disease 114,883	Cerebro-vascular 142,142
6	Placenta Cord. Membranes 841	Influenza & Pneumonia 103	Chronic Low. Respiratory Disease 68	Heart Disease 111	Congenital Anomalies 388	Liver Disease 925	Liver Disease 2,851	Diabetes Mellitus 6,267	Liver Disease 13,448	Diabetes Mellitus 56,452	Alzheimer's Disease 116,103
7	Bacterial Sepsis 583	Septicemia 70	Influenza & Pneumonia 48	Chronic Low Respiratory Disease 75	Diabetes Mellitus 211	Diabetes Mellitus 792	Diabetes Mellitus 2,049	Cerebro-vascular 5,353	Cerebro-vascular 12,310	Unintentional Injury 53,141	Diabetes Mellitus 80,058
8	Respiratory Distress 488	Perinatal Period 60	Septicemia 40	Cerebro-vascular 50	Chronic Low Respiratory Disease 206	Cerebro-vascular 575	Cerebro-vascular 1,851	Chronic Low. Respiratory Disease 4,307	Suicide 7,759	Influenza & Pneumonia 42,479	Influenza & Pneumonia 51,537
9	Circulatory System Disease 460	Cerebro-vascular 55	Cerebro-vascular 38	Influenza & Pneumonia 39	Influenza & Pneumonia 189	HIV 546	HIV 971	Septicemia 2,472	Septicemia 5,941	Nephritis 41,095	Nephritis 50,046
10	Neonatal Hemorrhage 398	Chronic Low Respiratory Disease 51	Benign Neoplasms 31	Septicemia 31	Complicated Pregnancy 184	Complicated Pregnancy 472	Septicemia 897	Homicide 2,152	Nephritis 5,650	Septicemia 30,405	Suicide 44,965

Injuries in Childhood

Compared to other stages of the life span, childhood for most children is uneventful in terms of overall health. In fact, during the school years, children in developed nations are the healthiest people of any age, being least likely to die or become seriously injured or ill (WHO, 2010d). Even so, an estimated 9,000 children and teens die each year in the United States as a result of unintentional injury (CDC, 2015a). For children ages 1 to 4, the leading causes of injury-related death are drowning and motor-vehicle accidents. From 5 to 9 years of age, about half of all injury-related deaths occur in motor-vehicle crashes, and most of the remainder are caused by fire/burns (just over 14%) and drowning (12.6%). For children ages 10 to 14, over half of all injury-related deaths occur in motor vehicles (56.6%).

Each year, millions of children are treated in hospital emergency departments for fall-related injuries. For children younger than age 2, many of these injuries are the result of falls from cribs and playpens (Yeh, Rochette, McKenzie, & Smith, 2011). Among older children, many nonfatal fall-related injuries are the result of playground accidents that

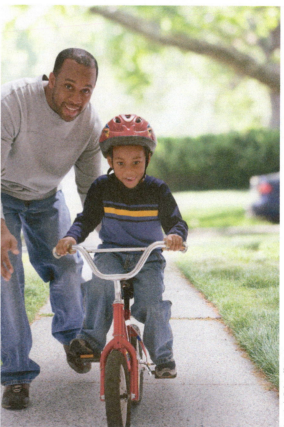

Most childhood injuries are predictable and preventable. Adult supervision and the use of safety equipment go a long way in keeping children safe.

lead to fractures, concussions, and internal injuries. Childhood falls occur largely as a result of children's evolving physical and cognitive development, especially their innate curiosity about their surroundings and increasing levels of independence. Although inadequate adult supervision is often cited as a risk factor, the circumstances are often complex, interacting with poverty, single parenthood, and environments that are particularly hazardous. For instance, several studies have found that playgrounds in low-income areas had more maintenance-related hazards than those in more affluent neighborhoods. These hazards included rusty play equipment, trash, and damaged fall surfaces.

Although most early childhood injuries are not deliberate, public health experts increasingly choose not to call them "accidents," which would imply that they are random and unpredictable. Instead of accident prevention, experts prefer the term **injury control** (or harm reduction). Minor injuries are an inevitable part of any normal, active childhood, but serious injury is unlikely if efforts aimed at prevention are sound.

injury control Systematic efforts to prevent injuries from occurring and to limit the consequences of those that have already occurred.

Injuries in Adolescence and Emerging Adulthood

Unintentional injury is the leading cause of death for adolescents and young adults, with motor-vehicle accidents far and away the most prevalent type of injury resulting in death in these age groups (Murphy and others, 2017). This sobering statistic is true despite the fact that reflexes are faster and vision is better at these ages than at any other point in the life span. What accounts for this seemingly illogical fact? Many experts believe the answer is simple: Adolescents and young adults are prone to thoughtless impulses and poor decisions that lead to risky driving practices, including speeding, driving under the influence of alcohol, and driving while distracted—texting or talking on a cell phone, for instance.

Poor decision making is partly the result of the fact that different parts of the brain grow at different rates. The limbic system, including the amygdala (where fear, excitement, and other intense emotions originate) matures before the prefrontal cortex (where emotional regulation, impulse control, and thoughtful analysis occur). As a result, the emotional areas of the brain develop ahead of the executive, analytic areas. Add to this the fact that the surge of hormones that accompanies puberty strongly affects the amygdala, while the cortex "matures" more as a result of the experiences that accompany aging. For many teens and emerging adults, this is a dangerous time when emotional rushes, unchecked by caution, are common (Blakemore, 2008).

Neurological research finds that during adolescence, brain areas that respond to excitement and pleasure are much more active than brain areas that control inhibition and urge caution (Van Leijenhorst and others, 2010). This is evident in functional magnetic resonance imaging (fMRI) scans of the brains of people in different age groups. When compared with 18- to 23-year-olds, 14- to 15-year-olds show dramatically increased arousal in the brain's limbic areas, making them especially susceptible to excitement and the strong sensations provided by driving fast, participating in extreme sports, and using alcohol and strong drugs (Van Leijenhorst and others, 2010). This may partly explain why younger drivers are more likely to speed than older drivers. As shown in Figure 7.3, the percentage of fatal motor-vehicle crashes caused by speeding is highest, for both male and female drivers, between age 15 and age 20 and decreases throughout adulthood (National Highway Traffic Safety Administration [NHTSA], 2016).

FIGURE 7.3 Speeding Drivers in Fatal Crashes by Age and Sex For drivers involved in fatal crashes, young males are the most likely to be speeding. The relative proportion of speeding-related crashes to all crashes decreases with driver age.

Data from: National Highway Traffic Safety Administration. (NHTSA.) (2018). *Traffic safety facts: Speeding, 2016 data.*

Young adults are prone to poor decisions that lead to risky driving practices, including driving while distracted.

A pertinent example of the cautious part of the brain being overwhelmed by the emotions of the moment comes from studies showing the hazards of texting and other distractions while driving. In 2015, 10% of fatal crashes and 15% of injury crashes were due to distracted driving. Drivers in their twenties had the largest proportion of distracted drivers of any age group (National Center for Statistics and Analysis, 2017). Other examples of poor impulse control and faulty reasoning while driving abound. Consider the following data from the CDC (2015a):

- Teens are more likely than older drivers to underestimate dangerous situations and may be unable to recognize hazardous situations.

- Teens are more likely than older drivers to speed and to allow shorter headways (the distance from the front of one vehicle to the front of the next). Interestingly, the presence of male passengers increases the likelihood of this risky driving behavior.

- Compared with other age groups, teens have the lowest rate of seat belt use.

- At all levels of blood alcohol concentration, the risk of involvement in a motor-vehicle crash is greater for teens than for older drivers.

Because the immature brains of young drivers play such a large role in causing motor-vehicle accidents, it is not surprising that four preventive measures have saved hundreds of lives: (1) graduated driver licensing (GDL), which requires more time between issuing a learner's permit and granting a full license; (2) restricted driving at night; (3) no teenage passengers; and (4) zero tolerance for driving under the influence of alcohol (Fell, Fisher, Voas, Blackman, & Tippetts, 2011). Consider the impact of GDL, which is designed to delay full licensure while allowing a greater period of time for young drivers with a learner's permit to practice and gain initial driving experience under supervised, low-risk conditions. Research studies demonstrate that comprehensive GDL programs are associated with reductions of 38% and 40% in fatal and nonfatal injury crashes, respectively, among 16-year-old drivers (Baker, Chen, & Li, 2007).

Injuries in Adulthood

Injuries remain the leading cause of death in adults ages 35 to 44; but then they become less prevalent as chronic illnesses such as cardiovascular disease and cancer begin to cause more deaths in older adults (Murphy and others, 2017). For people who have reached age 65, injuries have dropped to the ninth-leading cause of death.

The types of injuries that people suffer and from which they sometimes die also change as people get older. In adults aged 25 to 34, car accidents are the leading cause of injury-related death, followed by poisoning and homicide. Between ages 35 and 54, poisoning causes the most injury-related fatalities, followed by motor-vehicle crashes and suicides. Car accidents, suicides, and poisoning, in that order, cause the most injury-related fatalities between ages 55 and 64. For those aged 65 and older, falls are the leading cause of injury-related death, followed by car accidents and suicide.

Poisoning

Unintentional poisoning death rates—which include deaths from drug overdoses—have been increasing steadily since 1992 and have become second only to motor-vehicle crashes as a cause of accidental death. In 2013, unintentional poisonings caused 98,000 deaths worldwide (GBD, 2015). Most unintentional deaths from poisoning (91%) are caused by drugs; of these, prescription painkillers, including hydrocodone, oxycodone, and methadone, are most commonly involved, followed by cocaine and heroin.

Among adults treated in hospital emergency departments for nonfatal poisoning involving drugs, the use of pain medications and central nervous system (CNS)–depressant benzodiazepines (such as Valium) is reported most often. Men are twice as likely as women to die from poisoning, and the prevalence of poison-related deaths varies with ethnicity. In the United States, Native Americans have the highest death rates by poisoning, followed by European Americans, and then African Americans (Murphy and others, 2017).

Homicide

The low rate of chronic illness among people between ages 18 and 25 is offset by a high rate of severe injuries and violent deaths, with males being more than twice as vulnerable as females. The high rate of violent death is evident particularly among young males. Violent deaths are more common than disease deaths during these years even in nations with rampant infection and malnutrition (Patton and others, 2012).

In 2015, there were 17,793 homicides in the United States. Of these, 12,979 (72.94%) involved the use of a firearm (Murphy and others, 2017). More people are murdered during emerging adulthood than at any other period, with people aged 18 to 24 years consistently having the highest rate of homicide.

The epidemiology of gun violence in the United States reveals the importance of several factors, including gender, ethnicity/race, geographical region, and public policy (NPR, 2013). Briefly put, white people who die by gunfire are much more likely to be male, to live in rural areas, and to commit suicide; black people who die by gunfire are more likely to be male, to live in urban areas, and to be victims of homicide. Males are nearly seven times more likely to die by homicide than females, and African Americans are twice as likely to die by homicide as whites. Homicide is one reason why African Americans have a shorter average life expectancy than whites. Stated differently, for every white male shot in a homicide, five shoot themselves; and for every black male who kills himself with a gun, five are killed by homicide. The rates for women are much lower for both homicide and suicide.

Suicide

Homicide is most prevalent in people ages 18 to 24, whereas suicide is most likely among those of ages 45 to 54. Nearly 1 million people worldwide commit suicide each year, with prevalence rates varying from country to country (WHO, 2011b). For instance, suicide rates in Britain, Italy, and Spain are little more than half those of the United States, Canada, and Australia. The age-adjusted suicide rate for the total population of the United States is about

11.8 per 100,000 people, with the greatest number occurring between the ages of 45 and 54. Worldwide, women are more likely than men to attempt suicide, but men are four times more likely to actually end their lives; men represent nearly 80% of all U.S. suicides, probably because they are more likely to use a gun or some other lethal means (WHO, 2011b).

Firearms are the most commonly used method of suicide among males (55.7%), whereas poisoning is the most common method among females (40.2%). In the United States, whites and Native Americans commit suicide twice as often as blacks, Hispanics, and Asians (Murphy and others, 2017). Suicide rates are higher among people who are affluent, single, widowed, divorced, depressed, or alcohol-dependent. Suicidal thoughts also arise when people feel disconnected or that they are a burden to others (Joiner, 2010), when they feel trapped by an inescapable situation (Taylor, Gooding, Wood, & Tarrier, 2011), and when they are driven to reach a goal they believe is unattainable (Chatard & Selimbegovic, 2011). Among gay and lesbian youth, peer rejection and an unsupportive family have been associated with attempted suicide (Haas and others, 2011).

Because suicide is so often an impulsive act, environmental barriers such as preventing access to firearms, which are involved in 57% of U.S. suicides, are an important deterrent (Anderson, 2008). People who live in a house where a firearm is kept are five times as likely to die by suicide as people who live in gun-free homes. One massive study examined the association between firearm ownership and suicide across all 50 states (Miller, Lippmann, Azrael, & Hemenway, 2007). After taking into account poverty, unemployment, mental illness, and drug and alcohol abuse, the researchers found that people of all ages and both sexes are more likely to die from suicide when they live in a community in which more households own firearms.

Some people, especially adolescents and young adults, stop short of suicide by turning to *non-suicidal self-injury* (NSSI) behaviors such as cutting the skin, pulling out hair, inserting objects under the skin, and administering their own tattoos (Fikke, Melinder, & Landro, 2011). Although NSSI is a risk factor for future suicide attempts, those who engage in NSSI usually are *suicide gesturers,* not *suicide attempters* (Wilkinson & Goodyer, 2011). They are often extremely self-critical and have poor communication and problem-solving skills (Nock, 2010). Experts also suggest that NSSI behaviors may be an attempt to

- gain attention and ask others for help,
- get others to stop bullying them,
- use pain to distract from persistent negative thoughts and rumination,
- relieve guilt through self-punishment, or
- fit in with a peer group.

Falls

Falls are the second leading cause of unintentional injury deaths worldwide (WHO, 2012). Each year, an estimated 424,000 people globally die as a result of falls, of which over 80% are in low- and middle-income countries. Many more people suffer nonfatal fall-related injuries. In the United States, falls are the overall leading cause of injury, accounting for twice as many injuries as any other cause (see Figure 7.4).

In 2014, in the United States, 2.5 million nonfatal fall-related injuries among older adults were treated in hospital emergency departments, resulting in a direct medical cost of $34 billion (CDC, 2015a). Each year, one out of every three adults aged 65 and older

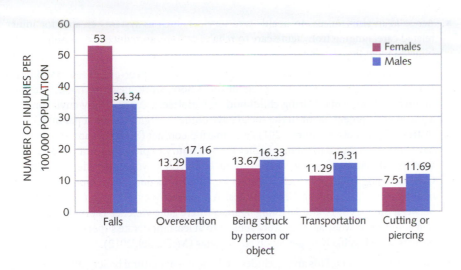

FIGURE 7.4 Falls Falls are the overall leading cause of injury, accounting for nearly 40% of all injuries in the United States each year.

Data from: Adams, P. F., Kirzinger, W. K., & Martinez, M. E. (2012). Summary health statistics for the U.S. population: National Health Interview Survey, 2011. National Center for Health Statistics. *Vital Health Stat 10*(255).

falls. The global result is approximately 37.3 million falls that do not result in death but are serious enough to require medical attention. Nonfatal falls are responsible for the loss of over 17 million *disability-adjusted life years* (DALYs), with the highest rates of morbidity occurring in people 65 and older, followed by young adults aged 15 to 29, and then by children 15 years and younger.

Among older adults, 20% to 30% of falls result in moderate to severe injuries such as bruises, hip fractures, and traumatic brain injuries. This risk level may be in part due to physical, sensory, and cognitive changes associated with aging, in combination with environments that are not optimized for older adults. Many people who fall, even if they are not injured, develop a fear of falling that may cause them to limit their activities. This leads to loss of physical fitness, which in turn increases their future risk of falling.

Injury Prevention

Because of the tremendous cost of injuries to individuals and society, health psychologists have an important role to play in developing interventions aimed at prevention. The premise of the ecological systems approach (discussed in Chapter 1) is that an individual does not act or develop in a vacuum, but rather in the presence of people, places, and situations that influence how the person thinks, behaves, and acts. From this perspective, a wide range of contextual factors influences the risk of an injury occurring. These factors vary in their influence across the life span and include societal, neighborhood and community, family, peer, and individual factors. Consistent with this perspective, *Healthy People 2020* identified the following areas as targets for interventions aimed at reducing the risk of unintentional injury and violence (CDC, 2010b):

- *Individual behaviors.* The choices people make, such as alcohol use, texting while driving, or risk-taking, can increase injuries. As another example, higher levels of activity and injury history are associated with more frequent injuries (Schwebel and others, 2011).

- *Physical environment.* Features such as lighting, smoke detectors, and fences can affect the rate of injuries related to falls, fires and burns, drowning, and violence.

■ *Access to services.* Access to health care services, such as systems created for injury-related care, ranging from acute care to rehabilitation, can reduce the consequences of injuries, including death and disability.

■ *Social environment.* This area includes adult supervision, peer-group associations, and family interactions, as well as aspects of the school, work, neighborhood, and community environments. During childhood and adolescence, the family environment is a particularly potent factor in the social environment. Higher levels of parental mental distress (Schwebel and others, 2011) and marital conflict (Schwebel and others, 2012) have both been found to predict higher rates of injury in preadolescent children. Conversely, *parental monitoring* can help reduce the risk of young people being injured. Consider gang violence, which accounts for as many as one in five murders in several of the largest cities in the United States. A recent survey of more than 4,000 teens between the ages of 14 and 18 living in areas where gang violence is prevalent reported that adolescents who said they were subject to at least moderate supervision from their parents were less likely to get involved in gangs (McDaniel, 2012).

■ *Societal-level factors.* This area includes such factors as cultural beliefs, attitudes, incentives and disincentives, and laws and regulations.

Harm reduction and injury control measures can be grouped into three types of prevention, beginning with *primary prevention*—changes in laws and other societal policies that are designed to make harm less likely for everyone. *Secondary prevention* is more specific, reducing the chance of injury in high-risk situations or for vulnerable individuals. *Tertiary prevention* begins after an injury has occurred, limiting the damage. Primary prevention is most effective because it begins long before someone does something that is careless, foolish, or neglectful.

Consider how the three levels of prevention might apply to childhood drowning, which is a leading cause of unintentional death among 1- to 4-year-olds. Primary prevention would include the enforcement of building codes and local laws that require all swimming pools to be surrounded completely by a locked fence. Secondary prevention might be the wise parent who puts good life jackets on children before they paddle a canoe on the lake. An example of tertiary prevention is the immediate delivery of cardiopulmonary resuscitation (CPR) to a submerged child who has been pulled from the water.

Other examples of primary prevention through societal changes include state and federal laws that restrict certain behaviors and mandate others. Many states now have laws mandating the use of age-appropriate restraints for children through 6 to 8 years of age, with some states also requiring that children sit in the back seat. As another example, a growing number of communities are banning the use of handheld cell phones and texting while driving. Still other examples of primary prevention are laws regarding alcohol use that are designed to prevent drunk driving; building codes and regulations that require smoke detectors in buildings; local ordinances requiring the wearing of bicycle helmets; and federal laws mandating air bags, the use of seat belts, and lower speed limits.

Some critics of public health policy say children today are overprotected, with more laws mandating child car seats, cushioned safety surfaces, fewer jungle gyms, and so forth. Consider

Age-appropriate safety seats and restraints are required for infants and children throughout the United States, though the details and criteria vary from state to state.

Blend Images/Alamy Stock Photo

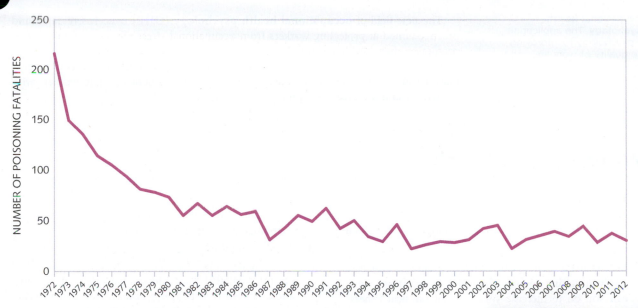

FIGURE 7.5 Childhood Poisoning Fatalities—1972 to 2012 Poisoning fatalities for U.S. children younger than age 5 dropped dramatically in the first decade after Congress enacted legislation requiring protective labeling and packaging of poisonous household products. At the same time, a public information campaign with a "Mr. Yuk" image raised awareness of childhood poisoning risks.

Data from: Qin, A. (2015). Pediatric poisoning fatalities from 1972 through 2012. Consumer Product Safety Commission.

another example of the effectiveness of primary prevention: accidental poisoning from drugs and household chemicals. In 1970, the U.S. Congress passed the Poison Prevention Packaging Act (PPPA), under which child-resistant packaging was for the first time mandated for 30 categories of medicines and hazardous household products. Since the PPPA became law, the number of childhood deaths from accidental poisoning decreased more than 80%, from about 500 that year to an average of about 36 in 2012 (Figure 7.5). Thanks to better awareness and prevention efforts at each of the three levels, when injuries of all types are considered, less than half as many 1- to 4-year-olds in the United States were fatally injured in 2010 as in 1980 (Hoyert, 2012).

Sound laws and policies work hand in hand with secondary prevention in preventing injuries. Even simple and inexpensive efforts such as keeping household chemicals, medications (in child-resistant containers), guns, and other dangerous objects in inaccessible, locked cabinets go a long way in reducing the likelihood of injuries.

Taking a prevention approach to injury control is a recent phenomenon. As recently as the 1980s, injury prevention was not even covered in most textbooks on community psychology. Community health psychologists generally focus on three accepted strategies in injury prevention programs: (1) *education and behavior change,* (2) *legislation and enforcement,* and (3) *engineering and technology.* Education and behavior-change strategies typically are aimed at reducing risk behaviors (anything that increases the likelihood that a person will be injured) and increasing protective behaviors (anything that reduces potential harm from a risk behavior).

occupational health psychology The application of psychology to improving the quality of work life, and to protecting and promoting the safety, health and well-being of workers.

The new field of **occupational health psychology (OHP)** concerns research and practice aimed at protecting workers from occupational stress, illness, and injury, and promoting their health and well-being. Occupational health psychologists work closely with the *National Institute for Occupational Safety and Health (NIOSH)* to reduce workplace hazards, and to develop primary prevention interventions to equip workers with knowledge and resources to improve their health.

Weigh In on Health

Respond to each question below based on what you learned in the chapter. (**Tip:** Use the items in "Summing Up" to take into account related biological, psychological, and social concerns.)

1. List as many benefits of physical fitness as you can. Are you getting enough physical activity? If not, what can you do to increase your level of physical fitness? What habits could you adopt to keep physically active throughout your life?

2. You have been asked to deliver a speech about the health hazards of sleep deprivation. Using the biopsychosocial model, prepare an outline of an effective speech on this topic. Then fill in the key research findings and other subpoints that support your central ideas.

3. Think about the last time that you suffered an unintentional injury. Was it truly an "accident," or could it have been prevented? How could you have changed the situation, or your own behavior, and avoided injury? What can you do in similar situations in the future to produce a different outcome?

Summing Up

Physical Activity, Exercise, and Fitness

1. Regular exercise and physical fitness increase physical strength, help maintain bone density and a healthy weight, and reduce risks for cardiovascular disease, cancer, osteoporosis, metabolic syndrome, and other chronic illnesses.

2. Exercise may also serve as an effective buffer against anxiety and stress; boost self-esteem and self-efficacy; help people feel more vigor and less fatigue; improve cognitive functioning; and offer protection against dementia, depression, and anxiety. The cognitive benefits of exercise are especially important for older adults.

3. Some older adults face several barriers to exercising, including ageist stereotypes, lack of confidence (exercise self-efficacy) and motivation, and myths that exercise can actually undermine their health.

4. Minority group members have lower physical activity levels than majority group members, with minority women being among the least active subgroups in the United States.

Physical activity levels are also low among people with lower socioeconomic status.

5. People are most likely to stick with exercise programs if they enjoy exercise, already have formed the habit of exercising regularly, grew up in families that exercised, have social support for exercising and a strong sense of self-efficacy toward exercising, and believe that individuals should take responsibility for their own health.

6. Interventions to promote physical activity work best when they are matched to the stage of readiness of individual participants; they emphasize behavioral strategies; and they target neighborhood, community, and societal barriers in a comprehensive ecological approach. Health psychologists have also developed interventions to assist nurses and other providers in promoting exercise to their patients.

7. Exercise can lead to injury and, if compulsive, can resemble addictive behavior. Compulsive exercise is sometimes used to manage personal or emotional problems.

Sleep

8. The sleeping brain operates according to a 90-minute biological rhythm, cycling through four distinct sleep stages. There are two broad types of sleep: non–rapid eye movement (NREM) and rapid eye movement (REM), distinguished by different brain waves, changes in breathing and muscle tension, and a few other bodily changes.

9. Newborns sleep 15 to 17 hours a day, in segments lasting 1 to 3 hours, because the brain areas that regulate sleep are immature. The number of hours that babies sleep decreases rapidly as their brains continue to develop.

10. Short sleep duration is linked to race/ethnicity, issues in the workplace and neighborhood, and other social factors. People who are coping with stressful events at work or in the home also report poorer sleep, especially when stressors are appraised as uncontrollable. About one third of adults experience sleep problems occasionally, and 1 in 10 adults (1 in 4 older adults) complains of insomnia.

11. Chronic sleep debt promotes increased body weight, suppresses immune functioning, and adversely affects our body's metabolic, neural, and endocrine functioning in ways that mimic accelerated aging. The brain uses sleep to repair damage; to replenish energy stores; and to promote neurogenesis, or the formation of new nerve cells.

12. *DSM-V* lists 11 categories of sleep disorders, including insomnia, narcolepsy, and sleep apnea. Cognitive behavioral therapy for insomnia (CBT-I) is an effective intervention for improving restful sleep without the use of sleeping pills.

13. Sleep hygiene focuses on improving lifestyle behaviors that influence sleep, such as drinking too much alcohol, consuming caffeine late in the day, or not getting regular exercise. It also includes training in ways to wind down before bedtime.

Injury Control and Prevention

14. The risk of injury as well as the likelihood of dying from an injury vary considerably across the life span. Most injury-related deaths are from unintentional injuries. In younger people, external causes account for more deaths than chronic conditions do. In older age groups, chronic conditions account for more deaths than external causes do.

15. Poor decision making during adolescence and emerging adulthood is partly the result of the fact that different parts of the brain grow at different rates. The limbic system, including the amygdala (where fear, excitement, and other intense emotions originate), matures before the prefrontal cortex (where emotional regulation, impulse control, and thoughtful analysis occur). As a result, the emotional areas of the brain develop ahead of the executive, analytic areas.

Key Terms and Concepts to Remember

physical activity, p. 196
physical exercise, p. 196
aerobic exercise, p. 196
anaerobic exercise, p. 196
basal metabolic rate (BMR), p. 196
calorie, p. 196
physical fitness, p. 199
cardiorespiratory endurance, p. 199
osteoporosis, p. 202
metabolic syndrome (MetS), p. 202

metabolic flexibility, p. 203
functional plasticity, p. 204
behavior change technique (BCT), p. 207
mHealth, p. 208
compulsive exercise, p. 211
short sleep duration, p. 211
sleep disorder, p. 211
circadian rhythm, p. 211
rapid eye movement (REM), p. 213

insomnia, p. 216
cognitive behavioral therapy for insomnia (CBT-I), p. 217
narcolepsy, p. 218
sleep apnea, p. 219
unintentional injury, p. 222
intentional injury, p. 222
injury control, p. 225
occupational health psychology (OHP), p. 232

 To accompany your textbook, you have access to a number of online resources, including quizzes for every chapter of the book, flashcards, critical thinking exercises, videos, and *Check Your Health* inventories. To access these resources, please visit the Straub Health Psychology LaunchPad at **launchpadworks.com**

Chapter **8**

Corina Marie Howell/Getty Images

Nutrition, Obesity, and Eating Disorders

LEARNING OUTCOMES
Once you have studied this chapter, you will be able to:
- Define a healthy diet and explain how diet and health are related,
- Explain the principles of weight regulation in relation to food consumption,
- Identify the hazards of obesity and the factors that contribute to it,
- Describe methods of preventing and treating obesity, and
- Define eating disorders and the treatments available to address them.

One of my former students (let's call her Jodi) had been an 800-meter track champion and an academic all-American during her high school and college years. At age 26, Jodi was hospitalized with serious coronary complications that resulted from her 12-year battle with disordered eating. She weighed only 78 pounds, yet she saw herself as bloated and obese.

Growing up in an upper-middle-class home, Jodi had a loving family, but she always felt pressure to live up to their high expectations. She found it particularly difficult to follow in the footsteps of her talented and popular sister and felt that she had to be perfect at everything.

In her view, her most significant imperfection was that she did not look like a swimsuit model. Jodi had a short, powerful build that was well suited for running fast. Even though she was the top runner on her high school and college teams, her coaches and trainers advised that she could run faster if only she would shed a few pounds.

Jodi tried her best to lose weight, but her body simply wouldn't cooperate. She tried several diets, all of which made her tired, hungry, and unable to concentrate on her schoolwork, and she never stayed on them very long. Her weight bounced up and down like a yo-yo.

Then Jodi found a terrible solution for her "problem": She would eat whatever she wanted and then either make herself vomit or take a large dose of laxatives. She also increased her daily running mileage and added cross-training workouts to her regular routine. She still felt tired, but she thought it was worth it to gain some control over her weight.

Jodi was able to hide her bingeing and purging during high school and college, but once she was living on her own, she started eating less and less, and her weight loss became obvious. One holiday, she was visiting her family when she fainted while playing basketball with her father. When he lifted her up off the pavement, he realized that she weighed little more than a child.

Jodi's parents insisted that she see a doctor, who quickly placed her into a treatment program in which she was force-fed for a week. Although Jodi's weight increased, the years of disordered eating had taken such a severe toll on her body that her prospects for regaining her health were not promising.

Throughout most of history, a full figure has been considered a sign of prosperity and health, and this is still true in developing countries. But today's Western culture idealizes a thin physique. We are bombarded with media images of thinness that shape our standards of attractiveness and strongly influence how we feel about our bodies. Several studies have shown that even children as young as 3 years of age have a negative body image (Professional Association for Childcare and Early Years [PACEY], 2016). As Jodi's heart-wrenching story illustrates, not everyone can have a thin figure. Yet the market is flooded with weight-loss "solutions," most of which are ineffective beyond the first few weeks.

Health psychology endeavors to help people attain and maintain a healthy weight, not necessarily to have people achieve the cultural ideal. Yet the ease with which we gain weight has led more of us to suffer serious health risks from being **overweight** (body mass index [BMI] equal to or greater than 25) or **obese** (BMI equal to or greater than 30) (see Figure 8.1).

The epidemic of overweight and obesity has spread worldwide, including Spain, France, Australia, Brazil, Mexico, Denmark, Italy, Russia—where more than half the populations are overweight—and Japan—which has a national law mandating maximum waistline measurements (33.5 inches for men and 35.4 inches for women) as part of annual physical exams for all adults ages 40 to 74 (Onishi, 2008). A global study of 188 countries revealed that since the mid-1980s, *no* country has reduced its obesity rate (Ng and others, 2014). The worldwide prevalence of obesity has nearly tripled since 1975, and for the first time in history, the global number

overweight Body weight that exceeds the desirable weight for a person of a given height, age, and body shape.

obesity Excessive accumulation of body fat.

FIGURE 8.1 Prevalence of Overweight and Obese Americans Data from the National Health and Nutrition Examination Survey (NHANES) reveal that 40 years ago, 47% of Americans were classified as overweight or obese (BMI > 25.0); today, 65% are overweight or obese. Americans are fatter today than their parents and grandparents ever were, and they are getting fatter every year.

Data from: Fryar, C. D., Carroll, M. D., & Ogden, C. L. (2014). Prevalence of overweight, obesity, and extreme obesity among adults: United States, trends 1960–1962 through 2011–2012. Centers for Disease Control and Prevention. National Center for Health Statistics.

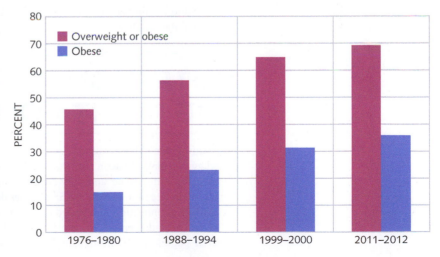

of overweight people (more than 1.9 billion) rivals the number of underfed and under-weight people (World Health Organization [WHO], 2018). Is it any wonder that the World Health Organization recognizes obesity as one of the top ten health problems in the world and one of the top five in developed countries?

In the United States, more people are treated for obesity than for all other health conditions combined (Carroll, Navaneelan, Bryan, & Ogden, 2015). The global scope of the problem is enormous, leading to more deaths each year than underweight (WHO, 2018).

The problem became so acute that in 2010 then–First Lady Michelle Obama announced a nationwide campaign (dubbed "Let's Move") to eliminate the problem of childhood obesity within one generation (Linshi, 2015). The Let's Move program reflects a biopsychosocial solution and emphasizes (1) getting nutrition and exercise information to parents, (2) improving the quality of food in schools, (3) making healthy foods more affordable and accessible, and (4) focusing more on physical education. The new standards for school lunches, which were phased in starting in the 2012–2013 school year, include requirements to double the amounts of vegetables and fruits available, switch all grains to whole grains, and offer milk in only fat-free or low-fat varieties.

More than seven years into the Let's Move campaign, the results were mixed. In 2017 in the United States, nearly one in five school-age children and teenagers (6 to 19 years) was obese (Centers for Disease Control [CDC], 2018). However, obesity among very young children (2 to 5 years) had dropped slightly, perhaps reflecting parental awareness of how to promote healthy weight in their children. One might also hope that kids who are taught healthy nutrition and exercise habits at a young age will be more likely to carry those habits into adolescence and adulthood. Meanwhile, in Canada, there is not a single province where a majority of adults are not overweight or obese (Young, 2017).

Psychologists have joined forces with molecular biologists, genetic engineers, nutritionists, and other health professionals to find answers to some puzzling questions: Why is obesity becoming more prevalent? Why is it relatively simple to lose weight but nearly impossible to keep it off? Why do some people gain weight more easily than others? Which foods are most healthful to consume, and how can we safely maintain a healthy weight? And why do social inequalities in overweight and obesity persist? In this chapter, we will address these and other important questions in our exploration of eating behavior and weight regulation. We begin by examining the components of food and their role in maintaining health.

NUTRITION: EATING THE RIGHT FOODS

In Framingham, Massachusetts, in 1948, a "healthy" breakfast consisted of a plate of fried eggs, a slab of bacon, and several pieces of white toast slathered with margarine. Residents spooned sugar and fatty cream from the top of milk bottles into their coffee. In this town, one in four men age 55 or older developed heart disease, but doctors hadn't yet made the connection to diet and often listed "acute indigestion" as the cause of death.

Researchers descended on the town, and after 50 years and over 1,000 scholarly research papers, the Framingham Heart Study (2018) has shown that poor nutrition is a leading risk factor for heart disease. We have learned that a diet focused on fruits, vegetables, and lean proteins, while limiting the consumption of saturated fat and entirely avoiding trans-fatty acids, provides the body with the nutrients it needs to protect and repair itself. We are, indeed, what we eat.

Healthy Eating and Adherence to a Healthy Diet

In addition to daily caloric energy, our bodies require 46 nutrients to remain healthy. Nutrients are grouped into five categories: proteins, fats, carbohydrates, minerals, and vitamins. Each group offers unique contributions to bodily function and health—and in the case of proteins, fats, and carbohydrates, the caloric energy our bodies need to meet the demands of daily living. Water is also a major source of nutrition, transporting nutrients throughout the bloodstream, removing wastes, and regulating the body's temperature. Most people in the United States drink less than the recommended amount of water each day (Kant, Graubard, & Atchinson, 2009). Although individual needs vary, most people can stay well hydrated by drinking six to eight 8-ounce glasses of water and other healthy fluids each day—enough so that there is the need to urinate every two to four hours and the urine is a light color.

The U.S. Department of Agriculture's guidelines, which are updated every five years (see *Diversity and Healthy Living: Acculturation in Nutrition Guidelines*), advocate a largely plant-based diet with an abundance of fruits and vegetables, whole grains, and seeds and nuts, along with low-fat dairy, seafood, and beans. The nutrition panel also emphasizes the importance of taking sustainability of food production into consideration when choosing what to eat. The 2015 government report raised the question, for instance, of whether it's sustainable to recommend 8 to 12 ounces of fish a week. This emphasis on sustainability—appearing for the first time in the 2015 guidelines—also circles back to the desirability of plant-based foods. The report states that "a diet higher in plant-based foods, such as vegetables....and lower in calories and animal-based foods is more health promoting and is associated with less environmental impact than is the current U.S. diet" (U.S. Department of Health and Human Services and U.S. Department of Agriculture, 2015).

U.S. Department of Agriculture's guidelines emphasize the importance of taking into consideration food production sustainability, with emphasis on plant-based foods, when choosing what to eat.

Earlier U.S. dietary guidelines put a strong emphasis on nutrients—which people don't generally think of as being what they eat—with recommendations such as "limit intake of saturated fat" and "get more calcium." The 2015 guidelines moved to an emphasis on actual foods and on the ways foods interact with each other based on a person's overall dietary pattern. Healthy dietary patterns such as the Mediterranean and DASH (Dietary Approach to Stop Hypertension) diets receive a great deal of attention in the 2015 guidelines.

One user-friendly resource that helps to disseminate the government guidelines is the "MyPlate/MiPlato" diagram, a quick visual reminder to make healthy choices

iStock/Getty Images

USDA Center for Nutrition Policy and Promotion

FIGURE 8.2 A Balanced Diet
MyPlate/MiPlato illustrates the five food groups that are the building blocks for a healthy diet. The latest guidelines place less emphasis on grains and serving sizes and cap fat and sugar at no more than 10% of calories each.

when choosing one's next meal. It depicts a place setting divided into five food groups of approximately 30% vegetables, 30% grains, 20% fruits, and 20% protein, accompanied by a small circle representing dairy, such as a glass of skim milk (Figure 8.2). The exact amount that you should eat from each food group depends on your age, gender, and level of physical activity. (For a quick estimate of your needs, see the online calculator at www.choosemyplate.gov.) By mid-2012, MyPlate information began to be displayed on food packaging and restaurant menus and used in nutrition education. Unfortunately, nutritional advice is frequently ignored, and adherence to healthy diets overall tends to be modest at best.

The Sugar–Fat Controversy

Government recommendations regarding consumption of fat and sugar are a high-profile cautionary tale about evaluating dietary data. An article in the prestigious *Journal of the American Medical Association* dropped a bombshell when its authors charged that five decades of dietary research and nutrition guidelines were largely shaped by the sugar industry (Kearns, Schmidt, & Glantz, 2016). Based on their review of 50-year-old industry documents, the authors claimed that the sugar industry commissioned *Project 226,* in which research scientists were paid to conduct a review of the literature to blame fat and cholesterol as the primary cause of heart disease, while downplaying the hazards of sugary foods and beverages. In addition to paying the scientists, sugar industry representatives may also have selected the articles to be included in the review and screened prepublication drafts of the final report. The 1967 report, which appeared in the highly respected *New England Journal of Medicine,* concluded that there was "no doubt" that reducing saturated fat and cholesterol were the only dietary interventions needed to prevent heart disease. Note that the article appeared at a time when journals did not typically require authors to disclose their funding sources and possible conflicts of interest, as they must do today.

Diversity and Healthy Living

Acculturation in Nutrition Guidelines

Every five years, the U.S. government issues a new set of dietary guidelines based on the input of a panel of experts who review the latest nutrition studies over a two-year period. The guidelines are important, not only because people look to them for authoritative evidence on how to make healthy food choices, but also because federal law requires that school lunches and other government nutrition programs be based on them. In late 2015, the panel submitted its latest guidelines, which differ significantly from the older guidelines in a number of ways.

- **Cultural Sensitivity and Acculturation**
  The report recognizes the large body of evidence that immigrants, who represent a significant proportion of the U.S. population, "adopt the dietary habits and disease patterns of host cultures." A separate subcommittee focused on the equally well-documented finding that immigrants' health tends to go downhill as they shift from traditional diets to the less healthy "typical American diet." For instance, among immigrant adults of Latino/Hispanic national origin—particularly persons of Mexican origin and women of all Latina/Hispanic ethnicities—higher acculturation is associated with lower intake of fruits and vegetables and higher intake of fast food. The guidelines recommend increased resources and policy changes for immigrant outreach programs such as the Supplemental Nutrition Assistance Program (SNAP)—to encourage the purchase of healthier foods.

- **Personal Responsibility and Societal Responsibility**
  The panel in the 2015 dietary guidelines followed an ecological-systems approach (see Chapter 1) by stating that it isn't enough for individuals to try to eat better; success will come only if attention is paid to the entire environment and context that shapes our food choices. To this end, separate subcommittees focused on the changes to support better nutrition that can be made (a) by small groups (such as families) on their own and (b) by society. Highlighting the importance of a systems approach, one expert asked, How can we expect people to make half their grains whole until half the grain choices at fast-food restaurants are whole?

Information from: U.S. Department of Health and Human Services and U.S. Department of Agriculture. (2015). *2015–2020 Dietary guidelines for Americans* (8th ed.).

These allegations are important because, for decades, dietary guidelines encouraged people to eat a low-fat, high-carbohydrate diet that some researchers now blame for contributing to the overweight/obesity crisis (O'Connor, 2016). Due to the considerable body of evidence linking added dietary sugar to hypertension, cardiovascular disease, and other conditions, the most significant recent change in the dietary guidelines is a much lower limit on sugar consumption, now set at no more than 10% of daily calories. (To put this into perspective, a single 12-ounce can of sugary cola exceeds this limit!) Although some experts believe that avoiding fat is not the key to a healthy diet, the debate about the relative dangers of fat and sugar in the diet continues today. Current nutrition guidelines specify limiting saturated fat to no more than 10% of daily calories (Taubes, 2016).

Controversy among industry groups, health science researchers, and government regulators is not limited to the aforementioned "bombshell" allegations against the sugar industry; experts with different backgrounds and goals often disagree on what constitutes a healthy diet. For example, the 2015 dietary guidelines from the U.S. Department of Agriculture quickly sparked criticism among a number of groups. The North American Meat Institute called the recommendations "flawed" and "nonsensical" for their failure to recognize the role that nutrient-dense meats can play in a balanced diet. The American Beverage Association was also critical of the report, especially statements such as "sugars should be reduced in the diet and not replaced with low-calorie sweeteners, but rather with healthy options, such as water in place of sugar-sweetened beverages" and

Processed foods marketed as fat free are often high in carbohydrates and sodium.

"some evidence links high caffeine intake in the form of energy drinks to certain adverse outcomes, such as caffeine toxicity and cardiovascular events" (U.S. Department of Health and Human Services and U.S. Department of Agriculture, 2015).

To be fair, the kinds of carbohydrates the authors of nutrition guidelines had in mind in the 1960s were fruits, vegetables, and whole grains. But the food industry quickly saw the low-fat, high-carb trend as an opportunity to create a new range of products that replaced fat with sugar. The consumption of added sugars in processed and prepared foods has increased the risk of cardiovascular disease. An estimated 16% of U.S. children and adolescents' total caloric intake comes from added sugars, most of which come from foods, not beverages, consumed at home (Ervin, Kit, Carroll, & Ogden, 2012).

How does the body react to ingesting sugar? The *glycemic index* (GI) ranks carbohydrates based on how quickly the body converts them to the naturally occurring blood sugar, *glucose*. The index ranges from 0 to 100, with higher values given to foods that cause the most rapid rise in glucose (see Table 8.1). The *glycemic load* (GL) of a food is a measure of how much the food will raise a person's blood glucose level. Paying attention to the GI and GL values of foods is important because your body performs best when blood sugar is relatively constant. When the blood sugar level drops too low, you feel lethargic and hungry; and when the level is too high, your pancreas produces more insulin, which brings your blood sugar back down by converting excess sugar to stored fat. High-GI foods tend to cause a surge of energy that is

TABLE 8.1 The Glycemic Index (GI) of Some Common Foods

Low-GI Foods (GI = 55 or less)		
Skim milk	Plums	Slow-cooked oatmeal
Soy beverages	Oranges	Lentils, kidney beans, and other legumes
Apples	Sweet potatoes	
Moderate-GI Foods (GI = 56–69)		
Bananas	Brown rice	Whole wheat bread
Pineapple	Basmati rice	Rye bread
Raisins		
High-GI Foods (GI = 70 or more)		
Watermelon	Instant rice	French fries
Dried dates	Sugary breakfast cereals	Table sugar (sucrose)
White potatoes and bread	Bagels	

Note: Not all carbohydrates are created equal! Foods that raise your blood glucose level quickly have a higher GI than foods that raise your blood glucose level more slowly. Choosing low- and moderate-GI foods—which are usually low in calories and fat, while rich in fiber, nutrients, and antioxidants—may help you keep your energy and cholesterol levels balanced, reduce inflammation, and lower your risk of heart disease and Type 2 diabetes.

Ted Foxx/Alamy Stock Photo

quickly followed by increased fat storage, lethargy—and more hunger! This balancing act is complicated, however: Different people show different rises and falls in blood sugar—even when they have eaten the exact same foods—suggesting that diets need to be tailored to our personal characteristics (Zeevi and others, 2015). Elevated *postprandial* (after eating) blood glucose levels are considered a global pandemic and a major risk factor for Type 2 diabetes.

Fast Food, Supersizing, and Mindless Eating

In recent decades, three counterproductive trends have emerged in the dietary habits of people in developed countries. The increased consumption of fast food, larger portion sizes (supersizing), and tendency to eat mindlessly have all contributed to the obesity epidemic and accompanying health risks.

Fast-food consumption has become a central part of many people's eating habits since the introduction of low-priced fast-food restaurant chains in the 1950s. Fast food can be defined as food that is prepared quickly (often pre-assembled) and sold inexpensively in restaurants that use a self-service and/or take-out style of serving. Usually, fast food is fried and therefore high in fat; it also tends to be high in sodium and carbohydrates, and it offers few essential vitamins and minerals in proportion to its calories. The classic fast-food meal of a hamburger, french fries, and a sugary cola drink contains about 1,000 to 1,500 calories (depending on portion size), is high in sodium and saturated fat, and is very low in fiber and vitamins. On average, children and adolescents in the United States consume 12.4% of their total daily calories from fast food (Vikraman, Fryar, & Ogden, 2015). Eating fast food more than once a week is linked to an increased risk of obesity; eating fast food twice a week or more is associated with a higher risk of metabolic syndrome, Type 2 diabetes, and death from coronary heart disease (Bahadoran, Mirmiran, & Azizi, 2015). Non-Hispanic Black adults consume a higher percentage of calories from fast food than non-Hispanic White and Hispanic adults. Among young adults, as income increases, the percentage of calories from fast food decreases. Among adults, the percentage of calories consumed from fast food varies with body weight. In every age group, obese adults consume the highest percentage of their calories from fast food (Figure 8.3).

The term *supersizing* originated in fast-food marketing, but the trend of increasing food portion sizes is prevalent in restaurants of all levels, as well as grocery products and even the servings suggested in cookbooks (Jou, 2017). Supersizing increases the risk of overweight and obesity because people eat more when given larger portions, a behavioral phenomenon known as *unit bias* (Geier, Roin, & Doros, 2006). In one study, Brian Wansink and his colleagues (Wansink, Van Ittersum, & Painter, 2006) found that even nutrition experts took 31% more ice cream when given a big bowl rather than a small one, ate 15% more when scooping the ice cream with a big scoop rather than a small one, and poured 37% more liquid when using a short, wide glass compared to a tall, narrow one of the same volume. Businesses such as self-serve frozen yogurt shops, which charge by weight, take full advantage of this phenomenon by offering "small" serving cups that hold 12 to 16 ounces. Most customers tend to fill these cups to the brim, and ultimately end up consuming far more of this supposedly "healthy" dessert alternative than they ought to.

Behavior such as this is an example of *mindless eating,* in which we allow situations to control our eating. Other examples include the tendency to eat more when eating with other people (Hetherington, 2007), to snack while watching TV, and to eat more when offered a variety of foods from a buffet (Remick, Polivy, & Pliner, 2009).

FIGURE 8.3 Percentage of Calories from Fast Food Among Adults by Age and Weight Status Between 2007 and 2010, adults consumed an average of 11.3% of their total daily calories from fast food. The percentage of calories consumed from fast food did not differ significantly between men (11.8%) and women (10.9%). However, in all age groups, overweight and obese individuals consumed a higher percentage of their daily calories from fast food than did underweight or normal-weight individuals.

Data from: Fryar, C. D., & Ervin, R. B. (2013). *Caloric intake from fast food among adults: United States, 2007–2010.* NCHS Data Brief No. 114. Hyattsville, MD: National Center for Health Statistics.

multiple chronic conditions (MCC) Two or more chronic conditions (lasting a year or more, requiring medical attention, and/or limiting daily activities) that affect a person at the same time.

Because people tend to eat more when offered a variety of foods, as on a buffet table, all-you-can-eat-buffet restaurants can promote unhealthy overeating.

All of these counterproductive dietary trends have a link to the mistaken belief that our stomachs will tell us when they are full and we will stop before overeating. In a remarkable study, Wansink fed participants from a "bottomless bowl" of soup that was pressure-fed under the table and slowly and subtly refilled. The results: Participants with bottomless bowls ate 73% more than those with normal bowls, yet when asked, they didn't realize they had eaten more. "The lesson is, don't rely on your stomach to tell you when you're full. It can lie," said Wansink (2011).

Diet and Disease

Among American adults, 6 in 10 have at least one chronic condition, and 4 in 10 have **multiple chronic conditions (MCC)** (Buttorff, Ruder, & Bauman, 2017 (Figure 8.4). The most prevalent combinations of chronic conditions are hypertension and diabetes, hypertension and heart disease, and hypertension and cancer. The prevalence of obesity—a clear risk factor for certain types of heart disease and cancer, hypertension, and diabetes—is likely a factor in this trend. Globally, poor diet is a factor in one in five deaths and in five of the ten leading causes of death (Naghavi, 2017).

ChiccoDodiFC/Getty Images

Excess dietary fat and sugar have been widely acknowledged as major health hazards. Researchers once thought that all fat was bad, but we now know that they were wrong. Fat is a major source of energy and also helps the body absorb essential vitamins. *Trans fats* are indeed unhealthful and in fact should be avoided altogether. *Saturated fats* should be consumed in moderation, but *monounsaturated fats* and *polyunsaturated fats* (especially *omega-3 fatty acids*) are actually healthful because they help provide satiety, prevent the overeating of other foods, reduce cholesterol levels in the blood, and have an anti-inflammatory effect (Brownlee, 2006). To help consumers sort through the complexities of choosing food products on the basis of their fat content, beginning in 2006, the FDA required food companies to list a product's total amount of trans fat, saturated fat, and cholesterol on its label.

Food Security

A USDA study focused on the relationship between **food security** and health (Gregory & Coleman-Jensen, 2017). By definition, a household that is "food secure" has access at all times to the kinds and amounts of foods needed for its members to enjoy an active, healthy life. In 2015, 12.7% of American households experienced *food insecurity* at some point; they could not afford to eat nutritious meals, and they sometimes skipped meals or cut the size of meals. Food insecurity was more common in households with incomes near or below the poverty level, in single-parent households, in Black- and Hispanic-headed households, and in households in which a single adult lived alone (Coleman-Jensen, Rabbitt, Gregory, & Singh, 2016). Using data from the National Health Interview Study, the researchers also reported that lower food security is associated with increased probability of each of the 10 chronic diseases examined: hypertension, coronary heart disease, hepatitis, stroke, cancer, asthma, diabetes, arthritis, chronic obstructive pulmonary disease, and kidney disease (see Figure 8.5).

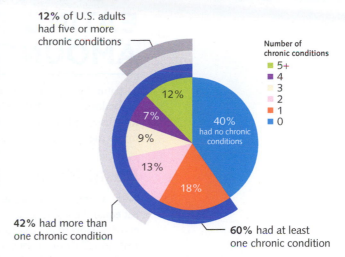

Percentage of U.S. Adults with Chronic Conditions, by Number of Chronic Conditions (2014)

12% of U.S. adults had five or more chronic conditions

Number of chronic conditions
- 5+
- 4
- 3
- 2
- 1
- 0

40% had no chronic conditions

12%

7%

9%

13%

18%

42% had more than one chronic condition

60% had at least one chronic condition

FIGURE 8.4 Percentage of U.S. Adults with Chronic Conditions, by Number of Chronic Conditions About 60% of U.S. adults have at least one chronic condition, and the prevalence increases with age. By middle age (the 45–64 age group), about half of adults have two or more chronic conditions.

Data from: Buttorff, C., Ruder, T., & Bauman, M. (2017). *Multiple chronic conditions in the United States.* Santa Monica, CA: Rand Corporation.

food security Having reliable access to a sufficient quantity of affordable, nutritious food.

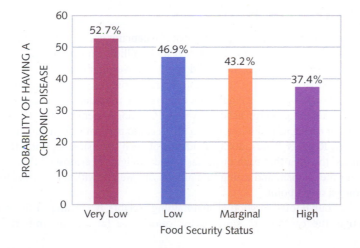

FIGURE 8.5 Food Insecurity and Chronic Illness The National Health Interview Study found that lower food security is associated with increased probability of chronic disease.

Data from: Coleman-Jensen, A., & Gregory, C. A. (2017). *Food Insecurity, Chronic Disease, and Health Among Working-Age Adults,* RR-235. U.S. Department of Agriculture, Economic Research Service.

WEIGHT DETERMINATION: EATING THE RIGHT AMOUNT OF FOOD

Naturally, it's not only what we eat, but also how much we eat in relation to the body's caloric needs, that determine our weight and our health. Before we discuss obesity—its causes and treatment—let's explore the basic mechanisms by which the body determines the type and amount of calories needed.

Basal Metabolic Rate and Caloric Intake

Body weight remains stable when the calories that your body absorbs from the food you eat equal the calories that your body expends for basic metabolic functions plus physical activity. How many calories does your body need to maintain bodily functions while at rest? Recall from Chapter 7 that this figure, called the *basal metabolic rate (BMR)*, is not easily determined, because it depends on a number of variables, including your age, gender, current weight, and activity level.

Individual differences in BMR help explain why it is possible for two people of the same age, height, and apparent activity level to eat the same diet (in the same quantities) and yet have significantly different body weights. Several factors determine BMR, including, first, heredity. Some people have a naturally higher metabolic rate than others, even when they're asleep. People with a lower metabolism need fewer calories for the same amount and level of physical activity. Second, younger people and those who are active generally have a higher BMR than do older adults and those who are sedentary. Third, fat tissue has a lower metabolic rate (burns fewer calories) than muscle does. Once you add fat to your body, you require less food to maintain your weight than you did to gain the weight in the first place. Finally, because men have proportionately more muscle, their bodies burn 10% to 20% more calories at rest than women's bodies do.

The Set-Point Hypothesis

Our bodies have an elegantly regulated way of balancing energy intake and expenditure. A typical adult consumes roughly 900,000 to 1 million calories a year. Subtract from this figure the energy costs of BMR, and you'll discover that less than 1% of the calories that you eat are stored as fat, a remarkable degree of precision in energy balance (Gibbs, 1996). Because of this precise regulation, experts have used data from national surveys to estimate that affecting energy balance by only 100 calories per day (as little as 15 minutes of walking, or eating just a bit less at each meal) could prevent weight gain in most people (Hill, Wyatt, Reed, & Peters, 2003). Evidence of such precision supports the **set-point hypothesis**, the idea that each of us has a body weight "thermostat" that continuously adjusts our metabolism and eating to maintain our weight within a genetically predetermined range, or set point.

Why are our bodies so good at maintaining weight? According to the evolutionary perspective, the capacity to store excess calories as fat was an important survival

set-point hypothesis The idea that each person's body weight is genetically set within a given range, or set point, that the body works hard to maintain.

Your Health Assets

Super Foods for a Super You

Given the pandemic of overweight and obesity, it is not surprising that many people are preoccupied with calories, mistakenly thinking that so long as they aren't gaining weight, it doesn't really matter what they eat. For optimal well-being, however, it is important to learn to eat for health, not weight. What you eat is as important as what you do not eat. Focus on eating foods that are minimally processed and as close to their natural state as possible.

Here are 10 everyday super foods that are easy to eat and packed with nutrients:

- Low-fat or fat-free plain yogurt is higher in calcium than many other dairy products and contains protein, potassium, and other important nutrients. Also, it can be enriched with heart-healthy plant stanols and probiotics to promote healthy bacteria in your gut.

- Eggs are nutritious, economical, and a great way to add quality protein to your diet. They also contain 12 vitamins and minerals—including choline, which is important for brain development and cognitive functioning.

- Nuts are a good source of protein, heart-healthy fats, fiber, and antioxidants. The key to nuts is portion control. In small doses, they can help lower cholesterol levels and promote weight loss.

- The kiwi is one of the most nutritionally dense fruits. Rich in antioxidants, one large kiwi contains a full day's supply of vitamin C and is a good source of potassium, fiber, and vitamins A and E.

- Quinoa (pronounced "keen-wa") is one of the healthiest grains that you can eat. One cup of cooked quinoa is high in protein (8 grams) and fiber (5 grams) and is a naturally good source of iron, zinc, vitamin E, and selenium (this last nutrient can help control weight and lower your risk for diabetes and heart disease).

- Beans are loaded with insoluble fiber, which helps lower cholesterol, as well as soluble fiber, which fills you up and helps the body remove waste. Beans are also an excellent, low-fat source of protein, carbohydrates, magnesium, and potassium. Edamame (whole soybeans) also contain heart-healthy omega-3 fatty acids.

- Salmon is rich in omega-3 fatty acids, protein, and iron, and it is very low in saturated fat. The American Heart Association recommends eating fatty fish such as salmon twice weekly because of the protective effects such fish have on heart health.

- Broccoli and other cruciferous vegetables (such as kale) are rich sources of vitamin A, vitamin C, and bone-building vitamin K. These super foods are also high in fiber, which helps fill you up and control weight.

- Sweet potatoes are part of the dark orange vegetable family, which leads all foods in vitamin A content. Sweet potatoes are also rich in potassium, which helps reduce bone loss, and low in sodium, which is good for keeping blood pressure levels healthy.

- Berries are low in calories and high in water and fiber content, which helps to control blood sugar and keep you feeling full longer. In addition, they are loaded with phytonutrients and are some of the best sources of antioxidants around. Especially important is the fact that berries satisfy our cravings for sweets—for a fraction of the calories and fat content of baked goods.

mechanism for our ancestors. Animals that hibernate and those that must endure periods of nutritional scarcity—as did the human species throughout much of our history—store internal energy reserves when food is plentiful and live off those reserves when food is in short supply. Natural selection favored those human ancestors who developed "thrifty genes"—genes that increased the humans' ability to store fat from each feast in order to sustain themselves until the next meal. Although those of us who live in well-stocked, developed countries no longer need to store so much fat, many of us continue to do so.

The Biological Basis of Weight Regulation

Our BMR determines how many calories we need to maintain bodily functioning, but what sets off the initial hunger pangs we all feel? What is it that triggers hunger and its opposite—*satiety*? Researchers have tackled this question by focusing on where in the brain the signals for hunger and satiety are processed. During the 1960s, researchers located appetite centers in two areas of the hypothalamus: a side region called the *lateral hypothalamus (LH),* which seemed to trigger hunger, and a lower area in the middle called the *ventromedial hypothalamus (VMH),* which seemed to trigger satiety. Animal experiments during the 1960s demonstrated that electrical stimulation of the LH causes an animal that has eaten to the point of fullness to begin eating again; when this area is lesioned, even an animal that has not eaten in days shows no signs of hunger. Conversely, when the VMH is stimulated, animals stop eating; when this area is destroyed, they overeat to the point of extreme obesity (Hoebel & Teitelbaum, 1966). We now know that the lateral hypothalamus secretes the hunger-triggering hormone *orexin* as time passes since a last meal and blood sugar level drops (Blundell, Gibbons, Caudwell, Finlayson, & Hopkins, 2015).

Increased feelings of hunger also have been linked to an increase in the number of fat cells, or **adipocytes**, in the body. When adipocytes reach their maximum storage capacity, they divide—a condition called *fat-cell hyperplasia.* People who are not obese have 25 billion to 30 billion fat cells, whereas those who are severely obese may have 200 billion or more (Hirsch, 2003). Periods of inactivity can also increase fat stores and the number of fat cells (Roberts, 2007). Once the number of fat cells increases in a person's body, it never decreases, even when the person loses weight (Spalding, 2008).

Researchers have discussed several other specific mechanisms for regulating how often and how much we eat on a given day and for regulating our body weight over months and years.

Short-Term Appetite Regulation

The pancreas produces the hormone insulin and assists the body in converting glucose into fat. When glucose levels fall, insulin production increases and we feel hunger. Conversely, when glucose levels rise, hunger and insulin levels decrease. In addition to insulin reduction, low blood glucose triggers a release of stored fat from body cells. As fat is depleted, the hypothalamus also arouses hunger, motivating us to replenish our fat and glucose stores by eating.

Researchers have also identified *cholecystokinin (CCK),* a satiety hormone released into the bloodstream by the intestine, which signals when we've had enough to eat. CCK suppresses appetite even when injected into starving animals (Thompson, 2000). Two other short-term appetite-regulating hormones that have been identified are *ghrelin,* an appetite stimulant, and *peptide YY (PYY),* an appetite suppressant. The stomach produces ghrelin, which causes the pituitary gland to release growth hormone and stimulates appetite. This discovery helped clear

adipocytes Collapsible body cells that store fat.

Adipocytes Typically, we each have about 30 billion of these fat cells, or adipocytes. They are like little storage tanks. In a thin person, the fat cells are relatively empty; as the person gains weight, the cells begin to fill up. Each of the cells in this electron photomicrograph is filled by a single lipid droplet, mostly formed by triglycerides. Connective tissue fibers surround and provide support for the fat cells.

Kateryna Kon/Shutterstock

up a mystery in appetite research: why people want to eat at specific times each day. David Cummings and his colleagues (Cummings, Foster-Schubert, & Overduin, 2005) discovered that ghrelin levels rise an hour or two before mealtimes and decrease afterward, stimulating appetite by activating neurons in the hypothalamus. Ghrelin also stimulates receptors on nerve cells in the hippocampus, a brain area involved in learning and memory (Diano and others, 2006). This finding makes evolutionary sense, because hungry animals need to remember where they found a food source. Most obese people have lower levels of ghrelin than those who are thinner, and ghrelin production increases in people who are dieting— explaining in part why dieters may find it increasingly difficult to stick to their regimen.

Long-Term Weight Regulation

Why do some people seem more prone than others to become fat? Molecular biologists speculate that genetic disorders may interfere with the body's ability to regulate the number of fat cells, thereby causing people to gain weight. In 1994, researchers discovered that laboratory mice with a defective gene for regulating the hormone **leptin** could not control their hunger and became obese. Leptin, produced by fat cells, is found at greater levels in people with more body fat and at lower levels in those with less body fat. Because they usually have higher body fat content, women generally have higher leptin levels than men do.

leptin The weight-signaling hormone monitored by the hypothalamus as an index of body fat.

As body fat increases, higher levels of leptin signal the normal brain to suppress hunger. Animals with defective leptin genes produce too little leptin, and thus they overeat. They become hugely obese and diabetic, and they have a substantially lower BMR than their genetically normal counterparts (Zhang, Proenca, Maffei, & Barone, 1994). When given daily injections of leptin, they eat less, they become more active, and their body weights eventually return to normal (Halaas and others, 1995).

The discovery of leptin renewed support for the set-point theory. According to this line of reasoning, if the body's set point is something like a thermostat, leptin acts as the thermometer. As a person gains weight, more leptin is produced. This shuts off appetite, increases energy expenditure, and triggers other mechanisms to restore body weight to the set point. Conversely, as a person loses weight (as in dieting), levels of leptin decrease, hunger increases, and metabolism falls until the person's weight returns to its targeted level.

Leptin's signaling ability also may explain why most dieters regain lost weight—a phenomenon frequently observed among contestants on the TV show *The Biggest Loser*. Once weight increases, obesity often seems to stamp in a new, higher set point that the body defends (Shungin and others, 2015). After dieting, less leptin is available to signal the brain, possibly increasing hunger and slowing metabolism. In normal mice, leptin levels dropped 40% after a three-day fast and dropped 80% after a six-day fast (Nakamura and others, 2000). Although the effects of leptin have made researchers enthusiastic about its possible use as a weight-loss drug, so far the scientists' efforts have not been successful (Madhusoodanan, 2017).

Other research studies point to a different function of leptin. Although some rare cases of human obesity are caused by defects in leptin production, most obese humans have higher-than-normal blood levels of the hormone (Marx, 2003). Some believe that the leptin receptors of obese people are simply less sensitive to leptin. Following this line of reasoning leads to the conclusion that leptin's main role may be to protect against weight loss in times of deprivation rather than against weight gain in times of plenty. Obese people simply produce the hormone at a greater rate to compensate for a faulty signaling process (Nakamura and others, 2000). Researchers have reported some success reducing obesity with supplements that reverse the *leptin resistance* that is often associated with obesity (Tam and others, 2012).

Although injections of leptin are not effective for treating most cases of obesity in humans, the discovery of the hormone helped pinpoint the neural pathways involved in weight regulation. In particular, a pathway in the hypothalamus called the *arcuate nucleus (ARC)* contains large numbers of receptors for leptin and other hormones involved in long-term weight control. The ARC also contains two major types of neurons with opposing actions. Activation of one type, which produces a neurotransmitter called *neuropeptide Y,* stimulates appetite and reduces metabolism. Activation of the other type causes the release of *melanocyte-stimulating hormone,* which reduces appetite. In addition, the ARC has a short-term response to ghrelin, stimulating appetite when mealtime is approaching. For these reasons, the ARC has been called the "master center" for both short- and long-term weight regulation (Marx, 2003).

OBESITY: A COMPLEX PHENOMENON

People are concerned about what they eat, and how much, for many reasons—including the negative physiological and psychological effects of obesity. Being overweight carries a social **weight stigma** (also called *weight bias*) in many parts of the world today, reflecting the importance that many societies place on physical appearance (Meadows & Daníelsdóttir, 2016). In fact, obese people are one of very few disabled groups who regularly endure public criticism. Obese children are teased and bullied more than their normal-weight peers and are more likely to experience social isolation, depression, and lower self-esteem (CDC, 2018b; Weir, 2012). Among adults, obesity is associated with lower psychological well-being, especially among women, and with a marked increase in depression (Mendes, 2010). Obese people are mistakenly stereotyped as being slow, lazy, and undisciplined (Puhl & Heuer, 2009). Compared to normal-weight women of equal intelligence, obese women earn less money, are less likely to be married, and are underrepresented among corporate CEOs (Roehling, Roehling, Vandlen, Bazek, & Guy, 2009).

Weight stigma is also expressed as *implicit bias,* in which some people automatically, and often unconsciously, favor one group over another (Carels and others, 2010; Greenwald, Banaji, & Nosek, 2015). A widely used tool for assessing people's unconscious attitudes and biases is the Implicit Association Test (IAT), which uses speed of response to measure how strongly participants associate a given image with a certain group. In one study using this test with adults who were obese and overweight themselves, the participants responded significantly faster to images of obese and thin people engaging in stereotype-consistent behaviors (e.g., obese people watching TV/eating junk food; thin people exercising/eating healthy food) than they did to photos depicting stereotype-inconsistent behaviors (Figure 8.6, Carels and others, 2013). Researchers have also found that health care professionals exhibit implicit weight bias to the same degree as do people in the general population (Fitzgerald & Hurst, 2017).

weight stigma Prejudice and discrimination directed at people based on their weight or body size.

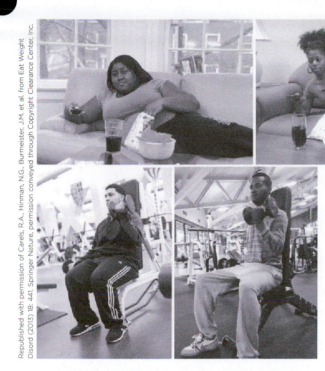

FIGURE 8.6 Sample Item from Implicit Association Test   The IAT is a widely used method for assessing implicit attitudes. In this test of implicit associations with obesity, participants were asked to rapidly categorize images related to two target concepts (Fat and Thin) and two attributes (snacking on the couch, and lifting weights). The target concepts Fat and Thin were paired with the stereotype-consistent and stereotype-inconsistent pictures. Faster responses to pairings are interpreted as indicative of stronger associations in memory, and thus implicit weight bias. In this study, people who were overweight or obese showed a significant anti-Fat/pro-Thin bias on the IAT.

How our weight affects our psychological well-being depends in great part on our gender. For instance, overweight women are more likely to be depressed, even suicidal, than their thinner counterparts (Carpenter, Hasin, Allison, & Faith, 2000). Interestingly, *underweight* men are more likely to be diagnosed with clinical depression than are their heavier counterparts.

How do we define *obesity*? In recent years, the definition of *obesity* has been refined to mean the presence of excess body fat. A person with an acceptable weight and figure but too much body fat could be considered obese, and his or her health could be at risk. Thus, at the same weight, you can be healthy or not—it all depends on your individual fat-to-muscle ratio.

The most frequently used measure of obesity today is the **body mass index (BMI)**, which is strongly correlated with percentage of body fat. Here's how to determine your BMI: Multiply your weight in pounds (without shoes or clothes) by 705. Divide this product by your height in inches. Then divide it again by your height. Alternatively, you could use the BMI calculator at the National Institutes of Health (NIH) Web site (https://www.nhlbi.nih.gov/health/educational/lose_wt/BMI/bmicalc.htm). For example, if you weigh 140 pounds and are 5 feet 6 inches tall, your BMI is 22.66, which is within the normal range (see Table 8.2). A BMI of 40 or greater is considered Class III (high-risk) obesity—the point where the excess body fat begins to interfere with day-to-day movement and even breathing. Class III obesity is equivalent to 294 pounds for a 6-foot man or 247 pounds for a woman 5 feet 6 inches tall.

body mass index (BMI)
A measure of obesity calculated by dividing body weight by the square of a person's height.

TABLE 8.2 Body Mass Index (BMI) and Weight

BMI Categories

- Underweight = <18.5
- Normal Weight = 18.5–24.9
- Overweight = 25–29.9
- Class I Obesity = 30–34.9
- Class II Obesity = 35.0–39.9
- Class III Obesity = 40+

Information from: Department of Health and Human Services (2015). Centers for Disease Control and Prevention.

Doug Pensinger/Getty Images

tommasolizzul/Getty Images

Body Mass Index Can Be Deceptive Because body mass index (BMI) does not take into account muscle mass, bone density, or overall body composition, it can be deceptive as an indicator of health. A professional male football player may have a BMI above 30, putting him well into the "obese" category, but he may actually have a great deal of lean muscle mass. At the other end of the scale, a very thin gymnast may have enough muscle mass to register his BMI as "overweight."

abdominal obesity Excess fat around the stomach and abdomen; also called *male-pattern obesity*.

It is important to realize, however, that there is no set ideal amount of body fat for all people, because the amount of body fat changes with age. In healthy adults, acceptable levels of body fat range from 25% to 30% in women and from 18% to 23% in men.

Furthermore, although the BMI provides a good estimate of body fat, it is an incomplete measure of health as it does not take into account muscle mass, bone density, or overall body composition. As a result, athletes with highly developed muscles and very little body fat can have BMIs in the overweight or even obese range.

The major problem with BMI is that it reflects total body fat without regard to how it is distributed. While the overall amount of body fat is important in assessing a person's health, evidence indicates that *where* body fat is distributed may be even more significant. The excess *visceral fat* associated with **abdominal obesity** (also called *male-pattern obesity*) has been linked to metabolic syndrome, inflammation, atherosclerosis, hypertension, and diabetes (Despres & Lemieux, 2006). Pound for pound, abdominal obesity is considered a greater overall health risk than fat that is concentrated on the hips and thighs (sometimes called *female-pattern obesity*). However, the health hazards of a high waist-to-hip ratio apply to both women and men and may even be a more accurate predictor of mortality from all causes than BMI. To measure your waist-to-hip ratio, perform the following steps:

1. Measure your waist at its slimmest point.
2. Measure your hips at their widest point.
3. Divide your waist measurement by your hip measurement—(waist in inches)/(hips in inches).

Thus, a woman with a waist measurement of 29 inches and a hip measurement of 37 inches would have a ratio of 0.78, while a man with a 34-inch waist measurement and a 40-inch hip measurement would have a ratio of 0.85. Both ratios fall within the healthy range. As a rule, the desirable waist-to-hip ratio is less than 0.8 for women and less than 0.95 for men. (See Table 8.3 for instructions on how to measure and interpret waist circumference.) The latest research shows that the chance of suffering a heart attack or a stroke increases steadily as a man's ratio rises above 0.95; for women, risk begins to rise when the ratio exceeds 0.85 (*Harvard Health Letter*, 2013).

TABLE 8.3 Interpreting Your Waist Circumference

An even simpler metric for measuring abdominal fat is waist circumference. To measure your waist circumference, take your shoes off and stand with your feet together. Relax and exhale. Using a cloth measuring tape that can't be stretched, keep the tape parallel to the ground and measure your bare waist at the navel to the nearest one-tenth of an inch.

	Men	Women
Low risk	37 inches and below	31.5 inches and below
Intermediate risk	37.1–39.9 inches	31.6–34.9 inches
High risk	40 inches and above	35 inches and above

Note: Harvard Health Publications does not endorse any products or medical procedures.

Information from: Waisted: Abdominal Obesity and Your Health in *Harvard Men's Health Watch*, January 2009. © 2009 Harvard University. Updated 2016.

Hazards of Obesity

The NIH cites obesity as second only to cigarette smoking in its importance as a behavioral factor in mortality rates (Berrington de Gonzales and others, 2010): As body fat accumulates, it crowds the space occupied by internal organs and contributes to many chronic health problems. For instance, obesity increases the risk of several problems related to metabolism and the body's ability to process sugars and fats. One of these conditions is *hyperinsulinemia*, an endocrine disorder in which insulin progressively loses its effectiveness in sweeping glucose from the bloodstream into the 60 trillion or so cells of our bodies. For this reason, obesity is a leading cause of Type 2 diabetes. In individuals with excess body weight, the liver manufactures more triglycerides (the most common form of dietary fat in the bloodstream) and cholesterol, which increases the risk of arthritis, gout, and gallbladder disease. The prevalence of *metabolic syndrome*, or MetS (the set of obesity-related factors that increase the risk for coronary artery disease, stroke, inflammation, and diabetes), increases with BMI. Overweight men are 6 times as likely and obese men are 32 times as likely as normal-weight men to meet the criteria for MetS. Overweight women are 5 times as likely and obese women are 17 times as likely to meet the criteria (Ervin, 2009).

Although we usually associate high blood pressure, high cholesterol, and heart disease with adults, these conditions are also found in children who are obese. Obese children are also more likely than their normal-weight peers to have breathing problems such as asthma and sleep apnea, fatty liver disease, and Type 2 diabetes—another ailment which historically only affected older adults (CDC, 2018b). Obese children as young as 8 years old may have enlarged hearts, a sign that the cardiac muscle is under strain (Beil, 2015). During adolescence, obesity and MetS are linked to impairments in brain structure, including reduced hippocampal volumes and reduced white matter (Yau, Castro, Tagani, Tsui, & Convit, 2012).

Given the health hazards that obesity poses, it will come as no surprise that being significantly overweight can cut life short (Figure 8.7; Adams and others, 2006). A large-scale study following more than 1 million Americans over a 14-year period reported that White men and women with the highest BMI (40 or higher) had two to six times the

FIGURE 8.7 Mortality Rates as a Function of Body Mass Index (BMI) Generally speaking, thinner women and men live longer. At a BMI of 40, a woman's risk of dying is approximately 50% higher than that of a person with a BMI of 24; for men with a BMI over 40, the risk of death is about 2.5 times higher. However, very thin people do not have the lowest mortality rates, indicating that the relationship between weight and poor health would actually be U-shaped, were the graph extended to BMIs below 18.

Data from: Calle, E. E., Thun, M. J., Petrelli, J. M., Rodriguez, C., & Heath, C. W. (1999). Body-mass index and mortality in a prospective cohort of U.S. adults. *New England Journal of Medicine, 341,* 1097–1105.

relative risk of premature death of their thinner counterparts with a BMI of 24 (Calle, Thun, Petrelli, Rodriguez, & Heath, 1999). Another large prospective study reported that adults who are overweight are likely to die three years earlier than their thinner counterparts (Peeters and others, 2003). A more recent examination of BMI and mortality in 1.46 million adults showed that mortality rates for all causes of death were lowest for people with a BMI of 20 to 24.9 (Berrington de Gonzalez and others, 2010).

However, researchers are still debating whether having a BMI between 25 and 30 is truly hazardous. Some experts suggest that people who are short, elderly, and African American, Hispanic American, or Asian American suffer no ill effects unless they become truly obese (Strawbridge, Wallhagen, & Shema, 2000). For instance, while the lowest mortality rates among European American women and men occur in those with a BMI of 24 to 25, the lowest mortality rates among African Americans occur in those with a BMI of 27 (Durazo-Arvizu, McGee, Cooper, Liao, & Luke, 1998).

Proponents of the Health at Every Size movement believe that health is the result of a nutritious diet, exercise, and other behaviors that are independent of body weight (Bacon & Aphramor, 2011). In support of this viewpoint, which remains controversial, they point to evidence that weight loss interventions do not always produce positive health outcomes, and instead may lead to rapid swings in body weight that inflict physical and psychological damage that is at least as harmful as obesity.

Another factor that complicates the obesity–health relationship is age. Being overweight increases the risk of premature death from all causes among young and middle-aged adults (Adams and others, 2006). After about age 65, however, being *underweight* is actually associated with increased risk of dying from all causes (Diehr and others, 2008), because losing weight in late adulthood generally leads to less muscle, thinner bones, and greater risk of accidents and chronic disease.

While being excessively underweight or overweight is hazardous to health, **weight cycling** (also called *yo-yo dieting*)—a pattern of repeated weight gain and loss often associated with *crash diets* and binge eating—may also be unhealthy (Stevens and others, 2012).

weight cycling Repeated weight gains and losses through repeated dieting.

The Biopsychosocial Model of Obesity

Although it is tempting to take the view that obesity is simply the result of overeating, research shows that this is an oversimplification. Those who are overweight often do *not* eat more than their thin friends do. Rather, obesity is a complex phenomenon involving biological, social, and psychological factors in both its causes and consequences (Hruby & Hu, 2015).

Biological Factors in Obesity

Research on the biological factors that contribute to obesity has focused on the roles of genes, the brain, and hormones in regulating appetite.

Genes Although individual variation in our susceptibility to obesity has a genetic component, body weight is influenced by many different genes, most of which, individually, seem to have small effects. For example, one global study of 40,000 people identified a variant of the FTO gene, which seems to double the risk of becoming obese (Frayling and others, 2007). How might the so-called *fat mass and obesity-associated gene* influence obesity? One possibility is that a variant of the gene might influence BMR, perhaps lowering it and thus promoting weight gain because the body does not burn as many calories as it normally would.

To find out, researchers measured the height, weight, and waist-to-hip ratios of 2,700 elementary school children in Scotland (Cecil, Tavendale, Watt, Hetherington, & Palmer, 2008). They also took saliva samples to check FTO genes. As expected, overweight and obese children were more likely to have the FTO gene variant. The most interesting part of the study involved a subgroup of 76 students who had their metabolism monitored for 10 days while eating special test meals at the school. The researchers weighed the available food before and after each meal to see how much the kids had eaten. The results showed that the FTO variant was not associated with reduced metabolism; rather, it was linked to eating more food, especially high-calorie food. So the FTO variant that confers a predisposition to obesity may be involved in food intake and food choice—especially a preference for energy-dense foods.

Another study suggests that the FTO gene may also be involved in how the body handles calories, functioning as a "genetic switch" that determines whether people will burn extra calories or store them as body fat. Interestingly, about 42% of Southeast Asians and 40% of Europeans but only 5% of Africans carry the obesity-risk variant of the FTO gene (Claussnitzer and others, 2015).

Destiny? Genetics Versus Environmental Factors Despite the evidence for the role of biological factors in obesity, it is important to recognize that specific genetic defects are involved in only about 4% of cases of human obesity (Walley, Asher, & Froguel, 2009). The role of genetic factors in obesity is complex and *polygenic* (affected by many genes) (Harvard University School of Public Health [HSPH], 2018), and each of the genes involved may have a relatively small effect. Rates of obesity have increased dramatically in recent years, which means that genes can't explain it all. Moreover, heredity alone does not predispose a person to be fat. Obesity is a product of genetic vulnerability and environmental factors or maladaptive behaviors (Morrison, 2008). What appears to be inherited is a *tendency* to be overweight; the amount overweight a person becomes is affected by diet and activity level. Regular activity and a healthy diet can limit genetic tendencies toward obesity.

Psychosocial Factors in Obesity

Hunger and eating behavior are not controlled by physiological factors alone. Psychosocial factors also come into play. One 32-year longitudinal study of over 12,000 people found that a person is most likely to become obese when a friend is obese (Christakis & Fowler, 2007), and if that friend is a close one, the odds almost triple. As another example, we are conditioned to associate eating with holidays, personal achievements, and most social occasions. And the giving of food is among the first symbols of love between a parent and child. Should we be surprised that people are conditioned to turn to food when they are upset, anxious, or under stress? The idea of **stress eating** is embodied in the familiar concept of *comfort food*. One study of college students demonstrated that being provided comfort food during childhood was an important predictor of later stress eating (Brown, Schiraldi, & Wrobleski, 2009).

stress eating Eating in the absence of hunger when we are upset, anxious, or under stress.

A growing body of evidence indicates that both acute and chronic stresses are associated with eating in the absence of hunger (Rutters, Nieuwenhuizen, Lemmens, Born, & Westertep-Plantenga, 2009). One study drew on data from the Health and Behavior in Teenagers Study (HABITS) to determine whether long-term stress is associated with unhealthy eating, particularly of fatty foods and snacks (Cartwright and others, 2003). The HABITS sample is a large, socioeconomically and ethnically diverse sample of 4,320 schoolchildren (mean age of 12 years) who completed questionnaires measuring their stress and dietary practices. Girls and boys who reported the highest levels of stress ate more fatty food and snacks than their less-stressed peers and were less likely to consume the recommended five or more daily fruits and vegetables or to eat breakfast.

Studies finding data such as these suggest that stress eating may contribute to long-term disease risk by triggering unhealthy patterns of food consumption. The classic *restraint theory* may help explain why. This theory contends that people who chronically follow a strict diet (restrained eating) will be more likely to eat and possibly overeat (unrestrained eating) when feeling stressed (Herman and Polivy, 1975). Because many obese people diet and attempt to restrain their eating, they may be prone to overeating in stressful situations (Wardle, Parmenter, & Waller, 2000).

Culture, Socioeconomic Status, and Gender Genes cannot explain why being overweight or obese is more prevalent today than in the past. Today, the average woman in the United States is 5 feet 4 inches tall, weighs between 140 and 150 pounds, has a waist size of 34 to 35 inches, and wears a size 12 to 14 dress. Women 50 years ago averaged the same height, but they weighed only about 120 pounds, had a waist size of approximately 24 to 25 inches, and wore a size 8 dress (Peeke, 2010). In the late 1980s, 47% of Americans were classified as overweight or obese; today this figure has jumped to 65% (Freking, 2006). Americans are fatter today than their parents and grandparents ever were, and they are getting fatter every year.

Genes also cannot explain why the increase in weight in our population is not evenly distributed; there has been a disproportionate increase in the number of massively obese people in recent years, especially in certain ethnic groups. Within the United States, obesity is more prevalent among African Americans, Hispanic Americans, Native Americans, and other minority groups (Figure 8.8). Socioeconomic factors may help explain this relationship. Particularly among women in developed countries, there is an inverse relationship between obesity and socioeconomic status (SES), with people of lower SES

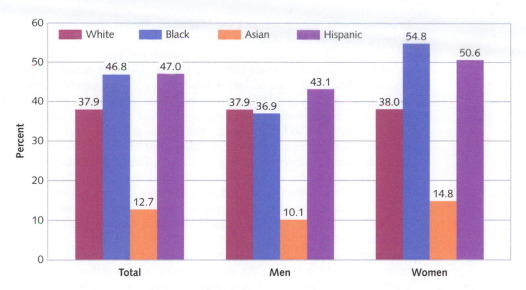

FIGURE 8.8 Percentage of U.S. Women and Men Who Are Obese by Racial and Ethnic Group. Among adults in the United States, the prevalence of obesity (BMI 30 or greater) shows significant variation by racial and ethnic groups.

Data from: Hales, C.M, Carroll M.D., Fryar C.D., & Ogden C.L. (2015). Prevalence of obesity among adults and youth: United States, 2015–2016. NCHS Data Brief No 288. Hyattsville, MD: National Center for Health Statistics. 2017.

more likely to be overweight than those who are more affluent. The fact that members of racial and ethnic minority groups are disproportionately represented among lower-SES groups helps explain why members of those minority groups are more likely to be overweight (Sanchez-Vaznaugh, Kawachi, Subramanian, Sanchez, & Acevedo-Garcia, 2009).

Low-SES children and adolescents are more likely to be obese than their higher-SES counterparts, although the relationship is not consistent across race and ethnicity groups (Ogden, Lamb, Carroll, & Flegal, 2010). Public health researchers commonly use the **poverty income ratio (PIR)**, defined as the ratio of household income to the poverty threshold after accounting for inflation and family size. The prevalence of obesity is 11.9% for boys living in households with income at or above 35% of the poverty level, while 21.1% of those who live below 13% of the poverty level are obese. Among girls, 12% of those living in households with income at or above 35% of the poverty level are obese, while 19.3% of those with income below 13% of the poverty level are obese (Ogden and others, 2010).

Being overweight or obese is also inversely related to education and occupation level. Among all young people between 16 and 24 years of age, those who are overweight tend not only to have lower personal incomes but also to have completed fewer years of education and to work in lower occupational categories than their normal-weight counterparts (Martin, Nieto, Ruiz, & Jimenez, 2008). Once again, these socioeconomic variables have a greater predictive value in women than in men. Men and women of all races with a college degree are less likely to be overweight than men and women with fewer than 12 years of education. Since the mid-1970s, however, the prevalence of being overweight or obese among men and women has increased steadily at all education levels (National Center for Health Statistics, 2012).

Why are less educated, lower-SES people at increased risk for obesity? Their risk factors include more limited access to health care services, less knowledge about the

poverty income ratio (PIR)
The ratio of household income to the poverty threshold after accounting for inflation and family size.

importance of a healthy diet and the hazards of obesity, lower perceived self-efficacy in being able to increase their fruit and vegetable intake, and less exercise (Steptoe and others, 2003). Data from the massive Monitoring the Future Study also suggest that social disparities in body weight may occur because African American women, Hispanic women, and men with lower SES are less likely to practice six important health behaviors regularly: eating breakfast, eating green vegetables, eating fruit, exercising, watching television in moderation, and sleeping seven hours each night (Clarke, O'Malley, & Johnston, 2009). It also has been suggested that the greater daily stress associated with poverty—resulting from prejudice, crowding, and crime, for example—may trigger increased eating as a defensive coping mechanism. Thus, it is not surprising that obesity is less prevalent among minority Americans who live in more affluent neighborhoods than among those living in lower-SES neighborhoods (Mays, Cochran, & Barnes, 2007). Higher-SES adolescents also display greater awareness of the social ideals of slimness and are more likely to have family and friends who are trying to lose weight (Wardle and others, 2004).

Accessibility of healthy foods can apparently offset the dietary hazards of low income. A study compared the dietary composition and food attitudes of a large sample of culturally diverse, low- to middle-income middle school students attending two schools. Students who attended a private school where nutritious lunch and snack food choices were available had significantly lower fat in their overall diets and greater awareness of the benefits of a healthy diet than did students attending a public school where food choices were more limited and less nutritious (Frenn & Malin, 2003). This was true despite the fact that, as a group, the private school students came from families with significantly lower incomes than those of the students attending the public school.

The issue of access to healthy foods and other barriers to adherence to a healthy-weight lifestyle comes into sharp focus when one considers the plight of residents of cities such as Detroit and Chicago, where a much higher-than-average percentage of citizens are obese. In these cities there are hundreds of fast-food restaurants and convenience stores that stock fatty snack foods but there are a limited number of supermarkets that sell fruits, vegetables, and other nutritious foods. To make matters worse, these sprawling cities have weak public transportation systems, making it difficult for many Detroiters and Chicagoans to escape the **food deserts** (Figure 8.9) of their neighborhoods in order to purchase healthy foods (Wehunt, 2009). However, more research is needed to determine how access influences the types of foods people actually purchase and consume (CDC, 2012c).

In the face of results such as these, health psychologists and legislators are calling for wide-scale public health and policy interventions. Among those being considered are bills that would extend nutrition labeling beyond packaged foods to include foods at fast-food restaurants and bills that would ban soft-drink and snack-food machines in schools. Some health psychologists and urban planners are also calling for a shift away from cities built around the automobile toward more "walkable cities" that reengineer physical activity back into daily routines. In support of this idea, researchers have found that people who live in sprawling cities such as Detroit, and who must therefore rely more on their cars to commute from distant homes to stores and places of employment, weigh more than people who live in more compact cities (Saelens, Sallis, & Frank, 2003). They also are more likely to suffer from hypertension, another risk factor for obesity.

food deserts Geographical areas with little or no access to foods needed to maintain a healthy diet.

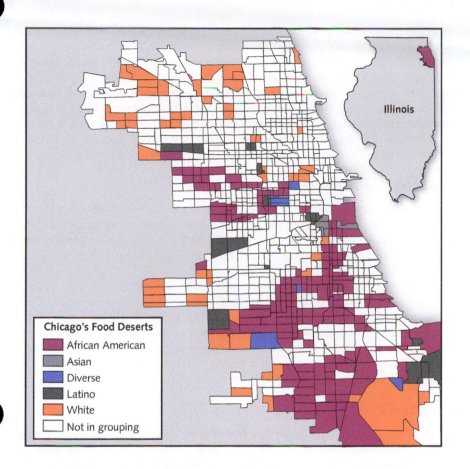

FIGURE 8.9 Urban Food Deserts Over half a million Chicagoans—most of them African Americans—live in the city's three food deserts **Data from:** Gallagher, 2006.

Chicago's Food Deserts
- African American
- Asian
- Diverse
- Latino
- White
- Not in grouping

Illinois

TREATMENT AND PREVENTION OF OBESITY

Attempts to address the serious health implications for the growing number of people who are obese, combined with the social prejudice against obesity, have led to a proliferation of different weight-reduction regimens.

Dieting

A stroll through any bookstore will give you a quick idea of the vast array of dieting strategies—everything from preplanned meals with strict calorie limits to single-food plans to hypnosis. It's easy to be cynical about the number of choices. If any of them were truly effective, there would not be a market for such variety. The main beneficiaries of most of these books are their authors.

Successful weight loss in adults is often defined as at least a 10% reduction of initial weight that is maintained for one year (Rich, 2004). Weight losses of this magnitude generally produce significant improvements in health in most overweight adults. However, many people are trying to shed pounds for reasons that have little or nothing to do with health. This is especially true for women who are not overweight—just look at a random issue of any of the leading women's magazines and you will almost surely find one or more articles on how to lose weight, along with many photographs of fashion models who are thin to an unhealthy degree. The increasing popularity of dieting has been attributed to the growing cultural pressure to be slim.

How Effective Are Diets?

Dieting alone usually does not work to take weight off and keep it off (Mann and others, 2007). The best way to lose weight and keep it off is to develop sound eating habits *and* to engage in regular physical exercise to raise the BMR. Studies also suggest that daily self-weighing can be an important factor for long-term weight control (LaRose and others, 2014).

Even though most diets fail, Americans spend billions of dollars each year on them. Nearly two thirds of adults say they are over their ideal weight; 55% say they would like to lose weight, yet only 27% say they are "seriously trying" to lose weight (Jones, 2009). The gap between the percentage of adults who would like to weigh less and the percentage who are actively making the attempt has existed for many years. Overall, 17% of teens aged 12 to 19 say they are actively trying to lose weight. This includes only about half of those who are actually overweight, 48% of whom say they are trying to lose weight (Saad, 2006).

Why Diets Fail

One reason that diets fail is that many people are not very good at calculating the number of calories their bodies need or the size of the food portions they are eating. Underestimating calorie consumption is a common problem in many failed diets. In one study, for example, obese dieters reported eating an average of 1,028 calories per day, but their actual intake averaged 2,081 calories, more than twice as many calories as reported.

Diets also fail because many people have unrealistic expectations and find it nearly impossible to comply with dietary restrictions for very long (Wadden, Butryn, & Wilson, 2007). Inconvenience and feelings of deprivation are often cited as factors that undermine adherence (Jeffery, Kelly, Rothman, Sherwood, & Boutelle, 2004). One randomized clinical trial assessed the effectiveness and adherence rates of four popular diets—Atkins, Zone, Weight Watchers, and Ornish. All four diets resulted in "modest, statistically significant weight loss," with no differences in effectiveness among diets. However, only one in four participants was able to sustain that weight loss one year later (Dansinger, Gleason, Griffith, Selker, & Schaefer, 2005).

The most successful diets are clinical interventions that include some form of post-treatment following weight loss, such as social support, exercise programs, or continued contact with the therapist. Commercial group programs like Weight Watchers typically promote social support, self-monitoring in the form of daily food diaries, and discussion about exercise and nutrition as key components. In one study, two thirds of the participants who enrolled in a group weight-loss program with friends kept their lost weight off six months after the program ended, compared to only one fourth of those who attended alone (Wing & Jeffery, 1999).

Your Health Assets

Lose Weight the Smart Way

If you are struggling with obesity, you should seek medical guidance. For those who just want to shed a few pounds, here are a few tips:

- **Set a weight-loss goal only if you are motivated and self-disciplined.** Losing weight and keeping it off require a lifestyle change that combines healthier eating habits with increased exercise.
- **Make healthy food choices.** Choose fresh fruits, vegetables, whole grains, legumes, and healthy fats.
- **Get more exercise.** Exercise burns calories, suppresses appetite, and helps lower your body's weight set point.
- **Keep tempting foods out of sight.** Buy mostly fresh, whole foods like fruits, vegetables, fish and other lean proteins, eggs, and low-fat or nonfat dairy products. Avoid processed packaged foods with long lists of ingredients, especially ingredients that are artificial and hard to pronounce.
- **Manage portion size.** Keep meals simple and modest in size, even when eating healthy foods.
- **Don't starve yourself in order to eat one big meal.** This eating pattern slows metabolism and causes calories to be stored as fat more readily.
- **Eat slowly, and beware of binge eating.** People who eat slowly tend to eat less. Conversely, eating quickly and eating when you drink alcohol or feel anxious can cause you to overeat.

Behavioral and Cognitive Therapy

Behavior modification, particularly in conjunction with cognitive intervention techniques, has become a mainstay of many contemporary weight-loss programs. Self-monitoring is considered the cornerstone of behavioral interventions, and up to 25% of weigh-control success is estimated to be due to consistent self-monitoring (Elfhag & Rossner, 2005; Peterson and others, 2014). In one classic study, researchers examined self-monitoring of eating behaviors during three holiday periods (Thanksgiving, Christmas/Hanukkah, and New Year's Eve). Compared with the controls, who gained weight, those participants who were the most thorough in recordkeeping actually lost weight during the holiday weeks (Baker & Kirschenbaum, 1998). Other researchers have pointed to the effectiveness of another aspect of self-monitoring in weight loss: memory of recent eating. One study examined the effect that being reminded of a recent eating episode has on subsequent food intake (Higgs, 2002). Participants ate less at dinner following exposure to a "lunch cue," in which they were simply asked to think about what they had eaten for lunch earlier that day.

Behavior modification programs also include some of the following components:

- *Stimulus control* procedures to identify and limit the number of cues that trigger eating (for example, confining eating to one particular place);
- *Self-control* techniques to slow the act of eating (for example, chewing each bite a set number of times or putting down silverware between bites);
- *Aerobic exercise* to boost metabolism, burn calories, and help curb appetite;

- *Contingency contracts* in which therapist-delivered or self-controlled reinforcement is made dependent upon reaching weight-loss goals (for example, the client puts up a sum of money to be earned back as goals are attained);

- *Social support* of family members and friends, who are enlisted to provide additional reinforcement for success and compliance; and

- *Relapse prevention therapy* to teach people who are trying to maintain changes in their behavior how to anticipate and cope with urges, cravings, and high-risk situations.

Advocates of behavioral treatments have broadened their focus beyond behavior to include concern with the types of foods consumed. Consumption of unhealthy food choices can be reduced by increasing the behavioral costs associated with obtaining those unhealthy foods—through decreased access, for instance—and by providing healthy alternative foods and enjoyable activities. Efforts to limit access to unhealthy foods are often controversial, as seen when New York City attempted to ban large, sugary sodas (Grynbaum, 2013). However, such efforts can have big payoffs. One study that tracked more than 6,000 students in 40 states reported that children in states with strict laws governing the sale of snacks and sodas in schools gained less weight from fifth grade to eighth grade than their peers in states with weaker or fewer school food regulations (Taber, Chriqui, & Chaloupka, 2012).

Behavioral methods are most successful when they are combined with cognitive techniques that recognize that overweight people often start treatment with unrealistic expectations and self-defeating thoughts. *Cognitive-behavioral therapy (CBT)* focuses on the reciprocal interdependence of feelings, thoughts, behavior, consequences, social context, and physiological processes. The underlying premise of these therapies is that eating habits and attitudes must be modified on a permanent basis for weight loss to occur and

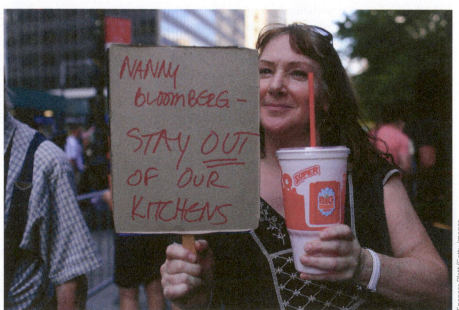

Efforts to limit access to unhealthy foods are often controversial, as seen when New York City attempted to ban large sugary sodas.

Spencer Platt/Getty Images

for that loss to be maintained. Rather than attempting to force quick and dramatic weight losses, CBT focuses on the gradual loss of one to two pounds per week, using a combination of conditioning, self-control, and cognitive restructuring techniques, in which the person learns to control self-defeating thoughts about body weight and dieting.

When it comes to weight loss and management in children, CBT generally focuses on prevention, including establishing healthy eating behaviors in the individual and family; reducing time spent in sedentary activities like television viewing, Internet surfing, and computer-game playing; and promoting positive attitudes toward food. Positive eating messages are critical, because studies have shown that dieting during childhood actually may promote weight gain and unhealthy eating behaviors later in life.

Fit Families, Fit Communities

The causes of obesity are as complex as its health hazards. Recall the ecological model that depicts a series of concentric circles, the central one of which is an individual person (see Figure 1.5 in Chapter 1). Moving outward, the circles represent ever-broader influences on a health behavior: the family, the culture, the neighborhood, the school, the community, and society at large.

In over 30 years of research, Leonard Epstein and his colleagues (Epstein and others, 2012; Epstein, Lin, Carr, & Fletcher, 2011) found that the most successful ways to help kids lose weight are *lifestyle interventions* that combine diet, physical activity, and behavioral control *and* that target both parents and children simultaneously. The trick is to help parents engineer healthy home environments by removing TVs from bedrooms, limiting computer time, teaching parents how to find and prepare nutritious foods on a budget, and making physical activity a routine for the entire family. Equally important is *social facilitation maintenance*, extending an intervention across the home, peer, and community environments to build social support and to help kids and families keep weight off after they've lost it. The school environment is particularly important since kids consume 35% to 50% of their total calories at school, many from **competitive foods** purchased from vending machines, school stores, and à la carte cafeteria offerings that typically include cookies, candy, and chips. Modifying school environments became easier in 2010 when the U.S. Congress passed the Healthy, Hunger-Free Kids Act, which set new school food policies that reduce fat and sugar and increase whole grains, fresh fruits, and vegetables.

Making healthy food choices, self-monitoring, and preventing obesity with other steps that people take on their own to maintain weight may be especially difficult today because too many of us live, work, and attend school in what has been described as an *obesigenic* (obesity-promoting) *environment* (Lowe, 2003). Unhealthy foods are everywhere, and our bodies are genetically programmed to eat when food is available. Consequently, experts have called for broader community strategies and public health measures in the war on obesity (Khan and others, 2009). These community strategies fall into six categories:

- *Promote the availability of affordable healthy food and beverages* by increasing the availability and affordability of healthier food and beverage choices in schools, day-care centers, city and county buildings, and other public service venues; offering incentives for supermarkets to relocate to underserved areas and offer healthier food choices; and providing incentives for the production, distribution, and purchase of food directly from farms.

competitive foods Foods and beverages that are often high in calories, sugar, fat, and sodium and are sold in schools in vending machines, à la carte lines, and student stores.

- *Support healthy food and beverage choices* by offering smaller portion-size options in public service venues, limiting advertising of less healthy foods and beverages, and discouraging the consumption of sugar-sweetened beverages.

- *Encourage breast-feeding of infants* by providing educational interventions; breast-feeding support programs; and increased availability of maternal care in hospitals, workplaces, and public service venues.

- *Encourage physical activity or limit sedentary activity among children and youth* by requiring time for physical education in schools, increasing community opportunities for extracurricular physical recreation, and reducing television and other sources of screen time in public service areas.

- *Create safe communities that support physical activity* by expanding access to outdoor recreational facilities; enhancing infrastructure to support bicycling and walking by creating safe, well-lit bike lanes, sidewalks, trails, and footpaths; and improving access to public transportation.

- *Encourage communities to organize for change* by creating partnerships to address obesity among health care professionals, educational institutions, government, industry, and the media.

EATING DISORDERS

eating disorders (EDs)
"Illnesses in which the people experience severe disturbances in their eating behaviors and related thoughts and emotions" (American Psychiatric Association, 2018a).

anorexia nervosa An eating disorder characterized by self-starvation; a distorted body image; and, in females, amenorrhea.

bulimia nervosa An eating disorder characterized by cycles of binge eating followed by purging through such techniques as vomiting or laxative abuse.

For some dieters, especially young, overachieving women like Jodi—the young woman we met at the beginning of the chapter—the search for the perfect body may turn into a serious eating disorder. An increasing number of men are also being diagnosed with **eating disorders (EDs)**, defined as "illnesses in which the people experience severe disturbances in their eating behaviors and related thoughts and emotions" (American Psychiatric Association, 2018a). The most common EDs are anorexia nervosa, bulimia nervosa, and binge-eating disorder.

Anorexia nervosa is characterized by an intense fear of becoming fat, a distorted body image in which the person falsely believes he or she is fat, and excessive dieting that leads to severe weight loss (American Psychiatric Association, 2018a). Anorexia nervosa is linked to many serious health consequences, including heart failure, kidney failure, osteoporosis, and early death. In fact, anorexia has the highest mortality rate of all psychological disorders (Civic Impulse, 2018).

Bulimia nervosa involves compulsive bingeing followed by purging through self-induced vomiting, fasting, or taking large doses of laxatives. Some sufferers purge regularly; others do so only after a binge. For example, they may consume as many as 5,000 to 10,000 calories at one time, eating until they are exhausted, in pain, or out of food. Often, people with bulimia also engage in compulsive exercise (see Chapter 7) to try to control their weight. Unlike those with anorexia, people with bulimia typically maintain a relatively normal weight (Wonderlich, Joiner, Keel, Williamson, & Crosby, 2007)—as Jodi initially did until she moved out on her own and began reducing her food intake.

People who engage in recurrent binge-eating episodes, followed by feelings of distress or guilt, but without the compensatory behaviors of purging, fasting, or excessive exercise that mark bulimia nervosa, are said to have **binge-eating disorder (BED)**. BED is the most common eating disorder in the United States and Canada, affecting three times the number of people with anorexia and bulimia combined (National Eating Disorders Association [NEDA], 2018). BED is often associated with depression and seems to run in some families. Some people with BED have also experienced emotional or physical abuse, or substance abuse disorders. BED may be treated with medications that reduce the urge to binge and with cognitive-behavioral therapy aimed at changing thoughts about eating and at understanding what triggers binges (NEDA, 2016).

Demographics of Eating Disorders

Anorexia and bulimia are unique among psychological disorders in having a strong gender bias (three out of four are females) and in their substantial increase during the past 50 years. Before the 1970s, eating disorders generally were found only among upper-middle-class women in Western cultures. Although anorexia nervosa is most common in non-Hispanic White women, its prevalence is increasing worldwide, among men, and in all ethnic groups (Saunders, Frazier, & Nichols-Lopez, 2016).

It is now estimated that 20 million women and 10 million men in the United States will have an eating disorder at some point in their lives (NEDA, 2018). Although the average age of onset in females is 12 or 13, college women are particularly at risk, as are 15- to 19-year-old females who attend ballet, gymnastics, or modeling academies (Swanson, Crow, Le Grange, Swendsen, & Merikangas, 2011). Athletes—both male and female— also are at increased risk, even those who participate in sports that do not emphasize appearance or an overly thin body. Despite the growing awareness of disordered eating, some experts believe that EDs actually are *under*diagnosed by health care professionals (Campbell & Peebles, 2014).

Eating Disorders in Men

Of the estimated 8 million Americans with an eating disorder, 20% to 30% are male (Davis, Guller, & Smith, 2016); in addition, disordered eating that is subclinical (not diagnosed as an ED) may be nearly as common in men as in women (NEDA, 2018). Males and females with eating disorders have similar issues with body image dissatisfaction, age of onset, morbidity, and prognosis, but they often differ in what pushed them toward disordered eating, their weight control behaviors, and the likelihood that they will seek help. For example, men are less likely to rely on purging than women, more likely to exercise or fast compulsively, and less likely to seek treatment for an ED (Davis, Guller, & Smith, 2016; Ricciardelli, McCabe, Williams, & Thompson, 2007).

Male athletes—especially swimmers, rowers, and wrestlers—are especially vulnerable to anorexia and bulimia (Weinberg & Gould, 2015). Sexual orientation may also be a factor. By one estimate, 20% of gay and bisexual men suffer from anorexia, and nearly 14% suffer from bulimia (Blashill, Goshe, Robbins, Mayer, & Safren, 2014). The age of onset of EDs in men is around puberty, but as is also true in women, EDs can be diagnosed in men at any age (National Eating Disorders Coalition [NEDC], 2017).

Some young men develop **muscle dysmorphia (MD)**, a disorder in which body image dissatisfaction is accompanied by an excessive desire to develop a more muscular build. Muscle dysmorphia, which appeared as an official diagnosis in *DSM-5,* is especially

binge-eating disorder (BED)
An eating disorder in which a person frequently consumes unusually large amounts of food.

muscle dysmorphia (MD)
A psychological disorder, more common in males, in which body image dissatisfaction is accompanied by an excessive desire to develop a more muscular build.

Begsteiger/agefotostock

Increasing numbers of men have a distorted body image, seeing themselves as "too fat" when they are actually underweight. Eating disorders are also becoming more common among men. A related disorder is muscle dysmorphia (MD), in which body image dissatisfaction is accompanied by an excessive desire to develop a more muscular build.

Kadeh Ferreira/Barcroft Images/Barcroft Media via Getty Images

common among male weight lifters, bodybuilders, and males involved in sports where body size and weight are competitive factors (American Psychiatric Association, 2013). In their efforts to "bulk up," men with MD sometimes use anabolic steroids and other dangerous drugs and supplements (Tod, Edwards, & Cranswick, 2016).

Applying the Biopsychosocial Model

As we have seen throughout this book, health and illness are best understood in terms of a combination of biological, psychological, and sociocultural factors. Let's take a look at how health psychologists have applied the biopsychosocial model to understand eating disorders.

Genes and Biology

Family, twin, and adoption studies of anorexia, bulimia, and binge-eating disorder consistently report significant genetic influences on eating disorders. People who have had a first-degree relative with an eating disorder are 7–12 times more likely to develop an eating disorder themselves (Thornton, Mazzeo, & Bulik, 2011). When one twin has bulimia, the chances of the other twin's sharing the disorder are substantially greater if they are identical twins rather than fraternal twins (Root and others, 2010).

Researchers are searching for specific genes that may influence susceptibility to eating disorders (Klump, Suisman, Burt, McGue, & Iacono, 2009). Several genes that may contribute to eating disorders are also associated with specific, highly heritable personality traits that often exist beforehand and persist after recovery (Wade & Bulik, 2007; Wilksch & Wade, 2009). These include a tendency toward obsessive thinking, perfectionism, neuroticism (emotional instability and hypersensitivity), rigidity and persistence (especially in anorexia nervosa), and impulsivity (especially in bulimia nervosa).

Genes also influence neurotransmitter systems that may contribute to eating disorders Dopamine activity appears to be altered in people who develop anorexia and bulimia, but in opposite ways that may explain why the disorders are associated with different weight control behaviors (Frank, Shott, Riederer, & Pryor, 2016). Similarly, differences in serotonin activity may explain why people who develop anorexia are able to inhibit their appetite, why those who develop binge-eating disorder are more vulnerable to overeating, and why people with bulimia are unable to control impulses to purge (Lee & Lin, 2010).

Using PET, fMRI, and other imaging techniques, researchers have discovered altered activity in areas of the brain that regulate reward, emotion, planning, and **interoception**—the sense that helps you understand and feel what's going on in your body. Children who struggle with interoception have trouble differentiating when they feel hungry, full, hot, cold, or thirsty. Imaging studies show that people with anorexia have altered activity in the *anterior insula,* an area of the brain associated with body self-awareness. Individuals with anorexia may literally not recognize when they are hungry (Kaplan, 2010).

interoception The sense that helps you understand and feel what's going on in your body.

Psychosocial Factors in Eating Disorders

The roots of eating disorders can be also found in certain psychological situations, such as the competitive, semiclosed social environments of some families, athletic teams, and college sororities. The families of people with anorexia tend to be high-achieving, competitive, overprotective, and characterized by intense interactions, poor communication and conflict resolution, and insecure attachments in social relationships (Ma, 2008). The families of people with bulimia have a higher-than-average incidence of alcoholism, drug addiction, obesity, and depression (Depestele, Lemmens, Dierckx, Baetens, & Claes, 2015). Researchers caution, however, against assuming that everyone who grew up in such a home is at risk for EDs.

Coping Skills and Traumatic Events People who develop EDs sometimes lack the coping skills needed to tolerate negative experiences. Disordered eating behaviors often develop in response to emotional pain, conflict, low self-esteem, anxiety, depression, or stress. In the absence of more positive coping skills, disordered eating may provide short-term relief but ultimately only serve to maintain a dangerous cycle of emotional dysregulation and numbed feelings. Many ED interventions teach mindfulness, self-soothing, journaling, and other positive coping techniques as part of a comprehensive treatment program (Ekern, 2016).

Traumatic events such as physical or sexual abuse sometimes contribute to the development of an eating disorder. Survivors—who may struggle with feelings of a loss of control, shame, or body image dissatisfaction—may use disordered eating behaviors in an attempt to regain control or cope with the traumatizing situation (Inniss, Steiger, & Bruce, 2011). As many as 50% of those with eating disorders may also be struggling with PTSD or another trauma-related disorder (Reyes-Rodriguez and others, 2011).

Body Image Dissatisfaction Despite living in a society that stigmatizes obesity and idealizes thinness, there are many more people who are overweight or obese than there are people who are thin. As a result of this disparity between the ideal and reality, body image dissatisfaction is so pervasive that it represents a "normative discontent" among adolescents of all shapes and sizes (Bell & Dittmar, 2010). The increased prevalence of eating disorders during the last half-century has coincided with this epidemic of body image dissatisfaction worldwide. Chinese teens express weight-gain anxiety similar to that of their peers in the United States and Canada (Chen & Jackson, 2009). A longitudinal study in South Korea found that body image dissatisfaction began at age 10, increasing depression and suicidal ideation (Kim & Kim, 2009).

Mattel/Splash News/Newscom

Barbie and the Female Body How much blame for girls' plump body image should be placed on the unrealistic body dimensions of Barbie and other popular dolls? By one estimate, to achieve "Barbie doll proportions," a female of average height would have to gain 12 inches in height, lose 5 inches from her waistline, and add 4 inches to her bustline! In recognition of the fact that girls and women don't come in one shape, toy manufacturer Mattel announced that the 2016 line of Barbie dolls would come in four body types, including tall, petite, and curvy, in addition to the original-size doll.

Society's current emphasis on thinness may be the clearest example of the power of advertising to influence cultural norms and individual behavior. Like clothing styles, body types go in and out of fashion and are promoted by advertising. Media images constantly reinforce the latest ideal, and the impact of the media in establishing role models is undeniable. With increasing Americanization and globalization, body image dissatisfaction is becoming more common among young women throughout the world, as well as among young men.

The ideal female weight—represented by actresses, supermodels, and Miss America titleholders—has progressively decreased to that of the thinnest 5% to 10% of American women. Consequently, over three fourths of normal-weight women think they weigh too much, and body image dissatisfaction is reported by 50% to 70% of adolescent girls (Wertheim & Paxton, 2011). When shown images of unnaturally thin models, women often report feeling depressed, ashamed, and dissatisfied with their own bodies—emotions and attitudes that are linked to increased risk of eating disorders (Grabe, Ward, & Hyde, 2008). Body image dissatisfaction is also common in young men, although the ideal body type for males is one that is muscular as well as lean (Wooldridge & Lemberg, 2016). Those who are most vulnerable to eating disorders are also those who idealize thinness (and, in men, muscularity) and have the greatest body dissatisfaction (Stice, Rohde, & Shaw, 2013).

Treatment of Eating Disorders

A number of different therapies have been used to treat anorexia, bulimia, and binge-eating disorder. These include force-feeding, family therapy, interpersonal therapy, dialectical behavior therapy, hypnosis, and psychodynamic approaches (Wilson, Grilo, & Vitousek, 2007). Experts agree that treatment must address both the behavior and the attitudes that perpetuate disordered eating.

Historically, many eating disorder interventions focused on providing information about the unhealthy effects of these conditions, with the hope that this would result in behavioral changes. However, *psychoeducational programs* of this type generally were not very successful (Stice, Shaw, & Marti, 2007). As you will see in subsequent chapters, interventions limited to education alone have also been largely unsuccessful in preventing other problems, including substance abuse, unprotected sex, and depression.

Restoring body weight is, of course, the first priority in treating anorexia. In extreme cases, inpatient treatment includes force-fed diets that gradually increase from about 1,500 to 3,500 calories per day. In many cases, a number of secondary biological and psychological disturbances are reduced once body weight is restored. Because motivational issues surrounding body image and food behavior must be addressed, interventions often must be maintained for long periods of time—one to two years of individual therapy is not uncommon in treating those with very low body weight (Wilson and others, 2007).

Family therapy is the most heavily researched treatment for anorexia nervosa, and in general, the results of a dozen or more clinical trials have been encouraging (Wilson and others, 2007). Particularly in adolescence, family-based therapy for eating disorders is more successful than therapy focused only on the individual (Couturier, Kimber, & Szatmari, 2013; Bass, 2015). The best known of these is a form of family therapy called the *Maudsley model*, an intervention applied to adolescent patients involving 10 to 20 family sessions spaced over 6 to 12 months. All family members are seen together, and initially, parents are coached to find effective ways to control their child's eating behavior. In the next phases, this external control gradually fades and—especially with older adolescents—autonomous eating behavior is explicitly linked to long-term resolution of the eating disorder.

Cognitive-behavioral therapy is the treatment of choice for bulimia nervosa and binge-eating disorder (Cardi & Treasure, 2010; Wilson and others, 2007). Treatment focuses on procedures designed to (a) enhance motivation for change, (b) replace unhealthy dieting with regular and flexible patterns of eating, (c) reduce an unhealthy concern with body weight and shape, and (d) prevent relapse. First, therapists monitor food intake, binge-eating episodes, and stimulus triggers of those episodes. They then use this information to gradually mold the patient's eating into a pattern of three or more meals per day; introduce feared foods into the diet; and change faulty thinking and distorted attitudes about food intake, weight, and body image. Treatment typically includes 16 to 20 sessions of individual therapy over four to five months.

How Effective Are Treatments for Eating Disorders?

Anorexia remains one of the most difficult behavior disorders to treat because many victims see nothing wrong with their eating behavior and resist any attempt to change (Agras and others, 2004). Christopher Fairburn, a leading bulimia researcher, has suggested that the long-term success rate of all eating disorder interventions is a function of two participant variables: self-esteem and body image. Regardless of the type of treatment used, patients with lower self-esteem and persistent body-image distortions tend to be less successful in terms of their long-term recovery (Fairburn, 2005).

Although there are relatively few controlled studies comparing the results of treatments for anorexia, most therapies result in some weight restoration in the short term but a high relapse rate (often in excess of 50%) and poor long-term outcome. Longer-term follow-up studies show that the majority of people with anorexia persist in their preoccupation with food and weight and that many continue to show psychological signs of the disorder, have low weight, and exhibit social or mood disturbances. Although anorexia has the highest mortality rate of any psychiatric disorder—about 3%—an estimated 75% of those with anorexia eventually recover (Keel & Brown, 2010).

In one study of the effectiveness of cognitive-behavioral therapy, researchers recruited college women with warning signs for eating disorders: low self-esteem, poor body image, perfectionism, and a history of repeated dieting. The students were randomly assigned to either a treatment group or a control group. The treatment group received training in cognitive strategies for increasing self-esteem, challenging self-defeating thinking, improving body image, and combating social pressures for thinness. After seven weeks, students in

Wendell Teodoro/Getty Images

The Thin Ideal Fashion models and beauty pageant contestants exemplify the Western idealization of the "slim" woman.

family therapy A type of psychotherapy in which individuals within a family learn healthier ways to interact with each other and resolve conflicts.

the treatment group showed greater improvement in self-esteem and body image than did students in the control group. They also reported significantly fewer disordered eating episodes (Kaminski & McNamara, 1996). Another study found that CBT typically eliminates binge eating and purging in about 30% to 50% of cases (Wilson and others, 2007).

Controlled studies of treatments for disordered eating show dropout rates ranging from 0% to 34% and long-term abstinence from disordered eating ranging from 20% to 76%. As Stewart Agras and his colleagues (2004) have noted, out of a treatment group of 100 binge eaters treated with CBT (generally the most effective treatment), 16 will probably drop out of treatment, and 40 will be abstinent by the end of treatment. A failure rate of 60% suggests that researchers have not yet found the ideal treatment for eating disorders. Even so, one meta-analysis of randomized controlled trials found that cognitive-behavioral interventions are effective in reducing binge eating (Vocks and others, 2010), and another reported that 70% of those with bulimia recover as a result of therapy (Keel & Brown, 2010). Researchers found guided self-help (Banasiak, Paxton, & Hay, 2005), and even CBT-based self-help interventions delivered by computer, to be effective with some bulimia nervosa and binge-eating patients, particularly if the programs are interactive and focused on girls over age 15 (Schmidt & Grover, 2007).

Cognitive dissonance–based interventions have emerged as effective prevention programs for dealing with eating disorders and body dissatisfaction (Halliwell & Diedrichs, 2014). *Cognitive dissonance (CD) theory* states that when our behavior is inconsistent with our thoughts, the behavior creates psychological discomfort (dissonance) that motivates us to change either our cognitions or our behaviors in order to restore consistency (Festinger, 1957). CD interventions use techniques such as role-playing, preparing and delivering speeches, and making a public commitment to reduce unhealthy behaviors. CD interventions have proven to be the most effective targeted programs to date for adolescents age 14 and older (Stice, Rohde, Durant, Shaw, & Wade, 2013; Stice and others, 2007).

The Body Project intervention targets the thin-ideal beauty standard. The reasoning is simple: If young women who endorse the "thin is beautiful" standard are given an opportunity to argue against it and the sociocultural forces behind it (e.g., the media, fashion industry, dieting industry), they may experience dissonance that would lead to a change in their attitudes toward this unrealistic ideal, thereby reducing body dissatisfaction and their risk for unhealthy weight-control behaviors. A growing body of research supports the effectiveness of dissonance-based interventions for eating disorders. Stice and his colleagues (Stice, Rohde, & Shaw, 2013) also have found that undergraduate peer leaders can effectively deliver a dissonance-based eating disorder prevention program.

There is also good news in the finding that some victims of eating disorders may recover on their own with the passage of time. One longitudinal study followed a cohort of 509 women and 206 men who were teenagers in the late 1970s and early 1980s. The researchers surveyed the participants' eating attitudes and behaviors while in college, and again 10 years later (Heatherton, Mahamedi, Striepe, & Field, 1997). The results showed that body dissatisfaction, chronic dieting, and eating disorder symptoms generally diminished among many of the women in the 10 years following college, with rates of apparent eating disorder dropping by more than half. However, a substantial number of the women, particularly those who were dissatisfied with their body weight or shape in college, continued to have eating problems 10 years after college. More than one in five of the women who met clinical criteria for an eating disorder in college also did so 10 years later.

These results suggest that some degree of disordered eating may be normative for college women and that diminution of these problems after graduation is also normative. However, body dissatisfaction and chronic dieting remain problems for a substantial number of women. Changes in maturation and gender role status may partly explain why eating problems diminish after college.

Along with greater awareness of disordered eating, today there is an increased emphasis on healthful eating and diets that are based on nutrient-dense, unprocessed foods rather than on diets that are just low in calories. Sociocultural messages about thinness have changed somewhat as well, again with greater emphasis on health and fitness and less on actual weight.

Health psychologists hope to continue this increased focus on overall good health rather than on attempting to achieve unattainably perfect physiques. This would help many of us avoid the dangers of obesity or eating disorders, as well as the anxiety and dissatisfaction caused by the disparity between our real bodies and an idealized, unhealthy body image.

Weigh In on Health

Respond to each question below based on what you learned in the chapter. (Tip: Use the items in "Summing Up" to take into account related biological, psychological, and social concerns.)

1. People typically enjoy eating the kinds of foods they ate as children. Think about the foods you most enjoy eating, as well as your normal daily diet. How have these choices been influenced by your family's diet when you were a child? What changes would be beneficial for your health? Why?

2. Suppose you are attending a conference about obesity in the United States with participants ranging in age from children to older adults and ranging in experience from those who struggle with obesity, to those with normal weight and low weight, to experts in the field. You have been chosen as a college student representative to participate in a panel discussion about obesity hazards, factors, and treatments. What are five points that you want to present to the panel about obesity and college life?

3. Your friend Tony has become a gym rat—so much so that he hardly does anything else. He's constantly thinking about losing weight and building his muscles. You suspect he might have an eating disorder, as well as a problem with body image, and one day Tony confides in you that this is true. What would you advise him to do? Based on what you've read in this chapter, what are some biological, psychological, and social or cultural influences that could be affecting Tony?

Summing Up

Nutrition: Eating the Right Foods

1. The prevalence of obesity has nearly tripled since 1975, and for the first time in history, the global number of overweight people rivals the number of underfed and underweight people.

2. Besides water and daily caloric energy, the body requires 46 nutrients, which are grouped into five categories: proteins, fats, carbohydrates, vitamins, and minerals. Poor nutrition has been implicated in 5 of the 10 leading causes of death: heart disease, cancer, stroke, diabetes, and atherosclerosis.

The debate about the relative dangers of fat and sugar in the diet continues today, although current guidelines recommend a limit of no more than 10% of total daily calories, each, from added sugar and saturated fat.

3. The number of people with multiple chronic conditions has increased for men and women, for all racial and ethnic groups, and for most income groups. The most prevalent combinations of chronic conditions are hypertension and diabetes, hypertension and heart disease, and hypertension and cancer.

Weight Determination: Eating the Right Amount of Food

4. Basal metabolic rate (BMR) depends on a number of variables, including age, gender, current weight, and activity level. Our bodies balance energy intake and expenditure quite closely, which supports the concept of a body weight set point. Once the number of fat cells in a person's body increases, it never decreases.

5. The arcuate nucleus may be the master center for short-term regulation of appetite and long-term regulation of body weight. Ghrelin and peptide Y (PYY) are hormones that have been linked to short-term feeding behaviors. Other hormones—including leptin and, to a lesser extent, insulin—are factors in long-term weight maintenance.

Obesity: A Complex Phenomenon

6. Obesity is a risk factor for many diseases and is second only to smoking in its importance as a behavioral factor in mortality rates. The most frequently used measure of obesity is the body mass index (BMI).

7. Distribution of fat is also important, with abdominal (male pattern) fat being less healthy than lower-body (female pattern) fat. Weight cycling may be more hazardous to health than a somewhat high but stable weight. The prevalence of *metabolic syndrome* increases as BMI increases.

8. Susceptibility to common obesity is *polygenic* (affected by many genes). The FTO gene may function as a "genetic switch" that determines whether people will burn extra calories or store them as body fat.

9. Stress eating may contribute to long-term disease risk by triggering unhealthy patterns of food consumption. Obesity is also inversely related to education and occupation level.

Research studies of food deserts and food security demonstrate that the accessibility of healthy foods can apparently offset the dietary hazards of low income.

Treatment and Prevention of Obesity

10. The most successful diets are clinical interventions that include some form of post-treatment following weight loss, such as social support, exercise programs, or continued contact with the therapist. Behavior modification, which focuses on techniques such as self-monitoring, is a mainstay of many contemporary weight-loss programs.

11. Making healthy food choices, self-monitoring, and preventing obesity with other steps that people take on their own to maintain weight may be especially difficult today because too many of us live, work, and attend school in an *obesigenic* (obesity-promoting) *environment.*

Eating Disorders

12. Anorexia nervosa is characterized by refusal to maintain healthy body weight, intense fear of weight gain, and disturbance of body image. Bulimia nervosa involves compulsive bingeing followed by purging through self-induced vomiting or ingestion of large doses of laxatives. The most prevalent eating disorder is binge-eating disorder, in which sufferers do not purge but feel out of control and distressed about their binge-eating episodes.

13. Although eating disorders are more common among women, they are also prevalent in men. Males and females with eating disorders have similar issues with body image dissatisfaction, age of onset, morbidity, and prognosis, but they often differ in what pushed them toward disordered eating, their weight control behaviors, and the likelihood that they will seek help.

14. Eating disorders are multifactorial—determined by the interaction of biological, psychological, social, and cultural factors. Eating disorders may be linked to abnormal levels of certain neurotransmitters in areas of the brain that regulate reward, emotion, planning, and interoception.

15. A range of therapies has been used to treat eating disorders. Experts agree that treatment must address both the behavior and the attitudes that perpetuate disordered eating. The most widely used therapy for anorexia and bulimia, cognitive-behavioral therapy, attacks faulty thinking about food intake, weight, and body image.

Key Terms and Concepts to Remember

overweight, p. 235

obesity, p. 235

multiple chronic conditions (MCC), p. 242

food security, p. 243

set-point hypothesis, p. 244

adipocytes, p. 246

leptin, p. 247

weight stigma, p. 248

body mass index (BMI), p. 249

abdominal obesity, p. 250

weight cycling, p. 252

stress eating, p. 254

poverty income ratio (PIR), p. 255

food deserts, p. 256

competitive foods, p. 261

eating disorder (ED), p. 262

anorexia nervosa, p. 262

bulimia nervosa, p. 262

binge-eating disorder (BED), p. 263

muscle dysmorphia (MD), p. 263

interoception, p. 265

family therapy, p. 267

 LaunchPad macmillan learning   To accompany your textbook, you have access to a number of online resources, including quizzes for every chapter of the book, flashcards, critical thinking exercises, videos, and *Check Your Health* inventories. To access these resources, please visit the Straub Health Psychology LaunchPad at **launchpadworks.com**

Chapter 9

VOISIN/PHANIE/AGE Fotostock

Substance Use, Abuse, and Addiction

LEARNING OUTCOMES

Once you have studied this chapter, you will be able to:

- Explain the basic mechanisms of substance use, abuse, and addiction;
- Differentiate the major models of substance use disorder;
- Describe the prevalence of alcohol use and the various methods of preventing and treating alcohol addiction;
- Evaluate the efficacy of tobacco cessation and prevention interventions; and
- Identify recent trends in substance use, including the rise of e-cigarette use and the resurgence of marijuana use.

Ryan, who is 24 years old, plays football for an amateur team sponsored by a local bar, where the players and fans regularly go to have drinks after games. One evening, teammates brought Ryan to the emergency room pale, sweating, in obvious pain, and near collapse. "It's my chest," he said to the resident on call and went on to explain that he'd been vomiting profusely for 3 days. Asked what might have brought this on, a sheepish-looking Ryan explained that his team had made it to the league final the previous weekend and he'd had "a fair bit to drink." Pressed for specifics, he admitted to drinking more than 20 cans of strong lager beer in the course of one evening of celebration.

Upon examination, Ryan had a fever, a rapid pulse of 120 beats per minute, and a raised white blood cell count; he was also dehydrated, with abnormal electrolyte levels. A chest X-ray and CT scan showed the presence of free air along the left border of Ryan's heart, apparently caused by a traumatic rupture of his esophagus. Spontaneous rupture of the esophagus is very rare, but it is life threatening and has a survival rate that quickly drops to as low as 11% if diagnosis and intervention are delayed by as little as 48 hours. Ryan had been vomiting profusely for 3 days.

Ryan's perforated esophageal wall was diagnosed as Boerhaave syndrome, the result of forceful vomiting and a sudden increase in pressure within the 12-inch passageway between his stomach and throat. His greatest danger was from extensive sepsis, which occurs when chemicals released into the bloodstream to fight an infection trigger inflammation that spreads throughout the body, potentially causing multiple organs to fail. Fortunately, after surgery and 10 days of hospitalization with broad-spectrum antibiotic treatment, Ryan was healthy enough to return home. One month later, he was able to resume playing football, this time swearing that he would never again risk the near-fatal effects that can occur with binge drinking.

Since antiquity, human beings have used alcohol and other substances to alter their moods, thought processes, and behaviors—often with significantly negative health effects. This chapter examines the different facets of substance use: its causes, effects, and prevention—including research pointing to a biopsychosocial common ground in the origins of addiction to many habit-forming substances.

UNDERSTANDING SUBSTANCE USE, ABUSE, AND ADDICTION

The American Psychiatric Association's *Diagnostic and Statistical Manual of Mental Disorders* (*DSM-5*) defines **substance use disorder (SUD)** as a behavior pattern characterized by impaired control, social impairment, and risky use of a drug (American Psychiatric Association, 2013). The severity of SUD varies from *mild* (the presence of two to three of the indicators listed in Table 9.1), to *moderate* (four to five indicators), to *severe* (six or more indicators). SUDs are identified for 10 classes of drugs: alcohol, caffeine, cannabis, hallucinogens, inhalants, opioids, sedatives, hypnotics (anxiolytics), stimulants, and tobacco. *DSM-5* also includes a new category of **behavioral addictions**, including gambling (see Your Health Assets: Social Media Addiction, on page 275).

Substance use disorders cause more deaths, illnesses, and disabilities than any other preventable health condition (United Nations Office on Drugs and Crime [UNODC], 2015). Alcohol, for instance, is implicated in 40% of all traffic deaths. Half of all murders in the United States involve alcohol or some other drug, and 80% of all suicide attempts occur after the person has been drinking alcohol. Each year, tobacco use causes nearly 6 million deaths globally (an estimated 8 million by the year 2030), and it results in a net loss of over $300 billion in the United States alone due to medical expenses and lost work time (World Health Organization [WHO], 2015i).

The most recent Monitoring the Future survey (Johnston and others, 2018) of high school students found that consumption of most substances—including alcohol, tobacco, stimulants, and prescription opioids—has fallen to the lowest levels in the past 40 years. By contrast, smoking marijuana and *vaping* have increased to the point that

substance use disorder (SUD) A pattern of behavior characterized by impaired control, social impairment, and risky use of a drug.

behavioral addiction A new category of behaviors such as gambling that display the characteristics of substance abuse disorders.

TABLE 9.1 When Is Drug Use a Disorder?

The severity of substance use disorder varies from *mild* (two to three of the following indicators) to *moderate* (four to five indicators) to *severe* (six or more indicators).

Diminished Control

1. Uses more substance, or for longer, than intended.
2. Tries unsuccessfully to regulate use of substance.
3. Spends much time acquiring, using, or recovering from effects of substance.
4. Craves the substance.

Diminished Social Functioning

5. Use disrupts commitments at work, school, or home.
6. Continues use despite social problems.
7. Causes reduced social, recreational, and work activities.

Hazardous Use

8. Continues use despite hazards.
9. Continues use despite worsening physical or psychological problems.

Drug Action

10. Experiences tolerance (needing more substance for the desired effect).
11. Experiences withdrawal when attempting to end use.

Information from: American Psychiatric Association. (2013). *Diagnostic and statistical manual of mental disorders* (5th ed.). Arlington, VA: American Psychiatric Publishing.

Opioid abuse has affected all levels of American society. The musician formerly known as Prince (pictured at the 2008 Grammy Awards) died in 2016 at age 57. His autopsy revealed very high amounts of fentanyl in his blood, liver, and stomach.

these substances are more popular than cigarettes (Johnston and others, 2018). Abuse of synthetic, so-called designer drugs has also increased. Among the most popular designer drugs are hallucinogens such as NBOMes (pronounced "en-bombs"), stimulants such as bath salts, and Spice—a synthetic drug that mimics the effects of marijuana. When a designer drug first appears for sale—often in convenience stores, gas stations, or online— it is technically not illegal, because its chemical makeup is slightly different from the illicit drug it is modeled after.

The misuse of and addiction to opioids—including prescription painkillers, heroin, and synthetic substances such as fentanyl—has become a serious national crisis with an economic burden of $78.5 billion a year. This includes the costs of health care, lost productivity, addiction treatment, and involvement of the criminal justice system (National Institute on Drug Abuse [NIDA], 2018).

Why, despite these enormous financial, health, and social costs, do people continue to abuse drugs? To answer this question, you first need to know how drugs move through and affect the body.

Mechanisms of Drug Action

Drugs are ingested, or administered, in one of five ways: orally, rectally, by injection, by inhalation, or by absorption through the skin or the mucous membranes. The manner in which a drug is administered can alter its physiological effects. For example, because they enter the bloodstream faster, drugs that are injected or inhaled usually have stronger and more immediate effects than those that are swallowed.

Within minutes after a drug is absorbed, it is distributed by the bloodstream to its site of action (receptors). How quickly a drug reaches its target receptors depends on the rate of blood flow and how easily the drug passes through cell membranes and other protective barriers. Blood flow to the brain is greater than to any other part of the body. Therefore, drugs that are able to pass through the network of cells that separates the blood and the brain—the **blood–brain barrier** (Figure 9.1)—move quickly into the central nervous system. The ease with which a drug passes through this barrier depends on its lipid (fat) solubility.

blood–brain barrier The network of tightly packed capillary cells that separates the blood and the brain.

Your Health Assets

Social Media Addiction

The use of social media has increased dramatically in recent years. In 2017, Facebook counted more than 184 million active daily users in the United States and Canada alone (Wagner & Molla, 2018). Media categories include online platforms for social and professional networking (such as Facebook and LinkedIn), video sharing (YouTube), and microblogging (Twitter and Instagram) (Balakrishnan & Griffiths, 2017).

Although one recent research study found that a small amount of social media use may promote well-being, evidence is mounting that extensive time on Twitter, Snapchat, or Facebook can be unhealthy and can be associated with low self-esteem and depression that may be a sign of a *behavioral addiction*. Although an estimated 3% of U.S. teens suffer from *Internet addiction*, this disorder does not appear in *DSM-5* (Jorgenson, Hsiao, & Yen, 2016).

How can you tell if your social media use may be bordering on a behavioral addiction? According to Baylor University's James Roberts, behavioral addictions have six core components: salience, euphoria, tolerance, withdrawal symptoms, conflict, and relapse. The follow six questions and statements can be used to gauge each of these components and to determine whether an attachment to social media could be an addiction.

1. Salience: Is your social media use deeply integrated into your daily life?
   I use social media like Twitter, Facebook, Snapchat, Instagram or Pinterest, throughout the entire day.
2. Euphoria: Do you depend on social media use for excitement throughout the day?
   I use social media when I am bored or alone.
3. Tolerance: Do you need to spend more time to get a "buzz" from social media?
   I find myself using social media more and more.
4. Withdrawal symptoms: Do you get nervous when you are not on social media?
   I'm afraid of missing out on something important when I am not on social media.
5. Conflict: Does your use of social media cause you trouble?
   My social media use has caused conflict with my friends, distracted me in class or while at work.
6. Relapse: Have you tried to cut back on your use of social media but failed?
   I have tried to cut back on my time on social media, but it didn't last very long.

Roberts says that answering yes to three or more of these questions might indicate a need to reconsider your use of social media, and to loosen its grip on your life by finding a "digital sweet spot" where you are still connected but make time for other activities as well.

Information from: Baylor University (2016, October 27). Are you addicted to social media? Six questions. *Science Daily*.

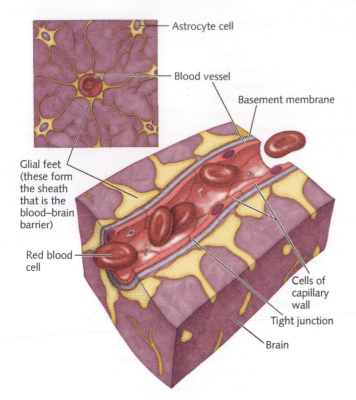

Astrocyte cell

Blood vessel

Basement membrane

Glial feet (these form the sheath that is the blood–brain barrier)

Red blood cell

Cells of capillary wall

Tight junction

Brain

FIGURE 9.1 The Blood–Brain Barrier Unlike the porous blood capillaries in most other parts of the body, those in the brain are tightly packed, forming a fatty glial sheath that provides a protective environment for the brain. The glial sheath develops from the nearby astrocyte cells. To reach the brain, a drug first must be absorbed through the capillary wall and then through the fatty sheath.

teratogens Drugs, chemicals, and environmental agents that can damage the developing person during fetal development.

agonist A drug that attaches to a receptor and produces neural actions that mimic or enhance those of a naturally occurring neurotransmitter.

antagonist A drug that blocks the action of a naturally occurring neurotransmitter or agonist.

Fat-soluble drugs that cross the blood–brain barrier are of particular concern to women who are pregnant, as these substances are usually also able to permeate the *placental barrier,* which separates maternal blood from that of the developing child. For this reason, alcohol, nicotine, or other drugs, as well as chemicals in cosmetics, foods, and the environment absorbed by the mother, can affect her unborn child. Scientists now understand a great deal about **teratogens**—drugs, pollutants, and other substances that cross the placental barrier and damage the developing person. The extent of damaging effects, however, depends on when exposure occurs; the greatest damage occurs during critical periods of development when specific organs and systems are developing most rapidly.

Drugs and Synapses

Once in the brain, drugs affect behavior by influencing the activity of neurons at their synapses. Drugs can achieve their effects in one of three ways: by mimicking or enhancing the action of a naturally occurring neurotransmitter, by blocking its action, or by affecting its reuptake (see Figure 9.2a).

Drugs that produce neural actions that mimic or enhance those of a naturally occurring neurotransmitter are **agonists** (see Figure 9.2b). Synaptic receptors function like cellular "locks" that wait for neurotransmitters with a particular shape to act as a key and trigger activity within the cell. *Partial agonists* are neurotransmitters that bind and activate receptors but elicit a smaller response than true or full agonists (see Figure 9.2c).

Drugs that produce their effects by blocking the action of neurotransmitters or agonist drugs are **antagonists** (see Figure 9.2d). Caffeine, for example, is an antagonist that blocks the effects of *adenosine,* a neurotransmitter that normally inhibits the release of other transmitters that excite postsynaptic cells (i.e., causes them to fire). Thus, the excitatory cells continue firing, resulting in the stimulation felt when caffeine is ingested.

Finally, drugs can alter neural transmission by enhancing or inhibiting the reuptake of neurotransmitters in the synapse (i.e., the natural breakdown or reabsorption of the neurotransmitter by the presynaptic neuron).

Addiction, Dependence, and Tolerance

Dependence is a state in which the body and mind have adjusted to the repeated use of a drug and require its presence in order to maintain "normal" functioning. In this context, *normal* refers to the absence of the withdrawal symptoms that will appear when use of a drug is discontinued. Drug **withdrawal** refers to the unpleasant physical and psychological symptoms that occur when a person abruptly ceases using a drug. The symptoms of withdrawal are generally the direct opposite of a drug's primary effects. Amphetamines, for example, create a rush of euphoria, and thus amphetamine withdrawal triggers the

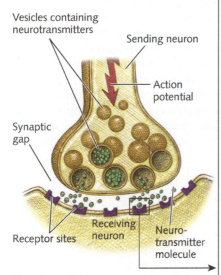

Neurotransmitters carry a message from a sending neuron across a synapse to receptor sites on a receiving neuron.

(a) This neurotransmitter molecule has a molecular structure that precisely fits the receptor site on the receiving neuron, much as a key fits a lock.

(b) This agonist molecule excites. It is similar enough in structure to the neuro-transmitter molecule that it mimics its effects on the receiving neuron. Morphine, for instance, mimics the action of endorphins by stimulating receptors in brain areas involved in mood and pain sensations.

(c) This partial antagonist molecule also excites, but it elicits a weaker response than does a true or full agonist. Buprenorphine, for instance, is a partial agonist of the receptor activated by morphine. For this reason, the drug is used clinically as an analgesic in pain management and as a treatment for morphine addiction.

(d) This antagonist molecule inhibits. It has a structure similar enough to the neurotransmitter to occupy its receptor site and block its action, but not similar enough to stimulate the receptor. Botulin poisoning paralyzes its victims by blocking acetylcholine (ACh) receptors involved in muscle movement.

FIGURE 9.2 Agonists, Partial Agonists, and Antagonists

opposing state of depression, along with vomiting, sleep disturbances, and anxiety. In extreme cases it can even lead to death.

Consistent with the biopsychosocial model, most drugs give rise to both physical and psychological dependence. For example, alcohol, which produces biochemical changes in the brain, also seems to improve mood and allow people to forget their problems. For people who are dependent on alcohol or some other drug, obtaining and using the substance can become the day's focus (refer back to Table 9.1). For someone who has overcome an addiction and is trying to abstain from the substance, memories of the "highs" once experienced fade slowly and are constant triggers for relapse.

dependence A state in which the use of a drug is required for a person to function normally.

withdrawal The unpleasant physical and psychological symptoms that occur when a person abruptly ceases using certain drugs.

The complementary effects of drug use and drug abstinence have led to a general theory—the *neural sensitization theory*—which proposes that addiction is the result of efforts by the body and brain to counteract the effects of a drug to maintain an optimal internal state. For example, nicotine—the key addictive substance in tobacco—accelerates heart rate. To compensate, the brain and nervous system respond by stimulating the vagus nerve, which slows the heart rate. Over time, the vagus nerve stimulation associated with smoking, vaping, or chewing tobacco seems to create a new, higher "set point" for vagus nerve activity. If the person quits using tobacco, vagal activity remains high because there is no nicotine in the system to increase the heart rate.

One sign of dependence is the development of *tolerance,* a state of progressively decreasing behavioral and/or physiological responsiveness to a frequently used drug. The drug user's brain chemistry adapts to offset the drug's effect (a process called *neuroadaptation*), and increased dosages are necessary to produce the effect formerly achieved by a smaller dose. With repeated use, some drugs are metabolized at a faster rate by the liver, so that more of the drug must be administered simply to maintain a constant level in the body. Also, brain receptors adapt to the continued presence of a particular drug either by increasing the number of receptor sites or by reducing their sensitivity to the drug.

Psychoactive Drugs

psychoactive drugs Drugs that affect mood, behavior, and thought processes by altering the functioning of neurons in the brain; they include stimulants, depressants, and hallucinogens.

Chemical substances that act on the brain to alter mood, behavior, and thought processes are known as **psychoactive drugs**. Psychoactive drugs are grouped into three major categories: hallucinogens, stimulants, and depressants.

Also called *psychedelic drugs, hallucinogens* such as marijuana and LSD alter sensory perception, induce visual and auditory hallucinations as they separate the user from reality, and disrupt thought processes.

Stimulants, including nicotine, caffeine, cocaine, and amphetamines, make people feel more alert and energetic by boosting activity in the central nervous system. At low doses, the moderate stimulants (nicotine and caffeine) reduce fatigue, elevate mood, and decrease appetite. However, in higher doses of the moderate drugs and with the more extreme drugs in any dosage, stimulants may cause irritability, insomnia, and anxiety. Like all psychoactive drugs, stimulants produce their effects by altering the action of neurotransmitters at synapses. They have a dramatic impact on acetylcholine, the catecholamines, dopamine, and, to a lesser extent, norepinephrine. Because of their powerful reward effects, stimulants are widely abused. Dependence and tolerance develop rapidly, forcing the addict to take progressively higher doses. Withdrawal symptoms associated with amphetamines include increased appetite, weight gain, fatigue, sleepiness, and, in some people, symptoms of paranoia.

Depressants (barbiturates, opiates, alcohol, general anesthetics, and antiepileptic drugs) dampen activity in the central nervous system. Low doses reduce responsiveness to sensory stimulation, slow thought processes, and lower physical activity. Higher doses result in drowsiness, lethargy, and amnesia and also can lead to death.

Barbiturates are used to block pain during surgery and to regulate high blood pressure. They are also popular street drugs because they produce a long-lasting sense of euphoria. They are highly addictive and considered particularly dangerous because, when taken in combination with another drug, they increase the effects of that drug, a reaction known as **drug potentiation**. In combination with alcohol, for example, a barbiturate may suppress the brain's respiratory centers and cause death.

drug potentiation The effect of one drug to increase the effects of another.

Another group of depressants, the *opiates* (morphine, heroin, and codeine), derive from the opium poppy. In this chapter we have also mentioned *opioids*, which are synthetically produced substances that act on the body in the same way as opiates. Opiates and opioids produce their effects by mimicking the body's natural opiates, the *endorphins,* which help regulate our normal experience of pain and pleasure. When the brain is flooded with an opiate or opioid, molecules of the drug bind to the receptor sites for the endorphins, and the brain stops producing its own naturally occurring opiates. If the drug is then discontinued, withdrawal symptoms soon occur, including rapid breathing, elevated blood pressure, severe muscle cramps, nausea and vomiting, panic, and intense cravings for the drug.

MODELS OF ADDICTION

The probability of substance abuse depends on both genetic and environmental influences. For example, the amount of alcohol use by parents correlates with that of both biological and adopted children, although more strongly with that of the biological children (McGue, Malone, Keyes, & Iacono, 2014). Further, children living in unstable environments are at increased risk of being diagnosed with an SUD, and that probability is even greater if they also have a particular gene that affects serotonin synapses (Windle and others, 2016).

Theories about how people become addicted to drugs can be grouped into three general categories: biomedical models, reward models, and social learning models.

Biomedical Models: Addiction as Disease

Biomedical models of addiction view physical dependence as a chronic brain condition caused by the biological effects of psychoactive drugs. The simplest model maintains that addicts inherit a biological vulnerability to physical dependence. Researchers point to evidence from studies that compare the **concordance rate**, or rate of agreement, of physical dependence among identical and fraternal twins. However, even though these studies suggest that genes play a role in physical dependence, researchers are cautious in interpreting the results because it is impossible to completely rule out possible confounding effects due to other variables. Moreover, twin studies do not pinpoint the specific gene or genes that might promote physical dependence.

concordance rate The rate of agreement between a pair of twins for a given trait; a pair of twins is concordant for the trait if both of them have it or if neither has it.

Another biomedical model points to altered neurochemistry as the basis for both physical and psychological dependence. According to the *withdrawal–relief hypothesis,* drug use serves to restore abnormally low levels of dopamine, serotonin, and other key neurotransmitters (Robinson & Berridge, 2003). Depression, anxiety, low self-esteem, and other unpleasant emotional states are indeed associated with neurotransmitter deficiencies and with substance use (Kim, Lim, & Kim, 2003). By elevating the release of presynaptic dopamine, drugs such as cocaine and the amphetamines restore neural functioning and produce a sense of psychological well-being.

The withdrawal–relief model, which was widely used for most of the twentieth century, was appealing because the idea that addicts need more of their drug to relieve physical distress made their intense determination to obtain drugs seem understandable—a rational response to their withdrawal sickness. However, the model does not explain why addicts begin taking a drug in sufficient dosages and with enough frequency to develop physical dependence in the first place. A second problem with this model is its inability to explain why many users suffer a relapse, even long after withdrawal symptoms have subsided.

Reward Models: Addiction as Pleasure Seeking

Researchers trying to explain the initial motivation for repeated use have focused on the pleasurable effects of psychoactive drugs. Recall from Chapter 3 that some experts believe that certain addictions may stem from a genetic *reward deficiency syndrome* in which the brain's reward circuitry malfunctions and leads to powerful cravings.

The Role of Dopamine

All major drugs of abuse overstimulate the brain's reward system, which also becomes active when a person engages in pleasurable behaviors that promote survival, such as eating or having sex. One neurotransmitter that plays a major role in each of these behaviors is dopamine. As a chemical messenger, dopamine is similar to adrenaline and affects neural processes that control movement, emotions, and the experiences of pleasure and pain. Cocaine, for example, produces its stimulating effect by binding to proteins that normally transport dopamine, thus blocking its reuptake. Because dopamine is not reabsorbed by the sending neuron, it remains in the synapse and continues to excite the receiving neuron. As more dopamine remains to stimulate neurons, the result may be prolonged feelings of pleasure and excitement.

Dopamine release may be an underlying mechanism for all addictions, including substance abuse. Amphetamines and other stimulants increase dopamine levels—as do opioids, nicotine, marijuana, and alcohol—and cause overstimulation of the *reward circuit,* the pleasure-pathway nerves in a region of brain called the **nucleus accumbens (NAC)** (Calipari & Ferris, 2013). This overstimulation causes the pleasurable "high" that leads some people to take a drug again and again. The NAC is involved in other reinforcing activities as well, including listening to music, enjoying food, being aroused sexually, and simply imagining something pleasant (Costa, Lang, Sabatinelli, Versace, & Bradley, 2010). Gambling and video-game playing also flood the NAC with dopamine in people who habitually engage in these activities (Ko and others, 2009).

nucleus accumbens (NAC) A brain region that plays a central role in pleasure and addiction.

Dopamine alone cannot explain addiction, however. If it could, anyone who uses drugs should become addicted, and addictive drugs should be interchangeable. Neither seems to be true. For example, less than 10% of people who use alcohol develop alcohol use disorder, and marijuana is not a substitute for cocaine for habitual users (Sack, 2012). The pharmaceutical industry has spent millions of dollars but failed to develop drugs that effectively treat addiction by affecting dopamine. Furthermore, drugs that block dopamine receptors in the brain do not reduce the reward properties, or use, of opioid drugs.

Shortcomings of the Reward Model

Despite its seeming logic, the reward model does not provide a definitive answer to the question of what causes addiction. It is true that cocaine, heroin, and other highly addictive drugs evoke the most powerful euphoria, but marijuana and other psychoactive drugs that are not considered physically addictive also produce feelings of well-being. In contrast, tobacco, which is highly addictive and as difficult to abstain from as cocaine or heroin, induces a very mild euphoria that is hardly on the same scale as that elicited by cocaine.

Another shortcoming of the reward model concerns the *gateway hypothesis*. Tobacco and alcohol use, for instance, have historically been considered powerful predictors of marijuana use. However, some newer research indicates that environmental factors may have a stronger influence on subsequent illicit drug use. A 12-year University of Pittsburgh study looked at a group of boys beginning at age 10, 214 of whom eventually used legal or illegal drugs. At 22 years of age, these 214 participants were categorized into three groups: those who had used only tobacco or alcohol, those who first used alcohol or tobacco and later used marijuana (**gateway drug** use), and those who used marijuana before using alcohol or tobacco. Nearly 25% of the participants reported using marijuana first. Three environmental factors differentiated these reverse pattern marijuana users: They were more likely to have lived in economically deprived neighborhood environments, had more exposure to drugs in these neighborhoods, and had less parental involvement when they were young children (Tarter, Vanyukov, Kirisci, Reynolds, & Clark, 2006). These data support what's known as **common liability to addiction**, which states that the likelihood a person will begin using illegal drugs is determined not by the preceding use of other specific legal drugs (gateway hypothesis), but instead by the particular tendencies and environmental circumstances of the drug user (Vanyukov, Tarter, & Ridenour, 2012).

In addition, reward models by themselves are unable to explain why drug use continues even when unpleasant side effects occur. Why don't alcohol abusers abstain, given the nausea and vomiting that they often experience? Kent Berridge and Terry Robinson's (2016) two-stage theory, known as the **wanting-and-liking theory** (also called the *incentive-sensitization theory*), provides a rationale for this. Rewarding behaviors are both "liked" and "wanted." In the first—"liking"—stage of addiction, good feelings from drug use prevail; in the second—"wanting"—stage, drug use becomes a habitual, automated behavior even as feelings of pleasure diminish or disappear. Evidence suggests that different brain circuits mediate these two stages, and that dopamine plays a larger role in the wanting or craving of a drug. Even though pleasure may not increase as drug use becomes habitual (and side effects may even be unpleasant), the reward systems continue to respond to the drug-related cues because they have become conditioned stimuli that evoke dopamine release and craving (Everitt & Heberlein, 2013). An addiction develops over time, "wanting" increases independently of "liking," and long-lasting changes in the underlying brain circuits occur due to neural sensitization (Figure 9.3).

gateway drug A drug that serves as a stepping-stone to the use of other, usually more dangerous, drugs.

common liability to addiction A model of addiction proposing that the likelihood a person will begin using illegal drugs is determined not by the preceding use of other specific legal drugs (gateway hypothesis), but instead by the particular tendencies and environmental circumstances of the drug user.

wanting-and-liking theory A two-stage theory of drug addiction. In the first stage, the original good feelings from drug use prevail; in the second stage, drug use becomes an automated behavior.

Social Learning Models: Addiction as Behavior

Although psychoactive drugs trigger neurochemical changes, and research points to hereditary risk factors in dependence, there is good reason to view addiction as a behavior that is shaped by learning as well as by sociocultural and cognitive factors. For instance, exposure to prosmoking media, such as point-of-sale displays, magazine advertising, and portrayals of smoking in movies, increases smoking in adolescence (Shadel, Martino, Setodji, & Scharf, 2012). As another example, smokers "learn" to smoke in a variety of situations, such as socializing with friends or after eating a meal. Through conditioning,

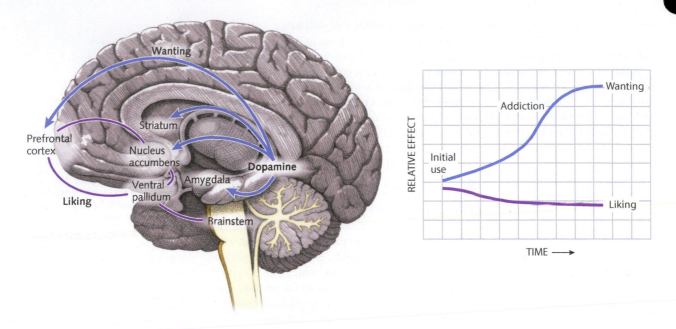

FIGURE 9.3 Brain Circuits of "Wanting" and "Liking"

Different brain circuits and neurotransmitters mediate the "liking" and "wanting" stages of addiction. In the first, "liking" stage, good feelings are common and reinforce the voluntary use of the drug. In the second stage, use of the drug becomes a habit, automatically triggering "wanting," even as feelings of pleasure diminish.

Information from: Berridge, K. C., & Robinson, T. E. (2016). Liking, wanting, and the incentive-sensitization theory of addiction. *American Psychologist 71*(8), 670–679. The model appears as Figure 1, p. 671, of the Berridge & Robinson (2016) publication. Underlying source as noted in published caption (This figure was adapted by Shannon Cole and Daniel Castro from Robinson & Berridge, 1993): Robinson, T. E., & Berridge, K. C. (1993). The neural basis of drug craving: An incentive-sensitization theory of addiction. *Brain Research Reviews 18*(3), 247–291.

the pleasurable physiological effects of nicotine, together with other rewarding aspects of social situations, transform these situations into powerful triggers for smoking.

A person's identification with a particular drug also plays a role in both the initiation and the maintenance of addiction. Adolescence is a time of pronounced self-concept development, and self-concept regulation strongly influences health behaviors (Shepperd, Rothman, & Klein, 2011). Adolescents are preoccupied with their public images and the social implications of their behaviors. Drinking and smoking, for example, may lead to the adoption of a certain lifestyle that makes abstinence a monumental task involving a new sense of self. Similarly, research studies have shown that the more adolescents feel that smoking is a defining aspect of who they are, the more likely they are to smoke (Hertel & Mermelstein, 2012). Conversely, adolescents who are encouraged to think about the positive social consequences of abstaining from alcohol use subsequently have lower levels of willingness to drink when opportunities arise (Moeller and others, 2002).

As another example of social influence on drug use, people—especially young people— may be protected by family, school, religion, and other social institutions. According to *social control theory,* the stronger a young person's attachment to such institutions, the less likely he or she will be to begin using drugs. Data from the Monitoring the Future study show that adolescents who do well in school are much more likely never to have used alcohol, tobacco, marijuana, or other drugs later in their lives than students who do poorly (Johnston and others, 2018).

The closely related *peer cluster theory* maintains that peer groups are strong enough to overcome the controlling influence of family, school, or religious values when it comes to the use of tobacco, alcohol, and some other drugs. For example, adolescents tend to change their smoking behavior to that of their friends, and the tendency to select friends based on similar smoking behavior is a strong predictor of smoking behavior (Mercken,

Steglich, Sinclair, Holliday, & Moore, 2012). This may be partly because some group settings, such as college campuses, induce false beliefs about social norms regarding drug use—specifically, giving the impression that "everybody" smokes cigarettes and engages in binge drinking and other drug use. Research studies have found that when students' illusions about peer drinking are corrected, alcohol use often subsides (Moreira, Smith, & Foxcroft, 2009).

Why Adolescence?

As we have seen, there seems to be a window of vulnerability in adolescence for risky behavior. Both the prevalence and incidence of drug use increase every year from age 10 to age 25 and then decrease. Substance *use* before age 18 is a strong predictor of later substance *abuse*, in part because adolescents are limited in their ability to analyze risks cognitively, partly because brain maturation is incomplete (see Chapter 3). For this reason, health psychologists are concerned with findings from the latest Monitoring the Future study. Although cigarette smoking, binge drinking, nicotine vaping, *hookah* use (breathing through a mouthpiece attached to a rubber hose in order to inhale tobacco smoke that passes through water), and the use of most illicit drugs all declined in 2017, the percentage of eighth-grade students who had ever used inhalants (fumes from glue, cleaning fluid, and aerosol containers) increased from 1.9% to 8.9% (Johnston and others, 2018). (Young adolescents may be most likely to try inhalant drugs because they are easy to obtain from supermarkets, drugstores, and hardware stores.)

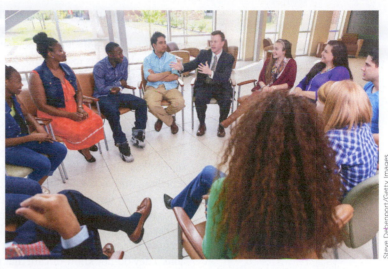

Social Support Self-help group meetings such as this one provide members with various types of help in overcoming drug dependence and abuse.

Drug use among adolescents varies markedly from place to place, again suggesting the influence of social-cultural factors. For example, the United States has a legal drinking age of 21, whereas many European countries have younger minimum drinking ages (as young as 16 in France and Italy and 18 in Ireland, Sweden, and the United Kingdom). Throughout most of Europe, alcohol is widely used, even by children. In much of the Middle East, however, alcohol use is illegal, and adolescents rarely drink. In many Asian countries, smoking is permitted everywhere. In the United States, smoking is widely advertised yet is banned in most schools and indoor public places. In Canada, cigarette advertising is banned. Could this be a factor in why fewer Canadian teens smoke?

Throughout the world, adolescent boys generally use more drugs than do girls, and they use them more often. Gender differences in substance use are tied to self-image and self-presentation and are reinforced by social constructions regarding appropriate male and female behavior. That is, they are influenced by teens' efforts to appear sophisticated, cool, or tough in the peer environment (Evans, Powers, Hersey, & Renaud, 2006). In the United States, boys and girls are similar in terms of *which* drugs they use, with two exceptions: Boys use more illegal drugs and steroids, whereas girls use more diet drugs (Johnston, O'Malley, Bachman, & Schulenberg, 2013).

Substance abuse among teens often occurs with other unhealthy behaviors as part of a problem behavior syndrome that also includes sexual intercourse in early adolescence, depressive symptoms, and general delinquency (Donahue, Lichtenstein, Langstrom, & D'Onofrio, 2013). Teens who display one or more of these behaviors often have high levels of family conflict and poor self-control and emotional regulation, which suggests that these behaviors may be emotional coping mechanisms in the face of a stressful environment (Goliath & Pretorius, 2016). For some teens, alcohol and other drugs allow for a momentary denial of problems. Too often, however, ignored problems don't go away, a drug is turned to more often, and the teenagers enter a vicious cycle that may lead to addiction.

Findings such as these have led some researchers to propose that the stress and strain of adolescence are contributing factors to drug use. In fact, however, prospective studies suggest that drug use *causes* more problems than it solves and often *precedes* depression, rebellion, and anxiety disorders (Meririnne and others, 2010). For example, teenagers who regularly use marijuana may become less motivated to achieve in school and then be more likely to develop other problem behaviors (Ansary & Luthar, 2009).

Fear of addiction may not persuade young adolescents to avoid drug use because of the *personal fable* phenomenon—a tendency for adolescents to believe that they are invulnerable. They do not know or care that psychoactive drugs excite emotional control centers in the brain's limbic system, while simultaneously interfering with analytical areas in the prefrontal cortex. These neurological effects make drug users more emotional than they otherwise would be, as well as less thoughtful. Every hazard of adolescence—including accidents, unsafe sex, depression, and suicide—is more common among those who are under the influence of a psychoactive drug. Yet educational campaigns and antidrug advertisements that use scare tactics may backfire and actually increase drug use, because of the personal fable and because savvy adolescents often recognize exaggerations and other partial truths used in such campaigns (Strasburger, Jordan, & Donnerstein, 2009).

Many parents and other adult caregivers are unaware of their children's drug use. In one study, less than 1% of the parents of U.S. sixth graders thought their children had ever tried alcohol, but 22% of the children said they had (O'Donnell, Brydon, Wright, & Steptoe, 2008). Parents may also fail to realize the extent to which they influence their children's substance use through their own behavior and the social context that they shape at home. Parents who quit smoking by the time their children reach the third grade have children who are more likely to have negative perceptions of smoking and, in turn, are less likely to smoke themselves (Wyszynski, Bricker, & Comstock, 2011). When parents forbid smoking in their homes, fewer adolescents smoke (Messer, Trinidad, Al-Delaimy, & Pierce, 2008). When parents are careful with their own drinking, fewer teenagers abuse alcohol (Van Zundert, Van Der Vorst, Vermulst, & Engels, 2006). When parents provide guidance about drinking, teenagers are less likely to get drunk or use other substances (Miller & Plant, 2010). Growing up with two married parents in the household reduces teenager cigarette and alcohol use, even when other influences such as parental smoking and family income are taken into account (Brown & Rinelli, 2010).

Changing the broader social context also has an impact. For example, higher prices, targeted warnings, and better law enforcement have led to a marked decline in cigarette smoking among younger adolescents. In 2016, only 2.6% of eighth graders had smoked cigarettes in the past month, compared with 21% 15 years earlier (Johnston and others, 2018).

Now that you understand more about addiction, let's turn to two of the most common addictions: alcohol and nicotine.

ALCOHOL USE AND ABUSE

Alcohol is a depressant that slows the functioning of the central nervous system in a manner similar to tranquilizers. When you drink an alcoholic beverage, approximately 20% of the alcohol is rapidly absorbed from the stomach directly into the bloodstream. The remaining 80% empties into the upper intestine, where it is absorbed at a pace that depends on whether the stomach is full or empty.

Once alcohol is absorbed, it is evenly distributed throughout body tissues and fluids. It takes a 175-pound man about 1 hour to metabolize the amount of alcohol contained in a 1-ounce glass of 80-proof liquor, a 4-ounce glass of wine, or a 12-ounce bottle of beer (Advokat, Comaty, & Julien, 2014). Drinking at a faster pace results in intoxication because a larger amount of alcohol remains in the bloodstream. Women metabolize alcohol more slowly because they produce less of the enzyme *alcohol dehydrogenase,* which breaks down alcohol in the stomach. Women also tend to weigh less than men. As a result of both of these factors, women have a higher blood alcohol content than men after consuming the same amount of alcohol.

The amount of alcohol in the bloodstream is your **blood alcohol level (BAL)**. In most states, a BAL of 0.08 grams per 100 milliliters of blood (0.08%) constitutes legal intoxication. It is illegal to attempt to drive an automobile when you have a BAL at this level or higher. A typical male college student would reach an illegal BAL after consuming one standard drink per hour for every 30 to 35 pounds of body weight. Women would reach an illegal BAL sooner. For some people, obvious intoxication may occur with BALs as low as 0.03% or 0.04%. Others develop a higher tolerance and are able to drink larger amounts of alcohol before becoming visibly impaired. Regardless of the visible effects, however, the legal regulation of BAL and the damaging internal, physiological effects are comparable for all drinkers.

blood alcohol level (BAL) The amount of alcohol in the blood, measured in grams per 100 milliliters.

The short-term effects of alcohol are dose-dependent. At BALs ranging from about 0.01 gpercent to 0.05 gpercent, a drinker usually feels relaxed and mildly euphoric. As the level increases to 0.10 gpercent, memory and concentration are dulled, and reaction time and motor functioning are impaired significantly. At 0.10 gpercent to 0.15 gpercent, walking and fine motor skills become extremely difficult. By 0.20 gpercent to 0.25 gpercent, vision becomes blurry, speech is slurred, walking without staggering is virtually impossible, and the drinker may lose consciousness. Death may occur at a BAL of 0.35 gpercent or more.

Prevalence of Alcohol Use

About 20% of college students meet the criteria for problem drinking. As Figure 9.4 shows, 59.4% of full-time college students in the United States ages 18 to 22 drank alcohol in the past month compared with 50.6% of other persons the same age. Nearly 40% of college students engaged in binge drinking (five or more drinks on one occasion) in the past month, compared with 33.4% of others the same age; and 12.7% engaged in heavy drinking (binge drinking on five or more occasions in the past month), compared with 9.3% of other nonstudents the same age (Centers for Disease Control and Prevention [CDC], 2016c; SAMHSA, 2015).

According to the Institute of Medicine, **at-risk drinking** can consist of two or more episodes of binge drinking in the past month, or of drinking an average of two or more

at-risk drinking Two or more episodes of binge drinking in the past month, or consuming an average of two or more alcoholic drinks per day in the past month.

FIGURE 9.4 Alcohol Use in the United States A total of 59.4% of full-time college students in the United States drank alcohol in the past month compared with 50.6% of others the same age. The same year, 39% of college students engaged in binge drinking (five or more drinks on one occasion) in the past month compared with 33.4% of others the same age. Finally, 12.7% engaged in heavy drinking (binge drinking on five or more occasions in the past month) compared with 9.3% of other nonstudents the same age.

Data from: SAMHSA. (2015). 2014 National Survey on Drug Use and Health (NSDUH). Table 6.88B—Alcohol use in the past month among persons aged 18 to 22, by college.

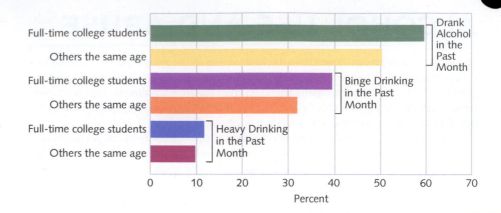

TABLE 9.2 Are You a Problem Drinker?

How will you know if you are drinking too much? Here are some key questions to ask:

Am I drinking alcohol as a beverage or using it as a drug?

- Do I need alcohol to relax or to relieve stress?
- Do I use alcohol to cope with negative reactions and emotions?
- Do I use alcohol to manage social functions or relationships?

How does alcohol fit into my life?

- Do I make sure there is always time for alcohol in my schedule?
- Has drinking become an important priority?

What do I expect from my alcohol consumption?

- An attitude adjustment?
- Solace and release from tension?

Can I honestly say that there are no negative consequences of my drinking?

- No impact on family or children?
- No physical effects (hangover, memory loss, loss of control)?
- No risky behavior (driving after drinking more than two or three drinks)?
- No family member or friend commenting on my drinking?
- No impact on my professional responsibilities (lateness, forgetting, poor judgment)?

Can I drink four or five drinks at a time and not feel negative effects?

Are there any occasions or circumstances when I feel I have to have a drink?

Do I have a spouse, friends, or family members who have a drinking problem?

If your answers to one or more of these statements or questions are positive, then you may be engaging either in risky drinking that puts you at risk for alcohol problems or in hazardous drinking that is already producing some negative consequences in your life.

Information from: DiClemente, C. C. (2005, September 28). Alcohol and problem drinking. Washington, DC: APA Practice Organization.

alcoholic drinks per day in the past month. At-risk drinking is a major public health concern because it is linked with poor health; with premature death; and with a variety of social consequences such as injury, unplanned and unprotected sex, and hostile encounters with police (see Table 9.2). About one in four college students report academic consequences from their drinking, including missing classes, falling behind, performing poorly on exams, and getting lower grades overall (National Institute on Alcohol Abuse and Alcoholism [NIAAA], 2015).

The prevalence of the various categories of drinking behavior varies by age, gender, education level, ethnicity, and culture. Adults between 25 and 44 years of age have the highest overall rates of drinking, but the 18-to-24 cohort has the highest rates of binge and heavy drinking (NIAAA, 2015). Alcohol use among adolescents ages 12 to 17 dropped substantially after the mid-1980s, when the legal age for purchasing alcohol was increased to 21 in most states. Rates of drinking are lowest among older adults (NIAAA, 2015). Compared with women, significantly more men are current drinkers, binge drinkers, and heavy drinkers (15 or more drinks per week for men or 8 or more drinks per week for women). European Americans have higher rates of drinking than African Americans, Asian Americans, or Hispanic Americans. African Americans are less likely to be heavy drinkers than European Americans and Hispanic Americans.

Although the specific causes of ethnic and cultural group differences in risk are not known, researchers have pointed to several possibilities. A powerful protective factor in the social-cultural environment is *racial identity (RI)*—an aspect of self-concept and social identity derived from the knowledge and value of group membership. Identifying as part of a group and having a sense of belonging and pride are associated with higher levels of psychological well-being and higher self-esteem among minority adolescents and young adults in ethnically diverse settings. Minority adolescents and young adults who have high levels of RI appear to be able to resist or delay substance use initiation, have a more negative attitude toward drugs, and are more likely to perceive substance use as being nonnormative, or atypical, among their racial group than are youths who have low levels of RI (Stock and others, 2013a).

The Physical Effects of Alcohol Consumption

Alcohol affects all parts of the body. At the most basic level, because cell membranes are permeable to alcohol, alcohol enters the cells and disrupts intracellular communication. Alcohol also affects genes that regulate cell functions such as the synthesis of dopamine, norepinephrine, and other important neurotransmitters.

The craving that some people develop for alcohol, the adverse reactions that occur during withdrawal, and the high rate of relapse are all due to biochemical changes in the brain brought on by heavy, long-term use of alcohol. Prolonged heavy drinking can cause the brain to shrink, especially in women (Mayo Clinic, 2006). Binge drinking inhibits *neurogenesis,* the process by which neurons are generated, as well as the formation of new synaptic connections (Crews, He, & Hodge, 2007). In addition, alcohol abuse may interfere with the body's absorption of thiamin, one of the B vitamins. The absence of thiamin may contribute to *Korsakoff's syndrome,* a neurological disorder most often caused by alcohol abuse and characterized by extreme difficulty with memory.

Alcohol has major effects on the hippocampus, a brain area associated with learning, memory, emotional regulation, sensory processing, appetite, and stress (see Chapter 3). It does so by inhibiting neurotransmitters that are strongly associated with emotional behavior and cravings. Dopamine transmission, in particular, is strongly associated with the rewarding properties of alcohol, nicotine, opiates, and cocaine.

Chronic alcohol abuse weakens the immune system, damages cellular DNA, interferes with normal endocrine system development, and disrupts the secretion of growth hormone—which may cause a problematic variety of other endocrine changes. Alcohol abuse has been linked to decreased testosterone levels in men, leading to impotence and

Science Source

Normal
43-year-old

Alcoholic
43-year-old

Alcohol abuse damages the brain These MRI scans show brain images of a normal patient (left) and a patient with damage from prolonged heavy alcohol use (right).

fetal alcohol syndrome (FAS) A cluster of birth defects—including facial abnormalities, low intelligence, and delayed body growth—caused by the mother's use of alcohol during pregnancy.

Fetal Alcohol Syndrome
If a woman drinks heavily during critical periods of fetal development, she puts her unborn child at risk of having fetal alcohol syndrome (FAS). Besides the specific facial structures seen here (including a thin upper lip and low nasal bridge), the child is also likely to be intellectually disabled.

decreased fertility. In women, menstrual disturbances, spontaneous abortions, and miscarriages increase with the level of alcohol consumption. Alcohol also may decrease estrogen levels in women, which may partly explain the association between alcohol use and increased risk of breast cancer (Allen, 2009).

Alcohol promotes the formation of fat deposits on heart muscle, which lowers the efficiency of the heart and contributes to cardiovascular disease. It also increases heart rate and causes blood vessels in the skin to dilate, resulting in a loss of body heat. Chronic abuse may increase blood pressure and serum cholesterol levels and accelerate the development of atherosclerotic lesions in coronary arteries. Although women experience alcohol-related heart damage at lower levels of consumption than men, both men and women who abuse alcohol are equally likely to suffer a fatal heart attack before age 55 (MMWR, 2004).

Excessive use of alcohol contributes to stomach inflammation and the formation of gastrointestinal ulcers. Severe inflammation of the liver (*hepatitis*) and the replacement of normal liver cells by fibrous tissue (*cirrhosis*) are two common chronic diseases caused by alcohol abuse. Chronic liver disease and cirrhosis cause approximately 36,000 deaths each year in the United States (CDC, 2015b).

Alcohol freely crosses the placenta of pregnant women, making alcohol a potent teratogen. Alcohol levels in a developing fetus quickly match those of the drinking mother. Pregnant women who drink during critical stages of fetal development place their infants at risk of developing **fetal alcohol syndrome (FAS)**. FAS causes severe birth defects, including low intelligence; microcephaly (small brain); intellectual disability;

Small palpebral fissures

Smooth philtrum

Thin upper lip

Microcephaly

Low nasal bridge

Epicanthal folds

Minor ear anomalies

Micrognathia

Centers for Disease Control and Prevention, National Center on Birth Defects and Developmental Disabilities delayed body growth; facial abnormalities such as malformed eyes, ears, nose, and cheekbones; and congenital heart defects.

The behavioral, psychological, and social effects of alcohol abuse are just as dangerous as its physical effects, as the next section will explain.

Psychosocial Consequences of Alcohol Use

As blood alcohol level initially rises, many drinkers feel cheerful, self-confident, and more sexually responsive. As levels continue to rise, however, higher-order cognitive functions are disrupted. Furthermore, alcohol impairs judgment and facilitates urges that otherwise might be resisted. This alcohol-induced sense of confidence and freedom from social constraints, which is known as **behavioral disinhibition**, often results in increased aggressiveness, risk-taking, or other behaviors the individual would normally avoid. When drinking, for example, both women and men are more disposed to casual sex, unprotected sex, and other high-risk behaviors (Ebel-Lam, MacDonald, Zanna, & Fong, 2009).

Alcohol also makes it difficult for drinkers to interpret complex or ambiguous stimuli; that is, they find it harder to attend to multiple cues and easier to focus on only the most salient ones. This **alcohol myopia** (nearsightedness) was demonstrated by Antonia Abbey and her colleagues (Abbey, Parkhill, Buck, & Saenz, 2007), who invited unacquainted college students (88 male–female pairs) to converse for 15 minutes after consuming either alcoholic or nonalcoholic drinks. Both men and women who drank alcohol perceived their partners and themselves as behaving more sexually and in a more disinhibited way than did those who did not drink. However, the effects also depended on the type of cue being evaluated. Intoxicated participants exaggerated the meaning of dating cues and *ignored* more ambiguous signals that were possibly indicating friendliness or sociability, rather than sexual interest. Thus, alcohol seems to make it even easier for people to concentrate on salient cues that fit their current beliefs (or hopes) and disregard more ambiguous cues that do not. Some researchers believe that these cognitive and perceptual changes are the very basis of alcohol's addictive capacity.

Alcohol-induced cognitive impairments are especially destructive during adolescence, perhaps because even low doses can impair the judgment of teens who are already distracted by the ongoing psychological, physiological, and social challenges of puberty. Hundreds of research studies have revealed the link between alcohol and risky sex—in particular, that students who use alcohol tend to have more sexual partners, to be less likely to use condoms, and to have more sexually transmitted infections and unwanted pregnancies than their nondrinking counterparts (Cooper, 2006). Frequent drinkers are also absent from school nearly four times more often than nondrinkers, more likely to ride in a car with a driver who has been drinking, and nearly three times as likely to engage in antisocial behaviors such as stealing and vandalizing property (Lammers, Ireland, Resnick, & Blum, 2000).

At all ages, alcohol abuse has been associated with a variety of other social problems, including difficulties in interpersonal relationships and various types of violence, including homicides, assault, robbery, suicides, and spousal abuse (Rogers, Boardman, Pendergast, & Lawrence, 2015; Davis, Norris, George, Martell, & Heiman, 2006). Half of all people convicted of rape or sexual assault were drinking before the commission of their crimes. Drinking also increases the chances of being a victim of crime. Approximately

behavioral disinhibition The false sense of confidence and freedom from social restraints that results from alcohol consumption.

alcohol myopia The tendency of alcohol to increase a person's concentration on immediate events and to reduce awareness of distant events.

72% of rapes committed on college campuses occur when victims are so intoxicated that they are unable to consent or refuse (Wechsler & Nelson, 2008).

Alcohol contributes to violence not only by loosening restraints due to behavioral disinhibition, but also by increasing a person's sensitivity to pain and frustration. In addition, brain imaging studies show that repeated heavy use of alcohol, stimulants, and other drugs disrupts frontal lobe activity, which impairs decision making and planning and lowers a person's normal threshold for violence.

Alcohol Use Disorder

alcohol use disorder (AUD) A maladaptive drinking pattern in which drinking interferes with role obligations.

For most adults, moderate alcohol use—no more than two drinks a day for men and one drink a day for women and older people—is relatively harmless. (A "drink" means 1.5 ounces of spirits, 5 ounces of wine, or 12 ounces of beer, all of which contain 0.5 ounces of alcohol.) Moderate use, however, is at one end of a range of drinking, and 15.1 million adults in the United States have an **alcohol use disorder (AUD)** (NIAAA, 2017). A person who meets 2 or more of the 11 problem-drinking criteria listed in Table 9.3 would be diagnosed as having an AUD.

TABLE 9.3 Alcohol Use Disorder (Based on *DSM-5* Criteria)

In the past year, have you:

1. Had times when you ended up drinking more, or longer, than you intended?
2. More than once wanted to cut down or stop drinking, or tried to, but couldn't?
3. Spent a lot of time drinking? Or being sick or getting over other after effects?
4. Wanted a drink so badly you couldn't think of anything else?
5. Found that drinking—or being sick from drinking—often interfered with taking care of your home or family? Or caused job troubles? Or school problems?
6. Continued to drink even though it was causing trouble with your family or friends?
7. Given up or cut back on activities that were important or interesting to you, or gave you pleasure, in order to drink?
8. More than once gotten into situations while or after drinking that increased your chances of getting hurt (such as driving, swimming, using machinery, walking in a dangerous area, or having unsafe sex)?
9. Continued to drink even though it was making you feel depressed or anxious or adding to another health problem? Or after having had a memory blackout?
10. Had to drink much more than you once did to get the effect you want? Or found that your usual number of drinks had much less effect than before?
11. Found that when the effects of alcohol were wearing off, you had withdrawal symptoms, such as trouble sleeping, shakiness, restlessness, nausea, sweating, a racing heart, or a seizure? Or sensed things that were not there?

In The presence of at least 2 of these symptoms indicates an *Alcohol Use Disorder (AUD)*.

The severity of the AUD is defined as follows:

Mild: the presence of 2 to 3 symptoms

Moderate: the presence of 4 to 5 symptoms

Severe: the presence of 6 or more symptoms

Information from: National Institute on Alcohol Abuse and Alcoholism (NIAAA). (2013a). *Alcohol Use Disorder*. NIH Pub. No.13-7999.

Various factors have been implicated in explaining why certain people are more likely than others to abuse alcohol, but no single factor or influence completely explains the origins of AUD.

Genes and Alcoholism

There is no single gene for alcoholism, but genes and alleles that make alcoholism more likely have been found on every chromosome except the Y (Epps & Holt, 2011). Some people inherit a greater tolerance for the aversive effects of alcohol, as well as a genetically greater sensitivity to the pleasurable effects. Both tendencies may be factors in early excessive drinking, leading to dependence. Consider the evidence:

- When either the mother or the father of a male child is alcohol-dependent, that child is significantly more likely to later abuse alcohol himself (Ball, 2008).

- Identical twins have twice the concordance rate (76%) of fraternal twins for AUD. This is true whether the twins were raised together or apart, and whether they grew up in the homes of their biological parents or with adoptive parents (Ball, 2008).

- The personalities of those most likely to abuse alcohol have several common traits, each of which is, at least in part, genetically determined: a quick temper, impulsiveness, intolerance of frustration, vulnerability to depression, and a general attraction to excitement (MacGregor and others, 2009).

Alcohol, Temperament, and Personality

Research studies that link temperament and personality to alcohol dependence provide another clear indication of the interaction of nature and nurture. Researchers no longer attempt to identify a single "alcoholic personality"; instead, they focus on specific personality traits that appear to be linked to alcohol dependence. One such trait is a temperament that includes attraction to excitement and intolerance of frustration. A second is **behavioral undercontrol**, characterized by aggressiveness, unconventionality, overactivity, and impulsive behavior. A third is **negative emotionality**, which is characterized by depression and anxiety. Marked by such traits, high-delinquent teens show consistently elevated numbers of alcohol-related problems (Allen & Gabbay, 2013).

Alcohol Expectancy Effects

As is true of all psychoactive drugs, alcohol's impact depends not only on the dose but also on the circumstances under which the drug is taken—the user's personality, mood, and **alcohol expectancy effects**. People who *believe* they have consumed alcohol behave just like those who have imbibed, whether or not they have (Heinz, de Wit, Lilje, & Kassel, 2013).

Several studies have also found that adolescents' and young adults' beliefs about their peers' alcohol use and attitudes predicted their own alcohol use. Those who are certain that many of their friends drink regularly—and enjoy doing so—are themselves more likely to begin using alcohol (Park, Klein, Smith, & Martell, 2009). As another example, people who believe that alcohol promotes sexual arousal become more responsive to sexual stimuli if they believe they have been drinking (Friedman, McCarthy, Förster, & Denzler, 2005).

behavioral undercontrol A general personality syndrome linked to alcohol dependence and characterized by aggressiveness, unconventionality, and impulsiveness; also called *deviance proneness*.

negative emotionality A state of alcohol abuse characterized by depression and anxiety.

alcohol expectancy effects The effects of an individual's beliefs about how alcohol affects behavior.

Treatment and Prevention of Alcohol Use Disorders

Although some people with AUDs do recover on their own, others continue to cycle in and out of alcohol problems throughout their lives. Those who seek treatment generally receive outpatient rather than inpatient care. The treatments generally involve the use of drugs or therapy, or some combination of the two.

Factors that influence the willingness of a person to enter treatment for an AUD include gender, age, marital status, and ethnicity. Among women, factors that predict entry into treatment include being older and unmarried and having a lower level of education, employment, and income. For men, factors that predict entry include having experienced alcohol-related social consequences, being older, and belonging to an ethnic minority. Although evaluations of the effectiveness of self-help groups are limited, drinking-related beliefs, readiness and motivation to change, and social support for abstinence are important predictors of the success or failure of treatment.

Drug Treatment for AUDs

Researchers working to understand the physiological mechanisms by which alcohol affects the brain have uncovered a number of pharmacological treatments for AUDs. Medications include detoxification agents to manage alcohol withdrawal, alcohol-sensitizing agents to deter future drinking, and anticraving agents to reduce the risks of relapse.

As noted, many people with an AUD also suffer from clinical depression. Antidepressants that increase serotonin levels are sometimes used to treat those in the early stages of abstinence from alcohol. The best known of these is *fluoxetine* (Prozac). Some researchers believe that deficiencies of serotonin may cause alcohol craving (Polina, Contini, Hutz, & Bau, 2009). Other researchers have focused instead on drug treatments that block the release of dopamine, which appears to decrease the reward properties of alcohol (Thompson, 2000).

Another approach involves the drug *naltrexone* (Revia), which binds to opiate receptors in the brain, prevents their activation, and also decreases the reward that comes from consuming alcohol. A number of studies have found that patients who received naltrexone as part of their treatment experienced less craving than patients who received a placebo, and those receiving naltrexone were more successful in maintaining their abstinence (Snyder & Bowers, 2008). For instance, the COMBINE project evaluated the effectiveness of naltrexone versus placebo for over 1,383 recently alcohol-abstinent volunteers. Over the 16-week duration of the study, different groups received either naltrexone or the placebo alone, or in combination with cognitive-behavioral therapy (CBT). Participants who received naltrexone combined with CBT remained abstinent longer than those who received placebos with or without CBT (Kreibel, 2010).

Researchers generally agree that treatment of AUDs is more successful when drugs are combined with behavioral and psychological therapy. One early technique, **aversion therapy**, associated a nauseating drug such as *disulfiram* (Antabuse) with alcohol. Although the drug does not reduce cravings for alcohol, if the patient takes a single drink within several days of ingesting Antabuse, a variety of unpleasant effects occur, including nausea, sweating, racing heart rate, severe headaches, and dizziness (NIAAA, 2013b). Drugs like Antabuse are designed to trigger a *conditioned aversion* to alcohol. When taken daily, Antabuse can result in total abstinence.

aversion therapy A behavioral therapy that pairs an unpleasant stimulus (such as a nauseating drug) with an undesirable behavior (such as drinking or smoking), causing the patient to avoid the behavior.

But it is very difficult to get patients to adhere to a daily Antabuse regimen, so some therapists prefer to conduct aversion therapy in a controlled clinical setting. The client drinks alcohol and then takes an *emetic drug,* which induces vomiting. Because the interval between the drink and the emetic drug is carefully timed, the latter functions as an unconditioned stimulus and becomes associated with the taste, smell, and act of taking a drink of alcohol. These stimuli thus become conditioned stimuli that trigger the unpleasant reaction of nausea.

Relapse Prevention Programs

Because of the unusually high rate of relapse in alcohol dependence, many treatments focus on enabling the person to deal with situations that tempt relapse, with emphasis on gaining control over situations that may precipitate a return to drinking.

One form of relapse prevention is based on the gradual *extinction* of drinking triggers. Treatments have been developed in which drinkers are exposed repeatedly to alcohol-related stimuli, such as the aroma of their favorite drink, but they are not allowed to drink. The patients' initially powerful, conditioned physical and psychological responses diminish with repeated exposure over a number of sessions (Witteman and others, 2015).

Many relapse prevention programs also incorporate *coping* and *social-skills* training, which helps "inoculate" drinkers by teaching specific strategies for coping with high-risk situations without the help of alcohol. Inoculation focuses on improving the person's assertiveness, listening skills, and ability to give and receive compliments and criticism, as well as on enhancing close relationships (Foxhall, 2001). In addition, the recovered drinkers are taught skills that permit them to abstain in drinking situations. *Drink refusal training* entails the modeling and rehearsal of skills needed to turn down offers to drink.

Controlled Drinking

Before 1970, virtually all interventions for alcohol dependency focused on total abstinence. Then, several research studies reported that a small percentage of recovered alcoholics were able to drink moderately without relapsing into problem drinking. Since that time, the issue has been highly controversial. It does appear that a small percentage of problem drinkers can become moderate drinkers, particularly those who are young, employed, and living in supportive and stable environments (Dawson and others, 2005). Although many intervention programs continue to insist upon total abstinence, they typically have very high dropout rates. For a small sector of problem drinkers, drinking in moderation may be a more realistic social goal than total abstinence. Some intervention programs teach *controlled drinking* skills to improve the individual's personal control over drinking. One technique, *placebo drinking,* involves consuming nonalcoholic beverages in place of, or in alternation with, alcohol-containing ones. The current consensus is that although controlled drinking treatment programs remain controversial, and abstinence is the safest treatment goal for AUD, reduced drinking approaches can be effective for some individuals (Mann, Aubin, & Witkiewitz, 2017).

Self-Help Groups

One of the most widely accepted nonmedical efforts to deal with alcohol dependence is Alcoholics Anonymous (AA). Founded in 1935, AA's 12-step approach suggests calling on a (not necessarily religious) higher power to help battle what is viewed as an incurable disease. Its theory is that "once an alcoholic, always an alcoholic," and it opposes "controlled drinking" and disagrees entirely with the belief that alcoholics can be reformed into moderate, responsible drinkers. AA counts more than 2 million members worldwide.

Self-help groups such as AA generally involve group discussions of members' experiences in recovering from alcohol abuse. Members benefit by connecting with a new, nondrinking network and sharing their fears and concerns about relapse. Another self-help group, Rational Recovery, offers a nonspiritual alternative to treating alcohol dependence.

Preventing Alcohol Problems

Given how difficult it is for those with AUD to break their habit, it seems logical to prevent alcohol abuse before it occurs. Alcohol prevention programs target individual drinkers, as well as the social environments in which drinking occurs. Preventive treatments aim to change attitudes about drinking, strengthen coping skills, and restructure environments to reduce the risk of alcohol-related problems.

Prevention programs are most effective when they target children and adolescents before people in those groups have succumbed to the habit. The efforts that have proved at least partly effective include strict enforcement of drunk-driving laws, higher prices of alcohol and cigarettes due to taxes on these items, and harsher punishments for those who sell (or make available) alcohol and cigarettes to minors; also effective have been classes that inform parents of the hazards of various drugs, help to improve parent–child communication, and/or realistically delineate the potential hazards of drug use.

Several primary prevention programs, including the Alcohol Misuse Prevention Study (AMPS), are based on correcting faulty reasoning about peers' drug use and improving social skills in targeted groups. The AMPS was designed to help preadolescent students resist social pressures that lead toward alcohol consumption. For instance, role-playing exercises allow students to practice declining alcohol, marijuana, and other drug offers in various social situations.

Realistically, however, health psychologists recognize that so long as drugs are available and are not perceived as serious threats to health, many young people will try them, and many will eventually abuse them. Following this line of reasoning, one strategy is to delay young people's experimentation as long as possible. Doing so will increase the odds that they are informed realistically about the hazards of the drug(s) in question and have the cognitive maturity to avoid the faulty reasoning that often leads to **drug abuse**.

drug abuse The use of a drug to the extent that it impairs the user's biological, psychological, or social well-being.

TOBACCO USE AND ABUSE

Along with caffeine and alcohol, nicotine is one of the three most widely used psychoactive drugs. Cigarette smoking in the United States peaked in the early 1960s, when half of all adult men and one third of adult women smoked. From the late 1960s until the present day, the number of U.S. smokers declined steadily—to about 15.5% of all adults (CDC, 2018d). However, the decline was not evenly distributed, with most of the decrease occurring among upper socioeconomic status (SES) groups and men. Lower-SES individuals continued to smoke, and the prevalence of smoking among women increased sharply. Smoking is most prevalent among non-Hispanic American Indian/Alaska natives

(31.8%), followed by non-Hispanic multiple race individuals (25.2%), non-Hispanic white adults (16.6%), African American adults (16.5%), Hispanic American adults (10.7%), and Asian American adults (9.0%).

Figure 9.5 shows that socioeconomic status also predicts smoking rates (CDC, 2018d). Smoking rates are highest among adults who have a General Education Development (GED) diploma (40.6%) and those with 9 to 11 years of education (24.1%). Smoking is least prevalent among those who have an undergraduate degree (7.7%) or a graduate degree (4.5%).

Data from the most recent Monitoring the Future study indicate that cigarette smoking among youth in the United States is now at the lowest level recorded in the 40-year history of the survey (Johnston and others, 2018). Overall increases in perceived risk and disapproval of smoking appear to have contributed to the downturn in cigarette use. Despite this good news, use of *electronic cigarettes* (e-cigarettes) has risen sharply worldwide, as will be discussed later in this chapter.

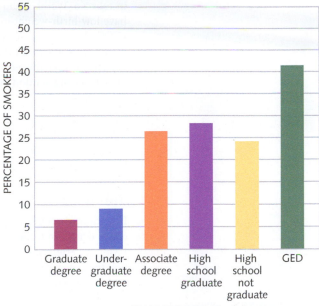

Physical Effects of Smoking

Cigarette smoking is the single most preventable cause of illness, disability, and premature death in this country and in much of the world. In the United States, cigarette smoking is responsible for one out of every five deaths—that's more than the combined number of deaths from murders, suicides, AIDS, automobile accidents, alcohol and other drug abuse, and fires (CDC, 2018d). Because each cigarette smoked reduces a person's life expectancy by an estimated 14 minutes, an adult who has smoked two packs of cigarettes a day (40 cigarettes) for 20 years can expect to lose about 8 years of life.

Each time a person lights up, 4,000 different chemical compounds are released. It is these chemicals that provide pleasure and energy, as well as disease and death. For example, the nicotine in cigarette smoke activates specific neural receptors, which in turn causes an increase in heart rate and blood pressure and the constriction of arteries, all of which contribute to the development of cardiovascular disease. The presence of nicotine also causes serum cholesterol levels to rise, hastening the formation of artery-blocking lesions.

Inhaling cigarette smoke leads to bronchial congestion by increasing the production of mucus in the throat and lungs while simultaneously damaging the hairlike cilia that line the respiratory tract. This leads to higher-than-normal incidence rates of bronchitis, emphysema, and respiratory infections.

The link between smoking and cancer is no longer a matter of debate. Benzo[a]pyrene (BPDE), a chemical in cigarette smoke, has been identified as a causative agent in lung cancer. BPDE damages a cancer suppressor gene, causing a mutation of lung tissue. Smoking is also a significant factor in cancers of the mouth, larynx, stomach, pancreas, esophagus, kidney, bladder, and cervix (CDC, 2008).

The risk for developing lung cancer is 20% to 70% higher in women than men at every level of exposure, indicating that women are more susceptible to the carcinogens

FIGURE 9.5 Who Smokes? Smoking is most prevalent among men and people with less than a high school education. About 15.5 % of American adults currently smoke.

Data from: CDC (2018d). Current cigarette smoking among adults in the United States. Centers for Disease Control and Prevention.

in tobacco. Women who smoke during pregnancy are also more likely to miscarry or to have low-birth-weight infants and infants who die from sudden infant death syndrome (CDC, 2008). Because cigarette smoke reduces the delivery of oxygen to the developing child's brain, the resulting *fetal hypoxia* can cause irreversible intellectual damage. School-children whose mothers smoked during pregnancy have lower IQs and an increased prevalence of attention deficit hyperactivity disorder (ADHD) (Kovess and others, 2015).

Why Do People Smoke?

To understand why people smoke, we need to consider each of the major stages of smoking behavior: initiation, maintenance, cessation, and relapse (Grunberg, Brown, & Klein, 1997).

Initiation

Initiation of drug use often occurs through social contacts. Initial use of many psycho-active drugs, with the exception of cocaine and amphetamines, is often unpleasant. As a result, a period of experimentation typically precedes the development of regular drug use, thus suggesting that factors other than physical effects are important in the initiation and maintenance of drug use until dependence develops.

Advertising is a powerful influence, and in 2015 tobacco companies spent $8.9 billion on it in the United States alone (Federal Trade Commission [FTC], 2017). Role-modeling and peer influence also lead many teenagers to start smoking. Celebrities who smoke create the image that smoking is linked with success, beauty, and even sexual arousal. Image, smoking among friends, relaxation, and pleasure are most often cited as reasons why teens begin smoking (Soldz & Cui, 2002). Having parents, older siblings, and friends who smoke is also predictive of teen smoking (Rodriguez, Romer, & Audrain-McGovern, 2007). In addition, low self-esteem, social isolation, and feelings of anger or depression all increase the likelihood of smoking (Repetto, Caldwell, & Zimmerman, 2005). Among adolescents whose parents and close friends do not smoke, smoking is rare.

The college years are a time when many young adults begin to smoke regularly. A four-year national study identified several personal and environmental factors as important predictors of smoking in college (Choi, Harris, Okuyemi, & Ahluwalia, 2003). Students who were more likely to begin smoking were those who did not like school as much and were more rebellious. High school students who had tried smoking were more likely to become regular smokers if they thought that their college peers approved of smoking and if they believed that experimentation with smoking was not dangerous. Finally, the longer a student avoided smoking, the less likely he or she was to experiment in college. Not surprisingly, students who lived in smoke-free dormitories were less likely to smoke than those

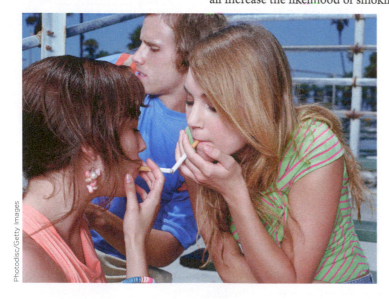

Peer Pressure Psychosocial factors such as peer pressure may contribute to smoking and experimentation with other drugs. The most promising new research takes a systems approach, recognizing that a person's choice to use drugs is the result of many interrelated factors.

Photodisc/Getty Images

who lived where smoking was permitted. The results of this study suggest that interventions that reinforce the message that nonsmoking is the norm and that increase access to smoke-free environments discourage initiation of smoking among college students.

In light of the evidence linking social influences with the initiation of smoking, the U.S. surgeon general has concluded that situational factors are more important than personality factors in explaining why people start smoking. Nevertheless, a number of *vulnerability factors* differentiate teens who are more likely to become dependent on nicotine and other psychoactive drugs. Smoking is especially prevalent among those who feel less competent and less in control of their future and who perceive a lack of social support (Camp, Klesges, & Relyea, 1993). This is particularly true among people of lower SES, who believe that their personal life and health can only be slightly controlled by their own behavior (Droomers, Schrijvers, & Mackenbach, 2002). In addition, rebelliousness; a strong need for independence; and perceptions of benefits such as weight control, increased alertness, and stress management are also linked to smoking initiation. Teenagers who smoke are also more likely to feel alienated from school, engage in antisocial behavior, have poor physical health, and feel depressed (Kandel & Davies, 1996). They also tend to spend more time in passive activities such as watching television and are more likely to be living with a single parent (Soldz & Cui, 2002).

Maintenance

Once a person has begun to smoke, a variety of biological, psychological, and social variables contribute to making it difficult for that individual to abstain.

Heavy smokers are physically dependent on nicotine, which has powerful properties as a reinforcer. Nicotine stimulates the sympathetic nervous system and causes the release of catecholamines, serotonin, corticosteroids, and pituitary hormones (Grunberg, Faraday, & Rahman, 2001). In addition, nicotine induces relaxation in the skeletal muscles and stimulates dopamine release in the brain's reward system (De Biasi & Dani, 2011).

Stanley Schachter and his colleagues (1977) first advanced the idea of the **nicotine-titration model**, suggesting that long-term smokers attempt to maintain a constant level of nicotine in their bloodstream. Schachter discovered that smokers smoke roughly the same amount day after day. When they are unknowingly forced to switch to lower-nicotine brands, they compensate by smoking more cigarettes, inhaling more deeply, and taking more puffs (Schachter, 1978). This *compensatory smoking* behavior has been confirmed in more recent studies and is generally considered to be one of many factors in how nicotine use promotes dependence and contributes to disease (U.S. Department of Health and Human Services [USDHHS], 2010).

Closely related to the idea of the nicotine-titration model, the *affect management model* proposes that smokers strive to regulate their emotional states. Accordingly, *positive affect smokers* are trying to increase stimulation, feel relaxed, or create some other positive emotional state. In contrast, *negative affect smokers* are trying to reduce anxiety, guilt, fear, or other negative emotional states. Evidence for this model comes from research showing that nicotine also affects levels of several neuroregulators, including dopamine, acetylcholine, norepinephrine, vasopressin, and endogenous opioids. Because of these effects, smoking may be used to boost mood, lower anxiety, reduce tension, increase concentration and alertness, and enhance memory temporarily.

nicotine-titration model The theory that smokers who are physically dependent on nicotine regulate their smoking to maintain a steady level of the drug in their bodies.

In support of the affect management model, researchers also have uncovered a link between nicotine use and depression, naturally leading to questions of whether one causes the other or whether some third factor contributes to both (Nauert, 2008). One longitudinal study of high school students suggests that smoking and depression have a reciprocal effect, triggering a vicious cycle of smoking and negative mood (Windle & Windle, 2001). Every six months, students completed questionnaires assessing their emotional state, cigarette smoking, family dynamics, and friends' drug use. Teens who were heavy smokers at the beginning of the 18-month study were more likely than those who smoked less to report symptoms of depression. In addition, students who had persistent symptoms of depression at the start of the study were more likely than other students to increase their smoking, even when other factors were taken into consideration.

Prevention Programs

Because it is so difficult for ex-smokers to remain nicotine-free, health psychologists have focused a great deal of energy on primary prevention. Their efforts have included educational programs in schools, public health messages, tobacco advertising bans, increasing tobacco taxes, and campaigns to ban smoking in public places. As of September 2012, the U.S. Food and Drug Administration (FDA) mandated that cigarette packages in the United States must carry new graphic warning labels showing cancerous lesions and other impacts of smoking. The warnings cover the upper portion of the cigarette pack, both front and back. In addition, at least 20% of most cigarette ads must also include the approved warnings. So far, the tobacco industry has managed to delay implementation of this rule (Cohen, 2016).

Researchers have found that neuroimaging data during antismoking messages can predict behavior change, above and beyond self-reporting (Falk, Berkman, Whalen, & Lieberman, 2011). A group of 31 heavy smokers who intended to quit donned liquid crystal display (LCD) goggles and were shown 16 professionally developed TV commercials designed to help smokers quit smoking, while neural activity was recorded using fMRI. The participants rated each ad on a 4-point scale, indicating the extent to which each ad promoted a sense of self-efficacy ("This ad makes me feel that I can quit"), increased intentions to quit ("This ad makes me more determined to quit"), and self-relevance ("I can relate to this ad"). One month later, the participants answered a series of questions regarding their efforts to quit smoking, and a biological verification (exhaled carbon monoxide [CO]) of their actual recent smoking. This outcome measure is important because self-reports of smoking behavior are often inaccurate due to poor recall, self-presentation concerns to appear consistent with stated intentions, and other cognitive biases (Pierce, 2009). The researchers found a positive relationship between neural activity in the medial prefrontal cortex (MPFC) and successful quitting (increased activity in the MPFC was associated with a greater decrease in exhaled CO).

Antismoking campaigns have been less effective with ethnic minorities, perhaps partly because tobacco companies have targeted a disproportionate amount

A proposal to ban smoking in parks and public spaces in London aims at improving the health of people living in the city and setting a better example for children.

Kathy deWitt/Alamy Stock Photo

of prosmoking advertising toward minority communities, especially the African American and Hispanic American communities.

Increasing Aversive Consequences

Successful primary prevention programs also strive to increase the aversive consequences of smoking. For example, increasing the tax paid on cigarettes is quite effective. Consider the experience of Canadian smokers, whose cigarette tax has increased more than 700% since 1980. When a pack of cigarettes costs more than $5, many teenagers think twice about smoking. The tax impact is the sharpest among teenagers, who have less disposable income and are in the age group most vulnerable to smoking behavior. According to a Health Canada survey, the smoking rate among 15- to 19-year-olds dropped to 18% in 2003 from 28% in 1999 after the tobacco tax was increased by $2.50 per carton (Canadian Tobacco Use Monitoring Survey, 2004).

Inoculation

Most effective for deterring smoking in adolescents have been "inoculation" programs that teach practical skills in resisting social pressures to smoke. Because smoking generally begins during the junior high and high school years, prevention programs are typically conducted in schools before children reach their teens.

The most successful programs are based on a *social learning model* that focuses on three variables: social pressure to begin smoking, media information, and anxiety. A program designed by Richard Evans (2003) used films, role-playing, and rehearsal to help young teens improve their social skills and refusal skills. In the films, same-age models were depicted encountering and resisting social pressure to smoke. The students also role-played situations, such as when someone is called "chicken" for not trying a cigarette. The students were instructed to give responses such as "I'd be a real chicken if I smoked just to impress you." After several sessions of "smoking inoculation" during the seventh and eighth grades, these students were only half as likely to start smoking as were those in a control group at another school, even though the parents of both groups had the same rate of smoking.

Cessation Programs

In contrast to information, cessation (quitting) programs aim to help smokers give up the habit. Since 1977, the American Cancer Society has sponsored the annual Great American Smokeout, in which smokers pledge to abstain from smoking for 24 hours. Campaigns such as these, along with print and broadcast ads, no-smoking pledge drives, smoking bans, and other programs—many of which have been funded from the $226 billion tobacco settlement in 1998—appear to be working (American Cancer Society, 2018a). The settlement originally was between the four largest tobacco companies in the United States and the attorneys general of 46 states. In exchange for exemption from additional, private lawsuits, the tobacco industry agreed to curtail certain tobacco marketing practices and to make annual payments to the states to compensate them for some of the medical costs of caring for persons with smoking-related illnesses.

Smoking cessation programs generally fall into two categories: those based on an addiction model and those with cognitive behavior approaches. Programs based on an addiction model of smoking emphasize the physiological effects and habitual behavior engendered by nicotine. Cognitive behavior models focus on helping smokers better understand the motivation, conditioning, and other psychological processes that trigger smoking. Intervention is aimed at helping smokers develop coping skills to gain control over smoking triggers and to deal with anxiety, stress, and other emotions without smoking.

Addiction Model Treatments

A variety of pharmacological replacement therapy programs have been developed for smokers, including transdermal nicotine patches, nicotine gum, and inhalers. These *nicotine replacement programs* have helped millions of smokers in their efforts to quit smoking. Once available only as expensive prescription drugs, most are now available over the counter.

People who smoke continuously, day in and day out, are good candidates for *transdermal nicotine patches,* which have become the most common pharmacological treatment for smoking. Worn during the day, the bandagelike patches release nicotine through the skin into the bloodstream. Users are able to reduce the daily dose gradually, in a series of steps that minimize withdrawal symptoms and help ensure success in remaining smoke-free.

However, nicotine patches are only moderately successful as a stand-alone treatment for smoking. Abstinence rates in patients using the nicotine patch have been found to be only about 1.9 times higher than those observed in patients using a placebo (Corelli & Hudmon, 2002). Like all pharmacological treatments, the effectiveness of nicotine gum varies with the strength of the smoker's dependency on nicotine and his or her particular smoking habits. Nicotine gum appears to be most helpful for smokers who tend to smoke many cigarettes in a short period of time. It may be most effective when used as part of a comprehensive behavioral treatment program. Some researchers believe that the relief of withdrawal symptoms and cravings is largely a *placebo effect,* rather than a pharmacological effect of the actual nicotine in the gum. Although less effective than the nicotine patch, nicotine gum improves cessation rates by about 50% compared with control interventions (Davies, Willner, James, & Morgan, 2004).

Another intervention is the oral inhaler, a plastic tube filled with 4 milligrams of nicotine that smokers can "puff" on 2 to 10 times a day. Patients who use the nicotine inhaler are 1.7 to 3.6 times more likely to remain abstinent than patients using a placebo inhaler (Rennard and others, 2006). Most effective is *combination therapy,* in which one intervention (such as the nicotine patch) provides steady levels of nicotine in the body and a second form (such as the nicotine agonist varenicline) is used as needed to control cravings and suppress nicotine withdrawal symptoms (Burke, Hays, & Ebbert, 2016).

Which Smoking Cessation Programs Are Effective?

There have been relatively few randomly controlled studies examining the effectiveness of smoking cessation programs for adolescents. In general, research studies support the viewpoint that younger smokers, especially those who are heavy tobacco users, are more likely to continue smoking than older smokers (Ferguson, Bauld, Chesterman, & Judge, 2005). A meta-analysis of teen smoking cessation programs revealed that the most effective programs are inexpensive, short-term interventions that include a motivational component, cognitive behavior techniques, and social influence education (Sussman, Sun, & Dent, 2006). More specifically, these programs

- enhanced the intrinsic and extrinsic motivation to quit with rewards and education designed to reduce ambivalence about quitting;

- were tailored to adolescents' developmental needs (rather than adult programs with only superficial changes) and made intervention programs fun;

- provided social support to help teens persevere and avoid relapse; and

- showed teens how to use community resources for remaining nicotine-free.

In contrast, there is an abundance of research on adult smoking cessation efforts. These studies have found that smoking treatment programs are most effective when two or more methods are used together. For example, treatment programs that combine behavioral methods with nicotine replacement are more effective than either approach used alone (Stead, Perera, Bullen, Mant, & Lancaster, 2008). A meta-analysis of over 100 combination therapy studies concluded that smoking treatment programs that include nicotine replacement have significantly higher quit rates than those that include placebos or no nicotine replacement therapy (Silagy, Lancaster, Stead, Mant, & Fowler, 2005).

Whichever combination of techniques is used, quitting smoking seems to be determined by three interacting factors: motivation to quit, level of physical dependence on nicotine, and barriers to or supports in remaining smoke-free. The extent of a smoker's physical dependence, for example, certainly will influence both readiness to quit and persistence. The presence or absence of a smoking spouse, workplace smoking bans, a child pressuring a parent to quit, and other barriers and supports also may influence motivation (Hammond, McDonald, Fong, Brown, & Cameron, 2004).

Valued Life Activities and Quitting

You may recall from Chapter 7 that I was able to quit smoking largely because it interfered with my desire to run a marathon and be identified as "a runner." Several lines of evidence suggest that the restriction of valued activities affects smoking and other health-compromising behaviors. First, low levels of engagement in valued activities (such as swimming, cycling, and running), restriction of valued activities due to physical condition (such as injuries), and the inability to find replacements for restricted valued activities have been linked to depressed mood (Manos, Kanter, & Busch, 2010). Depressed mood, in turn, is more common among smokers and interferes with efforts to quit. **Behavioral activation**, a counseling treatment that focuses on increasing engagement in valued life activities through guided goal setting, has shown promise as a tool in helping smokers quit (Banducci, Long, & MacPherson, 2014).

Smoking cessation among people with physical disabilities that cause impairment in mobility has been relatively neglected by researchers, despite the fact that cigarette smoking is more common among this group, with rates as high as 40% among nonelderly adults (Altman & Bernstein, 2008). Could it be that restriction of valued life activities due to physical limitations is a barrier to quitting in this population? The answer, according to the findings of a recent study of long-term smokers with physical disabilities, is yes. The study found that participants' readiness to quit smoking was enhanced by an educational intervention that helped identify satisfactory replacements for their most valued restricted activity (Busch & Borrelli, 2012).

behavioral activation A counseling treatment that focuses on increasing engagement in valued life activities through guided goal setting.

Relapse: Back to the Habit

Unfortunately, only a small percentage of people who quit remain smoke-free for very long. Attempts to quit, even within the first weeks of smoking, often fail (DiFranza, 2008). As with other addictions, smokers become *dependent,* and they develop *tolerance.* Quitting triggers withdrawal symptoms, including craving, anxiety, irritability, distractibility, and insomnia (Sayette, Loewenstein, Griffin, & Black, 2008). All it takes to relieve this unpleasant state is the negative reinforcement provided by a cigarette. Within 7 seconds, the rush of nicotine causes the brain to release epinephrine, norepinephrine, dopamine, and other neurotransmitters that boost alertness and calm anxiety.

The rewards that nicotine delivers keep people smoking, even among the 8 in 10 smokers who say they'd like to quit. Of these smokers, fewer than 1 in 10 are able to do so, and as many as 80% of smokers who quit smoking relapse within one year (USDHHS, 2012). Many factors are involved in relapse, the most fundamental being the severity of withdrawal symptoms and craving. In one study of 72 long-term smokers (38 men and 34 women), 48% relapsed within the first week of quitting. Participants who relapsed experienced greater distress and withdrawal symptoms during the first 24 hours of nicotine abstinence (al'Absi, Hatsukama, Davis, & Wittmers, 2004). Interestingly, the researchers found that stressful experiences affect men and women who are trying to quit smoking differently. For instance, cortisol responses before and after performing a public-speaking test were stronger in the men than in the women.

Ex-smokers may experience other side effects as well, which are immediately eliminated by a return to smoking. For example, some ex-smokers gain weight (perhaps because of slower metabolism, increased preference for sweet-tasting foods, or substituting eating for smoking), have trouble sleeping, are more irritable, and find it difficult to concentrate. Unfortunately, smoking is even used as a weight-control strategy—particularly by adolescents who are also likely to use other unhealthy strategies, such as diet pills and laxatives (Jenks & Higgs, 2007).

Another factor in relapse is the strength of previously conditioned associations to smoking. Smoking behaviors, as well as nicotine's physiological effects, become conditioned to a variety of environmental stimuli. Many ex-smokers relapse in the face of an irresistible urge (conditioned response) to smoke in certain situations or environments— for example, with that first cup of coffee in the morning or after a meal.

Because of this dismal prognosis for ex-smokers, smoking relapse has received considerable research attention in recent years. A working conference sponsored by the National Institutes of Health (NIH) took a first step in addressing the relapse problem by encouraging health experts to adopt a "stages of change" model (refer back to Figure 6.4 on page 167) in developing programs to prevent relapse. For example, rather than encouraging ex-smokers to attend an occasional follow-up session reminding them of the hazards of smoking, the NIH group encouraged training in relapse prevention strategies much earlier in the stages of quitting.

Efforts such as these are paying off, and smokers are getting the message that repeated attempts to quit can succeed, and success is equally likely whether they quit abruptly or gradually (USDHHS, 2012). After a year's abstinence from nicotine, only 1 in 10 will relapse in the next year (Hughes, 2010). Researchers will continue to study all aspects of substance abuse in an effort to help many more of us become "former users"—or, better yet, to avoid altogether the life disruption that substance abuse brings.

THE RISE OF E-CIGARETTES AND THE RESURGENCE OF MARIJUANA

In this final section of the chapter, we turn to two recent developments that merit special attention: the rise of electronic cigarettes and the resurgence of marijuana.

Electronic Cigarettes

Introduced in 2004, **e-cigarettes (EC)** are battery-powered vaporizers that simulate smoking without burning tobacco. Consisting of a liquid-filled cartridge (e-juice) and a heating element, e-cigarettes deliver nicotine, along with flavorings and other chemicals, as an aerosol instead of smoke. The user activates the device by taking a puff or pressing a button and inhaling the atomized nicotine (vaping).

Manufacturers of e-cigarettes make the devices in many shapes, including some that look like traditional cigarettes and pipes, but also some that look like everyday items such as pens and USB flash drives. E-cigarettes also come in more than 7,000 flavors, including some—such as mint, candy, and bubble gum—that likely are targeted to the tastes of younger users (Grana, Ling, Benowitz, & Glantz, 2014). This new industry has become an enormous business: Sales of e-cigarettes were about $3.5 billion in 2015 and are projected to exceed $20 billion by 2025 (Sussan and others, 2017). In 2017, 19% of high school seniors in the United States reported having used e-cigarettes to vape nicotine in the past year (Johnston and others, 2018) (see Figure 9.6).

E-cigarettes are cause for concern for several reasons. First, because they deliver vapor without burning tobacco, using e-cigarettes may appear to be safer and less toxic than smoking conventional cigarettes. Although e-cigarettes do not produce tobacco smoke and contain fewer harmful chemicals than regular cigarettes, they still contain nicotine—which is, as we have seen, a highly addictive drug with a wide range of harmful effects (Goniewicz and others, 2017). Another worry is that vaping exposes smokers to other harmful substances such as benzene, formaldehyde, and acetaldehyde—known carcinogens—as well as toxic metal nanoparticles released from the heating element (Pankow and others, 2017).

In addition to these issues, several studies suggest that e-cigarette use may encourage the use of other tobacco products, including conventional cigarettes (Miech, Patrick, O'Malley, & Johnston, 2017). That finding alone should create serious concerns about the rise of electronic cigarettes. Sadly, a Yale University study of teens who use e-cigarettes cited the low cost of the devices and the promise that vaping can help teens quit smoking as strong predictors of continued use (Barrington-Trimis and others, 2016).

e-cigarettes (EC) Battery-powered vaporizers that simulate smoking without burning tobacco.

Vaping exposes smokers to harmful substances such as formaldehyde and acetaldehyde—two known carcinogens.

diego_cervo/Getty Images

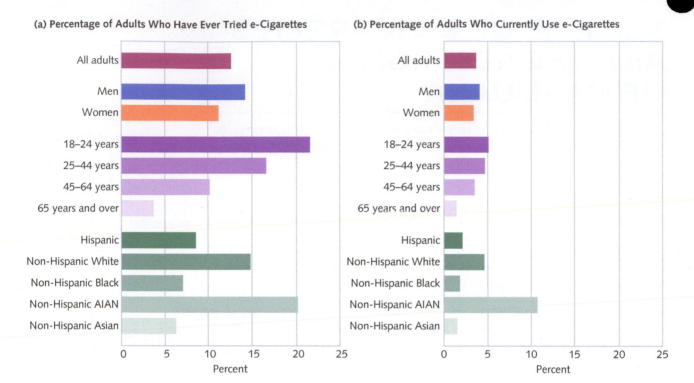

(a) Percentage of Adults Who Have Ever Tried e-Cigarettes

(b) Percentage of Adults Who Currently Use e-Cigarettes

FIGURE 9.6 E-Cigarette Usage Men are more likely than women to have ever tried e-cigarettes but are not more likely to be current users. Younger adults are more likely than older adults to have tried e-cigarettes and to currently use e-cigarettes. Both non-Hispanic AIAN (American Indian or Alaska native) and non-Hispanic White adults are more likely than non-Hispanic Black, non-Hispanic Asian, and Hispanic adults to have ever tried e-cigarettes and to be current e-cigarette users.

Data from: Schoenborn, C. A., & Gindi, R. M. (2015). *Electronic cigarette use among adults: United States, 2014.* NCHS Data Brief, No. 217. Hyattsville, MD: National Center for Health Statistics.

The Resurgence of Marijuana

According to the World Health Organization, cannabis is the most popular recreational drug worldwide (United Nations Office on Drugs and Crime [UNODC], 2015). Unlike many other recreational drugs, however, marijuana is also used as a medicine. Between 1996 and 2017, 29 states and Washington, D.C., passed laws allowing marijuana to be used for a variety of medical conditions, and 17 states reduced punishment for, or fully legalized, possession of small recreational amounts of the drug. From the 1960s until about 2010, public opinion polls showed that a majority of adults thought marijuana (or "pot") should remain illegal. Spurred by rising claims of its benign nature and medical benefits, by 2014 more than half of all adults in the United States said they supported the legalization of marijuana (see Figure 9.7). While many states have loosened older laws regarding marijuana, and others are seriously considering full legalization, marijuana use remains an offense under U.S. federal law.

Marijuana: Its Source, Its Use, and Its Physical Effects

Marijuana comes from the dried leaves, flowers, stems, and seeds of the hemp plant *Cannabis sativa,* all of which contain the mild hallucinogen THC (*delta-9-tetrahydrocannabinol*). A synthetic form of marijuana, called K2 or Spice, mimics THC. In addition to THC, marijuana contains more than 100 other chemical *cannabinoids*. Marijuana can be smoked in hand-rolled cigarettes (joints), water pipes (bongs), or emptied cigars refilled with the drug (blunts). It can also be inhaled from a vaporizer (vaping), added to food (edibles), and brewed as a tea. A dangerous new method, *dabbing,* involves smoking or

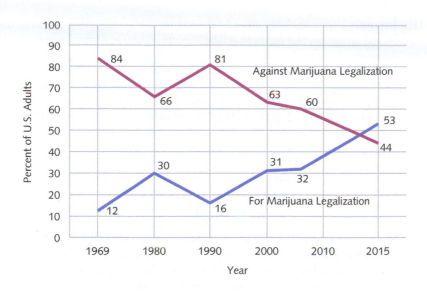

FIGURE 9.7 Growing Support for Legalization of Marijuana in the United States A 2017 Gallup survey reported that 64% of Americans now favor legalizing marijuana. As recently as 2006, just 32% supported marijuana legalization, while nearly twice as many (60%) were opposed.

Data from: McCarthy, J. (2017). Record-high support for legalizing marijuana use in U.S. Gallup News.

eating THC-rich resins that have been extracted from marijuana using butane (lighter fluid), which can cause serious burns, fires, and explosions.

Marijuana has both short- and long-term effects on the brain (see Figure 9.8). When inhaled, THC quickly passes from the lungs into the bloodstream, which carries the chemical to the brain (in under 10 seconds) and organs throughout the body. THC is absorbed more slowly when eaten, and its effects are typically felt after about 30 minutes to 1 hour. In the brain, THC binds to cannabinoid receptor type 1 (CB1) proteins that ordinarily react to natural THC-like chemicals in the brain. These natural chemicals, called *endocannabinoids*, are involved in pain perception, memory, mood, and appetite regulation, and they also play an important role in brain maturation. This brain maturation issue is of special concern to those who question the wisdom of legalizing marijuana, as explained in the next section.

FIGURE 9.8 How Marijuana Affects the Brain Marijuana has both short- and long-term effects on many regions of the brain. Additional research is needed to more fully understand these effects, particularly how marijuana use impacts brain maturation during adolescence.

Brain Area	Potential Effects of THC
Amygdala	altered emotions; anxiety and panic in some cases
Basal ganglia	impaired motor skills and learning
Cerebellum	impaired coordination and balance
Cortex	altered consciousness, perceptual distortions
Hippocampus	impaired memory storage recall
Hypothalamus	altered metabolic process such as increased appetite
Nucleus accumbens	euphoria; altered motivation and decision making

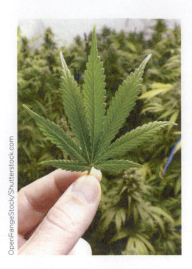

The leaves, flowers, stems, and seeds of the hemp plant *Cannabis sativa* (marijuana) all contain the mild hallucinogen THC (*delta-9-tetrahydrocannabinol*).

THC has many effects on the brain and behavior, including alterations in mood, time perception, and sensations (for example, seeing brighter colors) and impairment of thinking, problem-solving, and memory. Like alcohol, marijuana also relaxes, disinhibits, and may produce a euphoric high. Unlike alcohol, which is metabolized and eliminated from the body within hours, THC can remain in the body for more than a week. As a result, regular marijuana users are less likely to experience abrupt withdrawal from the drug and may get high with smaller drug amounts than they needed when they first used the drug.

The Debate over Legalization

Some people think pot is nothing less than a gift from nature: a nonaddictive drug that lifts the spirit, is safe at any dose, and has important medical applications. Others portray the drug as dangerous, addictive, and having a high potential for abuse. Who is right? Let's take a look at some of the evidence on both sides of the argument.

Medical marijuana refers to using the plant or its extracts to treat a disease or symptom. Although the FDA has not approved marijuana as a medicine, two THC-based drugs, *dronabinol* and *nabilone,* have been approved to relieve the pain and nausea caused by a variety of medical conditions, including AIDS and cancer, and to increase appetite in patients with AIDS wasting syndrome (Munsey, 2010). THC-based drugs may also help treat seizures and spasticity related to epilepsy and multiple sclerosis, while a related compound called *cannabidiol* (CBD) may be useful in treating autoimmune diseases, inflammation, pain, and substance use disorders (Seppa, 2010).

Advocates for legalizing marijuana (for medical or recreational use) argue that doing so may have important public health benefits, such as reducing the risk of overdoses from other drugs. They point to evidence that death rates from overdoses on prescription painkillers, heroin, and other illicit drugs average 24.8% lower in states with medical marijuana laws than in states without similar laws (Bachhuber, Saloner, Cunningham, & Barry, 2014).

Opponents of legalizing marijuana fear that wider recreational use will adversely affect public health. Case in point: driver safety. Marijuana use has been linked to increased accident risk, likely reflecting marijuana's disruptive effects on motor coordination and time perception. One study estimated that cannabis intoxication doubles a driver's risk of an automobile accident (Asbridge, Hayden, & Cartwright, 2012). Some states have expanded their DUI laws to include cannabis intoxication. Washington and Colorado, where recreational marijuana use was legalized in 2012, have a 5-nanogram limit on the level of THC in a driver's blood. Oregon doesn't use blood testing and instead relies on police officers' observations (Kullgren, 2014).

While most experts agree that marijuana is not nearly as addictive as alcohol, tobacco, and opioids, THC does seem to reduce the number of CB1 receptors in the brains of people who use marijuana daily. This may explain why about 1 user in 10 struggles to stop using marijuana and shows signs of becoming dependent on the drug (Hirvonen, Goodwin, & Innis, 2012). Among people who begin using pot as teens, the number showing signs of developing dependency seems to increase to about 1 in 6 (Lopez-Quintero and others, 2011). Heavy, regular users also show signs of developing tolerance for THC, as they need to increase their dose over time to experience the same effects. Some users also experience anxiety and irritability—two other features of addiction, according to *DSM-5*—after stopping heavy use of THC (NIDA, 2016).

As to the safety of marijuana, critics of the legalization movement argue that even though the drug may not be deadly, it is far from harmless. Marijuana smoke irritates the lungs and contributes to the same breathing problems that tobacco smokers experience, including more frequent lung infections and disease. THC also increases the heart rate for several hours after smoking, which may increase the risk of heart attacks. Marijuana use during pregnancy has been linked to increased risk of brain and behavior problems in babies (NIDA, 2016).

In Colorado, where marijuana laws have been loosened for both medical use and recreational use, emergency room doctors, law enforcement officers, and legalization opponents have pointed to recent problems—such as rising numbers of traffic citations for marijuana-impaired driving—as cautionary lessons for other states that are considering more lenient cannabis laws. Proponents of legalization note that the overall rate of crime in Colorado is down by 10% since legalization for recreational use went into effect in 2014, and they say that critics are cherry-picking statistics to undermine a new industry that is flourishing despite intense scrutiny (Healy, 2014).

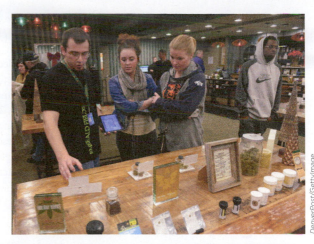

Shopping at the Marijuana Store An array of marijuana-infused products beckons, from energy shots and brownies to sour gummies. And if you're 21 or older, it's legal to buy in Colorado.

Opponents of legalization also note that the amount of THC in marijuana has been increasing steadily over the past few decades. Marijuana legally sold today in Colorado, for instance, contains three times as much THC as did plants grown in the 1980s (Mole, 2015). This greater potency may help explain the rise in emergency room visits involving marijuana. The growing popularity of marijuana edibles (cookies, brownies, candy, etc.) also increases the chance of harmful reactions. Because edibles take longer to produce a high, users may consume more to feel the effects faster, potentially leading to dangerous results.

Perhaps the biggest concern is the potential impact on teenagers, a decreasing number of whom believe that marijuana use is risky. In 2017, 10% of high school seniors in the United States engaged in *marijuana vaping* (Johnston and others, 2018). As we have seen, the adolescent brain is still growing and refining its neural networks—processes regulated in part by the natural endocannabinoid system in the cortex. Marijuana use at this vulnerable time may interfere with healthy brain development. Indeed, research has shown that young adults, ages 18 to 25, who use marijuana at least once a week are more likely than nonusers to have structural differences in two brain areas: the nucleus accumbens and the amygdala (Gilman, Kuster, & Breiter, 2014). Heavy use of THC for 20 years or more may also damage the corpus callosum (Rigucci and others, 2016), lead to a reduced volume of gray matter, and shrink the cortical areas that process memory (Filbey and others, 2014). However, other researchers are skeptical of the evidence that THC use harms the brain (Rogeberg, 2013; Weiland and others, 2015).

Marijuana use does seem to affect memory, language proficiency, and motivation—all of which are especially important during adolescence and emerging adulthood. Teens who use marijuana heavily are more likely to perform poorly in school and have other problems (Ansary & Luthar, 2009). One study reported that people who started using marijuana heavily as teenagers and had an ongoing cannabis use disorder lost an average of eight IQ points between ages 13 and 38 (Meier and others, 2012). In addition, the more often marijuana is used, especially during adolescence, the greater the risk of anxiety, depression, or addiction (Hurd, Michaelides, Miller, & Jutras-Aswad, 2014). Heavy cannabis use in early adolescence may even accelerate the onset of schizophrenia (Hill, 2015).

Although laws are changing, the biggest obstacle to truly understanding the potential risks and benefits of cannabis is the fact that research has been stifled by years of prohibition and by misconceptions about the plant and its active compounds (Grayson, 2015). Major gaps in knowledge continue to exist. For example, while a recent meta-analysis of cannabinoids for medical use supported their use in treating chronic pain and muscle spasticity, other claims about the benefits of THC and CBD were less well supported (Whiting and others, 2015). Until medical marijuana is made a public health priority and more research funding is made available, these knowledge gaps are unlikely to close. In addition to further research, the effects of the recent legalization of recreational marijuana in Colorado, Washington, and elsewhere will be instructive. The experiences of those states should provide a better sense of the social and public health impacts of this policy change.

Weigh In on Health

Respond to each question below based on what you learned in the chapter. (**Tip:** Use the items in "Summing Up" to take into account related biological, psychological, and social concerns.)

1. A classmate questions whether a mutual friend is addicted to cocaine. What would you be able to tell the classmate about what addiction is, and how a psychoactive drug like cocaine might affect your friend?

2. You just learned that your cousin, a senior in high school, started smoking cigarettes when she was a sophomore.

Now she's addicted to smoking but wants to quit before she starts college. Based on what you read in this chapter, how would you advise her? What if she asked you whether e-cigarette vaping was a safe alternative to smoking cigarettes?

3. Some states have attempted to criminalize drug use during pregnancy or treat it as grounds for terminating parental rights. Should it be illegal for a pregnant woman to purchase or use alcohol or tobacco products? Why or why not?

Summing Up

Understanding Substance Use, Abuse, and Addiction

1. Drugs affect behavior by influencing the activity of neurons at their synapses. Some (agonists and, to a lesser extent, partial agonists) do so by mimicking natural neurotransmitters, others (antagonists) by blocking their action, and still others by enhancing or inhibiting the reuptake of neurotransmitters in the synapse.

2. Substance use disorder is a behavior pattern characterized by overwhelming involvement with the use of a drug despite its adverse consequences.

Models of Addiction

3. Biomedical models propose that dependence is a chronic disease that produces abnormal physical functioning.

4. Reward models suggest that the pleasurable effects of psychoactive drugs provide the initial motivation for their

repeated use. All major drugs of abuse overstimulate the brain's reward system.

Alcohol Use and Abuse

5. Alcohol depresses activity in the nervous system, clouds judgment, and is linked to a variety of diseases. Genes play a role in alcohol dependence, especially in men. Psychosocial factors such as peer pressure, a difficult home environment, and tension reduction may contribute to problem drinking. Individuals who exhibit behavioral undercontrol and negative emotionality are especially prone to alcohol dependence.

6. Alcohol use disorder (AUD) is defined by several specific behaviors, including the need for daily use of alcohol, the inability to cut down on drinking despite repeated efforts to do so, binge drinking, loss of memory while intoxicated, and continued drinking despite known health problems.

7. Alcohol treatment usually begins with detoxification from alcohol under medical supervision. Counseling, psychotherapy, and support groups such as Alcoholics Anonymous (AA) also may help. Pharmacological treatments for alcohol dependence include aversion therapy, which triggers nausea if alcohol is consumed. Antidepressants such as Prozac may help reduce alcohol cravings.

Tobacco Use and Abuse

8. Cigarette smoking is the single most preventable cause of death in the Western world today. Nicotine, a stimulant that affects virtually every physical system in the body, induces powerful physical dependence and a withdrawal syndrome. Social pressures most often influence the initiation of smoking.

9. Once a person begins smoking, a variety of psychological, behavioral, social, and biological variables contribute to making it difficult to abstain from nicotine. According to the nicotine-titration model, long-term smokers may smoke to maintain a constant level of nicotine in their bodies.

10. Smoking prevention programs that focus on refusal skills and other inoculation techniques prior to the eighth grade may be the best solution to the public health problems associated with smoking. The most successful antismoking advertisements provide culturally sensitive nonsmoking peer role models that shift people's overall image of what behaviors are "normal" and valuable within one's peer group.

11. No single treatment has proved most effective in helping smokers quit smoking. Most programs have an extremely high relapse rate. Modern treatments for smoking deal with psychological factors through relapse prevention and with physiological factors through nicotine replacement.

The Rise of E-Cigarettes and the Resurgence of Marijuana

12. E-cigarettes are battery-powered vaporizers that simulate smoking without burning tobacco. Because they deliver vapor without burning tobacco, using e-cigarettes may appear to be safer and less toxic than smoking conventional cigarettes.

13. Vaping e-cigarettes exposes smokers to other harmful substances, including formaldehyde and acetaldehyde—two known carcinogens—as well as toxic metal nanoparticles released from the heating element.

14. Marijuana comes from the hemp plant *Cannabis sativa*, which contains the mild hallucinogen THC (*delta-9-tetrahydrocannabinol*). THC has many effects on the brain and on behavior, including alterations in mood, time perception, and sensations, along with impaired thinking, problem-solving, and memory.

15. Marijuana use may adversely affect memory, language proficiency, and motivation—all of which are especially important during adolescence and emerging adulthood. Heavy use of TCH for 20 years or more may also damage the corpus callosum, lead to a reduced volume of gray matter, and shrink the cortical areas that process memory.

Key Terms and Concepts to Remember

substance use disorder (SUD), p. 273
behavioral addiction, p. 273
blood–brain barrier, p. 275
teratogens, p. 276
agonist, p. 276
antagonist, p. 276
dependence, p. 277
withdrawal, p. 277
psychoactive drugs, p. 278
drug potentiation, p. 278

concordance rate, p. 279
nucleus accumbens (NAC), p. 280
gateway drug, p. 281
common liability to addiction, p. 281
wanting-and-liking theory, p. 281
blood alcohol level (BAL), p. 285
at-risk drinking, p. 285
fetal alcohol syndrome (FAS), p. 288
behavioral disinhibition, p. 289
alcohol myopia, p. 289

alcohol use disorder (AUD), p. 290
behavioral undercontrol, p. 291
negative emotionality, p. 291
alcohol expectancy effects, p. 291
aversion therapy, p. 292
drug abuse, p. 294
nicotine-titration model, p. 297
behavioral activation, p. 301
e-cigarettes (EC), p. 303

LaunchPad macmillan learning — To accompany your textbook, you have access to a number of online resources, including quizzes for every chapter of the book, flashcards, critical thinking exercises, videos, and *Check Your Health* inventories. To access these resources, please visit the Straub Health Psychology LaunchPad at **launchpadworks.com**

Part **4** CHRONIC AND LIFE-THREATENING ILLNESSES

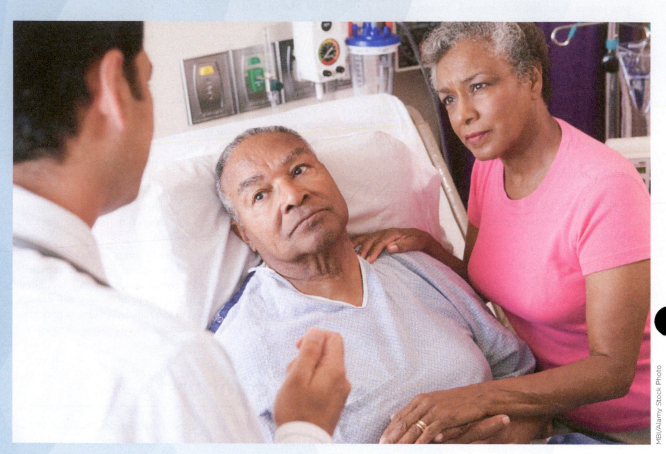

MBI/Alamy Stock Photo

Cardiovascular Disease and Diabetes

LEARNING OUTCOMES

Once you have studied this chapter, you will be able to:

- Define cardiovascular disease and explain its causes,
- Differentiate uncontrollable and controllable risk factors for cardiovascular disease,
- Identify and describe psychosocial factors that relate to cardiovascular disease,
- Identify strategies for reducing the risk of cardiovascular disease and preventing its recurrence, and
- Define diabetes and describe the role of health psychologists in its prevention and management.

Bryan McIver, M.D., a dedicated young endocrinologist at the Mayo Clinic, was driving to his laboratory to check on an experiment. He thought nothing of the mild case of indigestion that he'd been feeling since having a curry dinner with some friends. Mild stomach acidity was something he often experienced, so it seemed like a normal night.

When he arrived at the hospital, he again felt some discomfort in his chest, but he ignored it. When he walked past the emergency room three minutes later, however, things changed dramatically. In his words, "The world went blank . . . and I died."

What happened was a sudden and complete blockage of one of his heart's main coronary blood vessels. Within seconds, McIver's heart floundered into a chaotic rhythm, his blood pressure dropped to zero, the oxygen supply to his brain was cut off, and he passed into unconsciousness.

When the brain is deprived of oxygen, it begins to die within about three minutes. After six minutes, brain death occurs, and there is almost no chance for recovery. This would almost certainly have happened to McIver had his heart attack happened a minute earlier, as he strolled through the darkened parking lot, or a minute later, once he'd reached the seclusion of his laboratory. Miraculously, he collapsed in the hospital corridor, just a few feet from the emergency room.

As a 37-year-old nonsmoker with no history of high blood pressure, vascular disease, or diabetes, McIver hardly fit the typical profile of a cardiac patient. Although one of his grandmothers had died of a stroke (in her eighties), his family is generally long-lived. McIver did have some risk factors. Although he was not overweight (6 feet 1 inch tall, 197 pounds), he rarely exercised, had a high-stress job, and had unhealthy cholesterol levels. Even so, less than a month before his heart attack, McIver had been given a clean bill of health during a thorough physical exam. He was told only to try to exercise a bit more and lose a pound or two. Yet here he was, being resuscitated from the near-death experience of a massive heart attack.

Although he continues his high-pressure work as a medical researcher, McIver has taken steps to improve his coronary risk factor profile to increase his chances of living a long, healthy life. Many other people, however, are far less fortunate, and cardiovascular disease remains the number one cause of death in the United States and in the developed world.

This chapter examines the biological, psychological, and social risk factors in two major chronic illnesses: cardiovascular disease (including high blood pressure, stroke, and heart disease) and diabetes. Many of the risk factors in these diseases reflect lifestyle choices that are modifiable. However, it is important to remember that people also suffer from chronic illnesses that were not caused by their behavior and are beyond their control (other than learning to cope as well as possible). For example, I have a friend who died from lung cancer when he was in his mid-forties, despite being a fit nonsmoker who exercised regularly and ate a healthy diet. His family believes their loved one "basically just lost the genetic lottery," and that nothing he could have done would have prevented the disease. Cancer was not his "fault," yet he often received unsolicited, highly annoying advice from people who assumed he should be doing something more to get rid of his disease.

HEART HEALTH AND DISEASE

Because each of these disorders involves the circulatory system, let's first review how the heart and circulatory system should work, and then take a look at what goes wrong when each of these diseases strikes. As described in Chapter 3, the cardiovascular system comprises the blood, the blood vessels of the circulatory system, and the heart. About the size of your clenched fist and weighing on average only about 11 ounces, the heart consists of three layers of tissue: a thin outer layer, called the *epicardium;* a thin inner layer, called the *endocardium;* and a thicker middle layer, the heart muscle itself, or *myocardium* (derived from the Greek roots *myo* [muscle] and *kardia* [heart]). The myocardium is separated into four chambers that work in coordinated fashion to bring blood into the heart and then to pump it throughout the body. Like all muscles in the body, the myocardium needs a steady supply of oxygen and nutrients to remain healthy. And the harder the heart is forced to work to meet the demands of other muscles in the body, the more nutrients and oxygen it needs.

In one of nature's greatest ironies, the heart's blood supply comes not from the five or more quarts of blood pumped each minute through the internal chambers of the heart, but rather from two branches of the aorta (the major artery from the heart) lying on the surface of the epicardium. These left and right *coronary arteries* branch into smaller and smaller blood vessels called *arterioles* until they become the capillaries that supply the myocardium with the blood it needs to function. (See Figure 3.10 on p. 71 for a diagram of the heart and the flow of blood through it.) When the blood supply from the coronary arteries is impeded beyond a critical point, the risk of developing cardiovascular disease increases substantially.

More than 90 million Americans suffer from some kind of disorder of the heart and blood vessel system, collectively referred to as **cardiovascular disease (CVD)**. Leading all diseases in killing one of every three people each year in the United States, CVD appears in many guises, including stroke and **coronary heart disease (CHD)**, a chronic illness in which the arteries that supply the heart become narrowed or clogged and cannot supply enough blood to the heart (Benjamin and others, 2018). Before discussing the biological, social, and psychological factors that contribute to the onset of these diseases, we need to describe their underlying physical causes: atherosclerosis and arteriosclerosis.

Causes of Cardiovascular Disease: Atherosclerosis and Arteriosclerosis

Most cases of CVD result from **atherosclerosis**, a condition in which the linings of the arteries thicken with an accumulation of cholesterol and other fats. As these **atheromatous plaques** develop, the arterial passageways become narrowed, impeding the flow of blood through the coronary arteries (Figure 10.1). Although plaques tend to develop in most people in their thirties and forties, these plaques will not threaten their health—at least not until age 70 or older. Those not so fortunate, like Bryan McIver, may develop damaging plaques as early as their twenties or thirties—or even younger.

Inflammation in the circulating blood (*systemic inflammation*) can contribute to **atherogenesis**—the development of atherosclerosis that can help trigger heart attacks and strokes. Although the mechanism that triggers atherogenesis is unclear, the process begins with damage to the blood vessel wall that results in the formation of *fatty streaks,* which act as a "call for help" from the body's immune system. As we saw in Chapter 3, inflammation is the body's response to injury, and blood clotting is often part of that response. Although researchers are not certain what causes the low-grade inflammation that seems to put otherwise healthy people at increased risk for atherosclerosis, many believe that a chronic bacterial or viral infection might be the underlying cause.

One of the proteins that increase during the inflammatory response, *C-reactive protein (CRP)*, is used to assess a person's risk of CVD. CRP is a proinflammatory cytokine that is produced in the liver and released into the bloodstream when inflammation is present. The risk for heart attack in people with the highest CRP levels is twice that of people whose CRP levels are at the lowest levels (Welsh, Grassia, Botha, Sattar, & Maffia, 2017).

cardiovascular disease (CVD) Disorders of the heart and blood vessel system, including stroke and coronary heart disease (CHD).

coronary heart disease (CHD) A chronic disease in which the arteries that supply the heart become narrowed or clogged; results from either atherosclerosis or arteriosclerosis.

atherosclerosis A chronic disease in which cholesterol and other fats are deposited on the inner walls of the coronary arteries, reducing circulation to heart tissue.

atheromatous plaques Buildups of fatty deposits within the wall of an artery; occur in atherosclerosis.

atherogenesis The process of forming atheromatous plaques in the inner lining of arteries.

FIGURE 10.1 Atherosclerosis
Atherosclerosis is a common disease in which cholesterol and other fats are deposited on the walls of coronary arteries. As the vessel walls become thick and hardened, they narrow, reducing the circulation to areas normally supplied by the artery. Atherosclerotic plaques cause many disorders of the circulatory system. How atherosclerosis begins is not clear; possibly, injury to the artery causes scavenger macrophages to attack cholesterol deposits.

Artery

Cholesterol particles (lipoproteins)

Cholesterol deposited on lining of artery (fatty streaks)

Buildup begins

Plaque forms (atherosclerosis)

arteriosclerosis Also called "hardening of the arteries," a disease in which blood vessels lose their elasticity.

Closely related to atherosclerosis is **arteriosclerosis**, or "hardening of the arteries" (Figure 10.2). In this condition, the coronary arteries lose their elasticity, making it difficult for them to expand and contract. (Imagine trying to stretch a dried-out rubber band.) This makes it difficult for them to handle the large volumes of blood needed during physical exertion. In addition, a blood clot is much more likely to form in and block a coronary artery that has lost its elasticity due to arteriosclerosis.

FIGURE 10.2 Arteriosclerosis
In arteriosclerosis, the coronary arteries lose their elasticity and are unable to expand and contract as blood flows through them.

Although one might assume that CVD is an artifact of dietary and exercise habits in modern society, in fact atherosclerosis and arteriosclerosis appear to have been common 4,000 years ago among pre-agricultural hunter-gatherers. Whole-body CT scans of 137 mummies showed evidence of atherosclerosis in more than one-third of mummies from populations of ancient Egyptians, Peruvians, and ancestral Puebloans of southwest America (Thompson and others, 2014).

angina pectoris A condition of extreme chest pain caused by a restriction of the blood supply to the heart.

Cardiovascular Diseases: Angina Pectoris, Myocardial Infarction, and Stroke

Left unchecked, atherosclerosis and arteriosclerosis may advance for years before a person experiences any symptoms. This was the case with Dr. McIver. Once the process gets underway, however, the risk of developing one of three diseases increases with time.

The first begins with a gradual narrowing of the blood vessels. Any part of the body that depends on blood flow from an obstructed artery is subject to damage. For example, if the narrowing affects arteries in the legs, a person may experience leg pain while walking. When the arteries that supply the heart are narrowed with plaques, restricting blood flow to the heart—a condition called *ischemia*—the person may experience a sharp, crushing pain in the chest, called **angina pectoris**. Although most angina attacks usually pass within a few minutes without causing permanent damage, ischemia is a significant predictor of future coronary incidents.

Angina attacks can occur anytime—including while a person is sleeping—but they typically occur during moments of unusual exertion. In such circumstances, such as when a casual runner tries to complete a 26.2-mile marathon, the body demands that the heart pump more oxygenated blood than it is accustomed to handling. Angina may also occur

Egyptian Mummy Being Scanned by CT Whole-body scans of mummies show that atherosclerosis was common thousands of years ago.

ZEPHYR/Science Source

FIGURE 10.3 Stroke Damages the Brain This CT scan of the brain of a 54-year-old stroke patient shows that when blood flow to the brain is blocked, cells in the brain may be destroyed. The darkened area on the left shows where brain tissue has died because of an inadequate blood supply. The lack of blood may be due to an obstruction in a cerebral artery or to the hemorrhaging of a weakened artery wall. The result is paralysis or weakness on the right side of the body (since the tissue destroyed is on the left side of the brain).

myocardial infarction (MI) A heart attack; the permanent death of heart tissue in response to an interruption of blood supply to the myocardium.

stroke A cerebrovascular accident that results in damage to the brain due to lack of oxygen; usually caused by atherosclerosis or arteriosclerosis.

during strong emotional arousal or exposure to extreme cold or heat. Mental stress during daily life, including feelings of tension, frustration, and depression, increases the risk of ischemia (Rosenfeldt and others, 2004).

The second, much more serious cardiac disorder occurs when a plaque ruptures within a blood vessel, releasing a sticky mass that can further reduce blood flow or even obstruct it completely. Within seconds of the complete obstruction of a coronary artery, a heart attack, or **myocardial infarction (MI)**, occurs, and a portion of the myocardium begins to die (an *infarct* is an area of dead tissue). Unlike angina, which lasts only a brief time, MI involves a chronic deficiency in the blood supply and thus causes permanent damage to the heart.

The third possible manifestation of cardiovascular malfunction is cerebrovascular disease, or **stroke**. Stroke is the fifth leading cause of death in the United States, killing about 140,000 people each year (Centers for Disease Control and Prevention [CDC], 2017j). The most common type of stroke—*ischemic stroke*—occurs when plaques or a clot obstruct an artery, blocking the flow of blood to an area of the brain (Figure 10.3). *Hemorrhagic stroke* occurs when a blood vessel bursts inside the brain, increasing pressure on the cerebrum and damaging it by pressing it against the skull. Hemorrhagic stroke is associated with high blood pressure, which stresses the artery walls until they break or exposes a weak spot in an artery wall (*aneurysm*), which balloons out because of the pressure of the blood circulating inside.

The effects of stroke may include loss of speech or difficulty understanding speech; numbness, weakness, or paralysis of a limb or in the face; headaches; blurred vision; and dizziness. Strokes usually damage neural tissue on one side of the brain, with a resulting loss of sensation on the opposite side of the body. An estimated 10% to 20% of adults in the United States have experienced *silent brain infarction,* or "silent strokes," which damage tiny clusters of cells inside the brain but cause no immediately obvious symptoms. These strokes tend not to be detected until, over time, memory loss, dizziness, slurred speech, and other classic stroke symptoms begin to appear (Fanning, Wong, & Fraser, 2014).

RISK FACTORS FOR CARDIOVASCULAR DISEASE

What causes plaque to form in the coronary arteries? Why do the coronary arteries of some people escape the buildup of scar tissue while those of others become obstructed when the people are still at a young age?

Research has identified a number of risk factors linked to CVD. Much of this knowledge comes from the Framingham Heart Study, one of the most celebrated epidemiological studies in the history of medicine. When the Framingham study began, in 1948, the mortality rate due to CVD in the United States was nearly 500 cases per 100,000 people. This rate increased to a peak of 586.8 cases per 100,000 in 1950, but it has dropped steadily ever since. Much of the credit for this dramatic improvement in early-mortality rates is due to "healthy heart" initiatives that stem from the Framingham study. The results of this remarkable study have undoubtedly extended the lives of millions.

Before Framingham, epidemiologists studied disease by examining medical records and death certificates. Framingham set a new standard for epidemiological research by inaugurating the concept of studying the health of living persons over time with a *prospective design* that included 5,209 healthy people in the Boston suburb of Framingham, Massachusetts.

Every two years, the original participants received a complete physical exam that included an electrocardiogram, a blood pressure test, and more than 80 separate medical tests. (Their children have exams every four years.) In addition, each participant completed a battery of psychological tests and health questionnaires. The researchers asked questions about the participants' level of anxiety, sleeping habits, nervousness, alcohol and tobacco use, level of education, and typical response to anger.

Two large-scale studies followed the Framingham study and extended our knowledge of cardiovascular health. One is the ongoing Nurses' Health Study, established in 1976, which has followed more than 200,000 nurse-participants to assess women's risk factors for CVD, cancer, diabetes, and other conditions (Nurses' Health Study [NHS], 2015). The other is the Canadian-led INTERHEART study, which included nearly 30,000 participants in 52 countries: 15,152 cases of people hospitalized for an MI, matched by age and sex with 14,820 control participants with no history of heart disease (Yusuf and others, 2004). Concluded in 2004, INTERHEART is the largest case–control study of cardiovascular disease to date.

The findings of these three landmark studies identified two categories of *risk factors* for CVD: those that are largely uncontrollable, such as family history, age, and gender; and those that are more controllable, such as obesity, hypertension, cholesterol level, and tobacco use. A key finding from the INTERHEART study is that the risk factors for CVD are the same throughout the world (Anand and others, 2008).

Uncontrollable Risk Factors

A number of risk factors for CVD stem from genetic or biological conditions that are largely beyond our control.

Family History, Age, and Race

Family history strongly predicts CVD. This is especially true for those who have a close male relative who suffered a heart attack before age 55 or a close female relative who had a heart attack before age 65. Advancing age is also a risk factor for CVD. Indeed, approximately half of all CVD patients are over the age of 65.

Heredity plays a role in the CVD risk factor of **hypertension** (high blood pressure), as evidenced by the fact that the prevalence of hypertension varies widely among racial and ethnic groups. For instance, the prevalence of hypertension among African American women and men in the United States is among the highest in the world. Compared with European Americans, African Americans develop hypertension at a younger age, and their average blood pressures are much higher (Flack and others, 2010).

hypertension A sustained elevation of diastolic and systolic blood pressure (exceeding 140/90).

Gender

Cardiovascular disease is the leading cause of death across most sociodemographic groups in the United States, including both women and men (CDC, 2017c). The risk of CVD rises sharply in men after age 40. Except in women who smoke cigarettes, the risk of CVD remains low until menopause, when, as we will explain, it begins to accelerate. However, the risk is still much higher among men until about age 65. In fact, men have roughly the same rate of CVD as women who are 10 years older (American Heart Association, 2015). Although the gap narrows with advancing age, this gender difference explains in part why women live longer than men. In all developed countries and most developing countries, women outlive men by as many as 10 years. In the United States, life expectancy at birth is currently 81 years for women and 76 years for men (Kochanek, Murphy, Xu, & Arias, 2017).

Some experts believe that the gender difference in CVD mortality may be caused by differences in the sex hormones testosterone and estrogen. Testosterone has been linked with aggression, competitiveness, and other behaviors that are thought to contribute to heart disease (Morris & Channer, 2012). Coincidentally, testosterone levels increase during early adulthood, just when the difference in mortality between men and women is at its peak.

However, if gender is truly a risk factor for CVD, then the differences between women and men should be similar throughout the world. This does not appear to be the case. Gender differences in CVD mortality are much greater in some countries than in others, especially in Eastern Europe (Mosca, Barrett-Conner, & Wenger, 2011). It is likely that lifestyle factors, rather than biology, may be at work. As noted earlier in the text, masculinity norms have been implicated in the so-called crisis in men's health. Men are less likely than women to visit their general practitioner, more likely to be overweight and drink more alcohol, and more likely to make poorer dietary choices (Gough, 2013).

Although women may be at lower risk for CVD than men, heart disease takes the lives of more American women than does any other cause, affecting one of about every three women (as opposed to one in eight for breast cancer). Still, many women believe that breast cancer is the biggest threat to their health, despite the fact that CVD takes the lives of five times as many women as breast cancer (Figure 10.4). One study reported that minority women and those with lower socioeconomic status (SES) were more likely to believe that breast cancer causes more deaths in women than heart disease does (Kapp, Oliver, & Simoes, 2016).

FIGURE 10.4 Mortality Rates for Cardiovascular Disease and Breast Cancer in Women by Race Although women may be at lower risk for CVD than men, heart disease takes the lives of more American women than any other cause.

Data from: Mehta, L. S, Watson, K. E., Barac, A., Beckie, T. M, Bittner, V., . . . Volgman, A. S. (2018). Cardiovascular disease and breast cancer: Where these entities intersect. *Circulation, 137,* e30–e66. Figure 1, p. e32.

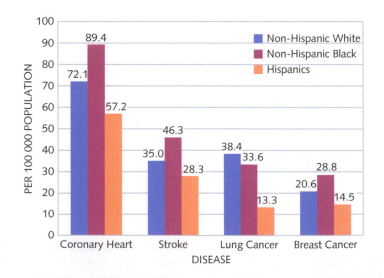

Controllable Risk Factors

Uncontrollable risk factors do not necessarily doom a person to death by heart attack. Knowing one's inherent risk profile is an important step in reducing the risk of CVD, however, because it allows high-risk individuals to minimize their total risk profile by changing those things they *can* control. Even with a family history of heart disease, for example, a person can reduce overall risk by working toward lowering blood pressure, eating a healthy diet, exercising regularly, and maintaining a normal body weight. These efforts can reap huge benefits. For instance, the Chicago Heart Association Detection Project evaluated the health outcomes for men between ages 18 and 39, men between ages 40 and 59, and women between ages 40 and 59. Younger men with the healthiest lifestyles had a life expectancy 9.5 years longer than other men in their age group. For healthy men aged 40 to 59 years, life expectancy was extended by 6 years. For women with the healthiest lifestyles, life was extended by 5.8 years (Yano and others, 2015).

Hypertension

Blood pressure is the force exerted by blood as it pushes out against the walls of the arteries. When pressure is too high, it can damage the vessels and lead to atherosclerosis. Systolic blood pressure (BP) less than 120 mmHg (millimeters of mercury), and diastolic BP less than 80 mmHg, is considered normal. When blood pressure rises above these levels, it is categorized as "elevated" (systolic between 120 and 129 or diastolic less than 80), Stage 1 hypertension (systolic between 130 and 139 and diastolic between 80 and 89), Stage 2 hypertension (systolic above 140 or diastolic above 90), or hypertensive crisis (systolic above 180 and/or diastolic above 120) (Whelton and others, 2017).

Hypertension is the result of the interaction of biological, psychological, and social factors. Obesity, lack of exercise, dietary salt, and excessive stress—all influences that the individual can control, to some extent—can produce hypertension in biologically predisposed people. Hypertension is also related to anxiety and anger, especially in middle-aged men (Player, King, Mainous, & Geesey, 2007). Stress is also linked with hypertension, particularly among people who have poor coping mechanisms or limited coping resources. Exposure to environmental stressors at a young age can be particularly harmful. Adolescents who report experiencing large numbers of chronic, uncontrollable negative family stressors exhibit greater systolic blood pressure throughout the day, regardless of their gender, ethnicity, body mass index, and activity level (Brady & Matthews, 2006). These early experiences may increase their risk of developing hypertension later in life.

Cardiovascular Reactivity, Hemostasis, and Inflammation

Although genes may create a biological predisposition to hypertension, heredity alone cannot explain the widespread variation in the prevalence of hypertension among different ethnic and cultural groups. Within the African American community, for instance, rates of hypertension vary substantially. Those with the highest rates are more likely to be middle-aged or older, overweight or obese, physically inactive, less educated, and to have diabetes (Yoon, Fryar, & Carroll, 2015). A number of researchers have suggested that the prevalence of hypertension among African Americans might reflect greater **cardiovascular reactivity (CVR)** to social stress—especially the stress of racial discrimination—in

cardiovascular reactivity (CVR) An individual's characteristic reaction to stress, including changes in heart rate, blood pressure, and hormones.

the form of larger increases in heart rate and blood pressure and a greater outpouring of epinephrine, cortisol, and other stress hormones.

Researchers have found that acute exposure to stressors such as mental arithmetic tasks (Arthur, Katkin, & Mezzacappa, 2004), racially provocative speeches (Merritt, Bennett, Williams, Edwards, & Sollers, 2006), on-the-job training exercises (Webb and others, 2011), and role-playing scenarios such as being accused of shoplifting (Lepore and others, 2006) are associated with increases in cardiovascular activation (see Huang, Webb, Zourdos, & Acevedo, 2013, for a review). Interestingly, low-SES African American men tend to display greater CVR to racial stressors than high-SES African American men *or women.* They also report significantly greater firsthand experience with racial prejudice (Williams, Priest, & Anderson, 2016). These findings are important because people who display elevated cardiovascular responses to and delayed recovery from psychosocial stressors are at greater risk of cardiovascular disease in the future (Chida & Steptoe, 2010; Panaite, Salomon, Jin, & Rottenberg, 2015). As noted in Chapter 5, however, the impact of a stressor such as racism may depend on the individual's past experience and coping resources. The presence of other factors, including anger, defensiveness, interpersonal skills, and coping style, all are potential mediators and moderators of CVR (Rutledge & Linden, 2003).

Hemostasis One biological mechanism that may link stress to CHD is **hemostasis**—the process that causes bleeding to stop via the aggregation of *platelets* and the *coagulation* of blood from a liquid to gel state. The hemostatic system requires close regulation to function properly. If the blood does not clot well, it may be due to a bleeding disorder such as *hemophilia.* Overactive clotting can also cause problems, including *thrombosis,* which occurs when blood clots form abnormally and potentially break off to cause *embolisms* that block blood flow in an artery or vein.

Many hemostatic factors are independently associated with coronary heart disease. Elevated concentrations of *fibrinogen,* for instance, are prospectively associated with MI and stroke, independently of other risk factors for cardiovascular disease (von Känel, Malan, Hamer, van der Westhuizen, & Malan, 2014). Fibrinogen is a protein in plasma that plays an important role in determining blood viscosity and platelet aggregation. Elevated fibrinogen levels cause a *hypercoagulable state*—a dangerous situation in which blood clots too easily, increasing the risk of a coronary or cerebrovascular incident. Conversely, low fibrinogen levels have been associated with a low risk of acute coronary events, even when serum cholesterol levels are high (Borissof, Spronk, & ten Cate, 2011).

The link to stress, which is a process of appraisal, is what puts hemostasis (to a certain extent) under the individual's control. Remarkably, as part of his "fight-or-flight" research, Walter Cannon noted more than a century ago that activation of the sympathetic nervous system influences hemostasis. Because acute stress is also associated with hypercoagulability, stressful events could conceivably trigger a heart attack or stroke (von Känel, 2015).

hemostasis The process that causes bleeding to stop via the aggregation of *platelets* and the *coagulation* of blood.

Coronary Angiography In this method of diagnosis, a small cardiac catheter is threaded through an artery into the aorta, then to the coronary artery suspected of blockage. The dye injected through the catheter enables the surgeon to x-ray the artery (see video monitor in the photo) and locate the blockage.

BSIP SA/Alamy Stock Photo

Inflammation As you learned in Chapter 3, inflammation is a nonspecific response of the immune system to tissue damage. When damage occurs, white blood cells rush to the injury site and defend against infection and further damage by engulfing bacteria and other potential invaders through the process of phagocytosis. As we've seen, the plaques that can lead to atherogenesis are simply fatty deposits of cholesterol-filled white blood cells.

Chronic inflammation increases the risk of atherosclerosis by affecting the development of plaques (Libby, 2012). Factors that promote inflammation may increase the likelihood of a stroke or MI by making plaques more likely to rupture into artery-blocking clots (Abi-Saleh, Iskandar, Elgharib, & Cohen, 2008). Some of these factors are controllable to some extent: chronic stress (Miller & Blackwell, 2006), depression (Kop and others, 2010), and metabolic syndrome (Vlachopoulos, Rokkas, Ioakeimidis, & Stefanadis, 2007)—each of which is associated with increased risk of CHD.

Obesity Excess body weight increases a person's risk of hypertension and all CVD, in part because of its association with high cholesterol. The risk of excess fat depends somewhat on how the fat is distributed. *Abdominal obesity* associated with excess fat in the midsection (the "beer belly") promotes the greatest risk of CVD, perhaps because it is often associated with lower levels of HDL cholesterol and higher triglyceride levels. People who carry excess weight in their midsections also have thicker artery walls, increasing blood pressure and the risk of stroke (De Michele and others, 2002). Indeed, waist circumference may be a more accurate predictor of hypertension than body mass index (Battie and others, 2016). Differences in where body fat is distributed may help to explain why men have higher rates of CVD than women, at least until menopause, as abdominal obesity is more common in men than in women of child-bearing age.

Cholesterol Level Doctors have known for years that people with a genetically high level of cholesterol also have a high rate of CVD, beginning at a young age. Before the Framingham Heart Study, however, there was no prospective evidence that excess dietary cholesterol was a coronary risk factor. The Framingham study found that people with low serum cholesterol rarely developed CVD, whereas those with high levels had a high risk. A blood cholesterol level lower than 200 milligrams per deciliter (mg/dl) is generally associated with a low risk of CVD. A level of 240 mg/dl or greater doubles the risk.

Total cholesterol is only part of the story, however. A more complete picture comes from comparing the relative amounts of *high-density lipoprotein cholesterol (HDL-C)*, *low-density lipoprotein cholesterol (LDL-C)*, and *triglycerides*. Total blood (or *serum*) cholesterol is calculated by adding together a person's HDL-C and LDL-C levels and 20% of the person's triglyceride levels. People with high triglyceride levels often have elevated serum and LDL-C levels and low HDL-C levels. Many people with heart disease or diabetes also have high triglyceride levels. Elevated triglycerides, and therefore serum cholesterol, can be the result of several behavioral factors, including overweight and obesity, physical inactivity, tobacco use, a high-carbohydrate diet, and excessive alcohol consumption (American Heart Association, 2018). In 2016, nearly 13% of adults in the United States had high serum cholesterol and 18% had low HDL-C (National Center for Health Statistics [NCHS], 2017).

For many years, doctors used ranges to evaluate the health significance of cholesterol. High serum cholesterol (≥ 240 mg/dL) and low HDL-C (< 40 mg/dL), for instance, are traditional risk factors for cardiovascular disease (Hamer, O'Donovan, & Stamatakis, 2018). Increasingly, health care professionals today think in broader terms in which cholesterol

Checking Blood Pressure
Blood pressure screening is provided by a nonprofit that donates medical care to uninsured individuals. Knowing one's blood pressure can lead to better choices regarding diet, exercise, and stress management.

metabolic syndrome A cluster of conditions that occur together—including elevated blood pressure and insulin levels, excess body fat, and unhealthy cholesterol ratios—that increase a person's risk for heart disease, stroke, and diabetes.

is viewed as just one factor of many in determining a person's cardiovascular disease risk. However, the relationships among cholesterol, fat consumption, cardiovascular disease, and early mortality continue to spark controversy.

The Prospective Urban Rural Epidemiology (PURE) study is the largest prospective observational study to date to assess the association between macronutrient consumption and cardiovascular disease and early mortality. The results from this massive study, which involved more than 200 researchers and 135,000 participants from 18 countries across 5 continents over a 7-year period, showed—surprisingly—that total fat intake and types of fat (saturated, unsaturated, etc.) were not associated with CVD, myocardial infarction, or CVD mortality. Higher saturated fat consumption was actually associated with a *reduced* risk of stroke. Based on their findings, the PURE researchers concluded that global dietary guidelines should be reconsidered, and that removing restrictions on fat intake (but avoiding high carbohydrate intake) might improve health (Dehghan and others, 2017).

Metabolic Syndrome People with **metabolic syndrome** (MetS) have a significantly higher risk of developing CVD and diabetes (Gurka, Filipp, & DeBoer, 2018). As defined in Chapter 7, *MetS* is a cluster of CVD risk factors that include abdominal obesity, high blood pressure, high triglycerides, low HDL-C, and high fasting blood glucose (commonly found in those suffering from diabetes, as we will see).

An estimated 35% of all adults in the United States, and 50% of those 60 years of age and older, meet the criteria for MetS. Since the mid-1980s, the prevalence of MetS has increased among every sociodemographic group in the United States (Moore, Chaudhary, & Akinyemiju, 2017).

Tobacco Use Smoking more than doubles the chances of having a heart attack and is linked to one of every five deaths due to CHD. Smokers have twice the risk of having a stroke and are less likely to survive an MI than are nonsmokers. On the positive side, one year after a person quits smoking, the risk of CVD decreases by 50%. In the United States, adult smoking rates have fallen from about 43% in 1965 to about 15% today (CDC, 2018d). However, as noted in Chapter 9, use of e-cigarettes and hookahs has increased significantly and continues to rise, particularly among teenagers.

PSYCHOSOCIAL FACTORS IN CARDIOVASCULAR DISEASE

The 52-country INTERHEART study identified nine risk factors that together accounted for over 90% of the statistical variability in cases of myocardial infarction. The study found that, after elevated lipids and smoking, psychosocial factors were the third leading risk factor for CHD (Yusuf and others, 2004). But the first clue that psychosocial factors were strongly related to CHD came decades earlier.

The Type A Personality

Puzzled by the fact that many coronary patients were *not* obese middle-aged men with elevated cholesterol, researchers decided that they must have been overlooking something. So they broadened their search for risk factors that might offer an explanation. In the late 1950s, cardiologists Meyer Friedman and Ray Rosenman (1959) began to study personality traits that might predict coronary events. They proposed a coronary-prone behavior pattern that included competitiveness, a strong sense of time urgency, and hostility; they labeled the behavior **Type A**. In contrast, people who are more relaxed and who are not overly pressured by time considerations tend to be coronary disease–resistant; Friedman and Rosenman called this behavior **Type B**.

Although hundreds of studies were conducted that initially seemed to support the association between Type A behavior and risk of future CVD, the research had serious limitations. For instance, Friedman and Rosenman's original sample included only middle-aged men, and later research challenging their findings caused the theory to fall out of favor.

Negative Affect, Depression, and Type D Personality

More recently, researchers have focused on *negative affect*—the tendency to experience negative emotions such as hostility—as the toxic core of Type A behavior, especially in men (Player and others, 2007). Hostility has been characterized as a chronic negative outlook that encompasses feelings (anger), thoughts (cynicism and mistrust of others), and overt actions (aggression). (See Table 10.1 to find out how you measure up when it comes to hostility.) Hostility may be as dangerous to the heart as smoking, a high-fat diet, or obesity (Mittleman & Mostofsky, 2011). In one study, hostile people were twice as likely to die of CVD as people who were low in hostility (Wong, Sin, & Whooley, 2014).

Depression is also a risk factor in the development and progression of CVD and metabolic syndrome (Räikkönen, Matthews, & Kuller, 2007). In one study, young women who had a previous episode of depression were twice as likely to develop MetS later on (Kinder, Carnethon, Palaniappan, King, & Fortmann, 2004). Even after controlling for other risk factors such as cholesterol and smoking, depression and anxiety predict the development of CVD (Goldston & Baillie, 2008; Shen and others, 2008). Although many patients become depressed because of a diagnosis of heart disease, it is important to note that depression is not simply an aftereffect of diagnosis; rather, it is an independent risk factor in its own right that likely has both genetic and environmental causes (McCaffery and others, 2006). By some estimates, depression rivals regular exposure to secondhand smoke as a risk factor for CVD (Wulsin & Singal, 2003). Evidence of the relationship between depression and the development and progression of CVD is sufficiently strong that it is now generally recommended that at-risk patients be assessed and, if necessary, treated for depression (Davidson and others, 2006). Unfortunately, however, depression remains an underdiagnosed and often untreated condition in many people with CVD (Hare, Toukhsati, Johansson, & Jaarsma, 2014). Researchers have reported prevalence rates of major depression as high as 27% among patients hospitalized with CVD (Glassman, 2007).

Type A A personality type found in competitive, hurried, hostile people who may be at increased risk for developing cardiovascular disease.

Type B A personality type found in more relaxed people who are not pressured by time considerations and thus tend to be coronary disease–resistant.

TABLE 10.1 Measuring Hostility

For each of the following items, circle the answer that most closely fits how you would respond.

1. A teenager drives by my yard blasting the car stereo.
   a. I begin to understand why teenagers can't hear.
   b. I can feel my blood pressure starting to rise.

2. A boyfriend/girlfriend calls me at the last minute, "too tired to go out tonight." I'm stuck with two $15 tickets.
   a. I find someone else to go with.
   b. I tell my friend how inconsiderate he or she is.

3. I am waiting in a long express checkout line at the supermarket, where a sign says, "No more than 10 items, please."
   a. I pick up a magazine and pass the time.
   b. I glance to see if anyone has more than 10 items.

4. Most homeless people in large cities:
   a. are down and out because they lack ambition.
   b. are victims of illness or some other misfortune.

5. At times when I've been very angry with someone:
   a. I was able to stop short of hitting him or her.
   b. I have, on occasion, hit or shoved him or her.

6. When I am stuck in a traffic jam:
   a. I am usually not particularly upset.
   b. I quickly start to feel irritated and annoyed.

7. When there's a really important job to be done:
   a. I prefer to do it myself.
   b. I am apt to call on my friends to help.

8. The cars ahead of me start to slow and stop as they approach a curve.
   a. I assume that there is a construction site ahead.
   b. I assume that someone ahead had a fender-bender.

9. An elevator stops for a long time at the floor above where I'm waiting.
   a. I soon start to feel irritated and annoyed.
   b. I start planning the rest of my day.

10. When a friend or co-worker disagrees with me:
    a. I try to explain my position more clearly.
    b. I am apt to get into an argument with him or her.

11. At times in the past, when I was really angry:
    a. I never threw things or slammed a door.
    b. I sometimes threw things or slammed a door.

12. Someone bumps into me in a store.
    a. I pass it off as an accident.
    b. I feel irritated at their clumsiness.

13. When my significant other is fixing a meal:
    a. I keep a close watch on things to make sure nothing burns.
    b. I talk about my day or read the paper.

14. Someone is hogging the conversation at a party.
   a. I look for an opportunity to put him or her down.
   b. I soon move to another group.

15. In most arguments:
   a. I am the angrier one.
   b. the other person is angrier than I am.

To score your responses, give yourself one point for each of the following answers:
1. b; 2. b; 3. b; 4. a; 5. b; 6. b; 7. a; 8. b; 9. a; 10. b; 11. b; 12. b; 13. a; 14. a; 15. a. Scores of 4 or higher indicate a tendency toward hostility.

Information from: Williams, R. B., & Williams, V. (1994). *Anger kills: Seventeen strategies for controlling the hostility that can harm your health* (pp. 5–11). New York: Harper Perennial.

Suppressing negative emotions may also be hazardous to health (Jorgensen & Kolodziej, 2007). People who score high in measures of **social inhibition** have difficulty expressing their feelings and seem to be driven by a need to avoid negative interactions with other people, especially conflict. Taken together, research findings on negative affect and social inhibition have led some researchers to propose a **Type D**, or *distressed*, behavior pattern, which may put people at an even greater risk for CVD than Type A behavior (Yu, Chen, Zhang, & Liu, 2011). Type D individuals are inclined to experience negative emotions and interpersonal difficulties that create a state of unease, tension, worry, and feelings of insecurity and a sense of being socially distant from other people (Bagherian-Sararoudi, Sanei, Attari, & Afshar, 2012).

> **social inhibition** A characteristic of people who have difficulty expressing their feelings and seem to be driven by a need to avoid negative interactions with other people.
>
> **Type D** A personality type found in people who tend to experience negative emotions and have difficulty expressing their feelings.

John Henryism

The fact that African Americans are two to three times more likely than those of European ancestry to develop hypertension by age 50 has motivated some researchers to study a phenomenon known as **John Henryism (JH)**, named after a poor African American steel driver in American folklore who beat a mechanical steam drill in a steel-driving contest, only to drop dead from exhaustion. Individuals who score high on measures of JH engage in high-effort coping with psychosocial demands, trying harder and harder in a pattern of relentless striving against odds that may be insurmountable.

> **John Henryism (JH)** An active style of coping with psychosocial stressors by expending high levels of effort; a syndrome that may promote hypertension and has been especially documented among lower-SES individuals.

More than three decades ago, Sherman James and his colleagues (James, Hartnett, & Kalsbeek, 1983) suggested that the stressful environments in which many African Americans live and work trigger JH. John Henry, as James wrote, "is a metaphor of the African American experience. It tells the struggle of black Americans to be a part of mainstream America. It is a struggle that has played out against great odds and against very powerful forces of marginalization that continue to create wear and tear on the bodies and minds of African Americans." As James saw it, John Henry both won and lost his battle.

Although JH has generally been viewed as a hazardous coping style, it does not appear to apply equally to all African American subgroups, especially those whose financial and educational attainments provide them with the greatest range of economic and social resources for coping with stress (James and others, 2006). However, the combination of high JH and low socioeconomic status appears to be linked to increased risk for hypertension in response to elevated stress hormones and persistent activation of the hypothalamic-pituitary-adrenocortical axis (see Chapter 4), promoting increased cardiovascular reactivity and slower recovery to psychosocial stressors (Merritt, Bennett, Williams,

Sollers, & Thayer, 2004). This pattern of relentless striving against the odds with limited resources may also be linked with increased risk of developing diabetes (Brody, Yu, Miller, & Chen, 2016) and faster aging of immune cells (Miller, Yu, Chen, & Brody, 2015).

Despite the origins of its name, John Henryism may not be unique to Black men (Hamblin, 2017). One study of over 1,400 middle-aged White men in Finland reported that the risk of myocardial infarction among low-SES men was twice as high in those who scored high in JH compared to men who scored low on measures of this coping style (Mujahid, James, Kaplan, & Salonen, 2017). However, the limited research on John Henryism among African American women suggests that JH may have fewer negative physical effects in women than in men (Stevens-Watkins, Sharma, Knighton, Oser, & Leukefeld, 2014).

How Does Negative Affect Promote Cardiovascular Disease?

An angry, hostile, or depressive behavior pattern predicts an increased risk of CVD, but how do these tendencies work their damage? The key theoretical models differ in their relative emphasis on biological, psychological, and social factors.

Psychosocial Vulnerability

Some theorists maintain that hostile adults lead more stressful lives and have lower levels of social support than their nonhostile peers. This combination, over time, exerts a toxic effect on cardiovascular health. In support of this *psychosocial vulnerability hypothesis*, researchers have found that chronic family conflict, unemployment, social isolation, and job-related stress are all linked to increased risk of CVD (Kop, Gottdiener, & Krantz, 2001).

The Health Behavior Explanation

We have seen that hostility, anger, job strain, and social isolation may affect health directly. Some researchers believe that these factors may have an indirect effect on health as well. For example, people with poor support may not take care of themselves as well as those who have someone to remind them to exercise, eat in moderation, or take their medicine. Similarly, a person with a cynical attitude may perceive health-enhancing behaviors, such as adhering to a healthy diet and an active lifestyle, as unimportant and may ignore warnings about smoking and other health-compromising behaviors.

The Cardiovascular Reactivity Model

Stress, hostility, depression, and social inhibition may act slowly over a period of years to damage the arteries and the heart. When we vent our anger, our pulse quickens, our heart pounds more forcefully, and our blood forms clots more quickly. In addition, blood vessels constrict, blood pressure surges, and blood levels of free fatty acids increase. Our immunity also decreases as adrenaline, cortisol, and other stress hormones suppress the activity of disease-fighting lymphocytes. The Healthy Women Study (University of Pittsburgh, 2000) showed that women who frequently express anger and also manifest symptoms of anxiety and depression have impaired functioning in the endothelial cells lining the internal surface of the coronary arteries. Normally, these cells promote vascular health by releasing substances that cause the blood vessels to relax or contract as needed to promote homeostasis. When these cells do not work properly, this delicate balance is disrupted. Consequently, the coronary arteries may become constricted and inflamed, which facilitates the deposit of lipids and the development of atherosclerotic lesions, thus promoting the development of CHD (Harris, Matthews, Sutton-Tyrrell, & Kuller, 2003).

However, the association between anger expression and cardiovascular reactivity is far from perfect, and it varies with such factors as a person's tendency to dwell on anger-provoking events and a person's tendency to forgive others. Hypertensive women and men who ruminate—that is, agree with such statements as "I think repeatedly about what I really would have liked to have done but did not"—tend to have higher resting blood pressure levels (Gerin and others, 2012; Hogan & Linden, 2004). Conversely, college students who have a generally forgiving personality and are therefore less likely to ruminate have lower blood pressure levels and lower cardiovascular reactivity during interviews about times when they felt betrayed by a parent or friend (Lawler and others, 2003).

Depression may be linked to elevated levels of inflammatory biomarkers such as interleukin-6 and C-reactive protein, which have been implicated in atherogenesis (Matthews and others, 2007; Vaccarino and others, 2007). Depression is also associated with decreased heart rate variability, especially following a heart attack, which may be another pathway between the two conditions (Glassman, Bigger, Gaffney, & Van Zyl, 2007). More generally, researchers have found that the Type D behavior pattern is associated with a marked response to social stressors, including higher levels of cortisol, greater arousal of the sympathetic nervous system, and increased inflammation (Conden and others, 2017). Moreover, Type D individuals are more likely to also have other risk factors, including increased anxiety, less social support, and depression (Pedersen, van Domburg, Theuns, Jordaens, & Erdman, 2004).

Education, Income, and the Work Environment

Low socioeconomic status, defined by lower educational level and/or low income, is another psychosocial risk factor for CVD (de Mestral & Stringhini, 2017). A massive European study that followed 60,000 men and women over a 23-year period reported that people of lower SES were more likely to smoke, eat an unhealthy diet, and live a sedentary life than those with more education (Ilanne-Parikka and others, 2008). Interestingly, the inverse relationship between SES and CVD risk factors is greater in countries with larger class discrepancies in education and income than in countries with smaller social-class divisions (Kim, Kawachi, Vander Hoorn, & Ezzati, 2008). The SES–CVD risk factor connection also can be observed early in life, occurring even in children and adolescents (Seo and others, 2018).

The work environment can be an important source of satisfaction or stress. As we saw in Chapter 4, jobs associated with high productivity demands, excessive overtime work, and conflicting requirements accompanied by little personal control tend to be especially stressful. Data from the 20-year CARDIA study reveal that *job strain*, defined as high job demands and low decision latitude, predicts the incidence of hypertension, even after adjusting for baseline blood pressure, education, body mass index, and age (Markovitz, Matthews, Whooley, Lewis, & Greenlund, 2004). Over time, then, it is not surprising that assembly-line workers, as well as those workers who wait tables and perform similarly stressful jobs, are especially susceptible to coronary disease. Workers who feel they have been promoted too slowly, those who feel insecure about their jobs, and those who feel that their ambitions are thwarted are also more likely to report stress and to show higher rates of illness, especially coronary disease (Sara and others, 2018).

Social Support

As we saw in Chapter 5, coping with stressful events is especially difficult when an individual feels cut off from others. Considerable prospective research shows that loneliness and the perception of little social support in one's life are risk factors for cardiovascular disease (Caspi, Harrington, Moffitt, Milne, & Poulton, 2006). This risk becomes even more hazardous as we age (Hawkley & Cacioppo, 2007). Interestingly, Julianne Holt-Lunstad and her colleagues (Holt-Lunstad, Uchino, Smith, Olson-Cerny, & Nealey-Moore, 2003) have found that the quality of people's relationships with others actually predicts their blood pressure during everyday social interactions with these people. Interactions with family members and friends for whom the participants reported generally positive, supportive ties were accompanied by lower systolic blood pressure (measuring the force of the heart's contraction), while interactions with people for whom participants reported ambivalent feelings (both positive and negative emotions) were associated with elevations in systolic blood pressure. Low perceived support at work or at home is associated with more rapid development of atheromatous plaques and coronary artery blockage (Wang, Mittleman, Leineweber, & Orth-Gomer, 2008).

The Biopsychosocial Model

Health psychologists have combined the insights of these findings to provide a biopsychosocial explanation for how hurriedness, hostility, and anger contribute to cardiovascular disease. This model suggests that for a chronic disease such as CVD to develop, a person first must have a physiological predisposition (Figure 10.5). This is determined by family history of CVD and previous health history (other diseases, poor diet, tobacco use, and so on). Whether CVD develops then depends on a variety of psychosocial factors in the

FIGURE 10.5 A Biopsychosocial Model of CVD For CVD to develop, a hostile person first must have a biological predisposition toward it. Then CVD may be more likely to develop because the hostile person's attitude has chased away social support people and continues to elicit negative responses from others, which leads to more hostility and damaging cardiac reactivity.

Biological Influences
- Uncontrollable risk factors such as age, gender, ethnicity
- Family history of CVD and other diseases
- Controllable risk factors such as hypertension, obesity, tobacco use, MetS, hemostasis, unhealthy cholesterol profile

Coping with and managing stress effectively

Psychosocial Influences
- Hostility, negative affect, depression, Type D personality, social inhibition, John Henryism
- Stressful life events
- Absence of social support

person's life, including the level of stress from the work and home environments and the availability of social support. For example, hostile individuals tend to elicit aggressive behaviors from others, producing interpersonal conflict and more hostility. This in turn leads to a reduction in social support, more negative affect, and artery-damaging cardiovascular reactivity. Thus, hostile attitudes create a self-fulfilling prophecy for the mistrusting, hostile person by producing a hostile environment.

REDUCING RISK AND PREVENTING RECURRENCE OF CARDIOVASCULAR DISEASE

Although epidemiological research has provided a wealth of information that should help prevent cardiovascular disease—limit fat intake, do not smoke, maintain a healthy weight, and get regular exercise—millions of us persist in making heart-unhealthy choices. Working from an evolutionary perspective, some researchers believe that our poor decisions are made by brains that were shaped to cope with an environment substantially different from the one that our species now inhabits. On the African savanna, where our species originated, those who had a tendency to consume large amounts of usually scarce fat were more likely to survive famines that killed their thinner companions. Those with a rapid-fire fight-or-flight reaction had a clear advantage in hunting and reacting to hostile threats and were more likely to survive and pass on these traits to their offspring. And we, their descendants, still carry these evolved urges and hostile tendencies.

Health psychology aims to help us overcome these evolved tendencies by establishing heart-healthy habits and modifying behaviors that increase the risk of CVD. Lifelong behavioral habits such as a poor diet, tobacco use, and a sedentary lifestyle are particularly difficult to modify. Studies of high-risk children (those with elevated cholesterol, obesity, and hypertension) typically reveal that such children remain at increased risk of developing CVD throughout adulthood. Yet perception of control is also a factor. Patients who have experienced an MI or angina and who report the highest levels of *perceived behavioral control* (see Chapter 6) over being able to exercise regularly, give up smoking, and modify other CVD risk behaviors are more likely, one year later, to report having done so (Johnston, Johnston, Pollard, Kinmouth, & Mant, 2004).

In the next section, we focus on interventions aimed at controlling hypertension, reducing elevated serum cholesterol, and reversing atherosclerosis. The most serious behavioral risk factor in CVD, cigarette smoking, was discussed in Chapter 9.

Controlling Hypertension

For every one-point drop in diastolic blood pressure, which measures the pressure between heartbeats, there is an estimated 2% to 3% reduction in the risk of an MI (Massey, Hupp, Kreisberg, Alpert, & Hoff, 2000). Interventions aimed at lowering high blood pressure

Risk Reduction—and Preventing Recurrence

Regular exercise and good nutrition are significant factors in preventing CVD and in preventing recurrence of CVD. A former heart attack victim (above left) saw his illness as a wake-up call and changed his life, beginning with a medically supervised program of aerobic exercise. A plant-based diet and moderate consumption of red wine (above right) can improve cholesterol ratios.

typically begin with pharmacological treatment. However, because hypertension is often symptom-free, many patients fail to adhere to prescribed treatment regimens.

Apart from taking drugs, changing behavior also can go a long way toward lowering blood pressure. For example, lowering sodium intake can bring about significant improvement in blood pressure readings. Many people with hypertension are sodium sensitive, meaning that excess sodium raises their blood pressure. Because there is no test for sodium sensitivity, almost everyone with hypertension should restrict dietary sodium to 2,000 mg per day.

Reducing Cholesterol

Numerous studies have shown that even moderate amounts of physical activity can help lower the resting blood pressure of people with hypertension (Ishikawa-Takata, Ohta, & Tanaka, 2003). Even when exercise fails to reduce hypertension, it conveys a heart-protecting benefit: Physically fit hypertensives with elevated cholesterol actually have a lower overall risk of CVD than unfit individuals who have normal blood pressure and cholesterol. Most impressively, data from the CARDIA study reveal that even after adjustment for age, race, sex, smoking, family history of hypertension, diabetes, and CHD, participants with low fitness levels (below the 20th percentile in performance on a treadmill test) were three to six times more likely to develop hypertension, diabetes, and the metabolic syndrome than participants with high fitness levels (above the 60th percentile) (Carnethon and others, 2003; Seeman and others, 2009). Regular exercise is also associated with significant reductions in the risk of ischemic and hemorrhagic strokes (Lee, Folsom, & Blair, 2003).

Findings from several epidemiological studies indicate that cardiorespiratory fitness may even protect against the health hazards of a high body mass index. Researchers identified one subgroup of obese individuals that has a substantially lower risk of hypertension, MetS, and CVD than other obese individuals. This group has been described as having *metabolically healthy obesity (MHO)*. Although the concept of MHO is controversial, its key aspects seem to be an absence of abdominal obesity and a high level of cardiorespiratory fitness (Stefan, Haring, & Schulze, 2013).

To be most beneficial, physical exertion should occur in the context of leisure and not work. In a case–control study of 312 patients with stable CHD, researchers found that participants who engaged in regular *leisure-time* physical activity also had lower levels of C-reactive protein—a protein that we have seen to be linked to the inflammatory response—and interleukin-6, a proinflammatory cytokine linked with immunosuppression (Rothenbacher, Hoffmeister, Brenner, & Koenig, 2003). By contrast, *work-related* physical exertion (e.g., entailed in such occupations as construction, cleaning, landscaping, and agriculture) was strongly associated with *increased* risk of CHD. These results suggest that one mechanism of the heart-protective effects of regular exercise is a beneficial effect on the body's inflammatory response.

Even if a person has had a heart attack, preventive behaviors can play an important role in controlling the negative effects of CVD. For example, exercise improves the heart's ability to pump blood to working muscles, as well as the muscles' ability to extract and use oxygen from the blood. Dozens of research studies involving thousands of heart attack patients demonstrate that patients who participated in cardiac rehabilitation exercise programs are significantly less likely to die from CVD (Stephens, 2009).

After CVD: Preventing Recurrence

Most people who survive an MI recover well enough to resume near-normal lives within a few weeks or months. However, they remain high-risk individuals and need to make lifestyle adjustments in order to improve their chances of living a long life and avoiding a recurrence of CHD. Perceived social support, dispositional optimism, low hostility, and religious involvement have all been shown to have beneficial effects in the recovery of heart surgery patients (Mavros and others, 2011).

Patients who participate in *cardiac rehabilitation (CR)* programs—comprising medically supervised exercise, education on heart-healthy life habits, and counseling to reduce stress—generally fare better and have lower morbidity and mortality rates. Such patients also show improvements in their control of such CHD risk factors as anxiety, stress, hostility, and depression and in their quality of life (Acevedo and others, 2013; Hsu and others, 2011; Lavie & Milani, 2005). Despite the benefits of CR, however, only 10% to 20% of patients who survive an MI enter a CR program (Yohannes, Yalfani, Doherty, & Bundy, 2007). Patients who smoke, those who have been physically inactive, and those with low scores on surveys assessing body pain, social functioning, and general health are less likely to begin or fully adhere to CR programs following a cardiac event (Bustamante and others, 2015).

One study of a diverse group of 77 cardiac patients demonstrated that irrational health beliefs also predict adherence to CR programs. Participants completed a 20-item survey that consisted of health-related vignettes such as the following:

> During a routine check-up, your doctor emphasized the importance of exercise and eating right to prevent health problems. You notice that the doctor is quite overweight. You think to yourself, "If good eating habits and exercise were really important, he would lose weight himself." (Christensen, Moran, & Wiebe, 1999)

Those who were most likely to agree with statements such as this one were more likely to drop out of their CR program prematurely (Anderson & Emery, 2014). The results of this study suggest that nonadherence may also be linked with a tendency to rely on beliefs that are not grounded in medical science.

Managing Stress, Anxiety, and Hostility

A heart attack or stroke can cause substantial distress to both the patient and his or her family members. Although many patients make a complete recovery and are able to resume most of their previous activities, some remain psychologically impaired for a long time. A major goal of many intervention programs is to deal with the approximately one third of the patients who experience significant stress, anxiety, depression, or hostility after their hospitalization (De Jonge & Ormel, 2007). One study of 477 acute-MI patients found that those with the most clinical symptoms of anxiety and depression two months after hospitalization had the worst prognosis in terms of recurrent MI and early mortality (Roest, Martens, de Jonge, & Denollet, 2014).

Interventions aimed at reducing hostility are based on two premises:

- Hostile people are more likely to encounter stress, which increases the prevalence of atherosclerosis-promoting experiences involving anger.

- Hostile people are less likely to have stress-busting resources such as social support, partly as a result of their antagonistic behavior.

Intervention studies focus on helping hostile people gain control over their anger. In the typical program, the psychologist first attempts to gain insight into the triggers of anger-inducing incidents by having participants self-monitor their behavior. Next, the participants develop strategies for coping with aggravation—for example, by avoiding especially stressful situations such as rush-hour traffic and controlling their reactions, perhaps by counting to 10 before reacting to a provoking incident. As the participants become increasingly able to cope with problem situations, the psychologist turns to a more cognitive intervention, helping participants learn to challenge cynical attitudes and modify unrealistic beliefs and expectations about life. Dozens of studies have supported the efficacy of these interventions.

Clinical health psychologists have used a variety of other strategies to help individuals cope with anger. One effective strategy is relaxation training, an effective means of coping with stress (see Chapter 5). Another method involves teaching angry persons new social and communication skills in which they learn to be more civilly assertive and to become aware of cues from other people that would normally provoke anger in them. Teaching participants to avoid provocative situations and to take themselves less seriously are also common goals of anger-intervention programs.

benefit finding The experience of identifying positive outcomes in the face of adversity.

Road Rage Hostility and anger, such as that displayed in extreme cases of aggressive driving, are powerful psychosocial influences on hypertension and cardiovascular disease. Road rage can also lead to assaults and collisions that result in injuries and even deaths.

Chris Rout/Alamy Stock Photo

Poor lifestyle behaviors and lifestyle-related risk factors are major contributors to cardiovascular disease. Fortunately, lifestyle modifications and comprehensive interventions, such as cognitive-behavior therapy, that combine stress management, exercise, relaxation training, and hostility reduction with nonsmoking and a healthy diet can significantly reduce a person's risk of CVD (Gulliksson and others, 2011).

Finally, another factor that has been associated with better psychosocial well-being and improved adherence in CVD and many other chronic illnesses is **benefit finding** (see *Your Health Assets: Benefit Finding*). Defined as the experience of identifying positive outcomes in the face of adversity, benefit finding is based on the idea that adversity can lead to a new sense of meaning and self-worth.

Your Health Assets

Benefit Finding

People who have cardiovascular disease, diabetes, or other serious conditions sometimes feel that their experiences have made positive contributions to their lives as well as causing problems. If you (or a loved one) have gone through something like this, circle the appropriate number to indicate how often you (or that other person) experienced each of the following benefits. Total up the numbers of the answers. Higher scores indicate higher levels of benefit.

Having had _____ has:	Not at all	A little	Moderately	Quite a Bit	Extremely
shown me that all people need to be loved.	1	2	3	4	5
made me more sensitive to family issues.	1	2	3	4	5
led me to be more accepting of things.	1	2	3	4	5
taught me that everyone has a purpose in life.	1	2	3	4	5
made us more in charge of ourselves as a family.	1	2	3	4	5
made me more aware and concerned for the future of humankind.	1	2	3	4	5
taught me how to adjust to things I cannot change.	1	2	3	4	5
given my family a sense of continuity, a sense of history.	1	2	3	4	5
made me a more responsible person.	1	2	3	4	5
made me realize the importance of planning for my family's future.	1	2	3	4	5
given my life better structure.	1	2	3	4	5
brought my family closer together.	1	2	3	4	5
made me more productive.	1	2	3	4	5
helped me take things as they come.	1	2	3	4	5
helped me to better budget my time.	1	2	3	4	5
made me more grateful for each day.	1	2	3	4	5
taught me to be patient.	1	2	3	4	5
taught me to control my temper.	1	2	3	4	5
renewed my interest in participating in different activities.	1	2	3	4	5
led me to cope better with stress and problems.	1	2	3	4	5

Information from: Tomich, P. L., & Helgeson, V. S. (2004). Is finding something good in the bad always good? Benefit finding among women with breast cancer. *Health Psychology, 23*, 16–23; Tran, V. H. (2010). *Benefit finding, negative affect, and daily diabetes management among adolescents with Type 1 diabetes.* Doctoral dissertation. Retrieved from https://repositories.tdl.org/utswmed-ir/bitstream/handle/2152.5/819/tranvincent.pdf?sequence=3

DIABETES

Cardiovascular disease has a very important risk factor that we have not yet discussed: *diabetes mellitus*, which involves the body's inability to produce or properly use insulin, a crucial hormone that helps convert sugar and starches from food into energy. There is no cure for diabetes, and its cause remains a mystery, although both heredity and lifestyle factors appear to play roles. Diabetes mellitus affects 30.3 million Americans (9.4% of the population), is the seventh leading cause of death in the United States, and has an annual cost of $245 billion. Overall, the risk of death among people with diabetes is twice that of people of the same age but without diabetes. Adding to the health burden caused by this chronic condition, medical expenses for people with diabetes average more than twice those for people without diabetes (CDC, 2017i).

It is estimated that 84.1 million Americans aged 20 years and older have *prediabetes*, characterized by blood glucose levels that are higher than normal but have not yet risen to the level that indicates a diagnosis of diabetes. People with prediabetes have an increased risk of developing diabetes, heart disease, and stroke (CDC, 2017i).

The number of people with diabetes has increased from 108 million in 1980 to over 400 million today. Prevalence rates for diabetes vary markedly around the world: The disease is absent or rare in some indigenous communities in developing countries in Africa, the Eastern Mediterranean, and the Western Pacific, but prevalence rates rise to as high as 14%–20% in some Arab, Asian Indian, Chinese, and Hispanic American populations (World Health Organization [WHO], 2017). Like numerous other chronic conditions, diabetes is distributed unequally across ethnic groups. The percentage of adults with diagnosed diabetes in the United States is highest among American Indians/Alaska Natives (15.1%), followed by non-Hispanic Blacks (12.7%), people of Hispanic ethnicity (12.1%), Asian Americans (8.0%), and non-Hispanic Whites (7.4%) (CDC, 2017g) (Figure 10.6).

Type 1 diabetes An autoimmune disorder in which insulin-producing cells of the pancreas are destroyed.

Type 2 diabetes A metabolic illness in which the body fails to produce enough insulin or fails to use insulin properly.

FIGURE 10.6 Estimated Age-Adjusted Prevalence of Diabetes in the United States by Ethnicity, 2013–2015 Diabetes takes a greater toll on some ethnic groups than on others; especially vulnerable are American Indians, Alaska Natives, non-Hispanic blacks, and Hispanic-Americans.

Data from: Centers for Disease Control and Prevention (CDC). (2017g). *National diabetes statistics report: Estimates of diabetes and its burden in the United States*. Figure 1 (p. 4). Atlanta, GA: U.S. Department of Health and Human Services.

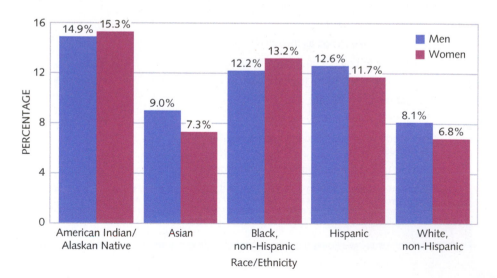

Types of Diabetes

There are two basic types of diabetes. **Type 1 diabetes (T1D)** is an autoimmune disease in which the person's immune system attacks the insulin- and glucagon-producing *islet cells* of the pancreas. In a healthy person, the opposing actions of these hormones help regulate the blood level of the sugar glucose. Glucagon stimulates the release of glucose, causing blood sugar levels to rise, and insulin decreases blood sugar levels by causing cells to take up glucose more freely from the bloodstream. Without functioning islet cells, the body is unable to regulate blood sugar levels, and the individual becomes dependent on insulin delivered by injections or a pump. The symptoms of T1D, which include excessive thirst and urination, craving for sweets, weight loss, fatigue, and irritability, are largely the result of the body's inability to metabolize glucose for energy, which forces it to begin feeding off its own fats and proteins.

Type 2 diabetes (T2D)—a milder form of the disease, which usually appears after age 30—is found in 90% to 95% of all people with diabetes. It results from *insulin resistance* (also called *glucose intolerance*—a condition in which the islet cells of the pancreas fail to make enough insulin) and/or an insensitivity to insulin caused by a decrease in the number of insulin receptors in target cells. The symptoms of T2D include frequent urination; irregular menstruation in women; fatigue; slow healing of cuts and bruises; dryness of the mouth; and pain or cramps in the legs, feet, and fingers. T2D is more common among women, overweight people, members of certain ethnic groups, and those of low socioeconomic status.

In both types of diabetes, two types of blood sugar problems can develop: *hypoglycemia* (blood sugar level that is too low) and *hyperglycemia* (blood sugar level that is too high). An estimated 50% to 75% of individuals with diabetes develop one or more long-term health complications as a result of their body's inability to regulate blood sugar (CDC, 2017i). Figure 10.7 illustrates these health complications. Elevated levels of glucose, for instance, cause the walls of arteries to thicken, accelerating the development of atherosclerosis and CVD. Men and women with diabetes have CHD mortality rates that are up to two times higher than for adults without diabetes. Because unregulated glucose levels in the blood can damage the retinas of the eyes, diabetes is also the leading cause of blindness among adults. Diabetes is also the leading cause of end-stage renal (kidney) disease and is associated with cancer of the pancreas, damage to the nervous system that may cause memory impairments (especially among older adults), and loss of sensation or pain in the extremities. In severe cases of poor circulation and loss of sensation in the extremities, amputation of the toes or feet may be required. The average life expectancy of a 50-year-old person with diabetes is about six years shorter than before someone without the disease (Baena-Diaz and others, 2016).

FIGURE 10.7 Health Complications Associated with Diabetes Over time, consistently high blood sugar can cause complications that affect the eyes, teeth and gums, heart, kidneys, nerves, feet, and other parts of the body. Poor blood sugar control during pregnancy increases the risk of premature birth, miscarriage, and birth defects.

Data from: Centers for Disease Control and Prevention (CDC). (2014c). *National diabetes statistics report: Estimates of diabetes and its burden in the United States, 2014.* Atlanta, GA: U.S. Department of Health and Human Services.

Causes of Diabetes

Like other chronic illnesses, diabetes seems to be caused by multiple factors, including viral or bacterial infections that damage the islet cells of the pancreas, an overactive immune system, and genetic vulnerability (see Table 10.2).

Obesity has been historically known as a major risk factor for T2D. Today, about 30% of overweight people have T2D, and 85.2% of those who have diabetes are overweight (Bhupathiraju & Hu, 2016). Researchers have discovered two critical links between obesity and diabetes. Both are based on the fact that, generally speaking, the more fat tissue a person has, the less sensitive the person becomes to insulin. First, it appears that fat cells release a protein called *pigment epithelium-derived factor (PEDF)* into the bloodstream, which causes muscle cells and the liver to become desensitized to insulin. In response, the pancreas works harder to produce more insulin. As fat accumulates, the pancreas eventually may slow or even stop the release of insulin, thus leading to T2D.

A second line of research implicates immune factors in the relationship between obesity and diabetes and suggests that obesity can be uncoupled from insulin resistance.

TABLE 10.2 Characteristics and Risk Factors of Type 1 and Type 2 Diabetes

Type 1	Type 2
Autoimmune disorder in which insulin-producing cells of the pancreas are destroyed	Chronic illness in which the body fails to produce enough insulin or fails to use insulin properly
Peak incidence occurs during puberty, around 10 to 12 years of age in girls and 12 to 14 in boys	Onset occurs after age 30
Accounts for 5%–10% of all cases of diabetes	Accounts for 90%–95% of all cases of diabetes
Symptoms may mimic flu, including excessive thirst, frequent urination, unusual weight loss, extreme fatigue, and irritability	Symptoms include any of the Type 1 symptoms and blurred vision, frequent infections, cuts that are slow to heal, tingling or numbness in hands or feet
Requires insulin injections	Requires strict diet and exercise
Who Is at Greater Risk?	**Who Is at Greater Risk?**
Children of parents with Type 1 diabetes	People over age 45 with a family history of diabetes
Siblings of people with Type 1 diabetes	Affects more women than men
Affects women and men equally	People who are overweight
Higher prevalence among European Americans than other ethnic groups	Women who had gestational diabetes or who had a baby weighing 9 pounds or more at birth
	People who don't exercise regularly
	People with low HDL cholesterol or high triglycerides
	African Americans, Native Americans, Hispanic Americans, Asians, and Pacific Islanders
	People of low socioeconomic status

Researchers studied mice that were genetically engineered to lack *T-bet,* a protein that regulates the differentiation and function of immune cells. They found that the mice had improved insulin sensitivity despite being obese. Although the mice had more abdominal fat, that fat contained fewer immune cells and was less inflamed than that of normal mice. The researchers also found that by transferring immune cells lacking T-bet to young, lean mice, they were able to improve insulin-sensitive obesity (Stolarczyk and others, 2013).

Not all diabetes cases are linked to weight. Genetics and environmental factors such as *nutritional Westernization*, which includes a diet high in fat and processed foods as well as total calories, also may be contributing factors in diabetes. Increased television watching associated with reduced physical activity and poor nutrition may also contribute to T2D. One study found that participants with T2D were more likely to watch more than four hours of TV per day compared to control participants (Huffman and others, 2012).

Stress has also been suggested as a precipitating factor in diabetes. People who have already been diagnosed with diabetes, as well as those at high risk for the disease, react to laboratory and environmental stressors with abnormally greater changes in their blood glucose levels than do people who are not at risk for diabetes (Weisli and others, 2005). Following the *diathesis–stress* model of disease (see Chapter 4), some investigators have suggested that abnormal blood sugar responses to challenging events (a symptom of an overreactive sympathetic nervous system), in conjunction with long-term exposure to high levels of stress, may be a *direct* path to the development of diabetes. Indirectly, stress also may promote the development of diabetes by adversely affecting the individual's diet, level of compliance with treatment regimens, and tendency to exercise.

Prevention and Self-Management of Diabetes

People at high risk for diabetes can use strategies to prevent or delay the development of the disease. The Diabetes Prevention Program (DPP), a large prevention study of people at high risk for diabetes conducted through the National Institutes of Health, showed that lifestyle interventions to lose weight and increase physical activity reduced the development of T2D by 58% during a 3-year period (National Institute of Diabetes and Digestive and Kidney Diseases [NIDDK], 2008). The reduction was even greater, 71%, among adults aged 60 years and older. Prevention or delay with lifestyle intervention was effective in all racial and ethnic groups studied and has been shown to persist for at least 10 years. Research also has found that lifestyle interventions are more cost-effective than medications (NIDDK, 2008).

Once an individual is diagnosed with diabetes, a crucial aspect of treatment is self-management. Fortunately, most people with diabetes are able to control their disease through lifestyle modifications—by changing their diet, regulating their weight, and exercising regularly, for example—and, in some cases, with daily injections of insulin. The goal of treatment, of course, is tight **glycemic control**—keeping blood sugar at a stable, healthy level—as revealed through a finger prick or venipuncture test measuring *HbA1c* (glycated hemoglobin) levels in the bloodstream, specifically in red blood cells, which contain the molecule hemoglobin. Glucose sticks to hemoglobin, forming HbA1c. The more glucose in the blood, the higher the HbA1c levels will be. Because red blood cells live for 8 to 12 weeks before they are replaced, the HbA1c test reveals how high blood glucose has been on average for this period of time.

glycemic control The action of monitoring glucose levels to keep blood sugar at a stable, healthy level.

Diversity and Healthy Living

Cultural Adaptations to Evidence-Based Interventions for Type 2 Diabetes

Women of Hispanic heritage (Latinas) living in the United States have a prevalence of T2D that is almost twice that found for non-Latina White women (National Diabetes Statistics Report, 2014). If current trends continue, by 2031 over 20% of the Latino population overall is expected to have diabetes.

To delay or prevent the numerous health problems associated with diabetes, people with the chronic condition must maintain tight glycemic control. Latinos with T2D, however, often exhibit poorer glycemic control, and thus, more frequent health complications, greater disease severity, and worse outcomes than non-Latino Whites (Fortmann and others, 2011).

One approach to the development of interventions for at-risk ethnic groups such as Latinos is the cultural adaptation of evidence-based interventions that have proven effective with other groups or health conditions (Castro, Barrera, & Holleran Streiker, 2010). A Spanish-language public education campaign called *¡Viva Bien!* was launched in 2005 by the American Diabetes Association, the American Heart Association, and the American Cancer Society. Aimed specifically at Latina women, the campaign was designed to help them make everyday choices that can improve their own health, as well as that of others in their community. The television commercials featured Latino families making healthy lifestyle choices such as taking a walk in the park, planting vegetables with their kids, and buying fruits at the market.

One study recruited 280 Latina women, 30 to 75 years of age, living in the Denver, Colorado, area, who had been diagnosed with Type 2 diabetes for at least six months. Extending the *¡Viva Bien!* program, health psychologists adapted the *Mediterranean Lifestyle Program,* which has proven effective in promoting diabetes self-management behaviors in non-Latina White women (Osuna and others, 2011). The intervention included a two and one-half-day retreat that introduced the components of the program and provided time for participants to practice new skills, including (1) following a Mediterranean-style diet adapted for Latino cultures, (2) daily stress-management techniques, (3) 30 minutes of daily physical activity, (4) smoking cessation, and (5) participation in problem-solving–based support groups. Following the retreat, weekly meetings continued for the next 6 months, followed by twice-monthly meetings for an additional 6 months.

Follow-up assessments of body mass index, physical activity, and saturated fat consumption were made at 6 months and 12 months. Statistically significant intervention effects were found for each of these outcome variables. Interestingly, the researchers found an interaction between participants' acculturation and several of the dependent variables. Specifically, Latina orientation was associated with both lower saturated fat intake (a protective factor) and less physical activity (a risk factor).

Diabetes self-management, a prerequisite for tight glycemic control, involves a daily regimen of several behaviors, including healthy eating, physical activity, blood glucose monitoring, foot care, taking medications, problem solving, and active coping (American Diabetes Association, 2010b). Completing these tasks day after day is demanding and often requires significant lifestyle modifications. Doing so, however, pays off. Researchers have consistently found an inverse association between diabetes self-management and HbA1c levels (Fortmann, Gallo, and Philis-Tsimikas, 2011).

Diabetes self-management training programs are especially critical for people who lack access to health care services, which is the case for many ethnic minorities (Anders and others, 2008). For instance, fewer than 60% of Latino adults with T2D receive annual eye and foot exams and participate in daily blood glucose monitoring (CDC, 2011a). To make matters worse, Latinos with T2D perceive self-monitoring of blood glucose as more difficult, and have more negative perceptions about their future well-being, than do

African Americans, Asian Americans, and non-Latino Whites with diabetes (Misra and Lager, 2009). To address this concern, the American Diabetes Association partnered with other organizations to develop a Spanish-language outreach (See *Diversity and Healthy Living: Cultural Adaptations to Evidence-Based Interventions for Type 2 Diabetes*). Passage of the Affordable Care Act in 2010 authorized the creation of the National Diabetes Prevention Program (NDPP) with the goal of "eliminat[ing] the preventable burden of diabetes." Based on the Diabetes Prevention Program study discussed earlier, the NDPP is a project of the federal Centers for Disease Control and Prevention and is designed to bring evidence-based lifestyle change programs for preventing T2D to communities throughout the country (Burge & Schade, 2014).

Diabetes self-management typically occurs in a social context of family, friends, health care providers, and the community, each of which can influence adherence (Barrera, Toobert, Angell, Glasgow, & MacKinnon, 2006). Individuals with T2D who report receiving greater support resources for their disease management exhibit greater physical activity (measured as caloric expenditure from exercise), better dietary outcomes (fat and fiber intake), greater adherence to blood glucose monitoring, and tighter glycemic control than do people with less support (D. K. King and others, 2010; Brody, Kogan, Mury, Chen, & Brown, 2008).

The medical community is currently debating whether both types of diabetes should be treated in the same way, including medication for precise glucose control, or differently. T1D treatment requires insulin management, while T2D treatment could focus on weight control, exercise, and diet—in particular, reducing sugar and carbohydrate intake and keeping the total number of calories consumed each day within a narrow range. In practice, a combination of treatments is used with T1D, depending on the severity of the individual case and the effectiveness of dietary and exercise modifications. For preventing diabetes, moderate exercise, improved diet, and other lifestyle interventions win hands down over medications (Zepf, 2005).

Health Psychology and Diabetes

The knowledge, beliefs, and behavior of patients strongly affect their ability to manage their diabetes and its impact on every domain of their health. This makes the health psychologist's role in the care and treatment of people with diabetes particularly important, as underscored by the standards of treatment recommended by the American Diabetes Association (ADA). Educational interventions are vitally important, but not sufficient on their own to promote adherence to healthier lifestyle regimens (Garcia-Perez, Alvarez, Dilla, Gil-Guillen, & Orozco-Beltran, 2013; Rutten, 2005). People with diabetes often have deficits in their knowledge about diabetes and about their increased risk for heart disease and other chronic conditions (Wagner, Lacey, Abbott, de Groot, & Chyun, 2006). The ADA also emphasizes that *self-management* is the cornerstone of treatment for all people with diabetes. As a result, psychologists are increasingly becoming involved in the primary care of people with diabetes (Gillies and others, 2007).

The primary diabetes outcome around which self-management interventions are based is **glycemic control**, as measured by a blood test that indicates average plasma glucose for the previous two to three months. The primary self-care tasks that help to maintain glycemic control, such as monitoring blood glucose levels, injecting insulin, and dosing insulin according to meter results, must be carried out several times per day, often around meals, and in varied contexts such as school, the workplace, home, and restaurants. Given the

RIA Novosti/Science Source

Self-Management of Diabetes
The goal of diabetes treatment is to keep blood sugar at a stable, healthy level. Here, a health care professional instructs a young child with diabetes on how to draw blood safely, to monitor blood sugar level.

illness intrusiveness The extent to which a chronic illness disrupts an individual's life by interfering with valued activities and interests and reducing perceptions of personal control, self-efficacy, and self-esteem.

frequency and nature of these tasks, it is not surprising that adherence rates are often suboptimal (Greening, Stoppelbein, Konishi, Jordan, & Moll, 2007).

Increasingly, smart phones and tablets are being used to sample behaviors and experiences in real time, and as the basis of interventions to promote adherence to self-care behaviors in managing chronic conditions such as diabetes (Mulvaney and others, 2012). This type of *ecological momentary assessment (EMA)* may be particularly effective with adolescents because an estimated 93% of 13- to 17-year-olds use cell phones (Lenhart, Purcell, Smith, & Zickuhr, 2010). Diabetes self-care behaviors measured via EMA include completion of blood glucose monitoring, timing of blood glucose monitoring, and timing and dosing of insulin.

Promoting Adjustment to Diabetes

A patient who receives a diagnosis of diabetes may experience a range of emotions, including shock, denial, anger, and depression. Helping patients accept their diagnoses is the first step in promoting self-management. Even after accepting their diagnoses, many patients with diabetes continue to struggle with **illness intrusiveness**, which refers to the disruptive effect of diabetes on their lives. Illness intrusiveness can affect an individual's well-being adversely in at least two ways: directly, when the condition interferes with valued activities and interests, and indirectly, as a result of perceptions of reduced personal control, self-efficacy, and self-esteem. However, research has shown that having strong social support and good personal coping resources—including high self-esteem, a sense of mastery, and feelings of self-efficacy in the face of adversity—are associated with fewer depressive symptoms in people with diabetes (Rassart and others, 2015).

Psychologists have designed interventions to help people who do not have the support or resources needed to cope with diabetes. These professionals reduce diabetes intrusiveness on daily living by teaching people to redefine personal priorities, increase participation in enjoyable activities, and restructure irrational expectations regarding the intrusiveness of the disease. They also help patients mobilize social support and improve personal coping skills.

Blood Glucose Awareness

Diabetes patients often lack proper understanding of their disease and its symptoms. As a result, they may overlook some potentially serious symptoms or overreact to other, irrelevant ones. Health psychologists have reported impressive results from *blood glucose awareness training,* in which patients learn to gauge their blood sugar levels from environmental cues (such as time of day or ongoing activity), physical symptoms (such as nausea and mouth dryness), and mood (such as fatigue and irritability). Through such training, which is similar in many ways to biofeedback training, most people with diabetes can learn to reliably recognize various cognitive and behavioral indicators of different blood glucose levels (Gebel, 2013). Compared with untrained control patients, those patients trained in blood glucose awareness have achieved these additional health benefits:

- improved glucose control and fewer long-term health complications
- fewer automobile and other accidents resulting from states of hypoglycemia
- fewer hospitalizations for blood sugar level abnormalities

Treating Diabetes-Related Psychological Disorders

Clinical disorders such as major depression, anxiety, and eating disorders are more prevalent among adults with diabetes than they are in the general population (Lustman & Clouse, 2005). Prevalence rates for major depressive disorder, for example, which range from 5% to 25% in the general population, have been found to range from 22% to 60% among those with diabetes (American Diabetes Association, 2010a). In one study, over 30% of Latino participants with diabetes reported depressive symptoms in the moderate to severe range (Gross and others, 2005).

The mechanisms underlying the link between depression and glycemic control are likely to involve a combination of behavioral and physiological factors. Behaviorally, the low energy levels that characterize depression may interfere with a person's ability to follow the self-management regimen. Physiologically, depression is associated with activation of the hypothalamic-pituitary-adrenal axis, sympathetic nervous system, and pro-inflammatory responses, each of which can induce insulin resistance and contribute to poorer diabetes-related health outcomes (Golden, 2007).

Many health professionals have suggested that individuals with diabetes should have psychosocial evaluations at some point during their medical treatment, preferably soon after the time of diagnosis (Gonzalez and others, 2008). Health psychologists who are involved in the primary care of people diagnosed with diabetes are in a good position to refer them to appropriate clinical psychologists, if needed.

Managing Weight and Stress

Effective weight management is particularly important for patients with diabetes, because lower weight improves the body's ability to regulate glucose and thereby reduces the need for medication. Weight-loss programs often produce substantial success among people with diabetes by using a multimodal approach that combines nutrition, education, low-calorie diets, and regular exercise. As with all weight-loss programs, however, the main problem has been in maintaining the loss.

Regular exercise can also help prevent T2D. Several research studies have found that physically active women and men have a much lower incidence of T2D than those who are sedentary (CDC, 2010a). This protective effect remains even after researchers control for other major diabetes risk factors, including obesity, hypertension, and family history of the disease. Interestingly, people with T2D have the greatest difficulty maintaining healthy concentrations of blood sugar in March and April, perhaps because the preceding months of cold weather have promoted inactivity (Doro, Benko, Matuz, & Soos, 2006).

Equally important is stress management. In people with diabetes, reactions to stress strongly influence whether and how well they follow a particular regimen. For example, stress may begin the vicious cycle of overeating, poor control over diabetes, more stress, more overeating, and so on. Relaxation training and other stress-management techniques appear to be beneficial for many individuals with diabetes.

Increasing Adherence to Diabetes Treatment Regimens

Health psychologists have approached the issue of adherence in two ways: by seeking to identify factors that predict compliance or noncompliance and by developing interventions to improve adherence to different aspects of a treatment regimen. Sociodemographic factors such as age, gender, ethnicity, and personality do not predict adherence to diabetes treatment regimens. Several factors contribute to noncompliance, including the sheer complexity of a lifelong regimen of self-care. Patients with diabetes also may perceive prescribed treatment as recommended and discretionary rather than mandatory, and they fail to comply. Those newly diagnosed with diabetes often feel no ill effects—severe medical complications of diabetes may not arise for a decade or more—and may find their current lifestyle too enjoyable to change. Social and environmental circumstances are also factors in poor adherence. During periods of unusual stress or social pressure to behave in unhealthy ways, for instance, dietary and exercise compliance often decreases among those with diabetes (Cramer, 2004).

Working from the transtheoretical model discussed in Chapter 6, health psychologists might try to get diabetes patients to adhere to treatment regimens by helping them cycle through the stages of precontemplation, contemplation, preparation, action, and maintenance. For example, the psychologist almost certainly would tell an obese woman newly diagnosed with T2D to lose weight. However, since she probably does not feel sick, she sees no reason to change from her delicious high-calorie, high-carbohydrate diet (precontemplation). To move her to the stage of contemplation, the psychologist would try to explain the connection between diet and diabetes. (She perceives a link, but she still isn't ready to give up her favorite foods.) Further education and support for change (family members are enlisted to help her modify her diet, for instance) may nudge the patient into the stage of preparation (she knows she will diet), and then to action (the patient works hard at dieting). Finally, during the maintenance stage (working to avoid relapse to unhealthy eating habits), she is likely to benefit from interventions that focus on how to maintain the treatment regimen in the face of circumstances that undermine it (such as unusual stress or social pressure to eat unhealthy foods).

Enhancing Communication and Increasing Social Support

Empowering individuals with diabetes (or any chronic illness) to participate actively in decision making in their treatment regimen produces a variety of benefits. Among these are an increased perception of control, enhanced doctor–patient communication, greater confidence in prescribed treatment regimens, and improved compliance. In one classic study, diabetes patients who were taught to be more assertive in acquiring knowledge about the disease and in using that information to negotiate treatment decisions with their physicians showed significant increases in their perceived self-efficacy, regulation of blood glucose, and satisfaction with their treatment regimen (Greenfield, Kaplan, Ware, Yano, & Frank, 1988).

The problems of managing diabetes extend beyond the individual to members of the family, who may react in ways that adversely (or favorably) affect the patient. The quality of marital relationships, for example, is an accurate predictor of diabetes regimen adherence (Trief, Ploutz-Snyder, Britton, & Weinstock, 2004). Among adolescents, elevated family conflict and weak parental monitoring are risk factors for poorer glycemic control (Hilliard and others, 2013). Family therapy is often helpful. Therapy often begins with education about diabetes, what must be done to achieve control, and how the behaviors of family members—including parental monitoring—affect the individual's control. This can be particularly important in the management of T1D in children and adolescents. Parents, for example, may become overly protective of a teenager newly diagnosed with diabetes, unnecessarily restricting activities and promoting a sense of helplessness.

Several studies have found that benefit finding, mentioned earlier in the chapter, is an important resource for adolescents who face heightened stress while dealing with an illness such as diabetes. One study reported that benefit finding was associated with both better adherence to diabetes management behaviors and fewer depressive symptoms among a group of 252 adolescents diagnosed with T1D (Tran, Wiebe, Fortenberry, Butler, & Berg, 2011).

From our biopsychosocial perspective, we have seen that many factors play a role in the development of chronic conditions such as cardiovascular disease and diabetes. Healthy living helps many people avoid or significantly delay the development of chronic conditions. Even those who are already suffering chronic disease still may improve their health by following better health practices, including eating well, exercising, maintaining normal weight, and avoiding tobacco. And physical and psychological coping strategies help many people limit the life disruption of chronic conditions.

Weigh In on Health

Respond to each question below based on what you learned in the chapter. (Tip: Use the items in "Summing Up" to take into account related biological, psychological, and social concerns.)

1. How does hostility influence biological, psychological, and social or cultural aspects of cardiovascular disease risk?

2. A friend, who knows that you are studying health psychology, wants to understand the relationship between practicing health psychology and reducing the risk of diabetes. Based on what you read in this chapter, how will you explain this relationship?

3. Diverse populations have not experienced improvements in health status uniformly. What factors do you think may contribute to health disparities in cardiovascular disease and diabetes among different racial/ethnic, socioeconomic, and cultural groups? What individual actions, programs, or policies could be put in place to reduce these disparities?

Summing Up

The Healthy Heart

1. The cardiovascular system consists of the blood, the blood vessels of the circulatory system, and the heart. The heart consists of three layers of tissue: a thin outer layer, called the *epicardium;* a thin inner layer, called the *endocardium;* and a thicker middle layer, the heart muscle itself, or *myocardium.* The myocardium is separated into four chambers that work in coordinated fashion to bring blood into the heart and then to pump it throughout the body.

Cardiovascular Disease

2. Cardiovascular disease (CVD), which includes coronary heart disease (CHD) and stroke, is the leading cause of death in the United States and most developed countries. CVD results from atherosclerosis, a chronic condition in which coronary arteries are narrowed by fatty deposits and atheromatous plaques that form over microscopic lesions in the walls of blood vessels, and from arteriosclerosis, or hardening of the arteries.

3. When the arteries that supply the heart are narrowed with plaques, restricting blood flow to the heart (ischemia), the person may experience chest pain, called angina pectoris. When severe atherosclerosis or a clot causes a coronary artery to become completely obstructed, a heart attack, or myocardial infarction (MI), occurs, and a portion of the myocardium begins to die. A third possible manifestation

of cardiovascular malfunction is a stroke, which occurs when a blood clot obstructs an artery in the brain.

Risk Factors for Cardiovascular Disease

4. The Framingham Heart Study, the Nurses' Health Study, and the global INTERHEART study identified a number of coronary risk factors. The "uncontrollable risk factors" for CVD include family history of heart disease, age, gender, and ethnicity. The risk of CVD increases with age, is much higher among men than among women, and varies across racial and ethnic groups. Economic and social factors may be the actual causes of racial and ethnic variation in CVD.

5. The major "controllable risk factors" for CVD are hypertension, biological reactivity and inflammation, hemostasis, obesity, elevated serum cholesterol, MetS, and smoking.

6. The relationships among cholesterol, fat consumption, cardiovascular disease, and mortality continue to spark controversy. The recent PURE study found that total fat intake and types of fat (saturated, unsaturated, etc.) were not associated with CVD, myocardial infarction, or CVD mortality.

Psychosocial Factors in Cardiovascular Disease

7. Characterized by a competitive, hurried, hostile nature, the Type A behavior pattern was linked to increased risk of CVD in early research studies. Researchers now point to hostility and anger as key factors in this relationship. Research studies on negative affect and social inhibition have led some researchers to propose a Type D, or *distressed,* personality that may put people at an even greater risk for CVD than Type A behavior does.

8. According to the psychosocial vulnerability model, hostile people have more stressful life events and low levels of social support. The health behavior model proposes that hostile people are more likely to develop cardiovascular disease because they have poorer health habits than less hostile people. The cardiovascular reactivity model maintains that frequent episodes of anger produce elevated cardiovascular and stress hormone responses that damage arteries and contribute to coronary disease.

9. The biopsychosocial model suggests that, for CVD to develop, a hostile person first must have a biological predisposition toward it. CVD then may be more likely to develop because the hostile person's attitude has chased away social support and continues to elicit negative responses from others, which leads to more hostility and damaging cardiac reactivity.

Reducing the Risk of Cardiovascular Disease

10. Lifestyle modifications can significantly reduce a person's risk of cardiovascular disease. Interventions include reducing weight, limiting salt and alcohol intake, increasing exercise, and improving cholesterol ratios. Eating more fiber, fruits, vegetables, grains, and mono- and polyunsaturated fats and less saturated fat can reduce serum cholesterol levels and improve the ratio of HDL cholesterol to LDL cholesterol.

After CVD: Preventing Recurrence

11. Lifestyle modifications and comprehensive interventions such as cognitive-behavior therapy—which combine stress management, exercise, relaxation training, and negative affect reduction—can significantly reduce a person's risk of CVD.

12. Interventions for hostility help people gain control of environmental triggers for their anger and learn to modify their negative emotions and cynical thought processes. Reducing hostility can substantially reduce the risk of future ischemia in cardiac patients.

Diabetes

13. Diabetes mellitus is a chronic disease in which the body is unable to produce or properly use the hormone insulin. Diabetes can develop in childhood (Type 1) or in adulthood (Type 2). Many individuals with diabetes also suffer from psychological disorders, including major depression, anxiety, and eating disorders. Health psychology's role has included studying factors in adjusting to the disease, such as psychological distress, personal coping skills, and social support, as well as factors that affect compliance with treatment regimens.

14. Health psychologists are becoming increasingly involved in the primary care of diabetes by reducing illness intrusiveness, increasing weight control and stress management, enhancing communication, and increasing compliance with complex treatment regimens.

15. Glycemic control, the primary diabetes outcome that self-management interventions are based around, is measured by a blood test that indicates average plasma glucose for the previous two to three months. Diabetes self-management, a prerequisite for tight glycemic control, involves a daily regimen of several behaviors, including healthy eating, physical activity, blood glucose monitoring, foot care, taking medications, problem solving, and active coping.

Key Terms and Concepts to Remember

cardiovascular disease (CVD), p. 313
coronary heart disease (CHD), p. 313
atherosclerosis, p. 313
atheromatous plaques, p. 313
atherogenesis, p. 313
arteriosclerosis, p. 314
angina pectoris, p. 315
myocardial infarction (MI), p. 316

stroke, p. 316
hypertension, p. 317
cardiovascular reactivity (CVR), p. 319
hemostasis, p. 320
metabolic syndrome, p. 322
Type A, p. 323
Type B, p. 323
social inhibition, p. 325

Type D, p. 325
John Henryism (JH), p. 325
benefit finding, p. 332
Type 1 diabetes, p. 334
Type 2 diabetes, p. 334
glycemic control, p. 337
illness intrusiveness, p. 340

 LaunchPad
macmillan learning

To accompany your textbook, you have access to a number of online resources, including quizzes for every chapter of the book, flashcards, critical thinking exercises, videos, and *Check Your Health* inventories. To access these resources, please visit the Straub Health Psychology LaunchPad at **launchpadworks.com**

Chapter 11

Phelan M. Ebenhack/AP Images

Cancer

LEARNING OUTCOMES
Once you have studied this chapter, you will be able to:

- Define cancer and identify several types of cancer,
- Identify major susceptibility factors and risk factors for cancer,
- Describe cancer diagnosis and treatment, and
- Explain various coping strategies used by cancer patients and survivors

"Dad, can we go home now? I don't feel sick, and I don't want to be poked anymore." So said my 6-year-old son, Jeremy, at the end of a very long day in which he was diagnosed with cancer. It was the day my family's world seemed to turn upside down.

It began in a relatively uneventful manner, as childhood health problems often do: soreness and swelling on the left side of Jeremy's neck that seemed to appear overnight and wouldn't go away. An almost-casual visit to the family pediatrician revealed that the discomfort was due to swollen lymph glands, yet it did not seem to be a cause for alarm. Just to be safe, Jeremy was referred to the university's pediatric hospital for a few more tests to rule out any (unlikely) serious health problems. We grew increasingly worried after a morning of blood tests; physical examinations by a stream of nurses, doctors, and interns; and finally magnetic resonance imaging (MRI) of Jeremy's neck. We were ushered into a small waiting room in the pediatric oncology wing of the hospital, where we were stunned by the diagnosis: non-Hodgkin's lymphoma.

Our immediate reaction was disbelief. How? Why? As a health psychologist, I knew there were probably no simple answers to those questions. There had been no warning signs or symptoms. Jeremy had always been a healthy, active kid. He wasn't overweight, he ate a nutritious diet, and, to my mind, he had no known risk factors for cancer (other than several relatives who'd battled skin cancer). Just as our son's life was beginning, it seemed, inexplicably, to be in danger of ending.

Fortunately, we were not defenseless against this disease, which only a few decades earlier would almost certainly have been fatal. We immediately enacted a full biopsychosocial assault, including state-of-the-art biomedical interventions that arrested the cancer, a diet and exercise program tailored to Jeremy's needs, and relaxation training to ease the discomfort of chemotherapy and promote a positive outlook. Jeremy's family, friends, classmates, primary care physician, and especially nurses provided extensive social support, and Jeremy himself showed incredible strength of character—especially for a young child. He was stoic throughout his treatment, which was sometimes painful (as in the needle pokes) and included many nausea-inducing bouts of chemotherapy. But his stoicism was not accompanied by emotional withdrawal. He shared his feelings, fears, and determination to beat the disease with us, and we grew stronger because of his strength. At times, he could even laugh at himself and turn adversity into an apparent asset. When chemotherapy caused his hair to fall out, Jeremy—who remains an ardent *Star Trek: The Next Generation* fan—joked that he looked like a young Captain Picard!

Today, many years later, Jeremy is a healthy adult who graduated from college, went on to earn a PhD in scientific computing, and directs a university laboratory that develops software for small satellites. He travels extensively, pilots his own plane, and credits his survival to early detection, a marvelous health care team, and the powers of mind–body medicine.

While I wouldn't wish this painful chapter of our lives on anyone, our family survived and thrived after bringing Jeremy back to health. We all became more health-conscious . . . and more aware of the interconnections among the physical, psychological, and social aspects of our well-being.

WHAT IS CANCER?

Few of us have avoided the life-changing effects of cancer—either in ourselves or in a loved one. Indeed, **cancer** is the second-leading cause of death globally, where it causes nearly one in six deaths, and many more suffer through nonfatal varieties, as Jeremy did (World Health Organization [WHO], 2018). It is not one disease, but a set of more than 100 related diseases in which abnormal body cells multiply and spread in uncontrolled fashion, forming a tissue mass called a *tumor*.

Not all tumors are cancerous. *Benign* (noncancerous) tumors tend to remain localized and usually do not pose a serious threat to health. In contrast, *malignant* (cancerous) tumors consist of renegade cells that do not respond to the body's genetic controls on growth and division. In addition to growing at the site where they originated (*in situ*), malignant cells often have the ability to migrate and attack, invade, and destroy surrounding body tissues. If this process of **metastasis** is not stopped, body organs and systems will be damaged, and death may result. Although some malignant cells remain

cancer A set of diseases in which abnormal body cells multiply and spread in uncontrolled fashion, often forming a tissue mass called a *tumor*.

metastasis The process by which malignant body cells proliferate in number and spread to surrounding body tissues.

as localized tumors and do not spread automatically, they still pose a threat to health and need to be surgically removed.

In the next section, we examine some of the many risk factors for cancer. Throughout the chapter, we discuss psychosocial risk factors in cancer—especially the significance of stress and negative emotions both as risk factors and as consequences of living with cancer. Then we take a look at medical treatment options, including surgery, radiation, and chemotherapy. Finally, we investigate how people adjust to a diagnosis of cancer, including the nature and effectiveness of interventions designed by health psychologists.

Types of Cancer

Most cancers can be classified as one of four types:

carcinoma Cancer of the epithelial cells that line the outer and inner surfaces of the body; includes breast, prostate, lung, and skin cancer.

- **Carcinomas** attack the *epithelial cells* that line the outer and inner surfaces of the body. Carcinomas are the most common type of cancer; they include cancer of the breast, prostate, colon, lungs, pancreas, and skin. Affecting one out of every five people in the United States, skin cancer is the most common (and most rapidly increasing) type of cancer in America (National Cancer Institute [NCI], 2018f).

sarcoma Cancer that strikes muscles, bones, and cartilage.

- **Sarcomas** are malignancies of cells in muscles, bones, and cartilage. Much rarer than carcinoma, sarcomas account for only about 2% of all cancers in adults.

lymphoma Cancer of the body's lymph system; includes Hodgkin's disease and non-Hodgkin's lymphoma.

- **Lymphomas** are cancers that form in the lymphatic system. Included in this group are *Hodgkin's disease,* a rare form of lymphoma that spreads from a single lymph node; and Jeremy's *non-Hodgkin's lymphoma,* in which malignant cells are found at several sites. An estimated 83,180 people living in the United States will be diagnosed with lymphoma in 2018 (8,500 cases of Hodgkin's lymphoma [NCI, 2018a] and 74,680 cases of non-Hodgkin's lymphoma [NCI, 2018c]).

leukemia Cancer of the blood and blood-producing system.

- **Leukemias** are cancers that attack the blood and blood-forming tissues, such as the bone marrow. Leukemia leads to a proliferation of white blood cells in the bloodstream and bone marrow, which impairs the immune system. Although often considered a childhood disease, leukemia strikes far more adults than children. It is estimated that 60,300 people will be diagnosed with leukemia in 2018 (NCI, 2018b).

A Malignant Tumor Normal and cancerous colon tissue samples.

Cancer Susceptibility: Demographic Aspects

Many individual factors, such as gender, age, and ethnic background, affect susceptibility to cancer. For example, over the course of a lifetime more men (just under one in two) develop cancer than women (just over one in three), but women are more likely to develop any cancer before age 60. Although women are more commonly diagnosed with breast cancer and men with prostate cancer, lung cancer accounts for 25.3% of all cancer deaths (Figure 11.1) (ACS, 2018a).

The strongest risk factor for cancer is advancing age (see Figure 11.2). As is true for many other chronic diseases, the older people become, the greater their chances of developing and dying of cancer. But in the United States, cancer is also the second-leading cause of death (after accidents) among children between 1 and 14 years of age.

Variations in the distribution of cancers by race and ethnicity add to the complexity of cancer's epidemiology. Among men, African Americans have the highest incidence of cancer, followed by European American, Hispanic American, Asian/Pacific Islander, and American Indian/Alaska Native men (Centers for Disease Control and Prevention [CDC], 2017a). Among women, European Americans have the highest rate of cancer incidence, followed by African American, Hispanic American, Asian/Pacific Islander, and American Indian/Alaska Native women. African American men are also more likely to die of cancer than other men, followed by European American, Hispanic American, American

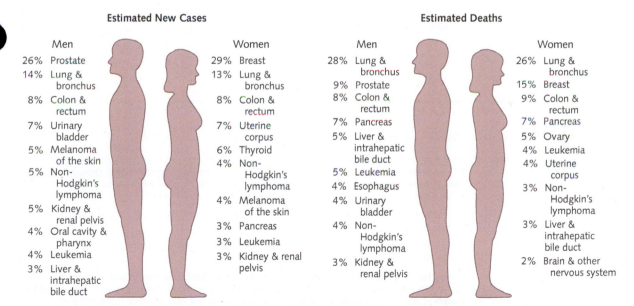

Estimated New Cases				Estimated Deaths			
Men		**Women**		**Men**		**Women**	
26%	Prostate	29%	Breast	28%	Lung & bronchus	26%	Lung & bronchus
14%	Lung & bronchus	13%	Lung & bronchus	9%	Prostate	15%	Breast
8%	Colon & rectum	8%	Colon & rectum	8%	Colon & rectum	9%	Colon & rectum
7%	Urinary bladder	7%	Uterine corpus	7%	Pancreas	7%	Pancreas
5%	Melanoma of the skin	6%	Thyroid	5%	Liver & intrahepatic bile duct	5%	Ovary
5%	Non-Hodgkin's lymphoma	4%	Non-Hodgkin's lymphoma	5%	Leukemia	4%	Leukemia
5%	Kidney & renal pelvis	4%	Melanoma of the skin	4%	Esophagus	4%	Uterine corpus
4%	Oral cavity & pharynx	3%	Pancreas	4%	Urinary bladder	3%	Non-Hodgkin's lymphoma
4%	Leukemia	3%	Leukemia	4%	Non-Hodgkin's lymphoma	3%	Liver & intrahepatic bile duct
3%	Liver & intrahepatic bile duct	3%	Kidney & renal pelvis	3%	Kidney & renal pelvis	2%	Brain & other nervous system

FIGURE 11.1 Estimated New Cancer Cases and Deaths by Type and Gender, 2018   Although the breasts in women and the prostate in men are the leading sites of new cases of cancer (left), lung cancer continues to be the leading cause of cancer deaths in both men and women (right).

Data from: American Cancer Society (ACS). (2018a). *Cancer facts and figures, 2018*. Atlanta, GA: American Cancer Society.

FIGURE 11.2 The Risk of Cancer Increases with Age
Percent of New Cancers by Age Group: All Cancer Sites.

Data from: National Cancer Institute (NCI). (2015a). *Age and cancer risk.*

Indian/Alaska Native, and Asian/Pacific Islander men. Among women, cancer mortality rates are highest for African Americans, followed by European American, American Indian/Alaska Native, and Asian/Pacific Islander women. However, Asian Americans have the lowest cancer incidence and death rates when compared to non-Hispanic Whites, African Americans, Hispanics, and American Indian/Alaska Natives.

As noted in Chapter 1, several variables contribute to ethnic disparities in chronic disease incidence and mortality, and cancer is no exception. Among these variables are socioeconomic status (SES), knowledge about cancer and its treatment, and attitudes toward the disease, which may affect access to health care and adherence to medical advice. For example, compared to other ethnic groups, Latino men have lower rates of participation in prostate cancer screening and less knowledge about risk factors for the disease (Glenn and others, 2012). As another example, although White women are more likely than African American women to develop breast cancer, African American women are more likely to die of the disease. African American women historically have been less likely to obtain mammograms, the most effective means of early detection (American Cancer Society [ACS], 2018b). (Table 11.1 highlights key screening tests that have proven effective in reducing deaths from cancer.)

TABLE 11.1 Screening Tests Shown to Reduce Cancer Deaths

Type of Screening Test	Effectiveness
Colonoscopy, sigmoidoscopy, and high-sensitivity fecal occult blood tests (FOBTs)	These tests reduce deaths from colorectal cancer. Colonoscopy and sigmoidoscopy also help prevent colorectal cancer because they can detect abnormal colon growths (polyps) that can be removed before they develop into cancer. People who are at average risk for colorectal cancer should be screened between 50 and 75 years of age.
Low-dose helical computed tomography (CT)	This test to screen for lung cancer has been shown to reduce lung cancer deaths among heavy smokers.
Mammography	This test reduces mortality from breast cancer disease among women ages 40 to 74, especially those age 50 or older.
Pap test and human papillomavirus (HPV) testing	These tests reduce the incidence of cervical cancer because they allow abnormal cells to be identified and treated before they become cancerous. Testing is recommended to begin at age 21 and to end at age 65, as long as recent results have been normal.
Breast MRI	This imaging test is often used for women who carry a harmful mutation in the BRCA1 gene or the BRCA2 gene; such women have a high risk of breast cancer, as well as increased risk for other cancers.

Information from: National Cancer Institute (NCI). (2016). Screening tests that have been shown to reduce cancer deaths.

Historically, members of ethnic minorities in the United States have also had less access to health insurance and health care facilities and greater distrust of the medical establishment, which they may perceive as insensitive and even racist. This explains why cancer of all types is generally diagnosed in later (usually more serious) stages in racial and ethnic minorities than it is in European Americans (ACS, 2018b).

African American cancer patients are also less likely than their European American counterparts to complete treatment and receive optimal treatment (DeSantis, Naishadham, & Jemal, 2013). This has been partially attributed to the less informative patterns of communication between African American cancer patients and health care providers (HCPs) (Song, Hamilton, & Moore, 2012). During medical visits, HCPs tend to be more verbally dominant, to use less patient-centered communication, and to be less likely to understand the cultural values and beliefs of African American patients. African American patients are often perceived as less effective communicators and are treated more contentiously than other patients, all of which makes them feel that they are treated unfairly and with disrespect by HCPs (Street & Haidet, 2011).

The issue of culturally competent health care extends to other groups (Lu, Zheng, Young, Kagawa-Singer, & Loh, 2012). Despite the fact that an estimated 20 million U.S. residents identify themselves as Asian (Lopez, Ruiz, & Patten, 2017), their quality of life and overall health during cancer survivorship have largely been overlooked (Yoo, Aviv, Levine, Ewing, & Au, 2010). As another example, the few studies that focus on Latinas have demonstrated that Latina cancer patients are less likely than non-Hispanic women to participate in the decision-making process and that they have higher treatment decision regret, greater dissatisfaction with treatment, and poorer quality of life after treatment (Hawley and others, 2008). In addition to facing language barriers, Latinas often interact with HCPs who have limited understanding of Latino culture and who tend to provide more psychosocial support with patients who are more educated and affluent (Yanez, Stanton, & Maly, 2012).

Finally, ethnic differences in diet, tobacco use, and other risk factors for cancer also play a role. For example, American Indian/Alaska Natives (31.8%) and Multiple-Race (non-Hispanics) (25.2%) tend to smoke more than African Americans (16.5%), European Americans (16.6%), and Asian Americans (9.0%) (CDC, 2018a).

RISK FACTORS FOR CANCER

It is interesting to speculate about the number of cancer cases that would arise naturally in a population of otherwise healthy people who completely avoided all **carcinogens** (agents that cause cancer). By one estimate, epidemiologists suggest that less than 25% of all cancers would develop anyway as a result of uncontrollable genetic and biological processes (Lindor, Lindor, & Greene, 2006). In most cases of cancer, behavioral risk factors such as smoking, poor diet, and physical inactivity play the most important role. About 4 out of every 10 cancer cases and cancer deaths in the United States are linked to behavioral risk factors—and thus could be preventable—such as tobacco use, an unhealthy diet, and physical inactivity (Islami and others, 2018). Globally, one third of cancer deaths are due to five behavioral and dietary risks: high body mass index, low fruit and vegetable intake, lack of physical activity, tobacco use, and alcohol use (WHO, 2018).

carcinogen A cancer-causing agent such as tobacco, ultraviolet radiation, or an environmental toxin.

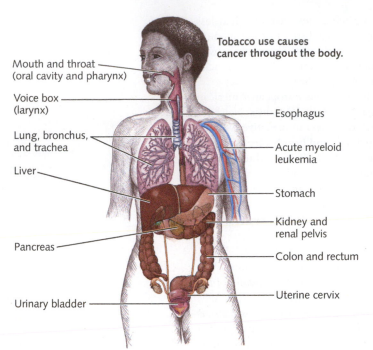

Tobacco use causes cancer througout the body.

Mouth and throat (oral cavity and pharynx)

Voice box (larynx)

Lung, bronchus, and trachea

Liver

Pancreas

Urinary bladder

Esophagus

Acute myeloid leukemia

Stomach

Kidney and renal pelvis

Colon and rectum

Uterine cervix

FIGURE 11.3 12 Different Types of Cancer Associated with Tobacco Use Tobacco use is associated with multiple types of cancer, including cancers of the lungs, mouth, stomach, larynx (voice box), esophagus, pancreas, uterus, cervix, kidney, and bladder.

Information from: Centers for Disease Control and Prevention (CDC). (2018a). *Burden of tobacco use in the U.S.*

consideration of future consequences The extent to which individuals consider and are influenced by the potential future outcomes of their behavior.

As we examine risk factors in this section, it is important to keep in mind that although risk factors increase a person's chance of developing cancer, not every person with those risk factors will develop the disease. Many people with one or more risk factors never develop cancer, whereas others who develop the disease have no known risk factors.

Tobacco Use

As we saw in Chapter 9, smoking is the most preventable cause of death in our society. The American Cancer Society estimates that about one in every five deaths in the United States is caused by tobacco, and most of those tobacco-related deaths were the result of cancer. Tobacco is a lethal carcinogen, and the majority of smoking-related cancer deaths are from lung cancer. Figure 11.3 shows 12 different types of cancer associated with tobacco use, including cancers of the lungs, mouth, stomach, larynx (voice box), esophagus, pancreas, uterus, cervix, kidney, and bladder (CDC, 2018).

Exposure to prosmoking media, such as to point-of-sale displays, magazine advertising, and portrayals of smoking in movies, is one factor that increases smoking in adolescents and young adults. In one study, researchers used ecological momentary assessment (EMA) to examine short-term changes in 135 college students' future smoking risk in response to prosmoking media. The students, who consisted of *never smokers* (never smoked, even a puff) and *ever smokers* (reported any level of past smoking), carried handheld computers for 21 days and recorded their exposures to all forms of prosmoking media. They also responded to random control prompts during each day of the assessment period. After each media exposure event and control prompt, the students answered questions that measured their risk of future smoking. The EMA data showed that all participants reported significantly higher future smoking risk following exposure to prosmoking messages (Shadel, Martino, Setodji, & Scharf, 2012).

These findings are consistent with other data showing that consideration of immediate consequences may be a more important determinant of health behaviors than **consideration of future consequences**, particularly for young people (Adams, 2012). One study of 160 smokers found that a simple intervention that presented feedback regarding expired-air carbon monoxide levels just before and again just after smoking a cigarette increased perceptions of susceptibility to smoking-related illnesses and was associated with a greater intention to quit smoking (Shahab, West, & McNeill, 2011).

We now know that cancer morbidity and mortality reflect smoking patterns of years earlier. Because North American men have been quitting for decades, lung cancer deaths for 55- to 64-year-old males are about half what they were in 1970 (CDC, 2018). Because few women smoked at the start of the twentieth century and because their smoking increased later in the century, lung cancer mortality rates for women doubled during this same time period.

Although cancer mortality is decreasing in most developed nations, including the United States, about one third of adults in Japan, Turkey, and the Netherlands still smoke. In India and China, more than half of all men smoke, and rates of smoking and cancer continue to increase, particularly for women. These trends led the World Health Organization in 2010 to call tobacco "the single largest preventable cause of death and chronic disease in the world" (Blas & Kurup, 2010).

Up to 20% of lung cancer patients who smoked prior to diagnosis continue to do so (see Schnoll and others, 2003, for a review). Continued use of tobacco after a cancer diagnosis increases the risk of recurrence and the development of additional tumors, reduces the effectiveness of chemotherapy and other cancer treatments, and exacerbates the unpleasant side effects of treatment.

Diet

A great deal of research has investigated the possibility that specific foods or macronutrients can increase or decrease cancer risk. The cancers that have been most directly linked to foods are those that affect the cells that line bodily tissues, including those in the lungs, colon, bladder, stomach, rectum, and, to a lesser degree, the uterus, prostate, breasts, and kidneys.

Studies of cancer cells in the laboratory and in animals have provided some evidence that some isolated food components may be carcinogenic, while others seem to have anti-cancer properties. With few exceptions, however, studies of human populations have not definitively demonstrated that any particularly dietary component causes cancer or, for that matter, prevents cancer.

Some retrospective epidemiological studies that have compared people with and without a certain type of cancer have pointed to dietary differences in the two groups. However, results such as these show only that the dietary component is correlated with a difference in cancer risk, not a causal link. Recall from Chapter 2 that when correlational evidence emerges linking a variable (such as a certain food) with a change in disease risk, a randomized trial is needed to test the possibility of a causal relationship. For ethical reasons, however, randomized trials are generally not conducted when there is evidence that a certain dietary component may be associated with a heightened risk of disease.

Charred and Processed Meat

Two food products that do appear to cause cancer are meat that has been cooked, or charred, at high temperatures and meat that has been highly processed. Certain chemicals, called *heterocyclic amines (HCAs)* and *polycyclic aromatic hydrocarbons (PAHs)*, are formed when beef, pork, fish, or poultry are prepared using high-temperature methods, such as pan frying or grilling over an open flame. In many experiments, animals fed a diet supplemented with HCAs have developed tumors of the colon, liver, lung, prostate, breast, and other organs (NCI, 2015b). Rodents fed PAHS also developed cancers, including leukemia and tumors of the gastrointestinal tract and lungs (NCI, 2015b). In addition, a number of prospective epidemiological studies have reported that high consumption of well-done, fried, or barbecued meats is associated with increased risks of colorectal, pancreatic, and prostate cancer (see, for example, Cross and others, 2010).

Numerous research studies have also linked processed meat—such as bacon, hot dogs, and salami—to colorectal cancer. Processed meats are altered through salting,

2/3 vegetables, fruits, whole grains, and or beans

1/3 lean meat

FIGURE 11.4 A Model Plate for Cancer Prevention The American Institute for Cancer Research (AICR) recommends aiming for meals comprising at least two thirds vegetables, fruits, whole grains, and/or beans, and no more than one third animal protein.

Information from: American Institute for Cancer Research (AICR). (2018). *A model plate for a cancer preventive diet.*

curing, fermenting, or smoking. So consistent is the evidence that, after reviewing more than 800 epidemiological studies, the World Health Organization designated processed meats as a *Group 1 carcinogen* (Bouvard and others, 2015). This group of cancer-causing agents also includes asbestos and cigarette smoking. The significance of the ranking is that it means that the evidence linking processed meat to colorectal cancer is as strong as the evidence that links smoking to cancer.

Dietary Recommendations

We often hear that a healthy diet is important for cancer prevention, but exactly what does that mean? The American Institute for Cancer Research (AICR) offers several dietary recommendations that people can follow to help reduce their risk of developing cancer:

- reducing intake of foods and drinks that promote weight gain—namely, foods high in saturated fats and sugary drinks;

- eating mostly plant-based foods;

- limiting intake of red meat, and avoiding processed meat;

- limiting consumption of alcoholic beverages and salt; and

- reducing intake of oat-based, corn-based, wheat-based, and rice-based breakfast cereals—such as Cheerios, Cornflakes, Total, and Rice Krispies—which may contain *ochratoxin*—a potentially cancer-causing by-product of mold.

The AICR's *model plate* for a cancer preventive diet (Figure 11.4) aims for meals that are made up of at least two thirds plant-based foods, and one third (or less) animal protein (American Institute for Cancer Research [AICR], 2018).

Good nutrition is important at all times, including for people who are being treated for cancer. *Nutrition therapy* is used to help cancer patients get the nutrients they need to fight infection and keep up their strength. Good nutrition may benefit people living with cancer in several ways, including providing support for their immune systems, improving tolerance to treatment, and promoting faster recuperation after treatment, all of which may yield a better chance of recovery.

Alcohol Use

Heavy or regular alcohol use increases the risk of developing cancers of the oral cavity, pharynx (throat), larynx (voice box), esophagus, liver, breast, colon, and rectum (NCI, 2015a). The risk of developing cancer increases with the amount of alcohol a person drinks. Women who consume two or more alcohol-containing drinks a day have at least a 25% greater risk of developing breast cancer than women who do not use alcohol (Nurses' Health Study [NHS], 2010). Alcohol-related cirrhosis is a frequent cause of liver cancer and may place the immune system in overdrive, even when no threat (other than excessive alcohol) is present. However, we must be cautious in drawing conclusions about alcohol and immunocompetence. People who abuse alcohol may also suffer from poor nutrition and sleep deprivation and may be exposed to other pathogens that compromise their health.

Physical Activity

A sedentary lifestyle increases the risk of many types of cancer, including colon cancer, breast cancer, endometrial cancer, stomach cancer, pancreatic cancer, lung cancer, and cancers of the head and neck, rectum, and bladder. Thus, physical activity can reduce risks for these cancers (NCI, 2017). American Cancer Society researchers examined 26 cancer types to find out which ones had the biggest link to preventable, behavioral risk factors. Physical inactivity accounted for 26.7% of uterine cancers, 16.3% of colorectal cancers, and 3.9% of female breast cancers (Islami and others, 2018).

Overweight and Obesity

As we saw in Chapter 7, physical activity is important for maintaining a healthy body weight and body mass index, both of which are risk factors for a number of cancers. In 2015, an estimated 40% of adult men and 30% of adult women in the United States were overweight. Almost as many were obese (35% of men and 37% of women) (Yang & Colditz, 2015).

Until recently, the relationship between being overweight and having an increased risk of death (from all causes) remained uncertain. However, the massive NIH–AARP Diet and Health Study monitored the health status of over half a million Americans ages 50 to 71 years, from 1995 through 2005, by using mailed questionnaires and surveying death records. Among nonsmokers, the risk of mortality at age 50 among those who were overweight increased by 20% to 40%. For obese participants, the mortality risk doubled or tripled (NCI, 2010c).

The exact mechanisms by which obesity and being overweight increase cancer risk are not known and may be different for different cancers. Possible mechanisms in obese people include alterations in sex hormones (estrogen, progesterone, and testosterone) as well as in insulin and IGF-1 (a hormone similar to insulin) that may cause increased risk for cancers of the breast, endometrium, and colon (NCI, 2010c). We do know that obesity increases the risk of cancers of the endometrium (the lining of the uterus), colon, kidney, esophagus, pancreas, ovaries, and gallbladder (NCI, 2015c). But, as an example of potential complexities in these relationships, the effect of obesity on the risk of breast cancer has been found to depend on a woman's menopausal status. Before menopause, obese women have a lower risk of developing breast cancer than do women who are not obese. After menopause, obese women have 1.5 times greater risk of developing breast cancer than women who are not obese. The relationship between obesity and breast cancer risk is strongest in women with a large amount of abdominal fat.

Family History

Across all forms of cancer, an estimated 5% to 10% are caused by inherited mutations of genes, with breast, prostate, ovarian, and colorectal cancers being most likely to arise from family history (ACS, 2015b). Still, having a relative with one of these cancers does not automatically mean that one is destined to have that cancer.

Genetic vulnerability can, however, interact with other risk factors to increase an individual's risk. For example, approximately one third of the 175,000 women diagnosed with breast cancer each year in the United States have a family history of the disease.

Evidence comes from the Nurses' Health Study, which found that the daughters of women diagnosed with breast cancer before age 40 were more than twice as likely to develop breast cancer, as compared to women whose mothers had no history of the disease. The daughters of women with breast cancer after age 70 were one and a half times more likely to develop breast cancer. Participants who had a sister with breast cancer were more than twice as likely to develop this cancer themselves; when both mother *and* sister were diagnosed with breast cancer, the risk increased to two and a half times (NHS, 2010).

Families in which breast cancer is inherited typically demonstrate the following characteristics:

- breast cancer in two or more close relatives, such as a mother and two sisters;
- early onset—often before age 50—of breast cancer in family members;
- history of breast cancer in more than one generation;
- cancer in both breasts in one or more family members;
- frequent occurrence of ovarian cancer; and
- Ashkenazi (Eastern and Central European) Jewish ancestry, with a family history of breast and/or ovarian cancer.

Nevertheless, the ACS (2015b) advises that only a small percentage of breast cancer cases are directly inherited. The vast majority (nearly 95%) are linked to a combination of genetic and nongenetic risk factors. Nongenetic risk factors include obesity, younger age at menarche (first menstruation), lack of exercise, smoking, poor diet, use of oral contraceptives, the presence of other diseases of the breast, radiation exposure, and use of alcohol.

Environmental and Occupational Hazards

The degree of cancer hazard posed by environmental toxins depends on the concentration of the carcinogen and the amount of exposure to the toxin. However, even low-dose exposure can represent a significant public health hazard when a large segment of the population is involved.

Toxic Chemicals

Various chemicals are clearly carcinogenic, including asbestos, vinyl chloride, and arsenic. In addition, some researchers believe that exposure to chlorine-containing compounds found in some household cleaning and pest-control products may increase the risk of breast cancer and, possibly, other hormone-related cancers. Although the popular media have focused on the dangers of pesticides, the very low concentrations found in some foods are generally well within established safety levels and pose minimal risks.

Environmental toxins in the air, soil, and water are estimated to contribute to about 2% of fatal cancers, mainly of the bladder and the lungs. Although long-term exposure to high levels of air pollution—including second-hand smoke generated by smokers—may increase the risk of lung cancer by as much as 50%, this pales in comparison to the 2000% increased risk caused by heavy smoking itself.

Although a few studies have linked water chlorinating and fluoridation with bladder cancer, most experts believe that the potential health risk is small and is outweighed by the greater danger of the spread of diseases such as cholera and typhoid fever by germs in unchlorinated water. Moreover, fluoride in drinking water is an effective agent in preventing tooth decay (NCI, 2010a).

Ultraviolet Radiation

Beginning in the 1950s and 1960s, a well-tanned complexion became fashionable. However, we now know that a serious long-term effect of sun exposure is skin cancer. In those earlier decades, when skin-protective sunscreens were generally unknown, sunbathing was especially risky. Is it any wonder that one in every five Americans will develop skin cancer (ACS, 2015c)? An estimated 73,870 new cases of invasive melanoma were diagnosed in 2015 (ACS, 2015c).

High-frequency radiation, ionizing radiation (IR), and ultraviolet (UV) radiation are proven carcinogens. Ultraviolet B rays, which can damage DNA, cause more than 90% of all skin cancers, including **melanoma**, a potentially deadly form of cancer that forms in skin cells. For over 30 years, the incidence rate of melanoma has been increasing in the United States (ACS, 2018d). American Cancer Society researchers estimate that UV radiation exposure accounts for more than 90% of melanomas of the skin in the United States (Islami and others, 2018). The rise in melanoma cases can be attributed to three factors:

melanoma A potentially deadly form of cancer that strikes the melatonin-containing cells of the skin.

- the overall frequency of sunburns during childhood;
- the thinning of the earth's ozone layer, which filters skin-damaging UV radiation; and
- the increase in suntanning and use of tanning booths, which has exposed people to greater amounts of UV radiation. In 2014, UV tanning devices were reclassified by the Food and Drug Administration from Class 1 (low to moderate risk) to Class II (moderate to high risk) devices (Ogden, 2015).

Suntans Are Unhealthy
Ultraviolet radiation, whether from the sun or the tanning booth, injures the skin and ages it prematurely (a 20-year-old who tans frequently may look 10 years older). In addition, frequent tanning may contribute to skin cancer.

Given the evidence that the sun's UV rays can cause cancer, why do so many people continue to bask in the sun? In one classic study, researchers interviewed sunbathers at California beaches about their decision to lie in the sun (Keesling & Friedman, 1987). Those with the deepest tans (who also reported spending the largest amounts of time in the sun) were least knowledgeable about skin cancer. They also were more relaxed, more sensitive to the influence of peers who valued a good tan, more likely to take other risks, and more focused on their appearance. A more recent study of Australian teenagers reported that people with "medium" tans were perceived as healthier and more attractive than people with no tan (Broadstock, Borland, & Gason, 2006). Interestingly, this has not always been so. The tanning business skyrocketed in the 1990s, mostly in Western cultures. In some other parts of the world, fair skin remains the standard of beauty.

Another factor in why people tan appears to be a hopeful belief that their risk of skin cancer is minimal. In one study, 211 sixth-, seventh-, and eighth-grade students were shown pictures of either tanned or fair-skinned models and then responded to a questionnaire that included an assessment of their *comparative optimism*

Stockbyte/Getty Images

Your Health Assets

What Is Your Risk of Developing Skin Cancer?

Most experts agree that the following things affect a person's risk of melanoma. Which of them apply to you?

- Older age
- Light or fair physical features
- Childhood sunburns
- Immunosuppressive medications
- Family history

Age As with most cancers, the risk of melanoma goes up with age. However, melanoma tends to develop earlier in life than many other cancers. The average age at diagnosis is 57.

Physical Features People who have fair skin and naturally light-colored hair and eyes have a higher risk of melanoma. This is because people with these features often have lower levels of pigment in their skin and are more likely to get sunburned. Pigment gives skin its color. Higher levels of pigment make skin darker and help protect it from the sun. People with many moles on their skin also have a higher risk of melanoma than do people with fewer moles.

Sunburn People who had repeated, severe sunburns as children have a higher risk of melanoma. Radiation from the sun can cause abnormal changes in skin cells that develop into cancer later in life. Sun damage in adulthood also increases the risk of skin cancer.

Immunosuppressive Medications People who have taken immunosuppressive medication have a higher risk of melanoma. Immunosuppressive medications are very important in the treatment of many medical conditions. However, they can interfere with the body's ability to respond to abnormal cell changes, which increases the risk of abnormal cell growth and cancer.

Family History People who have a mother, father, brother, or sister with melanoma have a higher risk of developing skin cancer. This is because some cases of melanoma are linked to mutations in the DNA of body cells that can be passed from generation to generation.

Information from: Siteman Cancer Center. (2015). *Your disease risk*. St. Louis, MO: Washington University School of Medicine.

---

comparative optimism The tendency to think that one will experience more positive and fewer negative events than others do.

regarding skin cancer later in life. **Comparative optimism** for a negative event refers to the tendency for people to believe that their personal risk is lower than that of their peers (Harris, Griffin, & Murray, 2008). For some individuals (those who avoid tanning), this belief may be accurate for certain health outcomes (such as skin cancer) because these people are in fact at a lower risk than their peers (people who do not avoid tanning). To gauge your risk and possibly make a decision about your sun exposure, see *Your Health Assets: What Is Your Risk of Developing Skin Cancer?*

Occupational Carcinogens and Pollution

People whose work involves exposure to certain chemicals have long been known to be at greater risk of developing cancer than others. *Occupational cancers* mostly affect the lungs, skin, bladder, and blood-forming systems of the body (National Institute for Occupational Safety and Health [NIOSH], 2015). For example, those who work with asbestos, chromium, and chromium compounds are much more likely than other workers to develop lung cancer. Workers exposed to benzene, a solvent used in making varnishes and dyes, are at high risk for developing leukemia.

Other substances now known to be carcinogenic include diesel exhaust and radon. In recent years, however, strict control measures in the workplace (at least in the developed world) have reduced the proportion of cancer deaths caused by job-related carcinogens to less than 5%. Unfortunately, such control measures generally lag behind the pace of industrialization in developing countries, where job-related cancers are still likely to increase.

Cancer and Infectious Disease

An estimated 15% to 20% of new cancers worldwide each year are attributable to infection (ACS, 2015a). This percentage is higher in developing countries where certain infections are more prevalent. Cancer-causing infections, such as hepatitis and human papilloma virus (HPV), cause 25% of cancer cases in low- and middle-income countries (WHO, 2018). HPVs are the main causes of cervical cancer, and they also contribute to some cancers of the mouth and throat. All types of HPV are spread by contact. More than 40 types of HPV can be spread through sexual contact. Hepatitis B virus and hepatitis C virus cause viral hepatitis, which is a type of liver infection that increases a person's chance of developing liver cancer.

Bacterial infections can also cause cancer. For example, long-term infection of the stomach with *Helicobacter pylori* (*H. pylori*) can damage the inner layer of the stomach and lead to cancer over time. About two in three adults worldwide are infected with *H. pylori,* with the rate of infection being higher in developing countries and in older age groups. *H. pylori* is spread in several ways, including fecal–oral contact, such as through water contaminated with human waste.

Infections can increase a person's risk of developing cancer in at least three ways:

- Some viruses can insert their own genes into healthy cells, causing them to grow out of control.
- Some infections trigger chronic inflammation in a part of the body, leading to changes in affected cells that can lead to cancer.
- Some infections can suppress the immune system and reduce its ability to protect the body from cancer.

Even though some bacterial and viral infections increase the risk of certain types of cancer, most people with these infections do not develop cancer. Infection with *H. pylori,* for example, may increase your risk of stomach cancer, but whether you smoke, what you eat, and other factors are also important factors.

Stress and Immunocompetence

With advances in *psychoneuroimmunology (PNI),* researchers are paying more attention to psychological risk factors—in particular, the role of stress—in the development of cancer. In Chapter 4, we saw how PNI researchers study the relationships among the mind, the body, and immunity. **Immunocompetence**—our immune system's ability to mount an effective defense against disease and harmful foreign agents—depends on many factors, including our overall health, the nature of the health-threatening disease or foreign agent, and perceived stress.

immunocompetence The overall ability of the immune system, at any given time, to defend the body against the harmful effects of foreign agents.

immune surveillance theory The theory that cells of the immune system play a monitoring function in searching for and destroying abnormal cells such as those that form tumors.

How might perceived stress promote the development of cancer? According to the **immune surveillance theory**, cancer cells, which develop spontaneously in the body, are prevented from spreading and developing into tumors by natural killer (NK) cells and other agents of the immune system. However, when the immune system is overwhelmed by the number of cancer cells or weakened by stress or some other factor, the immune system's surveillance is suppressed, and cancer may develop.

Although the *immunosuppression model* dominated the thinking of PNI researchers for years and continues to be influential, the concept of broad decreases in immunity does not make sense to some researchers as a species' response to all stressors. They reason that if the stress-immune response did indeed evolve, a healthy person should not be adversely affected when it is triggered because this would be maladaptive; natural selection would have selected against this over the course of evolution. Indeed, studies done over the past 40 years, examining the relationship between stress and cancer risk, have produced conflicting results (Segerstrom & Miller, 2004). Some studies have reported an indirect relationship between stress and certain types of virus-related cancers, such as Kaposi's sarcoma and some lymphomas (NCI, 2010b). And although many studies have demonstrated that stress can affect neuroendocrine function and immune function adversely, the clinical significance of these changes for cancer patients is not clear (Luecken & Compas, 2002). One reason for the inconsistency in results in the examination of cancer risk is that it is difficult to separate stress from other factors such as smoking, using alcohol, becoming overweight, and even growing older.

To address this problem, the *biphasic model* proposes that only the most chronic stressors cause global immunosuppression. Short-term stressors that trigger our fight-or-flight response either have no effect on immunity or might actually *enhance* immunity to help prepare us to defend against possible infection or injury (Dhabhar & McEwen, 2001; Segerstrom & Miller, 2004). Examples of acute stressors that enhance natural immunity include challenging computer tasks, mental arithmetic, and loud noises. In contrast, chronic stressors such as bereavement, long-term caregiving, and suffering a traumatic injury produce global suppression of most measures of immune function.

Childhood Adversity

Childhood adversity has been associated with greater emotional and physiological sensitivity to stress (McLaughlin and others, 2010). For example, individuals who experienced adversity as children are more likely to report difficulties when they encounter stressors in adulthood than those who did not have these experiences earlier in life (Fagundes, Glaser, Malarkey, & Kiecolt-Glaser, 2013). They also have more pronounced cortisol and autonomic responses to stress (Heim, Newport, Mletzko, Miller, & Nemeroff, 2008). Stressful early-life events also may disrupt cellular immune function. One study found that adolescents who were abused or institutionalized had higher antibody responses to the herpes simplex virus, reflecting poorer cellular immune system control compared to those who did not experience these adversities (Shirtcliff, Coe, & Pollak, 2009). Another found that children growing up in poverty had elevated cytomegalovirus (CMV) antibody titers compared to those from higher-income families (Dowd, Palermo, & Aiello, 2012). These studies suggest that childhood adversity may have an impact on whether cancer develops later in life.

Childhood stressors also may promote long-term immune system dysregulation. In addition, childhood adversity seems to heighten the impact of later-life caregiving stress, being associated with elevated inflammation, shorter telomere length, and poorer localized immune response to tumors (Kiecolt-Glaser and others, 2011). A recent study found that breast cancer survivors who had experienced more adversities as children had higher Epstein-Barr virus and CMV antibody titers, as well as more depressive symptoms and poorer sleep quality, than those with fewer childhood adversities (Fagundes and others, 2013).

Depression: Both Risk and Result

Depression reduces a person's overall quality of life and subjective well-being, and it can also adversely affect physical health (Wang, Cai, Qian, & Peng, 2014). As such, depression can contribute to an individual's susceptibility to cancer. And a cancer diagnosis and cancer treatments can themselves cause depression. In fact, periodic or long-term clinical depression is relatively common among people adjusting to cancer, with estimated prevalence rates ranging between 13% and 40% (Walker and others, 2013).

Many of the symptoms of cancer, as well as the side effects of cancer treatment, have similarities to symptoms of depression: disturbances of sleep and appetite, fatigue, concentration difficulties, and pain. Further, these may be aggravated by stress hormones such as cortisol (Thornton, Andersen, & Blakely, 2010).

Cancer patients who are members of ethnic minorities may also be at increased risk for depression. One meta-analysis of 21 studies reported that Hispanic cancer patients in the United States had significantly higher levels of distress, depressive symptoms, and lower health-related quality of life than European American cancer patients (Luckett and others, 2011). Similar findings were obtained from a sample of Afro-Caribbean and Latino immigrant cancer patients (Costas & Gany, 2013).

Depression has also been linked to a higher risk of early death among people with cancer. One review of 76 prospective studies reported that a diagnosis of clinical depression and higher levels of depressive symptoms before or after cancer diagnosis were associated with elevated cancer-related mortality (Pinquart and Duberstein, 2010). Patients who are depressed may be less likely to adhere to recommended preventive screening procedures, cancer treatments, and other recommendations for maintaining their health. For instance, depressed patients may be less likely to exercise, may be more likely to smoke or drink alcohol to excess, and may skip medication regimens or miss therapy appointments.

Results such as these strongly suggest that screening for depression should be a routine part of cancer treatment. In addition, these findings raise the question of whether effective treatment for depression could not only enhance quality of life, but also extend survival among cancer patients.

CANCER TREATMENT

When cancer does develop, early detection and treatment can prevent death and perhaps reduce overall treatment time. Unfortunately, however, access to effective diagnosis and treatment is often limited or nonexistent for patients who live in low- and middle-income countries. In 2017, only 26% of low-income countries reported having cancer diagnosis and treatment services that are found in more than 90% of high-income countries such as the United States and Canada (WHO, 2018).

Early Diagnosis

Cancer develops over time, as neoplastic cells grow into tumors that may metastasize to surrounding tissues. Detecting this process early on, before malignant cells have gained a strong foothold, can dramatically improve a person's chances of survival (Table 11.2). Yet, even in the United States, the number of people who follow recommended screening schedules for cancer of the prostate, breasts, colon, rectum, and cervix is relatively low (Table 11.3). A growing body of health psychology research demonstrates that the perception of risk and feelings of vulnerability ("I'd rather not know!") are key reasons why people fail to follow recommended screening schedules (Fagerlin and others, 2010). These feelings and risk perception can be influenced by tailored educational interventions (Dillard, Ferrer, Ubel, & Fagerlin, 2012).

TABLE 11.2 Five-Year Relative Survival Rates (%) by Stage at Diagnosis

Five-year relative survival rates are commonly used to monitor progress in the early detection and treatment of cancer. This data includes all survivors, whether in remission, disease-free, or under treatment. The term *localized* refers to a malignant tumor confined entirely to the organ of origin. *Regional* refers to a malignant tumor that has extended beyond the limits of the organ of origin into the surrounding organs or tissues and/or involves regional lymph nodes by way of the lymphatic system. *Distant* refers to a malignant cancer that has spread to parts of the body remote from the primary tumor—either by direct extension or by metastasis, or via the lymphatic system to distant lymph nodes. The earlier the detection, the greater the likelihood that the tumor will be localized; thus, survival increases markedly the earlier the cancer is diagnosed.

	All stages	Local	Regional	Distant		All stages	Local	Regional	Distant
Breast (female)	90%	99%	85%	27%	Oral cavity & pharynx	65%	84%	64%	39%
Colon & rectum	65%	90%	71%	14%	Ovary	47%	93%	73%	29%
Colon	64%	91%	72%	14%	Pancreas	8%	32%	12%	3%
Rectum	67%	88%	70%	15%	Prostate	99%	>99%	>99%	30%
Esophagus	19%	43%	23%	5%	Stomach	31%	67%	31%	5%
Kidney	74%	93%	67%	12%	Testis	95%	99%	96%	73%
Larynx	61%	77%	45%	34%	Thyroid	98%	>99%	98%	56%
Liver	18%	31%	11%	3%	Urinary bladder	77%	70%	35%	5%
Lung & bronchus	18%	56%	29%	5%	Uterine cervix	67%	92%	57%	17%
Melanoma of the skin	92%	99%	63%	20%	Uterine corpus	81%	95%	69%	16%

Data from: American Cancer Society (ACS) (2018a). *Cancer facts & figures, 2018.* Table 8, page 21. Atlanta, GA: American Cancer Society.

TABLE 11.3 Prevalence of Cancer Screening among Five Racial and Ethnic Groups

Cancer Screening	European American	African American	Hispanic American	Native American	Asian/Pacific Islander
Prostate test (protoscopy) within the past five years	30.4%	28.2%	22.4%	27.6%	California*: 24.3%; Hawaii*: 40.7%
Colorectal test	18.2%	20.3%	14.2%	12.3%	California*: 2.6%; Hawaii*: 23.8%
Mammogram within the past two years	73.7%	76.1%	63.5%	Alaska*: 93.5% Hawaii*: 80.7%	
Cervical/uterine test within the past three years	84.7%	91.1%	80.9%	90.5%	Hawaii*: 84.2%

*Indicates state-specific prevalence estimates available for the corresponding race/ethnic group.

Data from: Centers for Disease Control and Prevention (CDC). (2016a). *Behavioral risk factor surveillance system: Summary data quality report (rev.).* National Center for Chronic Disease Prevention and Health Promotion.

For individuals with family histories of cancer, genetic screening has become a useful method of early detection. A simple blood test can detect genetic mutations linked to an increased risk of many types of cancer. Such tests, however, have raised a host of ethical and practical questions. On the practical side, many laboratories administering these tests do not follow the (admittedly vague and inadequate) regulatory controls that help ensure the validity of genetic tests. And some labs market tests to physicians, obstetricians, and primary care providers who lack expertise in medical genetics.

The more significant problem has to do with the ethics of genetic testing and the knowledge that it provides—about cancer and many other illnesses and conditions. The ability to predict someone's genetic future raises a host of psychosocial concerns, both for the individual being tested and for other family members who might be at risk. If your genes predisposed you to develop cancer, would you want to know? What would you do in response? Providing people with a diagnosis of a life-threatening disease raises concerns, especially when dealing with children who may not fully understand the implications of the tests. Others fear that children identified as carriers of serious diseases will be discriminated against. A related concern is the real possibility that insurance companies will deny coverage to individuals who have a predisposition toward developing a particular disease. An important goal of the Affordable Care Act was to prevent this by requiring insurance companies to cover people with preexisting conditions.

Detecting Skin Cancer Most important in the treatment of cancer is early detection. Here, a health care provider examines a blemish on a patient's back. An unusual sore, lump, marking, or change in the way that an area of skin looks or feels may be a sign of skin cancer or a warning that cancer might occur there.

Treatment Options

Until recent decades, the treatment options for most forms of cancer were severely limited, and cancer was often a death sentence. Today, there are many effective treatment options that have reduced death rates from most types of cancer. These options include surgery, chemotherapy, radiation therapy, hormone therapy, adoptive T-cell and gene therapy, and combination regimens, such as those involving both bone marrow transplantation and radiation therapy. In 2017 alone, the FDA approved a record 18 new cancer therapies (American Society of Clinical Oncology [ASCO], 2018).

Surgery

Surgery is the oldest form of cancer treatment, and it generally offers the greatest chance of cure for most types of cancer. Surgery is usually recommended to achieve one or more of the following goals:

- *Diagnostic* surgery is used to obtain a tissue sample for laboratory testing to confirm a diagnosis and identify the specific cancer. A procedure to remove all or part of a tumor for diagnostic tests is called a *biopsy.*

- *Preventive* surgery is performed to remove a growth that is not presently malignant but is likely to become so if left untreated. Sometimes, preventive surgery is used to remove an organ when a person has an inherited condition that makes development of a cancer likely.

- *Staging* surgery is used to determine the extent of disease. In *laparoscopy,* for example, a tube is passed through a tiny incision in the abdomen to examine the abdomen's contents and remove tissue samples.

- *Curative* surgery involves the removal of a tumor when the tumor appears to be localized and there is hope of taking out all of the cancerous tissue.

- *Restorative* (or reconstructive) surgery is used to restore a person's appearance or the function of an organ or body part. Examples include breast reconstruction after mastectomy and the use of bone grafts or *prosthetic* (metal or plastic) bone or joint replacements after surgical treatment of bone cancer.

Chemotherapy

Unlike surgery, which can destroy or damage cancer cells in a specific area, *chemotherapy*—medicines to treat cancer—can destroy cancer cells that have spread, or metastasized, to parts of the body far from the original, or primary, tumor. These *systemic drugs* travel through the bloodstream to reach all areas of the body.

Depending on the type of cancer and its stage of development, chemotherapy can be used to cure cancer, to keep the cancer from spreading, to slow the cancer's growth, to kill cancer cells that may have spread from the original tumor to other parts of the body, or to relieve symptoms caused by the cancer. In one of the newest forms of chemotherapy, **immunotherapy**, medications are used to enhance the immune system's ability to selectively target cancer cells.

immunotherapy Chemotherapy in which medications are used to support or enhance the immune system's ability to selectively target cancer cells.

Anticancer chemotherapy drugs are made to kill fast-growing cells; however, because these drugs travel throughout the body, they can also affect normal, healthy cells. The normal cells most likely to be affected are blood cells that form in the bone marrow and cells in the digestive tract, reproductive system, and hair follicles (which is why my son, Jeremy, temporarily lost his hair). Some anticancer drugs also can damage cells of the heart, kidneys, bladder, lungs, and nervous system.

The most common side effects of chemotherapy are nausea and vomiting, hair loss, and fatigue. Less common side effects include bleeding, infections, and anemia. Although side effects are not always as bad as expected, their reputation makes chemotherapy an anxiety-provoking treatment.

Radiation Therapy

All cells, cancerous and healthy, grow and divide. But cancer cells grow and divide more rapidly than many of the normal cells around them. Radiation therapy delivers high doses of x-rays, gamma rays, or alpha and beta particles to cancerous tumors, killing or damaging them so that they cannot grow, multiply, or spread. Although some normal cells may be affected by radiation, most of these appear to repair themselves and recover fully after the treatment. Unlike chemotherapy, which exposes the entire body to cancer-fighting chemicals, radiation therapy is usually targeted to only the tumor and surrounding area.

Radiation therapy is the preferred treatment for cancer in almost any part of the body, including head and neck tumors; early-stage Hodgkin's disease; non-Hodgkin's lymphomas; and cancers of the lungs, breasts, cervix, prostate, testes, bladder, thyroid, and brain. Radiation therapy also can be used to shrink a tumor prior to surgery (so that it can be removed more easily) or after surgery to stop the growth of any cancer cells that remain.

Like chemotherapy, radiation is often associated with side effects, including temporary or permanent loss of hair in the area being treated, fatigue, loss of appetite, skin rashes, and loss of white blood cells. On the positive side, thousands of people have become cancer-free after receiving radiation treatments alone or in combination with surgery or chemotherapy.

Complementary and Alternative Treatments

When Apple Computer Company founder Steve Jobs was diagnosed with pancreatic cancer, which has a low survival rate for conventional medical treatments, he initially refused his doctor's recommendation for surgery and tried a vegan diet, acupuncture, and herbal remedies (Isaacson, 2011). Other nontraditional treatment modalities used by some cancer patients include aromatherapy, biofeedback, meditation, music therapy, prayer and spiritual practices, yoga, tai chi (an exercise-based form of "moving meditation"), art therapy, massage therapy, and herbal treatments (see Chapter 15).

Although these kinds of alternative therapies are generally unproven and have not been scientifically tested, many *can* be used safely as a complement to standard biomedical treatment, as they often help relieve symptoms or side effects, ease pain, and improve a patient's overall quality of life.

Courtesy of KIDSCOPE; Concept by Mitchell McGough

When child psychologist Elizabeth King was diagnosed with cancer, her son created a story and illustration about a character named "Kemo Shark," who swam around in his mother's body eating cancer cells (and sometimes healthy ones by mistake, which caused her to feel sick). When King completed her treatment, she developed her son's story into a children's comic book and funded the nonprofit organization KIDSCOPE to raise money to distribute the book at no cost.

BSIP SA/Alamy Stock Photo

Alternative therapies—like relational touch, shown here—can be used as a complement to standard biomedical treatment, as they often help to improve a patient's overall quality of life.

COPING WITH CANCER

Life-threatening chronic diseases such as cancer create unique stresses for both victims and their families. Cancer is a dreaded disease, which most people realize can be intensely painful and lead to disability, disfigurement, or death. An estimated 20% to 40% of all cancer patients report elevated levels of affective distress (Holland & Alici, 2010;

Hart & Charles, 2013). At diagnosis, during treatment, and even years after treatment, people with a history of cancer often report higher levels of anxiety, anger, hostility, and depression than do their nonaffected same-age peers (Hinz and others, 2010). However, this varies with the age of the individual. Older age generally is associated with less distress among both cancer patients and cancer survivors (Brant and others, 2011). Importantly, although the numbers and types of stressful events that cancer survivors experience seem similar to those experienced by the general population, some studies show that cancer survivors may perceive stressors as somewhat more severe and disruptive, particularly when the stressors involve interpersonal tension (Costanzo, Stawski, Ryff, Coe, & Almeida, 2012).

Health Psychology and Coping

As patients' expectations of survival have increased in recent years, so has the need for psychosocial supports aimed at restoring or maintaining quality of life. Health psychologists are helping focus attention and resources on enabling patients and their families to cope with the adverse effects of cancer treatment. They also are helping health care professionals recognize that the course of adjustment to cancer is not the same for all patients.

Research on the emotional and behavioral responses of cancer patients who undergo surgery consistently shows high levels of anxiety both before and after the operation. Compared with patients who are having surgery for benign conditions, cancer surgery patients have higher overall levels of distress and slower rates of emotional recovery. In one study, breast cancer patients' presurgery expectations were significant predictors of their *postsurgery* pain, fatigue, and nausea (Montgomery, 2004).

Even when cancer treatment is successful and the disease is in remission, the fear, stress, and uncertainty do not go away. The threat of recurrence looms, for some patients for the rest of their lives. In fact, the distress associated with cancer recurrence is often greater than that following the initial diagnosis (Vickberg, 2003). The words of one breast cancer survivor poignantly illustrate this anxiety:

> This is what cancer is about to me, living with possible recurrence. Cancer is not about two months of treatment and a couple of minor surgeries. … I think the hardest thing for women like me who have found their cancers early and kept their breasts is to believe we are going to get away with all this. Am I really going to be OK? (Vickberg, 2003)

Feelings such as these argue for educating cancer patients about what's normal following treatment and for improving the quality of life of cancer patients. Unfortunately, many health insurance providers do not distinguish between mental illness and psychosocial interventions for cancer patients. As a result, many patients find that psychological healing is not covered by their health insurance.

Emotions, Masculinity, and Ethnicity

Health psychologists are paying increasing attention to the experiences and coping techniques of ethnically diverse samples of people following the diagnosis of cancer, as well as those of men and of people who vary in their ability to regulate emotions.

Emotions and Coping

Although the link between personality traits and the development of cancer is tenuous, some personality factors do predict how well a person copes with cancer. For instance, expression of both positive and negative emotions can be beneficial in adjusting to a diagnosis of cancer (Quartana, Laubmeier, & Zakowski, 2006). In a sense, then, emotion-focused coping and denial of the diagnosis may be *positive* traits for cancer victims.

Some researchers have found that an optimistic disposition at the time the cancer is diagnosed is associated with an active, engaged coping style and less psychological distress over time (Carver and others, 2005). However, the relationship between optimism and long-term outcome in cancer patients remains unclear (Segerstrom, 2007), perhaps because optimists may have more difficulty adjusting to disappointing outcomes than those who are less optimistic but more realistic (Winterling, Glimelius, & Nordin, 2008). Similarly, while research studies have shown that maintaining a "fighting spirit" predicts better adjustment in early-stage cancer (O'Brien & Moorey, 2010), the evidence for its long-term benefits is questionable (Hoffman, 2015; Coyne & Tennen, 2010).

More generally, a growing body of research indicates that emotional regulation is critical to coping with traumatic events such as a diagnosis of cancer (Chuah, 2006). People who are good at identifying and articulating emotions, therefore, might be expected to fare better at coping with traumatic events than people who lack these skills. One dispositional characteristic that psychologists have focused on is *emotional intelligence (EI)*, defined as the ability to perceive, understand, express, and regulate emotions accurately (Mayer, Salovey, Caruson, & Sitarenios, 2001).

In one study, John Schmidt and Michael Andrykowski (2004) investigated the relationships among several social and dispositional variables and adjustment to breast cancer among 302 members of five Internet-based breast cancer support groups. In all cases, women who scored higher on a 30-item dispositional measure of EI reported less anxiety, depression, and overall distress than women who scored lower on the dispositional measure for EI. The beneficial effects of EI were especially pronounced among participants who perceived weaker social support and more social constraints that discouraged them from sharing their thoughts and feelings regarding their cancer. The researchers suggest that the presence of social constraints and absence of social support may have caused the women to actively avoid thinking about their cancer experience, thus inhibiting active processing and coping. Women who score low in EI may be less able to identify, communicate, and control their emotions effectively; thus, they "may be seen as irrational, demanding, or aversive" by others around them, who then respond in a manner that further discourages discussion (Schmidt & Andrykowski, 2004, p. 264). Those who have low EI also might be less effective in eliciting social support from others and less capable of recognizing and responding to supportive responses that others may make.

Cancer and Masculinity

Higher levels of aspects of masculinity, gender role conflict, and gender-linked personality characteristics are related to poorer outcomes in men with cancer. Consider men being treated for cancer of the prostate, a male organ which plays important roles in sexual and

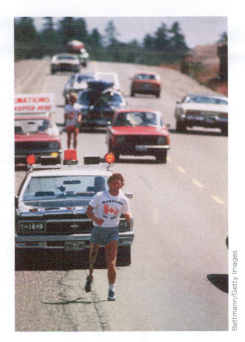

Bettmann/Getty Images

True "Fighting Spirit"
Canadian Terry Fox's refusal to be defeated by cancer has inspired several generations. In this photo, Terry, who lost his right leg to cancer, runs along a highway just before reaching the halfway mark in his cross-Canada run. Terry ran coast to coast on an artificial limb—often as far as a 26-mile marathon each day—to raise money to fight the killer disease. The annual "Terry Fox Run," first held shortly after his 1981 death, has grown in size to involve millions of participants in over 60 countries. It is the world's largest one-day fundraiser for cancer research.

urinary function. For men, prostate cancer is the most common cancer and the second leading cause of cancer death, accounting for an estimated 9.5% of all new cancer cases and 4.8% of all cancer deaths among men in the United States in 2018 (NCI, 2018d).

Common symptoms associated with prostate cancer treatment—such as erectile dysfunction, loss of libido, pain, fatigue, and feelings of vulnerability and fear—are linked to traditional gender role expectations and threatened masculine self-image (Storey and others, 2011). Prostate cancer patients often describe difficulties maintaining their social and family role functions, and they often report experiencing bodily changes that cause embarrassment, frustration, and feelings of weakness.

Aware of such concerns, researchers have developed a questionnaire to measure *cancer-related masculine threat (CMT)* in prostate cancer patients. Consisting of statements such as "Cancer makes me feel like less of a man," "Cancer makes me feel inferior to other men," and "Cancer is taking away my masculinity," the CMT questionnaire was used in a longitudinal study of 66 men who underwent radical prostatectomy and/or radiation therapy for prostate cancer. After controlling for baseline health and age, the researchers found that men who scored high in CMT had poorer prostate-related functioning over time, including sexual, urinary, and bowel functioning. Men with higher CMT were also less likely to process their cancer-related emotions and more likely to engage in rumination and other less constructive forms of emotional processing (Hoyt, Stanton, Irwin, & Thomas, 2013).

Many men who are coping with cancer treatment are particularly concerned about its effect on their ability to fulfill work-related roles. One qualitative study of 50 prostate cancer survivors, conducted during a semistructured interview following completion of their treatment, revealed several common themes. The first theme concerned the importance of work to the survivors' self-identity. Consider the following comments from one 52-year-old survivor:

> The only way I know how to live my life is if I work and my work is my life. And therefore when I'm not doing my work my life is obviously, unfortunately not full. My work/life balance is tipped more toward work, than life, I guess. That's just how it is. (Grunfield, Drudge-Coates, Rixon, Eaton, & Cooper, 2013)

Another difficulty for men coping with prostate and other cancers is that role models may not be as readily available to men as they are to female cancer survivors. Men are less likely than women to disclose a cancer diagnosis, and male cancers are underrepresented in the media in comparison to female cancers (Gough, 2006). Fortunately, this is beginning to change. There is a growing amount of literature on masculinity and health, with a move away from a strongly gender-typed view of masculinity toward a more dynamic construct that changes from one context to another (Evans, Frank, Oliffe, & Gregory, 2011).

Once prostate cancer has been diagnosed, masculinities may affect treatment, including men's attitudes toward *active surveillance (AS)*. Following the AS protocol, men diagnosed with low-grade, early-stage prostate cancer are monitored, and treatment is deferred until disease markers indicate that active treatment is warranted. During this period of "watchful waiting," no medical treatment—medications, surgery, or radiation—is delivered. The benefits of AS include avoiding comorbidities such as impotence and incontinence, and the reduced quality of life often associated with treatment for prostate cancer (Tosoian and others, 2011). Despite these benefits, some research suggests that less than 10% of eligible American men opt for AS, in part because the perception of "doing nothing" is difficult for men to accept (Mroz, Oliffe, & Davison, 2013).

Ethnicity and Coping

Health psychologists are paying increasing attention to the experiences of ethnically diverse samples of people following the diagnosis of cancer. As an example, among breast cancer survivors, African Americans report more difficulties with physical functioning and activities of daily living than do European Americans; European Americans report more sexual difficulties than do African Americans; Latinas score higher than the other groups on measures of distress; and Filipina patients report the most difficulties with emotional functioning (see Giedzinska, Meyerowitz, Ganz, & Rowland, 2004, for a review).

Other researchers have found that women of lower SES, as well as African American and Hispanic women, are more likely than European Americans to perceive *benefits* from a diagnosis of breast cancer, such as a renewed focus on relationships in their lives (Tomich & Helgeson, 2004). The researchers suggest that impoverished and minority women are more likely to have faced discrimination in their everyday lives before they developed cancer, and this adversity has prepared them to derive benefits from traumatic events.

Because ethnicity is often linked to other sociodemographic variables, such as income, education, and the nature of the medical treatment received, interpreting differences in coping such as these is difficult. At the very least, however, these findings demonstrate that psychologists and health care providers should not assume that the experiences of one ethnic group can be generalized to all others.

The idea that people can overcome challenges to experience a more hardy state is relatively new in health and disease research. Positive change among patients coping with chronic illness has been referred to as **post-traumatic growth (PTG)**, but also as *benefit finding* (see Chapter 10) or *thriving*. PTG is theorized as occurring when an adverse life event, such as cancer, disrupts a person's view of the world and his or her place in it (Arpawong, Richeimer, Weinstein, Elghamrawy, & Milam, 2013). Disruption in turn may cause cognitive restructuring, a search for meaning, and the rebuilding of a more positive life perspective. Those who experience PTG after being diagnosed and treated for cancer often report several types of benefits, including greater appreciation for life, personal strength, relationships with others, recognition for new possibilities in life, and spiritual understanding (Lelorain, Bonnaud-Antignac, & Florin, 2010; Schroevers, Kraaij, & Garnefski, 2011). One cross-sectional study of 114 adult outpatients in active cancer treatment reported that 87% of the participants reported at least one positive life change over the course of treatment (Arpawong and others, 2013).

A number of studies have found that the ability to find positive meaning from stressful life events, including a diagnosis of cancer, is associated with improved psychological adjustment, muted neuroendocrine stress responses, and enhanced immunity (Gonzalez and others, 2016). In one study, Julienne Bower and her colleagues (Bower, Kemeny, Taylor, & Fahey, 2003) asked women who had lost a close relative to breast cancer to write about the death (cognitive processing/disclosure group) or about non-emotional topics weekly for four weeks. Women in the cognitive processing/disclosure group who placed greater importance on goals such as cultivating relationships and striving for meaning in their lives following the intervention had stronger measures of immune functioning.

post-traumatic growth (PTG)
Positive psychological change experienced as the result of struggle with a highly challenging life circumstance. Also referred to as *benefit finding*, or *thriving*.

Knowledge, Control, Social Comparison, and Social Support

Considering the stress associated with being treated for cancer, most patients display remarkable physical and psychological resilience. Important factors in adjusting to cancer treatment include having access to information, perceiving some degree of control over treatment, and being able to express emotions while feeling supported by others.

Knowledge and Control

Health psychologists have made considerable progress in understanding the psychological reactions of patients to cancer treatment and the types of interventions and information that are effective in assisting their adjustment. They have found, for example, that procedural information (e.g., how the surgery, radiation, or chemotherapy regimen will be administered; what the patient can expect before and after treatment) has wide-ranging benefits. Among these are fewer negative emotions, reduced pain, and briefer hospitalization (e.g., Flowers & Birnie, 2015). Information presented in narrative form, as compared to nonnarrative (usually statistical) form, may be particularly effective (McQueen, Kreuter, Kalesan, & Alcaraz, 2011).

Also beneficial are interventions that focus on preventing patients from feeling helpless during their treatment. Even something as simple as encouraging patients to make choices about the hospital environment can improve a patient's well-being. For this reason, patients often are encouraged to decorate their rooms with pictures, photographs, and other personal items from home. Interventions aimed at *self-presentation* can help patients overcome difficulties in managing social relationships with family, friends, and coworkers that result from changes in their physical appearance (Davies & Batehup, 2010). Such interventions can range from the use of wigs by patients who have lost their hair to cognitive-behavior therapy to improve self-esteem.

Social Comparison

Another source of information that can affect how people cope with cancer is *social comparison* with other cancer patients (Brakel, Dijkstra, Buunk, & Siero, 2012). Listening to testimonials of fellow patients can have a reassuring effect and help patients develop a more positive perspective (Buunk and others, 2009). Whether such information is beneficial for a person coping with cancer depends, first, on how the person perceives the other individual. Is this other individual perceived as doing better (*upward comparison*) or worse (*downward comparison*) than the patient? Second, it depends on the extent to which the person feels similar to the comparison person (*identification*) or feels different, and therefore it represents a state that is not a possible future (*contrast*). *Upward identification* may lead to positive feelings and improved quality of life, while *upward contrast* may lead to negative consequences in which the patient feels inferior. People also differ in their sensitivity to social comparison information. One recent study of 139 Dutch cancer survivors found that those with good health status and a strong social comparison orientation reported a significant improvement in quality of life two months after listening to audio interviews with cancer survivors who talk about the use of active coping strategies, expression of emotion, and seeking social support (Brakel and others, 2012).

Social Support

Key to any effective intervention is providing cancer patients with support and an opportunity to discuss their fears about the disease and its treatment. A great deal of research demonstrates the protective value of social relationships on health in general and on cancer-related stress in particular. A spouse or significant other provides an important source of social support for many cancer patients. When this relationship is perceived as solid and supportive, the patient's physical and emotional well-being benefits greatly (Kamen and others, 2015). This is partly because married patients—often because of input from their spouses—generally detect cancer and other diseases at an earlier stage of development, and they are more likely to seek early treatment. Among women with breast cancer, for example, spousal support is associated with lower levels of depression and anxiety, improved psychological adjustment to cancer, greater feelings of intimacy, and improved quality of life (Belcher and others, 2011).

The benefits of social support extend beyond marriage. Women with breast cancer (Nausheen, Gidron, Peveler, & Moss-Morris, 2009) and men with prostate cancer (Zhou and others, 2010) who have larger social support networks have slower cancer progression than women and men with less social support. However, cancer patients also report unsupportive, negative behaviors from family, friends, and acquaintances: minimizing the patient's problem, forced cheerfulness, insensitive comments, and so forth. Such negative experiences have been associated with poorer adjustment to certain cancers (Gremore and others, 2011).

A limited number of studies also have suggested that behavioral and psychosocial interventions may lower stress hormone levels and improve immune function in cancer patients and people coping with cancer in a loved one. For instance, among breast cancer patients, biofeedback training, cognitive therapy, relaxation training, guided imagery, and stress management all have been associated with significant decreases in cortisol levels and increases in the number of circulating lymphocytes (e.g., Cruess and others, 2000). Although a few studies have even shown lower recurrence rates among cancer patients who participate in psychosocial interventions relative to waiting-list control participants, as noted earlier, the potential effects of such interventions on clinical outcomes remain speculative (see Luecken & Compas, 2002, for a review).

Cognitive-Behavioral Interventions

Health psychologists have made considerable progress in developing cognitive-behavioral interventions in comprehensive cancer care (Lau and others, 2018; do Carmo, Paiva, de Oliveira, Nascimento, & Paiva, 2017). During and following treatment, a variety of interventions have been used. For adults, the interventions have focused on depression, stress, fatigue, pain, control of aversive reactions to treatment (such as nausea during chemotherapy), and enhancement of emotional well-being. For children, they have focused on increasing adherence to medical advice and reducing suffering. Although the question of whether such interventions can prolong life for people with cancer remains controversial (Coyne, Stefanek, & Palmer, 2007), it is clear that such interventions can be successful in helping cancer patients manage their distress levels

Social Support Women and men who feel socially connected to a network of caring friends are less likely to die of all types of cancer than their socially isolated counterparts.

MBI/Alamy Stock Photo

systematic desensitization A form of behavior therapy, commonly used for overcoming phobias, in which the person is exposed to a series of increasingly fearful situations while remaining deeply relaxed.

(Manne & Andrykowski, 2006). Among the most widely used interventions are progressive muscle relaxation with guided imagery, systematic desensitization, hypnosis, biofeedback, and cognitive distraction. For instance, returning to the chapter-opening story, before Jeremy's attending physician performed a *lumbar puncture* (spinal tap) to sample my son's spinal fluid, the nurse engaged Jeremy in a detailed (and distracting) discussion of the most recent *Star Trek* program. (Biofeedback and hypnosis will be discussed in Chapter 15; guided imagery—covered in greater depth below—encompasses **systematic desensitization**.)

Many of these interventions stem from the field of psychoneuroimmunology (PNI). PNI researchers believe that the risk for many diseases (including cancer), the course that a particular disease follows, and the remission and recurrence of symptoms are all influenced by the interaction of behavioral, neuroendocrine, and immune responses.

Mindfulness-based stress-reduction interventions are being used with increasing frequency (Bartley, 2012; Gregoire, 2013). In one early study of prostate and breast cancer patients, a mindfulness intervention that focused on cultivating conscious awareness through relaxation, meditation, and yoga resulted in increased quality of life among participants, as well as a healthy shift in neuroendocrine response (Carlson, Speca, Patel, & Goodey, 2003). A meta-analysis of 22 studies found that mindfulness-based therapies—which included yoga, meditation, breathing exercises, and cognitive training—were associated with significantly reduced symptoms of anxiety and depression in pre- and postcancer treatment (Piet, Wurtzen, & Zachariae, 2012).

Exercise is also increasingly recommended as a general intervention to improve the well-being of cancer patients (Floyd & Moyer, 2010). Several studies have reported that physical exercise improved the physical functioning, quality of life, self-efficacy, and emotional well-being of cancer patients (McAuley, White, Rogers, Motl, & Courneya, 2010; Milne, Wallman, Gordon, & Courneya, 2008). One of the most consistent outcomes of physical activity is self-efficacy, or the individual's belief in his or her personal capabilities. Self-efficacy expectations may well enhance the effects of exercise on depression and fatigue in cancer survivors (McAuley and others, 2010).

Below, we'll describe two of the more common techniques in use today: (1) emotional disclosure and expressive writing and (2) guided imagery.

Emotional Disclosure and Expressive Writing

Emotional disclosure can have a beneficial effect for people coping with chronic illness. Annette Stanton and her colleagues (2000) examined the importance to patients of being able to actively process and express the emotions involved in coping with breast cancer. The participants were recruited within 20 weeks of completing surgery, chemotherapy, or radiation. Over the next three months, women who expressed their emotions about cancer had fewer medical appointments for cancer-related health problems and reported significantly lower stress levels than their less expressive and less socially receptive counterparts. The researchers suggest that by openly expressing one's fears—for instance, a loss of perceived control—"one may begin to distinguish what one can and cannot control [in order] to channel energy toward attainable goals, and to generate alternate pathways for bolstering control" (Stanton and others, 2000, p. 880). They also suggest that repeated expression of emotions may decrease negative emotions and the physiological arousal that comes with them, leading cancer patients to believe that their situation is not as dire as originally thought and to derive some benefit from their adversity.

In another study, Stanton and her colleagues (Stanton, Thompson, Crespi, Link, & Waisman, 2013) evaluated an intervention to teach patients with cancer how to use blogging to chronicle their experiences and communicate with their social networks via the Internet. The study gathered 88 women with breast cancer and assigned them randomly to participate either in Project Connect Online (PCO)—a 3-hour workshop for hands-on creation of personal Web sites—or in a control group. Participants in the PCO group developed their own Web sites using a template consisting of six functions:

- a journal (blog) that could contain photos;

- a section for Web site links, to be populated by each participant (for instance, the oncology clinic, National Cancer Institute);

- a How You Can Help page, in which participants could convey actions visitors could undertake (such as meal provision, written cards);

- choice of privacy settings;

- instructions for visitors to post messages and subscribe for automatic notification of Web site updates; and

- an online survey to assess visitors' reactions to PCO.

Over the six-month period of the research trial, women in the blogging (PCO) group showed significant benefit—relative to control-group women—in symptoms of depression and overall appreciation of life.

Numerous, randomized, controlled trials have arrived at conflicting conclusions regarding the efficacy of *expressive writing (EW)* as a therapeutic intervention for people living with cancer. One meta-analysis of 13 controlled studies reported some positive effects of EW on patients' pain levels, sleep, and general physical and psychological symptoms (Merz, Fox, & Malcarne, 2014). However, another meta-analysis of 16 randomized controlled trials found no statistically significant effects of EW on any psychological or physical outcomes in cancer patients (Zachariae & O'Toole, 2015). A third meta-analysis of 11 randomized controlled trials evaluating an EW intervention in breast cancer patients concluded that EW may have a significant positive impact on self-reported physical symptoms, but this benefit may not last very long (Zhou, Wu, An, & Li, 2015).

EW seems to benefit some patients more than others, leading some researchers to conclude that its efficacy may depend more on social support and other factors in the lives of cancer patients than on the intervention itself (Zachariae & O'Toole, 2015). One such factor seems to be the level of social support a patient perceives. To date, until more research is completed, the conclusion that can be most safely drawn is that EW is a simple, low-cost, self-administered intervention that may have a therapeutic effect in some subgroups of patients.

Guided Imagery

Guided imagery draws on patients' psychophysiological reactions to the environment to help them optimize physiological activity in various body systems and thus relieve pain or discomfort. For example, a patient who views an impending surgery as a life-threatening

guided imagery The use of one or more external devices to assist in relaxation and the formation of clear, strong, positive mental images.

trauma may exhibit hypertension, cardiac arrhythmia, and other health-compromising responses prior to surgery. Conversely, a patient who looks forward to the same operation as a lifesaving event is more likely to remain relaxed before, during, and following treatment.

In guided imagery, the therapist uses one or more external devices to help the patient relax and then form clear, strong, positive images to replace the symptoms. Effective images draw on several sensory modalities, including vision, hearing, touch, and even smell or taste and may be stimulated by taped music, sounds of nature, verbal suggestions, pictures of objects or places, aromas from scented candles, or a variety of other devices.

Guided imagery begins with the patient assuming a comfortable position, either lying down or sitting, with eyes closed or open. After taking several slow, deep breaths, the person begins a process of systematically attending to and then relaxing any areas of bodily tension. A variety of techniques may be used to assist relaxation, including progressive muscle relaxation and biofeedback training.

Once a relaxed state is reached, the person visualizes a safe, peaceful place and strives to make the image as clear and intense as possible by focusing on sights, sounds, smells, and other sensory aspects of the moment. At this point, the patient follows taped suggestions (or a nurse's or therapist's verbal suggestions) and forms a mental image of a symptom, such as pain or nausea. The patient then imagines the symptom changing. For example, the "red" fiery pain changes to a cool shade of blue, or queasiness is expelled from the body with each exhalation.

After a few minutes of focusing on the altered symptom (sometimes describing its changed appearance to the nurse or therapist), the patient is instructed to relax, breathe deeply, and return to the peaceful place. After several sessions, which may last only 5 or 10 minutes each, most patients are able to perform imagery without assistance.

Imagery may be beneficial for several reasons:

- Imagery triggers a state of relaxed concentration that enhances the person's sensitivity to health-promoting images.

- Imagery gives the patient an increased sense of control and a decreased sense of helplessness over stressful aspects of disease or treatment.

- Imagery also may work through the *placebo effect*. In fact, people who believe that imagery and relaxation have the potential to improve their health may experience physiological changes that enhance their ability to fight disease.

The intervention studies that we have discussed in this chapter provide substantial evidence that psychosocial factors can influence a cancer patient's response to treatment and, quite possibly, the course of recovery (or the likelihood of recurrence). Those studies that have reported longer survival for cancer patients are especially vivid demonstrations of the value of such interventions.

Weigh In on Health

Respond to each question below based on what you learned in the chapter. (**Tip:** Use the items in "Summing Up" to take into account related biological, psychological, and social concerns.)

1. What have you learned in this chapter about cancer that helps you better understand your risks as you move forward in your life, as well as what you can do now to try to prevent an occurrence of cancer in the future?

2. Testing for inherited cancer risk and hundreds of other disease genes is increasingly available to patients through health care providers and, in some cases, without medi-

cal supervision. For treatable conditions, genetic testing is rarely controversial. But for untreatable conditions, genetic testing raises many ethical questions. For instance, should all people have equal access to genetic tests? Under what circumstances should the results of genetic tests be shared with others? What other ethical issues does genetic testing raise?

3. Use what you have learned in this chapter to write a checklist about positive ways in which people have learned how to cope with cancer. One day this checklist could be a valuable resource for someone you know (or even for yourself).

Summing Up

What Is Cancer?

1. Globally, cancer is the second leading cause of death. It is actually more than 100 different but related diseases. There are four general types of cancer: Carcinomas are cancers of the epithelial cells, which line the outer and inner surfaces of the body. Lymphomas are cancers of the lymph system. Sarcomas are cancers that develop in muscle, bone, fat, and other connective tissue. Leukemias are cancers of the blood and blood-forming system.

2. Several variables contribute to ethnic differences in cancer, including socioeconomic status, knowledge about cancer, and attitudes toward the disease, which may affect access to health care and adherence to medical advice. In addition, health care providers do not always provide culturally competent medical care.

Risk Factors for Cancer

3. Globally, one third of cancer deaths are due to five behavioral and dietary risks: high body mass index, low fruit and vegetable intake, lack of physical activity, tobacco use, and alcohol use. Several environmental factors are linked to cancer, including ultraviolet light, toxic chemicals, and occupational carcinogens.

4. Cancer-causing infections, such as hepatitis and human papilloma virus (HPV), cause 25% of cancer cases in low- and middle-income countries (WHO, 2018).

5. Prolonged stress may compromise the immune system and allow malignant cells to spread. Reduced immunocompetence has been demonstrated following exams, divorce, bereavement, unemployment, and occupational stress. Childhood adversity has been associated with greater emotional and physiological sensitivity to stress. Childhood stressors also may promote long-term immune system dysregulation, which influences cancer morbidity.

Cancer Treatment

6. When cancer does develop, its impact on health nearly always can be minimized through early detection and treatment. For many types of cancer, advances in genetic screening, mammography, and other detection technologies have dramatically improved people's survival rates. However, many people fail to heed early warning signs of cancer.

7. Biomedical treatments for cancer include surgery, chemotherapy, and radiation therapy. Surgery generally offers the greatest chance for cure for most types of cancer. Chemotherapy is used to destroy fast-growing cancer cells that have spread to parts of the body far from the primary tumor. Unlike chemotherapy, radiation therapy affects only the tumor and the surrounding area.

8. Many cancer patients try one or more alternative treatments (such as meditation, biofeedback, or herbal treatments) to relieve side effects and to improve their overall quality of life.

Coping with Cancer

9. Cancer and cancer treatment create unique stresses both for patients and for their families. Even when treatment is successful, the threat of the disease's recurrence looms. Although cancer survivors seem to experience similar numbers and types of stressful events as the general population, some studies show that cancer survivors may perceive stressors as somewhat more severe and disruptive.

10. Many psychosocial interventions have been used to assist patients in coping with cancer. Effective interventions enhance patients' knowledge about what to expect from treatment, increase patients' perception of having some control over their lives, and offer a supportive social environment in which to share fears and concerns.

11. Higher levels of masculinity, gender role conflict, and gender-linked personality characteristics are related to poorer outcomes in men with cancer.

12. Interventions that provide health education and teach specific skills for solving problems and managing stress are also beneficial to patients' well-being. Information presented in narrative, as compared to nonnarrative (usually statistical), form may be particularly effective. Another source of information that can affect how people cope with cancer is *social comparison* with other cancer patients. Guided imagery effectively helps patients control the side effects of chemotherapy and other cancer treatments.

Key Terms and Concepts to Remember

cancer, p. 347
metastasis, p. 347
carcinoma, p. 348
sarcoma, p. 348
lymphoma, p. 348
leukemia, p. 348

carcinogen, p. 351
consideration of future consequences, p. 352
melanoma, p. 357
comparative optimism, p. 358
immunocompetence, p. 359

immune surveillance theory, p. 360
immunotherapy, p. 364
post-traumatic growth (PTG), p. 369
systematic desensitization, p. 372
guided imagery, p. 373

 LaunchPad
macmillan learning
To accompany your textbook, you have access to a number of online resources, including quizzes for every chapter of the book, flashcards, critical thinking exercises, videos, and *Check Your Health* inventories. To access these resources, please visit the Straub Health Psychology LaunchPad at **launchpadworks.com**

Chapter 12

Sexually Transmitted Infections: HIV/AIDS and Other Communicable Conditions

Justin Sullivan/Getty Images

LEARNING OUTCOMES

Once you have studied this chapter, you will be able to:

- Differentiate communicable and noncommunicable diseases and discuss their global impact,
- Define *sexually transmitted infection* and identify the most common STIs,
- Trace the history of the AIDS pandemic and the stages of HIV infection,
- Discuss the impact of living with a chronic illness on a person, and
- Explain health psychology's role in battling STIs.

Six months before the start of the 1988 summer Olympics, 28-year-old diving champion Greg Louganis received an HIV-positive diagnosis, which at that time was widely viewed as a death sentence. Although his first inclination was to "lock myself away in my house and wait to die" (Louganis, 2014), he continued to train. He also began taking AZT, the first effective pharmaceutical weapon against the virus—a drug that had been fast-tracked over a mere 25 months of clinical trials and approved by the FDA one year earlier.

His decisions paid off later that summer in Seoul, South Korea. Although Louganis was injured when he struck his head on the board during a preliminary dive, he made a remarkable comeback. Only 30 minutes later and after receiving stitches for his wound, he returned to the 3-meter board competition, won gold for this event, and later won gold for the men's 10-meter platform. In doing so, he became the only diver in history to win two gold medals in back-to-back Olympic Games.

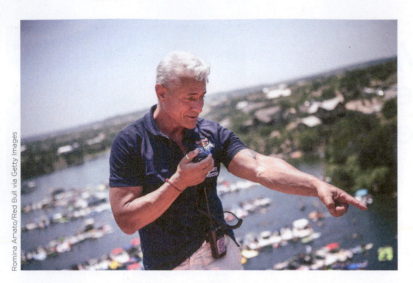

Olympic champion Greg Louganis as he looks today—healthy, with HIV under control.

Despite this remarkable athletic achievement, Greg didn't expect to live to see age 30. Before the advent of today's carefully calibrated "cocktail" of antiviral drugs, success in stopping the progression of HIV infection into AIDS was rare. A year after his Olympic triumph, Louganis officially retired from diving to become a sports commentator and a national speaker on such issues as LGBT rights, HIV/AIDS, domestic violence, and overcoming adversity. In 2011, he returned to diving to help coach the latest generation of U.S. divers. Twenty-eight years after winning his gold medals, 56-year-old Louganis said in an interview, "I am still here! I didn't allow my HIV [to] take over as an obsession; it's a mere part of me that I've lived with" (Louganis, 2014).

Louganis, who at 5 feet 9 inches and 175 pounds looks fitter than many people half his age, acknowledges that HIV is "a smart virus. It mutates over time, and they have to change up your treatments to be effective" (Ain, 2016). Throughout the years since his diagnosis, he has followed an aggressive program to maintain his overall health: In addition to anti-HIV medications, he takes nutritional supplements; eats a carefully planned diet; and stays active with daily workouts that include swimming, spin classes, weight lifting, and yoga-based mindful meditation. These aspects of his lifestyle, he says, are as important to his well-being as his medication regimen. All of his practices continue to pay off. "The HIV virus may remain in my body," he says, "but it's now undetectable" (Ain, 2016).

Although AIDS and some other sexually transmitted diseases seem to be recent phenomena, health experts believe that they actually are thousands of years old. AIDS became a global problem because of the dramatic increase in mobility of most of the world's population, which allowed the disease to spread from continent to continent. Although the initial panic created by the outbreak of the HIV virus has subsided in developed countries, where early screening and successful drug treatments have turned AIDS into a survivable, manageable, chronic disease, the picture remains bleak in developing countries.

This chapter focuses on chronic illness, with emphasis on HIV/AIDS and other STIs. We begin by discussing the nature of communicable diseases, including their means of transmission, global burden, and primary measures of control. Next, we'll examine AIDS, including its impact on the body and how the virus is spread. The chapter concludes with a discussion of health psychology's role in the design and implementation of programs to prevent the development and spread of STIs, and to provide support for those living with a chronic illness or condition.

COMMUNICABLE AND NONCOMMUNICABLE DISEASES

People in much of the world are living longer than ever before. Due to improved infection control and the aging of populations, the global burden of disease has shifted increasingly toward **noncommunicable diseases (NCDs)** such as heart disease, cancer, chronic respiratory disease, and diabetes (World Health Organization [WHO], 2017). Unlike NCDs, which are noninfectious and nontransmissible, **communicable diseases (CDs)** are caused by infections, such as tuberculosis (TB), or by parasites, such as hookworm. Many CDs manifest in acute, short-term symptoms, but—as we will see later in this chapter—some are long-term chronic conditions. And some are symptomatic only sporadically, like the chicken pox virus, typically contracted in childhood, which remains in the body and can flare up later in life as the painful shingles infection.

Communicable diseases can be transmitted from one person to another, from an animal to a person, and from a person to an animal. Transmission can occur directly, such as through respiration, or indirectly through a *vector*, such as a mosquito in the case of malaria or the *Zika virus.*

Examples of communicable diseases and their methods of transmission include these:

- *Waterborne*—cholera, rotavirus
- *Sexual or blood-borne*—HIV, hepatitis
- *Food-borne*—salmonella, *E. coli*
- *By traumatic contact*—rabies
- *By inhalation*—meningitis, influenza, tuberculosis
- *Vector-borne*—malaria, Zika virus

Communicable diseases can be controlled in many ways. Vaccination is the primary control measure for infections such as smallpox, meningitis, tetanus, and influenza. Improved treatment and caregiving are primary control measures for respiratory infections, HIV/AIDS, and tuberculosis. Cleaner water, better hygiene, and healthier sanitation measures are the primary control measure for diarrheal diseases. Vector control and containment are primary control measures for malaria, West Nile virus, avian influenza, and the Zika virus. Finally, behavioral change (such as consistent condom use) is a primary control measure for sexually transmitted infections, Ebola virus, and HIV.

The Epidemiological Transition

The **epidemiological transition** occurs over time as a developing country or region gains increased control over the acute infectious diseases of childhood. Within that population, the CDs of childhood are gradually overtaken by the chronic NCDs typical of adulthood. In North America, Western Europe, and other parts of the industrialized world, this transition has occurred gradually over a century or more. In some countries,

noncommunicable disease A noninfectious disease; one that is nontransmissible.

communicable disease A disease that is transmitted from a human to another human, from a human to an animal, or from an animal to a human.

epidemiological transition A shift in the disease pattern of a population as mortality falls: acute, infectious diseases are reduced, while chronic, noncommunicable diseases increase in prevalence.

Interpreting Data

Causes of Death in Four Categories of World Economies

The World Health Organization (WHO) operates within the United Nations' system, working with policymakers, governmental and nongovernmental organizations, and the private sector to promote global health. The WHO's work includes collecting statistics on health, diseases, and causes of death around the world. In the four graphs shown here, the top ten causes of death are compared in countries with high-income economies, upper-middle-income economies, lower-middle-income economies, and low-income economies.

The data displayed on the Y-axis of these graphs makes it clear that people tend to die of very different causes, depending on how rich or poor their country's economy is. More than half of all deaths in low-income countries were caused by communicable diseases, conditions arising in pregnancy and childbirth, and nutritional deficiencies. By contrast, less than 7% of deaths in high-income countries were due to such causes. What factor(s) might explain this difference? Low-income countries had the highest mortality

rate due to road traffic injuries. What hypotheses would you suggest to pinpoint factor(s) that might account for this difference? And why do you suppose lower respiratory infections are among the leading causes of death across all income groups?

Examining the X-axis data brings up new questions. Notice that the number of deaths per 100,000 population is significantly different from one graph to another. In high-income economies, ischemic heart disease kills more than 145 people per 100,000, whereas in lower-middle-income economies it kills fewer than 120 per 100,000. Yet it is the top cause of death in both. Does this mean that fewer people are dying in lower-middle-income countries than in rich countries? If not, why not?

As this discussion demonstrates, simply eyeballing a set of graphs can be deceptive. To make sure you are not comparing "apples and oranges," it is important to examine both axes of a graph, and to ask questions about the underlying data.

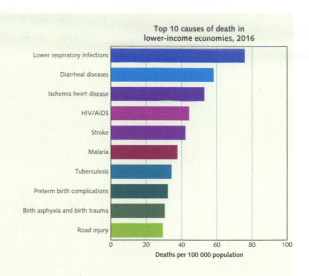

FIGURE 12.1 Top 10 Causes of Death

Data from: World Health Organization. (2017). *Global health estimates 2016: Estimated deaths by cause and region, 2000 and 2016.*

such as Mexico, it has taken place in just a few decades. Although the number of deaths caused by CDs is falling worldwide, these diseases and related conditions still account for nearly half of deaths in low-income countries (Ritchie & Roser, 2018).

Experts once believed that, as countries develop, NCD replaced communicable disease as the main source of ill health. However, there is now evidence that the poorest populations in developing countries face the double burden of high rates of both communicable and noncommunicable disease. In low-income countries, the rates of cardiovascular disease, cancers, injuries, and other NCDs have risen, yet CDs also persist (see *Interpreting Data: Causes of Death in Four Categories of World Economies*). In poor countries, the three leading causes of death are communicable diseases: lower respiratory infections, HIV/AIDs, and diarrheal diseases. In high-income countries, the three leading causes of death are NCDs: stroke, ischemic heart disease, and lung cancer.

People living in affluent countries are more likely to have the knowledge and ability to protect themselves from diarrhea and parasitic diseases that are often spread by unsafe water. They are less likely to live in overcrowded conditions, which can spread diseases such as tuberculosis, and they are more likely to be able to immunize their children against vaccine-preventable diseases. Although there are safe, effective, and inexpensive treatments for many communicable diseases, those treatments are still underused in low- and middle-income countries (Skolnik, 2016).

The impact of specific communicable diseases varies by age group. For example, the impact of diarrheal disease, lower respiratory infections, measles, and malaria is greatest on young children, while the impact of HIV/AIDS and TB is greatest on people between 15 and 59 years of age (Hay and others, 2017). The economic and social costs of communicable disease are also especially high for infants and children, often adversely affecting their schooling and productivity throughout life (Skolnik, 2016). For example, AIDS, which often impacts young adults in low-income countries, can reduce average life expectancy by up to 20 years. As another example, treatment for malaria, which most often impacts children in low-income countries, can easily cost up to 25% of a family's income (HEAL, 2016).

The global burden of communicable disease is generally about the same for females as it is for males. Two exceptions are tuberculosis, which affects more males than females, and HIV/AIDS, which globally now ranks higher as a cause of death for women than for men (Hay and others, 2017).

Emerging and Reemerging Communicable Diseases

Throughout history, new communicable diseases have periodically emerged, sometimes with catastrophic effects. For example, the first major *bubonic plague* that swept through the Mediterranean world in the sixth century was transmitted by black rats that traveled aboard grain ships and transmitted the virus that killed nearly 25% of the European population (Horgan, 2014). As another example, since 1976, there have been more than two dozen outbreaks of the Ebola virus in 10 African countries, as well as in parts of Europe and the United States. Believed to originally have been animal-borne, Ebola now has human fatality rates in the range of 25% to 90%. The World Health Organization estimates that about 5,000 people died in the outbreak of Ebola in West Africa that began in 2014 (WHO, 2016b).

HIV, which we'll discuss in detail later in this chapter, emerged in the 1980s. A decade later, *severe acute respiratory syndrome (SARS)* spread to more than two dozen countries in North America, South America, Europe, and Asia before being contained in 2003 (Reperant & Osterhaus, 2017). Caused by a respiratory virus, SARS spread from Hong Kong to infect over 8,000 people in 37 countries within a matter of weeks. Of those infected, 774 died.

Two recently emerging infectious diseases are the avian influenza H5N1, commonly called "bird flu," and the Zika virus. Unlike other types of flu, H5N1, which is deadly to poultry, usually does not spread between people. Zika, which is spread to people primarily through the bite of an infected *Aedes* species mosquito, generally causes only mild symptoms in adults. However, Zika may cause *microcephaly,* a serious birth defect of the brain, as well as other poor birth outcomes in mothers who were infected with the virus while pregnant (Centers for Disease Control and Prevention [CDC], 2016d).

Antimicrobial Resistance

A growing global health concern is the emergence of drug-resistant forms of communicable disease. All microbes have the ability to develop resistance to drugs

Prevention of Infectious Disease Public education is an important strategy in preventing and containing infectious diseases. A poster in Singapore reminds residents to make their homes and property inhospitable to mosquitoes that may be carrying dengue fever.

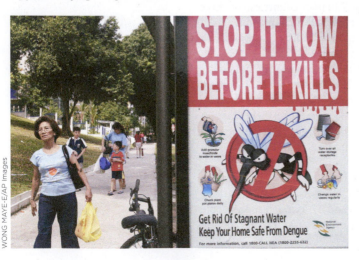

WONG MAYE-E/AP Images

that are used to kill them and thus become drug-resistant organisms. **Antimicrobial resistance** is the ability of bacteria, viruses, and parasites to change and resist the effect of drugs as a result of mutation or the exchange of genetic material among different strains.

antimicrobial resistance The ability of bacteria, viruses, and other microbes to resist the effect of drugs.

The use of antibiotics is the single most important factor in the development of antimicrobial resistance. Only a few years after penicillin was introduced, for example, strains of bacteria that were resistant to the antibiotic emerged. Similarly, malaria can no longer be treated effectively with the drug *chloroquine* because the virus is now resistant to it.

Tuberculosis

Tuberculosis is another case in point. TB is caused by the bacterium *Mycobacterium tuberculosis* and spreads through aerosolized droplets that people inhale from others who are already infected with the disease. An untreated person with active TB may infect 10 to 15 other people each year, about 10% of whom will develop the disease themselves. Two thirds of those who develop the active disease will die if they do not receive proper treatment (Skolnik, 2016). Among the conditions that increase susceptibility to TB are living in crowded circumstances and having a weakened immune system. In 2016, 10.4 million people fell ill with TB, and 1.7 million died from the disease (WHO, 2018b).

Most people with TB are cured by a strictly followed, six-month treatment regimen with first-line antimicrobial drugs such as isoniazid and rifampicin. However, in recent decades *multidrug-resistant TB (MDR-TB)*—tuberculosis that does not respond to first-line anti-TB drugs—has developed. Today, this strain is often what is transmitted from one person to another. Globally, in 2016, an estimated 490,000 developed MDR-TB (WHO, 2018b).

Because the mere use of antibiotics creates resistance, these drugs should be used only to treat infections. Unfortunately, however, antibiotics are misused as much as 50% of the time, including being prescribed when not needed, dosed incorrectly, or taken for the wrong amount of time (CDC, 2014b). The use of counterfeit or poor-quality medicines that do not contain the correct ingredients also contributes to global drug resistance (Skolnik, 2016).

Another important factor in the development of antimicrobial resistance is the spread of resistant strains of bacteria from person to person in crowded settings such as hospitals, nursing homes, schools, and prisons. In such settings, poor sanitation and hygiene and weak infection control often contribute to this danger.

Breakdowns in public health measures can also promote the reemergence of diseases. For example, from the end of World War II until the beginning of the HIV/AIDs pandemic, in many affluent countries, there was a general sense that the most dangerous infectious diseases had been conquered. As a result, many nations loosened their measures to control communicable diseases such as TB. Small wonder that there was a resurgence of TB and MDR-TB in many areas, including New York City in the 1980s (Snowden, 2008).

Food Contamination

Figure 12.2 illustrates another way antibiotic resistance can spread. The microbes that contaminate food can also become resistant due to the use of antibiotics. For some germs, such as the bacterium *Salmonella*, the primary factor in increased resistance is that antibiotics are being fed to animals that are raised for food. Antibiotics that are medically important to treating infections in humans should be used in food-producing animals only to treat infectious disease, not to promote growth.

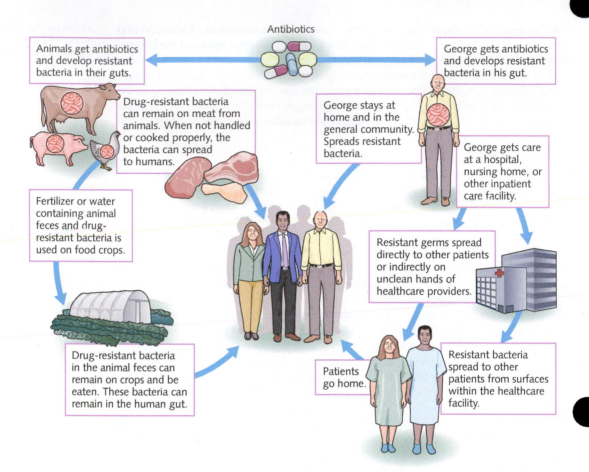

Antibiotics

Animals get antibiotics and develop resistant bacteria in their guts.

George gets antibiotics and develops resistant bacteria in his gut.

Drug-resistant bacteria can remain on meat from animals. When not handled or cooked properly, the bacteria can spread to humans.

George stays at home and in the general community. Spreads resistant bacteria.

George gets care at a hospital, nursing home, or other inpatient care facility.

Fertilizer or water containing animal feces and drug-resistant bacteria is used on food crops.

Resistant germs spread directly to other patients or indirectly on unclean hands of healthcare providers.

Drug-resistant bacteria in the animal feces can remain on crops and be eaten. These bacteria can remain in the human gut.

Patients go home.

Resistant bacteria spread to other patients from surfaces within the healthcare facility.

FIGURE 12.2 How Antibiotic Resistance Spreads Simply taking antibiotic drugs, or giving them to animals, creates drug-resistant bacteria.

sexually transmitted infections (STIs) Infections that are spread primarily through person-to-person sexual contact.

SEXUALLY TRANSMITTED INFECTIONS

Diseases that are spread through sexual contact are often called *sexually transmitted diseases,* or *STDs.* Some, such as chlamydia and gonorrhea, are spread mainly by sexual contact with an infected person. Others, such as Ebola and Zika, can be spread sexually; but more often they are spread in other ways, such as through direct contact with the blood or body fluids of an infected person (Ebola) or through the bite of an infected mosquito (Zika).

In recent years, public health experts have suggested replacing STD with the term *sexually transmitted infection,* or **STI.** Why the change? One reason is that the concept of disease, as in STD, suggests a major medical problem, usually with some clear symptoms.

But several common STDs have no symptoms, or have only signs that can easily be over-looked in the majority of those who are infected. So the sexually transmitted virus or bacterium is best described as creating an infection, which may or may not result in disease.

Identifying and Understanding STIs

According to the Centers for Disease Control and Prevention, young people (ages 15–24) account for half of all new cases of STIs, even though they make up only 25% of the sexually experienced population (CDC, 2013c). Many STIs are particularly hazardous for women during pregnancy and childbirth, because they can increase the risk of miscarriage and premature or low-birthweight delivery or they can be passed along to the newborn. For these reasons, it is especially important that the college-age population be knowledgeable about the means of transmission, the signs and symptoms, and the available treatments for STIs.

Although there are dozens of STIs, and although the course of how they infect the body can vary greatly, epidemiological research has provided data that health psychologists and other healthcare providers can use in public education and screening to control the spread of these conditions. One thing to keep in mind is that it is very common for infected people to be unaware that they have an STI, because symptoms are either entirely absent or are minor enough not to be noticeable. As such, the medical standard of care for sexually active patients—and especially women who are pregnant or planning to become pregnant—is to routinely screen for STIs by means of laboratory tests as well as a physical examination and medical interview questions about the patient's sexual behavior and history. In this section we examine those STIs that are most common or prevalent.

Genital Human Papillomavirus (HPV)

Genital human papillomavirus (HPV) is actually a group of more than 100 different viruses that are passed on by an infected person through genital contact, most often during vaginal or anal sex but also through oral sex. Although the highest prevalence rates for HPV infection have been found among women ages 20 to 24, anyone who is having (or has ever had) sex can get HPV. HPV is so common that nearly all sexually active women and men become infected at some point in their lives (CDC, 2013a). Most people with HPV never develop symptoms or health problems, but the virus can cause serious health problems, including genital warts and certain cancers.

Chlamydia

Chlamydia is caused by a bacterium that is known to create infections in the throat, genitals, and anus. With over 1.2 million cases reported annually, chlamydia is the most frequently reported bacterial STI in the United States (CDC, 2017a). Chlamydia spreads through contact with infected semen and vaginal fluids during unprotected vaginal sex, anal sex, and oral sex. Although women do not usually show symptoms of this STI, some may experience pain during sex or urination. Men usually do show symptoms, including a discharge or itchy feeling in the penis, painful urination, or an infection of the throat or anus. If untreated, chlamydia infection may cause infertility and arthritis in both women and men. In women, the infection may also cause pelvic pain, pelvic inflammatory disease, and ectopic pregnancy.

Trichomoniasis

Trichomoniasis is caused by infection with a protozoan parasite, *Trichomonas vaginalis*. Most people who have the parasite cannot tell they are infected. Symptoms may appear within one to four weeks after a person becomes infected, or much later; and symptoms can be intermittent over a period of years. In men, symptoms include itching or irritation inside the penis, burning upon urination or ejaculation, and discharge from the penis. Women may experience itching or soreness of the genitals, discomfort upon urination, and a vaginal discharge with an unusual "fishy" odor. Although untreated trichomoniasis is not known to have the serious long-term complications that some other STIs can cause, by irritating the genital tract it can make individuals more vulnerable to infection with other STIs.

Gonorrhea

Gonorrhea is caused by a bacterium that commonly infects the genitals, anus, and throat. This STI is also spread by infected semen and vaginal fluids during unprotected vaginal sex, anal sex, and oral sex. Most women with gonorrhea show either no symptoms or some vaginal discharge or pain while urinating. Men usually notice a thick yellow-green discharge from the penis, and they may experience pain while urinating. If infected in the rectum, men and women have pain, bleeding, and discharge. In both women and men, untreated gonorrhea may cause arthritis, infertility, and other complications such as infections of the brain, heart muscle, or liver.

Genital Herpes

Genital herpes is caused by the *herpes simplex virus*. It is spread through unprotected vaginal, anal, or oral sex in the form of direct skin-to-skin touch. The symptoms of genital herpes typically come and go sporadically. They include fatigue; fever; and painful blisters that redden the skin, itch, ulcerate, and may cause scarring. The virus is especially contagious if the infected person is having an outbreak of blisters at the time of sexual contact, but it can also be transmitted in the absence of symptoms. Over time, the virus can hide in nerve endings, causing pain in remote parts of the body such as the legs.

Syphilis

Syphilis is caused by a spiral-shaped form of bacteria called a spirochete. Unlike many other STIs, untreated syphilis follows a predictable course of stages: primary, secondary, latent, and tertiary. In the primary stage, the infected person has a sore (usually painless, round, and hard) called a *chancre* at the site of infection, usually the penis, vagina or vulva, anus, or mouth. In the secondary stage, the person may develop a skin rash on the palms of the hands and soles of feet, swollen lymph nodes, and fever. Syphilis then goes into the latent stage, when symptoms disappear. Until the twentieth century, patients and their physicians commonly believed that the disease was cured when, instead, it was just latent. After a symptom-free incubation period that may last for several years, tertiary syphilis develops. It manifests in severe problems, including dementia and other brain conditions, and damage to the nerves, eyes, heart, blood vessels, liver, bones, and/or joints.

Hepatitis

Hepatitis is an inflammation of the liver, most often caused by a virus. There are five main hepatitis viruses, referred to as types A, B, C, D, and E. Hepatitis A (HAV) and hepatitis E (HEV) are usually spread via contaminated food or water, not sexual contact. However, hepatitis B (HBV), hepatitis C (HCV), and hepatitis D (HDV) viruses are most commonly spread through contact with the blood, semen, or other body fluids of an infected person, or by sharing needles and even toiletries such as toothbrushes and razors (since they can come in contact with blood and open sores). Unlike hepatitis A and E, which are acute, short-term illnesses, hepatitis B, C, and D are more likely to become chronic conditions and can lead to scarring of the liver (fibrosis, and in its later stages, cirrhosis) and liver cancer. These chronic forms of hepatitis develop slowly, so their signs and symptoms often go unnoticed.

HIV/AIDS

Human immunodeficiency virus (HIV) attacks the body's immune system and leaves it vulnerable to infection. Left untreated, HIV infection develops into **acquired immunodeficiency syndrome (AIDS)**. As the HIV infection develops into AIDS, its victims usually struggle with infections that otherwise would be handled with relative ease if their immune systems were not compromised. In this way, AIDS increases its victims' vulnerability to *opportunistic infections,* such as pneumonia and certain cancers, which prey on the weakened immune system.

Present in high concentration in the blood and semen of HIV-positive individuals, HIV can enter the body through any tear in the skin or mucous membranes, including tears not visible to the human eye. More specifically, HIV can be spread through any of these:

- *Unprotected sex*—primarily vaginal and anal intercourse
- *Blood exchange*—including by accidental needle sticks or by needle-sharing
- *Mother-to-child transmission*—during birth or through breast feeding

More of the virus is found in ejaculate than in vaginal and cervical secretions, so unprotected vaginal sex is much riskier for HIV for women than for men, and unprotected anal sex is even riskier for women than unprotected vaginal sex (CDC, 2018c). After intercourse, the infected lymphocytes in semen may remain in the vagina and cervix for many days, thus giving the virus more time to infect the woman. By contrast, secretions from an HIV-positive (HIV1) vagina and cervix are washed from the penis easily. Male-to-female transmission of HIV through vaginal intercourse is far more common than is female-to-male transmission.

Of the 2.1 million children worldwide living with HIV, most were infected by their HIV-positive mothers during pregnancy, childbirth, or breast feeding. For many countries around the world, interventions to eliminate mother-to-child transmission are the most important HIV prevention strategy (Avert, 2018a). Fortunately, progress is being made in this area. Globally, the annual incidence of new infections among children has been reduced by nearly 50% since 2010 (Avert, 2018a).

A less common route of HIV infection involves a transfusion of infected blood. In the early years of the AIDS epidemic, HIV spread rapidly through transfusions of infected blood to victims of **hemophilia**. Since 1985, however, blood banks have been screening

human immunodeficiency virus (HIV) A virus that infects cells of the immune system, destroying or impairing their function.

acquired immunodeficiency syndrome (AIDS) The most advanced stages of HIV infection, defined by a T cell count of less than 200 and the occurrence of opportunistic infections or HIV-related cancers that take advantage of a weakened immune system.

hemophilia A genetic disease in which the blood fails to clot quickly enough, causing uncontrollable bleeding from even the smallest cut.

Gideon Mendel/Getty Images

AIDS in Africa Six weeks after she gave birth, 29-year-old Mathato Notsi discovered that both she and her baby were HIV positive. At the time, pediatric doses of antiretroviral drugs were available to only one in four children living in Lesotho, South Africa. Luckily, Mathato's daughter was able to receive this lifesaving treatment.

all donor blood for HIV antibodies, and the risk of contracting HIV through transfusion has all but disappeared. Fortunately, HIV is transmitted less easily than most other less deadly viruses (such as malaria). Without a supportive environment of blood, semen, or the cytoplasm of a host cell, the virus quickly dies, usually within 30 minutes. We will examine HIV/AIDS in greater detail later in this chapter.

Prevention and Treatment of STIs

Some STIs can be fully cured by a course of antibiotics or other drugs, especially when the STIs are diagnosed and treated early. Other STIs, unfortunately, have no cure and can only be managed as chronic conditions. Millions of people in the United States and around the world are living with these conditions, a topic we will return to later in this chapter.

Primary Prevention

The surest way to avoid contracting an STI is to abstain from sexual contact with any partner who might be carrying one of these infections. This is easier said than done, however, since a partner may be unaware of being infected or may be less than honest about his or her health status. Thus, mechanical means of prevention offer an important source of protection. The American College of Obstetricians and Gynecologists (2017) recommends that people use a latex condom every time they engage in vaginal, oral, or anal sex. In addition, individuals are advised to avoid sexual behavior that may tear or abrade the skin or vaginal tissue.

Open communication and limiting one's sexual partners are also important ways of reducing STI exposure. When two people are in the formative stages of an intimate relationship, they should discuss their sexual health; ideally, they may agree to each be tested for STIs before having unprotected sex.

Vaccination and Prophylaxis

Preventive vaccines exist for some STIs, including hepatitis A, hepatitis B, and HPV. Because HPV is so prevalent—as mentioned earlier, it is likely to affect virtually all sexually active men and women at some point in their lives—the availability of a vaccine is extremely important. Moreover, HPV vaccines are safe, effective, and widely available. The CDC recommends that 11- or 12-year-old boys and girls be vaccinated before their first sexual encounter as part of standard medical care. In the first 10 years after the vaccine became available in 2006, it reduced HPV infections by 64% among teenage girls in the United States. Yet the use of the vaccine is uneven and controversial: Only 42% of girls and 22% of boys between 13 and 17 years of age have received the recommended three doses of the vaccine (Markowitz and others, 2016). Compare this with the rates of vaccination among adolescents and young adults for meningitis (60%), tetanus (87.6%), and other viruses (MMWR, 2015, July 31).

Why is the HPV vaccine so underutilized? Health psychologists have found that among the barriers to HPV vaccination are beliefs about sexuality, including parental concerns that getting the vaccine will encourage their adolescent son or daughter to have sex. Other barriers include the cost, perceived effectiveness, possible negative health consequences,

TABLE 12.1 Treatment of Sexually Transmitted Infections

STI	Testing	Treatment	Cure Likelihood	Complications / Comments
HPV	Pap smear and follow-up HPV test if risk is indicated; visual examination of genital warts	Cryotherapy and other excision techniques to remove genital warts and/or abnormal cells	No cure, but high rate of recovery without treatment	Vaccine is safe, effective, and widely available; untreated, can lead to infertility, cervical cancer, and other cancers
Chlamydia	Swab of genital area	Antibiotics	Very high	Untreated, can lead to infertility, pelvic inflammatory disease, and ectopic pregnancy
Trichomoniasis	Swab of genital area	Antibiotics	Very high	Untreated, the parasite remains in the body
Gonorrhea	Swab of genital area or discharge fluid	Antibiotics	Very high	Untreated, can lead to infertility, pelvic inflammatory disease, and ectopic pregnancy
Genital Herpes	Swab of blister fluid; blood test if risk is indicated	Antiviral drugs to reduce symptoms	No cure	Virus remains in the body, but outbreaks tend to be less frequent over time; can be passed from mother to infant during childbirth
Syphilis	Blood test; test of fluid from sores, if any	Penicillin or other antibiotics in early stages	Very high in early stages	Tertiary syphilis can cause stillbirth or be passed from mother to infant; can damage the brain, nervous system, and other organs
Hepatitis B	Blood test, liver ultrasound, liver biopsy	Antiviral drugs to reduce symptoms	No cure, but high rate of recovery without treatment; some people become "carriers"	Vaccine is safe, effective, and widely available; untreated, high risk of transmission from mother to infant during pregnancy
HIV	Blood test	Antiretroviral drugs to lower the amount of HIV in blood and prevent development of AIDS	No cure	Untreated, highly likely to be fatal within a decade after infection; can be passed from mother to infant

Information from: American College of Obstetrics and Gynecology (ACOG) (2017). *Sexually transmitted infections: Resource overview*. Mayo Clinic (1998–2018). *Diseases and conditions*. Planned Parenthood (2018). *STDs*. WebMD (2005–2018). *Sexual conditions health center*.

and safety of the vaccine. Another barrier is the lack of information about the timing of vaccination relative to sexual activity (Gerend, Shepherd, & Shepherd, 2013). In addition, racial disparities exist, including a finding that Hispanic Americans and African Americans are less likely to be vaccinated than European Americans (Gelman and others, 2013). Patients who choose to get the HPV vaccination are likely to do so upon a doctor's recommendation, and are likely to hold subjective norms in favor of vaccinations (Krawczyk and others, 2012).

Ever since HIV and AIDS were first identified, scientists have been working to develop a vaccine for this life-threatening virus. This goal has not yet been attained, but some drugs have been found to have a preventive effect. Accordingly, individuals at high risk for HIV exposure are advised to take *pre-exposure prophylaxis*, or *PrEP*, a pharmacological treatment that can reduce the risk of becoming infected with the virus. Patients who report recent exposure to HIV (within the past 72 hours) are sometimes advised to take *post-exposure prophylaxsis*, or *PEP*, a related pharmacological treatment designed to reduce the risk of infection.

Treatment of STIs

Once someone becomes infected with an STI, treatment will vary according to the particular type of infection and how far it has progressed before the patient received medical attention. As shown in Table 12.1, some STIs can be treated with antibiotics and have a high likelihood of cure, especially when caught early. Others are difficult or impossible to cure, but they can be treated to some extent. Because of the likelihood of passing an infection on to sex partners, when patients are diagnosed with an STI they often are encouraged to have recent partners seek medical attention, and to avoid unprotected sex until treatment is completed.

THE AIDS EPIDEMIC

Most of today's college students are young enough that they don't remember a time when HIV and AIDS were unknown, but their parents and grandparents have such memories.

A Brief History of HIV/AIDS

In the late 1970s, unrecognized cases of what we now know to be AIDS began to appear. Although no one knows exactly how the AIDS virus infected the first human, it appears to have originated in west-central Africa, spreading quickly through neighboring countries. HIV is one of a family of primate viruses similar to a harmless virus found in certain subspecies of chimpanzees and green monkeys. Of particular interest in the investigation into the origins of AIDS is the *simian immunodeficiency virus (SIV)*, which affects monkeys. This virus is believed to be at least 32,000 years old and closely resembles HIV1 and HIV2, the two types of HIV (Worobey and others, 2010).

The disease was first documented in humans around 1980, when several dozen young men were diagnosed with a cluster of similar symptoms with an unknown cause. Their symptoms were indicative of **Kaposi's sarcoma**, a rare cancer usually found only among the elderly. Epidemiologists suspected that the cause of the unexpected illness was a weakened immune system. Since most of the first reported victims were gay men and injection drug users, it appeared that the disease was being transmitted sexually or through the exchange of infected blood.

In 1983, the National Institutes of Health (NIH) in the United States and the Pasteur Institute in France concluded that a new virus was the probable cause of the disease. A year later, in the spring of 1984, the U.S. Department of Health announced that it had isolated the new virus—HIV. A public health initiative of massive proportions followed.

Kaposi's sarcoma A rare cancer of the blood vessels that serve the skin, mucous membranes, and other glands in the body.

By 1987, the CDC had established the National AIDS Clearinghouse, which provided telephone service to deliver accurate information to health practitioners and the general public, disseminated millions of copies of health education publications, and helped to coordinate the efforts of thousands of local and regional research projects and public health organizations (Sinnock, Murphy, Baker, & Bates, 1991).

Previously limited mostly to White gay men and injection drug users in the United States, AIDS began surfacing among other demographic groups during the late 1980s and through the 1990s. As the disease continued to grow exponentially, it reached 400,000 cases worldwide by 1994, with increased incidence among women and still no effective drug treatments.

As the millennium approached, new anti-HIV drugs were finally proving to be effective, and death rates from AIDS declined sharply in the United States (UNAIDS, 2007). However, these drugs weren't available to everyone who needed them, and worldwide the AIDS **pandemic** continued to spiral out of control (see Table 12.2). Now, four decades into the pandemic, HIV has reached every corner of the globe, causing about 35 million deaths from AIDS-related causes so far, the majority in low- and middle-income countries (Figure 12.3). Of the 36.7 million people living with HIV/AIDS worldwide, 30% do not know that they are infected. This number includes 1.8 million people who became infected in 2016. The same year, 1 million people died of AIDS-related illnesses (WHO, 2018a). Fortunately, things have begun to improve. Since 2010, new HIV infections among adults and children have

Isaac Brekken/Getty Images for Global Gaming Expo

AIDS Awareness NBA superstar Earvin "Magic" Johnson stunned the world in 1991 by announcing that he was HIV positive. Because of Johnson's fame and popularity, this statement was a major factor in reducing AIDS stigma both in the United States and around the world. In addition to decades of HIV/AIDS advocacy, Johnson has pursued a highly successful career as chairman and CEO of the billion-dollar investment conglomerate Magic Johnson Enterprises, and as owner or co-owner of business ventures in professional sports, entertainment, financial services, and other industries.

pandemic A worldwide epidemic such as AIDS.

TABLE 12.2 Regional HIV/AIDS Statistics, End of 2016

Region	Adults and Children Living with HIV/AIDS	Adults and Children Newly Infected	Main Mode(s) of Transmission*
Eastern and southern Africa	19.4 million	790,000	Hetero
Western and central Africa	6.1 million	370,000	IDU, Hetero
Middle East and North Africa	230,000	18,000	IDU, Hetero
Asia and the Pacific	5.1 million	270,000	IDU, Hetero, MSM
Latin America	1.8 million	97,000	MSM, IDU, Hetero
Caribbean	310,000	18,000	Hetero, MSM
Eastern Europe and Central Asia	1.6 million	190,000	IDU, MSM
Western and central Europe and North American	2.1 million	73,000	MSM, IDU, Hetero
Total	36.7 million	1.8 million	

* MSM (sexual transmission among men who have sex with men); IDU (transmission through injection drug use); Hetero (heterosexual transmission)

Data from: UNAIDS Data 2017.

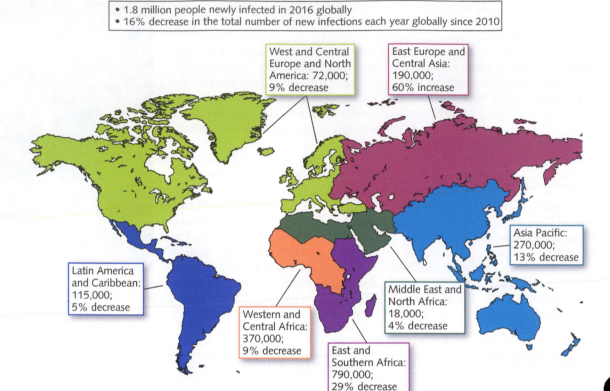

- 1.8 million people newly infected in 2016 globally
- 16% decrease in the total number of new infections each year globally since 2010

West and Central Europe and North America: 72,000; 9% decrease

East Europe and Central Asia: 190,000; 60% increase

Asia Pacific: 270,000; 13% decrease

Latin America and Caribbean: 115,000; 5% decrease

Western and Central Africa: 370,000; 9% decrease

Middle East and North Africa: 18,000; 4% decrease

East and Southern Africa: 790,000; 29% decrease

FIGURE 12.3 Number of New HIV Infections in 2016 and Change Since 2010 Although new HIV infections have decreased since 2010 in most regions of the world, they have increased dramatically in East Europe and Central Asia.

Information from: Avert. (2017, August 23). *New HIV infections around the world in 2016.* Infographic.

Data from: UNAIDS Data 2017.

decreased by an estimated 11% and 47%, respectively; AIDS-related deaths have fallen by 48%; and the United Nations has set the goal of ending the AIDS pandemic by 2030 (UNAIDS, 2018).

The Epidemiology of AIDS

As you learned in Chapter 2, the first step in fighting and preventing a chronic disease like AIDS is taken by epidemiologists, who investigate the factors that contribute to the prevalence and incidence of the disease in a particular population. Keeping track of the distribution of AIDS by demographic traits is a difficult job because of the fluidity of the disease, but the disease is most prevalent among certain populations. In the United States, the AIDS epidemic has taken the greatest toll on gay, bisexual, and other men who have sex with men (MSM), particularly young African Americans (Figure 12.4). An estimated 1.1 million people in the United States are living with HIV, with the largest number of diagnoses occurring in people 20–29 years of age (CDC, 2018f). This number may be misleading, however, due to the long incubation period associated with the HIV virus. Many people with AIDS who are now in their twenties undoubtedly were infected while still in their teens. Nearly one in seven HIV+ individuals in the United States (14.3%) are unaware of their infection (CDC, 2017d).

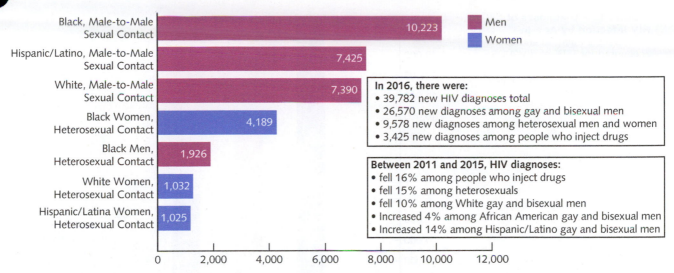

In 2016, there were:
- 39,782 new HIV diagnoses total
- 26,570 new diagnoses among gay and bisexual men
- 9,578 new diagnoses among heterosexual men and women
- 3,425 new diagnoses among people who inject drugs

Between 2011 and 2015, HIV diagnoses:
- fell 16% among people who inject drugs
- fell 15% among heterosexuals
- fell 10% among White gay and bisexual men
- Increased 4% among African American gay and bisexual men
- Increased 14% among Hispanic/Latino gay and bisexual men

FIGURE 12.4 New HIV Diagnoses in the United States Among the Most-Affected Groups, 2016 The estimated incidence of HIV has remained stable in recent years, at about 40,000 new cases each year. Some groups are affected more than others, especially men who have sex with men (MSM); injection drug users (IDUs); and, among races/ethnicities, African Americans.

Data from: CDC. (2017d). HIV in the United States: At a glance.

The initial spread of the HIV virus among injection drug users and gay men in the United States and other Western countries is believed to have occurred because these are relatively small, closed populations in which an individual is more likely to be exposed to the virus repeatedly. Since that time, AIDS has had a devastating effect on minority populations in the United States. For instance, although African Americans make up around 12% of the U.S. population, they account for 44% of all new HIV cases (CDC, 2017d). Hispanics/Latinos represent 18% of the U.S. population, but they account for about 25% of all new cases of HIV infection (CDC, 2017d). The main transmission route for HIV in these groups is high-risk sexual contact (e.g., unprotected sex and sex with multiple partners)—behavior that may be made more likely by alcohol and drug use.

Ethnic and racial differences in rates of HIV transmission are thought to reflect sociocultural differences in drug use. For example, in impoverished minority communities, injection drug users commonly share needles; of course, when they share those needles with HIV-positive drug users, they almost certainly become infected themselves and expose their sexual partners. In 2016, about 9% of new HIV diagnoses in the United States were attributable to injection drug use (IDU) (CDC, 2018e).

HIV is increasingly affecting older adults (see Figure 12.5). In 2016, people aged 50 and older accounted for 17.1% (6,812) of the estimated 39,660 HIV diagnoses in the United States (CDC, 2017d). The increase in HIV among those over age 50 is partly due to advanced HIV therapy, which has increased life expectancy. However, research suggests that it is also because older people, as well as their health care providers, incorrectly perceive older adults as having little risk of contracting HIV and other sexually transmitted infections and therefore recognize it less often (or more slowly) when people in this age group do get such diseases. Adding to the problem is the fact that HIV infection is harder to detect among older adults because the symptoms are sometimes masked by normal signs of aging. As a result, older adults are more likely than younger people to be diagnosed late in the course of HIV infection, which means they start treatment later and possibly have a poorer prognosis.

FIGURE 12.5 Diagnoses of HIV Infection by Age In 2016, people aged 50 and over accounted for 17.1% of HIV/AIDS diagnoses in the United States.

Data from: CDC. (2017b). *HIV in the United States: At a glance.*

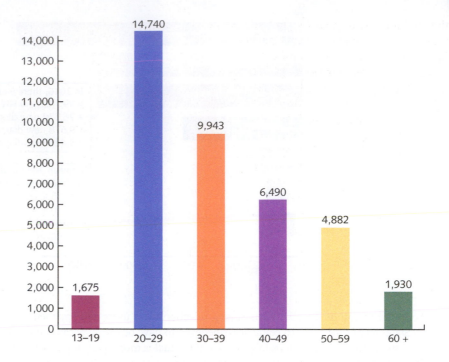

Although HIV diagnoses among women declined 16% between 2011 and 2015, 7,529 women (19% of all new cases) received a diagnosis of HIV infection in the United States in 2016 (CDC, 2018c). Among all women who received an HIV diagnosis, 61% were African American, 19% were European American, and 16% were Hispanic/Latina. Although most of the exposure (87%) was from heterosexual contact, 28% of HIV diagnoses among White women were due to injection drug use.

How HIV Progresses

HIV infects mostly lymph tissues, where *lymphocytes* develop and are stored. Recall from Chapter 3 that lymphocytes are immune cells that help prevent cancer and other chronic illnesses by controlling cell growth. They also guard against infection by producing antibodies. HIV invades and destroys a type of lymphocyte called the T cell, which is a crucial player in the immune response because it recognizes harmful microbes and triggers the production of antibodies. It also coordinates the release of natural killer (NK) cells.

HIV is classified as a **retrovirus** because it works by injecting a copy of its own genetic material, or genome, into the DNA of the T cell (the host cell). The infected DNA may remain dormant in the chromosome of the host lymphocyte for a period of time. Eventually, however, the infected lymphocyte is certain to become activated against another virus or some other foreign substance. At that point, it divides, replicating HIV along with itself. As infected cells continue to divide, vast numbers of HIV particles emerge from the infected host and invade other lymphocytes.

HIV progresses through four stages of infection, which vary in length from person to person (see Figure 12.6). During the first stage, which lasts from one to eight weeks,

retrovirus A virus that copies its genetic information onto the DNA of a host cell.

the immune system destroys most HIV, so people experience only mild symptoms that are similar to those of many other illnesses, such as swollen lymph glands, sore throat, fever, chronic diarrhea, skeletal pain, gynecological infection in women, neurological problems, and, in some cases, a skin rash. These symptoms are often so mild that they go unnoticed or unremembered.

The second stage, which may last for months or years, appears to be a period of latency. The person has no obvious symptoms except perhaps for swollen lymph nodes, which may go unnoticed; nevertheless, the HIV infection is far from inactive. In fact, during stage 2, as T cell concentration falls, HIV is constantly replicating.

Within five years, 30% of infected people move to stage 3, when T cells are further reduced, immune function is impaired, and opportunistic infections occur. Among the most common are Kaposi's sarcoma (a cancer of blood vessels that causes purplish spots in the skin, mouth, and lungs); lymphoma; parasitic gastrointestinal infections; and *pneumocystis carinii pneumonia (PCP),* a bacterial disease that caused 60% of all AIDS deaths prior to the development of the effective treatments available today.

During stage 4, the number of T cells (sometimes called CD4 cells) drops from a healthy count of 1,000 to 200 cells or less per cubic milliliter of blood, and almost all natural immunity is lost. At this point, HIV has developed into AIDS. As T cell levels

National Cancer Institute/Science Source

The AIDS Virus HIV is classified as a retrovirus because it destroys lymphocytes by injecting a copy of its own genetic material into the host cell's DNA.

Stage 1: Soon after the initial HIV infection, the immune system destroys most of the virus; symptoms are mild or nonexistent.	Stage 2 (latency period): The T cell concentration falls and HIV concentration rises, accompanied by symptoms such as swollen lymph nodes.	Stage 3: As T cells are reduced further, immune function is impaired, and opportunistic infections occur.	Stage 4: Finally, almost all natural immunity is lost and full-blown AIDS occurs.

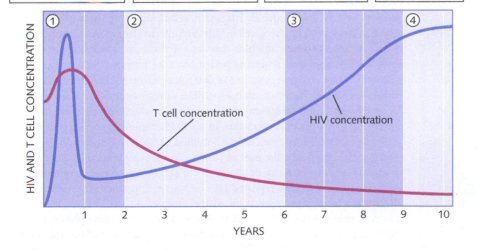

FIGURE 12.6 The Course of HIV/AIDS HIV infection may be carried for years in Stage 1 before symptoms appear or become severe enough that medical attention is sought. Unfortunately, this "dormant" period often means that carriers who are unaware of their infection are likely to spread HIV to others unwittingly.

drop below 100, the balance of power in the immune system shifts to favor the invading virus. HIV levels soar, and microorganisms that the immune system normally would destroy easily begin to proliferate. Without treatment, death generally occurs within a year or two.

Factors in the Progression of AIDS

The period from diagnosis of full-blown AIDS until death is notoriously unpredictable—as short as several months or as long as five years. Although the average time from HIV infection to AIDS is about 10 years, people with HIV who start treatment with anti-AIDS drugs have life expectancies only about 20% shorter than that of the general population, provided they start treatment before their CD4 count drops below 200 cells per microliter (Johnson, 2013). Several factors are thought to play a role in the prognosis of AIDS.

One factor is the strength of the initial immune response. HIV progresses much more slowly among patients whose immune systems mount strong lymphocyte activity in the acute stage of HIV sickness (stage 2). This strong defense apparently helps preserve the body's later ability to produce the T cells that target HIV.

Genetic vulnerability also may affect the rate at which AIDS develops. Viruses require collaboration from the body, which in the case of AIDS is the existence of the protein receptor to which HIV particles bind. AIDS researchers suspect that some people have genes that protect against the development of this receptor. Indeed, it appears that 1% of people of Northern European descent inherit a gene from both parents that blocks this development, giving them apparent immunity to HIV infection. Another 20% inherit the protective gene from only one parent and, while not immune to HIV, display a much slower progression of symptoms (Ring, 2012).

Globally, access to treatment is a major factor in the progression of AIDs (see Figure 12.7). As described in the chapter's opening vignette, Greg Louganis was fortunate to have access to the latest treatments from the time he was first diagnosed as HIV positive, whereas many patients do not. Fortunately, the number of people receiving HIV treatment has increased dramatically in recent years, particularly in low-income countries. Today's optimum HIV treatment regimen is *combination antiretroviral therapy (cART),* which involves several antiretroviral drugs that attack different parts of HIV or stop the virus from entering cells. Although the treatment does not get rid of HIV, it slows the pace at which the virus reproduces. The cART regimen used to be complicated, requiring patients to take a series of pills at varying times of the day. At a cost of up to $15,000 a year, many AIDS patients simply couldn't afford it. However, as competition among generic manufacturers increases, the cost of treatment continues to fall, which has been especially significant in low-income countries. In 2016, 19.5 million people living with HIV received cART, up from only 7.5 million in 2010 (Avert, 2018b).

After HIV exposure, the pace at which clinical symptoms of AIDS begin to appear and the severity of illness at all stages can vary tremendously. Poor nutrition, drug use, repeated HIV exposure, and other viral infections all can accelerate the progression of the disease. As with other diseases, however, epidemiologists have discovered that even after these physical risk factors are accounted for, there is still a tremendous amount of unexplained variability in the course of AIDS.

AIDS Intervention Until the past few years, AIDS patients were required to take a variety of pills each day on a very strict timetable. However, with research advances, more streamlined pharmacological regimens have been used and have proven equally effective.

Veronique Burger/Science Source

Discrimination, Social Exclusion, and HIV Risk

Researchers have begun to focus on psychosocial factors that may contribute to ethnic/racial disparities in HIV risk (Stock, Gibbons, Peterson, & Gerard, 2013b). In particular, racial discrimination and social exclusion have been suggested as important contributing factors in health-risk behaviors and HIV infection (see *Diversity and Healthy Living: HIV Stigma and Living with AIDS Around the World*). Data from the Family and Community Health Study (FACHS) have shown that experiences of discrimination at ages 10 to 11 were associated with greater sexual risk-taking at ages 18 to 19, even after controlling for neighborhood risk, socioeconomic status (SES), gender, age, the absence of a father, and other variables. These data also demonstrate that discrimination is often associated with heightened perceived norms for deviant behavior among peers, which in turn predict higher levels of substance use and risky sex behaviors (Roberts and others, 2012).

Research indicates that there is a profound need for preventive interventions that target substance use and risky sex behaviors in reducing HIV risk, particularly among young Black adults, for whom the incidence of HIV/AIDS is 14 times higher than it is for other racial groups in the United States (CDC, 2013b). Interventions that focus on the effects of substance use on sexual risk-taking in response to discrimination and other stressors seem especially warranted. In addition, parenting that involves communication, warmth, and discipline (Gibbons and others, 2010), as well as racial identity and socialization (Stock and others, 2013b), may buffer the adverse effects of discrimination on HIV risk-taking.

FIGURE 12.7 Global Access to Treatment The number of people living with HIV globally has stabilized and access to treatment is on the rise, but millions still lack access to treatment.

Data from: Avert. (2018b). *Global HIV and AIDS statistics.*

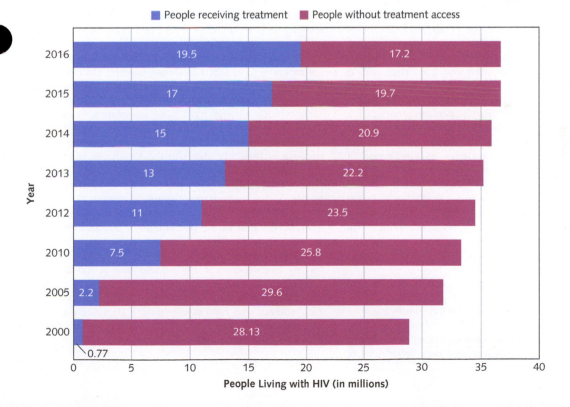

Diversity and Healthy Living

HIV Stigma and Living with AIDS Around the World

Besides the physical suffering caused by their chronic illness, people living with HIV/AIDS (PLWHA) have other challenges to overcome, including stigmatization. *Public stigma* occurs when a group of people is subjected to negative stereotypes, prejudice, and discrimination that cause them to be devalued and cut off from society. Stigma is often directed at specific groups because they are associated with a disease, lifestyle, or behavior. To experience *self-stigma*, a member of a marginalized group must become aware of hurtful stereotypes (for example, that people with AIDS are entirely to blame for their illness) and agree with the stereotypes ("That's right, I am to blame for my illness").

In Canada, for example, homeless youth are a highly marginalized population who have reduced access to healthcare, are more likely to become involved with the criminal justice system, are more often exposed to food insecurity, and have limited job and education opportunities. Compared to the general Canadian youth population, they also are more likely to be sexually active, have multiple sex partners, experience sexual debut at an earlier age, report low rates of condom use, and engage in sex work (Zivanovic and others, 2016). These factors place street-involved young people at an elevated risk of acquiring STIs. Indeed, the incidence of both chlamydia and gonorrhea among street-involved youth in Canada is ten times that of their peers, and the prevalence of HIV is three times that of the Canadian adult population (Karamouzian and others, 2017).

HIV-related stigmatization was prevalent worldwide during the early years of the AIDS pandemic, when the increasing incidence and prevalence of new cases of HIV seemed unstoppable, even in resource-rich, affluent countries such as the United States, Canada, and those of Western Europe. Fortunately, today PLWHA who live in countries where access to medical treatment is good, and who also have sufficient personal resources to facilitate their care—people like Greg Louganis, whom we met in the chapter opening—are less likely to experience HIV-related stigmatization (Stangl, 2017).

PLWHA suffer from stigma due to cultural rejection of their sexual orientation, their gender identities, their behavior (such as drug use and sex work), or simply because they are HIV positive. One meta-analysis of 64 separate research studies of PLWHA reported significant associations between perceived HIV-related stigma and higher rates of depression, lower social support, and lower levels of adherence to antiretroviral medications and other health and social services (Rueda and others, 2016).

HIV-related stigma and discrimination is a global phenomenon, although its manifestations vary from country to country and across different communities and individuals. HIV stigma remains high in South Africa and Zambia, where PLWHA often become objects of scorn, hatred, and even violence (Hargreaves and others, 2018). Research by the ICRW (Stangl, 2017) recently identified numerous consequences of HIV-related stigma for PLWHA in these countries:

- loss of hope and feelings of worthlessness
- loss of reputation
- loss of income and livelihood
- loss of marriage and childbearing options
- poor care within the health sector
- wariness of other people for fear of HIV status being discovered

In addition to its negative psychological impact on people, stigma is a significant public health problem because of the barriers it creates for PLWHA in obtaining treatment, housing, education, and employment, all of which are essential to health. The United Nations' People Living with HIV Stigma Index measures stigma and discrimination reported by PLWHA. In 22 of the 65 countries in which Stigma Index surveys have been completed, more than 10% of PLWHA reported they had been denied health care, or had been refused employment or a work opportunity because of their HIV status in the 12 months before the survey (UNAIDS, 2016).

HIV-related stigma also blocks access to condoms, HIV testing, and adherence to antiretroviral therapy (Galea and others, 2018). In one remarkable study, UNAIDS researchers reported that as the percentage of people living in a region who report discriminatory attitudes toward PLWHA increases, the percentage of people who are screened for HIV decreases. Is it any wonder that in sub-Saharan Africa an estimated 49% of adults living with HIV do not know their HIV status? Fear of social rejection and health care workers who hold discriminatory attitudes were the most commonly cited reasons for avoiding HIV screening (Stangl, Lloyd, Brady, Holland, & Baral, 2013).

HIV stigmatization has persisted despite improvements, as a result of cART, in the quality of life and life expectancy of people living with HIV/AIDS. Although many countries have nondiscrimination laws to protect people living with HIV, these laws are often poorly enforced. In some countries, HIV-related stigma is even facilitated by laws and policies that are overly broad in criminalizing PLWHA (Bernard & Cameron, 2016). As of 2016, for example, 73 countries criminalized same-sex activity (Carroll, 2016).

In March 2016, UNAIDS and the World Health Organization launched the Agenda for Zero Discrimination in Healthcare. This initiative works toward a world where all people, everywhere, are able to receive the health care they need with no discrimination. Until that goal is achieved, health psychologists can play an important role by helping to design interventions that address the behavioral and social aspects of HIV/AIDS, and by informing public policy professionals, health care professionals who treat PLWHA, and society at large about HIV stigma. As with other aspects of STI prevention, it is easy for people to become complacent. For example, a recent meta-analysis reported significant regional variation in scientists' approach to the problem of HIV/AIDS. The researchers found that proximity to the HIV/AIDS problem was strongly correlated with the extent to which scientists investigate the behavioral and social aspects of HIV/AIDS rather than the biomedical aspects (Lakeh & Ghaffarzadegan, 2017).

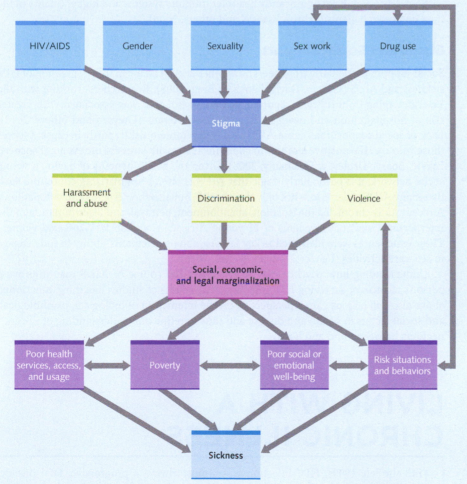

FIGURE 12.8 How Stigma Leads to Sickness

Information from: Avert. (2017, January 27). *How HIV stigma leads to sickness. HIV-related stigma and discrimination have wide-ranging consequences.* Based on United Nations Development Programme stigma–sickness slope.

Stress and Negative Emotions

Stress, negative emotions, and social isolation may influence the pace at which AIDS progresses, perhaps by altering hormonal and immune environments that affect the resistance of host cells to the invading virus. One recent study of 117 HIV-positive African American men found that participants' history of psychosocial trauma predicted levels of stress-related biomarkers in their urine, including cortisol, epinephrine, norepinephrine, and dopamine (Glover, Williams, & Kisler, 2013).

Several researchers have reported that low self-esteem, a pessimistic outlook, chronic depression, and other negative emotions may influence the production of proinflammatory cytokines (Pala and others, 2012). They also are linked with a decline in T cells and a more rapid course of illness and the development of opportunistic infections among HIV-infected individuals (Cole, 2008). Interventions that reduce depression are also valuable in the fight against AIDS, because depression increases the severity of many immune-related disorders (Safen, Reisner, Herrick, Mimiaga, & Stall, 2010). Patients without depression have significantly healthier immune systems and higher quality of life than depressed patients (Schroecksnadel and others, 2008).

Stress and Social Support

Social support, particularly from peers, is another critical factor in the progression of HIV sickness and AIDS (Galvan, Davis, Banks, & Bing, 2008). Researchers working with the Veterans Aging Cohort Study reported that social isolation was associated with greater risk of hospitalization and death in HIV-positive veterans (Greysen and others, 2013). Lack of social support may cause AIDS to develop more quickly, partly because it leaves those who are HIV positive less able to cope effectively with stressful life events (Deichert, Fekete, Boarts, Druley, & Delahanty, 2008). Given the health benefits of having a strong social network, it is particularly tragic that AIDS is often a stigmatizing condition, such that many AIDS patients lose not only their health, but also their friends and companions. A recent study chronicled the isolation, abandonment, betrayal, and discrimination in the interpersonal and social systems of 11 young African American HIV-infected women. These experiences were identified as key factors in the participants' ability to fully engage in self-care activities (Peltzer, Domian, & Teel, 2016).

Understanding how psychosocial factors affect the course of AIDS may improve a person's chances of surviving HIV infection. The results of studies like those mentioned above also will help us gain a perspective on the interaction of biological, psychological, and social factors in health and disease and thus to refine our understanding of the connections between mind and body.

LIVING WITH A CHRONIC ILLNESS

Until the late 1990s, HIV infection was almost always a progressive, fatal disease. Medical interventions focused almost exclusively on treating the opportunistic diseases that resulted from immune failure, not on eliminating (or even controlling) the

HIV virus. Today, however, scientists have a much better understanding of how the virus behaves, and treatment advances have transformed AIDS into a manageable chronic illness; people like Greg Louganis are living with HIV for longer periods of time.

Chronic illnesses such as HIV/AIDS are the leading cause of disability throughout the world, including in the United States where they cause 7 of every 10 deaths and account for most of the nation's annual health care expenditures (USDHHS, 2017). Half of all Americans have at least one chronic illness, and one third have multiple chronic conditions. As discussed in Chapter 8, NCDs account for the most prevalent combinations of chronic conditions: hypertension and diabetes, hypertension and heart disease, and hypertension and cancer.

Some chronic conditions can't be ignored and are felt every day; one example is the progressive loss of muscle control that accompanies the *amyotrophic lateral sclerosis (ALS)* that the famous physicist and cosmologist Stephen Hawking lived with for most of his life, Other conditions, such as hypertension or insulin resistance, are less noticeable but nevertheless dangerous. In addition to its effects on a person's physical well-being, chronic illness can have a substantial impact on cognition, emotions, self-esteem, and interpersonal relationships.

A diagnosis of a chronic illness often releases a flood of psychological and emotional responses, including fear and uncertainty about the future, anxiety, sadness, grief, or anger (Kwakkenbos & others, 2014; Stanton & Revenson, 2011). For some chronic illnesses, such as STIs and diabetes, diagnosis may be accompanied by feelings of guilt and shame (Nash, 2013). Depression is also common, as 56-year-old Greg Louganis noted in a recent interview. "At the time I was diagnosed [in 1988], we thought of HIV as a death sentence. . . . I did suffer from depression; if we had a day off [from Olympic training], I couldn't get out of bed. I would just pull the covers over my head." People who are experiencing a number of stressful life events before diagnosis and therefore have a high allostatic load, as well as people who have a history of depression, may be at particular risk of psychological distress when they learn they have a chronic illness (Bourdeau & Walters, 2013).

Although the experience of chronic disease often provokes significant distress and life disruption, many individuals, such as Stephen Hawking and Greg Louganis, eventually report positive adjustment. Psychological adjustment has a major impact on chronic disease health outcomes, and researchers have sought to determine why some people who face the enduring stress of a chronic illness adjust well, whereas others experience significant emotional and interpersonal decline. To answer this question we must first ask, what does it mean to adjust to chronic disease?

As Figure 12.9 shows, acute and ongoing stressors; cognitive, emotional and behavioral responses; personal background; and social and environmental background are important factors in how well a person adjusts to a chronic condition such as ALS or HIV/AIDS. Chronic disease often triggers acute stressors, (becoming aware of a disease diagnosis, undergoing treatment, experiencing relapse, etc.), as well as ongoing stressors (fear about the future, threats to social

FIGURE 12.9 Adjusting to a Chronic Condition Individuals living with chronic conditions have to cope with a range of acute and ongoing stressors, including cognitive, emotional and behavioral responses; personal background; and social and environmental background.

Information from: Dekker, J., & DeGroot, V. (2016). Psychological adjustment to chronic disease and rehabilitation—An exploration. *Disability and Rehabilitation, 40*(1):116–120. National Center for Biotechnology Information, National Institutes of Health.

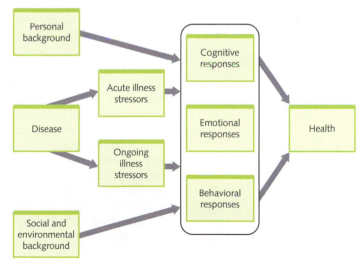

relationships, disruption of lifestyle, etc.). **Psychological adjustment** refers to a person's cognitive, emotional, and behavioral responses to these stressors, which can be beneficial and contribute to improved health, or detrimental and contribute to worsening health (Dekker & de Groot, 2016). An example of a cognitive response leading to good health is self-efficacy (confidence in one's ability to perform activities such as adherence to medical treatment), while wishful thinking is a thought process that is less likely to be effective. Sticking with one's workout routine, as Olympic diver Greg Louganis has done in the decades since his HIV diagnosis, is a behavioral response that may improve health, whereas avoiding physical activity is more likely to result in worsening health in the long run. As we've seen throughout this book, personal background factors such as early life experiences, socioeconomic status, personality (e.g., negative affectivity), and neighborhood quality also influence how people adjust to chronic disease. These factors moderate the impact of illness stressors, as well as our cognitive, emotional, and behavioral responses to these stressors.

Health Psychologists' Roles in Battling STIs

In the 1980s, once HIV was understood to be sexually transmitted, health psychologists played a key role in designing a major public education campaign to prevent new cases of HIV. This campaign focused on delivering several messages, including the importance of condom use and other safer sex practices, testing blood donors so that HIV wouldn't be spread by transfusions, and discouraging needle-sharing among injection drug users. This watershed moment represents the first major health epidemic for which behavioral strategies and educational interventions had the potential to ameliorate the incidence of new cases.

Health psychologists play a number of roles in battling STIs, including both primary and secondary prevention interventions. Primary prevention includes counseling people about being tested for infection and helping individuals modify high-risk behaviors. Secondary prevention includes helping patients cope with treatment regimen, as well as emotional and cognitive disturbances related to infection.

Since the beginning of the AIDS epidemic, many different psychosocial interventions have been implemented to promote prevention and screening for STIs. The earliest programs targeted high-risk groups such as gay men or injection drug users, using behavior modification and educational interventions to try to change attitudes and behaviors. Programs at the high school and college levels have typically focused on increasing students' knowledge of AIDS and promoting safe sex. Mass media campaigns have emphasized awareness of how AIDS is transmitted—and they have been quite successful. Despite a slow beginning, AIDS education and other intervention programs skyrocketed during the 1990s, thanks initially to the efforts of the gay community in the United States. As a result, public awareness of AIDS increased, and a corresponding reduction in risk-related behaviors occurred, accompanied by a sharp decline in the number of new cases of HIV infection. Globally, however, threat of HIV/AIDS continues to be a major health concern (see *Diversity and Healthy Living*).

Let's take a look at the theories on which health psychology's intervention programs are based. Then we'll examine some of the interventions that have proven to be effective in reducing HIV/AIDS risk-related behavior.

The Basis for Psychosocial Interventions

Many of the theoretical models described in Chapter 6 have been used to predict whether and when people will change a risky health-related behavior, so those models often form the basis for HIV/AIDS intervention programs.

Social-cognitive theory, which focuses on the interaction of environmental events, our internal processes, and our behaviors, has served as the framework for a number of interventions (Kelly & Kalichman, 2002). Three factors addressed by this model appear to be particularly important in successful intervention programs: (1) *perceived social norms* regarding peer acceptance of HIV risk-reducing behaviors; (2) *self-efficacy beliefs* controlling one's own thoughts, emotions, and behaviors in order to avoid unsafe behaviors; and (3) *social skills,* the ability to respond assertively in negotiating risky behaviors. The relevance of the social-cognitive model was demonstrated by Seth Kalichman (2008), who found that gay men who practice high-risk behaviors also score lower on measures of perceived safer-sex norms, safer-sex self-efficacy, and social skills.

The health belief model, which is based on the idea that beliefs predict behavior, has achieved modest success with a variety of high-risk groups in predicting condom use, the number of sexual partners, and knowledge of partners' past sexual history. The theory of planned behavior, which links beliefs and behavior, has achieved greater success, probably due to the influence of social norms on the sexual activity of many at-risk populations, including teenagers (Davis and others, 2016). Researchers have consistently found that people with more favorable attitudes toward condoms, as well as those who believe their friends are supportive of condom use, are more likely to engage in protected sex. The researchers have also found that individuals in high-risk groups, such as young men who have sex with men, often have overly optimistic beliefs about their risk, which does little to deter their risk behaviors (MacKellar and others, 2007). These dangerous beliefs, perhaps fomented by the success of antiretroviral therapy, may create a form of *AIDS optimism:* HIV-negative men who have sex with men are less concerned about contracting HIV; HIV-positive men who have sex with men are less concerned about transmitting it; and both groups are more likely to engage in unsafe sex—resulting in more HIV infection (Pham, 2007).

Support for stage models comes from evidence that certain individuals may profit more than others from a specific intervention. For example, younger, less knowledgeable individuals tend to benefit from educational interventions that close gaps in knowledge about how AIDS is transmitted, while older individuals in certain high-risk groups may be more likely to profit from interventions that stir them into preventive action.

Educational Programs

An important motivational factor in many models of health behavior (see Chapter 6) is *outcome expectancy,* as a person balances the pros and cons of a specific action, such as using a condom. In one study of 410 men who have sex with men (MSM) recruited at different gay venues in Hong Kong, participants completed a questionnaire about the costs and benefits of condom use that tapped a range of different consequences that could occur if people use condoms with their partners (see *Your Health Assets*). The items were rated on a six-point Likert scale, from *(1) extremely unlikely* to *(6) extremely likely.* The results showed that the perceived benefits of condom use were significantly and most

Your Health Assets

Costs and Benefits of Condom Use for MSM

How likely do you think it is that condom use can:

1. protect both of you against HIV?
2. show your concern for your partner's well-being?
3. offend your partner?
4. provide variety in your sex life?
5. reduce sexual pleasure?
6. interrupt foreplay?
7. reduce the intimacy of sex?
8. destroy the spontaneity of sex?
9. reduce trust between you and your partner?

Information from: Teng, Y., & Mak, W. W. S. (2011). The role of planning and self-efficacy in condom use among men who have sex with men: An application of the Health Action Process Approach Model. *Health Psychology, 30*(1), 119–128.

strongly related to condom use intentions, underscoring the importance of emphasizing these issues in STI-prevention campaigns (Teng & Mak, 2011).

All these results suggest that the frequency of unprotected sex can be dramatically reduced with a few steps: help people to improve their outlook on life, their feelings of self-efficacy, and their sense of personal control; encourage them to talk more openly about safe sex; and always take the following precautions:

- Stay sober. Alcohol and many other drugs lower inhibitions and increase the likelihood of high-risk behaviors.

- Be selective in choosing partners, and limit the number of partners in the *sexual network*. Avoid sexual contacts with people who are known to engage in high-risk sexual or drug-use behaviors.

- Use latex condoms during vaginal, anal, and oral sex. These barriers block nearly all sexually transmitted microorganisms, including HIV. Doctor-prescribed and -fitted vaginal diaphragms or cervical caps that block semen and spermicides that paralyze sperm (and lymphocytes) are also advisable.

- Never share hypodermic needles, razors, cuticle scissors, or other implements that may be contaminated with another person's blood or bodily fluids.

- Do not be lulled into a sense of complacency about STIs by media reports about treatment breakthroughs. There is still no cure for AIDS or many other STIs.

Promoting Adherence to Treatment

Another way that health psychologists have become involved in the war on AIDS is by designing interventions to promote adherence to medical treatment regimens. Poor adherence remains a substantial problem for many chronic illnesses. In the case of those undergoing cART, poor adherence can lead to significantly decreased life expectancy; it also increases the likelihood of HIV transmission. Poor adherence is particularly problematic among adolescents living in low- and middle-income countries (Hudelson & Cluver, 2015).

Online interventions have been shown to promote adherence to treatment and to modify a variety of health behaviors (Webb, Joseph, Yardley, & Michie, 2010). As with other education interventions, tailoring online content to individual users improves outcomes by easing the delivery of information and making it more relevant. **Dynamic tailoring**, which refers to the delivering of individualized health messages over multiple time periods to provide unique feedback based on the individual's status at that moment in time, is particularly effective (Johnson, Cummins, & Evers, 2008). In one study, researchers delivered dynamically tailored messages via mobile phone to 52 HIV-positive MSM. For participants who had reported nonadherence to their regimens, as well as those who were just beginning antiretroviral therapy, the reminder messages were delivered one to three times each day (e.g., "Stop, drop, and pop. Take your meds now."). Participants who were adherent received weekly messages that encouraged them to keep taking medications (e.g., "He shoots! He scores! Perfect med adherence. Great job!"). Over the three-month intervention period, participants reported reading and enjoying the text messages, as well as missing significantly fewer days, and researchers found a significant decrease in viral load and increase in CD4 cell counts (Lewis and others, 2013).

dynamic tailoring The delivery of individualized and targeted health messages over multiple periods of time.

A critical factor in tailored interventions that are delivered via smartphones, tablets, and other digital devices is **eHealth literacy**, or how well a person navigates, understands, and uses electronic health information (Horvath & Bauermeister, 2017). Tailoring online content is most likely to benefit those with moderate or high levels of eHealth literacy because of their familiarity and skill in using digital devices and in navigating and evaluating Web site–delivered information. Conversely, those who have lower eHealth literacy are more likely to have difficulty navigating and integrating tailored information into their lifestyles and knowledge base (Clark & Mayer, 2016).

eHealth literacy How well a person navigates, understands, and uses electronic health information.

Cognitive Behavioral Stress Management (CBSM)

One of the roles of health psychology in helping people cope with HIV and other STIs is helping people live with their infection and illness. Coping with a life-threatening illness is especially challenging for people with the greatest risk for HIV infection, since they are more likely to have a history of trauma and comorbid mental health problems, including anxiety disorders, depression, and substance abuse (Gaynes, Pence, Eron, & Miller, 2008). This is significant because it indicates that they may lack good coping skills (Whetten, Reif, Whetten, & Murphy-McMillan, 2008).

As we have seen, the neuroendocrine consequences of stress may contribute to health problems, including a more rapid course of illness in people with AIDS and an increased likelihood of developing opportunistic infections (Cole, 2008). A growing body of research demonstrates that comprehensive cognitive-behavioral intervention programs focused on increasing positive coping skills are effective in improving the quality of life and emotional and physiological well-being of HIV-positive individuals. A meta-analysis

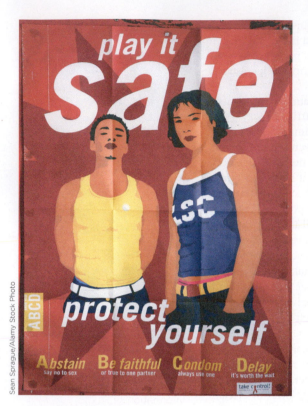

Education Aimed at Prevention In the absence of a vaccine, preventing HIV infection remains our best weapon against AIDS. Throughout the world, educational campaigns are the major means of primary prevention.

of 35 randomized, controlled trials found that CBSM interventions were successful in reducing anxiety, depression, distress, and fatigue in HIV-positive adults (Scott-Sheldon, Kalichman, Carey, & Fielder, 2008). In a more recent clinical trial involving racial/ethnic minority women with HIV and HPV, a 10-week CBSM intervention was associated with increased positive affect, positive states of mind, benefit finding, and spiritual well-being (Jensen and others, 2013). Women who most increased their confidence in stress-management skills showed the largest changes in positive well-being.

Community-Wide Interventions

Intensive, coordinated, community-wide interventions have proved to be the best way to educate people about STIs such as HIV and to change social norms that influence high-risk behaviors. As noted earlier, the AIDs epidemic in the United States was the first major health epidemic for which behavioral strategies and educational interventions were implemented. The largest AIDS prevention program of this kind to date was implemented in San Francisco in 1982, where the initial impact of AIDS was most strongly felt (Blair, 2016). (It is no coincidence that the nation's first department of health psychology was established around this time at the University of California, San Francisco.) The San Francisco Model involved seven different organizations chosen to reach people at different levels of risk: the mass media, schools, family planning centers, drug abuse clinics, health care organizations, churches, and clubs.

Each organization developed an educational program that was appropriate for its clientele. At each site, classes, videos, and models were used to teach safer-sex practices. In addition, mass media motivational messages and social action groups focused on increasing awareness of high-risk behaviors and reducing the social stigma attached to HIV-positive persons.

The program was an immediate success, with reported high-risk behavior among the sample population dropping from 60% to 30% within five years. The continuing success of the program indicates that HIV/AIDS interventions need to strike on several fronts. Effective interventions are those that

- target high-risk behaviors among at-risk individuals;
- teach specific skills to reduce risk (such as proper condom use and needle cleaning);
- promote interpersonal assertiveness and other communication skills necessary to initiate and maintain lower-risk sexual relationships;
- address social and cultural norms that surround sexual activity;
- focus on improving self-esteem and feelings of self-efficacy regarding how to practice safer sex;
- address faulty, even "magical," thinking regarding HIV transmission and personal vulnerability; and
- involve coordinated, community-level education.

Psychosocial Barriers to AIDS Intervention

Campaigns such as this are having an impact. Nationwide, the proportion of high school students who have ever had sexual intercourse decreased significantly from 46.8% in 2005 to 41.2% in 2015 (Ethier, Kann, & McManus, 2018). Health psychologists see this as a positive change among adolescents, because early initiation of sexual activity is linked to having more sexual partners, to not using condoms, and to increased risk of developing an STI. Still, the news is not all good. For one thing, significant decreases occurred among all sex and race/ethnicity subgroups except European American students. For another, reported sexual activity decreased among ninth- and tenth-grade students, but not eleventh- and twelfth-grade students. Finally, despite massive efforts to educate the public and discourage high-risk behaviors, condom use remains startlingly low. Among high school students who are sexually active, 43% did not use a condom the last time they had sex (Ethier, Kann, & McManus, 2018).

Media depictions of sexual encounters, which almost never include the use of a condom, do little to promote interventions aimed at promoting safe sex. This is particularly damaging for teenagers, who acquire a misleading personal script of how things are supposed to progress and attempt to follow that script during their first intimate experiences. Feeding into this is poor communication between sexual partners. One study of 701 sexually active African American females ages 14 to 20 found that partner communication was the strongest predictor of condom use (DePadilla, Windle, Wingood, Cooper, & DiClemente, 2011).

Ironically, a significant impediment to STI prevention programs is the success of advances in medical treatment, which has brought new hope and optimism for HIV-infected people but at the cost of greater public complacency regarding the dangers of the disease. Those who perceive a reduced threat of HIV/AIDS are more likely to engage in high-risk sexual behaviors, as are people who suppress HIV-related thoughts during intimate encounters (Hoyt, Nemeroff, & Huebner, 2006).

Another common example of faulty reasoning about STIs is the belief that the danger of infection depends on the depth of the relationship with the HIV-positive person. This line of thinking causes many people to worry needlessly about casual, nonsexual contact with HIV-positive coworkers and strangers—such as shaking hands or sitting in an adjoining theater seat—but to behave recklessly with people they know more intimately. Among college students, for instance, condom use appears to drop off abruptly over the time of a relationship (Pluhar, Frongillo, Stycos, & Dempster-McClain, 2003). Our faulty HIV/AIDS thinking is partly the result of believing that we are somehow less vulnerable to infection than others are. *Optimistic bias* and *perceived invincibility* contribute to our tendency to underestimate the possible consequences of engaging in high-risk behaviors.

Health psychologists play an important role in battling STIs. In the early years of the AIDS pandemic, psychologists were key players in designing and implementing primary and secondary prevention efforts to reduce the spread of HIV and to help those who were HIV positive cope with their illness. These efforts included interventions to reduce risky behaviors for AIDS and to help those who were HIV positive adhere to complex treatment regimens. More recently, health psychologists have teamed up with immunologists and other scientists to study how psychosocial factors—such as social support, coping style, and possible symptoms of anxiety and depression—influence risk behaviors for STIs and the course of illnesses such as AIDS. Based on the growing evidence from these investigations, psychologists are designing interventions that not only improve the quality of life of people living with a chronic illness such as AIDS, but also increase their chances of long-term survival.

Weigh In on Health

Respond to each question below based on what you learned in the chapter. (**Tip:** Use the items in "Summing Up" to take into account related biological, psychological, and social concerns.)

1. You've been asked to prepare a short talk on the global burden of disease. What are the most important communicable diseases in terms of deaths around the world? What are some of the concerns about drug resistance for these diseases?

2. Among a group of friends, the topic of STIs comes up. Anthony says that there's not much to worry about

anymore, because these kinds of infections are not as common as they used to be and treatments are available. What would you say to him about why it's important for everyone at every life stage to remain vigilant against STIs?

3. Imagine that you and your friends who had the conversation about HIV/AIDS decided that students at your college should be more aware of this disease, plus other STIs. What aspects of intervention and coping with HIV/AIDS or STIs (biological, psychological, and social or cultural) do you think all college students should know about?

Summing Up

Communicable and Noncommunicable Diseases

1. A communicable disease (CD) is a one that is transmitted from a human to another human, from a human to an animal, or from an animal to a human. A communicable disease can be transmitted directly, such as through respiratory means, or indirectly through a *vector,* such as a mosquito in the case of malaria or the Zika virus.

2. The epidemiological transition occurs as the death rate in a country declines and a higher proportion of children survive into adulthood. Over time, chronic, degenerative noncommunicable diseases become more prevalent, but CDs also persist in poorer countries.

3. The use of antibiotics is the single most important factor in the development of antimicrobial resistance. Another factor is the spread of resistant strains of bacteria from person to person in crowded settings such as hospitals, nursing homes, schools, and prisons.

Sexually Transmitted Infections

4. Diseases such as gonorrhea and syphilis that are spread mainly by sexual contact are called sexually transmitted diseases (STDs). Sexually transmitted viruses and bacteria that trigger no symptoms, or only signs that can easily be overlooked, are best described as sexually transmitted infections (STIs), which may or may not result in disease. This is the case for genital human papillomavirus (HPV),

chlamydia, trichomoniasis, gonorrhea, genital herpes, and hepatitis.

5. HIV is a retrovirus that causes host cells to reproduce the virus's genetic code. In doing so, HIV destroys T cells, progressively reduces immunocompetence, and leaves its victims vulnerable to a host of opportunistic infections. HIV sickness progresses through four stages, which vary in length from person to person.

6. Preventive vaccines exist for some STIs, notably HPV and hepatitis B. Subjective norms and social influence are of particular importance in promoting vaccination.

7. Many STIs can be easily treated by antibiotics and have a high cure rate, but others are incurable and must be managed as lifelong chronic conditions.

The AIDS Epidemic

8. In the United States, the AIDS epidemic has taken the greatest toll on gay, bisexual, and other men who have sex with men (MSM), particularly young African Americans and Hispanics/Latinos. For a variety of biological, economic, and sociocultural reasons, women are more vulnerable than men to HIV infection and tend to contract AIDS at a younger age and a lower HIV viral load.

9. HIV is transmitted primarily through the sharing of virus-infected lymphocytes in bodily fluids—blood, semen, vaginal and cervical secretions, and breast milk. High-risk

behaviors that promote HIV infection include having un-protected sex with multiple partners, using injected drugs, and sharing needles. HIV also may be transmitted from an infected mother to her unborn child during pregnancy, as well as from mother to child during breast feeding.

10. Globally, access to treatment is a major factor in the pro-gression of AIDs. Stress, negative emotions, and social iso-lation also influence the pace at which AIDS progresses, perhaps by altering hormonal and immune environments that affect the resistance of host cells to the invading virus. Interventions that target social and behavioral factors are valuable in the fight against AIDS but are often overlooked by scientists.

11. Racial discrimination and HIV-related stigma may be con-tributing factors to health-risk behaviors and HIV infec-tion. Discrimination often is associated with heightened perceived norms for certain behaviors, which in turn pre-dict reduced feelings of belonging and higher levels of sub-stance use and risky sex behaviors. Findings such as these highlight the potential for reducing STI risk through pre-ventive interventions that target substance abuse and risky sex behaviors.

Living with a Chronic Illness

12. Chronic illnesses are the leading cause of disability throughout the world. Until the late 1990s, HIV infection

was almost always a progressive, fatal disease. Today, com-bination antiretroviral therapy drugs have transformed AIDS into a manageable chronic condition.

13. A diagnosis of a chronic illness often releases a flood of psychological and emotional responses, including fear and uncertainty about the future, anxiety, sadness, grief, or anger. Acute and ongoing stressors; cognitive, emotional and behavioral responses; personal background; and social and environmental background are important factors in how well a person adjusts to a chronic illness.

14. Health psychologists play important roles in the battle against STIs, including counseling people about being tested for STIs, helping individuals modify high-risk be-haviors, and helping AIDS patients cope with emotional and cognitive disturbances.

15. A critical factor in tailored, digitally delivered interventions is how well a person navigates, understands, and uses elec-tronic health information. A particularly effective way to package stress-management interventions for HIV-positive patients seems to be a multimodal, cognitive-behavioral stress management (CBSM) approach.

16. Although STI prevention programs have had some success, many barriers to prevention remain. Misinformation, feel-ings of personal invulnerability, cultural norms, and per-sonal resources are all factors in the success (or failure) of AIDS prevention measures.

Key Terms and Concepts to Remember

noncommunicable disease (NCD), p. 379
communicable disease (CD), p. 379
epidemiological transition, p. 379
antimicrobial resistance, p. 383

sexually transmitted infection (STI), p. 384
human immunodeficiency virus (HIV), p. 387
acquired immunodeficiency syn-drome (AIDS), p. 387

hemophilia, p. 387
Kaposi's sarcoma, p. 390
pandemic, p. 391
retrovirus, p. 394
dynamic tailoring, p. 405
eHealth literacy, p. 405

 LaunchPad macmillan learning   To accompany your textbook, you have access to a number of online resources, including quizzes for every chapter of the book, flashcards, critical thinking exercises, videos, and *Check Your Health* inventories. To access these resources, please visit the Straub Health Psychology LaunchPad at **launchpadworks.com**

Part 5 SEEKING TREATMENT

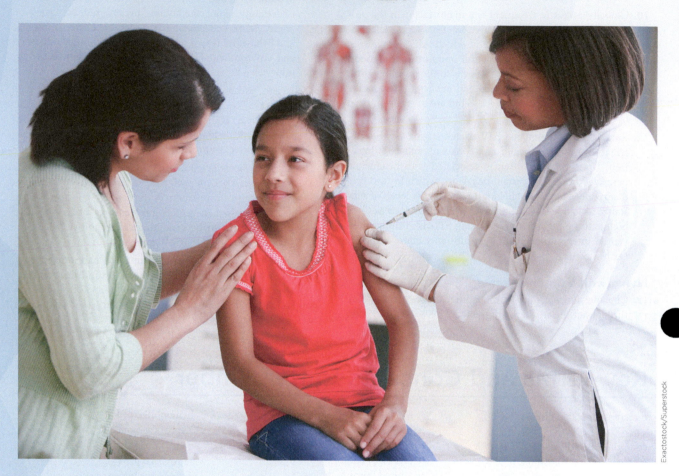

The Role of Health Psychology in Seeking and Obtaining Health Care

Chapter 13

Calaimage/Robert Daly/Getty Images

LEARNING OUTCOMES

Once you have studied this chapter, you will be able to:

- Identify factors that should prompt people to seek medical treatment;
- Describe factors that influence how people seek, access, and adhere to medical treatment;
- Identify factors that influence the patient–provider relationship; and
- Describe characteristics of health care systems in the United States and around the world.

E ven though the event happened over 40 years ago, it is as vivid in my mind today as it was on that unusually warm afternoon in April when one of my fraternity brothers was nearly blinded. A bunch of us were watching the Detroit Tigers battle the St. Louis Cardinals in a spring training baseball exhibition game. "Anybody want to play handball?" asked Bruce, bounding through the lobby. I declined, as did everyone but Chris. "I'll play," he said, "but only for about half an hour. I've got a chemistry final tomorrow."

The rest of us turned our attention back to the game and thought nothing more about handball until about 45 minutes later, when a worried-looking Chris came through the door with a woozy Bruce leaning heavily on him for support. It was easy to see that Bruce had been hurt—his left eye was discolored and growing puffy.

"Bruce took a handball right in the eye," Chris explained. "I wanted to take him right over to the health center, but he refused."

"It's nothing," Bruce said shakily. "I'll probably have a black eye tomorrow, but I'll be fine. Just get me some ice and a couple of aspirin."

As Bruce stretched out on a couch, somebody ran for the ice and aspirin. The rest of us looked at one another doubtfully. As the minutes passed, Bruce's eye was looking angry and red, and the swelling was starting to force his eyelid closed. He was clearly in pain, wincing with every word he spoke. Vision was not something to mess around with, even if you were trying to keep up a stoic front for a bunch of college buddies and especially if, like Bruce, you were hoping one day to become an airline pilot.

For all of these reasons, I knew what we had to do. In less than five minutes, Glenn, Jack, and I had phoned Campus Safety, the Health Center, and Bruce's parents. Following their instructions, we drove Bruce to the emergency room at County Medical Hospital, paced by a police cruiser with siren blaring and lights flashing. Half an hour after being hit by the handball, Bruce was rushed into the operating room, where a board-certified surgeon sutured his ruptured eyeball and saved his vision.

Why was Bruce reluctant to seek medical care? Why wasn't the severe pain in his eye sufficient to sound the alarm that his health was in jeopardy? In considering why people do or do not seek treatment and how they interact with the health care system, we shift our focus from *primary* prevention to *secondary* prevention—that is, from actions designed to prevent a disease or injury to actions intended to identify and treat an illness early in its course.

Collaborative Care Today, the health care system is increasingly focused on *collaborative care*, the combined efforts of physicians, psychologists, and other health care people, such as this team talking with a patient.

Caiaimage/Robert Daly/Getty Images

This chapter explores the role of health psychology in the relationships between patients and the health care system. Social and psychological factors have both a direct and an indirect impact on those relationships. First, such factors strongly influence when and how people initially decide they are sick. Second, the confidence that people have in their health care providers influences their satisfaction with treatment, as well as how they respond to it. Third, the extent and quality of communication between patients and health care providers indirectly influence almost every aspect of health care, including how patients decide when they need medical attention, why people sometimes choose to ignore health-related symptoms, and why people carefully follow their provider's instructions at some times but not at other times.

As a result of our improved understanding of these psychosocial influences, a significantly increasing number of psychologists now work in general health care settings, and medical school curricula include a greater focus on the behavioral and social sciences. In addition, a growing number of medical centers are encouraging greater use of **collaborative care** (also called *integrated care* or *primary care behavioral health*), in which physicians, psychologists (sometimes called *behavioral consultants*), and other health care providers join forces to improve patient care. Optimum health care is not achieved by defining the separate responsibilities of patients and health care providers, but through their harmonious interaction.

collaborative care A cooperative form of health care in which physicians, psychologists, and other health care providers join forces to improve patient care.

RECOGNIZING AND INTERPRETING SYMPTOMS

How and when do we decide that we are sick? At what point does a nagging headache, upset stomach, or other symptom become serious enough for us to recognize a problem that needs professional attention? The criteria that people use to recognize and interpret symptoms vary enormously. However, certain broad psychosocial factors play an important role in the process.

Illness Representations

Our personal views of health and illness, called **illness representations**, affect our health in at least two ways: by influencing our preventive health behaviors and by affecting how we react when symptoms appear. Researchers have studied several components of how we represent illnesses. Each component by itself can affect substantially our motivation to seek medical care.

illness representation How a person views a particular illness, including its label and symptoms, perceived causes, timeline, consequences, and controllability.

Identity of the Illness

There appears to be a symmetrical bond between the two elements that constitute a disease's identity: its label and its symptoms. Thus, a person who has symptoms will seek a diagnostic label for those symptoms; a person who has been diagnosed (labeled) will seek symptoms that are consistent with that label. A classic study provides a vivid example of this symmetry (Baumann, Cameron, Zimmerman, & Leventhal, 1989). The researchers found that research participants who were told that they had hypertension (high blood pressure) were more likely than others to report symptoms commonly associated with this illness. This was true regardless of whether or not they really were hypertensive. In this era of direct-to-consumer advertising, many skeptics suspect that pharmaceutical companies capitalize on the human tendency to seek labels for ambiguous symptoms by marketing expensive medications for conditions such as irritable bowel syndrome, fibromyalgia, and restless leg syndrome.

All medical conditions are at least partly *social constructions*, meaning that their identity and diagnosis are shaped by culture, advertising, and other nonbiological forces. German physicians, for example, are far more likely than their counterparts in France, Britain, and the United States to diagnose and treat low blood pressure.

Another example is the epidemic of *attention deficit hyperactivity disorder* (ADHD) in the United States. Nowhere in the world are the behaviors associated with this disorder treated with the same intensity as in the United States. The point to remember: People in different places can experience the same biological phenomena in very different ways.

Causes

Individuals tend to attribute symptoms to external factors, such as infection or injury, or internal factors, such as genetic predisposition. A student who interprets her tension headache as a by-product of cramming for an exam will react quite differently from the student who interprets the same symptoms as signs of a brain tumor.

Timeline

A disease's timeline is the duration and rate of its development. For example, 4 out of 10 patients being treated for hypertension believe that their condition is *acute* (that is, short in duration, caused by temporary agents, and not a serious threat to long-term health). In contrast, *chronic illnesses* are long in duration, are caused by multiple factors, and represent potentially serious threats to long-term health. Patients who believe their illness is acute often drop out of treatment earlier than those who believe it to be chronic.

Consequences

The consequences of an illness are manifested in its physical, social, and economic impact. We are far more likely to ignore symptoms that minimally disrupt our daily lives (such as minor muscle soreness following a strenuous workout) than we are to ignore symptoms that have a serious disruptive effect (such as a severe muscular strain that prevents a laborer from earning a paycheck).

Controllability

Our illness representations also include our beliefs regarding whether the illness can be prevented, controlled, and/or cured. If we view our disease or condition as incurable, we may skip appointments, neglect treatment, or even behave in self-destructive ways because we feel helpless and lack hope.

Note that the key to all of these illness representation components is not the actual facts about the disease, but our *perception* of the symptoms. How we initially react to a stomachache, for example, depends not on its actual cause, about which we are unaware, but on what we *believe* is causing the pain.

Explanatory Style and Psychological Disturbances

Explanatory style (optimistic or pessimistic) and psychological health also influence the reporting of symptoms. People who have a more positive outlook on life generally report fewer symptoms than do people who are more negative. Those in a good mood also have

Psychological disorders
- Negative emotional states and traits
- Mood and anxiety disorders

Biological pathways
- Sympatho-adreno-medullary arousal
- Hypothalamic-pituitary-adrenal arousal

Behavioral pathways
- Poor health practices
- Misuse of health services
- Poor medical adherence

Cognitive pathways
- Faulty interpretation of physical stimuli
- Inaccurate illness representations
- Focus on health decision processes

Social pathways
- Interference with daily life and social roles
- Isolation from others

Physical disorders
- Onset
- Progression
- Increased severity

Illness behaviors
- Reporting symptoms
- Seeking care
- Pain and disability

FIGURE 13.1 Psychological Disorders, Physical Disorders, and Illness Behavior
Psychological disorders can predispose physical disorders and illness behavior via a number of biological, behavioral, cognitive, and social pathways.

Information from: Cohen, S., & Rodriguez, M. S. (1995). Pathways linking affective disturbances and physical disorders. *Health Psychology, 14,* 374–380.

comorbidity The simultaneous occurrence of two or more physical and/or psychological disorders or symptoms.

higher *self-reported health* and consider themselves less vulnerable to future illness than do people in bad moods (Winter, Lawton, Langston, Ruckdeschel, & Sando, 2007).

People who are anxious and those who score low on tests of emotional stability tend to report more physical symptoms, perhaps because they tend to exaggerate the seriousness of minor complaints that other people may ignore. In addition, symptoms of psychological or emotional disorders sometimes are misattributed to physical problems. Actually, there is substantial **comorbidity** of psychological and physical disorders—physical and psychological symptoms and disorders occurring simultaneously. Psychological disorders such as anxiety or depression can predispose physical disorders through biological, behavioral, cognitive, and social pathways (Figure 13.1). For example, depression might trigger poor health practices, such as alcohol abuse, and a general apathy regarding treatment regimens. Anxiety and depression also can lead to an excessive focus on bodily symptoms.

SEEKING TREATMENT

The presence of symptoms is not always enough to get us into the health care system. Why do some of us keep up our normal activities even in the face of undeniable evidence that something is wrong, while others take time off work in response to the slightest symptom?

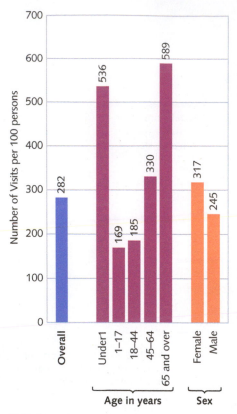

FIGURE 13.2 Age, Gender, and Physician Contact In general, young children and older adults are more likely than adolescents and young adults to use health services. Starting in adolescence, women contact their physicians more than men do.

Information from: NCHS, National Ambulatory Medical Care Survey, 2014.

Data from: Ashman, J. J., Rui, M. P. H., and Okeyode, T. (2017). *Characteristics of office-based physician visits, 2014.* NCHS Data Brief No. 292. U.S. Department of Health and Human Services. National Center for Health Statistics.

We fail to respond to potentially serious medical symptoms for many reasons. We may avoid seeing a doctor because we believe that our symptoms are not serious and that all we need is a day or two of rest, an over-the-counter medication, or some other form of self-care. We may avoid the use of health services because we lack health insurance or are afraid we can't afford treatment. We may be fearful that our symptoms *are* a sign of a serious condition, and our inaction is a result of denial. Finally, we may avoid medical care because we are suspicious of the health care system and we doubt its ability to treat our condition effectively.

Several demographic and sociocultural factors play important roles in determining whether a person will take the next step and seek medical treatment.

Age and Gender

Overall, the very young and the elderly use health services more often than do adolescents and young adults (Centers for Medicare and Medicaid Services [CMS], 2017). As any parent knows, young children are vulnerable to many different infectious diseases as their immune systems are developing. They need checkups, vaccinations, and regular health services. In general, however, our younger years are among the healthiest of the entire life span. The frequency of illness and the need to visit physicians decline steadily throughout late childhood, adolescence, and young adulthood. Health services begin to increase again in middle age and late adulthood as a result of the increasing prevalence of chronic, age-related diseases (Figure 13.2).

During late adulthood, ageist stereotypes can be significant barriers to achieving and maintaining good health. Old age often is viewed as a period of inevitable decline in which elderly people are unable or unwilling to change lifestyle behaviors, adhere to treatment regimens, or gain much benefit from health interventions. This is unfortunate, because most people aged 65 years or older suffer from at least one chronic health condition that, in many cases, may be cured or at least controlled. Ageist stereotypes may also prevent older adults from seeking (or receiving) optimal preventive health care, such as cancer screenings, and serve as a barrier to adopting healthier lifestyles aimed at increasing overall health expectancy. Fortunately, research studies indicate that many seniors remain optimistic about their health status—which is a good thing because self-reported health is known to predict mortality and other health outcomes better than objective ratings, and it is the strongest predictor of life satisfaction during old age (Winter and others, 2007).

Gender is another factor in the way that health services are used. Beginning in adolescence and continuing throughout adulthood, women are more likely than men to report symptoms and to use health services (CMS.gov, 2017), due in large part to pregnancy and childbirth. New mothers are staying in the hospital about half a day longer than they did in the mid-1990s, when insurance companies cut childbirth stays to 24 hours, sparking outcries about "drive-by deliveries" (Organization for Economic Cooperation and Development [OECD], 2017). However, even when medical visits for pregnancy and childbirth are not counted, women still visit their physicians more often than do men.

Historically, women have also paid more for health care than men. The practice of *gender rating*—charging women more for the same coverage—was widespread prior to implementation of the Affordable Care Act (ACA). A large-scale study conducted by the National Women's Law Center found that women "are continuously charged more for health coverage simply because they are women, and individual market health plans often exclude coverage for services that women need, like maternity coverage" (National Women's Law Center [NWLC], 2012). Fortunately, as of 2014, the ACA eliminated gender rating in the insurance market, requiring all insurance plans to provide maternity coverage. However, the threat of "repeal and replace" legislation that might eliminate this protection and roll back American health care coverage to an era of gender disparities remains very real (Niehans, 2017).

Men, especially low-income young men, more often dodge the doctor, even when faced with potentially serious problems. Large-scale surveys conducted by the Kaiser Family Foundation (2015) revealed that, of those sampled:

- About 72% of men report they have a usual source of heath care, compared to 86% of women. Only 62% of low-income men (those living with less than 200% of the federal poverty level) have a regular place to go for care.

- More than one third of the men wouldn't go to a doctor immediately, even if experiencing severe chest pains (34%) or shortness of breath (37%).

- In the past two years, 91% of women report having seen a health care provider, compared with only 75% of men.

- Men are less likely than women to get recommended screening services, including a general checkup, and tests for high blood pressure and cholesterol (see Figure 13.3).

- Gender differences in office visits vary by age, with the largest gap among men and women 18 to 44 years of age, while narrowing among middle-aged adults and disappearing among the oldest age group.

Why are women generally more likely than men to seek health care? It may be because they are exposed to more illness as a result of caring for the elderly and children, who have the highest incidence of being sick. Women also are more likely to be nurses, elementary school teachers, and day-care providers—all occupations that increase their risk of exposure to infectious agents.

Gender difference in the seeking of health care also may be due in part to social factors. For instance, women visit doctors more than men do because their health care tends to be more fragmented. For a routine physical exam, most men are "one-stop shoppers." That is, they visit a general practitioner or nurse-practitioner who is able to perform most, if not all, of the tests they need. In contrast, a woman may need to visit three or more specialists or clinics for a thorough checkup: an internist for her physical, a gynecologist for a Pap smear, a mammography specialist to screen for breast tumors, and so forth. Some researchers see this fragmentation

FIGURE 13.3 Percentages of Women and Men Receiving Recommended Health Screenings In general, women are more likely than men to get recommended health screening services.

Data from: Kaiser Family Foundation. (2015). Gender differences in health care, status, and use: Spotlight on men's health. Findings from the 2013 Kaiser Men's Health Survey and 2013 Kaiser Women's Health Survey.

ivanastar/Getty Images

Behavior of Sick Women and the Elderly In general, women are more likely than men to seek health care, and women over age 65 are more likely than younger women to seek health care.

lay referral system An informal network of family members, friends, and other nonprofessionals who offer their own impressions, experiences, and recommendations regarding a set of bodily symptoms.

as an indication that Western medicine is male-biased and not well structured to meet women's basic needs.

Socioeconomic Status and Cultural Factors

Socioeconomic status (SES) predicts both symptom reporting and the seeking of health care. High-income people generally report fewer symptoms and better health than do low-income people (Grzywacz, Almeida, Neupert, & Ettner, 2004). However, high-SES people are more likely to seek health care when it's needed. In contrast, poor people are less likely to use health services, simply because they can- not afford to do so (Adler & Stewart, 2010). People in lower-SES groups also tend to wait longer before seeking treatment, making it more likely that they will become seriously ill and require hospitalization. In addition, people with lower family incomes are more likely to use outpatient clinics and hospital emergency rooms for medical care because they are less likely than their financially advantaged counterparts to have health insurance and regular physicians (Kaiser Family Foundation, 2015). This helps explain why morbidity and mortality are highest among people at the lowest SES levels.

Cultural factors also influence a person's tendency to seek treatment. People who hold beliefs that conflict with Western medicine are less likely to seek traditional biomedical care and more likely to rely on a **lay referral system**—an informal social network of family, friends, and other nonprofessionals who offer their own impressions and experiences regarding a set of symptoms. A member of the referral system might help interpret a symptom or give advice about seeking treatment.

Several researchers have studied ethnic and cultural variations in the lay referral system. They have found, for example, that ethnic groups differ widely in the degree to which they believe that human intervention in health outcomes is possible or desirable. Some groups attribute disease to nonphysical factors, such as God's will. In such cases, people may be more inclined to employ non-Western practices for treatment (see Chapter 15). This poses an interesting problem for Western health care providers, because the closer a patient's cultural or ethnic background is to that of Western physicians, the more the patient's reported symptoms will approximate those that are recognizable as signs of disease.

Upbringing is a related cultural factor in determining the likelihood that a person will seek treatment for a particular symptom. People whose parents paid close attention to physical symptoms and sought regular health care may be more likely to do the same. Conversely, those whose parents were suspicious of doctors and more likely to rely on self-care or some form of alternative treatment may be more likely to carry that suspicion with them.

Delay Behavior

Clearly, for medical emergencies such as heart attack or stroke, getting help as quickly as possible is of the utmost importance. Although other chronic diseases and conditions may not present this kind of minute-by-minute urgency in survival, seeking timely care when symptoms first appear can make the difference between dying from the disease or condition and discovering it when it still may be treatable. For example, beginning treatment for certain types of cancer while it is still localized and before it has metastasized to other areas of the body often makes the difference between a long, full life and one that is shortened prematurely.

Despite the benefits of seeking care when symptoms first appear, many people, like my friend Bruce whom you met at the beginning of the chapter, ignore their symptoms and do not seek medical help. This is called **delay behavior**.

Why do people delay seeking medical attention for serious conditions? There is no single answer, but delay is often related to people misinterpreting their symptoms or being reluctant to discuss them (Oberoi, Jiwa, McManus, & Hodder, 2015). According to one model, there are five stages in the decision-making process for seeking medical care (Walter, Webster, Scott, & Emery, 2012) (see Figure 13.4). The model predicts that people will avoid seeking medical care because

- symptoms go unnoticed (*appraisal delay*),
- sickness seems unlikely (*illness delay*),
- professional help is deemed unnecessary (*behavioral delay*),
- the individual procrastinates in making an appointment (*scheduling delay*), or
- the perceived costs of treatment outweigh the perceived benefits (*treatment delay*).

delay behavior The tendency to avoid seeking medical care because symptoms go unnoticed (*appraisal delay*), sickness seems unlikely (*illness delay*), professional help is deemed unnecessary (*behavioral delay*), the individual procrastinates in making an appointment (*scheduling delay*), or the perceived costs of treatment outweigh the perceived benefits (*treatment delay*).

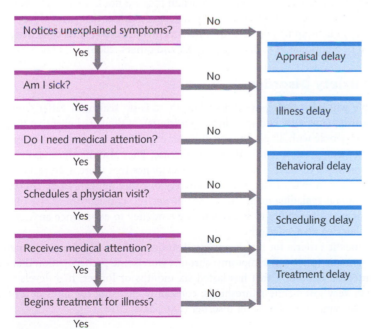

FIGURE 13.4 Stages of Delay in Seeking Medical Attention The Andersen model of patient delay shows that noticing symptoms does not automatically lead to treatment. People have to make a concerted effort to take each step, so it's possible for intervening factors to interrupt the process.

Information from: Walter, F., Webster, A., Scott, S., & Emery, J. (2012). The Andersen Model of Total Patient Delay: A systematic review of its application in cancer diagnosis. *Journal of Health Services Research & Policy, 17*(2), 110–118; Anderson, B. L., Cacioppo, J. T., & Roberts, D. C. (1995). Delay in seeking a cancer diagnosis: Delay stages and psychophysiological comparison processes. *British Journal of Social Psychology, 34,* 33–52.

At each of these stages, a person can exhibit delay behavior.

During the appraisal delay stage, the sensory prominence of the symptoms is the most important factor in determining the amount of delay. Patients seeking care at hospital clinics indicated delaying less when they were in pain or bleeding. Myocardial infarction patients who stopped to research their symptoms by consulting books and other sources delayed more than five times as long as patients who did not do research. Initial pain led to a short delay, whereas talking with others about one's symptoms resulted in a significantly longer delay (Waller, 2006).

In the illness delay stage, patients who had previously experienced similar symptoms were more likely than those who experienced symptoms for the first time to delay seeking medical attention. For example, with *carpal tunnel syndrome*, a nerve disorder caused by repetitive motion, the symptoms may come and go over a long period of time, so people tend to ignore them. Only when the symptoms become persistent and acute will the person start moving through the stages toward seeking treatment. In addition, patients who spent more time imagining the consequences of being sick were more likely to delay seeking medical attention.

In the last three stages, delay was longest for patients who were more concerned about the cost of treatment, had little pain, and were doubtful that their symptoms could be cured. The association between not feeling pain and delaying medical care is unfortunate because pain is not a major symptom in the early stages of a number of chronic diseases, including cancer, hypertension, and diabetes.

Overusing Health Services

At the opposite extreme from those who avoid or postpone medical treatment are people who misuse health services by seeking care when they do not have a diagnosable health condition. So pervasive is this problem that physicians estimate that as much as two thirds of their time is taken up by people with problems that are either medically insignificant or the result of emotional disturbances (Franko and others, 2005).

Illness Anxiety Disorder

illness anxiety disorder The condition of experiencing abnormal anxiety over one's health, often including imaginary symptoms.

Some people who visit their physicians when there is no real need suffer from **illness anxiety disorder** (formerly known as *hypochondriasis*), or the false belief that they have a disease. Most people with illness anxiety disorder experience vague or ambiguous symptoms that they exaggerate and misattribute to disease. They also may have an exaggerated fear of contracting a disease, even in the face of evidence that there is no real danger. An underlying factor in many cases of illness anxiety disorder appears to be *neuroticism*, a state of emotional maladjustment that encompasses self-consciousness; the inability to inhibit cravings; vulnerability to stress; and the tendency to experience anxiety, depression, and other negative emotions.

The diagnostic criteria for illness anxiety disorder include, but are not limited to, an absence of somatic (physical) symptoms; chronic, worrisome preoccupation that one has a serious medical condition that has lasted six months or longer; high levels of *health anxiety,* with very low sickness thresholds; constantly checking for signs of illness; and the absence of symptoms of another disorder (Dimsdale, 2018).

Malingering

Some patients who report hard-to-verify symptoms such as pain are feigning illness, or **malingering**, in order to derive some benefit from their behavior—sympathy from others, time off from work, insurance compensation, or a prescription for drugs, among other motivations. If the physical examination is not consistent with the patient's description of symptoms and an incentive is evident, malingering may be suspected (McDermott & Feldman, 2008).

People who score high on emotional instability and neuroticism average two to three times as many physical complaints as those who score low on these traits (Goodwin & Friedman, 2006). But does this prove that neuroticism causes illness anxiety disorder? As we have seen, correlational evidence such as this cannot pinpoint causality. Even if it could, we would be unable to discern the *direction* of causality. It could be that having many aches, pains, and illnesses causes an excessive preoccupation with one's health.

Stress and anxiety often create a number of physical symptoms that may resemble the symptoms of a biologically based disorder (Martin & Brantley, 2004). For example, anxiety (perhaps about upcoming exams) may disrupt sleeping and concentration, trigger diarrhea and nausea, suppress appetite, and/or result in a state of general agitation.

malingering Making believe that one is ill in order to benefit from sick role behavior.

Patient Adherence

Surprisingly, even when people seek health care, many simply ignore (or fail to follow closely) the treatment that is prescribed for them. Every health care professional can tell stories about this phenomenon: the patient who cheats on a special diet; the coronary case who, without consulting her doctor, stops taking her hypertension medication; or the accident victim who misuses a prescribed painkiller.

Adherence is broadly defined as "closely following the advice of a health care provider." This includes advice pertaining to medications and lifestyle changes (e.g., losing weight or quitting smoking), as well as recommendations about preventive measures (e.g., avoiding fatty foods or starting an exercise program). Adherence is both an attitude and a behavior. As an attitude, it entails a willingness to follow health advice; as a behavior, it is related to the actual carrying out of specific recommendations.

When patients do not follow the treatment regimens that their health care providers recommend, the result is **nonadherence**, or noncompliance, which includes the refusal to adhere to a treatment regimen or the lack of sustained effort in following a treatment regimen. The costs associated with nonadherence are potentially enormous. In patients with organ transplants, for example, failure to adhere to immunosuppressant drug regimens can lead to organ rejection. On a monetary level, it is estimated that nonadherence has an annual economic impact of $100 billion to $300 billion in avoidable treatment and hospitalization costs (Neiman and others, 2017).

adherence A patient both agreeing to and then closely following a treatment regimen as advised by his or her health care provider.

nonadherence The condition in which a patient refuses to complete a prescribed therapeutic regimen.

How Widespread Is Nonadherence?

Estimating the prevalence of nonadherence is difficult because the problem takes so many different forms. For example, a patient may not show up for a scheduled appointment, fail to complete the course of an antibiotic, or fail to follow some other treatment regimen.

In other words, there are many degrees of nonadherence. Beyond that, some types of nonadherence, such as not taking every dose of medication, are done by the patient in private, so the doctor has no way of discovering them. In broad terms, a meta-analysis of 569 studies over a 50-year span found an average rate of nonadherence of about 25%— only three out of every four patients follow their treatment regimens closely (van Dulmen and others, 2007).

What Factors Predict Adherence?

Are some people more likely than others to comply with treatment? Is adherence more likely for certain kinds of treatment than for others? In their search for answers to these questions, biomedical researchers have examined two broad categories of variables: *patient variables* and *treatment regimen variables*.

Patient and Provider Variables Although a substantial amount of adherence research has focused on age, gender, ethnicity, education, and income, it is now generally understood that sociodemographic factors are not very accurate predictors of adherence. In general, this is because people are inconsistent in their adherence behaviors. A patient may follow a medication regimen but not necessarily a dietary regimen. Among some patients, alcohol or drug use (Weitzman, Ziemnik, Huang, & Levy, 2015) and depression, anxiety, and other mental health problems (Tucker and others, 2004) have been associated with nonadherence. Among other patients, it is memory and cognitive deficits (Stilley, Bender, Dunbar-Jacob, Sereika, & Ryan, 2010) or a disorganized lifestyle (Schreier & Chen, 2010) that contribute to nonadherence.

At the consumer level, what promotes adherence? Being in a good mood, having optimistic expectations, and having trust in one's care provider are important factors (Thom, Hall, & Pawlson, 2004). Having the support of family and friends is also important. For instance, studies have shown that marital support improves adherence to diabetes care regimens that include food purchase and preparation, medication administration, glucose testing, and exercise (Trief, Ploutz-Snyder, Britton, & Weinstock, 2004).

Perceived control and preference for control of treatments also help to explain adherence. Patients who express greater preference for control and involvement in their health care demonstrate better adherence to medical treatments that are largely self-directed and that take place in the home. However, greater preference for control predicts *poorer* adherence when treatments take place in a clinic or hospital (Cvengros, Christensen, & Lawton, 2004).

Provider variables, such as level of job satisfaction, the number of patients seen per week, and communication style, can have a powerful influence on patient adherence. In addition, personal characteristics of health care providers are very important to patients. At the top of the list are a provider's display of empathy and confidence, in addition to a forthright and respectful manner (Bendapudi, Berry, Frey, Parish, & Rayburn, 2006). Perhaps because female physicians spend more time with patients—and ask and encourage more questions—their care promotes higher rates of adherence than that of male physicians (Roter & Hall, 2004).

Promoting Adherence
Patients are more likely to follow recommendations that they believe in and that they are capable of carrying out.

Jose Luis Pelaez Inc/Getty Images

Interventions that target these and other provider variables are highly effective in increasing patient adherence (Conn, Ruppar, Enriquez, Cooper, & Chan, 2015).

Treatment Regimen Variables Patients are more likely to follow recommendations that they believe in and are capable of carrying out. Researchers generally have found that the more complex a treatment regimen is, the less likely patients are to adhere to it completely. Health care providers can take several steps to improve adherence in their patients, including the following:

- Tailor the treatment to fit the patient's lifestyle. Adherence will increase in response to anything that makes a treatment regimen easier to follow.

- Simplify instructions with clear language to ensure that the patient understands the amount, timing, and duration of the treatment.

- Make sure that the patient understands enough of the treatment rationale to gain confidence in the treatment schedule.

- Involve family members, friends, and other patient supporters in the treatment and the explanation of its rationale.

- Provide feedback about progress.

THE PATIENT–PROVIDER RELATIONSHIP

The relationship between health care provider and patient is the backbone of all medical treatment. A full 60% to 80% of medical diagnoses and treatment decisions are made on the basis of information that arises from the medical consultation process alone. Yet patients and providers do not always share the same view of the effectiveness of the process. Too often, providers overestimate how well a consultation went and how likely it is that the patient will follow through on their advice. The quality of the patient–provider relationship plays an important role in promoting patient adherence to treatment instructions.

Factors Affecting the Patient-Provider Relationship

Research has demonstrated that the central elements of the patient–provider relationship are *continuity of care, communication*, and the overall *quality of consultations*. The same principles apply to this relationship regardless of the provider or the health care system. In one investigation of satisfaction with their family doctors, nearly 40% of patients cited issues, both positive and negative, concerning interpersonal relationships. Statements concerning competency (12.9%) and personal qualities (10.5%) of doctors were less common (Marcinowicz, Chlabicz, & Grebowski, 2009). One reason for this decrease in satisfaction is that half of all patients are convinced that treatment decisions are based strictly on what their health insurance will cover. General communication problems may result from a lack of continuity in care, but other factors—from both provider and patient perspectives—also play a role.

Provider Communication Problems

At the heart of the patient–provider relationship are the nature and quality of communication. Health care providers who are good communicators, are less businesslike, and meet patient expectations regarding the information that they are entitled to receive tend to have patients who are more likely to adhere to treatment recommendations. In contrast, a lack of information about and a poor understanding of medical advice and the recommended treatment tend to leave patients dissatisfied. Ideally, health care providers listen carefully to patients, ask questions to ensure that patients understand their condition and treatment, and fully inform patients about every aspect of their care. Stress levels are particularly high during difficult consultations, making it more challenging for patients to take in everything the doctor says. To improve the situation, communication-skills training is now an integral component of the medical education (Accreditation Council for Graduate Medical Education [ACGME], 2018).

Many health care providers today have "too little time, and too much to do" and do not spend enough time with patients. Research shows that the more time the physicians spend with their patients (even just to chat), the more satisfied the patients are and the more likely they are to follow treatment plans successfully. Doctors who rush more patients through their practice each day have less-satisfied patients who are also less likely to be up to date on immunizations, mammograms, and other health-enhancing procedures and tests (Chen, 2013).

Some health care providers also have communication issues with patients because they fail to listen carefully or they treat patients either like medical school faculty or children. In one classic study of 74 consultations, researchers reported that in nearly two thirds of the cases, the physician interrupted the patient's description of symptoms after only 18 seconds (Beckman & Frankel, 1984). Other studies show that far too often, the medical information provided was too detailed or complex for patients to understand or retain, and that patients and doctors frequently interpreted the same information in different ways. To make matters worse, doctors often use a patronizing tone that can leave patients feeling helpless (Castro, Wilson, Wang, & Schillinger, 2007).

The poor communication skills may be explained by the fact that medical training is based on technical expertise, not social skills. Until relatively recently, medical schools placed little emphasis on communication. Few providers were trained to deliver bad news, and many—out of sheer ignorance or in response to time pressures—say things to patients and families that cause unnecessary emotional pain and even may reduce the effectiveness of treatment. And the harm that stems from such poorly delivered bad news can be long-lasting, even permanent. In the worst instances, providers seemed to adopt coping strategies to minimize *their* discomfort with delivering bad news and failed to realize what was needed to minimize the trauma experienced by patients and their loved ones.

Discrimination, Prejudice, and Racism

Discrimination and prejudice adversely affect minority populations and the health care system in general. Discrimination and prejudice may be based on differences due to race, ethnicity, age, ability, gender, religion, sexual orientation, or any other characteristic by which people differ. In its landmark report *Unequal Treatment: Confronting Racial and Ethnic Disparities in Health Care*, the Institute of Medicine (IOM) concluded that there is ample evidence of racism within the U.S. health care system (*institutional racism*) and among health care providers (*personally mediated racism*) (Smedley, Stith, & Nelson, 2002). The report went on to say that institutional racism is an important factor in racial/ethnic differences in overall health due to differences in the quality of care that members of minority groups receive. Among diabetes patients, for example, African Americans are less likely to receive influenza vaccinations or have their hemoglobin and cholesterol tested (Peek, Cargill, & Huang, 2007). The IOM found that racial/ethnic differences in health care persisted even after adjusting for other variables such as gender and socioeconomic status.

As another example of institutional racism, consider that historically, minorities have been underrepresented in clinical trials (Fisher & Kalbaugh, 2011). This is significant because efforts to address racial and ethnic disparities in health will require physicians, physician assistants, nurses, and other health care professionals to develop new evidence-based approaches to treatment and education for diabetes, cancer, and other diseases that disproportionately affect minorities. It is crucial that the evidence from clinical trials be based on representative populations of study participants.

One impediment to minority participation in clinical trials is a lack of trust in the medical research system stemming from "experiments" such as the infamous Tuskegee Syphilis Study. Conducted by the U.S. Public Health Service from 1932 to 1972, this study aimed to observe the long-term effects of syphilis by withholding treatment from 399 poor African American men with the sexually transmitted disease. Although penicillin had been widely available since the 1940s and soon thereafter became accepted as the standard of care for syphilis, the participants were never made aware of or given this treatment. Sadly, three fourths of the men died from complications of the disease, and many of those who survived became blind and crippled. The experiment was conducted without the benefit of the patients' informed consent.

Institutionalized racism does not necessarily entail the personal bias commonly associated with the term *racism*. In contrast, personally mediated racism refers to prejudicial assumptions about people's abilities, motives, and intentions, as well as discriminatory actions toward others according to their race (Jones, 2005). Health care providers may be at increased risk of relying on stereotypes as cognitive shortcuts because of time pressure, limited resources, and other clinical demands. Stereotypes based on patient characteristics such as race may influence the interpretation of symptoms and, consequently, affect clinical decisions (Burgess, van Ryn, Dovidio, & Saha, 2007). For example, one study found that physicians were more likely, after controlling for confounding variables, to rate their African American patients as less educated, less intelligent, more likely to abuse drugs and alcohol, and less likely to adhere to treatment regimens (van Ryn & Burke, 2000).

Minorities also experience prejudice and discrimination in health care delivery in the form of disrespect and failure to communicate options (Peek and others, 2010). Several studies have reported that physicians provide less information to and are less supportive of African American and Hispanic patients and patients of lower SES than other patients in the same health care setting (Manfredi, Kaiser, Matthews, & Johnson, 2010). African American patients are often perceived as less effective communicators and may be treated more contentiously by health care providers (Street, Gordon, & Haidet, 2007). Health care providers are more verbally dominant and engage in less patient-centered communication with African American patients, and they are less likely to understand the cultural

Monkey Business Images/Shutterstock.com

Seeking Social Skills Medical school students now regularly participate in communication-skills training, along with all their technical learning. This will help them establish better patient–provider and other relationships as they move along in their careers.

beliefs attached to certain health conditions (Street & Haidet, 2011). In response, minority patients are apt to perceive ineffective communication as a form of disrespect and unfair treatment, which may jeopardize their trust in and strain their relationship with health care providers (Song, Hamilton, & Moore, 2012).

While the issue of how to best measure racism and prejudice in health care remains controversial (Kressin, Raymond, & Manze, 2008), most researchers rely upon patient reports of perceived discrimination. There is growing evidence that such perceptions are associated with adverse outcomes, such as less preventive health care (e.g., cancer screening, influenza vaccinations) (Hausmann, Jeong, Bost, & Ibrahim, 2008; Trivedi & Ayanian, 2006), poorer prescription medication adherence, and less medical testing/treatment (Van Houtven and others, 2005). Among diabetes patients, perceived health care discrimination is also associated with lower-quality physician interactions and worse diabetes care and outcomes (Ryan, Gee, & Griffith, 2008).

There is evidence that many physicians also have negative perceptions of the elderly and those seeking treatment for psychological disorders, and even worse perceptions of older patients who have difficulty communicating. Gender differences are also a factor in the physician–patient relationship. A number of studies have found that female physicians demonstrate more proficient clinical performance than do their male counterparts, conducting longer office visits, asking more questions, and showing significantly more verbal and nonverbal support (Roter & Hall, 2004). Patients often are most comfortable communicating and interacting with health care providers who are of the same gender and similar in other ways to themselves.

Patient Communication Problems

Health care providers are not to blame for all miscommunications. Patients themselves are often the ones who are uninformed and unprepared, at times giving faulty information or discussing symptoms offhandedly for fear that doctors either will not be fully forthcoming about serious conditions or will confirm patients' apprehensions.

The differing educational and social backgrounds of patient and provider also can adversely affect communication. Traditionally, physicians have been upper-middle-class and White, while their patients reflect a much more diverse and heterogeneous group. The provider may think that he or she is explaining a problem clearly, while the patient may get an altogether different (and incorrect) meaning. Research has shown that patients with the most extensive and complicated health care problems are at greatest risk for misunderstanding their diagnoses, medications, and treatment instructions (Parker, 2000). Low-level reading skills among many patients also contribute to this problem. The health care system needs reshaping, including providing nonwritten materials for health education and offering the services of surrogate readers, so that patients with low literacy levels have access to information.

health literacy The capacity to obtain and understand basic health information and services needed to make appropriate health decisions.

Low (or nonexistent) reading levels contribute to low levels of **health literacy**, the "ability to understand and use health care information to make decisions and follow instructions for treatment." The Institute of Medicine has said that eradicating low health literacy is the first public health movement of the twenty-first century (Hernandez, 2013). The National Assessment of Adult Literacy conducted by the U.S. Department of Education reported that more than 90 million people in the United States have difficulty reading, with approximately 40 million to 44 million being functionally illiterate (National Assessment of Adult Literacy [NAAL], 2003) and another 50 million being marginally illiterate (Centers for Disease Control and Prevention [CDC], 2012a).

One aspect of health literacy is *numeracy,* the "ability to think and express oneself effectively in quantitative terms." Numeracy is essential for the understanding of quantitative information about health (Garcia-Retamero & Galesic, 2010a). People with low numeracy skills have less accurate perceptions of the risks and benefits of health screening, are more susceptible to certain errors in judgment, and have greater difficulty following complicated treatment regimens than those with high numeracy skill (Garcia-Retamero & Galesic, 2010b).

Patients with low health literacy are more likely to have difficulty navigating through the health care system, are less likely to seek preventive care and adhere to prescribed treatment and self-care regimens, and are more likely to make medication and treatment errors (Paasche-Orlow, 2011). Patient difficulties with health literacy also place a huge financial burden on the health care system. Adults with low health literacy average more hospital visits, stay in the hospital longer, and have annual health care costs that are four times those of their counterparts with higher health literacy. (See *Your Health Assets: Health Literacy.*)

Improving Patient–Provider Communication

Health care providers increasingly realize that patients who are better informed about the potential consequences of their behaviors are more likely to follow instructions and respond well to treatment. Approximately half of all causes of morbidity and mortality in the United States are linked to behavioral and social factors (Morbidity and Mortality Weekly Report [MMWR], 2014; National Center for Health Statistics [NCHS], 2006), so doctors must treat these risk factors as well as physical symptoms, which requires the patients' active cooperation and good patient–provider communication.

Communication training for health care providers includes a focus on *active listening* skills in which providers echo, restate, and seek to clarify patients' statements to achieve a shared understanding of symptoms, concerns, and treatment expectations. It also includes training in developing good rapport with patients through appropriate eye contact and other responses designed to acknowledge patients' feelings and to help them talk freely. In addition, providers receive instruction about how to communicate with patients about sensitive or difficult health topics, as well as about how to give bad news.

A number of communication-enhancing interventions also have been directed at patients, especially those who are about to receive an important

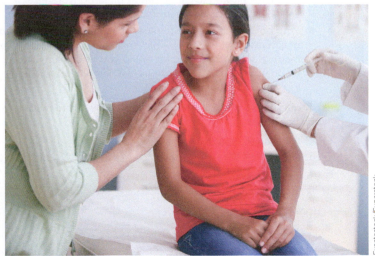

Children and Medical Procedures To get a child to undergo difficult or "scary" medical procedures, parents, nurses, and doctors should understand how the child appraises such situations. It is valuable for providers to use good communication skills with the child as well as with the parent or guardian.

Exactostock/Superstock

Your Health Assets

Health Literacy

Health literacy—the ability to read, understand, and act on health information—is critical to good outcomes in health care. Patients with low health literacy may not fully adhere to treatment instructions from physicians and other providers. Identifying people who are at risk for low health literacy allows providers to tailor their communication to promote patients' understanding.

The "Newest Vital Sign" (NVS) is a 3-minute tool administered by health care providers to test patients' literacy skills for information printed on an ice cream label. The ability to read and analyze nutrition labels requires the same analytical and conceptual skills needed to understand and follow medical instructions.

In May 2016, the Food and Drug Administration announced new requirements for nutrition facts labels designed to make it easier for consumers to make better-informed food choices. These new requirements include increasing the font size for "Calories," "Servings per container," and "Serving size," and bold-facing the number of calories and "Serving size" to highlight this information. In addition, product labels must disclose the actual amount—in addition to the percent Daily Value—of vitamin D, calcium, iron, and potassium.

Want to test your own literacy? Take a look at the label on the next page, which is on the back of a pint of ice cream. Then answer the questions below.

Is ice cream a healthy food choice? Food labels are an excellent place to test your own health literacy.

iStock/Getty Images

1. If you eat the entire container, how many calories will you eat?

2. If you are allowed to eat 60 grams of carbohydrates as a snack, how much ice cream could you have?

3. Your doctor advises you to reduce the amount of saturated fat in your diet. You usually have 42 grams of saturated fat each day, which includes one serving of ice cream. If you stop eating ice cream, how many grams of saturated fat would you be consuming each day?

4. If you usually eat 2,500 calories in a day, what percentage of your daily value of calories will you be eating if you eat one serving?

For questions 5 and 6, pretend that you are allergic to the following substances: penicillin, peanuts, latex gloves, and bee stings.

5. Is it safe for you to eat this ice cream?

6. (Ask only if the patient responds "No" to question 5) Why not?

Correct Answers

1. The correct answer is 1,000.

2. Either of the following is correct: 1 cup (or any amount up to 1 cup); half the container. Note: If the patient answers "two servings," ask "How much ice cream would that be if you were to measure it into a bowl?"

3. The only correct answer is 33.

4. The only correct answer is 10 percent.

5. No.

6. It isn't safe because it has peanut oil.

Scoring

Give yourself 1 point for each correct answer (maximum 6 points).

- A score of 0–1 suggests high likelihood (50% or greater) of limited literacy.

- A score of 2–3 indicates the possibility of limited literacy.

- A score of 4–6 almost always indicates adequate literacy.

Health literacy is so important to good health care outcomes that experts recommend that the patient's NVS score should be entered on his or her medical chart, along with blood pressure, body mass index, and other vital signs.

Nutrition Facts

Serving Size	1/2 cup
Servings per container	4

Amount per serving

Calories	250	Fat Cal	120
			%DV

Total Fat 13g	20%
Sat Fat 9g	40%
Cholesterol 28mg	12%
Sodium 55mg	2%
Total Carbohydrate 30g	12%
Dietary Fiber 2g	
Sugars 23g	
Protein 4g	8%

*Percentage Daily Values (DV) are based on a 2,000-calorie diet. Your daily values may be higher or lower depending on your calorie needs.

Ingredients: Cream, Skim Milk, Liquid Sugar, Water, Egg Yolks, Brown Sugar, Milk Fat, Peanut Oil, Sugar, Butter, Salt, Carrageenan, Vanilla Extract.

---

consultation. These interventions generally have focused on increasing patients' level of participation, specifically to ensure that their concerns will be heard clearly and that they leave the consultation with a clear understanding of the information that has been provided.

To help overly passive patients, some health psychologists recommend *assertiveness coaching*, beginning with a careful review of each patient's medical record. A psychologist helps patients formulate questions for the doctor and offers tips on entering the doctor's office with a clear sense of one's goals and telling the doctor about feelings, fears, and symptoms without being hindered by embarrassment or anxiety. Assertiveness coaching can pay huge dividends. By establishing a greater degree of control in their office visits, patients who have been coached obtain more information. Follow-up interviews reveal that these patients also miss fewer workdays, rate their overall health as better, and report fewer symptoms than patients who do not receive assertiveness coaching (T. Y. Lee and others, 2013).

The Internet and the Patient–Provider Relationship

The Internet has become a major vehicle for health care. Surveys of users indicate that most believe the Internet has made them better consumers of health information. In one survey, nearly half had urged a family member or friend to visit a doctor, changed their exercise

Brooks Kraft/Getty Images

Telemedicine: Making New Connections In addition to physicians and patients using e-mail for basic communications, advances in technology are providing greater access to health care, especially for people in remote areas. This orthopedic surgeon is using video technology to conduct a consultation with a primary care doctor and her patient.

telemedicine The delivery of medical information and clinical services through interactive audiovisual media.

or eating habits, or made a treatment decision for themselves as a result of online research (Hughes & Wareham, 2010). Patients who access authoritative medical information also visit emergency rooms and doctors' offices less frequently, cutting health care costs (Landro, 2001).

Telemedicine and *eHealth services* are now part of every health care provider's training. With this approach, many physicians use information technologies to provide clinical care at a distance for minor health problems such as common low back pain, upper respiratory infections, and urinary infections (Koutras, Bitsaki, Koutras, Nikolaou, & Heep, 2015). Using patients' test results from reliable home monitoring equipment, uploaded to sites that provide two-way video and audio communication, physicians prescribe and adjust doses of drugs, consult with other health care providers, send laboratory reports, and refer patients to other providers. Increasingly, health care professionals are expected to offer these services, and health insurers will cover them just as they cover medication, surgery, and other medical elements.

Some experts caution, however, that the patient–provider relationship may change for the worse in the wake of enhanced electronic communication, greater access to health and medical information online, and other changes in technology. E-mail or text message exchanges can be impersonal and mechanical and may not communicate emotional tone and context accurately. Nonverbal cues available during a face-to-face consultation may be lost with online care. However, more positive changes from advancing technologies such as VSee—which enables secure, encrypted video conferencing compliant with patient privacy laws—are already being seen in the area of telemedicine, which is especially valuable for people in remote areas (Tsuboi, 2013).

THE HEALTH CARE SYSTEM

The World Health Organization (WHO) defines a health care *system* as "all activities whose primary purpose is to promote, restore, or maintain health" (World Health Organization [WHO], 2006). Hospitals play an important role in the health care system by offering a range of diagnostic and curative services. How these services are implemented varies considerably from one country to another. In this section, we take a look at the impact of hospitalization on patients, variations in how health care is delivered around the world, and the factors driving the health care reform movement today.

Hospitalization

Although the word *hospital* comes from the same root as the word *hospitality*, many patients don't find hospitals to be very hospitable places. More than 36 million people are admitted each year to the 5,534 registered hospitals in the United States (American

Hospital Association, 2018), and too many of those people experience problems such as the staff providing them with conflicting information and tests, and procedures not being done on time. Furthermore, hospitalization is not as safe as it should be. Globally, millions of people die each year from medical errors and infections linked to health care. According to the WHO, going to the hospital is far riskier than flying (Nebehay, 2011).

Historically, the psychological well-being of the patient has not been a primary goal of health care. Rather, its goals were to bring together all the necessary medical staff and equipment to cure people who are seriously ill in the most efficient way possible. In fact, surveys from around the world consistently reveal that the single greatest stressor for health care providers is being behind schedule. This need for efficiency has prompted a somewhat one-dimensional, depersonalized view of hospitalized patients.

Loss of Control and Depersonalization

Upon entering the hospital, patients are expected to conform to the rules of the hospital, including its schedule for eating, sleeping, and receiving visitors, and to make their bodies available for examination and treatment whenever necessary. Throughout their hospitalization, patients are expected to remain cooperative, which often leads to passivity and feeling a loss of control.

Patients also often are treated as little more than bodies to be medicated, watched, and managed. Being referred to as "the appendectomy in Room 617" highlights the concept that nearly every aspect of a patient's identity disappears when the person enters the hospital. Sometimes this *depersonalization* is so complete that hospital staff converse among themselves about the patient in his or her presence, using medical jargon that excludes the patient. Although medical terminology was designed to allow physicians and nurses to telegraph their conversations to convey a great deal of information quickly, when health providers use it without translation, most patients are left feeling both helpless and anxious (Weitz, 2007).

A need for efficiency is only partly to blame for this depersonalized care. There is also a need to reduce the daily stress of the hospital environment. Hospital staff may attempt to distance themselves emotionally as a way to cope with the pressures of making life-or-death decisions, working in an environment with hazardous chemicals, being exposed to contagious illnesses, and treating patients who may not respond to care or who may die. Excessive waiting, communication problems, and being treated impersonally combine with other aspects of hospitalization to make it a stressful experience for many patients (Weingart and others, 2006).

Preparing for Hospitalization

Facing surgery, chemotherapy, and many other invasive procedures is especially daunting because it means confronting our vulnerability and mortality. Surgeons and anesthesiologists have an old saying: "The way a patient enters anesthesia is the way he or she will come out of it." In other words, patients who approach treatment with an optimistic demeanor, confidence, and a sense of being in control often do better after treatment than do highly anxious people who feel helpless and overwhelmed by the situation. For this reason, psychological interventions are increasingly used to prepare patients for stressful medical procedures, with the most effective interventions being those that increase patients' sense of control over their treatment and recovery. Although interventions often overlap in the types of control that they emphasize, most can be categorized as primarily promoting increased informational, cognitive, or behavioral control.

Increasing Informational Control

informational control Patients' knowledge regarding the particular procedures and physical sensations that accompany a medical treatment.

Informational control interventions focus on the particular procedures and physical sensations that accompany a medical treatment. Imagine that you are in the hospital for a minor operation that, although not dangerous, is likely to be followed by a painful recovery. What type of information would you want? Would you want a detailed description of the medical steps to be followed before, during, and after the surgery (procedural information); or would you like to know how you can expect to feel before, during, and after surgery (sensory information)? Sensory information allows you to make an accurate attribution for sensations that you actually experience. If you are told, for example, that it is customary to feel nauseated for a few days following a particular medical procedure, you will not be surprised when you actually do feel sick to your stomach. More important, armed with accurate information beforehand, you will not worry when the symptom appears. Unprepared, however, you might fear that your nausea is a sign that something has gone wrong and that you are not recovering properly. Procedural information, on the other hand, may reduce stress by giving patients an increased sense of control over what their bodies are experiencing. When procedures are expected and predictable, many patients develop greater confidence and become more relaxed.

The results of studies comparing the advantages of procedural and sensory information have been mixed, possibly due to differences in the way researchers define *improvement*. In a large-scale meta-analysis, researchers reported that although procedural information and sensory information are both beneficial, procedural information appears to help the greatest number of patients (Cordasco, 2013). In many instances, of course, providing both types of information produces the maximum benefits.

Interestingly, researchers have found that a patient's reaction to procedural or sensory information regarding a stressful medical procedure depends, in part, on the patient's style of coping. As might be expected, sensitizers tend to deal with stressful medical procedures with constant vigilance and anxious monitoring of the cues of discomfort, while repressors deny stress, actively suppress stressful thoughts, and do not appear to be anxious. Researchers have also discovered that sensitizers welcome as much detailed information as they can get, while repressors prefer to know as little as possible.

Cognitive-Behavioral Interventions

cognitive control Interventions that direct the patient's attention to the positive aspects of a procedure (such as improved health) rather than to feelings of discomfort.

behavioral control Interventions that teach techniques for controlling pain and speeding recovery during and after a medical procedure.

Health psychologists, behavioral consultants, and other collaborative care providers increasingly use cognitive-behavioral therapy (CBT) to help patients cope with anxiety and depression, as well as to help them prepare for surgery and other medical procedures. Aimed at improving **cognitive control**, CBT directs the patient's attention to the positive aspects of a procedure (such as improved health) rather than to feelings of discomfort. CBT interventions encourage patients to redefine their role—from that of an immobile body being operated on to that of an active participant. They also aim at improving patients' **behavioral control** by teaching techniques for controlling pain and speeding recovery during and after a medical procedure. These might include relaxation instructions, breathing exercises, and other techniques. Such interventions may provide patients with an even greater sense of control, because the patients focus on actual tools to influence how they are feeling.

Lamaze training, which is designed to prepare prospective parents for natural childbirth, is perhaps the most widely used intervention aimed at improving behavioral control. At the heart of the Lamaze technique is relaxation training that enhances the prospective mother's behavioral control over breathing and the muscles of the uterus, which push the baby out. Delivering mothers who are afraid tend to counteract the natural, rhythmic contractions of childbirth by tightening their muscles, which lengthens labor and makes it more painful. Cross-cultural research reveals that women in cultures in which childbirth is anticipated with less fear and apprehension generally report shorter, less painful deliveries, indicating that psychological preparation may play a role in easing the difficulty that some mothers experience during labor (Wong, 2009).

Interventions aimed at increasing behavioral control are most beneficial for medical procedures in which the patient's participation can assist progress. In delivering a baby, for example, the mother-to-be clearly *can* do something to make things run more smoothly. Conversely, behavioral control interventions may be useless when medical procedures require that the patient remain still and passive. For example, cardiac catheterization and dental surgery both require that patients be inactive. There is little the patient can do to make these procedures more pleasant or to assist the health care providers.

CBT has been successfully employed with patients waiting for many different medical procedures (Auerbach, Penberthy, & Kiesler, 2004), including coronary artery bypass graft surgery (CABG). In one study, a diverse group of 100 patients awaiting CABG were assigned randomly to either a treatment-as-usual (TAU) group or a CBT intervention group. Patients in the intervention group participated in four 60-minute treatment sessions, administered by psychologists and focused on education and enhancing cognitive and behavioral control. Table 13.1 provides an overview of the four sessions of CBT. Measures of both physical and

Lamaze training A natural childbirth process designed to prepare prospective parents by enhancing their informational, cognitive, and behavioral control over childbirth.

TABLE 13.1 Overview of Cognitive-Behavioral Therapy

Session Number	Duration (minutes)	When	Content
1	60	Before surgery	Overview of intervention Education about cardiovascular disease, surgery, depression, anxiety Overview of patient concerns
2	60	Before surgery	Review behavioral goals Introduce cognitive strategies
3	60	Three days after surgery	Review cognitive strategies Review cognitive distortions Continue to support and encourage
4	60	Five days after surgery	Review strategies Generate a plan for continued change Continue to support and encourage

Information from: Dao, T. K., Nagy, A. Y., Armsworth, M., Wear, E., Papathopoulos, K. N., & Gopaldas, R. (2011). Randomized controlled trial of brief cognitive behavioral intervention for depression and anxiety symptoms preoperatively in patients undergoing coronary artery bypass graft surgery. *Journal of Thoracic and Cardiovascular Surgery, 142*(3), e109–e115.

mental health were administered to both groups one week before their surgery and again during a follow-up appointment with their health care team three to four weeks afterward.

The results showed that CBT had beneficial effects on all outcome measures. Patients in the TAU group stayed in the hospital longer than those in the CBT group (9.2 days compared to 7.9 days). In addition, symptoms of depression in the TAU group increased at the time of their release from the hospital, whereas patients in the intervention group had decreased symptoms of depression at the time of discharge. Finally, patients in the CBT group had greater improvements in self-reported anxiety and quality of life at the follow-up than did those in the control group (Dao and others, 2011).

Health Care Around the World

Organized health systems barely existed anywhere in the world a century ago; until well into the nineteenth century, hospitals were little more than homes for the orphaned, crippled, destitute, or insane. But several discoveries made later that same century sparked the development of organized public health measures and eventually led to the creation of the first organized health care delivery systems. Among them was the need to combat and prevent diseases in the workforce. For example, during the construction of the Panama Canal, it was realized that malaria and yellow fever were transmitted by mosquitoes. In response, control of mosquito breeding sites became part of prevention efforts, as did providing clean water and basic living conditions for workers. Another discovery that had an impact was that soldiers who fought in combat (including those who fought in the Civil War) were more likely to be killed by disease than by the enemy.

In both rich countries and poor countries, health care needs today differ greatly from those that existed 100 or even 50 years ago. Expectations of access to some form of health care continue to increase, as do demands for measures to protect individuals against the financial cost of poor health. People today also turn to health care systems for a much more diverse array of problems than ever before—not just pain relief or a specified medical treatment, but also information on nutrition, substance abuse, child-rearing, mental health, and countless other issues.

Although physicians are the main providers of health care, other professionals are increasingly involved. **Nurse-practitioners** have completed graduate training programs in *advanced-practice nursing*, as well as training in primary care. They often work with physicians in private practice, seeing their own patients and providing all routine medical care, including prescribing treatments for various illnesses and conditions. **Physician assistants (PAs)** perform many of the routine tasks involved in health care, including taking medical histories, conducting physical examinations, ordering and interpreting diagnostic tests, and prescribing medications. PAs often take the same classes as medical students in their first year of training, after which they embark on a second year of training spent in clinical rotations with direct patient contact.

Global Health Care

Health care delivery systems around the world are modeled to varying degrees on one or more of a few basic designs that emerged and have been refined since the late nineteenth century: *national health service, national health insurance, "pay-as-you-go,"* and *pluralistic* health care (Skolnik, 2016). Table 13.2 gives us a brief look at each.

nurse-practitioner An advanced-practice nurse who, in addition to training in traditional nursing, received training in the delivery of primary health care.

physician assistant (PA) A graduate of a training program that teaches how to practice medicine under the direction of physicians and surgeons.

TABLE 13.2 Characteristics of Health Care Delivery Systems

System Type	Financing	Ownership	Private Insurance?
Single provider (United Kingdom, Italy, Spain, New Zealand, Greece, Portugal, Norway, Sweden, Denmark, Finland, Ireland)	General taxation, central government (United Kingdom) or local/regional government (Scandinavia)	Public	Yes
National health insurance/single-payer (Canada, South Korea, Taiwan)	General taxation, central government and/or regional government	Mixed public and private	No
Social insurance (France, Germany, Holland, Switzerland, Belgium, Luxembourg, Japan)	Mandated social insurance, typically funded by payroll taxes	Mixed public and private	Yes
Pay-as-you-go (developing countries)	Out of pocket	Mixed public and private	Yes
Pluralistic (United States, Australia, Singapore)	Mixed	Mixed public and private	Yes

Information from: Matthews, R. B., Jenkins, G. K., & Robertson, J. (2012). Health care reform: Why not best practices? *American Journal of Health Sciences, 3*(1), 97–113.

The national health service model is characterized by universal coverage, tax-based financing, and government ownership. Also called a *single-provider system*, this type of health care is based on the ideas of William Beveridge, a daring social reformer who in 1948 designed the National Health Service in the United Kingdom after the country's health infrastructure was destroyed by war. In this system, health care is provided and financed by the government through tax payments, just like a police force or the public library in a community. This may be done at the national level (as in the United Kingdom) or the regional/local level (as in many Scandinavian countries). Many hospitals and clinics, but not all, are owned by the government, and some doctors are government employees. There is also a private health care option, serviced by private doctors who collect their fees from the government. National health systems have low costs per capita because the government, as the sole payer, controls what doctors can do and what they can charge. Countries that follow a national health service model include Italy, Spain, Norway, Portugal, Greece, the United Kingdom, Ireland, Sweden, Finland, Denmark, and New Zealand. A variant of the single-provider model, called a *single-payer system*, follows the national health insurance model, except that private-sector health care providers are paid directly by a universal, government-run insurance program. Canada, South Korea, and Taiwan have single-payer health care systems.

The national health insurance (NHS) model is characterized by compulsory universal coverage paid for jointly by employers and employees through payroll deductions. This system uses multiple payers (numerous insurance funds that may be government or privately owned) and multiple providers (generally, private doctors and privately owned hospitals). The joint financing of health care by employers and employees and the risk-sharing nature of insurance pools are the advantages of this model. Participants generally have the right to supplement the basic insurance by purchasing policies from private insurers. People do so, for instance, if they prefer not to wait for NHS treatment

Phanie/Alamy Stock Photo

National Health Insurance
France enjoys high-quality health care, such as the rehabilitation services shown here, for less than the United States spends. In 2016 France spent 11% of its gross domestic product (GDP) on health care, compared with 17.2% in the United States. France has mandatory health insurance coverage for all its citizens. By contrast, recent estimates suggest that 27 million Americans are completely uninsured.

fee-for-service A payment model in which health care services are paid for by patients out of pocket at the time of treatment.

health maintenance organization (HMO) An organization that provides managed care, in which individuals pay a fixed monthly rate and use services as needed.

managed care A system of health care in which health insurance plans contract with providers and medical facilities to provide care for members at reduced rates.

preferred-provider organization (PPO) A managed-care network of physicians, hospitals, and other health care providers who agree to charge preestablished rates for specific services.

or if they want to be covered for services they can't get on the NHS (such as specialist treatment for sports-related injuries). In France, for example, which has the most highly ranked health care system in the world, over 99% of the population are covered by at least the basic level of insurance. Other countries that follow this model include Canada, Germany, and Japan.

Under the Canada Health Act, the country's health care system is built around the principle that all citizens should have access to "medically necessary hospital and physician services on a prepaid basis" (Health Canada, 2016). To accomplish this, each of Canada's ten provinces and three territories runs its own health insurance plan, all of which share common features and basic standards of coverage.

The pay-as-you-go, or **fee-for-service**, model is characterized by individual purchase of health care at the time of treatment. In most developing countries (approximately 160 countries out of 200), access to a doctor is available if and only if you can pay the bill out of pocket at the time of treatment. The main drawback of this model is its inequitable distribution of resources. In this type of system, it is often only the rich who get medical care. The poor stay sick or die. Only 40 or so of the industrialized, developed countries of the world have established health care systems that fall into the national health service or mandated insurance category. In remote regions of Africa, China, India, and South America, many people go their whole lives without ever seeing a licensed, conventional doctor.

The United States and several other countries (such as Australia and Singapore) are pluralistic systems that combine two or more of these approaches to health care. Until just a few decades ago, most Americans received their health care from private physicians, whom they paid directly at the time of treatment. Today, however, more than 90 million Americans receive their care through a **health maintenance organization (HMO)**, a prepaid delivery system in which an employer or employee pays a monthly rate and the individual is allowed to use health services at no additional (or greatly reduced) cost (Kaiser Family Foundation, 2018). In a variation of this type of **managed care**, called a **preferred-provider organization (PPO)**, a network of health care providers charges fixed rates for specific services.

The health care system of the United States traditionally has been a unique mixture of public, private nonprofit, and private for-profit hospitals, in which most physicians were compensated on a fee-for-service basis. Their compensation has come from a variety of sources—sometimes from insurance companies, sometimes directly from patients, and sometimes from government programs such as Medicare (for the elderly), Medicaid (for the poor), and the Veterans Health Administration. The health care system in the United States is unlike that of any other country, because it maintains so many separate systems for different groups of people and is a combination of several approaches. When it comes to treating Americans over age 65, who are on Medicare, the single-payer system is like that of Canada. For working Americans who have insurance on the job, the system is much like the social insurance system found in Germany. For military veterans, health care in the United States is a single-provider system that is much like that in Cuba or the United Kingdom. Finally, for those who have no health insurance and earn too much to be eligible for Medicaid, American health care is like that in rural India, with access available only to those who can pay out of pocket or who are sick enough to be admitted to the emergency department at a public hospital (R. B. Matthews, Jenkins, & Robertson, 2012).

Patient Dissatisfaction, Patient-Centered Care, and Health Care Reform

Spiraling health care costs, medical errors, and patient dissatisfaction are major reasons why health care in the United States is changing. Most importantly, the role of the physician is changing. New delivery systems under managed care and the increasing number of women in the medical profession have changed the role of the doctor from what was once an authoritarian, paternalistic arrangement to one that is patient-centered and more characterized by shared responsibility.

In **patient-centered health care**, patients become active participants in their own care and receive services designed to focus on their individual needs and preferences. Working with the American Academy of Family Physicians, the Roper and Harris polling organizations surveyed a large sample of patients, asking them to grade the importance of 40 attributes in physicians. Table 13.3 lists 10 things people want from their health care providers. These data show that doctors' training and knowledge of new medical treatments are less important to many patients than their ability to center their care on patients and their individual needs. So it's not surprising that one of the Institute of Medicine's six aims for twenty-first-century health care—as issued in its landmark report *Crossing the Quality Chasm* (Institute of Medicine, 2001)—is that it be centered around the patient.

The passage of the Affordable Care Act (ACA) in 2010 brought about significant changes in how health care is paid for and provided in the United States. Supporters of ACA frequently cited a 2000 World Health Organization comparison of global health care delivery systems in which American health care ranked only thirty-seventh among 191 member countries in its overall performance. In 2016, the United States spent about twice

patient-centered health care The delivery of health care services that are respectful of and responsive to individual patient preferences, needs, and values.

TABLE 13.3 10 Things People Want from Their Health Care Providers

1. To have a doctor who listens well
2. To have a doctor who is caring and compassionate
3. To have a doctor who explains information well and avoids medical jargon
4. To have convenient and quick access to health care
5. To have a doctor who treats them with dignity and respect, and as a partner in decision-making
6. To have a doctor who is willing to spend enough time with them
7. To have a doctor who makes eye contact
8. To have a doctor who asks good questions in order to understand their needs
9. To have a doctor who provides options, and explains each option
10. To have a doctor who does his or her homework and knows the patient's history

Information from: Wen, L. S., and Tucker, S. (2015). What do people want from their health care? A qualitative study. *Journal of Participatory Medicine, 7,* e10; NRC Health (2016). What do patients really want from their physician?

as much as 10 other affluent countries on medical care, yet performed less well on many population health outcomes (Papanicolas, Woskie, & Jha, 2018). Life expectancy in the United States was the lowest of the 11 countries at 78.8 years (mean of all countries = 81.7 years), and infant mortality was the highest (5.8 deaths per 1,000 live births compared to 3.6 per 1,000 for all 11 countries). In 2016, the United States spent 17.8% of its gross domestic product on health care, far more than that spent in the other countries (ranging from 9.6% in Australia to 12.4% in Switzerland).

Among the countries with the best overall health care are France, Italy, Japan, Canada, and the United Kingdom—all countries with national health systems. Skeptics of the ACA, who generally label the act "Obamacare," express concerns about whether its goals are feasible, whether its reforms represent a step backward instead of forward, and whether a single-payer or single-provider system is desirable or achievable (R. B. Matthews and others, 2012).

accountable care organization (ACO) An organization of health care providers who agree to be accountable for the quality, cost, and overall care of members.

A major part of health care reform under the ACA are **accountable care organizations (ACOs)**, in which groups of doctors, hospitals, and other health care providers come together to give coordinated, evidence-based care to their patients. The goal of this type of care is to ensure that patients receive high-quality and cost-effective care while avoiding the unnecessary duplication of services that often occurs when health care is not coordinated among primary care doctors, specialists, and other providers. Another key feature of ACOs is *accountability,* which is evaluated by ACOs using quality metrics to measure health care delivery processes. Designed to reduce medical errors, these measurements now include such statistics as the percentage of doctors in an ACO who use electronic prescriptions and patient medical records and the percentage of patients who receive screenings, vaccinations, and counseling about health risks (Meisel & Pines, 2011).

The core principles of the original ACA include (Kaiser Foundation, 2012):

- *Individual mandate.* Beginning in 2014, people not covered by Medicare or Medicaid were required to have health insurance or pay a tax penalty. In addition, insurance companies no longer were allowed to deny coverage to individuals with preexisting conditions, to impose lifetime limits on benefits, or to cancel coverage when a person gets sick. In December 2017, Congress passed a new tax law that will eliminate the penalty beginning in 2019, and thus effectively cancel the individual mandate.

- *Affordable coverage.* Under the ACA, lower- and some middle-income individuals and families receive financial assistance to help purchase health insurance. In addition, insurance companies are required to report each year on the dollars paid into the system as insurance premiums that were spent on actual medical care; they must provide rebates to their customers if this number is less than 80%.

- *Employer requirements.* There is no employer mandate to provide health care to all workers in the ACA, but those with more than 50 employees are assessed a fee of $2,000 per full-time employee if they do not offer coverage. A tax credit for employers at smaller-sized companies is designed to encourage them to provide health care to their employees.

- *Coverage for preventive health services.* New group and individual insurance plans are required to pay for certain screenings, immunizations, and other preventive care so that patients can get these services at no cost to themselves.

In 2017, Congress repeatedly failed to repeal and replace the Affordable Care Act. However, as with eliminating the individual mandate, it weakened the law through a series of regulatory actions and rules, causing an increase in insurance premiums and a decrease in the percentage of the population with health care insurance (Abutaleb, 2018).

In this chapter we have seen substantial evidence that psychosocial factors influence how people interact with the health care system. This includes how they interpret symptoms, whether they seek treatment (and how well they adhere to it), how they respond to hospitalization, and the quality of their relationships with health care providers. Today, health care around the world is under increasing pressure to become more accessible, accountable, and patient-centered. More than ever, health psychologists are valued members of health care teams.

Weigh In on Health

Respond to each question below based on what you learned in the chapter. (**Tip:** Use the items in "Summing Up" to take into account related biological, psychological, and social concerns.)

1. How have you or someone you know experienced illness? Using this chapter's discussions, explain the experience in terms of how you or the person you're thinking of were influenced psychologically and especially in terms of how symptoms were interpreted and reported.

2. Based on what you've read in this chapter, what are some biological, psychological, and social or cultural influences that affect how illnesses are treated and how people adhere to advice from health care providers?

3. Why is communication such an important element in the provider–patient relationship? Support your answer with research discussed in this chapter.

4. Health psychologists participate in health care in a variety of settings, including primary care programs and hospitals, as well as specialized programs for pain management, rehabilitation, and other services. It has been said that no matter what setting they are working in, health psychologists must be experts in human relations. Why do you think this is so, and what kinds of training would be most helpful in preparing for this role?

Summing Up

Recognizing and Interpreting Symptoms

1. Detecting physical symptoms and interpreting their medical significance are influenced strongly by psychological processes—including the individual's personality, culture, gender, and psychological health—as well as by the individual's focus of attention.

2. Illness representations regarding the type of disease, its causes, time frame, consequences, and controllability also influence how people react to and interpret physical symptoms.

Seeking Treatment

3. Social and demographic variables, such as cultural norms, age, gender, and socioeconomic status, influence whether a person seeks treatment. Delay behavior may result from a failure to notice symptoms (appraisal delay), a refusal to believe that one is actually sick (illness delay) or needs professional help (behavioral delay), procrastination in making an

appointment (scheduling delay), or a belief that the benefits of seeking treatment are not worth the costs (treatment delay).

4. Some people may use health services when there is no real need because they are feigning illness (malingering) or because they falsely believe they have a disease when they do not (illness anxiety disorder). In other people, bodily symptoms are an expression of emotional stress.

Patient Adherence

5. *Adherence* means closely following the advice of a health care provider, which less than half of patients do (nonadherence).

6. Patient adherence improves with perceived control (for those who prefer control), optimism, a good mood, trust in the care provider, a strong patient–provider relationship, a simple and clearly explained treatment regimen, and social support.

7. Provider variables, such as level of job satisfaction, the number of patients seen per week, and communication style, also have a powerful influence on patient adherence.

The Patient–Provider Relationship

8. The central elements of the essential relationship between health care provider and patient are continuity of care, communication, and the overall quality of consultations. Poor communication between health care providers and patients is common, given the time pressures of health care and the fact that providers may lack communication skills. Other factors in miscommunication include the attitudes and beliefs patients and providers have regarding their roles, as well as gender, cultural, and educational differences between providers and patients.

9. Discrimination, prejudice, and institutional racism adversely affect minority populations and the health care system in general. Historically, minorities have also been underrepresented in clinical trials.

10. Patients with low health literacy are more likely to have difficulty navigating the health care system, less likely to seek preventive care and adhere to prescribed treatment and self-care regimens, and more likely to make medication and treatment errors.

11. The quality of the patient–provider relationship may be challenged by enhanced electronic communication and greater access to Internet health and medical information.

The burgeoning field of telemedicine, however, has improved health care greatly in remote locations.

The Health Care System

12. One of the most persistent problems of hospitals is the depersonalization of patients as a result of a need for efficiency and the need of hospital staff to distance themselves emotionally from their stressful daily experiences. Cognitive-behavioral therapy (CBT) and other interventions often improve adjustment to hospitalization and to stressful medical procedures.

13. Although physicians are the main providers of health care, nurse-practitioners, physician assistants, and other professionals are increasingly involved in providing routine medical care, including prescribing treatments for various illness and conditions.

14. Health care delivery systems around the world are modeled to varying degrees on one or more of a few basic designs that emerged and have been refined since the late nineteenth century: *single-provider, single-payer, mandated insurance*, and *fee-for-service* health care. The United States and several other countries are pluralistic systems that combine two or more of these approaches to health care.

15. Increasing health care costs, medical errors, and patient dissatisfaction are major factors in why health care in the United States is changing. In patient-centered health care, patients become active participants in their own care and receive services designed to focus on their individual needs and preferences.

Key Terms and Concepts to Remember

collaborative care, p. 413
illness representations, p. 413
comorbidity, p. 415
lay referral system, p. 418
delay behavior, p. 419
illness anxiety disorder, p. 420
malingering, p. 421
adherence, p. 421
nonadherence, p. 421

health literacy, p. 426
telemedicine, p. 430
informational control, p. 432
cognitive control, p. 432
behavioral control, p. 432
Lamaze training, p. 433
nurse-practitioner, p. 434
physician assistant (PA), p. 434
fee-for-service, p. 436

health maintenance organization (HMO), p. 436
managed care, p. 436
preferred-provider organization (PPO), p. 436
patient-centered health care, p. 437
accountable care organization (ACO), p. 438

 LaunchPad
macmillan learning

To accompany your textbook, you have access to a number of online resources, including quizzes for every chapter of the book, flashcards, critical thinking exercises, videos, and *Check Your Health* inventories. To access these resources, please visit the Straub Health Psychology LaunchPad at **launchpadworks.com**

Managing Pain

Chapter 14

Clive Brunskill/Allsport Concepts/ Getty Images

LEARNING OUTCOMES

Once you have studied this chapter, you will be able to:

- Define pain and explain its epidemiology and significance,
- Identify various methods of measuring pain,
- Describe the physiology of pain,
- Enumerate several factors that influence pain, and
- Describe and evaluate various methods of treating pain.

At the 1976 Olympic Games in Montreal, the pressure was on the Japanese gymnastics team. Japan had won the gymnastics gold medal in four consecutive Olympics—Rome, Tokyo, Mexico City, and Munich—and now they were going for their fifth straight title. In the midst of the competition, Shun Fujimoto, their star competitor, broke his kneecap while performing the floor exercise. Remarkably, he didn't disclose the injury to his coaches or teammates. "I did not want to worry my teammates," he recalled. "The competition was so close, I didn't want them to lose their concentration with worry about me."

Blessed with incredible strength and a nearly perfect gymnastics physique, Fujimoto was a team leader whose buoyant spirit and national pride had rallied his teammates many times in previous competitions. But how could he continue? Although Olympic rules prohibited him from taking a painkiller, Fujimoto was determined to stay in the competition and endure the excruciating pain. Fortunately, the next apparatus was the pommel horse, an event in which the knees are mostly locked in place. Unless he fell, the pain might be tolerable. Fujimoto completed a nearly flawless performance, receiving a score of 9.5 out of a possible 10.

The final event, however, would be much more demanding. The high rings test arm strength, but vital points can also be lost during the dismount, when the gymnast descends from a great height after a swinging routine that propels him onto the mat at high velocity. "I knew when I descended from the rings, it would be the most painful moment," Fujimoto remembered. "I also knew that if my posture was not good when I landed, I would not receive a good score. I must try to forget the pain."

After another nearly perfect routine, Fujimoto landed, smiled for the judges, held his position for the required few seconds, and then fell to the mat as his injured leg buckled beneath him. Incredibly, his near-perfect score of 9.7 was enough to propel his team to gold medal victory!

Biological, psychological, and social factors contributed to Fujimoto's development as a gymnast, and those same factors played a role in his triumphant Olympic victory. The story also makes clear one of health psychology's most fundamental themes: that the mind and body are inextricably intertwined. Fujimoto's determination not to let his teammates down allowed him to endure a painful injury that in other circumstances most certainly would have been crippling.

Until recently researchers knew next to nothing about pain—what causes it and how to control it—and medical schools spent little time covering the topic. Since the 1980s, however, health psychologists have made considerable progress in filling in the gaps about the nature and treatment of this common, yet extraordinarily complex, phenomenon.

In this chapter, we discuss the components of pain: the ways in which it is experienced; how it is measured; and the biological, psychological, and social factors that influence the experience of pain. Many instances of pain begin with physical injury or a disruption to the normal functioning of human systems, so we will explore technical details about the biology of pain and how it starts from a full biopsychosocial health perspective. And we will take a look at how pain is treated within medicine and at the latest multidimensional interventions introduced by health psychology.

clinical pain Pain that requires some form of medical treatment.

Components of Pain Pain obviously has a strong physical component, as the face of this soccer player clearly reveals. It also has emotional and psychological components—his pain would probably be more bearable if his injury involved a kick that won the game for his team.

imageBROKER/Superstock

WHAT IS PAIN?

Few topics in health psychology are as elusive as pain. Pain is obviously a physical sensation. Yet the pain of losing a loved one or ending a long-term relationship, which is more psychological than physical in nature, often feels just as real. Pain is highly subjective, and sometimes not altogether unpleasant. After a hard workout on the track, for example, I often feel soreness that is definitely uncomfortable, yet somehow also warm and pleasant.

This chapter focuses on **clinical pain**, which is pain that requires some form of medical treatment. Let's begin by considering how many of us suffer pain and how often.

Epidemiology and Components of Pain

Pain is a major public health problem, affecting more than 1.5 billion people worldwide and an estimated 100 million Americans—more than the number affected by heart disease, cancer, and diabetes combined (American Academy of Pain

Medicine, 2013). Pain is a significant public health problem that costs the United States around $600 billion annually, or about $2,000 for every person living in the United States (Institute of Medicine [IOM], 2011b). Chronic pain affects at least 10% of the world's population, with prevalence estimates varying considerably in different regions and countries (Jackson, Stabile, & McQueen, 2014). In the United States, 25.3 million adults (11.2%) suffer from daily (chronic) pain (Nahin, 2015). Pain is the most common reason that people seek medical treatment and is so pervasive that it is considered a fifth vital sign, along with blood pressure, pulse, temperature, and respiration. No other class of health problems even approaches this level of impact.

Pain clearly illustrates the biopsychosocial model, which distinguishes among the biological mechanisms by which the body processes painful stimuli; the subjective, emotional experience of pain; and the social and behavioral factors that help shape our response to pain. For Shun Fujimoto, the gymnast highlighted at the start of this chapter, the biological mechanisms of his injury sparked an interplay of his emotions with his social perspective, based on principles of Japan's collectivist culture, which resulted in a triumphant performance despite the physical pain of a broken kneecap.

Significance and Types of Pain

Despite the discomfort and stress it can cause, pain is essential to our survival. It can be bothersome, but it is that bothersome nature that makes it highly adaptive. Pain sounds a warning that something is wrong and alerts you to try to prevent further physical damage. In fact, inability to feel pain would be hazardous to your health.

Types of Pain

In general, researchers divide pain into three broad categories: acute, recurrent, and chronic. **Acute pain** is sharp, stinging pain that is usually localized in an injured area of the body. It can last from a few seconds to several months, and it generally subsides as normal healing occurs. Examples include burns and fractures. **Recurrent pain** involves intermittent periods of discomfort that recur for more than three months. Periodic migraines and noncardiac chest pain, which is experienced by nearly 10% of school-age children (J. L. Lee and others, 2013), fall into this category.

Chronic pain, which is traditionally defined as pain that lasts six months or longer—long past the normal healing period—may be continuous or intermittent, moderate or severe, and felt in just about any of the body's tissues (Turk & Okifuji, 2002). Chronic pain lowers overall quality of life and increases vulnerability to infection and thus to a host of diseases. Chronic pain also can take a devastating psychological toll, triggering lowered self-esteem, insomnia, anger, hopelessness, depression, personality disorders, and many other signs of distress.

Hyperalgesia

Those with chronic pain may become even more sensitive to pain, a condition known as **hyperalgesia**. Hyperalgesia also happens during sickness or injury and may facilitate recovery by stimulating recuperative behaviors. For example, the flu makes you weak and achy and drives you back to bed, which is exactly where you need to be to recover.

acute pain Sharp, stinging pain that is short-lived and usually related to tissue damage.

recurrent pain Pain that involves episodes of discomfort that recur for more than three months interspersed with periods in which the individual is relatively pain-free.

chronic pain Dull, burning pain that is long-lasting.

hyperalgesia A condition in which a chronic pain sufferer becomes more sensitive to pain over time.

Painful Struggle Ashlyn Blocker's mother, shown here with Ashlyn (right) and her sister, struggles daily with Ashlyn's inability to sense pain, hot, and cold. "Pain's there for a reason. It lets your body know something's wrong and it needs to be fixed. I'd give anything for her to feel pain" (quoted in Bynum, 2004).

AP IMAGES/STEPHEN MORTON

Hundreds of experiments over more than 100 years have confirmed that hyperalgesia often occurs as a normal adaptation during sickness. Most kinds of internal pain are accompanied by increased sensitivity in nearby tissues. In the 1890s, physiologists Henry Head and Mames MacKensie proposed that signals from diseased parts of the body set up an "irritable focus" in the central nervous system that creates areas of enhanced pain sensitivity in nearby, otherwise healthy, body parts, suggesting that the signals originate in the central nervous system. In *opioid-induced hyperalgesia*, long-term use of opioids leads to an increasing sensitivity to noxious stimuli, even to the point at which common sensory stimuli become painful (Angst & Clark, 2006). Researchers believe this sensitization occurs because of a long-lasting enhancement of neural impulses (*long-term potentiation*) among cells in the spinal cord that are involved in relaying pain messages to the brain (Drdla, Gassner, Gingl, & Sandkuhler, 2009).

MEASURING PAIN

Because of its multidimensional and subjective nature, pain is not easily measured. Nevertheless, clinicians and researchers have developed a number of ways to assess pain: *physical measures, behavioral measures,* and *self-report measures.*

Physical Measures

We know of no objective measures of pain, despite the efforts of clinicians and researchers to find them. In fact, more than a century ago the problem of measuring pain set the stage for the very earliest *psychophysical studies* in the new field of psychology. These studies highlight the familiar *mind–body problem*: How does conscious awareness derive from and affect the physical sensations of the body?

One way to assess pain is to measure the specific physiological changes that accompany pain. For example, *electromyography* (EMG) assesses the amount of muscle tension experienced by patients suffering from headaches or lower back pain. Researchers have also recorded changes in heart rate, breathing rate, blood pressure, skin temperature, and skin conductance—all indicators of the *autonomic arousal* that may accompany pain. But these measures have not demonstrated any consistent differences between those with and those without a specific type of pain. This failure may well be because pain is only one of many factors that contribute to autonomic changes; other factors include diet, attention, activity level, stress, and the presence of illness.

Behavioral Measures

Another assessment technique measures signs of pain in a patient's behavior. Relatives and friends of the patient or health care professionals can do this in structured clinical sessions. Wilbert Fordyce (1982), a pioneer in pain research, developed a pain-behavior training program in which an observer is asked to monitor 5 to 10 behaviors—the amount of time the patient spends in bed and the number of requests for painkillers, for example—that frequently signal the onset of pain.

In clinical settings, nurses and other health professionals are trained to observe patients' pain behaviors systematically during routine care procedures. One frequently used pain inventory is the Pain Behavior Scale, which consists of a series of target behaviors, including verbal complaints, facial grimaces, awkward postures, and mobility (Feuerstein & Beattie, 1995). Observers rate the occurrence of each target behavior on a three-point scale: "frequent," "occasional," and "none."

The Pain Response Preference Questionnaire (PRPQ) is used to assess the degree to which a range of potential pain-related responses are desired from a spouse or partner (McWilliams, Saldanha, Dick, & Watt, 2009). The PRPQ includes items that fall into four separate scales: *solicitude* ("treat me with extra care and concern"; "ask me about my pain"); *management* ("encourage me to rest"; "tell me to take it easy"); *encouragement* ("tell me I can do things despite pain"; "tell me to keep active"); and *suppression* ("help me ignore the pain"; "act like I'm not in pain") (McWilliams, Dick, Bailey, Verrier, & Kowal, 2012).

With children, there is growing consensus that measuring emotional responses to pain is a core outcome measure (McGrath and others, 2008). Fear in children is common and can increase the perception of pain (Mathews, 2011). Needle fears are particularly prevalent. Several scales have been developed to capture the dimensions of pain and fear in children, including the Children's Anxiety and Pain Scales (CAPS) and the Children's Fear Scale (CFS) (McMurtry, Noel, Chambers, & McGrath, 2011).

Self-Report Measures

The simplest way to measure pain is to have people use a numeric rating scale (NRS) to assign a number—typically from 1 ("no pain") to 10 ("worst possible pain")—to describe their current discomfort level. Another widely used technique, the visual analog scale (VAS), has people locate the level of their pain at a point along a horizontal or vertical line that is about 10 centimeters in length and anchored by two extremes: "no pain" and "worst possible pain" (Figure 14.1). The advantage of the VAS is that the scale is continuous and does not take discrete jumps from one level to the next. Patient and research participant reports using the VAS and NRS for assessment of pain intensity agree well and are equally sensitive. Both scales are more powerful in detecting changes in pain intensity than verbal rating scales in

(a) Visual Analog Scale (VAS)

No pain ← → Worst possible pain

(b) Wong-Baker FACES® Pain Rating Scale

0	2	4	6	8	10
No Hurt	Hurts Little Bit	Hurts Little More	Hurts Even More	Hurts Whole Lot	Hurts Worst

FIGURE 14.1 Basic Pain Scales A visual analog scale, such as the scale shown in (a), allows people to identify the intensity of their pain at the appropriate point on a continuum. For children ages 3 and over, seniors, and some other adults, using the Wong-Baker FACES Pain Rating Scale, the scale shown in (b), may be more helpful. (Instructions on the use of the latter scale are available from www.wongbakerfaces.org.)

which people choose from a list the word that most accurately describes the pain (for example, "none," "mild," "moderate," and "severe") (Hjermstad and others, 2011).

Many years ago, pain research pioneer Ronald Melzack developed a system for categorizing pain along three dimensions (Melzack & Torgerson, 1971). The first dimension, *sensory quality*, highlighted the tremendous variations that occur in the sensation of pain. The second dimension, *affective quality*, focuses on the many different emotional reactions that pain can trigger. The final dimension is *evaluative quality*, which refers to the sufferer's judgment of the severity of the pain, as well as its meaning or significance. From this multidimensional model of pain, Melzack derived the McGill Pain Questionnaire (MPQ), which has become the most widely used pain inventory today.

THE PHYSIOLOGY OF PAIN

You slip on an icy sidewalk and fall hard on your elbow. In the instant before you feel the pain, a cascade of biochemical and electrical reactions occurs. The processing of all sensory information begins when *sensory receptors* in your skin convert a physical stimulus into neural impulses. The pressure of striking the ground activates the receptors in your elbow, which stimulates the peripheral nervous system to relay the message to your brain. Only when the brain registers and interprets this neural input is pain experienced. What happens in between the stimulation of sensory receptors and the brain's interpretation has been the subject of a great deal of exciting research.

Pain Pathways

Pain is not triggered by only one type of stimulus—nor does it have a single type of receptor. Tissue injury isn't the only thing that will produce pain. The corneas of your eyes, for instance, are exquisitely sensitive. Almost any stimulus, from a speck of dust to the application of a bit too much pressure when inserting a contact lens, will be experienced as pain, even though the cornea suffers no damage. All of these stimuli trigger the pain response in the brain through different receptors.

Pain Receptors

For more than a century, researchers have been on a quest to find the definitive sensory receptors for pain. A *receptor* is a neuron that is specialized for *transduction*, which is the conversion of a physical stimulus from the environment, such as pressure, warmth, or cold, into a neural impulse. Unlike *efferent (motor) neurons*, which stimulate organs and glands and cause muscles to contract, receptors are *afferent (sensory) neurons* that relay information from the skin, eye, ear, and other sense organs toward the central nervous system. A third type of neuron—the *interneuron*—connects afferent to efferent neurons. Among the candidates as pain receptors are **free nerve endings**, which are found throughout the body: in the skin, muscles (cramps), internal organs of the viscera (stomachaches), membranes that surround joints and bones (arthritic pain), and even the pulp of teeth (toothaches).

free nerve endings Sensory receptors found throughout the body that respond to temperature, pressure, and painful stimuli.

Free nerve endings are simple, yet they are poorly understood. We know that they respond primarily to temperature change and pressure, and also to certain chemicals secreted in damaged tissues. However they are aroused, it appears that free nerve endings begin a process that ends when the brain registers and interprets the sensation as pain. For this reason, researchers refer to free nerve endings that are activated by *noxious* (painful) stimuli as **nociceptors**.

nociceptor A specialized neuron that responds to painful stimuli.

Pain Nerve Fibers

The pain process begins when neural signals from free nerve endings are routed to the central nervous system via three types of nerve fibers that differ in several ways, including their size, the speed at which they are able to carry neural impulses, and the type of messages they send to the brain (see Table 14.1). **A-delta** (fast) **fibers** are relatively large and have axons that are coated with *myelin*, an insulating layer of fatty tissue that increases the speed of neural conduction to 15 to 30 meters per second. **C** (slow) **fibers** are smaller, unmyelinated fibers that conduct electrical impulses at only 0.5 to 2 meters per second. **A-beta fibers**, which are also large and myelinated, conduct rapidly and may be involved in inhibiting other pain messages from reaching the brain.

A-delta fibers Small, afferent fibers involved in the experience of acute pain.

C fibers Small, afferent fibers that are involved in the experience of chronic pain.

A-beta fibers Large, afferent fibers that may inhibit the transmission of pain messages to the brain.

Type A-delta and C fibers are the messengers for two pain systems in the brain. The *fast pain system* (involving the A-delta fibers) appears to serve only the skin and mucous membranes; the *slow pain system* (involving the C fibers) serves all body tissues except the brain itself, which does not experience pain. The fast pain system carries pain that is perceived as stinging and localized in one area, whereas slow nerve fibers signal dull, aching pain that may be generalized throughout the body.

Strong mechanical pressure or extreme temperatures normally stimulate fast nerve fibers, whereas slow nerve fibers are typically activated by chemical changes in damaged tissues. These chemical changes make both types of nerves more responsive to further stimulation. This is why even the lightest touch on an injured area of skin can be extremely painful.

To get a feeling for the practical differences in the speed of the two pain systems, consider that slow fibers relaying a painful message from your foot could take as long as 2 seconds to reach the brain. In contrast, the faster fibers relay their messages in a fraction of a second. This explains a familiar experience. Sticking your toe in unbearably hot bath water will stimulate the fast pain fibers, producing an immediate sharp pain. The message is carried from the skin to the spinal cord, where it is passed via a single interneuron to motor neurons that cause you to jerk your toe out of the water. But this highly adaptive *spinal reflex* is completed well before you experience the deeper, dull pain that really hurts.

TABLE 14.1 Pain Nerve Fibers

Type of Fiber	Characteristics	Pain Signal
A-delta	large, myelinated	fast, acute pain
C-fiber	small, unmyelinated	slow, burning pain
A-beta	large, myelinated	inhibition of pain

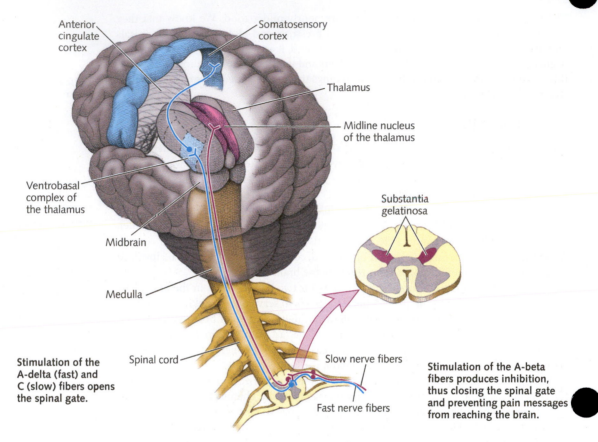

Anterior cingulate cortex

Somatosensory cortex

Thalamus

Midline nucleus of the thalamus

Ventrobasal complex of the thalamus

Midbrain

Medulla

Substantia gelatinosa

Stimulation of the A-delta (fast) and C (slow) fibers opens the spinal gate.

Spinal cord

Slow nerve fibers

Fast nerve fibers

Stimulation of the A-beta fibers produces inhibition, thus closing the spinal gate and preventing pain messages from reaching the brain.

FIGURE 14.2 Pain Pathways The blue line illustrates the pathway for fast, acute pain, which originates with fast nerve fibers in the spinal cord and projects to the somatosensory cortex. The red line illustrates the pathway for slow, chronic pain, which begins with slow nerve fibers in the spinal cord.

substantia gelatinosa The dorsal region of the spinal cord where both fast and slow pain fibers synapse with sensory nerves on their way to the brain.

referred pain Pain manifested in an area of the body that is sensitive to pain but caused by disease or injury in an area of the body that has few pain receptors.

After leaving the skin, the sensory fibers of the fast and slow pain systems group together as nerves to form *sensory tracts* that funnel information up the spinal cord to the brain (Figure 14.2). Both types of pain fibers enter through the back of the spinal cord, where they synapse with neurons in the **substantia gelatinosa**. In the spinal cord, the pain fibers link up with sensory nerves that carry touch, pressure, and limb movement sensations to the thalamus, the brain's sensory switchboard.

On its way to the thalamus, the fast pain pathway triggers neural activity in the reticular formation, which is the brain's mechanism for arousing the cortex in response to important messages and for reducing our awareness of unimportant stimuli. Once in the thalamus, incoming messages are routed to the *somatosensory area* of the cerebral cortex, the area that receives input from all the skin senses.

The amount of somatosensory cortex allotted to various regions of the body determines our sensitivity in that region. For example, even though your face has a much smaller surface area than your back, it has much more somatosensory cortex dedicated to it, making it capable of sensing weaker touch stimuli than your back (see Figure

14.3). The internal organs of the body are not mapped in the cortex in the same way as the skin, making it difficult to pinpoint pain from the body's interior. In fact, visceral (internal) pain often becomes **referred pain**, in that it feels as though it originates on the surface of the body rather than in the organ that produced the pain. So reliable is this phenomenon that referred pain is often used to diagnose serious medical conditions. A patient complaining of pain in the shoulder, for example, is often scheduled for an electrocardiogram (EKG) stress test because that type of pain often accompanies advanced heart disease.

The slow pain system follows roughly the same pathway as the fast system up the spinal cord to the brainstem (refer back to Figure 14.2). In the brainstem, slow pain messages are reprocessed; from there, they travel to the hypothalamus (the rear portion of the thalamus) and then to the amygdala of the limbic system.

The Neurochemistry of Pain

Like all neurons, those that carry pain messages depend on several types of chemical neurotransmitters to relay information across synapses. One neurotransmitter, called **substance P**, works with another neurotransmitter, called *glutamate,* to continuously stimulate nerve endings at the site of an injury and within your spinal cord, increasing pain messages.

A third group of neurotransmitters, called **enkephalins** (the smallest member of the brain's natural opiates, the endorphins), binds to receptors in the brain to deaden pain sensations. Through their synapses with slow fibers, enkephalin-containing neurons are believed to regulate how much substance P is released. If substance P is not released or is released in small quantities, an incoming pain message may be reduced or completely blocked.

The search for what activates enkephalin neurons has led researchers to the **periaqueductal gray (PAG)** area of the midbrain. When this area is stimulated, pain is reduced almost immediately, with the *analgesia* (pain relief) continuing even after stimulation is discontinued (Goffaux, Redmond, Rainville, & Marchand, 2007). The PAG is also believed to be the primary site at which drugs such as morphine exert their analgesic effects. Sensory neurons in the PAG project into the medulla, a lower brain structure also involved in the perception of pain (Fairhurst, Wiech, Dunckley, & Tracey, 2007).

Recent functional magnetic resonance imaging (fMRI) studies have implicated another brain region, the dorsal **anterior cingulate cortex (ACC)**, as being specifically involved in the cognitive modulation of pain (Chapin and others, 2013). The ACC is known to be involved in other areas of self-regulation as well (Anderson, 2013). Interestingly, chronic pain patients are often deficient in self-regulatory skills, such as self-control (Flor, 2014; Solberg Nes, Roach, & Segerstrom, 2009).

substance P A neurotransmitter secreted by pain fibers in the spinal cord that stimulates the transmission cells to send pain signals to the brain.

enkephalins Endogenous (naturally occurring) opioids found in nerve endings of cells in the brain and spinal cord that bind to opioid receptors.

periaqueductal gray (PAG) A region of the midbrain that plays an important role in the perception of pain; electrical stimulation in this region activates a descending neural pathway that produces analgesia by "closing the pain gate."

anterior cingulate cortex (ACC) The front part of the cingulate cortex, which resembles a collar in surrounding the corpus callosum and plays a role in pain processing and many self-regulating functions.

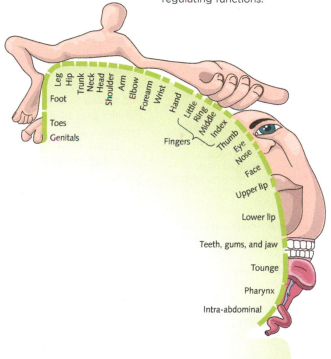

FIGURE 14.3 Mapping the Somatosensory Cortex The brain devotes more cortical tissue to sensitive areas and to areas requiring precise control. For instance, the fingers have a greater representation in the cortex than does the upper arm.

Midbrain

Periaqueductal gray ——
(PAG)

Inhibitory interneuron,
which releases enkephalin

Slow nerve
fibers

Ascending pain
signal from spinal
cord

Spinal cord

**FIGURE 14.4 The Pain-
Inhibiting System** Neural
activity resulting from
stimulation of the midbrain's
periaqueductal gray (PAG) area
activates inhibitory neurons in
the spinal cord. These in turn act
directly on incoming slow nerve
fibers to block pain signals
from being relayed to the brain.
The slow nerve fibers contain
substance P and glutamate.
When the nerve fibers' release
of substance P is inhibited,
as it is here, the ascending
pain signal is aborted (that is,
prevented from traveling to the
brain).

endogenous opiate peptides
Opiatelike substances naturally
produced by the body.

stress-induced analgesia (SIA)
A stress-related increase in
tolerance to pain, presumably
mediated by the body's
endorphin system.

Thus, it appears that the brain is capable of "turning off" pain through a *descending neural pathway*—the ACC to the PAG down to neurons in the medulla and then to the substantia gelatinosa of the spinal cord. This descending pain control pathway uses the neurotransmitter *serotonin* to activate enkephalin-containing spinal neurons, which, in turn, inhibit pain information coming from substance P fibers (Figure 14.4).

But what turns on the pain-inhibiting cells in the PAG? While still a graduate student, Candace Pert, a pioneer in the field of psychoneuroimmunology, discovered that neural chemicals called **endogenous opiate peptides** function as information messengers that affect the mind, emotions, immune system, and other body systems simultaneously. One of the peptides that she identified was *endorphin*, a natural opioid powerful enough to produce pain relief comparable to that of morphine and other opiates (Julien, Advokat, & Comaty, 2011). It turns out that the PAG has numerous opiate/endorphin receptors.

Research is ongoing, but a variety of events have been demonstrated to increase the level of endorphins. One is stress. **Stress-induced analgesia (SIA)** refers to the pain relief that results from the body's production of endorphins in response to stress. In one study, 14 healthy participants became less sensitive to electrical pain simulation while completing a stressful color word interference test (Stroop task), as indicated by reductions in their heart rate and blood pressure (Fechir and others, 2012). However, participants injected with an endorphin-blocking drug called naloxone before the noise did not show the SIA, indicating clearly that the pain-relieving effect depends on endorphins.

In addition to endorphins, proteins produced by the immune system called *proinflammatory cytokines* are involved in the experience of pain (Watkins and others, 2007). Recall from Chapter 3 that cytokines trigger a range of sickness responses, including fatigue and increased sensitivity to pain. Cytokines may also be involved in the development of chronic pain by increasing the sensitivity of structures in the spinal cord that affect the message that ascending pain pathways transmit to the brain.

Similar neurochemical effects may account for the *placebo effect* (see Chapter 9) in pain relief. Many research studies have demonstrated that one quarter to one third of people suffering pain receive significant relief simply by taking a placebo. A classic field study of dental pain (Levine, Gordon, & Fields, 1978) was the first to suggest that endorphins might mediate SIA and thus produce the placebo effect. Three hours after having a major tooth pulled (ouch!), one half of a group of dental patients were given a placebo, which they referred to as a "painkiller." The remaining subjects received an injection of naloxone. One hour later, subjects who had received the placebo were injected with naloxone, and those who had received naloxone were injected with the placebo. After each injection, the participants were asked to indicate on a standard pain-rating scale the degree of pain that they were experiencing.

Under the "influence" of the placebo painkiller, patients reported some relief from their pain, which provides additional support for the validity of the placebo effect. Under the influence of naloxone, patients reported feeling increased pain compared to that reported in the placebo condition, indicating that the placebo effect is at least partly the result of the body mustering its own mechanisms of pain relief. Injections of a drug that blocks cholecystokinin, a hormone that inhibits the action of endorphins, enhance the placebo effect in pain relief (Sullivan, Paice, & Benedetti, 2004). Other studies using fMRI have found that when patients expect to feel reduced pain after taking a placebo, their brains also display decreased activity in pain-processing regions (Wager and others, 2004). As we'll see later in the chapter, some other nonmedical techniques for producing analgesia may also work because they trigger the release of endorphins.

Genes and Pain

Chronic pain conditions, as well as sensitivity to pain, have been shown to have a considerable genetic component (Vehof, Zavos, Lachance, Hammond, & Williams, 2014). Several rare but serious pain disorders are caused by mutations in a gene called SCN9A, which encodes instructions for sodium channels that help nerve cells that relay painful sensations in the body's tissues to the central nervous system. In two of the disorders, people have faulty alleles of the gene and suffer intense pain because their sodium channels either open too easily or can't close (Markovic, Jankovic, & Vesilinovic, 2015). In another disorder, which leaves people completely unable to feel pain, SCN9A produces a protein that cannot function (Thompson, Knapp, Feeg, Madden, & Shenkman, 2010).

Studies of twins have reported heritability of about 50% for different pain traits, including variation in how people respond to painful stimuli such as skin heating (Norbury, MacGregor, Urwin, Spector, & McMahon, 2007). These studies suggest that genes may exert their influence in at least two ways: by mediating anxiety and depression—both of which have been linked to individual variation in the prevalence and experience of pain—and by affecting individual sensitivity to painful stimuli (Robinson and others, 2013). One study of patients suffering from *fibromyalgia* (FM), a chronic form of generalized musculoskeletal pain, found that those with one variation of the COMT gene displayed the most severe psychological and functional impact scores of FM pain (Desmeules and others, 2012). COMT, or catechol-o-methyl-transferase, is one of several enzymes involved in the metabolism of catecholamine neurotransmitters (dopamine, epinephrine, and norepinephrine). The results of other studies suggest that COMT genetic variations influence the severity of pain reports, as well as the length of physical and psychological recovery from traumatic events such as car accidents that cause the musculoskeletal pain associated with whiplash (McLean and others, 2011).

Gate Control Theory

In the past, several theories were proposed to explain pain perception. Most, however, fell short in accounting for all aspects of pain—biological, psychological, and social. In 1965, Ronald Melzack and Peter Wall outlined a **gate control theory (GCT)** that overcame some of the shortcomings of earlier theories. Although the theory has received its share of criticism, it was the impetus for the biopsychosocial model of pain, which is the dominant theory of pain today (Gatchel, Peng, Peters, Fuchs, & Turk, 2007).

The GCT first introduced the idea that the pain experience is not the result of a straight-through sensory channel that begins with the stimulation of a skin receptor and ends with the brain's perception of pain. Rather, as we have seen, incoming sensations that *potentially* signal pain are modulated in the spinal cord as they are conducted to the

gate control theory (GCT) The idea that there is a neural "gate" in the spinal cord that regulates the experience of pain.

FIGURE 14.5 The Gate Control Theory of Pain In Melzack and Wall's gate control theory, excitatory signals (pluses) tend to open the gate; inhibitory signals (minuses) tend to close the gate. The drawing on the left illustrates the conditions that might exist when the pain gate remains open and strong pain is felt. The drawing to the right illustrates the conditions that might exist when the pain gate is closed as a result of strong inhibitory stimulation from the brain and peripheral nerve fibers. In both situations, messages from fast pain fibers tend to close the gate, and messages from slow pain fibers tend to open it.

Information from: Melzack, R., & Wall, P. D. (1988). *The challenge of pain.* New York: Basic Books.

brain. They are also subject to modification under the influence of descending pathways from the brain.

The theory proposed the existence of neural structures in the spinal cord and brainstem that function like a gate (see Figure 14.5), swinging open to increase the flow of transmission from nerve fibers or swinging shut to decrease the flow (Melzack & Wall, 1965). With the gate open, signals arriving in the spinal cord stimulate sensory neurons called *transmission cells,* which, in turn, relay the signals upward to reach the brain and trigger pain. With the gate closed, signals are blocked from reaching the brain, and no pain is felt.

Melzack and Wall (1988) suggested that the mechanism for opening and closing the gate is found in the substantia gelatinosa (the "gatekeeper") of the spinal cord, where both small and large pain fibers have synapses (refer back to Figure 14.2). Activity in the fast pain fiber system tends to close the gate, whereas activity in the slow pain fiber system tends to force the gate open.

To account for the influence of thoughts and feelings on the perception of pain, Melzack and Wall also described a *central control mechanism* by which signals from the brain can shut the gate. Through this mechanism, anxiety or fear may amplify the experience of pain, whereas the distraction of other activities, such as athletic competition, can dampen the experience of pain.

Melzack (2005) later proposed that a widely distributed network of neurons, which ultimately determine a person's perceptual experience, further processes messages reaching the brain. This network of cells, called the **neuromatrix**, also seems to operate even in the absence of sensory input, placing still greater emphasis on the role of the brain in our experience of pain (as in the phantom limb sensation described in the *Diversity and Healthy Living* box), as well as in reducing pain. One example is **neuropathic pain** (nerve pain), a type of chronic pain that occurs when somatosensory nerve fibers (see Chapter 3) begin to send incorrect signals to the pain centers of the brain. Neuropathic pain is experienced by 30% of cancer patients, and may be caused by the treatment itself (Davis, 2018).

neuromatrix The neural network that integrates sensory information with emotional and cognitive states to determine a person's experience of pain.

neuropathic pain Pain caused by damaged nerve fibers that send incorrect signals to the brain.

Diversity and Healthy Living

Phantom Limb Pain

Sometimes people experience pain that has no apparent physical cause. One example is **phantom limb pain**, which is the experience of pain in an amputated body part. Most amputees experience some sort of phantom sensations, but between 65% and 85% actually report severe phantom pain (Williams, 1996). The pain may be occasional or continuous, and it is usually described as "cramping," "shooting," "burning," or "crushing."

Phantom pain develops most often in patients who experienced pain in the limb prior to amputation. In addition, phantom pain often resembles the type of pain that was present before the amputation. Ronald Melzack (1993) describes a patient who continued to report a painful sensation from a splinter in his hand long after he had lost the hand in an industrial accident. Phantom limb sensations are incredibly "real" in their sensory qualities and their precise location in space—so real that an amputee may try to step off the bed onto a phantom foot. Even minor sensations, such as the presence of a wedding ring on a phantom finger, are felt. Parkinson's patients may even continue to perceive "tremors" like those that occurred prior to an amputation.

The Search for a Cause While the underlying cause of phantom limb pain remains a mystery, recent studies have shed light on a possible mechanism—evidence that neurons in the brain "rewire" themselves to seek input from other sources after a limb is amputated. A team of researchers led by Michael Merzenich surgically amputated the middle fingers from a group of adult owl monkeys. After the monkeys recovered, the researchers electrically stimulated the remaining fingers on each monkey's paw while recording electrical activity from the somatosensory area of the monkeys' brains. Remarkably, Merzenich found that cortical neurons that originally fired in response to stimulation of the amputated fingers responded every time he touched the remaining fingers of the monkeys' paws. The neurons had not responded to stimulation of these fingers before the amputation (cited in Ranadive, 1997).

Vilayanur Ramachandran conducted experiments on people who had lost a finger or a hand (Ramachandran & Rogers-Ramachandran, 2000). Blindfolding his patients, Ramachandran applied pressure to different parts of their bodies and discovered that several subjects reported

TANG CHHIN SOTHY/GETTY IMAGES

An amputee uses a mirror during a therapy session to relieve pain by tricking the brain into "moving" the missing limb, allowing the pain to subside.

phantom hand sensations as areas of their faces were touched. Ramachandran suggested that his findings made sense because the cortical areas that once served the missing finger or hand are adjacent to those that serve the face. Perhaps neurons in these adjacent areas invade those areas that are left fallow because sensations are no longer received from the missing limb.

But what actually accounts for phantom limb pain? One hypothesis is that the brain forms a neural representation of a limb, and that presentation becomes stronger after the limb is lost. One study used fMRI to measure and compare changes in brain activity in three groups of people: people with one hand amputated, people born without one hand, and people with an intact pair of hands. When amputees who were experiencing phantom limb pain "moved" their missing hand, their brains displayed the same activity as the brains of people with two intact hands (Makin and others, 2013).

Treatment Phantom limb pain is a condition that often is extremely resistant to conventional pain therapies. Among the treatments that have been tried, with varying degrees of success, are the fitting of prosthetic limbs, ultrasound, transcutaneous electrical nerve stimulation (TENS) (see p. 460 of this chapter), anti-inflammatory and anticonvulsant drugs, and nerve blocks such as injections of local anesthetics into trigger points (Williams, 1996).

Researchers have also found that blocking glutamate receptors may prevent abandoned cortical neurons, which are no longer communicating with a missing limb, from forming new synapses with neurons linked to other parts of the body (Subedi & Grossberg, 2011). When the blockage to the spinal cord subsides, the original cortical connections and functions remain intact. Researchers are also testing whether blocking glutamate receptors will prevent neural reorganization in those with amputated limbs, thereby reducing phantom limb pain.

In the meantime, Ramachandran has devised a simpler therapy: a mirror box that allows a person to "see" the phantom limb. For example, when James Peacock, a security guard whose right arm was amputated, slips his intact left arm into the box, mirrors make it appear as if his missing right arm is there as well. The box has provided the only relief Peacock knows from wrenching spasms in his phantom hand. "When I move my left hand," he says, "I can feel it moving my phantom hand" (quoted in Brownlee, 1995, p. 76).

phantom limb pain Pain following amputation of a limb; false pain sensations that appear to originate in the missing limb.

FIGURE 14.6 Neuromatrix According to neuromatrix theory, the experience of pain occurs in the brain as an integrated response, or *neurosignature,* to sensory input (such as tissue damage), as well as a person's memories, fears, and other subjective experiences.

The concept of the neuromatrix underscores two important points. First, the experience of pain occurs in the brain and nowhere else (Institute for Chronic Pain [ICP], 2017). Second, the pain gate responds not only to physical factors such as injury, but also to emotional factors—including anxiety, depression, and stress—as well as cognitive factors such as attention or boredom (Figure 14.6).

FACTORS THAT INFLUENCE THE EXPERIENCE OF PAIN

The experience of pain is a complex, multidimensional phenomenon involving not only physical events but also psychological factors and social learning (Reimann and others, 2010). All pain patients are unique individuals who are acting (and reacting) members of social groups. In this section, we take a look at how such factors influence the experience of pain.

Age

The National Health and Aging Trends Study (NHATS) investigated pain and other aspects of the health of older adults through in-person interviews of over 7,000 Medicare beneficiaries aged 65 years and older (Patel, Guralnik, Dansie, & Turk, 2013). The overall prevalence of bothersome pain among participants was 52.9%, with the majority of these (74.9%) reporting pain in multiple locations, such as in the back, knees, and hips. Pain reports did not vary after the researchers accounted for differences in cognitive performance, dementia, proxy responses, and residential-care living status. Pain prevalence was higher in women and in people with obesity, musculoskeletal conditions, and depressive symptoms. The NHATS also found that pain was strongly associated with decreased physical capacity. Older adults with pain, particularly those with pain in multiple locations, had weaker muscle strength, slower walking speed, and poorer overall function than those without pain.

But before we conclude that aging is inevitably accompanied by a world of pain, we would do well to ask ourselves whether other factors—such as overall health, differences in socialization, and coping resources—might account for age-related differences in pain experiences. As we have seen, it is very easy for researchers examining differences between groups of people (such as age cohorts) to overlook such factors. For example, older adults who feel a greater sense of overall well-being complain less about pain than others the same age. Pain perceptions are also influenced by social comparisons with people in other reference groups. For example, adults who reported that their parents had experienced frequent severe pain were themselves more likely to report substantial back, muscle, and joint pain. Older people are also generally more vigilant than young people in monitoring their health status, and they see themselves as more vulnerable. This may help explain why there is a progressive increase in reports of pain and a decrease in tolerance to experimentally induced pain as individuals grow older (Molton & Terrill, 2014).

Gender

Gender differences in health behavior are already apparent in adolescence, with boys being less likely than girls to seek medical care. As adults, women are more likely to report medical symptoms to a doctor, to experience more frequent episodes of pain, and to report lower pain thresholds and less tolerance to painful stimuli than are men (Bartley & Fillingim, 2013).

Women may also feel pain more intensely than men do. A massive Stanford University study of over 12,000 patients investigated gender differences in reported pain for more than 250 diseases and conditions. For almost every diagnosis, including diabetes, arthritis, respiratory infections, and fibromyalgia, women's pain scores averaged 20% higher than men's scores (Ruau, Liu, Clark, Angst, & Butte, 2012).

Gender differences extend to the types of pain most commonly reported by women and men. Women seem to suffer more than men from migraines and tension headaches, as well as from pelvic pain, facial pain, and lower back pain (Henderson, Gandevia, & Macefield, 2008).

Gender disparities are also apparent in how the medical community treats pain (Leresche, 2011). The Institute of Medicine's report, *Relieving Pain in America,* found not only that women report suffering from more pain than men, but also that women's reports of pain were more likely to be dismissed or treated less aggressively when diagnosed, and women's pain was more likely to be characterized as "emotional" and therefore not real (Institute of Medicine [IOM], 2011b).

A number of researchers believe that gender differences in treating pain reflect stereotyped views about women and men rather than specific symptoms (Edwards, 2013). This line of reasoning was explored in a study in which subjects immersed a hand and forearm in icy water for several minutes (Levine & DeSimone, 1991). The results showed that women reported more pain than men did. More interesting was the fact that men reported significantly lower pain ratings to a female experimenter than to a male experimenter. However, there was no difference in the female subjects' self-reports of pain to experimenters of either sex. These and other researchers have suggested that gender differences reflect traditional gender roles, with men responding to female experimenters with a more stoic, "macho" image (Fillingim, 2000). Consistent with this view, men who identify more strongly with traditional gender roles are less likely than others of either gender to admit feeling pain (Pool, Schwegler, Theodore, & Fuchs, 2007). Interestingly, a recent study involving the response of 172 women to a similar pain discomfort task found that lesbian and bisexual women reported lower pain intensity ratings and had higher pain threshold and tolerance levels than did heterosexual women (Vigil, Rowell, & Lutz, 2014).

Sociocultural Factors

Why would two patients undergoing the same surgical procedure report vastly different levels of postoperative pain? The answer is that pain is a variable personal experience not closely linked to tissue damage. In this section, we examine social and cultural factors that are the foundation of how pain is conceptualized and experienced.

Socioeconomic Status and Stress

As we have seen, people at lower levels of socioeconomic status (SES) have greater morbidity and mortality across many diseases when compared with those at higher SES levels (Bacon, Bouchard, Loucks, & Lavoie, 2009). They also experience more stressful life events (Hatch & Dohrenwend, 2007), live in environments that expose them to more chronic stressors (Gee & Payne-Sturges, 2004), and have fewer psychosocial resources for managing stressful experiences (Gallo & Matthews, 2003). Lower SES is also associated with more frequent reports of musculoskeletal pain, pain intensity, and physical disability (Jablonska, Soares, & Sundin, 2006).

The challenges associated with lower SES also make those who suffer chronic pain more vulnerable to the harmful effects of stress on health and physical functioning. A study of 250 women with osteoarthritis, fibromyalgia, or both found that participants with greater levels of economic hardship reported greater pain severity in response to daily financial worries than their counterparts with little or no economic hardship (Rios & Zautra, 2011). Interestingly, the effect of day-to-day financial worry was moderated by employment. Having a job, even a part-time position, was a psychological resource that protected against the adverse effects of day-to-day financial worries on pain.

Culture and Ethnicity

Cultural and ethnic groups differ greatly in their responses to pain, suggesting that different groups establish their own norms for both the degree to which suffering should be expressed openly and the form that pain behaviors should take (Pillay, van Zyl, & Blackbeard, 2014). The sociocultural context also influences how pain is conceptualized, which, in turn, affects the relationship between pain patients and their health care providers. With increased global migration and diversity within most countries, health care providers need to develop increased sensitivity to the influence of culture on pain perceptions and behaviors (Kposowa & Tsunokai, 2002).

The pain responses of patients and research participants are sometimes divided into two culturally related categories: *stoic* and *emotive*. Stoic people tend to "grin and bear" pain. They are less expressive than emotive people and more likely to turn inward and withdraw socially when feeling discomfort, perceiving pain as a private and personal experience. In contrast, emotive people and cultures are more likely to verbalize and in other ways openly express pain. They also prefer to have others around to respond to their discomfort, perhaps to validate it (Carteret, 2012).

Childbirth provides a vivid example of cultural variation in the experience of pain. In some stoic cultures, childbirth is treated as an almost run-of-the-mill activity that brings little pain and is treated with quiet acceptance. When questioned, women who have given birth in such cultures say that they felt pain but they felt that to express that fact openly was wrong (Callister, 2003). In contrast to this matter-of-fact approach, women in other, expressive cultures view childbirth as a more dangerous and painful process. In these cultures, women are more likely to openly express their pain during their labor and delivery (Wall, 2000).

Some clinicians and researchers have made the broad generalization that people who are more likely to be expressive in the face of pain often have Hispanic, Middle Eastern, and Mediterranean backgrounds, while those who are stoic often come from Asian and Northern European backgrounds (Carteret, 2012). It has been suggested that patients from "stoic cultures" may exemplify stoicism as a reflection of cultural values about proper self-conduct. In Asian cultures, for instance, behaving in a dignified manner is generally considered very important. People who openly complain, even when feeling great discomfort, may be perceived as having poor social skills (Callister, 2003). Researchers have also suggested that the underreporting of pain in other stoic groups, such as older Irish adults, might reflect cultural beliefs related to self-blame and guilt (Cornally & McCarthy, 2011).

As with age and gender differences, however, we should be very cautious in interpreting cultural variations in reported pain. For one thing, not all studies have found these group differences in pain expressiveness. Cross-cultural studies are typically correlational in design, making it difficult to rule out differences in socioeconomic pressure, social support, coping resources, education level, and other underlying factors.

A second reason for caution is that cross-cultural studies often lack ease of comparison. For example, while English has at least four basic words to describe

The Culture of Childbirth Pain
Childbirth is not feared as a painful event in all societies. Prepared childbirth that takes place in a calm and comfortable environment—such as in this home birth, in which loved ones surround the new mother—can greatly reduce both anxiety and the pain that it often causes.

AMELIE-BENOIST/BSIP/AGE Fotostock

pain—*ache, sore, hurt,* and *pain*—Japanese has three words for pain, and Thai has only two, making it difficult to equate subjective pain reports across groups.

A final reason for caution in generalizing about group differences is that although culture influences behavior, not everyone necessarily conforms to behavioral norms to the same degree. People's experience of pain reflects not only their culture, but also their unique personal history and perceptions (Jarrett, 2011).

Personality and Mood State

Researchers have used a variety of tests, especially the Minnesota Multiphasic Personality Inventory (MMPI), to determine whether there is such a thing as a *pain-prone personality*. The MMPI contains 10 clinical scales, and acute and chronic pain patients often show elevated scores on two of them: hysteria (the tendency to exaggerate symptoms and behave emotionally) and hypochondriasis (the tendency to be overly concerned about health and to overreport symptoms).

Research also demonstrates that mood disturbances are linked with the experience of pain (Beesdo and others, 2010). People who are anxious, worried, fearful, depressed, and negative in outlook report more pain (Leeuw and others, 2007). In fact, depression is more prevalent among lower back pain patients than among the general population (Williams, Jacka, Pasco, Dodd, & Berk, 2006) and among children coping with certain types of pain (J. L. Lee and others, 2013). However, these results could simply be reflecting the challenges of dealing with pain. Similarly, people who are experiencing pain are more likely to report anxiety and/or depression, with those reporting the highest levels of these emotions also reporting the highest levels of pain (Mok & Lee, 2008).

Because the research linking depression, anxiety, and pain is correlational in nature, it is impossible to conclude that there is a causal relationship between mood state and pain, or if there is, whether depression causes chronic pain or chronic pain causes depression. One study found that patients undergoing dialysis who initially reported symptoms of depression were more likely to develop severe pain during the 2-and-one-half year follow-up period (Yamamoto and others, 2010).

Social Learning

Social and cultural factors can influence people's experience of pain and actually lead to the *social construction* of an illness (Lucire, 2003). But how do these factors exert their influence? Many health psychologists believe that social learning and social comparison play a critical role in determining future processing of the pain experience, with the family and the surrounding culture acting as the earliest models for pain behavior. Observing family members and other people in the reference group helps a person determine what pain behaviors are appropriate in a given situation.

The social environment also shapes an individual's pain experience by way of operant conditioning. The expression of pain serves an adaptive function by capturing the attention of others and triggering caregiving and helping behaviors (Vervoort and others, 2011; Vervoort, Caes, Trost, Notebaert, & Goubert, 2012). Pioneering researcher Wilbert Fordyce's *operant conditioning model of pain* suggests that chronic pain sufferers receive social reinforcement for **pain behaviors** from the attention that they receive from

pain behaviors Actions that are a response to pain, such as taking drugs, grimacing, or taking time off from school or work.

Psychosocial Influences on Pain The experience of pain is shaped by the meanings that we attach to events. In some cultures and religions, tattooing and seemingly excruciating body piercing are perceived as benign and bring great honor. In many Western cultures today, tattooing, body piercing, and "branding" are not only acceptable behaviors but also are desirable in certain age and social groups.

Photodisc/Getty Images

family and friends (Butler, 2010). In some social and cultural groups, a person who grimaces or moans in response to pain is reinforced for that response by receiving attention from others. In other groups, open expressions of pain are either ignored or received with hostility and therefore not reinforced.

As with many behaviors, how we learn to respond to pain begins in childhood. Children whose parents disregard their pain behavior may grow up more stoic in their approach to pain than children whose parents pay undue attention to every minor ache and pain (Langer, Romano, Manci, & Levy, 2014).

TREATING PAIN

The treatment of pain is big business. The global market for pain management is predicted to reach $77 billion by 2023, driven mostly by the demand for drugs for pain treatment and the aging of the population (Business Wire, 2018). There are two broad categories of pain treatment: (1) medical interventions and (2) nonmedical interventions, which include cognitive-behavioral treatments such as hypnosis and biofeedback. Although health care professionals once scoffed at most nonmedical treatments, the proven effectiveness of using psychological techniques with pain patients—as well as evidence that some techniques, such as the placebo effect, work partly by mobilizing the body's physical system of analgesia—has increasingly led to the realization that there is no sharp dividing line between physical and nonphysical pain treatments.

In this section, we look first at the better-known pharmacological, surgical, and electrical stimulation treatments, then at the cognitive-behavioral treatments now widely used in pain control. Finally, we examine how pain treatments are evaluated.

Pharmacological Treatments

For most patients, analgesic drugs are a mainstay in pain control. Analgesics fall into two general classes. The first includes *opioid* (centrally acting) drugs such as morphine. The second category consists of *nonopioid* (peripherally acting) chemicals that produce their pain-relieving and anti-inflammatory effects at the actual site of injured tissue.

Opioid Analgesics

Formerly called *narcotics* (from the Greek word *narke,* which means "numbness"), opioids are *agonists* (excitatory chemicals) that act on specific receptors in the spinal cord and brain to reduce either the intensity of pain messages or the brain's response to pain messages.

The most powerful and most widely used opioid for treating severe pain is morphine. After binding to receptors in the PAG, the thalamus, and cells at the back of the spinal cord, morphine produces intense analgesia and indifference to pain, a state of relaxed euphoria, reduced apprehension, and a sense of tranquility.

Because of morphine's powerful effects, however, regular users predictably develop tolerance so quickly that doctor-prescribed doses of morphine sometimes have to be increased to retain their effectiveness—from clinical doses of 50 to 60 milligrams per day to doses as high as 500 milligrams per day, over as short a period as 10 days (Advokat, Comaty, & Julien, 2014). And there is another drawback to the powerful effects of morphine: Its effectiveness makes it highly addictive. Long-term use may eventually lead to opioid-induced hyperalgesia (mentioned earlier in the chapter), a condition in which the nervous system responds to painful stimuli with increasing sensitivity when opioids are withdrawn. For these reasons, the use of opioids to control pain is controversial and some patients who are experiencing pain are left undermedicated (Jamison & Mao, 2015).

One alternative to the use of prescription opioids stems from the finding that many chronic pain patients have lower-than-normal levels of endorphins in their spinal fluid. Clinicians have used synthetic endorphins to boost these stores. Patients have, for example, reported excellent, long-lasting pain relief after receiving injections of a synthetic form of endorphin called *beta-endorphin* (Paungmali and others, 2018).

Nonopioid Analgesics

The nonopioid analgesics include aspirin, acetaminophen, and ibuprofen. Also called *nonsteroidal anti-inflammatory drugs (NSAIDs),* these drugs produce several effects, including pain reduction without sedation, reduction of inflammation, and reduction of body temperature when fever is present.

NSAIDs relieve pain by blocking a chemical chain reaction that is triggered when tissue is injured. Consider sunburn pain. One of the chemicals produced at the site of the burn is called *arachidonic acid,* which the body converts into **prostaglandin**, the substance responsible for sunburn pain (or other localized pain) and inflammation. NSAIDs work their magic by blocking production of the enzyme needed to convert arachidonic acid into prostaglandin.

prostaglandin The chemical substance responsible for localized pain and inflammation; prostaglandin also causes free nerve endings to become more and more sensitized as time passes.

Surgery, Electrical Stimulation, and Physical Therapy

For centuries, healers have used surgery in their attempts to relieve severe pain. Their reasoning made sense: If pain is a simple *stimulus–response* connection between peripheral pain receptors and the brain, why not simply cut, or lesion, pain fibers so that the messages don't get through?

Sometimes surgery is helpful. For example, destroying thalamic cells of the slow pain system has been demonstrated to alleviate some deep, burning pain without altering the sense of touch or the more acute, stinging pain of the fast pain system. More often, however, surgery has unpredictable results, and its effects are short-lived, perhaps because of the nervous system's remarkable regenerative ability. As a result, some pain patients have endured numerous "hit-or-miss" surgeries that provide only short-term relief. And in some cases, patients actually experience *worse* pain due to the cumulative damage of repeated surgeries. For these reasons, surgery is rarely used to control pain today and only as a last-ditch effort.

More effective than surgery is **counterirritation**, which involves stimulating one area of the body to reduce pain in another. For example, spinal stimulation has proven effective in controlling the lower back pain of many patients (De Andres & Van Buyten, 2006). In **transcutaneous electrical nerve stimulation (TENS)**, brief pulses of electricity are applied to nerve endings under the skin near the painful area or where nerve fibers enter the back of the spinal cord, and patients can administer treatment themselves. TENS can produce a feeling of numbness that overcomes the sensation of pain, and it has yielded excellent

counterirritation Analgesia in which one pain (for example, a pulled muscle) is relieved by creating another counteracting sensation (such as rubbing near the site of the injury).

transcutaneous electrical nerve stimulation (TENS) A counterirritation form of analgesia involving electrically stimulating spinal nerves near a painful area.

local pain relief for some chronic pain patients. Consistent with gate control theory, counterirritation seems to activates A-beta fibers, which decode the stimulus as irritating but not urgent, thus closing the pain gate and preventing the pain message from reaching the brain (Tashani & Johnson, 2009).

For more widespread and severe pain (such as that associated with some advanced cancers), another electrical form of analgesia, called *stimulation-produced analgesia (SPA),* involves delivering mild electrical pulses through electrodes that are surgically implanted in the brain and appears to work by stimulating endorphin neurons. Accordingly, SPA electrodes are implanted in brain sites known to be rich in opioid receptors. Once again, patients self-administer treatment, determining when and how much stimulation is needed. Although SPA is expensive and risky, many patients report that their pain seems to melt away when they use it (Kotze & Simpson, 2008).

People who are in pain, as well as those who are suffering disability as a result of disease, injury, or surgery, also may be referred to a physical therapist for assistance. Physical therapists are rehabilitation professionals who promote optimal health and functional independence through their efforts to identify, correct, or prevent movement dysfunction, physical disability, and pain. Physical therapy often begins in the hospital and continues as long as needed.

Biofeedback

First described by Neal Miller in the late 1960s, **biofeedback** is a technique for converting certain supposedly involuntary physiological responses—such as brain waves (*neurofeedback*), skin temperature, muscle activity, heart rate, and blood pressure—into electrical signals and providing visual or auditory feedback about them (Miller, 1969). It is based on the principle that we learn to perform a specific response when we receive information (feedback) about the consequences of that response and then make appropriate adjustments.

Using an electronic monitoring device that detects and amplifies internal responses, biofeedback training begins by helping the person gain awareness of a maladaptive response, such as tense forehead muscles. Next, the person focuses attention on a tone, a light, or some other signal that identifies desirable changes in the internal response. By attempting to control this biofeedback signal, the patient learns to control his or her physiological state. Finally, the individual learns to transfer control from the laboratory setting to everyday life.

The most common biofeedback technique in clinical use today is *electromyography (EMG) feedback.* EMG biofeedback detects skeletal muscle activity by measuring muscle tension via the electrical discharge of muscle fibers. Electrodes are attached to the skin over the muscles to be monitored. The biofeedback machine responds with an auditory signal that reflects the electrical activity (tension) of the muscle being measured. EMG biofeedback to decrease muscle tension has been used to treat facial tics, spasmodic movements, and other muscular disorders. In addition, it has been used to treat headaches and lower back pain.

Hilary Morgan/Alamy Stock Photo

TENS Back pain can be relieved with transcutaneous electrical nerve stimulation (TENS). Portable TENS machines help relieve the pain of thousands of sufferers. After the person logistically places the pads shown here on either side of the painful area, he or she can hook the small electrical conduit to a belt and continue with daily activities while pulses are delivered to the body.

biofeedback A system that provides audible or visible feedback information regarding involuntary physiological states.

leezsnow/iStock/Getty Images

Biofeedback for the brain In a neurofeedback session, a client monitors, and attempts to gain control over, his ongoing brainwave (EEG) activity. This type of training may help people who are living with a neurological problem such as stroke, anxiety, pain, or PTSD.

Another common technique, *thermal biofeedback,* is based on the principle that skin temperature tends to vary in relation to a person's perceived level of stress. The rationale for this technique is that high stress, which often causes blood vessels in the skin to constrict, may be linked to cooler surface skin temperatures. Accordingly, by placing a temperature-sensitive instrument on the skin's surface (most often the fingertips), people sometimes are able to raise their skin temperature by monitoring an auditory or visual feedback signal. Thermal biofeedback is often used to help people cope with stress and pain. It is also frequently used with migraine and tension headache patients (National Center for Complementary and Integrative Health [NCCIH], 2016b).

Although biofeedback is widely used within the field of pain medicine, particularly in conjunction with relaxation training, empirical support for its effectiveness beyond the general effects of relaxation strategies has not been widely demonstrated except in the treatment of tension headaches, migraine headaches, and low back pain (Benzon, Raja, Liu, Fishman, & Cohen, 2018). Even so, for patients who have difficulty recognizing physical changes that may accompany pain or stress, such as grimacing or tensing other muscles, biofeedback may be useful in helping them to recognize these changes, and this in turn may enhance the effect of other pain management interventions.

Cognitive-Behavioral Therapy

Because no single pain control technique has proved to be the most effective in relieving chronic pain, many health care providers today use an eclectic, or "cafeteria," approach to helping their patients manage pain. This means that treatment is tailored to each individual case and that patients are taught several pain-management strategies from which they may choose as needed.

cognitive-behavioral therapy (CBT) A multidisciplinary pain-management program that combines cognitive, physical, and emotional interventions.

One such program is **cognitive-behavioral therapy (CBT)**, an umbrella term for a variety of multidisciplinary interventions aimed, in this context, at changing people's experience of pain by changing their thought processes and behaviors and teaching them to employ such strategies as distraction, imagery, meditation, exercising, and deep breathing. CBT has become the dominant model for treating chronic pain (Ehde, Dillworth, & Turner, 2014). Although specific components of CBT vary, most programs include (1) education and goal-setting that focus on the factors influencing pain and that clarify the client's expectations for treatment, (2) cognitive interventions to enhance patients' self-efficacy and sense of control over pain, (3) teaching new skills for responding to pain triggers, and (4) promoting increased exercise and activity levels.

Education and Goal-Setting

CBT counselors often begin by briefly explaining the differences between acute pain and chronic pain; the mechanisms of gate control theory; and the contributions of depression, anxiety, lack of activity, and other controllable factors to pain. Patients are encouraged to generate examples from their own pain experiences, perhaps by keeping a daily diary that records pain frequency, duration, and intensity; medication use; and mood and activity levels. The diary almost always gives clients new insights into some of the factors that affect their pain experience, and these insights are invaluable in promoting an increased sense of control over pain.

This phase is most useful for establishing specific goals for the intervention. Goals need to be specific and measurable in order to prevent miscommunication and the development of unrealistic expectations; they also should be phrased in a way that downplays the common tendency to dwell on pain. For example, rather than saying, "I would like to be able to resume my normal activities without feeling pain," a better goal is "I would like to take a brisk, 30-minute walk four times a week."

Cognitive Interventions

Our emotions, attitudes, and beliefs are powerful influences on our health. Faulty reasoning often contributes to poor health outcomes and interferes with treatment. Negative emotions such as anxiety, anger, and depression intensify pain, which in turn intensifies negative emotions (Gilliam and others, 2010). Negative emotions also intensify pain behaviors and complicate treatment (Burns and others, 2008). For this reason, depression and thought processes often need to be targeted along with pain management (Teh, Zasylavsky, Reynolds, & Cleary, 2010). *Cognitive restructuring* challenges maladaptive thought processes and helps pain sufferers to redefine pain as an experience that is more manageable than they once believed. It also helps correct irrational beliefs.

Health psychologists recognize a general pattern of cognitive errors in the thinking of chronic pain patients, including the following:

- *Catastrophizing.* Many pain sufferers overestimate the distress and discomfort caused by an unfortunate experience, such as being injured. They also tend to focus excessively on the negative aspects of pain and use more pain medication than those who think less catastrophically (Wideman & Sullivan, 2011).

- *Overgeneralizing.* Some pain victims believe that their pain will never end and that it will ruin their lives completely, often leading to depression and poorer health outcomes.

- *Victimization.* Some chronic pain patients feel that they have experienced an injustice that consumes them, with many unable to get beyond the "Why me?" stage.

- *Self-blame.* In contrast, some chronic pain patients come to feel worthless and blame themselves for not being able to carry on with their responsibilities.

- *Dwelling on the pain.* Some pain sufferers can't stop thinking about their pain problem, often replaying painful episodes and negative thoughts in their minds.

A growing body of evidence demonstrates that cognitive errors and other individual differences in how people cope with pain are important contributors to variability in the pain experience, in part because of neurobiological effects (Edwards, Campbell, Jamison, & Wiech, 2009). For instance, several fMRI studies using standardized pain stimuli have reported that higher levels of catastrophizing are associated with enhanced neural activity in the anterior cingulate cortex and amygdala (Strigo, Simmons, Matthews, Craig, & Paulhus, 2008); these brain regions are intimately involved in processing the pain experience. Moreover, among healthy subjects exposed to mildly painful electrical stimulation, there was a positive relationship between the degree of catastrophizing about pain and pain-related responses in cortical pain-processing regions of the brain (Seminowicz & Davis, 2006).

Catastrophic thinking also may intensify pain because of its effects on blood pressure reactivity and muscle tension (Shelby and others, 2009; Wolff and others, 2008). Correlational research also links catastrophizing to stronger inflammatory responses to stress and pain (Edwards, Bingham, Bathon, & Haythornthwaite, 2006). This association appears to be specific to catastrophizing. One study of rheumatoid arthritis patients suggested that helplessness (a key component of catastrophizing) was associated with elevated levels of *C-reactive protein (CRP),* a protein produced during the inflammatory response, while anxiety and depression were unrelated to CRP levels (Edwards and others, 2008). Catastrophizing during an acute pain experience also has been associated with elevations in *interleukin-6,* a proinflammatory cytokine that regulates immune functions and inflammation (Edwards and others, 2009a). Catastrophizing and other cognitive errors probably exert their influence through descending, or "top-down," cortical circuits, rather than by directly affecting peripheral pain pathways (Wiech, Ploner, & Tracey, 2008b). Researchers speculate that catastrophizing and other cognitive errors may interfere with activation of opioid-mediated descending pain modulatory systems. Some experts have called for the clinical appraisal of catastrophizing as an indicator of problematic recovery from surgery and other medical treatments, and for the development of routine clinical interventions that target this type of thinking (Wideman & Sullivan, 2011).

In contrast with catastrophizing, victimization, and other cognitive errors, pain-coping strategies—such as distraction, efforts to increase the perception of self-control over pain, and reappraising or reinterpreting pain sensations—provide potential benefits in terms of reduced pain and improved function (Van Damme, Crombez, & Eccleston, 2008).

Cognitive Distraction

Does *cognitive distraction* have any practical usefulness in pain control? Many CBT therapists think so. Music is frequently used to help burn victims distract their attention from painful treatments, such as having wound dressings changed. In addition, verbal suggestions that distract people with pleasant images ("Think of a warm, comfortable environment") or drawing attention away from painful stimulation ("Count backward by 3s") are especially effective ways to activate pain-inhibiting processes and increase pain tolerance (Edwards and others, 2009a).

One study using spinal fMRI demonstrated that the pain-relieving effects of cognitive distraction are not merely a psychological phenomenon, but that they also involve the actual inhibition of the central nervous system's response to incoming pain signals. Participants in the study were asked to complete either an easy or a difficult memory task while a painful level of heat was applied to their arms. Not only did participants who were more distracted by the harder of the two memory tasks perceive less pain, but also their experience was reflected in lower levels of neural activity in their spinal cords (Sprenger and others, 2012).

The pain-relieving effects of cognitive distraction appear to be mediated by the body's production of endogenous opioids. When the study was repeated, this time giving participants an injection of the opioid antagonist naloxone or a saline solution, the amount of pain relief experienced by participants during the distracting memory task dropped by 40% (Sprenger and others, 2012).

Diverting attention away from a painful stimulus can diminish self-reported pain intensity by 30% to 40%, and doing so also seems to reduce activity in pain-processing regions of the cortex (the anterior cingulate cortex) by well over 50% (Edwards and others, 2009a)—an amount comparable to the effects of potent analgesic drugs. Distraction from pain also may engage some of the descending pain-inhibitory pathways that catastrophizing seems to disrupt (Wiech and others, 2008b). Some researchers have reported that combining analgesic medication with a virtual-reality video game distractor task can have analgesic effects, illustrating the potential benefits of multimodal interventions in clinical settings (H. G. Hoffman and others, 2007).

Sensory Focus and ACT

Another short-term cognitive technique for coping with acute pain, *sensory focus*, involves attending directly to the sensations of a painful stimulus without necessarily trying to change those reactions. Although it may seem counterintuitive that directing attention *toward* a painful stimulus would increase the ability to cope with it, that is what sometimes seems to occur. For people who score high on measures of health anxiety, sensory focus seems to be more effective than cognitive distraction in coping with acute pain.

In one study, chronic pain patients were instructed to think about their children, relaxing on the beach, the upcoming weekend, or another source of cognitive distraction during their often-painful physical therapy sessions. Other patients were encouraged to focus directly on the concrete sensations they were experiencing as they completed each physical therapy exercise. The results showed that cognitive distraction was the more effective strategy for participants who scored low in measures of overall health anxiety. For those characterized by high health anxiety, however, sensory focus was associated with greater reduction in pain (Hadjistavropoulos, Hadjistavropoulos, & Quine, 2000). Sensory focus has also proven effective in helping patients manage the pain associated with burns, dental procedures, labor and childbirth, and other conditions (Ebert & Kerns, 2010).

Other research studies have shown that being accepting of pain, rather than attempting to suppress it, seems to mitigate its intensity (Masedo & Rosa, 2007). Attempting to suppress pain seems to actually increase pain levels: Ironically, such attempts may actually prolong pain-related thoughts and increase physiological arousal (Burns, 2006). *Acceptance and commitment therapy (ACT)* is a therapeutic tool that has been applied to many conditions, including chronic pain. As with sensory focus, ACT emphasizes observing thoughts and feelings as they are, without trying to change them, and behaving in ways consistent with valued goals and life directions. The basic premise of ACT as applied to chronic pain is that while pain hurts, it is the struggle with pain that causes suffering. Two aspects of pain acceptance appear to be important: (1) being willing to experience pain and (2) continuing to engage in valued life activities even in the face of pain.

A growing body of evidence demonstrates that acceptance of pain is often associated with lower self-rated pain intensity, less self-rated depression and pain-related anxiety, greater physical and social ability, less pain avoidance, and better work status (McCracken & Vowles, 2014). Laboratory studies with clinical and nonclinical populations have also shown that techniques used in ACT (such as observing and accepting thoughts and feelings as they are) produce greater tolerance of acute pain and discomfort than more traditional techniques of pain control, such as distraction and cognitive restructuring (Simpson, Mars, & Esteves, 2017).

Guided Imagery

Guided imagery (GI) is a pain control technique that is designed to promote changes in perception by combining a mental process (as in *imagining*) and a procedure (as in *guided*). GI is actually a form of self-hypnosis, because it involves focused concentration and attention. It is incorporated into relaxation techniques that involve suggestions (for example, "Your hands are heavy") and into *mental rehearsal*, which helps patients prepare for an uncomfortable medical treatment and relieves the anxiety, pain, and side effects that are exacerbated by heightened emotional reactions.

GI techniques are based on the concept that our attention and awareness have a limited capacity and that different stimuli compete for our attention. The purpose of the intervention is to teach patients to switch their attention from pain to other stimuli. For example, a pain patient may be taught to construct a vivid, multisensory image, such as strolling through a meadow on a beautiful day, focusing intently on the surrounding sights, sounds, textures, and smells. The elaborated features of the image presumably compete with the painful stimulus and lower its impact.

How effective is GI in controlling pain? One review of randomized clinical trials (RCTs) reported that eight of nine studies provided evidence of the effectiveness of GI as a stand-alone therapy in reducing musculoskeletal pain (lower back pain, tendonitis, and muscle pain) (Posadzki & Ernst, 2012). A separate review of RCTs testing the effectiveness of GI in reducing nonmusculoskeletal pain (that is, pain from the skin, cardiovascular system, and other structures outside the musculoskeletal system) similarly reported that 11 of 15 studies provided evidence of GI's effectiveness (Posadzki, Lewandowski, Terry, Ernst, & Stearns, 2011). Despite these encouraging results, the researchers concluded that the methodological quality of many of the RCTs was poor. Thus far, it seems that GI works best with low to medium levels of pain intensity. Patients who have been trained in the use of positive imagery may experience benefits such as reduced anxiety and pain during medical procedures, reduced use of pain medication, fewer side effects, and increased pain tolerance (Burhenn, Olausson, Vilegas, & Kravits, 2014).

Cognitive Reappraisal

As noted earlier, chronic pain patients are often deficient in self-regulatory skills such as self-control and the ability to reappraise situations, which may exacerbate their feelings of pain (Solberg Nes, Roach, & Segerstrom, 2009). A key component of CBT is helping individuals *reinterpret* pain-related sensations (for example, labeling a noxious stimulus as "pressure" rather than pain), *restructure* maladaptive thought patterns ("this pain will never get better"), and make *positive self-statements* ("I can handle this"). For example, writing interventions that help pain patients express their emotions and find meaning in their experience have been effective in reducing both pain and distress (Graham, Lobel, Glass, & Lokshina, 2008).

A growing body of evidence demonstrates that these pain-coping strategies, collectively referred to as **cognitive reappraisal**, are associated with reduced activation of key regions of the pain-processing areas of the brain. For example, naloxone, a drug that

cognitive reappraisal A key component of CBT that focuses on helping individuals *reinterpret* pain-related sensations, *restructure* maladaptive thought patterns, and make *positive self-statements.*

blocks the binding of endorphins and other opiates to neural receptor sites, disrupts the beneficial effects of cognitive reappraisal; this finding strongly suggests that these internal biochemical pathways are involved in these beneficial effects (Edwards and others, 2009a). These findings dovetail with those on the neurobiology of distraction, suggesting that CBT interventions that enhance these cognitive processes function by activating descending pain-inhibiting systems that originate in the prefrontal cortex (Sprenger and others, 2012).

Meditation

In hundreds of studies, researchers have studied the use of meditation as a treatment for pain, finding that meditation often helps relieve pain, sometimes significantly, though it does not cure it (Steiner, 2014). A University of North Carolina study performed MRI scans on the brains of 15 healthy participants while inducing pain. Over the next three days, the participants were taught *mindfulness meditation* (learning to focus on a single sense and breathing, while accepting transient thoughts). On the fourth day, the researchers scanned the participants' brains again, once while the participants were not meditating and another time while they were meditating, with pain induced by an electrical stimulus to the skin during both sessions. The results showed a 40% reduction in pain intensity ratings during meditation when compared with nonmeditation (Zeidan, Gordon, Merchant, & Goolkasian, 2009).

Like other aspects of CBT, meditation seems to work best with chronic pain, which, as we have seen, is not the same as the tissue-damaging pain caused by an injury (acute pain). Although it often begins with an injury, chronic pain is perpetuated by stress and environmental and emotional effects long after a reasonable recovery time for physical healing has passed.

Four areas of the brain that are involved in processing pain and regulating emotional and behavioral responses appear to be affected by meditation (see Figure 14.7):

- *Primary somatosensory cortex.* This is the brain area directly involved in processing painful stimuli. If a woman burns her hand, this area of the brain figures out where the pain is and what the initial pain level is.

- *Anterior insula.* By monitoring heart rate, blood pressure, and other indicators of arousal, this brain region appraises pain in the body. After a person's hand has been burned, the insula judges how painful the resulting injury is.

- *Anterior cingulate cortex.* This area regulates a person's emotional response to a stimulus such as heat. The person who burns her hand may then feel frustrated, scared, or angry as a result of the injury.

- *Prefrontal cortex.* As the brain's command center, this area takes information and guides a person's subsequent thoughts and actions. After first feeling angry, the woman who burned her hand may suppress unhelpful thoughts and focus on seeking treatment for her burn.

Research studies have shown that meditation can alter activity in each of these areas of the brain. Decreasing activity in the primary somatosensory cortex and increasing activity in the three other regions can often reduce pain. In the above example, imagine that the woman who burned her hand meditates regularly. Neuroimaging studies show that

Prefrontal cortex

Somatosensory cortex

Anterior cingulate cortex

Anterior insula

FIGURE 14.7 Areas of the Brain Involved in Processing Pain and Regulating Emotional and Behavioral Responses The areas of the brain shown here, which are related to processing and responding to pain, are those that seem most affected by meditation.

the effects of meditation on the brain mean that the burn won't hurt as much from the beginning, the pain won't be judged to be as strong, and the focus will be on regulating the emotional and behavioral reaction to the injury.

Thus, meditation may activate the same descending pain-inhibitory pathways that are involved in distraction and cognitive reappraisal. Experienced meditation practitioners have enhanced thickness in regions of the anterior cingulate cortex, and they have about half the activation of pain-processing brain regions compared to nonmeditators. Similar effects have been observed in new meditation practitioners after only 5 months of training (Orme-Johnson, Schneider, Son, Nidich, & Cho, 2006).

Exercise

Many types of pain are made worse by a lack of flexibility and by weak muscles. For this reason, exercise and physical therapy can be effective as pain-management interventions. Both aerobic exercise and resistance (strength) training can help decrease pain. Researchers in one study compared the effectiveness of four common self-management strategies in women with fibromyalgia (Rooks and others, 2007). The participants were randomly assigned to a 16-week program of either aerobic and flexibility training; strength training, aerobic, and flexibility training; a fibromyalgia self-help course; or a combination of strength training and the self-help course. The results showed that women who completed *any* of the types of exercise training reported significantly greater improvements in terms of reduced pain and enhanced functioning than their counterparts who received only the self-help program.

As we discussed in Chapter 7, people who exercise regularly also have lower levels of disability. In another study, researchers randomly assigned fibromyalgia patients to either a 12-week program of 60-minute tai chi sessions twice a week or a control group that received wellness education training and participated in light stretching for the same amount of time (Wang and others, 2010). *Tai chi* is an ancient Chinese form of exercise consisting of graceful and slow movements (see Chapter 15). At the end of the 6-month follow-up period, participants in the tai chi group displayed significant clinical improvement in fibromyalgia symptoms, as well as in their quality of life.

The use of technology to promote and motivate increased physical activity among people with chronic pain shows encouraging results. For example, smartphone apps for self-management often include information about pain and how increasing physical activity can reduce pain. Some apps include demonstrations of exercises for increasing strength and promoting relaxation through mindfulness meditation and other techniques. Other apps log data and enable the monitoring of key variables such as mood and pain, and they provide reminders such as for medication, daily mindfulness moments, and other pain-management activities. Movement games using consoles such as the Nintendo Wii and Microsoft Kinect have also been used to promote greater physical activity in older adults, as well as those recovering from strokes and other conditions (Singh and others, 2014).

Apps and games provide multimodal feedback and are inexpensive and accessible, but are they effective in increasing physical activity? In a recent study, 215 adults participated in an evaluation of a smartphone app designed to reduce sedentary time through prompts to interrupt periods of sitting (Kendzor and others, 2016). For 7 days, participants carried smartphones and wore accelerometers that measured their movement. Those in the intervention group also received text reminders about the health risks of sitting too much that also encouraged them to get up and move around. Participants in the control group did not receive reminders. Over the course of the week, those who received the reminders were 3% more active (engaging in about 25 minutes more daily activity) than those in the control group (Kendzor and others, 2016).

Reshaping Pain Behavior

The mainstay of the behavioral aspect of CBT is the targeting of specific pain behaviors that are associated with continued pain and disability for modification. Although pain may initially be caused by an injury or underlying organic pathology, its expression over time often is maintained by social and environmental reinforcement. In some cases, treatment may not progress because of the "benefits" (attention, lots of rest, not having to work, etc.) of being a pain patient. Comprehensive treatment programs, therefore, try to modify pain behaviors, such as excessive sleeping and use of pain medication. Stemming from a conditioning model, the intervention begins by identifying the events (stimuli) that precede targeted pain behaviors (responses) as well as the consequences that follow (reinforcers). Treatment then involves changing the *contingencies* between responses and reinforcers to increase the frequency of more adaptive ways of coping with discomfort.

Religious/Spiritual Coping

Religious and spiritual coping activities are widely used among chronic pain patients, although their effectiveness is controversial. Some research studies report positive pain-related effects; other studies have actually found more negative outcomes among spiritual copers, including higher levels of pain. One possible explanation for the inconsistent results

Managing Pain with Your Phone As shown in this example, there are a variety of smartphone apps for monitoring and recording pain. An app such as this can help to promote effective self-management of pain.

Copyright My Pain Diary

is that spiritual coping techniques that encourage passivity may be ineffective, while those that include active coping efforts may engage the same descending pain-inhibiting pathways as do distraction and cognitive reappraisal (Edwards and others, 2009a). One interesting fMRI study found that contemplation of a picture of the Virgin Mary by practicing Catholics was associated with increased activity in the prefrontal cortex and decreased perceived intensity of a painful stimulus (Wiech and others, 2008a). Non-Catholic participants viewing the same image showed no pain reduction or increased prefrontal activity, and Catholics viewing a similar but nonreligious image also showed no beneficial effects. The researchers suggested that Catholics viewing the religious image were able to achieve a calm, distracted state and activate descending pain-inhibitory systems.

Evaluating the Effectiveness of Pain Treatments

Which approach to pain control works best? The most effective pain-management programs are multidisciplinary ones that combine the cognitive, physical, and emotional interventions of CBT therapy with judicious use of analgesic drugs (American Pain Society, 2016). Most important, effective programs encourage patients to develop (and rehearse) a specific, individualized **pain-management program** for coping when the first signs of pain appear and as pain intensifies. In doing so, patients learn to be active and resourceful participants in managing their pain, rather than passive victims. The increased feelings of self-efficacy that follow from these steps are an important element in determining the patient's degree of pain and overall well-being. Individualized CBT programs have proven effective in treating lower back pain (Ostelo and others, 2005), rheumatoid arthritis (Astin, 2004), headaches (Martin, Forsyth, & Reece, 2007), fibromyalgia (Lami and others, 2018), and pain associated with various types of cancer (Mendoza and others, 2017).

pain-management program
An individualized, multimodal intervention aimed at modifying chronic pain through neurological, cognitive, and behavioral strategies.

With all of these applications, the goals of CBT include reducing pain and psychological distress, identifying and correcting maladaptive thoughts and beliefs, and increasing self-efficacy for pain management (Ehde and others, 2014). Many people with chronic pain also have mood, anxiety, and sleep disorders, and CBT is also used to treat these conditions (Gore, Sadosky, Stacey, Tai, & Leslie, 2012).

A number of meta-analyses have evaluated the efficacy of CBT for treating chronic pain, generally concluding that CBT, compared with treatment-as-usual conditions, has statistically significant but small effects on pain and disability, as well as moderate effects on mood and catastrophizing (Williams, Eccleston, & Morley, 2012). For example, one meta-analysis of 22 randomized controlled trials of chronic back pain management found that CBT had positive effects on pain, pain-related interference with activities, health-related quality of life, and depression (B. M. Hoffman, Papas, Chatkoff, & Kerns, 2007).

Another meta-analysis of headache pain management concluded that CBT-based interventions (relaxation, biofeedback, and cognitive therapy) effectively reduced headaches 30% to 60% on average (Andrasik and others, 2007). These benefits surpassed those of control conditions and typically persisted over time, including years after treatment. Biofeedback, in particular, is effective in treating chronic headaches, either as a stand-alone treatment or in conjunction with other CBT techniques (Turk, Swanson, & Tunks, 2008).

Meta-analyses provide evidence of significant effects of biofeedback on reducing the frequency and duration of migraine and tension-type headaches, when compared to control conditions (Nestoriuc, Rief, & Martin, 2008).

Other meta-analyses have supported the efficacy of CBT in reducing arthritis pain (Knittle, Maes, & de Gucht, 2010) and fibromyalgia pain (Glombiewski and others, 2010). Taken together, the body of research evidence supports the efficacy of CBT, as compared with control conditions, in treating pain-related problems, with small to medium effects on pain intensity, mood, and cognitive errors such as catastrophizing; and small but beneficial effects on pain-related disability and activity interference. Although average effect sizes are small to moderate across pain outcomes, another benefit of CBT is that it is not associated with the risks of chronic pain medication, surgery, and other medical interventions.

The Joint Commission (2016), which sets standards and accredits nearly 21,000 health care programs in the United States, has underscored the psychological effects of pain by establishing new guidelines for the assessment and management of pain. Under the guidelines, health care facilities (including nursing homes) are required to:

- recognize the right of patients, residents, or clients to appropriate assessment and management of pain;

- screen patients, residents, or clients for pain during their initial assessments and, when clinically required, during ongoing, periodic reassessments; and

- educate patients, residents, or clients suffering from pain, as well as their families, about pain management.

The goals of pain-management programs extend beyond controlling pain. They seek to restore the patient's overall quality of life—by decreasing the reliance on medication, by restoring activity levels, and by enhancing psychological and social well-being.

Weigh In on Health

Respond to each question below based on what you learned in the chapter. (**Tip:** Use the items in "Summing Up" to take into account related biological, psychological, and social concerns.)

1. Think about a time or an incident that caused you to feel pain. How do you understand that experience differently now that you've read about what pain is and how it is measured? Using what you learned, describe the components of pain you experienced. Also, explain your pain experience according to the gate control theory.

2. Imagine that a friend of your family is going to seek treatment for pain. According to research, what does his gender, age of 65 years, and Latino background suggest about his pain experience?

3. Compare and contrast biomedical and cognitive therapies used to treat pain. Name two kinds of biomedical and cognitive therapies. What pain experiences does each kind of therapy seem to treat best?

Summing Up

What Is Pain?

1. Pain involves our total experience in reacting to a damaging event, including the physical mechanism by which the body reacts; our subjective, emotional response (suffering); and our observable actions (pain behavior). Pain is categorized in terms of its duration as acute, recurrent, or chronic.

2. People who have chronic pain may become even more sensitive to pain over time (hyperalgesia). In *opioid-induced hyperalgesia*, the long-term use of opioids leads to an increasing sensitivity to noxious stimuli, even to the point to which common sensory stimuli become painful.

Measuring Pain

3. Because of pain's subjective nature, researchers have to rely on behavioral measures, visual and numerical rating scales, and pain inventories to measure pain.

The Physiology of Pain

4. Pain typically begins when free nerve endings in the skin, called *nociceptors*, are stimulated. The nociceptors relay this input to fast A-delta nerve fibers that signal sharp, acute pain or to slower C fibers that signal slow, burning pain. Pain signals travel from these peripheral nerve fibers to the spinal cord, and from there to the thalamus, a message-sorting station that relays the pain message to the cerebral cortex, the reasoning part of the brain.

5. Endorphins and enkephalins produced in the brain act as neurotransmitters and inhibit pain by acting on cells in the substantia gelatinosa of the spinal cord and the periaqueductal gray region of the brain. In addition, fMRI studies have implicated the dorsal anterior cingulate cortex as being specifically involved in the cognitive modulation of pain.

6. The gate control theory suggests that a pain gate exists in the spinal cord. Stimulation of the fast pain fiber system may close the pain gate, whereas activity in the slow pain system tends to open the gate. The neuromatrix integrates sensory information with emotional and cognitive states to determine a person's experience of pain.

Factors That Influence the Experience of Pain

7. Although older people and women are more likely to report higher levels of pain than younger people and men, the relationships among pain, gender, and aging are complex. They may also reflect faulty reasoning that exaggerates the relatively few differences among age groups, women, and men, while ignoring their similarities.

8. The mechanisms underlying ethnic differences in pain experiences are unclear. They may reflect environmental factors that disproportionately affect minority populations. Cross-cultural studies are typically correlational, making it difficult to rule out differences in socioeconomic pressure, social support, coping resources, education level, and other underlying factors.

9. There seems not to be a "pain-prone personality," though people who are anxious, worried, fearful, and negative in outlook—in addition to those who score high in depression—report more pain.

Treating Pain

10. The most common biomedical method of treating pain is the use of analgesic drugs, including opioids such as morphine. A less addictive class of analgesics, the nonsteroidal anti-inflammatory drugs (NSAIDs), produce their pain-relieving effects by blocking the formation of prostaglandin at the site of injured tissue. Electrical stimulation techniques, such as TENS, deliver mild electrical impulses to tissues near the pain-producing area to close the pain gate in the spinal cord.

11. Biofeedback is a technique for converting certain supposedly involuntary physiological responses into electrical signals and providing visual or auditory feedback about them. In this way, the person learns to perform a specific response to the feedback and then make appropriate adjustments.

12. Health psychologists recognize a general pattern of cognitive errors in the thinking of chronic pain patients, including catastrophic thinking, overgeneralizing, victimization, self-blame, and dwelling on pain. Cognitive errors are associated with abnormal patterns of neural activity in the anterior cingulate cortex, greater blood pressure reactivity, and elevations in certain proinflammatory cytokines.

13. By diverting attention away from a painful stimulus, therapies such as guided imagery, CBT, and meditation can diminish self-reported pain intensity. Another form of therapy, ACT, proposes that while pain hurts, it is the struggle with pain that causes suffering.

14. Because many types of pain are made worse by a lack of flexibility and weak muscles, exercise and physical therapy can be effective as pain-management interventions. Many

pain patients use religious and spiritual coping activities, although their effectiveness is controversial.

15. The most successful pain treatment programs are multidisciplinary, combining the use of analgesic drugs with eclectic cognitive behavioral programs. These programs use a mix of techniques to develop individualized pain-management programs, including cognitive restructuring of pain beliefs, distraction, imagery, and relaxation training.

Key Terms and Concepts to Remember

clinical pain, p. 442
acute pain, p. 443
recurrent pain, p. 443
chronic pain, p. 443
hyperalgesia, p. 443
free nerve endings, p. 446
nociceptor, p. 447
A-delta fibers, p. 447
C fibers, p. 447
A-beta fibers, p. 447
substantia gelatinosa, p. 448

referred pain, p. 448
substance P, p. 449
enkephalins, p. 449
periaqueductal gray (PAG), p. 449
anterior cingulate cortex (ACC), p. 449
endogenous opiate peptides, p. 450
stress-induced analgesia (SIA), p. 450
gate control theory (GCT), p. 451
neuromatrix, p. 452
neuropathic pain, p. 452

phantom limb pain, p. 454
pain behaviors, p. 458
prostaglandin, p. 460
counterirritation, p. 460
transcutaneous electrical nerve stimulation (TENS), p. 460
biofeedback, p. 461
cognitive-behavioral therapy (CBT), p. 462
cognitive reappraisal, p. 466
pain-management program, p. 470

To accompany your textbook, you have access to a number of online resources, including quizzes for every chapter of the book, flashcards, critical thinking exercises, videos, and *Check Your Health* inventories. To access these resources, please visit the Straub Health Psychology LaunchPad at **launchpadworks.com**

Chapter **15**

The Image Bank/Getty Images

Complementary and Alternative Medicine

LEARNING OUTCOMES
Once you have studied this chapter, you will be able to:
- Define complementary and alternative medicine,
- Identify what constitutes evidence of a treatment's effectiveness,
- Evaluate claims of the effectiveness of complementary and alternative treatments, and
- Describe future expectations and predictions for complementary and alternative medicine.

In August 2003, a 53-year-old woman—call her Cynthia—visited an Oregon clinic to undergo chelation therapy. Although she was in good health, Cynthia opted for the unconventional treatment (against the advice of her doctor) because of its reputed health and antiaging effects. Proponents claim that chelation, which involves intravenous infusions of the drug ethylenediaminetetraacetic acid (EDTA), removes heavy metals and other environmental toxins from the body. Although there were no apparent adverse effects from the earlier treatments, about 15 minutes into her fourth infusion Cynthia lost consciousness. She was rushed to the emergency room of a local hospital, where cardiopulmonary resuscitation was initiated, but it failed, and Cynthia died. The medical examiner determined the cause of death to be cardiac arrhythmia resulting from abnormally low levels of calcium in Cynthia's body (Quackwatch, 2006).

Cynthia's tragic story signals caution for those considering the use of health modalities outside the purview of conventional medicine, but it should not be taken as a wholesale condemnation of all complementary and alternative treatments. The medical professional increasingly recognizes the role of such treatments in helping people stay healthy and recover from illness. Even patients with serious conditions such as cancer can benefit from guides like the National Cancer Institute's (2005) booklet on complementary and alternative treatments.

The National Institutes of Health (NIH) estimates that less than one third of the world's health care is delivered by biomedically trained doctors and nurses (National Center for Complementary and Integrative Health [NCCIH], 2017a). The remainder comes from self-care and traditional indigenous approaches. This may mean a trip to the acupuncturist, massage therapist, faith healer, or chiropractor; purchases of aromatherapy ingredients, herbal medicines, or megavitamins; or a daily hour of yoga or meditation.

But how well do these methods work? Unconventional treatments must be subjected to the same rules of **evidence-based medicine** that traditional biomedical interventions undergo, including rigorous testing and careful evaluation of alleged health benefits. In earlier chapters, we discussed several unconventional techniques, including guided imagery, stress management, and cognitive reappraisal. In this chapter, we focus on larger-scale, unconventional therapies that encompass some of these techniques: *acupuncture, mind–body therapies, chiropractic, biofeedback,* and *naturopathy.* In addition to describing such modalities, we will report what we know about their tested effectiveness.

evidence-based medicine An approach to health care that promotes the collection, interpretation, and integration of the best research-based evidence in making decisions about the care of individual patients.

WHAT IS COMPLEMENTARY AND ALTERNATIVE MEDICINE?

Our consideration of alternative approaches to health care prompts this question: What is traditional medicine? The answer depends to a large extent on our belief systems and culture. **Conventional medicine** (also called Western or *allopathic* medicine) is health care as practiced by holders of MD (medical doctor) and DO (doctor of osteopathic medicine) degrees and by allied professionals, including physical therapists, psychologists, and registered nurses.

Osteopathic medicine is a branch of American medicine with a distinct philosophy and approach to patient care. A doctor of osteopathy (DO) receives the same basic four years of medical education as a doctor of medicine (MD), followed by three to eight years of graduate medical education consisting of internships, residencies, and fellowships. DOs practice a "whole-person" approach to health care and receive special training in the musculoskeletal system to understand better how that system influences the condition of all other body systems. In addition, DOs are trained to identify and correct structural problems, which presumably assists the body's natural tendency toward health and self-healing. Both DOs and MDs can practice in any specialty of medicine, such as surgery, pediatrics, or family medicine.

The term *alternative medicine* has been used to identify a broad range of therapeutic modalities that are generally defined as health care practices that are not taught widely in medical schools, not generally used in hospitals, and not usually reimbursed by insurance

conventional medicine Biomedically based medicine as practiced by holders of the MD (medical doctor) or DO (doctor of osteopathy) degrees and their allied health professionals.

osteopathic medicine A form of medical practice that provides all the benefits of conventional allopathic medicine, including prescription drugs and surgery, and emphasizes the interrelationship between the structure and function of the human body.

alternative medicine A broad range of health care practices that are not taught in medical schools, not generally used in hospitals, and not usually reimbursed by insurance companies.

complementary medicine The use of "alternative medicines" in conjunction with—rather than instead of—regular medicine. For example, the combined effect of drug *and* relaxation-training interventions for hypertension exceeds that of either the drug or relaxation by itself, and relaxation may reduce the doses of the drug needed.

holistic medicine An approach to medicine that considers not only physical health but also the emotional, spiritual, social, and psychological well-being of the person.

complementary and alternative medicine (CAM) The use and practice of therapies or diagnostic techniques that fall outside conventional biomedicine.

Scott Mc Kiernan/ZUMA Press/Newscom

Navajo Healing
Complementary and alternative medicine (CAM) includes a wide variety of practices, some more or less accepted in Western civilization. Here, Jones Benally, a Navajo medicine man, treats a patient. (Jones Benally was the first American Indian medicine man to be hired [in 1997] by a U.S. government Indian Health Services [IHS] hospital.)

companies. More recently, **complementary medicine** has become a preferred way of referring to such practices, as they are increasingly used in conjunction with, rather than instead of, conventional medical treatments. For example, the combined effect of drug and relaxation-training interventions for hypertension exceeds that of either the drug or relaxation by itself, and relaxation may reduce the doses of the drug needed. A number of alternative or complementary practices are considered a part of a **holistic medicine** approach, in which the practitioner addresses the physical, mental, emotional, and spiritual needs of the whole client. The boundaries between alternative medicine and conventional medicine are not absolute and may change over time, as specific interventions are subjected to clinical trials and become widely accepted.

Establishing a Category for Unconventional Medicine

Some "alternative" methods have been around for a very long time. For example, the Chinese practice of acupuncture is documented to have existed more than 2,000 years ago. I myself consulted an MD who is also a licensed acupuncturist when I needed to heal from a running injury. In addition to several sessions of acupuncture, she incorporated treatments that a "regular" doctor might also have recommended: rest (time off from running), daily ice massage, and a moderate course of oral ibuprofen every four to six hours.

The National Center for Complementary and Integrative Health (NCCIH) was established in 1998 as part of the U.S. federal government's National Institutes of Health. The NCCIH developed the classification scheme depicted in Table 15.1, which separates **complementary and alternative medicine (CAM)** practices into five major domains.

Three Ideals of Complementary and Alternative Medicine

Despite the endless variety of alternative therapies, most forms of alternative medicine *do* share several features that distinguish them from traditional medicine. Most work from three fundamental ideals: to provide health treatment that is natural, that is holistic, and that promotes wellness.

Natural Medicine

During most of the twentieth century, the public seemed to have an undying faith in modern technology, science, and biomedicine. However, from the 1960s onward evidence increasingly indicated that advances in health-related technology were not always healthy—and things began to change.

The current popularity of CAM seems to indicate a growing desire for more "natural" treatments. Immunization is a powerful example. Although vaccinations are an essential component of pediatric well-child care and are required for entering school, there has been controversy over the possibility of adverse side effects and the use of multiple-antigen vaccines (Bonhoeffer, 2007). How "natural" is it, skeptics ask, to inject a person with a disease virus or bacterium—even when it has been rendered harmless in the laboratory before it is administered?

TABLE 15.1 Domains of Complementary and Alternative Medicine

Medicine Type	Approach
Whole medical systems	Complete health care systems that evolved independently of Western biomedicine. Examples include traditional Chinese medicine, ayurveda, and homeopathy.
Mind and body medicine	Techniques designed to affect the mind's capacity to influence bodily functions and symptoms. Examples include meditation, yoga, acupuncture, deep-breathing exercises, guided imagery, hypnosis, progressive relaxation, qi gong, and tai chi.
Natural products	This area of CAM includes use of a variety of herbal medicines (also known as *botanicals*), vitamins, minerals, and other "natural products." Many are sold over the counter as dietary supplements. CAM natural products also include probiotics—live microorganisms (usually bacteria) that are similar to microorganisms normally found in the human digestive tract and that may have beneficial effects. Probiotics are available in foods (e.g., yogurt) and as dietary supplements.
Manipulative and body-based practices	Techniques that focus primarily on the structures and systems of the body, including the bones and joints, soft tissues, and circulatory and lymphatic systems. Two commonly used therapies fall within this category: ■ Massage therapy ■ Spinal manipulation as practiced by chiropractors, osteopathic physicians, naturopathic physicians, and physical therapists
Other CAM practices	CAM also encompasses movement therapies—a broad range of Eastern and Western movement-based approaches such as Pilates, used to promote physical, mental, emotional, and spiritual well-being. Traditional healers use methods based on indigenous beliefs and experiences handed down from generation to generation. A familiar example in the United States is the Native American healer/medicine man/woman. Other CAM practices involve manipulation of various energy fields to affect health (e.g., magnet therapy and light therapy). Practices based on putative energy fields (also called biofields) generally reflect the concept that human beings are infused with subtle forms of energy; qi gong, Reiki, and healing touch are examples of such practices.

Information from National Center for Complementary and Integrative Health (NCCIH). (2017e). *Types of complementary health approaches.*

The antivaccine movement started gaining traction in 1997, after a U.K. doctor published an article in which he claimed to have found evidence that the measles, mumps, and rubella (MMR) vaccine had caused autism in 12 children (Ziv, 2015). This purported evidence was later debunked, and the doctor was stripped of his medical license for ethical violations; the original research article was retracted, and a wealth of authoritative evidence shows no link between the MMR vaccine and autism (Jain and others, 2015).

Nevertheless, vaccination rates plummeted, and a 2014 National Consumers League survey reported that one third of parents with children under 18 years of age continue to mistakenly believed that vaccinations cause autism (NCL Communications, 2014). Vaccination rates have continued to vary from region to region, and MMR vaccination coverage among kindergarten children in the United States during the 2016–2017 school year was only 94% (MMWR, 2017, October 13).

Holistic Medicine

In addition to seeking "natural" solutions, CAM also aims to avoid the narrow specialization of conventional biomedicine. As physician Patch Adams, a pioneer of holistic medicine, noted, "Treat a disease and you win or lose, treat the person and you win every time" (Adams & Mylander, 1998, p. 22). Many patients seek out alternative care because they prefer to work with practitioners who will see (and treat) them as a whole person. The physician and author Steven Bratman (2007) describes one extreme case of a man whose various symptoms eventually led to treatment by six medical specialists: a neurologist (for cognitive symptoms stemming from a stroke), an orthopedist (for bone degeneration), an ophthalmologist (for eye pain), a dermatologist (for skin lesions), a urologist (for bladder problems), and a cardiologist (for heart valve leakage). Until an elderly neighbor (who happened to be a retired general practitioner) realized that the seemingly independent symptoms were similar to the syphilis cases that he had often seen 40 years earlier, no one suspected that what the man actually needed was a program of penicillin shots to rid him of this sexually transmitted infection.

Specialization and fragmentation are predictable consequences of the analytical nature of biomedicine, which encourages doctors to focus on the fine details of the symptoms that each patient presents. As a backlash against the overspecialization of conventional medicine, many alternative practitioners broaden their analysis of each patient's complaints to examine diet, emotions, and lifestyle as well as the specific symptoms of the disease or condition. This is especially true of traditional Chinese medicine, the ancient system of ayurveda from India, and homeopathy. Homeopathy is a largely unproven system of so-called energy medicine developed in the nineteenth century.

Promoting Wellness

Given Western biomedicine's historical focus on battling disease, it is understandable that the concept of wellness was long considered too vague for medical science to rally around. Instead, biomedicine orbited around disease; in contrast, the primary focus of many alternative treatments is to strengthen the individual, even if the person currently has no serious symptoms. However, conventional medicine practitioners have increasingly embraced the wellness ideal in the twenty-first century.

Alternative practitioners believe that medication, surgery, and other mainstream interventions can fight illness but generally cannot produce an optimal state of healthy vitality. Indeed, although most medical interventions eliminate major symptoms, they often entail adverse side effects, such as an upset stomach or a headache.

Many alternative treatments do make the person "feel like a million bucks" and can even relieve the symptoms of serious illnesses, if only temporarily (Fellowes, Barnes, & Wilkinson, 2004). Acupuncture, aromatherapy, and massage therapy may produce feelings of relaxation, while chiropractic generates a feeling of being energized. Whether these feelings are due to positive suggestion, a placebo effect, the patient's expectations, or an actual physiological effect doesn't matter—the patient still benefits.

Many CAM practitioners acknowledge that both disease-focused and wellness-focused approaches are needed, depending on the circumstances. Health care providers who practice **integrative medicine** combine traditional biomedical interventions with CAM therapies for which there is evidence of both effectiveness and safety (NCCIH, 2017a). For example, the University of California, San Francisco's Osher Center for Integrative Medicine includes cancer treatment with integrative oncologists on its staff.

For many varieties of CAM, the concept of wellness is closely connected with belief in the existence of a "life energy" or "vital force," known as **vitalism**. In **traditional Chinese medicine (TCM)**, as you'll recall from Chapter 1, the life force of *qi* (pronounced *chee* in Chinese and *kee* in Japanese) is believed to flow through every cell of the body. Acupuncture, herbal therapy, and other interventions supposedly restore vitality by correcting blockages, deficiencies, and isolated excesses of qi. Ayurveda, one of the world's oldest medical systems, originated in India more than 3,000 years ago and remains one of that country's traditional health care practices. Ayurveda concepts about health and disease promote the use of herbal compounds, minerals, special diets, and other nonallopathic health treatments.

How Widespread Is Complementary and Alternative Medicine?

Health care in the United States remains primarily based on allopathic medicine; yet, according to a survey conducted by the National Center for Complementary and Integrative Health, more than 30% of adults and 12% of children regularly use some form of CAM (NCCIH, 2017a). In 2012, Americans spent $30.2 billion out-of-pocket on complementary health approaches—nearly 30% of what they spent out-of-pocket on conventional medicine (NCCIH, 2016b). The most popular uses of CAM are for self-care therapies such as nonvitamin and nonmineral dietary supplements, homeopathic products, and yoga (see Figure 15.1). Some people are more likely than others to use CAM.

integrative medicine A multidisciplinary approach to medicine that involves traditional biomedical interventions, as well as complementary and alternative medical practices that have been proven both safe and effective.

vitalism The concept of a general life force, popular in some varieties of complementary and alternative medicine.

traditional Chinese medicine An ancient, integrated herb- and acupuncture-based system of healing founded on the principle that internal harmony is essential for good health.

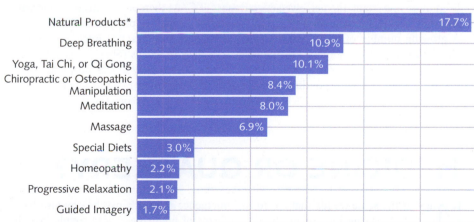

FIGURE 15.1 Ten Most Common Complementary Health Approaches Among Adults, 2012

Data from Clarke, T. C., Black, L., Stussman, B. J., Barnes, P. M., & Nahin, R. L. (2015). *Trends in the use of complementary health approaches among adults: United States, 2002–2012.* National Health Statistics Reports No. 79. Hyattsville, MD: National Center for Health Statistics.

*Dietary supplements other than vitamins and minerals.

TABLE 15.2 Percentage of Physicians Responding to Questions Regarding CAM Treatments

Treatment	Understand treatment but are uncomfortable counseling patients (%)	Understand treatment and are comfortable counseling patients (%)
Acupuncture	45	21
Biofeedback	48	47
Megavitamin therapy	25	30
Chiropractic	29	38
Massage	27	41
Homeopathy	23	16
Herbal medicine	35	21
Spiritual healing	28	22
Aromatherapy	29	8
Energy healing	12	5
Magnetic therapy	14	12
Naturopathy	12	7
Relaxation	24	38

Data from Wahner-Roedler, D. L., Vincent, A., Elking, P. L., Loehrer, L. L., Cha, S. S., & Bauer, B. A. (2006). Physicians' attitudes toward complementary and alternative medicine and their knowledge of specific therapies: A survey at an academic medical center. *Evidence-Based Complementary and Alternative Medicine, 3*(4), 495–501.

Overall, CAM is used more by women than by men, by people with higher education levels, and by people who have been hospitalized during the previous year primarily for back problems, anxiety or depression, sleeping problems, and headaches.

The use of unconventional medical therapies is increasing throughout the world. Even more important, the perceived effectiveness of CAM therapies seems to be increasing among both the general public and traditional allopathic physicians (Table 15.2). A growing number of traditionally trained physicians now practice integrative medicine by incorporating some CAM therapies into their practices (Shere-Wolfe, Tilburt, D'Adamo, Berman, & Chesney, 2013). In addition, a 2011 survey of U.S. hospitals found that more than 42% of responding hospitals indicated they offer one or more alternative medicine therapies, up from 37% in 2007 (American Hospital Association [AHA], 2011).

MEDICINE OR QUACKERY?

Many of the same trends that led to the emergence of health psychology also have fueled increasing interest in alternative forms of medicine. These trends include increasing public concern about

- the costly and impersonal nature of modern medical care;
- the adverse effects of treatment; and
- the seemingly profit-driven nature of health care and medical research that ignores unpatentable (and unprofitable) treatment options, such as herbal medicines.

Ironically, the surge in popularity of CAM also is due, at least in part, to the success of Western biomedicine. Today, people living in developed countries are less likely to die from infectious diseases such as smallpox. But as average life expectancy has increased, so have the rates of chronic diseases for which biomedicine has, as of yet, no cure. CAM therapies give people something else to try as they battle such diseases and strive to make their lives not just longer, but also healthier and more comfortable.

What Constitutes Evidence?

One reason it is difficult to determine the effectiveness of CAM is that its advocates and conventional physicians and scientists have different views of what constitutes an acceptable research design and which kinds of evidence are needed to demonstrate effectiveness. Biomedical researchers demand evidence from controlled clinical trials, in which treatments that are effective in eradicating or controlling individual pathogens are isolated. CAM practitioners, whose therapies are based on a more holistic philosophy, claim that treatment variables cannot always be studied independently. Many practitioners of herbal medicine, for example, claim that certain tonics and combinations of plant medicines are effective precisely *because* of the interactions among the various substances. According to this view, any attempt to isolate one ingredient from another would render the treatment useless.

As a result of such differences in perspective, many alternative practitioners are willing to endorse interventions even when the evidence backing their claims is far from convincing based on conventional standards of scientific reasoning. Health food stores, for example, have shelf after shelf of impressive-sounding literature that is largely unsupported. As always, one should keep this in mind when evaluating statements made by alternative practitioners.

Finally, the two groups differ in their focus. Rather than just seeking to remove a pathogen or to "cure" a physical condition, as biomedical practitioners do, CAM therapists emphasize the overall quality of a patient's life, broadening their focus to include important psychological, social, emotional, and spiritual aspects. Consequently, many CAM studies appear vague, do not use hypothesis testing or large samples, and tend to rely more on verbal reports from patients as evidence of effectiveness. It is not surprising that the quality of many CAM studies, as judged by Western scientists, is considered poor.

Participant Selection and Outcome Measures

As noted in Chapter 2, scientists have established specific criteria for the proper design of a clinical trial. Besides the obvious need to use the scientific method, researchers must begin by selecting large, representative samples of research participants, grouped by gender, age, socioeconomic status, and similarity of medical condition. Then these people are assigned randomly to groups so that each has an equal chance of either receiving or not receiving the treatment of interest.

For both practical and ethical reasons, however, randomized clinical trials (RCTs) sometimes present problems for medical researchers, especially for CAM researchers.

Many CAM trials include too few people in a group to allow researchers to determine whether results are statistically significant or are due to chance alone. Furthermore, CAM practitioners often find it difficult (or morally unacceptable) to persuade volunteers to participate in a study in which they may be "randomized" into a no-treatment control group. For this reason, CAM evidence is often based on informal case studies. This type of *anecdotal evidence,* based as it is on subjective opinions regarding diagnosis and treatment outcomes, does little to advance the credibility of unconventional treatments.

Another weakness in CAM research is the use of incomplete, biased, or invalidated treatment outcome measures. Many CAM studies rely on self-reporting. Although within certain guidelines, self-reporting can yield useful information, skeptics are naturally concerned about the accuracy of self-report data. Answers can be influenced by the research participants' desire to please the researchers, to appear "normal," and to persuade themselves that they are experiencing symptom relief. This criticism is made all the more important by the fact that CAM studies too often rely on single-outcome measures rather than on several different measures that might or might not provide converging lines of evidence. For example, several panels of scientists evaluating research on acupuncture concluded that there were too few acceptable studies comparing the effectiveness of acupuncture with either placebo or sham controls. These scientists encouraged future researchers to provide accurate descriptions of protocols for the types and number of treatments, subject enrollment procedures, and methods of diagnosing outcomes (NCCIH, 2016a).

Participant Expectancy, the Placebo Effect, and the Meaning Response

These controversies fundamentally raise the question: How, and why, does healing occur? Whenever patients are treated for an illness or a health condition, any improvement may be due to one of four explanations:

- The treatment may actually be effective.

- The illness simply improved on its own over time. This is true of most illnesses, including pain, which tend to be cyclical, **self-limiting conditions**. Because most people seek help when they are symptomatic, any intervention that occurs—whether inert or otherwise—is likely to be followed by improvement, often creating a powerful illusory correlation that it is the intervention rather than the passage of time and the body's self-healing, autonomous responses that caused the improvement.

- The patients were misdiagnosed and in fact did not have an illness at all.

- Patients improve on their own because of some nonspecific effect, such as their belief that the treatment will be beneficial (*placebo effect*).

Medical students are often taught the story of "Mr. Wright," a California cancer patient who was given only a few days to live. After hearing that scientists had discovered that a horse serum called *Krebiozen* might be effective against cancer, he begged his doctor to administer it. Reluctantly, the patient's physician gave Mr. Wright an injection. Three days later, the doctor found to his amazement that the patient's golf-ball-sized tumors "had melted like snowballs on a hot stove." Two months later, after reading a medical report that the serum was actually a quack remedy, Mr. Wright suffered an immediate relapse and died. Although many doctors dismiss this story as an anecdote, researchers have long

self-limiting conditions A condition that tends to improve with the passage of time, even in the absence of treatment recognized that part of medicine's power to heal is derived from the expectations that both patients and practitioners bring to therapy.

Placebos are physiologically inert substances that have been shown to treat a variety of conditions successfully due to the patient's expectations of healing. According to one survey of 1,200 physicians in the United States, half believe placebos are potentially beneficial, prescribe them regularly to their patients, and believe that doing so is ethical (Tilburt, Emanuel, Kaptchuk, Curlin, & Miller, 2008).

Inert substances can, however, also have adverse health effects. When they do, they are called *nocebos*. A **nocebo** (Latin for "I will harm," in contrast to *placebo*, which means "I will please") is a harmless substance or treatment that ends up creating a harmful effect. A *nocebo response* occurs, for example, when a participant in a controlled clinical trial of a drug reports uncomfortable side effects after taking a placebo.

The same substance or treatment can work as both a placebo and a nocebo. In one study, researchers gave participants who believed they were allergic to various foods an injection that they were told contained the allergen. Although the injection contained only salt water, a number of participants experienced allergic reactions. Then the researchers injected salt water again, this time telling participants it would neutralize the effects of the previous injection. In many cases, it did (Barsky, Saintfort, Rogers, & Borus, 2002).

Why do placebos work? According to one explanation, the medical treatments that we receive over the course of our lives are like conditioning trials, and we still may experience a therapeutic benefit as a *conditioned response* to the same medical stimuli. Another explanation is that placebos tap into the body's natural "inner pharmacy" of self-healing substances. For instance, placebos may reduce levels of cortisol, norepinephrine, and other stress hormones. Researchers also strongly suspect that at least part of placebo-based pain relief occurs because placebos stimulate the release of *endorphins*, morphine-like neurotransmitters produced by the brain. In one remarkable study, Fabrizio Benedetti (1996) asked 340 healthy people to squeeze hand exercisers repeatedly while tourniquets on their arms limited blood flow, causing pain that increased over time (Figure 15.2). Throughout the ordeal, the participants periodically rated their pain on a 10-point scale that ranged from 1 (no pain) to 10 (unbearable). When participants reached 7 on the scale, one of several drugs or saline solution was administered through an intravenous line, either fully within their view or surreptitiously.

Benedetti's results were important for several reasons. First, because only a *visible* placebo reduced pain, it was clearly not the placebo itself that reduced the pain, but rather the *knowledge* of the placebo that did the trick. Second, placebo-induced analgesia (pain relief) clearly was mediated by the body's autonomous production of endorphins in response to the expectation that a treatment (a visible injection) would be beneficial: Pharmacological interventions that blocked endorphin production (naloxone) disrupted placebo-induced analgesia, whereas those that enhanced the activity of endorphins (proglumide) strengthened placebo-induced analgesia.

According to *expectancy theory*, the anticipated consequences of treatment play a crucial role in health outcomes because people tend to feel and act in ways that they think they should. Like Mr. Wright, research participants respond to placebos according to what they are told. Depending whether they are told the treatment will relieve their pain or depression, or that it contains alcohol or another sedative, they will predictably report a decrease in pain or an elevation in mood or they will act as if they are intoxicated (Hyland, 2011). Conversely, people who do not know what to expect from a treatment—or are who unaware that they are being given a treatment at all—do not benefit as much as those who are told what to expect (Colloca, Lopiano, Lanette, & Benedetti, 2004).

nocebo A harmless substance that nevertheless creates harmful effects in a person who takes it.

FIGURE 15.2 Placebo Analgesia Visible injections of placebos were significantly more effective in reducing pain than hidden injections—suggesting that it was not the placebo itself, but rather knowledge of the placebo, that produced analgesia. In addition, injections that blocked endorphin production (naloxone) disrupted placebo-induced analgesia, whereas those that enhanced the activity of endorphins (proglumide) strengthened placebo-induced analgesia.

Data from Benedetti, F. (1996). The opposite effects of the opiate antagonist naloxone and the cholecystokinin antagonist proglumide on placebo analgesia. *Pain, 64*(3), 540.

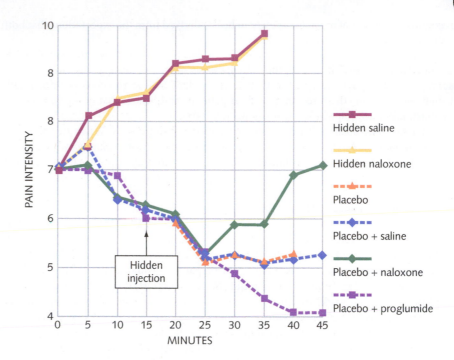

According to *meaning response theory,* every health care intervention, from taking a pill to undergoing surgery, is imbued with symbolism that conveys meaning and determines its efficacy (Moerman & Jonas, 2002). Because they are by definition inert, placebos cannot cause the *placebo effect* on their own. What they can cause—and what other treatments, from drugs to surgery, can also cause—is a *meaning response* based on how a person interprets the intervention. Studies of patient responses to placebos have found that name-brand pills produce a stronger response than do generic ones, that two pills work better than one, and that the more expensive the pill, the more effective it is assumed to be (Moerman, 2002). As another example, patients in cultures that place greater faith in conventional medical interventions display stronger responses to placebos that resemble a medical intervention, such as a pill or injection, than they do to treatments that do not (Moerman, 2011). The point is that people respond to the meaning that surrounds the placebo, thus shaping their anticipation of effects and, in turn, their perception of experience and behavior (Moerman, personal communication, 2017).

Although any medical procedure—from drugs to surgery—can have a placebo effect, critics contend that CAM is entirely placebo-based. When conventional therapies fail to help, the acupuncturist, chiropractor, or herbalist presents a powerful belief system designed to give the suffering patient hope that help is available. It is ironic that biomedicine's insistence on rigorous standards of scientific "proof" of the efficacy of a new drug or alternative therapy actually may be the strongest testimony for the prevalence of the placebo effect. "Scientific proof" requires the use of a double-blind RCT (see Chapter 2). The method is based on the premise that if either the patient or the researcher knows which treatment is "supposed to work," it would indeed work. Paradoxically, the working assumption of the double-blind method is that the placebo effect occurs routinely.

DOES COMPLEMENTARY AND ALTERNATIVE MEDICINE WORK?

If we know that the placebo effect can have an important influence on complementary and alternative medicine, how do we evaluate such treatments? How do we determine what works and what doesn't? In this section, we will try to answer these questions for several of the most widely used alternative treatments: acupuncture, mind–body therapies, therapeutic manipulation, and naturopathic medicine.

Acupuncture

Acupuncture was first practiced during the Bronze Age in ancient China as part of an integrated system of healing that was founded on the principle that internal harmony is essential for good health. In the West, it was recognized only 100 years ago or so. Although Asian-Americans have a long history with acupuncture, general interest in acupuncture in the United States did not increase noticeably until 1971, when a *New York Times* reporter underwent an emergency operation in China, was later treated with acupuncture for complications, and then wrote all about it for the newspaper (Reston, 1971). Since then, acupuncture schools have begun springing up, and there are currently about 30,000 licensed acupuncturists in the United States (Council of Colleges of Acupuncture and Oriental Medicine [CCAOM], 2016).

An acupuncture session typically involves inserting thin needles superficially or as deep as one or more inches, depending on the particular site and the practitioner's style of treatment. Which of the approximately 2,000 acupuncture points are selected, along with the angle and depth of the needle insertion, varies with the symptom. Needles are sometimes twirled, heated, or electrically stimulated to maximize their effects. Acupuncturists often also incorporate herbal medicine and dietary recommendations in their treatment regimens—two other common components of traditional Chinese medicine.

acupuncture A component of traditional Chinese medicine in which fine needles are inserted into the skin to relieve pain, treat addiction and illness, and promote health.

How Is Acupuncture Supposed to Work?

No one really knows the mechanism by which acupuncture operates. Traditional acupuncturists believe that every part of the body corresponds to the whole, whether it's the ear or the sole of the foot. Classical acupuncture theory identifies 14 "lines of energy" (qi) on the body, called *meridians*. Most acupuncture points, believed to allow for corrections of blockages or deficiencies in qi, lie on these meridians. Inserting needles at one or more points along a meridian is intended to produce effects elsewhere on that meridian.

Early researchers tried unsuccessfully to match the meridian lines with physical structures in the body. But many conventional doctors, including those who practice acupuncture, find it hard to accept the concept of an invisible energy path, or qi.

Acupuncture Acupuncture, originally practiced only in China, has become increasingly popular throughout Western industrialized nations. It has proved most successful in treating pain, although practitioners contend that it rejuvenates the body as well.

Andrey_Popov/Shutterstock.com

Brain scan during acupuncture treatment Studies comparing actual needle acupuncture to "sham" (or pseudo) acupuncture found different patterns in activation of brain regions associated with modulating the perception of pain.

Instead, they may explain treatment success as an example of the placebo effect. Others maintain that the pain of inserting acupuncture needles simply distracts the patient from his or her original pain, or that acupuncture triggers the release of the body's own natural painkillers (endorphins) and anti-inflammatory agents. None of these explanations, however, is widely accepted.

Today, using tools such as functional magnetic resonance imaging (fMRI) and positron emission tomography (PET), researchers are probing the brain in search of specific acupuncture sites and effects. A meta-analysis of 34 studies using fMRI to investigate the effect of acupuncture on the brain reported that acupuncture modulates neural activity in brain regions that are involved not only in somatosensory processing, but also in affective and cognitive processing. Some of the studies in this meta-analysis compared actual needle acupuncture to "sham" acupuncture, in which the patient falsely believed acupuncture was being performed. In such studies, needle acupuncture was associated with greater activation in the basal ganglia, brain stem, and cerebellum, and greater deactivation in limbic brain areas such as the amygdala and hippocampus (Huang and others, 2012). These results suggest that acupuncture-induced analgesia may result from activation of descending pain pathways and other brain structures that modulate the perception of pain (see Chapter 14). The hypothesis that acupuncture triggers the release of opioid peptides (natural painkillers) is supported by the fact that the analgesic effects of acupuncture are reversed by the drug naloxone, which blocks neural receptor sites for endorphins and other opiates (Gardea, Gatchel, & Robinson, 2004).

Evaluating Acupuncture

The only scientific way to determine the effectiveness of interventions such as acupuncture is through controlled studies. But such studies are difficult to perform for several reasons. First, the highly individualized nature of acupuncture does not lend itself well to standardized tests. Acupuncturists themselves disagree about the appropriate acupuncture needle sites for a given medical condition. Some studies allow acupuncturists to choose their own points of stimulation, to control the number of sessions, and to use electrical stimulation if desired. For these reasons, it is very difficult for researchers to isolate independent variables or to compare study results.

Double-blind controls, the mainstay of clinical trials, are even more problematic. Needles can be inserted at points that are inappropriate to a patient's health problem, making the patient blind to treatment, but the acupuncturist has to know whether the points are sham or real, so the study can't be double-blind. As noted above, research trials that use sham acupuncture often show that it has some effect—and in some cases, the effect is as strong as genuine acupuncture (Ernst, Pittler, Wider, & Boddy, 2007). Needless to say, the idea that stabbing patients at random points may be nearly as effective as using real acupuncture points is quite disturbing to acupuncturists who spend years memorizing locations.

Yet another difficulty is that operational definitions of successful acupuncture treatments have been inconsistent at best, and woefully vague at worst. In the case of addiction research, success has been defined variously as complete abstinence, decreased use, decreased cravings, diminished withdrawal symptoms, improved outlook, and increased productivity. Thus, one study may characterize an intervention as successful because substance use decreased overall even though more than half the participants relapsed, while another may report similar findings as indicating a failed intervention. Such variations make it impossible to compare one study to another.

Acupuncture and Pain

Hundreds of randomized clinical trials have been conducted testing acupuncture's effectiveness on 10 painful conditions. These studies provide evidence, although not statistically conclusive, that acupuncture provides *some* patients with *some* relief from painful conditions such as osteoarthritis, fibromyalgia, neck and lower back pain, migraine headaches, tennis elbow, and postoperative dental and hemorrhoid pain (Vickers & Linde, 2014).

Excluding 12-step programs, acupuncture is the most widely used CAM method for the treatment of substance abuse, especially of nicotine, alcohol, heroin, and cocaine (Carter, Olshan-Perlmutter, Norton, & Smith, 2011). More than 2,000 alcohol and drug treatment programs in the United States and 40 other countries have added ear acupuncture to their protocols (Smith, 2012). The goals of acupuncture treatment include reducing the symptoms of withdrawal, including drug craving; keeping abusers in treatment programs; and continued abstinence from drug use.

In 1996, the U.S. Food and Drug Administration (FDA) classified acupuncture needles as a type of medical device, boosting the credibility of acupuncturists and increasing the likelihood that an insurance provider will pay for acupuncture treatments. Although the American Medical Association (AMA) does not officially sanction acupuncture, more than 2,000 of the 12,000 acupuncturists in the United States are MDs. As another sign of growing recognition, the World Health Organization has identified some 50 diseases for which it considers acupuncture an appropriate treatment (World Health Organization [WHO], 2013a).

Despite the evidence that acupuncture holds some promise in treating pain, addiction, and depression, its overall effectiveness remains controversial (NCCIH, 2016a). One meta-analysis concluded that while the number of controlled clinical trials had increased for 13 of the 26 conditions studied, the evidence was favorable for only 7 of them (Ernst and others, 2007). Despite the inconsistency of research evidence for acupuncture's effectiveness, acupuncture's success rate is among the highest of all alternative medical interventions, and for some individuals its effectiveness with some conditions compares favorably with conventional treatments.

Mind–Body Therapies

The basic premise of mind–body therapies is that cognitive, emotional, and spiritual factors can have profound effects on one's health (NCCIH, 2017b). In this section, we'll examine four of the most popular mind–body therapies: hypnosis, relaxation and meditation (including tai chi and yoga), biofeedback, and spiritual healing and prayer.

Hypnosis

hypnosis A social interaction in which one person (the hypnotist) suggests to another person that certain thoughts, feelings, perceptions, or behaviors will occur.

Hypnosis is a psychological state that results from a social interaction in which one person (the hypnotist) suggests to another (the hypnotized person) that certain thoughts, feelings, perceptions, or behaviors will occur. Hypnotists often caution that some people are more hypnotizable than others; anecdotally, such individuals are said to be highly suggestible, fantasy-prone, and responsive to authority figures. Brain imaging studies have indeed shown differences in frontal lobe and temporal lobe activity between individuals who are high and low in hypnotizability. Research conducted at Stanford University's Center for Integrative Medicine has suggested that some people have a robust connection between the brain's executive (decision-making) and salience (attention-focusing) functions that could account for this difference (Hoeft and others, 2012).

Depending on the hypnotherapist, a variety of cognitive processes may come into play during a hypnosis session, including focused attention, relaxation, imagery, expectation, and role-playing. The most salient feature of hypnosis is the hypnotic trance, which is a waking state of attentive and focused concentration in which the subject becomes detached from his or her surroundings and becomes absorbed by the hypnotist's suggestions.

Hypnosis and Pain Hypnosis is most often used to treat pain, and it seems to be most effective in helping people manage acute pain rather than chronic pain. A typical hypnosis intervention for pain involves several overlapping stages:

- a prehypnotic stage, in which the therapist builds rapport with the subject;
- the use of suggestions and imagery to induce relaxation and the focused attention of the hypnotic trance;
- the treatment stage, which may involve various kinds of suggestions and imagery to reduce the experience of pain;
- a consolidation phase, which may incorporate *posthypnotic suggestions* to be carried out after the hypnosis session has ended; and
- a posthypnotic stage, in which the patient is awakened, given additional instructions, and released. In addition, the hypnotherapist may train patients in self-hypnosis so they can practice the therapy at home.

Evaluating Hypnosis Physiologically, hypnosis is accompanied by a generalized decrease in sympathetic nervous system activity, a decrease in oxygen consumption and carbon dioxide elimination, a lowering of blood pressure and heart rate, and an increase in certain kinds of brain-wave activity. This suggests that hypnotic phenomena reflect the workings of normal consciousness. We all probably flow naturally in and out of hypnotic-like states all the time—for example, while watching a mind-numbing television program. People often move into trancelike states of focused concentration when they are under stress, such as when they are about to experience an uncomfortable treatment. During such moments, when a person in a position of authority issues an instruction, it may have as strong an effect as a posthypnotic suggestion.

For highly hypnotizable people, hypnosis does appear to be more powerful than a placebo for coping with pain (Patterson, Jensen, & Montgomery, 2010), including pain from migraine and tension headaches (Milling, 2008), the care of burn wounds

(Askay, Patterson, Jensen, & Sharar, 2007), surgery and other invasive medical procedures, and childbirth (Cyna, McAuliffe, & Andrew, 2004). For people who are low in hypnotizability, however, hypnotic suggestions of analgesia are no more effective than drug placebos (Miller, Barabasz, & Barabasz, 1991).

One meta-analysis of fMRI studies of hypnotic analgesia points to possible neurological mechanisms of pain relief. The study found that hypnotic suggestions are linked to specific changes in activation in several brain areas within the "pain matrix." Compared with control conditions (normal wakefulness, or hypnosis with no suggestions of analgesia), hypnotic suggestions of analgesia during experimental pain are associated with increased activation in the right anterior cingulate cortex and insula and with decreased activation in the thalamus. Activation of this bilateral cortical network may result in reductions in pain intensity (Del Casale and others, 2016).

Relaxation and Meditation

As noted in other chapters, relaxation and meditation are related therapies that have proved successful in helping some patients cope with and recover from a number of medical conditions. *Meditation* refers to a variety of techniques or practices intended to focus or control attention (NCCIH, 2017b). Those who practice **mindfulness meditation** learn to pay nonjudgmental, in-the-moment attention to changing perceptions and thoughts. Conversely, in *transcendental meditation,* the person focuses awareness on a single object or on a word or short phrase, called a *mantra.* Proponents of meditation claim that its practice can influence the experience of chronic illness positively and can serve as a primary, secondary, and/or tertiary prevention strategy.

mindfulness meditation The practice of paying nonjudgmental, in-the-moment attention to changing perceptions and thoughts.

In his classic experiment on relaxation, Herbert Benson (1993) fitted experienced practitioners of transcendental meditation with measurement devices to record changes in a number of physiological functions, including oxygen consumption—a reliable indicator of the body's overall metabolic state. After recording the participants' physiological state for a 20-minute baseline period during which they simply sat in a quiet resting position, Benson instructed the participants to begin meditating. The participants were not permitted to change their posture or activity; they simply changed their thoughts to maintain a meditative focus. Following the meditation period, which also lasted 20 minutes, they were instructed to return to their normal state of thinking. The participants consumed significantly less oxygen while meditating than they did in the premeditation period (Figure 15.3). Other changes occurred during meditation as well: Breathing slowed from a rate of 14 or 15 breaths per minute to approximately 10 or 11 breaths, and brain-wave patterns included more low-frequency alpha, theta, and delta waves—waves associated with rest and relaxation—and significantly fewer high-frequency beta waves associated with higher states of alertness. In addition, during meditation, the level of lactate (a chemical that has been linked to anxiety) in the participants' bloodstream decreased dramatically.

Relaxation, meditation, and other physiological self-regulation techniques are effective in helping to manage a variety of disorders (NCCIH, 2017b). Recall from Chapter 5 that *mindfulness-based stress reduction (MBSR)* has been used to improve people's ability to self-regulate negative reactions to stress. MBSR has been extensively tested in randomized clinical trials using a standard eight-week instructional format focused on three somatically focused techniques in meditation: body scan, sitting meditation, and mindful yoga

Radius/Superstock

Mind–Body Interventions
Relaxation, meditation, and other physiological self-regulation techniques are effective in helping to manage a variety of disorders.

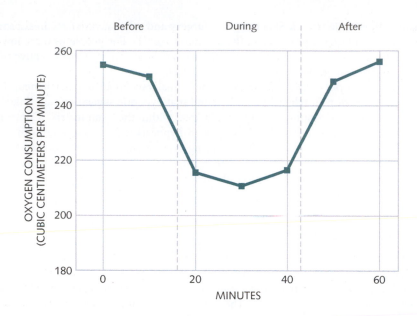

FIGURE 15.3 Oxygen Consumption during Transcendental Meditation
The body's metabolic rate, reflected in the amount of oxygen consumed, decreased significantly in experienced meditators when they switched from simply resting (Before) to meditating (During); it rose when they stopped meditating (After).

Data from Benson, H. (1993). The relaxation response. In D. Goleman & J. Gurin (Eds.), *Mind–Body Medicine* (pp. 233–257). New York: Consumer Reports Books.

(Fjorback, Arendt, Ornbol, Fink, & Walach, 2011). For instance, the first two weeks of the eight-week *standardized mindfulness (ST-mindfulness)* training program involves practice devoted to a meditative body scan of "moving a focused spotlight of attention from one part of the body to another." This exercise presumably enables practitioners to learn to "control the attention spotlight" even when focusing on painful sensations.

Research has shown that the benefits of mindfulness meditation are far-reaching, from minimizing pain sensitivity to helping people regulate their emotions. Indeed, for patients with chronic pain, meditation is effective, according to a National Institutes of Health review (Lebovits, 2007). One study demonstrated the pain-relieving benefits of mindfulness training for people with inflammatory rheumatic joint diseases (Zangl and others, 2011). The study included 73 people with rheumatoid arthritis between ages 20 and 70. Half were randomly assigned to perform mindfulness exercises in 10 group sessions for 15 weeks, as well as another session 6 months after the 10 sessions were completed. The remaining participants received conventional treatment for the condition, as well as a CD that taught them how to do mindfulness exercises. In this particular study, mindfulness training aimed to help people concentrate on their own thoughts, experiences, and pain in the moment, without actively trying to avoid them or evaluate them. At the end of the study, the people who had the group mindfulness training scored significantly lower in measurements of pain, stress, and fatigue than people who didn't have the training.

Based on multiple RCTs, mindfulness training is also effective in preventing depression (Piet & Hougaard, 2011) and in improving quality of life in chronic pain conditions such as fibromyalgia (Schmidt and others, 2011) and lower back pain (Morone, Greco, & Weiner, 2008); in chronic functional disorders such as irritable bowel syndrome (IBS) (Gaylord and others, 2011); and in illnesses such as cancer (Speca, Carlson, Goodey, & Angen, 2000) and multiple sclerosis (Grossman and others, 2013). One remarkable study reported that mindfulness meditation also slows the progression of HIV infection, as measured by CD4 T cell count (Creswell, Myers, Cole, & Irwin, 2009). ST-mindfulness also helps people cope with difficult life situations such as caring for a loved one with Alzheimer's disease (Epstein-Lubow, Miller, & McBee, 2006).

Tai Chi and Yoga Sometimes called "moving meditation," **tai chi** originated in China hundreds of years ago and is a component of traditional Chinese medicine. A blend of exercise, dance, and concentration, tai chi is practiced in a series of slow, circular, continuous, smooth, and controlled movements in which weight is shifted regularly from one foot to the other (NCCIH, 2017d). Groups of people practicing the rhythmical, dancelike movements of tai chi are a common sight in parks and other public places throughout China.

Yoga, a Sanskrit word meaning "union," has strong ties to spiritual and mystical traditions originating in India, where it has been practiced for thousands of years. Yoga encompasses a global lifestyle—consisting of diet, meditation, and physical exercise—that is now practiced by more than 20 million people in the United States on a regular basis (Li & Goldsmith, 2012). The two primary forms practiced in the West are *hatha yoga* (physical postures and breathing) and *raja yoga* (relaxation and mental and spiritual mastery).

It is widely believed that yoga and tai chi provide some of the physical and psychological benefits of more strenuous exercise without straining the muscles or the cardiovascular system. Tai chi has been shown to improve balance and stability in older adults and in those with Parkinson's disease; reduce back and knee pain due to osteoarthritis; and generally improve well-being in people with cancer, heart disease, and other chronic diseases. Yoga is also used to treat fatigue, chronic pain, and many ailments related to stress and anxiety. Because stress and anxiety contribute to many chronic conditions, yoga and tai chi are nondrug treatment options that many people find improve their quality of life (NCCIH, 2017g).

Tai chi and yoga may offer no special advantages over other forms of relaxation and exercise, and evidence of their effectiveness may have limited generalizability because most studies failed to use randomized trials with control groups. Nevertheless, they are growing in popularity, largely because health benefits *are* often demonstrated when a participant's pre- and postintervention status are compared.

How Might Relaxation and Meditation Promote Health? Just how relaxation or meditation might promote health is the subject of ongoing debate. One suggestion is that the relaxation at the center of these therapies relieves stress, muscle tension, anxiety, and negative emotionality, all of which might exacerbate physical symptoms and increase a person's vulnerability to ill health.

Researchers also have suggested that relaxation and meditation may alter a person's emotional response to symptoms such as pain. "I'm still in constant pain," notes one woman, who joined the pain reduction program at the University of Massachusetts after a bad fall left her with neck and back injuries and fibromyalgia. "Meditation makes the pain more bearable. I have less pain, muscles are more relaxed, and I have much better mobility" (Eisenberg and others, 1998). This makes sense, according to mind–body therapy advocates, because these techniques alter the way that pain sufferers respond to painful sensations and the way that they feel about them. Relaxation interventions often teach pain sufferers to reinterpret painful sensations, regarding them as "warm, even pleasant" rather than "burning and unpleasant" (Eisenberg and others, 1998).

In addition, relaxation and meditation may bolster the immune system. In one randomized trial, 40 adults between the ages of 55 and 85 were divided into two groups. One

tai chi A form of "moving meditation" that blends exercise, dance, and concentration, and is a component of traditional Chinese medicine.

yoga A movement-based form of relaxation and meditation that combines diet, physical postures, and breathing to promote physical and spiritual well-being.

practiced mindfulness-based stress reduction that involved attending two-hour weekly meetings, meditating at home daily for 30 minutes, and attending a day-long retreat. A control group did not meditate. Researchers took blood samples at the start and end of the study to measure gene expression and levels of inflammation. MBSR participants reported reduced feelings of loneliness, and their blood tests indicated a significant drop in the expression of inflammation-related genes. These included the marker C-reactive protein (CRP), a strong risk factor for heart disease; and a group of genes regulated by the transcription factor NF-κB—a molecular signal that activates inflammation (Creswell and others, 2012).

Other studies have shown that MBSR training significantly reduced levels of a pro-inflammatory cytokine (interleukin-6) (Tomfohr, Pung, Mills, & Edwards, 2015), as well as other markers of inflammation (Rosenkranz and others, 2013). In one randomized clinical trial, a 12-week yoga intervention significantly reduced fatigue and inflammation by altering gene expression in a group of breast cancer survivors (Bower and others, 2014).

Despite the growing body of evidence that mindfulness interventions can improve a broad range of health outcomes, the biological pathways linking mindfulness and health are not well understood. Noting that mindfulness-based health effects seem to most often occur in high-stress populations, some researchers have suggested that mindfulness training produces its effects on health indirectly by altering a person's cognitive appraisal processes when potential stressors are encountered (see Chapter 5). According to this view, as stressors arise, mindfulness facilitates a person's capacity to observe them with acceptance and equanimity, which in turn buffers initial threat appraisals and increases secondary appraisals of coping resources. Consequently, mindfulness may decrease the likelihood of rumination about potential stressors and increase the likelihood of using problem-focused, approach-oriented coping strategies (Creswell & Lindsay, 2014).

Using fMRI and other neuroimaging techniques, other research studies have begun to assemble the brain mechanisms by which meditation modulates the experience of pain. These studies indicate that mindfulness meditation engages several brain mechanisms that subjectively influence the pain experience. For instance, mindfulness training may trigger changes in limbic areas involved in emotional regulation. One study reported decreased amygdala activation after mindfulness training in social anxiety patients who were exposed to socially threatening stimuli (Goldin & Gross, 2010).

Other scientists believe that mindfulness practices are accompanied by reduced pain-related activation of areas in the somatosensory cortex and increased activity in the anterior cingulate cortex (ACC), which, as we have seen, are brain areas involved in pain processing. In one study, mindfulness meditation in the presence of painful stimuli reduced pain intensity ratings significantly (by 40%) compared to control conditions (Zeidan and others, 2011). Meditation also was associated with *thalamic deactivation*, suggesting a gating effect between incoming sensory signals and executive-order brain areas. In another study, mindfulness practitioners were able to reduce the unpleasantness and anxiety associated with painful stimuli significantly by 22% and 29%, respectively, compared to controls (Gard and others, 2011). These benefits were associated with decreased activation in the prefrontal cortex during painful stimuli and increased activation in the ACC while anticipating pain.

According to other researchers, mindfulness practice—the ability to observe one's thoughts and feelings from an objective distance—works as something of a "volume control" for sensations, giving experienced practitioners better control over how the brain processes pain and emotions. In one study, Brown University scientists observed that when people focused their attention on sensations in the left hand, the corresponding "map" for the hand in the cortex showed a significant decrease in the amplitude of alpha brain waves. When the participants shifted their attention away from the body part, the alpha wave amplitude increased. Subsequent studies showed that participants who received eight weeks of mindfulness training produced quicker and larger changes in alpha wave amplitude during the attention shift than did untrained control participants (Orenstein, 2013).

Perhaps most remarkable of all, scientists have reported that mindfulness meditation is linked to actual physical changes in the brain—beneficial changes that enhance the transmission of neural signals (Tang, Lu, Fan, Yang, & Posner, 2012). Brain imaging researchers from the University of Oregon reported that two weeks after practicing mindfulness meditation, the study participants had an increase in axonal density in their brain's ACC. After a month, there were even more increases in neural connections, as well as an increase in the myelin coating of axons in the ACC.

Thus, mindful people seem to remain unfazed by potential stressors for two reasons. First, they recruit increased activity in brain regions that aid emotion regulation and show less activity in brain regions, such as the amygdala, that are linked to stressful responses (Way, Creswell, Eisenberger, & Lieberman, 2010). Second, their sympatho-adrenal-medullary (SAM) and hypothalamic-pituitary-adrenal (HPA) axes do not go into overdrive when potential stressors are encountered. Mindful people recognize and accept stress, which buffers them from increased heart rate or excessive secretion of cortisol and other stress hormones (Nyklíček, Mommersteeg, Van Beugen, Ramakers, & Van Boxtel, 2013).

Biofeedback

As discussed in earlier chapters, biofeedback is a technique for converting certain supposedly involuntary physiological responses—such as skin temperature, muscle activity, heart rate, and blood pressure—into electrical signals and providing visual or auditory feedback about them. Biofeedback has proved to be somewhat beneficial in treating stress-related health problems in some people. For example, research support is relatively strong for alleviation of tension headaches (presumed to involve chronic muscle tension in the neck and head) and migraine headaches (Nestoriuc & Martin, 2007). Other disorders for which there is at least some research support to justify the therapeutic use of biofeedback include asthma, fibromyalgia, irritable bowel syndrome, urinary incontinence, tinnitus, epileptic seizures, and motion sickness (Moss & Gunkelman, 2002).

Despite some promising results, several important questions remain about the medical effectiveness of biofeedback. To date, there have been relatively few well-controlled clinical outcome trials using large numbers of patients who have confirmed medical conditions. Two limitations have emerged in clinical evaluations of biofeedback. First, people often cannot generalize the biofeedback training that they receive in clinical settings to everyday situations. Second, research has not confirmed that biofeedback itself

Biofeedback monitoring for stress Biofeedback has proved to be somewhat beneficial for stress-related conditions, though it is not clear why.

Will & Deni McIntyre/Science Source/Getty Images

enables people to control their internal, involuntary responses. Even when biofeedback is effective, it is not clear why, which raises the possibility that relaxation, suggestion, an enhanced sense of control, or even a placebo effect may be operating.

The few available studies on the use of biofeedback for maladies such as lower back pain and hypertension have produced mixed results. For instance, although biofeedback alone may be no more effective than simple relaxation training or a drug placebo in treating lower back pain and other conditions, when biofeedback is combined with cognitive-behavioral therapy, it may convey some short-term advantages (NCCIH, 2017a). However, because stress is often linked to either momentary or long-term increases in systolic and diastolic blood pressure, biofeedback has been shown to be an effective *complementary* therapy—combined with lifestyle modifications in diet, weight, and exercise—for reducing patients' dependence on medication in managing hypertension (Goebel, Viol, & Orebaugh, 1993).

Other researchers have suggested that relaxation and meditation are no more effective than placebos in modulating physiological responses. The National Center for Complementary and Integrative Health (NCCIH, 2017b) considers biofeedback a mind–body therapy that can offer benefits similar to hypnosis, relaxation training, and meditation. Even though researchers aren't sure exactly how or why biofeedback works, most people who benefit have conditions that appear to be brought on or worsened by stress. Moreover, as with other CAM therapies, some people choose to try biofeedback instead of drugs because of its lack of side effects.

Spirituality and Prayer

As noted in Chapter 1, through much of history, religion and medicine have been closely connected as healing traditions. Indeed, spiritual and physical healing were frequently conducted by the same person. As Western biomedicine matured, however, the two traditions diverged. Rather than consulting a spiritual healer to cure infection and prevent disease, people began turning to vaccines, antibiotics, and the growing number of new disease-fighting weapons in the modern medical arsenal.

There are signs, however, that the wall between medicine and spiritual healing—which never was nearly as high in some countries as in the United States—is toppling. Medical conferences and centers for research on spirituality and healing are cropping up at many universities, and over 90% of U.S. medical schools now offer spirituality-in-medicine coursework, up from only three schools in 1992 (Koenig, Hooten, Lindsay-Calkins, & Meador, 2010). Several surveys of family physicians have reported that a majority agree that prayer, meditation, and other spiritual and religious practices can increase the effectiveness of medical treatment (AMA, 2008; Greenberg, 2014).

But is there scientific evidence to support this growing movement? Does spirituality promote health, as four of every five Americans believe (Dembner, 2005)? As is often the case with nontraditional interventions, the evidence is mixed. To be sure, there is evidence that faith and spirituality are correlated with health. A number of studies have reported that devotees of various religions have lower illness and mortality rates than the general population. However, most of those studies were uncontrolled, making them vulnerable to mistaken interpretation and unable to pinpoint causation. For example, ill health may prevent many individuals from attending services in the first place. As another example, if religious people shared other health-promoting traits—say, they exercised as much as they worshipped, or they avoided smoking or excessive alcohol use—religion might have nothing to do with their improved health.

Although correlation does not prove causality, one study that followed more than 5,000 Californians over a 28-year period reported that even after ruling out differences due to gender, ethnicity, age, and education, people who were religiously active were 36% less likely to die in any given year than their less-religious counterparts (Oman, Kurata, Strawbridge, & Cohen, 2002). In another study, which controlled for the age, race, and gender of the participants, researchers reported that those who rarely attended religious services were 1.87 times more likely to die during the eight-year study than were those who attended frequently (Hummer, Rogers, Nam, & Ellison, 1999).

What accounts for the correlation between strong religious practices and longevity? At least three intervening factors remain strong candidates: lifestyle, social support, and positive emotions. First, compared with people in the general population, those who are religiously active tend to smoke less, consume alcohol more moderately, eat less fat, be more active, and be less likely to engage in high-risk sexual behaviors (Masters & Hooker, 2013). Second, because religion tends to be a communal experience, those who are religiously active may benefit from more social ties than those in the general population. Throughout this book, we have seen the beneficial effects of social support on each domain of health. Third, religious activity may promote health by fostering more positive emotions, including an optimistic and hopeful worldview, a feeling of acceptance and personal control, and a sense that life itself is meaningful (Chida, Steptoe, & Powell, 2009).

Therapeutic Manipulation

Two of the most common forms of therapeutic manipulation today—*chiropractic* and *osteopathy*—are the only major forms of CAM originally developed in the United States (osteopathy was described earlier in this chapter). Another form of manipulation is massage.

Chiropractic

The word **chiropractic** is derived from the Greek roots *cheir* ("hand") and *praktikos* ("done by"). Its actual practice can be traced back to September 1895, when a healer named Daniel David Palmer supposedly cured a patient's deafness by realigning the man's spine. Two years later, Palmer founded the first school of chiropractic, based on his belief that the human body has an innate self-healing power and seeks a state of *homeostasis,* or balance. Imbalance is believed to be caused by misalignments of bones within joints or by abnormal movements that interfere with the flow of nervous impulses. By manipulating the bones, muscles, and joints, particularly in the spine, chiropractors work to improve the function of the neuromusculoskeletal system and restore homeostasis.

chiropractic A complementary and alternative medicine approach to healing that is concerned with the diagnosis, treatment, and prevention of disorders of the neuromusculoskeletal system.

According to the National Health Interview Survey (NCHS, 2016b), which included a comprehensive survey of CAM use by Americans, in 2012 about 8% of adults and nearly 3% of children had received chiropractic manipulation in the previous 12 months.

Before performing any type of adjustment, the chiropractor will *palpate,* or feel, the patient's vertebrae to detect misalignment of bones or muscular weaknesses. He or she may test the patient's reflexes to check neural functioning. Also, x-rays may be taken to reveal any underlying joint problems that might interfere with treatment or be worsened by chiropractic adjustment.

During a treatment, the chiropractor will adjust the joints one at a time, using a slight thrusting movement that moves a restricted joint just beyond its limited range of motion. The patient may be asked to lie on a padded table for a spinal adjustment or to sit or stand for an adjustment of the neck and other joints. Although the treatments are usually painless, it is not uncommon to hear joints crack during an adjustment.

Evaluating Chiropractic Critics charge that chiropractic treatments are at best useless, because misaligned vertebrae are common and harmless, and the misalignment usually clears up on its own; and at worst, chiropractic manipulation can cause severe damage to the body if fractures or tumors are present. Others question the premise that a sound nervous system is the foundation of overall health, pointing to quadriplegics, who often have healthy internal organs despite extensive nerve damage. Some critics accept chiropractic treatment as effective for back pain but argue that it should be restricted to this disorder because there is insufficient evidence to support its efficacy in treating other conditions. Some people use chiropractors as their primary care gatekeepers, which is a cause for concern because not all chiropractors are trained to diagnose all medical conditions.

Despite such criticism, chiropractic remains very popular with the general public, causing Congress, in 1974, to pass legislation requiring Medicare to pay for chiropractic services. Although still considered a form of alternative medicine by many conventional doctors, chiropractic has achieved mainstream acceptance and is licensed in all 50 states. As another testimonial to the growing acceptability of chiropractic, the services of chiropractors generally are covered not only by Medicare and Medicaid, but also by about 85% of major insurance plans.

Evidence for chiropractic's effectiveness in treating back pain has been accumulating since 1952, when a Harvard study reported that this was the most common reason for visiting a chiropractor and that one fifth of back pain sufferers have used chiropractic successfully (Eisenberg and others, 1993). There have been many controlled clinical trials of *spinal manipulation*, but their results are inconsistent and the studies are often of poor quality (Ernst & Canter, 2006). A 2010 review of evidence on the efficacy of chiropractic concluded that spinal manipulation may be helpful for several conditions, including back pain, migraine headaches, neck pain, upper- and lower-extremity joint conditions, and whiplash-associated disorders. The review also identified a number of conditions for which spinal manipulation appears not to be an effective therapy (including asthma and hypertension), or where the evidence to date is inconclusive (fibromyalgia, premenstrual syndrome, sciatica, and temporomandibular joint disorders) (Bronfort, Haas, Evans, Leininger, & Triano, 2010).

Massage

While chiropractic focuses on the joints and spine, massage manipulates soft tissue. There are several different types of therapeutic massage. Swedish massage promotes relaxation through the therapist's use of light strokes moving in one direction on the skin, together with the deeper kneading of muscles in the opposite direction (NCCIH, 2017a). Other forms of therapeutic massage are derived from other systems of medicine, including TCM, ayurveda, and naturopathy. **Acupressure**, also known by the Japanese name *shiatsu*, is similar to acupuncture in that it is based on a system of meridians. As the name implies, it involves the application of pressure (rather than needles) to the meridian points.

Massage was once considered a luxury or a purely rehabilitative part of physical therapy, but it is now an accepted alternative treatment to relieve stress, anxiety, and many

acupressure The application of pressure rather than needles to the points used in acupuncture; shiatsu is a major form of acupressure.

types of pain. For example, massage may be beneficial for patients in managing pain following surgery (Kukimoto, Ooe, & Ideguchi, 2017) and, when combined with exercise, for managing fibromyalgia (Toprak and others, 2017).

Naturopathic Medicine

Naturopathic medicine aims to provide holistic, or whole-body, health care by returning humans to their "natural state." This "back-to-nature" movement has been traced to German doctors such as Vincent Preissnitz (1799–1851), who balked at the harsh treatment used by medical doctors. While medical doctors were "treating" their patients with mercury, bloodletting, and other "modern cures," Preissnitz and other German "nature doctors" were taking patients for walks in the woods and recommending fasting to "detoxify the body," followed by a simple diet and the healing powers of fresh air, sunlight, and bathing in natural hot springs.

At about the same time, a variation of naturopathic medicine called the *hygienic movement* was becoming popular in the United States. This movement, founded by Sylvester Graham (originator of the graham cracker), advocated a strict vegetarian diet, herbal treatments, and an abundance of whole grains. Another dietary mogul who regarded conventional medicine as a fundamentally wrongheaded attempt to improve on nature through artificial means was John Harvey Kellogg, best known as the founder of Kellogg's cereal company.

Benedict Lust (1872–1945), another advocate of natural treatments, coined the word *naturopath*. Lust also opened the world's first health food store in New York City around 1920. From then until the start of World War II, naturopathic medicine was a popular alternative to conventional medicine. By the 1950s, however, naturopathy was forced out of popularity by the increasingly powerful American Medical Association and by the discovery of penicillin and other potent antibiotics that were effective against many life-threatening diseases.

Naturopaths follow six basic principles, which are in keeping with the major ideals of CAM: *help nature heal, do no harm, find the underlying cause, treat the whole person, encourage prevention,* and *act as a teacher.* Naturopathic medicine integrates herbal medicine, clinical nutrition, homeopathy, and sometimes other CAM therapies with modern medical methods of diagnosis and treatment.

There are only six accredited naturopathic medical schools in the United States. Elements of naturopathic medicine, therefore, seem destined either to be absorbed into conventional medicine or to become a separate branch of it (Romeyke, Nöhammer, Scheuer, & Stummer, 2017). Although naturopathic physicians are licensed to practice in 23 states and U.S. territories, the majority of other states allow them to practice in limited ways (Association of Accredited Naturopathic Medical Colleges [AANMC], 2018). Naturopathic practice is regulated by state law, but only a few insurance providers cover naturopathic health care.

> **naturopathic medicine** The system that aims to provide holistic health care by drawing from several traditional healing systems, including homeopathy, herbal remedies, and traditional Chinese medicine.

Herbs and Other Natural Products

People have used plants to treat physical, mental, and behavioral conditions since the dawn of time, and all known cultures have ancient histories of folk medicine that include the use of herbs. This knowledge was often grouped into a collection called a *pharmacopoeia.*

Herbal Medicines Medicine sellers, like this one in Menghan, Yunan Province, China, set up stalls in the open market—displaying the many herbs used to treat anything from a toothache to lower back pain to cancer.

probiotics Bacteria that help maintain the natural balance of organisms (microflora) in the intestines and help promote a healthy digestive system.

shaman A general term used for the practitioner of folk medicine who often uses herbs and a range of rituals to effect cures; also referred to as "medicine man" or "medicine woman."

The ancient Greek and Roman cultures developed extensive pharmacopoeias. In Europe, *herbology* was traditionally a woman's profession until the practice of healing was taken over by male-dominated medical schools as early as the thirteenth century. Herbology then lost favor, and many women herbalists were persecuted as witches.

In the United States, physicians relied on medicinal plants as primary medicines through the 1930s. In fact, botany was once an important part of the medical school curriculum. But during the second half of the twentieth century, the use of medicinal plants declined due to developments in the ability to produce pharmaceuticals synthetically.

Today, some pharmacists create herbal compounds based on prescriptions written by doctors or naturopaths, but most herbs are marketed as food supplements because it is illegal for doctors to recommend an herb as a treatment for anything. Doing so is considered the same as prescribing an illegal drug. In practice, of course, herbs are widely used as treatments for numerous health conditions, with annual sales reaching into the billions of dollars.

Another natural product that is especially popular today is **probiotics**—live microorganisms (e.g., bacteria) that are either the same as or similar to microorganisms found naturally in the human body and that may have health benefits. Also referred to as "good bacteria," probiotics are available in oral products such as capsules, tablets, powders, and yogurts, as well as in other products such as creams. Although some probiotic formulations have shown promise in research (Avadhani & Steefel, 2015) and probiotics usually have few side effects, strong empirical evidence to support specific uses of probiotics for most conditions is lacking, and the U.S. Food and Drug Administration (FDA) has not approved any health claims for probiotics (National Center for Complementary and Alternative Medicine [NCCAM], 2013).

Types of Herbs Derived from the leaves, stems, roots, bark, flowers, fruits, seeds, and sap of plants, herbs (also called *botanicals*) can be prepared or marketed in different forms—as supplements, medicines, or teas—depending on their intended use. Herbs can be used as tonics and remedies for virtually every known ailment and condition. Herbal teas can be steeped to varying strengths. Roots, bark, and other plant parts can be simmered into potent solutions called *decoctions*. Today, many herbs (in the form of tablets and capsules) are available in health food stores, pharmacies, and even grocery stores. Highly concentrated alcohol-based herb extracts called *tinctures* are also popular.

Herbs play a central role in botanical medicine, Chinese medicine, ayurvedic medicine, and Native American medicine. Although many Native Americans prefer to consult an allopathic doctor for health conditions that require antibiotics or surgery, botanical remedies continue to play a major role in the treatment of various ailments. The herbs prescribed by Native American medicine practitioners, or **shamans**, vary from tribe to tribe, depending on the condition being treated and what herbs are locally available. Some shamans direct that herbs be eaten; others instruct that they be brewed as a tea. In most healing rites, sage, sweet grass, cedar, or other herbs are burned over the patient, allowing the restorative smoke to drift over the person's body.

In Western herbal medicine, herbs are categorized in several ways. They may be grouped according to their potency. *Tonics,* or normalizers, have a gentle, healing effect on the body, whereas *effectors* have potent actions and are used to treat illness. In addition, herbs are often grouped according to their effects on the body. These categories include anti-inflammatories, diuretics, and laxatives, as well as other, lesser-known classes such as diaphoretics, which promote perspiration and nervousness, allegedly to strengthen the nervous system. Herbs also are often grouped according to which of the body's systems they affect. The cardiovascular system, for example, is said to respond to ginkgo, buckwheat, linden, and other herbs that are touted as being able to strengthen blood vessels.

Evaluating Herbs Although roughly 25% of our pharmaceutical drugs are derived from herbs, many physicians believe that herbs in general are ineffective and potentially dangerous (McCarthy, 2001). Still, there is at least some evidence that plant-based medicines are effective in treating certain conditions. For example, ginger's proven anti-inflammatory and antirheumatic properties, coming from both human and animal trials, suggest that it may be effective in treating arthritis and perhaps the pain associated with other inflammatory conditions (Rahnama, Montazeri, Fallah Huseini, Kianbakht, & Naseri, 2012). As another example, capsaicin, an extract from the cayenne pepper, is effective in relieving the pain of osteoarthritis. As a third example, aloe vera is a succulent plant that is effective in promoting healing, especially of burns (Maenthaisong, Chaiyakunapruk, Niruntraporn, & Kongkaew, 2007).

On the other hand, the evidence for the effectiveness of some popular herbs is mixed at best. The safest conclusion seems to be that certain herbs may be beneficial for certain conditions. In general, however, there simply is not enough good evidence that herbs work as well as many people would like to believe (Gardea and others, 2004). Furthermore, compared to the often-dramatic power of pharmaceutical drugs, herbs usually have fairly subtle effects. *Standardized extracts,* which have long been available in Europe and are increasingly available in the United States, do seem to be more effective, perhaps because the dosages used are generally higher than those found in dried herbs.

Many advocates of herbal medicine claim that the presence of many different active and inactive ingredients in synthetic drugs—known and unknown—means that botanical products are comparatively safer and more effective. This is mostly speculation, however, because there have been few clinical trials directly comparing herbs and pharmaceuticals in their effectiveness in treating specific diseases and conditions. Furthermore, advocates of herbal medicine typically neglect to mention the possible adverse side effects created by the lack of purity and standardization of some herbal products.

Food Supplement Therapy

The use of vitamins and food supplements is a second major emphasis of naturopathy and is perhaps the best known of all CAM treatments. Look through nearly any popular magazine, and you are sure to find a discussion of at least one recommended supplement, such as vitamin E, to deter atherosclerosis and prevent premature aging of the skin, or folic acid, to support the immune system. Although most medical experts have yet to fully endorse dietary supplements, an estimated 76% of adults in the United States take them regularly (Council for Responsible Nutrition [CRN], 2017).

There is little doubt that food supplements can have important health benefits. A large body of convincing research evidence shows that materials derived from foods can

Alex Segre/Alamy Stock Photo

Natural Product Therapies
Supplements and other forms of
CAM seem especially effective
with cyclical conditions that
naturally improve over time,
perhaps because people
seek out a supplement when
symptoms are worst and
presume that it worked when
they feel better.

be effective in treating a number of diseases. For example, niacin is effective in lowering cholesterol levels, and glucosamine sulfate is effective in reducing the pain of arthritis. Moreover, food supplements often trigger fewer adverse side effects than do drugs of comparable effectiveness.

Food supplements are generally used in two ways: to correct dietary deficiencies (*nutritional medicine*) or in immense doses to trigger a specific therapeutic effect (*megadose therapy*). As nutritional medicine, they are useful in correcting fairly common deficiencies in many essential nutrients, including deficiencies in calcium; folic acid; iron; magnesium; zinc; and vitamins A, B_6, C, D, and E. Although conventional biomedicine supports eating a balanced diet or, short of that, using nutritional medicine to correct deficiencies in vitamins and minerals, the use of megadose therapy is more controversial. Linus Pauling's famous recommendation to take 4,000 to 10,000 milligrams per day of vitamin C is a prime example (Linus Pauling Institute, 2016). According to naturopaths, this huge dose—equivalent to eating 40 to 100 oranges per day, or 10 to 15 times the official recommended daily allowance (RDA)—is needed because the stresses of modern life and the effects of environmental toxins cause nutritional needs to increase beyond what a normal diet can provide. This claim remains controversial among nutritionists.

Similarly, claims about the health benefits of fish oil–derived omega-3 fatty acid supplements, which are taken by nearly 1 in 10 adults in the United States, have come under fire. A 2018 meta-analysis of studies involving 78,000 participants with a history of coronary heart disease (66%), stroke (28%), or diabetes (37%) compared fish oil with placebo or no supplement over the past four years. All told, fish oil did not reduce the risk of coronary heart disease (CHD) deaths, nonfatal heart attacks, strokes, or deaths due to any cause among the full study population (Abbasi, 2018).

Dietary Medicine

Naturopaths have always believed that fruits, vegetables, nuts, and whole grains are "natural foods," and that any refinement of these foods reduces their natural vitality and health-promoting properties. In contrast, conventional biomedicine paid little attention to diet until recently. Only since the 1980s have medical researchers begun to take seriously the idea that what people eat has a major impact on their health. As discussed in Chapter 8, the overwhelming evidence from large-scale epidemiological research has shown that diet plays a central role in preventing most of the major chronic diseases, including heart disease; strokes; and cancer of the breast, colon, and prostate.

Despite this agreement, naturopaths typically go well beyond conventional medicine's recommendations regarding diet. In addition to calling for dramatic reductions in the consumption of meat and saturated fat, they decry the use of food preservatives and the artificial fertilizers, pesticides, and hormones used in modern farming. Instead, they recommend eating organic foods that are produced without these adulterations.

Another popular dietary concept in naturopathic medicine has to do with the idea of *food allergy* or, more accurately, *food sensitivity*. Diets based on avoiding "trigger" foods such as sugar, wheat, or dairy products are prescribed for many conditions, from arthritis to irritable bowel syndrome to chronic fatigue (NCCIH, 2017a). When a food sensitivity is suspected, naturopaths typically place the patient on a highly restricted elimination diet of a small number of foods (including rice, sweet potatoes, turkey, and applesauce) known to seldom cause allergic reactions. If symptoms begin to clear up after several weeks on the restricted diet, foods are gradually added back into the diet, one at a time, while the patient keeps a journal of symptoms such as sneezing or headaches.

But even naturopaths disagree about the elements of a healthy diet. Proponents of *raw food theory*, a naturopathic concept dating back more than 100 years, believe that cooking foods destroys the "vital life force" (along with the vitamins, enzymes, and micronutrients) found in food. In contrast, *macrobiotics*—a system of combining foods believed to maximize their nutritional value—condemns raw foods as unhealthy, considering them a cause of multiple sclerosis, rheumatoid arthritis, and other diseases. Macrobiotic nutritionists insist that all foods, including vegetables, should be cooked.

Evaluating Dietary Modifications and Food Supplements Epidemiological and experimental studies in animals and humans have provided substantial evidence that diet (in the form of foods or as supplements) can have a major effect on risk factors for certain diseases and the progression of disease. For example, since the early twenty-first century, plant-based diets, dietary fiber supplementation, and antioxidant supplementation have become increasingly accepted treatments for managing cardiovascular disease. In fact, along with low-fat diets, aerobic exercise, and stress reduction, these treatments, formerly considered alternative therapies, are accepted as either complementary or a part of standard medical practice for reducing the risk of cardiovascular disease (NCCIH, 2017a).

Similarly, low-fat, high-fiber, basically vegetarian diets such as the Pritikin diet and the Ornish diet have been demonstrated to be effective in lowering blood glucose levels in people with diabetes. In one study, 60% of people with Type 2 diabetes on the Ornish diet no longer required insulin (McGrady & Horner, 1999). A number of epidemiological studies (for example, Ornish and others, 2008) also have suggested a possible decrease in the prevalence of cancer in people who consume higher amounts of fruits and vegetables, perhaps due to the antioxidant effects of these foods.

Elimination diets, megavitamin supplementation, and diets that focus on replacing trace elements are popular forms of CAM therapy that have been used to treat *attention deficit hyperactivity disorder (ADHD)*. The Feingold diet, for example, eliminates food colorings, artificial flavors, and highly processed foods from the ADHD child's diet, with mixed results in improving symptoms (Millichap & Yee, 2012). Despite the inconsistency in research results, the American Academy of Pediatrics concluded that a low-additive diet is a valid intervention for children with ADHD (American Academy of Pediatrics [AAP], 2015).

The value of food supplements, on the other hand, is not so clear. Certain supplements have been proved to be reasonably effective in treating certain conditions—for example, glucosamine sulfate for osteoarthritis and zinc for prostate enlargement. Despite these successes, however, megadose supplements rarely are as powerful as synthetic drugs, and supplement therapy alone usually is inadequate to manage serious health conditions. For instance, a review of clinical trials in the treatment of colds with small and large doses of vitamin C concluded that there is no evidence for the efficacy of this vitamin (Hemila, Chalker, & Douglas, 2010).

Safety Concerns As with herbal medicines, the FDA cautions consumers that some unregulated dietary supplements may contain hazardous substances. For example, in January 1999, the FDA asked dietary supplement manufacturers to recall supplements that contained gamma butyrolactone (GBL), which were sold via the Internet and in health food stores and health clubs. Marketed under such brand names as Blue Nitro, GH Revitalizer, and Revivarant, the popular supplement was supposed to build muscles, reduce weight, and improve athletic and sexual performance. In fact, GBL contains a chemical also found in commercial floor strippers that affects the central nervous system; slows breathing and heart rate; and can lead to seizures, unconsciousness, and coma. GBL has been linked to at least six deaths and to adverse health effects in hundreds of other people (Casciani, 2009).

The FDA also warns against the use of certain herbs and food supplements by those who are also taking prescription medications. For instance, in a February 2000 public health advisory, the FDA cautioned that St. John's wort had been found to reduce the effectiveness of the AIDS drug indinavir by 57% (Piscitelli, Burstein, Chaitt, Alfaro, & Falloon, 2000). The FDA also cited a Zurich, Switzerland, study reporting that this popular herbal remedy for depression reduced levels of a transplant rejection drug (ciclosporin), increasing the odds that a heart transplant patient might reject a donated heart (Fugh-Berman, 2000).

What to Expect from a Visit to a Naturopath

The herbal medicines, food supplements, and dietary medicines discussed in this section are provided by naturopaths, who function as primary, preventive care doctors. A visit to a naturopath generally begins with a standard physical exam, possibly one that includes conventional blood and urine tests and even radiology. In addition, naturopaths will spend considerable time recording the patient's medical history, focusing on the patient's lifestyle—including diet, exercise level, stress, and even emotional and spiritual issues.

After this initial examination, the patient and naturopath work together to establish a treatment program. Usually, the program emphasizes noninvasive therapies and lifestyle changes such as eliminating unhealthy behaviors. Then the naturopath may prescribe dietary changes, food supplements, and/or herbal medicine for any specific complaints. Depending on where the naturopath practices, conventional drugs, vaccinations, or even surgery may also be recommended.

Evaluating Naturopathy Diseases that are strongly affected by lifestyle and environment are among those for which naturopathic treatment most often is reported to be effective. For example, *naturopathy* has been used effectively to treat allergies, chronic infections, fatigue, arthritis, asthma, headache, hypertension, and depression, to name only a few conditions (NCCIH, 2017c). In a typical case of hypertension, for example, a naturopathic doctor might prescribe a multifaceted treatment that includes dietary changes, vitamin and mineral supplements, herbal medicine, and lifestyle changes designed to reduce stress. For an arthritis sufferer, the regimen might include dietary modifications, herbal medicine, and massage.

Critics of naturopathic medicine raise several concerns. Chief among these is that unsuspecting consumers are flooded with inaccurate or deceptive information carrying extreme claims about the effectiveness of herbs. In addition, herbal therapy is criticized for being untested according to pharmaceutical standards. Herbalists reply that because herbs are natural products (and therefore cannot be patented), the extremely expensive testing required of pharmaceutical drugs is unlikely to happen. Proponents point out that the modern pharmaceutical industry grew out of herbal medicine and that many drugs—from the digitalis used to treat heart disease (derived from the foxglove plant) to morphine (from the opium poppy)—still are made from plant extracts. Another concern is safety. For this reason, most herbalists recommend purchasing herbs rather than harvesting them in the wild. Plants have natural variations that can be misleading, and this has caused more than one death from a person's ingesting a toxic plant that he or she believed to be a beneficial herb.

LOOKING AHEAD: COMPLEMENTARY AND ALTERNATIVE MEDICINE IN OUR FUTURE

Growing interest in CAM is viewed by some as one of several indications of a major paradigm shift in medicine and health care in the United States. One of the changes is a shift from the traditional view of the provider–patient relationship, in which patients are willing, passive, and dependent, to one in which patients are activist health consumers. These days, patients are more likely to demand and seek out accurate and timely health information on their own, not likely to blindly accept their doctors' recommendations, and more likely to be critical of traditional medicine and to consider (and use) alternative forms of treatment.

Armed with unprecedented access to health information from the Internet, self-help books, and other media, today's patients are becoming more empowered to manage their own health. Turning to CAM practitioners is a predictable manifestation of this sense of empowerment—choosing one's own treatment approach despite what a physician might suggest.

This assessment of changed patient behavior is evident in data from the most recent National Health Interview Survey on the growing use of CAM in the United States (NCCIH, 2017e). The report indicated that 33% of U.S. adults used complementary health approaches, and most patients did so because they believed that CAM would improve their health when used in combination with conventional medical treatments. As shown in Figure 15.1, on p. 479, the most commonly used CAM approaches were dietary supplements (especially fish oil, melatonin, probiotics, and prebiotics) and mind-body therapies (especially yoga, chiropractic, meditation, and massage).

The NCCIH, part of the NIH, has funded numerous research studies to explore, among other topics, CAM and aging, arthritis, cancer, and cardiovascular disease; chiropractic; botanical supplements and women's health; and acupuncture.

The Best of Both Worlds

In the end, no single approach to health care has all the answers; the search for the best solution to a medical condition often requires a willingness to look beyond one remedy or system of treatment. Many insurance companies cover certain alternative methods, including acupuncture. And conventional doctors are incorporating alternative therapies into their treatment regimens. A survey of American physicians' knowledge and use of, training in, and acceptance of CAM as legitimate yielded the range of attitudes summarized in Table 15.2. Diet and exercise, biofeedback, and counseling or psychotherapy were used most often.

Thus, health care practitioners in the United States are moving toward a more open-minded view of unconventional medicine. Even the AMA has shifted its views toward greater tolerance. In the mid-1970s, the AMA's official position was that "the fakes, the frauds, and the quackeries need to be identified, exposed, and, if possible, eradicated" (AMA, 1973). By 1995, however, the AMA had substituted "alternative medicine" for "quackery" and passed a resolution encouraging its members to "become better informed regarding the practices and techniques of alternative or complementary medicine" (AMA, 1995). In November 1998, the prestigious *Journal of the American Medical Association* devoted an entire issue to the subject of alternative medicine. And where there once were none, there are now eight peer-reviewed journals devoted to alternative medicine.

Healthy Skepticism

The growing acceptability of CAM, however, should not be construed as an indication of its complete acceptance by the biomedical community. One survey of 1,150 patients, 333 primary care physicians (PCPs), and 241 CAM practitioners revealed growing acceptance of CAM but differing expectations regarding its use in primary care settings (Ben-Ayre & Frenkel, 2008). Patients expected their family physician to refer them to CAM, to have updated knowledge about CAM, and to offer CAM treatment based on appropriate training. When asked about CAM integration into medical care, more patients expected to receive CAM in a primary care setting (62%) compared to PCPs' expectations of prescribing CAM (30%).

"Let the buyer beware" is sound advice for consumers considering CAM therapies. A recent national survey of physicians who specialize in treating allergies revealed that 81% had patients who were using CAM therapies instead of conventional treatments, and many (60% of the respondents) had patients who experienced adverse reactions (Land & Wang, 2018). Among the reported adverse events were liver failure from the use of herbal medication, malnutrition from extreme food avoidance, worsening of eczema and other skin conditions from the use of "natural" skin care products, and an intensification of asthma symptoms from delayed use of conventional medication. Of particular concern was the finding that more than 80% of the allergists had patients using CAM who discontinued conventional treatment despite their physician's advice. Another study estimated that 23,000 visits to hospital emergency departments in the United States each year are attributable to adverse events related to dietary supplements (Geller and others, 2015).

Both alternative and conventional medicine are guilty of discounting one another's approach to health care, and both conventional medicine and alternative medicine are mixtures of good and bad health practices. The best course is to be an informed consumer and to be skeptical about unsupported claims.

Clearly, the best result would be for patients to have access to the "best of both worlds." Following a conventional medical evaluation and discussion of conventional allopathic options, patients may choose a CAM consultation. But before doing so, the physician (according to Eisenberg, 1997) should

■ ensure that the patient recognizes and understands his or her symptoms;

■ maintain a record of all symptoms, including the patient's own opinions;

- review any potential for harmful interactions; and
- plan for a follow-up visit to review CAM effectiveness.

This approach is designed to help keep communication channels open between patient and provider so that the patient receives the most effective and safest treatment.

Weigh In on Health

Respond to each question below based on what you learned in the chapter. (**Tip:** Use the items in "Summing Up" to take into account related biological, psychological, and social concerns.)

1. What general opinion did you have about complementary and alternative medicine before you read the chapter? How have the discussions of CAM in this chapter changed your opinion, if at all, on any CAM methods? In particular, what did you read about research on CAM that influenced how you now think about it?

2. Your roommate suffers from chronic headaches, and her medical doctor has not yet been able to diagnose their cause. She is tempted to try hypnosis, acupuncture, a form of meditation and relaxation, or naturopathy. What can you tell her about these methods of CAM from a biopsychosocial perspective? What has research shown about the efficacy of these approaches?

3. Using what you learned about CAM in this chapter, predict a way in which CAM will influence the way that people and providers in the future approach the prevention or treatment of illness, or the maintenance of well-being.

Summing Up

What Is Complementary and Alternative Medicine?

1. Complementary and alternative medicine (CAM) refers to the range of health-promoting interventions that fall outside of conventional, Western biomedicine. Most CAM practitioners work from three fundamental ideals: to provide health treatment that is natural, is holistic, and promotes wellness. Various forms of what we now call CAM have been around for thousands of years, but they were eclipsed during most of the twentieth century by the success of biomedicine.

2. CAM is used more by women than men, by people with higher education levels, and by people who have been hospitalized during the past year primarily for back problems, anxiety or depression, sleeping problems, and headaches.

Medicine or Quackery?

3. Skeptics of CAM raise several concerns about unconventional treatments. Foremost among these is that many CAM therapies never have been subjected to rigorous empirical scrutiny regarding their effectiveness or safety. When CAM studies are conducted, critics contend, the methods often are poor and the conclusions questionable. Another concern is that people who rely on CAM therapies instead of conventional medicine may delay or lose the opportunity to benefit from scientifically based treatment.

4. CAM skeptics also contend that when conventional therapies fail to help, the acupuncturist, chiropractor, or naturopath presents a powerful belief system, and the CAM techniques then seem to work due to the placebo effect. Inert substances can also have adverse health effects. When they do, they have been called *nocebos*.

Does Complementary and Alternative Medicine Work?

5. Acupuncture was originally practiced as part of an integrated system of healing. Today, its use is sanctioned in the United States primarily for the treatment of pain and addiction. Brain imaging studies suggest that acupuncture

modulates neural activity in brain regions involved not only in somatosensory processing, but also in affective and cognitive processing.

6. The basic premise of mind–body therapies is that cognitive, emotional, and spiritual factors can have profound effects on one's health. Among the mind–body therapies are hypnosis, relaxation training and meditation (including tai chi and yoga), biofeedback, and spiritual healing.

7. Relaxation and meditation also may promote health by bolstering the immune system, reducing pain, and lowering stress hormones. Some researchers have suggested that mindfulness training produces its effects on health indirectly by altering a person's cognitive appraisal processes when potential stressors are encountered.

8. Research has shown that the benefits of mindfulness meditation are far-reaching, from minimizing pain sensitivity to preventing depression to helping people regulate their emotions. Mindfulness training may trigger changes in limbic areas involved in emotional regulation, as well as reduced pain-related activation of areas in the somatosensory cortex and increased activity and axonal density in the anterior cingulate cortex (ACC).

9. Several studies have found that people who are religiously active are healthier and live longer lives than their less spiritual or less religious counterparts, perhaps due to differences in lifestyle, social support, and positive emotions.

10. Chiropractic spinal manipulation may be helpful for several conditions, including back pain, migraine headaches, neck pain, upper- and lower-extremity joint conditions, and whiplash-associated disorders. Massage may be effective for stress, anxiety, and many types of pain.

11. Naturopathic medicine aims to provide holistic, or whole-body, health care by returning us to our "natural state." Modern naturopathy draws from several CAM traditions, especially herbal medicine, food supplement therapy, and dietary modification.

12. Roughly 25% of our modern-day pharmaceutical drugs are derived from herbs. Certain herbs may be beneficial for certain conditions, but caution must be exercised because many herbs remain untested and may have harmful effects.

13. There is substantial evidence from epidemiological and experimental studies on animals and humans that diet (in the form of foods or as supplements) can have a major effect on risk factors for certain diseases and the progression of disease.

Looking Ahead: Complementary and Alternative Medicine in Our Future

14. Growing interest in CAM is viewed by some as one of several indications of a major paradigm shift in medicine and health care in the United States. Even so, a large survey of patients, primary care physicians, and CAM practitioners revealed a growing acceptance of CAM but differing expectations regarding its use in primary care settings.

Key Terms and Concepts to Remember

evidence-based medicine, p. 475
conventional medicine, p. 475
osteopathic medicine, p. 475
alternative medicine, p. 475
complementary medicine, p. 476
holistic medicine, p. 476
complementary and alternative
  medicine (CAM), p. 476

integrative medicine, p. 479
vitalism, p. 479
traditional Chinese medicine (TCM),
  p. 479
self-limiting conditions, p. 482
nocebo, p. 483
acupuncture, p. 485
hypnosis, p. 488

mindfulness meditation, p. 489
tai chi, p. 491
yoga, p. 491
chiropractic, p. 495
acupressure, p. 496
naturopathic medicine, p. 497
probiotics, p. 498
shaman, p. 498

LaunchPad macmillan learning   To accompany your textbook, you have access to a number of online resources, including quizzes for every chapter of the book, flashcards, critical thinking exercises, videos, and *Check Your Health* inventories. To access these resources, please visit the Straub Health Psychology LaunchPad at **launchpadworks.com**

Health Psychology Today and Tomorrow

Epilogue

I wasn't always interested in health. When I enrolled at Columbia University in the fall of 1975, I was blessed with a sound mind and body that I took for granted, as many students do. I rarely exercised, ate too much fast food, slept too little, and even began smoking cigarettes—to "cope" with the stress of college, I rationalized. I had little interest in what psychology might contribute to our understanding of health. My schedule of classes and research focused on learning theory, neurobiology, and cognition.

Things began to change, however, when I decided to branch out and study applied social psychology with Professor Stanley Schachter. His distinctive approach to research was breaking new ground in the study of emotions, obesity, and addiction. Unlike most of his peers, Schachter always focused on the broader context in which social behaviors were embedded. Nowhere is this more evident than in his effort to understand the biological processes involved in seemingly social phenomena, such as increased cigarette smoking at parties or in response to stress. Much of the emerging field of health psychology was rooted in Schachter's work. I began to see a clearer path toward the contributions to humanity that I was hoping to make. Psychology for me became a tool to promote health.

As my professional interests shifted, my personal interests followed. I recall one seminar when Stan, who himself was

Christopher Futcher/Getty Images

struggling to quit smoking, asked me when I was going to take up the battle against nicotine addiction. "Why don't you apply what you've learned here to your own life?" he asked. So I began to do so, and I've tried to be faithful to Schachter's challenge ever since. It was tough, but I did quit smoking many years ago. Along with kicking that habit, I also formed some new habits: exercising regularly, eating a more nutritious diet, and following a healthier sleep schedule. As new research findings have come along, I've tried to incorporate them into how I cope with stress; the efforts I make to keep strong, positive, social connections with others; and how I appraise the events around me.

My hope is that this book has sparked your interest in the field of health psychology—either as a profession, or as a tool in promoting your own better health and the health of those in your life whom you care about!

Health psychology has traveled a long way since the American Psychological Association first recognized it in 1978. My goal in this Epilogue is to look back—to review what has been accomplished along the way—and to look ahead to the most pressing challenges of the future. Although this book focuses on health psychologists' contributions to various health-related goals, it is important to remember that those psychologists are not working alone. Medical professionals and others involved in delivering health care all work together to achieve these ends.

HEALTH PSYCHOLOGY'S MOST IMPORTANT LESSONS

The science of health psychology remains in its infancy, and its contributions are still unfolding. Thus, much work remains to be done. Yet virtually all health psychologists agree that lessons have been learned during the past four decades of research that all of us should heed.

Lesson 1: Psychological and Social Factors Interact with Biology in Health

As we have seen, for many diseases, heredity plays a role, but not every person with the same genetic vulnerability to a disease eventually gets that disease. Bacteria, viruses, and other microorganisms cause some diseases, but being exposed doesn't guarantee that a person will become ill. Stress, negative emotions, coping resources, healthy behaviors, and a number of other factors affect our susceptibility to disease, the progression of disease, and how quickly we recover (if at all).

Behavior, mental processes, social influences, and health are intimately connected. This is the fundamental message of the biopsychosocial model of health. Even those among us with "hardy" genes and healthy immune systems can become ill if we engage in risky health behaviors, live in unhealthy social and physical environments, and develop a negative emotional style and poor stress-management techniques.

Unhealthy Behaviors and Social Alienation

Nearly nine out of ten college students report that their health is good, very good, or excellent (American College Health Association [ACHA], 2017). Morbidity and mortality data confirm this perception. As we learned in Chapter 6, young adults have a lower prevalence of chronic disease and premature death than older adults. Although feeling good about one's health can be beneficial, we have also seen that it can be hazardous if it causes people to be unrealistically optimistic that their good health will continue in spite of their lifestyle behaviors. And as we discussed in Chapter 6, this illusion is dangerous and may increase the risk of unintentional injury (accidents) and exposure to other serious health hazards.

The evidence is clear: Unhealthy behaviors such as smoking, alcohol and drug use, poor nutrition, high-risk sexual behavior, and physical inactivity lead to or at least accelerate the occurrence of illness, injury, and other adverse chronic conditions. For example, extensive research has eliminated any doubt that smoking is causally related to lung cancer and that alcohol use is related both to diseases of the liver and to traffic fatalities. Similarly, a low-fiber, high-fat diet increases a person's risk of developing cardiovascular disease and some forms of cancer. And, of course, a sedentary life increases the risk of cardiovascular disease and certain kinds of cancer and results in poorer immune functioning.

Numerous studies suggest that psychosocial factors can also affect the development and progression of diseases ranging from a simple cold to chronic conditions such as cardiovascular disease, cancer, and HIV/AIDS. Among the psychosocial factors that affect cardiovascular health are socioeconomic status (SES), gender, race, employment, acute and chronic stress, social support versus isolation, anger, and depression (Khayyam-Nekouei, Neshatdoost, Yousefy, Sadeghi, & Manshaee, 2013).

Social Integration Versus Isolation

Life expectancy in the United States reached an all-time high of 78.9 years in 2014, but has fallen each year since to today's average of 78.6 years (Kochanek, Murphy, Xu, & Arias, 2017). As we have seen, many deaths are preventable, premature, and linked in part to psychosocial factors such as social support (Liao and others, 2015). In a large body of research, Lisa Berkman (2010) has investigated how social networks affect health. In one study of 16,699 French workers, she determined a social integration score for each participant based on marital status, contacts with friends and relatives, church membership, and other group memberships. Over a seven-year follow-up and after adjustment for age, smoking, alcohol consumption, body mass index (BMI), and depressive symptoms, men with low social integration scores had a risk of dying that was 2.7 times greater than that of men with high scores; for women, the rate was 3.64 times greater.

Researchers cannot yet state exactly why social integration protects against chronic disease. So far, the most valid hypotheses proposed include the following: Social support may buffer the effects of stress on the body; social support may influence positively health behaviors associated with disease (such as diet and exercise); and social support may directly affect the underlying physical mechanisms associated with disease (Berkman, 2010). In support of the physical mechanisms hypothesis, researchers have found that social integration is negatively correlated with several inflammatory and immune system markers of cardiovascular disease. In fact, the link between close relationships and immune function is one of the most robust findings in the psychoneuroimmunology literature (Fagundes, Bennett, Derry, & Kiecolt-Glaser, 2011).

Conversely, relationship conflict and the perception of weak social support in one's life can effectively modulate proinflammatory cytokine secretion both directly (via central nervous system/neural/endocrine/immune biobehavioral pathways) and indirectly (by promoting depression, emotional stress responses, and unhealthy behaviors) (Kiecolt-Glaser, Gouin, & Hantsoo, 2010). People also expect to live longer when they perceive strong social and emotional support in their lives (Umberson & Montez, 2010).

Stress

Since Hans Selye's pioneering research on stress (discussed in Chapter 4), there has been mounting evidence that poor stress management can take a negative toll on health, both directly and indirectly, increasing the risk of many chronic diseases, altering the progression of those diseases, and undermining the effectiveness of treatment (Figure EP.1).

FIGURE EP.1 Direct and Indirect Effects of Stress on the Disease Process Stress affects health directly by elevating blood pressure and serum cholesterol levels and by decreasing immunity. The indirect effects of stress include reduced adherence to treatment instructions, an increase in smoking, and a variety of other unhealthy behaviors.

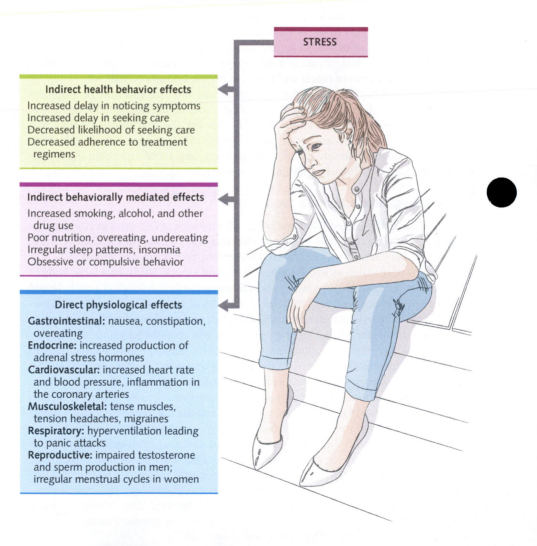

STRESS

Indirect health behavior effects

Increased delay in noticing symptoms
Increased delay in seeking care
Decreased likelihood of seeking care
Decreased adherence to treatment regimens

Indirect behaviorally mediated effects

Increased smoking, alcohol, and other drug use
Poor nutrition, overeating, undereating
Irregular sleep patterns, insomnia
Obsessive or compulsive behavior

Direct physiological effects

Gastrointestinal: nausea, constipation, overeating
Endocrine: increased production of adrenal stress hormones
Cardiovascular: increased heart rate and blood pressure, inflammation in the coronary arteries
Musculoskeletal: tense muscles, tension headaches, migraines
Respiratory: hyperventilation leading to panic attacks
Reproductive: impaired testosterone and sperm production in men; irregular menstrual cycles in women

Health psychologists have delineated the various possible consequences of how a person responds to daily hassles, occupational demands, environmental stressors, and other challenging events and situations. We now understand many of the physiological mechanisms by which stress adversely affects health and increases the likelihood of illness. For example, poorly managed stress can result in elevated blood pressure and serum cholesterol levels (Rosenthal & Alter, 2012). In addition, the evidence base for the relationship between stress and inflammatory processes has mounted significantly (Gianaros & Manuck, 2010).

Some of health psychology's most dramatic findings have focused on immune function. For example, temporary psychological stress, including exam-taking or daily hassles, can decrease immune function (Goliszek, 2014), especially in people who have poor coping skills and in those who magnify the impact of potential stressors and appraise them as uncontrollable. In addition, chronic stress, such as that arising from natural disasters or caring for a spouse or parent with Alzheimer's disease, can reduce immunocompetence (Haley, Roth, Howard, & Stafford, 2010). These findings are part of the burgeoning field of psychoneuroimmunology. When we have a calm sense of being in control, we tend to have a comparable emotional and physiological reaction. When we become angry or fearful or feel hopeless because we believe a situation is out of our control, we tend to become emotionally aroused, and consequently, our physiological response is more dramatic. Because we know that reactions such as these, if repeated and chronic, can promote illness, it is important for us to learn to manage our thoughts and emotional reactions.

Lesson 2: It Is Our Own Responsibility to Promote and Maintain Our Health

Our society has become increasingly health conscious. As a result, more of us realize that the responsibility for our health does not rest solely in the hands of health care professionals; rather, we ourselves have a major role to play in determining our overall well-being.

Americans and Canadians have become well informed over recent decades about the hazards of smoking, substance abuse, poor dietary practices, and sedentary living. We know, too, that stress, our emotional temperament, the quality of interpersonal relationships, and coping resources are important factors in health. We have learned about the importance of having regular checkups, adhering to our prescribed treatment, and seeking early detection screening for various chronic illnesses, especially if our age, gender, race, or ethnicity places us in the "high-risk" group for these conditions. And today, people can inquire about health issues and communicate with health providers by tapping into the computer-driven resources of telemedicine.

This awareness does not guarantee that people will follow through on what they know to be the healthiest course of action. As of March 2014, a series of midcourse reviews of progress toward the 26 leading objectives of *Healthy People 2020* demonstrated mixed progress for Americans (Figure EP.2). Progress has been made for a number of objectives. For example,

- fewer adults smoke cigarettes;
- fewer children are exposed to secondhand smoke;

An Informed Consumer
Each of us plays a major role in determining our own well-being, including knowing the ingredients of the foods we choose to eat.

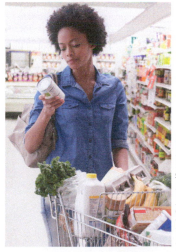

512   EPILOGUE | Health Psychology Today and Tomorrow

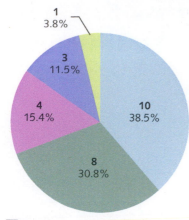

- Improving: 10 indicators (38.5%)
- Little or no detectable change: 8 indicators (30.8%)
- Target met: 4 indicators (15.4%)
- Getting worse: 3 indicators (11.5%)
- Baseline data only: 1 indicator (3.8%)

FIGURE EP.2 Status of the 26 *HP2020* Leading Health Indicators Progress has been generally positive toward achieving *Healthy People 2020* targets. As of 2014, 14 of the 26 indicators (53.9%) either met the target or showed improvement.

Data from: *Healthy People 2020.* (2014). *Healthy People 2020 leading health indicators: progress update.* Washington, DC: U.S. Department of Health and Human Services, Office of Disease Prevention and Health Promotion.

- more adults are meeting targets for physical activity;

- fewer adolescents are using alcohol or illicit drugs;

- more people have medical insurance, access to health services, and a usual primary care provider;

- more people have access to clinical preventive services, including recommended cancer screening and blood pressure control services;

- more children are receiving recommended vaccinations;

- injury deaths and homicides have declined; and

- indices of maternal, infant, and child health have improved, including continued declines in the number of infant deaths and preterm births.

In other areas, however, there has been little or no improvement. For example,

- the percentage of overweight and obese children, adolescents, and adults has increased;

- more people have been diagnosed with diabetes;

- trends in the area of mental health are worsening, including the number of suicides and adolescents with major depressive episodes;

- there has been little or no change in the status of most objectives for healthier dietary intake;

- the number of people who have regular dental checkups has declined; and

- the number of adults who engage in binge drinking has not declined.

Clearly, Americans have made some gains in improving their health habits. Yet as much as 40% of annual deaths from each of the five leading causes (heart disease, cancer, chronic lower respiratory diseases, stroke, and unintentional injuries) are preventable. Taken together, mortality from these causes accounts for about 63% of all deaths each year in the United States (Centers for Disease Control and Prevention [CDC], 2016b). Many deaths from these causes are avoidable if people make changes in personal behaviors and if disparities can be reduced that result from the social, environmental, and economic attributes of the communities and neighborhoods in which people live and work. If health disparities were eliminated, as called for in *Healthy People 2020*, the United States would be much closer to achieving the lowest possible mortality rates for the leading causes of death.

Still, it is important to remember that many illnesses and health conditions are not caused by people's behavioral choices but rather by heredity, environmental exposure, and other factors—including unknown ones we might simply call bad luck—alone or in combination. Each of us can probably think of people who were highly health conscious and followed a health-promoting lifestyle, yet died at an early age or were diagnosed with a chronic ailment. The role of health psychologists in such cases is not to look for things the patient may have done "wrong," but rather to help the person find the best possible strategies to cope with the adverse health condition.

Lesson 3: Unhealthy Lifestyles Are Harder to Change Than to Prevent

Health psychology has, of course, identified many lifestyle interventions that promote good health, but although these often meet with initial success, too many people "fall off the wagon." Ex-smokers, former heavy drinkers, weight-loss program participants, and those who are new to exercise regimens too often lapse back into their old bad habits, a problem that must continue to be a focus for future health psychologists.

Good nutrition; cardiovascular fitness; responsible drinking; and healthy management of body weight, stress, and social relationships are lifelong challenges that are best begun at a young age. Most smokers, for example, take up the habit during adolescence, usually before they graduate from high school. But as we have seen, preventing smoking, like preventing certain risky sexual activities, is a daunting challenge. Many people, especially young people, are more heavily influenced by the immediate "rewards" of smoking—the stimulating "kick" from nicotine, the self-image of doing something that seems mature or perhaps rebellious, the desire to fit in with their peers who are trying smoking—than by worries about long-term health consequences.

Preventing poor health habits from developing in the first place will continue to be a high priority for health psychology. New research will investigate the most effective and efficient interventions for reaching the largest number of people in the workplace, schools and universities, and the community. The use of **behavioral immunization** programs, such as those targeting adolescents most likely to engage in risky sex, smoking, drug abuse, undereating or overeating, and other unhealthy behaviors, also will continue to grow. For some health behaviors, interventions will probably need to target even younger "at-risk" individuals. Among these are pediatric "well-parent/well-child" programs designed to teach new parents how to minimize the risks of accidents in the home and car and how to start their youngsters off on a lifetime of healthy eating and cardiopulmonary fitness.

behavioral immunization Efforts to inoculate people against unhealthy habits by exposing them to mild versions of messages that try to convince them to engage in the adverse behavior.

Lesson 4: Positive Stress Appraisal and Management Are Essential to Good Health

One of health psychology's most important contributions in the area of stress and health has been the resolution of the controversy regarding whether stress is external or internal. Research has clearly revealed that it is both: Stress is a transaction in which each of us must adjust continually to daily challenges. As you learned in Chapters 4 and 5, each of life's stressful events can be appraised as either a motivating challenge or a threatening obstacle. Viewing life's stressors as challenges that we can handle helps us maintain a sense of control and minimizes the impact of stress on our health.

Learning to manage the stress that we encounter is crucial to our physical, psychological, and emotional well-being. Research has revealed the benefits of several stress-management strategies: keeping stress at manageable levels; preserving our physical resources by following a balanced diet, exercising, and drinking responsibly; establishing a stress-busting social network; increasing our psychological hardiness; disclosing our feelings when something is bothering us; cultivating a sense of humor; reducing hostile behaviors and negative emotions; and learning to relax.

HEALTH PSYCHOLOGY'S FUTURE CHALLENGES

Most of health psychology's challenges stem from two major research agendas. The most recent is the U.S. Department of Health and Human Services report *Healthy People 2020* (2014), which, as we have seen, outlined the nation's highest priorities for promoting health and preventing disease among all Americans. The report was based on the best judgments of a large group of health experts from the scientific community, professional health organizations, and the corporate world. The report's health objectives were organized under four overarching goals:

- attaining high-quality, longer lives free of preventable disease, disability, injury, and premature death;

- achieving health equity, eliminating disparities, and improving the health of all groups;

- creating social and physical environments that promote good health for all; and

- promoting quality of life, healthy development, and healthy behaviors across all life stages.

The second research agenda, produced more than 20 years ago by the American Psychological Association, Science Directorate (1995) in collaboration with the National Institutes of Health (NIH) and 21 other professional societies, focused more specifically on health psychology's role in health care reform. *Doing the Right Thing: A Research Plan for Healthy Living* identified four research tasks, out of which emerge the five challenges that we will discuss in this section.

compression of morbidity Efforts to limit the time that an older person spends ill or disabled.

A Century of Living! One of health psychology's key challenges is helping older adults optimize their well-being later in life.

Thomas Fricke/First Light/Getty Images

Challenge 1: To Increase the Span of Healthy Life for All People

Although people are living longer lives than ever before, the rapid aging of the population draws our attention to a crucial challenge: developing effective interventions that will enable older adults to maintain the highest possible level of functioning, or to improve it, for the greatest number of years.

Healthy life is a combination of average life expectancy and quality of life. The challenge for health psychology is to increase the average number of years that a person can expect to live in full health, along with a **compression of morbidity**—which refers to a shortening of the amount of time that people spend disabled, ill, or in pain. To illustrate, consider twin brothers who, although genetically identical and exposed to the same health hazards while growing up, have had very different health experiences since adolescence. The first brother smokes two packs of cigarettes a day, has an obesity-indicating BMI of 30.2, never exercises, has an angry and pessimistic outlook on life, and eats foods containing excessive amounts of animal fat and sugar. The second brother pursues a much healthier lifestyle, avoiding tobacco and excessive stress, exercising regularly, watching his diet, and enjoying the social support of a close-knit circle of family and friends. As Figure EP.3 shows, although the two brothers have the same genetic vulnerabilities to lung, circulatory, and cardiovascular disease, the unhealthy lifestyle of the first brother dooms him to an extended period of adulthood morbidity beginning at about age 45. In contrast, the healthier brother's lifestyle postpones disease until much later in life. If he does contract any of the ill-nesses, they are likely to be less severe, and recovery will be quicker. In some cases, the illness, such as lung cancer, may be "postponed" right out of his life.

We have achieved some success, but there is room for much additional improvement. One mea-sure of a nation's health is average life expectancy. The higher the life expectancy, the better the health status of a country. Globally, 72 years is the average life expectancy for people born today. In Canada, Australia, and New Zealand, and most of western Europe, life expectancy currently averages above 80 years, whereas in the United States it is 78.5. In a middle-income country such as Jordan, life expec-tancy drops to 74 years; and in a very poor country, such as Sierra Leone, life expectancy is only about 46 years (World Health Organization [WHO], 2018b).

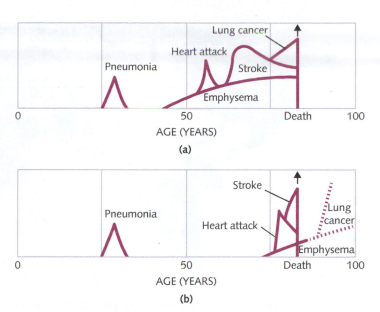

FIGURE EP.3 Compression of Morbidity In focusing on the individual's quality-adjusted life years (QALYs), health psychologists seek to limit the time that a person spends ill or infirm, as illustrated in this diagram of the illnesses and eventual deaths of identical twin brothers. Although the brothers carry the same disease vulnerabilities and life-span-limiting genetic clocks, the health lifestyle of one (b) keeps disease and disability at bay until an advanced age. In contrast, the unhealthy lifestyle of his brother (a) takes its toll at a much younger age.

Another measure of a nation's health is **health-adjusted life expectancy (HALE)**, the number of healthy, *well years* that people can expect to live free from disease and disability. The degree of discrepancy between life expectancy and HALE is quite variable when we compare various socioeconomic groups and countries of the world. Lower SES is associated with shorter average life expectancy, but even more so with fewer well years (WHO, 2018a; see Figure EP.4). Around the world, the percentage of life expectancy lost to disability ranges from less than 9% in the healthiest regions to more than 14% in the least healthy areas (Skolnik, 2016).

Positive Health

For health psychologists working within the positive psychology movement, an important challenge is to place greater emphasis on a strength-based, preventive approach to research and interventions, rather than use psychology's more traditional approach of tackling prob-lems after they have occurred. Enhancing people's opportunities to not only be well, but also to attain a state of optimal human functioning is a priority for health psychology in the future.

Positive health is the scientific study of *health assets:* behaviors, traits, thoughts, and emotions associated with longer life, reduced morbidity, lower health care expenditure, and greater recuperative power and better prognosis when illness does strike. Martin Seligman and his colleagues (2016) have suggested that the field of positive health gener-ates two broad hypotheses, one modest and one bold. The modest hypothesis is that assets such as positive emotions, self-regulation, cardiorespiratory fitness, and social engage-ment predict good health. The evidence for the modest proposal is already strong, and for many of these factors, there are evidence-based interventions that pay health dividends.

The second, bolder hypothesis is that there exist health states that have been described as thriving, resilience, or flourishing—that are associated with measurable outcomes such as less frequent and briefer ailments, enhanced recuperative ability when illness does occur, and greater physiological reserves. To date, much of the evidence for this hypoth-esis comes from anecdotes about people who never miss a day of work, people who stay

health-adjusted life expectancy (HALE) The number of healthy, well years a person can expect to live free from disease and disability.

positive health The scientific study of behaviors and traits that are associated with longer life, reduced morbidity, lower health care expenditure, and greater recuperative power.

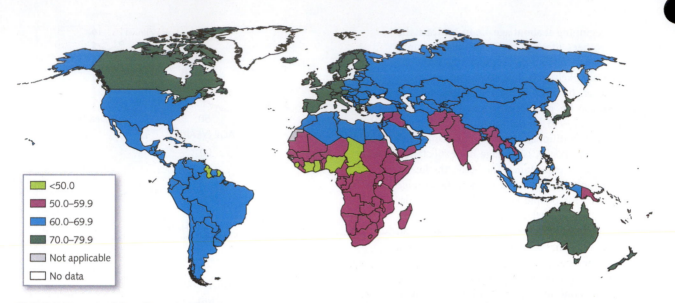

FIGURE EP.4 Health-Adjusted Life Expectancy (HALE) The World Health Organization and other health advocates increasingly focus not just on life expectancy, but on how many years people can expect to live in good health. This map shows HALE for people of both sexes born in 2016.

Data from: World Health Organization. (2018a). *Global Health Observatory (GHO) data. Healthy life expectancy (HALE) at birth.*

physically active long after others in their age cohort retire, people who lead a flourishing life despite serious illness or trauma, and people who are off-the-chart with respect to their physiological capabilities.

An ongoing Robert Wood Johnson study seeks to identify biological, psychological, and functional factors that may lead to these states of super health, if indeed they exist. Biological health assets include high heart rate variability, high VO_2 max (maximal oxygen uptake), greater telomere (DNA segment) length, and low body mass index (BMI). Psychological assets include optimism, personal control, subjective well-being, and curiosity. Functional health assets include such things as indicators of exceptional physical function (such as great strength, endurance, and motor coordination); a good match between a person's abilities and the requirements of his or her chosen roles and lifestyle; and close friends, meaningful work, and integration within a strong social community (Seligman and others, 2016). These assets are desirable in their own right. The challenge for positive health researchers is to expand the evidence base concerning whether and how such assets contribute to health-related outcomes.

Challenge 2: To Reduce Health Discrepancies and Increase Our Understanding of the Effects of Race, Gender, Culture, and Socioeconomic Status on Health

Historically, several measures of health have shown substantial differences among various ethnic and sociodemographic groups, as well as between the genders. For example, life expectancy at birth for African Americans has risen since 1950 but remains

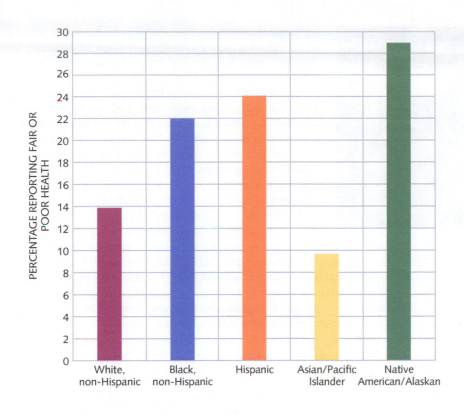

FIGURE EP.5 Quality of Health by Ethnic Group
When asked to describe their health, a surprisingly high percentage of all ethnic groups used "fair" or "poor." Especially telling are the differences between ethnic groups, with Asian Americans and European Americans having the most positive view of their health and Native Americans being least positive.

Data from CDC. (2016a). *Behavioral Risk Factor Surveillance System (BRFSS)*. Atlanta, GA: Centers for Disease Control and Prevention.

noticeably lower than that for European Americans (Kochanek and others, 2017). Compared with European Americans, African Americans have higher mortality rates in every age group and are more likely to suffer from many chronic health conditions—including heart disease, cancer, and diabetes—as well as fatal on-the-job injuries. Research studies focused on Hispanics/Latinos and Native Americans reveal similar disparities. Asking people about their health reveals even greater differences by ethnic group, as shown in Figure EP.5. The reasons for these discrepancies are undoubtedly complex, but they may include unequal access to health care, genetic susceptibility to specific diseases, and lifestyle differences.

The negative effects of ethnicity and poverty on health may be the result of factors such as poor nutrition, crowded and unsanitary environments, inadequate medical care, stressful life events, and subjective perceptions that environmental stressors are beyond one's ability to cope. Another factor is less effective use of health screening among certain groups. For example, African American women delay longer than White women in seeking care for breast symptoms, and older women, who frequently are at increased risk of breast cancer, are less likely to seek preventive care.

However, ethnic group disparities in health are not completely attributable to the social conditions in which people live. For example, Hispanic Americans generally fare as well as or better than European Americans on most measures of health, actually having a lower death rate than European Americans from heart disease, lung cancer, and stroke. This is paradoxical, given the high rates of hypertension, obesity, and tobacco use among Hispanic Americans. Some researchers believe that this puzzling fact reflects a

Pat Greenhouse/The Boston Globe/Getty Images

Education and Health On average, achieving a higher level of education leads to a longer life and better overall health.

lag in acculturation, because the same trend can be found in all immigrant groups: As immigrants adopt an American life-style, they eventually develop the same patterns of illness and mortality as earlier immigrant groups.

Another factor that may be important is education. Regard-less of ethnicity, people who have achieved higher levels of education live longer and have better overall health than those with less education, most likely because people with fewer years of education generally are more likely to engage in unhealthy behaviors such as smoking and eating a high-fat diet than those with more years of education. Recognizing the importance of education to health, *Healthy People 2020* (2014) set "increasing the number of U.S. students awarded a high school diploma four years after starting the ninth grade" as one of its leading social health indicators. A midcourse review showed that while this number has improved to just over 78%, there is still room for improvement (National Center for Health Statistics, 2016c).

Health psychologists have not been able to pinpoint the reasons for the discrepancies because, until fairly recently, what they knew about health and disease derived from research that was disproportionately concentrated on young, relatively healthy, European American research participants. Health psychologists have begun to widen the scope of their research to include a more diverse pool of people and, in many cases, to focus spe-cifically on understudied groups. For example, they have found that women and men have very different psychological, social, and biological characteristics and vulnerabilities, so they differ in their susceptibility to various diseases and in their coping reactions to stress. The same seems to be true of many different ethnic and racial groups.

Clearly, much more research is needed before health psychologists can confidently explain why there are health discrepancies among traditionally understudied groups. One attempt to fill this void was provided by the Women's Health Initiative (2010), a long-term national health study launched in 1991 that focused on the prevention of heart disease, breast and colorectal cancer, and osteoporosis in postmenopausal women. The prospec-tive study included three components:

- a randomized, controlled clinical trial of 64,500 women, testing the impact of a low-fat diet, hormone replacement therapy, and calcium–vitamin D supplementation;

- an observational study of another 100,000 women, examining the biological and psy-chological determinants of these chronic diseases in women; and

- a massive study evaluating eight different model education/prevention programs in communities throughout the United States.

As Neil Grunberg, my friend and former classmate, and a renowned NIH researcher, noted more than 25 years ago:

> Research on health and behavior should consider men and women—not because it is discriminatory not to do so—but because it is good science. The study of women and men, of young, and old, of African Americans and Caucasians, Asians, Latinos, and American Indians will all help to reveal psychosocial and biological mechanisms that are critical to understanding mortality, morbidity, and quality of life. (Baum & Grunberg, 1991, p. 84)

Challenge 3: To Achieve Equal Access to Preventive Health Care Services for All People

As we have seen throughout this book, many minorities and impoverished Americans of every ethnicity and race have historically had limited access to preventive health care. And there is a disproportionate concentration of certain minority groups in unhealthy neighborhoods. These are some of the reasons why minorities and the poor tend to suffer more health problems and have a higher mortality rate. Health psychology faces the continuing challenge of understanding barriers that limit access to health care and assisting in their removal.

Health care costs have risen sharply since the mid-twentieth century. In 1960, health care costs represented only 5.1% of the U.S. gross domestic product (GDP). By 2017, the amount spent on health care had more than tripled to 17.9% (about $10,348 per person) (Centers for Medicare and Medicaid Services [CMS], 2018). Although this amount is much higher than that of most developed nations in the world, the United States has a lower average life expectancy than that in other affluent countries, fewer physicians, and fewer hospital beds per person. In fact, the United States has, for years, ranked dead last among 11 industrialized nations as measured by such factors as access, equity, and health care outcomes, according to the 2017 Commonwealth Fund Survey (see Figure EP.6). The United Kingdom ranked best in this survey, followed by Australia (Schneider, Sarnak, Squires, Shah, & Doty, 2017).

As we have seen, one reason for these low rankings is the tremendous disparity in access and delivery of health care. The United States has the most inequitable health care system with the poorest health outcomes compared to the other Commonwealth Fund nations, each of which provides universal health care. So long as some people have access to quality health care while others have no access, we will have a two-tiered health care system in this country: state-of-the-art, high-tech care for those who have managed to get health insurance, and substandard care (or no care) for everyone else. Health care reform remains a continuing challenge—for health psychology as well as for the national political agenda.

On March 23, 2010, President Barack Obama signed into law the Patient Protection and Affordable Care Act (PPACA), the most significant overhaul of U.S. health care in nearly 50 years. The primary goals of the law were to decrease the number of people who do not have health insurance and to lower the costs of health care. This legislation was starting to make a dent in some of the equity and outcome issues but is now in danger of being repealed with no serious plan for how to replace it (Salber, 2017).

Telehealth

As discussed in Chapter 13, the digital technologies that comprise telemedicine are rapidly transforming how health care providers remotely deliver clinical services. More broadly, **telehealth** (or *eHealth)* is clinical care that is delivered remotely, and also the use of virtual tools to conduct health research, track wellness, and deliver health care education (Siddiqui and others, 2017). People increasingly are using their smartphones, digital tablets, and computers to "see" healthcare providers. At the Cleveland Clinic, for example, patients

telehealth Clinical care that is delivered remotely and the use of virtual tools to conduct health research, track wellness, and to deliver education.

COUNTRY RANKINGS	AUS	CAN	FRA	GER	NETH	NZ	NOR	SWE	SWIZ	UK	US
OVERALL RANKING (2013)	4	10	9	5	5	7	7	3	2	1	11
Quality Care	2	9	8	7	5	4	11	10	3	1	5
Effective Care	4	7	9	6	5	2	11	10	8	1	3
Safe Care	3	10	2	6	7	9	11	5	4	1	7
Coordinated Care	4	8	9	10	5	2	7	11	3	1	6
Patient-Centered Care	5	8	10	7	3	6	11	9	2	1	4
Access	8	9	11	2	4	7	6	4	2	1	9
Cost-Related Problem	9	5	10	4	8	6	3	1	7	1	11
Timeliness of Care	6	11	10	4	2	7	8	9	1	3	5
Efficiency	4	10	8	9	7	3	4	2	6	1	11
Equity	5	9	7	4	8	10	6	1	2	2	11
Healthy Lives	4	8	1	7	5	9	6	2	3	10	11
Health Expenditures/Capita, 2011**	$3,800	$4,522	$4,118	$4,495	$5,099	$3,182	$5,669	$3,925	$5,643	$3,405	$8,508

Legend: Top 2* / Middle / Bottom 2*

Notes: *Includes ties. **Expenditures shown in $US PPP (purchasing power parity); Australian $ data are from 2010.
Source: Calculated by The Commonwealth Fund based on 2011 International Health Policy Survey of Sicker Adults; 2012 International Health Policy Care Physicians; 2013 International Health Policy Survey; Commonwealth Fund *National Scorecard 2011*; World Health Organization; and Organization for Economic Cooperation and Development, *OECD Health Data, 2013* (Paris OECD, Nov. 2013).
Credit: Puwadol Jaturawutthichai/Shutterstock

Puwadol Jaturawutthichai/Shutterstock.com

FIGURE EP.6 Health Care Rankings of 11 Developed Countries Among the 11 nations compared, the U.S. health care system ranks last, as it did in 2014, 2010, 2007, 2006, and 2004. Most troubling, the U.S. system is last or near last on dimensions of access, outcomes, and equity.

Information from Schneider, E. C., Sarnak, D. O., Squires, D., Shah, A., & Doty, M. M. (2017). *Mirror, Mirror 2017: International comparison reflects flaws and opportunities for better U.S. health care.* New York: The Commonwealth Fund.

Simon Price/Alamy Stock Photo

Telehealth Patients are increasingly offered ways to interact with health care professionals via computer, cell phone, and other personal computing devices.

can receive a diagnosis or a prescription from a health care provider for nonemergency concerns, night or day, in a 10-minute virtual visit. In addition to being fast and convenient, virtual consultations generally cost less than an urgent care or emergency room visit (Cleveland Clinic, 2018).

Virtual care clinics and remote patient monitoring are proving effective at improving access to health care services and reducing health care disparities among certain populations, especially patients living in rural areas—where 46% of the world's population live (Lewis, 2016; Sabesan, 2015; World Bank, 2018). Although most patients value/prefer face-to-face contact, health care professionals increasingly report feeling comfortable with virtual consultations, and both patients and providers generally report high levels of satisfaction with health care that is delivered virtually (Gorst and others, 2016).

Challenge 4: To Adjust the Focus of Research and Intervention to Maximize Health Promotion with Evidence-Based Approaches

In the past, health psychology followed biomedicine's lead in focusing on mortality rather than on morbidity. Even when prevention was stressed, health psychologists tended to focus on those chronic diseases that were the leading causes of death. Although reducing mortality will continue to be a priority, health psychology also must devote greater attention to conditions such as arthritis, which have a minimal impact on mortality rates but a dramatic impact on wellness among the elderly.

A related challenge is to place more emphasis on health-enhancing behaviors and factors that may delay mortality and reduce morbidity. In the past, health psychologists focused more of their research on studying risk factors for chronic disease and less of their research on learning about health-promoting behaviors that help prevent people from developing illnesses. The positive psychology movement is working to address this imbalance as researchers pay greater attention to promoting healthy individuals, healthy families and communities, and healthy workplaces.

A continuing challenge for health psychology is to employ evidence-based approaches through documentation of the effectiveness of various interventions. This issue comes into sharp relief as the debate continues over the extent to which psychological interventions should be covered by managed health insurance. Even the most exciting new intervention—if backed only by weak or poorly conducted research studies—is likely to meet with the same skeptical reaction from health care professionals that many complementary and alternative therapies have faced (see Chapter 15). Complicating the research picture is the fact that true primary prevention studies often take decades to complete, and they require expensive, long-term funding. Fortunately, the Centers for Disease Control and Prevention (CDC) has shown considerable interest in continuing behavioral intervention research.

Despite health psychology's successes, much remains to be done before the goals of *Healthy People 2020* are fully met. Although health psychologists continue to focus on eliminating health disparities among various sociocultural groups, greater emphasis is also being placed on improving the health of all Americans.

Challenge 5: To Assist in Health Care Reform

Historically, health care in the United States has faced three fundamental problems: It has been far too expensive, not all citizens have had equal access to high-quality health care, and its services often have been used inappropriately. For many years, researchers therefore predicted a major revolution in the U.S. health care system. Among the issues needing to be addressed has been universal access to health care, comprehensive mandated health benefits, cost containment, quality, accountability, and a shift in emphasis from secondary prevention to primary prevention. Although the PPACA addresses many of these issues, unfortunately health care in this country continues to focus much more on expensive inpatient care (and other efforts at secondary prevention) than on cost-effective primary prevention and health promotion.

To improve health care while cutting costs is among the most pressing of needs. One of health psychology's most fundamental messages is that prevention and health promotion are effective **cost containment** strategies, and that they must be made as important in the

cost containment A systematic effort to reduce or hold down the cost of health care.

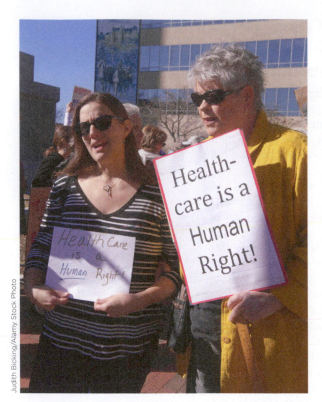

Judith Bicking/Alamy Stock Photo

Health Care as a Social Issue
As the Affordable Care Act has continued to be politically controversial, health psychologists, health professionals, and other concerned citizens have engaged in advocacy for their various points of view.

cost effectiveness Determining the efficacy of a healthcare intervention relative to its cost, and relative to the cost of alternative treatments.

quality-adjusted life year (QALY) One year of good health, free from disease and disability.

health care system as disease treatment is now. As the Institute of Medicine (IOM) (2011a) itself has noted, health promotion has substantial **cost effectiveness** and should be a standard part of medical practice; in addition, mounting evidence demonstrates the importance of shifting from a model of tertiary care to primary care. Health care also must be defined more broadly so that it doesn't focus solely on the services provided by doctors, nurses, clinicians, and hospitals. Many health psychologists emphasize the importance of patients taking responsibility for their own well-being, while also recognizing the significant roles played by the individual's family, friends, and community. More effective health care will recognize that schools, places of worship, and workplaces are major sites for promoting health and should become part of the network of interconnected services in the nation's health care system.

The role that psychologists play in improving physical health through enhancing treatment outcomes now has been firmly established (Clay, 2016). This has led to a significant increase in the number of psychologists working in general health care settings. One way to estimate the benefits of preventive actions is with combined measures of life expectancy and **quality-adjusted life years (QALY)**. One QALY equates to one year in perfect health. QALYs can be used to calculate the cost-effectiveness of various primary and secondary prevention efforts. For example, a pharmaceutical treatment, medical screening procedure, or behavior intervention that improves the quality of life by half (0.5) for two people will result in the equivalent of one QALY over a period of one year. As an example, researchers have found that regular exercise produces one QALY for as little as $2,500—a modest expenditure relative to many biomedical interventions (Wu, Cohen, Shi, Pearson, & Sturm, 2011). As another example, it is highly cost-effective to reduce distracted driving by getting people to stop texting, eating, and in other ways multitasking, but much less cost-effective to save the lives of people who have had car accidents. It is cost-effective to promote the health of children by ensuring their access to healthy food. It is much less cost-effective to provide care for the additional morbidity that may occur from pneumonia, measles, and other diseases that may occur in children who are deficient in vitamin A and other key nutrients (Skolnik, 2016).

Health care policy is not solely to blame. Several studies argue that health psychologists have not always adapted well to new integrated-care models (Clay, 2016). Although health psychologists and primary care providers generally share goals and wish to collaborate, they too often are held back from greater collaboration because of differences in their educations, clinical styles, and reimbursement systems.

Psychosocial Interventions

Health psychologists perform a wide range of activities, including training future doctors and nurses on the importance of psychosocial factors in patient adherence and recovery and directly intervening to assist patients who are facing difficult procedures and adjusting to chronic illness. Treatment interventions cover every domain of health. In the biological domain, treatment is designed to directly change specific physiological responses involved in the illness. Examples include relaxation to reduce hypertension, hypnosis to alleviate pain, and systematic desensitization to reduce the nausea that often occurs in anticipation of chemotherapy. In the psychological domain, health psychologists have applied both cognitive and behavioral interventions. Cognitive interventions include stress inoculation to decrease anxiety about an upcoming medical procedure, cognitive-behavioral treatment for depression, and anger management for hostile cardiovascular disease patients. Behavioral interventions include teaching skills to improve patient–provider communication, to develop a behavioral-change program to modify unhealthy habits, and to help train patients in self-management skills such as daily injections of insulin. Social interventions include establishing support groups for those suffering from chronic illness, providing counseling for families of the terminally ill, and conducting role-playing exercises with young children to socially "inoculate" them against being pressured by peers into risky behaviors.

Such psychosocial interventions actually can yield significant cost savings, particularly when used to prepare patients for surgery and other anxiety-producing medical procedures (Novotney, 2010b). Patients who are overly anxious when facing hospitalization and invasive procedures such as surgery often experience a disintegration of normal coping skills. Relaxation training, postsurgical exercises, distraction techniques, and control-enhancing techniques can reduce the length of hospitalization and the need for pain-relieving medication and can help prevent disruptive patient behavior. In addition, psychosocial interventions are perceived as effective and desirable both by patients and by their families (Clay, 2016).

The challenge of cost containment is likely to continue because cardiovascular disease and cancer—chronic, age-related diseases that are extraordinarily costly to treat—probably will remain the leading causes of death for some time to come. Health psychology's emphasis on prevention, if widely employed, would help contain overall expenses despite the initial cost of additional health personnel. One of the best ways to contain these costs is to help people improve their health behaviors so they avoid getting sick and to help those who become sick to recover as quickly as possible.

Integrated Primary Care

As further testimony to health psychology's future role in helping the health care system's efforts to contain costs, the Human Capital Initiative (American Psychological Association, Science Directorate, 1995) has called for greater use of integrated care (also called collaborative care or integrated care; see Chapter 13). This interdisciplinary model, in which treatment teams approach diseases from biological, psychological, and sociocultural perspectives, shows great promise in improving treatment while simultaneously cutting costs (Table EP.1).

One medical trend that affects health psychology is the use of **integrated primary care (IPC)** in treating chronic conditions (Hewitt, 2017). IPC combines medical and behavioral health services by bringing all available treatments together into an individualized intervention plan for a patient (APA, 2017b). A good example of this approach is the coordinated care available to dying patients in hospice settings. This includes palliative care for pain control; symptom management for comfort; and counseling, bereavement,

integrated primary care Care that combines medical and behavioral health services by bringing all available treatments together into an individualized intervention plan for a patient.

TABLE EP.1 Reduction in Treatment Frequency with Integrated Care

Total ambulatory care visits	−17%
Visits for minor illnesses	−35%
Pediatric acute illness visits	−25%
Office visits for acute asthma	−49%
Office visits by arthritis patients	−40%
Average length of stay in hospital for surgical patients	−1.5 days
Cesarean sections	−56%
Epidural anesthesia during labor and delivery	−85%

Information from American Psychological Association, Science Directorate. (1995). *Doing the right thing: A research plan for healthy living—A Human Capital Initiative strategy report.* Washington, DC: American Psychological Association. Human Capital Initiative Coordinating Committee.

and education for patients and families. IPC allows patients to feel that for any problem they have, they are in the right place.

As we have seen, the potential benefits of integrating health psychology into primary care include better patient retention, higher treatment adherence rates, improved outcomes, and lower cost. However, challenges remain. There is a pressing need for more research focused on health psychology interventions in real-world treatment settings. And, as with any research study that attempts to study one variable while controlling others, key issues are determining the degree of penetration of health psychology into primary care settings and clarifying the specific roles of health psychologists in integrated care (Thielke, Thompson, & Stuart, 2011).

The success of integrated care reflects health psychology's growing acceptance by traditional biomedicine over the past 30 years—a trend that is likely to continue (Clay, 2016). One sign of its acceptance is the increase in the number of psychologists working in medical schools and academic health centers—the single largest area of placement of psychologists in recent years (Association of Psychologists in Academic Health Centers (APAHC), 2016). Increasingly, medical schools recognize that a complete medical education must include, alongside the biological and physical sciences, the perspectives and research findings that have emerged from behavioral and social sciences. Psychologists have become key members of multidisciplinary clinical and research teams in many medical specialties, including family practice, pediatrics, rehabilitation, cardiology, oncology, and anesthesiology. Another sign is the growing role of nurses in delivering psychological services. An increasing number of nurses are obtaining advanced degrees in psychology, and the nursing profession has established the National Institute for Nursing Research (NINR), which focuses on controlled studies of psychological variables in nursing.

Paradoxically, as medical care has grown more specialized and more complex, it also has begun to broaden its scope, incorporating more complementary and alternative aspects of healing. Relaxation training, imagery, and some of the spiritual aspects of non-Western healing traditions are beginning to be accepted by some managed care programs because these methods are typically inexpensive and yet often effective in helping patients cope with a variety of stress-related symptoms. With ever-rising medical costs, the cost-effectiveness ratio of such interventions can't be ignored.

International Reform

As we have seen, there is great variability in the prevalence of specific diseases throughout the world. Poverty, lack of health care, and ignorance generally contribute to a higher incidence of infectious diseases in developing countries than in developed countries. Noninfectious diseases also follow this trend: For example, as smoking continues to decline in Canada and the United States, its prevalence is increasing in developing parts of the world, resulting in rising rates of lung cancer, cardiovascular disease, and emphysema.

Health psychology can take the lead in carrying the messages of the thousands of research studies from developed nations to other parts of the world in which similar health problems are just beginning to emerge. But the transmission of information can flow in both directions. Health psychologists can help reform the U.S. health care system by helping policymakers understand those things that other countries do better than we do. As an example, consider one aspect of the Australian system: well-woman/well-man clinics. The aim of these clinics is to promote the health of the total woman and man—wellness rather than treating and curing disease. These clinics, staffed by nurse-practitioners and providing care free of charge to patients, are found throughout the country. They focus not just on medicine but also on education, assessment, and nonmedicinal management of personal and family stress problems (Well Men & Women Too, 2016).

CONCLUSION

Health psychology's outlook as a profession is bright. The field has made impressive advances in its brief history, though there is much more to learn. Future health psychologists will face many challenges as they work to improve individual and community health and to help reform the health care system. I hope that your increasing understanding of health psychology will be as motivating to you—both personally and professionally—as it has been to me.

Weigh In on Health

Respond to each question below based on what you learned in the Epilogue and the entire text.

1. After having read this textbook, identify some ways that you think you could improve your health related to its biological, psychological, and social or cultural components.

2. Some friends of yours know that you have taken a class in health psychology. They want you to share your insights on the future of health care, especially how it will be influenced by the work of health psychologists. What will you tell them? What research did you read about that supports your thinking?

3. After finishing this course in health psychology, you decide to pursue health psychology as your career. What subfield of health psychology will you choose, and why: teacher, research scientist, or clinician (see Chapter 1)? Identify a goal that you would hope to accomplish in your chosen career.

Summing Up

Health Psychology's Most Important Lessons

1. The fundamental message of the biopsychosocial model of health is that behavior, mental processes, social influences, and health are intimately connected.

2. The responsibility for our health does not rest solely in the hands of health care professionals; rather, we ourselves have a major role to play in determining our overall well-being.

3. Unhealthy lifestyles are harder to change than to prevent. Good health habits are lifelong challenges that are best begun at a young age.

4. Learning to manage the stress that we encounter is crucial to our physical, psychological, and emotional well-being.

Health Psychology's Future Challenges

5. A first challenge for health psychology is to increase the average number of years that a person can expect to live in full health.

6. Historically, several measures of health have shown substantial differences among various ethnic and sociodemographic groups, as well as between the genders. Health psychology's second challenge is to reduce these discrepancies and increase our understanding of the effects of race, gender, culture, and socioeconomic status on health.

7. Many minorities and impoverished Americans of every ethnicity and race have historically had limited access to preventive health care. A third challenge for health psychology is to promote equal access to preventive health care services for all people.

8. A fourth challenge is to shift research and intervention away from a focus on chronic illness and mortality, and toward more directly promoting health and an understanding morbid conditions that greatly impact well-being.

9. A final challenge for health psychology is to assist in health care reform. Among the issues needing to be addressed are access to health care, cost containment, quality, accountability, and a shift in emphasis from secondary prevention to primary prevention.

Key Terms and Concepts to Remember

behavioral immunization, p. 513
compression of morbidity, p. 514
health-adjusted life expectancy
  (HALE), p. 515

positive health, p. 515
telehealth, p. 519
cost containment, p. 521
cost effectiveness, p. 522

quality-adjusted life years (QALY),
  p. 522
integrated primary care, p. 523

 LaunchPad macmillan learning To accompany your textbook, you have access to a number of online resources, including quizzes for every chapter of the book, flashcards, critical thinking exercises, videos, and *Check Your Health* inventories. To access these resources, please visit the Straub Health Psychology LaunchPad at **launchpadworks.com**

Glossary

abdominal obesity. Excess fat around the stomach and abdomen; also called male-pattern obesity.

A-beta fibers. Large, afferent fibers that may inhibit the transmission of pain messages to the brain.

accountable care organization (ACO). An organization of health care providers who agree to be accountable for the quality, cost, and overall care of members.

acquired immunodeficiency syndrome (AIDS). The most advanced stages of HIV infection, defined by a T cell count of less than 200 and the occurrence of opportunistic infections or HIV-related cancers that take advantage of a weakened immune system.

acupressure. The application of pressure rather than needles to the points used in acupuncture; shiatsu is a major form of acupressure.

acupuncture. A component of traditional Chinese medicine in which fine needles are inserted into the skin to relieve pain, treat addiction and illness, and promote health.

acute disorder. An illness or other medical problem that occurs over a short period of time.

acute pain. Sharp, stinging pain that is short-lived and usually related to tissue damage.

A-delta fibers. Small, afferent fibers involved in the experience of acute pain.

adherence. A patient both agreeing to and then closely following a treatment regimen as advised by his or her health care provider.

adipocytes. Collapsible body cells that store fat.

adrenal glands. Lying above the kidneys, the pair of endocrine glands that secrete epinephrine, norepinephrine, and cortisol, which are hormones that arouse the body during moments of stress.

aerobic exercise. Light- to moderate-intensity exercise performed for an extended period of time; examples include swimming, cycling, and running.

affective neuroscience. The scientific study of the neural mechanisms of emotion.

agonist. A drug that attaches to a receptor and produces neural actions that mimic or enhance those of a naturally occurring neurotransmitter.

alcohol expectancy effects. The effects of an individual's beliefs about how alcohol affects behavior.

alcohol myopia. The tendency of alcohol to increase a person's concentration on immediate events and to reduce awareness of distant events.

alcohol use disorder (AUD). A maladaptive drinking pattern in which drinking interferes with role obligations.

allostatic load (allostasis). The cumulative long-term effects of the body's physiological response to stress.

allostatic overload. The consequences of long-term elevations of stress-related catabolic hormones, including hypertension, wasted muscles, ulcers, fatigue, and increased risk of chronic disease.

alternative medicine. A broad range of health care practices that are not taught in medical schools, not generally used in hospitals, and not usually reimbursed by insurance companies.

amygdala. Two clusters of neurons in the limbic system that are linked to emotion, especially aggression.

anaerobic exercise. High-intensity exercise performed for short periods of time; examples include weight training and sprinting.

angina pectoris. A condition of extreme chest pain caused by a restriction of the blood supply to the heart.

anorexia nervosa. An eating disorder characterized by self-starvation; a distorted body image; and, in females, amenorrhea.

antagonist. A drug that blocks the action of a naturally occurring neurotransmitter or agonist.

anterior cingulate cortex (ACC). The front part of the cingulate cortex, which resembles a collar in surrounding the corpus callosum and plays a role in pain processing and many self-regulating functions.

antigen. A foreign substance that stimulates an immune response.

antimicrobial resistance. The ability of bacteria, viruses, and other microbes to resist the effect of drugs.

appraised meaning. How a particular stressor is cognitively perceived—for instance, as a challenge or threat.

arteries. Blood vessels that carry blood away from the heart to other organs and tissues; a small artery is called an arteriole.

arteriosclerosis. Also called "hardening of the arteries," a disease in which blood vessels lose their elasticity.

association cortex. Areas of the cerebral cortex that integrate multisensory information and higher mental functions such as thinking and speaking.

atherogenesis. The process of forming atheromatous plaques in the inner lining of arteries.

atheromatous plaques. Buildups of fatty deposits within the wall of an artery; occur in atherosclerosis.

atherosclerosis. A chronic disease in which cholesterol and other fats are deposited on the inner walls of the coronary arteries, reducing circulation to heart tissue.

at-risk drinking. Two or more episodes of binge drinking in the past month, or consuming an average of two or more alcoholic drinks per day in the past month.

attributable risk. The actual amount that a disease can be attributed to exposure to a particular risk factor. Attributable risk is determined by subtracting the incidence rate of a disease in people who have been exposed to a risk factor from the incidence rate of the disease in people who have not been exposed to the risk factor.

aversion therapy. A behavioral therapy that pairs an unpleasant stimulus (such as a nauseating drug) with an undesirable behavior (such as drinking or smoking), causing the patient to avoid the behavior.

basal metabolic rate (BMR). The minimum number of calories the body needs to maintain bodily functions while at rest.

behavior change technique (BCT). A theory-based method for changing one or more determinants of a health behavior, such as self-efficacy.

behavioral activation. A counseling treatment that focuses on increasing engagement in valued life activities through guided goal setting.

behavioral addiction. A new category of behaviors such as gambling that display the characteristics of substance abuse disorders.

behavioral control. Interventions that teach techniques for controlling pain and speeding recovery during and after a medical procedure.

behavioral disinhibition. The false sense of confidence and freedom from social restraints that results from alcohol consumption.

behavioral immunization. Efforts to inoculate people against unhealthy habits by exposing them to mild versions of messages that try to convince them to engage in the adverse behavior.

behavioral intention. In theories of health behavior, the rational decision to engage in a health-related behavior or to refrain from engaging in the behavior.

behavioral undercontrol. A general personality syndrome linked to alcohol dependence and characterized by aggressiveness, unconventionality, and impulsiveness; also called deviance proneness.

benefit finding. The experience of identifying positive outcomes in the face of adversity.

binge-eating disorder (BED). An eating disorder in which a person frequently consumes unusually large amounts of food.

biofeedback. A system that provides audible or visible feedback information regarding involuntary physiological states.

biological embedding. The processes by which the structure and functioning of the brain are shaped by feedback from neuroendocrine systems as they are engaged as part of the body's effort to maintain homeostasis.

biomedical model. The dominant view of twentieth-century medicine that maintains that illness always has a physical cause.

biopsychosocial model. The viewpoint that health and other behaviors are determined by the interaction of biological mechanisms, psychological processes, and social influences.

birth cohort. A group of people who, because they were born at about the same time, experience similar historical and social conditions.

blood alcohol level (BAL). The amount of alcohol in the blood, measured in grams per 100 milliliters.

blood–brain barrier. The network of tightly packed capillary cells that separates the blood and the brain.

body mass index (BMI). A measure of obesity calculated by dividing body weight by the square of a person's height.

brainstem. The oldest and most central region of the brain; includes the medulla, pons, and reticular formation.

bronchi. The pair of respiratory tubes that branch into progressively smaller passageways, the bronchioles, culminating in the air sacs within the right and left lungs (the alveoli).

buffering hypothesis. A theory that social support produces its stress-busting effects indirectly by helping the individual cope more effectively.

bulimia nervosa. An eating disorder characterized by cycles of binge eating followed by purging through such techniques as vomiting or laxative abuse.

burnout. A job-related state of physical and psychological exhaustion.

C fibers. Small, afferent fibers that are involved in the experience of chronic pain.

calorie. A measure of food energy equivalent to the amount of energy needed to raise the temperature of 1 gram of water 1 degree Celsius.

cancer. A set of diseases in which abnormal body cells multiply and spread in uncontrolled fashion, often forming a tissue mass called a tumor.

carcinogen. A cancer-causing agent such as tobacco, ultraviolet radiation, or an environmental toxin.

carcinoma. Cancer of the epithelial cells that line the outer and inner surfaces of the body; includes breast, prostate, lung, and skin cancer.

cardiorespiratory endurance. The ability of the heart, blood vessels, and lungs to supply oxygen to working muscles during physical activity for prolonged periods of time.

cardiovascular disease (CVD). Disorders of the heart and blood vessel system, including stroke and coronary heart disease (Chd).

cardiovascular reactivity (CVR). An individual's characteristic reaction to stress, including changes in heart rate, blood pressure, and hormones.

cardiovascular system. Consists of the heart, blood, and blood vessels that supply oxygen to the body.

case–control studies. A retrospective epidemiological study in which people with a disease or condition (cases) are compared with people who are not affected by the disease or condition (controls).

cell. The basic unit of structure and function in living things.

cerebellum. Located at the rear of the brain, this brain structure coordinates voluntary movement and balance.

cerebral cortex. The thin layer of cells that covers the cerebrum; the seat of conscious sensation, skilled motor responses, language, and information processing.

chiropractic. A complementary and alternative medicine approach to healing that is concerned with the diagnosis, treatment, and prevention of disorders of the neuromusculoskeletal system.

chronic illness. An illness that lasts a long time and is usually irreversible.

chronic pain. Dull, burning pain that is long-lasting.

cilia. Tiny hairs; those that line the air passageways in the nose, mouth, and trachea move in wavelike fashion, trapping germs and forcing them out of the respiratory system.

circadian rhythm. A biological clock that operates on a 24-hour cycle.

clinical pain. Pain that requires some form of medical treatment.

cognitive behavioral stress management (CBSM). A multimodal intervention that combines relaxation training, visualization, cognitive restructuring, reinforcement, and other techniques to help people cope with a range of stressors.

cognitive behavioral therapy for insomnia (CBT-I). A structured treatment for insomnia aimed at replacing thoughts and behaviors that cause or worsen sleep problems with habits that promote sound sleep without the use of medication.

cognitive control. Interventions that direct the patient's attention to the positive aspects of a procedure (such as improved health) rather than to feelings of discomfort.

cognitive reappraisal. A key component of CBT that focuses on helping individuals *reinterpret* pain-related sensations, restructure maladaptive thought patterns, and make *positive self-statements*.

cognitive-behavioral interventions. Health interventions that focus on the conditions that elicit health behaviors and the factors that help to maintain and reinforce them.

cognitive-behavioral therapy (CBT). A multidisciplinary pain-management program that combines cognitive, physical, and emotional interventions.

cognitive-behavioral therapy. The use of principles from learning theory to change unhealthy patterns of thinking and behavior.

collaborative care. A cooperative form of health care in which physicians, psychologists, and other health care providers join forces to improve patient care.

common liability to addiction. A model of addiction proposing that the likelihood a person will begin using illegal drugs is determined not by the preceding use of other specific legal drugs (gateway hypothesis), but instead by the particular tendencies and environmental circumstances of the drug user.

communicable disease (CD). A disease that is transmitted from a human to another human, from a human to an animal, or from an animal to a human.

comorbidity. The simultaneous occurrence of two or more physical and/or psychological disorders or symptoms.

comparative optimism. The tendency to think that one will experience more positive and fewer negative events than others do.

competitive foods. Foods and beverages that are often high in calories, sugar, fat, and sodium and are sold in schools in vending machines, à la carte lines, and student stores.

complementary and alternative medicine (CAM). The use and practice of therapies or diagnostic techniques that fall outside conventional biomedicine.

complementary medicine. The use of "alternative medicines" in conjunction with—rather than instead of—regular medicine. For example, the combined effect of drug and relaxation-training interventions for hypertension exceeds that of either the drug or relaxation by itself, and relaxation may reduce the doses of the drug needed.

compression of morbidity. Efforts to limit the time that an older person spends ill or disabled.

compulsive exercise. Physical activity that becomes obsessive and causes dysfunction in a person's life.

concordance rate. The rate of agreement between a pair of twins for a given trait; a pair of twins is concordant for the trait if both of them have it or if neither has it.

confirmation bias. A form of faulty reasoning in which our expectations prevent us from seeing alternative explanations for our observations.

consideration of future consequences. The extent to which individuals consider and are influenced by the potential future outcomes of their behavior.

contingency contract. A formal agreement between a person attempting to change a health behavior and another individual, such as a therapist, regarding the consequences of target behaviors.

conventional medicine. Biomedically based medicine as practiced by holders of the MD (medical doctor) or DO (doctor of osteopathy) degrees and their allied health professionals.

coping. The cognitive, behavioral, and emotional ways in which we manage stressful situations.

coronary heart disease (CHD). A chronic disease in which the arteries that supply the heart become narrowed or clogged; results from either atherosclerosis or arteriosclerosis.

correlation coefficient. A statistical measure of the strength and direction of the relationship between two variables, and thus of how well one predicts the other.

corticosteroids. Hormones produced by the adrenal cortex that fight inflammation, promote healing, and trigger the release of stored energy.

cost containment. A systematic effort to reduce or hold down the cost of health care.

cost effectiveness. Determining the efficacy of a healthcare intervention relative to its cost, and relative to the cost of alternative treatments.

counterirritation. Analgesia in which one pain (for example, a pulled muscle) is relieved by creating another counteracting sensation (such as rubbing near the site of the injury).

critical thinking. A skeptical attitude that encourages health care providers and researchers to evaluate evidence and scrutinize conclusions.

cross-sectional study. A type of observational study in which data are collected from a population, or representative subset, *at one specific point in time.*

cytokines. Protein molecules produced by immune cells that act on other cells to regulate immunity (including the interferons, interleukins, and tumor necrosis factors).

debrief. The process in which research participants are given more details about the study following its completion.

delay behavior. The tendency to avoid seeking medical care because symptoms go unnoticed (appraisal delay), sickness seems unlikely (illness delay), professional help is deemed unnecessary (behavioral delay), the individual procrastinates in making an appointment (scheduling delay), or the perceived costs of treatment outweigh the perceived benefits (treatment delay).

dependence. A state in which the use of a drug is required for a person to function normally.

descriptive study. A research method in which researchers observe and record participants' behaviors, often forming hypotheses that are later tested more systematically; includes case studies, interviews and surveys, focus groups, and observational studies.

diathesis–stress model. The model that proposes that two interacting factors determine an individual's susceptibility to stress and illness: predisposing factors in the person (such as genetic vulnerability) and precipitating factors from the environment (such as traumatic experiences).

digestive system. The body's system for digesting food; includes the digestive (gastrointestinal, or GI) tract, salivary glands, pancreas, liver, and gallbladder.

direct effect hypothesis. A theory that social support produces its beneficial effects during both stressful and nonstressful times by enhancing the body's physical responses to challenging situations.

discriminative stimuli. Environmental signals that certain behaviors will be followed by reinforcement.

disengagement. A coping strategy aimed at distancing oneself from a stressful situation.

dispositional affect. A person's coping style or personality dimension consisting of a tendency toward chronic negative emotions and distress (negative affectivity), or positive emotions and subjective well-being (positive affectivity).

drug abuse. The use of a drug to the extent that it impairs the user's biological, psychological, or social well-being.

drug potentiation. The effect of one drug to increase the effects of another.

dynamic tailoring. The delivery of individualized and targeted health messages over multiple periods of time.

eating disorder (ED). "Illnesses in which the people experience severe disturbances in their eating behaviors and related thoughts and emotions" (American Psychiatric Association, 2018).

e-cigarettes (EC). Battery-powered vaporizers that simulate smoking without burning tobacco.

ecological momentary assessment (EMA). A method of measuring stress that involves repeated sampling of people's behaviors and experiences in real time and in their natural environments.

ecological-systems approach. The viewpoint that nature is best understood as a hierarchy of systems, in which each system is simultaneously composed of smaller subsystems and larger, interrelated systems.

eHealth literacy. How well a person navigates, understands, and uses electronic health information.

emotional cascade. Becoming so focused on an upsetting event that one gets worked into an intense, painful state of negative emotion.

emotional disclosure. A therapeutic activity in which people express their strong, often stress-related, emotions by writing or talking about the events that triggered the emotions.

emotional-approach coping (EAC). The process of working through, clarifying, and understanding the emotions triggered by a stressor.

emotion-focused coping. A coping strategy in which we try to control our emotional response to a stressor.

endocrine system. Consists of glands that secrete hormones, chemical messengers that regulate bodily functions.

endogenous opiate peptides. Opiatelike substances naturally produced by the body.

enkephalins. Endogenous (naturally occurring) opioids found in nerve endings of cells in the brain and spinal cord that bind to opioid receptors.

epidemic. Literally, among the people; an epidemic disease is one that spreads rapidly among many individuals in a community at the same time.

epidemiological transition. A shift in the disease pattern of a population as mortality falls: acute, infectious diseases are reduced, while chronic, noncommunicable diseases increase in prevalence.

epidemiology. The scientific study of the frequency, distribution, and causes of a particular disease or other health outcome in a population.

epigenetic. The effects of environmental forces on how genes are expressed.

etiology. The scientific study of the causes or origins of specific diseases.

evidence-based medicine. An approach to health care that promotes the collection, interpretation, and integration of current best evidence in making decisions about the care of individual patients or the delivery of health services.

expressive writing. A technique that promotes emotional disclosure through writing, or journaling, about our feelings.

family therapy. A type of psychotherapy in which individuals within a family learn healthier ways to interact with each other and resolve conflicts.

fee-for-service. A payment model in which health care services are paid for by patients out of pocket at the time of treatment.

fetal alcohol syndrome (FAS). A cluster of birth defects—including facial abnormalities, low intelligence, and delayed body growth—caused by the mother's use of alcohol during pregnancy.

food deserts. Geographical areas with little or no access to foods needed to maintain a healthy diet.

food security. Having reliable access to a sufficient quantity of affordable, nutritious food.

free nerve endings. Sensory receptors found throughout the body that respond to temperature, pressure, and painful stimuli.

functional plasticity. The brain's ability to move functions from damaged areas to undamaged ones.

gain-framed message. A health message that focuses on attaining positive outcomes or avoiding undesirable ones by adopting a health-promoting behavior.

gate control theory (GCT). The idea that there is a neural "gate" in the spinal cord that regulates the experience of pain.

gateway drug. A drug that serves as a stepping-stone to the use of other, usually more dangerous, drugs.

general adaptation syndrome (GAS). Selye's term for the body's reaction to stress, which consists of three stages: alarm, resistance, and exhaustion.

genome. The complete instructions for making an organism, including all the genetic material found in that organism's chromosomes.

genomics. The study of the structure, function, and mapping of the genetic material of organisms.

genotype. The sum total of all the genes present in an individual.

glucocorticoid receptor (GCR) resistance model. The idea that chronic stress promotes the development and progression of disease by reducing the sensitivity of immune system receptors to glucocorticoid hormones such as cortisol, thereby interfering with the body's ability to regulate the inflammatory response.

glycemic control. The action of monitoring glucose levels to keep blood sugar at a stable, healthy level.

guided imagery. The use of one or more external devices to assist in relaxation and the formation of clear, strong, positive mental images.

health behavior. A health-enhancing behavior or habit.

health belief model (HBM). A nonstage theory that identifies four factors that influence decision making regarding health behavior: perceived susceptibility to a health threat, perceived severity of the disease or condition, perceived benefits of and barriers to the behavior, and cues to action.

health disparities. Preventable differences in the burden of disease, injury, violence, or opportunities to achieve optimal health that are experienced by socially disadvantaged populations.

health habit. An automatic health behavior that has become a firmly established part of everyday life.

health literacy. The capacity to obtain and understand health information and services, and to use them to make appropriate decisions about one's health.

health maintenance organization (HMO). An organization that provides managed care, in which individuals pay a fixed monthly rate and use services as needed.

health psychology. The application of psychological principles and research to the enhancement of health and the prevention and treatment of illness.

health. A state of complete physical, mental, and social well-being.

health-adjusted life expectancy (HALE). The number of healthy, well years a person can expect to live free from disease and disability.

hemophilia. A genetic disease in which the blood fails to clot quickly enough, causing uncontrollable bleeding from even the smallest cut.

hemostasis. The process that causes bleeding to stop via the aggregation of platelets and the coagulation of blood.

hippocampus. A structure in the brain's limbic system linked to spatial orientation, learning, and memory.

holistic medicine. An approach to medicine that considers not only physical health but also the emotional, spiritual, social, and psychological well-being of the person.

homeostasis. The tendency to maintain a balanced or constant internal state; the regulation of any aspect of body chemistry, such as the level of glucose in the blood, around a particular set point.

hormones. Chemical messengers released into the bloodstream by endocrine glands, which have an effect on distant organs.

human immunodeficiency virus (HIV). A virus that infects cells of the immune system, destroying or impairing their function.

humoral theory. A concept of health proposed by Hippocrates that considered wellness a state of perfect equilibrium among four basic body fluids, called humors. Sickness was believed to be the result of disturbances in the balance of humors.

hyperalgesia. A condition in which a chronic pain sufferer becomes more sensitive to pain over time.

hypertension. A sustained elevation of diastolic and systolic blood pressure (exceeding 140/90).

hypnosis. A social interaction in which one person (the hypnotist) suggests to another person that certain thoughts, feelings, perceptions, or behaviors will occur.

hypothalamic-pituitary-adrenocortical (HPA) axis. The body's delayed response to stress, involving the secretion of corticosteroid hormones from the adrenal cortex.

hypothalamus. Lying just below the thalamus, the region of the brain that influences hunger, thirst, body temperature, and sexual behavior; helps govern the endocrine system via the pituitary gland.

illness anxiety disorder. The condition of experiencing abnormal anxiety over one's health, often including imaginary symptoms.

illness intrusiveness. The extent to which a chronic illness disrupts an individual's life by interfering with valued activities and interests and reducing perceptions of personal control, self-efficacy, and self-esteem.

illness representations. How a person views a particular illness, including its label and symptoms, perceived causes, timeline, consequences, and controllability.

immigrant paradox. The finding that, although low socioeconomic status usually predicts poor health, this is not true for some ethnic groups, such as Hispanics, in the United States.

immune surveillance theory. The theory that cells of the immune system play a monitoring function in searching for and destroying abnormal cells such as those that form tumors.

immunocompetence. The overall ability of the immune system, at any given time, to defend the body against the harmful effects of foreign agents.

immunotherapy. Chemotherapy in which medications are used to support or enhance the immune system's ability to selectively target cancer cells.

incidence. The number of new cases of a disease or condition that occur in a specific population within a defined time interval.

informational control. Patients' knowledge regarding the particular procedures and physical sensations that accompany a medical treatment.

informed consent. Permission granted by a client, patient, or research participant with full knowledge of the potential risks involved in a treatment, procedure, or research study.

injury control. Systematic efforts to prevent injuries from occurring and to limit the consequences of those that have already occurred.

insomnia. A persistent problem in falling or staying asleep.

integrated primary care. Care that combines medical and behavioral health services by bringing all available treatments together into an individualized intervention plan for a patient.

integrative medicine. A multidisciplinary approach to medicine that involves traditional biomedical interventions, as well as complementary and alternative medical practices that have been proven both safe and effective.

integumentary system. Includes the skin, hair, nails, and sweat glands.

intentional injury. Harm that results from behaviors designed to hurt oneself or others.

interoception. The sense that helps you understand and feel what's going on in your body.

John Henryism (JH). An active style of coping with psychosocial stressors by expending high levels of effort; a syndrome that may promote hypertension and has been especially documented among lower-SES individuals.

Kaposi's sarcoma. A rare cancer of the blood vessels that serve the skin, mucous membranes, and other glands in the body.

Lamaze training. A natural childbirth process designed to prepare prospective parents by enhancing their informational, cognitive, and behavioral control over childbirth.

lay referral system. An informal network of family members, friends, and other nonprofessionals who offer their own impressions, experiences, and recommendations regarding a set of bodily symptoms.

leptin. The weight-signaling hormone monitored by the hypothalamus as an index of body fat.

leukemia. Cancer of the blood and blood-producing system.

limbic system. A network of neurons surrounding the central core of the brain; associated with emotions such as fear and aggression; includes the hypothalamus, the amygdala, and the hippocampus.

longitudinal study. A study in which a single group of people is observed over a long span of time.

loss-framed message. A health message that focuses on a negative outcome from failing to perform a health-promoting behavior.

lymphocytes. Antigen-fighting white blood cells produced in the bone marrow.

lymphoma. Cancer of the body's lymph system; includes Hodgkin's disease and non-Hodgkin's lymphoma.

malingering. Making believe that one is ill in order to benefit from sick role behavior.

managed care. A system of health care in which health insurance plans contract with providers and medical facilities to provide care for members at reduced rates.

massification. The transformation of a product or service that once was available to only the wealthy such that it becomes accessible to everyone. Applied to education and health, it is the idea that college can benefit everyone.

matching hypothesis. The idea that social support is beneficial to the extent that it meets an individual's specific needs.

meaning-focused coping. A coping strategy in which a person attempts to find meaning in a stressful situation or traumatic event, rather than trying to change the situation or event or alter the distress associated with it.

medulla. The brainstem region that controls heartbeat and breathing.

melanoma. A potentially deadly form of cancer that strikes the melatonin-containing cells of the skin.

meta-analysis. A quantitative technique that combines the results of many studies examining the same effect or phenomenon.

metabolic flexibility. The body's ability to switch fuel sources, from carbohydrates to fats, when needed.

metabolic syndrome (MetS). A cluster of conditions—including increased blood pressure, high blood sugar level, abdominal obesity, low HDL ("good") cholesterol level, and high triglyceride level—that occur together and increase a person's risk of heart disease, stroke, and diabetes.

metastasis. The process by which malignant body cells proliferate in number and spread to surrounding body tissues.

mHealth. The use of smartphones and other mobile technologies to promote health and well-being.

microaggressions. Insults, indignities, and marginalizing messages sent by well-intentioned people who seem unaware of the hidden messages that they are sending.

microbiota (microbiome). The bacteria and other micro-organisms of a particular habitat, such as the gastrointestinal tract.

microbiota-gut-brain axis (MGBA). A bidirectional communication system that links the central nervous system with the enteric nervous system.

mindfulness meditation. The practice of paying nonjudgmental, in-the-moment attention to changing perceptions and thoughts.

mindfulness-based stress reduction (MBSR). A form of therapy that focuses on using structured meditation to promote mindfulness—a moment-to-moment, nonjudgmental awareness.

minority stress theory. The concept that proposes that health disparities among minority individuals are due to chronically high levels of stress experienced by members of stigmatized groups.

morbidity. As a measure of health, the number of cases of a specific illness, injury, or disability in a given group of people at a given time.

mortality. As a measure of health, the number of deaths due to a specific cause in a given group of people at a given time.

motor cortex. Lying at the rear of the frontal lobes, the region of the cerebral cortex that controls voluntary movements.

multiple chronic conditions (MCC). Two or more chronic conditions (lasting a year or more, requiring medical attention, and/or limiting daily activities) that affect a person at the same time.

muscle dysmorphia (MD). A psychological disorder, more common in males, in which body image dissatisfaction is accompanied by an excessive desire to develop a more muscular build.

muscular system. Includes the body's skeletal, cardiac, and visceral muscle tissues.

myocardial infarction (MI). A heart attack; the permanent death of heart tissue in response to an interruption of blood supply to the myocardium.

narcolepsy. A sleep disorder characterized by uncontrollable sleep attacks.

naturopathic medicine. The system that aims to provide holistic health care by drawing from several traditional healing systems, including homeopathy, herbal remedies, and traditional Chinese medicine.

negative emotionality. A state of alcohol abuse characterized by depression and anxiety.

nervous system. Consists of all the neurons in the body; the central nervous system includes the brain and spinal cord, and the peripheral nervous system includes the body's other nerves.

neuromatrix. The neural network that integrates sensory information with emotional and cognitive states to determine a person's experience of pain.

neuropathic pain. Pain caused by damaged nerve fibers that send incorrect signals to the brain.

neurotransmitters. Chemical messengers released by a neuron at synapses that communicate across the synaptic gap and alter the electrical state of a receiving neuron.

nicotine-titration model. The theory that smokers who are physically dependent on nicotine regulate their smoking to maintain a steady level of the drug in their bodies.

nocebo. A harmless substance that nevertheless creates harmful effects in a person who takes it.

nociceptor. A specialized neuron that responds to painful stimuli.

nonadherence. The condition in which a patient refuses to complete a prescribed therapeutic regimen.

noncommunicable disease (NCD). A noninfectious disease; one that is nontransmissible (not passed from person to person); often a chronic disease, such as cardiovascular disease, cancer, or diabetes.

nucleus accumbens (NAC). A brain region that plays a central role in pleasure and addiction.

nurse-practitioner. An advanced-practice nurse who, in addition to training in traditional nursing, received training in the delivery of primary health care.

obesity. Excessive accumulation of body fat.

observational studies. A nonexperimental research method in which a researcher observes and records the behavior of a research participant.

occupational health psychology (OHP). The application of psychology to improving the quality of work life, and to protecting and promoting the safety, health and well-being of workers.

organ. A group of tissues working together to perform a specific function.

osteopathic medicine. A form of medical practice that provides all the benefits of conventional allopathic medicine, including prescription drugs and surgery, and emphasizes the interrelationship between the structure and function of the human body.

osteoporosis. A disease of the bones involving a loss of bone mineral density that leads to an increased risk of fracture.

overweight. Body weight that exceeds the desirable weight for a person of a given height, age, and body shape.

pain behaviors. Actions that are a response to pain, such as taking drugs, grimacing, or taking time off from school or work.

pain-management program. An individualized, multimodal intervention aimed at modifying chronic pain through neurological, cognitive, and behavioral strategies.

pandemic. A disease or ailment that affects people over a large geographical area, such as multiple continents or worldwide; for example, the global HIV/AIDS epidemic.

pathogen. A virus, bacterium, or some other microorganism that causes a particular disease.

Patient Protection and Affordable Care Act (PPACA). A federal law aimed at reducing the number of people in the United States who do not have health insurance, as well as lowering the costs of health care.

patient-centered health care. The delivery of health care services that are respectful of and responsive to individual patient preferences, needs, and values.

periaqueductal gray (PAG). A region of the midbrain that plays an important role in the perception of pain; electrical stimulation in this region activates a descending neural pathway that produces analgesia by "closing the pain gate."

phantom limb pain. Pain following amputation of a limb; false pain sensations that appear to originate in the missing limb.

phenotype. A person's observable characteristics; determined by the interaction of the individual's genotype with the environment.

physical activity. Bodily movement produced by skeletal muscles that requires expenditure of energy.

physical exercise. Physical activity that is planned, repetitive, and purposeful in the sense that it is intended to improve or maintain one or more aspects of physical fitness.

physical fitness. A set of attributes relating to the ability to perform physical activity that includes muscular strength, endurance, flexibility, and healthy body composition.

physician assistant (PA). A graduate of a training program that teaches how to practice medicine under the direction of physicians and surgeons.

pituitary gland. Controlled by the hypothalamus, this gland releases a variety of hormones that act on other glands throughout the body.

positive health. The scientific study of health assets, which are factors that produce longer life, reduce illness, and increase overall well-being.

positive health. The scientific study of behaviors and traits that are associated with longer life, reduced morbidity, lower health care expenditure, and greater recuperative power.

positive psychology. The study of optimal human functioning and the healthy interplay between people and their environments.

post-traumatic growth (PTG). Positive psychological change experienced as the result of struggle with a highly challenging life circumstance. Also referred to as *benefit finding, or thriving*.

post-traumatic stress disorder (PTSD). A psychological disorder triggered by exposure to an extreme traumatic stressor, such as combat or a natural disaster. Symptoms of PTSD include haunting memories and nightmares of the traumatic event, extreme mental distress, and unwanted flashbacks.

poverty income ratio (PIR). The ratio of household income to the poverty threshold after accounting for inflation and family size.

preferred-provider organization (PPO). A managed-care network of physicians, hospitals, and other health care providers who agree to charge preestablished rates for specific services.

prevalence. The total number of diagnosed cases of a disease or condition that exist at a given time.

primary appraisal. A person's initial determination of an event's meaning, whether irrelevant, benign-positive, or threatening.

primary prevention. Health-enhancing efforts to prevent disease or injury from occurring.

probiotics. Bacteria that help maintain the natural balance of organisms (microflora) in the intestines and help promote a healthy digestive system.

problem-focused coping. A coping strategy for dealing directly with a stressor, in which we either reduce the stressor's demands or increase our resources for meeting its demands.

progressive muscle relaxation. A form of relaxation training that reduces muscle tension through a series of tensing and relaxing exercises involving the body's major muscle groups.

prospective study. A forward-looking longitudinal study that begins with a healthy group of subjects and follows the development of a particular disease in that sample.

prostaglandin. The chemical substance responsible for localized pain and inflammation; prostaglandin also causes free nerve endings to become more and more sensitized as time passes.

psychoactive drugs. Drugs that affect mood, behavior, and thought processes by altering the functioning of neurons in the brain; they include stimulants, depressants, and hallucinogens.

psychological control. The belief that we make our own decisions and determine what we do and what others do to us.

psychoneuroimmunology (PNI). The field of research that emphasizes the interaction of psychological, neural, and immunological processes in stress and illness.

psychosomatic medicine. A branch of psychiatry that developed in the 1900s and focused on the diagnosis and treatment of certain diseases believed to be caused by emotional conflicts.

qualitative research. Research that focuses on qualities instead of quantities. Participants' expressed ideas are often part of qualitative studies.

quality-adjusted life years (QALY). One year of good health, free from disease and disability.

quasi-experiment. A study comparing two groups that differ naturally on a specific variable of interest.

randomized clinical trial. A true experiment that tests the effects of one independent variable (such as a particular drug or treatment) on individuals or on groups of individuals (community field trials).

rapid eye movement (REM). Rapid eye movement sleep; a sleep stage during which vivid dreams occur.

reactivity. Our physiological reaction to stress, which varies by individual and affects our vulnerability to illness.

reactivity hypothesis. The hypothesis that individuals who show large changes in blood pressure and vascular resistance to stress have increased risk of developing heart disease.

recurrent pain. Pain that involves episodes of discomfort that recur for more than three months interspersed with periods in which the individual is relatively pain-free.

referred pain. Pain manifested in an area of the body that is sensitive to pain but caused by disease or injury in an area of the body that has few pain receptors.

regulatory control. The various ways in which we modulate our thinking, emotions, and behavior over time and across changing circumstances.

relapse prevention. Training in coping skills and other techniques intended to help people resist falling back into old health habits following a successful behavioral intervention.

relative risk. A statistical indicator of the likelihood of a causal relationship between a particular health risk factor and a health outcome; computed as the ratio of the incidence (or prevalence) of a health condition in a group exposed to the risk factor to its incidence (or prevalence) in a group not exposed to the risk factor.

relaxation response. A meditative state of relaxation in which metabolism slows and blood pressure lowers.

repressive coping. An emotion-focused coping style in which we attempt to inhibit our emotional responses, especially in social situations, so we can view ourselves as imperturbable.

reproductive system. The organs that make procreation possible; includes the male and female gonads and genitals.

resilience. The quality that allows some people to bounce back from difficult events that might otherwise disrupt their well-being.

resilience. The capacity of the brain and body to withstand challenges to homeostasis.

respiratory sinus arrhythmia (RSA). Variability in heart rate in synchrony with breathing.

respiratory system. Consists of the lungs and airway through which we inhale air and exhale carbon dioxide.

reticular formation. A network of neurons running through the brainstem involved with sleep, alertness, and arousal.

retrospective studies. A longitudinal study that looks back at the history of a group of people, often one suffering from a particular disease or condition.

retrovirus. A virus that copies its genetic information onto the DNA of a host cell.

rumination. Repetitive focusing on the causes, meanings, and consequences of stressful experiences.

sarcoma. Cancer that strikes muscles, bones, and cartilage.

scatterplot. A graphed cluster of data points, each of which represents the values of two variables in a descriptive study.

secondary appraisal. A person's determination of whether his or her own resources and abilities are sufficient to meet the demands of an event that is appraised as potentially threatening or challenging.

secondary prevention. Actions taken to identify and treat an illness or disability early in its course.

self-limiting conditions. A condition that tends to improve with the passage of time, even in the absence of treatment.

self-monitoring. People keeping track of their own target behavior that is to be modified, including the stimuli associated with it and the consequences that follow it.

sensory cortex. Lying at the front of the parietal lobes, the region of the cerebral cortex that processes body sensations such as touch.

set-point hypothesis. The idea that each person's body weight is genetically set within a given range, or set point, that the body works hard to maintain.

sexually transmitted infection (STI). Infections that are spread primarily through person-to-person sexual contact.

shaman. A general term used for the practitioner of folk medicine who often uses herbs and a range of rituals to effect cures; also referred to as "medicine man" or "medicine woman."

short sleep duration. Sleeping less than 7 hours each night.

skeletal system. Consists of 206 bones and the body's network of cartilage, ligaments, and tendons.

sleep apnea. A sleep disorder characterized by temporary cessations of breathing.

sleep disorder. Any problem with sleeping.

social inhibition. A characteristic of people who have difficulty expressing their feelings and seem to be driven by a need to avoid negative interactions with other people.

social integration. The number of social roles a person participates in.

social-evaluative threat. A stressor in which people fear negative evaluation by others of their appearance or ability.

socioeconomic status (SES). A person's position in society as determined by education, income, and occupation.

statistical literacy. The ability to read and interpret statistics and to think critically about arguments that use statistics as evidence.

stem cells. Early, undifferentiated biological cells with the potential to develop into any other type of specialized cell.

stereotype threat. The experience of stress in a situation where a person's ability, appearance, or other characteristic has the potential to confirm a negative viewpoint about his or her social group.

stimulus-control intervention. A behavioral intervention aimed at modifying the environmental discriminative stimuli that control a target behavior by signaling its reinforcement.

stress eating. Eating in the absence of hunger when we are upset, anxious, or under stress.

stress inoculation training. A cognitive behavioral treatment in which people identify stressors in their lives and learn skills for coping with them so that when those stressors occur, the people are able to put those skills into effect.

stress management. The various psychological methods designed to reduce the impact of potentially stressful experiences.

stress. The process by which we perceive and respond to events, called stressors, that we appraise as threatening or challenging.

stress-induced analgesia (SIA). A stress-related increase in tolerance to pain, presumably mediated by the body's endorphin system.

stressor. Any event or situation that triggers coping adjustments.

stroke. A cerebrovascular accident that results in damage to the brain due to lack of oxygen; usually caused by atherosclerosis or arteriosclerosis.

subjective norm. An individual's interpretation of the views of other people regarding a particular health-related behavior.

subjective well-being. The cognitive and emotional evaluations of a person's life.

substance P. A neurotransmitter secreted by pain fibers in the spinal cord that stimulates the transmission cells to send pain signals to the brain.

substance use disorder (SUD). A pattern of behavior characterized by impaired control, social impairment, and risky use of a drug.

substantia gelatinosa. The dorsal region of the spinal cord where both fast and slow pain fibers synapse with sensory nerves on their way to the brain.

sympatho-adreno-medullary (SAM) axis. The body's initial, rapid-acting response to stress, involving the release of epinephrine and norepinephrine from the adrenal medulla under the direction of the sympathetic nervous system.

systematic desensitization. A form of behavior therapy, commonly used for overcoming phobias, in which the person is exposed to a series of increasingly fearful situations while remaining deeply relaxed.

tai chi. A form of "moving meditation" that blends exercise, dance, and concentration, and is a component of traditional Chinese medicine.

telehealth. Clinical care that is delivered remotely; the use of virual tools to conduct health research, track wellness, and to deliver education.

telemedicine. The delivery of medical information and clinical services through interactive audiovisual media.

tend and befriend. The human tendency to respond to stress by seeking the company of other people and nurturing offspring.

teratogens. Drugs, chemicals, and environmental agents that can damage the developing person during fetal development.

tertiary prevention. Actions taken to contain damage once a disease or disability has progressed beyond its early stages.

thalamus. The brain's sensory switchboard; located on top of the brainstem, this brain structure routes messages to the higher brain regions.

theory of planned behavior (TPB). A theory that predicts health behavior on the basis of three factors: personal attitude toward the behavior, the subjective norm regarding the behavior, and perceived degree of control over the behavior.

thriving. A paradoxical outcome in which adversity somehow leads people to greater psychological and/or physical well-being.

tissue. A group of similar cells organized into a functional unit.

traditional Chinese medicine (TCM). An ancient, integrated herb- and acupuncture-based system of healing founded on the principle that internal harmony is essential for good health.

transactional model. Lazarus's theory that the experience of stress depends as much on the individual's cognitive appraisal of a potential stressor's impact as it does on the event or situation itself.

transcutaneous electrical nerve stimulation (TENS). A counterirritation form of analgesia involving electrically stimulating spinal nerves near a painful area.

transtheoretical model (TTM) (stages of change model). A stage theory that contends that people pass through five stages in altering health-related behavior: precontemplation, contemplation, preparation, action, and maintenance.

Type 1 diabetes. An autoimmune disorder in which insulin-producing cells of the pancreas are destroyed.

Type 2 diabetes. A metabolic illness in which the body fails to produce enough insulin or fails to use insulin properly.

Type A. A personality type found in competitive, hurried, hostile people who may be at increased risk for developing cardiovascular disease.

Type B. A personality type found in more relaxed people who are not pressured by time considerations and thus tend to be coronary disease–resistant.

Type D. A personality type found in people who tend to experience negative emotions and have difficulty expressing their feelings.

unintentional injury. Harm that is accidental, not meant to occur.

urinary (renal) system. Includes the kidneys, bladder, ureters, and urethra.

veins. Blood vessels that carry blood back to the heart from the capillaries.

vitalism. The concept of a general life force, popular in some varieties of complementary and alternative medicine.

wanting-and-liking theory. A two-stage theory of drug addiction. In the first stage, the original good feelings from drug use prevail; in the second stage, drug use becomes an automated behavior.

weight cycling. Repeated weight gains and losses through repeated dieting.

weight stigma. Prejudice and discrimination directed at people based on their weight or body size.

withdrawal. The unpleasant physical and psychological symptoms that occur when a person abruptly ceases using certain drugs.

yoga. A movement-based form of relaxation and meditation that combines diet, physical postures, and breathing to promote physical and spiritual well-being.

References

Abbasi, J. (2018). Another nail in the coffin for fish oil supplements. *Journal of the American Medical Association, 319*(18), 1851–1852.

Abbey, A., Parkhill, M. R., Buck, P. O., & Saenz, C. (2007). Condom use with a sexual partner: What distinguishes college students' use when intoxicated? *Psychology of Addictive Behaviors, 21*(1), 76–83.

Abele, A. E., & Vollmer, J. (2011). Dual-career couples: Specific challenges for work-life integration. In S. Kaiser, M. J. Ringlstetter, D. R. Eikhof, & M. Pina e Cunha (Eds.), *Creating balance: International perspectives on the work-life integration of professionals* (pp. 173–192). Berlin, Germany: Springer-Verlag.

Abi-Saleh, B., Iskandar, S. B., Elgharib, N., & Cohen, M. V. (2008). C-reactive protein: The harbinger of cardiovascular diseases. *Southern Medical Journal, 101*, 525–533.

Abraido-Lanza, A. F. (2004). Social support and psychological adjustment among Latinas with arthritis: A test of a theoretical model. *Annals of Behavioral Medicine, 27*(3), 162–171.

Abutaleb, Y. (2018, February 14). U.S. healthcare spending to climb 5.3 percent in 2018. *Reuters.* Retrieved from https://www.reuters.com/article/us-usa-healthcare-spending/u-s-healthcare-spending-to-climb-5-3-percent-in-2018-agency-idUSKCN1FY2ZD

Accreditation Council for Graduate Medical Education (ACGME). (2017). *Common program requirements.* Retrieved from http://www.acgme.org/What-We-Do/Accreditation/Common-Program-Requirements

Accreditation Council for Graduate Medical Education (ACGME). (2018). *Common program requirements.* Retrieved from http://www.acgme.org/What-We-Do/Accreditation/Common-Program-Requirements

Acevedo, M., Kramer, V., Bustamante, M. J., Yanez, F., Guidi, D., Corbalan, R., ... Fernandez, M. (2013). Exercise and cardiac rehabilitation in secondary cardiovascular prevention. *Revista Medica de Chile, 141*(10), 1307–1314.

Adams, J. (2012). Consideration of immediate and future consequences, smoking status, and body mass index. *Health Psychology, 31*(2), 260–263.

Adams, K. F., Schatzkin, A., Harris, T. B., Kipnis, V., Mouw, T., & Ballard-Barbash, R. (2006). Overweight, obesity, and mortality in a large prospective cohort of persons 50 to 71 years old. *The New England Journal of Medicine, 355*, 763–778.

Adams, M. A., Norman, G. J., Hovell, M. F., Sallis, J. F., & Patrick, K. (2009). Reconceptualizing decisional balance in an adolescent sun protection intervention: Mediating effects and theoretical interpretations. *Health Psychology, 28*(2), 217–225.

Adams, P., & Mylander, M. (1998). *Gesundheit! Bringing good health to you, the medical system, and society through physician service, contemporary therapies, humor, and joy.* Rochester, NY: Inner Traditions International.

Adams, P. F., Kirzinger, W. K., & Martinez, M. E. (2012). Summary health statistics for the U.S. population: National Health Interview Survey, 2011. Hyattsville, MD: National Center for Health Statistics. *Vital and Health Statistics, 10*(255). Retrieved from http://www.cdc.gov/nchs/data/series/sr_10/sr10_255.pdf

Ader, R., & Cohen, N. (1985). CNS-immune system interactions: Conditioning phenomena. *Behavioral and Brain Sciences, 8,* 379–394.

Adler, N. E., & Rehkopf, D. H. (2008). U.S. disparities in health: Descriptions, causes, and mechanisms. *Annual Review of Public Health, 29,* 235–252.

Adler, N. E., & Stewart, J. (2010). Preface to the biology of disadvantage: Socioeconomic status and health. *Annals of the New York Academy of Sciences, 1186*(1), 1–4.

Advokat, R. M., Comaty, J. E., & Julien, R. M. (2014). *Julien's primer of drug action* (13th ed.). New York, NY: Worth.

Agras, W. S., Brandt, H. A., Bulik, C. M., Dolan-Sewell, R., Fairburn, C. G., & Halmi, K. A. (2004). Report of the National Institutes of Health workshop on overcoming barriers to treatment research in anorexia nervosa. *International Journal of Eating Disorders, 35,* 506–521.

Ain, M. (2016, June 23). "I didn't think I'd see 30," says Greg Louganis. *ESPN The Magazine: Body Issue 2016.* Retrieved from http://www.espn.com/olympics/story/_/page/bodygreglouganis/olympic-diver-greg-louganis-living-hiv-staying-fit-56-body-issue-2016

al'Absi, M., Hatsukama, D., Davis, G. L., & Wittmers, L. E. (2004). Prospective examination of effects of smoking abstinence on cortisol and withdrawal symptoms as predictors of early smoking relapse. *Drug and Alcohol Dependence, 73*(3), 267–278.

Ala-Mursula, L., Buxton, J. L., Ek, E., Koiranen, M., Taanila, A., & Blakemore, A. I. (2013). Long-term unemployment is associated with short telomeres in 31-year-old men: An observational study in the Northern Finland Birth Cohort 1966. *PLOS ONE, 8*(11), e80094. Retrieved from http://journals.plos.org/plosone/article?id=10.1371/journal.pone.0080094

Alashwal, H., Dosunmu, R., & Zawia, N. H. (2012). Integration of genome-wide expression and methylation data: Relevance to aging and Alzheimer's disease. *Neurotoxicology, 33*(6), 1450–1453.

Alba, R. D., Logan, J. R., & Stults, B. J. (2000). How segregated are middle-class African Americans? *Social Problems, 47*(4), 543–558.

Albert, C. M., Mittleman, M. A., Chae, C. U., Lee, I. M., Hennekens, C. H., & Manson, J. E. (2000). Triggering of sudden death from cardiac causes by vigorous exertion. *New England Journal of Medicine, 343,* 1355–1361.

Alexander, E. (1950). *Psychosomatic medicine.* New York, NY: Norton.

Alfieri, D. W., Costanzo, S., & Borgogni, T. (2011). Biological resilience of older adults against frailty. *Medical Hypotheses, 76*(2), 304–305.

Allen, K. J. D., & Gabbay, F. H. (2013). The amphetamine response moderates the relationship between negative emotionality and alcohol use. *Alcoholism: Clinical and Experimental Research, 37*(2), 348–360.

Allen, N. E. (2009). Moderate alcohol intake and cancer incidence in women. *Journal of the National Cancer Institute, 101*(5), 296–305.

Altarum Institute. (2014, September 18). Clarifying feasible procedures for reinvesting health care cost savings. Retrieved from http://altarum.org/publications/clarifying-feasible-procedures-for-reinvesting-health-care-cost-savings

Altbach, P. G. (2010). The realities of mass higher education in a globalized world. In D. B. Johnstone, M. B. d'Ambrosio, & P. J. Yakoboski (Eds.), *Higher education in a global society* (pp. 25–41). Cheltenham, UK: Edward Elgar.

Altman, B., & Bernstein, A. (2008). *Disability and health in the United States, 2001–2005.* Hyattsville, MD: National Center for Health Statistics.

American Academy of Pain Medicine (AAPM). (2013). *AAPM facts and figures.* Retrieved from http://www.painmed.org/patientcenter/facts_on_pain.aspx#refer

American Academy of Pediatrics (AAP). (2015). *AAP recommends whole diet approach to children's nutrition.* Retrieved from https://www.aap.org/en-us/about-the-aap/aap-press-room/Pages/AAP-Recommends-Whole-Diet-Approach-to-Children's-Nutrition.aspx

American Academy of Sleep Medicine (AASM). (2017). *Healthy sleep habits.* Retrieved from http://www.sleepeducation.org/essentials-in-sleep/healthy-sleep-habits

American Cancer Society (ACS). (2015a). *Cancer facts and figures 2015.* Atlanta, GA: Author. Retrieved from http://www.cancer.org/acs/groups/content/@editorial/documents/document/acspc-044552.pdf

American Cancer Society (ACS). (2015b). *Family cancer syndromes.* Retrieved from http://www.cancer.org/cancer/cancercauses/geneticsandcancer/heredity-and-cancer

American Cancer Society (ACS). (2015c). *Skin cancer.* Retrieved from http://www.cancer.org/cancer/skincancer/index

American Cancer Society (ACS). (2018a). *Cancer facts and figures, 2018.* Atlanta, GA: Author. Retrieved from https://www.cancer.org/content/dam/cancer-org/research/cancer-facts-and-statistics/annual-cancer-facts-and-figures/2018/cancer-facts-and-figures-2018.pdf

American Cancer Society (ACS). (2018b). *Cancer facts and figures for African-Americans 2016–2018.* Retrieved from https://www.cancer.org/content/dam/cancer-org/research/cancer-facts-and-statistics/cancer-facts-and-figures-for-african-americans/cancer-facts-and-figures-for-african-americans-2016-2018.pdf

American Cancer Society (ACS). (2018c). *The great American smokeout.* Retrieved from https://www.cancer.org/healthy/stay-away-from-tobacco/great-american-smokeout.html

American Cancer Society (ACS). (2018d). *Key Statistics for Melanoma Skin Cancer.* Retrieved from https://www.cancer.org/cancer/melanoma-skin-cancer/about/key-statistics.html

American College Health Association. (2017). *National College Health Assessment.* Retrieved from http://www.acha-ncha.org/pubs_rpts.html

American College of Obstetricians and Gynecologists (ACOG). (2017). *Sexually transmitted infections: Resource overview.* Retrieved from https://www.acog.org/Womens-Health/Sexually-Transmitted-Infections

American Diabetes Association (ADA). (2010a). Living with diabetes: Depression. Retrieved April 5, 2010, from http://www.diabetes.org/living-with-diabetes/women/depression.html

American Diabetes Association (ADA). (2010b). Standards of medical care in diabetes—2010. *Diabetes Care, 33* (Supplement 1), S11–S61.

American Heart Association (AHA). (2015). *Heart disease and stroke statistics—2015 update.* Dallas, TX: Author. Retrieved from https://www.heart.org/idc/groups/ahamah-public/@wcm/@sop/@smd/documents/downloadable/ucm_470707.pdf

American Heart Association (AHA). (2018). *What your cholesterol levels mean.* Retrieved from http://www.heart.org/HEARTORG/Conditions/Cholesterol/AboutCholesterol/What-Your-Cholesterol-Levels-Mean_UCM_305562_Article.jsp#.WuwOHxSUdWY

American Hospital Association (AHA). (2011, September 7). *More hospitals offering complementary and alternative medicine services.* Retrieved from http://www.aha.org/presscenter/pressrel/2011/110907-pr-camsurvey.pdf

American Hospital Association (AHA). (2018). *Fast facts on U.S. hospitals.* Retrieved from https://www.aha.org/system/files/2018-02/2018-aha-hospital-fast-facts.pdf

American Institute for Cancer Research (AICR). (2018). A model plate for a cancer preventive diet. Retrieved from http://www.aicr.org/new-american-plate/cancer-preventive-diet-model-plate.html

American Medical Association (AMA). (1973). *Proceedings of the House of Delegates.* New York: Author.

American Medical Association (AMA). (1995). *Proceedings of the House of Delegates.* Chicago: Author.

American Medical Association (AMA). (2008, March 10). *More schools teaching spirituality in medicine.* Retrieved from Amednews.com/article/20080310/profession/303109968/7/

American Pain Society. (2016). *Interdisciplinary pain management.* Retrieved from http://americanpainsociety.org/uploads/about/position-statements/interdisciplinary-white-paper.pdf

American Psychiatric Association. (2013). *Diagnostic and statistical manual of mental disorders—DSM-V* (5th ed.). Arlington, VA: American Psychiatric Association.

American Psychiatric Association. (2018a). *What are eating disorders?* Retrieved from https://www.psychiatry.org/patients-families/eating-disorders/what-are-eating-disorders

American Psychiatric Association. (2018b). *What is posttraumatic stress disorder?* Retrieved from https://www.psychiatry.org/patients-families/ptsd/what-is-ptsd

American Psychological Association (APA). (2009). *2009 doctoral psychology workforce fast facts.* Washington, DC: Author. Retrieved from http://www.apa.org/workforce/snapshots/2009/fast-facts.pdf

American Psychological Association (APA). (2010, November 9). *Stress in America findings.* Washington, DC: American Psychological Association.

American Psychological Association (APA). (2017a). *Ethical principles of psychologists and code of conduct.* Retrieved from http://www.apa.org/ethics/code/ethics-code-2017.pdf

American Psychological Association (APA). (2017b). *Psychology essential to achieving goals of patient-centered medial homes.* Retrieved from http://www.apa.org/news/press/releases/2017/01/medical-homes.aspx

American Psychological Association (APA). (2018). *What is resilience? The road to resilience.* Retrieved from http://www.apa.org/helpcenter/road-resilience.aspx

American Psychological Association, Science Directorate. (1995). *Doing the right thing: A research plan for healthy living—A Human Capital Initiative strategy report.* Washington, DC: American Psychological Association Human Capital Initiative Coordinating Committee.

American Society of Clinical Oncology (ASCO). (2018). *Advances in cancer treatment.* Retrieved from https://www.asco.org/research-progress/reports-studies/clinical-cancer-advances-2018/advances-cancer-treatment

Amick, B. C., McDonough, P., Chang, H., Rodgers, W. H., Pieper, C. F., & Duncan, G. (2002). Relationship between all-cause mortality and cumulative working life course psychosocial and physical exposure in the United States labor market from 1968 to 1992. *Psychosomatic Medicine, 64,* 370–381.

Amigo, I., Buceta, J. M., Becona, E., & Bueno, A. M. (1991). Cognitive behavioral treatment for essential hypertension: A controlled study. *Stress Medicine, 7,* 103–108.

Anand, S., Islam, S., Rosengren, A., Franzosi, M. G., Steyn, K., Yusufali, … Yusuf, S. (2008). Risk factors for myocardial infarction in women and men: Insights from the INTERHEART study. *European Heart Journal, 29*(7), 932–940.

Anders, R. L., Olson, T., Wiebe, J., Bean, N. H., DiGregorio, R., Guillermina, M., & Ortiz, M. (2008). Diabetes prevalence and treatment adherence in residents living in a colonia located on the West Texas, USA/Mexico border. *Nursing and Health Sciences, 10,* 195–202.

Anderson, B. L., Cacioppo, J. T., & Roberts, D. C. (1995). Delay in seeking a cancer diagnosis: Delay stages and psychophysiological comparison processes. *British Journal of Social Psychology, 34,* 33–52.

Anderson, D. R., & Emery, C. F. (2014). Irrational health beliefs predict adherence to cardiac rehabilitation. *Health Psychology, 33,* 1614–1617.

Anderson, P. (2013). Where is pain in the brain? *Medscape Medical News,* April 18. Retrieved from http://www.medscape.com/viewarticle/782732

Anderson, R. J., & Brice, S. (2011). The mood-enhancing benefits of exercise: Memory biases augment the effect. *Psychology of Sport and Exercise, 12,* 79–82.

Anderson, S. (2008, July 8). The urge to end it. *The New York Times.* Retrieved from http://www.nytimes.com

Andrasik, F., Grazzi, L., Usai, S., D'Amico, D., Kass, S., & Bussone, G. (2007). Disability in chronic migraine with medication overuse: Treatment effects at 3 years. *Headache, 47*(9), 1277–1281.

Angel, R., Angel, J., & Hill, T. (2008). A comparison of the health of older Hispanics in the United States and Mexico. *Journal of Aging and Health, 20,* 1, 3–31.

Angst, M. S., & Clark, D. J. (2006). Opioid-induced hyperalgesia: A qualitative systematic review. *Anesthesiology, 104,* 570–587.

Ansary, N. S., & Luthar, S. S. (2009). Distress and academic achievement among adolescents of affluence: A study of externalizing and internalizing problem behaviors and school performance. *Development and Psychopathology, 21*(1), 319–341.

Antoni, M. H., Ironson, G., & Scheiderman, N. (2007). *Cognitive-behavioral stress management workbook.* New York, NY: Oxford University Press.

Antoni, M. H., Lechner, S., Diaz, A., Vargas, S., Holley, H., Phillips, K., … Blomberg, B. (2009). Cognitive behavioral stress management effects on psychosocial and physiological adaptation in women undergoing treatment for breast cancer. *Brain, Behavior and Immunity, 23,* 580–591.

Antoni, M. H., Lehman, J. M., Kilbourn, K. M., Boyers, A. E., Culver, J. L., Alferi, S. M., … Carver, C. S. (2001). Cognitive-behavioral stress management intervention decreases the prevalence of depression and enhances benefit finding among women under treatment for early-stage breast cancer. *Health Psychology, 20*(1), 20–32.

Appleton, A. A., Buka, S. L., McCormick, M. C., Koenen, K. C., Loucks, E. B., & Kubzansky, L. D. (2012). The association between childhood emotional functioning and adulthood inflammation is modified by early-life socioeconomic status. *Health Psychology, 31*(4), 413–422.

Arbour-Nicitopoulos, K. P., Duncan, M. J., Remington, G., Cairney, J., & Faulkner, G. E. (2017). The utility of the health action process approach model for predicting physical activity intentions and behavior in schizophrenia. *Frontiers in Psychiatry, 8,* 135. doi.org/10.3389/fpsyt.2017.00135

Armitage, C. J. (2009). Is there utility in the transtheoretical model? *British Journal of Health Psychology, 14*(Pt 2), 195–210.

Armitage, C. J., Sheeran, P., Conner, M., & Arden, M. A. (2004). Stages of change or changes of stage? Predicting transitions in transtheoretical model stages in relation to healthy food choice. *Journal of Consulting and Clinical Psychology, 72,* 491–499.

Arnett, J. J., & Schwab, J. (2012). The Clark University Poll of emerging adults: Thriving, struggling & hopeful. Retrieved from clarku.edu/clarkpoll

Arnst, C. (2009, November 12). 10 ways to cut health-care costs right now. *Bloomberg Business Week.* Retrieved from http://www.bloomberg.com/news/articles/2009-11-12/10-ways-to-cut-health-care-costs-right-now

Aronoff, J., Stollak, G. E., & Woike, B. A. (1994). Affect regulation and the breadth of interpersonal engagement. *Journal of Personality and Social Psychology, 67,* 105–114.

Arpawong, T. E., Richeimer, S. H., Weinstein, F., Elghamrawy, A., & Milam, J. E. (2013). Posttraumatic growth, quality of life, and treatment symptoms among cancer chemotherapy outpatients. *Health Psychology, 32*(4), 397–408.

Arthur, C. M., Katkin, E. S., & Mezzacappa, E. S. (2004). Cardiovascular reactivity to mental arithmetic and cold pressor in African Americans, Caribbean Americans, and white Americans. *Annals of Behavioral Medicine, 27*(1), 31–37.

Asbridge, M., Hayden, J. A., & Cartwright, J. L. (2012). Acute cannabis consumption and motor vehicle collision risk: Systematic review of observational studies and meta-analysis. *British Medical Journal, 344.* Retrieved from http://www.bmj.com/content/344/bmj.e536

Askay, S. W., Patterson, D. R., Jensen, M. P., & Sharar, S. R. (2007). A randomized controlled trial of hypnosis for burn wound care. *Rehabilitation Psychology, 52,* 247–253.

Aslund, C., Nordquist, N., Comasco, E., Leppert, J., Oreland, L., & Nilsson, K. W. (2011). Maltreatment, MAOA, and delinquency: Sex differences in gene-environment interaction in a large population-based cohort of adolescents. *Behavior Genetics, 41,* 262–272.

Association of Accredited Naturopathic Medical Colleges (AANMC). (2018). *Naturopathic doctor licensure.* Retrieved from https://aanmc.org/resources/licensure/

Association of Psychologists in Academic Health Centers (APAHC). (2016). *APAHC task force on behavioral and social science foundations for physicians.* Retrieved from http://www.div12.org/section8/index.html

Astin, J. A. (2004). Mind-body therapies for the management of pain. *Clinical Journal of Pain, 20*, 27–32.

Auerbach, S. M., Penberthy, A. R., & Kiesler, D. J. (2004). Opportunity for control, interpersonal impacts, and adjustment to a long-term invasive health care procedure. *Journal of Behavioral Medicine, 27*, 11–29.

Aughinbaugh, A., Robles, O., & Sun, H. (2013, October). Marriage and divorce: Patterns by gender, race, and educational attainment. *Monthly Labor Review*. Washington, DC: Bureau of Labor Statistics. Retrieved from http://www.bls.gov/opub/mlr/2013/article/marriage-and-divorce-patterns-by-gender-race-and-educational-attainment.htm#

Austin, A. W., Wissman, T., & Von Känel, R. (2013). Stress and hemostasis: An update. *Seminars in Thrombosis and Hemostasis, 39*(9), 902–912.

Auter, Z. (2018, January 16). U.S. uninsured rate steady at 12.2% in fourth quarter of 2017. *Gallup Well-Being*. Retrieved from http://news.gallup.com/poll/225383/uninsured-rate-steady-fourth-quarter-2017.aspx

Avadhani, A., & Steefel, L. (2015). Probiotics: A review for NPs. *Nurse Practitioner, 40*(8), 50–54.

Avert. (2017, January 27). *How HIV stigma leads to sickness. HIV-related stigma and discrimination have wide-ranging consequences*. Retrieved from https://www.avert.org/infographics/how-hiv-stigma-leads-sickness

Avert. (2017, August 23). *New HIV infections around the world in 2016*. Infographic. https://www.avert.org/infographics/new-hiv-infections-around-world-2016

Avert. (2018a). *Children, HIV, and AIDS*. Retrieved from https://www.avert.org/professionals/hiv-social-issues/key-affected-populations/children

Avert. (2018b). *Global HIV and AIDS statistics*. Retrieved from https://www.avert.org/global-hiv-and-aids-statistics

Bachhuber, M. A., Saloner, B., Cunningham, C. O., & Barry, C. L. (2014). Medical cannabis laws and opioid analgesic overdose mortality in the United States, 1999–2010. *Journal of the American Medical Association Internal Medicine, 174*(10), 1668–1673.

Bacon, L., & Aphramor, L. (2011). Weight science: Evaluating the evidence for a paradigm shift. *Nutrition Journal, 10*(9). Retrieved from https://nutritionj.biomedcentral.com/articles/10.1186/1475-2891-10-9

Bacon, S. L., Bouchard, A., Loucks, E. B., & Lavoie, K. L. (2009). Individual-level socioeconomic status is associated with worse asthma morbidity in patients with asthma. *Respiratory Research*. Retrieved from http://respiratory-research.biomedcentral.com/articles/10.1186/1465-9921-10-125

Baena-Diaz, J. M., Peñafiel, J., Subirana, I., Ramos, R., Elosua, R., Marin-Ebañez, A., … Grau, M. (2016). Risk of cause-specific death in individuals with diabetes: A competing risk analysis. *Diabetes Care, 39*(11), 1987–1995.

Bagherian-Sararoudi, R., Sanei, H., Attari, A., & Afshar, H. (2012). Type D personality is associated with hyperlipidemia in patients with myocardial infarction. *Journal of Research in Medical Sciences: The Official Journal of Isfahan University of Medical Sciences, 17*(6), 543–547.

Bagot, R. C., Zhang, T. Y., Wen, X., Nguyen, T. T., Nguyen, H. B., Diorio, J., & Meaney, M. J. (2012). Variations in postnatal maternal care and the epigenetic regulation of metabotropic glutamate receptor 1 expression and hippocampal function in the rat. *Proceedings of the National Academy of Sciences of the United States of America, 109*(Suppl. 2), 17200–17207.

Bahadoran, Z., Mirmiran, P., & Azizi, F. (2015). Fast food pattern and cardiometabolic disorders: A review of current studies. *Health Promotion Perspectives, 5*(4), 231–240.

Baker, R., & Kirschenbaum, D. S. (1998). Weight control during the holidays: Highly consistent self-monitoring as a potentially useful coping mechanism. *Health Psychology, 17*, 367–370.

Baker, S. P., Chen, L., & Li, G. (2007). *Nationwide review of graduated driver licensing*. Washington, DC: AAA Foundation for Traffic Safety. Retrieved from http://www.aaafoundation.org/pdf/NationwideReviewOfGDL.pdf

Balakrishnan, J., & Griffiths, M. D. (2017). Social media addiction: What is the role of content in YouTube? *Journal of Behavioral Addictions, 6*(3), 364+. Retrieved from http://0-link.galegroup.com.wizard.umd.umich.edu/apps/doc/A509894501/HRCA?u=lom_umichdearb&sid=HRCA&xid=2ccbd92a

Ball, D. (2008). Addiction science and its genetics. *Addiction, 103*, 360–367.

Balsam, K. F., Molina, Y., Beadnell, B., Simoni, J., & Walters, K. (2011). Measuring multiple minority stress: The LGBT people of color microaggressions scale. *Cultural Diversity & Ethnic Minority Psychology, 17*(2), 163–174.

Banasiak, S. J., Paxton, S. J., & Hay, P. (2005). Guided self-help for bulimia nervosa in primary care: A randomized controlled trial. *Psychological Medicine, 35*, 1283–1294.

Banducci, A. N., Long, K. E., & MacPherson, L. (2014). A case series of a behavioral activation-enhanced smoking cessation program for inpatient substance users with elevated depressive symptoms. *Clinical Case Studies, 14*(1), 61–77.

Bandura, A. (1997). *Self-efficacy: The exercise of control*. New York, NY: W. H. Freeman.

Bandura, A., Taylor, C. B., Williams, S. L., Mefford, I. N., & Barchas, J. D. (1985). Catecholamine secretion as a function of perceived coping self-efficacy. *Journal of Consulting and Clinical Psychology, 53*(3), 406–414.

Barger, S. D., & Gallo, L. C. (2008). Ability of ethnic self-identification to partition modifiable health risk among U.S. residents of Mexican ancestry. *American Journal of Public Health, 98*(11), 1971–1978.

Barker, E. T., Greenberg, J. S., Seltzer, M. M., & Almeida, D. M. (2012). Daily stress and cortisol patterns in parents of adult children with a serious mental illness. *Health Psychology, 31*(1), 130–134.

Barker, F., Atkins, L., & de Lusignan, S. (2016, July). Applying the COM-B behavior model and behavior change wheel to develop an intervention to improve hearing-aid use in adult auditory rehabilitation. *International Journal of Audiology, Supplement 3*, S90–S98.

Barnes, P. M., Bloom, B., & Nahin, R. (2008). Complementary and alternative medicine use among adults and children: United States, 2007. *National Health Statistics Reports* (12). Hyattsville, MD: National Center for Health Statistics.

Barrera, M., Toobert, D. J., Angell, K. L., Glasgow, R. E., & MacKinnon, D. P. (2006). Social support and social-ecological resources as mediators of lifestyle intervention effects for type 2 diabetes. *Journal of Health Psychology, 11*, 483–495.

Barrington-Trimis, J. L., Urman, R., Leventhal, A. M., Gauderman, J., Cruz, T. B., Gilreath, T. D., … McConnell, R. (2016, August 8). E-cigarettes, cigarettes, and the prevalence of adolescent tobacco use. *Pediatrics, 138*(2). Retrieved from http://pediatrics .aappublications.org/content/pediatrics/138/2/e20153983.full.pdf

Barsky, A. J., Saintfort, R., Rogers, M. P., & Borus, J. F. (2002). Nonspecific medication side effects and the nocebo phenomenon. *Journal of the American Medical Association, 287*(5), 622–627.

Bartholow, B. D., Sher, K. J., & Krull, J. L. (2003). Changes in heavy drinking over the third decade of life as a function of collegiate fraternity and sorority involvement: A prospective, multilevel analysis. *Health Psychology, 22*(6), 616–625.

Bartley, E. J., & Fillingim, R. B. (2013). Sex differences in pain: A brief review of clinical and experimental findings. *Medicine and Health, 111*(1), 52–58.

Bartley, T. (2012). *Mindfulness-based cognitive therapy for cancer*. West Sussex, England: Wiley.

Bass, P. F. (2015). Family-based therapy for eating disorders. *Contemporary Pediatrics*. Retrieved from http://contemporarypediatrics .modernmedicine.com/contemporary-pediatrics/news/family -based-therapy-eating-disorders?page=full

Battie, C. A., Borja-Hart, N., Ancheta, I. B., Flores, R., Rao, G., & Palaniappan, L. (2016). Comparison of body mass index, waist circumference, and waist to height ratio in the prediction of hypertension and diabetes mellitus: Filipino-American women cardiovascular study. *Preventive Medicine Reports, 4*, 608–613.

Baum, A., & Grunberg, N. E. (1991). Gender, stress, and health. *Health Psychology, 10*, 80–85.

Baumann, L. J., Cameron, L. D., Zimmerman, R. S., & Leventhal, H. (1989). Illness representations and matching labels with symptoms. *Health Psychology, 8*, 449–469.

Baylor University. (2016, October 27). Are you addicted to social media? Six questions. *Science Daily*. Retrieved from www .sciencedaily.com/releases/2016/10/161027115714.htm

Bech, P. (2004). Measuring the dimensions of psychological general well-being by the WHO-5. *Quality of Life Newsletter, 32*, 15–16.

Beck, K. H., & Frankel, A. (1981). A conceptualization of threat communications and protective health behavior. *Social Psychology Quarterly, 44*, 204–217.

Beckett, L. (2014, March 4). Why hospitals are failing civilians who get PTSD. *ProPublica*. Retrieved from https://0-search-proquest-com.wizard.umd.umich.edu/docview/1830794959/fulltext/ C22592F376204F3BPQ/1?accountid=14578

Beckman, H. B., & Frankel, R. M. (1984). The effect of physician behavior on the collection of data. *Annals of Internal Medicine, 101*, 692–696.

Beesdo, K., Hoyer, J., Jacobi, F., Low, N. C. P., Hofler, M., & Wittchen, H. U. (2010). Association between generalized anxiety levels and pain in a community sample: Evidence for diagnostic specificity. *Journal of Anxiety Disorders, 24*(2), 290–291.

Beil, L. (2015). Typical American diet can damage immune system. *Science News, 187*(11). Retrieved from https://www.sciencenews .org/article/typical-american-diet-can-damage-immune-system

Belar, C. D., & Deardorff, W. W. (1996). *Clinical health psychology in medical settings: A practitioner's guidebook*. Washington, DC: American Psychological Association.

Belcher, A. J., Laurenceau, J. P., Graber, E. C., Cohen, L. H., Dasch, K. B., & Siegel, S. D. (2011). Daily support in couples coping with early stage breast cancer: Maintaining intimacy during adversity. *Health Psychology, 30*(6), 665–673.

Bell, B., & Dittmar, H. (2010). Does media type matter? The role of identification in adolescent girls' media consumption and the impact of different thin-ideal media on body image. *Sex Roles, 65*(7/8), 478–490.

Bellavance, M.-A., & Rivest, S. (2014). The HPA–immune axis and the immunomodulatory actions of glucocorticoids in the brain. *Frontiers in Immunology, 5*, 136.

Ben-Ayre, E., & Frenkel, M. (2008). Referring to complementary and alternative medicine: A possible tool for implementation. *Complementary Therapies in Medicine, 16*, 325–330.

Bendapudi, N. M., Berry, L. L., Frey, K. A., Parish, J. T., & Rayburn, W. L. (2006). Patients' perspectives on ideal physician behaviors. *Mayo Clinic Proceedings, 81*, 338–344.

Benedetti, F. (1996). The opposite effects of the opiate antagonist naloxone and the cholecystokinin antagonist proglumide on placebo analgesia. *Pain, 64*(3), 540.

Benjamin, E. J., Virani, S. S., Callaway, C. W., Chamberlain, A. M., Chang, A. R., Cheng, S., … Muntner, P. (2018). Heart disease and stroke statistics—2018 update: A report from the American Heart Association. *Circulation, 137*(12), e67–e492.

Benson, H. (1993). The relaxation response. In D. Goleman & J. Gurin (Eds.), *Mind–Body Medicine* (pp. 233–257). New York: Consumer Reports Books.

Benson, H. (1996). *Timeless healing: The power and biology of belief*. New York, NY: Scribner.

Benzon, H., Raja, S., Liu, S. S., Fishman, S. M., & Cohen, S. P. (2018). *Essentials of pain medicine* (4th ed.). Philadelphia, PA: Elsevier.

Berkman, L. F. (2010). Social networks and health. Presented at *Ageing and health: From evidence to policy*. Meeting of the Study on global AGEing and adult health (SAGE), June 10. Geneva, Switzerland: World Health Organization. Retrieved from http:// www.who.int/healthinfo/systems/sage/en/index3.html

Berkman, L. F., Buxton, O., Ertel, K., & Okechukwu, C. (2010). Managers' practices related to work-family balance predict employee cardiovascular risk and sleep duration in extended care settings. *Journal of Occupational Health Psychology, 15*(3), 316–329.

Berkman, L. F., & Syme, L. S. (1994). Social networks, host resistance, and mortality: A nine-year follow-up study of Alameda County residents. In A. Steptoe & J. Wardle (Eds.), *Psychosocial processes and health: A reader* (pp. 43–67). Cambridge, England: Cambridge University Press.

Berkman, L. F., & Syme, S. L. (1979). Social networks, host resistance, and mortality: A nine-year follow-up of Alameda County residents. *American Journal of Epidemiology, 109*(2), 190.

Bernard, E. J., & Cameron, S. (2016). *Advancing HIV justice 2: Building momentum in global advocacy against HIV criminalisation*. Brighton, England, and Amsterdam, Netherlands: HIV Justice Network and Global Network of People Living with HIV. Retrieved from https://hivlawcommission.org/wp-content/ uploads/2017/06/312008825-Advancing-HIV-Justice-2-Building-momentum-in-global-advocacy-against-HIV-criminalisation-1.pdf

Berridge, K. C., & Robinson, T. E. (2016). Liking, wanting, and the incentive-sensitization theory of addiction. *American Psychologist, 71*(8), 670–679.

Berrington de Gonzales, A. G., Hartge, P., Cerhan, J. R., Flint, A. J., Hannan, L., MacInnis, R. J. … Thun, M. J. (2010). Body-mass index and mortality among 1.46 million white adults. *New England Journal of Medicine, 363*, 2211–2219.

Berry, J. W., & Worthington, E. L. (2001). Forgiveness, relationship quality, stress while imagining relationship events, and physical and mental health. *Journal of Counseling Psychology, 48*(4), 447–455.

Best, J. (2002). *Damned lies and statistics: Untangling numbers from the media, politicians, and activists.* Berkeley: University of California Press.

Bhupathiraju, S. N., & Hu, F. B. (2016). Epidemiology of obesity and diabetes and their cardiovascular complications. *Circulation Research, 118*(11), 1723–1735.

Bianchi, S. M., & Milkie, M. A. (2010). Work and family research in the first decade of the 21st century. *Journal of Marriage and Family, 72*(3), 705–725.

Blair, T. R. (2016). Plague doctors in the HIV/AIDS epidemic: Mental health professionals and the "San Francisco model," 1981–1990. *Bulletin of the History of Medicine, 90*(2), 279–311. Retrieved from http://0-search.proquest.com.wizard.umd.umich.edu/docview/1811918752?accountid=14578

Blakemore, S.-J. (2008). Development of the social brain during adolescence. *Quarterly Journal of Experimental Psychology, 61*, 40–49.

Blanchard, C. M., Fortier, M., Sweet, S., O'Sullivan, T., Hogg, W., Reid, R. D., & Sigal, R. J. (2007). Explaining physical activity levels from a self-efficacy perspective: The physical activity counseling trial. *Annals of Behavioral Medicine, 34*, 323–328.

Blas, E., & Kurup, A. S. (Eds.). (2010). *Equity, social determinants, and public health programmes.* Geneva, Switzerland: World Health Organization.

Blascovich, J., Seery, M. D., Mugridge, C. A., Norris, R. K., & Weisbuch, M. (2004). Predicting athletic performance from cardiovascular indexes of challenge and threat. *Journal of Experimental Social Psychology, 40*, 683–688.

Blashill, A. J., Goshe, B. M., Robbins, G. K., Mayer, K. H., & Safren, S. A. (2014). Body image disturbance and health behaviors among sexual minority men living with HIV. *Health Psychology, 33*, 667–680.

Blundell, J. E., Gibbons, C., Caudwell, P., Finlayson, G., & Hopkins, M. (2015). Appetite control and exergy balance: Impact of exercise. *Obesity Reviews, 16*(Suppl. 1), 67–76.

Bolt, M. (2004). *Pursuing human strengths: A positive psychology guide.* New York, NY: W. H. Freeman.

Bonaz, B. L., & Bernstein, C. N. (2012). Brain-gut interactions in inflammatory bowel disease. *Reviews in Basic and Clinical Gastroenterology and Hepatology, 144*(1), 36–49.

Bonhoeffer, H. J. (2007). Adverse events following immunization: Perception and evidence. *Current Opinions Infectious Disease, 20*(3), 237–246.

Bonita, R., Beaglehole, R., & Kjellstrom, T. (2006). *Basic epidemiology* (2nd ed.). Geneva, Switzerland: World Health Organization.

Booij, L., Wang, D., Levesque, M. L., Tremblay, R. E., & Szf, M. (2013). Looking beyond the DNA sequence: The relevance of DNA methylation processes for the stress-diathesis model of depression. *Philosophical Transactions of the Royal Society of Biological Sciences, 368*(1615). Retrieved from http://rstb.royalsocietypublishing.org/content/current

Boone-Heinonen, J., Diez Roux, A. V., Kiefe, C. I., Lewis, C. E., Guilkey, D. K., & Gordon-Larsen, P. (2011). Neighborhood socioeconomic status predictors of physical activity through young to middle adulthood: The CARDIA study. *Social Science & Medicine, 72*(5), 641–649.

Borissoff, J. I., Spronk, H. M. H., & ten Cate, H. (2011). The hemostatic system as a modulator of atherosclerosis. *The New England Journal of Medicine, 364*(18), 1746–1760.

Bourdeau, T. L., & Walters, A. (2013). *Coping with a diagnosis of chronic illness.* American Psychological Association. Retrieved from http://www.apa.org/helpcenter/chronic-illness.aspx

Bourgeois, B., & Owens, J. W. (2014). The influence of hurricanes Katrina and Rita on the inflammatory cytokine response and protein expression in A549 cells exposed to PM2.5 collected in the Baton Rouge-Port Allen industrial corridor of Southeastern Louisiana in 2005. *Toxicology Mechanisms and Methods, 24*(3), 220–242.

Bouvard, V., Loomis, D., Guyton, K. Z., Grosse, Y., Ghissassi, F. E., Benbrahim-Tallaa, L., … Straif, K. (2015). Carcinogenicity of red and processed meat. *The Lancet Oncology, 16*(16), 1599–1600.

Bowen, S., Witkiewitz, K., Dillworth, T. M., Chawla, N., Simpson, T. L., Ostafin, B. D., Larimer, M. E., Blume, A. W., Parks, G. A., & Marlatt, G. A. (2006). Mindfulness meditation and substance use in an incarcerated population. *Psychology of Addictive Behaviors, 20*(3), 343–347.

Bower, J. E., Greendale, G., Crosswell, A. D., Garet, D., Sternlieb, B., Ganz, P. A., … Cole, S. W. (2014). Yoga reduces inflammatory signaling in fatigued breast cancer survivors: A randomized controlled trial. *Psychoneuroendocrinology, 43*, 20–29.

Bower, J. E., Kemeny, M. E., Taylor, S. E., & Fahey, J. L. (2003). Finding positive meaning and its association with natural killer cell cytotoxicity among participants in a bereavement-related disclosure intervention. *Annals of Behavioral Medicine, 25*(2), 146–155.

Bowling, N. A., Eschleman, K. J., & Wang, Q. (2010). A meta-analytic examination of the relationship between job satisfaction and subjective well-being. *Journal of Occupational and Organizational Psychology, 83*, 915–934.

Bracizewski, J. M. (2010). *Family environment and psychological distress: A longitudinal study of at-risk youth.* WorldCat Dissertations and Theses. Udini by ProQuest. Retrieved from http://udini.proquest.com/view/family-environment-and-goid:305231554/

Brady, S. S., & Matthews, K. A. (2006). Chronic stress influences ambulatory blood pressure in adolescents. *Annals of Behavioral Medicine, 31*(1), 80–88.

Brakel, T. M., Dijkstra, A., Buunk, A. P, & Siero, F. W. (2012). Impact of social comparison on cancer survivors' quality of life: An experimental field study. *Health Psychology, 31*(5), 660–670.

Brant, J. M., Beck, S., Dudley, W. N., Cobb, P., Pepper, G., & Miaskowski, C. (2011). Symptom trajectories in posttreatment cancer survivors. *Cancer Nursing, 34*, 67–77.

Bratman, S. (2007). *Complementary and alternative health: The scientific verdict on what really works.* New York, NY: Harper Collins.

Brembo, E. A., Kapstad, H., Van Dulmen, S., & Eide, H. (2017). Role of self-efficacy and social support in short-term recovery after total hip replacement: A prospective cohort study. *Health and Quality of Life Outcomes, 15*(1), 68.

Breslow, L., & Breslow, N. (1993). Health practices and disability: Some evidence from Alameda County. *Preventive Medicine, 22*, 86–95.

Broadbent, E., Kahokeher, A., Booth, R. J., Thomas, J., Windsor, J. A., Buchanan, C. M., & Hill, A. G. (2012). A brief relaxation intervention reduces stress and improves surgical wound healing response: A randomized trial. *Brain, Behavior, and Immunity, 26*, 212–217.

Broadbent, E., Petrie, K. J., Alley, P. G., & Booth, R. J. (2003). Psychological stress impairs early wound repair following surgery. *Psychosomatic Medicine, 65*(5), 865–869.

Broadstock, M., Borland, R., & Gason, R. (2006). Effects of suntan on judgments of healthiness and attractiveness by adolescents. *Journal of Applied Social Psychology, 22*(2), 157–172.

Brody, G. H., Kogan, S. M., Mury, V. M., Chen, Y. F., & Brown, A. C. (2008). Psychological functioning, support for self-management, and glycemic control among rural African American adults with diabetes mellitus type 2. *Health Psychology, 27*(Suppl. 1), S83–S90.

Brody, G. H., Yu, T., Miller, G. E., & Chen, E. (2016). Resilience in adolescence, health, and psychosocial outcomes. *Pediatrics, 138*(6). Retrieved from http://pediatrics.aappublications.org/content/138/6/e20161042

Brody, J. E. (2002, November 26). When the eyelids snap shut at 65 miles an hour. *The New York Times*. Retrieved from http://www.nytimes.com

Bromberg, M. H., Gil, K. M., & Schanberg, L. E. (2012). Daily sleep quality and mood as predictors of pain in children with juvenile polyarticular arthritis. *Health Psychology, 31*(2), 202–209.

Bronfort, G., Haas, M., Evans, R., Leininger, B., & Triano, J. (2010). Effectiveness of manual therapies: The UK evidence report. *Chiropractic and Osteopathy, 18*(3). Retrieved from http://chiromt.biomedcentral.com/articles/10.1186/1746-1340-18-3

Brooks, K. P., Gruenewald, T., Karlamangla, A., Hu, P., Koretz, B., & Seeman, T. E. (2014). Social relationships and allostatic load in the MIDUS study. *Health Psychology, 33*, 1373–1381.

Broom, D. R., Batterham, R. L., King, J. A., & Stensel, D. J. (2009). Influence of resistance and aerobic exercise on hunger, circulating levels of acylated ghrelin, and peptide YY in healthy males. *American Journal of Physiology. Regulatory, Integrative, and Comparative Physiology, 296*(1), R29–R35.

Brown, G. D. A., Gardner, J., Oswald, A. J., & Qian, J. (2008). Does wage rank affect employees' well-being? *Industrial Relations, 47*, 355–389.

Brown, S. L., Nesse, R. M., Vinokur, A. D., & Smith, D. M. (2003). Providing social support may be more beneficial than receiving it: Results from a prospective study of mortality. *Psychological Science, 14*(4), 320–327.

Brown, S. L., & Rinelli, L. N. (2010). Family structure, family processes, and adolescent smoking and drinking. *Journal of Research on Adolescence, 20*(2), 259–273.

Brown, S. L., Schiraldi, G. R., & Wrobleski, P. P. (2009). Association of eating behaviors and obesity with psychosocial and familial influences. *American Journal of Health Education, 40*(2), 80–89.

Browning, L., Ryan, C. S., Greenberg, M. S., & Rolniak, S. (2006). Effects of cognitive adaptation on the expectation-burnout relationship among nurses. *Journal of Behavioral Medicine, 29*, 139–150.

Brownlee, C. (2006). Eat smart. Foods may affect the brain as well as the body. *Science News, 169*, 136–137.

Brownlee, S. (1995). The route of phantom pain. *U.S. News & World Report, 119*, 76.

Broyles, L. C. (2005). *Resilience: Its relationship to forgiveness in older adults* (Doctoral dissertation). Retrieved from gradworks.umi.com

Burge, M. R., & Schade, D. S. (2014). Diabetes and the Affordable Care Act. *Diabetes Technology and Therapeutics, 16*(7), 399–413.

Burgess, D., van Ryn, M., Dovidio, J., & Saha, S. (2007). Reducing racial bias among health care providers: Lessons from social-cognitive psychology. *Journal of General Internal Medicine, 22*(6), 882–887.

Burhenn, P., Olausson, J., Vilegas, G., & Kravits, K. (2014). Guided imagery for pain control. *Clinical Journal of Oncology Nursing, 18*(5), 501–503.

Burke, M. V., Hays, J. T., & Ebbert, J. O. (2016). Varenicline for smoking cessation: A narrative review of efficacy, adverse effects, use in at-risk populations, and adherence. *Patient Preference and Adherence, 10*, 435–441.

Burns, J. W. (2006). The role of attentional strategies in moderating links between acute pain induction and subsequent psychological stress: Evidence for symptom-specific reactivity among patients with chronic pain versus healthy nonpatients. *Emotion, 6*(2), 180–192.

Burns, J. W., Holly, A., Quartana, P., Wolff, M. S., Gray, E., & Bruehl, S. (2008). Trait anger management style moderates effects of actual ("state") anger regulation on symptom-specific reactivity and recovery among chronic low back pain patient. *Psychosomatic Medicine, 70*(8), 898–905.

Busch, A. M., & Borrelli, B. (2012). Valued life activities and readiness to quit smoking among mobility-impaired smokers. *Health Psychology, 31*(1), 122–125.

Business Wire. (2018, June 8). *Global pain management drugs market analysis & industry forecast, 2017–2023*. Retrieved from https://www.businesswire.com/news/home/20180608005405/en/Global-Pain-Management-Drugs-Market-Analysis-Industry

Bustamante, M. J., Valentino, G., Kramer, V., Adasme, M., Guidi, D., Ibara, C., … Acevedo, M. (2015). Patient adherence to a cardiovascular rehabilitation program: What factors are involved? *International Journal of Clinical Medicine, 6*, 605–614.

Butler, E. A., Egloff, B., Wilhelm, F. H., Smith, N. C., Erickson, E. A., & Gross, J. J. (2003). The social consequences of expressive suppression. *Emotion, 3*(1), 48–67.

Butler, S. (2010). A personal experience learning from two pain pioneers, J. J. Bonica and W. Fordyce: Lessons surviving four decades of pain practice. *Scandinavian Journal of Pain, 1*(1), 34–37.

Buttorff, C., Ruder, T., & Bauman, M. (2017). *Multiple chronic conditions in the United States*. Santa Monica, CA: Rand Corporation. Retrieved from https://www.rand.org/pubs/tools/TL221.html

Buunk, A. P., Brakel, T. M., Bennenbroek, F. T. C., Stiegelis, H., Sanderman, R., Van den Bergh, A. C. M., & Hagedoorn, M.

(2009). Neuroticism and responses to social comparison among cancer patients. *European Journal of Personality, 23*, 475–487.

Bynum, R. (2004, November 1). Rare disease makes girl unable to feel pain. *NBCNEWS.com*. Retrieved from http://www.nbcnews.com/id/6379795/ns/health-childrens_health/t/rare-disease-makes-girl-unable-to-feel-pain/#.V2FYt1fzglI

Cahill, K., Lancaster, T., & Green, N. (2010). Stage-based interventions for smoking cessation. *Cochrane Database of Systematic Reviews, 11*. Retrieved from http://cochranelibrary-wiley.com/doi/10.1002/14651858.CD004492.pub4/abstract

Caldwell, J. A. (2012). Crew schedules, sleep deprivation, and aviation performance. *Current Directions in Psychological Science, 21*(2), 85–89.

Calipari, E. S., & Ferris, M. J. (2013) Amphetamine mechanisms and actions of the dopamine terminal revisited. *Journal of Neuroscience, 33*(21), 8923–8925.

Calle, E. E., Thun, M. J., Petrelli, J. M., Rodriguez, C., & Heath, C. W. (1999). Body-mass index and mortality in a prospective cohort of U.S. adults. *New England Journal of Medicine, 341*(15), 1097–1105.

Callister, L. C. (2003). Cultural influences on pain perceptions and behaviors. *Home Health Care Management and Practice, 15*(3), 207–211.

Calsyn, M., & Rosenthal, L. (2013, May 20). How the Affordable Care Act helps young adults. *Center for American Progress*. Retrieved from http://www.americanprogress.org/issues/healthcare

Caltabiano, M. L., & Caltabiano, N. J. (2006). Resilience and health outcomes in the elderly. *Proceedings of the 39th Annual Conference of the Australian Association of Gerontology*, Sydney, Australia.

Camp, D. E., Klesges, R. C., & Relyea, G. (1993). The relationship between body weight concerns and adolescent smoking. *Health Psychology, 12*, 24–32.

Campbell, K., & Peebles, R. (2014). Eating disorders in children and adolescents: State of the art review. *Pediatrics, 134*(3), 582–592.

Canadian Tobacco Use Monitoring Survey. (2004). *Health Canada*. Retrieved from http://www.hc-sc.gc.ca/hl-vs/tobac-tabac/research-recherche/stat/ctums-esutc/2004/index_e.html

Cannon, W. (1932). *The wisdom of the body*. New York, NY: Norton.

Carabotti, M., Scirocco, A., Maselli, M. A., & Severi, C. (2015). The gut-brain axis: Interactions between enteric microbiota, central and enteric nervous systems. *Annals of gastroenterology, 28*(2), 203–209.

Cardi, V., & Treasure, J. (2010). Treatments in eating disorders: Towards future directions. *Minerva Psichiatrica, 51*(3), 191–206.

Carels, R. A., Hinman, N. G., Burmeister, J. M., Hoffmann, D. A., Ashrafioun, L., & Koball, A. M. (2013). Stereotypical images and implicit weight bias in overweight/obese people. *Eating and Weight Disorders, 18*(4), 441–445. doi:10.1007/s40519-013-0072-5

Carels, R. A., Wott, C. B., Young, K. M., Gumble, A., Koball, A., & Oehlhof, M. W. (2010). Implicit, explicit, and internalized weight bias and psychosocial maladjustment among treatment-seeking adults. *Eating Behavior, 11*(3):180–185.

Carlson, L. E., Speca, M., Faris, P., & Patel, K. D. (2007). One year pre-post intervention follow-up of psychological, immune, endocrine and blood pressure outcomes of mindfulness-based stress reduction (MBSR) in breast and prostate cancer outpatients. *Brain, Behavior, and Immunity, 21*(8), 1038–1049.

Carlson, L. E., Speca, M., Patel, K. D., & Goodey, E. (2003). Mindfulness-based stress reduction in relation to quality of life, mood, symptoms of stress, and immune parameters in breast and prostate cancer outpatients. *Psychosomatic Medicine, 65*, 571–581.

Carnegie Mellon University. (2012, April 2). *How stress influences disease: Carnegie Mellon study reveals stress as the culprit* (Press release). Retrieved from https://www.cmu.edu/news/stories/archives/2012/april/april2_stressdisease.html

Carnethon, M. R., Gidding, S. S., Nehgme, R., Sidney, S., Jacobs, D. R. Jr., & Liu, K. (2003). Cardiorespiratory fitness in young adulthood and the development of cardiovascular disease risk factors. *Journal of the American Medical Association, 290*(23), 3092–3100.

Carnethon, M. R., Knutson, K. L., Kim, K., de Chavez, P. J., Goldberger, J. J., Ng, J., … Zee, P. (2012). Racial/ethnic differences in sleep duration and quality in a population sample. Presented at the annual meeting of the Associated Professional Sleep Societies. *Journal of Sleep and Sleep Disorders Research, 35*(Abstract suppl.), A342.

Carpenter, K. M., Hasin, D. S., Allison, D. B., & Faith, M. S. (2000). Relationships between obesity and DSM-IV major depressive disorder, suicide ideation, and suicide attempts: Results from a general population study. *American Journal of Public Health, 90*, 251–257.

Carpenter, S. (2013). Awakening to sleep. *Monitor on Psychology, 44*(1), 40–45.

Carroll, A. (2016). *State sponsored homophobia: A world survey of sexual orientation laws: Criminalization, protection and recognition* (11th ed.). Geneva, Switzerland: International Lesbian, Gay, Bisexual, Trans and Intersex Association [ILGA]. Retrieved from https://ilga.org/downloads/02_ILGA_State_Sponsored_Homophobia_2016_ENG_WEB_150516.pdf

Carroll, D. (2011). A brief commentary on cardiovascular reactivity at a crossroads. *Biological Psychology, 86*(2), 149–151.

Carroll, J. E., Roux, A. V. D., Fitzpatrick, A. L., & Seeman, T. (2013). Low social support is associated with shorter leukocyte telomere length in late life: Multi-ethnic study of atherosclerosis. *Psychosomatic Medicine, 75*, 171–177.

Carroll, M. D., Navaneelan, T., Bryan, S., & Ogden, C. L. (2015). *Prevalence of obesity among children and adolescents in the United States and Canada (NCHS Data Brief No. 211)*. Hyattsville, MD: National Center for Health Statistics.

Carter, K. O., Olshan-Perlmutter, M., Norton, H. J., & Smith, M. O. (2011). NADA acupuncture prospective trial in patients with substance use disorders and seven common health symptoms. *Journal of Medical Acupuncture, 23*(3), 131–135.

Carteret, M. (2012). Cultural aspects of pain management. *Dimensions of Culture*. Retrieved from http://www.dimensionsofculture.com/2010/11/cultural-aspects-of-pain-management/

Cartwright, M., Wardle, J., Steggles, N., Simon, A. E., Croker, H., & Jarvis, M. J. (2003). Stress and dietary practices in adolescents. *Health Psychology, 22*(4), 362–369.

Carver, C. S. (1997). You want to measure coping but your protocol's too long: Consider the Brief COPE. *International Journal of Behavioral Medicine, 4*, 92–100. Table 1, p. 96.

Carver, C. S., & Connor-Smith, J. (2010). Personality and coping. *Annual Review of Psychology, 61,* 679–704.

Carver, C. S., & Scheier, M. F. (2002). Optimism. In C. R. Snyder & S. J. Lopez (Eds.), *Handbook of positive psychology* (pp. 231–243). New York, NY: Oxford University Press.

Carver, C. S., Smith, R. G., Antoni, M. H., Petronis, V. M., Weiss, S., & Derhagopian, R. P. (2005). Optimistic personality and psychosocial well-being during treatment predict psychosocial well-being among long-term survivors of breast cancer. *Health Psychology, 24*(5), 508–515.

Casciani, D. (2009). GBL drug death identified by UK doctors. *BBC News.* Retrieved from http://news.bbc.co.uk/2/hi/uk_news/8428802.stm

Caspi, A., Harrington, H., Moffitt, T. E., Milne, B. J., & Poulton, R. (2006). Socially isolated children 20 years later. *Archives of Pediatric Adolescent Medicine, 160,* 805–811.

Cassetta, J. A., Boden-Albala, B., Sciacca, R. R., & Giardina, E.-G. (2007). Association of education and race/ethnicity with physical activity in insured urban women. *Journal of Women's Health, 16*(6), 902–908.

Castillo-Garzon, M. J., Ruiz, J. R., Ortega, F. B., & Gutierrez, A. (2006). Anti-aging therapy through fitness enhancement. *Journal of Clinical Interventions in Aging, 1*(3), 213–220.

Castro, C. M., Wilson, C., Wang, F., & Schillinger, D. (2007). Babel babble: Physicians' use of unclarified medical jargon with patients. *American Journal of Health Behavior, 31,* S85–S95.

Castro, F. G., Barrera, M., Jr., & Holleran Streiker, L. K. (2010). Issues and challenges in the design of culturally adapted evidence-based interventions. *Annual Review of Clinical Psychology, 6,* 213–239.

Cecil, J. E., Tavendale, R., Watt, P., Hetherington, M. M., & Palmer, C. N. A. (2008). An obesity-associated FTO gene variant and increased energy intake in children. *New England Journal of Medicine, 359,* 2558–2566.

Center for Behavioral Health Statistics and Quality. (2015). *Behavioral health trends in the United States: Results from the 2014 National Survey on Drug Use and Health* (HHS Publication No. SMA 15-4927, NSDUH Series H-50). Retrieved from http://www.samhsa.gov/data/

Centers for Disease Control and Prevention (CDC). (2008). Cigarette smoking among adults—United States, 2007. *Morbidity and Mortality Weekly Report, 57*(45), 1221–1226.

Centers for Disease Control and Prevention (CDC). (2010a). *Diabetes public health resource.* Retrieved from http://www.cdc.gov/diabetes/consumer/beactive.htm

Centers for Disease Control and Prevention (CDC). (2010b). *Healthy youth!* Retrieved from http://www.cdc.gov/HealthyYouth/index.htm

Centers for Disease Control and Prevention (CDC). (2011a). *National diabetes fact sheet: National estimates and general information on diabetes and prediabetes in the United States, 2011.* Retrieved from http://www.cdc.gov/diabetes/pubs/pdf/ndfs_2011.pdf

Centers for Disease Control and Prevention (CDC). (2011b). Youth risk behavior surveillance—United States, 2011. *Morbidity and Mortality Weekly Report, 61*(SS-4).

Centers for Disease Control and Prevention (CDC). (2012a). *Health literacy: Accurate, accessible and actionable health information for all.* Retrieved from http://www.cdc.gov/healthliteracy/

Centers for Disease Control and Prevention (CDC). (2012b). *A look inside food deserts.* Retrieved from http://www.cdc.gov/features/FoodDeserts/

Centers for Disease Control and Prevention (CDC). (2013a). *Genital HPV infection—Fact sheet.* Retrieved from http://www.cdc.gov/std/hpv/stdfact-hpv.htm

Centers for Disease Control and Prevention (CDC). (2013b). *HIV surveillance report, 2011* (Vol. 23). Retrieved from http://www.cdc.gov/hiv/library/reports/surveillance/index.html

Centers for Disease Control and Prevention (CDC). (2013c). *Incidence, prevalence, and cost of sexually transmitted infections in the United States. Fact sheet.* Retrieved at https://www.cdc.gov/std/stats/STI-Estimates-Fact-Sheet-Feb-2013.pdf

Centers for Disease Control and Prevention (CDC). (2014a). All injuries. *Centers for Disease Control and Prevention FastStats.* Retrieved from http://www.cdc.gov/nchs/fastats/injury.htm

Centers for Disease Control and Prevention (CDC). (2014b). *Antibiotic resistance threats in the United States, 2013.* Retrieved from http://www.cdc.gov/drugresistance/threat-report-2013/

Centers for Disease Control and Prevention (CDC). (2014c). *National diabetes statistics report: Estimates of diabetes and its burden in the United States, 2014.* Atlanta, GA: U.S. Department of Health and Human Services.

Centers for Disease Control and Prevention (CDC). (2015a). Accidents or unintentional injuries. *Centers for Disease Control and Prevention FastStats.* Retrieved from http://www.cdc.gov/nchs/fastats/accidental-injury.htm

Centers for Disease Control and Prevention (CDC). (2015b). Chronic liver disease and cirrhosis. *Center for Disease Control and Prevention FastStats.* Retrieved from http://www.cdc.gov/nchs/fastats/liver-disease.htm

Centers for Disease Control and Prevention (CDC). (2015c). *Sleep and sleep disorders.* Retrieved from http://www.cdc.gov/sleep/index.html

Centers for Disease Control and Prevention (CDC). (2015d). *Work, stress, and health: Help us plan the next 25 years.* Retrieved from http://blogs.cdc.gov/niosh-science-blog/2015/07/01/workplace-stress/

Centers for Disease Control and Prevention (CDC). (2016a). *Behavioral risk factor surveillance system (BRFSS).* Atlanta, GA: Author. Retrieved from http://www.cdc.gov/brfss/annual_data/2000/pdf/2000summarydataquality report.pdf

Centers for Disease Control and Prevention (CDC). (2016b). *CDC estimates preventable deaths from 5 leading causes.* Retrieved from https://www.cdc.gov/media/releases/2016/p1117-preventable-deaths.html

Centers for Disease Control and Prevention (CDC). (2016c). *Fact sheet—Alcohol use and your health.* Retrieved from http://www.cdc.gov/alcohol/pdfs/alcoholyourhealth.pdf

Centers for Disease Control and Prevention (CDC). (2016d). *Ten leading causes of death and injury.* National Center for Injury Prevention and Control. Retrieved from http://www.cdc.gov/injury/wisqars/leadingcauses.html

Centers for Disease Control and Prevention (CDC). (2017a). *Cancer rates by race/ethnicity and sex.* Retrieved from https://www.cdc.gov/cancer/dcpc/data/race.htm

Centers for Disease Control and Prevention (CDC). (2017b). *Chlamydia—CDC fact sheet.* Retrieved from https://www.cdc.gov/std/chlamydia/stdfact-chlamydia-detailed.htm

Centers for Disease Control and Prevention (CDC). (2017c). *Heart disease facts.* Retrieved from https://www.cdc.gov/heartdisease/facts.htm

Centers for Disease Control and Prevention (CDC). (2017d). *HIV in the United States: At a glance.* Retrieved from https://www.cdc.gov/hiv/pdf/statistics/overview/cdc-hiv-us-ataglance.pdf

Centers for Disease Control and Prevention. CDC. (2017e). *Health equity.* Retrieved from https://www.cdc.gov/minorityhealth/index.html

Centers for Disease Control and Prevention (CDC). (2017f). *HIV Surveillance Report, 2016* (Vol. 28). Retrieved from http://www.cdc.gov/hiv/library/reports/hiv-surveillance.html

Centers for Disease Control and Prevention (CDC). (2017g). *National diabetes statistics report: Estimates of diabetes and its burden in the United States.* Atlanta, GA: U.S. Department of Health and Human Services.

Centers for Disease Control and Prevention (CDC). (2017h). *Short sleep duration among U.S. adults.* Retrieved from https://www.cdc.gov/sleep/data_statistics.html

Centers for Disease Control and Prevention (CDC). (2017i). *A snapshot: Diabetes in the United States.* Retrieved from https://www.cdc.gov/diabetes/library/socialmedia/infographics.html

Centers for Disease Control and Prevention (CDC). (2017j). *Stroke facts.* Retrieved from https://www.cdc.gov/stroke/facts.htm

Centers for Disease Control and Prevention (CDC). (2018a). *Burden of tobacco use in the U.S.* Retrieved from https://www.cdc.gov/tobacco/campaign/tips/resources/data/cigarette-smoking-in-united-states.html

Centers for Disease Control and Prevention (CDC). (2018b). *Childhood obesity facts.* Retrieved from https://www.cdc.gov/healthyschools/obesity/facts.htm

Centers for Disease Control and Prevention (CDC). (2018c). *HIV among women.* Retrieved from https://www.cdc.gov/hiv/group/gender/women/index.html

Centers for Disease Control and Prevention (CDC). (2018d). Current cigarette smoking among adults in the United States. Retrieved from https://www.cdc.gov/tobacco/data_statistics/fact_sheets/adult_data/cig_smoking/index.htm

Centers for Disease Control and Prevention (CDC). (2018e). *HIV among people who inject drugs.* Retrieved from https://www.cdc.gov/hiv/group/hiv-idu.html

Centers for Disease Control and Prevention (CDC). (2018f). *HIV among youth.* Retrieved from https://www.avert.org/professionals/hiv-social-issues/key-affected-populations/children

Centers for Disease Control and Prevention (CDC). (2018g). *Smoking and tobacco use fast facts.* Retrieved from https://www.cdc.gov/tobacco/data_statistics/fact_sheets/fast_facts/index.htm

Centers for Medicare and Medicaid Services (CMS). (2017). *Age and gender.* Retrieved from http://www.cms.gov/Research-Statistics-Data-and-Systems/Statistics-Trends-and-Reports/NationalHealthExpendData/Age-and-Gender.html

Cha, F. S., Doswell, W. M., Kim, K. H., Charron-Prochownik, D., & Patrick, T. E. (2007). Evaluating the Theory of Planned Behavior to explain intention to engage in premarital sex amongst Korean college students: A questionnaire survey. *International Journal of Nursing Studies, 4,* 1147–1157.

Champion, V., Skinner, C. S., Hui, S., Monahan, P., Julian, B., & Daggy, J. (2007). The effect of telephone versus print tailoring for mammography adherence. *Patient Education and Counseling, 65,* 416–423.

Chapin, H., Bagarinao, E., Hubbard, E. K., Dixon, E. A., Glover, G. H., & Mackey, S. (2013). *Neural correlates of effective cognitive modulation of pain.* Poster presented at the Meetings of the American Academy of Pain Medicine.

Chassin, L., Presson, C. C., Sherman, S. J., & Kim, K. (2003). Historical changes in cigarette smoking and smoking-related beliefs after 2 decades in a midwestern community. *Health Psychology, 22*(4), 347–353.

Chatard, A., & Selimbegovic, L. (2011). When self-destructive thoughts flash through the mind: Failure to meet standards affects the accessibility of suicide-related thoughts. *Journal of Personality and Social Psychology, 100,* 587–605.

Chen, E., Fisher, E. B., Bacharier, L. B., & Strunk, R. C. (2003). Socioeconomic status, stress, and immune markers in adolescents with asthma. *Psychosomatic Medicine, 65,* 984–992.

Chen, E. H., Shofer, F. S., Dean, A. J., Hollander, J. E., Baxt, W. G., Robey, J. L., … Millis, A. M. (2008). Gender disparity in analgesic treatment of emergency department patients with acute abdominal pain. *Academic Emergency Medicine, 15*(5), 414–418.

Chen, H., & Jackson, T. (2009). Predictors of changes in weight esteem among mainland Chinese adolescents: A longitudinal analysis. *Developmental Psychology, 45*(6), 1618–1629.

Chen, J. Y., Fox, S. A., Cantrell, C. H., Stockdale, S. E., & Kagawa-Singer, M. (2007). Health disparities and prevention: Racial/ethnic barriers to flu vaccinations. *Journal of Community Health 32,* 5–20.

Chen, P. W. (2013, May 30). For new doctors, 8 minutes per patient. *The New York Times.* Retrieved from http://well.blogs.nytimes.com/2013/05/30/for-new-doctors-8-minutes-per-patient/?_r=0

Chen, X., Beydoun, M. A., & Wang, Y. (2008). Is sleep duration associated with childhood obesity? A systematic review and meta-analysis. *Obesity, 16,* 265–274.

Chen, Y-F., Huang, X-Y, Chien, C-H., & Cheng, J-F. (2016). The effectiveness of diaphragmatic breathing relaxation training for reducing anxiety. *Perspectives in Psychiatric Care, 53*(4), 329–336.

Chiaramonte, G. R., & Friend, R. (2006). Medical students' and residents' gender bias in the diagnosis, treatment, and interpretation of coronary heart disease symptoms. *Health Psychology, 25*(3), 255–266.

Chida, Y., & Steptoe, A. (2008). Positive psychological well-being and mortality: A quantitative review of prospective observational studies. *Psychosomatic Medicine, 70*(7), 741–756.

Chida, Y., & Steptoe, A. (2010). Greater cardiovascular responses to laboratory mental stress are associated with poor subsequent cardiovascular risk status. *Hypertension, 55,* 1026–1032.

Chida, Y., Steptoe, A., & Powell, L. H. (2009). Religiosity/spirituality and mortality: A systematic quantitative review. *Psychotherapy and Psychosomatics, 78*(2), 81–90.

Chilet-Rosell, E. (2014). Gender bias in clinical research, pharmaceutical marketing, and the prescription of drugs. *Global Health Action, 7,* 10.3402/gha.v7.25484. doi.org/10.3402/gha.v7.25484

Choi, H., Meininger, J. C., & Roberts, R. E. (2006). Ethnic differences in adolescents' mental distress, social stress, and resources. *Adolescence, 41,* 263–283.

Choi, W. S., Harris, K. J., Okuyemi, K., & Ahluwalia, J. S. (2003). Predictors of smoking initiation among college-bound high school students. *Annals of Behavioral Medicine, 26*(1), 69–74.

Choshen-Hillel, S., & Yaniv, I. (2011). Agency and the construction of social preference: Between inequality aversion and prosocial behavior. *Journal of Personality and Social Psychology, 101*(6), 1253–1261.

Christakis, N. A., & Fowler, J. H. (2007). The spread of obesity in a large social network over 32 years. *New England Journal of Medicine, 357*, 370–379.

Christensen, A. J., Moran, P. J., & Wiebe, J. S. (1999). Assessment of irrational health beliefs: Relation to health practices and medical regimen adherence. *Health Psychology, 18*(2), 169–176.

Christiansen, D. M. (2015). Sex differences in PTSD: Mediation and moderation effects. *Comprehensive Guide to Post-Traumatic Stress Disorder*, 1–15. Retrieved from http://link.springer.com/referenceworkentry/10.1007/978-3-319-08613-2_4-1

Chuah, B. L. P. (2006). *The influence of coping and emotional intelligence on psychological adjustment to cancer: A longitudinal study of patients calling a cancer helpline*. Melbourne, Australia: University of Melbourne.

Churilla, J. R., Johnson, T. M., Magyari, P. M., & Crouter, S. E. (2012). Descriptive analysis of resistance exercise and metabolic syndrome. *Diabetes and Metabolic Syndrome: Clinical Research and Reviews, 6*(1), 42–47.

Civic Impulse. (2018). *H.R. 36 —112th Congress: Eating Disorders Awareness, Prevention, and Education Act of 2011*. Retrieved from https://www.govtrack.us/congress/bills/112/hr36

Clark, N. M., Mitchell, H. E., & Rand, C. S. (2009). Effectiveness of educational and behavioral asthma interventions. *Pediatrics, 123*(3), S185–S192.

Clark, R. C., & Mayer, R. E. (2016). *E-learning and the science of instruction: Proven guidelines for consumers and designers of multimedia learning*. Hoboken, NJ: Wiley.

Clarke, T. C., Black, L. Stussman, B. J., Barnes, P. M., & Nahin, R. L. (2015). *Trends in the use of complementary health approaches among adults: United States, 2002–2012* (National Health Statistics Reports No. 79). Hyattsville, MD: National Center for Health Statistics.

Clarke, T. C., Norris, T., & Schiller, J. S. (2017). *Early release of selected estimates based on data from 2016 National Health Interview Survey*. National Center for Health Statistics. Retrieved from https://www.cdc.gov/nchs/data/nhis/earlyrelease/earlyrelease201705.pdf

Clarke, P. J., O'Malley, P. M., & Johnston, L. D. (2009). Differential trends in weight-related health behaviors among American young adults by gender, race/ethnicity, and socioeconomic status: 1984–2006. *American Journal of Public Health, 99*(10), 1893–1901.

Claussnitzer, M., Dankel, S. N., Kim, K-H., Quon, G., Meuleman, W., Haugen, C., … Kellis, M. (2015). FTO variant circuitry and adipocyte browning in humans. *The New England Journal of Medicine, 373*(10), 895–907.

Clay, R. A. (2016, February). Adventures in integrated care. *Monitor on Psychology, 47*(2), 32–35.

Cleveland Clinic. (2018). *Express care online*. Retrieved from https://my.clevelandclinic.org/online-services/express-care-online?gclid=EAIaIQobChMI3oyqltiZ3AIVHLbACh2CtQphEAAYBCAAEgIx2fD_BwE

CMS. (2017). Age and gender. *Centers for Medicare and Medicaid Services*. Retrieved from http://www.cms.gov/Research-Statistics-Data-and-Systems/Statistics-Trends-and-Reports/NationalHealthExpendData/Age-and-Gender.html

CMS. (2018). National Health Expenditure Accounts. *Centers for Medicare and Medicaid Services*. Retrieved from https://www.cms.gov/Research-Statistics-Data-and-Systems/Statistics-Trends-and-Reports/NationalHealthExpendData/NationalHealthAccountsHistorical.html

Cochran, S. D., Mays, V. M., & Sullivan, J. G. (2003). Prevalence of mental disorders, psychological distress, and mental health services use among lesbian, gay, and bisexual adults in the United States. *Journal of Consulting and Clinical Psychology, 71*(1), 53–61.

Cohen, D. A., Wang, W., Wyatt, J. K., Kronauer, R. E., Dijk, D-J., Czeisler, C. A., & Klerman, E. B. (2010). Uncovering residual effects of chronic sleep loss on human performance. *Science Translational Medicine, 2*(14), 14ra3.

Cohen, F., Kemeny, M. E., Zegans, L. S., Johnson, P. Kearney, K. A., & Stites, D. P. (2007). Immune function declines with unemployment and recovers after stressor termination. *Psychosomatic Medicine, 69*, 225–234.

Cohen, J. (2016, June 3). Let smokers see the warning they need. *The New York Times*. Retrieved from http://www.nytimes.com/2016/06/03/opinion/let-smokers-see-the-warning-they-need.html?_r=1

Cohen, S., Alper, C. M., Doyle, W. J., Treanor, J. J., & Turner, R. B. (2006). Positive emotional style predicts resistance to illness after experimental exposure to rhinovirus or influenza A virus. *Psychosomatic Medicine, 68*, 809–815.

Cohen, S., Doyle, W., & Baum, A. (2006). Socioeconomic status is associated with stress hormones. *Psychosomatic Medicine, 68*, 414–420.

Cohen, S., Doyle, W. J., Turner, R., Alper, C. M., & Skoner, D. P. (2003). Sociability and susceptibility to the common cold. *Journal of the American Medical Association, 277*, 1940–1944.

Cohen, S., Janicki-Deverts, D., Doyle, W. J., Miller, G. E., Frank, E., Rabin, B. S., & Turner, R. B. (2012). Chronic stress, glucocorticoid receptor resistance, inflammation, and disease risk. *Proceedings of the National Academy of Sciences, 109*(16), 5995–5999. Retrieved from http://www.pnas.org/content/early/2012/03/26/1118355109.abstract

Cohen, S., & McKay, G. (1984). Social support, stress and the buffering hypothesis: A theoretical analysis. In A. Baum, S. E. Taylor, & J. E. Singer (Eds.), *Handbook of psychology and health* (pp. 253–268). Hillsdale, NJ: Erlbaum.

Cohen, S., & Pressman, S. D. (2006). Positive affect and health. *Current Directions in Psychological Science, 15*(3), 122–125.

Cohen, S., & Rodriguez, M. S. (1995). Pathways linking affective disturbances and physical disorders. *Health Psychology, 14*, 374–380.

Cohen, S., Sherrod, D. R., & Clark, M. S. (1986). Social skills and the stress-protective role of social support. *Journal of Personality and Social Psychology, 50*, 963–973.

Cohen, S., & Wills, T. A. (1985). Stress, social support, and the buffering hypothesis. *Psychological Bulletin, 93*, 310–357.

Cole, S. W. (2008). Psychosocial influences on HIV-1 disease progression: Neural, endocrine, and virologic mechanisms. *Psychosomatic Medicine, 70*, 562–568.

Coleman-Jensen, A., & Gregory, C. A. (2017). *Food insecurity, chronic disease, and health among working-age adults* (RR-235).

U.S. Department of Agriculture, Economic Research Service. Retrieved from https://www.ers.usda.gov/publications/pub-details/?pubid=84466

Coleman-Jensen, A., Rabbitt, M. P., Gregory, C. A., & Singh, A. (2016, September). *Household food security in the United States*. U.S. Department of Agriculture, Economic Research Service. Retrieved from https://www.ers.usda.gov/webdocs/publications/79761/err215_summary.pdf?v=42636

Collins, N. L., Dunkel-Schetter, C., Lobel, M., & Scrimshaw, S. C. (1993). Social support in pregnancy: Psychosocial correlates of birth outcomes and postpartum depression. *Journal of Personality and Social Psychology, 65*, 1243–1258.

Colloca, L., Lopiano, L., Lanette, M., & Benedetti, F. (2004). Overt versus covert treatment for pain, anxiety, and Parkinson's disease. *The Lancet Neurology, 3*(11), 679–684.

Conden, E., Rosenblad, A., Wagner, P., Leppert, J., Ekselius, L., & Aslund, C. (2017). Is Type D personality an independent risk factor for recurrent myocardial infarction or all-cause mortality in post-acute myocardial infarction patients? *European Journal of Preventive Cardiology, 24*(5), 522–533.

Congressional Budget Office (CBO). (2010). *Patient protection and the Affordable Care Act*. Retrieved from http://www.cbo.gov

Conn, V. S. (2010). Depressive symptom outcomes of physical activity interventions. Meta-analysis findings. *Annals of Behavioral Medicine, 39*, 128–138.

Conn, V. S., Hafdahl, A. R., & Mehr, D. R. (2011). Interventions to increase physical activity among healthy adults: Meta-analysis of outcomes. *American Journal of Public Health, 104*(4), 751–758.

Conn, V. S., Ruppar, T. M., Enriquez, M., Cooper, P. S., & Chan, K. C. (2015). Healthcare provider targeted interventions to improve medication adherence: Systematic review and meta-analysis. *International Journal of Clinical Practice, 69*(8), 889–899.

Conner, M., Norman, P., & Bell, R. (2002). The theory of planned behavior and healthy eating. *Health Psychology, 21*(2), 194–201.

Conroy, D. E., Hyde, A. L., Doerksen, S. E., & Riebeiro, N. F. (2010). Implicit attitudes and explicit motivation prospectively predict physical activity. *Annals of Behavioral Medicine, 39*, 112–118.

Cooper, M. L. (2006). Does drinking promote risky sexual behavior? A complex answer to a simple question. *Current Directions in Psychological Science, 15*, 19–23.

Cordasco, K. M. (2013). Obtaining informed consent from patients: Brief update. In *Making health care safer II: An updated critical analysis of the evidence for patient safety practices* (Evidence Reports/Technology Assessments No. 211). Rockville, MD: Agency for Healthcare Research and Quality.

Corelli, R. L., & Hudmon, K. S. (2002). Medications for smoking cessation. *Western Journal of Medicine, 176*(2), 131–135.

Cornally, N., & McCarthy, G. (2011). Chronic pain: The help-seeking behavior, attitudes, and beliefs of older adults living in the community. *Pain Management Nursing, 12*(4), 206–217.

Cornelis, M. C., El-Sohemy, A., Kabagambe, E. K., & Campos, H. (2006). Coffee, CYP1A2 genotype, and risk of myocardial infarction. *Journal of the American Medical Association, 295*(1), 1135–1141.

Costa, V. D., Lang, P. J., Sabatinelli, D., Versace, F., & Bradley, M. M. (2010). Emotional imagery: Assessing pleasure and arousal in the brain's reward circuitry. *Human Brain Mapping, 31*, 1446–1457.

Costanzo, E. S., Stawski, R. S., Ryff, C. D., Coe, C. L., & Almeida, D. M. (2012). Cancer survivors' responses to daily stressors: Implications for quality of life. *Health Psychology, 31*(3), 360–370.

Costas, R., & Gany, F. (2013). Depressive symptoms in a sample of Afro-Caribbean and Latino immigrant cancer patients: A comparative analysis. *Supportive Care in Cancer, 21*(9), 2461–2468.

Council of Colleges of Acupuncture and Oriental Medicine (CCAOM). (2016). *Acupuncture: Frequently asked questions*. Retrieved from http://www.ccaom.org/faqs.asp

Council for Responsible Nutrition (CRN). (2017). *CRN 2017 survey on dietary supplements*. Retrieved from https://www.crnusa.org/resources/crn-2017-annual-survey-dietary-supplements

Couturier, J., Kimber, M., & Szatmari, P. (2013). Efficacy of family-based treatment for adolescents with eating disorders: A systematic review and meta-analysis. *International Journal of Eating Disorders, 46*(1), 3–11.

Coyne, J. C., Stefanek, M., & Palmer, S. C. (2007). Psychotherapy and survival in cancer: The conflict between hope and evidence. *Psychological Bulletin, 133*, 367–394.

Coyne, J. C., & Tennen, H. (2010). Positive psychology in cancer care: Bad science, exaggerated claims, and unproven medicine. *Annals of Behavioral Medicine, 39*, 16–26.

Craciun, C., Schuz, N., Lippke, S., & Schwarzer, R. (2012). Facilitating sunscreen use in women by a theory-based online intervention: A randomized controlled trial. *Health Psychology, 17*, 207.

Cramer, J. A. (2004). A systematic review of adherence with medications for diabetes. *Diabetes Care, 27*, 1218–1224.

Cramer, H., Haller, H., Lauche, R., & Dobos, G. (2012). Mindfulness-based stress reduction for low back pain. A systematic review. *BMC Complementary and Alternative Medicine, 12*, 162. Retrieved from https://www.ncbi.nlm.nih.gov/pmc/articles/PMC3520871/pdf/1472-6882-12-162.pdf

Creswell, J. D., Irwin, M. R., Burklund, L. J., Lieberman, M. D., Arevalo, J. M. G., Ma, J., Breen, E. C., & Cole, S. W. (2012). Mindfulness-based stress reduction training reduces loneliness and pro-inflammatory gene expression in older adults: A small randomized controlled trial. *Brain, Behavior, and Immunity, 26*, 1095–1101.

Creswell, J. D., & Lindsay, E. K. (2014). How does mindfulness training affect health? A mindfulness stress buffering account. *Current Directions in Psychological Science, 23*(6), 401–407.

Creswell, J. D., Myers, H. F., Cole, S. W., & Irwin, M. R. (2009). Mindfulness meditation training effects on CD4+ T lymphocytes in HIV-1 infected adults: A small randomized controlled trial. *Brain, Behavior, & Immunology, 23*(2), 184–188.

Creswell, J. D., Way, B. M., Eisenberger, N. I., & Lieberman, M. D. (2007). Neural correlates of dispositional mindfulness during affect labeling. *Psychosomatic Medicine, 69*, 560–565.

Crews, F., He, J., & Hodge, C. (2007). Adolescent cortical development: A critical period of vulnerability for addiction. *Pharmacology, Biochemistry and Behavior, 86*, 189–199.

Crittenden, C. N., Pressman, S., Cohen, S., Janicki-Deverts, D., Smith, B. W., & Seeman, T. E. (2014). Social integration and pulmonary function in the elderly. *Health Psychology, 33*(6), 535–543.

Crosnoe, R. (2002). Academic and health-related trajectories in adolescence: The intersection of gender and athletics. *Journal of Health and Social Behavior, 43*, 317–335.

Cross, A. J., Ferrucci, L. M., Risch, A., Graubard, B. I., Ward, M. H., Park, Y., … Sinha, R. (2010). A large prospective study of meat consumption and colorectal cancer risk: An investigation of potential mechanisms underlying this association. *Cancer Research, 70*(6), 2406–2414.

Cruess, D. G., Antoni, M. H., McGreagor, B. A., Kilbourn, K. M., Boyers, A. E., Alferi, S. M., … Kumar, M. (2000). Cognitive-behavioral stress management reduces serum cortisol by enhancing benefit finding among women being treated for early stage breast cancer. *Psychosomatic Medicine, 62*(3), 304–308.

Cummings, D. E., Foster-Schubert, K. E., & Overduin, J. (2005). Ghrelin and energy balance: Focus on current controversies. *Current Drug Targets, 6*(2), 153–169.

Cunningham, T. J., Wheaton, A. G., Ford, E. S., & Croft, J. B. (2016). Racial/ethnic disparities in self-reported short sleep duration among US-born and foreign-born adults. *Ethnicity and Health, 21,* 628–638.

Cunningham, T. J., Wheaton, A. G., & Giles, W. H. (2015). The association between psychological distress and self-reported sleep duration in a population-based sample of women and men. *Sleep Disorders, 2015,* 172064.

Curhan, K. B., Sims, T., Markus, H. R., Kitayama, S., Karasawa, M., Kawakami, N., … Ryff, C. D. (2014). Just how bad negative affect is for your health depends on culture. *Psychological Science, 25*(12), 2277–2280.

Cvengros, J. A., Christensen, A. J., & Lawton, W. J. (2004). The role of perceived control and preference for control in adherence to a chronic medical regimen. *Annals of Behavioral Medicine, 27*(3), 155–161.

Cyna, A. M., McAuliffe, G. L., & Andrew, M. I. (2004). Hypnosis for pain relief in labour and childbirth: A systematic review. *British Journal of Anaesthesia, 93*(4), 505–511.

Daley, A. (2008). Exercise and depression: A review of reviews. *Journal of Clinical Psychology in Medical Settings, 15*(2), 140–147.

Daly, M., Delaney, L., Doran, P. P., Harmon, C., & MacLachlan, M. (2010). Naturalistic monitoring of the affect-heart rate relationship: A day reconstruction study. *Health Psychology, 29*(2), 186–195.

Dansinger, M. L., Gleason, J. A., Griffith, J. L., Selker, H. P., & Schaefer, E. J. (2005). Comparison of the Atkins, Ornish, Weight Watchers, and Zone diets for weight loss and heart disease risk reduction. *Journal of the American Medical Association, 293*(1), 43–53.

Dao, T. K., Nagy, A. Y., Armsworth, M., Wear, E., Papathopoulos, K. N., & Gopaldas, R. (2011). Randomized controlled trial of brief cognitive behavioral intervention for depression and anxiety symptoms preoperatively in patients undergoing coronary artery bypass graft surgery. *Journal of Thoracic and Cardiovascular Surgery, 142*(3), e109–e115.

Daruna, J. H. (2004). *Introduction to psychoneuroimmunology.* Burlington, MA: Elsevier Academic Press.

Davidson, K. W., Kupfer, D. J., Biggeer, T., Califf, R. M., Carney, R. M., Coyne, J. C., … Suis, J. M. (2006). Assessment and treatment of depression in patients with cardiovascular disease: National Heart, Lung, and Blood Institute working group report. *Psychosomatic Medicine, 68,* 645–650.

Davidson, K. W., & Mostovsky, E. (2010). Anger expression and risk of coronary disease: Evidence from the Nova Scotia Health Survey. *American Heart Journal, 159*(2), 199–206.

Davidson, R. J., Kabat-Zinn, J., Schumacher, J., Rosenkranz, M., Muller, D., Santorelli, S. F., … Sheridan, J. F. (2003). Alterations in brain and immune function produced by mindfulness meditation. *Psychosomatic Medicine, 65*(4), 564–570.

Davies, N. J., & Batehup, L. (2010). Self-management support for cancer survivors: Guidance for developing interventions. An update of the evidence. *National Cancer Survivorship Initiative.* Retrieved from http://www.ncsi.org.uk/wp-content/uploads/Guidance-for-Developing-Cancer-Specific-Self-Management-Programmes.pdf

Davies, G. M., Willner, P., James, D. L., & Morgan, M. J. (2004). Influence of nicotine gum on acute cravings for cigarettes. *Journal of Psychopharmacology, 18*(1), 83–87.

Davis, C. D., & Uthus, E. O. (2004). DNA methylation, cancer susceptibility, and nutrient interactions. *Experimental Biology and Medicine, 229*(10), 988–995.

Davis, C. L., Tomporowski, P. D., McDowell, J. E., Austin, B. P., Miller, P. H., Yanasak, N. E., … Naglieri, J. A. (2011). Exercise improves executive function and achievement and alters brain activation in overweight children: A randomized, controlled trial. *Health Psychology, 30*(1), 91–98. doi:10.1037/a0021766

Davis, H. A., Guller, L., & Smith, G. T. (2016). Developmental trajectories of boys' driven exercise and fasting during the middle school years. *Journal of Abnormal Child Psychology, 44*(7), 1309–1319.

Davis, K. C., Jacques-Tiura, A. J., Stappenbeck, C. A., Danube, C. L., Morrison, D. M., Norris, J., & George, W. H. (2016). Men's condom use resistance: Alcohol effects on Theory of Planned Behavior constructs. *Health Psychology, 35*(2), 178–186.

Davis, K. C., Norris, J., George, W. H., Martell, J., & Heiman, J. R. (2006). Men's likelihood of sexual aggression: The influence of alcohol, sexual arousal, and violent pornography. *Aggressive Behavior, 32,* 581–589.

Davis, M. P. (2018). Cancer-related neuropathic pain. *Hematology/Oncology Clinics of North America, 32*(3), 417–431.

Davison, K. K., Schmalz, D., & Downs, D. S. (2010). Hop, skip … no! Explaining adolescent girls' disinclination for physical activity. *Annals of Behavioral Medicine, 29,* 290–302.

Dawson, D. A., Grant, B. F., Stinson, F. S., Chou, P. S., Huang, B., & Ruan, W. J. (2005). Recovery from DSM-IV alcohol dependence: United States, 2001–2002. *Addiction, 100,* 281–292.

De Andres, J., & Van Buyten, J. P. (2006). Neural modulation by stimulation. *Pain Practice, 6,* 39–45.

De Biasi, M., & Dani, J. A. (2011). Reward, addiction, withdrawal to nicotine. *Annual Review of Neuroscience, 34,* 105–130.

de Jong, A. E., & Gamel, C. (2006). Use of a simple relaxation technique in burn care: Literature review. *Journal of Advanced Nursing, 54*(6), 710–721. doi:10.1111/j.1365-2648.2006.03858.x

De Jonge, P., & Ormel, J. (2007). Depression and anxiety after myocardial infarction. *British Journal of Psychiatry, 190,* 272–273.

De la Herrán-Arita, A. K., Kornum, B. R., Mahlios, J., Jiang, W., Lin, L., Hou, T., … Mignot, E. (2013). CD4+ T cell autoimmunity to hypocretin/orexin and cross-reactivity to a 2009 H1N1 influenza A epitope in narcolepsy. *Science Translational Medicine, 5*(216). Retrieved from http://stm.sciencemag.org/content/5/216/216ra176

De Mestral, C., & Stringhini, S. (2017). Socioeconomic status and cardiovascular disease: An update. *Current Cardiology Reports, 19*(11), 115. doi:10.1007/s11886-017-0917-z

De Michele, M., Panico, S., Iannuzzi, A., Celentano, E., Ciardullo, A. V., Galasso, R., ... Rubba, P. (2002). Association of obesity and central fat distribution with carotid artery wall thickening in middle-aged women. *Stroke, 33*(12), 2923–2928.

de Ridder, D. T. D., Bertha, J., & de Wit, F. (2006). *Self-regulation in health behavior.* Hoboken, NJ: Wiley.

Dean, A. J., Walters, J., & Hall, A. (2010). A systematic review of interventions to enhance medication adherence in children and adolescents with chronic illness. *Archives of Disease in Childhood, 95,* 717–723.

Debnam, K. J., Milam, A. J., Mullen, M. M., Lacey, K., & Bradshaw, C. P. (2018). The moderating role of spirituality in the association between stress and substance use among adolescents. *Journal of Youth and Adolescence, 47*(4), 818–828.

Dehghan, M., Mente, A., Zhang, X., Swaminathan, S., Li, W., Mohan, V., ... Yusuf, S. (2017). Associations of fats and carbohydrate intake with cardiovascular disease and mortality in 18 countries from five continents (PURE): A prospective cohort study. *The Lancet, 390*(10107), 2050–2062.

Deichert, N., Fekete, E., Boarts, J., Druley, J., & Delahanty, D. (2008). Emotional support and affect: Associations with health behaviors and active coping efforts in men living with HIV. *AIDS and Behavior, 12*(1), 139–145.

Dekker, J., & DeGroot, V. (2016). Psychological adjustment to chronic disease and rehabilitation—An exploration. *Disability and Rehabilitation, 40*(1):116–120. Retrieved from https://www.ncbi.nlm.nih.gov/pubmed/27830936

Del Casale, A., Ferracuti, S., Rapinesi, C., De Rossi, P., Angeletti, G., Sani, G., Kotsalidis, G. D., & Girardi, P. (2016). Hypnosis and pain perception: An activation likelihood estimation (ALE) meta-analysis of functional neuroimaging studies. *Journal of Physiology.* Retrieved from http://www.sciencedirect.com/science/article/pii/S0928425716300018

Dembner, A. (2005, July 25). A prayer for health: Scientists attempt to measure what religions accept on faith. *The Boston Globe.* Retrieved from http://www.boston.com/news/globe/health_science/articles/2005/07/25/a_prayer_for_health

Dempsey, M. (2002). Negative coping as mediator in the relation between violence and outcomes: Inner-city African American youth. *American Journal of Orthopsychiatry, 72*(1), 102–109.

Dentato, M. P. (2012). The minority stress perspective. *Psychology and AIDS Exchange Newsletter.* Retrieved from http://www.apa.org/pi/aids/resources/exchange/2012/04/minority-stress.aspx

DePadilla, L., Windle, M., Wingood, G., Cooper, H., & DiClemente, R. (2011). Condom use among young women: Modeling the theory of gender and power. *Health Psychology, 30*(3), 310–319.

Department for Professional Employees (DPE). (2009). *Fact sheet 2009, Professional women: Vital statistics.* Retrieved from http://www.dpeaflcio.org/programs/factsheets/fs_2009_Professional_Women.htm

Depestele, L., Lemmens, G. M. D., Dierckx, E., Baetens, I., & Claes, L. (2015). The role of non-suicidal self-injury and binge-eating/purging is in the caregiving experience among mothers and fathers of adolescents with eating disorders. *European Eating Disorders Review, 24*(3), 257–260. Retrieved from http://onlinelibrary.wiley.com/doi/10.1002/erv.2428/abstract

DeSantis, C., Naishadham, D., & Jemal, A. (2013). Cancer statistics for African Americans, 2013. *CA: A Cancer Journal for Clinicians, 63*(3), 151–166.

Deshpande, S., Basil, M. D., & Basil, D. Z. (2009). Factors influencing healthy eating habits among college students: An application of the health belief model. *Health Marketing Quarterly, 26*(2), 145–164.

Desmeules, J., Piguet, V., Besson, M., Chabert, J., Rapiti, E., Rebsamen, M., ... Cedraschi, C. (2012). Psychological distress in fibromyalgia patients: A role for catechol-O-methyl-transferase Va1158Met polymorphism. *Health Psychology, 31*(2), 242–249.

Despres, J.-P., & Lemieux, I. (2006). Abdominal obesity and metabolic syndrome. *Nature, 444,* 881–887.

Dew, M. A., Hoch, C. C., Busse, D. J., Monk, T. H., Begley, A. E., Houck, P. R., Hall, M., Kupfer, D. J., & Reynolds, C. F. (2003). Healthy older adults' sleep predicts all-cause mortality at 4 to 19 years of follow-up. *Psychosomatic Medicine, 65,* 63–73.

Dhabhar, F. S. (2014). Effects of stress on immune function: The good, the bad, and the beautiful. *Immunologic Research, 58*(2–3), 193–210.

Dhabhar, F. S., & McEwen, B. S. (2001). Bidirectional effects of stress and glucocorticoid hormones on immune function: Possible explanations for paradoxical observations. In R. Ader, D. L. Felten, & N. Cohen (Eds.), *Psychoneuroimmunology* (3rd ed.). San Diego: Academic Press.

Diano, S., Farr, S. A., Benoit, S. C., McNay, E. C., da Silva, I., Horvath, B. ... Horvath, T. L. (2006). Ghrelin controls hippocampal spine synapse density and memory performance. *Nature Neuroscience, 9*(3), 381–388.

Dickerson, S. S., Gruenewald, T. L., & Kemeny, M. E. (2004). When the social self is threatened: Shame, physiology, and health. *Journal of Personality, 72*(6), 1192–1216.

Dickerson, S. S., & Kemeny, M. F. (2004). Acute stressors and cortisol response: A theoretical integration and synthesis of laboratory research. *Psychological Bulletin, 130,* 355–391.

DiClemente, C. C. (2005, September 28). *Alcohol and problem drinking.* Washington, DC: APA Practice Organization.

Diehr, P., O'Meara, E. S., Fitzpatrick, A., Newman, A. B., Kuller, L., & Burke, G. (2008). Weight, mortality, years of healthy life and active life expectancy in older adults. *Journal of the American Geriatrics Society, 56*(1). doi:10.1111/j.1532-5415

DiFranza, J. R. (2008, May). Hooked from the first cigarette. *Scientific American,* 82–87.

Dillard, A. J., Ferrer, R. A., Ubel, P. A., & Fagerlin, A. (2012). Risk perception measures' associations with behiavor intentions, affect, and cognition following colon cancer screening measures. *Health Psychology, 31*(1), 106–113.

Dimsdale, J. E. (2018). Illness anxiety disorder. In *Merck Manual (Professional Version).* Retrieved from https://www.merckmanuals.com/professional/psychiatric-disorders/somatic-symptom-and-related-disorders/illness-anxiety-disorder

Ding, D., Lawson, K. D., Kolbe-Alexander, T. L., Finkelstein, E. A., Katzmarzyk, P. T., van Mechelen, W., & Pratt, M. (2016). The economic burden of physical inactivity: A global analysis of major non-communicable diseases. *The Lancet, 388*(10051), 1311–1324.

Direito, A., Carraca, E., Rawstorn, J., Whittaker, R., & Maddison, R. (2017). Health technologies to influence physical activity and sedentary behaviors: Behavior change techniques, systematic review, and meta-analysis of randomized controlled trials. *Annals of Behavioral Medicine, 51,* 226–239.

Dishman, R. K., Berthoud, H-R., Booth, F. W., Cotman, C. W., Edgerton, R., … & Zigmond, M. J. (2006a). Neurobiology of exercise. *Obesity, 14,* 345–356.

do Carmo, T. M., Paiva, B. S. R., de Oliveira, C. Z., Nascimento, M. S. D. A., & Paiva, C. E. (2017). The feasibility and benefit of a brief psychosocial intervention in addition to early palliative care in patients with advanced cancer to reduce depressive symptoms: A pilot randomized controlled clinical trial. *BMC Cancer, 17*(1). Retrieved from http://0-link.galegroup.com.wizard.umd.umich.edu/apps/doc/A511273016/AONE?u=lom_umichdearb&sid=AONE&xid=a53abdcc

Dobson, K. S. (Ed.). (2010). *Handbook of cognitive behavioral therapies.* New York, NY: Guilford Press.

Dohrenwend, B. P., Turner, J. B., Turse, N. A., Adams, B. G., Koenen, K. C., & Marshall, R. (2006). The psychological risks of Vietnam for U.S. veterans: A revisit with new data and methods. *Science, 255,* 946–956.

Doll, R., Peto, R., Boreham, J., & Sutherland, I. (2004). Mortality in relation to smoking: 50 years' observations on British male doctors. *British Medical Journal, 328,* 1519–1528.

Donahue, K. L., Lichtenstein, P., Langstrom, N., & D'Onofrio, B. M. (2013). Why does early sexual intercourse predict subsequent maladjustment? Exploring potential familial confounds. *Health Psychology, 32*(2), 180–189.

Doro, P., Benko, R., Matuz, M., & Soos, G. (2006). Seasonality in the incidence of type 2 diabetes: A population-based study. *Diabetes Care, 29*(1), 173–184.

Dowd, J. B., Palermo, T. M., & Aiello, A. E. (2012). Family poverty is associated with cytomegalovirus antibody titers in U.S. children. *Health Psychology, 31,* 5–10.

Dowd, J. B., Simanek, A. M., & Aiello, A. E. (2009). Socio-economic status, cortisol and allostatic load: A review of the literature. *International Journal of Epidemiology, 38*(5), 1297–1309.

Dowda, M., Dishman, R. K., Porter, D., Saunders, R. P., & Pate, R. R. (2009). Commercial facilities, social cognitive variables, and physical activity of 12th-grade girls. *Annals of Behavioral Medicine, 37,* 70–87.

Drdla, R., Gassner, M., Gingl, E., & Sandkuhler, J. (2009). Induction of synaptic long-term potentiation after opioid withdrawal. *Science, 325*(5937), 207–210.

Droomers, M., Schrijvers, C. T., & Mackenbach, J. P. (2002). Why do lower educated people continue smoking? Explanations from the longitudinal GLOBE study. *Health Psychology, 21*(3), 263–272.

Dunkel Schetter, C., & Dolbier, C. (2011). Resilience in the context of chronic stress and health in adults. *Social and Personality Psychology Compass, 5,* 634–652.

Dunn, M. J., Rodriguez, E. M., Barnwell, A. S., Grossenbacher, J. C., Vannatta, K., Gerhardt, C. A., & Compas, B. (2012). Posttraumatic stress symptoms in parents of children with cancer within six months of diagnosis. *Health Psychology, 31*(2), 176–185.

Dunton, G. F., & Vaughan, E. (2008). Anticipated affective consequences of physical activity adoption and maintenance. *Health Psychology, 27,* 703–710.

Durazo-Arvizu, R. A., McGee, D. L., Cooper, R. S., Liao, Y., & Luke, A. (1998). Mortality and optimal body mass index in a sample of the U.S. population. *American Journal of Epidemiology, 147,* 739–749.

Durmer, J. S., & Dinges, D. F. (2005). Neurocognitive consequences of sleep deprivation. *Seminars in Neurology, 25*(1), 117–129.

Ebel-Lam, A. P., MacDonald, T. K., Zanna, M. P., & Fong, G. T. (2009). An experimental investigation of the interactive effects of alcohol and sexual arousal on intentions to have unprotected sex. *Basic and Applied Social Psychology, 31,* 226–233.

Ebert, M. H., & Kerns, R. D. (Eds.). (2010). *Behavioral and psychopharmacologic pain management.* Cambridge, England: Cambridge University Press.

Editorial: The government's 'karoshi' report [Editorial]. (2016, October 12). *Japan Times.* Retrieved from https://www.japantimes.co.jp/opinion/2016/10/12/editorials/governments-karoshi-report/#.WrFfYGrwbcs

Edwards, L. (2013, March 16). The gender gap in pain. *The New York Times.* Retrieved from http://www.nytimes.com/2013/03/17/opinion/sunday/women-and-the-treatment-of-pain.html?_r=0

Edwards, L. M., & Romero, A. J. (2008). Coping with discrimination among Mexican-descent adolescents. *Hispanic Journal of Behavioral Sciences, 30,* 24–39.

Edwards, R. R., Bingham, C. O., Bathon, J., & Haythornthwaite, J. A. (2006). Catastrophizing and pain in arthritis, fibromyalgia, and other rheumatic diseases. *Arthritis & Rheumatism, 55*(2), 325–332.

Edwards, R. R., Campbell, C., Jamison, R. N., & Wiech, K. (2009). The neurobiological underpinnings of coping with pain. *Current Directions in Psychological Science, 18,* 237–241.

Edwards, R. R., Kronfli, T., Haythornthwaite, J. A., Smith, M. T., McGuire, L., & Page, G. G. (2008). Association of catastrophizing with interleukin-6 responses to acute pain. *Pain, 140*(1), 135–144.

Ehde, D. M., Dillworth, T. M., & Turner, J. A. (2014). Cognitive-behavioral therapy for individuals with chronic pain. *American Psychologist, 69*(2), 153–166.

Eijsvogels, T. M. H., Molossi, S., Duck-chul, L., Emery, M. S., & Thompson, P. D. (2016). Exercise at the extremes: The amount of exercise to reduce cardiovascular events. *Journal of the American College of Cardiology 67*(3), 316–329.

Eisenberg, D. M. (1997). Advising patients who use alternative medical therapies. *Annals of Internal Medicine, 127,* 61–69.

Eisenberg, D. M., Davis, R. B., Ettner, S. L., Appel, S., Wilkey, S., Van Rompay, M., & Kessler, R. C. (1998). Trends in alternative medicine use in the United States, 1990–1997: Results of a follow-up national survey. *Journal of the American Medical Association, 280,* 1569–1575.

Eisenberg, D. M., Delbanco, T. L., Berkey, C. S., Kaptchuk, T. J., Kupelnick, B., Kuhl, J., & Chalmers, T. C. (1993). Cognitive behavioral techniques for hypertension: Are they effective? *Annals of Internal Medicine, 118*(12), 964–972.

Eisenberger, N. I., Inagaki, T. K., Mashal, N. M., & Irwin, M. R. (2010). Inflammation and social experience: An inflammatory challenge induces feelings of social disconnection in addition to depressed mood. *Brain, Behavior, and Immunity, 24,* 558–563.

Ekern, J. (2016). *Effective coping skills: Eating disorder self-soothing.* Eating Disorder Hope. Retrieved from https://www

.eatingdisorderhope.com/recovery/self-help-tools-skills-tips/self-soothing-advice

Elfhag, K., & Rossner, S. (2005). Who succeeds in maintaining weight loss? A conceptual review of factors associated with weight loss maintenance and weight regain. *Obesity Review, 6*(1), 67–85.

Eller, N. H., Netterstrom, B., & Hansen, A. M. (2006). Psychosocial factors at home and at work and levels of salivary cortisol. *Biological Psychology, 73*, 280–287.

Elsing, E., Datson, N. A., van den Maagdenberg, A., & Ferrari, M. D. (2013). Epigenetic mechanisms in migraine: A promising avenue? *BMC Medicine, 11*(26). Retrieved from doi.org/10.1186/1741-7015-11-26

Emmons, R. A., & McCullough, M. E. (2003). Personality processes and individual differences—counting blessings versus burdens: An experimental investigation of gratitude and subjective well-being in daily life. *Journal of Personality & Social Psychology, 84*(2), 377–389.

Emmons, R. A., & Mishra, A., (2011). Why gratitude enhances well-being: What we know, what we need to know. In K. Sheldon, T. Kashdan, & M. F. Steger (Eds.), *Designing the future of positive psychology: Taking stock and moving forward* (pp. 248–264). New York, NY: Oxford University Press.

Epel, E. S., Blackburn, E. H., Lin, J., Dhabhar, F. S., Adler, N. E., Morrow, J. D., & Cawtho, R. M. (2004). Accelerated telomere shortening in response to life stress. *Proceedings of the National Academy of Sciences, 101*(49), 17312–17315.

Epps, C., & Holt, L. (2011). The genetic basis of addiction and relevant cellular mechanisms. *International Anesthesiology Clinics, 49*(1), 3–14.

Epstein, L. H., Jankowiak, N., Nederkoorn, C., Raynor, H. A., French, S. A., & Finkelstein, E. (2012). Experimental research on the relation between food price changes and food-purchasing patterns: A targeted review. *American Journal of Clinical Nutrition, 95*(4), 789–809.

Epstein, L. H., Lin, H., Carr, K. A., & Fletcher, K. D. (2011). Food reinforcement and obesity: Psychological moderators. *Appetite, 58*, 157–162.

Epstein-Lubow, G. P., Miller, I. W., & McBee, L. (2006). Mindfulness training for caregivers. *Psychiatric Services, 57*(3), 421.

Ernst, A. (2017). Self-disclosure as therapy: The benefits of expressive writing. *Current Psychiatry, 16*(10), 33–34.

Ernst, E., & Canter, P. H. (2006). A systematic review of systematic reviews of spinal manipulation. *Journal of the Royal Society of Medicine, 99*(4), 192–196.

Ernst, K. K., Pittler, E. E., Wider, B., & Boddy, K. (2007). Acupuncture: Its evidence-base is changing. *American Journal of Chinese Medicine, 35*(1), 21–25.

Ervin, R. B. (2009). Prevalence of metabolic syndrome among adults 20 years of age and over, by sex, age, race and ethnicity, and body mass index: United States, 2003–2006. *National Health Statistics Reports, 5*(13) 1–7.

Ervin, R. B., Kit, B. K., Carroll, M. D., & Ogden, C. L. (2012). *Consumption of added sugar among U.S. children and adolescents, 2005–2008 (NCHS Data Brief No. 87)*. Hyattsville, MD: National Center for Health Statistics.

Ethier, K. A., Kann, L., & McManus, T. (2018, January 5). Sexual intercourse among high school students—29 states and United States overall, 2005–2015. *Morbidity and Mortality Weekly Report, 66*(51 and 52). Retrieved from https://www.cdc.gov/mmwr/volumes/66/wr/pdfs/mm665152a1-H.PDF

Evans, J., Frank, B., Oliffe, J. L., & Gregory, D. (2011, March). Health, illness, men and masculinities (HIMM): A theoretical framework for understanding men and their health. *American Journal of Men's Health, 8*(1), 7–15.

Evans, R. I. (2003). Some theoretical models and constructs generic to substance abuse prevention programs for adolescents: Possible relevance and limitations for problem gambling. *Journal of Gambling Studies, 19*(3), 287–302.

Evans, W. D., Powers, A., Hersey, J., & Renaud, J. (2006). The influence of social environment and social image on adolescent smoking. *Health Psychology, 25*, 26–33.

Everitt, B. J., & Heberlein, U. (2013). Addiction. *Current Opinion in Neurobiology, 4*, 463–466.

Fabes, R. A., & Eisenberg, N. (1997). Regulatory control and adults' stress-related responses to daily life events. *Journal of Personality and Social Psychology, 73*(5), 1107–1117.

Fabian D., & Flatt T. (2011). The evolution of aging. *Nature Education Knowledge, 2*, 9.

Fagerlin, A., Zikmund-Fisher, B. J., Nair, V., Derry, H. A., McClure, J. B., Greene, S., & Ubel, P. A. (2010). Women's decisions regarding tamoxifen for breast cancer prevention: Responses to a tailored decision aid. *Breast Cancer Research & Treatment, 119*, 613–620.

Fagundes, C. P., Bennett, J. M., Alfano, C. M, Glaser, R., Povoski, S. P., Lipari, A. M., … Kiecolt-Glaser, J. K. (2012). Social support and socioeconomic status interact to predict Epstein-Barr virus latency in women awaiting diagnosis or newly diagnosed with breast cancer. *Health Psychology, 31*(1), 11–19.

Fagundes, C. P., Bennett, J. M., Derry, H. M., & Kiecolt-Glaser, J. K. (2011). Relationships and inflammation across the lifespan: Social developmental pathways to disease. *Social and Personality Psychology Compass, 5*(11), 891–903.

Fagundes, C. P., Glaser, R., Malarkey, W. B., & Kiecolt-Glaser, J. K. (2013). Childhood adversity and Herpesvirus latency in breast cancer survivors. *Health Psychology, 32*(3), 337–344.

Fairburn, C. G. (2005). Evidence-based treatment of anorexia nervosa. *International Journal of Eating Disorders, 37*(Suppl.), S26–S30.

Fairhurst, M., Wiech, K., Dunckley, P., & Tracey, I. (2007). Anticipatory brainstem activity predicts neural processing of pain in humans. *Pain, 128*, 101–110.

Falk, E. B., Berkman, E. T., Whalen, D., & Lieberman, M. D. (2011). Neural activity during health messaging predicts reductions in smoking above and beyond self-report. *Health Psychology, 30*(2), 177–185.

Fanning, J. P., Wong, A. A., & Fraser, J. F. (2014). The epidemiology of silent brain infarction: A systematic review of population-based cohorts. *BMC Medicine, 12*(119). Retrieved from https://bmcmedicine.biomedcentral.com/articles/10.1186/s12916-014-0119-0

Fassler, J. (2015, October 15). How doctors take women's pain less seriously. *The Atlantic.* Retrieved from https://www.theatlantic.com/health/archive/2015/10/emergency-room-wait-times-sexism/410515/

Fechir, M., Breimhorst, M., Kritzmann, S., Geber, C., Schlereth, T., Baier, B., & Birklein, F. (2012). Naloxone inhibits not only stress-induced analgesia but also sympathetic activation and baroreceptor-reflex sensitivity. *European Journal of Pain, 16*(1), 82–92.

Federal Trade Commission (FTC). (2017). *Federal Trade Commission cigarette report for 2015.* Retrieved from https://www.ftc.gov/system/files/documents/reports/federal-trade-commission-cigarette-report-2015-federal-trade-commission-smokeless-tobacco-report/2015_cigarette_report.pdf?utm_source=govdelivery%20

Feldman, P. J., & Steptoe, A. (2004). How neighborhoods and physical functioning are related: The roles of neighborhood socioeconomic status, perceived neighborhood strain, and individual health risk factors. *Annals of Behavioral Medicine, 27*(2), 91–99.

Felitti, V. J., Anda, R. F., Nordenberg, D., Williamson, D. F., Spitz, A. M., Edwards, V., Koss, M. P., & Marks, J. S. (1998). Relationship of childhood abuse and household dysfunction to many of the leading causes of death in adult. The Adverse Childhood Experiences (ACE) Study. *American Journal of Preventive Medicine, 14*(4), 245–258.

Fell, J. C., Fisher, D. A., Voas, R. B., Blackman, K., & Tippetts, A. S. (2011). The relationship of underage drinking laws to reductions in drinking drivers in fatal crashes in the United States. *Accident Analysis & Prevention, 40*, 1430–1440.

Fellowes, D., Barnes, K., & Wilkinson, S. (2004). Aromatherapy and massage for symptom relief in patients with cancer. *Cochrane Database of Systematic Reviews (Online), 2004*(2): CD002287.

Ferguson, J., Bauld, L., Chesterman, J., & Judge, K. (2005). The English smoking treatment services: One-year outcomes. *Addiction, 100*(Suppl. 2), 59–69.

Fernandez-Mendoza, J., Vela-Bueno, A., Vgontzas, A. N., Ramos-Platon, M. J., Olavarrieta-Bernardono, S., Bixler, E. O., & de la Cruz-Troca, J. J. (2010). Cognitive-emotional hyperarousal as a premorbid characteristic of individuals vulnerable to insomnia. *Psychosomatic Medicine, 72*, 397–403.

Ferri, P., Guadi, M., Marcheselli, L., Balduzzi, S., Magnani, D., & Di Lorenzo, R. (2016). The impact of shift work on the psychological and physical health of nurses in a general hospital: A comparison between rotating night shifts and day shifts. *Risk Management and Healthcare Policy, 9*, 203–211.

Ferris, P. A., Kline, T. J. B., & Bourdage, J. S. (2012). He said, she said: Work, biopsychosocial, and lifestyle contributions to coronary heart disease risk. *Health Psychology, 31*(4), 503–511.

Festinger, L. (1957). *A theory of cognitive dissonance.* Stanford, CA: Stanford University Press.

Feuerstein, M., & Beattie, P. (1995). Biobehavioral factors affecting pain and disability in low back pain: Mechanisms and assessment. *Physical Therapy, 75*, 267–280.

Fikke, L. T., Melinder, A., & Landro, N. I. (2011). Executive functions are impaired in adolescents engaging in non-suicidal self-injury. *Psychological Medicine, 41*, 601–610.

Fiksenbaum, L., Greenglass, E., & Eaton, J. (2006). Perceived social support, hassles, and coping among the elderly. *Journal of Applied Gerontology, 25*(1), 17–30.

Filbey, F. M., Aslan, S., Calhoun, V. D., Spence, J. S., Damaraju, E., Caprihan, A., & Segall, J. (2014). *Proceedings of the National Academy of Sciences, 111*(47), 16913–16918.

Fillingim, R. B. (2000). Sex, gender, and pain: Women and men really are different. *Current Review of Pain, 4*, 24–30.

Fincham, F. D., & Beach, S. R. H. (2010). Marriage in the new millennium: A decade in review. *Journal of Marriage and Family, 72*, 630–649.

Fisher, J. A., & Kalbaugh, C. A. (2011). Challenging assumptions about minority participation in U.S. clinical research. *American Journal of Public Health, 101*(12), 2217–2222.

FitzGerald, C., & Hurst, S. (2017). Implicit bias in healthcare professionals: A systematic review. *BMC Medical Ethics, 18*(1), 19.

Fitzgerald, S. T., Haythornthwaite, J. A., Suchday, S., & Ewart, C. K. (2003). Anger in young black and white workers: Effects of job control, dissatisfaction, and support. *Journal of Behavioral Medicine, 26*, 283–296.

Fjorback, L. O., Arendt, M., Ornbol, E., Fink, P., & Walach, H. (2011). Mindfulness-based stress reduction and mindfulness-based cognitive therapy: A systematic review of randomized controlled trials. *Acta Psychiatrica Scandinavica, 124*, 102–119.

Flack, J. M., Sica, D. A., Bakris, G., Brown, A. L., Ferdinand, K. C., Grimm, R. H., … Jamerson, K. A. (2010). Management of high blood pressure in blacks: An update of the International Society on Hypertension in Blacks Consensus Statement. *Hypertension, 56*, 780–800.

Flor, H. (2014). Psychological pain interventions and neurophysiology. *American Psychologist, 69*(2), 188–196.

Flowers, S. R., & Birnie, K. A. (2015). Procedural preparation and support as a standard of care in pediatric oncology. *Pediatric Blood and Cancer, 62*(S5), s694–s723.

Floyd, A., & Moyer, A. (2010). Group versus individual exercise interventions for women with breast cancer: A meta-analysis. *Health Psychology Review, 4*, 22–41.

Floyd, D. L., Prentice-Dunn, S., & Rogers, R. W. (2000). A meta-analysis of research on protection motivation theory. *Journal of Applied Social Psychology, 30*, 407–429.

Ford, E. S., Cunningham, T. J., & Croft, J. B. (2015). Trends in self-reported sleep duration among US adults from 1985 to 2012. *Sleep, 8*(5), 829–832.

Fordyce, W. E. (1982). A behavioural perspective on chronic pain. *British Journal of Clinical Psychology, 21*, 313–320.

Forman, T. A. (2002). The social psychological costs of racial segmentation in the workplace: A study of African Americans' well-being. *Journal of Health and Social Behavior, 44*(3), 332–352.

Fortmann, A. L., Gallo, L. C., & Philis-Tsimikas, A. (2011). Glycemic control among Latinos with Type 2 diabetes: The role of social-environmental support resources. *Health Psychology, 30*(3), 251–258.

Foster, J. A., & McVey Neufeld, K. A. (2013). Gut-brain axis: How the microbiome influences anxiety and depression. *Trends in Neurosciences, 36*(5), 305–312.

Foxhall, K. (2001). Preventing relapse. *Monitor on Psychology, 32*(special issue on substance abuse), 46–47.

Framingham Heart Study. (2018). *History of the Framingham Heart Study.* National Heart Lung and Blood Institute. Retrieved from https://www.framinghamheartstudy.org/fhs-about/history/

Frank, G. K. W., Shott, M. E., Riederer, J., & Pryor, T. L. (2016). Altered structural and effective connectivity in anorexia and bulimia nervosa in circuits that regulate energy and reward homeostasis. *Translational Psychiatry, 6*(11), e932.

Frankenhaeuser, M. (1975). Sympathetic-adreno-medullary activity behavior and the psychosocial environment. In P. H. Venables & M. J. Christie (Eds.), *Research in psychophysiology* (pp. 71–94). New York, NY: Wiley.

Franko, D. L., Striegel-Moore, R. H., Bean, J., Tamer, R., Kraemer, H. C., Dohm, F. A., … Daniels, S. R. (2005). Psychosocial and health consequences of adolescent depression in black and white young adult women. *Health Psychology, 24*, 586–593.

Frayling, T. M., Timpson, N. J., Weedon, M. N., Zeggini, E., Freathy, R. M., Lindgren, C. M., … McCarthy, M. I. (2007). A common variant in the FTO gene is associated with body mass index and predisposes to childhood and adult obesity. *Science, 316*, 889–894.

Freking, K. (2006, August 30). Rise in obesity weighs on health care experts. *The Detroit News*. Retrieved from http://www.detroitnews.com

Frenn, M., & Malin, S. (2003, October 24). Obesity risk factor: Access to low-fat foods increases health eating among adolescents. *Drug Week*, 273.

Frerichs, R. R. (2000). *John Snow: A portrait*. UCLA Department of Epidemiology. Retrieved from http://www.ph.ucla.edu/epi/snow.html

Friedman, M., & Rosenman, R. H. (1959). Association of specific overt pattern with blood and cardiovascular findings. *Journal of the American Medical Association, 169*, 1286–1296.

Friedman, R., McCarthy, D., Förster, J., & Denzler, M. (2005). Automatic effects of alcohol cues on sexual attraction. *Addiction, 100*(5), 672–681.

Fries, J. F. (2001). *Living well: Taking care of your health in the middle and later years*. New York, NY: Perseus Publishing.

Frisina, P. G., Borod, J. C., & Lepore, S. J. (2004). A meta-analysis of the effects of written emotional disclosure on the health outcomes of clinical populations. *Journal of Nervous and Mental Disease, 192*, 629–634.

Fritz, H. L., Russek, L. N., & Dillon, M. M. (2017). Humor use moderates the relation of stressful life events with psychological distress. *Personality and Social Psychology Bulletin, 43*(6), 845–859.

Fryar, C. D., Carroll, M. D., & Ogden, C. L. (2014). Prevalence of overweight, obesity, and extreme obesity among adults: United States, trends 1960–1962 through 2011–2012. Atlanta, GA: Centers for Disease Control and Prevention. National Center for Health Statistics.

Fryar, C. D., & Ervin, R. B. (2013). *Caloric intake from fast food among adults: United States, 2007–2010* (NCHS Data Brief No. 114). Hyattsville, MD: National Center for Health Statistics.

Fugh-Berman, A. (2000). Herb-drug interactions. *The Lancet, 355*(9198), 134–138.

Gaissmaier, W., Wegwarth, O., Skopec, E., Muller, A., Broschinski, S., & Politi, M. C. (2012). Numbers can be worth a thousand pictures: Individual differences in understanding graphical and numerical representations of health-related information. *Health Psychology, 31*(3), 286–296.

Gajilan, A. C. (2008). Iraq vets and post-traumatic stress: No easy answers. *The Utah Veteran*. Retrieved from http://www.utvet.com/IraqVet&PTSD.htm

Galea, J. T., Wong, M., Munoz, M., Valle, E., Leon, S.R., Diaz Perez, D., … & Franke, M. (2018). Barriers and facilitators to antiretroviral therapy adherence among Peruvian adolescents living with HIV: A qualitative study. *PLOS ONE, 13*(2), e0192791. Retrieved from http://journals.plos.org/plosone/article?id=10.1371/journal.pone.0192791

Galea, S., Nandi, A., & Vlahov, D. (2005). The epidemiology of post-traumatic stress disorder after disasters. *Epidemiologic Reviews, 27*(1), 78–91.

Gallagher, M. (2006). Examining the impact of food deserts on public health in Chicago. Retrieved from http://www.marigallagher.com/site_media/dynamic/project_files/Chicago_Food_Desert_Report.pdf

Gallo, L. C., & Matthews, K. A. (2003). Understanding the association between socioeconomic status and physical health: Do negative emotions play a role? *Psychological Bulletin, 129*, 10–51.

Galvan, F., Davis, E., Banks, D., & Bing, E. (2008). HIV stigma and social support among African Americans. *AIDS Patient Care and Standards, 22*(5), 423–436.

Gan, Y., Zheng, L., Wang, Y., & Li, W. (2017). An extension of the meaning making model using data from Chinese cancer patients: The moderating effect of resilience. *Psychological Trauma: Theory, Research, Practice, and Policy, 10*(5), 594–601. doi:10.1037/tra0000325

Gangwisch, J. E., Babiss, L. A., Malaspina, D., Turner, J. B., Zammit, G. K., & Posner, K. (2010). Earlier parental set bedtimes as a protective factor against depression and suicidal ideation. *Sleep, 33*(1), 97–106.

Gao, X., Chen, H., Schwarzschild, M. A., & Ascherio, A. (2011). Use of ibuprofen and risk of Parkinson disease. *Neurology, 76*(10), 863–869. doi:10.1212/WNL.0b013e31820f2d79

Gapen, M., Cross, D., Ortigo, K., Graham, A., Johnson, E., Evces, M., … Bradley, B. (2011). Perceived neighborhood disorder, community cohesion, and PTSD symptoms among low-income African Americans in an urban health setting. *American Journal of Orthopsychiatry, 81*(1), 31–37.

García Coll, C., & Marks, A. K. (2012). *The immigrant paradox in children and adolescents: Is becoming American a developmental risk?* Washington, DC: American Psychological Association.

Garcia-Perez, L. E., Alvarez, M., Dilla, T., Gil-Guillen, V., & Orozco-Beltran, D. (2013). Adherence to therapies in patients with type 2 diabetes. *Diabetes Therapy, 4*(2), 175–194.

Garcia-Retamero, R., & Galesic, M. (2010a). How to reduce the effects of framing on messages about health. *Journal of General Internal Medicine, 25*, 1323–1329.

Gard, T., Holzel, B. K., Sack, A. T., Hempel, H., Lazar, S. W., Vaitl, D., & Ott, U. (2011). Pain attenuation through mindfulness is associated with decreased cognitive control and increased sensory processing in the brain. *Cerebral Cortex*. Retrieved from http://cercor.oxfordjournals.org/content/early/2011/12/14/cercor.bhr352.full.pdf+html

Gardea, M. A., Gatchel, R. J., & Robinson, R. C. (2004). Complementary health care. In T. J. Boll, R. G. Frank, A. Baum, & J. L. Wallander (Eds.), *Handbook of clinical health psychology, Volume 3: Models and perspectives in health psychology* (pp. 341–375). Washington, DC: American Psychological Association.

Gatchel, R. J., Peng, Y. B., Peters, M. L., Fuchs, P. N., & Turk, D. C. (2007). The biopsychosocial approach to chronic pain: Scientific advances and future directions. *Psychological Bulletin, 133*, 581–624.

Gawwad, E. S. F. (2008). Stages of change in physical activity, self-efficacy and decisional balance among Saudi university students. *Journal of Family and Community Medicine, 15*(3), 107–115.

Gaylord, S. A., Palsson, O. S., Garland, E. L., Faurot, K. R., Coble, R. S., Mann, J. D., … Whitehead, W. E. (2011). Mindfulness training reduces the severity of irritable bowel syndrome in women: A randomized controlled trial. *American Journal of Gastroenterology, 106*, 1678–1688.

Gaynes, B. N., Pence, B. W., Eron, J. J., & Miller, W. C. (2008). Prevalence and comorbidity of psychiatric diagnoses based on reference standard in an HIV+ patient population. *Psychosomatic Medicine, 70*, 505–511.

GBD. (2015). Global burden of disease. *Institute for Health Metrics and Evaluation*. Retrieved from http://www.healthdata.org/sites/default/files/files/Projects/GBD/GBDcause_list.pdf

Gebel, E. (2013). Diabetes distress. *Diabetes forecast*. American Diabetes Association. Retrieved from http://www.diabetes.org/living-with-diabetes/complications/mental-health/diabetes-distress.html

Gee, G. C., & Payne-Sturges, D. C. (2004). Environmental health disparities: A framework integrating psychosocial and environmental concepts. *Environmental Health Perspectives, 112*, 1645–1653.

Geier, A. B., Roin, P., & Doros, G. (2006). Unit bias: A new heuristic that helps explain the effects of portion size on food intake. *Psychological Science, 17*, 521–525.

Geller, A. I., Shehab, N., Weidle, N. J., Lovegrove, M. C., Wolpert, B. J. III, & Budnitz, D. S. (2015). Emergency department visits for adverse events related to dietary supplements. *New England Journal of Medicine, 373*, 1531–1540.

Gelman, A., Miller, E., Schwarz, E. B., Akers, A. Y., Jeong, K., & Borrero, S. (2013). Racial disparities in human papillomavirus vaccination: Does access matter? *Journal of Adolescent Health, 53*(6), 756–762.

Gerend, M. A., Shepherd, M. A., & Shepherd, J. E. (2013). The multidimensional nature of perceived barriers: Global versus practical barriers to HPV vaccination. *Health Psychology, 32*(4), 361–369.

Gerin, W., Zawadzki, M. J., Brosschot, J. F., Thayer, J. F., Christenfeld, N. J. S., Campbell, T. S., & Smyth, J. M. (2012). Rumination as a mediator of chronic stress effects on hypertension: A causal model. *International Journal of Hypertension*. doi.org/10.1155/2012/453465

Gianaros, P. J., & Manuck, S. B. (2010). Neurobiological pathways linking socioeconomic position and health. *Psychosomatic Medicine, 72*, 450–461.

Gibbons, F. X., Etcheverry, P. E., Stock, M. L., Gerrard, M., Weng, C., & O'Hara, R. (2010). Exploring the link between racial discrimination and substance use: What mediates and what buffers? *Journal of Personality and Social Psychology, 99*, 785–801.

Gibbs, W. W. (1996). Gaining on fat. *Scientific American, 275*, 88–95.

Giedzinska, A. S., Meyerowitz, B. E., Ganz, P. A., & Rowland, J. H. (2004). Health-related quality of life in a multiethnic sample of breast cancer survivors. *Annals of Behavioral Medicine, 28*(1), 39–51.

Gill, J. M., Saligan, K., Woods, S., & Page, G. (2009). PTSD is associated with an excess of inflammatory immune activities. *Perspectives in Psychiatric Care, 45*(4), 262–277.

Gilliam, W., Burns, J. W., Quartana, P., Matsuura, J., Nappi, C., & Wolff, B. (2010). Interactive effects of catastrophizing and suppression on responses to acute pain: A test of an appraisal x emotion regulation model. *Journal of Behavioral Medicine, 33*, 191–199.

Gillies, C. L., Abrams, K. R., Lambert, P. C., Cooper, N. J., Sutton, A. J., & Hsu, R. T. (2007). Pharmacological and lifestyle interventions to prevent or delay Type 2 diabetes in people with impaired glucose tolerance: Systematic review and meta-analysis. *British Medical Journal, 334*, 299–302.

Gilman, J. M., Kuster, J. K., & Breiter, H. C. (2014). Cannabis use is quantitatively associated with nucleus accumbens and amygdala abnormalities in young adult recreational users. *Journal of Neuroscience, 34*(16), 5529–5538.

Glanz, K., Geller, A. C., Shigaki, D., Maddock, J. E., & Isnec, M. R. (2002). A randomized trial of skin cancer prevention in aquatic settings: The PoolCool program. *Health Psychology, 21*(6), 579–587.

Glassman, A. H. (2007). Depression and cardiovascular comorbidity. *Dialogues in Clinical Neuroscience, 9*(1), 9–17.

Glassman, A. H., Bigger, J. T., Gaffney, M., & Van Zyl, L. T. (2007). Heart rate variability in acute coronary syndrome patients with major depression, influence of sertraline and mood improvement. *Archives of General Psychiatry, 64*(9), 1025–1031.

Glenn, B. A., Bastani, R., Maxwell, A. E., Mojica, C. M., Herrmann, A. K., Gallardo, N. V., … Chang, L. C. (2012). Prostate cancer screening among ethnically diverse first-degree relatives of prostate cancer cases. *Health Psychology, 31*(5), 562–570. http://dx.doi.org/10.1037/a0028626

Glombiewski, J. A., Sawyer, A. T., Gutermann, J., Koenig, K., Rief, W., & Hoffmann, S. G. (2010). Psychological treatments for fibromyalgia: A meta-analysis. *Pain, 151*(2), 280–295.

Glover, V. (2011). The effects of prenatal stress on child behavioural and cognitive outcomes start at the beginning. In R. E. Tremblay, M. Boivin, & R. Peters (Eds), *Encyclopedia on early child development*. Retrieved from http://www.child-encyclopedia.com/stress-and-pregnancy-prenatal-and-perinatal/according-experts/effects-prenatal-stress-child

Glover, D. A., Williams, J. K., & Kisler, K. A. (2013). Using novel methods to examine stress among HIV-positive African American men who have sex with men and women. *Journal of Behavioral Medicine, 36*, 283–294.

Goebel, M., Viol, G. W., & Orebaugh, C. (1993). An incremental model to isolate specific effects of behavioral treatments in essential hypertension. *Biofeedback and Self-Regulation, 18*(4), 255–280.

Goel, N., Workman, J. L., Lee, T. T., Innala, L., & Viau, V. (2014). Sex differences in the HPA axis. *Comprehensive Physiology, 4*(3), 1121–1155.

Goffaux, P., Redmond, W. J., Rainville, P., & Marchand, S. (2007). Descending analgesia: When the spine echoes what the brain expects. *Pain, 130*, 137–143.

Golden, S. H. (2007). A review of the evidence for a neuroendocrine link between stress, depression, and diabetes mellitus. *Current Diabetes Review, 3*, 252–259.

Goldin, P. R., & Gross, J. J. (2010). Effects of mindfulness-based stress reduction (MBSR) on emotion regulation in social anxiety disorder. *Emotion, 10*(1), 83–91.

Goldring, A. B., Taylor, S. E., Kemeny, M. E., & Anton, P. A. (2002). Impact of health beliefs, quality of life, and the physician-patient relationship on the treatment intentions of inflammatory bowel disease patients. *Health Psychology, 21*(3), 219–228.

Goldstein, A., Clement, S., & Guo, J. (2015, September 17). Proportion of Americans without health insurance dropped in 2014. *The Washington Post.* Retrieved from https://www.washingtonpost.com/

Goldston, K., & Baillie, A. J. (2008). Depression and coronary heart disease: A review of the epidemiological evidence, explanatory mechanisms, and management approaches. *Clinical Psychology Review, 28,* 289–307.

Goliath, V., & Pretorius, B. (2016). Peer risk and protective factors in adolescence: Implications for drug use prevention. *Social Work, 52*(1), 113–129.

Goliszek, A. (2014, November 12). How stress affects the immune system. *Psychology Today.* Retrieved from https://www.psychologytoday.com/blog/how-the-mind-heals-the-body/201411/how-stress-affects-the-immune-system

Goniewicz, M. L., Gawron, M., Smith, D. M., Peng, M., Jacob, P., & Benowitz, N. L. (2017). Exposure to nicotine and selected toxicants in cigarette smokers who switched to electronic cigarettes: A longitudinal within-subjects observational study. *Nicotine & Tobacco Research, 19*(2), 160–167.

Gonzalez, J. S., Safren, S. A., Delanhanty, L. M., Cagliero, E., Wexler, D. J., Meigs, J. B., & Grant, R. W. (2008). Symptoms of depression prospectively predict poorer self-care in patients with Type 2 diabetes. *Diabetes Medicine, 9,* 1102–1107.

Gonzalez, P., Nunez, A., Wang-Letzkus, M., Lim, J., Flores, K. F., & Napoles, A. M. (2016). Coping with breast cancer: Reflections from Chinese American, Korean American, and Mexican American women. *Health Psychology, 35,* 19–28.

Goodwin, R., & Friedman, H. (2006). Health status and the five-factor personality traits in a nationally representative sample. *Health Psychology, 11*(5), 643–654.

Gordon, A. M., & Chen, S. (2014). The role of sleep in interpersonal conflict: Do sleepless nights mean worse fights? *Social Psychological and Personality Science, 5,* 168–175.

Gore, M., Sadosky, A., Stacey, B., Tai, K.-S., & Leslie, D. (2012). The burden of chronic low back pain: Clinical comorbidities, treatment patterns, and health care costs in usual care settings. *Spine, 37*(11), E668–E677.

Gorst, S. L., Gargon, E., Clarke, M., Blazeby, J. M., Altman, D. G., & Williamson, P. R. (2016). Choosing important health outcomes for comparative effectiveness research: An updated review and user survey. *PLOS ONE, 11*(1): e0146444.

Gottholmseder, G., Nowotny, K., Pruckner, G. J., & Theurl, E. (2009). Stress perception and commuting. *Health Economics, 18*(5), 559–576.

Gough, B. (2006). Try to be healthy, but don't forgo your masculinity: Deconstructing men's health discourse in the media. *Social Science and Medicine, 63,* 2476–2488.

Gough, B. (2013). The psychology of men's health: Maximizing masculine capital. *Health Psychology, 32*(1), 1–4.

Gough, B., & Deatrick, J. A. (2015). Qualitative health psychology research: Diversity, power, and impact. *Health Psychology, 34*(4), 289–292.

Gould, G. S., Bar-Zeev, Y., Bovill, M., Atkins, L., Gruppetta, M., Clarke, J. J., & Bonevski, B. (2017). Designing an implementation intervention with the Behaviour Change Wheel for health care provider smoking cessation care for Australian Indigenous pregnant women. *Implementation Science, 12,* 114–127.

Grabe, S., Ward, L. M., & Hyde, J. S. (2008). The role of the media in body image concerns among women: A meta-analysis of experimental and correlational studies. *Psychological Bulletin, 134,* 460–476.

Graham, J. E., Lobel, M., Glass, P., & Lokshina, I. (2008). Effects of written anger expression in chronic pain patients: Making meaning from pain. *Journal of Behavioral Medicine, 31,* 201–212.

Grana, R. A., Ling, P. M., Benowitz, N., & Glantz, S. (2014). Electronic cigarettes. *Circulation, 129*(19), e490–e492.

Grant, N., Wardle, J., & Steptoe, A. (2009). The relationship between life satisfaction and health behavior: A cross-cultural analysis of young adults. *International Journal of Behavioral Medicine, 16,* 259–268.

Gray, S. A. O., Jones, C. W., Theall, K. P., Glacken, E., & Drury, S. S. (2017). Thinking across generations: Unique contributions of maternal early life and prenatal stress to infant physiology. *Journal of the American Academy of Child & Adolescent Psychiatry, 56*(11), 922–929.

Grayling, A. C. (2009). Sleep, the elixir of health? *New Scientist, 201,* 44.

Grayson, M. (2015). Cannabis. *Nature, 525,* S1. Retrieved from http://www.nature.com/nature/journal/v525/n7570_supp/full/525S1a.html

Greenberg, R. (2014, March). More than a diagnosis: Medical schools and teaching hospitals address patients' spiritual needs. *AAMC Reporter* [Association of American Medical Colleges]. Retrieved from https://www.aamc.org/newsroom/reporter/march2014/374624/spiritual.html

Greenfield, S., Kaplan, S. H., Ware, J. E., Yano, E. M., & Frank, H. J. (1988). Patients' participation in medical care: Effects on blood sugar control and quality of life in diabetes. *Journal of General Internal Medicine, 3,* 448–457.

Greening, L., Stoppelbein, L., Konishi, C., Jordan, S. S., & Moll, G. (2007). Child routines and youths' adherence to treatment for Type 1 diabetes. *Journal of Pediatric Psychology, 32,* 437–447.

Greenwald, A. G., Banaji, M. R., & Nosek, B. A. (2015). Statistically small effects of the Implicit Association Test can have societally large effects. *Journal of Personality and Social Psychology, 108*(4), 553–561.

Gregoire, C. (2013, April 17). Mindfulness-based therapies may help ease stress of cancer treatment. *The Huffington Post.* Retrieved from http://www.huffingtonpost.com/2013/04/17/mindfulness-cancer-treatment-therapies-stress_n_3095435.html

Gregory, C. A., & Coleman-Jensen, A. (2017). *Food insecurity, chronic disease, and health among working-age adults.* Economic Research Service. Retrieved from https://www.ers.usda.gov/webdocs/publications/84467/err-235_summary.pdf?v=42942

Gremore, T. M., Baucom, D. H., Porter, L. S., Kirby, J. S., Atkins, D. C., & Keefe, F. J. (2011). Stress buffering effects of daily spousal support on women's daily emotional and physical experiences in the context of breast cancer concerns. *Health Psychology, 30*(1), 20–30.

Greysen, S. R., Horwitz, L. I., Covinsky, K. E., Gordon, K., Ohl, M. E., & Justice, A. C. (2013). Does social isolation predict hospitalization and mortality among HIV+ and uninfected older veterans? *The American Geriatrics Society, 61*, 1456–1463.

Gross, R., Olfson, M., Gameroff, M. J., Carasquillo, O., Shea, S., Feder, A., & Weissman, M. M. (2005). Depression and glycemic control in Hispanic primary care patients with diabetes. *Journal of General Internal Medicine, 20*, 460–466.

Grossman, P., Kappos, L, Gensicke, H., D'Souza, M., Mohr, D. C., Penner, I. K., … Liu, S. (2013). The effect of electroacupuncture on extinction responding of heroin-seeking behavior and FosB expression in the nucleus accumbens core. *Neuroscience Letters, 534*(8), 252–257.

Grossman, P., Niemann, L., Schmidt, S., & Walach, H. (2004). Mindfulness-based stress reduction and health benefits: A meta-analysis. *Journal of Psychosomatic Research, 57*, 35–43.

Grunberg, N. E., Brown, K. J., & Klein, L. C. (1997). Tobacco smoking. In A. Baum, S. Newman, J. Weinman, R. West, & C. McManus (Eds.), *Cambridge handbook of psychology, health, and medicine* (pp. 606–611). Cambridge, England: Cambridge University Press.

Grunberg, N. E., Faraday, M. M., & Rahman, M. A. (2001). The psychobiology of nicotine self-administration. In A. Baum, T. A. Revenson, & J. E. Singer (Eds.), *Handbook of health psychology* (pp. 249–261). Mahwah, NJ: Erlbaum.

Grunfield, E. A., Drudge-Coates, L., Rixon, L., Eaton, E., & Cooper, A. F. (2013). "The only way I know how to live is to work": A qualitative study of work following treatment for prostate cancer. *Health Psychology, 32*(1), 75–82.

Grynbaum, M. M. (2013, March 11). Judge blocks New York City's limits on big sugary drinks. *The New York Times*. Retrieved from http://www.nytimes.com/2013/03/12/nyregion/judge-invalidates-bloombergs-soda-ban.html?pagewanted=all&_r=0

Grzywacz, J. G., Almeida, D. M., Neupert, S. D., & Ettner, S. L. (2004). Socioeconomic status and health: A micro-level analysis of exposure and vulnerability to daily stressors. *Journal of Health and Social Behavior, 45*(1), 1–16.

Gu, F., Han, J., Laden, F., Pan, A., Caporaso, N. E., Stampfer, M. J., … Schernhammer, E. S. (2015). Total and cause-specific mortality of U.S. nurses working rotating night shifts. *American Journal of Preventive Medicine, 48*(3), 241–252.

Gu, J., Strauss, C., Bond, R., & Cavanagh, K. (2015). How do mindfulness-based cognitive therapy and mindfulness-based stress reduction improve mental health and wellbeing? A systematic review and meta-analysis of mediation studies. *Clinical Psychology Review, 37*, 1–12.

Gulliksson, M., Burell, G., Vessby, B., Lundin, L., Toss, H., & Svärdsudd, K. (2011). Randomized controlled trial of cognitive behavioral therapy vs standard treatment to prevent recurrent cardiovascular events in patients with coronary heart disease: Secondary Prevention in Uppsala Primary Health Care project (SUPRIM). *Archives of Internal Medicine, 171*(2), 134–140.

Gurka, M. J., Filipp, S. L., & DeBoer, M. D. (2018). Geographical variation in the prevalence of obesity, metabolic syndrome, and diabetes among U.S. adults. *Nutrition and Diabetes, 8*(1), 14. https://doi.org/10.1038/s41387-018-0024-2

Haack, M., & Mullington, J. M. (2007). Shorter habitual sleep duration is associated with higher increase in subjective estimation of pain in response to a total sleep deprivation (TSD) challenge. *Sleep, 129*, A133.

Haas, A., Eliason, M., Mays, V., Mathy, R., Cochran, S., D'Angelli, A., & Clayton, P. (2011). Suicide and suicide risk in lesbian, gay, bisexual, and transgender populations: Review and recommendations. *Journal of Homosexuality, 58*(1), 10–51.

Haas, V. K., Kohn, M. R., Clarke, S. D., Allen, J. R., Madden, S., Muller, J. J., & Gaski, K. J. (2009). Body composition changes in female adolescents with anorexia nervosa. *American Journal of Clinical Nutrition, 89*(4), 1005–1010.

Hadhazy, A. (2010, February 12). Think twice: How the gut's "second brain" influences mood and well-being. *Scientific American*. Retrieved from https://www.scientificamerican.com/article/gut-second-brain/

Hadjistavropoulos, H. D., Hadjistavropoulos, T., & Quine, A. (2000). Health anxiety moderates the effects of distraction versus attention to pain. *Behaviour Research and Therapy, 38*(5), 425–438.

Hakim, I. A., Harris, R. B., Garland, L. L., Cordova, C., Mikhael, D. M., & Sherry Crow, H. H. (2012). Gender difference in systematic oxidative stress and antioxidant capacity in current and former heavy smokers. *Cancer Epidemiology, Biomarkers & Prevention, 21*(12), 2193–2200.

Halaas, J. L., Gajiwala, K. S., Maffei, M., Cohen, S. L., Chait, B. T., Rabinowitz, D., … Friedman, J. M. (1995). Weight-reducing effects of the plasma protein encoded by the obese gene. *Science, 269*, 543–545.

Hale, C. J., Hannum, J. W., & Espelage, D. L. (2005). Social support and physical health: The importance of social support. *Journal of American College Health, 53*, 276–284.

Hales, C. M, Carroll M. D., Fryar C. D., & Ogden C. L. (2017). *Prevalence of obesity among adults and youth: United States, 2015–2016* (NCHS Data Brief No. 288). Hyattsville, MD: National Center for Health Statistics.

Haley, W. E., Roth, D. L., Howard, G., & Stafford, M. M. (2010). Caregiving strain and estimated risk for stroke and coronary heart disease among spouse caregivers: Differential effects by race and sex. *Stroke, 41*, 331–336.

Halliwell, E., & Diedrichs, P. C. (2014). Brief report: Testing a dissonance body image intervention among young girls. *Health Psychology, 33*, 201–204.

Hamblin, J. (2017, January 27). Why succeeding against the odds can make you sick. *The New York Times*. Retrieved from https://www.nytimes.com/2017/01/27/opinion/sunday/why-succeeding-against-the-odds-can-make-you-sick.html

Hamer, M., O'Donovan, G., & Stamatakis, E. (2018). High-density lipoprotein cholesterol and mortality: Too much of a good thing? *Arteriosclerosis, Thrombosis, and Vascular Biology, 38*(3), 669–672. doi:10.1161/ATVBAHA.117.310587

Hammond, D., McDonald, P. W., Fong, G. T., Brown, K. S., & Cameron, R. (2004). The impact of cigarette warning labels and smoke-free bylaws on smoking cessation: Evidence from former smokers. *Canadian Journal of Public Health, 95*(3), 201–204.

Han, F., Faraco, J., Dong, X. S., Ollila, H. M., Lin, L., Li, J., … Mignot, E. (2013). Genome wide analysis of narcolepsy in China implicates novel immune loci and reveals changes in association prior to versus after the 2009 H1N1 influenza pandemic. *PLOS Genetics*. Retrieved from http://journals.plos.org/plosgenetics/article?id=10.1371/journal.pgen.1003880

Hansen, A. M., Blangsted, A. K., Hansen, E. A., Sogaard, K., & Sjogaard, G. (2010). Physical activity, job demand-control, perceived stress energy, and salivary cortisol in white-collar workers. *International Archives of Occupational and Environmental Health, 83*(2), 143–153.

Hardy, J. D., & Smith, T. W. (1988). Cynical hostility and vulnerability to disease: Social support, life stress, and physiological response to conflict. *Health Psychology, 7*, 447–459.

Hare, D. L., Toukhsati, S. R., Johansson, P., & Jaarsma, T. (2014). Depression and cardiovascular disease: A clinical review. *European Heart Journal, 35*(21), 1365–1372.

Hargreaves, J. R., Krishnaratne, S., Matherma, H., Lilleston, P. S., Sievwright, K., Mandla, N., & … Stangl, A. (2018). Individual and community-level risk factors for HIV stigma in 21 Zambian and South African communities: Analysis of data from the HPTNO71 (PopART) study. *AIDS, 32*(6), 783–793.

Harris, J. L., Bargh, J. A., & Brownell, K. D. (2009). Priming effects of television food advertising on eating behavior. *Health Psychology, 28*(4), 404–413.

Harris, K. F., Matthews, K. A., Sutton-Tyrrell, K., & Kuller, L. H. (2003). Associations between psychological traits and endothelial function in postmenopausal women. *Psychosomatic Medicine, 65*(3), 402–409.

Harris, P. R., Griffin, D. W., & Murray, S. (2008). Testing the limits of optimistic bias: Event and person moderators in a multilevel framework. *Journal of Personality and Social Psychology, 95*, 1225–1237.

Hart, S. L., & Charles, S. T. (2013). Age-related patterns in negative affect and appraisals about colorectal cancer over time. *Health Psychology, 32*(3), 302–310.

Harvard Health Letter. (2013). *Abdominal obesity and your health.* Retrieved from http://www.health.harvard.edu/fhg/updates/abdominal-obesity-and-your-health.shtml

Harvard Health Publications. (2013). *Exercise and depression.* Retrieved from http://www.health.harvard.edu/newsweek/Exercise-and-Depression-report-excerpt.htm

Harvard Heart Letter. (2015). *Exercise-free activities that work your muscles and heart.* Retrieved from http://www.health.harvard.edu/heart-health/exercise-free-activities-that-work-your-muscles-and-heart

Harvard Men's Health Watch. (2009, January). *Abdominal obesity and your health.* Harvard Health Publishing. Boston, MA: Harvard Medical School.

Harvard University School of Public Health (HSPH). (2018). *Genes are not destiny: Obesity-promoting genes in an obesity-promoting world.* Retrieved from https://www.hsph.harvard.edu/obesity-prevention-source/obesity-causes/genes-and-obesity/

Hatch, S. L., & Dohrenwend, B. P. (2007). Distribution of traumatic and other stressful life events by race/ethnicity, gender, SES, and age: A review of the research. *American Journal of Community Psychology, 40*, 313–332.

Hausmann, L. R. M., Jeong, K., Bost, J. E., & Ibrahim, S. A. (2008). Perceived racial discrimination in health care: A comparison of veterans affairs and other patients. *American Journal of Public Health, 99*(Suppl. 3), S718–S724.

Hawkley, L. C., & Cacioppo, J. T. (2007). Aging and loneliness: Downhill quickly? *Current Directions in Psychological Science, 16*, 187–191.

Hawkley, L. C., Thisted, R. A., & Cacioppo, J. T. (2009). Loneliness predicts reduced physical activity: Cross-sectional and longitudinal analyses. *Health Psychology, 28*, 354–363.

Hawley, S. T., Janz, N. K., Hamilton, A., Griggs, J. J., Alderman, A. K., Mujahid, M., & Katz, S. J. (2008). Latina patient perspectives about informed treatment decision making for breast cancer. *Patient Education and Counseling, 73*, 363–370.

Hay, S. I., Amanuel, A. A., Kalkidan, H. A., Abbafati, C., Abbas, K. M., Abd-Allah, F., … Murray, C. J. L. (2017). Global, regional, and national disability-adjusted life-years (DALYs) for 333 diseases and injuries and healthy life expectancy (HALE) for 195 countries and territories, 1990–2016: A systematic analysis for the global burden of disease study 2016. *The Lancet, 390*(10100), 1260–1344.

Hayasaki, E. (2016, September 2). How poverty affects the brain. *Newsweek.* Retrieved from http://www.newsweek.com/2016/09/02/how-poverty-affects-brains-493239.html

Haynes, W. C., Van Tongeren, D. R., Aten, J., Davis, E. B., Davis, D. E., Hook, J. N., … Johnson, T. (2017). The meaning as a buffer hypothesis: Spiritual meaning attenuates the effect of disaster-related resource loss on posttraumatic stress. *Psychology of Religion and Spirituality, 9*(4), 446–453.

HEAL. (2016). *Communicable diseases.* Bronx, NY: Health & Ecosystems: Analysis of Linkages. Retrieved from http://www.wcs-heal.org/global-challenges/public-health-issues-and-costs/communicable-diseases

Health Canada. (2016). *Canada Health Act—Frequently asked questions.* Retrieved from http://www.hc-sc.gc.ca/hcs-sss/medi-assur/faq-eng.php

Healthy People 2020. (2013). Washington, DC: U.S. Department of Health and Human Services, Office of Disease Prevention and Health Promotion. Retrieved from https://www.healthypeople.gov

Healthy People 2020. (2014). *Healthy People 2020 leading health indicators: Progress update.* Washington, DC: U.S. Department of Health and Human Services, Office of Disease Prevention and Health Promotion. Retrieved from https://www.healthypeople.gov/2020/leading-health-indicators/Healthy-People-2020-Leading-Health-Indicators%3A-Progress-Update

Healy, J. (2014, May 31). After 5 months of sales, Colorado sees the downside of a legal high. *The New York Times.* Retrieved from http://nyti.ms/1kjtwf8

Heatherton, T. F., Mahamedi, F., Striepe, M., & Field, A. E. (1997). A 10-year longitudinal study of body weight, dieting, and eating disorder symptoms. *Journal of Abnormal Psychology, 106*, 117–125.

Heim, C., Ehlert, U., & Hellhammer, D. H. (2000). The potential role of hypocortisolism in the pathophysiology of stress-related bodily disorders. *Psychoneuroendocrinology, 25*(1), 1–24.

Heim, C., Newport, D. J., Mletzko, T., Miller, A. H., & Nemeroff, C. B. (2008). The link between childhood trauma and depression: Insights from HPA axis studies in humans. *Psychoneuroendocrinology, 33*, 693–710.

Heinz, A. J., de Wit, H., Lilje, T. C., & Kassel, J. D. (2013). The combined effects of alcohol, caffeine, and expectancies on subjective experience, impulsivity, and risk-taking. *Experimental and Clinical Psychopharmacology, 21*(3), 222–234.

Hellsten, R., Johansson, M., Dahlman, A., Sterner, O., & Bjartell, A. (2011). Galiellalactone inhibits stem cell-like ALDH-positive prostate cancer cells. *PLOS ONE, 6*(7), e22118. doi:10.1371/journal.pone.0022118

Hemila, H., Chalker, E., & Douglas, B. (2010). Vitamin C for preventing and treating the common cold. *Cochrane Database of Systematic Reviews.* Retrieved from http://mrw.interscience.wiley.com/cochrane/clsysrev/articles/CD000980/frame.html

Henderson, L. A., Gandevia, S. C., & Macefield, V. G. (2008). Gender differences in brain activity evoked by muscle and cutaneous pain: A retrospective study of single-trial fMRI data. *NeuroImage, 39*, 1867–1876.

Henig, R. M. (2010, August 18). What is it about 20-somethings? *The New York Times Magazine.* Retrieved from http://www.nytimes.com/2010/08/22/magazine/22Adulthood-t.html?pagewanted=all

Heo, E. H., Kim, S., Park, H. J., & Kil, S. Y. (2016). The effects of a simulated laughter programme on mood, cortisol levels, and health-related quality of life among hemodialysis patients. *Complementary Therapies in Clinical Practice, 25*, 1–7.

Herman, J. P., McKlveen, J. M., Ghosal, S., Kopp, B., Wulsin, A., Makinson, R., … Myers, B. (2016). Regulation of the hypothalamic-pituitary-adrenocortical stress response. *Comprehensive Physiology, 6*(2), 603–621.

Herman, C. P., & Polivy, J. (1975). Anxiety, restraint, and eating behavior. *Journal of Abnormal Psychology, 84*, 208–225.

Hernandez, L. M. (2013). *Health literacy: Improving, health, health systems, and health policy around the world.* Washington, DC: National Academies Press.

Hershner, S. D., & Chervin, R. D. (2014). Causes and consequences of sleepiness among college students. *Nature and Science of Sleep, 6*, 73–84.

Hertel, A. W., & Mermelstein, R. J. (2012). Smoker identity and smoking escalation among adolescents. *Health Psychology, 31*(4), 467–475.

Herzog, T. (2008). Analyzing the transtheoretical model using the framework of Weinstein, Rothman, and Sutton (1998). *Health Psychology, 27*, 548–556.

Hetherington, M. M. (2007). Cues to overeat: Psychological factors influencing overconsumption. *Proceedings—Nutrition Society of London, 66*(1), 113.

Hewitt, A. A. (2017, July). The role of psychologists in integrated primary care. *Psychology Today.* Retrieved from https://www.psychologytoday.com/us/blog/you-empowered/201707/the-role-psychologists-in-integrated-primary-care

Higgs, S. (2002). Memory for recent eating and its influence on subsequent food intake. *Appetite, 39*(2), 139–166.

Hill, J. O., Wyatt, H. R., Reed, G. W., & Peters, J. C. (2003). Obesity and the environment: Where do we go from here? *Science, 299*(5608), 853–855.

Hill, K. (2015). Medical marijuana does not increase adolescent marijuana use. *The Lancet Psychiatry, 2*(7), 572–573.

Hilliard, M. E., Holmes, C. S., Chen, R., Maher, K., Robinson, E., & Streisand, R. (2013). Disentangling the roles of parental monitoring and family conflict in adolescents' management of Type 1 diabetes. *Health Psychology, 32*(4), 388–396.

Hind, K., & Burrows, M. (2007). Weight-bearing exercise and bone mineral accrual in children and adolescents: A review of controlled trials. *Bone, 40*(1), 14–27.

Hindin, S. B., & Zelinski, E. M. (2012). Extended practice and aerobic exercise interventions benefit untrained cognitive outcomes in older adults: A meta-analysis. *Journal of the American Geriatrics Society, 60*(1), 136–141.

Hinz, A., Krauss, O., Hauss, J. P., Hockel, M., Kortmann, R. D., Stolzenburg, J. U., & Schwartz, R. (2010). Anxiety and depression in cancer patients compared with the general population. *European Journal of Cancer Care, 19*, 522–529.

Hirsch, J. (2003). Obesity: Matter over mind? *Cerebrum: The Dana Forum on Brain Science, 5*(1), 16.

Hirvonen, J., Goodwin, R. S., & Innis, R. B. (2012). Reversible and regionally selective downregulation of brain cannabinoid CB1 receptors in chronic daily cannabis smokers. *Molecular Psychiatry, 17*(6), 642–649.

Hjermstad, M. J., Fayers, P. M., Haugen, D. F., Caraceni, A., Hanks, G. W., Loge, J. H., … Kaasa, S. (2011). Studies comparing numerical rating scales, verbal ratings scales, and visual analogue scales for assessment of pain intensity in adults: A systematic literature review. *Journal of Pain and Symptom Management, 41*(6), 1073–1093.

Hoebel, B. G., & Teitelbaum, P. (1966). Effects of forcefeeding and starvation on food intake and body weight in a rat with ventromedial hypothalamic lesions. *Journal of Comparative and Physiological Psychology, 61*, 189–193.

Hoeft, F., Gabrieli, J. D. E., Whitfield-Gabrieli, S., Haas, B. W., Bammer, R., Menon, V., & Spiegel, D. (2012). Functional brain basis of hypnotizability. *Archives of General Psychiatry, 69*(10), 1064–1072. doi:10.1001/archgenpsychiatry.2011.2190

Hoffman, B. M., Papas, R. K., Chatkoff, D. K., & Kerns, R. D. (2007). Meta-analysis of psychological interventions for chronic low back pain. *Health Psychology, 26*, 1–9.

Hoffman, H. G., Richards, T. L., Van Oostrom, T., Coda, B. A., Jensen, M. P., Blough, D. K., & Sharar, S. R. (2007). The analgesic effects of opioids and immersive virtual reality distraction: Evidence from subjective and functional brain imaging assessments. *Anesthesia & Analgesia, 105*, 1776–1783.

Hoffman, K. (2015). Positivity and cancer—myth or reality? *Medivizor.* Retrieved from https://medivizor.com/blog/2015/04/30/positive-thinking-and-cancer/

Hofmann, S. G., Sawyer, A. T., Witt, A. A., & Oh, D. (2010). The effect of mindfulness-based therapy on anxiety and depression: A meta-analytic review. *Journal of Consulting and Clinical Psychology, 78*(2), 169–183.

Hogan, B. E., & Linden, W. (2004). Anger response styles and blood pressure: At least don't ruminate about it! *Annals of Behavioral Medicine, 27*(1), 38–49.

Hoge, C. W., Terhakopian, A., Castro, C. A., Messer, S. C., & Engel, C. C. (2007). Association of posttraumatic stress disorder with somatic symptoms, health care visits, and absenteeism among Iraq War veterans. *American Journal of Psychiatry, 164*, 150–153.

Holahan, C. J., Holahan, C. K., Moos, R. H., & Brennan, P. L. (1997). Psychosocial adjustment in patients reporting cardiac illness. *Psychology and Health, 12*, 345–359.

Holland, J. C., & Alici, Y. (2010). Management of distress in cancer patients. *Journal of Supportive Oncology, 8*, 4–12.

Holmes, T. H., & Rahe, R. H. (1967). The social readjustment rating scale. *Journal of Psychosomatic Research, 11*(2), 213–221.

Holt-Lunstad, J., Uchino, B. N., Smith, T. W., Olson-Cerny, C., & Nealey-Moore, J. B. (2003). Social relationships and ambulatory blood pressure: Structural and qualitative predictors of cardiovascular function during everyday social interactions. *Health Psychology, 22*(4), 388–397.

Holzel, B. K., Carmody, J., Vangel, M., Congleton, C., Yerramsetti, T. G., & Lazar, S. W. (2011). Mindfulness practice leads to increases in regional brain gray matter density. *Psychiatry Research: Neuroimaging, 91*(1), 36–43.

Hor, H., & Tafti, M. (2009). How much sleep do we need? *Science, 325,* 825–826.

Horgan, J. (2014). Justinian's plague. *Ancient history encyclopedia.* Retrieved from http://www.ancient.eu/article/782/

Horton, G. E., & Luna, N. (2016). Spirituality in the treatment of substance use disorders: Proposing the three-legged stool as a model for intervention. *Journal of Religion & Spirituality in Social Work: Social Thought, 35*(3), 179–199.

Horvath, K. J., & Bauermeister, J. A. (2017). eHealth literacy and intervention tailoring impacts the acceptability of HIV/STI testing intervention and sexual decision making among young gay and bisexual men. *AIDS Education and Prevention, 29*(1), 14–23.

House, J. S., Lepkowski, K. D., Williams, R., Mero, R. P., Lantz, P. M., Robert, S. A., & Chen, J. (2000). Excess mortality among urban residents: How much, for whom, and why? *American Journal of Public Health, 90*(12), 1898–1904. Retrieved from http://www.ncbi.nlm.nih.gov/pubmed/11111263

Housman, J., & Dorman, S. (2005). The Alameda County study: A systematic, chronological review. *American Journal of Health Education, 33*(5), 302–308.

Hoyert, D. L., & Xu, J. (2012, October 12). Deaths: Preliminary data for 2011. *National Vital Statistics Reports, 61*(6). Hyattsville, MD: National Center for Health Statistics.

Hoyt, M. A., Nemeroff, C. J., & Huebner, D. M. (2006). The effects of HIV-related thought suppression on risk behavior: Cognitive escape in men who have sex with men. *Health Psychology, 25*(4), 455–461.

Hoyt, M. A., Stanton, A. L., Irwin, M. R., & Thomas, K. S. (2013). Cancer-related masculine threat, emotional approach coping, and physical functioning following treatment for prostate cancer. *Health Psychology, 32*(1), 66–74.

Hruby, A., & Hu, F. B. (2015). The epidemiology of obesity: A big picture. *Pharmacoeconomics, 33*(7), 673–689.

Hsee, C. K., Yang, A. X., & Wang. L. (2010). Idleness aversion and the need for justifiable busyness. *Psychological Science, 21,* 926–930.

Hsu, C. J., Chen, S. Y., Su, S., Yang, M. C., Lan, C., Chou, N. K., … Wang, S. S. (2011). The effect of early cardiac rehabilitation on health-related quality of life among heart transplant recipients and patients with coronary artery bypass graft surgery. *Transplantation Proceedings, 43*(7), 2714–2717.

Hsu, M., Anen, C., & Quartz, S. R. (2008). The right and good: Distributive justice and neural encoding of equity and efficiency. *Science, 320*(5879), 1092–1095.

Huang, C. J., Webb, H. E., Zourdos, M. C., & Acevedo, E. O. (2013). Cardiovascular reactivity, stress, and physical activity. *Frontiers in Physiology, 4.* Retrieved from http://journal.frontiersin.org/article/10.3389/fphys.2013.00314/full

Huang, W., Pach, D., Napadow, V., Park, K., Long, X., Neumann, J., … Witt, C. M. (2012). Characterizing acupuncture stimuli using brain imaging with fMRI—A systematic review and meta-analysis of the literature. *PLOS ONE, 7*(4).

Hudelson, C., & Cluver, L. (2015). Factors associated with adherence to antiretroviral therapy among adolescents living with HIV/AIDS in low- and middle-income countries: A systematic review. *AIDS Care, 27*(7), 805–816.

Huffman, F. G., Vaccaro, J. A., Exebio, J. C., Zarini, G. G., Katz, T., & Dixon, Z. (2012). Television watching, diet quality, and physical activity and diabetes among three ethnicities in the United States. *Journal of Environmental and Public Health, 2012.* Retrieved from http://www.hindawi.com/journals/jeph/2012/191465/

Hughes, B., & Wareham, J. (2010). Knowledge arbitrage in global pharma: A synthetic view of absorptive capacity and open innovation. *R & D Management Special Issue: The Future of Open Innovation, 40*(3), 324–343.

Hughes, J. R. (2010). Craving among long-abstinent smokers: An Internet survey. *Nicotine & Tobacco Research, 12,* 459–462.

Hughes, J. W., Fresco, D. M., Myerscough, R., van Dulmen, M., Carlson, L. E., & Josephson, R. (2013). Randomized controlled trial of mindfulness-based stress reduction for prehypertension. *Psychosomatic Medicine, 75*(8), 721–728.

Hughes, M. E., & Waite, L. J. (2002). Health in household context: Living arrangements and health in late middle age. *Journal of Health and Social Behavior, 43,* 1–21.

Hummer, R. A., Rogers, R. G., Nam, C. B., & Ellison, C. G. (1999). Religious involvement and U.S. adult mortality. *Demography, 36,* 273–285.

Humpel, N., Marshall, A. L., Leslie, E., Bauman, A., & Own, N. (2004). Changes in neighborhood walking are related to changes in perceptions of environmental attributes. *Annals of Behavioral Medicine, 27,* 60–67.

Hurd, Y. L., Michaelides, M., Miller, M. L., & Jutras-Aswad, D. (2014). Trajectory of adolescent cannabis use on addiction vulnerability. *Neuropharmacology, 76,* 416–424.

Hustad, J. T. P., Carey, K. B., Carey, M. P., & Maisto, S. A. (2009). Self-regulation, alcohol consumption, and consequences in college heavy drinkers: A simultaneous latent growth analysis. *Journal of Studies on Alcohol and Drugs, 70*(3), 373–382.

Hyland, M. E. (2011). Motivation and placebos: Do different mechanisms occur in different contexts? *Philosophical Transactions of the Royal Society B: Biological Sciences, 366*(1572), 1828–1837.

Iarmarcovai, G., Bonassi, S., Botta, A., Baan, R. A., & Orsiere, T. (2008). Genetic polymorphisms and micronucleus formation: A review of the literature. *Mutation Research, 658*(3), 215–233.

Ilanne-Parikka, P., Laaksonen, D. E, Eriksson, J. G., Lakka, T. A., Lindstr, J., Peltonen, M., … Tuomilehto, J. (2010). Leisure-time physical activity and the metabolic syndrome in the Finnish diabetes prevention study. *Diabetes Care, 33*(7), 1610–1617.

Immordino-Yang, M. H., & Gotlieb, R. (2017). Embodied brains, social minds, cultural meaning: Integrating neuroscientific and educational research on social-affective development. *American Educational Research Journal, Centennial Issue, 54*(1), 344S–367S.

Infurna, F. J., & Gerstorf, D. (2014). Perceived control relates to better functional health and lower cardio-metabolic risk: The mediating role of physical activity. *Health Psychology, 33*(1), 85–94.

Infurna, F. J., Gerstorf, D., Ram, N., Schupp, J., & Wagner, G. G. (2011). Long-term antecedents and outcomes of perceived control. *Psychology and Aging, 26*(3), 559–575.

Inniss, D., Steiger, H., & Bruce, K. (2011). Threshold and subthreshold post-traumatic stress disorder in bulimic patients: Prevalences and clinical correlates. *Eating and Weight Disorders, 16*(1), e30–e36.

Institute for Chronic Pain (ICP). (2017). *What is the neuromatrix of pain?* Retrieved from http://www.instituteforchronicpain.org/understanding-chronic-pain/what-is-chronic-pain/neuromatrix-of-pain

Institute for Health Metrics and Evaluation (IHME). (2018). *Causes of death.* Retrieved from http://www.healthdata.org/causes-death

Institute of Medicine (IOM). (2001). *Crossing the quality chasm: A new health system for the 21st century.* Washington, DC: National Academies Press.

Institute of Medicine (IOM). (2011a). *Informing the future: Critical issues in health* (6th ed.). Washington, DC: National Academies Press.

Institute of Medicine (IOM). (2011b). *Relieving pain in America: A blueprint for transforming prevention, care, education, and research.* Washington, DC: National Academies Press.

International Human Genome Sequencing Consortium (IHGSC). (2001). Initial sequencing and analysis of the human genome. *Nature, 409*, 860–921. doi:10.1038/35057062

Inzlicht, M., & Schmader, T. (2012). *Stereotype threat: Theory, process, and application.* New York, NY: Oxford University Press.

Irwin, M. R. (2008). Human psychoneuroimmunology: 20 years of discovery. *Brain, Behavior, and Immunity, 22*, 129–139.

Isaacson, W. (2011). *Steve Jobs.* New York, NY: Simon and Schuster.

Ishikawa-Takata, K., Ohta, T., & Tanaka, H. (2003). How much exercise is required to reduce blood pressure in essential hypertensives: A dose-response study. *American Journal of Hypertension, 16*(8), 629–633.

Islami, F., Goding Sauer, A. G., Miller, K. D., Siegel, R. L., Fedewa, S. A., Jacobs, E. J., … Jemal, A. (2018). Proportion and number of cancer cases and deaths attributable to potentially modifiable risk factors in the United States. *CA: A Cancer Journal for Clinicians, 68*(1), 31–54.

Jablonska, B., Soares, J. J. F., & Sundin, O. (2006). Pain among women: Associations with socioeconomic status and work conditions. *European Journal of Pain, 10*, 435–447.

Jackson, C., Eliasson, L., Barber, N., & Weinman, J. (2014). Applying COM-B to medication adherence. *European Health Psychology, 16*, 7–17.

Jackson, T. P., Stabile, V. S., & McQueen, K. A. (2014). The global burden of chronic pain. *American Society of Anesthesiologists Newsletter, 78*(6), 24–27.

Jacobson, E. (1938). *Progressive relaxation.* Chicago, IL: University of Chicago Press.

Jain, A., Marshall, J., Buikema, A., Bancroft, T., Kelly, J. P., & Newachaffer, C. J. (2015). Autism occurrence by MMR vaccine status among US children with older siblings with and without autism. *Journal of the American Medical Association, 313*(15), 1534–1540.

Jakulj, F., Zernicke, K., Bacon, S. L., van Wielingen, L. E., Key, B. L., West, S. G., & Campbell, T. S. (2007). A high-fat meal increases cardiovascular reactivity to psychological stress in healthy young adults. *The Journal of Nutrition, 137*(4), 935–939.

James, S. A., Hartnett, S. A., & Kalsbeek, W. D. (1983). John Henryism and blood pressure differences among black men. *Journal of Behavioral Medicine, 6*(3), 259–278.

James, S. A., Van Hoewyk, J., Belli, R. F. Strogatz, D. S., Williams, D. R., & Raghunathan, T. E. (2006). Life-course socioeconomic position and hypertension in African American men: The Pitt County Study. *American Journal of Public Health, 96*(5), 812–817.

Jamison, R. N., & Mao, J. (2015). Opioid analgesics. *Mayo Clinic Proceedings, 90*(7), 957+. Retrieved from http://0-link.galegroup.com.wizard.umd.umich.edu/apps/doc/A423235468/AONE?u=lom_umichdearb&sid=AONE&xid=e938dec8

Janis, I. L., & Feshbach, S. (1953). Effects of fear-arousing communications. *Journal of Abnormal and Social Psychology, 48*, 78–92.

Jarrett, C. (2011). Ouch! The different ways people experience pain. *The British Psychological Society, 24*, 416–420.

Jeffery, R. W., Kelly, K. M., Rothman, A. J., Sherwood, N. E., & Boutelle, K. N. (2004). The weight loss experience: A descriptive analysis. *Annals of Behavioral Medicine, 27*(2), 100–106.

Jenks, R. A., & Higgs, S. (2007). Associations between dieting and smoking-related behaviors in young women. *Drug and Alcohol Dependence, 88*, 291–299.

Jensen, S., Pereira, D. B., Whitehead, N., Buscher, I., McCalla, J., Andrasik, M., Rose, R., & Antoni, M. H. (2013). Cognitive-behavioral stress management and psychological well-being in HIV+ racial/ethnic minority women with human papillomavirus. *Health Psychology, 32*(2), 227–230.

Jiang, H., Kuriakose, J. S., Miller, R. L., Moors, K., Niedzwiecki, M. M., & Perera, F. F. (2012). Reproducibility and intraindividual variation over days in buccal cell DNA methylation of two asthma genes, interferon [gamma] (IFN[gamma]) and inducible nitric oxide synthase (iNOS). *Clinical Epigenetics, 4*, 3.

Jiang, Y., Ekono, M., & Skinner, C. (2016). Basic facts about low income children: Children under 6 years 2014. New York, NY: National Center for Children in Poverty, Mailman School of Public Health, Columbia University. Retrieved from http://www.nccp.org/publications/pub_1099.html

Jiang, Y., Granja, M. R., & Koball, H. (2017). *Basic facts about low-income children: Children under 3 years, 2015.* New York, NY: National Center for Children in Poverty, Mailman School of Public Health, Columbia University.

Jobin, J., Wrosch, C., & Scheier, M. F. (2014). Associations between dispositional optimism and diurnal cortisol in a community sample: When stress is perceived as higher than normal. *Health Psychology, 33*(4), 382–391.

Johnson, K. W., Anderson, N. B., Bastida, E., Kramer, B. J., Williams, D., & Wong, M. (1995). Panel III: Macrosocial and environmental influences on minority health. *Health Psychology, 14*, 601–612.

Johnson, L. F. (2013). Treatment timing tied to longer life expectancy in HIV patients. *PLOS Medicine.* Retrieved from http://www.healio.com/infectious-disease/hiv-aids/news/online/%7Bc6ea4748-efe3-4e3b-bdf4-32c029327601%7D/treatment-timing-tied-to-longer-life-expectancy-in-hiv-patients

Johnson, N. G. (2004). Future directions for psychology and health. In R. H. Rozensky, N. G. Johnson, C. D. Goodheart, & W. R. Hammond (Eds.), *Psychology builds a healthy world: Opportunities for research and practice.* Washington, DC: American Psychological Association.

Johnson, S., Cummins, C., & Evers, K. (2008). The impact of Transtheoretical Model–based multiple behavior interventions on nutrition. In N. E. Bernhardt & A. M. Kasko (Eds.), *Nutrition for the middle aged and elderly* (pp. 195–212). New York, NY: Nova Science.

Johnson, V. C., Walker, L. G., Heys, S. D., Whiting, P. H., & Eremin, O. (1996). Can relaxation training and hypnotherapy modify the immune response to stress, and is hypnotizability relevant? *Contemporary Hypnosis, 13*(2), 100–108.

Johnston, D. W., Johnston, M., Pollard, B., Kinmouth, A. L., & Mant, D. (2004). Motivation is not enough: Prediction of risk behavior following diagnosis of coronary heart disease from the theory of planned behavior. *Health Psychology, 23*(5), 533–538.

Johnston, L. D., Miech, R. A., O'Malley, P. M., Bachman, J. G., Schulenberg, J. E., & Patrick, M. E. (2018). *Monitoring the future national survey results on drug use: 1975–2017: Overview, key findings on adolescent drug use.* Ann Arbor, MI: Institute for Social Research, University of Michigan.

Johnston, L. D., O'Malley, P. M., Bachman, J. G., & Schulenberg, J. E. (2013). *Monitoring the future: National results on drug use: 2012 overview: Key findings on adolescent drug use.* Ann Arbor, MI: Institute for Social Research, University of Michigan.

Joiner, T. E., Jr. (2010). *Myths about suicide.* Cambridge, MA: Harvard University Press.

Joint Commission. (2016). *Hospital national patient safety goals.* Retrieved from https://www.jointcommission.org/assets/1/6/2016_NPSG_HAP_ER.pdf

Jones, C. P. (2005). Naming racism as a threat to the health and well-being of the nation. *Program and abstracts of the 26th annual meeting of the Society of Behavioral Medicine.* April 13–16, 2005. Boston, Massachusetts.

Jones, C. N., You, S., & Furlong, M. J. (2013). A preliminary examination of covitality as integrated well-being in college students. *Social Indicators Research, 111*(2), 511–526.

Jones, J. M. (2009, November 20). In U.S., more would like to lose weight than are trying to. *Gallup News Service.* Retrieved from http://www.gallup.com/poll/124448/In-U.S.-More-Lose-Weight-Than-Trying-To.aspx

Jorgensen, R. S., & Kolodziej, M. E. (2007). Suppressed anger, evaluative threat, and cardiovascular reactivity: A tripartite profile approach. *International Journal of Psychophysiology, 66,* 102–108.

Jorgenson, A. G., Hsiao, R. C., & Yen, C. F. (2016). Internet addiction and other behavioral addictions. *Child and Adolescent Psychiatric Clinics, 25*(3), 509–520.

Jou, C. (2017). *Supersizing urban America. How inner cities got fast food with government help.* Chicago, IL: University of Chicago Press.

Julien, R. M., Advokat, C. D., & Comaty, J. E. (2011). *Primer of drug action* (12th ed.). New York, NY: Worth.

Kabat-Zinn, J. (2005). *Coming to our senses.* New York, NY: Hyperion.

Kain, J., & Jex, S. (2010). Karasek's (1979) job demands-control model: A summary of current issues and recommendations for future research. In P. L. Perrewé & D. C. Ganster (Eds.), *Research in occupational stress and well-being: Vol. 8. New developments in theoretical and conceptual approaches to job stress* (pp. 237–268). Bingley, England: Emerald Publishing Group.

Kaiser Family Foundation. (2015). *Gender differences in health care, status, and use: Spotlight on men's health. Findings from the 2013 Kaiser Men's Health Survey and 2013 Kaiser Women's Health Survey.* Retrieved from http://kff.org/womens-health-policy/fact-sheet/gender-differences-in-health-care-status-and-use-spotlight-on-mens-health/

Kaiser Family Foundation. (2017). *Key facts about the uninsured population.* Retrieved from http://files.kff.org/attachment/Fact-Sheet-Key-Facts-about-the-Uninsured-Population

Kaiser Family Foundation. (2018). *Total HMO enrollment.* Retrieved from https://www.kff.org/other/state-indicator/total-hmo-enrollment/?currentTimeframe=0&selectedRows=%7B%22wrapups%22:%7B%22united-states%22:%7B%7D%7D%7D&sortModel=%7B%22colId%22:%22Location%22,%22sort%22:%22asc%22%7D

Kaiser Foundation. (2010). *Assessing the effectiveness of public education campaigns.* Retrieved from http://www.kff.org/entmedia/entmedia042706pkg.cfm

Kaiser Foundation. (2012). *Summary of coverage provisions in the Affordable Care Act.* Retrieved from http://kaiserfamilyfoundation.files.wordpress.com/2013/01/8023-r.pdf

Kaiser Foundation. (2015). *Key facts about the uninsured population.* Retrieved from http://kff.org/uninsured/fact-sheet/key-facts-about-the-uninsured-population/

Kalichman, S. C. (2008). Co-occurrence of treatment nonadherence and continued HIV transmission risk behaviors: Implications for positive prevention interventions. *Psychosomatic Medicine, 70*(5), 593.

Kamarck, T. W., & Lichtenstein, E. (1998). Program adherence and coping strategies as predictors of success in a smoking treatment program. *Health Psychology, 7,* 557–574.

Kamen, C., Mustian, K. M., Heckler, C., Janelsins, M. C., Peppone, L. J., Mohile, S., … Morrow, G. R. (2015). The association between partner support and psychological distress among prostate cancer survivors in a nationwide study. *Journal of Cancer Survivorship: Research and Practice, 9*(3), 492–499.

Kaminski, P. L., & McNamara, K. (1996). A treatment for college women at risk for bulimia: A controlled evaluation. *Journal of Counseling and Development, 74,* 288–374.

Kandel, D. B., & Davies, M. (1996). High school students who use crack and other drugs. *Archives of General Psychiatry, 53,* 71–80.

Kann, L., McManus, T., Harris, W. A., Shanklin, S. L., Flint, K. H., Hawkins, J., … Zaza, S. (2016). Youth risk behavior surveillance—United States, 2015. *Morbidity and Mortality Weekly Report, Surveillance Summaries, 65*(6), 1–174. Retrieved from https://www.cdc.gov/healthyyouth/data/yrbs/pdf/2015/ss6506_updated.pdf

Kanner, A. D., Coyne, J. C., Schaefer, C., & Lazarus, R. S. (1981). Comparison of two modes of stress measurement: Daily hassles and uplifts versus major life events. *Journal of Behavioral Medicine, 4,* 1–39.

Kant, A. K., Graubard, B. I., & Atchinson, E. A. (2009). Intakes of plain water, moisture in foods and beverages, and total water in the adult US population—nutritional, meal pattern, and body weight correlates: National Health and Nutrition Examination Surveys 1999–2006. *American Journal of Clinical Nutrition, 90*(3), 655–663.

Kaplan, A. (2010). Anorexia and brain imaging. *Psychiatric Times, 27*(2). Retrieved from http://www.psychiatrictimes.com/eating-disorders/anorexia-and-brain-imaging

Kaplan, R. M., & Kronick, R. G. (2006). Marital status and longevity in the United States population. *Journal of Epidemiology and Community Health, 60,* 760–765.

Kapp, J. M., Oliver, D. P., & Simoes, E. J. (2016). A strategy for addressing population health management. *Journal of Public Health Management and Practice, 22*(5), e21–e28.

Karamouzian, M., Shoveller, J., Dong, H., Gilbert, M., Kerr, T., & DeBeck, K. (2017). Perceived devaluation and STI testing uptake among a cohort of street-involved youth in a Canadian setting. *Archives of Sexual Behavior, 46,* 2165–2172.

Karasek, R. A. (1979). Job demands, job decision latitude, and mental strain: Implications for job re-design. *Administrative Science Quarterly, 24,* 285–306.

Karatoreos, I. N., & McEwen, B. S. (2013). Annual research review: The neurobiology and physiology of resilience and adaptation across the life course. *Journal of Child Psychology and Psychiatry, 54*(4), 337–347.

Karlamangla, A. S., Singer, B. H., & Seeman, T. E. (2006). Reduction in allostatic load in older adults is associated with lower all-cause mortality risk: MacArthur studies of successful aging. *Psychosomatic Medicine, 68,* 662–668.

Kasai, K., Yamasue, H., Gilbertson, M. W., Shenton, M. E., Rauch, S. L., & Pitman, R. K. (2008). Evidence for acquired pregenual anterior cingulate gray matter loss from a twin study of combat-related posttraumatic stress disorder. *Biological Psychiatry 63,* 550–556.

Kashdan, T. B., & Silvia, P. J. (2008). Curiosity and interest: The benefits of thriving on novelty and change. In C. R. Snyder & S. J. Lopez (Eds.), *Oxford handbook of positive psychology* (2nd ed., pp. 367–375). New York, NY: University of Oxford Press.

Kashdan, T. B., & Steger, M. F. (2007). Curiosity and pathways to well-being and meaning in life: Traits, states, and everyday behaviors. *Motivation & Emotion, 31,* 159–173.

Kassem, N. O., & Lee, J. (2004). Understanding soft drink consumption among male adolescents using the theory of planned behavior. *Journal of Behavioral Medicine, 27,* 273–296.

Kawaharada, M., Yoshioka, E., Saijo, Y., Fukui, T., Ueno, T., & Kishi, R. (2009). The effects of a stress inoculation training program for civil servants in Japan: A pilot study of a non-randomized controlled trial. *Industrial Health, 47*(2), 173–182.

Kazak, A. E., Bosch, J., & Klonoff, E. A. (2012). Editorial: Health Psychology special series on health disparities. *Health Psychology, 31*(1), 1–4.

Kearns, C. E., Schmidt, L. A., & Glantz, S. A. (2016). Sugar industry and coronary heart disease research: A historical analysis of internal industry documents. *Journal of the American Medical Association Internal Medicine, 176*(11), 1680–1685.

Keel, P. K., & Brown, T. A. (2010). Update on course and outcome in eating disorders. *International Journal of Eating Disorders, 43*(3), 195–204.

Keesling, B., & Friedman, H. S. (1987). Psychosocial factors in sunbathing and sunscreen use. *Health Psychology, 6,* 477–493.

Keller, T., Hader, C., De Zeeuw, J., & Rasche, K. (2007). Obstructive sleep apnea syndrome: The effect of diabetes and autonomic neuropathy. *Journal of Physiology and Pharmacology, 58*(S5), 313–318.

Kelly, J. A., & Kalichman, S. C. (2002). Behavioral research in HIV/AIDS primary and secondary prevention: Recent advances and future directions. *Journal of Consulting and Clinical Psychology, 70,* 626–639.

Kemeny, M. (2003). The psychobiology of stress. *Current Directions in Psychological Science, 12,* 124–129.

Kemp, M., and Kissane, B. (2010). A five-step framework for interpreting tables and graphs in their contexts. In C. Reading (Ed.), *Data and context in statistics education: Towards an evidence-based society. Proceedings of the Eighth International Conference on Teaching Statistics.* Voorburg, The Netherlands: International Statistical Institute.

Kempen, G. I., Jelicic, M., & Ormel, J. (1997). Personality, chronic medical morbidity, and health-related quality of life among older persons. *Health Psychology, 16,* 539–546.

Kendzor, D., Businelle, M. S., Mazas, C. A., Cofta-Woerpel, L. M., Reitzel, L. R., Vidrine, J. I., Costello, T. J., Cinciripini, P. M., Ahluwalia, J. S., & Wetter, D. W. (2009). Pathways between socioeconomic status and modifiable risk factors among African American smokers. *Journal of Behavioral Medicine, 32*(6), 545–557.

Kendzor, D. E., Shuval, K., Gabriel, K. P., Businelle, M. S., Ma, P., High, R. R., … Wetter, D. W. (2016). Impact of a mobile phone intervention to reduce sedentary behavior in a community sample of adults: A quasi-experimental evaluation. *Journal of Medical Internet Research, 18*(1). Retrieved from http://www.jmir.org/2016/1/e19/

Kenrick, D. T., Griskevicius, V., Neuberg, S. L., & Schaller, M. (2010). Renovating the pyramid of needs: Contemporary extensions built upon ancient foundations. *Perspectives on Psychological Science, 5,* 292–314.

Khan, L. K., Sobush, K., Keener, Goodman, D., Lowry, K., Kakietek, J., & Zaro, S. (2009). Recommended community strategies and measurements to prevent obesity in the United States. *Morbidity and Mortality Weekly Report, 58*(RR07), 1–26.

Khayyam-Nekouei, Z., Neshatdoost, H., Yousefy, A., Sadeghi, M., & Manshaee, G. (2013). Psychological factors and coronary heart disease. *Atherosclerosis, 9*(1), 102–111.

Khurshid, K. A. (2015). A review of changes in DSM-5 sleep-wake disorders. *Psychiatric Times.* Retrieved from https://psychiatry.ufl.edu/files/2015/10/Psychiatric_Times_Khurshid.pdf

Kibby, M., Pavawalla, S., Fancher, J., Naillon, A., & Hynd, G. (2009). The relationship between cerebral hemisphere volume and receptive language functioning in dyslexia and attention-deficit hyperactivity disorder (ADHD). *Journal of Child Neurology, 24*(4), 438–448.

Kiecolt-Glaser, J. K., Gouin, J.-P., & Hantsoo, L. (2010). Close relationships, inflammation, and health. *Neuroscience and Biobehavioral Reviews, 35*(1), 33–38.

Kiecolt-Glaser, J. K., Gouin, J., Weng, N., Malarkey, W., Beversdorf, D., & Glaser, R. (2011). Childhood adversity heightens the impact of later-life caregiving stress on telomere length and inflammation. *Psychosomatic Medicine, 73,* 16–22.

Kiecolt-Glaser, J. K., Loving, T. J., Stowell, J. R., Malarkey, W. B., Lemesow, S., Dickinson, S. L., & Glaser, R. (2005). Hostile marital interactions, proinflammatory cytokine production, and wound healing. *Archives of General Psychiatry, 62,* 1377–1384.

Kiecolt-Glaser, J. K., Preacher, K. J., MacCallum, R. C., Atkinson, C., Malarkey, W. B., & Glaser, R. (2003). Chronic stress and age-related increases in the proinflammatory cytokine IL-6. *Proceedings of the National Academy of Sciences, 100*(15), 9090–9095.

Kim, D., Kawachi, I., Vander Hoorn, S., & Ezzati, M. (2008). Is inequality at the heart of it? Cross-country associations of income inequality with cardiovascular diseases and risk factors. *Social Science & Medicine, 66*, 1719–1732.

Kim, D. K., Lim, S. W., & Kim, H. (2003). Serotonin transporter gene polymorphisms in depression. *European Neuropsychopharmacology, 13*(4), S239.

Kim, D. S., & Kim, H. S. (2009). Body-image dissatisfaction as a predictor of suicidal ideation among Korean boys and girls in different stages of adolescence: A two-year longitudinal study. *Journal of Adolescent Health, 45*(1), 47–54.

Kim, S., Roth, W. T., & Wollburg, E. (2015). Effects of therapeutic relationship, expectancy, and credibility in breathing therapies for anxiety. *Bulletin of Menninger Clinic, 79*(2), 116–130. doi:10.1521/bumc.2015.79.2.116

Kinder, L. S., Carnethon, M. R., Palaniappan, L. P., King, A. C., & Fortmann, S. P. (2004). Depression and the metabolic syndrome in young adults: Findings from the Third National Health and Nutrition Examination Survey. *Psychosomatic Medicine, 66*(3), 316–322.

King, A. C., Goldberg, J. H., Salmon, J., Owen, N., Dunstan, D., Weber, D., … Robinson, T. N. (2010). Identifying subgroups of U.S. adults at risk for prolonged television viewing to inform program development. *American Journal of Preventive Medicine, 38*(1), 17–26.

King, D. K., Glasgow, R. E., Toobert, D. J., Strycker, L. A., Estabrooks, P. A., Osuna, D., & Faber, A. J. (2010). Self-efficacy, problem solving, and social-environmental support are associated with diabetes self-management behaviors. *Diabetes Care, 33*, 751–753.

King, K. R. (2005). Why is discrimination stressful? The mediating role of cognitive appraisal. *Cultural Diversity & Ethnic Minority Psychology, 11*(3), 202–212.

Kinnunen, M.-L., Kaprio, J., & Pulkkinen, L. (2005). Allostatic load of men and women in early middle age. *Journal of Individual Differences, 26*(1), 20–28.

Kirkcaldy, B. D., Shephard, R. J., & Siefen, R. (2002). The relationship between physical activity and self-image and problem behavior among adolescents. *Social Psychiatry and Psychiatric Epidemiology, 37*(11), 544–550.

Kivimaki, M., Head, J., Ferried, J. E., Brunner, E., Marmot, M. G., Vahtera, J., & Shipley, M. J. (2006). Why is evidence on job strain and coronary heart disease mixed? An illustration of measurement challenges in the Whitehall II study. *Psychosomatic Medicine, 68*, 398–401.

Kivimaki, M., Nyberg, S. T., Batty, G. D., Fransson, E., Heikkila, K., Alfredsson, L., … Theorell, T. (2012). Job strain as a risk factor for coronary heart disease: A collaborative meta-analysis of individual participant data. *The Lancet, 380*(9852), 1491–1497.

Kiviruusu, O., Huurre, T., & Aro, H. (2007). Psychosocial resources and depression among chronically ill young adults: Are males more vulnerable? *Social Science & Medicine, 65*(2), 173–186.

Klaus, S. F., Ekerdt, D. J., & Gajewski, B. (2012). Job satisfaction in birth cohorts of nurses. *Journal of Nursing Management, 20*(4), 461–471.

Klein, D. A., Bennett, A. S., Schebendach, J., Foltin, R. W., Devlin, M. J., & Walsh, B. T. (2004). Exercise "addiction" in anorexia nervosa: Model development and pilot data. *CNS Spectrums, 9*, 531–537.

Klein, S., & Alexander, D. A. (2007). Trauma and stress-related disorders. *Psychiatry, 5*(7), 225–227.

Klump, K. L., Suisman, J. L., Burt, S. A., McGue, M., & Iacono, W. G. (2009). Genetic and environmental influences on disordered eating: An adoption study. *Journal of Abnormal Psychology, 118*(4), 797–805.

Knabb, J. J., & Vasquez, V. E. (2018). A randomized controlled trial of a 2-week internet-based contemplative prayer program for Christians with daily stress. *Spirituality in Clinical Practice, 5*(1), 37–53.

Knittle, K., Maes, S., & de Gucht, V. (2010). Psychological interventions for rheumatoid arthritis: Examining the role of self-regulation with a systematic review and meta-analysis of randomized controlled trials. *Arthritis Care and Research, 62*(10), 1460–1472.

Ko, C. H., Liu, G. C., Hsiao, S., Yen, J. Y., Yang, M. J., Lin, W. C., … Chen, C. S. (2009). Brain activities associated with gambling urge of online gaming addiction. *Journal of Psychiatric Research, 43*, 739–747.

Kochanek, K. D., Murphy, S. L., & Xu, J. (2015). Deaths: Final data for 2011. *National Vital Statistics Reports, 63*(3). Hyattsville, MD: National Center for Health Statistics.

Kochanek, K. D., Murphy, S. L., Xu, J. Q., & Arias, E. (2014). *Mortality in the United States, 2013* (NCHS Data Brief No. 178). Hyattsville, MD: National Center for Health Statistics.

Kochanek, K. D., Murphy, S. L., Xu, J. Q., & Arias, E. (2017). *Mortality in the United States, 2016* (NCHS Data Brief No. 293). Hyattsville, MD: National Center for Health Statistics.

Koenig, H. G., Hooten, E. G., Lindsay-Calkins, E., & Meador, K. G. (2010). Spirituality in medical school curricula: Findings from a national survey. *International Journal of Psychiatry in Medicine, 40*(4), 391–398.

Kohn, M., Belza, B., Petrescu-Prahova, M., & Miyawaki, C. E. (2016). Beyond strength: Participant perspectives on the benefits of an older adult exercise program. *Health Education & Behavior, 43*(3), 305–312.

Koinis, A., Giannou, V., Drantaki, V., Angelaina, S., Stratou, E., & Saridi, M. (2015). The impact of healthcare workers job environment on their mental-emotional health coping strategies: The case of a local general hospital. *Health Psychology Research, 3*(1), 1984.

Kop, W. J., Gottdiener, J. S., & Krantz, D. S. (2001). Stress and silent ischemia. In A. Baum, T. A. Revenson, & J. E. Singer (Eds.), *Handbook of health psychology* (pp. 669–682). Mahwah, NJ: Erlbaum.

Kop, W. J., Stein, P. K., Tracy, R. P., Barzilay, J. I., Shulz, R., & Gottdiener, J. S. (2010). Autonomic nervous system dysfunction and inflammation contribute to the increased cardiovascular mortality risk associated with depression. *Psychosomatic Medicine, 72*, 626–635.

Korb, A. (2015). *The upward spiral: Using neuroscience to reduce the course of depression, one small change at a time.* Oakland, CA: New Harbinger Publications.

Kotze, A., & Simpson, K. H. (2008). Stimulation-produced analgesia: Acupuncture, TENS, and related techniques. *Anaesthesia and Intensive Care Medicine, 9*(1), 29–32.

Koutras, C., Bitsaki, M., Koutras, G., Nikolaou, C., & Heep, H. (2015, August 17). Socioeconomic impact of e-health services in major joint replacement: A scoping review. *Technology and Health Care, 23*(6), 809–817.

Kovess, V., Keyes, K. M., Hamilton, A., Pez, O., Bitfoi, A., Koç, C., … Susser, E. (2015). Maternal smoking and offspring inattention and hyperactivity: Results from a cross-national European survey. *European Child & Adolescent Psychiatry, 24*(8), 919–929.

Kozo, J., Sallis, J. F., Conway, T. L., Kerr, J., Cain, K., Saelens, B. E., … Owen, N. (2012). Sedentary behaviors of adults in relation to neighborhood walkability and income. *Health Psychology, 31*(6), 704.

Kposowa, A. J., & Tsunokai, G. T. (2002). Searching for relief: Racial differences in treatment of patients with back pain. *Race and Society, 5*(2), 193–223.

Krawczyk, A. L., Perez, S., Lau, E., Holcroft, C. A., Amsel, R., Knauper, B., & Rosberger, Z. (2012). Human papillomavirus vaccination intentions and uptake in college women. *Health Psychology, 31*(5), 685–693.

Kreibel, J. (2010, April 30). Behavioral and drug therapy together help treat alcoholism. National Institute on Alcohol Abuse and Alcoholism. Retrieved from http://www.niaaa.nih.gov/research/niaaa-research-highlights/behavioral-and-drug-therapy-together-help-treat-alcoholism

Kressin, N. R., Raymond, K. L., & Manze, M. (2008). Perceptions of race/ethnicity-based discrimination: A review of measures and evaluation of their usefulness for the health care setting. *Journal of Health Care for the Poor and Underserved, 19*(3), 697–730.

Krohne, H. W., & Slangen, K. E. (2005). Influence of social support on adaptation to surgery. *Health Psychology, 24,* 101–105.

Krok, D. (2015). Religiousness, spirituality, and coping with stress among late adolescents: A meaning-making perspective. *Journal of Adolescence, 45,* 196–203.

Krueger, P. M., & Chang, V. W. (2008). Being poor and coping with stress: Health behaviors and the risk of death. *American Journal of Public Health, 98*(5), 889–896.

Kudielka, B. M., & Kirschbaum, C. (2005). Sex differences in HPA axis response to stress: A review. *Biological Psychology, 69,* 113–132.

Kukimoto, Y., Ooe, N., & Ideguchi, N. (2017). The effects of massage therapy on pain and anxiety after surgery: A systematic review and meta-analysis. *Pain Management Nursing, 18*(6), 378–390.

Kullgren, I. K. (2014, August 29). If Oregon legalizes marijuana, how will it keep roads safe? *The Oregonian.* Retrieved from http://www.oregonlive.com/politics/index.ssf/2014/08/if_oregon_legalizes_marijuana.html

Kumari, M., Shipley, M., Stafford, M., & Kivimaki, M. (2011). Association of diurnal patterns in salivary cortisol with all-cause and cardiovascular mortality: Findings from the Whitehall II study. *Journal of Clinical Endocrinology and Metabolism, 96,* 1478–1485.

Kurl, S., Laukkanen, J. A., Rauramaa, R., Lakka, T. A., Sivenius, J., & Salonen, J. T. (2003). Cardiorespiratory fitness and the risk for stroke in men. *Archives of Internal Medicine, 163*(14), 1682–1688.

Kwakkenbos, L., Willems, L. M., van den Hoogen, F. H., van Lankveld, W. G., Beenackers, H., van Helmond, T. F., … van den Ende, C. H. (2014). Cognitive-behavioural therapy targeting fear of progression in an interdisciplinary care program: A case study in systemic sclerosis. *Journal of Clinical Psychology in Medical Settings, 21*(4), 297–312.

LaBrie, J. W., Hummer, J. F., & Pedersen, E. R. (2007). Reasons for drinking in the college student context: The differential role and risk of the social motivator. *Journal of Studies on Alcohol, 68*(3), 393–398.

Lachman, M. E., & Weaver, S. L. (1998). The sense of control as a moderator of social class differences in health and well-being. *Journal of Personality and Social Psychology, 74,* 763–773.

Lakeh, A. B., & Ghaffarzadegan, N. (2017). Global trends and regional variations in studies of HIV/AIDS. *Nature Scientific Reports, 7*(4170). Retrieved from https://www.nature.com/articles/s41598-017-04527-6.pdf

Lami, M. J., Martínez, M. P., Miró, E., Sánchez, A. I., Prados, G., Cáliz, R., & Vlaeyen, J. W. S. (2018). Efficacy of combined cognitive-behavioral therapy for insomnia and pain in patients with fibromyalgia: A randomized controlled trial. *Cognitive Therapy and Research, 42*(1), 63–79.

Lammers, C., Ireland, M., Resnick, M., & Blum, R. (2000). Influences on adolescents' decision to postpone onset of sexual intercourse: A survival analysis of virginity among youths aged 13 to 18 years. *Journal of Adolescent Health, 26,* 42–48.

Land, M. H., & Wang, J. (2018). Complementary and alternative medicine use among allergy practices: Results of a nationwide survey of allergists. *Journal of Allergy and Clinical Immunology, 6,* 95–98.

Landolfi, E. (2013). Exercise addiction. *Sports Medicine, 43*(2), 111–119.

Landro, L. (2001, February 2). Health groups push "information therapy" to help treat patients. *The Wall Street Journal,* p. B1.

Langer, S. L, Romano, J. M., Manci, L., & Levy, R. L. (2014). Parental catastrophizing partially mediates the association between parent-reported child pain behavior and parental protective responses. *Pain Research and Treatment.* Retrieved from http://www.hindawi.com/journals/prt/2014/751097/

LaRocca, T. J., Seals, D. R., & Pierce, G. L. (2010). Leukocyte telomere length is preserved with aging in endurance-trained adults and related to maximal aerobic capacity. *Mechanisms of Ageing and Development, 131*(2), 165.

LaRose, J. G., Fava, J. L., Steeves, E. A., Hecht, J., Wing, R. R., & Raynor, H. A. (2014). Daily self-weighing within a lifestyle intervention: Impact on disordered eating symptoms. *Health Psychology, 33*(3), 297–300.

Lau, B. H., Chow, A. Y. M., Wong, D. F. K., Chan, J. S. M., Chan, C. H. Y., Ho, R. T. H., … Chan, C. L. W. (2018). Study protocol of a randomized controlled trial comparing integrative body-mind-spirit intervention and cognitive behavioral therapy in fostering quality of life in patients with lung cancer and their family caregivers. *Journal of Evidence-Informed Social Work, 15*(3), 258–276.

Lauver, D. R., Henriques, J. B., Settersten, L., & Bumann, M. C. (2003). Psychosocial variables, external barriers, and stage of mammography adoption. *Health Psychology, 22*(6), 649–653.

Lavie, C. J., & Milani, R. V. (2005). Prevalence of hostility in young coronary artery disease patients and effects of cardiac rehabilitation and exercise training. *Mayo Clinic Proceedings, 80*(3), 335–342.

Lawler, K. A., Younger, J. W., Piferi, R. L., Billington, E., Jobe, R., Edmondson, K., & Jones, W. H. (2003). A change of heart: Cardiovascular correlates of forgiveness in response to interpersonal threat. *Journal of Behavioral Medicine, 26*(5), 373–393.

Laws, H. B., Sayer, A. G., Pietromonaco, P. R., & Powers, S. I. (2015). Longitudinal changes in spouses' HPA responses: Convergence in cortisol patterns during the early years of marriage. *Health Psychology, 34,* 1076–1089.

Lawton, R., Conner, M., & Parker, D. (2007). Beyond cognition: Predicting health risk behaviors from instrumental and affective beliefs. *Health Psychology, 26,* 259–267.

Lazarus, R. S., & Folkman, S. (1984). *Stress, appraisal, and coping.* New York, NY: Springer.

Lebovits, A. (2007). Cognitive-behavioral approaches to chronic pain. *Primary Psychiatry, 14*(9), 48–50.

Lee, C. D., Folsom, A. R., & Blair, S. N. (2003). Physical activity and stroke risk: A meta–analysis. *Stroke, 34*(1), 2475–2481.

Lee, I. M., Bauman, A. E., Blair, S. N., Heath, G. W., Kohl, H. W., Pratt, M., & Hallal, P. C. (2013). Annual deaths attributable to physical inactivity: Whither the missing 2 million? *The Lancet, 381*(9871), 992–993.

Lee, J. L., Gilleland, J., Campbell, R. M., Simpson, P., Johnson, G. L., Dooley, K. J., & Blount, R. L. (2013). Health care utilization and psychosocial factors in pediatric noncardiac chest pain. *Health Psychology, 32*(3), 320–327.

Lee, T. Y., Chang, S. C., Chu, H., Yang, C. Y., Ou, K. L., Chung, M. H., & Chou, K. R. (2013). The effects of assertiveness training in patients with schizophrenia: A randomized, single-blind, controlled study. *Journal of Advanced Nursing, 69*(11), 2549–2559.

Lee, Y., & Lin, P. Y. (2010). Association between serotonin transporter gene polymorphism and eating disorders: A meta-analytic study. *International Journal of Eating Disorders, 43*(6), 498–504.

Leeuw, M., Goossens, M. E. J. B., Linton, S. J., Crombez, G., Boersma, K., & Vlaeyen, J. W. S. (2007). The fear-avoidance model of musculoskeletal pain: Current state of scientific evidence. *Journal of Behavioral Medicine, 30,* 77–94.

Lelorain, S., Bonnaud-Antignac, A., & Florin, A. (2010). Long-term posttraumatic growth after breast cancer: Prevalence, predictors, and relationships with psychological health. *Journal of Clinical Psychology in Medical Settings, 17,* 14–22.

Lenhart, A., Purcell, K., Smith, A., & Zickuhr, K. (2010). *Social media and mobile Internet use among teens and young adults.* Washington, DC: Pew Internet & American Life Project.

Leonhard, C., & Randler, C. (2009). In sync with the family: Children and partners influence the sleep-wake circadian rhythm and social habits of women. *Chronobiology International, 26,* 510–525.

Lepore, S. J., Revenson, T. A., Weinberger, S. L., Weston, P., Frisina, P. G., Robertson, R., ... Cross, W. (2006). Effects of social stressors on cardiovascular reactivity in black and white women. *Annals of Behavioral Medicine, 31*(2), 120–127.

Leproult, R., Copinschi, G., Buxton, O., & Van Cauter, E. (1997). Sleep loss results in an elevation of cortisol levels the next evening. *Sleep, 20,* 865–870.

Leresche, L. (2011). Defining gender disparities in pain management. *Clinical Orthopaedics and Related Research, 7,* 1871–1877.

Lestideau, O. T., & Lavallee, L. F. (2007). Structured writing about current stressors: The benefits of developing plans. *Psychology and Health, 22,* 659–676.

Levine, F. M., & DeSimone, L. L. (1991). The effect of experimenter gender on pain report in male and female subjects. *Pain, 44,* 69–72.

Levine, J. D., Gordon, N. C., & Fields, H. L. (1978). The mechanism of placebo analgesia. *The Lancet, 8091,* 654–657.

Lewandowski, A. S., Palermo, T. M., De la Mott, S., & Fu, R. (2010). Temporal daily associations between pain and sleep in adolescents with chronic pain versus healthy adolescents. *Pain, 15,* 220–225.

Lewis, M. A., Uhrig, J. D., Bann, C. M., Harris, J. L., Furberg, R. D., Coomes, C., & Kuhns, L. M. (2013). Tailored text messaging intervention for HIV adherence: A proof-of-concept study. *Health Psychology, 32*(3), 248–253.

Lewis, N. (2016). *Telehealth helps close health care disparity gap in rural areas.* Association of American Medical Colleges. Retrieved from https://news.aamc.org/patient-care/article/telehealth-health-care-disparity-gap/

Lewis, R. J., Derlega, V. J., Berndt, A., Morris, L. M., & Rose, S. (2002). An empirical analysis of stressors for gay men and lesbians. *Journal of Homosexuality, 42,* 63–88.

Li, A. W., & Goldsmith, C. A. (2012). The effects of yoga on anxiety and stress. *Alternative Medicine Review, 17*(1), 21–35.

Li, Y., Baer, D., Friedman, G. D., Udaltsova, N., Shim, V., & Klatsky, A. L. (2009). Wine, liquor, beer and risk of breast cancer in a large population. *European Journal of Cancer, 45*(5), 843–850.

Liao, C. C., Yeh, C. J., Lee, S. H., Liao, W. C., Liao, M. Y., & Lee, M. C. (2015). Providing instrumental support is more beneficial to reduce mortality risk among the elderly with low educational level in Taiwan: A 12-year follow-up national longitudinal study. *Journal of Nutrition, Health, and Aging, 19*(4), 447–453.

Libby, P. (2012). Inflammation in atherosclerosis. *Arteriosclerosis, Thrombosis, and Vascular Biology, 32*(9), 2045–2051. Retrieved from https://www.ahajournals.org/doi/10.1161/ATVBAHA.108.179705

Libin, E. (2017, March 3). Coping intelligence: Efficient life stress management. *Frontiers in Psychology.* doi.org/10.3389/fpsyg.2017.00302

Lichtenstein, M. B., Hinze, C. J., Emborg, B., Thomsen, F., & Hemmingsen, S. D. (2017). Compulsive exercise: Links, risks and challenges faced. *Psychology Research and Behavior Management, 10,* 85–95.

Lick, D. J., Durso, L. E., & Johnson, K. L. (2013). Minority stress and physical health among sexual minorities. *Perspectives on Psychological Science, 8,* 521–548.

Lim, J., & Dinges, D. F. (2010). A meta-analysis of the impact of short-term sleep deprivation on cognitive variables. *Psychological Bulletin, 136,* 375–389.

Lindor, N. M., Lindor, C. J., & Greene, M. H. (2006). Hereditary neoplastic syndromes. In D. Schottenfeld & J. F. Fraumeni Jr. (Eds.), *Cancer epidemiology and prevention* (pp. 562–576). New York, NY: Oxford University Press.

Linshi, J. (2015, February 9). This chart shows how hard it is to end childhood obesity. *Time.* Retrieved from http://time.com/3700930/childhood-obesity-michelle-obama-lets-move/

Linus Pauling Institute (LPI). (2016). *Linus Pauling Institute micronutrient information center*. Retrieved from http://lpi .oregonstate.edu/mic/vitamins/vitamin-C

Liston, C., Miller, M. M., Goldwater, D. S., Radley, J. J., Rocher, A. B., Hof, P. R., Morrison, J. H., & McEwen, B. S. (2006). Stress-induced alterations in prefrontal cortical dendritic morphology predict selective impairments in perceptual attentional set-shifting. *Journal of Neuroscience, 26*(30), 7870–7874.

Liu-Ambrose, T., Nagamatsu, L. S., Voss, M. W., Khan, K. M., & Handy, T. C. (2012). Resistance training and functional plasticity of the aging brain: A 12-month randomized controlled trial. *Neurobiology of Aging, 33*(8), 1690–1698.

Livermore, M. M., & Powers, R. S. (2006). Unfulfilled plans and financial stress: Unwed mothers and unemployment. *Journal of Human Behavior in the Social Environment, 13*, 1–7.

LoConte, N. K., Brewster, A. M., Kaur, J. S., Merrill, J. K., & Alberg, A. J. (2018). Alcohol and cancer: A statement of the American Society of Clinical Oncology. *Journal of Clinical Oncology, 36*(1), 83–93.

Logie, C. H., James, L., Wangari, T., & Loutfy, M. R. (2012). "We don't exist": A qualitative study of marginalization experienced by HIV-positive lesbian, bisexual, queer and transgender women in Toronto, Canada. *Journal of the International AIDS Society*. Retrieved from http://www.jiasociety.org/index.php/jias/article/view/17392

Lopez, G., Ruiz, N. G., & Patten, E. (2017, September 8). *Key facts about Asian Americans, a diverse and growing population*. Pew Research Center FacTank. Retrieved from http://www.pewresearch.org /fact-tank/2017/09/08/key-facts-about-asian-americans/

Lopez-Quintero, C., Pérez de los Cobos, J., Hasin, D. S, Okuda, M., Wang, S., Grant, B. F., & Blanco, C. (2011). Probability and predictors of transition from first use to dependence on nicotine, alcohol, cannabis, and cocaine: Results of the National Epidemiologic Survey on Alcohol and Related Conditions (NESARC). *Drug and Alcohol Dependence, 115*(1–2), 120–130.

Louganis, G. (2014, September 20). Living with HIV: New horizons. *The Huffington Post*. Retrieved from http://www.huffingtonpost .com/greg-louganis/living-with-hiv-new-horizons_b_5844824 .html

Low, C. A., Matthews, K. A., & Hall, M. (2013). Elevated C-reactive protein in adolescents: Roles of stress and coping. *Psychosomatic Medicine, 75*(5), 449–452.

Lowe, M. R. (2003). Self-regulation of energy intake in the prevention and treatment of obesity: Is it feasible? *Obesity Research, 11*(S10), 44S–59S.

Lu, Q., Zheng, D., Young, L., Kagawa-Singer, M., & Loh, A. (2012). A pilot study of expressive writing intervention among Chinese-speaking breast cancer survivors. *Health Psychology, 31*(5), 548–551.

Lucire, Y. (2003). *Constructing RSI: Belief and desire*. Sydney, Australia: University of New South Wales Press.

Luckett, T., Goldstein, D., Butow, P. N., Gebski, V., Aldridge, L. J., McGrane, J., … King, M. T. (2011). Psychological morbidity and quality of life of ethnic minority patients with cancer: A systematic review and meta-analysis. *The Lancet Oncology, 12*, 1240–1248.

Luecken, L. J., & Compas, B. E. (2002). Stress, coping, and immune function in breast cancer. *Annals of Behavioral Medicine, 24*, 336–344.

Luo, Y., Xu, J., Granberg, E., & Wentworth, W. M. (2012). A longitudinal study of social status, perceived discrimination, and physical and emotional health among older adults. *Research on Aging, 34*(3), 237–301.

Lustman, P. J., & Clouse, R. E. (2005). Depression in diabetic patients: The relationship between mood and glycemic control. *Journal of Diabetes and Its Complications, 19*, 113–122.

Luthans, F., Avolio, B. J., Avey, J. B., & Norman, S. M. (2007). Positive psychological capital: Measurement and relationship with performance and satisfaction. *Personnel Psychology, 60*, 541–572.

Lyons, A. C., Goodwin, I., McCreanor, T., & Griffin, C. (2015). Social networking and young adults' drinking practices: Innovative qualitative methods for health behavior research. *Health Psychology, 34*(4), 293–302.

Lyubomirsky, S., Caldwell, N. D., & Nolen-Hoeksema, S. (1998). Effects of ruminative and distracting responses to depressed mood on retrieval of autobiographical memories. *Journal of Personality and Social Psychology, 75*, 166–177.

Ma, J. L. (2008). Eating disorders, parent-child conflicts, and family therapy in Shenzhen, China. *Qualitative Health Research, 18*(6), 803–810.

Maas, J. B. (2013). *Sleep to Win!* Bloomington, IN: AuthorHouse

MacGregor, S., Lind, P. A., Bucholz, K. K., Hansell, N. K., Madden, P. A., Richter, M. M., Montgomery, G. W., Martin, N. G., Heath, A. C., & Whitfield, J. B. (2009). Associations of ADH and ALDH2 gene variation with self-report alcohol reactions, consumption and dependence: An integrated analysis. *Human Molecular Genetics, 18*(3), 580–593.

MacKellar, D. A., Valleroy, L. A., Secura, G. M., Behel, S., Bingham, T., Celentano, D. D., … Torian, L. V. (2007). Perceptions of lifetime risk and actual risk for acquiring HIV among young men who have sex with men. *AIDS and Behavior, 11*, 263–270.

Madhusoodanan, J. (2017). Hungering for obesity treatments. *Chemical and Engineering News, 95*(13), 19–21.

Maenthaisong, R., Chaiyakunapruk, N., Niruntraporn, S., & Kongkaew, C. (2007). The efficacy of aloe vera used for burn wound healing: A systematic review. *Burns, 33*(6), 713–718.

Mahler, H. I. M., Kulik, J. A., Gibbons, F. X., Gerrard, J., & Harrell, J. (2003). Effects of appearance-based interventions on sun protection intentions and self-reported behaviors. *Health Psychology, 22*, 99–209.

Maier, K. J., Waldstein, S. R., & Synowski, S. J. (2003). Relation of cognitive appraisal to cardiovascular reactivity, affect, and task engagement. *Annals of Behavioral Medicine, 26*(1), 32–41.

Maisel, N. C., & Gable, S. L. (2009) The paradox of received social support: The importance of responsiveness. *Psychological Science, 20*(8), 928–932.

Makin, T. R., Scholz, J., Filippini, N., Slater, D. H., Tracey, I., & Johansen-Berg, H. (2013). Phantom pain is associated with preserved structure and function in the former hand area. *Nature Communications, 4*, 1570.

Manco, M. (2012). Gut microbiota and developmental programming of the brain: From evidence in behavioral endophenotypes to novel perspective in obesity. *Frontiers in Cellular Infectious Microbiology, 2*, 109.

Manfredi, C., Kaiser, K., Matthews, A. K., & Johnson, T. P. (2010). Are racial differences in patient-physician cancer communication and information explained by background, predisposing, and enabling factors? *Journal of Health Communication, 15,* 272–292.

Mann, K., Aubin, H. J., & Witkiewitz, K. (2017). Reduced drinking in alcohol dependence treatment, what is the evidence? *European Addiction Research, 23*(5), 219–230.

Mann, T., Sherman, D., & Updegraff, J. (2004). Dispositional motivations and message framing: A test of the congruency hypothesis in college students. *Health Psychology, 23*(3), 330–334.

Mann, T., Tomiyama, A. J., Westling, E., Lew, A.-M., Samuels, B., & Chatman, J. (2007). Medicare's search for effective obesity treatments: Diets are not the answer. *American Psychologist, 62,* 220–233.

Mann, T., & Ward, A. (2007). Attention, self-control, and health behaviors. *Current Directions in Psychological Science, 16*(5), 280–283.

Manne, S. L., & Andrykowski, M. A. (2006). Are psychological interventions effective and accepted by cancer patients? Using empirically supported therapy guidelines to decide. *Annals of Behavioral Medicine, 32,* 98–103.

Manos, R. C., Kanter, J. W., & Busch A. M. (2010). Attempts to measure activation as conceptualized within behavioral activation treatments. *Clinical Psychology Review, 30,* 547–561.

Marchand, A., Durand, P., & Lupien, S. (2012, June 9). Work hours and cortisol variation from non-working to working days. *International Archives of Occupational and Environmental Health, 86*(5), 553–559.

Marcinowicz, L., Chlabicz, S., & Grebowski, R. (2009). Patient satisfaction with healthcare by family doctors: Primary dimensions and an attempt at typology. *BMC Health Services Research, 9,* 63–67.

Markovic, D., Jankovic, R., & Vesilinovic, I. (2015). Mutations in sodium channel gene SCN9A and the pain perception disorders. *Advances in Anesthesiology.* Retrieved from http://www.hindawi.com/journals/aan/2015/562378/

Markovitz, J. H., Matthews, K. A., Whooley, M., Lewis, C. E., & Greenlund, K. J. (2004). Increases in job strain are associated with incident hypertension in the CARDIA Study. *Annals of Behavioral Medicine, 28*(1), 4–9.

Markowitz, L. E., Liu, G., Hariri, S., Steinau, M., Dunne, E. F., & Unger, E. R. (2016, February 22). Prevalence of HPV after introduction of the vaccination program in the United States. *Pediatrics Online, 137*(2). Retrieved from http://pediatrics.aappublications.org/content/early/2016/02/19/peds.2015-1968

Marquié, J. C., Tucker, P., Folkard, S., Gentil, C., & Ansiau, D. (2015). Chronic effects of shift work on cognition: Findings from the VISAT longitudinal study. *Occupational and Environmental Medicine, 72*(4), 258–264.

Martin, A. R., Nieto, J. M., Ruiz, J. P., & Jimenez, L. E. (2008). Overweight and obesity: The role of education, employment, and income in Spanish adults. *Appetite, 51*(2), 266–272.

Martin, P. D., & Brantley, P. J. (2004). Stress, coping, and social support in health and behavior. In J. M. Raczynsky & L. C. Leviton (Eds.), *Handbook of clinical health psychology* (Vol. 2; pp. 233–267). Washington, DC: American Psychological Association.

Martin, P. R., Forsyth, M., & Reece, J. E. (2007). Cognitive-behavioral therapy versus temporal pulse amplitude biofeedback training for recurrent headache. *Behavior Therapy, 38,* 350–363.

Marx, J. (2003). Cellular warriors at the battle of the bulge. *Science, 299*(5608), 846–849.

Masedo, A. L., & Rosa, E. M. (2007). Effects of suppression, acceptance, and spontaneous coping on pain tolerance, pain intensity and distress. *Behaviour Research and Therapy, 45*(2), 199–209.

Masic, I., Miokovic, M., & Muhamedagic, B. (2008). Evidence based medicine—New approaches and challenges. *Acta Informatica Medica, 16*(4), 219–225.

Maslach, C. (2003). Job burnout: New directions in research and intervention. *Current Directions, 12,* 189–192.

Massey, C. V., Hupp, C. H., Kreisberg, M., Alpert, M. A., & Hoff, C. (2000). Estrogen replacement therapy is underutilized among postmenopausal women at high risk for coronary heart disease. *American Journal of the Medical Sciences, 320,* 124–127.

Masters, K. S., & Hooker, S. A. (2013). Religiousness/spirituality, cardiovascular disease, and cancer: Cultural integration for health research and intervention. *Journal of Consulting and Clinical Psychology, 81*(2), 206–216.

Matarazzo, J. (1982). Behavioral health's challenge to academic, scientific, and professional psychology. *American Psychologist, 37*(1), 1–14.

Mather, M., & Thayer, J. (2018). How heart rate variability affects emotion regulation brain networks. *Current Opinion in Behavioral Sciences, 19,* 98–104.

Mathews, L. (2011). Pain in children: Neglected, unaddressed and mismanaged. *Indian Journal of Palliative Care, 17,* S70–S73.

Matthews, K. A., Dahl, R. E., Owens, J. F., Lee, L., & Hall, M. (2012). Sleep duration and insulin resistance in healthy black and white adolescents. *Sleep, 35*(10), 1353–1358.

Matthews, K. A., Raikkonen, K., Sutton-Tyrrell, K., & Kuller, L. H. (2004). Optimistic attitudes protect against progression of carotid atherosclerosis in healthy middle-aged women. *Psychosomatic Medicine, 66*(5), 640–644.

Matthews, K. A., Schott, L. L., Bromberger, J. T., Cyranowski, J., Everson-Rose, S., & Sowers, M. F. (2007). Associations between depressive symptoms and inflammatory/hemostatic markers in women during the menopausal transition. *Psychosomatic Medicine, 69,* 124–130.

Matthews, K. A., Woodall, K. L., & Allen, M. T. (1993). Cardiovascular reactivity to stress predicts future blood pressure status. *Hypertension, 22*(4), 479–485.

Matthews, R. B., Jenkins, G. K., & Robertson, J. (2012). Health care reform: Why not best practices? *American Journal of Health Sciences, 3*(1), 97–113.

Matthews, T. J., MacDorman, M. F., & Thoma, M. E. (2015). Infant mortality statistics from the 2013 period linked birth/infant death data set. *National Vital Statistics Reports, 64*(9). Hyattsville, MD: National Center for Health Statistics.

Mavros, M. N., Athanasiou, S., Gkegkes, I. O., Polyzos, K. A., Peppas, G., & Falagas, M. E. (2011). Do psychological variables affect early surgical recovery? *PLOS ONE, 6*(5). Retrieved from http://www.ncbi.nlm.nih.gov/pmc/articles/PMC3102096/#__ffn_sectitle

Mayer, J. D., Salovey, P., Caruson, D. R., & Sitarenios, G. (2001). Emotional intelligence as a standard intelligence. *Emotion, 1*(3), 232–242.

Mayo Clinic. (1998–2018). *Diseases and conditions.* Retrieved from https://www.mayoclinic.org/diseases-conditions

Mayo Clinic. (2006). Alcohol: Even a drink a day can adversely affect women's health. Retrieved from http://www.mayoclinic.org/news2006-mchi/3271.html

Mayo Clinic. (2011). Aerobic exercise: Top 10 reasons to get physical. Retrieved from http://www.mayoclinic.com/health/aerobic-exercise/EP00002

Mayo Clinic. (2015). Sleep disorders. Retrieved from http://www.mayoclinic.org/diseases-conditions/sleep-disorders/basics/definition/con-20037263

Mays, V. M., Cochran, S. D., & Barnes, N. W. (2007). Race, race-based discrimination, and health outcomes among African Americans. *Annual Review of Psychology, 58*, 201–225.

McAlonan, G. M., Cheung, V., Cheung, C., Chua, S. E., Murphy, D. G., Suckling, J., Tai, K. S., Yip, L. K., Leung, P., & Ho, T. P. (2007). Mapping brain structure in attention-deficit hyperactivity disorder: A voxel-based MRI study of regional grey and white matter volume. *Psychiatry Research, 154*(2), 171–180.

McAuley, E., Jerome, D. X., Marquez, S., Elavsky, S., & Blissmer, B. (2003). Exercise self-efficacy in older adults: Social, affective, and behavioral influences. *Annals of Behavioral Medicine, 25*(1), 1–7.

McAuley, E., White, S. M., Rogers, L. Q., Motl, R. W., & Courneya, K. S. (2010). Physical activity and fatigue in breast cancer and multiple sclerosis: Psychosocial mechanisms. *Psychosomatic Medicine, 72*, 88–96.

McBride, C. M., & Emmons, K. M. (2003). Understanding the potential of teachable moments: The case of smoking cessation. *Health Education Research, 18*(2), 156–170.

McCaffery, J. M., Frasure-Smith, N., Dube, M. P., Theroux, P., Rouleau, G. A., Duan, Q., & Lesperance, F. (2006). Common genetic vulnerability to depressive symptoms and coronary artery disease: A review and development of candidate genes related to inflammation and serotonin. *Psychosomatic Medicine, 68*(2), 187–200.

McCarthy, J. (2001). Superfoods or superfrauds? *Shape, 20*, 104–106.

McCarthy, J. (2017, October 25). Record-high support for legalizing marijuana use in U.S. *Gallup News.* Retrieved from https://news.gallup.com/poll/221018/record-high-support-legalizing-marijuana.aspx

McCracken, L. M., & Vowles, K. E. (2014). Acceptance and commitment therapy and mindfulness for chronic pain. *American Psychologist, 69*(2), 178–187.

McCright, A. M., & Dunlap, R. E. (2011). Cool dudes: The denial of climate change among conservative white males in the United States. *Global Environmental Change, 21*(4), 1163–1172.

McDaniel, D. D. (2012). Risk and protective factors associated with gang affiliation among high-risk youth: A public health approach. *Injury Prevention.* Retrieved from http://injuryprevention.bmj.com/content/early/2012/01/04/injuryprev-2011-040083.full

McDermott, B., & Feldman, M. (2008). Malingering in the medical setting. *Psychiatric Clinics of North America, 30*(4), 645–662. doi:10.1016/j.psc.2007.07.007

McEachan, R. R. C., Conner, M., Taylor, N. J., & Lawton, R. J. (2011). Prospective predictions of health-related behaviours with the Theory of Planned Behaviour: A meta-analysis. *Health Psychology Review, 5*(2), 97–144.

McEwen, B. S. (2011). Neurobiology of stress and adaptation: Implications for health psychology, behavioral medicine, and beyond. In M. A. Gernsbacher, R. W. Pew, L. M. Hough, & J. R. Pomerantz (Eds.), *Psychology and the real world: Essays illustrating fundamental contributions to society* (pp. 24–30). New York, NY: Worth.

McEwen, B. S. (2007). Physiology and neurobiology of stress and adaptation. *Physiological Review, 87*, 873–904.

McEwen, B. S., & Gianaros, P. J. (2011). Stress- and allostasis-induced brain plasticity. *Annual Review of Medicine, 62*, 431–445.

McGrady, A., & Horner, J. (1999). Role of mood in outcome of biofeedback assisted relaxation therapy in insulin dependent diabetes mellitus. *Applied Psychophysiology and Biofeedback, 24*, 79–88.

McGrath, J. (2003). Pediatric cardiovascular reactivity: Evidence for stable individual differences and differentiation of higher- and lower-risk children. *Dissertation Abstracts International, 63*(10-B), 4913.

McGrath, P. J., Walco, G. A., Turk, D. C., Dworkin, R. H., Brown, M. T., Davidson, K., … Zeltzer, L. (2008). Core outcome domains and measures for pediatric acute and chronic/recurrent pain clinical trials: PedIMMPACT recommendations. *Journal of Pain, 9*, 771–783.

McGue, M., Malone, S., Keyes, M., & Iacono, W. G. (2014). Parent–offspring similarity for drinking: A longitudinal adoption study. *Behavior Genetics, 44*(6), 620–628.

McLaughlin, K. A., Green, J. G., Gruber, M. J., Sampson, N. A., Zaslavsky, A. M., & Kessler, R. C. (2010). Childhood adversities and adult psychiatric disorders in the national comorbidity survey replication II: Associations with persistence of DSM-IV disorders. *Archives of General Psychiatry, 67*, 124–132.

McLean, S. A., Diatchenko, L., Lee, Y. M., Swor, R. A., Domeier, R. M., Jones, J. S., … Liberzon, I. (2011). Catechol-o-methyltransferase haplotype predicts immediate musculoskeletal neck pain and psychological symptoms after motor vehicle collision. *Journal of Pain, 12*, 101–107.

McMaster, S. K., Paul-Clark, M. J., Walters, M., Fleet, M., Anandarajah, J., Sriskandan, S., & Mitchell, J. A. (2008). Cigarette smoke inhibits macrophage sensing of gram-negative bacteria and lipopolysaccharide: Relative roles of nicotine and oxidant stress. *British Journal of Pharmacology, 153*(3), 536–543.

McMurtry, C. M., Noel, M., Chambers, C. T., & McGrath, P. J. (2011). Children's fear during procedural pain: Preliminary investigation of the Children's Fear Scale. *Health Psychology, 30*(6), 780–788.

McNulty, J. K., & Fincham, F. D. (2012). Beyond positive psychology? Toward a contextual view of psychological processes and well-being. *American Psychologist, 67*(2), 101–110.

McQueen, A., Kreuter, M. W., Kalesan, B., & Alcaraz, K. (2011). Understanding narrative effects: The impact of breast cancer survivor stories on message processing, attitudes, and beliefs among African American women. *Health Psychology, 30*(6), 674–682.

McWilliams, L. A., Dick, B. D., Bailey, K., Verrier, M. J., & Kowal, J. (2012). A psychometric evaluation of the pain response preference questionnaire in a chronic pain patient sample. *Health Psychology, 31*(3), 343–351.

McWilliams, L. A., Saldanha, K. M., Dick, B. D., & Watt, M. C. (2009). Development and psychometric evaluation of a new measure of pain-related support preferences: The Pain Response Preference Questionnaire. *Pain Research Management, 14*, 461–469.

Mead, G. E., Morley, W., Campbell, P., Greig, C. S., McMurdo, M., & Lawlor, D. A. (2010). Exercise for depression. *Cochrane Database of Systematic Reviews, 2010*(1).

Meadows, A., & Daníelsdóttir, S. (2016). What's in a word? On weight stigma and terminology. *Frontiers in Psychology, 7*, 1527. doi.org/10.3389/fpsyg.2016.01527

Mehta, L. S., Watson, K. E., Barac, A., Beckie, T. M, Bittner, V., Cruz-Flores, S., … Volgman, A. S. (2018). Cardiovascular disease and breast cancer: Where these entities intersect. *Circulation, 137*(8), e30–e66. doi:10.1161/CIR.0000000000000556

Meichenbaum, D. (2007). Stress inoculation training: A preventative and treatment approach. In P. M. Lehrer, R. L. Woolfolk, W. S. Sime, & D. H. Barlow (Eds.), *Principles and practice of stress management* (3rd ed., pp. 497–516). New York, NY: Guilford Press.

Meier, M. H., Caspi, A., Ambler, A., Harrington, H., Houts, R., Keefe, R. S., McDonald, K., Ward, A., Poulton, R., & Moffitt, T. E. (2012). Persistent cannabis users show neuropsychological decline from childhood to midlife. *Proceedings of the National Academy of Sciences, 109*(40), E2657–E2664.

Meisel, Z., & Pines, J. (2011, May 31). Post-HMO health care: Are ACOs the answer? *Time Medical Insider*. Retrieved from http://www.time.com/time/health/article/0,8599,2074816,00.html

Meit, M., Knudson, A., Gilbert, T., Yu, A. T., Tanenbaum, E., Ormson, E., … Popat, S. (2014). *The 2014 update of the rural–urban chartbook.* Rural Health Reform Policy Research Center. Retrieved from https://ruralhealth.und.edu/projects/health-reform-policy-research-center/pdf/2014-rural-urban-chartbook-update.pdf

Melzack, R. (1993). Pain: Past, present, and future. *Canadian Journal of Experimental Psychology, 47*, 615–629.

Melzack, R. (2005). Evolution of the neuromatrix theory of pain. *Pain Practice, 5*(2), 85–94.

Melzack, R., & Torgerson, W. S. (1971). On the language of pain. *Anesthesiology, 34*, 50–59.

Melzack, R., & Wall, P. D. (1965). Pain mechanisms: A new theory. *Science, 150*, 971–979.

Melzack, R., & Wall, P. D. (1988). *The challenge of pain.* New York, NY: Basic Books.

Mendes, E. (2010, February 9). Six in 10 overweight or obese in U.S., more in '09 than in '08. *Gallup News Service.*

Mendoza, M. E., Capafons, A., Gralow, J. R., Syrjala, K. L., Suárez-Rodríguez, J. M., Fann, J. R., & Jensen, M. P. (2017). Randomized controlled trial of the Valencia model of waking hypnosis plus CBT for pain, fatigue, and sleep management in patients with cancer and cancer survivors. *Psycho-oncology, 26*(11), 1832–1838.

Mercken, L., Steglich, C., Sinclair, P., Holliday, J., & Moore, L. (2012). A longitudinal social network analysis of peer influence, peer selection, and smoking behavior among adolescents in British schools. *Health Psychology, 31*(4), 450–459.

Meririnne, E., Kiviruusu, O., Karlsson, L., Pelkonen, M., Ruuttu, T., Tulsku, V., & Marttunen, M. (2010). Brief report: Excessive alcohol use negatively affects the course of adolescent depression: One-year naturalistic follow-up study. *Journal of Adolescence, 33*(1), 221–226.

Merritt, M. M., Bennett, G. G., Williams, R. B., Edwards, C. L., & Sollers, J. J. (2006). Perceived racism and cardiovascular reactivity and recovery to personally relevant stress. *Health Psychology, 25*(3), 364–369.

Merritt, M. M., Bennett, G. G., Williams, R. B., Sollers, J. J., & Thayer, J. F. (2004). Low educational attainment, John Henryism and cardiovascular reactivity to and recovery from personally relevant stress. *Psychosomatic Medicine, 66*(1), 49–55.

Merz, E. L., Fox, R. S., & Malcarne, V. L. (2014). Expressive writing interventions in cancer patients: A systematic review. *Health Psychology Review, 8*(3), 339–361.

Messer, K., Trinidad, D. R., Al-Delaimy, W. K., & Pierce, J. P. (2008). Smoking cessation rates in the United States: A comparison of young adult and older smokers. *American Journal of Public Health, 98*(2), 317–322.

Meyer, I. H. (2003). Prejudice, social stress, and mental health in lesbian, gay, and bisexual populations: Conceptual issues and research evidence. *Psychological Bulletin, 129*(5), 674–697.

Michie, S., Abraham, C., Whittington, C., McAteer, J., & Gupta, S. (2009). Effective techniques in healthy eating and physical activity interventions: A meta-regression. *Health Psychology, 28*, 690–701.

Michie, S., van Stralen, M., & West, R. (2011). The behavior change wheel: A new method for characterizing and designing behavior change interventions. *Implementation Science, 6*, 42.

Miech, R. A., Patrick, M. E., O'Malley, P. M., & Johnston, L. D. (2017). E-cigarette use as a predictor of cigarette smoking: Results from a 1-year follow-up of a national sample of 12th grade students. *Tobacco Control, 26*(e2), e106–e111.

Milad, M. R., Wright, C. I., Orr, S. P., Pitman, R. K., Quirk, G. J., & Rauch, S. L. (2007). Recall of fear extinction in humans activates the ventromedial prefrontal cortex and hippocampus in concert. *Biological Psychiatry, 62*, 446–454.

Miles, C., Tait, E., Schure, M. B., & Hollis, M. (2016). Effect of laughter yoga on psychological well-being and physiological measures. *Advances in Mind-Body Medicine, 30*(1), 12–20.

Miller, G. E., & Blackwell, E. (2006). Turning up the heat: Inflammation as a mechanism linking chronic stress, depression, and heart disease. *Current Directions in Psychological Science, 15*, 269–272.

Miller, G. E., Chen, E., & Parker, K. J. (2011). Psychological stress in childhood and susceptibility to the chronic diseases of aging: Moving toward a model of behavioral and biological mechanisms. *Psychological Bulletin, 137*(6), 959–997.

Miller, G. E., & Cohen, S. (2001). Psychological interventions and the immune system: A meta-analytic review and critique. *Health Psychology, 20*, 47–63.

Miller, G. E., Cohen, S., & Ritchey, A. K. (2002). Chronic psychological stress and the regulation of pro-inflammatory cytokines: A glucocorticoid-resistance model. *Health Psychology, 21*(6), 531–541.

Miller, G. E., & Wrosch, C. (2007). You've gotta know when to fold 'em. *Psychological Science, 18*, 773–777.

Miller, G. E., Yu, T., Chen, E., & Brody, G. H. (2015). Self-control forecasts better psychosocial outcomes but faster epigenetic aging in low-SES youth. *Proceedings of the National Academy of Sciences, 112*(33), 10325–10330. Retrieved from http://www.pnas.org/content/112/33/10325

Miller, K., & Miller, P. M. (2001). *Journey of hope: The story of Irish immigration to America.* New York, NY: Chronicle Books.

Miller, M., Lippmann, S. J., Azrael, D., & Hemenway, D. (2007). Household firearm ownership and rates of suicide across the 50 United States. *Journal of Trauma, Injury, Infection, and Critical Care, 62*, 1029–1035.

Miller, M. F., Barabasz, A. F., & Barabasz, M. (1991). Effects of active alert and relaxation hypnotic inductions on cold pressor pain. *Journal of Abnormal Psychology, 100*, 223–226.

Miller, N. E. (1969). Psychosomatic effects of specific types of training. *Annals of the New York Academy of Sciences, 159*(3), 1025–1040.

Miller, P., & Plant, M. (2010). Parental guidance about drinking: Relationship with teenage psychoactive substance use. *Journal of Adolescence, 33*(1): 55–68.

Millichap, J. G., & Yee, M. M. (2012). The diet factor in attention-deficit/hyperactivity disorder. *Pediatrics, 129*(2), 330–337.

Milling, L. (2008). Is high hypnotic suggestibility necessary for successful hypnotic pain intervention? *Current Pain and Headache Reports, 12*(2), 98–102.

Milne, H. M., Wallman, K. E., Gordon, S., & Courneya, K. S. (2008). Impact of a combined resistance and aerobic exercise program on motivational variables in breast cancer survivors: A randomized-controlled trial. *Annals of Behavioral Medicine, 36*, 158–166.

Mirescu, C., & Gould, E. (2006). Stress and adult neurogenesis. *Hippocampus, 16*, 233–238.

Misra, R., & Lager, J. (2009). Ethnic and gender differences in psychosocial factors, glycemic control, and quality of life among adult type 2 diabetic patients. *Journal of Diabetes and Its Complications, 23*, 54–64.

Mitchell, M. D., Gehrman, P., Perlis, M., & Umscheid, C. A. (2012). Comparative effectiveness of cognitive behavioral therapy for insomnia: A systematic review. *BMC Family Practice, 13*, 40.

Mittleman, M. A., & Mostofsky, E. (2011). Physical, psychological, and chemical triggers of acute cardiovascular events: Preventive strategies. *Circulation, 124*(3), 346–354.

Miyazaki, T., Ishikawa, T., Iimori, H., Miki, A., Wenner, M., Fukunishi, I., ... Kawamura, N. (2003). Relationship between perceived social support and immune function. *Stress and Health, 19*, 3–7.

MMWR. (2004). Alcohol-attributable deaths and years of potential life lost—United States, 2001. *Morbidity and Mortality Weekly Report, 53*(37), 866–870.

MMWR. (2012). Cancer screening—United States, 2010. *Morbidity and Mortality Weekly Report, 61*(3), 41–45.

MMWR. (2014, October 31). CDC National Health Report: Leading causes of morbidity and mortality and associated behavioral risk and protective factors [Supplement]. *Morbidity and Mortality Weekly Report, 63*(4), 3–27. Retrieved March 19, 2016, from http://www.cdc.gov/mmwr/preview/mmwrhtml/su6304a2.htm

MMWR. (2015, January 9). Indicators for chronic disease surveillance—United States, 2013. *Morbidity and Mortality Weekly Report, 64*(1). Retrieved from https://www.cdc.gov/mmwr/pdf/rr/rr6401.pdf

MMWR. (2015, July 31). National, regional, state, and selected local area vaccination coverage among adolescents aged 13–17 years—United States, 2014. *Morbidity and Mortality Weekly Report, 64*(29), 784–792.

MMWR. (2017, October 13). Vaccination coverage for selected vaccines, exemption rates, and provisional enrollment among children in kindergarten—United States, 2016–17 school year. *Morbidity and Mortality Weekly Report, 66*(40), 1073–1080.

Moberly, N. J., & Watkins, E. R. (2008). Ruminative self-focus, negative life events, and negative affect. *Behaviour Research and Therapy, 46*(9), 1034–1039.

Moeller, F. G., Dougherty, D. M. Barratt, E. S., Oderinde, V., Mathias, C. W., Harper, R. A., & Swann, A. C. (2002). Increased impulsivity in cocaine dependent subjects independent of antisocial personality disorder and aggression. *Drug and Alcohol Dependence, 68*(1), 105–112.

Moerman, D. E. (2002). *Meaning, medicine and the "placebo effect."* Cambridge, England: Cambridge University Press.

Moerman, D. E. (2011). Meaningful placebos—Controlling the uncontrollable. *New England Journal of Medicine, 365,* 171–172.

Moerman, D. E, & Jonas, W. B. (2002). Deconstructing the placebo effect and finding the meaning response. *Annals of Internal Medicine, 136*(6), 471–476.

Mok, L. C., & Lee, I. (2008). Anxiety, depression, and pain intensity in patients with low back pain who are admitted to acute care hospitals. *Journal of Clinical Nursing, 17*(11), 1471–1480.

Mole, B. (2015, March 24). Today's pot is more potent, less therapeutic. *Science News.* Retrieved from https://www.sciencenews.org/blog/science-ticker/today's-pot-more-potent-less-therapeutic?mode=topic&cont ext=45

Moller-Levet, C. S., Archer, S. N., Bucca, G., Laing, E. E., Slak, A., Kabiljo, R., Lo, J., Santhi, N., von Schantz, M., Smith, C. P., & Dijk, D. (2013). Effects of insufficient sleep on circadian rhythmicity and expression amplitude of the human blood transcriptome. *Proceedings of the National Academy of Sciences.* Retrieved from http://www.pnas.org/content/110/12/E1132.full.pdf

Molton, I. R., & Terrill, A. L. (2014). Overview of persistent pain in older adults. *American Psychologist, 69*(2), 197–207.

Mommersteeg, P. M. C., Keijsers, G. P. J., Heijnen, C. J., Verbraak, M. J. P. M., & van Doornen, L. J. P. (2006). Cortisol deviations in people with burnout before and after psychotherapy: A pilot study. *Health Psychology, 25*, 243–248.

Montanaro, E. A., & Bryan, A. D. (2014). Comparing theory-based condom interventions: Health belief model versus theory of planned behavior. *Health Psychology, 33*(10), 1251–1260.

Monteil-Castro, A. J., Gonzalez-Cervantes, R. M., Bravo-Ruiseco, G., & Pacheco-Lopez, G. (2013). The microbiota-gut-brain axis: Neurobehavioral correlates, health, and sociality. *Frontiers in Integrative Neuroscience, 7,* 70.

Montgomery, G. H. (2004). Presurgery distress and specific response expectancies predict postsurgery outcomes in surgery patients confronting breast cancer. *Health Psychology, 23*(4), 381–387.

Montpetit, M. A., & Bergeman, C. S. (2007). Dimensions of control: Mediational analyses of the stress-health relationship. *Personality and Individual Differences, 43*, 2237–2248.

Moore, J. X., Chaudhary, N., & Akinyemiju, T. (2017). Metabolic syndrome prevalence by race/ethnicity and sex in the United States, National Health and Nutrition Examination Survey, 1988–2012. *Preventing Chronic Disease, 14.* Retrieved from https://www.cdc.gov/pcd/issues/2017/16_0287.htm

Moreira, M. T., Smith, L. A., & Foxcroft, D. (2009). Social norms interventions to reduce alcohol misuse in university or college students. *Cochrane Database of Systematic Reviews, 2009*(3), CD006748.

Morey, J. N., Boggero, I. A., Scott, A. B., & Segerstrom, S. C. (2015). Current directions in stress and immune function. *Current Opinion in Psychology, 5,* 13–17.

Morgan, C. A., Wang, S., Rasmusson, A., Hazlett, G., Anderson, G., & Charney, D. S. (2001). Relationship among plasma cortisol, catecholamines, neuropeptide Y, and human performance during exposure to uncontrollable stress. *Psychosomatic Medicine, 63*(3), 412–422.

Moriarty, D. G., Kobau, R., Zack, M. M., & Zahran, H. S. (2005). Tracking healthy days—A window on the health of older adults. *Preventing Chronic Disease, 2*(3), 5.

Morojele, N. K., & Stephenson, G. M. (1994). Addictive behaviours: Predictors of abstinence intentions and expectations in the theory of planned behavior. In D. R. Rutter & L. Quine (Eds.), *Social psychology and health: European perspectives* (pp. 47–70). Aldershot, England: Avebury.

Morone, N. E., Greco, C. M., & Weiner, D. K. (2008). Mindfulness meditation for the treatment of chronic low back pain in older adults: A randomized controlled pilot study. *Pain, 134,* 310–319.

Morris, P. D., & Channer, K. S. (2012). Testosterone and cardiovascular disease in men. *Asian Journal of Andrology, 14*(3), 428–435.

Morrison, C. D. (2008). Leptin resistance and the response to positive energy balance. *Physiology and Behavior, 94,* 660–663.

Mosca, L., Barrett-Conner, E., & Wenger, N. K. (2011). Sex/gender differences in cardiovascular disease prevention: What a difference a decade makes. *Circulation, 124,* 2145–2154.

Mosconi, M. W., Cody-Hazlett, H., Poe, M. D., Gerig, G., Gimpel-Smith, R., & Piven, J. (2009). Longitudinal study of amygdala volume and joint attention in 2- to 4-year-old children with autism. *Archives of General Psychiatry, 65*(5), 509–516.

Moss, D., & Gunkelman, J. (2002). Task force report on methodology and empirically supported treatments. *Applied Psychophysiology and Biofeedback, 27*(4), 271–272.

Motivala, S. J., & Irwin, M. R. (2007). Sleep and immunity: Cytokine pathways linking sleep and health outcomes. *Current Directions in Psychological Science, 16*(1), 21–25.

Mroz, L. W., Oliffe, J. L., & Davison, B. J. (2013). Masculinities and patient perspectives of communication about active surveillance for prostate cancer. *Health Psychology, 32*(1), 83–90.

Mueller, C. E., Bridges, S. K., & Goddard, M. S. (2011). Sleep and parent-family connectedness: Links, relationships and implications for adolescent depression. *Journal of Family Studies, 17*(1), 9–23.

Mujahid, M. S., James, S. A., Kaplan, G. A., & Salonen, J. T. (2017). Socioeconomic position, John Henryism, and incidence of acute myocardial infarction in Finnish men. *Social Science and Medicine, 173,* 54–62.

Mulvaney, S. A., Rothman, R. L., Dietrich, M. S., Wallston, K. A., Grove, E., Elasy, T. A., & Johnson, K. B. (2012). Using mobile phones to measure adolescent diabetes adherence. *Health Psychology, 31*(1), 43–50.

Mund, M., & Mitte, K. (2012). The costs of repression: A meta-analysis on the relation between repressive coping and somatic diseases. *Health Psychology, 31*(5), 640–649.

Munsey, C. (2010). Medicine or menace? Psychologists' research can inform the growing debate over legalizing marijuana. *Monitor on Psychology, 41*(6), 50.

Murphy, S. L., Kochanek, K. D., Xu, J. Q., & Heron, M. (2015). Deaths: Final data for 2012. *National Vital Statistics Reports, 63*(9). Hyattsville, MD: National Center for Health Statistics.

Murphy, S. L., Xu, J., Kochanek, K. D., Curtin, S. C., & Arias, E. (2017). Deaths: Final data for 2015. *National Vital Statistics Reports, 66*(6). Hyattsville, MD: National Center for Health Statistics.

Myers, L. B. (2010). The importance of the repressive coping style: Findings from 30 years of research. *Anxiety, Stress, and Coping, 23*(1), 3–17.

Myers, L. B., Burns, J. W., Derakshan, N., Elfant, E., Eysenck, M. W., & Phipps, S. (2008). Current issues in repressive coping and health. In A. Vingerhoet (Ed.), *Emotion regulation: Conceptual and clinical issues* (pp. 69–86). New York, NY: Springer.

Myrin, B., & Lagerstrom, M. (2006). Health behaviour and sense of coherence among pupils aged 14–15. *Scandinavian Journal of Caring Sciences, 20*(3), 339–346.

Nabel, E. G. (2000). Coronary heart disease in women—An ounce of prevention. *New England Journal of Medicine, 343,* 572–574. doi:10.1056/NEJM200008243430809

Naghavi, M., and others. (2017). Global, regional, and national age-specific mortality for 264 causes of death, 1980–2016: A systematic analysis for the Global Burden of Disease Study. *The Lancet, 390*(10100), 1151–1210.

Nahin, R. L. (2015). Estimates of pain prevalence and severity in adults: United States, 2012. *The Journal of Pain, 16*(8), 769–780.

Nakamura, M., Tanaka, M., Kinukawa, N., Abe, S., Itoh, K., Imai, K., Masuda, T., & Nakao, H. (2000). Association between basal serum and leptin levels and changes in abdominal fat distribution during weight loss. *Journal of Atherosclerosis and Thrombosis, 6,* 28–32.

Nash, J. (2013). Dealing with diagnosis. In *Diabetes and wellbeing: Managing the psychological and emotional challenges of diabetes types 1 and 2* (pp. 23–48). Chichester, England: Wiley-Blackwell.

National Assessment of Adult Literacy (NAAL). (2003). *What is NAAL?* National Center for Education Statistics. Retrieved from http://nces.ed.gov/naal/

National Cancer Institute (NCI). (2005, April). *Thinking about complementary & alternative medicine: A guide for people with cancer.* U.S. Department of Health and Human Services, National Institutes of Health, National Cancer Institute, National Center for Complementary and Alternative Medicine (NIH Publication No. 04-5541). Retrieved from https://www.cancer.gov/publications/patient-education/367NCINewV2.pdf

National Cancer Institute (NCI). (2010a). *Fluoridated water: Questions and answers.* Retrieved from http://www.cancer.gov/cancertopics/factsheet/Risk/fluoridated-water

National Cancer Institute (NCI). (2010b). *Psychological stress and cancer: Questions and answers.* Retrieved from http://www.cancer.gov/cancertopics/factsheet/Risk/stress

National Cancer Institute (NCI). (2010c). *Quitting smoking: Why to quit and how to get help.* Retrieved from http://www.cancer.gov/cancertopics/factsheet/Tobacco/cessation

National Cancer Institute (NCI). (2015a). *Age and cancer risk.* Retrieved from https://www.cancer.gov/about-cancer/causes-prevention/risk/age

National Cancer Institute (NCI). (2015b). *Chemicals in meat cooked at high temperatures and cancer risk.* Retrieved from http://

www.cancer.gov/about-cancer/causes-prevention/risk/ diet/ cooked-meats-fact-sheet

National Cancer Institute (NCI). (2015c). *Obesity and cancer risk*. Retrieved from http://www.cancer.gov/about-cancer/causes-prevention/risk/obesity/obesity-fact-sheet

National Cancer Institute (NCI). (2015d). *Physical activity and cancer*. Retrieved from http://www.cancer.gov/about-cancer/causes-prevention/risk/obesity/physical-activity-fact-sheet

National Cancer Institute (NCI). (2016). *Screening tests that have been shown to reduce cancer deaths*. Retrieved from http://www.cancer.gov/about-cancer/screening/screening-tests#screening-test

National Cancer Institute (NCI). (2017). *Physical activity and cancer*. Retrieved from https://www.cancer.gov/about-cancer/causes-prevention/risk/obesity/physical-activity-fact-sheet

National Cancer Institute (NCI). (2018a). *Cancer stat facts: Hodgkin lymphoma*. Surveillance, Epidemiology, and End Results (SEER) Program. Retrieved from https://seer.cancer.gov/statfacts/html/hodg.html

National Cancer Institute (NCI). (2018b). *Cancer stat facts: Leukemia*. Surveillance, Epidemiology, and End Results (SEER) Program. Retrieved from https://seer.cancer.gov/statfacts/html/leuks.html

National Cancer Institute (NCI). (2018c). *Cancer stat facts: Non-Hodgkin lymphoma*. Surveillance, Epidemiology, and End Results (SEER) Program. Retrieved from https://seer.cancer.gov/statfacts/html/nhl.html

National Cancer Institute (NCI). (2018d). *Cancer stat facts: Prostate cancer*. Surveillance, Epidemiology, and End Results (SEER) Program. Retrieved from https://seer.cancer.gov/statfacts/html/prost.html

National Cancer Institute (NCI). (2018e). *Cancer statistics*. Retrieved from https://www.cancer.gov/about-cancer/understanding/statistics

National Cancer Institute (NCI). (2018f). *Physical activity and cancer*. Retrieved from https://www.cancer.gov/about-cancer/causes-prevention/risk/obesity/physical-activity-fact-sheet

National Center for Complementary and Alternative Medicine (NCCAM). (2013). *Oral probiotics: An introduction*. Retrieved from http://nccam.nih.gov/health/probiotics/ introduction.htm

National Center for Complementary and Integrative Health (NCCIH). (2016a). *Acupuncture: In depth*. Retrieved March 2, 2016, from https://nccih.nih.gov/health/acupuncture/introduction#hed1

National Center for Environmental Health. (2017a). *Asthma*. Centers for Disease Control and Prevention. Retrieved from https://www.cdc.gov/asthma/default.htm

National Center for Environmental Health. (2017b). *2015 previous most recent asthma data*. Centers for Disease Control and Prevention. Retrieved from https://www.cdc.gov/asthma/archivedata/2015/2015_data.html

National Center for Health Statistics (NCHS). (2006). *Health, United States, 2006*. Hyattsville, MD: U.S. Department of Health and Human Services.

National Center for Health Statistics (NCHS). (2012). *Health, United States, 2011: With special feature on socioeconomic status and health*. Hyattsville, MD: U.S. Department of Health and Human Services.

National Center for Health Statistics (NCHS). (2016). *Progress reviews for Healthy People 2020*. Retrieved from http://www.cdc.gov/nchs/healthy_people/hp2020/hp2020_progress_reviews.htm

National Center for Health Statistics (NCHS). (2017). *Health, United States, 2016*. Hyattsville, MD: Author.

National Center for PTSD. (2018). *How common is PTSD?* Retrieved from https://www.ptsd.va.gov/public/PTSD-overview/basics/how-common-is-ptsd.asp

National Center for Statistics and Analysis. (2017, March). *Traffic safety facts research note: Distracted driving 2015* (Report No. DOT HS 812 381). Washington, DC: National Highway Traffic Safety Administration.

National Diabetes Statistics Report. (2014). Centers for Disease Control and Prevention. Retrieved from http://www.cdc.gov/diabetes/pubs/statsreport14/national-diabetes-report-web.pdf

National Eating Disorders Association (NEDA). (2016). *Binge eating disorder. National Eating Disorders Association*. Retrieved from https://www.nationaleatingdisorders.org/binge-eating-disorder

National Eating Disorders Association (NEDA). (2018). *Statistics and research on eating disorders*. Retrieved from https://www.nationaleatingdisorders.org/statistics-research-eating-disorders

National Eating Disorders Coalition (NEDC). (2017). *Eating disorders in males*. Retrieved from http://www.nedc.com.au/eating-disorders-in-males

National Highway Traffic Safety Administration (NHTSA). (2018). *Traffic safety facts: Speeding, 2016 data*. Washington, DC: National Center for Statistics and Analysis.

National Institute for Occupational Safety and Health (NIOSH). (2015). *Occupational cancer*. Retrieved from http://www.cdc.gov/niosh/topics/cancer/

National Institute for Occupational Safety and Health (NIOSH). (2018). *Work schedules: Shift work and long hours*. Retrieved from https://www.cdc.gov/niosh/topics/workschedules/default.html

National Institute of Diabetes and Digestive and Kidney Diseases (NIDDK). (2008, October). *Diabetes prevention program (DPP)* (NIH Publication No. 09-5099). U.S. Dept. of Health and Human Services. Retrieved from http://www.niddk.nih.gov/about-niddk/research-areas/diabetes/diabetes-prevention-program-dpp/Pages/default.aspx

National Institute on Alcohol Abuse and Alcoholism (NIAAA). (2006). *College students and drinking*. Retrieved from http://pubs.niaaa.nih.gov/publications/aa29.htm

National Institute on Alcohol Abuse and Alcoholism (NIAAA). (2012). *A family history of alcoholism: Are you at risk?* (NIH Publication No. 03-5340). Hyattsville, MD: U.S. Government Printing Office.

National Institute on Alcohol Abuse and Alcoholism (NIAAA). (2013a). *Alcohol Use Disorder* (NIH Pub. No. 13-7999). Hyattsville, MD: U.S. Government Printing Office.

National Institute on Alcohol Abuse and Alcoholism (NIAAA). (2013b). *Moderate and binge drinking*. Retrieved from http://www.niaaa.nih.gov/alcohol-health/overview-alcohol-consumption/moderate-binge-drinking

National Institute on Alcohol Abuse and Alcoholism (NIAAA). (2015). *A snapshot of annual high-risk college drinking consequences*. Retrieved from http://www.collegedrinkingprevention.gov/statssummaries/snapshot.aspx

National Institute on Alcohol Abuse and Alcoholism (NIAAA). (2017). *Alcohol facts and statistics*. Retrieved from https://www.niaaa.nih.gov/alcohol-health/overview-alcohol-consumption/alcohol-facts-and-statistics

National Institute on Drug Abuse (NIDA). (2016). *Can marijuana use during and after pregnancy harm the baby?* Retrieved from https://www.drugabuse.gov/publications/research-reports/marijuana/can-marijuana-use-during-pregnancy-harm-baby

National Institute on Drug Abuse (NIDA). (2018). *Opioid overdose crisis.* Retrieved from https://www.drugabuse.gov/drugs-abuse/opioids/opioid-overdose-crisis

National Sleep Foundation. (2013). Adult sleep habits and styles. In Johnston, L. D., O'Malley, P. M., Miech, R. A., Bachman, J. G., & Schulenberg, J. E. (2015). *Monitoring the future national survey results on drug use: 1975–2015: 2015 overview: Key findings on adolescent drug use.* Ann Arbor, MI: Institute for Social Research, The University of Michigan.

National Women's Law Center (NWLC). 2012. New NWLC report: Discriminatory health insurance practices cost women $1 billion a year. Washington, DC: National Women's Law Center. Retrieved from http://nwlc.org/press-releases/new-nwlc-report-discriminatory-health-insurance-practices-cost-women-1-billion-year/

Nauert, R. (2008, April 25). Smoking ups risk of depression. *PsychCentral.* Retrieved from http://psychcentral.com/news/2008/04/25/smoking-ups-risk-of-depression/2190.html

Nausheen, B., Gidron, Y., Peveler, R., & Moss-Morris, R. (2009). Social support and cancer progression: A systematic review. *Journal of Psychosomatic Research, 67,* 403–415.

NCCIH. (2016b). *Americans spent $30.2 billion out-of-pocket on complementary health approaches.* National Center for Complementary and Integrative Health. Retrieved from https://nccih.nih.gov/news/press/cost-spending-06222016

NCCIH. (2017a). *Complementary, alternative, or integrative health: What's in a name?* National Center for Complementary and Integrative Health. Retrieved from https://nccih.nih.gov/health/integrative-health

NCCIH. (2017b). *Mind and body practices.* National Center for Complementary and Integrative Health. Retrieved from https://nccih.nih.gov/health/mindbody

NCCIH. (2017c). *Naturopathy.* National Center for Complementary and Integrative Health. Retrieved from https://nccih.nih.gov/health/naturopathy

NCCIH. (2017d). *Tai chi and qi gong.* National Center for Complementary and Integrative Health. Retrieved from https://nccih.nih.gov/health/taichi

NCCIH. (2017e). *Types of complementary health approaches.* National Center for Complementary and Integrative Health. https://nccih.nih.gov/health/integrative-health?nav=gsa#types

NCCIH. (2017f). *Use of complementary health approaches in the U.S.: National Health Interview Survey (NHIS).* National Center for Complementary and Integrative Medicine. Retrieved from https://nccih.nih.gov/research/statistics/NHIS/2012

NCCIH. (2017g). *Yoga.* National Center for Complementary and Integrative Health. Retrieved from https://nccih.nih.gov/health/yoga

NCL Communications. (2014). Survey: One-third of American parents mistakenly link vaccines to autism. *National Consumers League.* Retrieved from http://www.nclnet.org/survey_one_third_of_american_parents_mistakenly_link_vaccines_to_autism

Nebehay, S. (2011, July 21). *Going into hospital far riskier than flying: WHO.* Retrieved from http://www.reuters.com/article/2011/07/21/us-safety-idUSTRE76K45R20110721

Nedeltcheva, A. V., Kilkus, J. M., Imperial, J., Kasza, K., Schoeller, D. A., & Penev, D. V. (2009). Sleep curtailment is accompanied by increased intake of calories from snacks. *American Journal of Clinical Nutrition, 89*(1), 126–133.

Neiman, A. B., Ruppar, T., Ho, M., Garber, L., Weidle, P. J., Hong, Y., … Thorpe, P. G., 2017. CDC grand rounds: Improving medication adherence for chronic disease management—Innovations and opportunities. *MMWR (Morbidity and Mortal Weekly Report), 66*(45). https://www.cdc.gov/mmwr/volumes/66/wr/mm6645a2.htm

Nelson, S. K., & Lyubomirsky, S. (2016). Gratitude. In Howard Friedman (Ed.), *Encyclopedia of mental health* (Vol. 2, pp. 277–280). New York, NY: Academic Press.

Nestoriuc, Y., & Martin, A. (2007). Efficacy of biofeedback for migraine: A meta-analysis. *Pain, 128,* 111–127.

Nestoriuc, Y., Rief, W., & Martin, A. (2008). Meta-analysis of biofeedback for tension-type headache: Efficacy, specificity, and treatment moderators. *Journal of Consulting and Clinical Psychology, 76*(3), 379–396.

Ng, M., Fleming, T., Robinson, M., Thompson, B., Graetz, N., Margono, C., … Gakidou, E. (2014). Global, regional, and national prevalence of overweight and obesity in children and adults during 1980–2013: A systematic analysis for the Global Burden of Disease Study 2013. *The Lancet, 384*(9945), 766–782.

Niederhoffer, K. G., & Pennebaker, J. W. (2002). Sharing one's story: On the benefits of writing or talking about emotional expression. In Snyder, C. R., & S. J. Lopez (Eds.), *Oxford handbook of positive psychology* (pp. 573–583). New York, NY: Oxford University Press.

Niehans, A. (2017, October 23). Disparities in healthcare detrimental for American women. *Badger Herald.* Retrieved from https://badgerherald.com/opinion/2017/10/23/disparities-in-healthcare-detrimental-for-american-women/

Nock, M. K. (2010). Self-injury. *Annual Review of Clinical Psychology, 6,* 339–363.

Norbury, T. A., MacGregor, A. J., Urwin, J., Spector, T. D., & McMahon, S. B. (2007). Heritability of responses to painful stimuli in women: A classical twin study. *Brain, 130,* 3041–3049.

North, H. (2011). *Endometriosis Diagnosis Survey 2011. Endometriosis UK.* Retrieved from https://www.endometriosis-uk.org/sites/default/files/files/Endometriosis%20Diagnosis%20Survey%20Feb2011%20Report%20final.pdf

Novotney, A. (2010a). Integrated care is nothing new for these psychologists. *Monitor on Psychology, 41*(1), 41–45.

Novotney, A. (2010b). A prescription for empathy. *Monitor on Psychology, 41*(1), 47–49.

NPR. (2013, March 26). The epidemiology of gun violence: Race, region and policy. *Talk of the Nation.* National Public Radio. Retrieved from http://www.wbur.org/npr/175378043/the-epidemiology-of-gun-violence-race-region-and-policy

NRC Health. (2016). *What do patients really want from their physician?* Retrieved from https://nrchealth.com/10-things-patients-wantfrom-their-doctors/

Nurses' Health Study (NHS). (2010). *The nurses' health study.* Retrieved from http://www.channing.harvard.edu/nhs

Nurses' Health Study (NHS). (2015). *The nurses' health study.* Retrieved from http://www.channing.harvard.edu/nhs/

Nygren, B., Alex, L., Jonsen, E., Gustafson, Y., Norberg, A., & Lundman, B. (2005). Resilience, sense of coherence, purpose in life and transcendence in relation to perceived physical and mental health among the oldest old. *Aging and Mental Health, 9*(4), 354–362.

Nyklíček, I., Mommersteeg, P. M. C., Van Beugen, S., Ramakers, C., & Van Boxtel, G. J. (2013). Mindfulness-based stress reduction and physiological activity during acute stress: A randomized controlled trial. *Health Psychology, 32*, 1110–1113.

O'Brien, C. W., & Moorey, S. (2010). Outlook and adaptation in advanced cancer: A systematic review. *Psycho-Oncology, 19*, 1239–1249.

O'Connor, A. (2016, September 13). Sugar backers paid to shift blame to fat. *The New York Times*, p. A1.

O'Donnell, K., Brydon, L., Wright, C. E., & Steptoe, A. (2008). Self-esteem levels and cardiovascular and immunity responses to acute stress. *Brain, Behavior, and Immunity, 22*(8), 1241–1247.

Oberoi, D. V., Jiwa, M., McManus, A., & Hodder, R. (2015). Men's help-seeking behavior with regards to lower bowel symptoms. *American Journal of Health Behavior, 39*(2), 212–221.

Occupational Safety and Health Administration (OSHA). (2016). *Guidelines for preventing workplace violence for healthcare and social service workers* (OSHA 3148-06R 2016). Retrieved from https://www.osha.gov/Publications/osha3148.pdf

Office of Disease Prevention and Health Promotion (ODPHP). (2018). *Genomics*. Retrieved from https://www.healthypeople.gov/2020/topics-objectives/topic/genomics

Office of Minority Health (OMH). (2015). *HHS promotores de salud initiative*. U.S. Department of Health and Human Services. Retrieved from http://minorityhealth.hhs.gov/omh/content.aspx?ID=8929

Office of the Surgeon General. (2011). *National prevention strategy*. National Prevention, Health Promotion, and Public Health Council. Rockville, MD: Author. Retrieved from http://www.surgeongeneral.gov/initiatives/prevention/strategy

Ogden, C. L., Lamb, M. M., Carroll, M. D., & Flegal, K. M. (2010). *Obesity and socioeconomic status in children and adolescents: United States, 2005–2008* (NCHS Data Brief No. 51). Hyattsville, MD: National Center for Health Statistics.

Ogden, N. (2015). General and plastic surgery devices: Reclassification of ultraviolet lamps for tanning: A rule by the Food and Drug Administration. *Federal Register*. Retrieved from https://www.federalregister.gov/articles/2014/06/02/2014-12546/general-and-plastic-surgery-devices-reclassification-of-ultraviolet-lamps-for-tanning-henceforth-to

Olds, J., & Milner, P. (1954). Positive reinforcement produced by electrical stimulation of the septal area and other regions of rat brain. *Journal of Comparative and Physiological Psychology, 47*, 419–427.

Oman, D., Kurata, J. H., Strawbridge, W. J., & Cohen, R. D. (2002). Religious attendance and cause of death over 31 years. *International Journal of Psychiatry in Medicine, 32*, 69–89.

Onishi, N. (2008, June 13). Japan, seeking trim waists, measures millions. *The New York Times*. Retrieved from http://www.nytimes.com

Open Science Collaboration. (2015). Estimating the reproducibility of psychological science. *Science, 349*(6251). Retrieved from http://science.sciencemag.org/content/349/6251/aac4716.full

Orenstein, D. (2013, February 13). A neural basis for benefits of meditation. *News from Brown* [Brown University]. Retrieved from http://news.brown.edu/pressreleases/2013/02/mindfulness

Organization for Economic Cooperation and Development (OECD). (2017). *Health at a glance 2017: Average length of hospital stay for normal delivery, 2015*. Retrieved from https://www.oecd-ilibrary.org/social-issues-migration-health/health-at-a-glance-2017/average-length-of-stay-for-normal-delivery-2015-or-nearest-year_health_glance-2017-graph163-en

Orme-Johnson, D. W., Schneider, R. H., Son, Y. D., Nidich, S., & Cho, Z. (2006). Neuroimaging of meditation's effect on brain reactivity to pain. *NeuroReport, 17*(12), 1359–1363.

Ornish, D., Magbanua, M. J., Weidner, G., Weinberg, V., Kemp, C., Green, C., … Carroll, P. R. (2008). Changes in prostate gene expression in men undergoing an intensive nutrition and lifestyle intervention. *Proceedings of the National Academy of Sciences, 105*(24), 8369–8374.

Ostelo, R. W. J. G., van Tulder, M. W., Vlaeyen, J. W. S., Linton, S. J., Morley, S. J., & Assendelft, W. J. J. (2005). Behavioural treatment for chronic low-back pain. *Cochrane Database of Systematic Reviews*, Cochrane AN: CD002014. Retrieved from http://www.ncbi.nlm.nih.gov/pubmed/15674889

Osuna, D., Barrera, M., Jr., Strycker, L. A., Toobert, D. J., Glasgow, R. E., Geno, C. R., … Doty, A. T. (2011). Methods for the cultural adaptation of a diabetes lifestyle intervention for Latinas: An illustrative project. *Health Promotion Practice, 12*(3), 341–348.

Paasche-Orlow, M. (2011). Caring for patients with limited health literacy. *Journal of the American Medical Association, 306*(10), 1122–1129.

Pagoto, S., McChargue, D., & Fuqua, R. W. (2003). Effects of a multi-component intervention on motivation and sun protection behaviors among Midwestern beachgoers. *Health Psychology, 22*(4), 429–433.

Pala, A. N., Steca, P., Varani, S., Calza, L, Colangeli, V., & Viale, P. (2012). Emotions may influence the production of pro-inflammatory cytokines in HIV positive individuals. *European Journal of Psychotraumatology, 3*(1), 1.

Panaite, V., Salomon, K., Jin, A., & Rottenberg, J. (2015). Cardiovascular recovery from psychological and physiological challenge and risk for adverse cardiovascular outcomes and all-cause mortality. *Psychosomatic Medicine, 77*(3), 215–226.

Pankow, J. F., Kim, K., McWhirter, K. J., Luo, W., Escobedo, J. O., Strongin, R. M., … Peyton, D. H. (2017). Benzene formation in electronic cigarettes. *PLOS ONE, 12*(3), e0173055.

Papanicolas, I., Woskie, L. R., & Jha, A. K. (2018). Health care spending in the United States and other high-income countries. *Journal of the American Medical Association, 319*(10), 1024–1039.

Paquet, C., Dube, L., Gauvin, L., Kestens, Y., & Daniel, M. (2010). Sense of mastery and metabolic risk: Moderating role of the local fast-food environment. *Psychosomatic Medicine, 72*, 324–331.

Park, H. S., Klein, K. A., Smith, S., & Martell, D. (2009). Separating subjective norms, university descriptive and injunctive norms, and U.S. descriptive and injunctive norms for drinking behavior intentions. *Health Communication, 24*, 746–751.

Parker, R. (2000). Health literacy: A challenge for American patients and their health care providers. *Health Promotion International, 15*, 277–283.

Parkinson's Disease Foundation. (2010). What is Parkinson's disease? Retrieved from http://www.pdf.org

Paruthi, S., Brooks, L. J., D'Ambrosio C., Hall, W.A., Kotagal, S., Lloyd, R. M., … Wise, M. A. (2016). Recommended amount of sleep for pediatric populations: A consensus statement of the American Academy of Sleep Medicine. *Journal of Clinical Sleep Medicine, 12*(6), 785–786.

Pascoe, E. A., & Richman, L. S. (2009). Perceived discrimination and health: A meta-analytic review. *Psychological Bulletin, 135,* 531–554.

Pasquali, R. (2012). The hypothalamic-pituitary-adrenal axis and sex hormones in chronic stress and obesity: Pathophysiological and clinical aspects. *Annals of the New York Academy of Sciences, 1264*(1), 20–35.

Patel, K. V., Guralnik, J. M., Dansie, E. J., & Turk, D. C. (2013). Prevalence and impact of pain among older adults in the United States: Findings from the 2011 National Health and Aging Trends Study (NHATS). *Pain, 154*(12). Retrieved from http://www.ncbi .nlm.nih.gov/pmc/articles/PMC3843850/

Patel, N. P., Grandner, M. A., Xie, D., Branas, C. C., & Gooneratne, N. (2010). "Sleep disparity" in the population: Poor sleep quality is strongly associated with poverty and ethnicity. *BMC Public Health, 10*(475). Retrieved from http://www.biomedcentral .com/1471-2458/10/475

Patterson, D. R., Jensen, M. P., & Montgomery, G. H. (2010). Hypnosis for pain control. In S. J. Lynn, J. W. Rhue, & I. Kirsch (Eds.), *Handbook of clinical hypnosis* (2nd ed.). Washington, DC: American Psychological Association.

Patton, G. C., Coffey, C., Cappa, C., Currie, D., Riley, L., Gore, F., Degenhardt, L., Richardson, D., Astone, N., Sangowawa, A. O., Mokdad, A., & Ferguson, J. (2012). Health of the world's adolescents: A synthesis of internationally comparable data. *The Lancet, 379,* 1665–1675.

Paul, K., Boutain, D., Manhart, L., & Hitti, J. (2008). Racial disparity in bacterial vaginosis: The role of socioeconomic status, psychosocial stress, and neighborhood characteristics, and possible implications for preterm birth. *Social Science and Medicine, 67*(5), 824–833.

Paungmali, A., Joseph, L. H., Punturee, K., Sitilertpisan, P., Pirunsan, U., & Uthaikhup, S. (2018). Immediate effects of core stabilization exercise on β-endorphin and cortisol levels among patients with chronic nonspecific low back pain: A randomized crossover design. *Journal of Manipulative and Physiological Therapeutics, 41*(3), 181–188.

Pawlyck, A. C., Ferber, M., Shah, A., Pack, A., & Naidoo, N. (2007). Proteomic analysis of the effects and interactions of sleep deprivation and aging in mouse cerebral cortex. *Journal of Neurochemistry, 103*(6), 2301–2313.

Pearsall, P. (2004). *The Beethoven factor: The new psychology of hardiness, happiness, healing, and hope.* New York, NY: Hampton Roads Publishing.

Pedersen, S. S., van Domburg, R. T., Theuns, D. A., Jordaens, L., & Erdman, R. A. (2004). Type D personality is associated with increased anxiety and depressive symptoms in patients with an implantable cardioverter defibrillator and their partners. *Psychosomatic Medicine, 66*(5), 714–719.

Peek, M. E., Cargill, A., & Huang, E. S. (2007). Diabetes health disparities: A systematic review of health care interventions. *Medical Care Research and Review, 64*(5), 101–156.

Peek, M. E., Odoms-Young, A., Quinn, M. T., Gorwara-Bhat, R., Wilson, S. C., & Chin, M. H. (2010). Racism in healthcare: Its

relationship to shared decision-making and health disparities: A response to Brady. *Social Science & Medicine, 71*(1), 13–17.

Peeke, P. (2010, January 25). Just what is an average woman's size anymore? *WebMD Everyday Fitness.* Retrieved from http://blogs .webmd.com/pamela-peeke-md/2010/01/just-what-is-average-womans-size.html

Peeters, A., Barendregt, J. J., Willekens, F., Mackenbach, J. P., Mamun, A. A., & Bonneux, L. (2003). Obesity in adulthood and its consequences for life expectancy: A life-table analysis. *Annals of Internal Medicine, 138,* 24–32.

Peltzer, J. N., Domian, E. W., & Teel, C. S. (2016). Infected lives: Experiences of young African American HIV-positive women. *Western Journal of Nursing Research, 38*(2), 216–230.

Penedo, F. J., Dahn, J. R., Molton, I., Gonzalez, J. S., Kinsinger, D., Roos, B. A., … Antoni, M. H. (2004). Cognitive-behavioral stress management improves stress-management skills and quality of life in men recovering from treatment of prostate carcinoma. *Cancer, 100*(1), 192–200.

Penfield, W. (1952). Memory mechanisms. *AMA Archives of Neurology & Psychiatry, 67,* 178–198.

Pennebaker, J. W., & Susman, J. R. (1988). Disclosure of traumas and psychosomatic processes. *Social Science and Medicine, 26*(3), 327–332.

Peralta-Ramirez, M. I., Jimenez-Alonzo, J., Godoy-Garcia, J. F., & Perez-Garcia, M. (2004). The effects of daily stress and stressful life events on the clinical symptomology of patients with lupus erythematosus. *Psychosomatic Medicine, 66,* 788–794.

Perkinson-Gloor, N., Lemola, S., & Grob, A. (2013). Sleep duration, positive attitude toward life, and academic achievement: The role of daytime tiredness, behavioral persistence, and school start times. *Journal of Adolescence, 36*(2), 311–318.

Perry, W. G. (1999). *Forms of ethical and intellectual development in the college years.* San Francisco: Jossey-Bass.

Perry-Jenkins, M., Repetti, R. L., & Crouter, A. C. (2000). Relationship processes: Work and family in the 1990s. *Journal of Marriage and the Family, 62*(4), 981–997.

Pert, C. B. (2003). *Molecules of emotion: The science behind mind-body medicine.* New York, NY: Simon & Schuster.

Peterson, N. D., Middleton, K. R., Nackers, L. M., Medina, K. E., Milsom, V. A., & Perri, M. G. (2014). Dietary self-monitoring and long-term success with weight management. *Obesity (Silver Spring, Md.), 22*(9), 1962–1967.

Pew Research Center. (2018). *Mobile fact sheet.* Retrieved from http:// www.pewinternet.org/fact-sheet/mobile/

Pham, T. (2007). *AIDS optimism and condom usage among men who have sex with men in Australia, the Netherlands, and United States (Independent Study Project [ISP] Collection Paper 152).* Retrieved from http://digitalcollections.sit.edu/isp_collection/152/?utm_source=digitalcollections.sit.edu%2Fisp_collection%2F152&utm_medium=PDF&utm_campaign=PDFCoverPages

Phillips, A. C., & Hughes, B. M. (2011). Introductory paper: Cardiovascular reactivity at a crossroads: Where are we now? *Biological Psychology, 86*(2), 95–97.

Phillips, K. M., Antoni, M. H., Carver, C. S., Lechner, S. C., Penedo, F. J., McCullough, M. E., & Blomberg, B. B. (2011). Stress management skills and reductions in serum cortisol across the year after surgery for non-metastatic breast cancer. *Cognitive Therapy and Research, 35*(6), 595–600.

Pierce, J. P. (2009). Electronic recording, self-report, and bias in measuring cigarette consumption. *Health Psychology, 28,* 527–528.

Piet, J., & Hougaard, E. (2011). The effect of mindfulness-based cognitive therapy for prevention of relapse in recurrent major depressive disorder: A systematic review and meta-analysis. *Clinical Psychology Review, 31,* 1032–1040.

Piet, J., Wurtzen, H., & Zachariae, R. (2012). The effect of mindfulness-based therapy on symptoms of anxiety and depression in adult cancer patients and survivors: A systematic review and meta-analysis. *Journal of Consulting and Clinical Psychology, 80*(6), 1007–1020.

Pilisuk, M., Boylan, R., & Acredolo, C. (1987). Social support, life stress, and subsequent medical care utilization. *Health Psychology, 6,* 273–288.

Pillay, T., van Zyl, H. A., & Blackbeard, B. (2014). Chronic pain perception and cultural experience. *Procedia—Social and Behavioral Sciences, 113*(7), 151–160.

Pinquart, M., & Duberstein, P. R. (2010). Depression and cancer mortality: A meta-analysis. *Psychological Medicine, 40*(11), 1797–1810.

Piscitelli, S. C., Burstein, A. H., Chaitt, D., Alfaro, R. M., & Falloon, J. (2000). Indinavir concentrations and St. John's wort. *The Lancet, 355,* 547–548.

Planned Parenthood. (2018). *STDs.* Retrieved from https://www.plannedparenthood.org/learn/stds-hiv-safer-sex

Player, M. S., King, D. E., Mainous, A. G., & Geesey, M. E. (2007). Psychosocial factors and progression from prehypertension to hypertension or coronary heart disease. *Annals of Family Medicine, 5*(5), 403–411.

Pluhar, E. I., Frongillo, E. A., Stycos, J. M., & Dempster-McClain, D. (2003). Changes over time in college students' family planning knowledge, preference, and behavior and implications for contraceptive education and prevention of sexually transmitted infections. *College Students Journal, 37*(3), 420–434.

Poetz, A., Eyles, J. D., Elliott, S., Wilson, K., & Keller-Olaman, S. (2007). Path analysis of income, coping and health at the local level in a Canadian context. *Health and Social Care in the Community, 15*(6), 542–552.

Polina, E. R., Contini, V., Hutz, M. H., & Bau, C. H. (2009). The serotonin 2A receptor gene in alcohol dependence and tobacco smoking. *Drug and Alcohol Dependence, 101*(1), 128.

Polk, D. E., Coen, S., Doyle, W. J., Skoner, D. P., & Kirschbaum, C. (2005). State and trait affect as predictors of salivary cortisol in healthy adults. *Psychoneuroendocrinology, 30*(3), 261–272.

Ponniah, K., & Hollon, S. D. (2009). Empirically supported psychological treatments for acute stress disorder and posttraumatic stress disorder: A review. *Depression and Anxiety, 26*(12), 1086–1090.

Pool, G. J., Schwegler, A. F., Theodore, B. R., & Fuchs, P. N. (2007). Role of gender norms and group identification on hypothetical and experimental pain tolerance. *Pain, 129,* 122–129.

Posadzki, P., & Ernst, E. (2012). Guided imagery for non-musculoskeletal pain: A systematic review of randomized clinical trials. *Journal of Pain and Symptom Management, 44*(1), 95–104.

Posadzki, P., Lewandowski, W., Terry, R., Ernst, E., & Stearns, A. (2011). Guided imagery for musculoskeletal pain: A systematic review. *Clinical Journal of Pain, 27*(7), 648–653.

Potenza, M. N. (2014). Non-substance addictive behaviors in the context of DSM-5. *Addictive Behavior, 39*(1), 1–2.

Powell, K. E., Paluch, A. E., & Blair, S. N. (2011). Physical activity for health: What kind? How much? How intense? On top of what? *Annual Review of Public Health, 32,* 349–365.

Pressman, S. D., & Bowlin, S. (2014). Positive affect: A pathway to better physical health. In J. Gruber & J. Moskowitz (Eds.), *Positive emotion: Integrating the light sides and dark sides.* New York, NY: Oxford University Press.

Pressman, S. D., Gallagher, M., & Lopez, S. (2013). Is the emotion-health connection a "First World" problem? *Psychological Science, 24,* 544–549.

Prince-Embury, S., & Saklofske, D. H. (2013). *Resilience in children, adolescents, and adults: Translating research into practice.* New York, NY: Springer.

Professional Association for Childcare and Early Years (PACEY). (2016). *Children as young as 3 unhappy with their bodies.* Retrieved from https://www.pacey.org.uk/news-and-views/news/archive/2016-news/august-2016/children-as-young-as-3-unhappy-with-their-bodies/

Proper, K. L., van de Langenberg, D., Rodenburg, W., Vermeulen, R. C. H., van der Beek, A. J., van Steeg, H., & van Kerkhof, L. W. M. (2016). The relationship between shift work and metabolic risk factors: A systematic review of longitudinal studies. *American Journal of Preventive Medicine, 50*(5), e147–3157

Proxmire, C. A. (2015). Study: Health risks high for LGBT people. *Between the Lines News.* Retrieved from http://www.pridesource.com/article.html?article=63234

PsychoNeuroImmunology Research Society (PNIRS). (2010). *Mission statement.* Retrieved from https://www.pnirs.org

Puhl, R. M., & Heuer, C. A. (2009). The stigma of obesity: A review and update. *Obesity, 17,* 941–964.

Puska, P. (1999). The North Karelia project: From community intervention to national activity in lowering cholesterol levels and CHD risk. *European Heart Journal Supplements, 1,* S1–S4.

Qin, A. (2015). *Pediatric poisoning fatalities from 1972 through 2012.* U.S. Consumer Product Safety Commission.

Quackwatch. (2006). *Implausibility of EDTA chelation therapy.* Retrieved from http://www.quackwatch.org

Quartana, P. J., Laubmeier, K. K., & Zakowski, S. G. (2006). Psychological adjustment following diagnosis and treatment of cancer: An examination of the moderating role of positive and negative emotional expressivity. *Journal of Behavioral Medicine, 29,* 487–498.

Quick, J. C., & Quick, J. D. (2004). *Organizational stress and preventive management.* New York, NY: McGraw-Hill.

Quigley, K. S., Barrett, L. F., & Weinstein, S. (2002). Cardiovascular patterns associated with threat and challenge appraisals: A within-subjects analysis. *Psychophysiology, 39*(3), 292–302.

Quinn, J. M., Pascoe, A., Wood, W., & Neal, D. T. (2010). Can't control yourself? Monitor those bad habits. *Personality and Social Psychology Bulletin, 36,* 499–511.

Raaijmakers, L. G., Martens, M. K., Hesselink, A. E., de Weerdt, I., de Vries, N. K., & Kremens, S. P. (2014). Mastery and perceived autonomy support are correlates of Dutch diabetes patients' self-management and quality of life. *Patient Education and Counseling, 97*(1), 75–81.

Rahe, R. H., Mahan, J. L., & Arthur, R. J. (1970). Prediction of near-future health changes from subjects' preceding life changes. *Journal of Psychosomatic Research, 14,* 401–406.

Rahnama, P., Montazeri, A., Fallah Huseini, H., Kianbakht, S., & Naseri, M. (2012). Effect of *Zingiber officinale* R. rhizomes (ginger) on pain relief in primary dysmenorrhea: A placebo randomized trial. *BMC Complementary and Alternative Medicine, 12,* 92. Retrieved from http://www.biomedcentral.com/1472-6882/12/92

Räikkönen, K., Matthews, K. A., & Kuller, L. H. (2007). Depressive symptoms and stressful life events predict metabolic syndrome among middle-aged women: A comparison of World Health Association, adult treatment panel III, and international diabetes foundation definitions. *Diabetes Care, 30*(4), 872–877.

Ramachandran, V. S., & Rogers-Ramachandran, D. (2000). Phantom limbs and neural plasticity. *Archives of Neurology, 57,* 317–320.

Ranadive, U. (1997). Phantom limbs and rewired brains. *Technology Review, 100,* 17–18.

Randler, C., & Frech, D. (2009). Young people's time-of-day preferences affect their school performance. *Journal of Youth Studies, 12,* 653–667.

Rasmussen, H. N., Scheier, M. F., & Greenhouse, J. B. (2009). Optimism and physical health: A meta-analytic review. *Annals of Behavioral Medicine, 37*(3), 239–256.

Rasmusson, A. M., Vythilingam, M., & Morgan, C. A. (2003). The neuroendoctrinology of posttraumatic stress disorder: New directions. *CNS Spectrums, 8,* 651–667.

Rassart, J., Luyckx, K., Berg, C. A., Bijttbier, P., Moons, P., & Weets, I. (2015). Psychosocial functioning and glycemic control in emerging adults with type 1 diabetes: A 5-year follow-up study. *Health Psychology, 34*(11), 1058–1065.

Reese, C., Pedersen, T., Avila, S., Joseph, K., Nagy, K., Dennis, A., … Bokhari, F. (2012). Screening for traumatic stress among survivors of urban trauma. *Journal of Trauma and Acute Care Surgery, 73*(2), 462–467.

Regoeczi, W. C. (2003). When context matters: A multilevel analysis of household and neighbourhood crowding on aggression and withdrawal. *Journal of Environmental Psychology, 23,* 457–470.

Reimann, F., Cox, J. J., Belfer, I., Diatchenko, L., Zaykin, D. V., McHale, D. P., … Woods, C. G. (2010). Pain perception is altered by a nucleotide polymorphism in SCN9A. *Proceedings of the National Academy of Sciences, 107,* 5148–5153.

Remick, A. K., Polivy, J., & Pliner, P. (2009). Internal and external moderators of the effect of variety on food intake. *Psychological Bulletin, 135,* 434–451.

Rennard, S., Glover, E. D., Leischow, S., Daughton, D. M., Glover, P. N., Muramoto, M., Franzon, M., Danielsson, T., Landfeldt, B., & Westin, A. (2006). Efficacy of the nicotine inhaler in smoking reduction: A double-blind randomized trial. *Nicotine and Tobacco Research, 8*(4), 555–564.

Renner, M. J., & Mackin, R. S. (1998). A life stress instrument for classroom use. *Teaching of Psychology, 25*(47), 46–48.

Reperant, L. A., & Osterhaus, A. (2017). AIDS, Avian flu, SARS, MERS, Ebola, Zika … What next? *Vaccine, 35*(35), 4470–4474.

Repetti, R. L., Taylor, S. E., & Seeman, T. E. (2002). Risky families: Family social environments and the mental and physical health of offspring. *Psychological Bulletin, 128*(2), 330–338.

Repetti, R. L., Wang, S.-W., & Saxbe, D. (2009). Bringing it all back home: How outside stressors shape families' everyday lives. *Current Directions in Psychological Science, 18,* 106–111.

Repetto, P. B., Caldwell, C. H., & Zimmerman, M. A. (2005). A longitudinal study of the relationship between depressive symptoms and cigarette use among African American adolescents. *Health Psychology, 24,* 209–219.

Reston, J. (1971, July 26). Now, about my operation in Peking. *The New York Times,* pp. 1, 6.

Reyes-Rodriguez, M. L., Von Holle, A., Ulman, T. F., Thornton, L. M., Klump, K. L., Brandt, H., … Bulik, C. M. (2011). Posttraumatic stress disorder in anorexia nervosa. *Psychosomatic Medicine, 73*(6), 491–497.

Reynolds, G. (2009, September 16). Phys ed: What sort of exercise can make you smarter? *The New York Times.* Retrieved from http://well.blogs.nytimes.com/2009/09/16/what-sort-of-exercise-can-make-you-smarter/

Ricciardelli, L. A., McCabe, M. P., Williams, R. J., & Thompson, J. K. (2007). The role of ethnicity and culture in body image and disordered eating among males. *Clinical Psychology Review, 27*(5), 582–606.

Rich, L. E. (2004). Bringing more effective tools to the weight-loss table. *Monitor on Psychology, 35*(1), 52–55.

Riddihough, G., & Zahn, L. M. (2010). What is epigenetics? *Science, 330*(6004), 611.

Rigucci, S., Marques, T. R., Di Forti, M., Taylor, H., Dell'Aqua, F., Mondell, V. … Dazzan, P. (2016). Effect of high-potency cannabis on corpus callosum microstructure. *Psychological Medicine, 46*(4), 841–854.

Riley, K. E., & Kalichman, S. (2015). Mindfulness-based stress reduction for people living with HIV/AIDS: Preliminary review of intervention trial methodologies and findings. *Health Psychology Review, 9*(2), 224–243.

Ring, T. (2012). Is anyone immune to HIV? *HIV Plus.* Retrieved from https://www.hivplusmag.com/research-breakthroughs/2016/3/23/anyone-immune-hiv

Rios, R., & Zautra, A. J. (2011). Socioeconomic disparities in pain: The role of economic hardship and daily financial worry. *Health Psychology, 30*(1), 58–66.

Ritchie, H., & Roser, M. (2018). *Causes of death.* Our World in Data. Retrieved from https://ourworldindata.org/causes-of-death

Rix, S. E. (2012). *The employment situation, April 2012: Little encouraging news for older workers (Fact Sheet 257).* Washington, DC: AARP Public Policy Institute.

Robert Wood Johnson Foundation. (2018). *Socioeconomics and obesity.* Retrieved from https://stateofobesity.org/socioeconomics-obesity/

Roberts, C. K. (2007). Inactivity and fat cell hyperplasia: Fat chance? *Journal of Applied Physiology, 102*(4), 1308–1309.

Roberts, M. E., Gibbons, F. X., Gerrard, M., Weng, C., Murry, V. M., Simons, L. G., & Simons, R. L. (2012). From racial discrimination to risky sex: Prospective relations involving peers and parents. *Developmental Psychology, 48,* 89–102.

Robertson, T., Beveridge, G., & Bromley, C. (2017). Allostatic load as a predictor of all-cause and cause-specific mortality in the general population: Evidence from the Scottish Health Survey. *PLOS ONE, 12*(8), e0183297. Retrieved from doi.org/10.1371/journal.pone.0183297

Robinson, H., Jarrett, P., Vedhara, K., & Broadbent, E. (2017). The effects of expressive writing before or after bunch biopsy on wound healing. *Brain, Behavior, and Immunity, 61,* 217–227.

Robinson, R. L., Kroenke, K., Williams, D. A., Mease, P., Chen, Y., Faries, D., ... McCarberg, B. (2013). Longitudinal observation of treatment patterns and outcomes for patients with fibromyalgia: 12-month findings from the REFLECTIONS Study. *Pain Medicine, 14*(9), 1400–1415.

Robinson, T. E., & Berridge, K. C. (1993). The neural basis of drug craving: An incentive sensitization theory of addiction. *Brain Research Reviews, 18*(3), 247–291.

Robinson, T. E., & Berridge, K. C. (2003). Addiction. *Annual Review of Psychology, 54*, 25–53.

Rodriguez, D., Romer, D., & Audrain-McGovern, J. (2007). Beliefs about the risks of smoking mediate the relationship between exposure to smoking and smoking. *Psychosomatic Medicine, 69*, 106–113.

Roehling, P. V., Roehling, M. V., Vandlen, J. D., Bazek, J., & Guy, W. C. (2009). Weight discrimination and the glass ceiling effect among top US CEOs. *Equal Opportunities International, 28*, 179–196.

Roelfs, D. J., Davidson, K. W., & Schwartz, J. E. (2011). Losing life and livelihood: A systematic review and meta-analysis of unemployment and all-cause mortality. *Social Science and Medicine, 72*(6), 840–854.

Roemer, L., Orsillo, S. M., & Salters-Pedneault, K. (2008). Efficacy of an acceptance-based behavior therapy for generalized anxiety disorder: Evaluation in a randomized controlled trial. *Journal of Consulting and Clinical Psychology, 76*(6), 1083–1089.

Roenneberg, T., Allebrandt, K. V., Merrow, M., & Vetter, C. (2012). Social jetlag and obesity. *Current Biology, 22*(10), 939–943.

Roenneberg, T., Kuehnle, T., Pramstaller, P. P., Ricken, J., Havel, M., Guth, A., & Merrow, M. (2004). A marker for the end of adolescence. *Current Biology, 14*, R1038–R1039.

Roest, A. M., Martens, E. J., de Jonge, P., & Denollet, J. (2014). Anxiety and risk of incident coronary heart disease: A meta-analysis. *Journal of the American College of Cardiology, 56*(1), 38–46.

Rogeberg, O. (2013). Correlations between cannabis use and IQ change in the Dunedin cohort are consistent with confounding from socioeconomic status. *Proceedings of the National Academy of Sciences, 110*(11), 4251–4254.

Rogers, C. J., Colbert, L. H., Greiner, J. W., Perkins, S. N., & Hursting, S. D. (2008). Physical activity and cancer prevention: Pathways and targets for intervention. *Sports Medicine, 38*, 271–296.

Rogers, P. A. W., D'Hooghe, T. M., Fazleabas, A., Giudice, L. C., Montgomery, G. W., Petraglia, F., & Taylor, R. N. (2013). Defining future directions for endometriosis research: Workshop report from the 2011 World Congress of Endometriosis in Montpellier, France. *Reproductive Sciences, 20*(5), 483–499.

Rogers, R. G., Boardman, J. D., Pendergast, P. M., & Lawrence, E. M. (2015). Drinking problems and mortality risk in the United States. *Drug and Alcohol Dependence, 151*, 38–46.

Rogers, R. W. (1983). Cognitive and physiological appraisals in fear appeals and attitude change: A revised theory of protection motivation. In J. Cacioppo & R. Petty (Eds.), *Social psychophysiology.* New York, NY: Guilford Press.

Romero, S. A., Li, Q. S., & Mao, L. J. (2017, January). *Factors and barriers associated with changes in physical activity after cancer diagnosis.* Paper presented at the meeting of the American Society of Clinical Oncology, San Francisco.

Romeyke, T., Nöhammer, E., Scheuer, H. C. M., & Stummer, H. (2017). Integration of naturopathic medicine into acute inpatient care: An approach for patient-centred medicine under diagnosis-related groups. *Complementary Therapies in Clinical Practice, 28*, 9–17.

Roohafza, H., Sadeghi, M., Shirani, S., Bahonar, A., Mackie, M., & Sarafzadegan, N. (2009). Association of socioeconomic status and life-style factors with coping strategies in Isfahan Healthy Heart Program, Iran. *Croatian Medical Journal, 50*(4), 380–386. doi:org/10.3325/cmj.2009.50.380

Rooks, D. S., Gautam, S., Romeling, M., Cross, M. L., Stratigakis, D., Evans, B., & Katz, J. N. (2007). Group exercise, education, and combination self-management in women with fibromyalgia: A randomized trial. *Archives of Internal Medicine, 167*, 2192–2200.

Root, T. L., Thornton, L. M., Lindroos, A. K., Stunkard, A. J., Lichtenstein, P., Pedersen, N. L., ... Bulik, C. M. (2010). Shared and unique genetic and environmental influences on binge eating and night eating: A Swedish twin study. *Eating Behaviors, 11*, 92–98.

Rosemberg, M.-A. S., Li, Y., & Seng, J. (2017). Allostatic load: A useful concept for advancing nursing research. *Journal of Clinical Nursing, 26*, 5191–5205. doi:10.1111/jocn.13753

Rosen, C. S. (2000). Is the sequencing of change processes by stage consistent across health problems? A meta-analysis. *Health Psychology, 19*(6), 593–604.

Rosenfeldt, F., Miller, F., Nagley, P., Hadj, A., Marasco, S., Quick, D., ... Pepe, S. (2004). Response of the senescent heart to stress: Clinical therapeutic strategies and quest for mitochondrial predictors of biological age. *Annals of the New York Academy of Sciences, 1019*, 78–84.

Rosengren, A., Wilhelmsen, L., & Orth-Gomer, K. (2004). Coronary disease in relation to social support and social class in Swedish men: A 15-year follow-up in the study of men born in 1933. *European Heart Journal, 25*(1), 56–63.

Rosenkranz, M. A., Davidson, R. J., Maccoon, D. G., Sheridan, J. F., Kalin, N. H., & Lutz, A. (2013). A comparison of mindfulness-based stress reduction and an active control in modulation of neurogenic inflammation. *Brain, Behavior, & Immunity, 27*(1), 174–184.

Rosenthal, T., & Alter, A. (2012). Occupational stress and hypertension. *Journal of the American Society of Hypertension, 6*(1), 2–22.

Roshania, R., Narayan, K. M., & Oza-Frank, R. (2008). Age at arrival and risk of obesity among U.S. immigrants. *Obesity, 16*(12), 2669–2675.

Roter, D. L., & Hall, J. A. (2004). Physician gender and patient-centered communication: A critical review of empirical research. *Annual Review of Public Health, 25*, 497–519.

Rothbaum, B. O., Kearns, M. C., Reiser, E., Davis, J. S., Kerley, K. A., Rothbaum, A. O., ... Ressler, K. J. (2014). Early intervention following trauma may mitigate genetic risk for PTSD in civilians: A pilot prospective emergency department study. *Journal of Clinical Psychiatry, 75*(12), 1380–1387. doi:10.4088/JCP.13m08715

Rothenbacher, D., Hoffmeister, A., Brenner, H., & Koenig, W. (2003). Physical activity, coronary heart disease, and inflammatory response. *Archives of Internal Medicine, 163*(10), 1200–1205.

Rothman, A. J. (2000). Toward a theory-based analysis of behavioral maintenance. *Health Psychology, 19*, 64–69.

Roy, B., Diez-Roux, A. V., Seeman, T., Ranjit, N., Shea, S., & Cushman, M. (2010). Association of optimism and pessimism with inflammation and hemostasis in the multi-ethnic study of atherosclerosis (MESA). *Psychosomatic Medicine, 72,* 134–140.

Ruau, D., Liu, L. Y., Clark, J. D., Angst, M. S., & Butte, A. J. (2012). Sex differences in reported pain across 11,000 patients captured in electronic medical records. *The Journal of Pain, 13*(3), 228–234.

Ruby, M. B., Dunn, E. W., Perrino, A., Gillis, R., & Viel, S. (2011). The invisible benefits of exercise. *Health Psychology, 30*(1), 67–74.

Rueda, S., Mitra, S., Chen, S., Gogollishvili, D., Globerman, J., Chambers, L., … Rourke, S. B. (2016). Examining the associations between HIV-related stigma and health outcomes in people living with HIV/AIDS: A series of meta-analyses. *British Medical Journal Open, 6*(7), e011453. doi:10.1136/bmjopen-2016-01145

Rueggeberg, R., Wrosch, C., & Miler, G. E. (2012). The different roles of perceived stress in the association between older adults' physical activity and physical health. *Health Psychology, 32*(2), 164–171.

Rugaber, C. S. (2017, January 12). Pay gap between college grads and everyone else at a record. *USA Today.* Retrieved from https://www.usatoday.com/story/money/2017/01/12/pay-gap-between-college-grads-and-everyone-else-record/96493348/

Russo, S. J., Murrough, J. W., Han, M.-H., Charney, D. S., & Nestler, E. J. (2012). Neurobiology of resilience. *Nature Neuroscience, 15,* 1475–1484.

Rutledge, T., & Linden, W. (2003). Defensiveness and 3-year blood pressure levels among young adults: The mediating effect of stress reactivity. *Annals of Behavioral Medicine, 25*(1), 34–40.

Rutledge, T., Matthews, K., Lui, L. Y., Stone, K. L., & Cauley, J. A. (2003). Social networks and marital status predict mortality in older women: Prospective evidence from the Study of Osteoporotic Fractures (SOF). *Psychosomatic Medicine, 65*(4), 688–694.

Rutten, G. (2005). Diabetes patient education: Time for a new era. *Diabetic Medicine, 22,* 671–673.

Rutters, F., Nieuwenhuizen, A. G., Lemmens, S. G., Born, J. M., & Westertep-Plantenga, M. S. (2009). Acute stress-related changes in eating in the absence of hunger. *Obesity, 17*(1), 72–77.

Ryan, A. M., Gee, G. C., & Griffith, D. (2008). The effect of perceived discrimination on diabetes management. *Journal of Health Care for the Poor and Underserved, 19*(1), 149–163.

Ryff, C. D., Singer, B. H., Wing, E., & Love, G. D. (2001). Elective affinities and uninvited agonies: Mapping emotion with significant others onto health. In C. D. Ryff & B. H. Singer (Eds.), *Emotion, social relationships, and health* (pp. 133–175). New York, NY: Oxford University Press.

Saad, L. (2006, February 13). Nearly one in five teens is overweight. *Gallup News Service.* Retrieved from http://www.gallup.com/poll/21409/Nearly-One-Five-Teens-Overweight.aspx

Sabesan, S. (2015). Specialist cancer care through telehealth models. *Australian Journal of Rural Health, 23*(1), 19–23.

Sack, D. (2012, July 12). Rethinking everything we thought about addiction. *Psychology Today.* Retrieved from https://www.psychologytoday.com/us/blog/where-science-meets-the-steps/201207/rethinking-everything-we-thought-about-addiction

Sadeh, A., Mindel, J. A., Luedtke, K., & Wiegand, B. (2009). Sleep and sleep ecology in the first 3 years: A Web-based study. *Journal of Sleep Research, 18*(1), 60–73.

Saelens, B. E., Sallis, J. F., & Frank, L. D. (2003). Environmental correlates of walking and cycling: Findings from the transportation, urban design, and planning literatures. *Annals of Behavioral Medicine, 25*(2), 80–91.

Safen, S. A., Reisner, S. L., Herrick, A., Mimiaga, M. J., & Stall, R. (2010). Mental health and HIV risk in men who have sex with men. *Journal of Acquired Immune Deficiency Syndromes, 55*(Suppl. 2), S74–S77.

Salber, P. (2017). US healthcare ranks dead last compared to 10 other countries. *The Doctor Weighs In.* Retrieved from https://thedoctorweighsin.com/u-s-healthcare-ranks-dead-last-compared-to-11-high-income-countries/

Salovey, P. (2011). Framing health messages. In M. A. Gernsbacher, R. W. Pew, L. M. Hough, & J. R. Pomerantz (Eds.), *Psychology and the real world* (pp. 214–223). New York, NY: Worth.

SAMHSA. (2015). 2014 National Survey on Drug Use and Health (NSDUH). Table 6.88B—Alcohol use in the past month among persons aged 18 to 22, by college enrollment status and demographic characteristics: Percentages, 2013 and 2014. Retrieved from http://pubs.niaaa.nih.gov/publications/CollegeFactSheet/CollegeFactSheet.pdf

Sanchez-Vaznaugh, E., Kawachi, I., Subramanian, S. V., Sanchez, B. N., & Acevedo-Garcia, D. (2009). Do socioeconomic gradients in BMI vary by race/ethnicity, gender, and birthplace? *American Journal of Epidemiology, 169*(9), 1102–1112.

Sander, R. (2009). Musical therapy to reduce sleep problems. *Nursing Older People, 21*(7), 13.

Sanger-Katz, M. (2014, October 26). Is the Affordable Care Act working? *The New York Times.* Retrieved from http://www.nytimes.com/interactive/2014/10/27/us/is-the-affordable-care-act-working.html?_r=0#/

Sapolsky, R. M. (1990). Glucocorticoids, hippocampal damage, and the glutamatergic synapse. *Progress in Brain Research, 86,* 13–20.

Sapolsky R. M. (2004a). Organismal stress and telomeric aging: An unexpected connection. *Proceedings of the National Academy of Sciences, 101*(50), 17323–17324.

Sapolsky, R. M. (2004b). *Why zebras don't get ulcers* (3rd ed.). New York, NY: Holt.

Sapolsky, R. M. (2005). The influence of social hierarchy on primate health. *Science, 308,* 648–652.

Sapolsky, R. M. (2010, November 14). This is your brain on metaphors. *The New York Times.* Retrieved from http://www.nytimes.com

Sara, J. D., Prasad, M., Eleid, M. F., Zhang, M., Widmer, R. J., & Lerman, A. (2018). Association between work-related stress and coronary heart disease: A review of prospective studies through the job strain, effort-reward balance, and organizational justice models. *Journal of the American Heart Association, 7*(9), e008073. Retrieved from https://www.ncbi.nlm.nih.gov/pmc/articles/PMC6015274/

Sarly, B. (2017, December 30). Obamacare barely survived 2017. How's 2018 look? *NBC News.* Retrieved from https://www.nbcnews.com/politics/white-house/obamacare-barely-survived-2017-how-s-2018-look-n832936

Saunders, J. F., Frazier, L. D., & Nichols-Lopez, K. A. (2016). Self-esteem, diet self-efficacy, body mass index, and eating disorders: Modeling effects in an ethnically diverse sample. *Eating and Weight Disorders, 21*(3), 459–468.

Sayette, M. A., Loewenstein, G., Griffin, K. M., & Black, J. J. (2008). Exploring the cold-to-hot empathy gap in smokers. *Psychological Science, 19*, 926–932.

Schachter, S. (1978). Pharmacological and psychological determinants of smoking. *Annals of Internal Medicine, 88*, 104–114.

Schachter, S., Silverstein, B., Kozlowski, L. T., Perlick, D., Herman, C. P., & Liebling, B. (1977). Studies of the interaction of psychological and pharmacological determinants of smoking. *Journal of Experimental Psychology General, 106*, 3–12.

Schernhammer, E. (2005). Taking their own lives—The high rate of physician suicide. *New England Journal of Medicine, 352*, 2473–2476.

Schield, M. (2010). Assessing statistical literacy: Take CARE. In P. Bidgood, N. Hunt, & F. Jolliffe (Eds.), *Assessment methods in statistical education: An international perspective* (pp. 133–152). West Sussex, England: Wiley.

Schieman, S., Bierman, A., & Ellison, C. G. (2013). Religion and mental health. In C. S. Aneshensel, J. C. Phelan, & A. Bierman (Eds.), *Handbook of the sociology of mental health* (pp. 457–478). Netherlands: Springer.

Schmidt, J. E., & Andrykowski, M. A. (2004). The role of social and dispositional variables associated with emotional processing in adjustment to breast cancer: An Internet-based study. *Health Psychology, 23*(3), 259–266.

Schmidt, S., Grossman, P., Schwarzer, B., Jena, S., Naumann, J., & Walach, H. (2011). Treating fibromyalgia with mindfulness-based stress reduction: Results from a 3-armed randomized controlled trial. *Pain, 152*, 361–369.

Schmidt, U., & Grover, M. (2007). Computer-based intervention for bulimia nervosa and binge eating. In J. Latner & G. T. Wilson (Eds.), *Self-help approaches for obesity and eating disorders: Research and practice* (pp. 166–174). New York, NY: Guilford Press.

Schneider, E. C., Sarnak, D. O., Squires, D., Shah, A., & Doty, M. M. (2017). *Mirror, Mirror 2017: International comparison reflects flaws and opportunities for better U.S. health care.* New York: Commonwealth Fund. Retrieved from http://www.commonwealthfund.org/interactives/2017/july/mirror-mirror/

Schneider, R. H., Alexander, C. N., Staggers, F., Rainforth, M., Salerno, J. W., Hartz, A., Arndt, S., Barnes, V. A., & Nicich, S. (2005). Long-term effects of stress reduction on mortality in persons > or = 55 years of age with systemic hypertension. *American Journal of Cardiology, 95*, 1060–1064.

Schnittker, J. (2007). Working more and feeling better: Women's health, employment, and family life. *American Sociological Review, 72*, 221–238.

Schnoll, R. A., James, C., Malstrom, M., Rothman, R. L., Wang, H., Babb, J., … Goldberg, M. (2003). Longitudinal predictors of continued tobacco use among patients diagnosed with cancer. *Annals of Behavioral Medicine, 25*(3), 214–221.

Schoenborn, C. A., & Gindi, R. M. (2015). *Electronic cigarette use among adults: United States, 2014* (NCHS Data Brief No. 217). Hyattsville, MD: National Center for Health Statistics.

Scholz, U., Keller, R., & Perren, S. (2009). Predicting behavioral intentions and physical exercise: A test of the health action process approach at the intrapersonal level. *Health Psychology, 28*, 702–708.

Schpero, W. L., Morden, N. E., Sequest, T. D., Rosenthal, M. B., Gottlieb, D. J., & Colla, C. H. (2017). For selected services, Blacks and Hispanics more likely to receive low-value care than Whites. *Health Affairs, 36*(6), 1065–1069.

Schreier, H. M. C., & Chen, E. (2010). Longitudinal relationships between family routines and biological profiles among youth with asthma. *Health Psychology, 29*, 82–90.

Schroecksnadel, K., Sarcletti, M., Winkler, C., Mumelter, B., Weiss, G., Fuchs, D., … Zengerle, R. (2008). Quality of life and immune activation in patients with HIV-infection. *Brain, Behavior, and Immunity, 22*(6), 881–889.

Schroevers, M. J., Kraaij, V., & Garnefski, N. (2011). Cancer patients' experience of positive and negative changes due to the illness: Relationships with psychological well-being, coping, and goal reengagement. *Psycho-Oncology, 20*, 165–172.

Schulman, K. A., Berlin, J., Harless, W., Kerner, J. F., Sistrunk, S. H., Gersh, B. J., … Escarce, J. J. (1999). The effect of race and sex on physicians' recommendations for cardiac catheterization. *New England Journal of Medicine, 340*(8), 618–625.

Schuz, B., Wurm, S., Ziegelmann, J. P., Wolff, J. K., Warner, L. M., Schwarzer, R., & Tesch-Romer, C. (2012). Contextual and individual predictors of physical activity: Interactions between environmental factors and health cognitions. *Health Psychology, 31*(6), 714–723.

Schwarzer, R. (2008). Modeling health behavior change: How to predict and modify the adoption and maintenance of health behaviors. *Applied Psychology: International Review, 57*(1), 1–29.

Schwarzer, R. (2016). Health Action Process Approach (HAPA) as a theoretical framework to understand behavior change. *Actualidades en Psicologia, 30*(121), 119–130. Retrieved from http://www.scielo.sa.cr/pdf/ap/v30n121/2215-3535-ap-30-121-00119.pdf

Schwarzer, R., & Luszczynska, A. (2015). Health action process approach. In M. Conner & P. Norman (Eds.), *Predicting and changing health behaviour* (3rd ed., pp. 252–278). New York, NY: McGraw-Hill Open University Press.

Schwebel, D. C., Roth, D. L., Elliott, M. N., Chien, S. A. T., Mrug, S., Shipp, E., Dittus, P., Zlomke, K., & Schuster, M. A. (2012). Marital conflict and fifth-graders' risk for injury. *Accident Analysis and Prevention, 47*, 30–35.

Schwebel, D. C., Roth, D. L., Elliott, M. N., Windle, M., Grunbaum, J. A., Low, B., Cooper, S. P., & Schuster, M. A. (2011). The association of activity level, parent mental distress, and parental involvement and monitoring with unintentional injury risk in fifth graders. *Accident Analysis and Prevention, 43*, 848–852.

Scott-Sheldon, L. A. J., Kalichman, S. C., Carey, M. P., & Fielder, R. L. (2008). Stress management interventions for HIV positive adults: A meta-analysis of randomized controlled trials, 1989 to 2006. *Health Psychology, 27*, 129–139.

Searle, A., & Bennett, P. (2001). Psychological factors and inflammatory bowel disease: A review of a decade of literature. *Psychology, Health, and Medicine, 6*, 121–135.

Sears, S. F., Urizar, G. G., & Evans, G. D. (2000). Examining a stress-coping model of burnout and depression in extension agents. *Journal of Occupational Health Psychology, 5*, 56–62.

Seeman, T. E., Gruenewald, T., Sidney, S., Liu, K., Schwartz, J., McEwen, B., & Karlamangla, A. S. (2009). Modeling multi-system biological risk in young adults: Coronary Artery Risk Development in Young Adults Study (CARDIA). *American Journal of Human Biology*. December 28, 2009 [Epub ahead of print]. PMID: 20039257.

Segerstrom, S. C. (2006). Optimism and resources: Effects on each other and on health over 10 years. *Journal of Research in Personality, 41*, 772–786.

Segerstrom, S. C. (2007). Stress, energy, and immunity: An ecological view. *Current Directions in Psychological Science, 16*, 326–330.

Segerstrom, S. C., & Miller, G. E. (2004). Psychological stress and the immune system: A meta-analytic study of 30 years of inquiry. *Psychological Bulletin, 130*(4), 601–630.

Segerstrom, S. C., & Sephton, S. E. (2010). Optimistic expectancies and cell-mediated immunity: The role of positive affect. *Psychological Science, 21*, 448–455.

Segerstrom, S. C., Taylor, S. E., Kemeny, M. E., & Fahey, J. (1998). Optimism is associated with mood, coping, and immune change in response to stress. *Journal of Personality and Social Psychology, 74*(6), 1646–1655.

Seidman, E., Allen, L., Aber, J. L., Mitchell, C., Feinman, J., Yoshikawa, H., Comtois, K. A., Golz, J., Miller, R. L., Ortiz-Torres, B., & Roper, G. C. (1995). Development and validation of adolescent-perceived microsystem scales: Social support, daily hassles, and involvement. *American Journal of Community Psychology, 23*(3), 355–388.

Selby, E. A., Anestis, M. D., Bender, T. W., & Joiner, T. E. (2009). An exploration of the emotional cascade model in borderline personality disorder. *Journal of Abnormal Psychology, 118*(2), 375–387.

Selby, E. A., Franklin, J., Carson-Wong, A., & Rizvi, S. L. (2013). Emotional cascades and self-injury: Investigating instability of rumination and negative emotion. *Journal of Clinical Psychology, 69*(12), 1213–1227. doi:10.1002/jclp.21966

Self, C. A., & Rogers, R. W. (1990). Coping with threats to health: Effects of persuasive appeals on depressed, normal, and antisocial personalities. *Journal of Behavioral Medicine, 13*, 343–358.

Seligman, M. E. P. (2002). Positive psychology, positive prevention, and positive therapy. In C. R. Snyder & S. J. Lopez (Eds.), *Oxford handbook of positive psychology* (pp. 3–9). New York, NY: Oxford University Press.

Seligman, M. E. P., & Csikszentmihalyi, M. (2000). Positive psychology: An introduction. *American Psychologist, 55*, 5–14.

Seligman, M. E. P., Peterson, C., Barsky, A. J., Boehm, J. K., Kubzansky, L. D., Park, N., & Labarthe, D. (2016). *Positive health and health assets: Re-analysis of longitudinal data sets*. Robert Wood Johnson Foundation. Retrieved from http://positivehealthresearch.org/sites/positivehealthresearch.org/files/PH_Whitepaper_Layout_Web.pdf

Selye, H. (1974). *The stress of life*. New York, NY: McGraw-Hill.

Seminowicz, D. A., & Davis, K. D. (2006). A re-examination of pain-cognition interactions: Implications for neuroimaging. *Pain, 130*(1), 8–13.

Semmer, N. K. (2007, February 14). *Recognition and respect (or lack thereof) as predictors of occupational health and well-being*. Presentation at meeting of the World Health Organization, Geneva, Switzerland. Retrieved from http://www.who.int/occupational_health/topics/stressatwp/en/

Seo, Y. G., Chol, M. K., Kang, J. H., Lee, H. J., Jang, H. B., Park, S. I., … Park, K. H. (2018). Cardiovascular disease risk factor clustering in children and adolescents: A prospective cohort study. *Archives of Disease in Childhood, 103*(10), 968–973. doi:10.1136/archdischild-2017-313226

Seo, Y. G., Yates, B., LaFramboise, L., Pozehl, B., Norman, J. F., & Hertzog, M. (2016). A home-based diaphragmatic breathing retraining in rural patients with heart failure. *Western Journal of Nursing Research, 38*(3), 270–291. doi:10.1177/0193945915584201

Seppa, N. (2010). Not just a high. Scientists test medical marijuana against MS, inflammation and cancer. *Science News, 177*(13), 16–19.

Shadel, W. B., Martino, S. C., Setodji, C., & Scharf, D. (2012). Momentary effects of exposure to prosmoking media on college students' future smoking risk. *Health Psychology, 31*(4), 460–466.

Shadyab, A. H., Macera, C. A., Shaffer, R. A., Jain, S., Gallo, L. C., LaMonte, M. J., … & LaCroix, A. Z. (2017). Associations of accelerometer-measured and self-reported sedentary time with leukocyte telomere length in older women. *American Journal of Epidemiology, 185*(3), 172–184.

Shahab, L., West, R., & McNeill, A. (2011). A randomized, controlled trial of adding expired carbon monoxide feedback to brief stop smoking advice: Evaluation of cognitive and behavioral effects. *Health Psychology, 30*(1), 49–57.

Shankar, A., Hamer, M., McMunn, A., & Steptoe, A. (2013). Social isolation and loneliness: Relationships with cognitive function during 4 years of follow-up in the English Longitudinal Study of Ageing. *Psychosomatic Medicine, 75*(2), 161–170.

Shelby, R. A., Somers, T. J., Keefe, F. J., Silva, S. G., McKee, D. C., She, L., … Johnson, P. (2009). Pain catastrophizing in patients with noncardiac chest pain: Relationships with pain, anxiety, and disability. *Psychosomatic Medicine, 71*, 816–868.

Sheline, Y. I. (2000). 3D MRI studies of neuroanatomic changes in unipolar major depression: The role of stress and medical comorbidity. *Biological Psychiatry, 48*(8), 791–800.

Shen, B. J., Avivi, Y. E., Todaro, J. F., Spiro, A., Laurenceau, J. P., Ward, K. D., & Niaura, R. (2008). Anxiety characteristics independently and prospectively predict myocardial infarction in men: The unique contribution of anxiety among psychologic factors. *Journal of the American College of Cardiology, 51*, 113–119.

Shen, L., Yang, L., Zhang, J., & Zhang, M. (2018). Benefits of expressive writing in reducing test anxiety: A randomized controlled trial in Chinese samples. *PLOS ONE, 13*(2): e0191779. doi.org/10.1371/journal.pone.0191779

Shepperd, J. A., Rothman, A. J., & Klein, W. M. P. (2011). Using self- and identity-regulation to promote health: Promises and challenges. *Self and Identity, 10*, 407–416.

Shere-Wolfe, K. D., Tilburt, J. C., D'Adamo, C., Berman, B., & Chesney, M. A. (2013). Infectious diseases physicians' attitudes and practices related to complementary and integrative medicine: Results of a national survey. *Evidence-based Complementary and Alternative Medicine (eCAM), 2013*, 1–8.

Shiels, P. G., Stenvinkel, P., Kooman, J. P., & McGuinness, D. (2017). Circulating markers of ageing and allostatic load: A slow train coming. *Practical Laboratory Medicine, 7*, 49–54.

Shiffman, S., Stone, A. A., & Hufford, M. R. (2008). Ecological momentary assessment. *Annual Review of Clinical Psychology, 4*, 1–32.

Shirom, A., Toker, S., Berliner, S., & Shapira, I. (2008). The Job Demand-Control-Support model and micro-inflammatory responses among healthy male and female employees: A longitudina l study. *Work & Stress, 28*(2), 661–669.

Shirtcliff, E. A., Coe, C. L., & Pollak, S. D. (2009). Early childhood stress is associated with elevated antibody levels to herpes simplex virus type 1. *Proceedings of the National Academy of Sciences, 106*, 2963–2967.

Shlisky, J. D., Hartman, T. J., Kris-Etherton, P. M., Rogers, C. J., Sharkey, N. A., & Nickols-Richardson, S. M. (2012). Partial sleep deprivation and energy balance in adults: An emerging issue for consideration by dietetics practitioners. *Journal of the Academy of Nutrition and Dietetics, 112*(11), 1785–1797.

Shockey, T. M., & Wheaton, A. G. (2017, March 3). Short sleep duration by occupation group—29 states, 2013–2014. *Morbidity and Mortality Weekly Report, 66*(8), 207–213.

Shuger, S. L., Sui, X., Church, T. S., Meriwether, R. A., & Blair, S. N. (2008). Body mass index as a predictor of hypertension incidence among initially healthy normotensive women. *American Journal of Hypertension, 21*(6), 613–619.

Shungin, D., Winkler, T. W., Croteau-Chonka, D. C., Ferreira, T., Locke, A. E., Mägi, R., … Mohlke, K. L. (2015). New genetic loci link adipose and insulin biology to fat distribution. *Nature, 518*, 187–196.

Shwartz, M. (2007, March 7). Robert Sapolsky discusses physiological effects of stress. *Stanford News*. Retrieved from http://news.stanford.edu/news/2007/march7/sapolskysr-030707.html

Siddiqui, J., Herchline, T., Kahlon, S., Moyer, K. J., Scott, J. D., Wood, B. R., & Young, J. (2017). Infectious Diseases Society of America position statement on telehealth and telemedicine as applied to the practice of infectious diseases. *Clinical Infectious Diseases, 64*(3), 237–242.

Silagy, C., Lancaster, T., Stead, L., Mant, D., & Fowler, G. (2005). Nicotine replacement therapy for smoking cessation. *Cochrane Database of Systematic Reviews*. Retrieved from http://www2.cochrane.org/reviews/en/ab000146.html

Silber, M. H., Ancoli-Israel, S., Bonnet, M. H., Chokroverty, S., Grigg-Damberger, M. M., Hirshkowitz, M., … Iber, C. (2008). The visual scoring of sleep in adults. *Journal of Clinical Sleep Medicine, 3*, 121–131.

Silver, R. C., Holman, E. A., Andersen, J. P., Poulin, M., McIntosh, D. N., & Gil-Rivas, V. (2013). Mental- and physical-health effects of acute exposure to media images of the September 11, 2001, attacks and the Iraq war. *Psychological Science*. Retrieved from http://pss.sagepub.com/content/early/2013/08/01/0956797612460406.full.pdf+html

Simpson, P. A., Mars, T., & Esteves, J. E. (2017). A systematic review of randomised controlled trials using acceptance and commitment therapy as an intervention in the management of non-malignant, chronic pain in adults. *International Journal of Osteopathic Medicine, 24*, 18–31.

Sin, N. L., Moskowitz, J. T., & Whooley, M. A. (2015). Positive affect and health behaviors across five years in patients with coronary heart disease: The Heart and Soul Study. *Psychosomatic Medicine, 77*(9), 1058–1066.

Singh, A., Klapper, A., Jia, J., Fidalgo, A., Tajadura Jimenez, A., Kanakam, N., Bianchi-Berthouze, N., & Williams, N. (2014). Motivating people with chronic pain to do physical activity: Opportunities for technology design. *Proceedings of the SIGCHI Conference on Human Factors in Computing Systems*. Retrieved from https://www.researchgate.net/publication/261174870_Motivating_People_with_Chronic_Pain_to_do_Physical_Activity_Opportunities_for_Technology_Design

Singh, T., & Newman, A. B. (2011). Inflammatory markers in population studies of aging. *Aging Research Review, 10*, 319–329.

Sinnock, P., Murphy, P. E., Baker, T., & Bates, R. (1991). First 3 years of the national AIDS clearinghouse. *Public Health Reports (1974-), 106*(6), 634–639. Retrieved from http://www.jstor.org/stable/4597028

Siteman Cancer Center. (2015). *Your disease risk*. St. Louis, MO: Washington University School of Medicine. Retrieved from http://www.yourdiseaserisk.wustl.edu/YDRDefault.aspx?ScreenControl=YDRGeneral&ScreenName=YDRCancer_Index

Skipper, M. (2011). Epigenomics: Epigenetic variation across the generations. *Nature Reviews Genetics, 12*, 740.

Skolnik, R. (2016). *Global health 101* (3rd ed.). Burlington, MA: Jones & Bartlett.

Slatcher, R. B., & Robles, T. F. (2012). Preschoolers' everyday conflict at home and diurnal cortisol patterns. *Health Psychology, 31*(6), 834–838.

Slatcher, R. B., Selcuk, E., & Ong, A. D. (2015). Perceived partner responsiveness predicts diurnal cortisol profiles 10 years later. *Psychological Science, 26*(7), 972–982.

Sloan, R. P., Bagiella, E., & Powell, T. (1999). Religion, spirituality, and medicine. *The Lancet, 353*, 664–667.

Smedley, B. D., Stith, A. Y., & Nelson, A. R. (2002). *Unequal treatment: Confronting racial and ethnic disparities in health care*. Institute of Medicine. Washington, DC: National Academies Press.

Smith, J. C. (2005). *Relaxation, meditation, and mindfulness: A mental health practitioner's guide to new and traditional approaches*. New York, NY: Springer.

Smith, M. O. (2012, July 16). The use of acupuncture in addiction treatment programs. *The Huffington Post*. Retrieved from http://www.huffingtonpost.com/dr-michael-o-smith/addiction-acupuncture_b_1665796.html

Smith, T. W., Birmingham, W., & Uchino, B. N. (2012). Evaluative threat and ambulatory blood pressure: Cardiovascular effects of social stress in daily experience. *Health Psychology, 31*(6), 763–766.

Smith, W. A., Hung, M., & Franklin, J. D. (2011). Racial battle fatigue and the miseducation of black men: Racial microaggressions, societal problems, and environmental stress. *Journal of Negro Education, 80*(1), 63–82.

Snodgrass, S. E. (1998). Thriving: Broadening the paradigm beyond illness (personal experience with breast cancer). *Journal of Social Issues, 54*(2), 373–378.

Snowden, F. M. (2008). Emerging and reemerging diseases: A historical perspective. *Immunological Reviews, 225*, 9–26.

Solberg Nes, L., Roach, A. R., & Segerstrom, S. C. (2009). Executive functions, self-regulation, and chronic pain: A review. *Annals of Behavioral Medicine, 37*(2), 173–183.

Soldz, S., & Cui, X. (2002). Pathways through adolescent smoking: A 7-year longitudinal grouping analysis. *Health Psychology, 21*(5), 495–594.

Solomon, G. F., & Moos, R. H. (1964). Emotions, immunity, and disease: A speculative theoretical integration. *Archives of General Psychiatry, 11*, 657–674.

Sommestad, T., Karlzen, H., & Halberg, J. (2015). A meta-analysis of studies on Protection Motivation Theory and information security behaviour. *International Journal of Information Security and Privacy, 9*(1), 26–46.

Song, L., Hamilton, J. B., & Moore, A. D. (2012). Patient-healthcare provider communication: Perspectives of African American cancer patients. *Health Psychology, 31*(5), 539–547.

Southwick, S. M., & Charney, D. S. (2018). *Resilience: The science of mastering life's greatest challenges* (2nd ed). Cambridge, England: Cambridge University Press.

Spalding, K. L. (2008). Dynamics of fat cell turnover in humans. *Nature, 453*, 783–787.

Spasojevic, J., & Alloy, L. B. (2001). Rumination as a common mechanism relating depressive risk factors to depression. *Emotion, 1*, 25–37.

Speca, M., Carlson, L. E., Goodey, E., & Angen, M. (2000). A randomized, wait-list controlled trial: The effect of a mindfulness meditation-based stress reduction program on mood and symptoms of stress in cancer outpatients. *Psychosomatic Medicine, 62*(5), 613–622.

Spiegel, D. (1996). Psychological stress and disease course for women with breast cancer: One answer, many questions. *Journal of the National Cancer Institute, 88*(1), 629–631.

Sprenger, C., Eippert, F., Finsterbusch, J., Bingel, U., Rose, M., & Buchel, C. (2012). Attention modulates spinal cord responses to pain. *Current Biology, 22*(11), 1019–1022.

Stacy, A. W., Bentler, P. M., & Flay, B. R. (1994). Attitudes and health behavior in diverse populations: Drunk driving, alcohol use, binge eating, marijuana use, and cigarette use. *Health Psychology, 13*, 73–85.

Stamatakis, E., Hamer, M., & Dunstan, D. W. (2011). Screen-based entertainment time, all-cause mortality, and cardiovascular events: Population-based study with ongoing mortality and hospital events follow-up. *Journal of the American College of Cardiology, 57*(3), 292–299.

Stanford Center for Narcolepsy. (2015). *About narcolepsy.* Retrieved from http://med.stanford.edu/narcolepsy/symptoms.html

Stangl, A. (2017). *HIV-related stigma and discrimination.* International Centre for Research on Women [ICRW]. Retrieved from https://www.icrw.org/publications/impact-case-study-stigma-framework-measurement-strive/

Stangl, A. L., Lloyd, J. K., Brady, L. M., Holland, C. E., & Baral, S. (2013). A systematic review of interventions to reduce HIV-related stigma and discrimination from 2002 to 2013: How far have we come? *Journal of the International AIDS Society, 16*(3Suppl 2), 18734. http://doi.org/10.7448/IAS.16.3.18734

Stanovich, K. E., & West, R. F. (1998). Individual differences in rational thought. *Journal of Experimental Psychology: General, 127*(2), 161–188.

Stanton, A. L. (2010). Regulating emotions during stressful experiences: The adaptive utility of coping through emotional approach. In S. Folkman (Ed.), *Oxford handbook of stress, health and coping* (pp. 369–386). New York, NY: Oxford University Press.

Stanton, A. L., Danoff-Burg, S., Cameron, C. L., Bishop, M., Collins, C. A., Kirk, S. B., ... Twillman, R. (2000). Emotionally expressive coping predicts psychological and physical adjustment to breast cancer. *Journal of Consulting and Clinical Psychology, 68*(5), 875–882.

Stanton, A. L., & Revenson, T. A. (2011). Adjustment to chronic disease: Progress and promise in research. In H. S. Friedman (Ed.), *The Oxford handbook of health psychology* (pp. 241–268). New York, NY: Oxford University Press.

Stanton, A. L., Thompson, E. H., Crespi, C. M., Link, J. S., & Waisman, J. R. (2013). Project Connect Online: Randomized trial of an Internet-based program to chronicle the cancer experience and facilitate communication. *American Society of Clinical Oncology, 33*(25), 2763–2771.

Starr, J. M., Shields, P. G., Harris, S. E., Pattie, A., Pearce, M. S., Relton, C. L., & Deary, I. J. (2008). Oxidative stress, telomere length and biomarkers of physical aging in a cohort aged 79 years from the 1932 Scottish Mental Survey. *Mechanisms of Ageing and Development, 129*(12), 745–751.

Stead, L. F., Perera, R., Bullen, C., Mant, D., & Lancaster, T. (2008). Nicotine replacement therapy for smoking cessation. *Cochrane Database of Systematic Reviews*, Cochrane AN: CD000146.

Stefan, N., Haring, H. U., & Schulze, M. B. (2013). Metabolically healthy obesity: Epidemiology, mechanisms, and clinical implications. *The Lancet Diabetes and Endocrinology, 1*(2), 152–162.

Steiner, B. (2014, April 1). Treating chronic pain with meditation. *The Atlantic.* Retrieved from http://www.theatlantic.com/health/archive/2014/04/treating-chronic-pain-with-meditation/284182/

Stephens, M. B. (2009). Cardiac rehabilitation. *American Family Physician, 80*(9), 955–959.

Steptoe, A., Hamer, M., & Chida, Y. (2007). The effects of acute psychological stress on circulating inflammatory factors in humans: A review and meta-analysis. *Brain, Behavior, and Immunity, 21*, 901–912.

Steptoe, A., O'Donnell, K., & Badrick, E. (2008). Neuroendocrine and inflammatory markers associated with positive affect in healthy men and women: The Whitehall II study. *American Journal of Epidemiology, 167*(1), 96–102.

Steptoe, A., Perkins-Porras, L., McKay, C., Rink, E., Hilton, S., & Cappuccio, F. P. (2003). Psychological factors associated with fruit and vegetable intake and with biomarkers in adults from a low-income neighborhood. *Health Psychology, 22*(2), 148–155.

Steptoe, A., Siegrist, J., Kirschbaum, C., & Marmot, M. (2004). Effort-reward imbalance, overcommitment, and measures of cortisol and blood pressure over the working day. *Psychosomatic Medicine, 66*, 323–329.

Steptoe, A. D., & Ayers, S. (2004). Stress, health and illness. In S. Sutton, A. Baum, & M. Johnston (Eds.), *The Sage handbook of health psychology* (pp. 169–196). Thousand Oaks, CA: Sage Publications.

Steptoe, A. D., de Oliveira, C., Demakakos, P., & Zaninotto, P. (2014). Enjoyment of life and declining physical function at older ages:

A longitudinal cohort study. *Canadian Medical Association. Journal, 186*(4), E150-6.

Sternberg, E. M. (2001). *The balance within: The science connecting health and emotions.* New York, NY: W. H. Freeman.

Stevens, V. L., Jacobs, E. J., Sun, J., Patel, A. V., McCullough, M. L., Teras, L. R., & Gapstur, S. M. (2012). Weight cycling and mortality in a large prospective US study. *American Journal of Epidemiology, 175*(8), 785–792.

Stevens-Watkins, D., Sharma, S., Knighton, J., Oser, C., & Leukefeld, C. (2014). Examining cultural correlates of active coping among African American female trauma survivors. *Psychological Trauma: Theory, Research, Practice, & Policy, 6*(4), 328–336.

Stewart, D. E., Abbey, S. E., Shnek, Z. M., Irvine, J., & Grace, S. L. (2004). Gender differences in health information needs and decisional preferences in patients recovering from an acute ischemic coronary event. *Psychosomatic Medicine, 66,* 42–48.

Stewart, L. K., Flynn, M. G., Campbell, W. W., Craig, B. A., Robinson, J. P., & Timmerman, K. L. (2007). The influence of exercise training on inflammatory cytokines and C-reactive protein. *Medicine and Science in Sports and Exercise, 39,* 1714–1719.

Stice, E., Rohde, P., & Shaw, H. (2013). *The Body Project: A dissonance-based eating disorder prevention intervention.* New York, NY: Oxford University Press.

Stice, E., Rohde, P., Durant, S., Shaw, H., & Wade, E. (2013). Effectiveness of peer-led dissonance-based eating disorder prevention groups: Results from two randomized pilot trials. *Behaviour Research and Therapy, 51*(4–5), 197–206.

Stice, E., Shaw, H., & Marti, C. N. (2007). A meta-analytic review of eating disorder prevention programs: Encouraging findings. *Annual Review of Clinical Psychology, 3,* 207–231.

Stickgold, R. (2009). The simplest way to reboot your brain. *Harvard Business Review, 87*(10), 36.

Stilley, C. S., Bender, C. M., Dunbar-Jacob, J., Sereika, S., & Ryan, C. M. (2010). The impact of cognitive function on medication management: Three studies. *Health Psychology, 21,* 131–138.

Stock, M. L., Gibbons, F. X., Gerrard, M., Houlihan, A. E., Weng, C.-Y., Lorenz, F. O., & Simons, R. L. (2013a). Racial identification, racial composition, and substance use vulnerability among African American adolescents and young adults. *Health Psychology, 32*(3), 237–247.

Stock, M. L., Gibbons, F. X., Peterson, L. M., & Gerrard, M. (2013b). The effects of racial discrimination on the HIV-risk cognitions and behaviors of black adolescents and young adults. *Health Psychology, 32*(5), 543–550.

Stolarczyk, E., Vong, C. T., Perucha, E., Jackson, I., Cawthorne, M. A., Wargent, E. T., ... Howard, J. K. (2013). Improved insulin sensitivity despite increased visceral adiposity in mice deficient for the immune cell transcription factor T-bet. *Cell Metabolism, 17*(4), 520–533.

St-Onge, M. P., Roberts, A. L., Chen, J., Kellerman, M., O'Keefe, M., RoyChoudhury, A., & Jones, P. J. (2011). Short sleep duration increases energy intakes but does not change energy expenditure in normal-weight individuals. *American Journal of Clinical Nutrition, 94*(2), 410–416.

Stone, A. A., Mezzacappa, E. S., Donatone, B. A., & Gonder, M. (1999). Psychosocial stress and social support are associated with prostate-specific antigen levels in men: Results from a community screening program. *Health Psychology, 18*(5), 485.

Stone, R. (2005). In the wake: Looking for keys to posttraumatic stress. *Science, 310,* 1605.

Storey, D. J., McLaren, D. B., Atkinson, M. A., Butcher, I., Liggatt, S., O'Dea, R., & Sharpe, M. (2011). Clinically relevant fatigue in recurrence-free prostate cancer survivors. *Annals of Oncology, 23,* 65–72.

Stowe, R. P., Peek, M. K., Perez, N. A., Yetman, D. L., Cutchin, M. P., & Goodwin, J. S. (2010). Herpes virus reactivation and socioeconomic position: A community-based study. *Journal of Epidemiology and Community Health, 64*(8), 666–671.

Strasburger, V. C., Jordan, A. B., & Donnerstein, E. (2009). Health effects of media on children and adolescents. *Pediatrics, 125*(4), 756–767.

Straub, R. H., & Kalden, J. R. (2009). Stress of different types increases the proinflammatory load in rheumatoid arthritis. *Arthritis Research and Therapy, 11*(3), 114–115.

Strawbridge, W. J., Wallhagen, M. I., & Shema, S. J. (2000). New NHLBI clinical guidelines for obesity and overweight: Will they promote health? *American Journal of Public Health, 90,* 340–343.

Strecher, V. J., & Rosenstock, I. M. (1997). The health belief model. In A. Baum, S. Newman, J. Weinman, R. West, & C. McManus (Eds.), *Cambridge handbook of psychology, health, and medicine* (pp. 113–117). Cambridge, England: Cambridge University Press.

Street, R. L, Jr., Gordon, H., & Haidet, P. (2007). Physicians' communication and perceptions of patients: Is it how they look, how they talk, or is it just the doctor? *Social Science & Medicine, 65,* 586–598.

Street, R. L., Jr., & Haidet, P. (2011). How well do doctors know their patients? Factors affecting physician understanding of patients' health beliefs. *Journal of General Internal Medicine, 26,* 21–27.

Strigo, I. A., Simmons, A. N., Matthews, S. C., Craig, A. D., & Paulhus, M. P. (2008). Association of major depressive disorder with altered functional brain response during anticipation and processing of heat pain. *Archives of General Psychiatry, 65*(11), 1275–1284.

Strully, K. W. (2009). Job loss and health in the U.S. labor market. *Demography, 46*(2), 221–246.

Subedi, B., & Grossberg, G. T. (2011). Phantom limb pain: Mechanisms and treatment approaches. *Pain Research and Treatment, 2011,* 864605. doi.org/10.1155/2011/864605

Sue, D. W. (2011). Microaggressions, marginality, and oppression: An introduction. In D. Sue (Ed.), *Microaggressions and marginality: Manifestation, dynamics, and impact* (pp. 3–22). Hoboken, NJ: Wiley.

Sue, D. W., Capodilupo, C. M., Torino, G. C., Bucceri, J. M., Holder, A. M. B., Nadal, K. L., & Esquilin, M. (2007). Racial microaggressions in everyday life: Implications for clinical practice. *American Psychologist, 62*(4), 271–286.

Suhr, J., Demireva, P., & Heffner, K. (2008). The reaction of salivary cortisol to patterns of performance on a word list learning task in healthy older adults. *Psychoneuroimmunology, 33*(9), 1293–1296.

Sullivan, M., Paice, J. A., & Beneditti, F. (2004). Placebos and treatment of pain. *Pain Medicine, 5*(3), 325–328.

Surtees, P. G., Wainwright, N. W., Luben, R., Khaw, K. T., & Day, N. E. (2006). Mastery, sense of coherence, and mortality: Evidence of independent associations from the EPIC-Norfolk Prospective Cohort Study. *Health Psychology, 25*(1), 102–110.

Sussan, T. E., Shahzad, F. G., Tabassum, E., Cohen, J. E., Wise, R. A., Blaha, M. J., ... Biswal, S. (2017). Electronic cigarette use behaviors and motivations among smokers and non-smokers. *BMC Public Health, 17*(686). doi.org/10.1186/s12889-017-4671-3

Sussman, S., Sun, P., & Dent, C. W. (2006). A meta-analysis of teen cigarette smoking cessation. *Health Psychology, 25*, 549–557.

Sutton, S. R. (1997). The theory of planned behavior. In A. Baum, S. Newman, J. Weinman, R. West, & C. McManus (Eds.), *Cambridge handbook of psychology, health, and medicine.* Cambridge, England: Cambridge University Press.

Suurland, J., van der Heijden, K. B., Smaling, H. J., Huijbregts, S. C., van Goozen, S. H., & Swaab, H. (2016). Infant autonomic nervous system response and recovery: Associations with maternal risk status and infant emotion regulation. *Developmental Psychopathology, 29,* 1–15.

Swan, G. E., & Carmelli, D. (1996). Curiosity and mortality in aging adults: A 5-year follow-up of the Western Collaborative Group Study. *Psychology and Aging, 11*, 449–453.

Swanson, S. A., Crow, S. J., Le Grange, D., Swendsen, J., & Merikangas, K. R. (2011). Prevalence and correlates of eating disorders in adolescents. Results from the national comorbidity survey replication adolescent supplement. *Archives of General Psychiatry, 68*(7), 714–723.

Szapary, P. O., Bloedon, L. T., & Foster, B. D. (2003). Physical activity and its effects on lipids. *Current Cardiology Reports, 5*, 488–492.

Szeto, A. C. H., & Dobson, K. S. (2013). Mental disorders and their association with perceived work stress: An investigation of the 2010 Canadian Community Health Survey. *Journal of Occupational Health Psychology, 18*(2), 191–197.

Taber, D. R., Chriqui, J. F., & Chaloupka, F. J. (2012). Differences in nutrient intake associated with state laws regarding fat, sugar, and caloric content of competitive foods. *Pediatrics, 166*(5), 452–458.

Taheri, S., Lin, L., Austin, D., Young, T., & Mignot, E. (2004). Short sleep duration is associated with reduced leptin, elevated ghrelin, and increased body mass index. *PLOS Medicine,* Retrieved from http://www.plosmedicine.org/article/info%3Adoi%2F10.1371%2Fjournal.pmed.0010062

Tam, J., Cinar, R., Liu, J., Godlewski, G., Wesley, D, Jordan, T., … Kunos, G. (2012). Peripheral cannabinoid-1 receptor inverse agonism reduces obesity by reversing leptin resistance. *Cell Metabolism, 16*(2), 167–179.

Tang, W. W., Wang, Z., Levison, B. S., Koeth, R. A., Britt, E. B., Fu, X., … Hazen, S. L. (2013). Intestinal microbial metabolism of phosphatidylcholine and cardiovascular risk. *New England Journal of Medicine, 368,* 1575–1584.

Tang, Y.-Y., Lu, Q., Fan, M., Yang, Y., & Posner, M. I. (2012). Mechanisms of white matter changes induced by meditation. *Proceedings of the National Academy of Sciences*, Early Edition. Retrieved from http://www.pnas.org/content/early/2012/06/05/1207817109.abstract?sid=0229e3f4-0b13-4a40-bbfe-67990e8c8468

Tapper, K., Shaw, C., Illsey, J., Hill, A. J., Bond, F. W., & Moore, L. (2009). Exploratory randomized controlled trial of a mindfulness weight loss intervention for women. *Appetite, 52*(2), 396–404.

Tarpey, M. D. (2017). Skeletal muscle autophagy and mitophagy in endurance-trained runners before and after a high-fat meal. *Molecular Metabolism, 6*(12), 1597–1609.

Tarter, R. E., Vanyukov, M., Kirisci, L., Reynolds, M., & Clark, D. B. (2006). Predictors of marijuana use in adolescents before and after illicit drug use: Examination of the gateway hypothesis. *American Journal of Psychiatry, 163*(12), 2134–2140.

Tashani, O., & Johnson, M. I. (2009). Transcutaneous electrical nerve stimulation (TENS): A possible aid for pain relief in developing countries? *Libyan Journal of Medicine, 4*(2), 62–65.

Taubes, G. (2016). *The case against sugar.* New York, NY: Alfred A. Knopf.

Taylor, P. J., Gooding, P., Wood, A. M., & Tarrier, N. (2011). The role of defeat and entrapment in depression, anxiety, and suicide. *Psychological Bulletin, 137*, 391–420.

Taylor, S. E. (2011). Social support: A review. In H. S. Friedman (Ed.), *Oxford handbook of health psychology* (pp. 189–214). New York, NY: Oxford University Press.

Taylor, S. E., & Broffman, J. I. (2011). Psychosocial resources: Functions, origins, and links to mental and physical health. In J. M. Olson & M. P. Zanna (Eds.), *Advances in experimental social psychology* (pp. 1–57). New York, NY: Academic Press.

Taylor, S. E., Cousino, L., Lewis, B. P., Grunewald, T. L., Gurung, R. A., & Updegraff, J. A. (2000). Biobehavioral responses to stress in females: Tend-and-befriend, not fight-or-flight. *Psychological Review, 107*(3), 411–429.

Taylor, S. E., Gonzaga, G., Klein, L. C., Hu, P., Greendale, G. A., & Seeman, S. E. (2006). Relation of oxytocin to psychological stress responses and hypothalamic-pituitary-adrenocortical axis activity in older women. *Psychosomatic Medicine, 68*, 238–245.

Taylor, S. E., Lerner, J. S., Sherman, D. K., Sage, R. M., & McDowell, N. K. (2003). Are self-enhancing cognitions associated with healthy or unhealthy biological profiles? *Journal of Personality and Social Psychology, 85*(4), 605–615.

Taylor, S. E., Seeman, T. E., Eisenberger, N. I., Kozanian, T. A., Moore, A. N., & Moons, W. G. (2010). Effects of a supportive or unsupportive audience on biological and psychological responses to stress. *Journal of Personality and Social Psychology, 98*, 47–56.

Taylor, S. E., & Stanton, A. L. (2007). Coping resources, coping processes, and mental health. *Annual Review of Clinical Psychology, 3,* 377–401.

Teasdale, J. D., Segal, Z. V., Williams, J. M. G., Ridgeway, V. A., Soulsby, J. M., & Lau, M. A. (2000). Prevention of relapse/recurrence in major depression by mindfulness-based cognitive therapy. *Journal of Consulting and Clinical Psychology, 68*(4), 615–623.

Teh, C. F., Zasylavsky, A. M., Reynolds, C. F., & Cleary, P. D. (2010). Effect of depression treatment on chronic pain outcomes. *Psychosomatic Medicine, 72*, 61–67.

Templeton, S. (2004, January 11). Up in smoke: Our hopes for health. Finland beat heart disease by changing the nation's diet. *The Sunday Herald*. Retrieved from http://business.highbeam.com/61222/article-1P2-10000665/up-in-smoke-our-hopes-health-obesity-finland-beat-heart

Teng, Y., & Mak, W. W. S. (2011). The role of planning and self-efficacy in condom use among men who have sex with men: An application of the Health Action Process Approach Model. *Health Psychology, 30*(1), 119–128.

Thayer, J. F., & Lane, R. D. (2007). The role of vagal function in the risk for cardiovascular disease and mortality. *Biological Psychology,74*, 224–242.

Thielke, S., Thompson, A., & Stuart, R. (2011). Health psychology in primary care: Recent research and future directions. *Journal of Psychology Research and Behavior Management, 4*, 59–68.

Thom, D. H., Hall, M. A., & Pawlson, L. G. (2004). Measuring patients' trust in physicians when assessing quality of care. *Health Affairs, 23*(4), 124–132.

Thompson, L. A., Knapp, C. A., Feeg, V., Madden, V. L., & Shenkman, E. A. (2010). Pediatricians' management practices for chronic pain. *Journal of Palliative Medicine, 13*(2), 171–178.

Thompson, R. (2000). *The brain: A neuroscience primer* (3rd ed.). New York, NY: Worth.

Thompson, R. C., Allam, A. H., Zink, A., Wann, L. S., Lombardi, G. P., Cox, S. L., … Thomas, G. S. (2014). Computed tomographic evidence of atherosclerosis in the mummified remains of humans from around the world. *Global Heart, 9*(2), 187–196.

Thornton, L. M., Andersen, B. L., & Blakely, W. P. (2010). The pain, depression, and fatigue symptom cluster in advanced breast cancer: Covariation with the hypothalamic-pituitary-adrenal axis and the sympathetic nervous system. *Health Psychology, 29*(3), 333–337.

Thornton, L. M., Mazzeo, S. E., & Bulik, C. M. (2011). The heritability of eating disorders: Methods and current findings. *Current Topics in Behavioral Neurosciences, 6*, 141–156. doi.org/10.1007/7854_2010_91

Thorp, A. A., Healy, G. N., Owen, N., Salmon, J., Ball, K., Shaw, J. E., … Dunstan, D. W. (2010). Deleterious associations of sitting time and television viewing time with cardiometabolic risk biomarkers: Australian diabetes, obesity, and lifestyle (AusDiab) study 2004–2005. *Diabetes Care, 33*(2), 327–334.

Thorsteinsen, K., Vittersø, J., & Svendsen, G. B. (2014). Increasing physical activity efficiently: An experimental pilot study of a website and mobile phone intervention. *International Journal of Telemedicine and Applications.* Retrieved from http://www.hindawi.com/journals/ijta/2014/746232/

Tilburt, J. C., Emanuel, E. J., Kaptchuk, T. J., Curlin, F. A., & Miller, F. G. (2008). Prescribing "placebo treatments": Results of a national survey of internists and rheumatologists. *BMJ, 337.* Retrieved from https://www.bmj.com/content/337/bmj.a1938.long

Tod, D., Edwards, C., & Cranswick, I. (2016). Muscle dysmorphia: Current insights. *Psychology Research and Behavior Management, 9*, 179–188.

Tolmunen, T., Lehto, S. M., Heliste, M., Kurl, S., & Kauhanen, J. (2010). Alexithymia is associated with increased cardiovascular mortality in middle-aged Finnish men. *Psychosomatic Medicine, 72*, 187–191.

Tomfohr, L. M., Pung, M. A., Mills, P. J., & Edwards, K. (2015). Trait mindfulness is associated with blood pressure and interleukin-6: Exploring interactions among subscales of the Five Facet Mindfulness Questionnaire to better understand relationships between mindfulness and health. *Journal of Behavioral Medicine, 38*(1), 28–38.

Tomich, P. L., & Helgeson, V. S. (2004). Is finding something good in the bad always good? Benefit finding among women with breast cancer. *Health Psychology, 23*, 16–23.

Toossi, M., & Morisi, T. L. (2017). *Women in the workforce before, during, and after the great recession. Spotlight on Statistics.* U.S. Bureau of Labor Statistics. Retrieved from https://www.bls.gov/spotlight/2017/women-in-the-workforce-before-during-and-after-the-great-recession/pdf/women-in-the-workforce-before-during-and-after-the-great-recession.pdf

Toprak Celenay, S., Anaforoglu Kulunkoglu, B., Yasa, M. E., Sahbaz Pirincci, C., Un Yildirim, N., Kucuksahin, O., … Akkus, S. (2017). A comparison of the effects of exercises plus connective tissue massage to exercises alone in women with fibromyalgia syndrome: A randomized controlled trial. *Rheumatology International, 37*(11), 1799–1806.

Torbeyns, T., Bailey, S., Bos, I., & Meeusen, R. (2014). Active workstations to fight sedentary behaviour. *Sports Medicine, 44*(9), 1261–1273.

Tosoian, J. J., Trock, B. J., Landis, P., Feng, Z., Epstein, J. I., Partin, A. W., & Carter, H. B. (2011). Active surveillance program for prostate cancer: An update of the Johns Hopkins experience. *Journal of Clinical Oncology, 29*, 2185–2190.

Tran, V. H. (2010). *Benefit finding, negative affect, and daily diabetes management among adolescents with Type 1 diabetes* (Doctoral dissertation). Retrieved from https://repositories.tdl.org/utswmed-ir/bitstream/handle/2152.5/819/tranvincent.pdf?sequence=3

Tran, V. H., Wiebe, D. J., Fortenberry, K. T., Butler, J. M., & Berg, C. A. (2011). Benefit finding, affective reactions to diabetes stress, and diabetes management among early adolescents. *Health Psychology, 30*(2), 212–219.

Trief, P. M., Ploutz-Snyder, R., Britton, K. D., & Weinstock, R. S. (2004). The relationship between marital quality and adherence to the diabetes care regimen. *Annals of Behavioral Medicine, 27*(3), 148–154.

Trivedi, A. N., & Ayanian, J. Z. (2006). Perceived discrimination and use of preventive health services. *Journal of General Internal Medicine, 21*(6), 553–558.

Tronick, E., Als, H., Adamson, L., Wise, S., & Brazelton, T. B. (1978). The infant's response to entrapment between contradictory messages in face-to-face interaction. *Journal of the American Academy of Child and Adolescent Psychiatry, 17*(1), 1–13.

Tsuboi, K. (2013, March 21). New telemedicine tech maintains patient privacy. *CNet.* Retrieved from http://news.cnet.com/8301-11386_3-57575658-76/new-telemedicine-tech-maintains-patient-privacy

Tucker, J. S., Orlando, M., Burnam, M. A., Sherbourne, C. D., Kung, F.-Y., & Gifford, A. (2004). Psychosocial mediators of antiretroviral nonadherence in HIV-positive adults with substance use and mental health problems. *Health Psychology, 23*(4), 363–370.

Turk, D. C., & Okifuji, A. (2002). Chronic pain. In A. J. Christensen & M. H. Antoni (Eds), *Chronic physical disorders: Behavioral medicine's perspective* (pp. 165–190). Malden, MA: Blackwell.

Turk, D. C., Swanson, K. S., & Tunks, E. R. (2008). Psychological approaches in the treatment of chronic pain patients—when pills, scalpels, and needles are not enough. *Canadian Journal of Psychiatry, 53*(4), 213–223.

Turner, R. J., & Avison, W. R. (2003). Status variations in stress exposure: Implications for the interpretation of research on race, socioeconomic status, and gender. *Journal of Health and Social Behavior, 44*, 488–505.

Turner-Cobb, J. M., Sephton, S. E., Koopman, C., Blake-Mortimer, J., & Spiegel, D. (2000). Social support and salivary cortisol in women with metastatic breast cancer. *Psychosomatic Medicine, 62*, 337–345.

U.S. Bureau of Labor Statistics. (2017). *Number of jobs, labor market experience, and earnings growth among Americans at 50: Results from a longitudinal study.* (Press release). Retrieved from https://www.bls.gov/news.release/pdf/nlsoy.pdf

U.S. Census Bureau (USCB). (2004). *Statistical abstract of the United States: 2004–2005* (124th ed.). Washington, DC: U.S. Department of Commerce.

U.S. Census Bureau (USCB). (2012). *Statistical abstract of the United States: 2011* (130th ed.). Washington, DC: U.S. Department of Commerce.

U.S. Census Bureau (USCB). (2015). Median age at first marriage: 1890 to present. *Decennial censuses, 1890 to 1940, and current population. Survey, annual social and economic supplements, 1947 to 2015.* Retrieved from https://www.census.gov/hhes/families/files/graphics/MS-2.pdf

U.S. Census Bureau (USCB). (2018). *Statistical abstract of the United States: 2018.* Washington, DC: U.S. Department of Commerce.

U.S. Department of Health and Human Services (USDHHS). (2001). *NIH policy and guidelines on the inclusion of women and minorities as subjects in clinical research (amended).* Retrieved from http://grants.nih.gov/grants/funding/women_min/guidelines_amended_10_2001.htm

U.S. Department of Health and Human Services (USDHHS). (2010). *How tobacco smoke causes disease: The biology and behavioral basis for smoking-attributable disease: A report of the surgeon general.* Atlanta, GA: U.S. Department of Health and Human Services, Centers for Disease Control and Prevention, National Center for Chronic Disease Prevention and Health Promotion, Office on Smoking and Health.

U.S. Department of Health and Human Services (USDHHS). (2012). *Preventing tobacco use among youth and young adults. A Report of the Surgeon General.* Atlanta, GA: U.S. Department of Health and Human Services, Centers for Disease Control and Prevention, National Center for Chronic Disease Prevention and Health Promotion, Office on Smoking and Health.

U.S. Department of Health and Human Services (USDHHS). (2015). *Body mass index (BMI) and weight.* Atlanta, GA: Centers for Disease Control and Prevention.

U.S. Department of Health and Human Services (USDHHS). (2017). *At a glance 2016: National Center for Chronic Disease Prevention and Health Promotion.* Atlanta, GA: Centers for Disease Control and Prevention. Retrieved from https://www.cdc.gov/chronicdisease/resources/publications/aag/pdf/2016/nccdphp-aag.pdf

U.S. Department of Health and Human Services and U.S. Department of Agriculture. (2015). *2015–2020 Dietary guidelines for Americans* (8th ed.). Retrieved from http://health.gov/dietaryguidelines/2015/guidelines/

U.S. Department of Labor. (2015). *What is workplace violence? OSHA fact sheet.* Retrieved from https://www.osha.gov/OshDoc/data_General_Facts/factsheet-workplace-violence.pdf

Uchino, B. N., Cawthon, F. M., Smith, T. W., Light, K. C., McKenzie, J., Carlisle, M., … Bowen, K. (2012). Social relationships and health: Is feeling positive, negative, or both (ambivalent) about your social ties related to telomeres? *Health Psychology, 31*(6), 789–796.

Umberson, D., & Montez, J. K. (2010). Social relationships and health: A flashpoint for health policy. *Journal of Health and Social Behavior, 51*, S54–S66.

UNAIDS. (2007). *AIDS epidemic update, 2007.* Geneva, Switzerland: Joint United Nations Programme on HIV/AIDS.

UNAIDS. (2016). *Global AIDS update.* Retrieved from http://www.afro.who.int/sites/default/files/2017-05/global-AIDS-update-2016_en.pdf

UNAIDS. (2018). *Global HIV statistics.* Retrieved from http://www.unaids.org/sites/default/files/media_asset/UNAIDS_FactSheet_en.pdf

United Nations Office on Drugs and Crime (UNODC). (2015). *World drug report.* Retrieved from https://www.unodc.org/documents/wdr2015/World_Drug_Report_2015.pdf

University of Bonn. (2008, March 26). Anxiety linked to blood clots: Fear that freezes the blood in your veins. *ScienceDaily.* Retrieved from http://www.sciencedaily.com/releases/2008/03/080325111800.htm

University of Pittsburgh. (2000). *Epidemiology of cardiovascular risk factors in women (Healthy Women Study).* Retrieved from https://clinicaltrials.gov/ct2/show/NCT00005160

Updegraff, J. A., Silver, R. C., & Holman, E. A. (2008). Searching for and finding meaning in a collective trauma: Results from a national longitudinal study of the 9/11 terrorist attacks. *Journal of Personality and Social Psychology, 95*(3), 709–722.

Vaccarino, V., Johnson, B. D., Sheps, D. S., Reis, S. E., Kelsey, S. F., Bittner, V., … Bairey-Merz, C. N. (2007). Depression, inflammation, and incident cardiovascular disease in women with suspected coronary ischemia: The National Heart, Lung, and Blood Institute-sponsored WISE Study. *Journal of the American College of Cardiology, 50*(21), 2044–2050.

Valero-Elizondo, J., Salami, J. A., Osundu, C. U., Ogunmoroti, O., Arrieta, A., Spatz, E. S., … Nasir, K. (2016). Economic impact of moderate-vigorous physical activity among those with and without established cardiovascular disease: 2012 Medical Expenditure Panel Survey. *Journal of the American Heart Association, 5*(9), 1–11.

Van Damme, S., Crombez, G., & Eccleston, C. (2008). Coping with pain: A motivational perspective. *Pain, 139*, 1–4.

Van De Ven, M. O. M., Engels, R. C. M., Otten, R., & Van Den Eijnden, R. J. J. (2007). A longitudinal test of the theory of planned behavior predicting smoking onset among asthmatic and non-asthmatic adolescents. *Journal of Behavioral Medicine, 30*, 435–445.

Van der Voorn, B., Hollanders, J. J., Ket, J. C. F., Rotteveels, J., & Finken, M. J. J. (2017). Gender-specific differences in hypothalamus-pituitary-adrenal axis activity during childhood: A systematic review and meta-analysis. *Biology of Sex Differences, 8*(3). Retrieved from https://bsd.biomedcentral.com/articles/10.1186/s13293-016-0123-5

Van Dulmen, S., Sluijis, E., van Dijk, L., de Ridder, D., Heerdink, R., & Bensing, J. (2007). Patient adherence to medical treatment: A review of reviews. *BMC Health Services Research, 17*(7). Retrieved from https://bmchealthservres.biomedcentral.com/articles/10.1186/1472-6963-7-55

Van Leijenhorst, L., Zanolie, K., Van Meel, C. S., Westenberg, P. M., Rombouts, S. A., & Crone, E. A. (2010). What motivates the adolescent? Brain regions mediating reward sensitivity across adolescence. *Cerebral Cortex, 20*(1), 61–69.

van Ryn, M., & Burke, J. (2000). The effect of patient race and socio-economic status on physicians' perceptions of patients. *Social Science & Medicine, 50*(6), 813–828.

van Stralen, M. M., De Vries, H., Mudde, A. N., Bolman, C., & Lechner, L. (2009). Determinants of initiation and maintenance of physical activity among older adults: A literature review. *Health Psychology Review, 3*, 147–207.

Van Zundert, R. M. P., Van Der Vorst, H., Vermulst, A. A., & Engels, R. C. (2006). Pathways to alcohol use among Dutch students in regular education and education for adolescents with behavioral problems: The role of parental alcohol use, general parenting practices, and alcohol-specific parenting practices. *Journal of Family Psychology, 20*(3), 456–467.

Vancampfort, D., Vansteenkiste, M., De Hert, M., De Herdt, A., Soundy, A., Stubbs, B., … Probst, M. (2014). Self-determination and stage of readiness to change physical activity behaviour in schizophrenia. *Mental Health and Physical Activity, 7*(3), 171–176.

Vanyukov, M. M., Tarter, R. E., & Ridenour, R. A. (2012). Common liability to addiction and "gateway hypothesis": Theoretical, empirical and evolutionary perspective. *Drug and Alcohol Dependence, 123*(S1), S3–S17.

Varni, J. W., Setoguchi, Y., Rappaport, L. R., & Talbot, D. (1992). Psychological adjustment and perceived social support in children with congenital/acquired limb deficiencies. *Journal of Behavioral Medicine, 15*(1), 31–44.

Vehof, J., Zavos, H. M., Lachance, G., Hammond, C. J., & Williams, F. M. (2014). Shared genetic factors underlie chronic pain syndromes. *Pain, 155*(8), 1562–1568.

Velicer, W. F., & Prochaska, J. O. (2008). Stages and non-stage theories of behavior and behavior change: A comment on Schwarzer. *Applied Psychology: An International Review, 57*, 75–83.

Verma, R., Balhara, Y., & Gupta, C. (2011). Gender differences in stress response: Role of developmental and biological determinants. *Industrial Psychiatry Journal, 20*, 4–10.

Vervoort, T., Caes, L., Crombez, G., Koster, E. H. W., Van Damme, S., De Witte, M., & Goubert, L. (2011). Parental catastrophizing about children's pain and selective attention to varying levels of facial expression of pain in children: A dot-probe study. *Pain, 152*, 1751–1757.

Vervoort, T., Caes, L., Trost, Z., Notebaert, L., & Goubert, L. (2012). Parental attention to their child's pain is modulated by threat-value of pain. *Health Psychology, 31*(5), 623–631.

Vickberg, S. M. (2003). The Concerns About Recurrence Scale (CARS): A systematic measure of women's fears about the possibility of breast cancer recurrence. *Annals of Behavioral Medicine, 25*(1), 16–24.

Vickers, A. J., & Linde, K. (2014). Acupuncture for chronic pain. *Journal of the American Medical Association, 311*(9), 955–956.

Vigil, J. M., Rowell, L. M., & Lutz, C. (2014). Gender expression, sexual orientation and pain sensitivity in women. *Pain Research and Management, 19*(2), 87–92.

Vikraman, S., Fryar, C. D., & Ogden, C. L. (2015). *Caloric intake from fast food among children and adolescents in the United States, 2011–2012* (NCHS Data Brief No. 213). Hyattsville, MD: National Center for Health Statistics.

Villella, C., Martinotti, G., Di Nicola, M., Cassano, M., La Torre, G., Gliubizzi, M. D., … Conte, G. (2011). Behavioural addictions in adolescents and young adults: Results from a prevalence study. *Journal of Gambling Studies, 27*(2), 203–214.

Vinokur, A. D., Schul, Y., Vuori, J., & Price, R. H. (2000). Two years after a job loss: Long-term impact of the JOBS program on reemployment and mental health. *Journal of Occupational Health Psychology, 5*, 32–47.

Visich, P. S., & Fletcher, E. (2009). Myocardial infarction. In J. K. Ehrman, P. M. Gordon, P. S. Visich, & S. J. Keleyian (Eds.), *Clinical exercise physiology* (2nd ed., pp. 281–300). Champaign, IL: Human Kinetics.

Vitaliano, P. P., Zhang, J., & Scanlan, J. M. (2003). Is caregiving hazardous to one's physical health? A meta-analysis. *Psychological Bulletin, 129*(6), 946–972.

Vitiello, M. V. (2009). Recent advances in understanding sleep and sleep disturbances in older adults: Growing older does not mean sleeping poorly. *Current Directions in Psychological Science, 18*, 316–320.

Vittinghoff, E., Shlipak, M. G., Varosy, P. D., Furberg, C. D., Ireland, C. C., Khan, S. S., … Hulley, S. (2003). Risk factors and secondary prevention in women with heart disease: The Heart and Estrogen/Progestin Replacement Study. *Annals of Internal Medicine, 13*, 81–89.

Vlachopoulos, C., Rokkas, K., Ioakeimidis, N., & Stefanadis, C. (2007). Inflammation, metabolic syndrome, erectile dysfunction, and coronary artery disease: Common links. *European Urology, 52*, 1590–1600.

Vocks, S., Tuschen-Caffier, B., Pietrowsky, R., Rustenbach, S. J., Kersting A., & Herpertz, S. (2010). Meta-analysis of the effectiveness of psychological and pharmacological treatments for binge eating disorder. *International Journal of Eating Disorder, 43*, 205–217.

von Känel, R. (2015). Acute mental stress and hemostasis: When physiology becomes vascular harm. *Thrombosis Research, 135*(S1), S52–S55.

von Känel, R., Bellingrath, S., & Kudielka, B. M. (2009). Association between longitudinal changes in depressive symptoms and plasma fibrinogen levels in school teachers. *Psychophysiology, 46*(3), 473–480.

von Känel, R., Dimsdale, J. E., Mills, P. J., Ancoli-Israel, S., Patterson, T. L., Mausbach, B. T., & Grant, I. (2006). Effect of Alzheimer caregiving stress and age on frailty markers Interleukin-6, C-reactive protein, and d-dimer. *Journals of Gerontology, Series A: Biological and Medical Sciences, 61A*, 963–969.

von Känel, R., Malan, N. T., Hamer, M., van der Westhuizen, F. H., & Malan, L. (2014). Leukocyte telomere length and hemostatic factors in a South African cohort: The SABPA Study. *Journal of Thrombosis and Haemostasis, 12*(12), 1975–1985.

Vorona, R. D., Szklo-Coxe, M., Wu, A., Dubnik, M., Zhao, Y., & Ware, J. C. (2011). Dissimilar teen crash rates in two neighboring southeastern Virginia cities with different high school start times. *Journal of Clinical Sleep Medicine, 7*(2), 145–151.

Wadden, T. A., Butryn, M. L., & Wilson, C. (2007). Lifestyle modification for the management of obesity. *Gastroenterology, 132*(6), 2226–2238.

Wade, T. D., & Bulik, C. M. (2007). Shared genetic and environmental risk factors between undue influence of body shape and weight on self-evaluation and dimensions of perfectionism. *Psychological Medicine, 37*(5), 635–644.

Wadhwa, P. D., Entringer, S., Buss, C., & Lu, M. C. (2011). The contribution of maternal stress to preterm birth: Issues and considerations. *Clinics in Perinatology, 38*(3), 351–384.

Wager, N., Fieldman, G., & Hussey, T. (2003). The effect on ambulatory blood pressure of working under favourably and unfavourably perceived supervisors. *Occupational and Environmental Medicine, 60*(7), 468–474.

Wager, T. D., Rilling, J. K., Smith, E. E., Sololik, A., Casey, K. L., Davidson, R. J., … Cohen, J. D. (2004). Placebo-induced changes in fMRI in the anticipation and experience of pain. *Science, 303,* 1162–1167.

Wagner, J., Lacey, K., Abbott, G., de Groot, M., & Chyun, D. (2006). Knowledge of heart disease risk in a multicultural community sample of people with diabetes. *Annals of Behavioral Medicine, 31*(3), 224–230.

Wagner, K., & Molla, R. (2018, January 31). Facebook lost daily users for the first time ever in the U.S. and Canada. *Recode.* Retrieved from https://www.recode.net/2018/1/31/16957122/facebook-daily-active-user-decline-us-canda-q4-earnings-2018

Wagnild, G. (2008). Resilience and depression among middle-aged and older adults. *Journal of Psychosocial Nursing and Mental Health Services, 47*(12), 28–33.

Wahner-Roedler, D. L., Vincent, A., Elking, P. L., Loehrer, L. L., Cha, S. S., & Bauer, B. A. (2006). Physicians' attitudes toward complementary and alternative medicine and their knowledge of specific therapies: A survey at an academic medical center. *Evidence-Based Complementary and Alternative Medicine, 3*(4), 495–501.

Walburn, J., Vedhara, K., Hankins, M., Rixon, L., & Weinman, J. (2009). Psychological stress and wound healing in humans: A systematic review and meta-analysis. *Journal of Psychosomatic Research, 67*(3), 253–271.

Walker, J., Holm Hansen, C., Martin, P., Sawhney, A., Thekkumpurath, P., Beale, C., … Sharpe, M. (2013). Prevalence of depression in adults with cancer: A systematic review. *Annals of Oncology, 24*(4), 895–900.

Wall, P. (2000). *Pain: The science of suffering.* New York, NY: Columbia University Press.

Waller, G. (2006). Understanding prehospital delay behavior in acute myocardial infarction in women. *Critical Pathways in Cardiology, 5*(4), 228–234.

Walley, A. J., Asher, J. E., & Froguel, P. (2009). The genetic contribution to non-syndromic human obesity. *Nature Reviews: Genetics, 10*(7), 431–442.

Walter, F., Webster, A., Scott, S., & Emery, J. (2012). The Andersen Model of Total Patient Delay: A systematic review of its application in cancer diagnosis. *Journal of Health Services Research & Policy, 17*(2), 110–118.

Wanberg, C. R. (2012). The individual experience of unemployment. *Annual Review of Psychology, 63*(1), 369–396.

Wang, C., Schmid, C. H., Rones, R., Kalish, R., Yinh, J., Goldenberg, D. L., … McAlindon, T. (2010). A randomized trial of tai chi for fibromyalgia. *New England Journal of Medicine, 363,* 743–754.

Wang, H. X., Mittleman, M. A., Leineweber, C., & Orth-Gomer, K. (2008). Depressive symptoms, social isolation, and progression of coronary artery atherosclerosis: The Stockholm Female Coronary Angiography Study. *Psychotherapy and Psychosomatics, 75,* 96–102.

Wang, J. L., Lesage, A., Schmitz, N., & Drapeau, A. (2008). The relationship between work stress and mental disorders in men and women: Findings from a population-based study. *Journal of Epidemiology and Community Health, 62,* 42–47.

Wang, X., Cai, L., Qian, J., & Peng, J. (2014). Social support moderates stress effects on depression. *International Journal of Mental Health Systems, 8,* 41–46.

Wansink, B. (2011). Modifying the food environment: From mindless eating to mindlessly eating better. Washington, DC: Annual Meeting of the American Psychological Association, August 5, 2011.

Wansink, B., van Ittersum, K., & Painter, J. E. (2006). Ice cream illusions: Bowls, spoons, and self-served portion sizes. *American Journal of Preventive Medicine, 31,* 240–243.

Ward, B. W., Clarke, T. C., Nugent, C. N., & Schiller, J. S. (2016). *Early release of selected estimates based on data from the 2015 National Health Interview Survey.* National Center for Health Statistics. Retrieved from http://www.cdc.gov/nchs/nhis.htm

Wardle, J., Parmenter, K., & Waller, J. (2000). Nutrition knowledge and food intake. *Appetite, 34*(3), 269–275.

Wardle, J., Robb, K. A., Johnson, F., Griffith, J., Brunner, E., Power, C., & Tovee, M. (2004). Socioeconomic variation in attitudes to eating and weight in female adolescents. *Health Psychology, 23*(3), 275–282.

Warner, R., & Griffiths, M. D. (2006). A qualitative thematic analysis of exercise addiction: An exploratory study. *International Journal of Mental Health and Addiction, 4,* 13–26.

Wasfy, M. M., Hutter, A. M., & Weiner, R. B. (2016). Sudden cardiac death in athletes. *Methodist DeBakey Cardiovascular Journal, 12*(2), 76–80.

Watkins, L. R., Hutchinson, M. R., Ledeboer, A., Wieseler-Frank, J., Milligan, E. D., & Maier, S. F. (2007). Glia as the "bad guys": Implications for improving clinical pain control and the clinical utility of opioids. *Brain, Behavior and Immunity, 21,* 131–146.

Watson, D., Clark, L. A., & Tellegen, A. (1988). Development and validation of brief measures of positive and negative affect: The PANAS Scales. *Journal of Personality and Social Psychology, 54*(6), 1063–1070.

Watson, N. F., Badr, M. S., Belenky, G., Bliwise, D. L., Buxton, O. M., Buysse, D., … Tasali, E. (2015). Joint consensus statement of the American Academy of Sleep Medicine and Sleep Research Society on the recommended amount of sleep for a healthy adult: Methodology and discussion. *Sleep, 38*(8), 1161–1183.

Way, B. M., Creswell, J. D., Eisenberger, N. I., & Lieberman, M. (2010). Dispositional mindfulness and depressive symptomatology: Correlations with limbic and self-referential neural activity during rest. *Emotion, 10*(1), 12–24.

Wearing, D. (2005, January 12). The man who keeps falling in love with his wife. *The Daily Telegraph.* Retrieved from http://www.telegraph.co.uk/news/health/3313452/The-man-who-keeps-falling-in-love-with-his-wife.html

Webb, J., Foster, J., & Poulter, E. (2016). Increasing the frequency of physical activity very brief advice for cancer patients. Development of an intervention using the behavior change wheel. *Public Health, 133,* 45–56.

Webb, H. E., Garten, R. S., McMinn, D. R., Beckman, J. L., Kamimori, G. H., & Acevedo, E. O. (2011). Stress hormones and vascular function in firefighters during concurrent challenges. *Biological Psychology, 87,* 152–160.

Webb, T. L., Joseph, J., Yardley, L., & Michie, S. (2010). Using the Internet to promote health behavior change: A systematic review and meta-analysis of the impact of theoretical basis, use of behavior change techniques, and mode of delivery on efficacy. *Journal of Medical Internet Research, 12*(1), e4. doi:10.2196/jmir.1376

WebMD. (2018). *Sexual conditions health center.* Retrieved from https://www.webmd.com/sexual-conditions/default.htm

Wechsler, H., & Nelson, T. F. (2008). What we have learned from the Harvard School of Public Health College Alcohol Study: Focusing attention on college student alcohol consumption and the environmental conditions that promote it. *Journal of Studies on Alcohol and Drugs, 69*(4), 481–490.

Wehunt, J. (2009, July). The "food desert." *Chicago Magazine.* Retrieved from http://www.chicagomag.com/Chicago-Magazine/July-2009/The-Food-Desert

Weiland, B. J., Thayer, R. E., Depue, B. E., Sabbineni, A., Bryan, A. D., & Hutchinson, K. E. (2015). Daily marijuana use is not associated with brain morphometric measures in adolescents or adults. *The Journal of Neuroscience, 35*(4), 1505–1512.

Weinberg, R. S., & Gould, D. (2015). *Foundations of sport and exercise psychology* (6th ed.). Champaign, IL: Human Kinetics.

Weingart, S. N., Pagovich, O., Sands, D. Z., Li, J. M., Aronson, M. D., Davis, R. B., … Bates, D. W. (2006). Patient-reported service quality on a medicine unit. *International Journal for Quality in Health Care, 18,* 95–101.

Weinstein, A. M., Voss, M. W., Prakash, R. S. Chaddock, L., Szabo, A., White, S. M., … Erickson, K. I. (2012). The association between aerobic fitness and executive function is mediated by prefrontal cortex volume. *Brain, Behavior, and Immunity, 26*(5), 811–819.

Weir, K. (2012). Big kids. *Monitor on Psychology, 43*(11), 58–63.

Weisli, P., Schmid, C., Kerwer, O., Nigg-Koch, C., Klaghofer, R., & Seifert, B. (2005). Acute psychological stress affects glucose concentrations in patients with Type I diabetes following food intake but not in the fasting state. *Diabetes Care, 28,* 1910–1915.

Weitz, R. (2007). *The sociology of health, illness, and health care: A critical approach* (4th ed.). Belmont, CA: Wadsworth.

Weitzman, E. R., Ziemnik, R. E., Huang, Q., & Levy, S. (2015). Alcohol and marijuana use and treatment nonadherence among medically vulnerable youth. *Pediatrics, 136*(3). Retrieved from http://pediatrics.aappublications.org/content/136/3/450

Well Men & Women Too. (2016). *The complete health program.* Retrieved from http://www.wellmen.com.au/site%20map.htm

Welsh, P., Grassia, G., Botha, S., Sattar, N., & Maffia, P. (2017). Targeting inflammation to reduce cardiovascular disease risk: A realistic clinical prospect? *British Journal of Pharmacology, 174(22),* 3898–3913. doi:10.1111/bph.13818

Wen, L. S., and Tucker, S. (2015). What do people want from their health care? A qualitative study. *Journal of Participatory Medicine, 7,* e10.

Wenze, S. J., & Miller, I. W. (2010). Use of ecological momentary assessment in mood disorders research. *Clinical Psychology Review, 30*(6), 794–804.

Wertheim, E. H., & Paxton, S. J. (2011). Body image development in adolescent girls. In T. F. Cash & T. Pruzinsky (Eds.), *Body image:*

A handbook of theory, research, and clinical practice (2nd ed., pp. 76–84). New York, NY: Guilford Press.

Wesley, J. (2003). *Primitive physic: An easy and natural method of curing most diseases.* Eugene, OR: Wipf and Stock.

Wheaton, A. G., Olsen, E. O., Miller, G. F., & Croft, J. B. (2016, April 8). Sleep duration and injury-related risk behaviors among high school students—United States, 2007–2013. *Morbidity and Mortality Weekly Report, 65*(13), 337–341.

Whelton, P. K., Carey, R. M., Aronow, W. S., Casey, D. E. Jr., Collins, K. J., Dennison Himmelfarb, C., …, Wright, J. T. Jr. (2017). 2017 guideline for the prevention, detection, evaluation, and management of high blood pressure in adults: A report of the American College of Cardiology/American Heart Association Task Force on Clinical Practice Guidelines (Table 6, p. 22). *Hypertension, 71*(6). Retrieved from https://www.ahajournals.org/doi/full/10.1161/HYP.0000000000000065

Whetten, K., Reif, S., Whetten, R., & Murphy-McMillan, L. K. (2008). Trauma, mental health, distrust, and stigma among HIV-positive persons: Implications for effective care. *Psychosomatic Medicine, 70,* 531–538.

White, H. R., Labouvie, E. W., & Papadaratsakis, V. (2005). Changes in substance use during the transition to adulthood: A comparison of college students and their noncollege-age peers. *Journal of Drug Issues, 35*(2), 281–305.

Whitehead, D. L., Perkins-Porras, L., Strike, P. C., Magid, K., & Steptoe, A. (2007). Cortisol awakening response is elevated in acute coronary syndrome patients with Type D personality. *Journal of Psychosomatic Research, 62,* 419–425.

Whiting, P. F., Wolff, R. F., Deshpande, S., Di Nisio, M., Duffy, S., Hernandez, A. V., … Kleijnen, J. (2015). Cannabinoids for medical use: A systematic review and meta-analysis. *Journal of the American Medical Association, 313*(24), 2456–2473.

Wideman, T. H., & Sullivan, M. J. (2011). Reducing catastrophic thinking associated with pain. *Pain Management, 1*(3), 249–256.

Wiech, K., Farias, M., Kahane, G., Shackel, N., Tiede, W., & Tracey, I. (2008a). An fMRI study measuring analgesia enhanced by religion as a belief system. *Pain, 139,* 467–476.

Wiech, K., Ploner, M., & Tracey, I. (2008b). Neurocognitive aspects of pain perception. *Trends in Cognitive Sciences, 12,* 306–313.

Wiest, M., Schüz, B., Webster, N., & Wurm, S. (2011). Subjective well-being and mortality revisited: Differential effects of cognitive and emotional facets of well-being on mortality. *Health Psychology, 30*(6), 728–735.

Wilcox, V. L., Kasl, S. V., & Berkman, L. F. (1994). Social support and physical disability in older people after hospitalization: A prospective study. *Health Psychology, 13,* 170–179.

Wilkinson, P., & Goodyer, I. (2011). Non-suicidal self-injury. *European Child and Adolescent Psychiatry, 20,* 103–108.

Wilksch, S. M., & Wade, T. D. (2009). An investigation of temperament endophenotype candidates for early emergence of the core cognitive component of eating disorders. *Psychological Medicine, 39*(5), 811–821.

Williams, A. C., Eccleston, C., & Morley, S. (2012). Psychological therapies for the management of chronic pain (excluding headache) in adults. *Cochrane Database of Systematic Reviews* 11:CD007407. doi:10.1002/14651858.CD007407.pub3

Williams, D. A. (1996). Acute pain management. In R. Gatchel & D. C. Turk (Eds.), *Psychological approaches to pain management: A practitioner's handbook* (pp. 55–77). New York, NY: Guilford Press.

Williams, D. R., Priest, N., & Anderson, N. (2016). Understanding associations between race, socioeconomic status and health: Patterns and prospects. *Health Psychology: Official Journal of the Division of Health Psychology, American Psychological Association, 35*(4), 407–411.

Williams, D. S. (2000). Racism and mental health: The African American experience. *Ethnicity & Health, 5*(3–4), 243–268.

Williams, L. J., Jacka, F. N., Pasco, J. A., Dodd, S., & Berk, M. (2006). Depression and pain: An overview. *Acta Neuropsychiatrica, 18*, 79–87.

Williams, R. B., & Williams, V. (1994). *Anger kills: Seventeen strategies for controlling the hostility that can harm your health* (pp. 5–11). New York: Harper Perennial.

Wilson, G. T., Grilo, C. M., & Vitousek, K. M. (2007). Psychological treatment of eating disorders. *American Psychologist, 62*(3), 199–216.

Wilson-Simmons, R., Jiang, Y., & Aratani, Y. (2017). *Strong at the broken places: The resiliency of low-income parents.* New York, NY: National Center for Children in Poverty, Columbia University Mailman School of Public Health.

Windle, G., Hughes, D., Linck, P., Russell, I., & Woods, B. (2010). Is exercise effective in promoting mental well-being in older age? A systematic review. *Aging and Mental Health, 14*, 652–669.

Windle, M., Kogan, S. M., Lee, S., Chen, Y. F., Lei, K. M., Brody, G. H. … Yu, T. Y. (2016). Neighborhood X serotonin transporter linked polymorphic region (5_HTTLPR) interactions for substance abuse from ages 10 to 24 years using a harmonized data set of African American children. *Development and Psychopathology, 28*(2), 415–431.

Windle, M., & Windle, R. C. (2001). Depressive symptoms and cigarette smoking among middle adolescents: Prospective associations and intrapersonal and interpersonal influences. *Journal of Consulting and Clinical Psychology, 69*, 215–226.

Winerman, L. (2006). Brain, heal thyself. *Monitor on Psychology, 37*(1), 56–57.

Winett, R. A. (1995) A framework for health promotion and disease prevention programs. *American Psychologist, 50*(5), 341–350.

Wing, R. R., & Jeffery, R. W. (1999). Benefits of recruiting participants with friends and increasing social support for weight loss and maintenance. *Journal of Consulting and Clinical Psychology, 67*(1), 132–138.

Winter, L., Lawton, M., Langston, C., Ruckdeschel, K., & Sando, R. (2007). Symptoms, affects, and self-rated health. *Journal of Aging and Health, 19*(3), 453–569.

Winterling, J., Glimelius, B., & Nordin, K. (2008). The importance of expectations on the recovery period after cancer treatment. *Psycho-Oncology, 17*, 190–198.

Wipfli, B. M., Rethorst, C. D., & Landers, D. M. (2008). The anxiolytic effects of exercise: A meta-analysis of randomized trials and dose-response analysis. *Journal of Sport and Exercise Psychology, 30*(4), 392–410.

Witteman, J., Post, H., Tarvainen, M., de Bruijn, A., Perna, E., Ramaekers, J. G., & Weirs, R. W. (2015). Cue reactivity and its relation to craving and relapse in alcohol dependence: A combined laboratory and field study. *Psychopharmacology, 232*(20), 3685–3696.

Wolf, L. D., & Davis, M. (2014). Loneliness, daily pain, and perceptions of interpersonal events in adults with fibromyalgia. *Health Psychology, 33*, 929–937.

Wolff, B., Burns, J. W., Quartana, P. J., Lofland, K., Bruehl, S., & Chung, O. Y. (2008). Pain catastrophizing, physiological indexes, and chronic pain severity: Tests of mediation and moderation models. *Journal of Behavioral Medicine, 31*, 105–114.

Women's Health Initiative (WHI). (2010). *Women's health initiative update.* Retrieved from http://www.nhlbi.nih.gov/whi/update.htm

Wonderlich, S. A., Joiner, Jr., T. E., Keel, P. K., Williamson, D. A., & Crosby, R. D. (2007). Eating disorder diagnoses: Empirical approaches to classification. *American Psychologist, 62*, 167–180.

Wong, C. A. (2009). Advances in labor analgesia. *International Journal of Women's Health, 1*, 139–154.

Wong, J. M., Sin, L. L., & Whooley, M. A. (2014). A comparison of Cook-Medley Hostility Subscales and mortality in patients with coronary heart disease: Data from the Heart and Soul Study. *Psychosomatic Medicine, 76*(4), 311–317.

Wood, S. (2012, January 13). Resveratrol scientists react to fraud scandal. *Medscape.* Retrieved from http://www.medscape.com/viewarticle/756905

Wooldridge, T., & Lemberg, R. (2016). Macho, bravado, and eating disorders in men: Special issues in diagnosis and treatment. *Psychiatric Times, 33*(5), 1–5.

World Bank. (2018). *Life expectancy at birth, total (years).* Retrieved from https://data.worldbank.org/indicator/SP.DYN.LE00.IN

World Cancer Research Fund International. (2017). *Continuous update project report: Diet, nutrition, physical activity and breast cancer.* World Cancer Research Fund International/American Institute for Cancer Research. Retrieved from wcrf.org/breast-cancer-2017

World Health Organization (WHO). (2006). *The world health report 2006: Working together for health.* Geneva, Switzerland: Author.

World Health Organization (WHO). (2010). *Global recommendations on physical activity for health.* Geneva, Switzerland: Author.

World Health Organization (WHO). (2011). *Suicide prevention.* Geneva, Switzerland: Author. Retrieved from http://www.who.int/mental_health/prevention/suicide/suicideprevent/en

World Health Organization (WHO). (2012). *Violence and injury prevention fact sheets.* Geneva, Switzerland: Author. Retrieved from http://www.who.int/violence_injury_prevention/violence/world_report/factsheets/en/index.html

World Health Organization (WHO). (2013). *Acupuncture: Review and analysis of reports on controlled clinical trials.* Geneva, Switzerland: Author. Retrieved from http://apps.who.int/medicinedocs/pdf/s4926e/s4926e.pdf

World Health Organization (WHO). (2015a). *Deaths from NCDs.* Geneva, Switzerland: Author. Retrieved February 28, 2016, from http://www.who.int/gho/ncd/mortality_morbidity/ncd_total_text/en/

World Health Organization (WHO). (2015b). *Noncommunicable diseases* (Fact Sheet No. 355). World Health Organization Media Centre. Retrieved from http://www.who.int/mediacentre/factsheets/fs355/en/

World Health Organization (WHO). (2015c). *Physical activity* (Fact Sheet No. 385). World Health Organization Media Centre. Retrieved from http://www.who.int/mediacentre/factsheets/fs385/en/

World Health Organization (WHO). (2015d). *World health statistics, 2015*. Geneva, Switzerland: Author. Retrieved from http://www.who.int/gho/publications/world_health_statistics/2015/en

World Health Organization (WHO). (2016). *Ebola virus disease* (Fact Sheet No. 103). Retrieved from http://www.who.int/mediacentre/factsheets/fs103/en/

World Health Organization (WHO). (2017a). *Asthma fact sheet*. Retrieved from http://www.who.int/mediacentre/factsheets/fs307/en/

World Health Organization (WHO). (2017b). *Diabetes: Key facts*. Retrieved from http://www.who.int/en/news-room/fact-sheets/detail/diabetes

World Health Organization (WHO). (2017c). *Global health estimates 2016: Estimated deaths by cause and region, 2000 and 2016*. Retrieved from http://www.who.int/healthinfo/global_burden_disease/estimates/en/

World Health Organization (WHO). (2017d). *Noncommunicable diseases: Key facts*. Retrieved from http://www.who.int/news-room/fact-sheets/detail/noncommunicable-diseases

World Health Organization (WHO). (2018a). *Cancer: Key facts*. Retrieved from http://www.who.int/news-room/fact-sheets/detail/cancer

World Health Organization (WHO). (2018b). *Global Health Observatory (GHO) data. Healthy life expectancy (HALE) at birth*. Retrieved from http://www.who.int/gho/mortality_burden_disease/life_tables/hale/en/

World Health Organization (WHO). (2018c). *HIV/AIDS*. Retrieved from http://www.who.int/gho/hiv/en/

World Health Organization (WHO). (2018d). *Immunization coverage fact sheet*. Retrieved from http://www.who.int/mediacentre/factsheets/fs378/en/

World Health Organization (WHO). (2018e). *Life expectancy*. Retrieved from http://www.who.int/gho/mortality_burden_disease/life_tables/situation_trends/en/

World Health Organization (WHO). (2018f). *Obesity and overweight*. Retrieved from http://www.who.int/mediacentre/factsheets/fs311/en/

World Health Organization (WHO). (2018g). *Tuberculosis: Key facts*. Retrieved from http://www.who.int/news-room/fact-sheets/detail/tuberculosis

Worobey, M., Telfer, P., Souquiere, S., Hunter, M., Coleman, C. A., Metzger, M. J., ... Marx, P. A. (2010). Island biogeography reveals the deep history of SIV. *Science, 329*, 1487.

Wrosch, C., Schulz, R., Miller, G. E., Lupien, S., & Dunne, E. (2007). Physical health problems, depressive mood, and cortisol secretion in old age: Buffer effects of health engagement control strategies. *Health Psychology, 26*, 341–349.

Wu, J. (2015, July 6). Dignity declared, yet still denied. *The Huffington Post*. Retrieved from http://www.huffingtonpost.com/janson-wu/dignity-declared-yet-stil-denied_b_7701954.html

Wu, S., Cohen, D., Shi, Y., Pearson, M., & Sturm, R. (2011). Economic analysis of physical activity interventions. *American Journal of Preventive Medicine, 40*(2), 149–158.

Wulsin, L. R., & Singal, B. M. (2003). Do depressive symptoms increase the risk for the onset of coronary disease? A systematic quantitative review. *Psychosomatic Medicine, 65*, 201–210.

Wyszynski, C. M., Bricker, J. B., & Comstock, B. A. (2011). Parental smoking cessation and child daily smoking: A 9-year longitudinal study of mediation by child cognitions about smoking. *Health Psychology, 30*(2), 171–176.

Xu, H., Xiao, T., Chen, C.-H., Li, W., Meyer, C. A., Wu, Q., ... Liu, S. X. (2015). Sequence determinants of improved CRISPR sgRNA design. *Genome Research, 25*(8), 1147–1157.

Yamamoto, Y., Hayashino, Y., Akiba, T., Akizawa, T., Akira, S., Kurokawa, K., & Fukuhara, S. (2010). Depressive symptoms predict the subsequent risk of bodily pain in dialysis patients: Japan dialysis outcomes and practice patterns study. *Pain Medicine, 10*(5), 883–889.

Yanez, B., Stanton, A. L., & Maly, R. C. (2012). Breast cancer treatment decision making among Latinas and non-Latina whites: A communication model predicting decisional outcomes and quality of life. *Health Psychology, 31*(5), 552–561.

Yang, L., & Colditz, G. A. (2015). Prevalence of overweight and obesity in the United States, 2007–2012. *Journal of the American Medical Association Internal Medicine, 175*(8), 1412–1413.

Yang, S. (2010). Racial disparities in training, pay-raise attainment, and income. *Research in Social Stratification and Mobility, 25*(4), 323–335.

Yano, Y., Stamler, J., Garside, D. B., Daviglus, M. L., Franklin, S. S., Carnethon, M. R., Liu, K., ... Lloyd-Jones, D. M. (2015). Isolated systolic hypertension in young and middle-aged adults and 31-year risk for cardiovascular mortality: The Chicago Heart Association Detection Project in Industry Study. *Journal of the American College of Cardiology, 65*(4), 327–335. doi:10.1016/j.jacc.2014.10.060

Yau, P. L., Castro, M. G., Tagani, A., Tsui, W. H., & Convit, A. (2012). Obesity and metabolic syndrome and functional and structural brain impairments in adolescence. *Pediatrics, 130*(4), 856–864.

Yeh, E. S., Rochette, L. M., McKenzie, L. B., & Smith, G. A. (2011). Injuries associated with cribs, playpens, and bassinets among young children in the U.S., 1990–2008. *Pediatrics, 127*, 479–486.

Yehuda, R. (2000). Biology of posttraumatic stress disorder. *Journal of Clinical Psychiatry, 61*(7), 14–21.

Yeo, M., Berzins, S., & Addington, D. (2007). Development of an early psychosis public education program using the precede/proceed model. *Health Education Research, 22*(5), 639–647.

Yohannes, A. M., Yalfani, A., Doherty, P., & Bundy, C. (2007). Predictors of drop-out from an outpatient cardiac rehabilitation programme. *Clinical Rehabilitation, 21*(3), 222–229.

Yoo, G., Aviv, C., Levine, E., Ewing, C., & Au, A. (2010). Emotion work: Disclosing cancer. *Supportive Care in Cancer, 18*(2), 205–213.

Yoon, S. S., Fryar, C. D., & Carroll, M. D. (2015). *Hypertension prevalence and control among adults: United States 2011–2014 (NCHS Data Brief No. 220)*. Hyattsville, MD: National Center for Health Statistics.

Young, L. (2017, August 1). Canadian obesity rates continue to climb, Saskatchewan takes top spot. *Global News Canada*. Retrieved from https://globalnews.ca/news/3639663/canadian-obesity-rates-continue-to-climb-saskatchewan-takes-top-spot/

Youth Risk Behavior Surveillance System (YRBSS). (2018). *Adolescent and school health.* Retrieved from https://www.cdc.gov/healthyyouth/data/yrbs/index.htm

Yu, X. N., Chen, Z., Zhang, J., & Liu, X. (2011). Coping mediates the association between Type D personality and perceived health in Chinese patients with coronary heart disease. *International Journal of Behavioral Medicine, 18*(3), 277–284.

Yusuf, S., Hawken, S., Ounpuu, S., Dans, T., Avezum, A., Lanas, F., … INTERHEART Study Investigators. (2004). Effect of potentially modifiable risk factors associated with myocardial infarction in 52 countries (the INTERHEART study): Case-control study. *The Lancet, 364*(9438), 937–952.

Zachariae, R., & O'Toole, M. S. (2015). The effect of expressive writing intervention on psychological and physical health outcomes in cancer patients—A systematic review and meta-analysis. *Psycho-Oncology, 24*(11), 1349–1359.

Zainal, N. Z., Booth, S., & Huppert, F. A. (2013). The efficacy of mindfulness-based stress reduction on mental health of breast cancer patients: A meta-analysis. *Psychooncology, 22*(7), 1457–1465.

Zakhari, S. (2006). Overview: How is alcohol metabolized by the body? *Alcohol Research and Health, 29,* 245–255.

Zangl, H. A., Mowinckel, P., Finset, A., Eriksson, L. R., Hoystad, T. O., Lunde, A. K., & Hagen, K. B. (2011). A mindfulness-based group intervention to reduce psychological distress and fatigue in patients with inflammatory rheumatic joint diseases: A randomized controlled trial. *Annals of the Rheumatic Diseases, 71*(6), 911–917.

Zanstra, Y. J., Schellekens, J. M. H., Schaap, C., & Kooistra, L. (2006). Vagal and sympathetic activity burnouts during a mentally demanding workday. *Psychosomatic Medicine, 68,* 583–590.

Zeevi, D., Korem, T., Zmora, N., Israeli, D., Rothschild, D., Weinberger, A., … Segal, E. (2015). Personalized nutrition by prediction of glycemic responses. *Cell, 163*(5), 1079–1094.

Zeidan, F., Gordon, N. S., Merchant, J., & Goolkasian, P. (2009). The effect of brief mindfulness training on experimentally induced pain. *The Journal of Pain, 11*(3), 199–209.

Zeidan, F., Martucci, K. T., Kraft, R. A., Gordon, N. S., McHaffie, J. G., & Coghill, R. (2011). Brain mechanisms supporting the modulation of pain by mindfulness meditation. *Journal of Neuroscience, 31*(14), 5540–5548.

Zen, A. L., Whooley, M. A., Zhao, S., & Cohen, B. E. (2012). Post-traumatic stress disorder is associated with poor health behaviors: Findings from the Heart and Soul Study. *Health Psychology, 31*(2), 194–201.

Zepf, B. (2005). Lifestyle changes most effective in preventing diabetes. *American Family Physician, 65*(11), 2338–2448.

Zhang, T. Y., Hellstrom, I. C., Bagot, R. C., Wen, X. Z., Diorio, J., & Meaney, M. J. (2010). Maternal care and DNA methylation of a glutamic acid decarboxylase 12 promoter in rat hippocampus. *Journal of Neuroscience, 30,* 13130–13137.

Zheng, Y., Plomin, R., & von Stumm, S. (2016). Heritability of intraindividual mean and variability of positive and negative affect: Genetic analysis of daily affect ratings over a month. *Psychological Science, 27*(12), 1611–1619.

Zhang, Y., Proenca, R., Maffei, M., & Barone, M. (1994). Positional cloning of the mouse obese gene and its human analogue. *Nature, 372,* 425–432.

Zhou, C., Wu, Y., An, S., & Li, X. (2015). Effect of expressive writing intervention on health outcomes in breast cancer patients: A systematic review and meta-analysis of randomized controlled trials. *PLOS ONE, 10*(7). Retrieved from http://journals.plos.org/plosone/article?id=10.1371/journal.pone.0131802

Zhou, E. S., Penedo, F. J., Lewis, J. E., Rasheed, M., Traeger, L., Lechner, S., … Antoni, M. H. (2010). Perceived stress mediates the effects of social support on health-related quality of life among men treated for localized prostate cancer. *Journal of Psychosomatic Research, 69,* 587–590.

Zhu, X., Han, Y., Du, J., Liu, R., Jin, K., & Yi, W. (2017). Microbiota-gut-brain axis and the central nervous system. *Oncotarget, 8*(32), 53829–53838.

Zijlstra, G. A., van Haastregt, J. C., van Rossum, E., van Eijk, J. T., Yardley, L., & Kempen, G. I. (2007). Interventions to reduce fear of falling in community-living older people: A systematic review. *Journal of the American Geriatrics Society, 55*(4), 603–615.

Zisser, H., Sueyoshi, M., Krigstein, K., Sziglato, A., & Riddell, M. C. (2012). Advances in exercise, physical activity, and diabetes mellitus. *International Journal of Clinical Practice, 66*(s175), 62–71.

Ziv, S. (2015, February 10). Andrew Wakefield, father of the anti-vaccine movement, responds to the current measles outbreak for the first time. *Newsweek.* Retrieved from http://www.newsweek.com/2015/02/20/andrew-wakefield-father-anti-vaccine-movement-sticks-his-story-305836.html

Zivanovic, R., Omura, J., Wood, E., Nguyen, P., Kerr, T., & DeBeck, K. (2016). Eviction and loss of income assistance among street-involved youth in Canada. *Journal of Public Health Policy, 37*(2), 244–259.

Zoccola, P. M., Dickerson, S. S., & Lam, S. (2009). Rumination predicts longer sleep onset latency after an acute psychosocial stressor. *Psychosomatic Medicine, 71,* 771–775.

Name Index

Subject Index

Note: Page numbers followed by f indicate figures; those followed by t indicate tables.

obesity in, 251, 261–262
pain assessment in, 445
resilient, 141–143, 184. *See also* Resilience
sleep in, 213–214
stress in, 84, 97–99, 118, 360–361
work-family conflict and, 103
Children's Anxiety and Pain Scales, 445
Children's Fear Scale, 445
Chinese medicine, traditional, 8f, 9–10, 478, 479, 485–487
Chiropractic, 495–496
Chlamydia, 385, 389t
Cholecystokinin, 246
Cholera, 43
Cholesterol
cardiovascular disease and, 313–315, 314f, 321–322
exercise and, 202, 330
reduction of, 330–331
Chromosomes, 82–83, 82f
Chronic illness, 18, 414
depression in, 401–402
exercise and, 200, 202–203, 209–210
living with, 400–407. *See also* Coping with chronic illness
with multiple illnesses, 242, 243f
prevalence of, 401
psychological factors in, 17–18
sleep deprivation and, 220–221, 220t
stress of, 401–402, 401f
Chronic pain, 443, 451. *See also* Pain
Chronic stress, 92, 107–108, 119, 120–121, 122. *See also* Stress
Cigarettes. *See also* Tobacco use and abuse
electronic, 295, 303, 304f
Cilia, 73, 77
Cingulate gyrus, 62f
Circadian rhythms, 211–212
shiftwork and, 105, 214–216
sleep-wake disorders and, 219t
Circulatory system, 68–69, 85–86. *See also under* Cardiovascular
Clinical health psychologists, 27
Clinical pain, 442
Clinical trials, 46
of complementary and alternative medicine, 481
evidence-based medicine and, 33–35, 475, 521
gender bias in, 22–23, 518
minorities in, 425
randomized, 46
Clitoris, 81f
Clotting, 68
stress and, 118–119, 320
Cocaine, 278, 280
Code of ethics, 35. *See also* Ethical issues
Codeine, 279
Cognitive appraisal
in pain management, 428–429

of stress, 17, 93, 124–125, 124f, 513
Cognitive control, 432. *See also* Control
Cognitive development, exposure to violence and, 126
Cognitive dissonance interventions, for eating disorders, 268
Cognitive distraction, in pain management, 464–465
Cognitive function
alcohol and, 289
exercise and, 203–204
Cognitive reappraisal, 466–467
Cognitive restructuring, 154, 154f
in pain management, 463–464
Cognitive-behavioral interventions
for cancer, 371–374
for eating disorders, 267–269
for hospitalization, 432–434, 433t
for insomnia, 217–218
in prevention, 178–179
Cognitive-behavioral stress management, 154–155
in HIV/AIDS, 405–406
for sexually transmitted infections, 405–406
Cognitive-behavioral therapy, 153–154
definition of, 153, 462
mindfulness-based, 151–153
for pain, 462–471. *See also* Pain management
for weight loss, 260–261
Collaborative care, 413
Collective trauma, 101
Collectivistic cultures, negative affectivity in, 139
College education. *See also* Education
health benefits of, 28
College students. *See* Adolescence; Emerging adulthood
College Undergraduate Stress Scale, 93–95, 94t
Colon, 74f, 75
cancer of, 350t, 355, 362t. *See also* Cancer
Colonoscopy, 350t, 363t
COM-B behavior change model, 209–210
Combination antiretroviral therapy, for HIV/AIDS, 389t, 396, 404–405
Comfort food, 254
Common liability to addiction, 281
Communicable diseases, 18, 379. *See also specific diseases*
age and, 381–382
antimicrobial resistance and, 382–383
in children, 381–382
definition of, 379
emerging and reemerging, 382
epidemic, 10
epidemiological transition and, 379–382
gender and, 382

immunization for. *See* Immunization
mortality from, 336t, 379–382
overview of, 379
socioeconomic status and, 379–381
Communication, provider-patient, 424, 426–428
Community health approaches
for HIV/AIDS, 406
for obesity, 261–262
for prevention, 174–176, 512
Community health education, 174–176
Community health psychologists, 27
Comorbidity, 182, 415, 415f
Comparative optimism, for health events, 357–358
Compensatory smoking, 297
Competitive foods, 261
Complementary and alternative medicine, 474–506. *See also specific practices*
acupressure in, 496–497
acupuncture in, 485–487
biofeedback in, 461–462, 493–494
for cancer, 365
chiropractic in, 495–496
clinical trials of, 481
controversial practices in, 476–478
cultural aspects of, 476, 477t, 479
definition of, 476
domains of, 477t
effectiveness of, 480–484
food supplements in, 499–500, 501–502
future directions for, 503–505
growing acceptance of, 503–504
healthy skepticism about, 504–505
herbs in, 497–499
historical perspective on, 7–9, 8f
holistic medicine and, 478
hypnosis in, 188, 488
ideals of, 476–479
massage in, 496–497
meditation in. *See* Meditation
mind-body therapies in, 487–495
natural medicine and, 478
naturopathic medicine in, 497–503
outcome measures for, 481–482
placebo effect in, 479, 482–484
popularity of, 479–480
regulation of, 503–504
relaxation techniques in, 218, 372, 489–493
safety of, 501–502, 503–504
spirituality and prayer in, 494–495
tai chi in, 491
traditional Chinese medicine in, 8f, 9–10, 478, 479, 485–487
use by allopathic physicians, 479–480, 480t, 503–504
yoga in, 491
Compliance. *See* Treatment adherence

Compression of morbidity, 169–170, 170f, 514–515, 515f
Compulsive exercise, 210–211
Computed tomography (CT) scan, 315f
  in lung cancer screening, 350t
COMT, in fibromyalgia, 451
Concordance rate, 279
Condom use, HIV/AIDS and, 397, 403–404, 407
Confirmation bias, 34
Connective tissue, 59, 85
Consent, informed, 53
Consideration of future consequences, health behaviors and, 352
Contingency contracts, 178, 179
Control
  adherence and, 422
  behavioral, 432–433
  cognitive, 432
  coping with cancer and, 370
  coping with stress and, 104–105, 140–141, 144
  health education and, 177
  hospitalization and, 431
  informational, 432
  personal, 370
  positive psychology and, 189–190
  psychological, 140–141
  regulatory (self-control), 113–114, 141
  work-related stress and, 104–105
Control group, 39–40
Controlled drinking, 293
Conventional medicine. See Allopathic medicine
Conversion disorders, 12
Coping intelligence, 136
Coping skills training, for alcohol use disorder, 293
Coping with cancer, 161–162, 365–374
  cognitive-behavioral interventions in, 371–374
  emotional aspects of, 367
  emotional disclosure in, 372–373
  expressive writing in, 373
  guided imagery in, 373–374
  health psychology and, 366
  information resources and, 370
  masculinity threat and, 368
  personal control and, 370
  personality factors and, 367
  post-traumatic growth and, 369
  race/ethnicity and, 369
  repressive coping in, 136
  social comparison and, 370
  social support in, 371
Coping with chronic illness, 400–407.
    See also Chronic illness
  benefit finding and, 332–333
  global aspects of, 398–399
  health psychologists' role in, 402–407

psychological adjustment and, 401–402, 401f
psychosocial interventions and, 402–407.
    See also HIV/AIDS intervention programs
  response to diagnosis and, 401
  stress and, 401–402, 401f
Coping with HIV/AIDS, 400–407. See also Coping with chronic illness; HIV/AIDS intervention programs
Coping with pain. See Pain management
Coping with stress, 17, 133–159
  avoidance coping in, 136, 141
  in cancer, 371–374. See also Coping with cancer
  cardiovascular reactivity and, 113–114, 125
  cognitive-behavioral therapy in, 153–154, 405–406
  college-sponsored programs for, 149
  control and, 104–105, 140–141, 144. See also Control
  cultural factors in, 139
  definition of, 135
  in diabetes, 341
  dispositional affectivity and, 138–139, 138t, 156
  emotional-approach coping in, 135–136
  emotion-focused coping in, 135, 136
  exercise and, 203
  gratitude in, 156–157
  humor in, 157
  interventions for, 149–157. See also Stress management
  meaning-focused coping in, 157
  optimism and, 139–140
  pessimism and, 154, 154f
  pets and, 157
  problem-focused coping in, 135, 136
  race/ethnicity and, 127–130, 129t, 140–141, 144–145
  repressive coping in, 136
  resilience and, 141–143, 515–516
  smoking and, 297–298
  social support and, 106–107
  socioeconomic status and, 140–141
  spirituality in, 157
  stress inoculation training in, 154–155
  vagal tone and, 98–99, 114, 142f
  writing in, 155–157
Coronary angiography, 320
Coronary arteries, 313
  in arteriosclerosis/atherosclerosis, 313–315, 314f
Coronary heart disease, 242, 313. See also Cardiovascular disease
Correlation, 37–38
Correlation coefficient, 37
Corticosteroids, 67, 109
Corticotropin-releasing hormone, 67, 109, 110f

Cortisol
  inflammation and, 121
  in post-traumatic stress disorder, 127
  in stress response, 67, 109–112, 118, 121, 127, 184, 187
Cortisol awakening response, 118
Cost containment strategies, 521–522
Cost effectiveness, of health promotion, 522
Coughing, 73
Counterirritation, for pain, 460
Covitality, 182
Crash diets, 252
C-reactive protein
  in cardiovascular disease, 313–314, 330, 464
  inflammation and, 139, 313, 330
  pain and, 464
Crime
  alcohol and, 289–290
  workplace, 180–181
Critical thinking, 34–35
Cross-sectional studies, 42
CT scan, 315f
  in cancer screening, 350t
Cultural aspects. See also Race/ethnicity
  of body image, 235–236
  of complementary and alternative medicine, 476, 477t, 478, 479
  of diabetes self-management, 338–339
  of diet, 241
  of eating disorders, 265–266, 268
  of folk medicine, 7–9, 8f
  of health beliefs and practices, 20–21
  of negative affectivity, 139
  of obesity, 235–236, 254–255
  of pain, 456–458
  of stress, 139
  of substance abuse, 283–284
  of treatment seeking, 418
Culture, definition of, 20
Curiosity, 188–189
Cytokines, 79, 121
  anti-inflammatory, 79
  neurotransmitters and, 115
  proinflammatory, 79, 121, 450
  stress and, 107, 121
Cytoplasm, 58

Dabbing, 304–305
Daily Hassles Microsystem Scale, 101
Daily hassles, stress and, 99–101, 100t
Data interpretation
  association vs. causation, 39
  risk measurement, 50
  tables and graphs, 47–48
Death and dying. See also Injuries; Mortality
  from injuries, 222–223, 223f
  leading causes of, 16, 16f, 18–19, 19t, 222–223, 223f
  social support during, 146

melanoma and, 357
stress and, 116–117, 120–121, 120f, 360, 511
Immunotherapy, for cancer, 364
Implicit bias, 248, 249f
Incentive-sensitization theory, 281
Incidence, 44
Independent variables, 39
India, traditional medicine in, 10, 478
Indigenous healers, historical perspective on, 8f, 9–10
Indirect effect hypothesis, 119
Individual mandate (ACA), 171, 172
Individualistic cultures, negative affectivity in, 139
Infant(s). See also Children
post-term, 82
preterm, 82, 97–99
sleep in, 213–214
Infant mortality, 18, 19f, 21
Infarct, 316
Infarction
brain, 316, 316f
myocardial, 316
Infectious diseases. See Communicable diseases
Inflammation, 78, 78f
cardiovascular disease and, 313–314, 321
cortisol and, 121
c-reactive protein and, 139, 313, 330
cytokines in. See Cytokines
sleep and, 221
stress and, 120–121
systemic effects of, 78
Influenza, avian, 382
Informational control, 432. See also Control
Informed consent, 53
Inhalant abuse, 283
Injection drug users, HIV/AIDS in, 393, 394
Injuries
in adulthood, 16f, 223f, 226–229
in childhood, 223f, 224–225
from exercise, 210–211
from falls, 224–225, 228–229, 229f
intentional, 223, 227–228
from motor vehicle accidents, 225–226, 226f
non-suicidal self-injury, 228
from poisoning, 227
prevention of, 4t, 225, 229–232, 231f
from suicide, 227–228
unintentional, 223
from violence, 227
Injury control, 225
Inoculation programs, for smoking prevention, 299
Insomnia, 217–218, 219t. See also Sleep loss
Institutional Review Boards (IRBs), 35, 53
Institutionalized racism, 425–426

Insulin, 68, 75, 240–241
appetite and, 246
exercise and, 203
obesity and, 203, 221, 251
Insulin resistance, 203, 221, 335, 336–337
Insulin therapy, 337–338
Insurance. See Health insurance
Integrated care, 413, 523–525, 524t
Integrative medicine, 479, 480t
Integumentary system, 85–86
Intelligence, emotional, 367
Intentional injuries, 223, 227–228
Interferons, 78–79
INTERHEART Study, 317, 322
Interleukins, 79, 216
pain and, 464
Internet
in disease self-management, 469
patient-provider relationship and, 429–430
Interoception, 265
Interviewing, in descriptive research, 36–37, 36t
Intestines, 74f, 75
Intoxication, 285. See also Alcohol use and abuse
Intravenous drug use, HIV/AIDS and, 393
Invincibility fable, 163
Ireland, health care in, 436
Ischemia, in coronary artery disease, 315
Ischemic stroke, 316, 316f
Islet cells, 335

Japan, health care in, 436
Japan, work-related stress in, 106
Jet lag, social, 214
Job strain, 104, 327. See also Work
John Henryism, 325–326
Journaling, 155–157

K2, 304
Kaposi's sarcoma, 45, 390
Karoshi, 106
Kidneys, 85
Korsakoff's syndrome, 287

Labor, 82
Lamaze training for, 433
pain in, 457
Laparoscopy, 364
Large intestine, 74f, 75
Lateral hypothalamus, in weight regulation, 246
Latinos. See Hispanic Americans; Race/ethnicity
Laughter, coping and, 157
Lay referral system, 418
Learned optimism, 140

Left atrium, 70, 70f
Left ventricle, 70, 70f
Leptin, 221, 247–248
Lesbians
discrimination against, 398–399
microaggression and, 101
stress and, 101, 130
"Let's Move" program, 236
Leukemia, 348. See also Cancer
Leukocytes, 68
LGBT People of Color Microaggressions Scale, 101
LGBT populations
discrimination against, 398–399
eating disorders in, 263
HIV/AIDS in, 392–393, 393f
microaggression and, 101
minority-stress model and, 130
Life change units, 93–95
Life expectancy
average, 514
compression of morbidity and, 169–170, 170f, 514–515, 515f
health-adjusted, 515
Life-course perspective, 16, 17t
Lifestyle interventions, 513
for diabetes, 337
for obesity, 261–262
Limbic system, 63, 63f
maturation of, 225
in pain pathway, 449
in stress response, 108
Lipids/lipoproteins. See also Cholesterol; Fat(s)
cardiovascular disease and, 313–315, 314f, 321–322
exercise and, 202, 330–331
Listening skills, 427
Literacy
graph, 47
health, 426–427
statistical, 39
Literature review, 46
Liver, 74f, 75
Liver disease, alcohol-related, 288, 354
Longevity. See Life expectancy
Longitudinal studies, 42
Long-term potentiation, 444
Loss-framed messages, 177–178
Low-density lipoproteins, 321. See also Lipids/lipoproteins
LSD, 278
Lung
smoking effects on, 295–296
structure and function of, 71–74, 71f
Lung cancer. See also Cancer
health education for, 175
screening for, 350t
smoking and, 50, 295–296
Lymph, 76